ALL GLORY TO ŚRĪ GURU AND GAURĀṄGA

ŚRĪMAD BHĀGAVATAM

of

KṚṢṆA - DVAIPĀYANA VYĀSA

ज्ञाने प्रयासमुदपास्य नमन्त एव
जीवन्ति सन्मुखरितां भवदीयवार्ताम् ।
स्थाने स्थिताः श्रुतिगतां तनुवाङ्मनोभिर्
ये प्रायशोऽजित जितोऽप्यसि तैस्त्रिलोक्याम् ॥ ३ ॥

jñāne prayāsam udapāsya namanta eva
jīvanti san-mukharitāṁ bhavadīya-vārtām
sthāne sthitāḥ śruti-gatāṁ tanu-vāṅ-manobhir
ye prāyaśo'jita jito'py asi tais tri-lokyām

(*Śrīmad-Bhāgavatam* 10.14.3)

Books by His Divine Grace
A. C. Bhaktivedanta Swami Prabhupāda:

Bhagavad-gītā As It Is
Śrīmad-Bhāgavatam (1st to 10th Cantos)
Śrī Caitanya-Caritāmṛta (9 vols.)
Kṛṣṇa, The Supreme Personality of Godhead
Teachings of Lord Caitanya
The Nectar of Devotion
The Nectar of Instruction
Śrī Īśopaniṣad
Light of the Bhāgavata
Easy Journey to Other Planets
The Science of Self-Realization
Kṛṣṇa Consciousness: The Topmost Yoga System
Perfect Questions, Perfect Answers
Teachings of Lord Kapila, the Son of Devahuti
Transcendental Teachings of Prahlāda Mahārāja
Teachings of Queen Kuntī
Kṛṣṇa, the Reservoir of Pleasure
The Path of Perfection
Life Comes from Life
Message of Godhead
The Perfection of Yoga
Beyond Birth and Death
On the Way to Kṛṣṇa
Rāja-vidyā: The King of Knowledge
Elevation to Kṛṣṇa Consciousness
Kṛṣṇa Consciousness: The Matchless Gift
Selected Verses from the Vedic Scriptures
Back to Godhead magazine (founder)

A complete catalogue is available upon request.
The Bhaktivedanta Book Trust, ISKCON Temple,
Hare Krishna Land, Juhu, Mumbai 400 049. India.
The above books are also available at ISKCON centers.
Please contact a center near to your place.

ŚRĪMAD BHĀGAVATAM

Tenth Canto

"The Summum Bonum"

(Part Two—Chapters 14–44)

With the Original Sanskrit Text, Its Roman Transliteration, Synonyms, Translation and Elaborate Purports

by disciples of

His Divine Grace
A. C. Bhaktivedanta Swami Prabhupāda
Founder-*Ācārya* of the International Society for Krishna Consciousness

THE BHAKTIVEDANTA BOOK TRUST

Readers interested in the subject matter of this book are invited by The Bhaktivedanta Book Trust to correspond with its secretary at the following address:

The Bhaktivedanta Book Trust
Hare Krishna Land,
Juhu, Mumbai 400 049, India.

Website / E-mail :
www.indiabbt.com
admin@indiabbt.com

Śrīmad Bhāgavatam Tenth Canto-Part Two (English)

First printing in India : 2,000 copies
Second to Eighteenth printings : 59,500 copies
Nineteenth printing, July 2020 : 5,000 copies

ISBN : 978-93-84564-13-1 (v.13)
ISBN : 978-93-84564-00-1 (18-volume set)

Published and Printed by
The Bhaktivedanta Book Trust.

SJ1K

Table of Contents

CHAPTER TWENTY–FIVE

Lord Kṛṣṇa Lifts Govardhana Hill 377

CHAPTER TWENTY–SIX

Wonderful Kṛṣṇa 403

CHAPTER THIRTY

The Gopīs Search for Kṛṣṇa 519

CHAPTER THIRTY–ONE

The Gopīs' Songs of Separation 557

CHAPTER THIRTY–SEVEN

The Killing of the Demons Keśi and Vyoma   695

CHAPTER THIRTY–EIGHT

Akrūra's Arrival in Vṛndāvana   715

CHAPTER FORTY–ONE

CHAPTER FORTY–TWO

Preface

nama oṁ viṣṇu-pādāya kṛṣṇa-preṣṭhāya bhū-tale
śrīmate bhaktivedānta-svāmin iti nāmine

I offer my most respectful obeisances at the lotus feet of His Divine Grace A. C. Bhaktivedanta Swami Prabhupāda, who is very dear to Lord Kṛṣṇa on this earth, having taken shelter at His lotus feet.

namas te sārasvate deve gaura-vāṇī-pracāriṇe
nirviśeṣa-śūnyavādi-pāścātya-deśa-tāriṇe

I offer my most respectful obeisances unto the lotus feet of His Divine Grace A. C. Bhaktivedanta Swami Prabhupāda, who is the disciple of Śrīla Bhaktisiddhānta Sarasvati Ṭhākura and who is powerfully distributing the message of Caitanya Mahāprabhu and thus saving the fallen Western countries from impersonalism and voidism.

Śrīmad-Bhāgavatam, with authorized translation and elaborate purports in the English language, is the great work of His Divine Grace Oṁ Viṣṇupāda Paramahaṁsa Parivrājakācārya Aṣṭottara-śata Śrī Śrīmad A. C. Bhaktivedanta Swami Prabhupāda, our beloved spiritual master. Our present publication is a humble attempt by his servants to complete his most cherished work of *Śrīmad-Bhāgavatam.* Just as one may worship the holy Ganges River by offering Ganges water unto the Ganges, similarly, in our attempt to serve our spiritual master, we are offering to him that which he has given to us.

Śrīla Prabhupāda came to America in 1965, at a critical moment in the history of America and the world in general. The story of Śrīla Prabhupāda's arrival and his specific impact on world civilization, and especially Western civilization, has been brilliantly documented by Satsvarūpa dāsa Goswami. From Satsvarūpa Goswami's authorized biography of Śrīla Prabhupāda, called *Śrīla Prabhupāda-līlāmṛta,* the reader can fully understand Śrīla Prabhupāda's purpose, desire and mission in presenting *Śrīmad-Bhāgavatam.* Further, in Śrīla Prabhupāda's own preface to the *Bhāgavatam* (reprinted as the foreword in this volume), he clearly states that this transcendental literature will provoke a cultural revolution in the world, and that is now underway. I do not wish to be redundant by repeating what Śrīla Prabhupāda has so eloquently stated in his preface, or that which has been so abundantly documented by Satsvarūpa Goswami in his authorized biography.

It is necessary to mention, however, that *Śrīmad-Bhāgavatam* is a completely transcendental, liberated sound vibration coming from the spiritual world. And, being absolute, it is not different from the Absolute Truth Himself, Lord Śrī Kṛṣṇa. By understanding *Śrīmad-Bhāgavatam,* consisting of twelve cantos, the reader acquires perfect knowledge, by which he or she may live peacefully and progressively on the earth, attending to all material necessities and simultaneously achieving supreme spiritual liberation. As we have worked to prepare this and other volumes of *Śrīmad-Bhāgavatam,* our intention has always been to faithfully serve the lotus feet of our spiritual master, carefully trying to translate and comment exactly as he would have, thus preserving the unity and spiritual potency of this edition of *Śrīmad-Bhāgavatam.* In other words, by our strictly following the disciplic succession, called in Sanskrit *guru-paramparā,* this edition of the *Bhāgavatam* will continue to be throughout its volumes a liberated work, free from material contamination and capable of elevating the reader to the kingdom of God.

Our method has been to faithfully follow the commentaries of previous *ācāryas* and exercise a careful selectivity of material based on the example and mood of Śrīla Prabhupāda. One may write transcendental literature only by the mercy of the Supreme Personality of Godhead, Śrī Kṛṣṇa, and the authorized, liberated spiritual masters coming in disciplic succession. Thus we humbly fall at the lotus feet of the previous *ācāryas,* offering special gratitude to the great commentators on the *Bhāgavatam,* namely Śrīla Śrīdhara Svāmī, Śrīla Jīva Gosvāmī, Śrīla Viśvanātha Cakravartī Ṭhākura and Śrīla Bhaktisiddhānta Sarasvatī Gosvāmī, the spiritual master of Śrīla Prabhupāda. We also offer our obeisances at the lotus feet of Śrīla Vīrarāghavācārya, Śrīla Vijayadhvaja Ṭhākura and Śrīla Vaṁśīdhara Ṭhākura, whose commentaries have also helped in this work. Additionally, we offer our humble obeisances at the lotus feet of the great *ācārya* Śrīla Madhva, who has made innumerable learned comments on *Śrīmad-Bhāgavatam.* We further offer our humble obeisances at the lotus feet of the Supreme Personality of Godhead, Śrī Kṛṣṇa Caitanya Mahāprabhu, and to all of His eternally liberated followers, headed by Śrīla Nityānanda Prabhu, Advaita Prabhu, Gadādhara Prabhu, Śrīvāsa Ṭhākura and the six Gosvāmīs, namely Śrīla Rūpa Gosvāmī, Śrīla Sanātana Gosvāmī, Śrīla Raghunātha dāsa Gosvāmī, Śrīla Raghunātha Bhaṭṭa Gosvāmī, Śrīla Jīva Gosvāmī and Śrīla Gopāla Bhaṭṭa Gosvāmī. Finally we offer our most respectful obeisances at the lotus feet of the Absolute Truth, Śrī Śrī Rādhā and Kṛṣṇa, and humbly beg for Their mercy so that this great work of *Śrīmad-Bhāgavatam* can be quickly finished. *Śrīmad-Bhāgavatam* is undoubtedly the most important book in the universe, and the sincere readers of *Śrīmad-Bhāgavatam* will undoubtedly achieve the highest perfection of life, Kṛṣṇa consciousness.

In conclusion, I again remind the reader that *Śrīmad-Bhāgavatam* is the great work of His Divine Grace A. C. Bhaktivedanta Swami Prabhupāda, and that the present volume is the humble attempt of his devoted servants.

Hare Kṛṣṇa

Hridayananda dāsa Goswami

Foreword

We must know the present need of human society. And what is that need? Human society is no longer bounded by geographical limits to particular countries or communities. Human society is broader than in the Middle Ages, and the world tendency is toward one state or one human society. The ideals of spiritual communism, according to *Śrīmad-Bhāgavatam,* are based more or less on the oneness of the entire human society, nay, of the entire energy of living beings. The need is felt by great thinkers to make this a successful ideology. *Śrīmad-Bhāgavatam* will fill this need in human society. It begins, therefore, with an aphorism of Vedānta philosophy, *janmādy asya yataḥ,* to establish the ideal of a common cause.

Human society, at the present moment, is not in the darkness of oblivion. It has made rapid progress in the fields of material comforts, education and economic development throughout the entire world. But there is a pinprick somewhere in the social body at large, and therefore there are large-scale quarrels, even over less important issues. There is need of a clue as to how humanity can become one in peace, friendship and prosperity with a common cause. *Śrīmad-Bhāgavatam* will fill this need, for it is a cultural presentation for the respiritualization of the entire human society.

Śrīmad-Bhāgavatam should be introduced also in the schools and colleges, for it is recommended by the great student-devotee Prahlāda Mahārāja in order to change the demoniac face of society.

kaumāra ācaret prājño
dharmān bhāgavatān iha
durlabhaṁ mānuṣaṁ janma
tad apy adhruvam artha-dam

(*Bhāg.* 7.6.1)

Disparity in human society is due to lack of principles in a godless civilization. There is God, or the Almighty One, from whom everything emanates, by whom everything is maintained and in whom everything is merged to rest. Material science has tried to find the ultimate source of creation very insufficiently, but it is a fact that there is one ultimate source of everything that be. This ultimate source is explained rationally and authoritatively in the beautiful *Bhāgavatam,* or *Śrīmad-Bhāgavatam.*

Śrīmad-Bhāgavatam is the transcendental science not only for knowing the ultimate source of everything but also for knowing our relation with Him and our duty toward perfection of the human society on the basis of this perfect knowledge. It is powerful reading matter in the Sanskrit language, and it is now rendered into English elaborately so that simply by a careful reading one will know God perfectly well, so much so that the reader will be sufficiently educated to defend himself from the onslaught of atheists. Over and above this, the reader will be able to convert others to accepting God as a concrete principle.

Śrīmad-Bhāgavatam begins with the definition of the ultimate source. It is a bona fide commentary on the *Vedānta-sūtra* by the same author, Śrīla Vyāsadeva, and gradually it develops into nine cantos up to the highest state of God realization. The only qualification one needs to study this great book of transcendental knowledge is to proceed step by step cautiously and not jump forward haphazardly as with an ordinary book. It should be gone through chapter by chapter, one after another. The reading matter is so arranged with the original Sanskrit text, its English transliteration, synonyms, translation and purports so that one is sure to become a God-realized soul at the end of finishing the first nine cantos.

The Tenth Canto is distinct from the first nine cantos because it deals directly with the transcendental activities of the Personality of Godhead, Śrī Kṛṣṇa. One will be unable to capture the effects of the Tenth Canto without going through the first nine cantos. The book is complete in twelve cantos, each independent, but it is good for all to read them in small installments one after another.

I must admit my frailties in presenting *Śrīmad-Bhāgavatam,* but still I am hopeful of its good reception by the thinkers and leaders of society on the strength of the following statement of *Śrīmad-Bhāgavatam* (1.5.11):

tad-vāg-visargo janatāgha-viplavo
yasmin prati-ślokam abaddhavaty api
nāmāny anantasya yaśo 'ṅkitāni yac
chṛṇvanti gāyanti gṛṇanti sādhavaḥ

"On the other hand, that literature which is full of descriptions of the transcendental glories of the name, fame, form and pastimes of the unlimited Supreme Lord is a transcendental creation meant for bringing about a revolution in the impious life of a misdirected civilization. Such transcendental literature, even though irregularly composed, is heard, sung and accepted by purified men who are thoroughly honest."

Oṁ tat sat

A. C. Bhaktivedanta Swami

Introduction

"This *Bhāgavata Purāṇa* is as brilliant as the sun, and it has arisen just after the departure of Lord Kṛṣṇa to His own abode, accompanied by religion, knowledge, etc. Persons who have lost their vision due to the dense darkness of ignorance in the age of Kali shall get light from this *Purāṇa*." (*Śrīmad-Bhāgavatam* 1.3.43)

The timeless wisdom of India is expressed in the *Vedas,* ancient Sanskrit texts that touch upon all fields of human knowledge. Originally preserved through oral tradition, the *Vedas* were first put into writing five thousand years ago by Śrīla Vyāsadeva, the "literary incarnation of God." After compiling the *Vedas,* Vyāsadeva set forth their essence in the aphorisms known as *Vedānta-sūtras. Śrīmad-Bhāgavatam (Bhāgavata Purāṇa)* is Vyāsadeva's commentary on his own *Vedānta-sūtras.* It was written in the maturity of his spiritual life under the direction of Nārada Muni, his spiritual master. Referred to as "the ripened fruit of the tree of Vedic literature," *Śrīmad-Bhāgavatam* is the most complete and authoritative exposition of Vedic knowledge.

After compiling the *Bhāgavatam,* Vyāsa imparted the synopsis of it to his son, the sage Śukadeva Gosvāmī. Śukadeva Gosvāmī subsequently recited the entire *Bhāgavatam* to Mahārāja Parīkṣit in an assembly of learned saints on the bank of the Ganges at Hastināpura (now Delhi). Mahārāja Parīkṣit was the emperor of the world and was a great *rājarṣi* (saintly king). Having received a warning that he would die within a week, he renounced his entire kingdom and retired to the bank of the Ganges to fast until death and receive spiritual enlightenment. The *Bhāgavatam* begins with Emperor Parīkṣit's sober inquiry to Śukadeva Gosvāmī: "You are the spiritual master of great saints and devotees. I am therefore begging you to show the way of perfection for all persons, and especially for one who is about to die. Please let me know what a man should hear, chant, remember and worship, and also what he should not do. Please explain all this to me."

Śukadeva Gosvāmī's answer to this question, and numerous other questions posed by Mahārāja Parīkṣit, concerning everything from the nature of the self to the origin of the universe, held the assembled sages in rapt attention continuously for the seven days leading up to the king's death. The sage Sūta Gosvāmī, who was present in that assembly when Śukadeva Gosvāmī first recited *Śrīmad-Bhāgavatam,* later repeated the *Bhāgavatam* before a gathering of sages in the forest of Naimiṣāraṇya. Those sages, concerned about the spiritual welfare of the people in general, had gathered to perform a long, continuous chain of sacrifices to counteract the degrading influence of the incipient age of Kali. In response to the sages' request that he speak the essence of Vedic wisdom, Sūta Gosvāmī repeated from memory the entire eighteen thousand verses of *Śrīmad-Bhāgavatam,* as spoken by Śukadeva Gosvāmī to Mahārāja Parīkṣit.

The reader of *Śrīmad-Bhāgavatam* hears Sūta Gosvāmī relate the questions of Mahārāja Parīkṣit and the answers of Śukadeva Gosvāmī. Also, Sūta Gosvāmī sometimes responds directly to questions put by Śaunaka Ṛṣi, the spokesman for the sages gathered at Naimiṣāraṇya. One therefore simultaneously hears two dialogues: one between Mahārāja Parīkṣit and Śukadeva Gosvāmī on the bank of the Ganges, and another at Naimiṣāraṇya between Sūta Gosvāmī and the sages at Naimiṣāraṇya forest, headed by Śaunaka Ṛṣi. Futhermore, while instructing King Parīkṣit, Śukadeva Gosvāmī often relates historical episodes and gives accounts of lengthy philosophical discussions between such great souls as Nārada Muni and Vasudeva. With this understanding of the history of the *Bhāgavatam,* the reader will easily be able to follow its intermingling of dialogues and events from various sources. Since philosophical wisdom, not chronological order, is most important in the text, one need only be attentive to the subject matter of *Śrīmad-Bhāgavatam* to appreciate fully its profound message.

The translators of this edition compare the *Bhāgavatam* to sugar candy—wherever you taste it, you will find it equally sweet and relishable. Therefore, to taste the sweetness of the *Bhāgavatam,* one may begin by reading any of its volumes. After such an introductory taste, however, the serious reader is best advised to go back to the First Canto and then proceed through the *Bhāgavatam,* canto after canto, in its natural order.

This edition of the *Bhāgavatam* is the first complete English translation of this important text with an elaborate commentary, and it is the first widely available to the English-speaking public. The first twelve volumes (Canto One through Canto Ten, Part One) are the product of the scholarly and devotional effort of His Divine Grace A. C. Bhaktivedanta Swami Prabhupāda, the founder-*ācārya* of the International Society for Krishna Consciousness and the world's most distinguished teacher of Indian religious and Philosophical thought.

Śrīla Prabhupāda began his *Śrīmad-Bhāgavatam* in mid-1962 in Vṛndavana, India, the land most sacred to Lord Kṛṣṇa. With no assistants and limited funds, but with an abundance of devotion and determination, he was able to publish the First Canto (then in three volumes) by early 1965. After coming to the United States later that year, Śrīla Prabhupāda continued his commentated translation of the *Bhāgavatam*, and over the next twelve years, while developing his growing Kṛṣṇa consciousness movement and traveling incessantly, he produced twenty-seven more volumes. These were all edited, illustrated, typeset, proofread and indexed by his disciples, members of the Bhaktivedanta Book Trust (BBT). Throughout all of these volumes (totaling twelve in the present edition), Śrīla Prabhupāda's pure devotion to Lord Kṛṣṇa, his consummate Sanskrit scholarship and his intimate familiarity with Vedic culture and thought, and with modern life, combine to reveal to the Western reader a magnificent exposition of this important classic.

After Śrīla Prabhupāda's departure from this world in 1977, his monumental work of translating and commenting on *Śrīmad-Bhāgavatam* was continued by his disciples, headed by Hridayānanda dāsa Goswami, Gopīparāṇadhana dāsa Adhikārī and Draviḍa dāsa Brahmacārī—all seasoned BBT workers. Relying on the same Sankrit editions of *Śrīmad-Bhāgavatam* that Śrīla Prabhupāda had used, Hridayānanda dāsa Goswami and Gopīparāṇadhana dāsa translated the Sanskrit text and added commentary. Then they turned over the manuscript to Draviḍa dāsa for final editing and production. In this way the concluding six volumes were published.

Readers will find this work of value for many reasons. For those interested in the classical roots of Indian civilization, it serves as a vast detailed reservoir of information on virtually every one of its aspects. For students of comparative philosophy and religion, the *Bhāgavatam* offers a penetrating view into the meaning of India's profound spiritual heritage. To sociologists and anthropologists, the *Bhāgavatam* reveals the practical workings of a peaceful, prosperous and scientifically organized Vedic culture, whose institutions were integrated on the basis of a highly developed spiritual world view. Students of literature will discover the *Bhāgavatam* to be a masterpiece of majestic poetry. For students of psychology, the text provides important perspectives on the nature of consciousness, human behavior and the philosophical study of identity. Finally, to those seeking spiritual insight, the *Bhāgavatam* offers simple and practical guidance for attainment of the highest self-knowledge and realization of the Absolute Truth. The entire multivolume text, presented by the Bhaktivedanta Book Trust, promises to occupy a significant place in the intellectual, cultural and spiritual life of modern man for a long time to come.

—The Publishers

His Divine Grace
A. C. Bhaktivedanta Swami Prabhupāda
Founder-Ācārya of ISKCON and greatest exponent of Kṛṣṇa consciousness in the modern world

With his mind fully concentrated and his body trembling, Lord Brahmā very humbly began offering praise to Lord Kṛṣṇa with faltering words.(10.13.64)

As the ass demons attacked, Kṛṣṇa and Balarāma easily seized them one after another by the hind legs, whirled them around and threw them into the tops of the palm trees. (10.15.37)

Five thousand years ago, Lord Kṛṣṇa, the Supreme Personality of Godhead, descended to earth in His original spiritual form and displayed His transcendental pastimes with His associates. Here Lord Kṛṣṇa (dressed in yellow), His brother Balarāma and Their cowherd friends enter the Vṛndāvana forest with their cows. The great sage Śukadeva Gosvāmī said, "The Supreme Personality of Godhead looked over the

forest, which resounded with the charming sounds of bees, animals and birds, and which was enhanced by a lake whose clear water resembled the minds of great souls and by a breeze carrying the fragrance of hundred-petaled lotuses. Seeing all this, Lord Kṛṣṇa decided to enjoy the auspicious atmosphere." (10.15.2–3)

Seeing the acute distress the residents of Gokula were feeling on account of their love for Him, Lord Kṛṣṇa rose up from the bonds of the Kāliya serpent and began to dance on his hoods. The Lord's wonderful, powerful dancing trampled and broke all the serpent's one thousand hoods. (10.16.26)

The residents of Vṛndāvana told Kṛṣṇa, "If this deadly fire overcomes us, we will be separated from Your lotus feet, and this is unbearable for us. Therefore, just so that we can go on serving Your lotus feet, please protect us." Seeing His devotees so disturbed, Śrī Kṛṣṇa, the infinite Lord of the universe and possessor of infinite power, then swallowed the terrible forest fire. (10.17.24–25)

When Lord Kṛṣṇa convinced his father, Nanda Mahārāja, to forego the sacrifice to Indra and instead use the collected paraphernalia to worship Govardhana Hill, the *brāhmaṇas* and the cows, Indra became furious and sent the devastating Saṁvārtaka clouds to harass the residents of Vraja with downpours of rain and hail. The cowherd community was very disturbed by this storm and approached Kṛṣṇa for shelter. Under-

standing that this trouble was Indra's work, Kṛṣṇa decided to smash the demigod's false prestige to pieces, and thus He lifted Govardhana Hill with one hand. He then invited the entire cowherd community to take shelter in the dry space beneath the mountain. For seven successive days He held up the hill, until Indra finally understood Kṛṣṇa's mystic power and ordered the clouds to withdraw. (10.25.1–23)

Thus smashed by Balarāma's fist, Pralamba's head immediately cracked open. The demon vomited blood from his mouth and lost all consciousness, and then with a great noise he fell lifeless on the ground, like a mountain devastated by Indra. (10.18.24–30)

When the *gopīs* saw that their dearmost Kṛṣṇa had returned to them, they became ecstatic, and out of their affection for Him their eyes bloomed wide. It was as if the air of life had reentered their bodies. (10.32.3)

In the festive *rāsa* dance, Lord Kṛṣṇa expanded Himself and entered between each pair of *gopīs*, and as that master of mystic power placed His arms around their necks, each girl thought He was standing next to her alone. The demigods and their wives were overwhelmed with eagerness to witness the *rāsa* dance, and they soon crowded the sky with their hundreds of celestial airplanes. Kettledrums then resounded

in the sky while flowers rained down and the chief Gandharvas and their wives sang Lord Kṛṣṇa's spotless glories. A tumultuous sound arose from the armlets, ankle bells and waist bells of the *gopīs* as they sported with their beloved Kṛṣṇa in the circle of the *rāsa* dance. In the midst of the dancing *gopīs*, Lord Kṛṣṇa appeared most brilliant, like an exquisite sapphire in the midst of golden ornaments. (10.33.19)

Increasingly agitated by ecstasy at seeing the Lord's footprints, his bodily hairs standing on end because of his pure love, and his eyes filled with tears, Akrūra jumped down from his chariot and began rolling about among those footprints, exclaiming, "Ah, this is the dust from my master's feet!" (10.38.1–26)

Kṛṣṇa and Balarāma approach the city of Mathurā. (10.41.19–23)

Lord Kṛṣṇa straddled Kaṁsa and began to strike him over and over again. Simply from the blows of Kṛṣṇa's fist, Kaṁsa lost his life. (10.44.37–38).

CHAPTER FOURTEEN

Brahmā's Prayers to Lord Kṛṣṇa

This chapter describes the prayers Brahmā offered to Lord Kṛṣṇa, who is also known as Nanda-nandana.

For His satisfaction, Brahmā first praised the beauty of the Lord's transcendental limbs and then declared that His original identity of sweetness is even more difficult to comprehend than His opulence. Only by the devotional process of hearing and chanting transcendental sounds received from Vedic authorities can one realize the Personality of Godhead. It is fruitless to try to realize God through processes outside the scope of Vedic authority.

The mystery of the Personality of Godhead, who is the reservoir of unlimited spiritual qualities, is inconceivable; it is even more difficult to understand than the impersonal Supreme. Thus only by the mercy of God can one understand His glories. Finally realizing this, Brahmā repeatedly condemned his own actions and recognized that Lord Śrī Kṛṣṇa, the ultimate shelter of the universe, is Brahmā's own father, the original Nārāyaṇa. In this way Brahmā begged the Lord's forgiveness.

Brahmā then glorified the inconceivable opulence of the Personality of Godhead and described the ways in which Brahmā and Śiva differ from Lord Viṣṇu, the reason for the Supreme Lord's appearance in various species of demigods, animals and so on, the eternal nature of the pastimes of the Personality of Godhead, and the temporality of the material world. By knowing the Supreme Personality in truth, the individual spirit soul can achieve liberation from bondage. In actuality, however, both liberation and bondage are unreal, for it is only from the living entity's conditioned outlook that his bondage and liberation are produced. Thinking the personal form of Lord Kṛṣṇa illusory, fools reject His lotus feet and look elsewhere to find the Supreme Self. But the futility of their search is the obvious proof of their foolishness. There is simply no way to understand the truth of the Personality of Godhead without His mercy.

Having established this conclusion, Lord Brahmā analyzed the great good fortune of the residents of Vraja and then personally prayed to be born there even as a blade of grass, a bush or a creeper. Indeed, the homes of the residents of Vṛndāvana are not prisons of material existence but rather abodes envied even by the *jñānīs* and *yogīs.* On the other hand, any home without a connection to Lord Kṛṣṇa is in fact a prison cell of material existence. Finally, Brahmā offered his whole self at the lotus feet of the Supreme Lord and, praising Him again and again, circumambulated Him and took his leave.

Lord Kṛṣṇa then gathered the animals Brahmā stole and led them to the place on the Yamunā's bank where the cowherd boys had been taking lunch. The same friends who had been present before were sitting there now. By the power of Kṛṣṇa's illusory energy, they were not at all aware of what had happened. Thus when Kṛṣṇa arrived with the calves, the boys told Him, "You've returned so quickly! Very good. As long as You were gone we couldn't take even a morsel of food, so come and eat."

Laughing at the words of the cowherd boys, Lord Kṛṣṇa began taking His meal in their company. While eating, Kṛṣṇa pointed out to His young friends the skin of the python, and the boys thought, "Kṛṣṇa has just now killed this terrible snake." Indeed, later they related to the residents of Vṛndāvana the incident of Kṛṣṇa's killing the Agha demon. In this way, the cowherd boys described pastimes that Lord Kṛṣṇa had performed in His *bālya* age (one to five), even though His *pauganda* age (six to ten) had begun.

Śukadeva Gosvāmī concludes this chapter by explaining how the *gopīs* loved Lord Kṛṣṇa even more than they loved their own sons.

TEXT 1

श्रीब्रह्मोवाच
नौमीड्य तेऽभ्रवपुषे तडिदम्बराय
गुञ्जावतंसपरिपिच्छलसन्मुखाय ।
वन्यस्रजे कवलवेत्रविषाणवेणु-
लक्ष्मश्रिये मृदुपदे पशुपांगजाय ॥ १ ॥

śrī-brahmovāca
naumīḍya te'bhra-vapuṣe taḍid-ambarāya
guñjāvataṁsa-paripiccha-lasan-mukhāya
vanya-sraje kavala-vetra-viṣāṇa-veṇu-
lakṣma-śriye mṛdu-pade paśupāṅgajāya

śrī-brahmā uvāca—Lord Brahmā said; *naumi*—I offer praise; *īḍya*—O most worshipable one; *te*—unto You; *abhra*—like a dark cloud; *vapuṣe*—whose body; *taḍit*—like lightning; *ambarāya*—whose garment; *guñjā*—made of small berries; *avataṁsa*—with ornaments (for the ears); *paripiccha*

—and peacock feathers; *lasat*—resplendent; *mukhāya*—whose face; *vanya-sraje*—wearing garlands of forest flowers; *kavala*—a morsel of food; *vetra*—a stick; *viṣāṇa*—a buffalo-horn bugle; *veṇu*—and a flute; *lakṣma*—characterized by; *śriye*—whose beauty; *mṛdu*—soft; *pade*—whose feet; *paśu-pa*—of the cowherd (Nanda Mahārāja); *aṅga-jāya*—unto the son.

TRANSLATION

Lord Brahmā said: My dear Lord, You are the only worshipable Lord, the Supreme Personality of Godhead, and therefore I offer my humble obeisances and prayers just to please You. O son of the king of the cowherds, Your transcendental body is dark blue like a new cloud, Your garment is brilliant like lightning, and the beauty of Your face is enhanced by Your guñjā earrings and the peacock feather on Your head. Wearing garlands of various forest flowers and leaves, and equipped with a herding stick, a buffalo horn and a flute, You stand beautifully with a morsel of food in Your hand.

PURPORT

In the previous chapter Brahmā, the creator of the universe, tried to bewilder the Supreme Personality of Godhead, Lord Kṛṣṇa, by stealing His cowherd boyfriends and calves. But by a slight exhibition of Kṛṣṇa's own mystic potency, Brahmā himself was completely bewildered, and now with great humility and devotion he offers his humble obeisances and prayers unto the Lord.

The word *kavala* in this verse refers to a morsel of rice mixed with yogurt that Kṛṣṇa held in His left hand. According to Sanātana Gosvāmī, the Lord held a cowherding stick and a buffalo horn pressed under His left arm, and His flute was placed under His belt. Beautiful young Kṛṣṇa, decorated with multicolored forest minerals, exhibited opulences far greater than those of Vaikuṇṭha. Although Brahmā had seen innumerable four-armed forms of the Lord, he now surrendered unto the lotus feet of the two-armed form of Kṛṣṇa, who appeared as the son of Nanda Mahārāja. Brahmā offered his prayers to that form.

TEXT 2

अस्यापि देव वपुषो मदनुग्रहस्य
स्वेच्छामयस्य न तु भूतमयस्य कोऽपि।
नेशे महि त्ववसितुं मनसान्तरेण
साक्षात्तवैव किमुतात्मसुखानुभूतेः ॥ २ ॥

asyāpi deva vapuṣo mad-anugrahasya
svecchā-mayasya na tu bhūta-mayasya ko'pi
neśe mahi tv avasituṁ manasāntareṇa
sākṣāt tavaiva kim utātma-sukhānubhūteḥ

asya—of this; *api*—even; *deva*—O Lord; *vapuṣaḥ*—the body; *mat-anugrahasya*—which has shown mercy to me; *sva-icchā-mayasya*—which appears in response to the desires of Your pure devotees; *na*—not; *tu*—on the other hand; *bhūta-mayasya*—a product of matter; *kaḥ*—Brahmā; *api*—even; *na īśe*—I am not able; *mahi*—the potency; *tu*—indeed; *avasitum*—to estimate; *manasā*—with my mind; *antareṇa*—which is controlled and withdrawn; *sākṣāt*—directly; *tava*—Your; *eva*—indeed; *kim uta*—what to speak; *ātma*—within Yourself; *sukha*—of happiness; *anubhūteḥ*—of Your experience.

TRANSLATION

My dear Lord, neither I nor anyone else can estimate the potency of this transcendental body of Yours, which has shown such mercy to me and which appears just to fulfill the desires of Your pure devotees. Although my mind is completely withdrawn from material affairs, I cannot understand Your personal form. How, then, could I possibly understand the happiness You experience within Yourself?

PURPORT

In *Kṛṣṇa, the Supreme Personality of Godhead,* Chapter Fourteen, Śrīla Prabhupāda explains that in the present verse Lord Brahmā expressed the following prayerful sentiment: "Your appearance as a cowherd child is for the benefit of the devotees, and although I have committed offenses at Your lotus feet by stealing away Your cows, boys and calves, I can understand that You are now showing me Your mercy. That is Your transcendental quality: You are very affectionate toward Your devotees. Yet in spite of Your affection for me, I cannot estimate the potency of Your bodily activities. It is to be understood that when I, Lord Brahmā, the supreme personality of this universe, cannot estimate the childlike body of the Supreme Personality of Godhead, then what to speak of others? And if I cannot estimate the spiritual potency of Your childlike body, then what can I understand about Your transcendental pastimes? Therefore, as it is said in the *Bhagavad-gītā,* anyone who can understand a little of the transcendental pastimes, appearance and disappearance of the Lord immediately becomes eligible to enter the kingdom of God after quitting the material body. This statement is confirmed in the *Vedas,* and it is stated simply: By understanding the Supreme Personality of Godhead, one can overcome the chain of repeated birth and death. I therefore recommend that people should not try to understand You by their speculative knowledge."

When Brahmā disrespected the supreme status of the Personality of Godhead, Lord Kṛṣṇa first bewildered him by exhibiting the Lord's own transcendental power. Then, having humbled His devotee Brahmā, Kṛṣṇa gave him His personal audience.

According to Śrīla Viśvanātha Cakravartī Ṭhākura, Lord Kṛṣṇa's transcendental body can also function through the agency of His plenary expansions, called *viṣṇu-tattva.* As stated by Brahmā himself in the *Brahma-saṁhitā* (5.32): *aṅgāni yasya sakalendriya-vṛttimanti.* This verse indicates not only that the Lord can perform any bodily function with any of His limbs but also that He can see through the eyes of His Viṣṇu expansions or, indeed, through the eyes of any living entity, and similarly that He can hear through the ears of any Viṣṇu or *jīva* expansion. Śrīla Viśvanātha Cakravartī Ṭhākura points out that although the Lord can perform any function with any one of His senses, in His transcendental pastimes as Śrī Kṛṣṇa He generally sees with His eyes, touches with His hands, hears with His ears and so on. Thus He behaves like the most beautiful and charming young cowherd boy.

The Vedic knowledge expands from Lord Brahmā, who is described in the first verse of *Śrīmad-Bhāgavatam* as *ādi-kavi,* the primeval Vedic scholar. Yet Brahmā could not understand the transcendental body of Lord Kṛṣṇa, because it is beyond the reach of ordinary Vedic knowledge. Among all the transcendental forms of the Lord, the two-armed form of Govinda — Kṛṣṇa — is original and supreme. Thus Lord Govinda's pastimes of stealing butter, drinking the *gopīs'* breast milk, tending the calves, playing His flute and playing childhood sports are extraordinary even in comparison with the activities of the Lord's Viṣṇu expansions.

TEXT 3

ज्ञाने प्रयासमुदपास्य नमन्त एव
जीवन्ति सन्मुखरितां भवदीयवार्ताम् ।
स्थाने स्थिताः श्रुतिगतां तनुवाङ्मनोभिर्
ये प्रायशोऽजित जितोऽप्यसि तैस्त्रिलोक्याम् ॥ ३ ॥

jñāne prayāsam udapāsya namanta eva
jīvanti san-mukharitāṁ bhavadīya-vārtām
sthāne sthitāḥ śruti-gatāṁ tanu-vāṅ-manobhir
ye prāyaśo'jita jito'py asi tais tri-lokyām

jñāne—for knowledge; *prayāsam*—the endeavor; *udapāsya*—giving up completely; *namantaḥ*—offering obeisances; *eva*—simply; *jīvanti*—live; *sat-mukharitām*—chanted by the pure devotees; *bhavadīya-vārtām*—topics related to You; *sthāne*—in their material position; *sthitāḥ*—remaining; *śruti-gatām*—received by hearing; *tanu*—with their body; *vāk*—words; *manobhiḥ*—and mind; *ye*—who; *prāyaśaḥ*—for the most part; *ajita*—O unconquerable one; *jitaḥ*—conquered; *api*—nevertheless; *asi*—You become; *taiḥ*—by them; *tri-lokyām*—within the three worlds.

TRANSLATION

Those who, even while remaining situated in their established social positions, throw away the process of speculative knowledge and with their body, words and mind offer all respects to descriptions of Your personality and activities, dedicating their lives to these narrations, which are vibrated by You personally and by Your pure devotees, certainly conquer Your Lordship, although You are otherwise unconquerable by anyone within the three worlds.

PURPORT

Here the word *udapāsya* clearly indicates that one should not even slightly endeavor to understand the Absolute Truth by the process of mental speculation, for it invariably carries one to an imperfect, impersonal understanding of God. The word *jīvanti* indicates that a devotee who always hears about Lord Kṛṣṇa will go back home, back to Godhead, even if he can do nothing except maintain his existence and hear topics concerning the Lord.

Śrīla Sanātana Gosvāmī has explained the words *tanu-vāṅ-manobhiḥ* ("by the body, words and mind") in three ways. In reference to devotees, through their body, words and mind they are able to conquer Lord Kṛṣṇa. Thus becoming perfect in Kṛṣṇa consciousness, they can touch His lotus feet with their hands, call Him to come with their words, and attain His direct audience within their mind simply by thinking about Him.

In the case of nondevotees, the words *tanu-vāṅ-manobhiḥ* refer to the word *ajita,* "unconquered," and indicate that those not engaged in the loving service of Lord Kṛṣṇa cannot conquer the Absolute Truth by their bodily strength, verbal expertise or mental power. Despite all their endeavors, the ultimate truth remains beyond their reach.

In reference to the word *jitaḥ,* "conquered," the words *tanu-vāṅ-manobhiḥ* indicate that the pure devotees of Lord Kṛṣṇa conquer His body, words and mind. Lord Kṛṣṇa's body is conquered because He always remains by the side of His pure devotees; Lord Kṛṣṇa's words are conquered because He always chants the glories of His devotees; and Lord Kṛṣṇa's mind is conquered because He always thinks about His loving devotees.

Śrīla Viśvanātha Cakravartī Ṭhākura has explained the words *tanu-vāṅ-manobhiḥ* in regard to the word *namantaḥ,* "offering obeisances." He explains that the devotees can take full advantage of the transcendental topics of the Lord by offering all respects to those topics with their body, words and mind. One should engage his body by touching the ground with his hands and head while offering obeisances to the topics of the Lord; one should engage his words by praising transcendental literatures such as *Bhagavad-gītā* and *Śrīmad-Bhāgavatam,* as well as the devotees who are preaching such literatures; and one should engage his mind by feeling great reverence and pleasure while hearing the transcendental topics of the Lord. In this way, a sincere devotee who has acquired even a small amount of transcendental knowledge about Lord Kṛṣṇa can conquer Him and thus go back home, back to Godhead, for eternal life at the Lord's side.

TEXT 4

श्रेयःसृतिं भक्तिमुदस्य ते विभो
क्लिश्यन्ति ये केवलबोधलब्धये ।
तेषामसौ क्लेशल एव शिष्यते
नान्यद् यथा स्थूलतुषावघातिनाम् ॥ ४ ॥

śreyaḥ-sṛtiṁ bhaktim udasya te vibho
kliśyanti ye kevala-bodha-labdhaye
teṣām asau kleśala eva śiṣyate
nānyad yathā sthūla-tuṣāvaghātinām

śreyaḥ—of supreme benefit; *sṛtim*—the path; *bhaktim*—devotional service; *udasya*—rejecting; *te*—they; *vibho*—O almighty Lord; *kliśyanti*—struggle; *ye*—who; *kevala*—exclusive; *bodha*—of knowledge; *labdhaye*—for the achievement; *teṣām*—for them; *asau*—this; *kleśalaḥ*—botheration; *eva*—merely; *śiṣyate*—remains; *na*—nothing; *anyat*—other; *yathā*—just as; *sthūla-tuṣa*—empty husks; *avaghātinām*—for those who are beating.

TRANSLATION

My dear Lord, devotional service unto You is the best path for self-realization. If someone gives up that path and engages in the cultivation of speculative knowledge, he will simply undergo a troublesome process and will not achieve his desired result. As a person who beats an empty husk of wheat cannot get grain, one who simply speculates cannot achieve self-realization. His only gain is trouble.

PURPORT

Loving service to the Supreme Person is the natural and eternal function of every living entity. If a person renounces his own constitutional function and instead laboriously seeks so-called enlightenment through impersonal, speculative knowledge, his result is simply the trouble and bother that come from following an artificial process. A fool may beat an empty husk, not knowing that the grain has already been removed. Similarly foolish is the person who throws his mind again and again into the pursuit of knowledge without surrendering to the Supreme Personality of Godhead, for it is the Supreme Personality of Godhead who is the very substance and goal of knowledge, just as grain is the substance and goal of the entire agricultural effort. Vedic knowledge or, indeed, material science without the Personality of Godhead is exactly like an empty and useless husk of wheat.

One may argue that by practicing *yoga* or cultivating impersonal knowledge one can acquire prestige, wealth, mystic powers or even impersonal liberation. But these so-called gains are actually useless, because they do not situate the living being in his constitutional position of loving service to the Supreme Lord. Therefore such results, being superfluous to the living being's essential nature, are impermanent. As stated in the *Nṛsiṁha Purāṇa, patreṣu puṣpeṣu phaleṣu toyeṣv akrīta-labhyeṣu vadaiva satsu/ bhaktyā su-labhye puruṣe purāṇe muktyai kim arthaṁ kriyate prayatnaḥ:* "Since the primeval Personality of Godhead is easily attained by offering Him such things as leaves, flowers, fruits and water, which are all found without difficulty, why does one need to endeavor for liberation separately?"

Although the process of devotional service to Lord Kṛṣṇa is very simple, it is extremely difficult for stubborn conditioned souls to completely humble themselves before the Supreme Personality of Godhead and absorb themselves twenty-four hours a day in His loving service. The mood of loving service is anathema to belligerent conditioned souls determined to defy God and enjoy. When such stubborn conditioned souls attempt to bypass surrendering to God through proud attempts at philosophical speculation, austerity, and *yoga,* they are turned back to the material platform by the powerful laws of God and violently merged into the heaving ocean of insignificance called the material world.

TEXT 5

पुरेह भूमन् बहवोऽपि योगिनस्
त्वदर्पितेहा निजकर्मलब्धया ।
विबुध्य भक्त्यैव कथोपनीतया
प्रपेदिरेऽञ्जोऽच्युत ते गतिं पराम् ॥ ५ ॥

pureha bhūman bahavo'pi yoginas
tvad-arpitehā nija-karma-labdhayā
vibudhya bhaktyaiva kathopanītayā
prapedire'ñjo'cyuta te gatiṁ parām

purā—previously; *iha*—in this world; *bhūman*—O almighty Lord; *bahavaḥ*—many; *api*—indeed; *yoginaḥ*—followers of the path of *yoga; tvat*—unto You; *arpita*—having offered; *īhāḥ*—all their endeavors; *nija-karma*—by their prescribed duties; *labdhayā*—which is achieved; *vibudhya*—coming to understand; *bhaktyā*—by devotional service; *eva*—indeed; *kathā-upanītayā*—cultivated through hearing and chanting topics about You; *prapedire*—they achieved by surrender; *añjaḥ*—easily; *acyuta*—O infallible one; *te*—Your; *gatim*—destination; *parām*—supreme.

TRANSLATION

O almighty Lord, in the past many yogīs in this world achieved the platform of devotional service by offering all their endeavors unto You and faithfully carrying out their prescribed duties. Through such devotional service, perfected by the processes of hearing and chanting about You, they came to understand You, O infallible one, and could easily surrender to You and achieve Your supreme abode.

TEXT 6

तथापि भूमन्महिमागुणस्य ते
विबोद्धुमर्हत्यमलान्तरात्मभिः ।

अविक्रियात् स्वानुभवादरूपतो
हृनन्यबोध्यात्मतया न चान्यथा ॥ ६ ॥

tathāpi bhūman mahimāguṇasya te
viboddhum arhaty amalāntar-ātmabhiḥ
avikriyāt svānubhavād arūpato
hy ananya-bodhyātmatayā na cānyathā

tathā api—nevertheless; *bhūman*—O limitless one; *mahimā*—the potency; *aguṇasya*—of Him who has no material qualities; *te*—of You; *viboddhum*—to understand; *arhati*—one is able; *amala*—spotless; *antaḥ-ātmabhiḥ*—with mind and senses; *avikriyāt*—not based on material differentiations; *sva-anubhavāt*—by perception of the Supreme Soul; *arūpataḥ*—without attachment to material forms; *hi*—indeed; *ananya-bodhya-ātmatayā*—as self-manifested, without the help of any other illuminating agent; *na*—not; *ca*—and; *anyathā*—otherwise.

TRANSLATION

Nondevotees, however, cannot realize You in Your full personal feature. Nevertheless, it may be possible for them to realize Your expansion as the impersonal Supreme by cultivating direct perception of the Self within the heart. But they can do this only by purifying their mind and senses of all conceptions of material distinctions and all attachment to material sense objects. Only in this way will Your impersonal feature manifest itself to them.

PURPORT

It is difficult for conditioned souls to understand all the transcendental features of the Supreme Lord. As confirmed in the First Canto of *Śrīmad-Bhāgavatam* (1.2.11): *brahmeti paramātmeti bhagavān iti śabdyate.* The transcendental existence of God is understood progressively as the impersonal effulgence, the localized Supersoul in one's heart, and finally the Supreme Personality of Godhead existing in His eternal abode. Lord Kṛṣṇa's transcendental existence is beyond the qualities of material nature. Thus here the Lord is referred to as *aguṇasya,* without material qualities.

Even by practicing *yoga* or engaging in advanced philosophical speculation, one will find it very difficult to understand clearly the transcendental existence beyond the modes of material nature. And these processes are virtually useless for understanding the Lord's own unlimited transcendental qualities, which are far beyond the impersonal conception of spiritual existence. Only by the mercy of the pure devotees of the Lord or by associating with the Lord Himself can one begin the process of realizing the personal feature of God—a process that culminates in pure Kṛṣṇa consciousness, the final and supreme perfection of knowledge.

TEXT 7

गुणात्मनस्तेऽपि गुणान् विमातुं
हितावतीर्णस्य क ईशिरेऽस्य ।
कालेन यैर्वा विमिताः सुकल्पैर्
भूपांशवः खे मिहिका द्युभासः ॥ ७ ॥

guṇātmanas te'pi guṇān vimātuṁ
hitāvatīrṇasya ka īśire'sya
kālena yair vā vimitāḥ su-kalpair
bhū-pāṁśavaḥ khe mihikā dyu-bhāsaḥ

guṇa-ātmanaḥ—of the possessor of all superior qualities; *te*—You; *api*—certainly; *guṇān*—the qualities; *vimātum*—to count; *hita-avatīrṇasya*—who have descended for the benefit of all living entities; *ke*—who; *īśire*—are able; *asya*—of the universe; *kālena*—in due course of time; *yaiḥ*—by whom; *vā*—or; *vimitāḥ*—counted; *su-kalpaiḥ*—by great scientists; *bhū-pāṁśavaḥ*—the atoms of an earthly planet; *khe*—in the sky; *mihikāḥ*—the particles of snow; *dyu-bhāsaḥ*—the illumination of stars and planets.

TRANSLATION

In time, learned philosophers or scientists might be able to count all the atoms of the earth, the particles of snow, or perhaps even the shining molecules radiating from the sun, the stars and other luminaries. But among these learned men, who could possibly count the unlimited transcendental qualities possessed by You, the Supreme Personality of Godhead, who have descended onto the surface of the earth for the benefit of all living entities?

PURPORT

Śrīla Sanātana Gosvāmī explains that Lord Kṛṣṇa is *guṇātmā,* "the soul of all superior qualities," because He gives them life. For example, one may discuss in an abstract way such qualities as generosity, intelligence and mercy, but they come to life only when a living person exhibits them. Thus Lord Kṛṣṇa is *guṇātmā* because He descends to the material world and reestablishes religious principles by exhibiting all godly qualities Himself and inspiring them in others. A living entity who develops the transcendental qualities found in the Lord receives immeasurable benefit and eventually goes with the Lord back to His own abode, where all living beings are liberated and fully endowed with the transcendental nature.

Śrīla Sanātana Gosvāmī further explains that the Lord manifests a specific spiritual quality for the benefit of each living entity. Since there are innumerable living entities within the confines of the material creation, the Lord manifests infinite qualities. Thus every conditioned soul can appreciate the Supreme Lord in a particular way.

The example is given here that even if the most learned scholars could someday count the particles of earth, snow and light, they would still fail to understand the qualities of the Lord. In this example earth, snow and light are progressively more subtle; thus it is to be understood that there is an increasing difficulty in counting their virtually infinite particles.

According to Śrīla Viśvanātha Cakravartī Ṭhākura, great personalities like Lord Saṅkarṣaṇa actually *have* counted the number of atoms on the earth, and even the molecules in the entire universe. Yet even such a personality as Saṅkarṣaṇa, who has been continuously chanting the glories of the Lord since time immemorial, has not even approached a final count of those glories.

Lord Kṛṣṇa exhibits His most astonishing qualities during His childhood pastimes in Vṛndāvana, where He steals butter from the cowherd ladies, dances with His girlfriends, and plays with His cowherd boyfriends as their most dear companion. Although appearing like ordinary human activities, such sublime pastimes embody Lord Kṛṣṇa's immeasurable and innumerable beautiful transcendental qualities, which are the life and soul of the pure devotees.

TEXT 8

तत्तेऽनुकम्पां सुसमीक्षमाणो
भुञ्जान एवात्मकृतं विपाकम् ।
हृद्वाग्वपुर्भिर्विदधन्नमस्ते
जीवेत यो मुक्तिपदे स दायभाक् ॥ ८ ॥

tat te'nukampāṁ su-samīkṣamāṇo
bhuñjāna evātma-kṛtaṁ vipākam
hṛd-vāg-vapurbhir vidadhan namas te
jīveta yo mukti-pade sa dāya-bhāk

tat—therefore; *te*—Your; *anukampām*—compassion; *su-samīkṣamāṇaḥ*—earnestly hoping for; *bhuñjānaḥ*—enduring; *eva*—certainly; *ātma-kṛtam*—done by himself; *vipākam*—the fruitive results; *hṛt*—with his heart; *vāk*—words; *vapurbhiḥ*—and body; *vidadhan*—offering; *namaḥ*—obeisances; *te*—unto You; *jīveta*—lives; *yaḥ*—anyone who; *mukti-pade*—to the position of liberation; *saḥ*—he; *dāya-bhāk*—the rightful heir.

TRANSLATION

My dear Lord, one who earnestly waits for You to bestow Your causeless mercy upon him, all the while patiently suffering the reactions of his past misdeeds and offering You respectful obeisances with his heart, words and body, is surely eligible for liberation, for it has become his rightful claim.

PURPORT

Śrīla Śrīdhara Svāmī explains in his commentary that just as a legitimate son has to simply remain alive to gain an inheritance from his father, one who simply remains alive in Kṛṣṇa consciousness, following the regulative principles of *bhakti-yoga,* automatically becomes eligible to receive the mercy of the Personality of Godhead. In other words, he will be promoted to the kingdom of God.

The word *su-samīkṣamāṇa* indicates that a devotee earnestly awaits the mercy of the Supreme Lord even while suffering the painful effects of previous sinful activities. Lord Kṛṣṇa explains in the *Bhagavad-gītā* that a devotee who fully surrenders unto Him is no longer liable to suffer the reactions of his previous *karma.* However, because in his mind a devotee may still maintain the remnants of his previous sinful mentality, the Lord removes the last vestiges of the enjoying spirit by giving His devotee punishments that may sometimes resemble sinful reactions. The purpose of the entire creation of God is to rectify the living entity's tendency to enjoy without the Lord, and therefore the particular punishment given for a sinful activity is specifically designed to curtail the mentality that produced the activity. Although a devotee has surrendered to the Lord's devotional service, until he is completely perfect in Kṛṣṇa consciousness he may maintain a slight inclination to enjoy the false happiness of this world. The Lord therefore creates a particular situation to eradicate this remaining enjoying spirit. This unhappiness suffered by a sincere devotee is not technically a karmic reaction; it is rather the Lord's special mercy for inducing His devotee to completely let go of the material world and return home, back to Godhead.

A sincere devotee earnestly desires to go back to the Lord's abode. Therefore he willingly accepts the Lord's merciful punishment and continues offering respects and obeisances to the Lord with his heart, words and body. Such a bona fide servant of the Lord, considering all hardship a small price to pay for gaining the personal association of the Lord, certainly becomes a legitimate son of God, as indicated here by the words *dāya-bhāk.* Just as one cannot approach the sun without becoming fire, one cannot approach the supreme pure, Lord Kṛṣṇa, without undergoing a rigid purificatory process, which may appear like suffering but which is in fact a curative treatment administered by the personal hand of the Lord.

TEXT 9

पश्येश मेऽनार्यमनन्त आद्ये
परात्मनि त्वय्यपि मायिमायिनि ।
मायां वितत्येक्षितुमात्मवैभवं
ह्यहं कियानैच्छमिवार्चिरग्नौ ॥ ९ ॥

paśyeśa me'nāryam ananta ādye
parātmani tvayy api māyi-māyini
māyāṁ vitatyekṣitum ātma-vaibhavaṁ
hy ahaṁ kiyān aiccham ivārcir agnau

paśya—just see; *īśa*—O Lord; *me*—my; *anāryam*—contemptible behavior; *anante*—against the unlimited; *ādye*—the primeval; *para-ātmani*—the Supersoul; *tvayi*—You; *api*—even; *māyi-māyini*—for the masters of illusion; *māyām*—(my) illusory potency; *vitatya*—spreading; *īkṣitum*—to see; *ātma*—Your; *vaibhavam*—power; *hi*—indeed; *aham*—I; *kiyān*—how much; *aiccham*—I desired; *iva*—just like; *arciḥ*—a small spark; *agnau*—in comparison to the whole fire.

TRANSLATION

My Lord, just see my uncivilized impudence! To test Your power I tried to extend my illusory potency to cover You, the unlimited and primeval

Supersoul, who bewilder even the masters of illusion. What am I compared to You? I am just like a small spark in the presence of a great fire.

PURPORT

A great fire produces many sparks, which are insignificant in comparison to it. Indeed, if one of the small sparks were to try to burn the original fire, the attempt would be simply ludicrous. Similarly, even the creator of the entire universe, Lord Brahmā, is an insignificant spark of the potency of God, and therefore Brahmā's attempt to bewilder the Supreme Lord was certainly ludicrous.

Brahmā here addresses Lord Kṛṣṇa as *īśa,* which indicates that Kṛṣṇa is not only the supreme master of everyone but is also specifically the master of Brahmā, who creates the universe directly under the guidance of the Lord and who, indeed, is born directly from the Lord's own body.

Brahmā felt ashamed of his impudent attempt at deluding Lord Kṛṣṇa, and he was therefore perfectly willing to be punished or forgiven by the Lord, according to His decision. If Lord Kṛṣṇa does not mercifully punish His devotees when they act improperly, their foolishness will simply increase and gradually completely overwhelm their devotional sentiments. Therefore Lord Kṛṣṇa kindly disciplines His devotees and maintains them on the progressive path back home, back to Godhead.

TEXT 10

अतः क्षमस्वाच्युत मे रजोभुवो
ह्यजानतस्त्वत्पृथगीशमानिनः ।
अजावलेपान्धतमोऽन्धचक्षुष
एषोऽनुकम्प्यो मयि नाथवानिति ॥ १० ॥

ataḥ kṣamasvācyuta me rajo-bhuvo
hy ajānatas tvat-pṛthag-īśa-māninaḥ
ajāvalepāndha-tamo-'ndha-cakṣuṣa
eṣo'nukampyo mayi nāthavān iti

ataḥ—therefore; *kṣamasva*—please excuse; *acyuta*—O infallible Lord; *me*—me; *rajaḥ-bhuvaḥ*—who have taken birth in the mode of passion; *hi*—indeed; *ajānataḥ*—being ignorant; *tvat*—from You; *pṛthak*—separate; *īśa*—a controller; *māninaḥ*—presuming myself; *aja*—the unborn creator; *avalepa*—the covering; *andha-tamaḥ*—by such darkness of ignorance;

andha—blinded; *cakṣuṣaḥ*—my eyes; *eṣaḥ*—this person; *anukampyaḥ*—should be shown mercy; *mayi*—Me; *nātha-vān*—having as his master; *iti*—thus thinking.

TRANSLATION

Therefore, O infallible Lord, kindly excuse my offenses. I have taken birth in the mode of passion and am therefore simply foolish, presuming myself a controller independent of Your Lordship. My eyes are blinded by the darkness of ignorance, which causes me to think of myself as the unborn creator of the universe. But please consider that I am Your servant and therefore worthy of Your compassion.

PURPORT

In his commentary, Śrīla Viśvanātha Cakravartī Ṭhākura explains that Brahmā wanted to present the following argument to the Lord: "My dear Lord, because I have acted so badly I certainly deserve to be punished. On the other hand, because I am so ignorant You should consider me an innocent fool and be merciful to me. Thus, although I deserve both punishment and forgiveness, I humbly beg You to exercise tolerance in this matter and simply forgive me and show me Your mercy."

The words *nāthavān iti* indicate that Lord Brahmā wanted to humbly remind Lord Kṛṣṇa that He was, after all, Brahmā's father and master and should therefore forgive the unfortunate transgressions of His humble servant. Every conditioned soul, whether he be Lord Brahmā or an insignificant ant, falsely identifies himself with the material world and in this way forgets his eternal relationship with the Supreme Personality of Godhead. Lord Brahmā, because of his prestigious position as the cosmic creator, also tends to identify himself as the lord of this world, and thus he sometimes forgets his position as an insignificant servant of the Supreme Lord. Now, by Lord Kṛṣṇa's mercy, this false identification is being rectified and Lord Brahmā is remembering his constitutional position as the eternal servant of God.

TEXT 11

क्वाहं तमोमहदहंखचराग्निवार्भू-
संवेष्टिताण्डघटसप्तवितस्तिकायः ।
क्वेदृग्विधाविगणिताण्डपराणुचर्या-
वाताध्वरोमविवरस्य च ते महित्वम् ॥ ११ ॥

kvāhaṁ tamo-mahad-ahaṁ-kha-carāgni-vār-bhū-
saṁveṣṭitāṇḍa-ghaṭa-sapta-vitasti-kāyaḥ
kvedṛg-vidhāvigaṇitāṇḍa-parāṇu-caryā-
vātādhva-roma-vivarasya ca te mahitvam

kva—where; *aham*—I; *tamaḥ*—the material nature; *mahat*—the total material energy; *aham*—false ego; *kha*—ether; *cara*—air; *agni*—fire; *vāḥ*—water; *bhū*—earth; *saṁveṣṭita*—surrounded by; *aṇḍa-ghaṭa*—a potlike universe; *sapta-vitasti*—seven spans; *kāyaḥ*—body; *kva*—where; *īdṛk*—such; *vidhā*—like; *avigaṇita*—unlimited; *aṇḍa*—universes; *para-aṇu*—like the atomic dust; *caryā*—moving; *vāta-adhva*—airholes; *roma*—of hair on the body; *vivarasya*—of the holes; *ca*—also; *te*—Your; *mahitvam*—greatness.

TRANSLATION

What am I, a small creature measuring seven spans of my own hand? I am enclosed in a potlike universe composed of material nature, the total material energy, false ego, ether, air, water and earth. And what is Your glory? Unlimited universes pass through the pores of Your body just as particles of dust pass through the openings of a screened window.

PURPORT

In the *Caitanya-caritāmṛta, Ādi-līlā,* Chapter Five, Text 72, Śrīla Prabhupāda gives the following purport for this verse: "When Lord Brahmā, after having stolen all Kṛṣṇa's cows and cowherd boys, returned and saw that the cows and boys were still roaming with Kṛṣṇa, he offered this prayer in his defeat. A conditioned soul—even one so great as Brahmā, who manages the affairs of the entire universe—cannot compare to the Personality of Godhead, for He can produce numberless universes simply by the spiritual rays emanating from the pores of His body. Material scientists should take lessons from the utterances of Śrī Brahmā regarding our insignificance in comparison with God. In these prayers of Brahmā there is much to learn for those who are falsely puffed up by the accumulation of power."

In *Kṛṣṇa, the Supreme Personality of Godhead,* Chapter Fourteen, Śrīla Prabhupāda further comments on this verse: "Lord Brahmā realized his actual position. He is certainly the supreme teacher of this universe, in charge of the production of material nature, which consists of the complete material elements, false ego, sky, air, fire, water and earth. Such a universe may be gigantic, but it can be measured, just as we measure our body as seven spans. Generally, everyone's personal bodily measurement is calculated to be seven spans of his hand. This particular universe may appear to be a very gigantic body, but it is nothing but the measurement of seven spans for Lord Brahmā."

Aside from this universe, there are unlimited other universes outside the jurisdiction of this particular Lord Brahmā. Just as innumerable atomic infinitesimal fragments pass through the holes of a screened window, so millions and trillions of universes in their seedling form are coming out from the bodily pores of Mahā-Viṣṇu, and that Mahā-Viṣṇu is but a part of the plenary expansion of Kṛṣṇa. Under these circumstances, although Lord Brahmā is the supreme creature within this universe, what is his importance in the presence of Lord Kṛṣṇa?

TEXT 12

उत्क्षेपणं गर्भगतस्य पादयोः
किं कल्पते मातुरधोक्षजागसे ।
किमस्तिनास्तिव्यपदेशभूषितं
तवास्ति कुक्षेः कियदप्यनन्तः ॥ १२ ॥

utkṣepaṇaṁ garbha-gatasya pādayoḥ
kiṁ kalpate mātur adhokṣajāgase
kim asti-nāsti-vyapadeśa-bhūṣitaṁ
tavāsti kukṣeḥ kiyad apy anantaḥ

utkṣepaṇam—the kicking; *garbha-gatasya*—of a child in the womb; *pādayoḥ*—of the legs; *kim*—what; *kalpate*—amounts to; *mātuḥ*—for the mother; *adhokṣaja*—O transcendental Lord; *āgase*—as an offense; *kim*—what; *asti*—it exists; *na asti*—it does not exist; *vyapadeśa*—by the designations; *bhūṣitam*—decorated; *tava*—Your; *asti*—there is, *kukṣeḥ*—of the abdomen; *kiyat*—how much; *api*—even; *anantaḥ*—external.

TRANSLATION

O Lord Adhokṣaja, does a mother take offense when the child within her womb kicks with his legs? And is there anything in existence—whether designated by various philosophers as real or as unreal—that is actually outside Your abdomen?

PURPORT

Śrīla Prabhupāda comments as follows on this verse in *Kṛṣṇa, the Supreme Personality of Godhead,* Chapter Fourteen: "Lord Brahmā therefore compared himself to a little child within the womb of his mother. If the child within the womb plays with his hands and legs, and while playing touches the body of the mother, is the mother offended with the child? Of course she isn't. Similarly, Lord Brahmā may be a very great personality, and yet not only Brahmā but everything that exists is within the womb of the Supreme Personality of Godhead. The Lord's energy is all-pervading: there is no place in the creation where it is not acting. Since everything is existing within the energy of the Lord, so the Brahmā of this universe or the Brahmās of the many other millions and trillions of universes are existing within the energy of the Lord. Therefore the Lord is considered to be the mother, and everything existing within the womb of the mother is considered to be the child. And the good mother is never offended with the child, even if he touches the body of the mother by kicking his legs."

TEXT 13

जगत्त्रयान्तोदधिसम्प्लवोदे
नारायणस्योदरनाभिनालात् ।
विनिर्गतोऽजस्त्विति वाङ् न वै मृषा
किंत्वीश्वर त्वन्न विनिर्गतोऽस्मि ॥ १३ ॥

jagat-trayāntodadhi-samplavode
nārāyaṇasyodara-nābhi-nālāt
vinirgato'jas tv iti vāṅ na vai mṛṣā
kintv īśvara tvan na vinirgato'smi

jagat-traya—of the three worlds; *anta*—in the dissolution; *udadhi*—of all the oceans; *samplava*—of the total deluge; *ude*—in the water; *nārāyaṇasya*—of the Supreme Personality of Godhead, Nārāyaṇa; *udara*—growing from the abdomen; *nābhi*—from the navel; *nālāt*—out of the lotus stem; *vinirgataḥ*—came out; *ajaḥ*—Brahmā; *tu*—indeed; *iti*—thus speaking; *vāk*—the words; *na*—are not; *vai*—certainly; *mṛṣā*—false; *kintu*—thus; *īśvara*—O Lord; *tvat*—from You; *na*—not; *vinirgataḥ*—specifically emanated; *asmi*—am I.

TRANSLATION

My dear Lord, it is said that when the three planetary systems are merged into the water at the time of dissolution, Your plenary portion,

Nārāyaṇa, lies down on the water, gradually a lotus flower grows from His navel, and Brahmā takes birth upon that lotus flower. Certainly, these words are not false. Thus am I not born from You?

PURPORT

Although every living being is a child of God, Lord Brahmā here makes a special claim because he takes birth on a lotus flower that emanates from the navel of Nārāyaṇa, the Personality of Godhead. Ultimately, all living beings are equally expansions of the transcendental body of the Supreme Lord. But Brahmā has an intimate relationship with the Lord because of the activities of universal creation, and so he uses the prefix *vi* in the word *vinirgata* to beg the Lord's special mercy. Lord Brahmā is called *aja* because he is not born from any mother but rather emanates directly from the body of the Lord. As Śrīla Prabhupāda states in *Kṛṣṇa, the Supreme Personality of Godhead:* "It is naturally concluded that the mother of Brahmā is Nārāyaṇa." On these grounds, Lord Brahmā is requesting special forgiveness for his offenses.

TEXT 14

नारायणस्त्वं न हि सर्वदेहिनाम्
आत्मास्यधीशाखिललोकसाक्षी ।
नारायणोऽङ्गं नरभूजलायनात्
तच्चापि सत्यं न तवैव माया ॥ १४ ॥

nārāyaṇas tvaṁ na hi sarva-dehinām
ātmāsy adhīśākhila-loka-sākṣī
nārāyaṇo 'ṅgaṁ nara-bhū-jalāyanāt
tac cāpi satyaṁ na tavaiva māyā

nārāyaṇaḥ—the Supreme Lord Nārāyaṇa; *tvam*—You; *na*—not; *hi*—whether; *sarva*—of all; *dehinām*—embodied living beings; *ātmā*—the Supersoul; *asi*—You are; *adhīśa*—O supreme controller; *akhila*—of all; *loka*—planets; *sākṣī*—the witness; *nārāyaṇaḥ*—Lord Śrī Nārāyaṇa; *aṅgam*—the expanded plenary portion; *nara*—from the Supreme Personality; *bhū*—originating; *jala*—of the water; *ayanāt*—because of being the manifesting source; *tat*—that (expansion); *ca*—and; *api*—indeed; *satyam*—true; *na*—not; *tava*—Your; *eva*—at all; *māyā*—illusory energy.

TRANSLATION

Are You not the original Nārāyaṇa, O supreme controller, since You are the Soul of every embodied being and the eternal witness of all created realms? Indeed, Lord Nārāyaṇa is Your expansion, and He is called Nārāyaṇa because He is the generating source of the primeval water of the universe. He is real, not a product of Your illusory Māyā.

PURPORT

In the *Caitanya-caritāmṛta, Ādi-līlā,* Chapter Two, Text 30, Śrīla Prabhupāda comments on this verse as follows: "This statement was spoken by Lord Brahmā in his prayers to Lord Kṛṣṇa after the Lord defeated him by displaying His mystic powers. Brahmā had tried to test Lord Kṛṣṇa to see if He was really the Supreme Personality of Godhead playing as a cowherd boy. Brahmā stole all the other boys and their cows from the pasturing grounds, but when he returned to the pastures he saw that all the boys and cows were still there, for Lord Kṛṣṇa, had created them all again. When Brahmā saw this mystic power of Lord Kṛṣṇa, he admitted defeat and offered prayers to the Lord, addressing Him as the proprietor and seer of everything in the creation and as the Supersoul who is within each and every living entity and is dear to all. Lord Kṛṣṇa is Nārāyaṇa, the father of Brahmā, because Lord Kṛṣṇa's plenary expansion Garbhodakaśāyī Viṣṇu, after placing Himself on the Garbha Ocean, created Brahmā from His own body. Mahā-Viṣṇu in the Causal Ocean and Kṣīrodakaśāyī Viṣṇu, the Supersoul in everyone's heart, are also transcendental expansions of the Supreme Truth."

In his commentary on this verse, Śrīla Sanātana Gosvāmī has elaborately explained the expansion of the Viṣṇu, or Nārāyaṇa, incarnations from the original form of Godhead, Lord Śrī Kṛṣṇa. The essence is that although Lord Brahmā was born from Lord Nārāyaṇa, Brahmā now understands that Nārāyaṇa is Himself a mere expansion of the original Personality of Godhead, Lord Śrī Kṛṣṇa.

TEXT 15

तच्चेज्जलस्थं तव सज्जगद्वपुः
किं मे न दृष्टं भगवंस्तदैव ।
किं वा सुदृष्टं हृदि मे तदैव
किं नो सपद्येव पुनर्व्यदर्शि ॥ १५ ॥

tac cej jala-sthaṁ tava saj jagad-vapuḥ
kiṁ me na dṛṣṭaṁ bhagavaṁs tadaiva
kiṁ vā su-dṛṣṭaṁ hṛdi me tadaiva
kiṁ no sapady eva punar vyadarśi

tat—that; *cet*—if; *jala-stham*—situated upon the water; *tava*—Your; *sat*—real; *jagat*—sheltering the entire universe; *vapuḥ*—the transcendental body; *kim*—why; *me*—by me; *na dṛṣṭam*—was not seen; *bhagavan*—O Supreme Lord; *tadā eva*—at that very time; *kim*—why; *vā*—or; *su-dṛṣṭam*—perfectly seen; *hṛdi*—within the heart; *me*—by me; *tadā eva*—just then; *kim*—why; *na*—not; *u*—on the other hand; *sapadi*—suddenly; *eva*—indeed; *punaḥ*—again; *vyadarśi*—was seen.

TRANSLATION

My dear Lord, if Your transcendental body, which shelters the entire universe, is actually lying upon the water, then why were You not seen by me when I searched for You? And why, though I could not envision You properly within my heart, did You then suddenly reveal Yourself?

PURPORT

Lord Brahmā here refers to his experience at the dawn of cosmic creation. As described in the Second Canto of *Śrīmad-Bhāgavatam,* Lord Brahmā took birth on the seat of a giant lotus whose stem emanated from the navel of Nārāyaṇa. Brahmā was bewildered as to his whereabouts, function and identity, and therefore he tried to trace out the source of the lotus stem, searching for clear information. Unable to find the Personality of Godhead, he returned to his seat and engaged in severe austerities, having been ordered to do so by the transcendental voice of the Lord, who could be heard but not seen. After long meditation, Brahmā saw the Lord but then again lost sight of Him. Thus Brahmā concludes that the transcendental body of the Personality of Godhead is not material but rather an eternal, spiritual form endowed with inconceivable mystic potencies. In other words, Lord Brahmā should not have challenged the Personality of Godhead, the Lord of all mystic power.

TEXT 16

अत्रैव मायाधमनावतारे
ह्यस्य प्रपञ्चस्य बहिः स्फुटस्य ।

कृत्स्नस्य चान्तर्जठरे जनन्या
मायात्वमेव प्रकटीकृतं ते ॥ १६ ॥

atraiva māyā-dhamanāvatāre
hy asya prapañcasya bahiḥ sphuṭasya
kṛtsnasya cāntar jaṭhare jananyā
māyātvam eva prakaṭī-kṛtaṁ te

atra—in this; *eva*—indeed; *māyā-dhamana*—O subduer of Māyā; *avatāre*—in the incarnation; *hi*—certainly; *asya*—of this; *prapañcasya*—created material manifestation; *bahiḥ*—externally; *sphuṭasya*—which is visible; *kṛtsnasya*—entire; *ca*—and; *antaḥ*—within; *jaṭhare*—Your abdomen; *jananyāḥ*—unto Your mother; *māyātvam*—Your bewildering potency; *eva*—indeed; *prakaṭī-kṛtam*—has been demonstrated; *te*—by You.

TRANSLATION

My dear Lord, in this incarnation You have proved that You are the supreme controller of Māyā. Although You are now within this universe, the whole universal creation is within Your transcendental body—a fact You demonstrated by exhibiting the universe within Your abdomen before Your mother, Yaśodā.

PURPORT

Lord Brahmā here describes the inconceivable spiritual potency of the Lord. We may find a pot within a house, but we can hardly expect to find the house within the same pot. By the Lord's spiritual potency, however, He can appear within this universe and simultaneously exhibit all the universes within His body. One may argue that since the universes seen by mother Yaśodā within Lord Kṛṣṇa's abdomen were within the Lord's body, they are different from the illusory material universes manifest externally. Here Lord Brahmā refutes that argument, however. Lord Kṛṣṇa is *māyā-dhamana,* the supreme controller of illusion. By the Lord's own supreme mystic potency, He can bewilder even illusion herself, and thus the Lord actually exhibited all the material universes within His body. This is *māyātvam,* the supreme bewildering potency of the Personality of Godhead.

TEXT 17

यस्य कुक्षाविदं सर्वं सात्मं भाति यथा तथा।
तत्त्वय्यपीह तत् सर्वं किमिदं मायया विना ॥ १७॥

yasya kukṣāv idaṁ sarvaṁ
sātmaṁ bhāti yathā tathā
tat tvayy apīha tat sarvaṁ
kim idaṁ māyayā vinā

yasya—of whom; *kukṣau*—within the abdomen; *idam*—this cosmic manifestation; *sarvam*—all; *sa-ātmam*—including Yourself; *bhāti*—is manifested; *yathā*—as; *tathā*—so; *tat*—that; *tvayi*—within You; *api*—although; *iha*—here externally; *tat*—that cosmic manifestation; *sarvam*—whole; *kim*—what; *idam*—this; *māyayā*—the influence of Your inconceivable energy; *vinā*—without.

TRANSLATION

Just as this entire universe, including You, was exhibited within Your abdomen, so it is now manifested here externally in the same exact form. How could such things happen unless arranged by Your inconceivable energy?

PURPORT

Śrīla Prabhupāda comments on this verse as follows in *Kṛṣṇa, the Supreme Personality of Godhead:* "Lord Brahmā stressed herein that without accepting the inconceivable energy of the Supreme Personality of Godhead, one cannot explain things as they are."

TEXT 18

अद्यैव त्वदृतेऽस्य किं मम न ते मायात्वमादर्शितम्
एकोऽसि प्रथमं ततो व्रजसुहृद्वत्साः समस्ता अपि ।
तावन्तोऽसि चतुर्भुजास्तदखिलैः साकं मयोपासितास्
तावन्त्येव जगन्त्यभूस्तदमितं ब्रह्माद्वयं शिष्यते ॥ १८ ॥

adyaiva tvad ṛte'sya kiṁ mama na te māyātvam ādarśitam
eko'si prathamaṁ tato vraja-suhṛd-vatsāḥ samastā api
tāvanto'si catur-bhujās tad akhilaiḥ sākaṁ mayopāsitās
tāvanty eva jaganty abhūs tad amitaṁ brahmādvayaṁ śiṣyate

adya—today; *eva*—just; *tvat ṛte*—apart from You; *asya*—of this universe; *kim*—what; *mama*—to me; *na*—not; *te*—by You; *māyātvam*—the basis in Your inconceivable potency; *ādarśitam*—shown; *ekaḥ*—alone; *asi*

—You are; *prathamam*—first of all; *tataḥ*—then; *vraja-suhṛt*—Your cowherd boyfriends of Vṛndāvana; *vatsāḥ*—and the calves; *samastāḥ*—all; *api*—even; *tāvantaḥ*—of the same number; *asi*—You became; *catuḥ-bhujāḥ*—four-handed forms of Lord Viṣṇu; *tat*—then; *akhilaiḥ*—by all; *sākam*—together with; *mayā*—myself; *upāsitāḥ*—being worshiped; *tāvanti*—of the same number; *eva*—also; *jaganti*—universes; *abhūḥ*—You became; *tat*—then; *amitam*—the unlimited; *brahma*—Absolute Truth; *advayam*—one without a second; *śiṣyate*—You now remain.

TRANSLATION

Have You not shown me today that both You Yourself and everything within this creation are manifestations of Your inconceivable potency? First You appeared alone, and then You manifested Yourself as all of Vṛndāvana's calves and cowherd boys, Your friends. Next You appeared as an equal number of four-handed Viṣṇu forms, who were worshiped by all living beings, including me, and after that You appeared as an equal number of complete universes. Finally, You have now returned to Your unlimited form as the Supreme Absolute Truth, one without a second.

PURPORT

As stated in the Vedic literature, *sarvaṁ khalv idaṁ brahma:* everything that exists is an expansion of the Supreme Personality of Godhead. Thus everything is ultimately part and parcel of the Lord's spiritual existence. By Lord Kṛṣṇa's causeless mercy, Lord Brahmā personally experienced that all existence, being the potency of God, is nondifferent from Him.

TEXT 19

अजानतां त्वत्पदवीमनात्मन्य्
आत्मात्मना भासि वितत्य मायाम्।
सृष्टाविवाहं जगतो विधान
इव त्वमेषोऽन्त इव त्रिनेत्रः ॥ १९ ॥

ajānatāṁ tvat-padavīm anātmany
ātmātmanā bhāsi vitatya māyām
sṛṣṭāv ivāhaṁ jagato vidhāna
iva tvam eṣo'nta iva trinetraḥ

ajānatām—to persons who are in ignorance; *tvat-padavīm*—of Your transcendental position; *anātmani*—in the material energy; *ātmā*—Yourself; *ātmanā*—by Yourself; *bhāsi*—appear; *vitatya*—expanding; *māyām*—Your inconceivable energy; *sṛṣṭau*—in the matter of creation; *iva*—as if; *aham*—I, Brahmā; *jagataḥ*—of the universe; *vidhāne*—in the maintenance; *iva*—as if; *tvam eṣaḥ*—Yourself; *ante*—in the annihilation; *iva*—as if; *tri-netraḥ*—Lord Śiva.

TRANSLATION

To persons ignorant of Your actual transcendental position, You appear as part of the material world, manifesting Yourself by the expansion of Your inconceivable energy. Thus for the creation of the universe You appear as me [Brahmā], for its maintenance You appear as Yourself [Viṣṇu], and for its annihilation You appear as Lord Trinetra [Śiva].

PURPORT

Although the impersonal Māyāvādī philosophers think that the demigods are illusory, Lord Brahmā, Lord Śiva and Lord Viṣṇu are stated here to be expansions of the Supreme Personality of Godhead and are thus real. Indeed, they are the extraordinarily powerful controllers of the universe. The ultimate truth is a supreme and beautiful person, and thus throughout the creation of God we will always find the personal touch.

TEXT 20

सुरेष्वृषिष्वीश तथैव नृष्वपि
तिर्यक्षु यादःस्वपि तेऽजनस्य ।
जन्मासतां दुर्मदनिग्रहाय
प्रभो विधातः सदनुग्रहाय च ॥ २० ॥

sureṣv ṛṣiṣv īśa tathaiva nṛṣv api
tiryakṣu yādaḥsv api te'janasya
janmāsatāṁ durmada-nigrahāya
prabho vidhātaḥ sad-anugrahāya ca

sureṣu—among the demigods; *ṛṣiṣu*—among the great sages; *īśa*—O Lord; *tathā*—as well as; *eva*—indeed; *nṛṣu*—among the human beings; *api*—and; *tiryakṣu*—among animals; *yādaḥsu*—among aquatics; *api*—also; *te*—of You; *ajanasya*—who never takes material birth; *janma*—the birth;

asatām—of the nondevotees; *durmada*—the false pride; *nigrahāya*—for the purpose of subduing; *prabho*—O master; *vidhātaḥ*—O creator; *sat*—to the faithful devotees; *anugrahāya*—for the purpose of showing mercy; *ca*—and.

TRANSLATION

O Lord, O supreme creator and master, You have no material birth, yet to defeat the false pride of the faithless demons and show mercy to Your saintly devotees, You take birth among the demigods, sages, human beings, animals and even the aquatics.

PURPORT

Among the demigods Lord Kṛṣṇa appears in such forms as Vāmana-deva, among the sages as Paraśurāma, among human beings as Lord Kṛṣṇa Himself and as Lord Rāmacandra, and among animals as the boar incarnation. Lord Kṛṣṇa appears among the aquatics as Matsya, the gigantic fish. Indeed, the plenary expansions of the Supreme Personality of Godhead are innumerable, as the Lord relentlessly comes down within the universes to smash the false pride of the atheists and show mercy to the saintly devotees.

In another sense, the Lord never appears, since He exists eternally. His appearance is like that of the sun, which is always present in the sky but which periodically appears to our vision.

TEXT 21

को वेत्ति भूमन् भगवन् परात्मन्
योगेश्वरोतीर्भवतस्त्रिलोक्याम् ।
क्व वा कथं वा कति वा कदेति
विस्तारयन् क्रीडसि योगमायाम् ॥ २१ ॥

ko vetti bhūman bhagavan parātman
yogeśvarotīr bhavatas tri-lokyām
kva vā kathaṁ vā kati vā kadeti
vistārayan krīḍasi yoga-māyām

kaḥ—who; *vetti*—knows; *bhūman*—O supreme great one; *bhagavan*—O Supreme Personality of Godhead; *para-ātman*—O Supreme Soul; *yoga-īśvara*—O master of mystic power; *ūtīḥ*—the pastimes; *bhavataḥ*—of Your Lordship; *tri-lokyām*—in the three worlds; *kva*—where; *vā*—or; *katham*—

how; *vā*—or; *kati*—how many; *vā*—or; *kadā*—when; *iti*—thus; *vistārayan*—expanding; *krīḍasi*—You play; *yoga-māyām*—Your spiritual energy.

TRANSLATION

O supreme great one! O Supreme Personality of Godhead! O Supersoul, master of all mystic power! Your pastimes are taking place continuously in these three worlds, but who can estimate where, how and when You are employing Your spiritual energy and performing these innumerable pastimes? No one can understand the mystery of how Your spiritual energy acts.

PURPORT

Brahmā previously stated that Lord Kṛṣṇa incarnates among the demigods, human beings, animals, fish and so on. This does not mean, however, that the Lord is degraded by His incarnations. As Brahmā clarifies here, no conditioned soul can understand the transcendental nature of the Lord's activities, which He enacts through His spiritual potency. Although the Lord is *bhūman,* the supremely great one, He is still Bhagavān, the supremely beautiful personality exhibiting pastimes of love in His own abode. At the same time He is Paramātmā, the all-pervading Supersoul, who witnesses and sanctions all the activities of conditioned souls. The Lord's multiple identity is explained by the term *yogeśvara.* The Absolute Truth is the master of all mystic potencies, and although He is one and supreme, He manifests His greatness and opulence in many different ways.

Such elevated spiritual matters can hardly be understood by foolish persons primitively identifying themselves with the insignificant material body. These conditioned souls, such as atheistic scientists, consider their own puffed-up intelligence supreme. Gullibly placing their firm faith in material illusion, they are captured by the modes of nature and driven far away from knowledge of God.

TEXT 22

तस्मादिदं जगदशेषमसत्स्वरूपं
स्वप्नाभमस्तधिषणं पुरुदुःखदुःखम्।
त्वय्येव नित्यसुखबोधतनावनन्ते
मायात उद्यदपि यत् सदिवावभाति ॥ २२ ॥

tasmād idaṁ jagad aśeṣam asat-svarūpaṁ
svapnābham asta-dhiṣaṇaṁ puru-duḥkha-duḥkham
tvayy eva nitya-sukha-bodha-tanāv anante
māyāta udyad api yat sad ivāvabhāti

tasmāt—therefore; *idam*—this; *jagat*—cosmic manifestation; *aśeṣam*—entire; *asat-svarūpam*—whose existence is unreal in the sense of temporary; *svapna-ābham*—like a dream; *asta-dhiṣaṇam*—wherein awareness becomes covered over; *puru-duḥkha-duḥkham*—full of repeated miseries; *tvayi*—within You; *eva*—indeed; *nitya*—eternal; *sukha*—happy; *bodha*—conscious; *tanau*—whose personal appearances; *anante*—who is unlimited; *māyātaḥ*—by the illusory energy; *udyat*—coming forth; *api*—although; *yat*—which; *sat*—real; *iva*—as if; *avabhāti*—appears.

TRANSLATION

Therefore this entire universe, which like a dream is by nature unreal, nevertheless appears real, and thus it covers one's consciousness and assails one with repeated miseries. This universe appears real because it is manifested by the potency of illusion emanating from You, whose unlimited transcendental forms are full of eternal happiness and knowledge.

PURPORT

As an object of enjoyment or a permanent residence for the conditioned souls, the material universe is certainly illusion, nothing more than a dream. One may give the analogy that the vision of abundant water in a desert is no more than a dream, although real water exists elsewhere. Similarly, the vision of home, happiness and reality within matter is certainly no better than a foolish dream in which repeated miseries appear.

In another sense, however, the universe is real. In his commentary on *Vedanta-sūtra,* Śrīla Madhvācārya has confirmed this by quoting the following statement from the Vedic *śruti-mantras: satyaṁ hy evedaṁ viśvam asṛjata.* "This universe, created by the Lord, is real." The perfect authority of the *Vedas* thus certifies this universe to be real; nevertheless, because our knowledge is stolen by illusion (as indicated here by the words *asta-dhiṣaṇam*), we cannot properly understand this universe or the Supreme Lord who has created it. As the expansion of Lord Kṛṣṇa, the universe is real and is meant for being engaged in His service. One who accepts the kingdom of God as home, the Lord Himself as the object of love, and the material universe as paraphernalia for being engaged in the Lord's service dwells within eternal reality wherever he may go within the material and spiritual worlds.

TEXT 23

एकस्त्वमात्मा पुरुषः पुराणः
सत्यः स्वयंज्योतिरनन्त आद्यः ।
नित्योऽक्षरोऽजस्रसुखो निरञ्जनः
पूर्णाद्वयो मुक्त उपाधितोऽमृतः ॥ २३ ॥

ekas tvam ātmā puruṣaḥ purāṇaḥ
satyaḥ svayaṁ-jyotir ananta ādyaḥ
nityo'kṣaro'jasra-sukho nirañjanaḥ
pūrṇādvayo mukta upādhito'mṛtaḥ

ekaḥ—one; *tvam*—You; *ātmā*—the Supreme Soul; *puruṣaḥ*—the Supreme Person; *purāṇaḥ*—the oldest; *satyaḥ*—the Absolute Truth; *svayam-jyotiḥ*—self-manifested; *anantaḥ*—without end; *ādyaḥ*—without beginning; *nityaḥ*—eternal; *akṣaraḥ*—indestructible; *ajasra-sukhaḥ*—whose happiness cannot be obstructed; *nirañjanaḥ*—devoid of contamination; *pūrṇa*—complete; *advayaḥ*—without a second; *muktaḥ*—free; *upādhitaḥ*—from all material designations; *amṛtaḥ*—deathless.

TRANSLATION

You are the one Supreme Soul, the primeval Supreme Personality, the Absolute Truth—self-manifested, endless and beginningless. You are eternal and infallible, perfect and complete, without any rival and free from all material designations. Your happiness can never be obstructed, nor have You any connection with material contamination. Indeed, You are the indestructible nectar of immortality.

PURPORT

Śrīla Śrīdhara Svāmī explains how the various terms of this verse demonstrate that the transcendental body of Lord Kṛṣṇa is free from the characteristics of material bodies. All material bodies go through six phases: birth, growth, maturity, reproduction, decline and destruction. But Lord Kṛṣṇa does not take material birth, since He is the original reality, a fact clearly indicated here by the word *ādya,* "original." We take our material birth within a particular material atmosphere, in material bodies that are amalgamations of various material elements. Since Lord Kṛṣṇa existed long before the creation of any material atmosphere or element, there is no question of material birth for His transcendental body.

Similarly, the word *pūrṇa,* meaning "full and complete," refutes the concept that Lord Kṛṣṇa could grow, since He is ever-existing in fullness. When one's material body becomes mature, one can no longer enjoy as in youth; but the words *ajasra-sukha,* "enjoying unobstructed happiness," indicate that Lord Kṛṣṇa's body never reaches so-called middle age, since it is always full of spiritual youthful bliss. The word *akṣara,* "undiminishing," refutes the possibility that Lord Kṛṣṇa's body grows old or declines, and the word *amṛta,* "immortal" negates the possibility of death.

In other words, Lord Kṛṣṇa's transcendental body is free from the transformations of material bodies. The Lord does, however, create innumerable worlds and expand Himself as innumerable living entities. But the Lord's so-called reproduction is completely spiritual and does not take place at a certain phase of bodily existence; rather, it constitutes the Lord's eternal proclivity to expand His spiritual bliss and glories.

As the Lord states in *śruti, pūrvam evāham ihāsam:* "I alone existed in the beginning." Therefore here the Lord is called *puruṣaḥ purāṇaḥ,* "the primeval enjoyer." This original *puruṣa* expands Himself as the Supersoul and enters every living being. Still, He is ultimately the Absolute Truth, Kṛṣṇa, as stated in the *Gopāla-tāpanī Upaniṣad: yaḥ sākṣāt para-brahmeti govindaṁ sac-cid-ānanda-vigrahaṁ vṛndāvana-sura-bhūruha-talāsīnam.* "The Absolute Truth Himself is Govinda, who has an eternal form of bliss and knowledge and who is sitting beneath the shady desire trees of Vṛndāvana." This Absolute Truth is beyond material ignorance and beyond even ordinary spiritual knowledge, as stated in the same *Gopāla-tāpanī śruti: vidyāvidyābhyāṁ bhinnaḥ.* Thus, in many ways the supremacy of Lord Kṛṣṇa has been established in the Vedic literature, and it is here confirmed by Lord Brahmā himself.

TEXT 24

एवंविधं त्वां सकलात्मनामपि
स्वात्मानमात्मात्मतया विचक्षते ।
गुर्वर्कलब्धोपनिषत्सुचक्षुषा
ये ते तरन्तीव भवानृताम्बुधिम् ॥ २४ ॥

evaṁ-vidhaṁ tvāṁ sakalātmanām api
svātmānam ātmātmatayā vicakṣate
gurv-arka-labdhopaniṣat-sucakṣuṣā
ye te tarantīva bhavānṛtāmbudhim

evam-vidham—as thus described; *tvām*—You; *sakala*—of all; *ātmanām*—souls; *api*—indeed; *sva-ātmānam*—the very Soul; *ātma-ātmatayā*—as the Supersoul; *vicakṣate*—they see; *guru*—from the spiritual master; *arka*—who is like the sun; *labdha*—received; *upaniṣat*—of confidential knowledge; *su-cakṣuṣā*—by the perfect eye; *ye*—who; *te*—they; *taranti*—cross over; *iva*—easily; *bhava*—of material existence; *anṛta*—which is not real; *ambudhim*—the ocean.

TRANSLATION

Those who have received the clear vision of knowledge from the sunlike spiritual master can see You in this way, as the very Soul of all souls, the Supersoul of everyone's own self. Thus understanding Your original personality, they are able to cross over the ocean of illusory material existence.

PURPORT

As confirmed in the *Bhagavad-gītā* (4.9):

janma karma ca me divyam
evaṁ yo vetti tattvataḥ
tyaktvā dehaṁ punar janma
naiti mām eti so'rjuna

"One who knows the transcendental nature of My appearance and activities does not, upon leaving the body, take his birth again in this material world, but attains My eternal abode, O Arjuna."

TEXT 25

आत्मानमेवात्मतयाविजानतां
तेनैव जातं निखिलं प्रपञ्चितम् ।
ज्ञानेन भूयोऽपि च तत् प्रलीयते
रज्ज्वामहेर्भोगभवाभवौ यथा ॥ २५ ॥

ātmānam evātmatayāvijānatāṁ
tenaiva jātaṁ nikhilaṁ prapañcitam

jñānena bhūyo'pi ca tat pralīyate
rajjvām aher bhoga-bhavābhavau yathā

ātmānam—Yourself; *eva*—indeed; *ātmatayā*—as the Supreme Soul; *avijānatām*—for those who do not understand; *tena*—by that; *eva*—alone; *jātam*—is generated; *nikhilam*—the entire; *prapañcitam*—material existence; *jñānena*—by knowledge; *bhūyaḥ api*—once again; *ca*—and; *tat*—that material existence; *pralīyate*—disappears; *rajjvām*—within a rope; *aheḥ*—of a snake; *bhoga*—of the body; *bhava-abhavau*—the apparent appearance and disappearance; *yathā*—just as.

TRANSLATION

A person who mistakes a rope for a snake becomes fearful, but he then gives up his fear upon realizing that the so-called snake does not exist. Similarly, for those who fail to recognize You as the Supreme Soul of all souls, the expansive illusory material existence arises, but knowledge of You at once causes it to subside.

PURPORT

Those submerged in illusion see material existence as infinite, just as one who is submerged in water sees only water all around him. For example, material scientists and philosophers, submerged deep within the ocean of material illusion, imagine that material nature extends infinitely in all directions. In fact, the material creation is a finite ocean of ignorance in which foolish living entities, such as material scientists, are unceremoniously dunked by the order of the Supreme Personality of Godhead.

To be trapped in a world in which all things are born and die is certainly a fearful experience. Anyone trapped in a dark place naturally becomes fearful. Since material life is always covered by the darkness of ignorance, every conditioned soul is fearful. The material nature is not ultimate reality, and thus analysis of matter can never provide answers to ultimate questions. This dark, snakelike existence called material life immediately disappears as soon as one opens his eyes to the bright light of Kṛṣṇa consciousness.

TEXT 26

अज्ञानसंज्ञौ भवबन्धमोक्षौ
द्वौ नाम नान्यौ स्त ऋतज्ञभावात् ।

अजस्रचित्यात्मनि केवले परे
विचार्यमाणे तरणाविवाहनी ॥ २६ ॥

ajñāna-saṁjñau bhava-bandha-mokṣau
dvau nāma nānyau sta ṛta-jña-bhāvāt
ajasra-city ātmani kevale pare
vicāryamāṇe taraṇāv ivāhanī

ajñāna—manifesting from ignorance; *saṁjñau*—which designations; *bhava-bandha*—bondage to material existence; *mokṣau*—and liberation; *dvau*—the two; *nāma*—indeed; *na*—not; *anyau*—separate; *staḥ*—are; *ṛta*—true; *jña-bhāvāt*—from knowledge; *ajasra-citi*—whose awareness is unimpeded; *ātmani*—the spirit soul; *kevale*—who is separate from matter; *pare*—who is pure; *vicāryamāṇe*—when he is properly distinguished; *taraṇau*—within the sun; *iva*—just as; *ahanī*—day and night.

TRANSLATION

The conception of material bondage and the conception of liberation are both manifestations of ignorance. Being outside the scope of true knowledge, they cease to exist when one correctly understands that the pure spirit soul is distinct from matter and always fully conscious. At that time bondage and liberation no longer have any significance, just as day and night have no significance from the perspective of the sun.

PURPORT

Material bondage is illusion because the living entity actually has no real relationship with the material world. Because of false ego, the conditioned soul identifies himself with matter. Therefore so-called liberation is simply the giving up of an illusion rather than release from actual bondage. Yet even if we think that the suffering of material illusion is real and that liberation is thus a meaningful release from suffering, the mere absence of material existence is still insignificant compared to the achievement of factual spiritual life, which is the positive eternal reality opposed to the negative illusion of material life. Ultimately, Kṛṣṇa consciousness, or pure love of Godhead, is the only significant, meaningful and permanent status for every living entity.

Since the darkness of night is caused by the absence of the sun, one would not experience night within the sun itself, nor would one experience individual days separated by nights. Similarly, within the pure living entity there is no material darkness and thus no experience of liberation from such darkness. When the conditioned soul comes to this platform of pure consciousness, he becomes fit to associate with the supreme pure, the Personality of Godhead Himself, in the Lord's own abode.

TEXT 27

त्वामात्मानं परं मत्वा परमात्मानमेव च।
आत्मा पुनर्बहिर्मृग्य अहोऽज्ञजनताज्ञता॥ २७॥

tvām ātmānaṁ paraṁ matvā
param ātmānam eva ca
ātmā punar bahir mṛgya
aho'jña-janatājñatā

tvām—You; *ātmānam*—the real self; *param*—something else; *matvā*—thinking; *param*—something else; *ātmānam*—Yourself; *eva*—indeed; *ca*—also; *ātmā*—the Supreme Self; *punaḥ*—again; *bahiḥ*—outside; *mṛgyaḥ*—must be searched out; *aho*—oh; *ajña*—ignorant; *janatā*—of persons; *ajñatā*—the ignorance.

TRANSLATION

Just see the foolishness of those ignorant persons who consider You to be some separated manifestation of illusion and who consider the self, which is actually You, to be something else, the material body. Such fools conclude that the supreme soul is to be searched for somewhere outside Your supreme personality.

PURPORT

Lord Brahmā is amazed at the gross ignorance of conditioned souls who consider Lord Kṛṣṇa's supreme spiritual body to be material. Ignorant of the spiritual form of the Lord, such persons also consider their own material bodies to be the self, and therefore they conclude that spiritual reality is to be found somewhere beyond the supreme personality of Lord Kṛṣṇa. Sometimes such fools consider Lord Kṛṣṇa to be one of many individual souls who together constitute a single impersonal spiritual entity. Unfortunately, such speculators are not inclined to hear from the Lord Himself or from the Lord's authorized representatives, such as Lord Brahmā. Because they whimsically speculate on the nature of the Supreme, their ultimate result is confusion and ignorance, which they euphemistically describe as "the mystery of life."

TEXT 28

अन्तर्भवेऽनन्त भवन्तमेव
ह्यतत्त्यजन्तो मृगयन्ति सन्तः ।
असन्तमप्यन्त्यहिमन्तरेण
सन्तं गुणं तं किमु यन्ति सन्तः ॥२८॥

antar-bhave'nanta bhavantam eva
hy atat tyajanto mṛgayanti santaḥ
asantam apy anty ahim antareṇa
santaṁ guṇaṁ taṁ kim u yanti santaḥ

antaḥ-bhave—within the body; *ananta*—O unlimited Lord; *bhavantam*—Yourself; *eva*—indeed; *hi*—certainly; *atat*—everything separate from You; *tyajantaḥ*—rejecting; *mṛgayanti*—search out; *santaḥ*—the saintly devotees; *asantam*—unreal; *api*—even; *anti*—present nearby; *ahim*—(the illusion of) a snake; *antareṇa*—without (negating); *santam*—real; *guṇam*—the rope; *tam*—that; *kim u*—whether; *yanti*—appreciate; *santaḥ*—persons who are spiritually situated.

TRANSLATION

O unlimited Lord, the saintly devotees seek You out within their own bodies by rejecting everything separate from You. Indeed, how can discriminating persons appreciate the real nature of a rope lying before them until they refute the illusion that it is a snake?

PURPORT

One may argue that a person should cultivate self-realization and at the same time pursue sense gratification for the material body. This proposition is herein refuted by the example of misidentifying a rope as a snake. One who mistakes a rope for a snake becomes fearful and thinks of the so-called snake. But upon discovering that the so-called snake is actually a rope, he experiences a different emotion—relief—and can then ignore the rope. Similarly, because we misunderstand the material body to be the self, we are experiencing many emotions in relation to the body. Upon discovering, however, that the body is simply a bag of material chemicals, we carefully note how this illusion was created and then lose interest in the body. Discovering that we are actually an eternal soul within the body, we naturally focus our attention on that real self.

Those who are saintly and wise always cultivate Kṛṣṇa consciousness, spiritual knowledge, having transcended the foolish misidentification of the body as the self. Such Kṛṣṇa conscious persons go on to realize the Supreme Personality of Godhead, who dwells within the material body as the Supersoul—the witness and guide of every living entity. Realization of the Supersoul and the individual soul is so pleasing and satisfying that a self-realized person automatically gives up everything irrelevant to his spiritual advancement.

TEXT 29

अथापि ते देव पदाम्बुजद्वय-
प्रसादलेशानुगृहीत एव हि ।
जानाति तत्त्वं भगवन्महिम्नो
न चान्य एकोऽपि चिरं विचिन्वन् ॥ २९ ॥

athāpi te deva padāmbuja-dvaya-
prasāda-leśānugṛhīta eva hi
jānāti tattvaṁ bhagavan-mahimno
na cānya eko'pi ciraṁ vicinvan

atha—therefore; *api*—indeed; *te*—Your; *deva*—my Lord; *pada-ambuja-dvaya*—of the two lotus feet; *prasāda*—of the mercy; *leśa*—by only a trace; *anugṛhītaḥ*—favored; *eva*—certainly; *hi*—indeed; *jānāti*—one knows; *tattvam*—the truth; *bhagavat*—of the Supreme Personality of Godhead; *mahimnaḥ*—of the greatness; *na*—never; *ca*—and; *anyaḥ*—another; *ekaḥ*—one; *api*—although; *ciram*—for a long period; *vicinvan*—speculating.

TRANSLATION

My Lord, if one is favored by even a slight trace of the mercy of Your lotus feet, he can understand the greatness of Your personality. But those who speculate to understand the Supreme Personality of Godhead are unable to know You, even though they continue to study the Vedas for many years.

PURPORT

This translation is quoted from Śrīla Prabhupāda's *Caitanya-caritāmṛta, Madhya-līla,* Chapter Six, Text 84.

Lord Kṛṣṇa is very eager to bestow His mercy upon the conditioned living beings, who are uselessly struggling with the Lord's illusory energy, Māyā. The conditioned soul struggles for happiness through sense gratification and for knowledge through mental speculation. Both processes ultimately bring him to a morose and hopeless condition. If the conditioned soul surrenders to the lotus feet of Lord Kṛṣṇa and thus acquires even a trace of His causeless mercy, the whole situation is changed, and the living entity can begin his real life of bliss and knowledge in Kṛṣṇa consciousness.

TEXT 30

तदस्तु मे नाथ स भूरिभागो
भवेऽत्र वान्यत्र तु वा तिरश्चाम् ।
येनाहमेकोऽपि भवज्जनानां
भूत्वा निषेवे तव पादपल्लवम् ॥ ३० ॥

tad astu me nātha sa bhūri-bhāgo
bhave'tra vānyatra tu vā tiraścām
yenāham eko'pi bhavaj-janānāṁ
bhūtvā niṣeve tava pāda-pallavam

tat—therefore; *astu*—may it be; *me*—my; *nātha*—O master; *saḥ*—that; *bhūri-bhāgaḥ*—greatest good fortune; *bhave*—in the birth; *atra*—this; *vā*—or; *anyatra*—in some other birth; *tu*—indeed; *vā*—or; *tiraścām*—among the animals; *yena*—by which; *aham*—I; *ekaḥ*—one; *api*—even; *bhavat*—or Your; *janānām*—devotees; *bhūtvā*—becoming; *niṣeve*—I may fully engage in serving; *tava*—Your; *pāda-pallavam*—lotus feet.

TRANSLATION

My dear Lord, I therefore pray to be so fortunate that in this life as Lord Brahmā or in another life, wherever I take my birth, I may be counted as one of Your devotees. I pray that wherever I may be, even among the animal species, I can engage in devotional service to Your lotus feet.

TEXT 31

अहोऽतिधन्या व्रजगोरमण्यः
स्तन्यामृतं पीतमतीव ते मुदा ।
यासां विभो वत्सतरात्मजात्मना
यत्तृप्तयेऽद्यापि न चालमध्वराः ॥ ३१ ॥

aho 'ti-dhanyā vraja-go-ramaṇyaḥ
stanyāmṛtaṁ pītam atīva te mudā
yāsāṁ vibho vatsatarātmajātmanā
yat-tṛptaye 'dyāpi na cālam adhvarāḥ

aho—oh; *ati-dhanyāḥ*—most fortunate; *vraja*—of Vṛndāvana; *go*—the cows; *ramaṇyaḥ*—and the *gopīs; stanya*—the breast milk; *amṛtam*—which is like nectar; *pītam*—has been drunk; *atīva*—fully; *te*—by You; *mudā*—with satisfaction; *yāsām*—of whom; *vibho*—O almighty Lord; *vatsatara-āt-maja-ātmanā*—in the form of the calves and the sons of the cowherd women; *yat*—whose; *tṛptaye*—for the satisfaction; *adya api*—even until now; *na*—not; *ca*—and; *alam*—sufficient; *adhvarāḥ*—the Vedic sacrifices.

TRANSLATION

O almighty Lord, how greatly fortunate are the cows and ladies of Vṛndāvana, the nectar of whose breast milk You have happily drunk to Your full satisfaction, taking the form of their calves and children! All the Vedic sacrifices performed from time immemorial up to the present day have not given You as much satisfaction.

TEXT 32

अहो भाग्यमहो भाग्यं नन्दगोपव्रजौकसाम् ।
यन्मित्रं परमानन्दं पूर्णं ब्रह्म सनातनम् ॥ ३२ ॥

aho bhāgyam aho bhāgyaṁ
nanda-gopa-vrajaukasām
yan-mitraṁ paramānandaṁ
pūrṇaṁ brahma sanātanam

aho—what great; *bhāgyam*—fortune; *aho*—what great; *bhāgyam*—fortune; *nanda*—of Mahārāja Nanda; *gopa*—of the other cowherd men; *vraja-okasām*—of the inhabitants of Vrajabhūmi; *yat*—of whom; *mitram*—the friend; *parama-ānandam*—the supreme bliss; *pūrṇam*—complete; *brahma*—the Absolute Truth; *sanātanam*—eternal.

TRANSLATION

How greatly fortunate are Nanda Mahārāja, the cowherd men and all the other inhabitants of Vrajabhūmi! There is no limit to their good

fortune, because the Absolute Truth, the source of transcendental bliss, the eternal Supreme Brahman, has become their friend.

PURPORT

This translation is quoted from Śrīla Prabhupāda's *Caitanya-caritāmṛta, Madhya-līlā,* Chapter Six, Text 149.

TEXT 33

एषां तु भाग्यमहिमाच्युत तावदास्ताम्
एकादशैव हि वयं बत भूरिभागाः ।
एतद्धृषीकचषकैरसकृत् पिबामः
शर्वादयोऽङ्घ्र्युदजमध्वमृतासवं ते ॥ ३३ ॥

eṣāṁ tu bhāgya-mahimācyuta tāvad āstām
ekādaśaiva hi vayaṁ bata bhūri-bhāgāḥ
etad-dhṛṣīka-caṣakair asakṛt pibāmaḥ
śarvādayo 'ṅghry-udaja-madhv-amṛtāsavaṁ te

eṣām—of these (residents of Vṛndāvana); *tu*—however; *bhāgya*—of the good fortune; *mahimā*—the greatness; *acyuta*—O infallible Supreme Lord; *tāvat*—so much; *āstām*—let it be; *ekādaśa*—the eleven; *eva hi*—indeed; *vayam*—we; *bata*—oh; *bhūri-bhāgāḥ*—are most fortunate; *etat*—of these devotees; *hṛṣīka*—by the senses; *caṣakaiḥ*—(which are like) drinking cups; *asakṛt*—repeatedly; *pibāmaḥ*—we are drinking; *śarva-ādayaḥ*—Lord Śiva and the other chief demigods; *aṅghri-udaja*—of the lotus feet; *madhu*—the honey; *amṛta-āsavam*—which is a nectarean, intoxicating beverage; *te*—of You.

TRANSLATION

Yet even though the extent of the good fortune of these residents of Vṛndāvana is inconceivable, we eleven presiding deities of the various senses, headed by Lord Śiva, are also most fortunate, because the senses of these devotees of Vṛndāvana are the cups through which we repeatedly drink the nectarean, intoxicating beverage of the honey of Your lotus feet.

TEXT 34

तद् भूरिभाग्यमिह जन्म किमप्यटव्यां
यद् गोकुलेऽपि कतमाङ्घ्रिरजोऽभिषेकम् ।

यज्जीवितं तु निखिलं भगवान्मुकुन्दस्
त्वद्यापि यत्पदरजः श्रुतिमृग्यमेव ॥ ३४ ॥

tad bhūri-bhāgyam iha janma kim apy aṭavyāṁ
yad gokule'pi katamāṅghri-rajo-'bhiṣekam
yaj-jīvitaṁ tu nikhilaṁ bhagavān mukundas
tv adyāpi yat-pada-rajaḥ śruti-mṛgyam eva

tat—that; *bhūri-bhāgyam*—the greatest good fortune; *iha*—here; *janma*—the birth; *kim api*—any whatsoever; *aṭavyām*—in the forest (of Vṛndāvana); *yat*—which; *gokule*—in Gokula; *api*—even; *katama*—of any (of the devotees); *aṅghri*—of the feet; *rajaḥ*—by the dust; *abhiṣekam*—bathing; *yat*—whose; *jīvitam*—life; *tu*—indeed; *nikhilam*—whole; *bhagavān*—the Supreme Personality of Godhead; *mukundaḥ*—Lord Mukunda; *tu*—but; *adya api*—even until now; *yat*—whose; *pāda-rajaḥ*—dust of the feet; *śruti*—by the *Vedas; mṛgyam*—sought after; *eva*—certainly.

TRANSLATION

My greatest possible good fortune would be to take any birth whatever in this forest of Gokula and have my head bathed by the dust falling from the lotus feet of any of its residents. Their entire life and soul is the Supreme Personality of Godhead, Mukunda, the dust of whose lotus feet is still being searched for in the Vedic mantras.

PURPORT

This verse indicates that Lord Brahmā desires to take birth even as the smallest blade of grass in Vṛndāvana so that the holy residents of the Lord's abode may walk upon his head and bless him with the dust of their feet. Being realistic, Lord Brahmā does not aspire to directly achieve the dust of Lord Kṛṣṇa's feet; rather, he aspires for the mercy of the Lord's devotees. Śrīla Viśvanātha Cakravartī Ṭhākura explains that Brahmā is willing to take birth even as a stone in a paved footpath in the Lord's abode. Since Brahmā is the creator of the entire universe, we can just imagine the glorious position of the residents of Vṛndāvana.

The Lord's devotees achieve their exalted position by unalloyed devotion and love. One cannot achieve such spiritual opulence by any puffed-up material process of personal improvement. In *Kṛṣṇa, the Supreme Personality of Godhead,* Śrīla Prabhupāda reveals the mind of Brahmā as follows: "But if I am not so fortunate as to take birth within the forest of Vṛndāvana, I beg to be allowed to take birth outside the immediate area of Vṛndāvana so that when the devotees go out they will walk over me. Even that would be a great fortune for me. I am just aspiring for a birth in which I will be smeared by the dust of the devotees' feet."

TEXT 35

एषां घोषनिवासिनामुत भवान् किं देव रातेति नश्
चेतो विश्वफलात् फलं त्वदपरं कुत्राप्ययन्मुह्यति ।
सद्वेषादिव पूतनापि सकुला त्वामेव देवापिता
यद्धामार्थसुहृत्प्रियात्मतनयप्राणाशयास्त्वत्कृते ॥ ३५ ॥

eṣāṁ ghoṣa-nivāsinām uta bhavān kiṁ deva rāteti naś
ceto viśva-phalāt phalaṁ tvad-aparaṁ kutrāpy ayan muhyati
sad-veṣād iva pūtanāpi sa-kulā tvām eva devāpitā
yad-dhāmārtha-suhṛt-priyātma-tanaya-prāṇāśayās tvat-kṛte

eṣām—to these; *ghoṣa-nivāsinām*—residents of the cowherd community; *uta*—indeed; *bhavān*—Your Lordship; *kim*—what; *deva*—O Supreme Personality of Godhead; *rātā*—will give; *iti*—thinking thus; *naḥ*—our; *cetaḥ*—mind; *viśva-phalāt*—than the supreme source of all benedictions; *phalam*—a reward; *tvat*—than You; *aparam*—other; *kutra api*—anywhere; *ayat*—considering; *muhyati*—becomes bewildered; *sat-veṣāt*—by disguising herself as a devotee; *iva*—indeed; *pūtanā*—the demoness Pūtanā; *api*—even; *sa-kulā*—along with her family members, Bakāsura and Aghāsura; *tvām*—You; *eva*—certainly; *deva*—O Lord; *āpitā*—was made to attain; *yat*—whose; *dhāma*—homes; *artha*—wealth; *suhṛt*—friends; *priya*—dear relatives; *ātma*—bodies; *tanaya*—children; *prāṇa*—life air; *āśayāḥ*—and minds; *tvat-kṛte*—dedicated to You.

TRANSLATION

My mind becomes bewildered just trying to think of what reward other than You could be found anywhere. You are the embodiment of all benedictions, which You bestow upon these residents of the cowherd community of Vṛndāvana. You have already arranged to give Yourself to Pūtanā and her family members in exchange for her disguising herself as a devotee. So what is left for You to give these devotees of Vṛndāvana,

whose homes, wealth, friends, dear relations, bodies, children and very lives and hearts are all dedicated only to You?

TEXT 36

तावद् रागादयः स्तेनास्तावत् कारागृहं गृहम् ।
तावन्मोहोऽङ्घ्रिनिगडो यावत् कृष्ण न ते जनाः ॥ ३६ ॥

tāvad rāgādayaḥ stenās
tāvat kārā-gṛhaṁ gṛham
tāvan moho'ṅghri-nigaḍo
yāvat kṛṣṇa na te janāḥ

tāvat—for that long; *rāga-ādayaḥ*—material attachment and so on; *stenāḥ*—thieves; *tāvat*—for that long; *kārā-gṛham*—a prison; *gṛham*—one's home; *tāvat*—for that long; *mohaḥ*—the bewilderment of family affection; *aṅghri*—upon their feet; *nigaḍaḥ*—shackles; *yāvat*—as long as; *kṛṣṇa*—O Lord Kṛṣṇa; *na*—do not become; *te*—Your (devotees); *janāḥ*—any persons.

TRANSLATION

My dear Lord Kṛṣṇa, until people become Your devotees, their material attachments and desires remain thieves, their homes remain prisons, and their affectionate feelings for their family members remain foot-shackles.

PURPORT

Apparently, the residents of Vṛndāvana, the abode of Lord Kṛṣṇa, are simple householders engaged in ordinary affairs such as herding cows, cooking, rearing children and performing religious ceremonies. However, all these activities are intensely engaged in the loving service of Lord Kṛṣṇa. The residents of Vṛndāvana perform all activities in pure Kṛṣṇa consciousness and thus exist on the most exalted platform of liberated life. Otherwise, the same activities performed without Kṛṣṇa consciousness constitute ordinary bondage to the material world.

Thus, one should not misunderstand the exalted position of the residents of Vṛndāvana, nor should one consider oneself highly religious simply because one performs ordinary domestic affairs very enthusiastically, but without Kṛṣṇa consciousness. By focusing our passionate attachment on our family and society, we are completely deviated from the progressive path of Kṛṣṇa consciousness. Conversely, if we engage our family in the loving service of the Lord, our endeavors to maintain our family become part and parcel of our progressive spiritual duties.

In conclusion, by studying the extraordinary status of the residents of Vṛndāvana, we can see that the essential quality of their lives is pure Kṛṣṇa consciousness—the rendering of loving service to the Lord without a trace of material desire or mental speculation. Such loving service to the original Personality of Godhead immediately creates the atmosphere of Śrī Vṛndāvana-dhāma, the kingdom of God.

TEXT 37

प्रपञ्चं निष्प्रपञ्चोऽपि विडम्बयसि भूतले ।
प्रपन्नजनतानन्दसन्दोहं प्रथितुं प्रभो ॥ ३७ ॥

prapañcaṁ niṣprapañco'pi
viḍambayasi bhū-tale
prapanna-janatānanda-
sandohaṁ prathituṁ prabho

prapañcam—that which is material; *niṣprapañcaḥ*—completely transcendental to material existence; *api*—although; *viḍambayasi*—You imitate; *bhū-tale*—on the surface of the earth; *prapanna*—who are surrendered; *janatā*—of people; *ānanda-sandoham*—the great variety of different kinds of ecstasies; *prathitum*—in order to spread; *prabho*—O master.

TRANSLATION

My dear master, although You have nothing to do with material existence, You come to this earth and imitate material life just to expand the varieties of ecstatic enjoyment for Your surrendered devotees.

PURPORT

Śrīla Viśvanātha Cakravartī Ṭhākura points out that just as a lamp does not seem to shine as brightly in sunlight as it does in the shade, or as a diamond does not seem as brilliant on a silver platter as it does on a plate of blue glass, the Lord's pastimes as Govinda do not seem as amazing in the transcendental abode of Vaikuṇṭha as they do within the material realm of Māyā. Lord Kṛṣṇa comes to the earth and acts toward His pure devotees exactly like a devoted son, boyfriend, husband, father, friend and so on, and within the darkness of material existence these brilliant, liberated pastimes give unlimited ecstasy to the surrendered devotees of the Lord.

In his *Kṛṣṇa, the Supreme Personality of Godhead,* Śrīla Prabhupāda quotes Lord Brahmā as follows: "I can also understand that Your appearance as a small cowherd boy, a child of the cowherd men, is not at all a material activity. You are so much obliged by their affection that You are here to enthuse them with more loving service by Your transcendental presence."

TEXT 38

जानन्त एव जानन्तु किं बहूक्त्या न मे प्रभो ।
मनसो वपुषो वाचो वैभवं तव गोचरः ॥ ३८ ॥

jānanta eva jānantu
kiṁ bahūktyā na me prabho
manaso vapuṣo vāco
vaibhavaṁ tava go-caraḥ

jānantaḥ—persons who think they are aware of Your unlimited potency; *eva*—certainly; *jānantu*—let them think like that; *kim*—what is the use; *bahu-uktyā*—with many words; *na*—not; *me*—my; *prabho*—O Lord; *manasaḥ*—of the mind; *vapuṣaḥ*—of the body; *vācaḥ*—of the words; *vaibhavam*—opulences; *tava*—Your; *go-caraḥ*—within the range.

TRANSLATION

There are people who say, "I know everything about Kṛṣṇa." Let them think that way. As far as I am concerned, I do not wish to speak very much about this matter. O my Lord, let me say this much: As far as Your opulences are concerned, they are all beyond the reach of my mind, body and words.

PURPORT

This translation is quoted from Śrīla Prabhupāda's *Caitanya-caritāmṛta, Madhya-līla,* Chapter Twenty-one, Text 27.

TEXT 39

अनुजानीहि मां कृष्ण सर्वं त्वं वेत्सि सर्वदृक् ।
त्वमेव जगतां नाथो जगदेतत्तवार्पितम् ॥ ३९ ॥

anujānīhi māṁ kṛṣṇa
sarvaṁ tvaṁ vetsi sarva-dṛk
tvam eva jagatāṁ nātho
jagad etat tavārpitam

anujānīhi—please give leave; *mām*—to me; *kṛṣṇa*—O Lord Kṛṣṇa; *sarvam*—everything; *tvam*—You; *vetsi*—know; *sarva-dṛk*—all-seeing; *tvam*—You; *eva*—alone; *jagatām*—of all the universes; *nāthaḥ*—the master; *jagat*—universe; *etat*—this; *tava*—to You; *arpitam*—is offered.

TRANSLATION

My dear Kṛṣṇa, I now humbly request permission to leave. Actually, You are the knower and seer of all things. Indeed, You are the Lord of all the universes, and yet I offer this one universe unto You.

PURPORT

In his *Kṛṣṇa, the Supreme Personality of Godhead,* Śrīla Prabhupāda has quoted Lord Brahmā as follows: "My dear Lord,althoughYou are the Supreme Lord of all creation, I sometimes falsely think that I am the master of this universe. I may be master of this universe, but there are innumerable universes, and there are also innumerable Brahmās who preside over these universes. But actually You are the master of them all. As the Supersoul in everyone's heart, You know everything. Please, therefore, accept me as Your surrendered servant. I hope that You will excuse me for disturbing You in Your pastimes with Your friends and calves. Now if You will kindly allow me, I will immediately leave so You can enjoy Your friends and calves without my presence."

The words *sarvaṁ tvaṁ vetsi sarva-dṛk* are very significant here. Lord Kṛṣṇa knows everything and sees everything, and therefore Lord Brahmā did not need to remain in Vṛndāvana to maintain his personal loving contact with the Lord. In fact, as the creator of the universe, Lord Brahmā was somewhat out of place in the simple, blissful atmosphere of Vṛndāvana, where Lord Kṛṣṇa was exhibiting His supreme opulences in herding cows, enjoying picnics, playing games, and so on.

Upon seeing the intense love the residents of Vṛndāvana had for Lord Kṛṣṇa, Brahmā felt unqualified to remain there. He was not eager to give up the Lord's association, but he felt it better to return to his personal devotional service in Brahmaloka. Somewhat embarrassed and unhappy over his foolish attempt at bewildering the Lord, Brahmā preferred to resume his transcendental loving service rather than try to enjoy the Lord's presence.

TEXT 40

श्रीकृष्ण वृष्णिकुलपुष्करजोषदायिन्
क्ष्मानिर्जरद्विजपशूदधिवृद्धिकारिन् ।
उद्धर्मशार्वरहर क्षितिराक्षसध्रुग्
आकल्पमार्कमर्हन् भगवन्नमस्ते ॥ ४० ॥

śrī-kṛṣṇa vṛṣṇi-kula-puṣkara-joṣa-dāyin
kṣmā-nirjara-dvija-paśūdadhi-vṛddhi-kārin
uddharma-śārvara-hara kṣiti-rākṣasa-dhrug
ā-kalpam ārkam arhan bhagavan namas te

śrī-kṛṣṇa—O Lord Kṛṣṇa; *vṛṣṇi-kula*—of the Yadu dynasty; *puṣkara*—to the lotus; *joṣa*—pleasure; *dāyin*—O You who bestow; *kṣmā*—of the earth; *nirjara*—the demigods; *dvija*—the *brāhmaṇas; paśu*—and of the animals; *udadhi*—of the great oceans; *vṛddhi*—the increase; *kārin*—O You who cause; *uddharma*—of atheistic principles; *śārvara*—of the darkness; *hara*—O dispeller; *kṣiti*—upon the earth; *rākṣasa*—of the demons; *dhruk*—the opponent; *ā-kalpam*—until the end of the universe; *ā-arkam*—as long as the sun shines; *arhan*—O supremely worshipable Deity; *bhagavan*—O Supreme Personality of Godhead; *namaḥ*—I offer my respectful obeisances; *te*—unto You.

TRANSLATION

My dear Śrī Kṛṣṇa, You bestow happiness upon the lotuslike Vṛṣṇi dynasty and expand the great oceans consisting of the earth, the demigods, the brāhmaṇas and the cows. You dispel the dense darkness of irreligion and oppose the demons who have appeared on this earth. O Supreme Personality of Godhead, as long as this universe exists and as long as the sun shines, I will offer my obeisances unto You.

PURPORT

According to Śrīla Sanātana Gosvāmī, Lord Brahmā is here engaged in the ecstasy of *nāma-saṅkīrtana,* glorifying various holy names of Lord Kṛṣṇa that indicate His variegated pastimes. Lord Kṛṣṇa expertly suppressed the demoniac population of the earth, which became unbearable with the advent of demoniac politicians like Kaṁsa, Jarāsandha and Śiśupāla. Similarly, in modern society there are many so-called God-fearing people who are actually attracted to demoniac existence. Such persons become enlivened with the setting of the sun and go out in the darkness to enjoy life in restaurants, nightclubs, discotheques, hotels and so on, which are all simply meant for illicit sex, intoxication, gambling and meat-eating. Then there are those who openly defy God and His laws, declaring themselves atheists and demons. Both the covert and the overt enemies of the Lord constitute an unholy burden for the earth, and Lord Kṛṣṇa descends to expertly remove this burden.

Here Lord Brahmā indirectly states that Lord Kṛṣṇa should remove Brahmā's own subtle atheism, which had led him to try to exert illusory power over Lord Kṛṣṇa. According to Śrīla Viśvanātha Cakravartī Ṭhākura, Lord Brahmā, in his shame, felt himself to be like a *brahma-rākṣasa* from Satyaloka who had come to the earth to disturb Lord Kṛṣṇa and His intimate friends and calves. Brahmā is lamenting that although Lord Kṛṣṇa is most exalted, the Lord of all lords, because He had appeared before Brahmā in such a simple and innocent feature—decorated with a stick, a conchshell, ornaments, red clay, a peacock feather and so on, and sporting with His cowherd boyfriends—Brahmā dared to challenge Him.

Concerning Brahmā's prayers, of which this verse is the conclusion, Śrīla Viśvanātha Cakravartī Ṭhākura states, "May these prayers of Brahmā, which take away all doubts and broadcast all the definitive conclusions of devotional service, become the expert craftsmanship of the foundation of my consciousness."

TEXT 41

श्रीशुक उवाच
इत्यभिष्टूय भूमानं त्रिः परिक्रम्य पादयोः ।
नत्वाभीष्टं जगद्धाता स्वधाम प्रत्यपद्यत ॥ ४१ ॥

śrī-śuka uvāca
ity abhiṣṭūya bhūmānaṁ
triḥ parikramya pādayoḥ
natvābhīṣṭaṁ jagad-dhātā
sva-dhāma pratyapadyata

śrī-śukaḥ uvāca—Śrī Śukadeva Gosvāmī said; *iti*—thus; *abhiṣṭūya*—offering praise; *bhūmānam*—to the unlimited Supreme Lord; *triḥ*—three times; *parikramya*—circumambulating; *pādayoḥ*—at His feet; *natvā*—bowing down; *abhīṣṭam*—desired; *jagat*—of the universe; *dhātā*—the creator; *sva-dhāma*—to his personal abode; *pratyapadyata*—returned.

TRANSLATION

Śukadeva Gosvāmī said: Having thus offered his prayers, Brahmā circumambulated his worshipable Lord, the unlimited Personality of Godhead, three times and then bowed down at His lotus feet. The appointed creator of the universe then returned to his own residence.

PURPORT

Although Lord Brahmā had prayed to take birth as a blade of grass in Vṛndāvana or even in the area surrounding Vṛndāvana, Lord Kṛṣṇa, by His silent response to Brahmā's prayers, indicated that Brahmā should return to his own abode. First Brahmā had to complete his personal devotional service of universal creation; then he could come to Vṛndāvana and get the mercy of the inhabitants there. In other words, a devotee should always be attentive to executing his personal devotional service properly. This is more important than trying to live in the Lord's abode.

TEXT 42

ततोऽनुज्ञाप्य भगवान् स्वभुवं प्रागवस्थितान् ।
वत्सान् पुलिनमानिन्ये यथापूर्वसखं स्वकम् ॥ ४२ ॥

tato'nujñāpya bhagavān
sva-bhuvaṁ prāg avasthitān
vatsān pulinam āninye
yathā-pūrva-sakhaṁ svakam

tataḥ—then; *anujñāpya*—giving permission; *bhagavān*—the Supreme Lord; *sva-bhuvam*—to His own son (Brahmā); *prāk*—from before; *avasthitān*—situated; *vatsān*—the calves; *pulinam*—to the shore of the river; *āninye*—He brought; *yathā-pūrva*—just as before; *sakham*—where the friends were present; *svakam*—His own.

TRANSLATION

After granting His son Brahmā permission to leave, the Supreme Personality of Godhead took the calves, who were still where they had been a year earlier, and brought them to the riverbank, where He had been taking His meal and where His cowherd boyfriends remained just as before.

PURPORT

The word *sva-bhuvam,* "to His own son," indicates that Lord Kṛṣṇa forgave the offense Brahmā had committed and treated him with affection, as His son. It is stated in this verse that the original cowherd boyfriends and calves were situated just as before: near the bank of the Yamunā River and in the forest, respectively. Previously the calves had disappeared within the forest and Lord Kṛṣṇa had gone to search for them. Not finding them, the Lord had returned to the riverbank to discuss the situation with His cowherd boyfriends, but they had also disappeared. Now the cows were once again in the forest and the boyfriends once again on the bank of the river, ready to take their lunch. According to Śrīla Sanātana Gosvāmī, the calves and boys remained in the forest and on the riverbank, respectively, for one full year. Lord Brahmā did not actually take them away to another place. By the Lord's omnipotent illusory energy, the *gopīs* and other residents of Vṛndāvana did not notice the calves and boys, nor did the calves and boys notice the passing of a year's time or feel any hunger, cold or thirst. All this was part of the pastime arranged by the Lord's illusory potency. Lord Brahmā thought, "I have kept all the boys and calves of Gokula sleeping on the bed of my mystic potency, and to this very day they have not risen. A similar number of boys and calves have been playing with Kṛṣṇa for one whole year, yet they are different from the ones illusioned by my mystic potency. Who are they? Where did they come from?"

Nothing is invisible to the Supreme Lord. Thus Lord Kṛṣṇa appeared to be searching for the calves and boys only to enact the dramatic pastime of bewildering Lord Brahmā. After Brahmā surrendered and offered prayers, Lord Kṛṣṇa returned to the original boys and calves, who appeared exactly as before, although their size had somewhat increased because of one year's growth.

According to Śrīla Viśvanātha Cakravartī Ṭhākura, since Lord Kṛṣṇa was playing exactly like an innocent young cowherd boy in Vṛndāvana, after four-headed Brahmā offered his prayers the Lord maintained His role as a young cowherd boy and thus remained silent before Brahmā. Kṛṣṇa's silence indicates the following thoughts: "Where did this four-headed Brahmā come from? What is he doing? What are these words he keeps on speaking? I am busy looking for My calves. I am just a cowherd boy and do not understand all this." Lord Brahmā had considered Lord Kṛṣṇa an ordinary cowherd boy and had treated Him as such. After accepting Brahmā's prayers, Kṛṣṇa continued to play as a cowherd boy and thus did not answer the four-headed Brahmā. Rather, Kṛṣṇa was more interested in rejoining His cowherd boyfriends for the picnic lunch on the bank of the Yamunā River.

TEXT 43

एकस्मिन्नपि यातेऽब्दे प्राणेशं चान्तरात्मनः ।
कृष्णमायाहता राजन् क्षणार्धं मेनिरेऽर्भकाः ॥ ४३ ॥

ekasminn api yāte'bde
prāṇeśaṁ cāntarātmanaḥ
kṛṣṇa-māyāhatā rājan
kṣaṇārdhaṁ menire'rbhakāḥ

ekasmin—one; *api*—although; *yāte*—having passed; *abde*—year; *prāṇa-īśam*—the Lord of their lives; *ca*—and; *antarā*—without; *ātmanaḥ*—of themselves; *kṛṣṇa*—of Lord Kṛṣṇa; *māyā*—by the illusory potency; *āhatāḥ*—covered; *rājan*—O King; *kṣaṇa-ardham*—half a moment; *menire*—they thought; *arbhakāḥ*—the boys.

TRANSLATION

O King, although the boys had passed an entire year apart from the Lord of their very lives, they had been covered by Lord Kṛṣṇa's illusory potency and thus considered that year merely half a moment.

TEXT 44

किं किं न विस्मरन्तीह मायामोहितचेतसः ।
यन्मोहितं जगत् सर्वमभीक्ष्णं विस्मृतात्मकम् ॥ ४४ ॥

kiṁ kiṁ na vismarantīha
māyā-mohita-cetasaḥ
yan-mohitaṁ jagat sarvam
abhīkṣṇaṁ vismṛtātmakam

kim kim—what indeed; *na vismaranti*—persons do not forget; *iha*—in this world; *māyā-mohita*—bewildered by illusion; *cetasaḥ*—whose minds; *yat*—by which; *mohitam*—bewildered; *jagat*—the world; *sarvam*—entire; *abhīkṣṇam*—constantly; *vismṛta-ātmakam*—making one forget even one's own self.

TRANSLATION

What indeed is not forgotten by those whose minds are bewildered by the Lord's illusory potency? By that power of Māyā, this entire universe

remains in perpetual bewilderment, and in this atmosphere of forgetfulness no one can understand his own identity.

PURPORT

It is clearly stated here that the entire universe is bewildered. Thus even great demigods like Indra and Brahmā are not exempt from the principle of forgetfulness. Since Lord Kṛṣṇa exercised His internal illusory potency over His cowherd boyfriends and calves, it is not at all astonishing that for one year they could not remember their position. Indeed, by the Lord's external illusory potency the conditioned souls forget their existence not only for one year but for many billions and billions of years as they transmigrate throughout the kingdom of ignorance called the material world.

TEXT 45

ऊचुश्च सुहृदः कृष्णं स्वागतं तेऽतिरंहसा ।
नैकोऽप्यभोजि कवल एहीतः साधु भुज्यताम् ॥ ४५ ॥

ūcuś ca suhṛdaḥ kṛṣṇaṁ
sv-āgataṁ te'ti-raṁhasā
naiko'py abhoji kavala
ehītaḥ sādhu bhujyatām

ūcuḥ—they spoke; *ca*—and; *suhṛdaḥ*—the friends; *kṛṣṇam*—to Lord Kṛṣṇa; *su-āgatam*—have come all the way back; *te*—You; *ati-raṁhasā*—very quickly; *na*—not; *ekaḥ*—one; *api*—even; *abhoji*—has been eaten; *kavalaḥ*—morsel; *ehi*—please come; *itaḥ*—here; *sādhu*—properly; *bhujyatām*—take Your meal.

TRANSLATION

The cowherd boyfriends said to Lord Kṛṣṇa: You have returned so quickly! We have not eaten even one morsel in Your absence. Please come here and take Your meal without distraction.

PURPORT

The words *sv-āgataṁ te'ti-raṁhasā* indicate that the cowherd boys were congratulating Lord Kṛṣṇa for having brought the calves back so quickly from the forest. Now Lord Kṛṣṇa's beloved friends urged Him to sit down properly and eat to His full satisfaction. According to Śrīla Prabhupāda's *Kṛṣṇa, the*

Supreme Personality of Godhead, the cowherd boyfriends felt quite jubilant and were eager to eat with their dear friend, Kṛṣṇa.

TEXT 46

ततो हसन् हृषीकेशोऽभ्यवहृत्य सहार्भकैः ।
दर्शयंश्चर्माजगरं न्यवर्तत वनाद् व्रजम् ॥ ४६ ॥

tato hasan hṛṣīkeśo
'bhyavahṛtya sahārbhakaiḥ
darśayaṁś carmājagaraṁ
nyavartata vanād vrajam

tataḥ—then; *hasan*—smiling; *hṛṣīkeśaḥ*—Lord Kṛṣṇa, the master of everyone's senses; *abhyavahṛtya*—taking lunch; *saha*—along with; *arbhakaiḥ*—the cowherd boys; *darśayan*—showing; *carma*—the skin; *ājagaram*—of the python Aghāsura; *nyavartata*—He returned; *vanāt*—from the forest; *vrajam*—to the village of Vraja.

TRANSLATION

Then Lord Hṛṣīkeśa, smiling, finished His lunch in the company of His cowherd friends. While they were returning from the forest to their homes in Vraja, Lord Kṛṣṇa showed the cowherd boys the skin of the dead serpent Aghāsura.

TEXT 47

बर्हप्रसूनवनधातुविचित्रितागंः
प्रोद्दामवेणुदलशृंगरवोत्सवाढ्यः ।
वत्सान् गृणन्ननुगगीतपवित्रकीर्तिर्
गोपीदृगुत्सवदृशिः प्रविवेश गोष्ठम् ॥ ४७ ॥

barha-prasūna-vana-dhātu-vicitritāṅgaḥ
proddāma-veṇu-dala-śṛṅga-ravotsavāḍhyaḥ
vatsān gṛṇann anuga-gīta-pavitra-kīrtir
gopī-dṛg-utsava-dṛśiḥ praviveśa goṣṭham

barha—with peacock feathers; *prasūna*—flowers; *vana-dhātu*—and forest minerals; *vicitrita*—decorated; *aṅgaḥ*—His transcendental body;

proddāma—great; *veṇu-dala*—made from the branch of a bamboo tree; *śṛṅga*—of the flute; *rava*—by the resounding; *utsava*—with a festival; *āḍhyaḥ*—resplendent; *vatsān*—the calves; *gṛṇan*—calling; *anuga*—by His companions; *gīta*—sung; *pavitra*—purifying; *kīrtiḥ*—His glories; *gopī*—of the cowherd women; *dṛk*—for the eyes; *utsava*—a festival; *dṛśiḥ*—the vision of Him; *praviveśa*—He entered; *goṣṭham*—the cow pasture.

TRANSLATION

Lord Kṛṣṇa's transcendental body was decorated with peacock feathers and flowers and painted with forest minerals, and His bamboo flute loudly and festively resounded. As He called out to His calves by name, His cowherd boyfriends purified the whole world by chanting His glories. Thus Lord Kṛṣṇa entered the cow pasture of His father, Nanda Mahārāja, and the sight of His beauty at once produced a great festival for the eyes of all the cowherd women.

PURPORT

According to Śrīla Jīva Gosvāmī and Śrīla Viśvanātha Cakravartī Ṭhākura, the *gopīs* mentioned here are the elder cowherd ladies such as mother Yaśodā, who loved Kṛṣṇa with parental affection. Kṛṣṇa's cowherd boyfriends were so proud of Kṛṣṇa's wonderful activities that while entering the village they all sang His glories.

TEXT 48

अद्यानेन महाव्यालो यशोदानन्दसूनुना ।
हतोऽविता वयं चास्मादिति बाला व्रजे जगुः ॥ ४८ ॥

adyānena mahā-vyālo
yaśodā-nanda-sūnunā
hato'vitā vayaṁ cāsmād
iti bālā vraje jaguḥ

adya—today; *anena*—by Him; *mahā-vyālaḥ*—a great serpent; *yaśodā*—of Yaśodā; *nanda*—and Mahārāja Nanda; *sūnunā*—by the son; *hataḥ*—has been killed; *avitāḥ*—have been saved; *vayam*—we; *ca*—and; *asmāt*—from that demon; *iti*—thus; *bālāḥ*—the boys; *vraje*—in Vṛndāvana; *jaguḥ*—sang.

TRANSLATION

As the cowherd boys reached the village of Vraja, they sang, "Today Kṛṣṇa saved us by killing a great serpent!" Some of the boys described Kṛṣṇa as the son of Yaśodā, and others as the son of Nanda Mahārāja.

PURPORT

Actually, Lord Kṛṣṇa had killed the demon Aghāsura one year earlier, but the boys, bewildered by the mystic potency of Brahmā for one year, did not notice the time passing and thus thought that on that very day Lord Kṛṣṇa had killed the demon Aghāsura and was now returning home with them.

TEXT 49

श्रीराजोवाच
ब्रह्मन् परोद्भवे कृष्णे इयान् प्रेमा कथं भवेत् ।
योऽभूतपूर्वस्तोकेषु स्वोद्भवेष्वपि कथ्यताम् ॥ ४९ ॥

śrī-rājovāca
brahman parodbhave kṛṣṇe
iyān premā kathaṁ bhavet
yo'bhūta-pūrvas tokeṣu
svodbhaveṣv api kathyatām

śrī-rājā uvāca—the King said; *brahman*—O *brāhmaṇa,* Śukadeva; *para-udbhave*—for the offspring of another; *kṛṣṇe*—Lord Kṛṣṇa; *iyān*—so much; *premā*—love; *katham*—how; *bhavet*—can be; *yaḥ*—which; *abhūta-pūrvaḥ*—unprecedented; *tokeṣu*—for the children; *sva-udbhaveṣu*—their own offspring; *api*—even; *kathyatām*—please explain.

TRANSLATION

King Parīkṣit said: O brāhmaṇa, how could the cowherd women have developed for Kṛṣṇa, someone else's son, such unprecedented pure love—love they never felt even for their own children? Please explain this.

TEXT 50

श्रीशुक उवाच
सर्वेषामपि भूतानां नृप स्वात्मैव वल्लभः ।
इतरेऽपत्यवित्ताद्यास्तद्वल्लभतयैव हि ॥ ५० ॥

śrī-śuka uvāca
sarveṣām api bhūtānāṁ
nṛpa svātmaiva vallabhaḥ
itare'patya-vittādyās
tad-vallabhatayaiva hi

śrī-śukaḥ uvāca—Śrī Śukadeva Gosvāmī said; *sarveṣām*—for all; *api*—indeed; *bhūtānām*—created living beings; *nṛpa*—O King; *sva-ātmā*—one's own self; *eva*—certainly; *vallabhaḥ*—dearmost; *itare*—others; *apatya*—children; *vitta*—wealth; *ādyāḥ*—and so on; *tat*—of that self; *vallabhatayā*—based on the dearness; *eva hi*—indeed.

TRANSLATION

Śrī Śukadeva Gosvāmī said: O King, for every created being the dearmost thing is certainly his own self. The dearness of everything else—children, wealth and so on—is due only to the dearness of the self.

PURPORT

Sometimes modern thinkers become puzzled when they study the psychology of moral behavior. Although every living entity is inclined toward self-preservation, as stated here, sometimes a person voluntarily sacrifices his own apparent interest through philanthropic or patriotic activities, such as giving his money for the benefit of others or giving his life for the national interest. Such so-called selfless behavior appears to contradict the principle of material self-centeredness and self-preservation.

As explained in this verse, however, a living entity serves his society, nation, family and so on only because these objects of affection represent the expanded concept of false ego. A patriot sees himself as a great servitor of a great nation, and thus he sacrifices his life to gratify his sense of egotism. Similarly, it is common knowledge that a man feels great pleasure by thinking that he is sacrificing everything to please his dear wife and children. A man derives great egotistic pleasure by seeing himself as a selfless well-wisher of his so-called family and community. Thus, to gratify his proud sense of false ego, a man is prepared even to lay down his life. This apparently contradictory behavior is yet another demonstration of the bewilderment of material life, which has neither rhyme nor reason, being a manifestation of gross ignorance of the nonmaterial soul.

TEXT 51

तद् राजेन्द्र यथा स्नेहः स्वस्वकात्मनि देहिनाम्।
न तथा ममतालम्बिपुत्रवित्तगृहादिषु ॥ ५१ ॥

tad rājendra yathā snehaḥ
sva-svakātmani dehinām
na tathā mamatālambi-
putra-vitta-gṛhādiṣu

tat—therefore; *rāja-indra*—O best of kings; *yathā*—as; *snehaḥ*—the affection; *sva-svaka*—of each individual; *ātmani*—for the self; *dehinām*—of the embodied beings; *na*—not; *tathā*—thus; *mamatā-ālambi*—for that which one identifies with as his possessions; *putra*—sons; *vitta*—wealth; *gṛha*—homes; *ādiṣu*—and so on.

TRANSLATION

For this reason, O best of kings, the embodied soul is self-centered: he is more attached to his own body and self than to his so-called possessions like children, wealth and home.

PURPORT

It is now common practice all over the world for a mother to kill her own child within the womb if the birth of that child represents any inconvenience for her. Similarly, grown children eagerly place their elderly parents in lonely institutions rather than be inconvenienced by their presence at home. These and innumerable other examples prove that people in general are more attached to their own body and self, which represent "I-ness," than to their family and other possessions, which represent "my-ness." Although conditioned souls are very proud of their so-called love for society, family and so forth, in reality every conditioned soul is acting on the platform of gross or subtle selfishness.

TEXT 52

देहात्मवादिनां पुंसामपि राजन्यसत्तम ।
यथा देहः प्रियतमस्तथा न ह्यनु ये च तम् ॥ ५२ ॥

dehātma-vādināṁ puṁsām
api rājanya-sattama

yathā dehaḥ priyatamas
tathā na hy anu ye ca tam

deha-ātma-vādinām—who ascribe to the view that the body is the self; *puṁsām*—for persons; *api*—indeed; *rājanya-sat-tama*—O best of kings; *yathā*—as; *dehaḥ*—the body; *priya-tamaḥ*—most dear; *tathā*—thus; *na*—not; *hi*—certainly; *anu*—relative; *ye*—which things; *ca*—and; *tam*—to that.

TRANSLATION

Indeed, for persons who think the body is the self, O best of kings, those things whose importance lies only in their relationship to the body are never as dear as the body itself.

TEXT 53

देहोऽपि ममताभाक् चेत्तर्ह्यसौ नात्मवत् प्रियः ।
यज्जीर्यत्यपि देहेऽस्मिन् जीविताशा बलीयसी ॥ ५३ ॥

deho'pi mamatā-bhāk cet
tarhy asau nātma-vat priyaḥ
yaj jīryaty api dehe'smin
jīvitāśā balīyasī

dehaḥ—the body; *api*—also; *mamatā*—of possessiveness; *bhāk*—the focus; *cet*—if; *tarhi*—then; *asau*—that body; *na*—not; *ātma-vat*—in the same way as the soul; *priyaḥ*—dear; *yat*—because; *jīryati*—when it is growing old; *api*—even; *dehe*—the body; *asmin*—this; *jīvita-āśā*—the desire to remain living; *balīyasī*—very strong.

TRANSLATION

If a person comes to the stage of considering the body "mine" instead of "me," he will certainly not consider the body as dear as his own self. After all, even as the body is growing old and useless, one's desire to continue living remains strong.

PURPORT

The word *mamatā-bhāk* is very significant here. An ordinary, foolish person thinks, "I *am* this body." A more discriminating, intelligent person thinks, "This is *my* body." In the literature and folklore of ordinary people we find the common theme of an old, decrepit person dreaming of obtaining a new, young body. Thus, even ordinary persons pick up the notion of self-realization, instinctively understanding that it is possible for the soul to exist in many different bodies.

As the body of an intelligent person becomes old and useless, he strongly desires to live, even when he knows that his body cannot live much longer. This indicates he is gradually becoming aware that his self is more important than his body. Thus simply the desire for life can indirectly bring one to a preliminary understanding of self-realization. And in this case as well, one's basic attachment is to one's own self and not to that which supposedly belongs to oneself.

It may be pointed out that the entire discussion between King Parīkṣit and Śukadeva Gosvāmī regarding the dearness of one's own self is ultimately meant for broaching the subject of why the cows and cowherd ladies of Vṛndāvana considered Kṛṣṇa more dear than their own selves and certainly more dear than their own offspring. The discussion proceeds as follows.

TEXT 54

तस्मात् प्रियतमः स्वात्मा सर्वेषामपि देहिनाम् ।
तदर्थमेव सकलं जगदेतच्चराचरम् ॥ ५४ ॥

tasmāt priyatamaḥ svātmā
sarveṣām api dehinām
tad-artham eva sakalaṁ
jagad etac carācaram

tasmāt—therefore; *priya-tamaḥ*—most dear; *sva-ātmā*—one's own self; *sarveṣām*—for all; *api*—indeed; *dehinām*—embodied living beings; *tat-artham*—for the sake of it; *eva*—certainly; *sakalam*—all; *jagat*—the created universe; *etat*—this; *cara-acaram*—with its moving and nonmoving entities.

TRANSLATION

Therefore it is his own self that is most dear to every embodied living being, and it is simply for the satisfaction of this self that the whole material creation of moving and nonmoving entities exists.

PURPORT

The word *carācaram* indicates moving living entities, such as animals, and nonmoving living entities, such as trees. Or the word may also refer to moving possessions, such as one's family and pets, and nonmoving possessions, such as one's house and household paraphernalia.

TEXT 55

कृष्णमेनमवेहि त्वमात्मानमखिलात्मनाम् ।
जगद्धिताय सोऽप्यत्र देहीवाभाति मायया ॥ ५५ ॥

kṛṣṇam enam avehi tvam
ātmānam akhilātmanām
jagad-dhitāya so'py atra
dehīvābhāti māyayā

kṛṣṇam—Lord Kṛṣṇa, the Supreme Personality of Godhead; *enam*—this; *avehi*—just try to understand; *tvam*—you; *ātmānam*—the Soul; *akhila-ātmanām*—of all living entities; *jagat-hitāya*—for the benefit of the whole universe; *saḥ*—He; *api*—certainly; *atra*—here; *dehī*—a human being; *iva*—like; *ābhāti*—appears; *māyayā*—by His internal potency.

TRANSLATION

You should know Kṛṣṇa to be the original Soul of all living entities. For the benefit of the whole universe, He has, out of His causeless mercy, appeared as an ordinary human being. He has done this by the strength of His internal potency.

PURPORT

In the *Caitanya-caritāmṛta, Madhya-līla,* Chapter Twenty, Text 162, Śrīla Prabhupāda comments on this verse as follows: "Parīkṣit Mahārāja asked Śukadeva Gosvāmī why Kṛṣṇa was so beloved by the residents of Vṛndāvana, who loved Him even more than their own offspring or life itself. At that time, Śukadeva Gosvāmī replied that everyone's *ātmā,* or soul, is very, very dear, especially to all living entities who have accepted material bodies. But that *ātmā,* the spirit soul, is part and parcel of Kṛṣṇa. For this reason, Kṛṣṇa is very dear to every living entity. Everyone's body is very dear to oneself, and one wants to protect the body by all means because within the body the soul is living. Due to the intimate relationship between the soul and the body, the body is important and dear to everyone. Similarly, the soul, being part and parcel of Kṛṣṇa, the Supreme Lord, is very, very dear to all living entities. Unfortunately, the soul forgets his constitutional position and thinks he is only the body (*dehātma-buddhi*). Thus the soul is subjected to the rules and regulations of material nature. When a living entity, by his intelligence, reawakens his attraction for Kṛṣṇa, he can understand that he is not the body but part and parcel of Kṛṣṇa. Thus filled with knowledge, he no longer labors under attachment to the body and everything related to the body (*janasya moho'yam ahaṁ mameti*). Material existence, wherein one thinks,'I am the body, and this belongs to me,' is also illusory. One must redirect his attraction to Kṛṣṇa. *Śrīmad-Bhāgavatam* (1.2.7) states:

vāsudeve bhagavati
bhakti-yogaḥ prayojitaḥ
janayaty āśu vairāgyaṁ
jñānaṁ ca yad ahaitukam

'By rendering devotional service unto the Personality of Godhead, Śrī Kṛṣṇa, one immediately acquires causeless knowledge and detachment from the world.'"

TEXT 56

वस्तुतो जानतामत्र कृष्णं स्थास्नु चरिष्णु च ।
भगवद्रूपमखिलं नान्यद् वस्त्विह किञ्चन ॥ ५६ ॥

vastuto jānatām atra
kṛṣṇaṁ sthāsnu cariṣṇu ca
bhagavad-rūpam akhilaṁ
nānyad vastv iha kiñcana

vastutaḥ—in fact; *jānatām*—for those who understand; *atra*—in this world; *kṛṣṇam*—Lord Kṛṣṇa; *sthāsnu*—stationary; *cariṣṇu*—moving; *ca*—and; *bhagavat-rūpam*—the manifest forms of the Personality of Godhead; *akhilam*—everything; *na*—nothing; *anyat*—else; *vastu*—substance; *iha*—here; *kiñcana*—at all.

TRANSLATION

Those in this world who understand Lord Kṛṣṇa as He is see all things, whether stationary or moving, as manifest forms of the Supreme Personality of Godhead. Such enlightened persons recognize no reality apart from the Supreme Lord Kṛṣṇa.

PURPORT

Everything exists within Lord Kṛṣṇa, and Lord Kṛṣṇa exists within everything. Still, the order of progression is always from the energetic to the expanded energy. Lord Kṛṣṇa is the original identity, from whom all other identities emanate. He is the supreme energetic, from whom all categories and dimensions of energy become manifest. Thus, our personal bodies, self, family, friends, nation, planet, universe and so on are all manifestations of the Supreme Lord, who expands Himself through His personal potencies. Lord Kṛṣṇa is certainly the supreme object of our love and attraction, and other objects, such as body, family and home, should be secondary objects of our affection. Moreover, a close analytic study of the actual situation will reveal that even the secondary objects of love are also manifestations of Lord Kṛṣṇa. The conclusion is that Lord Kṛṣṇa is our only friend and object of love.

In his *Kṛṣṇa, the Supreme Personality of Godhead,* Śrīla Prabhupāda comments on this verse as follows: "Without being an expansion of Kṛṣṇa, nothing can be attractive. Whatever is attractive within the cosmic manifestation is due to Kṛṣṇa. Kṛṣṇa is therefore the reservoir of all pleasure. The active principle of everything is Kṛṣṇa, and highly elevated transcendentalists see everything in connection with Him. In the *Caitanya-caritāmṛta* it is stated that a *mahā-bhāgavata,* a highly advanced devotee, sees Kṛṣṇa as the active principle in all movable and immovable living entities. Therefore he sees everything within this cosmic manifestation in relation to Kṛṣṇa."

TEXT 57

सर्वेषामपि वस्तूनां भावार्थो भवति स्थितः ।
तस्यापि भगवान् कृष्णः किमतद् वस्तु रूप्यताम्॥ ५७॥

sarveṣām api vastūnāṁ
bhāvārtho bhavati sthitaḥ
tasyāpi bhagavān kṛṣṇaḥ
kim atad vastu rūpyatām

sarveṣām—of all; *api*—indeed; *vastūnām*—entities; *bhāva-arthaḥ*—the original, unmanifested causal phase of material nature; *bhavati*—is; *sthitaḥ*—established; *tasya*—of that unmanifest nature; *api*—even; *bhagavān*—the Supreme Personality of Godhead; *kṛṣṇaḥ*—Lord Kṛṣṇa; *kim*—what; *atat*—separate from Him; *vastu*—thing; *rūpyatām*—may be ascertained.

TRANSLATION

The original, unmanifested form of material nature is the source of all material things, and the source of even that subtle material nature is the Supreme Personality of Godhead, Kṛṣṇa. What, then, could one ascertain to be separate from Him?

TEXT 58

समाश्रिता ये पदपल्लवप्लवं
महत्पदं पुण्ययशो मुरारेः ।
भवाम्बुधिर्वत्सपदं परं पदं
पदं पदं यद् विपदां न तेषाम् ॥ ५८ ॥

samāśritā ye pada-pallava-plavaṁ
mahat-padaṁ puṇya-yaśo murāreḥ
bhavāmbudhir vatsa-padaṁ paraṁ padaṁ
padaṁ padaṁ yad vipadāṁ na teṣām

samāśritāḥ—having taken shelter; *ye*—those who; *pada*—of the feet; *pallava*—like flower buds; *plavam*—which are a boat; *mahat*—of the total material creation, or of the great souls; *padam*—the shelter; *puṇya*—supremely pious; *yaśaḥ*—whose fame; *mura-areḥ*—of the enemy of the demon Mura; *bhava*—of the material existence; *ambudhiḥ*—the ocean; *vatsa-padam*—the hoof-print of a calf; *param padam*—the supreme abode, Vaikuṇṭha; *padam padam*—at every step; *yat*—where; *vipadām*—of material miseries; *na*—none; *teṣām*—for them.

TRANSLATION

For those who have accepted the boat of the lotus feet of the Lord, who is the shelter of the cosmic manifestation and is famous as Murāri, the enemy of the Mura demon, the ocean of the material world is like the water contained in a calf's hoof-print. Their goal is paraṁ padam, Vaikuṇṭha, the place where there are no material miseries, not the place where there is danger at every step.

PURPORT

This translation is taken from Śrīla Prabhupāda's commentary on the *Bhagavad-gītā As It Is*, Chapter Two, Text 51.

According to Śrīla Śrīdhara Svāmī, this verse summarizes the knowledge presented in this section of the *Śrīmad-Bhāgavatam.* Lord Kṛṣṇa's lotus feet are described as *pallava,* flower buds, because they are most tender and of a pinkish hue. According to Śrīla Sanātana Gosvāmī, the word *pallava* also indicates that Lord Kṛṣṇa's lotus feet are just like desire trees, which can fulfill all the desires of the Lord's pure devotees. Even exalted devotees like Śrī Nārada, who are themselves the great shelter for the conditioned souls in this universe, personally take shelter of the lotus feet of Lord Śrī Kṛṣṇa. Thus it is natural that when Lord Kṛṣṇa manifested Himself as all the young boys and calves of Vṛndāvana, their parents were more attracted to them than previously. Lord Kṛṣṇa is the reservoir of all pleasure and, being all-attractive, the ultimate object of everyone's love.

TEXT 59

एतत्ते सर्वमाख्यातं यत् पृष्टोऽहमिह त्वया ।
तत् कौमारे हरिकृतं पौगण्डे परिकीर्तितम् ॥ ५९ ॥

etat te sarvam ākhyātaṁ
yat pṛṣṭo'ham iha tvayā
tat kaumāre hari-kṛtaṁ
paugaṇḍe parikīrtitam

etat—this; *te*—unto you; *sarvam*—all; *ākhyātam*—described; *yat*—which; *pṛṣṭaḥ*—requested; *aham*—I; *iha*—in this regard; *tvayā*—by you; *tat*—that; *kaumāre*—in His early childhood (up to the end of His fifth year); *hari-kṛtam*—performed by Lord Hari; *paugaṇḍe*—in later childhood (beginning with His sixth year); *parikīrtitam*—glorified.

TRANSLATION

Since you inquired from me, I have fully described to you those activities of Lord Hari that were performed in His fifth year but not celebrated until His sixth.

TEXT 60

एतत् सुहृद्भिश्चरितं मुरारेर्
अघार्दनं शाद्वलजेमनं च ।
व्यक्तेतरद् रूपमजोर्वभिष्टवं
शृण्वन् गृणन्नेति नरोऽखिलार्थान् ॥ ६० ॥

etat suhṛdbhiś caritaṁ murārer
aghārdanaṁ śādvala-jemanaṁ ca
vyaktetarad rūpam ajorv-abhiṣṭavaṁ
śṛṇvan gṛṇann eti naro'khilārthān

etat—these; *suhṛdbhiḥ*—along with the cowherd friends; *caritam*—pastimes; *murāreḥ*—of Lord Murāri; *agha-ardanam*—the subduing of the demon Aghāsura; *śādvala*—on the grass in the forest; *jemanam*—the taking of lunch; *ca*—and; *vyakta-itarat*—supramundane; *rūpam*—the transcendental form of the Lord; *aja*—by Lord Brahmā; *uru*—elaborate; *abhiṣṭavam*—the offering of prayers; *śṛṇvan*—hearing; *gṛṇan*—chanting; *eti*—attains; *naraḥ*—any person; *akhila-arthān*—all desirable things.

TRANSLATION

Any person who hears or chants these pastimes Lord Murāri performed with His cowherd friends—the killing of Aghāsura, the taking of lunch on the forest grass, the Lord's manifestation of transcendental forms, and the wonderful prayers offered by Lord Brahmā—is sure to achieve all his spiritual desires.

PURPORT

According to Śrīla Sanātana Gosvāmī, even one who is only *inclined* to hear and chant the pastimes of Lord Kṛṣṇa will achieve spiritual perfection. Many devotees seriously engaged in propagating Kṛṣṇa consciousness are often so busy that they cannot chant and hear the pastimes of the Lord to their full satisfaction. However, simply by their intense desire to always chant and hear about Lord Kṛṣṇa, they will achieve spiritual perfection. Of course, as far as possible one should actually vibrate these transcendental pastimes of the Lord.

TEXT 61

एवं विहारैः कौमारैः कौमारं जहतुर्व्रजे ।
निलायनैः सेतुबन्धैर्मर्कटोत्प्लवनादिभिः ॥ ६१ ॥

evaṁ vihāraiḥ kaumāraiḥ
kaumāraṁ jahatur vraje
nilāyanaiḥ setu-bandhair
markaṭotplavanādibhiḥ

evam—thus; *vihāraiḥ*—with pastimes; *kaumāraiḥ*—of boyhood; *kaumāram*—the childhood age up to five years; *jahatuḥ*—they passed; *vraje*—in the land of Vṛndāvana; *nilāyanaiḥ*—with sports of chasing about; *setu-bandhaiḥ*—with the building of bridges; *markaṭa-utplavana*—with the jumping around of monkeys; *ādibhiḥ*—and so on.

TRANSLATION

In this way the boys spent their childhood in the land of Vṛndāvana playing hide-and-go-seek, building play bridges, jumping about like monkeys and engaging in many other such games.

PURPORT

According to Śrīla Sanātana Gosvāmī, the word *nilāyanaiḥ* refers to games such as hide-and-go-seek or cops and robbers. Sometimes the boys would jump around like the monkeys in Lord Rāmacandra's army and then enact the building of the bridge to Śrī Laṅkā by constructing play bridges in lakes or ponds. Sometimes the boys would imitate the pastime of churning the Ocean of Milk, and sometimes they would play catch with balls. We can find full pleasure in the spiritual world, with the simple condition that everything be performed in pure love of Godhead, Kṛṣṇa consciousness.

Thus end the purports of the humble servants of His Divine Grace A.C. Bhaktivedanta Swami Prabhupāda to the Tenth Canto, Fourteenth Chapter, of the Śrīmad-Bhāgavatam, *entitled "Brahmā's Prayers to Lord Kṛṣṇa."*

CHAPTER FIFTEEN

The Killing of Dhenuka, the Ass Demon

This chapter describes how Lord Balarāma and Lord Kṛṣṇa, while tending Their cows in the pastures of Vṛndāvana, killed Dhenukāsura, enabled the residents of Vṛndāvana to eat the fruits of the *tāla* trees and saved the young cowherds from Kāliya's poison.

Revealing Their boyhood (*paugaṇḍa*) phase of pastimes, Rāma and Kṛṣṇa were one day bringing the cows to pasture when They entered an attractive forest decorated with a clear lake. There They began playing forest sports along with Their friends. Pretending to tire, Lord Baladeva laid His head upon the lap of a cowherd boy and rested as Lord Kṛṣṇa helped relieve His elder brother's fatigue by massaging His feet. Then Kṛṣṇa also placed His head on the lap of a cowherd boy to rest, and another cowherd boy massaged His feet. In this way Kṛṣṇa, Balarāma and Their cowherd friends enjoyed various pastimes.

During this play, Śrīdāmā, Subala, Stoka-kṛṣṇa and other cowherd boys described to Rāma and Kṛṣṇa a wicked and irrepressible demon named Dhenuka, who had assumed the form of a jackass and was living in the Tālavana forest near Govardhana Hill. This forest was full of many varieties of sweet fruits. But fearing this demon, no one dared try to relish the taste of those fruits, and thus someone had to kill the demon and all his associates. Lord Rāma and Lord Kṛṣṇa, hearing of the situation, set off for this forest to fulfill the desire of Their companions.

Arriving at the Tālavana, Lord Balarāma shook many fruits out of the palm trees, and as soon as He did so the jackass demon, Dhenuka, ran swiftly to attack Him. But Balarāma grabbed his hind legs with one hand, whirled him around and threw him into the top of a tree, thus slaying him. All of Dhenukāsura's friends, overcome by fury, then rushed to attack, but Rāma and Kṛṣṇa took hold of them one by one, swung them around and killed them, until the disturbance was finally finished. When Kṛṣṇa and Balarāma returned to the cowherd community, Yaśodā and Rohiṇī placed Them on their respective laps. They kissed Their faces, fed Them with finely prepared food and then put Them to bed.

Some days later Lord Kṛṣṇa went with His friends, but without His older brother, to the banks of the Kālindī in order to tend the cows. The cows and cowherd boys became very thirsty and drank some water from the Kālindī. But it had been contaminated with poison, and they all fell unconscious on the riverbank. Kṛṣṇa then brought them back to life by the merciful rain of His glance, and all of them, regaining their consciousness, appreciated His great mercy.

TEXT 1

श्रीशुक उवाच
ततश्च पौगण्डवय:श्रितौ व्रजे
बभूवतुस्तौ पशुपालसम्मतौ ।
गाश्चारयन्तौ सखिभिः समं पदैर्
वृन्दावनं पुण्यमतीव चक्रतुः ॥ १ ॥

śrī-śuka uvāca
tataś ca pauganḍa-vayaḥ-śritau vraje
babhūvatus tau paśu-pāla-sammatau
gāś cārayantau sakhibhiḥ samaṁ padair
vṛndāvanaṁ puṇyam atīva cakratuḥ

śrī-śukaḥ uvāca—Śrī Śukadeva Gosvāmī said; *tataḥ*—then; *ca*—and; *paugaṇḍa vayaḥ*—the age of *paugaṇḍa* (years six to ten); *śritau*—attaining; *vraje*—in Vṛndāvana; *babhūvatuḥ*—They (Rāma and Kṛṣṇa) became; *tau*—the two of Them; *paśu-pāla*—as cowherds; *sammatau*—appointed; *gāḥ*—the cows; *cārayantau*—tending; *sakhibhiḥ samam*—along with Their friends; *padaiḥ*—with the marks of Their feet; *vṛndāvanam*—Śrī Vṛndāvana; *puṇyam*—auspicious; *atīva*—extremely; *cakratuḥ*—They made.

TRANSLATION

Śukadeva Gosvāmī said: When Lord Rāma and Lord Kṛṣṇa attained the age of paugaṇḍa [six to ten] while living in Vṛndāvana, the cowherd men allowed Them to take up the task of tending the cows. Engaging thus in the company of Their friends, the two boys rendered the land of Vṛndāvana most auspicious by imprinting upon it the marks of Their lotus feet.

PURPORT

Lord Kṛṣṇa wanted to encourage His cowherd boyfriends, who had been swallowed by Aghāsura and then stolen by Lord Brahmā. Therefore the Lord decided to bring them into the palm-tree forest called Tālavana, where there were many delicious ripe fruits. Since Lord Kṛṣṇa's spiritual body had apparently grown slightly in age and strength, the senior men of Vṛndāvana, headed by Nanda Mahārāja, decided to promote Kṛṣṇa from the task of herding calves to the status of a regular cowherd boy. He would now take care of the full-grown cows, bulls and oxen. Out of great affection, Nanda Mahārāja had previously considered Kṛṣṇa too small and immature to take care of full-grown cows and bulls. It is stated in the *Kārttika-māhātmya* section of the *Padma Purāṇa:*

śuklāṣṭamī kārttike tu
smṛtā gopāṣṭamī budhaiḥ
tad-dinād vāsudevo'bhūd
gopaḥ pūrvaṁ tu vatsapaḥ

"The eighth lunar day of the bright fortnight of the month of Kārttika is known by authorities as Gopāṣṭamī. From that day, Lord Vāsudeva served as a cowherd, whereas previously He had tended the calves."

The word *padaiḥ* indicates that Lord Kṛṣṇa blessed the earth by walking on her surface with His lotus feet. The Lord wore no shoes or other footgear but walked barefoot in the forest, giving great anxiety to the girls of Vṛndāvana, who feared that His soft lotus feet would be injured.

TEXT 2

तन्माधवो वेणुमुदीरयन् वृतो
गोपैर्गृणद्भिः स्वयशो बलान्वितः ।
पशून् पुरस्कृत्य पशव्यमाविशद्
विहर्तुकामः कुसुमाकरं वनम् ॥ २ ॥

tan mādhavo veṇum udīrayan vṛto
gopair gṛṇadbhiḥ sva-yaśo balānvitaḥ
paśūn puraskṛtya paśavyam āviśad
vihartu-kāmaḥ kusumākaraṁ vanam

tat—thus; *mādhavaḥ*—Lord Śrī Mādhava; *veṇum*—His flute; *udīrayan*—sounding; *vṛtaḥ*—surrounded; *gopaiḥ*—by the cowherd boys; *gṛṇadbhiḥ*

—who were chanting; *sva-yaśaḥ*—His glories; *bala-anvitaḥ*—accompanied by Lord Balarāma; *paśūn*—the animals; *puraskṛtya*—keeping in front; *paśavyam*—full of nourishment for the cows; *āviśat*—He entered; *vihartu-kāmaḥ*—desiring to enjoy pastimes; *kusuma-ākaram*—rich with flowers; *vanam*—the forest.

TRANSLATION

Thus desiring to enjoy pastimes, Lord Mādhava, sounding His flute, surrounded by cowherd boys who were chanting His glories, and accompanied by Lord Baladeva, kept the cows before Him and entered the Vṛndāvana forest, which was full of flowers and rich with nourishment for the animals.

PURPORT

Śrīla Sanātana Gosvāmī has explained the various meanings of the word *mādhava* as follows: *Mādhava* normally indicates Kṛṣṇa to be "the Lord, who is the consort of the goddess of fortune, Lakṣmī." This name also implies that Lord Kṛṣṇa descended in the dynasty of Madhu. Since the spring season is also known as Mādhava, it is understood that as soon as Lord Kṛṣṇa entered the Vṛndāvana forest, it automatically exhibited all the opulences of spring, becoming filled with flowers, breezes and a celestial atmosphere. Another reason Lord Kṛṣṇa is known as Mādhava is that He enjoys His pastimes in *madhu,* the taste of conjugal love.

Lord Kṛṣṇa would loudly sound His flute as He entered the forest of Śrī Vṛndāvana, thus giving inconceivable bliss to all the residents of His hometown, Vraja-dhāma. These simple pastimes of playfully entering the forest, playing on the flute and so forth were performed daily in the spiritual land of Vṛndāvana.

TEXT 3

तन्मञ्जुघोषालिमृगद्विजाकुलं
महन्मनःप्रख्यपयःसरस्वता ।
वातेन जुष्टं शतपत्रगन्धिना
निरीक्ष्य रन्तुं भगवान्मनो दधे ॥ ३ ॥

tan mañju-ghoṣāli-mṛga-dvijākulaṁ
mahan-manaḥ-prakhya-payaḥ-sarasvatā

vātena juṣṭaṁ śata-patra-gandhinā
nirīkṣya rantuṁ bhagavān mano dadhe

tat—that forest; *mañju*—charming; *ghoṣa*—whose sounds; *ali*—with bees; *mṛga*—animals; *dvija*—and birds; *ākulam*—filled; *mahat*—of great souls; *manaḥ*—the minds; *prakhya*—resembling; *payaḥ*—whose water; *sarasvatā*—with a lake; *vātena*—by the wind; *juṣṭam*—served; *śata-patra*—of hundred-petaled lotuses; *gandhinā*—with the fragrance; *nirīkṣya*—observing; *rantum*—to take pleasure; *bhagavān*—the Supreme Personality of Godhead; *manaḥ*—His mind; *dadhe*—turned.

TRANSLATION

The Supreme Personality of Godhead looked over that forest, which resounded with the charming sounds of bees, animals and birds, and which was enhanced by a lake whose clear water resembled the minds of great souls and by a breeze carrying the fragrance of hundred-petaled lotuses. Seeing all this, Lord Kṛṣṇa decided to enjoy the auspicious atmosphere.

PURPORT

Lord Kṛṣṇa saw that the Vṛndāvana forest was giving pleasure to all five senses. The bees, birds, and animals made charming sounds that brought sweet pleasure to the ears. The wind was faithfully rendering service to the Lord by blowing throughout the forest, carrying the cool moisture of a transparent lake and thus giving pleasure to the sense of touch. By the sweetness of the wind, even the sense of taste was being stimulated, and the fragrance of lotus flowers was bringing pleasure to the nostrils. And the entire forest was endowed with heavenly beauty, which was giving spiritual bliss to the eyes. Śrīla Viśvanātha Cakravartī Ṭhākura has thus explained the significance of this verse.

TEXT 4

स तत्र तत्रारुणपल्लवश्रिया
फलप्रसूनोरुभरेण पादयोः ।
स्पृशच्छिखान् वीक्ष्य वनस्पतीन्मुदा
स्मयन्निवाहाग्रजमादिपूरुषः ॥ ४ ॥

sa tatra tatrāruṇa-pallava-śriyā
phala-prasūnoru-bhareṇa pādayoḥ
spṛśac chikhān vīkṣya vanaspatīn mudā
smayann ivāhāgra-jam ādi-pūruṣaḥ

saḥ—He; *tatra tatra*—all around; *aruṇa*—reddish; *pallava*—of their buds; *śrīyā*—with the beauty; *phala*—of their fruits; *prasūna*—and flowers; *uru-bhareṇa*—with the heavy burden; *pādayoḥ*—at His two feet; *spṛśat*—touching; *śikhān*—the tips of their branches; *vīkṣya*—seeing; *vanaspatīn*—the lordly trees; *mudā*—with joy; *smayan*—laughing; *iva*—almost; *āha*—spoke; *agra-jam*—to His elder brother, Lord Balarāma; *ādi-pūruṣaḥ*—the primeval Supreme Lord.

TRANSLATION

The primeval Lord saw that the stately trees, with their beautiful reddish buds and their heavy burden of fruits and flowers, were bending down to touch His feet with the tips of their branches. Thus He smiled gently and addressed His elder brother.

PURPORT

The words *mudā smayann iva* indicate that Lord Kṛṣṇa was in a joking mood. He knew that the trees were actually bowing down to worship Him. But in the following verse the Lord, speaking in a friendly, lighthearted mood, gives the credit to His brother, Balarāma.

TEXT 5

श्रीभगवानुवाच
अहो अमी देववरामरार्चितं
पादाम्बुजं ते सुमनःफलार्हणम् ।
नमन्त्युपादाय शिखाभिरात्मनस्
तमोऽपहत्यै तरुजन्म यत्कृतम् ॥ ५ ॥

śrī-bhagavān uvāca
aho amī deva-varāmarārcitaṁ
pādāmbujaṁ te sumanaḥ-phalārhaṇam
namanty upādāya śikhābhir ātmanas
tamo-'pahatyai taru-janma yat-kṛtam

śrī-bhagavān uvāca—Lord Śrī Kṛṣṇa said; *aho*—oh; *amī*—these; *deva-vara*—O best of Lords (Śrī Balarāma); *amara*—by the immortal demigods; *arcitam*—worshiped; *pāda-ambujam*—to the lotus feet; *te*—of You; *sumanaḥ*—of flowers; *phala*—and fruits; *arhaṇam*—offerings; *namanti*—they are bowing down; *upādāya*—presenting; *śikhābhiḥ*—with their heads; *ātmanaḥ*—their own; *tamaḥ*—darkness of ignorance; *apahatyai*—for the purpose of eliminating; *taru-janma*—their birth as trees; *yat*—by which ignorance; *kṛtam*—created.

TRANSLATION

The Supreme Personality of Godhead said: O greatest of Lords, just see how these trees are bowing their heads at Your lotus feet, which are worshipable by the immortal demigods. The trees are offering You their fruits and flowers to eradicate the dark ignorance that has caused their birth as trees.

PURPORT

The trees of Vṛndāvana were thinking that because of past offenses they had now taken birth as trees and, being immovable, could not accompany Lord Kṛṣṇa in His wanderings throughout the Vṛndāvana area. In fact, all the creatures of Vṛndāvana, including the trees and cows, were great souls who could personally associate with the Supreme Personality of Godhead. But because of ecstatic sentiments of separation, the trees considered themselves in ignorance and thus tried to purify themselves by bowing down at the lotus feet of Kṛṣṇa and Balarāma. Lord Kṛṣṇa understanding their mentality, simultaneously glanced at them with affection and praised their devotional service before His older brother, Balarāma.

TEXT 6

एतेऽलिनस्तव यशोऽखिललोकतीर्थं
गायन्त आदिपुरुषानुपथं भजन्ते ।
प्रायो अमी मुनिगणा भवदीयमुख्या
गूढं वनेऽपि न जहत्यनघात्मदैवम् ॥ ६ ॥

ete'linas tava yaśo'khila-loka-tīrthaṁ
gāyanta ādi-puruṣānupathaṁ bhajante
prāyo amī muni-gaṇā bhavadīya-mukhyā
gūḍhaṁ vane'pi na jahaty anaghātma-daivam

ete—these; *alinaḥ*—bees; *tava*—Your; *yaśaḥ*—glories; *akhila-loka*—for all worlds; *tīrtham*—the place of pilgrimage; *gāyantaḥ*—are chanting; *ādi-puruṣa*—O original Personality of Godhead; *anupatham*—following You along the path; *bhajante*—they are engaged in worshiping; *prāyaḥ*—for the most part; *amī*—these; *muni-gaṇāḥ*—great sages; *bhavadīya*—among Your devotees; *mukhyāḥ*—the most intimate; *gūḍham*—hidden; *vane*—within the forest; *api*—even though; *na jahati*—they do not abandon; *anagha*—O sinless one; *ātma-daivam*—their own worshipable Deity.

TRANSLATION

O Original Personality, these bees must all be great sages and most elevated devotees of Yours, for they are worshiping You by following You along the path and chanting Your glories, which are themselves a holy place for the entire world. Though You have disguised Yourself within this forest, O sinless one, they refuse to abandon You, their worshipable Lord.

PURPORT

The word *gūḍham* is significant in this verse. It indicates that although the Supreme Personality of Godhead in His form of Kṛṣṇa or Balarāma appears like an ordinary human being within the material world, great sages always recognize the Lord as the Supreme Absolute Truth. All the transcendental forms of Godhead are eternal and full of bliss and knowledge, exactly the opposite of our material bodies, which are temporary and full of misery and ignorance.

One meaning of the word *tīrtha* is "the means for crossing beyond material existence." Simply by hearing the glories of the Supreme Lord or by chanting them, one immediately comes to the spiritual platform, beyond material existence. Thus the Lord's transcendental glories are here described as a *tīrtha* for everyone in the world. The word *gāyantaḥ* indicates that great sages give up their vows of silence and other selfish processes to glorify the activities of the Supreme Lord. Real silence means to not speak nonsense, to limit one's verbal activities to those sounds, statements and discussions relevant to the loving service of the Supreme Lord.

The word *anagha* indicates that the Supreme Lord never performs sinful or offensive activities. The word also indicates that the Lord immediately excuses a sin or offense committed by a sincere loving devotee who may accidentally deviate from the Lord's service. In the specific context of this verse, the word *anagha* indicates that Lord Balarāma was not disturbed by the bees who were constantly following Him (*anupatham*). The Lord blessed them by saying, "O bees, come into My confidential grove and feel free to taste its fragrance."

TEXT 7

नृत्यन्त्यमी शिखिन ईड्य मुदा हरिण्यः
कुर्वन्ति गोप्य इव ते प्रियमीक्षणेन ।
सूक्तैश्च कोकिलगणा गृहमागताय
धन्या वनौकस इयान् हि सतां निसर्गः ॥ ७ ॥

nṛtyanty amī śikhina īḍya mudā hariṇyaḥ
kurvanti gopya iva te priyam īkṣaṇena
sūktaiś ca kokila-gaṇā gṛham āgatāya
dhanyā vanaukasa iyān hi satāṁ nisargaḥ

nṛtyanti—are dancing; *amī*—these; *śikhinaḥ*—peacocks; *īḍya*—O worshipable Lord; *mudā*—with joy; *hariṇyaḥ*—the female deer; *kurvanti*—are making; *gopyaḥ*—the *gopīs; iva*—as if; *te*—for You; *priyam*—gratification; *īkṣaṇena*—by their glancing; *sūktaiḥ*—with Vedic prayers; *ca*—and; *kokila-gaṇāḥ*—the cuckoos; *gṛham*—to their home; *āgatāya*—who has arrived; *dhanyāḥ*—fortunate; *vana-okasaḥ*—the residents of the forest; *iyān*—such; *hi*—indeed; *satām*—of saintly personalities; *nisargaḥ*—the nature.

TRANSLATION

O worshipable one, these peacocks are dancing before You out of joy, these doe are pleasing You with affectionate glances, just as the gopīs do, and these cuckoos are honoring You with Vedic prayers. All these residents of the forest are most fortunate, and their behavior toward You certainly befits great souls receiving another great soul at home.

TEXT 8

धन्येयमद्य धरणी तृणवीरुधस्त्वत्-
पादस्पृशो द्रुमलताः करजाभिमृष्टाः ।
नद्योऽद्रयः खगमृगाः सदयावलोकैर्
गोप्योऽन्तरेण भुजयोरपि यत्स्पृहा श्रीः ॥ ८ ॥

dhanyeyam adya dharaṇī tṛṇa-vīrudhas tvat-
pāda-spṛśo druma-latāḥ karajābhimṛṣṭāḥ

nadyo'drayaḥ khaga-mṛgāḥ sadayāvalokair
gopyo'ntareṇae bhujayor api yat-spṛhā śrīḥ

dhanyā—fortunate; *iyam*—this; *adya*—now; *dharaṇī*—the earth; *tṛṇa*—her grasses; *vīrudhaḥ*—and bushes; *tvat*—Your; *pāda*—of the feet; *spṛśaḥ*—receiving the touch; *druma*—the trees; *latāḥ*—and creepers; *kara-ja*—by Your fingernails; *abhimṛṣṭāḥ*—touched; *nadyaḥ*—the rivers; *adrayaḥ*—and mountains; *khaga*—the birds; *mṛgāḥ*—and animals; *sadaya*—merciful; *avalokaiḥ*—by Your glances; *gopyaḥ*—the *gopīs; antareṇa*—in between; *bhujayoḥ*—Your two arms; *api*—indeed; *yat*—for which; *spṛhā*—maintains the desire; *śrīḥ*—the goddess of fortune.

TRANSLATION

This earth has now become most fortunate, because You have touched her grass and bushes with Your feet and her trees and creepers with Your fingernails, and because You have graced her rivers, mountains, birds and animals with Your merciful glances. But above all, You have embraced the young cowherd women between Your two arms—a favor hankered after by the goddess of fortune herself.

PURPORT

The word *adya,* "now," indicates the time of Lord Balarāma and Lord Kṛṣṇa's appearance on the earth. In His form of Varāha, Lord Kṛṣṇa personally saved the earth, and, indeed, the earth is understood to rest perpetually on the potency of Śeṣa. Both Varāha and Śeṣa are expansions of Balarāma, who is Himself an expansion of Lord Kṛṣṇa, the original Personality of Godhead. Lord Kṛṣṇa's statement that "this earth has now become most fortunate" (*dhanyeyam adya dharaṇī*) indicates that nothing can equal the blessings of the Supreme Personality of Godhead in His personal form as Kṛṣṇa, appearing simultaneously with His plenary expansion, Balarāma. The compound word *karajābhimṛṣṭāḥ,* "touched by Your fingernails," indicates that as Kṛṣṇa and Balarāma would move through the forest They would pick fruits and flowers from the trees, bushes and creepers and use this paraphernalia in Their pleasure pastimes. Sometimes They would break leaves off the plants and use them with the flowers to decorate Their bodies.

Kṛṣṇa and Balarāma would glance lovingly and mercifully at all the rivers, hills and creatures in Vṛndāvana. But the blessing received by the *gopīs*—being embraced directly between the Lord's arms—was the supreme benediction, desired even by the goddess of fortune herself. The goddess of fortune, who lives in Vaikuṇṭha on the chest of Lord Nārāyaṇa, once desired to be embraced on the chest of Śrī Kṛṣṇa, and thus she performed severe austerities to achieve this blessing. Śrī Kṛṣṇa informed her that her actual place was in Vaikuṇṭha and that it was not possible for her to dwell upon His chest in Vṛndāvana. Therefore she begged Kṛṣṇa to allow her to remain on His chest in the form of a golden line, and He granted her this benediction. Śrīla Viśvanātha Cakravartī Ṭhākura recounts this incident from the *Purāṇas.*

TEXT 9

श्रीशुक उवाच
एवं वृन्दावनं श्रीमत् कृष्णः प्रीतमनाः पशून् ।
रेमे सञ्चारयन्नद्रेः सरिद्रोधःसु सानुगः ॥ ९ ॥

śrī-śuka uvāca
evaṁ vṛndāvanaṁ śrīmat
kṛṣṇaḥ prīta-manāḥ paśūn
reme sañcārayann adreḥ
sarid-rodhaḥsu sānugaḥ

śrī-śukaḥ uvāca—Śrī Śukadeva Gosvāmī said; *evam*—in this way; *vṛndāvanam*—with the forest of Vṛndāvana and its inhabitants; *śrīmat*—beautiful; *kṛṣṇaḥ*—Lord Kṛṣṇa; *prīta-manāḥ*—being satisfied in His mind; *paśūn*—the animals; *reme*—He took pleasure; *sañcārayan*—making them graze; *adreḥ*—in the vicinity of the mountain; *sarit*—of the river; *rodhaḥsu*—upon the banks; *sa-anugaḥ*—together with His companions.

TRANSLATION

Śukadeva Gosvāmī said: Thus expressing His satisfaction with the beautiful forest of Vṛndāvana and its inhabitants, Lord Kṛṣṇa enjoyed tending the cows and other animals with His friends on the banks of the river Yamunā below Govardhana Hill.

TEXTS 10–12

क्वचिद् गायति गायत्सु मदान्धालिष्वनुव्रतैः ।
उपगीयमानचरितः पथि संकर्षणान्वितः ॥ १० ॥
अनुजल्पति जल्पन्तं कलवाक्यैः शुकं क्वचित् ।
क्वचित् सवल्गु कूजन्तमनुकूजति कोकिलम्

क्वचिच्च कलहंसानामनुकूजति कूजितम् ।
अभिनृत्यति नृत्यन्तं बर्हिणं हासयन् क्वचित् ॥ ११ ॥
मेघगम्भीरया वाचा नामभिर्दूरगान् पशून् ।
क्वचिदाह्वयति प्रीत्या गोगोपालमनोज्ञया ॥ १२ ॥

kvacid gāyati gāyatsu
madāndhāliṣv anuvrataiḥ
upagīyamāna-caritaḥ
pathi saṅkarṣaṇānvitaḥ

anujalpati jalpantaṁ
kala-vākyaiḥ śukaṁ kvacit
kvacit sa-valgu kūjantam
anukūjati kokilam

kvacic ca kala-haṁsānām
anukūjati kūjitam
abhinṛtyati nṛtyantaṁ
barhiṇaṁ hāsayan kvacit

megha-gambhīrayā vācā
nāmabhir dūra-gān paśūn
kvacid āhvayati prītyā
go-gopāla-manojñayā

kvacit—sometimes; *gāyati*—He sings; *gāyatsu*—when they are singing; *mada-andha*—blinded by intoxication; *aliṣu*—the bees; *anuvrataiḥ*—along with His companions; *upagīyamāna*—being chanted; *caritaḥ*—His pastimes; *pathi*—upon the path; *saṅkarṣaṇa-anvitaḥ*—accompanied by Lord Baladeva; *anujalpati*—He chatters in imitation; *jalpantam*—of the chattering; *kala-vākyaiḥ*—with broken speech; *śukam*—parrot; *kvacit*—sometimes; *kvacit*—sometimes; *sa*—with; *valgu*—charming; *kūjantam*—cuckooing; *anukū-jati*—He imitates the cuckooing; *kokilam*—of a cuckoo; *kvacit*—sometimes; *ca*—and; *kala-haṁsānām*—of the swans; *anukūjati kūjitam*—imitates the cooing; *abhinṛtyati*—He dances in front of; *nṛtyantam*—dancing; *barhiṇam*—a peacock; *hāsayan*—making laugh; *kvacit*—sometimes; *megha*—like clouds; *gambhirayā*—grave; *vācā*—with His voice; *nāmabhiḥ*—by name; *dūra-gān*—who had strayed far away; *paśūn*—the animals; *kvacit*—sometimes; *āhvayati*—He calls; *prītyā*—affectionately; *go*—to the cows; *gopāla*—and the cowherd boys; *manaḥ-jñayā*—which (voice) charms the mind.

TRANSLATION

Sometimes the honeybees in Vṛndāvana became so mad with ecstasy that they closed their eyes and began to sing. Lord Kṛṣṇa, moving along the forest path with His cowherd boyfriends and Baladeva, would then respond to the bees by imitating their singing while His friends sang about His pastimes. Sometimes Lord Kṛṣṇa would imitate the chattering of a parrot, sometimes, with a sweet voice, the call of a cuckoo, and sometimes the cooing of swans. Sometimes He vigorously imitated the dancing of a peacock, making His cowherd boyfriends laugh. Sometimes, with a voice as deep as the rumbling of clouds, He would call out with great affection the names of the animals who had wandered far from the herd, thus enchanting the cows and the cowherd boys.

PURPORT

Śrīla Sanātana Gosvāmī explains that Lord Kṛṣṇa would joke with His friends, saying, "Just look, this peacock does not know how to dance properly," whereupon the Lord would vigorously imitate the peacock's dancing, causing great laughter among His friends. The bees in Vṛndāvana would drink the sap of the forest flowers, and the combination of this nectar and the association of Śrī Kṛṣṇa made them mad with intoxication. Thus they closed their eyes in ecstasy and expressed their satisfaction by humming. And this humming was also expertly imitated by the Lord.

TEXT 13

चकोरक्रौञ्चचक्राह्वभारद्वाजांश्च बर्हिणः ।
अनुरौति स्म सत्त्वानां भीतवद् व्याघ्रसिंहयोः ॥ १३ ॥

cakora-krauñca-cakrāhva-
bhāradvājāṁś ca barhiṇaḥ
anurauti sma sattvānāṁ
bhīta-vad vyāghra-siṁhayoḥ

cakora-krauñca-cakrāhva-bhāradvājān ca—the *cakora, krauñca, cakrāhva* and *bhāradvāja* birds; *barhiṇaḥ*—the peacocks; *anurauti sma*—He would call out in imitation of; *sattvānām*—together with the other creatures; *bhīta-vat*—acting as if afraid; *vyāghra-siṁhayoḥ*—of the tigers and lions.

TRANSLATION

Sometimes He would cry out in imitation of birds such as the cakoras, krauñcas, cakrāhvas, bhāradvājas and peacocks, and sometimes He would run away with the smaller animals in mock fear of lions and tigers.

PURPORT

The word *bhīta-vat,* "as if afraid," indicates that Lord Kṛṣṇa played just like an ordinary boy and ran with the smaller forest creatures in mock fear of the lions and tigers. Actually, in Vṛndāvana, the abode of the Lord, the lions and tigers are not violent, and thus there is no reason to fear them.

TEXT 14

क्वचित् क्रीडापरिश्रान्तं गोपोत्संगोपबर्हणम्।
स्वयं विश्रमयत्यार्यं पादसंवाहनादिभिः ॥ १४॥

kvacit krīḍā-pariśrāntaṁ
gopotsaṅgopabarhaṇam
svayaṁ viśramayaty āryaṁ
pāda-saṁvāhanādibhiḥ

kvacit—sometimes; *krīḍā*—by playing; *pariśrāntam*—fatigued; *gopa*—of a cowherd boy; *utsaṅga*—the lap; *upabarhaṇam*—using as His pillow; *svayam*—personally; *viśramayati*—relieves Him from His fatigue; *āryam*—His elder brother; *pāda-saṁvāhana-ādibhiḥ*—by massaging His feet and offering other services.

TRANSLATION

When His elder brother, fatigued from playing, would lie down with His head upon the lap of a cowherd boy, Lord Kṛṣṇa would help Him relax by personally massaging His feet and offering other services.

PURPORT

The word *pāda-saṁvāhanādibhiḥ* indicates that Lord Kṛṣṇa would massage Balarāma's feet, fan Him and bring Him river water to drink.

TEXT 15

नृत्यतो गायतः क्वापि वल्गतो युध्यतो मिथः।
गृहीतहस्तौ गोपालान् हसन्तौ प्रशशंसतुः ॥ १५॥

nṛtyato gāyataḥ kvāpi
valgato yudhyato mithaḥ
gṛhīta-hastau gopālān
hasantau praśaśaṁsatuḥ

nṛtyataḥ—who were dancing; *gāyataḥ*—singing; *kva api*—sometimes; *valgataḥ*—moving about; *yudhyataḥ*—fighting; *mithaḥ*—with one another; *gṛhīta-hastau*—holding Their hands together; *gopālān*—the cowherd boys; *hasantau*—laughing; *praśaśaṁsatuḥ*—They offered praise.

TRANSLATION

Sometimes, as the cowherd boys danced, sang, moved about and playfully fought with each other, Kṛṣṇa and Balarāma, standing nearby hand in hand, would glorify Their friends' activities and laugh.

TEXT 16

क्वचित् पल्लवतल्पेषु नियुद्धश्रमकर्शितः ।
वृक्षमूलाश्रयः शेते गोपोत्संगोपबर्हणः ॥ १६ ॥

kvacit pallava-talpeṣu
niyuddha-śrama-karśitaḥ
vṛkṣa-mūlāśrayaḥ śete
gopotsaṅgopabarhaṇaḥ

kvacit—sometimes; *pallava*—made from new twigs and buds; *talpeṣu*—upon beds; *niyuddha*—from the fighting; *śrama*—by fatigue; *karśitaḥ*—worn out; *vṛkṣa*—of a tree; *mūla*—at the base; *āśrayaḥ*—taking shelter; *śete*—He lay down; *gopa-utsaṅga*—the lap of a cowherd boy; *upabarhaṇaḥ*—as His pillow.

TRANSLATION

Sometimes Lord Kṛṣṇa grew tired from fighting and lay down at the base of a tree, resting upon a bed made of soft twigs and buds and using the lap of a cowherd friend as His pillow.

PURPORT

The word *pallava-talpeṣu* implies that Lord Kṛṣṇa expanded Himself into many forms and lay down upon the many beds of twigs, leaves and flowers hastily constructed by His enthusiastic cowherd friends.

TEXT 17

पादसंवाहनं चक्रुः केचित्तस्य महात्मनः ।
अपरे हतपाप्मानो व्यजनैः समवीजयन् ॥ १७ ॥

pāda-saṁvāhanaṁ cakruḥ
kecit tasya mahātmanaḥ
apare hata-pāpmāno
vyajanaiḥ samavījayan

pāda-saṁvāhanam—the massaging of the feet; *cakruḥ*—did; *kecit*—some of them; *tasya*—of Him; *mahā-ātmanaḥ*—great souls; *apare*—others; *hata-pāpmānaḥ*—who were free from all sins; *vyajanaiḥ*—with fans; *samavījayan*—perfectly fanned Him.

TRANSLATION

Some of the cowherd boys, who were all great souls, would then massage His lotus feet, and others, qualified by being free of all sin, would expertly fan the Supreme Lord.

PURPORT

The word *samavījayan* indicates that the cowherd boys fanned the Lord very carefully and expertly, creating gentle and cooling breezes.

TEXT 18

अन्ये तदनुरूपाणि मनोज्ञानि महात्मनः ।
गायन्ति स्म महाराज स्नेहक्लिन्नधियः शनैः ॥ १८ ॥

anye tad-anurūpāṇi
manojñāni mahātmanaḥ
gāyanti sma mahā-rāja
sneha-klinna-dhiyaḥ śanaiḥ

anye—others; *tat-anurūpāṇi*—suitable for the occasion; *manaḥ-jñāni*—attractive to the mind; *mahā-ātmanaḥ*—of the great personality (Lord Kṛṣṇa); *gāyanti sma*—they would sing; *mahā-rāja*—O King Parīkṣit; *sneha*—by love; *klinna*—melted; *dhiyaḥ*—their hearts; *śanaiḥ*—slowly.

TRANSLATION

My dear King, other boys would sing enchanting songs appropriate to the occasion, and their hearts would melt out of love for the Lord.

TEXT 19

एवं निगूढात्मगतिः स्वमायया
गोपात्मजत्वं चरितैर्विडम्बयन् ।
रेमे रमालालितपादपल्लवो
ग्राम्यैः समं ग्राम्यवदीशचेष्टितः ॥ १९ ॥

evaṁ nigūḍhātma-gatiḥ sva-māyayā
gopātmajatvaṁ caritair viḍambayan
reme ramā-lālita-pāda-pallavo
grāmyaiḥ samaṁ grāmya-vad īśa-ceṣṭitaḥ

evam—in this way; *nigūḍha*—hidden away; *ātma-gatiḥ*—His personal opulence; *sva-māyayā*—by His own mystical potency; *gopa-ātmajatvam*—the status of being the son of a cowherd; *caritaiḥ*—by His activities; *viḍambayan*—pretending; *reme*—He enjoyed; *ramā*—by the goddess of fortune; *lālita*—attended; *pāda-pallavaḥ*—His feet, which are tender like new buds; *grāmyaiḥ samam*—together with village persons; *grāmya-vat*—like a village personality; *īśa-ceṣṭitaḥ*—although also displaying feats unique to the Supreme Lord.

TRANSLATION

In this way the Supreme Lord, whose soft lotus feet are personally attended by the goddess of fortune, concealed His transcendental opulences by His internal potency and acted like the son of a cowherd. Yet even while enjoying like a village boy in the company of other village residents, He often exhibited feats only God could perform.

TEXT 20

श्रीदामा नाम गोपालो रामकेशवयोः सखा ।
सुबलस्तोककृष्णाद्या गोपाः प्रेम्णेदमब्रुवन् ॥ २० ॥

śrīdāmā nāma gopālo
rāma-keśavayoḥ sakhā

subala-stokakṛṣṇādyā
gopāḥ premṇedam abruvan

śrīdāmā nāma—named Śrīdāmā; *gopālaḥ*—the cowherd boy; *rāma-keśavayoḥ*—of Lord Rāma and Lord Kṛṣṇa; *sakhā*—the friend; *subala-stokakṛṣṇa-ādyāḥ*—Subala, Stokakṛṣṇa and others; *gopāḥ*—cowherd boys; *premṇā*—with love; *idam*—this; *abruvan*—spoke.

TRANSLATION

Once, some of the cowherd boys—Śrīdāmā, the very close friend of Rāma and Kṛṣṇa, along with Subala, Stokakṛṣṇa and others—lovingly spoke the following words.

PURPORT

The word *premṇā,* "with love," indicates that the request the cowherd boys are about to place before Lord Kṛṣṇa and Lord Balarāma is motivated by love, not personal desire. The cowherd boys were eager for Kṛṣṇa and Balarāma to exhibit Their pastimes of killing demons and to enjoy the delicious fruits of the Tāla forest, and therefore they made the following request.

TEXT 21

राम राम महाबाहो कृष्ण दुष्टनिबर्हण ।
इतोऽविदूरे सुमहद् वनं तालालिसंकुलम् ॥ २१ ॥

rāma rāma mahā-bāho
kṛṣṇa duṣṭa-nibarhaṇa
ito'vidūre su-mahad
vanaṁ tālāli-saṅkulam

rāma rāma—O Rāma; *mahā-bāho*—O mighty-armed one; *kṛṣṇa*—O Kṛṣṇa; *duṣṭa-nibarhaṇa*—O eliminator of the miscreants; *itaḥ*—from here; *avidūre*—not far; *su-mahat*—very expansive; *vanam*—a forest; *tāla-āli*—with rows of palm trees; *saṅkulam*—filled.

TRANSLATION

[The cowherd boys said:] O Rāma, Rāma, mighty-armed one! O Kṛṣṇa, destroyer of the miscreants! Not far from here is a very great forest filled with rows of palm trees.

PURPORT

As stated in the Śrī Varāha Purāṇa:

asti govardhanaṁ nāma
kṣetraṁ parama-durlabham
mathurā-paścime bhāge
adūrād yojana-dvayam

"Not far from the western side of Mathurā, at a distance of two *yojanas* [sixteen miles], is the holy place named Govardhana, which is most difficult to attain." It is also stated in the *Varāha Purāṇa:*

asti tāla-vanaṁ nāma
dhenukāsura-rakṣitam
mathurā-paścime bhāge
adūrād eka-yojanam

"Not far from the western side of Mathurā, one *yojana* away [eight miles], is the forest known as Tālavana, which was guarded by Dhenukāsura." Thus it appears that the Tālavana forest is located midway between Mathurā and Govardhana Hill. The forest of Tālavana is described in the *Śrī Hari-vaṁśa* as follows:

sa tu deśaḥ samaḥ snigdhaḥ
su-mahān kṛṣṇa-mṛttikaḥ
darbha-prāyaḥ sthulī-bhūto
loṣṭra-pāṣāṇa-varjitaḥ

"The land there is even, smooth and very expansive. The earth is black, densely covered with *darbha* grass and devoid of stones and pebbles."

TEXT 22

फलानि तत्र भूरीणि पतन्ति पतितानि च।
सन्ति किन्त्ववरुद्धानि धेनुकेन दुरात्मना॥ २२॥

phalāni tatra bhūrīṇi
patanti patitāni ca
santi kintv avaruddhāni
dhenukena durātmanā

phalāni—the fruits; *tatra*—there; *bhūrīṇi*—very many; *patanti*—are falling; *patitāni*—have already fallen; *ca*—and; *santi*—they are; *kintu*—

however; *avaruddhāni*—kept under control; *dhenukena*—by Dhenuka; *durātmanā*—the evil one.

TRANSLATION

In that Tālavana forest many fruits are falling from the trees, and many are already lying on the ground. But all the fruits are being guarded by the evil Dhenuka.

PURPORT

The demon Dhenuka would not allow anyone to eat the delicious ripe palm fruits of the Tālavana, and Kṛṣṇa's young boyfriends protested this unjust usurpation of the right to enjoy the fruits of a public forest.

TEXT 23

सोऽतिवीर्योऽसुरो राम हे कृष्ण खररूपधृक् ।
आत्मतुल्यबलैरन्यैर्ज्ञातिभिर्बहुभिर्वृतः ॥ २३ ॥

so'ti-vīryo'suro rāma
he kṛṣṇa khara-rūpa-dhṛk
ātma-tulya-balair anyair
jñātibhir bahubhir vṛtaḥ

saḥ—he; *ati-vīryaḥ*—very powerful; *asuraḥ*—a demon; *rāma*—O Rāma; *he kṛṣṇa*—O Kṛṣṇa; *khara-rūpa*—the form of an ass; *dhṛk*—assuming; *ātma-tulya*—equal to himself; *balaiḥ*—whose strength; *anyaiḥ*—with others; *jñātibhiḥ*—companions; *bahubhiḥ*—many; *vṛtaḥ*—surrounded.

TRANSLATION

O Rāma, O Kṛṣṇa! Dhenuka is a most powerful demon and has assumed the form of an ass. He is surrounded by many friends who have assumed a similar shape and who are just as powerful as he.

TEXT 24

तस्मात् कृतनराहाराद् भीतैर्नृभिरमित्रहन् ।
न सेव्यते पशुगणैः पक्षिसङ्घैर्विवर्जितम् ॥ २४ ॥

tasmāt kṛta-narāhārād
bhītair nṛbhir amitra-han

na sevyate paśu-gaṇaiḥ
pakṣi-saṅghair vivarjitam

tasmāt—of him; *kṛta-nara-āhārāt*—who has eaten human beings; *bhītaiḥ*—who are afraid; *nṛbhiḥ*—by the human beings; *amitra-han*—O killer of enemies; *na sevyate*—is not resorted to; *paśu-gaṇaiḥ*—by the various animals; *pakṣi-saṅghaiḥ*—by the flocks of birds; *vivarjitam*—abandoned.

TRANSLATION

The demon Dhenuka has eaten men alive, and therefore all people and animals are terrified of going to the Tāla forest. O killer of the enemy, even the birds are afraid to fly there.

PURPORT

The cowherd boyfriends of Lord Kṛṣṇa and Lord Balarāma encouraged the two brothers to go at once to the Tāla forest and kill the ass demon. Indeed, here they address the brothers as *amitra-han,* "killer of the enemy." The cowherd boys were engaged in ecstatic meditation upon the potency of the Supreme Personality of Godhead and reasoned thus: "Kṛṣṇa has already killed terrible demons like Baka and Agha, so what is so special about this obnoxious jackass named Dhenuka, who has become public enemy number one in Vṛndāvana?"

The cowherd boys wanted Kṛṣṇa and Balarāma to kill the demons so that all the pious inhabitants of Vṛndāvana could enjoy the fruits in the Tāla forest. Thus they requested the special favor that the ass demons be killed.

TEXT 25

विद्यन्तेऽभुक्तपूर्वाणि फलानि सुरभीणि च ।
एष वै सुरभिर्गन्धो विषूचीनोऽवगृह्यते ॥ २५ ॥

vidyante'bhukta-pūrvāṇi
phalāni surabhīṇi ca
eṣa vai surabhir gandho
viṣūcīno'vagṛhyate

vidyante—are present; *abhukta-pūrvāṇi*—never before tasted; *phalāni*—fruits; *surabhīṇi*—fragrant; *ca*—and; *eṣaḥ*—this; *vai*—indeed; *surabhiḥ*—fragrant; *gandhaḥ*—aroma; *viṣūcīnaḥ*—spreading everywhere; *avagṛhyate*—is perceived.

TRANSLATION

In the Tāla forest are sweet-smelling fruits no one has ever tasted. Indeed, even now we can smell the fragrance of the tāla fruits spreading all about.

PURPORT

According to Śrīla Śrīdhara Svāmī, the sweet fragrance of the *tāla* fruits was carried by an easterly wind, which is conducive to rain in the Vṛndāvana area. This easterly wind generally blows in the month of Bhādra and thus indicates the excellent ripeness of the fruits, while the fact that the boys could smell them indicates the nearness of the Tāla forest.

TEXT 26

प्रयच्छ तानि नः कृष्ण गन्धलोभितचेतसाम् ।
वाञ्छास्ति महती राम गम्यतां यदि रोचते ॥ २६ ॥

prayaccha tāni naḥ kṛṣṇa
gandha-lobhita-cetasām
vāñchāsti mahatī rāma
gamyatāṁ yadi rocate

prayaccha—please give; *tāni*—them; *naḥ*—to us; *kṛṣṇa*—O Kṛṣṇa; *gandha*—by the fragrance; *lobhita*—made greedy; *cetasām*—whose minds; *vāñchā*—the desire; *asti*—is; *mahatī*—great; *rāma*—O Rāma; *gamyatām*—let us go; *yadi*—if; *rocate*—it appears like a good idea.

TRANSLATION

O Kṛṣṇa! Please get those fruits for us. Our minds are so attracted by their aroma! Dear Balarāma, our desire to have those fruits is very great. If You think it's a good idea, let's go to that Tāla forest.

PURPORT

Although neither man nor bird nor beast could even approach the Tāla forest, the cowherd boys had so much faith in Lord Kṛṣṇa and Lord Balarāma that they took it for granted the two Lords could effortlessly kill the sinful ass demons and acquire the delicious *tāla* fruits. Lord Kṛṣṇa's cowherd boyfriends are exalted, self-realized souls who would not ordinarily become greedy for sweet fruits. In fact, they are simply joking with the Lord and enthusing His pastimes, urging Him to perform unprecedented heroic feats in the Tāla forest. Innumerable demons disturbed the sublime atmosphere of Vṛndāvana during Lord Kṛṣṇa's presence there, and the Lord would kill such demons as a popular daily event.

Since Lord Kṛṣṇa had already killed many demons, on this particular day He decided to give first honors to Lord Balarāma, who would demolish the first demon, Dhenuka. By the words *yadi rocate,* the cowherd boys indicate that Lord Kṛṣṇa and Lord Balarāma need not kill the demon simply to satisfy them; rather, They should do so only if the Lords Themselves found the concept appealing.

TEXT 27

एवं सुहृद्वचः श्रुत्वा सुहृत्प्रियचिकीर्षया ।
प्रहस्य जग्मतुर्गोपैर्वृतौ तालवनं प्रभू ॥ २७ ॥

evaṁ suhṛd-vacaḥ śrutvā
suhṛt-priya-cikīrṣayā
prahasya jagmatur gopair
vṛtau tālavanaṁ prabhū

evam—thus; *suhṛt*—of Their friends; *vacaḥ*—the words; *śrutvā*—hearing; *suhṛt*—to Their friends; *priya*—pleasure; *cikīrṣayā*—desiring to give; *prahasya*—laughing; *jagmatuḥ*—the two of Them went; *gopaiḥ*—by the cowherd boys; *vṛtau*—surrounded; *tāla-vanam*—to the Tāla forest; *prabhū*—the two Lords.

TRANSLATION

Hearing the words of Their dear companions, Kṛṣṇa and Balarāma laughed and, desiring to please them, set off for the Tālavana surrounded by Their cowherd boyfriends.

PURPORT

Lord Kṛṣṇa was thinking, "How can a mere ass be so formidable?" And thus He smiled at the petition of His boyfriends. As stated by Lord Kapila in the *Śrīmad-Bhāgavatam* (3.28.32), *hāsaṁ harer avanatākhila-loka-tīvra-śokāśru-sāgara-viśoṣaṇam aty-udāram:* "The smile and laughter of the Supreme Lord Hari is most magnanimous. Indeed, for those who bow down to the Lord, His smile and laughter dry up the ocean of tears caused by the intense suffering of this world." Thus, to encourage Their boyfriends, Lord Kṛṣṇa and Lord Balarāma smiled, laughed and immediately set out with them for the Tāla forest.

TEXT 28

बलः प्रविश्य बाहुभ्यां तालान् सम्परिकम्पयन्।
फलानि पातयामास मतंगज इवौजसा ॥ २८ ॥

balaḥ praviśya bāhubhyāṁ
tālān samparikampayan
phalāni pātayām āsa
mataṅ-gaja ivaujasā

balaḥ—Balarāma; *praviśya*—entering; *bāhubhyām*—with His two arms; *tālān*—the palm trees; *samparikampayan*—making shake all around; *phalāni*—the fruits; *pātayām āsa*—He made fall; *matam-gajaḥ*—a maddened elephant; *iva*—just as; *ojasā*—by His strength.

TRANSLATION

Lord Balarāma entered the Tāla forest first. Then with His two arms He began forcefully shaking the trees with the power of a maddened elephant, causing the tāla fruits to fall to the ground.

TEXT 29

फलानां पततां शब्दं निशम्यासुररासभः ।
अभ्यधावत् क्षितितलं सनगं परिकम्पयन् ॥ २९ ॥

phalānāṁ patatāṁ śabdaṁ
niśamyāsura-rāsabhaḥ
abhyadhāvat kṣiti-talaṁ
sa-nagaṁ parikampayan

phalānām—of the fruits; *patatām*—which are falling; *śabdam*—the sound; *niśamya*—hearing; *asura-rāsabhaḥ*—the demon in the form of a jackass; *abhyadhāvat*—ran forward; *kṣiti-talam*—the surface of the earth; *sa-nagam*—together with the trees; *parikampayan*—making tremble.

TRANSLATION

Hearing the sound of the falling fruits, the ass demon Dhenuka ran forward to attack, making the earth and trees tremble.

TEXT 30

समेत्य तरसा प्रत्यग् द्वाभ्यां पद्भ्यां बलं बली ।
निहत्योरसि काशब्दं मुञ्चन् पर्यसरत् खलः ॥ ३० ॥

sametya tarasā pratyag
dvābhyāṁ padbhyāṁ balaṁ balī
nihatyorasi kā-śabdaṁ
muñcan paryasarat khalaḥ

sametya—meeting Him; *tarasā*—swiftly; *pratyak*—hind; *dvābhyām*—with the two; *padbhyām*—legs; *balam*—Lord Baladeva; *balī*—the powerful demon; *nihatya*—striking; *urasi*—upon the chest; *kā-śabdam*—an ugly braying sound; *muñcan*—releasing; *paryasarat*—ran around; *khalaḥ*—the jackass.

TRANSLATION

The powerful demon rushed up to Lord Baladeva and sharply struck the Lord's chest with the hooves of his hind legs. Then Dhenuka began to run about, braying loudly.

TEXT 31

पुनरासाद्य संरब्ध उपक्रोष्टा पराक् स्थितः ।
चरणावपरौ राजन् बलाय प्राक्षिपद् रुषा ॥ ३१ ॥

punar āsādya saṁrabdha
upakroṣṭā parāk sthitaḥ
caraṇāv aparau rājan
balāya prākṣipad ruṣā

punaḥ—again; *āsādya*—approaching Him; *saṁrabdhaḥ*—furious; *upakroṣṭā*—the ass; *parāk*—with his back toward the Lord; *sthitaḥ*—standing; *caraṇau*—two legs; *aparau*—hind; *rājan*—O King Parīkṣit; *balāya*—at Lord Balarāma; *prākṣipat*—he hurled; *ruṣā*—with anger.

TRANSLATION

Moving again toward Lord Balarāma, O King, the furious ass situated himself with his back toward the Lord. Then, screaming in rage, the demon hurled his two hind legs at Him.

PURPORT

The word *upakroṣṭā* indicates an ass and also one who is crying out nearby. Thus it is indicated herein that the powerful Dhenuka made horrible, angry sounds.

TEXT 32

स तं गृहीत्वा प्रपदोर्भ्रामयित्वैकपाणिना ।
चिक्षेप तृणराजाग्रे भ्रामणत्यक्तजीवितम् ॥ ३२ ॥

sa taṁ gṛhītvā prapador
bhrāmayitvaika-pāṇinā
cikṣepa tṛṇa-rājāgre
bhrāmaṇa-tyakta-jīvitam

saḥ—He; *tam*—him; *gṛhītvā*—seizing; *prapadoḥ*—by the hooves; *bhrāmayitvā*—whirling around; *eka-pāṇinā*—with a single hand; *cikṣepa*—He threw; *tṛṇa-rāja-agre*—into the top of a palm tree; *bhrāmaṇa*—by the whirling; *tyakta*—giving up; *jīvitam*—his life.

TRANSLATION

Lord Balarāma seized Dhenuka by his hooves, whirled him about with one hand and threw him into the top of a palm tree. The violent wheeling motion killed the demon.

TEXT 33

तेनाहतो महातालो वेपमानो बृहच्छिराः ।
पार्श्वस्थं कम्पयन् भग्नः स चान्यं सोऽपि चापरम् ॥ ३३ ॥

tenāhato mahā-tālo
vepamāno bṛhac-chirāḥ
pārśva-sthaṁ kampayan bhagnaḥ
sa cānyaṁ so'pi cāparam

tena—by that (body of the dead Dhenukāsura); *āhataḥ*—struck; *mahā-tālaḥ*—the great palm tree; *vepamānaḥ*—trembling; *bṛhat-śirāḥ*—which had a large top; *pārśva-stham*—another situated beside it; *kampayan*—making shake; *bhagnaḥ*—broken; *saḥ*—that; *ca*—and; *anyam*—another; *saḥ*—that; *api*—yet; *ca*—and; *aparam*—another.

TRANSLATION

Lord Balarāma threw the dead body of Dhenukāsura into the tallest palm tree in the forest, and when the dead demon landed in the treetop, the tree began shaking. The great palm tree, causing a tree by its side also to shake, broke under the weight of the demon. The neighboring tree caused yet another tree to shake, and this one struck yet another tree, which also began shaking. In this way many trees in the forest shook and broke.

PURPORT

Lord Balarāma threw the demon Dhenuka so violently into the great palm tree that a chain reaction was unleashed, and many towering palm trees shook and then broke with a great crashing sound.

TEXT 34

बलस्य लीलयोत्सृष्टखरदेहहताहताः ।
तालाश्चकम्पिरे सर्वे महावातेरिता इव ॥ ३४ ॥

balasya līlayotsṛṣṭa-
khara-deha-hatāhatāḥ
tālāś cakampire sarve
mahā-vāteritā iva

balasya—of Lord Balarāma; *līlayā*—as the pastime; *utsṛṣṭa*—thrown upward; *khara-deha*—by the body of the ass; *hata-āhatāḥ*—which were striking one another; *tālāḥ*—the palm trees; *cakampire*—shook; *sarve*—all; *mahā-vāta*—by a powerful wind; *īritāḥ*—blown; *iva*—as if.

TRANSLATION

Because of Lord Balarāma's pastime of throwing the body of the ass demon into the top of the tallest palm tree, all the trees began shaking and striking against one another as if blown about by powerful winds.

TEXT 35

नैतच्चित्रं भगवति ह्यनन्ते जगदीश्वरे ।
ओतप्रोतमिदं यस्मिंस्तन्तुष्वंग यथा पटः ॥ ३५ ॥

naitac citraṁ bhagavati
hy anante jagad-īśvare
ota-protam idaṁ yasmiṁs
tantuṣv aṅga yathā paṭaḥ

na—not; *etat*—this; *citram*—surprising; *bhagavati*—for the Personality of Godhead; *hi*—indeed; *anante*—who is the unlimited; *jagat-īśvare*—the Lord of the the universe; *ota-protam*—spread out horizontally and vertically; *idam*—this universe; *yasmin*—upon whom; *tantuṣu*—upon its threads; *aṅga*—my dear Parīkṣit; *yathā*—just as; *paṭaḥ*—a cloth.

TRANSLATION

My dear Parīkṣit, that Lord Balarāma killed Dhenukāsura is not such a wonderful thing, considering that He is the unlimited Personality of Godhead, the controller of the entire universe. Indeed, the entire cosmos rests upon Him just as a woven cloth rests upon its own horizontal and vertical threads.

PURPORT

Unfortunate persons cannot appreciate the blissful pastimes of the Supreme Lord. In this connection Śrīla Jīva Gosvāmī explains that the Supreme Lord possesses unlimited potency and strength, as expressed here by the word *anante.* The Lord exhibits a tiny fraction of His power according to the need of a particular situation. Lord Balarāma desired to vanquish the gang of demoniac asses who had unlawfully seized the Tālavana forest, and therefore He exhibited just enough divine opulence to easily kill Dhenukāsura and the other demons.

TEXT 36

ततः कृष्णं च रामं च ज्ञातयो धेनुकस्य ये ।
क्रोष्टारोऽभ्यद्रवन् सर्वे संरब्धा हतबान्धवाः ॥ ३६ ॥

tataḥ kṛṣṇaṁ ca rāmaṁ ca
jñātayo dhenukasya ye

kroṣṭāro'bhyadravan sarve
saṁrabdhā hata-bāndhavāḥ

tataḥ—then; *kṛṣṇam*—at Lord Kṛṣṇa; *ca*—and; *rāmam*—Lord Rāma; *ca*—and; *jñātayaḥ*—the intimate companions; *dhenukasya*—of Dhenuka; *ye*—who; *kroṣṭāraḥ*—the asses; *abhyadravan*—attacked; *sarve*—all; *saṁrabdhāḥ*—enraged; *hata-bāndhavāḥ*—their friend having been killed.

TRANSLATION

The other ass demons, close friends of Dhenukāsura, were enraged upon seeing his death, and thus they all immediately ran to attack Kṛṣṇa and Balarāma.

PURPORT

Śrīla Sanātana Gosvāmī makes the following comment on this verse: "It is stated here that the ass demons first attacked Kṛṣṇa and then Balarāma (*kṛṣṇaṁ ca rāmaṁ ca*). One reason for this is that the demons, having seen the prowess of Lord Balarāma, thought it wise to attack Kṛṣṇa first. Or it may be that out of affection for His elder brother, Lord Kṛṣṇa placed Himself between Balarāma and the ass demons. The words *kṛṣṇaṁ ca rāmaṁ ca* may also be understood to indicate that Lord Balarāma, out of affection for His younger brother, went to Lord Kṛṣṇa's side."

TEXT 37

तांस्तानापततः कृष्णो रामश्च नृप लीलया ।
गृहीतपश्चाच्चरणान् प्राहिणोत्तृणराजसु ॥ ३७ ॥

tāṁs tān āpatataḥ kṛṣṇo
rāmaś ca nṛpa līlayā
gṛhīta-paścāc-caraṇān
prāhiṇot tṛṇa-rājasu

tān tān—all of them, one by one; *āpatataḥ*—attacking; *kṛṣṇaḥ*—Lord Kṛṣṇa; *rāmaḥ*—Lord Balarāma; *ca*—and; *nṛpa*—O King; *līlayā*—easily; *gṛhīta*—seizing; *paścāt-caraṇān*—their hind legs; *prāhiṇot*—threw; *tṛṇa-rājasu*—into the palm trees.

TRANSLATION

O King, as the demons attacked, Kṛṣṇa and Balarāma easily seized them one after another by their hind legs and threw them all into the tops of the palm trees.

TEXT 38

फलप्रकरसंकीर्णं दैत्यदेहैर्गतासुभिः ।
रराज भूः सतालाग्रैर्घनैरिव नभस्तलम् ॥ ३८ ॥

phala-prakara-saṅkīrṇaṁ
daitya-dehair gatāsubhiḥ
rarāja bhūḥ sa-tālāgrair
ghanair iva nabhas-talam

phala-prakara—with heaps of fruits; *saṅkīrṇam*—covered; *daitya-dehaiḥ*—with the bodies of the demons; *gata-asubhiḥ*—which were lifeless; *rarāja*—shone forth; *bhūḥ*—the earth; *sa-tāla-agraiḥ*—with the tops of the palm trees; *ghanaiḥ*—with clouds; *iva*—as; *nabhaḥ-talam*—the sky.

TRANSLATION

The earth then appeared beautifully covered with heaps of fruits and with the dead bodies of the demons, which were entangled in the broken tops of the palm trees. Indeed, the earth shone like the sky decorated with clouds.

PURPORT

According to Śrīla Viśvanātha Cakravartī Ṭhākura, the bodies of the demons were dark, like dark blue clouds, and the large quantity of blood that had flowed from their bodies appeared like bright red clouds. Thus the whole scene was very beautiful. The Supreme Personality of Godhead in His various forms, such as Rāma and Kṛṣṇa, is always transcendental, and when He enacts His transcendental pastimes the result is always beautiful and transcendental, even when the Lord performs violent acts like killing the stubborn ass demons.

TEXT 39

तयोस्तत् सुमहत् कर्म निशम्य विबुधादयः ।
मुमुचुः पुष्पवर्षाणि चक्रुर्वाद्यानि तुष्टुवुः ॥ ३९ ॥

tayos tat su-mahat karma
niśamya vibudhādayaḥ
mumucuḥ puṣpa-varṣāṇi
cakrur vādyāni tuṣṭuvuḥ

tayoḥ—of the two brothers; *tat*—that; *su-mahat*—very great; *karma*—act; *niśamya*—hearing of; *vibudha-ādayaḥ*—the demigods and other elevated living beings; *mumucuḥ*—they released; *puṣpa-varṣāṇi*—downpours of flowers; *cakruḥ*—they performed; *vādyāni*—music; *tuṣṭuvuḥ*—they offered prayers.

TRANSLATION

Hearing of this magnificent feat of the two brothers, the demigods and other elevated living beings rained down flowers and offered music and prayers in glorification.

PURPORT

Śrīla Sanātana Gosvāmī comments that the demigods, great sages and other exalted beings were all astonished and ecstatic upon seeing the unusually swift and nonchalant way in which Kṛṣṇa and Balarāma killed the very powerful ass demons in the Tāla forest.

TEXT 40

अथ तालफलान्यादन्मनुष्या गतसाध्वसाः ।
तृणं च पशवश्चेरुर्हतधेनुककानने ॥ ४० ॥

atha tāla-phalāny ādan
manuṣyā gata-sādhvasāḥ
tṛṇaṁ ca paśavaś cerur
hata-dhenuka-kānane

atha—then; *tāla*—of the palm trees; *phalāni*—the fruits; *ādan*—ate; *manuṣyāḥ*—the human beings; *gata-sādhvasāḥ*—having lost their fear; *tṛṇam*—upon the grass; *ca*—and; *paśavaḥ*—the animals; *ceruḥ*—grazed; *hata*—killed; *dhenuka*—of the demon Dhenuka; *kānane*—in the forest.

TRANSLATION

People now felt free to return to the forest where Dhenuka had been killed, and without fear they ate the fruits of the palm trees. Also, the cows could now graze freely upon the grass there.

PURPORT

According to the *ācāryas,* low-class people such as the *pulindas* ate the fruits of the palm trees, but Kṛṣṇa's cowherd boyfriends considered them undesirable, since they had been tainted with the blood of the asses.

TEXT 41

कृष्णः कमलपत्राक्षः पुण्यश्रवणकीर्तनः।
स्तूयमानोऽनुगैर्गोपैः साग्रजो व्रजमाव्रजत्॥ ४१॥

kṛṣṇaḥ kamala-patrākṣaḥ
puṇya-śravaṇa-kīrtanaḥ
stūyamāno'nugair gopaiḥ
sāgrajo vrajam āvrajat

kṛṣṇaḥ—Lord Śrī Kṛṣṇa; *kamala-patra-akṣaḥ*—whose eyes are like lotus petals; *puṇya-śravaṇa-kīrtanaḥ*—hearing and chanting about whom is the most pious activity; *stūyamānaḥ*—being glorified; *anugaiḥ*—by His followers; *gopaiḥ*—the cowherd boys; *sa-agra-jaḥ*—together with His elder brother, Balarāma; *vrajam*—to Vraja; *āvrajat*—He returned.

TRANSLATION

Then lotus-eyed Lord Śrī Kṛṣṇa, whose glories are most pious to hear and chant, returned home to Vraja with His elder brother, Balarāma. Along the way, the cowherd boys, His faithful followers, chanted His glories.

PURPORT

When the glories of Śrī Kṛṣṇa are vibrated, both the speakers and the hearers are purified and become pious.

TEXT 42

तं गोरजश्छुरितकुन्तलबद्धबर्ह-
वन्यप्रसूनरुचिरेक्षणचारुहासम्।

वेणुं क्वणन्तमनुगैरुपगीतकीर्तिं
गोप्यो दिदृक्षितदृशोऽभ्यगमन् समेताः ॥ ४२ ॥

taṁ gorajaś-churita-kuntala-baddha-barha-
vanya-prasūna-rucirekṣaṇa-cāru-hāsam
veṇum kvaṇantam anugair upagīta-kīrtiṁ
gopyo didṛkṣita-dṛśo'bhyagaman sametāḥ

tam—Him; *go-rajaḥ*—with the dust raised by the cows; *churita*—smeared; *kuntala*—within His locks of hair; *baddha*—placed; *barha*—a peacock feather; *vanya-prasūna*—with forest flowers; *rucira-īkṣaṇa*—charming eyes; *cāru-hāsam*—and a beautiful smile; *veṇum*—His flute; *kvaṇantam*—sounding; *anugaiḥ*—by His companions; *upagīta*—being chanted; *kīrtim*—His glories; *gopyaḥ*—the *gopīs; didṛkṣita*—eager to see; *dṛśaḥ*—their eyes; *abhyagaman*—came forward; *sametāḥ*—in a body.

TRANSLATION

Lord Kṛṣṇa's hair, powdered with the dust raised by the cows, was decorated with a peacock feather and forest flowers. The Lord glanced charmingly and smiled beautifully, playing upon His flute while His companions chanted His glories. The gopīs, all together, came forward to meet Him, their eyes very eager to see Him.

PURPORT

Superficially, the *gopīs* were young married girls, and therefore they would naturally be ashamed and fearful of casting loving glances at a beautiful young boy like Śrī Kṛṣṇa. But Śrī Kṛṣṇa is the Supreme Personality of Godhead, and all living beings are His eternal servants. Thus the *gopīs,* although the most pure-hearted of all great souls, did not hesitate to come forward and satisfy their love-struck eyes by drinking in the sight of beautiful young Kṛṣṇa. The *gopīs* also relished the sweet sound of His flute and the enchanting fragrance of His body.

TEXT 43

पीत्वा मुकुन्दमुखसारघमक्षिभृंगैस्
तापं जहुर्विरहजं व्रजयोषितोऽह्नि ।
तत् सत्कृतिं समधिगम्य विवेश गोष्ठं
सव्रीडहासविनयं यदपांगमोक्षम् ॥ ४३ ॥

pītvā mukunda-mukha-sāragham akṣi-bhṛṅgais
tāpaṁ jahur viraha-jaṁ vraja-yoṣito'hni
tat sat-kṛtiṁ samadhigamya viveśa goṣṭhaṁ
savrīḍa-hāsa-vinayaṁ yad apāṅga-mokṣam

pītvā—drinking; *mukunda-mukha*—of the face of Lord Mukunda; *sāragham*—the honey; *akṣi-bhṛṅgaiḥ*—with their beelike eyes; *tāpam*—distress; *jahuḥ*—gave up; *viraha-jam*—based on separation; *vraja-yoṣitaḥ*—the ladies of Vṛndāvana; *ahni*—during the day; *tat*—that; *sat-kṛtim*—offering of respect; *samadhigamya*—fully accepting; *viveśa*—He entered; *goṣṭham*—the cowherd village; *sa-vrīḍa*—with shame; *hāsa*—laughter; *vinayam*—and humbleness; *yat*—which; *apāṅga*—of their sidelong glances; *mokṣam*—the release.

TRANSLATION

With their beelike eyes, the women of Vṛndāvana drank the honey of the beautiful face of Lord Mukunda, and thus they gave up the distress they had felt during the day because of separation from Him. The young Vṛndāvana ladies cast sidelong glances at the Lord—glances filled with bashfulness, laughter and submission—and Śrī Kṛṣṇa, completely accepting these glances as a proper offering of respect, entered the cowherd village.

PURPORT

In *Kṛṣṇa, the Supreme Personality of Godhead,* Śrīla Prabhupāda describes this incident as follows: "All the *gopīs* in Vṛndāvana remained very morose on account of Kṛṣṇa's absence. All day they were thinking of Kṛṣṇa in the forest or of Him herding cows in the pasture. When they saw Kṛṣṇa returning, all their anxieties were immediately relieved, and they began to look at His face the way drones hover over the honey of the lotus flower. When Kṛṣṇa entered the village, the young *gopīs* smiled and laughed. Kṛṣṇa, while playing the flute, enjoyed the beautiful smiling faces of the *gopīs.*"

The Supreme Lord, Śrī Kṛṣṇa, is the supreme master of romantic skills, and thus He expertly exchanged loving feelings with the young cowherd girls of Vṛndāvana. When a chaste young girl is in love, she glances at her beloved with shyness, jubilation and submission. When the beloved accepts her offering of love by receiving her glance and is thus satisfied with her, the loving young girl's heart becomes filled with happiness. These were exactly the romantic exchanges taking place between beautiful young Kṛṣṇa and the loving cowherd girls of Vṛndāvana.

TEXT 44

तयोर्यशोदारोहिण्यौ पुत्रयोः पुत्रवत्सले ।
यथाकामं यथाकालं व्यधत्तां परमाशिषः ॥ ४४ ॥

tayor yaśodā-rohiṇyau
putrayoḥ putra-vatsale
yathā-kāmaṁ yathā-kālaṁ
vyadhattāṁ paramāśiṣaḥ

tayoḥ—to the two; *yaśodā-rohiṇyau*—Yaśodā and Rohiṇī (the mothers of Kṛṣṇa and Balarāma, respectively); *putrayoḥ*—to their sons; *putra-vatsale*—who were very affectionate to their sons; *yathā-kāmam*—in accordance with Their desires; *yathā-kālam*—in accordance with the time and circumstances; *vyadhattām*—presented; *parama-āśiṣaḥ*—first-class enjoyable offerings.

TRANSLATION

Mother Yaśodā and mother Rohiṇī, acting most affectionately toward their two sons, offered all the best things to Them in response to Their every desire and at the various appropriate times.

PURPORT

The word *paramāśiṣaḥ* indicates the attractive blessings of a loving mother, which include wonderful food, beautiful clothes, jewelry, toys and constant affection. The words *yathā-kāmaṁ yathā-kālam* indicate that although Yaśodā and Rohiṇī satisfied all the desires of their sons, Kṛṣṇa and Balarāma, they also properly regulated the boys' activities. In other words, they prepared wonderful food for their children, but they saw to it that the boys ate at the proper time. Similarly, their children would play at the proper time and sleep at the proper time. The word *yathā-kāmam* does not indicate that the mothers indiscriminately allowed the boys to do whatever They liked, but in the proper, civilized way they showered their blessings upon their children.

Śrīla Sanātana Gosvāmī comments that the mothers loved their sons so much that as they embraced Them they would carefully check all Their limbs to see if They were healthy and strong.

TEXT 45

गताध्वानश्रमौ तत्र मज्जनोन्मर्दनादिभिः ।
नीवीं वसित्वा रुचिरां दिव्यस्रग्गन्धमण्डितौ ॥ ४५ ॥

gatādhvāna-śramau tatra
majjanonmardanādibhiḥ
nīvīṁ vasitvā rucirāṁ
divya-srag-gandha-maṇḍitau

gata—gone; *adhvāna-śramau*—whose weariness from being upon the road; *tatra*—there (in Their home); *majjana*—by bathing; *unmardana*—massaging; *ādibhiḥ*—and so on; *nīvīm*—in undergarments; *vasitvā*—being dressed; *rucirām*—charming; *divya*—transcendental; *srak*—with garlands; *gandha*—and fragrances; *maṇḍitau*—decorated.

TRANSLATION

By being bathed and massaged, the two young Lords were relieved of the weariness caused by walking on the country roads. Then They were dressed in attractive robes and decorated with transcendental garlands and fragrances.

TEXT 46

जनन्युपहृतं प्राश्य स्वाद्वन्नमुपलालितौ ।
संविश्य वरशय्यायां सुखं सुषुपतुर्व्रजे ॥ ४६ ॥

janany-upahṛtaṁ prāśya
svādy annam upalālitau
saṁviśya vara-śayyāyāṁ
sukhaṁ suṣupatur vraje

jananī—by Their mothers; *upahṛtam*—offered; *prāśya*—eating fully; *svādu*—delicious; *annam*—food; *upalālitau*—being pampered; *saṁviśya*—entering; *vara*—excellent; *śayyāyām*—upon bedding; *sukham*—happily; *suṣupatuḥ*—the two of Them slept; *vraje*—in Vraja.

TRANSLATION

After dining sumptuously on the delicious food given Them by Their mothers and being pampered in various ways, the two brothers lay down upon Their excellent beds and happily went to sleep in the village of Vraja.

TEXT 47

एवं स भगवान् कृष्णो वृन्दावनचरः क्वचित् ।
ययौ राममृते राजन् कालिन्दीं सखिभिर्वृतः ॥ ४७ ॥

evaṁ sa bhagavān kṛṣṇo
vṛndāvana-carah kvacit
yayau rāmam ṛte rājan
kālindīṁ sakhibhir vṛtaḥ

evam—thus; *saḥ*—He; *bhagavān*—the Supreme Personality of Godhead; *kṛṣṇaḥ*—Kṛṣṇa; *vṛndāvana-caraḥ*—wandering, and acting, in Vṛndāvana; *kvacit*—once; *yayau*—went; *rāmam ṛte*—without Lord Balarāma; *rājan*—O King Parīkṣit; *kālindīm*—to the river Yamunā; *sakhibhiḥ*—by His friends; *vṛtaḥ*—surrounded.

TRANSLATION

O King, the Supreme Lord Kṛṣṇa thus wandered about the Vṛndāvana area, performing His pastimes. Once, surrounded by His boyfriends, He went without Balarāma to the Yamunā River.

TEXT 48

अथ गावश्च गोपाश्च निदाघातपपीडिताः ।
दुष्टं जलं पपुस्तस्यास्तृष्णार्ता विषदूषितम् ॥ ४८ ॥

atha gāvaś ca gopāś ca
nidāghātapa-pīḍitāḥ
duṣṭaṁ jalaṁ papus tasyās
tṛṣṇārtā viṣa-dūṣitam

atha—then; *gāvaḥ*—the cows; *ca*—and; *gopāḥ*—the cowherd boys; *ca*—and; *nidāgha*—of the summer; *ātapa*—by the glaring sun; *pīḍitāḥ*—distressed; *duṣṭam*—contaminated; *jalam*—the water; *papuḥ*—they drank; *tasyāḥ*—of the river; *tṛṣa-ārtāḥ*—tormented by thirst; *viṣa*—by poison; *dūṣitam*—spoiled.

TRANSLATION

At that time the cows and cowherd boys were feeling acute distress from the glaring summer sun. Afflicted by thirst, they drank the water of the Yamunā River. But it had been contaminated with poison.

TEXTS 49–50

विषाम्भस्तदुपस्पृश्य दैवोपहतचेतसः ।
निपेतुर्व्यसवः सर्वे सलिलान्ते कुरूद्वह ॥ ४९ ॥
वीक्ष्य तान् वै तथाभूतान् कृष्णो योगेश्वरेश्वरः ।
ईक्षयामृतवर्षिण्या स्वनाथान् समजीवयत् ॥ ५० ॥

viṣāmbhas tad upaspṛśya
daivopahata-cetasaḥ
nipetur vyasavaḥ sarve
salilānte kurūdvaha

vīkṣya tān vai tathā-bhūtān
kṛṣṇo yogeśvareśvaraḥ
īkṣayāmṛta-varṣiṇyā
sva-nāthān samajīvayat

viṣa-ambhaḥ—the poisoned water; *tat*—that; *upaspṛśya*—simply touching; *daiva*—by the mystic potency of the Personality of Godhead; *upahata*—lost; *cetasaḥ*—their consciousness; *nipetuḥ*—they fell down; *vyasavaḥ*—lifeless; *sarve*—all of them; *salila-ante*—at the edge of the water; *kuru-udvaha*—O hero of the Kuru dynasty; *vīkṣya*—seeing; *tān*—them; *vai*—indeed; *tathā-bhūtān*—in such a condition; *kṛṣṇaḥ*—Lord Kṛṣṇa; *yoga-īśvara-īśvaraḥ*—the master of all masters of *yoga; īkṣayā*—by His glance; *amṛta-varṣiṇyā*—which is a shower of nectar; *sva-nāthān*—those who accepted only Him as their master; *samajīvayat*—brought back to life.

TRANSLATION

As soon as they touched the poisoned water, all the cows and boys lost their consciousness by the divine power of the Lord and fell lifeless at the water's edge. O hero of the Kurus, seeing them in such a condition, Lord Kṛṣṇa, the master of all masters of mystic potency, felt compassion for these devotees, who had no Lord other than Him. Thus He immediately brought them back to life by showering His nectarean glance upon them.

TEXT 51

ते सम्प्रतीतस्मृतयः समुत्थाय जलान्तिकात् ।
आसन् सुविस्मिताः सर्वे वीक्षमाणाः परस्परम् ॥ ५१ ॥

te sampratīta-smṛtayaḥ
samutthāya jalāntikāt
āsan su-vismitāḥ sarve
vīkṣamāṇāḥ parasparam

te—they; *sampratīta*—regaining perfectly; *smṛtayaḥ*—their memory; *samutthāya*—rising up; *jala-antikāt*—from out of the water; *āsan*—they became; *su-vismitāḥ*—very surprised; *sarve*—all; *vīkṣamāṇāḥ*—looking; *parasparam*—at one another.

TRANSLATION

Regaining their full consciousness, the cows and boys stood up out of the water and began to look at one another in great astonishment.

TEXT 52

अन्वमंसत तद् राजन् गोविन्दानुग्रहेक्षितम् ।
पीत्वा विषं परेतस्य पुनरुत्थानमात्मनः ॥ ५२ ॥

anvamaṁsata tad rājan
govindānugrahekṣitam
pītvā viṣaṁ paretasya
punar utthānam ātmanaḥ

anvamaṁsata—they subsequently thought; *tat*—that; *rājan*—O King Parīkṣit; *govinda*—of Lord Govinda; *anugraha-īkṣitam*—due to the merciful glance; *pītvā*—having drunk; *viṣam*—poison; *paretasya*—of those who have lost their lives; *punaḥ*—once again; *utthānam*—rising up; *ātmanaḥ*—on their own.

TRANSLATION

O King, the cowherd boys then considered that although they had drunk poison and in fact had died, simply by the merciful glance of Govinda they had regained their lives and stood up by their own strength.

Thus end the purports of the humble servants of His Divine Grace A.C. Bhaktivedanta Swami Prabhupāda to the Tenth Canto, Fifteenth Chapter, of the Śrīmad-Bhāgavatam, *entitled "The Killing of Dhenuka, the Ass Demon."*

CHAPTER SIXTEEN

Kṛṣṇa Chastises the Serpent Kāliya

This chapter describes Lord Śrī Kṛṣṇa's pastime of subduing the serpent Kāliya within the lake adjoining the river Yamunā and His showing mercy to Kāliya in response to the prayers offered by Kāliya's wives, the Nāgapatnīs.

To restore the purity of the Yamunā's waters, which had been contaminated by Kāliya's poison, Lord Kṛṣṇa climbed into a *kadamba* tree on the riverbank and jumped into the water. Then He began fearlessly playing within the water like a maddened elephant. Kāliya could not tolerate Kṛṣṇa's trespassing upon his personal residence, and the serpent quickly went up to the Lord and bit Him on the chest. When Kṛṣṇa's friends saw this, they fell down on the ground unconscious. At that time all sorts of evil omens appeared in Vraja, such as earth tremors, falling stars and the trembling of various creatures' left limbs.

The residents of Vṛndāvana thought, "Today Kṛṣṇa went to the forest without Balarāma, so we do not know what great misfortune may have befallen Him." Thinking in this way, they traced the path of Kṛṣṇa's footprints to the bank of the Yamunā. Within the water of the lake adjoining the river they saw Lord Kṛṣṇa, the very essence of their lives, enwrapped in the coils of a black snake. The residents thought the three worlds had become empty, and they all prepared to enter the water. But Lord Balarāma checked them, knowing well the power of Kṛṣṇa.

Then Lord Kṛṣṇa, seeing how disturbed His friends and relatives had become, expanded His body greatly and forced the serpent to loosen his grip and release Him. Next the Lord began playfully dancing about on the serpent's hoods. By this wonderful, boisterous dancing, Śrī Kṛṣṇa trampled the serpent's one thousand hoods until his body slackened. Vomiting blood from his mouths, Kāliya finally understood that Kṛṣṇa was the primeval personality, Lord Nārāyaṇa, the spiritual master of all moving and nonmoving creatures, and he took shelter of Him.

Seeing how very weary Kāliya had become, his wives, the Nāgapatnīs, bowed down at Lord Kṛṣṇa's lotus feet. Then they offered Him various prayers in hopes of gaining their husband's freedom: "It is quite fitting that You have brought our cruel husband to this condition. Indeed, by Your anger he has gained great benefit. What piety Kāliya must have amassed in his previous lives! Today he has borne upon his head the dust of the lotus feet of the Personality of Godhead, the attainment of which is difficult for even the mother of the universe, Goddess Lakṣmī. Please kindly forgive the offense Kāliya has committed out of ignorance, and allow him to live."

Satisfied by the Nāgapatnīs' prayers, Kṛṣṇa released Kāliya, who slowly regained his sensory and vital powers. Then Kāliya, in a distressed voice, acknowledged the offense he had committed, and finally he offered Kṛṣṇa many prayers and said he was ready to accept His command. Kṛṣṇa told him to leave the Yamunā lake with his family and return to Ramaṇaka Island.

TEXT 1

श्रीशुक उवाच

विलोक्य दूषितां कृष्णां कृष्णः कृष्णाहिना विभुः ।
तस्या विशुद्धिमन्विच्छन् सर्पं तमुदवासयत् ॥ १ ॥

śrī-śuka uvāca
vilokya dūṣitāṁ kṛṣṇāṁ
kṛṣṇaḥ kṛṣṇāhinā vibhuḥ
tasyā viśuddhim anvicchan
sarpaṁ tam udavāsayat

śrī-śukaḥ uvāca—Śrī Śukadeva Gosvāmī said; *vilokya*—seeing; *dūṣitām*—contaminated; *kṛṣṇām*—the river Yamunā; *kṛṣṇaḥ*—Lord Śrī Kṛṣṇa; *kṛṣṇa-ahinā*—by the black serpent; *vibhuḥ*—the almighty Lord; *tasyāḥ*—of the river; *viśuddhim*—the purification; *anvicchan*—desiring; *sarpam*—serpent; *tam*—that; *udavāsayat*—sent away.

TRANSLATION

Śukadeva Gosvāmī said: Lord Śrī Kṛṣṇa, the Supreme Personality of Godhead, seeing that the Yamunā River had been contaminated by the black snake Kāliya, desired to purify the river, and thus the Lord banished him from it.

TEXT 2

श्रीराजोवाच
कथमन्तर्जलेऽगाधे न्यगृह्णाद् भगवानहिम् ।
स वै बहुयुगावासं यथासीद् विप्र कथ्यताम् ॥ २ ॥

śrī-rājovāca
katham antar-jale'gādhe
nyagṛhṇād bhagavān ahim
sa vai bahu-yugāvāsaṁ
yathāsīd vipra kathyatām

śrī-rājā uvāca—King Parīkṣit said; *katham*—how; *antaḥ-jale*—within the water; *agādhe*—unfathomable; *nyagṛhṇāt*—subdued; *bhagavān*—the Supreme Personality of Godhead; *ahim*—the serpent; *saḥ*—he, Kāliya; *vai*—indeed; *bahu-yuga*—for many ages; *āvāsam*—having residence; *yathā*—how; *āsīt*—so became; *vipra*—O learned *brāhmaṇa; kathyatām*—please explain.

TRANSLATION

King Parīkṣit inquired: O learned sage, please explain how the Supreme Personality of Godhead chastised the serpent Kāliya within the unfathomable waters of the Yamunā, and how it was that Kāliya had been living there for so many ages.

TEXT 3

ब्रह्मन् भगवतस्तस्य भूम्नः स्वच्छन्दवर्तिनः ।
गोपालोदारचरितं कस्तृप्येतामृतं जुषन् ॥ ३ ॥

brahman bhagavatas tasya
bhūmnaḥ svacchanda-vartinaḥ
gopālodāra-caritaṁ
kas tṛpyetāmṛtaṁ juṣan

brahman—O *brāhmaṇa; bhagavataḥ*—of the Supreme Lord; *tasya*—of Him; *bhūmnaḥ*—the unlimited; *sva-chanda-vartinaḥ*—who acts according to His own desires; *gopāla*—as a cowherd boy; *udāra*—magnanimous; *caritam*—the pastimes; *kaḥ*—who; *tṛpyeta*—can be satiated; *amṛtam*—such nectar; *juṣan*—partaking of.

TRANSLATION

O brāhmaṇa, the unlimited Supreme Personality of Godhead freely acts according to His own desires. Who could be satiated when hearing the nectar of the magnanimous pastimes He performed as a cowherd boy in Vṛndāvana?

TEXT 4

श्रीशुक उवाच
कालिन्द्यां कालियस्यासीद् ह्रदः कश्चिद् विषाग्निना ।
श्रप्यमाणपया यस्मिन् पतन्त्युपरिगाः खगाः ॥ ४ ॥

śrī-śuka uvāca
kālindyāṁ kāliyasyāsīd
hradaḥ kaścid viṣāgninā
śrapyamāṇa-payā yasmin
patanty upari-gāḥ khagāḥ

śrī-śukaḥ uvāca—Śrī Śukadeva Gosvāmī said; *kālindyām*—within the river Yamunā; *kāliyasya*—of the serpent Kāliya; *āsīt*—there was; *hradaḥ*—lake; *kaścit*—a certain; *viṣa*—of his poison; *agninā*—by the fire; *śrapyamāṇa*—being heated and boiled; *payāḥ*—its water; *yasmin*—into which; *patanti*—would fall down; *upari-gāḥ*—traveling above; *khagāḥ*—the birds.

TRANSLATION

Śrī Śukadeva Gosvāmī said: Within the river Kālindī [Yamunā] was a lake inhabited by the serpent Kāliya, whose fiery poison constantly heated and boiled its waters. Indeed, the vapors thus created were so poisonous that birds flying over the contaminated lake would fall down into it.

PURPORT

In this regard the *ācāryas* explain that the Kāliya lake was situated apart from the main current of the river; otherwise the Yamunā's waters would have been poisonous even in cities like Mathurā and in other places farther away.

TEXT 5

विप्रुष्मता विषदोर्मिमारुतेनाभिमर्शिताः ।
म्रियन्ते तीरगा यस्य प्राणिनः स्थिरजंगमाः ॥ ५ ॥

vipruṣmatā viṣadormi-
mārutenābhimarśitāḥ
mriyante tīra-gā yasya
prāṇinaḥ sthira-jaṅgamāḥ

viprut-matā—containing droplets of the water; *viṣa-da*—poisonous; *ūrmi*—(having touched) the waves; *mārutena*—by the wind; *abhimarśitāḥ*—contacted; *mriyante*—would die; *tīra-gāḥ*—present upon the shore; *yasya*—of which; *prāṇinaḥ*—all living entities; *sthira-jaṅgamāḥ*—both nonmoving and moving.

TRANSLATION

The wind blowing over that deadly lake carried droplets of water to the shore. Simply by coming in contact with that poisonous breeze, all vegetation and creatures on the shore died.

PURPORT

The word *sthira,* "unmoving creatures," refers to various types of vegetation including trees, and *jaṅgama* refers to moving creatures such as animals, reptiles, birds and insects. Śrīla Śrīdhara Svāmī has quoted a further description of this lake from the *Śrī Hari-vaṁśa* (*Viṣṇu-parva* 11.42, 11.44 and 11.46):

dīrghaṁ yojana-vistāraṁ
dustaraṁ tridaśair api
gambhīram akṣobhya-jalaṁ
niṣkampam iva sāgaram

duḥkhopasarpaṁ tīreṣu
sa-sarpair vipulair bilaiḥ
viṣāraṇi-bhavasyāgner
dhūmena pariveṣṭitam

tṛṇeṣv api patatsv apsu
jvalantam iva tejasā
samantād yojanaṁ sāgraṁ
tīreṣv api durāsadam

"The lake was quite wide—eight miles across at some points—and even the demigods could not cross over it. The water in the lake was very deep and, like the immovable depths of the ocean, could not be agitated. Approaching the lake was difficult, for its shores were covered with holes in which serpents lived. All around the lake was a fog generated by the fire of the serpents' poison, and this powerful fire would at once burn up every blade of grass that happened to fall into the water. For a distance of eight miles from the lake, the atmosphere was most unpleasant."

Śrīla Sanātana Gosvāmī states that by the mystical science of *jala-stambha,* making solid items out of water, Kāliya had built his own city within the lake.

TEXT 6

तं चण्डवेगविषवीर्यमवेक्ष्य तेन
दुष्टां नदीं च खलसंयमनावतारः ।
कृष्णः कदम्बमधिरुह्य ततोऽतितुंगम्
आस्फोट्य गाढरशनो न्यपतद् विषोदे ॥ ६ ॥

taṁ caṇḍa-vega-viṣa-vīryam avekṣya tena
duṣṭāṁ nadīṁ ca khala-saṁyamanāvatāraḥ
kṛṣṇaḥ kadambam adhiruhya tato'ti-tuṅgam
āsphoṭya gāḍha-raśano nyapatad viṣode

tam—him, Kāliya; *caṇḍa-vega*—of fearsome power; *viṣa*—the poison; *vīryam*—whose strength; *avekṣya*—seeing; *tena*—by him; *duṣṭām*—contaminated; *nadīm*—the river; *ca*—and; *khala*—the envious demons; *saṁyamana*—for subduing; *avatāraḥ*—whose descent from the spiritual world; *kṛṣṇaḥ*—Lord Kṛṣṇa; *kadambam*—a *kadamba* tree; *adhiruhya*—climbing up on; *tataḥ*—from it; *ati-tuṅgam*—very high; *āsphoṭya*—slapping His arms; *gāḍha-raśanaḥ*—tying His belt firmly; *nyapatat*—He jumped; *viṣa-ude*—into the poisoned water.

TRANSLATION

Lord Kṛṣṇa saw how the Kāliya serpent had polluted the Yamunā River with his terribly powerful poison. Since Kṛṣṇa had descended from the spiritual world specifically to subdue envious demons, the Lord immediately climbed to the top of a very high kadamba tree and prepared Himself for battle. He tightened His belt, slapped His arms and then jumped into the poisonous water.

PURPORT

According to the *ācāryas,* Lord Kṛṣṇa also tied back the locks of His hair as He prepared to do battle with Kāliya.

TEXT 7

सर्पह्रदः पुरुषसारनिपातवेग-
सङ्क्षोभितोरगविषोच्छ्वसिताम्बुराशिः ।
पर्यक् प्लुतो विषकषायबिभीषणोर्मिर्
धावन् धनुःशतमनन्तबलस्य किं तत् ॥ ७॥

sarpa-hradaḥ puruṣa-sāra-nipāta-vega-
saṅkṣobhitoraga-viṣocchvasitāmbu-rāśiḥ
paryak pluto viṣa-kaṣāya-bibhīṣaṇormir
dhāvan dhanuḥ-śatam ananta-balasya kiṁ tat

sarpa-hradaḥ—the serpent's lake; *puruṣa-sāra*—of the most exalted Supreme Personality of Godhead; *nipāta-vega*—by the force of the fall; *saṅkṣobhita*—completely agitated; *uraga*—of the snakes; *viṣa-ucchvasita*—breathed upon with the poison; *ambu-rāśiḥ*—all of whose water; *paryak*—on all sides; *plutaḥ*—flooding; *viṣa-kaṣāya*—because of the contamination of the poison; *bibhīṣaṇa*—fearsome; *ūrmiḥ*—whose waves; *dhāvan*—flowing; *dhanuḥ-śatam*—the extent of one hundred bow-lengths; *ananta-balasya*—for Him whose strength is immeasurable; *kim*—what; *tat*—that.

TRANSLATION

When the Supreme Personality of Godhead landed in the serpent's lake, the snakes there became extremely agitated and began breathing heavily, further polluting it with volumes of poison. The force of the Lord's entrance into the lake caused it to overflow on all sides, and poisonous, fearsome waves flooded the surrounding lands up to a distance of one hundred bow-lengths. This is not at all amazing, however, for the Supreme Lord possesses infinite strength.

TEXT 8

तस्य ह्रदे विहरतो भुजदण्डघूर्ण-
वार्घोषमंग वरवारणविक्रमस्य ।
आश्रुत्य तत् स्वसदनाभिभवं निरीक्ष्य
चक्षुःश्रवाः समसरत्तदमृष्यमाणः ॥ ८॥

tasya hrade viharato bhuja-daṇḍa-ghūrṇa-
vār-ghoṣam aṅga vara-vāraṇa-vikramasya

āśrutya tat sva-sadanābhibhavaṁ nirīkṣya
cakṣuḥ-śravāḥ samasarat tad amṛṣyamāṇaḥ

tasya—of Him; *hrade*—in his lake; *viharataḥ*—who was playing; *bhuja-daṇḍa*—by His mighty arms; *ghūrṇa*—swirled about; *vāḥ*—of the water; *ghoṣam*—the resounding; *aṅga*—my dear King; *vara-vāraṇa*—like a great elephant; *vikramasya*—whose prowess; *āśrutya*—hearing; *tat*—that; *sva-sadana*—of his own residence; *abhibhavam*—the trespassing; *nirīkṣya*—taking note of; *cakṣuḥ-śravāḥ*—Kāliya; *samasarat*—came forward; *tat*—that; *amṛṣyamāṇaḥ*—being unable to tolerate.

TRANSLATION

Kṛṣṇa began sporting in Kāliya's lake like a lordly elephant—swirling His mighty arms and making the water resound in various ways. When Kāliya heard these sounds, he understood that someone was trespassing in his lake. The serpent could not tolerate this and immediately came forward.

PURPORT

According to the *ācāryas,* Lord Kṛṣṇa was producing wonderful musical sounds within the water simply by splashing His hands and arms.

TEXT 9

तं प्रेक्षणीयसुकुमारघनावदातं
श्रीवत्सपीतवसनं स्मितसुन्दरास्यम् ।
क्रीडन्तमप्रतिभयं कमलोदराङ्घ्रिं
सन्दश्य मर्मसु रुषा भुजया चछाद ॥ ९ ॥

taṁ prekṣaṇīya-sukumāra-ghanāvadātaṁ
śrīvatsa-pīta-vasanaṁ smita-sundarāsyam
krīḍantam apratibhayaṁ kamalodarāṅghriṁ
sandaśya marmasu ruṣā bhujayā cachāda

tam—Him; *prekṣaṇīya*—attractive to look at; *su-kumāra*—most delicate; *ghana*—like a cloud; *avadātam*—glowing white; *śrīvatsa*—wearing the Śrīvatsa mark; *pīta*—and yellow; *vasanam*—garments; *smita*—smiling; *sun-dara*—beautiful; *āsyam*—whose face; *krīḍantam*—playing; *aprati-bhayam*—without fear of others; *kamala*—of a lotus; *udara*—like the inside; *aṅghrim*

—whose feet; *sandaśya*—biting; *marmasu*—upon the chest; *ruṣā*—with anger; *bhujayā*—with his snake coils; *cachāda*—enveloped.

TRANSLATION

Kāliya saw that Śrī Kṛṣṇa, who wore yellow silken garments, was very delicate, His attractive body shining like a glowing white cloud, His chest bearing the mark of Śrīvatsa, His face smiling beautifully and His feet resembling the whorl of a lotus flower. The Lord was playing fearlessly in the water. Despite His wonderful appearance, the envious Kāliya furiously bit Him on the chest and then completely enwrapped Him in his coils.

TEXT 10

तं नागभोगपरिवीतमदृष्टचेष्टम्
आलोक्य तत्प्रियसखाः पशुपा भृशार्ताः ।
कृष्णेऽर्पितात्मसुहृदर्थकलत्रकामा
दुःखानुशोकभयमूढधियो निपेतुः ॥ १० ॥

taṁ nāga-bhoga-parivītam adṛṣṭa-ceṣṭam
ālokya tat-priya-sakhāḥ paśupā bhṛśārtāḥ
kṛṣṇe'rpitātma-suhṛd-artha-kalatra-kāmā
duḥkhānuśoka-bhaya-mūḍha-dhiyo nipetuḥ

tam—Him; *nāga*—of the serpent; *bhoga*—within the coils; *parivītam*—enveloped; *adṛṣṭa-ceṣṭam*—not exhibiting any movement; *ālokya*—seeing; *tat-priya-sakhāḥ*—His dear friends; *paśu-pāḥ*—the cowherds; *bhṛśa-ārtāḥ*—greatly disturbed; *kṛṣṇe*—unto Lord Kṛṣṇa; *arpita*—offered; *ātma*—their very selves; *su-hṛt*—their relations; *artha*—wealth; *kalatra*—wives; *kāmāḥ*—and all objects of desire; *duḥkha*—by pain; *anuśoka*—remorse; *bhaya*—and fear; *mūḍha*—bewildered; *dhiyaḥ*—their intelligence; *nipetuḥ*—they fell down.

TRANSLATION

When the members of the cowherd community, who had accepted Kṛṣṇa as their dearmost friend, saw Him enveloped in the snake's coils, motionless, they were greatly disturbed. They had offered Kṛṣṇa everything—their very selves, their families, their wealth, wives and all pleasures. At the sight of the Lord in the clutches of the Kāliya snake, their intelligence became deranged by grief, lamentation and fear, and thus they fell to the ground.

PURPORT

Śrīla Sanātana Gosvāmī explains that the cowherd boys, along with some cowherd men and farmers who happened to be in the vicinity and who were also devotees of Kṛṣṇa, fell to the ground just like trees that had been cut at the root.

TEXT 11

गावो वृषा वत्सतर्यः क्रन्दमानाः सुदुःखिताः ।
कृष्णे न्यस्तेक्षणा भीता रुदन्त्य इव तस्थिरे ॥ ११ ॥

gāvo vṛṣā vatsataryaḥ
krandamānāḥ su-duḥkhitāḥ
kṛṣṇe nyastekṣaṇā bhītā
rudantya iva tasthire

gāvaḥ—the cows; *vṛṣāḥ*—the bulls; *vatsataryaḥ*—the female calves; *krandamānāḥ*—crying loudly; *su-duḥkhitāḥ*—very much distressed; *kṛṣṇe*—upon Lord Kṛṣṇa; *nyasta*—fixed; *īkṣaṇāḥ*—their sight; *bhītāḥ*—fearful; *rudantyaḥ*—crying; *iva*—as if; *tasthire*—they stood still.

TRANSLATION

The cows, bulls and female calves, in great distress, called out piteously to Kṛṣṇa. Fixing their eyes on Him, they stood still in fear, as if ready to cry but too shocked to shed tears.

TEXT 12

अथ व्रजे महोत्पातास्त्रिविधा ह्यतिदारुणाः ।
उत्पेतुर्भुवि दिव्यात्मन्यासन्नभयशंसिनः ॥ १२ ॥

atha vraje mahotpātās
tri-vidhā hy ati-dāruṇāḥ
utpetur bhuvi divy ātmany
āsanna-bhaya-śaṁsinaḥ

atha—then; *vraje*—in Vṛndāvana; *mahā-utpātāḥ*—very ominous disturbances; *tri-vidhāḥ*—of the three varieties; *hi*—indeed; *ati-dāruṇāḥ*—most fearsome; *utpetuḥ*—arose; *bhuvi*—upon the earth; *divi*—in the sky; *ātmani*

—in the bodies of living creatures; *āsanna*—imminent; *bhaya*—danger; *saṁśinaḥ*—announcing.

TRANSLATION

In the Vṛndāvana area there then arose all three types of fearful omens—those on the earth, those in the sky and those in the bodies of living creatures—which announced imminent danger.

PURPORT

According to Śrīla Śrīdhara Svāmī, the omens were as follows: on the earth there were disturbing tremors, in the sky there were meteors falling, and in the bodies of creatures there was shivering, as well as quivering of the left eye and other parts of the body. These omens announce imminent danger.

TEXTS 13–15

तानालक्ष्य भयोद्विग्ना गोपा नन्दपुरोगमाः ।
विना रामेण गाः कृष्णं ज्ञात्वा चारयितुं गतम् ॥ १३ ॥
तैर्दुर्निमित्तैर्निधनं मत्वा प्राप्तमतद्विदः ।
तत्प्राणास्तन्मनस्कास्ते दुःखशोकभयातुराः ॥ १४ ॥
आबालवृद्धवनिताः सर्वेऽङ्ग पशुवृत्तयः ।
निर्जग्मुर्गोकुलाद्दीनाः कृष्णदर्शनलालसाः ॥ १५ ॥

tān ālakṣya bhayodvignā
gopā nanda-purogamāḥ
vinā rāmeṇa gāḥ kṛṣṇaṁ
jñātvā cārayituṁ gatam

tair durnimittair nidhanaṁ
matvā prāptam atad-vidaḥ
tat-prāṇās tan-manaskās te
duḥkha-śoka-bhayāturāḥ

ā-bāla-vṛddha-vanitāḥ
sarve'ṅga paśu-vṛttayaḥ
nirjagmur gokulād dīnāḥ
kṛṣṇa-darśana-lālasāḥ

tān—these signs; *ālakṣya*—seeing; *bhaya-udvignāḥ*—agitated by fear; *gopāḥ*—the cowherds; *nanda-puraḥ-gamāḥ*—headed by Nanda Mahārāja; *vinā*—without; *rāmeṇa*—Balarāma; *gāḥ*—the cows; *kṛṣṇam*—Kṛṣṇa; *jñātvā*—understanding; *cārayitum*—to herd; *gatam*—gone; *taiḥ*—from those; *durnimittaiḥ*—bad omens; *nidhanam*—destruction; *matvā*—considering; *prāptam*—attained; *atat-vidaḥ*—not knowing His opulences; *tat-prāṇāḥ*—having Him as their very source of life; *tat-manaskāḥ*—their minds being absorbed in Him; *te*—they; *duḥkha*—by pain; *śoka*—unhappiness; *bhaya*—and fear; *āturāḥ*—overwhelmed; *ā-bāla*—including the children; *vṛddha*—old persons; *vanitāḥ*—and ladies; *sarve*—all; *aṅga*—my dear King Parīkṣit; *paśu-vṛttayaḥ*—behaving as an affectionate cow does toward her calf; *nirjagmuḥ*—they went out; *gokulāt*—from Gokula; *dīnāḥ*—feeling wretched; *kṛṣṇa-darśana*—for the sight of Lord Kṛṣṇa; *lālasāḥ*—anxious.

TRANSLATION

Seeing the inauspicious omens, Nanda Mahārāja and the other cowherd men were fearful, for they knew that Kṛṣṇa had gone to herd the cows that day without His elder brother, Balarāma. Because they had dedicated their minds to Kṛṣṇa, accepting Him as their very life, they were unaware of His great power and opulence. Thus they concluded that the inauspicious omens indicated He had met with death, and they were overwhelmed with grief, lamentation and fear. All the inhabitants of Vṛndāvana, including the children, women and elderly persons, thought of Kṛṣṇa just as a cow thinks of her helpless young calf, and thus these poor, suffering people rushed out of the village, intent upon finding Him.

TEXT 16

तांस्तथा कातरान् वीक्ष्य भगवान्माधवो बलः ।
प्रहस्य किञ्चिन्नोवाच प्रभावज्ञोऽनुजस्य सः ॥ १६ ॥

tāṁs tathā kātarān vīkṣya
bhagavān mādhavo balaḥ
prahasya kiñcin novāca
prabhāva-jño 'nujasya saḥ

tān—them; *tathā*—in such a condition; *kātarān*—distressed; *vīkṣya*—seeing; *bhagavān*—the Supreme Personality of Godhead; *mādhavaḥ*—the master of all mystic knowledge; *balaḥ*—Lord Balarāma; *prahasya*—gently smiling; *kiñcit*—anything at all; *na*—did not; *uvāca*—say; *prabhāva-jñaḥ*—knowing the power; *anujasya*—of His younger brother; *saḥ*—He.

TRANSLATION

The Supreme Lord Balarāma, the master of all transcendental knowledge, smiled and said nothing when He saw the residents of Vṛndāvana in such distress, since He understood the extraordinary power of His younger brother.

PURPORT

Śrī Balarāma is the plenary expansion of Lord Kṛṣṇa and is thus nondifferent from Him. They are, in fact, the same Absolute Truth manifest in separate forms. According to Śrīla Viśvanātha Cakravartī Ṭhākura, Lord Balarāma was laughing because He thought, "Kṛṣṇa never cares to play with Me in My form of Śeṣa Nāga, but now He is playing with this ordinary, mundane snake named Kāliya."

The question may arise as to why Kṛṣṇa and Balarāma allowed Their loving devotees to suffer such great anguish during Kṛṣṇa's temporary imprisonment within the coils of Kāliya. It must be remembered that because the inhabitants of Vṛndāvana were completely liberated souls, they did not experience material emotions. When they saw their beloved Kṛṣṇa in apparent danger, their love for Him intensified to the highest degree, and thus they merged completely into the ecstasy of love for Him. The whole situation has to be seen from the spiritual point of view, or it will not be seen at all.

TEXT 17

तेऽन्वेषमाणा दयितं कृष्णं सूचितया पदैः ।
भगवल्लक्षणैर्जग्मुः पदव्या यमुनातटम् ॥ १७ ॥

te'nveṣamāṇā dayitaṁ
kṛṣṇaṁ sūcitayā padaiḥ
bhagaval-lakṣaṇair jagmuḥ
padavyā yamunā-taṭam

te—they; *anveṣamāṇāḥ*—searching out; *dayitam*—their dearmost; *kṛṣṇam*—Kṛṣṇa; *sūcitayā*—(along the path) which was marked; *padaiḥ*—by His footprints; *bhagavat-lakṣaṇaiḥ*—the symbolic markings of the Personality of Godhead; *jagmuḥ*—they went; *padavyā*—along the path; *yamunā-taṭam*—to the bank of the Yamunā.

TRANSLATION

The residents hurried toward the banks of the Yamunā in search of their dearmost Kṛṣṇa, following the path marked by His footprints, which bore the unique signs of the Personality of Godhead.

TEXT 18

ते तत्र तत्राब्जयवांकुशाशनि-
ध्वजोपपन्नानि पदानि विश्पतेः ।
मार्गे गवामन्यपदान्तरान्तरे
निरीक्षमाणा ययुरंग सत्वराः ॥ १८ ॥

te tatra tatrābja-yavāṅkuśāśani-
dhvajopapannāni padāni viś-pateḥ
mārge gavām anya-padāntarāntare
nirīkṣamāṇā yayur aṅga satvarāḥ

te—they; *tatra tatra*—here and there; *abja*—with the lotus flower; *yava*—barleycorn; *aṅkuśa*—elephant goad; *aśani*—thunderbolt; *dhvaja*—and flag; *upapannāni*—adorned; *padāni*—the footprints; *viṭ-pateḥ*—of Lord Kṛṣṇa, the master of the cowherd community; *mārge*—upon the path; *gavām*—of the cows; *anya-pada*—the other footprints; *antara-antare*—dispersed among; *nirīkṣamāṇāḥ*—seeing; *yuyuḥ*—they went; *aṅga*—my dear King; *sa-tvarāḥ*—rapidly.

TRANSLATION

The footprints of Lord Kṛṣṇa, the master of the entire cowherd community, were marked with the lotus flower, barleycorn, elephant goad, thunderbolt and flag. My dear King Parīkṣit, seeing His footprints on the path among the cows' hoofprints, the residents of Vṛndāvana rushed along in great haste.

PURPORT

Śrīla Sanātana Gosvāmī comments as follows: "Since Lord Kṛṣṇa had passed along the path some time previously, why weren't His footprints, which were surrounded by those of cows, cowherd boys and so on, smudged over and brushed away? Why hadn't His footprints been obliterated by those of the beasts and birds of Vṛndāvana forest? The answer is indicated by the word *viś-*

pati, master of the cowherd community. Since Lord Kṛṣṇa is actually the wealth of all living beings, all the inhabitants of the forest of Vraja would carefully preserve His footprints as great treasures, the very ornaments of the earth. Thus no creature within Vṛndāvana would ever walk upon Lord Kṛṣṇa's footprints."

TEXT 19

अन्तर्ह्रदे भुजगभोगपरीतमारात्
कृष्णं निरीहमुपलभ्य जलाशयान्ते ।
गोपांश्च मूढधिषणान् परितः पशूंश्च
संक्रन्दतः परमकश्मलमापुरार्ताः ॥ १९ ॥

antar hrade bhujaga-bhoga-parītam ārāt
kṛṣṇaṁ nirīham upalabhya jalāśayānte
gopāṁś ca mūḍha-dhiṣaṇān paritaḥ paśūṁś ca
saṅkrandataḥ parama-kaśmalam āpur ārtāḥ

antaḥ—within; *hrade*—the lake; *bhujaga*—of the serpent; *bhoga*—within the body; *parītam*—enveloped; *ārāt*—from a distance; *kṛṣṇam*—Lord Kṛṣṇa; *nirīham*—not moving; *upalabhya*—seeing; *jala-āśaya*—the body of water; *ante*—within; *gopān*—the cowherd boys; *ca*—and; *mūḍha-dhiṣaṇān*—unconscious; *paritaḥ*—surrounding; *paśūn*—the animals; *ca*—and; *saṅkrandataḥ*—crying out; *parama-kaśmalam*—the greatest bewilderment; *āpuḥ*—they experienced; *ārtāḥ*—being distressed.

TRANSLATION

As they hurried along the path to the bank of the Yamunā River, they saw from a distance that Kṛṣṇa was in the lake, motionless within the coils of the black serpent. They further saw that the cowherd boys had fallen unconscious and that the animals were standing on all sides, crying out for Kṛṣṇa. Seeing all this, the residents of Vṛndāvana were overwhelmed with anguish and confusion.

PURPORT

In their grief and panic, the residents of Vṛndāvana tried to find out whether Kāliya had forcibly dragged young Kṛṣṇa from the shore into the water, or whether Kṛṣṇa had Himself jumped from the shore and fallen into the clutches of the snake. They could not understand anything about the situation, and Kṛṣṇa's cowherd boyfriends, being unconscious, were unable to tell them anything. The cows and calves were crying out for Kṛṣṇa, and thus the whole situation was overwhelming and created a state of shock and panic among the residents of Vṛndāvana.

TEXT 20

गोप्योऽनुरक्तमनसो भगवत्यनन्ते
तत्सौहृदस्मितविलोकगिरः स्मरन्त्यः ।
ग्रस्तेऽहिना प्रियतमे भृशदुःखतप्ताः
शून्यं प्रियव्यतिहृतं ददृशुस्त्रिलोकम् ॥ २० ॥

gopyo'nurakta-manaso bhagavaty anante
tat-sauhṛda-smita-viloka-giraḥ smarantyaḥ
graste'hinā priyatame bhṛśa-duḥkha-taptāḥ
śūnyaṁ priya-vyatihṛtaṁ dadṛśus tri-lokam

gopyaḥ—the cowherd girls; *anurakta-manasaḥ*—their minds very much attached to Him; *bhagavati*—the Supreme Personality of Godhead; *anante*—the unlimited one; *tat*—His; *sauhṛda*—loving; *smita*—smiling; *viloka*—glances; *giraḥ*—and words; *smarantyaḥ*—remembering; *graste*—being seized; *ahinā*—by the serpent; *priya-tame*—their most dear; *bhṛśa*—extremely; *duḥkha*—by pain; *taptāḥ*—tormented; *śūnyam*—empty; *priya-vyatihṛtam*—deprived of their darling; *dadṛśuḥ*—they saw; *tri-lokam*—all the three worlds (the entire universe).

TRANSLATION

When the young gopīs, whose minds were constantly attached to Kṛṣṇa, the unlimited Supreme Lord, saw that He was now within the grips of the serpent, they remembered His loving friendship, His smiling glances and His talks with them. Burning with great sorrow, they saw the entire universe as void.

TEXT 21

ताः कृष्णमातरमपत्यमनुप्रविष्टां
तुल्यव्यथाः समनुगृह्य शुचः स्रवन्त्यः ।
तास्ता व्रजप्रियकथाः कथयन्त्य आसन्
कृष्णाननेऽर्पितदृशो मृतकप्रतीकाः ॥ २१ ॥

tāḥ kṛṣṇa-mātaram apatyam anupraviṣṭāṁ
tulya-vyathāḥ samanugṛhya śucaḥ sravantyaḥ
tās tā vraja-priya-kathāḥ kathayantya āsan
kṛṣṇānane'rpita-dṛśo mṛtaka-pratīkāḥ

tāḥ—those ladies; *kṛṣṇa-mātaram*—the mother of Kṛṣṇa (Yaśodā); *apatyam*—upon her son; *anupraviṣṭām*—fixing her vision; *tulya*—equally; *vyathāḥ*—pained; *samanugṛhya*—holding back firmly; *śucaḥ*—floods of sorrow; *sravantyaḥ*—spilling forth; *tāḥ tāḥ*—each of them; *vraja-priya*—of the darling of Vraja; *kathāḥ*—topics; *kathayantyaḥ*—speaking; *āsan*—they stood; *kṛṣṇa-ānane*—unto the face of Lord Kṛṣṇa; *arpita*—offered; *dṛśaḥ*—their eyes; *mṛtaka*—corpses; *pratīkāḥ*—resembling.

TRANSLATION

Although the elder gopīs were feeling just as much distress as she and were pouring forth a flood of sorrowful tears, they had to forcibly hold back Kṛṣṇa's mother, whose consciousness was totally absorbed in her son. Standing like corpses, with their eyes fixed upon His face, these gopīs each took turns recounting the pastimes of the darling of Vraja.

TEXT 22

कृष्णप्राणान्निर्विशतो नन्दादीन् वीक्ष्य तं ह्रदम् ।
प्रत्यषेधत् स भगवान् रामः कृष्णानुभाववित् ॥ २२ ॥

kṛṣṇa-prāṇān nirviśato
nandādīn vīkṣya taṁ hradam
pratyaṣedhat sa bhagavān
rāmaḥ kṛṣṇānubhāva-vit

kṛṣṇa-prāṇān—the men whose very life and soul was Kṛṣṇa; *nirviśataḥ*—entering; *nanda-ādīn*—headed by Nanda Mahārāja; *vīkṣya*—seeing; *tam*—that; *hradam*—lake; *pratyaṣedhat*—forbade; *saḥ*—He; *bhagavān*—the all-powerful Lord; *rāmaḥ*—Balarāma; *kṛṣṇa*—of Lord Kṛṣṇa; *anubhāva*—the power; *vit*—knowing well.

TRANSLATION

Lord Balarāma then saw that Nanda Mahārāja and the other cowherd men, who had dedicated their very lives to Kṛṣṇa, were beginning to enter

the serpent's lake. As the Supreme Personality of Godhead, Lord Balarāma fully knew Lord Kṛṣṇa's actual power, and therefore He restrained them.

PURPORT

Śrīla Sanātana Gosvāmī explains that Lord Balarāma checked some of the cowherd men by speaking to them, others by physically holding them and still others by casting upon them His potent smiling glance. Distraught over the situation, they were prepared to give up their lives for Lord Kṛṣṇa by entering the serpent's lake.

TEXT 23

इत्थं स्वगोकुलमनन्यगतिं निरीक्ष्य
सस्त्रीकुमारमतिदुःखितमात्महेतोः ।
आज्ञाय मर्त्यपदवीमनुवर्तमानः
स्थित्वा मुहूर्तमुदतिष्ठदुरंगबन्धात् ॥ २३ ॥

itthaṁ sva-gokulam ananya-gatiṁ nirīkṣya
sa-strī-kumāram ati-duḥkhitam ātma-hetoḥ
ājñāya martya-padavīm anuvartamānaḥ
sthitvā muhūrtam udatiṣṭhad uraṅga-bandhāt

ittham—in this fashion; *sva-gokulam*—His own community of Gokula; *ananya-gatim*—having no other goal or shelter (than Him); *nirīkṣya*—observing; *sa-strī*—including the women; *kumāram*—and children; *ati-duḥkhitam*—extremely distressed; *ātma-hetoḥ*—on His account; *ājñāya*—understanding; *martya-padavīm*—the way of mortals; *anuvartamānaḥ*—imitating; *sthitvā*—remaining; *muhūrtam*—for some time; *udatiṣṭhat*—He rose up; *uraṅga*—of the serpent; *bandhāt*—from the bonds.

TRANSLATION

The Lord remained for some time within the coils of the serpent, imitating the behavior of an ordinary mortal. But when He understood that the women, children and other residents of His village of Gokula were in acute distress because of their love for Him, their only shelter and goal in life, He immediately rose up from the bonds of the Kāliya serpent.

TEXT 24

तत्प्रथ्यमानवपुषा व्यथितात्मभोगस्
त्यक्त्वोन्नमय्य कुपितः स्वफणान् भुजंगः ।
तस्थौ श्वसञ्छ्वसनरन्ध्रविषाम्बरीष-
स्तब्धेक्षणोल्मुकमुखो हरिमीक्षमाणः ॥ २४ ॥

tat-prathyamāna-vapuṣā vyathitātma-bhogas
tyaktvonnamayya kupitaḥ sva-phaṇān bhujaṅgaḥ
tasthau śvasañ chvasana-randhra-viṣāmbarīṣa-
stabdhekṣaṇolmuka-mukho harim īkṣamāṇaḥ

tat—of Him, Lord Kṛṣṇa; *prathyamāna*—expanding; *vapuṣā*—by the transcendental body; *vyathita*—pained; *ātma*—his own; *bhogaḥ*—serpent body; *tyaktvā*—giving Him up; *unnamayya*—raising high; *kupitaḥ*—angered; *sva-phaṇān*—his hoods; *bhujaṅga*—the serpent; *tasthau*—stood still; *śvasan*—breathing heavily; *śvasana-randhra*—his nostrils; *viṣa-ambarīṣa*—like two vessels for cooking poison; *stabdha*—fixed; *īkṣaṇa*—his eyes; *ulmuka*—like firebrands; *mukhaḥ*—his face; *harim*—the Supreme Personality of Godhead; *īkṣamāṇaḥ*—observing.

TRANSLATION

His coils tormented by the expanding body of the Lord, Kāliya released Him. In great anger the serpent then raised his hoods high and stood still, breathing heavily. His nostrils appeared like vessels for cooking poison, and the staring eyes in his face like firebrands. Thus the serpent looked at the Lord.

TEXT 25

तं जिह्वया द्विशिखया परिलेलिहानं
द्वे सृक्वणी ह्यतिकरालविषाग्निदृष्टिम् ।
क्रीडन्नमुं परिससार यथा खगेन्द्रो
बभ्राम सोऽप्यवसरं प्रसमीक्षमाणः ॥ २५ ॥

taṁ jihvayā dvi-śikhayā parilelihānaṁ
dve sṛkvaṇī hy ati-karāla-viṣāgni-dṛṣṭim
krīḍann amuṁ parisasāra yathā khagendro
babhrāma so'py avasaraṁ prasamīkṣamāṇaḥ

tam—him, Kāliya; *jihvayā*—with his tongue; *dvi-śikhayā*—having two points; *parilelihānam*—repeatedly licking; *dve*—his two; *sṛkvaṇī*—lips; *hi*—indeed; *ati-karāla*—most terrible; *viṣa-agni*—full of poisonous fire; *dṛṣṭim*—whose glance; *krīḍan*—playing; *amum*—him; *parisasāra*—moved around; *yathā*—just as; *khaga-indraḥ*—the king of birds, Garuḍa; *babhrāma*—wandered around; *saḥ*—Kāliya; *api*—also; *avasaram*—the opportunity (to strike); *prasamīkṣamāṇaḥ*—carefully looking for.

TRANSLATION

Again and again Kāliya licked his lips with his bifurcated tongues as He stared at Kṛṣṇa with a glance full of terrible, poisonous fire. But Kṛṣṇa playfully circled around him, just as Garuḍa would play with a snake. In response, Kāliya also moved about, looking for an opportunity to bite the Lord.

PURPORT

Lord Kṛṣṇa moved around the serpent so skillfully that Kāliya could find no opportunity to bite Him. Thus the snake was defeated by Śrī Kṛṣṇa's transcendental agility.

TEXT 26

एवं परिभ्रमहतौजसमुन्नतांसम्
आनम्य तत्पृथुशिरःस्वधिरूढ आद्यः ।
तन्मूर्धरत्ननिकरस्पर्शातिताम्र-
पादाम्बुजोऽखिलकलादिगुरुर्ननर्त ॥ २६ ॥

evaṁ paribhrama-hataujasam unnatāṁsam
ānamya tat-pṛthu-śiraḥsv adhirūḍha ādyaḥ
tan-mūrdha-ratna-nikara-sparśāti-tāmra-
pādāmbujo'khila-kalādi-gurur nanarta

evam—in this way; *paribhrama*—because of the Lord's moving around him; *hata*—spoiled; *ojasam*—whose strength; *unnata*—raised high; *aṁsam*—whose shoulders; *ānamya*—making him bend down; *tat*—his; *pṛthu-śiraḥsu*—onto the broad heads; *adhirūḍhaḥ*—having climbed up; *ādyaḥ*—the ultimate origin of everything; *tat*—his; *mūrdha*—on the heads; *ratna-nikara*—the numerous jewels; *sparśa*—because of touching; *ati-tāmra*—very much reddened; *pāda-ambujaḥ*—whose lotus feet; *akhila-kalā*—of all arts; *ādi-guruḥ*—the original spiritual master; *nanarta*—began to dance.

TRANSLATION

Having severely depleted the serpent's strength with His relentless circling, Śrī Kṛṣṇa, the origin of everything, pushed down Kāliya's raised shoulders and mounted his broad serpentine heads. Thus Lord Śrī Kṛṣṇa, the original master of all fine arts, began to dance, His lotus feet deeply reddened by the touch of the numerous jewels upon the serpent's heads.

PURPORT

Śrī Hari-vaṁśa states, *śiraḥ sa kṛṣṇo jagrāha sva-hastenāvanamya:* "Kṛṣṇa grabbed Kāliya's head with His hand and forced it to bow down." Most people in this world are quite reluctant to bow down to the Supreme Person, the Absolute Truth. In the contaminated state called material consciousness, we conditioned souls become proud of our insignificant position and are thus reluctant to bow our heads before the Lord. Yet just as Lord Kṛṣṇa forcibly pushed Kāliya's heads down and thus defeated him, the Supreme Lord's energy in the form of irresistible time kills all conditioned souls and thus forces them to bow down their arrogant heads. We should therefore give up the artificial position of material life and become faithful servants of the Supreme Lord, enthusiastically bowing down at His lotus feet.

Śrīla Viśvanātha Cakravartī Ṭhākura explains that Lord Kṛṣṇa's lotus feet became red like copper because of their contact with the numerous hard jewels upon the heads of Kāliya. Lord Kṛṣṇa, with those glowing reddish feet, then began to demonstrate His artistic skill by dancing on the unsteady, moving surface of the serpent's hoods. This extraordinary demonstration of dancing skill was meant for the pleasure of the young women of Vṛndāvana, who at this phase of their relationship with Kṛṣṇa were seriously falling in love with Him.

TEXT 27

तं नर्तुमुद्यतमवेक्ष्य तदा तदीय-
गन्धर्वसिद्धमुनिचारणदेववध्वः ।
प्रीत्या मृदंगपणवानकवाद्यगीत-
पुष्पोपहारनुतिभिः सहसोपसेदुः ॥ २७ ॥

taṁ nartum udyatam avekṣya tadā tadīya-
gandharva-siddha-muni-cāraṇa-deva-vadhvaḥ
prītyā mṛdaṅga-paṇavānaka-vādya-gīta-
puṣpopahāra-nutibhiḥ sahasopaseduḥ

tam—Him; *nartum*—in dancing; *udyatam*—engaged; *avekṣya*—taking note of; *tadā*—then; *tadīya*—His servants; *gandharva-siddha*—the Gandharvas and Siddhas; *muni-cāraṇa*—the sages and the Cāraṇas; *deva-vadhvaḥ*—the wives of the demigods; *prītyā*—with great pleasure; *mṛdaṅga-paṇava-ānaka*—of various kinds of drums; *vādya*—with musical accompaniment; *gīta*—song; *puṣpa*—flowers; *upahāra*—other presentations; *nutibhiḥ*—and prayers; *sahasā*—immediately; *upaseduḥ*—arrived.

TRANSLATION

Seeing the Lord dancing, His servants in the heavenly planets—the Gandharvas, Siddhas, sages, Cāraṇas and wives of the demigods—immediately arrived there. With great pleasure they began accompanying the Lord's dancing by playing drums such as mṛdaṅgas, paṇavas and ānakas. They also made offerings of songs, flowers and prayers.

PURPORT

When the demigods and other residents of higher planetary systems became aware that Lord Śrī Kṛṣṇa was personally putting on a wonderful demonstration of the art of dancing, they immediately came to offer their services. Dancing becomes more enjoyable and beautiful to watch when it is accompanied by expert drum-playing, singing and the chanting of prayers. The artistic atmosphere was also enhanced by the showering of a multitude of flowers upon Lord Śrī Kṛṣṇa, who was blissfully engaged in dancing upon the hoods of the Kāliya serpent.

TEXT 28

यद् यच्छिरो न नमतेऽग शतैकशीर्ष्णस्
तत्तन्ममर्द खरदण्डधरोऽङ्घ्रिपातैः ।
क्षीणायुषो भ्रमत उल्बणमास्यतोऽसृङ्
नस्तो वमन् परमकश्मलमाप नागः ॥ २८ ॥

yad yac chiro na namate'ṅga śataika-śīrṣṇas
tat tan mamarda khara-daṇḍa-dharo'ṅghri-pātaiḥ
kṣīṇāyuṣo bhramata ulbaṇam āsyato'sṛṅ
nasto vaman parama-kaśmalam āpa nāgaḥ

yat yat—whichever; *śiraḥ*—heads; *na namate*—would not bow down; *aṅga*—my dear King Parīkṣit; *śata-eka-śīrṣṇaḥ*—of him who had 101 heads;

tat tat—those; *mamarda*—trampled down; *khara*—on those who are evil; *daṇḍa*—punishment; *dharaḥ*—the Lord who exerts; *aṅghri-pātaiḥ*—with the blows of His feet; *kṣīṇa-āyuṣaḥ*—of Kāliya, whose life was becoming depleted; *bhramataḥ*—who was still moving about; *ulbaṇam*—terrible; *āsyataḥ*—from his mouths; *asṛk*—blood; *nastaḥ*—from his nostrils; *vaman*—vomiting; *parama*—extreme; *kaśmalam*—trouble; *āpa*—experienced; *nāgaḥ*—the serpent.

TRANSLATION

My dear King, Kāliya had 101 prominent heads, and when one of them would not bow down, Lord Śrī Kṛṣṇa, who inflicts punishment on cruel wrong-doers, would smash that stubborn head by striking it with His feet. Then, as Kāliya entered his death throes, he began wheeling his heads around and vomiting ghastly blood from his mouths and nostrils. The serpent thus experienced extreme pain and misery.

TEXT 29

तस्याक्षिभिर्गरलमुद्वमतः शिरःसु
यद् यत् समुन्नमति निःश्वसतो रुषोच्चैः ।
नृत्यन् पदानुनमयन् दमयां बभूव
पुष्पैः प्रपूजित इवेह पुमान् पुराणः ॥ २९ ॥

tasyākṣibhir garalam udvamataḥ śirahsu
yad yat samunnamati niḥśvasato ruṣoccaiḥ
nṛtyan padānunamayan damayāṁ babhūva
puṣpaiḥ prapūjita iveha pumān purāṇaḥ

tasya—of him; *akṣibhiḥ*—from the eyes; *garalam*—poisonous waste; *udvamataḥ*—who was vomiting; *śirahsu*—among the heads; *yat yat*—whichever; *samunnamati*—would rise up; *niḥśvasataḥ*—who was breathing; *ruṣā*—out of anger; *uccaiḥ*—heavily; *nṛtyan*—while dancing; *padā*—with His foot; *anunamayan*—making bow down; *damayām babhūva*—He subdued; *puṣpaiḥ*—with flowers; *prapūjitaḥ*—being worshiped; *iva*—indeed; *iha*—on this occasion; *pumān*—the Personality of Godhead; *purāṇaḥ*—original.

TRANSLATION

Exuding poisonous waste from his eyes, Kāliya, would occasionally dare to raise up one of his heads, which would breathe heavily with anger. Then

the Lord would dance on it and subdue it, forcing it to bow down with His foot. The demigods took each of these exhibitions as an opportunity to worship Him, the primeval Personality of Godhead, with showers of flowers.

TEXT 30

तच्चित्रताण्डवविरुग्नफणासहस्रो
रक्तं मुखैरुरु वमन्नृप भग्नगात्रः ।
स्मृत्वा चराचरगुरुं पुरुषं पुराणं
नारायणं तमरणं मनसा जगाम ॥ ३० ॥

tac-citra-tāṇḍava-virugna-phaṇā-sahasro
raktaṁ mukhair uru vaman nṛpa bhagna-gātraḥ
smṛtvā carācara-guruṁ puruṣaṁ purāṇaṁ
nārāyaṇaṁ tam araṇaṁ manasā jagāma

tat—of Him; *citra*—amazing; *tāṇḍava*—by the powerful dancing; *virugna*—broken; *phaṇā-sahasraḥ*—his one thousand hoods; *raktam*—blood; *mukhaiḥ*—from his mouths; *uru*—profusely; *vaman*—vomiting; *nṛpa*—O King Parīkṣit; *bhagna-gātraḥ*—his limbs crushed; *smṛtvā*—remembering; *cara-acara*—of all moving and nonmoving beings; *gurum*—the spiritual master; *puruṣam*—the Personality of Godhead; *purāṇam*—ancient; *nārāyaṇam*—Lord Nārāyaṇa; *tam*—to Him; *araṇam*—for shelter; *manasā*—within his mind; *jagāma*—he approached.

TRANSLATION

My dear King Parīkṣit, Lord Kṛṣṇa's wonderful, powerful dancing trampled and broke all of Kāliya's one thousand hoods. Then the serpent, profusely vomiting blood from his mouths, finally recognized Śrī Kṛṣṇa to be the eternal Personality of Godhead, the supreme master of all moving and nonmoving beings, Śrī Nārāyaṇa. Thus within his mind Kāliya took shelter of the Lord.

PURPORT

In Chapter Sixteen of *Kṛṣṇa, the Supreme Personality of Godhead,* Śrīla Prabhupāda points out that whereas previously Kāliya was vomiting poison, now his poison was exhausted and he began to vomit blood. Thus he had been cleansed of the vile contamination within his heart that had manifested as serpent's venom. The word *smṛtvā,* "remembering," is very significant here. The wives of Kāliya were actually serious devotees of Lord Kṛṣṇa, and according to the *ācāryas* they had often tried to convince their husband to surrender to Him. Finally, finding himself in unbearable agony, Kāliya remembered his wives' advice and took shelter of the Lord. Śrīla Viśvanātha Cakravartī Ṭhākura explains that Kāliya's archrival had traditionally been Garuḍa, the carrier of Viṣṇu. But now Kāliya realized that he was fighting an opponent who was thousands of times stronger than Garuḍa and who therefore could be only the Supreme Personality of Godhead. Thus Kāliya took shelter of Lord Kṛṣṇa.

TEXT 31

कृष्णस्य गर्भजगतोऽतिभरावसन्नं
पार्ष्णिप्रहारपरिरुग्नफणातपत्रम् ।
दृष्ट्वाहिमाद्यमुपसेदुरमुष्य पत्न्य
आर्ताः श्लथद्वसनभूषणकेशबन्धाः ॥ ३१ ॥

kṛṣṇasya garbha-jagato'ti-bharāvasannaṁ
pārṣṇi-prahāra-parirugna-phaṇātapatram
dṛṣṭvāhim ādyam upasedur amuṣya patnya
ārtāḥ ślathad-vasana-bhūṣaṇa-keśa-bandhāḥ

kṛṣṇasya—of Lord Kṛṣṇa; *garbha*—in whose abdomen; *jagataḥ*—is found the entire universe; *ati-bhara*—by the extreme weight; *avasannam*—fatigued; *pārṣṇi*—of His heels; *prahāra*—by the striking; *parirugna*—shattered; *phaṇā*—his hoods; *ātapatram*—which were like umbrellas; *dṛṣṭvā*—seeing; *ahim*—the serpent; *ādyam*—the primeval Lord; *upaseduḥ*—approached; *amuṣya*—of Kāliya; *patnyaḥ*—the wives; *ārtāḥ*—feeling distressed; *ślathat*—disarrayed; *vasana*—their clothing; *bhūṣaṇa*—ornaments; *keśa-bandhāḥ*—and the locks of their hair.

TRANSLATION

When Kāliya's wives saw how the serpent had become so fatigued from the excessive weight of Lord Kṛṣṇa, who carries the entire universe in His abdomen, and how Kāliya's umbrellalike hoods had been shattered by the striking of Kṛṣṇa's heels, they felt great distress. With their clothing, ornaments and hair scattered in disarray, they then approached the eternal Personality of Godhead.

PURPORT

According to Śrīla Viśvanātha Cakravartī Ṭhākura, Kāliya's wives had been disgusted with their husband because of his demoniac activities. They had been thinking, "If this atheist is killed by the punishment of the Supreme Personality of Godhead, then let him be killed. We will become widows and engage in the worship of the Supreme Lord." But then the ladies noticed Kāliya's facial expression and other bodily features, and they understood that Kāliya had indeed taken shelter of the Lord within his mind. Seeing that he was manifesting symptoms of humility, remorse, regret and doubt, they thought, "Just see how fortunate we are! Our husband has now become a Vaiṣṇava. Therefore we must now endeavor to protect him." They felt affection for their repentant husband and severe distress because of his miserable position, and thus all together they went into the presence of the Supreme Lord.

TEXT 32

तास्तं सुविग्नमनसोऽथ पुरस्कृतार्भाः
कायं निधाय भुवि भूतपतिं प्रणेमुः ।
साध्व्यः कृताञ्जलिपुटाः शमलस्य भर्तुर्
मोक्षेप्सवः शरणदं शरणं प्रपन्नाः ॥ ३२ ॥

tās taṁ su-vigna-manaso'tha puraskṛtārbhāḥ
kāyaṁ nidhāya bhuvi bhūta-patiṁ praṇemuḥ
sādhvyaḥ kṛtāñjali-puṭāḥ śamalasya bhartur
mokṣepsavaḥ śaraṇa-daṁ śaraṇaṁ prapannāḥ

tāḥ—they, the wives of Kāliya; *tam*—to Him; *su-vigna*—very much agitated; *manasaḥ*—their minds; *atha*—then; *puraḥ-kṛta*—placing in front; *arbhāḥ*—their children; *kāyam*—their bodies; *nidhāya*—putting; *bhuvi*—upon the ground; *bhūta-patim*—to the Lord of all creatures; *praṇemuḥ*—they bowed down; *sādhvyaḥ*—the saintly ladies; *kṛta-añjali-puṭāḥ*—folding their hands in supplication; *śamalasya*—who was sinful; *bhartuḥ*—of their husband; *mokṣa*—the liberation; *īpsavaḥ*—desiring; *śaraṇa-dam*—He who grants shelter; *śaraṇam*—for shelter; *prapannāḥ*—they approached.

TRANSLATION

Their minds very much disturbed, those saintly ladies placed their children before them and then bowed down to the Lord of all creatures,

laying their bodies flat upon the ground. They desired the liberation of their sinful husband and the shelter of the Supreme Lord, the giver of ultimate shelter, and thus they folded their hands in supplication and approached Him.

TEXT 33

नागपत्न्य ऊचुः

न्याय्यो हि दण्डः कृतकिल्बिषेऽस्मिंस्
तवावतारः खलनिग्रहाय ।
रिपोः सुतानामपि तुल्यदृष्टिर्
धत्से दमं फलमेवानुशंसन् ॥ ३३ ॥

nāga-patnya ūcuḥ
nyāyyo hi daṇḍaḥ kṛta-kilbiṣe'smiṁs
tavāvatāraḥ khala-nigrahāya
ripoḥ sutānām api tulya-dṛṣṭir
dhatse damaṁ phalam evānuśaṁsan

nāga-patnyaḥ ūcuḥ—the wives of the serpent said; *nyāyyaḥ*—fair and just; *hi*—indeed; *daṇḍaḥ*—punishment; *kṛta-kilbiṣe*—to him who has committed offense; *asmin*—this person; *tava*—Your; *avatāraḥ*—descent into this world; *khala*—of the envious; *nigrahāya*—for the subjugation; *ripoḥ*—to an enemy; *sutānām*—to Your own sons; *api*—also; *tulya-dṛṣṭiḥ*—having equal vision; *dhatse*—You give; *damam*—punishment; *phalam*—the ultimate result; *eva*—indeed; *anuśaṁsam*—considering.

TRANSLATION

The wives of the Kāliya serpent said: The punishment this offender has been subjected to is certainly just. After all, You have incarnated within this world to curb down envious and cruel persons. You are so impartial that You look equally upon Your enemies and Your own sons, for when You impose a punishment on a living being You know it to be for his ultimate benefit.

TEXT 34

अनुग्रहोऽयं भवतः कृतो हि नो
दण्डोऽसतां ते खलु कल्मषापहः ।

यद्दन्दशूकत्वममुष्य देहिनः
क्रोधोऽपि तेऽनुग्रह एव सम्मतः ॥ ३४ ॥

anugraho'yaṁ bhavataḥ kṛto hi no
daṇḍo'satāṁ te khalu kalmaṣāpahaḥ
yad dandaśūkatvam amuṣya dehinaḥ
krodho'pi te'nugraha eva sammataḥ

anugrahaḥ—mercy; *ayam*—this; *bhavataḥ*—by You; *kṛtaḥ*—done; *hi*—indeed; *naḥ*—to us; *daṇḍaḥ*—punishment; *asatām*—of the evil; *te*—by You; *khalu*—indeed; *kalmaṣa-apahaḥ*—the dispelling of their contamination; *yat*—because; *dandaśūkatvam*—the condition of appearing as a serpent; *amuṣya*—of this Kāliya; *dehinaḥ*—the conditioned soul; *krodhaḥ*—anger; *api*—even; *te*—Your; *anugrahaḥ*—as mercy; *eva*—actually; *sammataḥ*—is accepted.

TRANSLATION

What You have done here is actually mercy for us, since the punishment You give to the wicked certainly drives away all their contamination. Indeed, because this conditioned soul, our husband, is so sinful that he has assumed the body of a serpent, Your anger toward him is obviously to be understood as Your mercy.

PURPORT

Śrīla Madhvācārya points out in this connection that when a pious person suffers in this world, he realizes, "The punishment the Supreme Lord is meting out to me is actually His causeless mercy." Envious persons, however, even after being punished by the Lord for their purification, continue to envy Him and be resentful, and this attitude is the reason for their continued failure to understand the Absolute Truth.

TEXT 35

तपः सुतप्तं किमनेन पूर्वं
निरस्तमानेन च मानदेन ।
धर्मोऽथवा सर्वजनानुकम्पया
यतो भवांस्तुष्यति सर्वजीवः ॥ ३५ ॥

tapaḥ sutaptaṁ kim anena pūrvaṁ
nirasta-mānena ca māna-dena

dharmo'tha vā sarva-janānukampayā
yato bhavāṁs tuṣyati sarva-jīvaḥ

tapaḥ—austerity; *su-taptam*—properly performed; *kim*—what; *anena*—by this Kāliya; *pūrvam*—in previous lives; *nirasta-mānena*—being free from false pride; *ca*—and; *māna-dena*—giving respect to others; *dharmaḥ*—religious duty; *atha vā*—or else; *sarva-jana*—to all persons; *anukampayā*—with compassion; *yataḥ*—by which; *bhavān*—Your good self; *tuṣyati*—is satisfied; *sarva-jīvaḥ*—the source of life for all beings.

TRANSLATION

Did our husband carefully perform austerities in a previous life, with his mind free of pride and full of respect for others? Is that why You are pleased with him? Or did he in some previous existence carefully execute religious duties with compassion for all living beings, and is that why You, the life of all living beings, are now satisfied with Him?

PURPORT

In this regard Śrīla Prabhupāda comments in his *Kṛṣṇa, the Supreme Personality of Godhead,* Chapter Sixteen: "The Nāgapatnīs confirm that one cannot come in contact with Kṛṣṇa without having executed pious activities in devotional service in his previous lives. As Lord Caitanya advised in His *Śikṣāṣṭaka,* one has to execute devotional service by humbly chanting the Hare Kṛṣṇa *mantra,* thinking oneself lower than the straw in the street and not expecting honor for himself but offering all kinds of honor to others. The Nāgapatnīs were astonished that, although Kāliya had the body of a serpent as the result of grievous sinful activities, at the same time he was in contact with the Lord to the extent that the Lord's lotus feet were touching his hoods. Certainly this was not the ordinary result of pious activities. These two contradictory facts astonished them."

TEXT 36

कस्यानुभावोऽस्य न देव विद्महे
तवाङ्घ्रिरेणुस्परशाधिकारः ।
यद्वाञ्छया श्रीर्ललनाचरत्तपो
विहाय कामान् सुचिरं धृतव्रता ॥ ३६ ॥

kasyānubhāvo'sya na deva vidmahe
tavāṅghri-reṇu-sparaśādhikāraḥ
yad-vāñchayā śrīr lalanācarat tapo
vihāya kāmān su-ciraṁ dhṛta-vratā

kasya—of what; *anubhāvaḥ*—a result; *asya*—of the serpent (Kāliya); *na*—not; *deva*—my Lord; *vidmahe*—we know; *tava*—Your; *aṅghri*—of the lotus feet; *reṇu*—of the dust; *sparaśa*—for touching; *adhikāraḥ*—qualification; *yat*—for which; *vāñchayā*—with the desire; *śrīḥ*—the goddess of fortune; *lalanā*—(the topmost) woman; *ācarat*—performed; *tapaḥ*—austerity; *vihāya*—giving up; *kāmān*—all desires; *su-ciram*—for a long time; *dhṛta*—upheld; *vratā*—her vow.

TRANSLATION

O Lord, we do not know how the serpent Kāliya has attained this great opportunity of being touched by the dust of Your lotus feet. For this end, the goddess of fortune performed austerities for centuries, giving up all other desires and taking austere vows.

TEXT 37

न नाकपृष्ठं न च सार्वभौमं
न पारमेष्ठ्यं न रसाधिपत्यम् ।
न योगसिद्धीरपुनर्भवं वा
वाञ्छन्ति यत्पादरजःप्रपन्नाः ॥ ३७ ॥

na nāka-pṛṣṭhaṁ na ca sārva-bhaumaṁ
na pārameṣṭhyaṁ na rasādhipatyam
na yoga-siddhīr apunar-bhavaṁ vā
vāñchanti yat-pāda-rajaḥ-prapannāḥ

na—not; *nāka-pṛṣṭham*—heaven; *na ca*—nor; *sārva-bhaumam*—supreme sovereignty; *na*—not; *pārameṣṭhyam*—the topmost position of Brahmā; *na*—not; *rasa-adhipatyam*—rulership over the earth; *na*—not; *yoga-siddhīḥ*—the perfections of yogic practice; *apunaḥ-bhavam*—freedom from rebirth; *vā*—or; *vāñchanti*—desire; *yat*—whose; *pāda*—of the lotus feet; *rajaḥ*—the dust; *prapannāḥ*—those who have attained.

TRANSLATION

Those who have attained the dust of Your lotus feet never hanker for the kingship of heaven, limitless sovereignty, the position of Brahmā or rulership over the earth. They are not interested even in the perfections of yoga or in liberation itself.

TEXT 38

तदेष नाथाप दुरापमन्यैस्
तमोजनिः क्रोधवशोऽप्यहीशः ।
संसारचक्रे भ्रमतः शरीरिणो
यदिच्छतः स्याद् विभवः समक्षः ॥ ३८ ॥

tad eṣa nāthāpa durāpam anyais
tamo-janiḥ krodha-vaśo'py ahīśaḥ
saṁsāra-cakre bhramataḥ śarīriṇo
yad-icchataḥ syād vibhavaḥ samakṣaḥ

tat—that; *eṣaḥ*—this Kāliya; *nātha*—O Lord; *āpa*—has achieved; *durāpam*—difficult to achieve; *anyaiḥ*—by others; *tamaḥ-janiḥ*—who was born in the mode of ignorance; *krodha-vaśaḥ*—who was under the sway of anger; *api*—even; *ahi-īśaḥ*—the king of serpents; *saṁsāra-cakre*—within the cycle of material existence; *bhramataḥ*—wandering; *śarīriṇaḥ*—for the embodied living entity; *yat*—by which (dust of Your lotus feet); *icchataḥ*—who has material desires; *syāt*—manifests; *vibhavaḥ*—all opulences; *samakṣaḥ*—before his eyes.

TRANSLATION

O Lord, although this Kāliya, the king of the serpents, has taken birth in the mode of ignorance and is controlled by anger, he has achieved that which is difficult for others to achieve. Embodied souls, who are full of desires and are thus wandering in the cycle of birth and death, can have all benedictions manifested before their eyes simply by receiving the dust of Your lotus feet.

PURPORT

It is very rare for a conditioned soul to free himself from the contamination of illusion and thus become established in perfect consciousness of the

Absolute Truth. And yet this benediction was achieved by the serpent Kāliya because the Lord personally danced upon the serpent's hoods with His lotus feet. Although we conditioned souls may not receive the mercy of having the Lord dance on our head, we can receive the dust of the lotus feet of the Absolute through the Lord's representative, the bona fide spiritual master, and thus go back home, back to Godhead, forever freed from the misery and ignorance of the mundane universe.

TEXT 39

नमस्तुभ्यं भगवते पुरुषाय महात्मने ।
भूतावासाय भूताय पराय परमात्मने ॥ ३९ ॥

namas tubhyaṁ bhagavate
puruṣāya mahātmane
bhūtāvāsāya bhūtāya
parāya paramātmane

namaḥ—obeisances; *tubhyam*—to You; *bhagavate*—the Supreme Personality of Godhead; *puruṣāya*—who are present within as the Supersoul; *mahā-ātmane*—who are all-pervasive; *bhūta-āvāsāya*—who are the shelter of the material elements (beginning with the ethereal sky); *bhūtāya*—who exist even prior to the creation; *parāya*—to the supreme cause; *parama-ātmane*—who are beyond all material cause.

TRANSLATION

We offer our obeisances unto You, the Supreme Personality of Godhead. Although present in the hearts of all living beings as the Supersoul, You are all-pervasive. Although the original shelter of all created material elements, You exist prior to their creation. And although the cause of everything, You are transcendental to all material cause and effect, being the Supreme Soul.

PURPORT

The beautiful Sanskrit poetry of this verse should be chanted out loud for the transcendental pleasure of the reciter and the hearer.

TEXT 40

ज्ञानविज्ञाननिधये ब्रह्मणेऽनन्तशक्तये ।
अगुणायाविकाराय नमस्ते प्राकृताय च ॥ ४० ॥

jñāna-vijñāna-nidhaye
brahmaṇe'nanta-śaktaye
aguṇāyāvikārāya
namas te prākṛtāya ca

jñāna—of consciousness; *vijñāna*—and spiritual potency; *nidhaye*—to the ocean; *brahmaṇe*—to the Absolute Truth; *ananta-śaktaye*—whose potencies are unlimited; *aguṇāya*—to Him who is never affected by the qualities of matter; *avikārāya*—who does not undergo any material transformation; *namaḥ*—obeisances; *te*—unto You; *prākṛtāya*—to the prime mover of material nature; *ca*—and.

TRANSLATION

Obeisances unto You, the Absolute Truth, who are the reservoir of all transcendental consciousness and potency and the possessor of unlimited energies. Although completely free of material qualities and transformations, You are the prime mover of material nature.

PURPORT

Those who consider themselves intellectual, philosophic or rational should carefully note here that the Absolute Truth, the Supreme Personality of Godhead, is the ocean of all knowledge and consciousness. Thus surrendering unto the Supreme Lord does not entail giving up the method of rationally comprehending reality. Rather, one merges into the ocean of rational, logical comprehension. The Supreme Lord is the perfection of all sciences and all forms of knowledge, and only envious and trivial minds would deny this obvious fact.

TEXT 41

कालाय कालनाभाय कालावयवसाक्षिणे ।
विश्वाय तदुपद्रष्ट्रे तत्कर्त्रे विश्वहेतवे ॥ ४१ ॥

kālāya kāla-nābhāya
kālāvayava-sākṣiṇe
viśvāya tad-upadraṣṭre
tat-kartre viśva-hetave

kālāya—unto time; *kāla-nābhāya*—unto Him who is the shelter of time; *kāla-avayava*—of the various phases of time; *sākṣiṇe*—to the witness; *viśvāya*

—to the form of the universe; *tad-upadraṣṭre*—to the observer of it; *tat-kartre*—to the creator of it; *viśva*—of the universe; *hetave*—to the total cause.

TRANSLATION

Obeisances unto You, who are time itself, the shelter of time and the witness of time in all its phases. You are the universe, and also its separate observer. You are its creator, and also the totality of all its causes.

PURPORT

The Supreme Personality of Godhead, although appearing in different incarnations, can never be limited by time, since He is time itself, the shelter of time, and the witness of time in all its phases.

TEXTS 42–43

भूतमात्रेन्द्रियप्राणमनोबुद्ध्याशयात्मने ।
त्रिगुणेनाभिमानेन गूढस्वात्मानुभूतये ॥ ४२ ॥
नमोऽनन्ताय सूक्ष्माय कूटस्थाय विपश्चिते ।
नानावादानुरोधाय वाच्यवाचकशक्तये ॥ ४३ ॥

bhūta-mātrendriya-prāṇa-
mano-buddhy-āśayātmane
tri-guṇenābhimānena
gūḍha-svātmānubhūtaye

namo'nantāya sūkṣmāya
kūṭa-sthāya vipaścite
nānā-vādānurodhāya
vācya-vācaka-śaktaye

bhūta—of the physical elements; *mātra*—the subtle basis of perception; *indriya*—the senses; *prāṇa*—the vital air of life; *manaḥ*—the mind; *buddhi*—the intelligence; *āśaya*—and of material consciousness; *ātmane*—to the ultimate soul; *tri-guṇena*—by the three modes of material nature; *abhimānena*—by false identification; *gūḍha*—who causes to become covered over; *sva*—one's own; *ātma*—of the self; *anubhūtaye*—perception; *namaḥ*—obeisances; *anantāya*—to the unlimited Lord; *sūkṣmāya*—to the supremely subtle; *kūṭa-sthāya*—who is fixed in the center; *vipaścite*—to the omniscient one; *nānā*—various; *vāda*—philosophies; *anurodhāya*—who sanctions; *vācya*—of expressed ideas; *vācaka*—and expressing words; *śaktaye*—who possesses the potencies.

TRANSLATION

Obeisances unto You, who are the ultimate soul of the physical elements, of the subtle basis of perception, of the senses, of the vital air of life, and of the mind, intelligence and consciousness. By Your arrangement the infinitesimal spirit souls falsely identify with the three modes of material nature, and their perception of their own true self thus becomes clouded. We offer our obeisances unto You, the unlimited Supreme Lord, the supremely subtle one, the omniscient Personality of Godhead, who are always fixed in unchanging transcendence, who sanction the opposing views of different philosophies, and who are the power upholding expressed ideas and the words that express them.

TEXT 44

नमः प्रमाणमूलाय कवये शास्त्रयोनये ।
प्रवृत्ताय निवृत्ताय निगमाय नमो नमः ॥ ४४ ॥

namaḥ pramāṇa-mūlāya
kavaye śāstra-yonaye
pravṛttāya nivṛttāya
nigamāya namo namaḥ

namaḥ—obeisances; *pramāṇa*—of authoritative evidence; *mūlāya*—to the basis; *kavaye*—to the author; *śāstra*—of the revealed scripture; *yonaye*—to the source; *pravṛttāya*—which encourages sense gratification; *nivṛttāya*—which encourages renunciation; *nigamāya*—to Him who is the origin of both kinds of scripture; *namaḥ namaḥ*—repeated obeisances.

TRANSLATION

We offer our obeisances again and again to You, who are the basis of all authoritative evidence, who are the author and ultimate source of the revealed scriptures, and who have manifested Yourself in those Vedic literatures encouraging sense gratification as well as in those encouraging renunciation of the material world.

PURPORT

If we did not have the powers of perception and cognition, evidence could not be transmitted, and if we had no tendency to believe in particular modes of evidence, persuasion could not take place. All of these processes—perception, cognition, persuasion and transmission—take place through the various potencies of the Supreme Lord. The Supreme Lord Kṛṣṇa is Himself the greatest scholar and intellectual being. He manifests the transcendental scriptures within the hearts of great devotees like Brahmā and Nārada, and in addition He incarnates as Vedavyāsa, the compiler of all Vedic knowledge. In multifarious ways the Lord generates a variety of religious scriptures, which gradually bring the conditioned souls through the various phases of re-entry into the kingdom of God.

TEXT 45

नमः कृष्णाय रामाय वसुदेवसुताय च ।
प्रद्युम्नायानिरुद्धाय सात्वतां पतये नमः ॥ ४५ ॥

namaḥ kṛṣṇāya rāmāya
vasudeva-sutāya ca
pradyumnāyāniruddhāya
sātvatāṁ pataye namaḥ

namaḥ—obeisances; *kṛṣṇāya*—to Lord Kṛṣṇa; *rāmāya*—to Lord Rāma; *vasudeva-sutāya*—the son of Vasudeva; *ca*—and; *pradyumnāya*—to Lord Pradyumna; *aniruddhāya*—to Lord Aniruddha; *sātvatām*—of the devotees; *pataye*—to the Lord; *namaḥ*—obeisances.

TRANSLATION

We offer our obeisances to Lord Kṛṣṇa and Lord Rāma, the sons of Vasudeva, and to Lord Pradyumna and Lord Aniruddha. We offer our respectful obeisances unto the master of all the saintly devotees of Viṣṇu.

TEXT 46

नमो गुणप्रदीपाय गुणात्मच्छादनाय च ।
गुणवृत्त्युपलक्ष्याय गुणद्रष्ट्रे स्वसंविदे ॥ ४६ ॥

namo guṇa-pradīpāya
guṇātma-cchādanāya ca

guṇa-vṛtty-upalakṣyāya
guṇa-draṣṭre sva-saṁvide

namaḥ—obeisances; *guṇa-pradīpāya*—to Him who manifests various qualities; *guṇa*—by the material modes; *ātma*—Himself; *chādanāya*—who disguises; *ca*—and; *guṇa*—of the modes; *vṛtti*—by the functioning; *upalakṣyāya*—who can be ascertained; *guṇa-draṣṭre*—to the separate witness of the material modes; *sva*—to His own devotees; *saṁvide*—who is known.

TRANSLATION

Obeisances to You, O Lord, who manifest varieties of material and spiritual qualities. You disguise Yourself with the material qualities, and yet the functioning of those same material qualities ultimately reveals Your existence. You stand apart from the material qualities as a witness and can be fully known only by Your devotees.

PURPORT

The word *guṇa* conveys various meanings: the three basic qualities of material nature, i.e., goodness, passion and ignorance; excellent qualities one manifests because of piety and spiritual achievement; or the internal senses, such as the mind and intelligence. The word *pradīpāya* means "unto Him who manifests or illumines." Thus here the Nāgapatnīs are addressing the Supreme Lord as "He who manifests all material and spiritual qualities and who causes the living entities to be conscious." One can see the Lord by going beyond the screen of material nature, and therefore He is called *guṇātma-cchādanāya.* If one methodically and intelligently studies the functioning of the material qualities, he will ultimately conclude that there is a Supreme Personality of Godhead and that He exhibits His illusory potency to bewilder those who do not surrender unto Him.

The Lord is never affected by the modes of nature, being their witness, and thus He is called *guṇa-draṣṭre.* The word *sva* indicates "one's own," and thus *sva-saṁvide* means that Lord Kṛṣṇa can be known only by His own people, the devotees, and also that ultimately only the Lord can know Himself perfectly. Therefore we should take Lord Kṛṣṇa's instructions in *Bhagavad-gītā* and immediately come to the right conclusion: full surrender to the Lord's lotus feet. Thus we should humbly glorify the Lord, following the example of the Nāgapatnīs.

TEXT 47

अव्याकृतविहाराय सर्वव्याकृतसिद्धये ।
हृषीकेश नमस्तेऽस्तु मुनये मौनशीलिने ॥ ४७ ॥

avyākṛta-vihārāya
sarva-vyākṛta-siddhaye
hṛṣīkeśa namas te'stu
munaye mauna-śīline

avyākṛta-vihārāya—to Him whose glories are unfathomable; *sarva-vyākṛta*—the creation and manifestation of all things; *siddhaye*—to Him who can be understood as existent on the basis of; *hṛṣīka-īśa*—O motivator of the senses; *namaḥ*—obeisances; *te*—unto You; *astu*—let there be; *munaye*—to the silent; *mauna-śīline*—to Him who acts in silence.

TRANSLATION

O Lord Hṛṣīkeśa, master of the senses, please let us offer our obeisances unto You, whose pastimes are inconceivably glorious. Your existence can be inferred from the necessity for a creator and revealer of all cosmic manifestations. But although Your devotees can understand You in this way, to the nondevotees You remain silent, absorbed in self-satisfaction.

TEXT 48

परावरगतिज्ञाय सर्वाध्यक्षाय ते नमः ।
अविश्वाय च विश्वाय तद्द्रष्ट्रेऽस्य च हेतवे ॥ ४८ ॥

parāvara-gati-jñāya
sarvādhyakṣāya te namaḥ
aviśvāya ca viśvāya
tad-draṣṭre'sya ca hetave

para-avara—of all things, both superior and inferior; *gati*—the destinations; *jñāya*—to Him who knows; *sarva*—of all things; *adhyakṣāya*—to the regulator; *te*—You; *namaḥ*—our obeisances; *aviśvāya*—to Him who is distinct from the universe; *ca*—and; *viśvāya*—in whom the illusion of material creation manifests; *tat-draṣṭre*—to the witness of such illusion; *asya*—of this world; *ca*—and; *hetave*—to the root cause.

TRANSLATION

Obeisances unto You, who know the destination of all things, superior and inferior, and who are the presiding regulator of all that be. You are distinct from the universal creation, and yet You are the basis upon which the illusion of material creation evolves, and also the witness of this illusion. Indeed, You are the root cause of the entire world.

PURPORT

The words *para* and *avara* indicate superior, subtle elements and inferior, gross ones. The words also indicate superior personalities—devotees of the Lord—and inferior personalities, who are unaware of the glories of God. Lord Kṛṣṇa knows the destiny of all superior and inferior entities, animate and inanimate, and as the Supreme Absolute Truth He remains in His unique position above everything, as indicated by the word *sarvādhyakṣāya.*

TEXT 49

त्वं ह्यस्य जन्मस्थितिसंयमान् विभो
गुणैरनीहोऽकृत कालशक्तिधृक् ।
तत्तत्स्वभावान् प्रतिबोधयन् सतः
समीक्षयामोघविहार ईहसे ॥ ४९ ॥

tvaṁ hy asya janma-sthiti-saṁyamān vibho
guṇair anīho 'kṛta-kāla-śakti-dhṛk
tat-tat-svabhāvān pratibodhayan sataḥ
samīkṣayāmogha-vihāra īhase

tvam—You; *hi*—indeed; *asya*—of this universe; *janma-sthiti-saṁyamān*—the creation, maintenance and destruction; *vibho*—O almighty Lord; *guṇaiḥ*—by the modes of nature; *anīhaḥ*—although uninvolved in any material endeavor; *akṛta*—beginningless; *kāla-śakti*—of the potency of time; *dhṛk*—the holder; *tat-tat*—of each of the modes; *sva-bhāvān*—the distinctive characteristics; *pratibodhayan*—awakening; *sataḥ*—which are already present in their dormant state; *samīkṣayā*—by Your glance; *amogha-vihāraḥ*—whose playful activities are impeccable; *īhase*—You act.

TRANSLATION

O almighty Lord, although You have no reason to become involved in material activity, still You act through Your eternal potency of time to

arrange for the creation, maintenance and destruction of this universe. You do this by awakening the distinct functions of each of the modes of nature, which before the creation lie dormant. Simply by Your glance You perfectly execute all these activities of cosmic control in a sporting mood.

PURPORT

Sceptics may question why the Supreme Lord has created the material world, which is full of birth, maintenance and death. Here the Nāgapatnīs point out that the Lord's pastimes are *amogha,* beyond any discrepancy. Śrī Kṛṣṇa actually desires that all conditioned souls live with Him in His eternal kingdom, but those forgetful souls who are inimical to their loving relationship with God must go to the material world and be subjected to the conditions of time. The fortunate conditioned souls are startled into remembrance of their actual position as loving servants of the Lord, and from within the heart the Lord then encourages them to come back home, back to Godhead, where time is conspicuous by its absence and where eternal, blissful existence supersedes the dramatic but disturbing functions of cosmic creation and annihilation.

TEXT 50

तस्यैव तेऽमूस्तनवस्त्रिलोक्यां
शान्ता अशान्ता उत मूढयोनयः ।
शान्ताः प्रियास्ते ह्यधुनावितुं सतां
स्थातुश्च ते धर्मपरीप्सयेहतः ॥ ५० ॥

tasyaiva te'mūs tanavas tri-lokyāṁ
śāntā aśāntā uta mūḍha-yonayaḥ
śāntāḥ priyās te hy adhunāvituṁ satāṁ
sthātuś ca te dharma-parīpsayehataḥ

tasya—of Him; *eva*—indeed; *te*—of You; *amūḥ*—these; *tanavaḥ*—material bodies; *tri-lokyām*—throughout the three worlds; *śāntāḥ*—peaceful (in the mode of goodness); *aśāntāḥ*—not peaceful (in the mode of passion); *uta*—and also; *mūḍha-yonayaḥ*—born in ignorant species; *śāntāḥ*—the peaceful persons in the mode of goodness; *priyāḥ*—dear; *te*—to You; *hi*—certainly; *adhunā*—now; *avitum*—to protect; *satām*—of the saintly devotees; *sthātuḥ*—who are present; *ca*—and; *te*—of You; *dharma*—their principles of religion; *parīpsayā*—with the desire of maintaining; *īhataḥ*—who is acting.

TRANSLATION

Therefore all material bodies throughout the three worlds—those that are peaceful, in the mode of goodness; those that are agitated, in the mode of passion; and those that are foolish, in the mode of ignorance—all are Your creations. Still, those living entities whose bodies are in the mode of goodness are especially dear to You, and it is to maintain them and protect their religious principles that You are now present on the earth.

TEXT 51

अपराधः सकृद् भर्त्रा सोढव्यः स्वप्रजाकृतः ।
क्षन्तुमर्हसि शान्तात्मन्मूढस्य त्वामजानतः ॥ ५१ ॥

aparādhaḥ sakṛd bhartrā
soḍhavyaḥ sva-prajā-kṛtaḥ
kṣantum arhasi śāntātman
mūḍhasya tvām ajānataḥ

aparādhaḥ—the offense; *sakṛt*—just once; *bhartrā*—by the master; *soḍhavyaḥ*—should be tolerated; *sva-prajā*—by Your own subject; *kṛtaḥ*—committed; *kṣantum*—to tolerate; *arhasi*—it is befitting for You; *śānta-ātman*—O You who are always peaceful; *mūḍhasya*—of the foolish one; *tvām*—You; *ajānataḥ*—who does not understand.

TRANSLATION

At least once, a master should tolerate an offense committed by his child or subject. O supreme peaceful Soul, You should therefore forgive our foolish husband, who did not understand who You are.

PURPORT

Because of their extreme anxiety, in this verse Kāliya's wives mention the same idea twice: that the Supreme Lord should kindly forgive their foolish husband. The Supreme Lord is *śāntātmā,* the supreme peaceful Soul, and therefore the Nāgapatnīs suggest it would be proper for Him to overlook, at least this once, the great offense committed by the ignorant Kāliya.

TEXT 52

अनुगृह्णीष्व भगवन् प्राणांस्त्यजति पन्नगः ।
स्त्रीणां नः साधुशोच्यानां पतिः प्राणः प्रदीयताम् ॥ ५२ ॥

anugṛhṇīṣva bhagavan
prāṇāṁs tyajati pannagaḥ
strīṇāṁ naḥ sādhu-śocyānāṁ
patiḥ prāṇaḥ pradīyatām

anugṛhṇīṣva—please show mercy; *bhagavan*—O Supreme Lord; *prāṇān*—his life airs; *tyajati*—is giving up; *pannagaḥ*—the serpent; *strīṇām*—for women; *naḥ*—us; *sādhu-śocyānām*—who are to be pitied by saintly personalities; *patiḥ*—the husband; *prāṇaḥ*—life itself; *pradīyatām*—should be given back.

TRANSLATION

O Supreme Lord, please be merciful. It is proper for the saintly to feel compassion for women like us. This serpent is about to give up his life. Please give us back our husband, who is our life and soul.

TEXT 53

विधेहि ते किंकरीणामनुष्ठेयं तवाज्ञया ।
यच्छ्रद्धयानुतिष्ठन् वै मुच्यते सर्वतो भयात् ॥ ५३ ॥

vidhehi te kiṅkarīṇām
anuṣṭheyaṁ tavājñayā
yac-chraddhayānutiṣṭhan vai
mucyate sarvato bhayāt

vidhehi—please order; *te*—Your; *kiṅkarīṇām*—by the maidservants; *anuṣṭheyam*—what should be done; *tava*—Your; *ājñayā*—by the command; *yat*—which; *śraddhayā*—with faith; *anutiṣṭhan*—executing; *vai*—certainly; *mucyate*—one will become freed; *sarvataḥ*—from all; *bhayāt*—fear.

TRANSLATION

Now please tell us, Your maidservants, what we should do. Certainly anyone who faithfully executes Your order is automatically freed from all fear.

PURPORT

The surrender of Kāliya's wives was now complete, and Lord Kṛṣṇa immediately gave them His mercy, as described in the following verses.

TEXT 54

श्रीशुक उवाच
इत्थं स नागपत्नीभिर्भगवान् समभिष्टुतः ।
मूर्च्छितं भग्नशिरसं विससर्जाङ्घ्रिकुट्टनैः ॥ ५४ ॥

śrī-śuka uvāca
itthaṁ sa nāga-patnībhir
bhagavān samabhiṣṭutaḥ
mūrcchitaṁ bhagna-śirasaṁ
visasarjāṅghri-kuṭṭanaiḥ

śrī-śukaḥ uvāca—Śrī Śukadeva Gosvāmī said; *ittham*—in this way; *saḥ*—He, Lord Kṛṣṇa; *nāga-patnībhiḥ*—by the wives of Kāliya; *bhagavān*—the Supreme Personality of Godhead; *samabhiṣṭutaḥ*—fully praised; *mūrcchitam*—who was unconscious; *bhagna-śirasam*—his heads crushed; *visasarja*—He let go; *aṅghri-kuṭṭanaiḥ*—by the striking of His feet.

TRANSLATION

Śukadeva Gosvāmī said: Thus praised by the Nāgapatnīs, the Supreme Personality of Godhead released the serpent Kāliya, who had fallen unconscious, his heads battered by the striking of the Lord's lotus feet.

PURPORT

According to Śrīla Viśvanātha Cakravartī Ṭhākura, Lord Kṛṣṇa, upon reaching His decision, immediately jumped down from Kāliya's hoods and stood before the serpent and his wives. We should remember that when Lord Kṛṣṇa executed these pastimes, He was just a young village boy in Vṛndāvana.

TEXT 55

प्रतिलब्धेन्द्रियप्राणः कालियः शनकैर्हरिम् ।
कृच्छ्रात् समुच्छ्वसन् दीनः कृष्णं प्राह कृताञ्जलिः ॥ ५५ ॥

pratilabdhendriya-prāṇaḥ
kāliyaḥ śanakair harim
kṛcchrāt samucchvasan dīnaḥ
kṛṣṇaṁ prāha kṛtāñjaliḥ

pratilabdha—regaining; *indriya*—the function of his senses; *prāṇaḥ*—and his vital force; *kāliyaḥ*—Kāliya; *śanakaiḥ*—gradually; *harim*—to the Supreme Personality of Godhead; *kṛcchrāt*—with difficulty; *samucchvasan*—breathing loudly; *dīnaḥ*—wretched; *kṛṣṇam*—to Lord Kṛṣṇa; *prāha*—spoke; *kṛta-añjaliḥ*—in humble submission.

TRANSLATION

Kāliya slowly regained his vital force and sensory functions. Then, breathing loudly and painfully, the poor serpent addressed Lord Kṛṣṇa, the Supreme Personality of Godhead, in humble submission.

TEXT 56

कालिय उवाच
वयं खलाः सहोत्पत्त्या तमसा दीर्घमन्यवः ।
स्वभावो दुस्त्यजो नाथ लोकानां यदसद्ग्रहः ॥ ५६ ॥

kāliya uvāca
vayaṁ khalāḥ sahotpattyā
tamasā dīrgha-manyavaḥ
svabhāvo dustyajo nātha
lokānāṁ yad asad-grahaḥ

kāliyaḥ uvāca—Kāliya said; *vayam*—we; *khalāḥ*—envious; *saha utpattyā*—by our very birth; *tāmasāḥ*—of ignorant nature; *dīrgha-manyavaḥ*—constantly angry; *svabhāvaḥ*—one's material nature; *dustyajaḥ*—is very difficult to give up; *nātha*—O Lord; *lokānām*—for ordinary persons; *yat*—because of which; *asat*—of the unreal and impure; *grahaḥ*—the acceptance.

TRANSLATION

The serpent Kāliya said: Our very birth as a snake has made us envious, ignorant and constantly angry. O my Lord, it is so difficult for people to give up their conditioned nature, by which they identify with that which is unreal.

PURPORT

Śrīla Sanātana Gosvāmī points out that because of his wretched condition, Kāliya was unable to compose original prayers to the Lord, and thus he paraphrased some of the prayers offered by his wives. The word *asad-graha* indicates that a conditioned soul seizes upon impermanent and impure things such as his own body, the bodies of others, and other countless varieties of material sense objects. The ultimate result of such material attachment is frustration, disappointment and anguish—a fact that has now become crystal clear to the poor serpent Kāliya.

TEXT 57

त्वया सृष्टमिदं विश्वं धातर्गुणविसर्जनम् ।
नानास्वभाववीर्यौजोयोनिबीजाशयाकृति ॥ ५७ ॥

tvayā sṛṣṭam idaṁ viśvaṁ
dhātar guṇa-visarjanam
nānā-svabhāva-vīryaujo-
yoni-bījāśayākṛti

tvayā—by You; *sṛṣṭam*—created; *idam*—this; *viśvam*—universe; *dhātaḥ*—O supreme provider; *guṇa*—of the material modes; *visarjanam*—the variegated creation; *nānā*—various; *sva-bhāva*—personal natures; *vīrya*—varieties of sensory strength; *ojaḥ*—and physical strength; *yoni*—wombs; *bīja*—seeds; *āśaya*—mentalities; *ākṛti*—and forms.

TRANSLATION

O supreme creator, it is You who generate this universe, composed of the variegated arrangement of the material modes, and in the process You manifest various kinds of personalities and species, varieties of sensory and physical strength, and varieties of mothers and fathers with variegated mentalities and forms.

PURPORT

Commenting on this verse, Śrīla Madhvācārya has quoted the *Nārada Purāṇa* as follows: "From Hiraṇyagarbha, Brahmā, comes the second creation of this universe, but the universe is primarily created by Viṣṇu Himself. Viṣṇu is thus the primary creator, and four-headed Brahmā is merely the secondary creator."

TEXT 58

वयं च तत्र भगवन् सर्पा जात्युरुमन्यवः ।
कथं त्यजामस्त्वन्मायां दुस्त्यजां मोहिताः स्वयम् ॥ ५८ ॥

vayaṁ ca tatra bhagavan
sarpā jāty-uru-manyavaḥ
kathaṁ tyajāmas tvan-māyāṁ
dustyajāṁ mohitāḥ svayam

vayam—we; *ca*—and; *tatra*—within that material creation; *bhagavan*—O Supreme Personality of Godhead; *sarpāḥ*—serpents; *jāti*—by species; *uru-manyavaḥ*—too much absorbed in anger; *katham*—how; *tyajāmaḥ*—we can give up; *tvat-māyām*—Your illusory potency; *dustyajām*—which is impossible to give up; *mohitāḥ*—bewildered; *svayam*—on our own.

TRANSLATION

O Supreme Personality of Godhead, among all the species within Your material creation, we serpents are by nature always enraged. Being thus deluded by Your illusory energy, which is very difficult to give up, how can we possibly give it up on our own?

PURPORT

Kāliya is here indirectly begging for the Lord's mercy, realizing that on his own he can never become free from illusion and suffering. Only by surrendering to the Lord and obtaining His mercy can one be released from the painful conditions of material life.

TEXT 59

भवान् हि कारणं तत्र सर्वज्ञो जगदीश्वरः ।
अनुग्रहं निग्रहं वा मन्यसे तद् विधेहि नः ॥ ५९ ॥

bhavān hi kāraṇaṁ tatra
sarva-jño jagad-īśvaraḥ
anugrahaṁ nigrahaṁ vā
manyase tad vidhehi naḥ

bhavān—Your good self; *hi*—certainly; *kāraṇam*—the cause; *tatra*—in that matter (the removal of illusion); *sarva-jñaḥ*—the knower of everything; *jagat-īśvaraḥ*—the supreme controller of the universe; *anugraham*—favor; *nigraham*—punishment; *vā*—or; *manyase*—(whatever) You consider; *tat*—that; *vidhehi*—arrange; *naḥ*—for us.

TRANSLATION

O Lord, since You are the omniscient Lord of the universe, You are the actual cause of freedom from illusion. Please arrange for us whatever You consider proper, whether it be mercy or punishment.

TEXT 60

श्रीशुक उवाच
इत्याकर्ण्य वचः प्राह भगवान् कार्यमानुषः ।
नात्र स्थेयं त्वया सर्प समुद्रं याहि मा चिरम् ।
स्वज्ञात्यपत्यदाराढ्यो गोनृभिर्भुज्यते नदी ॥ ६० ॥

śrī-śuka uvāca
ity ākarṇya vacaḥ prāha
bhagavān kārya-mānuṣaḥ
nātra stheyaṁ tvayā sarpa
samudraṁ yāhi mā ciram
sva-jñāty-apatya-dārāḍhyo
go-nṛbhir bhujyate nadī

śrī-śukaḥ uvāca—Śrī Śukadeva Gosvāmī said; *iti*—thus; *ākarṇya*—hearing; *vacaḥ*—these words; *prāha*—then spoke; *bhagavān*—the Supreme Personality of Godhead; *kārya-mānuṣaḥ*—who was acting like a human being; *na*—not; *atra*—here; *stheyam*—should remain; *tvayā*—you; *sarpa*—My dear serpent; *samudram*—to the ocean; *yāhi*—go; *mā ciram*—without delay; *sva*—your own; *jñāti*—by the companions; *apatya*—children; *dāra*—and wife; *āḍhyaḥ*—adequately accompanied; *go*—by the cows; *nṛbhiḥ*—and the humans; *bhujyate*—let it be enjoyed; *nadī*—the river Yamunā.

TRANSLATION

Śukadeva Gosvāmī said: After hearing Kāliya's words, the Supreme Personality of Godhead, who was acting the role of a human being, replied: O serpent, you may not remain here any longer. Go back to the ocean immediately, accompanied by your retinue of children, wives, other relatives and friends. Let this river be enjoyed by the cows and humans.

TEXT 61

य एतत् संस्मरेन्मर्त्यस्तुभ्यं मदनुशासनम् ।
कीर्तयन्नुभयोः सन्ध्योर्न युष्मद् भयमाप्नुयात्॥ ६१ ॥

ya etat saṁsmaren martyas
tubhyaṁ mad-anuśāsanam
kīrtayann ubhayoḥ sandhyor
na yuṣmad bhayam āpnuyāt

yaḥ—who; *etat*—this; *saṁsmaret*—remembers; *martyaḥ*—a mortal; *tubhyam*—to you; *mat*—My; *anuśāsanam*—command; *kīrtayan*—chanting; *ubhayoḥ*—at both; *sandhyoḥ*—junctures of the day; *na*—not; *yuṣmat*—from you; *bhayam*—fear; *āpnuyāt*—obtains.

TRANSLATION

If a mortal being attentively remembers My command to you—to leave Vṛndāvana and go to the ocean—and narrates this account at sunrise and sunset, he will never be afraid of you.

TEXT 62

योऽस्मिन् स्नात्वा मदाक्रीडे देवादींस्तर्पयेज्जलैः ।
उपोष्य मां स्मरन्नर्चेत् सर्वपापैः प्रमुच्यते ॥ ६२ ॥

yo'smin snātvā mad-ākrīḍe
devādīṁs tarpayej jalaiḥ
upoṣya māṁ smarann arcet
sarva-pāpaiḥ pramucyate

yaḥ—who; *asmin*—in this (Kāliya's lake in the Yamunā River); *snātvā*—bathing; *mat-ākrīḍe*—the place of My pastime; *deva-ādīn*—the demigods and other worshipable personalities; *tarpayet*—gratifies; *jalaiḥ*—with the water (of that lake); *upoṣya*—observing a fast; *mām*—Me; *smaran*—remembering; *arcet*—performs worship; *sarva-pāpaiḥ*—from all sinful reactions; *pramucyate*—he becomes freed.

TRANSLATION

If one bathes in this place of My pastimes and offers the water of this lake to the demigods and other worshipable personalities, or if one

observes a fast and duly worships and remembers Me, he is sure to become free from all sinful reactions.

PURPORT

According to the *ācāryas,* the Lord spoke this verse to make it clear to Kāliya that he could by no means remain in the Yamunā lake. Although the Lord had mercifully pardoned the serpent and ordered him to go to the ocean with all his associates, Kāliya should not even consider requesting to remain in the lake, because it was now to become a holy place for spiritual pilgrims.

TEXT 63

द्वीपं रमणकं हित्वा ह्रदमेतमुपाश्रितः ।
यद्भयात् स सुपर्णस्त्वां नाद्यान्मत्पादलाञ्छितम् ॥ ६३ ॥

dvīpaṁ ramaṇakaṁ hitvā
hradam etam upāśritaḥ
yad-bhayāt sa suparṇas tvāṁ
nādyān mat-pāda-lāñchitam

dvīpam—the great island; *ramaṇakam*—named Ramaṇaka; *hitvā*—abandoning; *hradam*—the small lake; *etam*—this; *upāśritaḥ*—taken shelter of; *yat*—of whom; *bhayāt*—because of the fear; *saḥ*—that; *suparṇaḥ*—Garuḍa; *tvām*—you; *na adyāt*—will not eat; *mat-pāda*—with My feet; *lāñchitam*—marked.

TRANSLATION

Out of fear of Garuḍa, you left Ramaṇaka Island and came to take shelter of this lake. But because you are now marked with My footprints, Garuḍa will no longer try to eat you.

TEXT 64

श्रीऋषिरुवाच
मुक्तो भगवता राजन् कृष्णेनाद्भुतकर्मणा ।
तं पूजयामास मुदा नागपत्न्यश्च सादरम् ॥ ६४ ॥

śrī-ṛṣir uvāca
mukto bhagavatā rājan
kṛṣṇenādbhuta-karmaṇā

taṁ pūjayām āsa mudā
nāga-patnyaś ca sādaram

śrī-ṛṣiḥ uvāca—the sage (Śukadeva) said; *muktaḥ*—freed; *bhagavatā*—by the Supreme Personality of Godhead; *rājan*—O King Parīkṣit; *kṛṣṇena*—by Lord Kṛṣṇa; *adbhuta-karmaṇā*—whose activities are very wonderful; *tam*—Him; *pūjayām āsa*—worshiped; *mudā*—with pleasure; *nāga*—of the serpent; *patnyaḥ*—the wives; *ca*—and; *sa-ādaram*—with reverence.

TRANSLATION

Śukadeva Gosvāmī continued: My dear King, having been released by Lord Kṛṣṇa, the Supreme Personality of Godhead, whose activities are wonderful, Kāliya joined his wives in worshiping Him with great joy and reverence.

PURPORT

Śrīla Viśvanātha Cakravartī Ṭhākura comments as follows on this verse: "The word *adbhuta-karmaṇā* indicates the Lord's wonderful activities of saving the residents of Vṛndāvana from Kāliya, saving Kāliya himself from Garuḍa, and bestowing grace upon both the victims of violence and the committer of that violence." The word *kṛṣṇena,* "by Kṛṣṇa," indicates that because Kāliya's wives were great devotees of the Lord and offered Him loving affection, Kṛṣṇa withdrew (*karṣaṇam*) both Kāliya's offense against the Lord's devotee Garuḍa and that against the residents of Vṛndāvana, who were very dear to Him.

TEXTS 65–67

दिव्याम्बरस्रङ्मणिभिः परार्ध्यैरपि भूषणैः ।
दिव्यगन्धानुलेपैश्च महत्योत्पलमालया ॥ ६५ ॥
पूजयित्वा जगन्नाथं प्रसाद्य गरुडध्वजम् ।
ततः प्रीतोऽभ्यनुज्ञातः परिक्रम्याभिवन्द्य तम् ॥ ६६ ॥
सकलत्रसुहृत्पुत्रो द्वीपमब्धेर्जगाम ह ।
तदैव सामृतजला यमुना निर्विषाभवत् ।
अनुग्रहाद् भगवतः क्रीडामानुषरूपिणः ॥ ६७ ॥

divyāmbara-sraṅ-maṇibhiḥ
parārdhyair api bhūṣaṇaiḥ

divya-gandhānulepaiś ca
mahatyotpala-mālayā

pūjayitvā jagan-nāthaṁ
prasādya garuḍa-dhvajam
tataḥ prīto 'bhyanujñātaḥ
parikramyābhivandya tam

sa-kalatra-suhṛt-putro
dvīpam abdher jagāma ha
tadaiva sāmṛta-jalā
yamunā nirviṣābhavat
anugrahād bhagavataḥ
krīḍā-mānuṣa-rūpiṇaḥ

divya—divine; *ambara*—with clothing; *srak*—garlands; *maṇibhiḥ*—and jewels; *para-ardhyaiḥ*—most valuable; *api*—also; *bhūṣaṇaiḥ*—ornaments; *divya*—divine; *gandha*—with scents; *anulepaiḥ*—and ointments; *ca*—as well; *mahatyā*—fine; *utpala*—of lotuses; *mālayā*—with a garland; *pūjayitvā*—worshiping; *jagat-nātham*—the Lord of the universe; *prasādya*—satisfying; *garuḍa-dhvajam*—Him whose flag is marked with the emblem of Garuḍa; *tataḥ*—then; *prītaḥ*—feeling happy; *abhyanujñātaḥ*—given permission to leave; *parikramya*—circumambulating; *abhivandya*—offering obeisances; *tam*—to Him; *sa*—along with; *kalatra*—his wives; *suhṛt*—friends; *putraḥ*—and children; *dvīpam*—to the island; *abdheḥ*—in the sea; *jagāma*—he went; *ha*—indeed; *tadā eva*—at that very moment; *sa-amṛta*—nectarean; *jalā*—her water; *yamunā*—the river Yamunā; *nirviṣā*—free from poison; *abhavat*—she became; *anugrahāt*—by the mercy; *bhagavataḥ*—of the Supreme Personality of Godhead; *krīḍā*—for pleasure pastimes; *mānuṣa*—humanlike; *rūpiṇaḥ*—manifesting a form.

TRANSLATION

Kāliya worshiped the Lord of the universe by offering Him fine garments, along with necklaces, jewels and other valuable ornaments, wonderful scents and ointments, and a large garland of lotus flowers. Having thus pleased the Lord, whose flag is marked with the emblem of Garuḍa, Kāliya felt satisfied. Receiving the Lord's permission to leave, Kāliya circumambulated Him and offered Him obeisances. Then, taking his wives, friends and children, he went to his island in the sea. The very

moment Kāliya left, the Yamunā was immediately restored to her original condition, free from poison and full of nectarean water. This happened by the mercy of the Supreme Personality of Godhead, who was manifesting a humanlike form to enjoy His pastimes.

PURPORT

Śrīla Viśvanātha Cakravartī Ṭhākura has commented extensively on this verse. To explain the word *maṇibhiḥ*—"(Kāliya worshiped the Lord) with jewels"—the *ācārya* has quoted from the *Śrī Rādhā-kṛṣṇa-gaṇoddeśa-dīpikā,* by Rūpa Gosvāmī, as follows:

kaustubhākhyo maṇir yena
praviśya hradam auragam
kāliya-preyasi-vṛnda-
hastair ātmopahāritaḥ

"The Lord had made His Kaustubha gem enter the serpent's lake, and then He arranged for it to be presented to Himself by the hands of Kāliya's wives." In other words, because Lord Kṛṣṇa wanted to act just like an ordinary human being, He made the transcendental Kaustubha gem invisible and caused it to enter within Kāliya's treasury. Then when the appropriate moment came for Kāliya to worship the Lord with many different jewels and ornaments, the serpent's wives, unaware of the Lord's transcendental trick, presented Him with the Kaustubha gem, thinking it was simply one of the jewels in their possession.

The *ācārya* has further commented that the reason Lord Kṛṣṇa is described in this verse as *garuḍa-dhvaja,* "He whose flag is marked by the symbol of His carrier, Garuḍa," is that Kāliya also desired to become Lord Kṛṣṇa's carrier. Garuḍa and the serpents are originally related as brothers, and therefore Kāliya wanted to indicate to Lord Kṛṣṇa, "If You ever have to go to a distant place, You should also think of me as Your personal carrier. I am the servant of Your servant, and in the wink of an eye I can travel hundreds of millions of *yojanas.*" Thus the *Purāṇas* narrate that in the course of Lord Kṛṣṇa's eternal cycle of pastimes, when Kaṁsa orders the Lord to come to Mathurā, He sometimes goes there mounted upon Kāliya.

Thus end the purports of the humble servants of His Divine Grace A.C. Bhaktivedanta Swami Prabhupāda to the Tenth Canto, Sixteenth Chapter, of the Śrīmad-Bhāgavatam, *entitled "Kṛṣṇa Chastises the Serpent Kāliya."*

CHAPTER SEVENTEEN

The History of Kāliya

This chapter describes how Kāliya left the island of the snakes and how the sleeping residents of Vṛndāvana were saved from a forest fire.

When King Parīkṣit inquired about Kāliya's leaving Ramaṇaka Island, the abode of the serpents, and about why Garuḍa acted inimically toward him, Śrī Śukadeva Gosvāmī replied as follows: All the serpents on the island were afraid of being devoured by Garuḍa. To placate him, every month they would leave various offerings for him at the foot of a banyan tree. But Kāliya, puffed-up as he was with false pride, would eat these offerings himself. Hearing of this, Garuḍa became furious and went to kill Kāliya, whereupon the snake began biting the great bird. Garuḍa fiercely beat him with his wing, sending Kāliya fleeing for his life to a lake adjoining the Yamunā River.

Prior to the above incident, Garuḍa had once come to the Yamunā and started eating some fish. Saubhari Ṛṣi had tried to stop him, but Garuḍa, agitated by hunger, had refused to heed the sage's prohibitions, and in response the sage had cursed Garuḍa that if he ever came there again he would immediately die. Kāliya had heard of this, and thus he lived there without fear. In the end, however, he was driven out by Śrī Kṛṣṇa.

When Lord Balarāma and all the residents of Vṛndāvana saw Śrī Kṛṣṇa rise up out of the lake, beautifully decorated with many different gems and ornaments, they embraced Him in great pleasure. The spiritual masters, priests and learned *brāhmaṇas* then told Nanda Mahārāja, the king of the cowherds, that although his son had been caught in the grips of Kāliya, it was by the king's good fortune that He was now free again.

Because the people of Vṛndāvana were quite worn out by hunger, thirst and fatigue, they spent that night on the banks of the Yamunā. In the middle of the night, a fire happened to blaze up within the forest, which had become dry during the hot season. As the fire surrounded the sleeping inhabitants of Vṛndāvana, they suddenly awoke and rushed to Śrī Kṛṣṇa for protection. Then the unlimitedly powerful Lord Śrī Kṛṣṇa, seeing His dear relatives and friends so distressed, immediately swallowed up the terrible forest fire.

TEXT 1

श्रीराजोवाच
नागालयं रमणकं कथं तत्याज कालियः ।
कृतं किं वा सुपर्णस्य तेनैकेनासमञ्जसम् ॥ १ ॥

śrī-rājovāca
nāgālayaṁ ramaṇakaṁ
kathaṁ tatyāja kāliyaḥ
kṛtaṁ kiṁ vā suparṇasya
tenaikenāsamañjasam

śrī-rājā uvāca—the King said; *nāga*—of the serpents; *ālayam*—the residence; *ramaṇakam*—the island named Ramaṇaka; *katham*—why; *tatyāja*—gave up; *kāliyaḥ*—Kāliya; *kṛtam*—was made; *kim vā*—and why; *suparṇasya*—of Garuḍa; *tena*—with him, Kāliya; *ekena*—alone; *asamañjasam*—enmity.

TRANSLATION

[Having thus heard how Lord Kṛṣṇa chastised Kāliya,] King Parīkṣit inquired: Why did Kāliya leave Ramaṇaka Island, the abode of the serpents, and why did Garuḍa become so antagonistic toward him alone?

TEXTS 2–3

श्रीशुक उवाच
उपहार्यैः सर्पजनैर्मासि मासीह यो बलिः ।
वानस्पत्यो महाबाहो नागानां प्राङ्निरूपितः ॥ २ ॥
स्वं स्वं भागं प्रयच्छन्ति नागाः पर्वणि पर्वणि ।
गोपीथायात्मनः सर्वे सुपर्णाय महात्मने ॥ ३ ॥

śrī-śuka uvāca
upahāryaiḥ sarpa-janair
māsi māsīha yo baliḥ
vānaspatyo mahā-bāho
nāgānāṁ prāṅ-nirūpitaḥ
svaṁ svaṁ bhāgaṁ prayacchanti
nāgāḥ parvaṇi parvaṇi

gopīthāyātmanaḥ sarve
suparṇāya mahātmane

śrī-śukaḥ uvāca—Śukadeva Gosvāmī said; *upahāryaiḥ*—who were qualified to make offerings; *sarpa-janaiḥ*—by the serpent race; *māsi māsi*—each month; *iha*—here (in Nāgālaya); *yaḥ*—which; *baliḥ*—offering of tribute; *vānaspatyaḥ*—at the base of a tree; *mahā-bāho*—O mighty-armed Parīkṣit; *nāgānām*—for the serpents; *prāk*—previously; *nirūpitaḥ*—ordained; *svam svam*—each his own; *bhāgam*—portion; *prayacchanti*—they present; *nāgāḥ*—the serpents; *parvaṇi parvaṇi*—once each month; *gopīthāya*—for the protection; *ātmanaḥ*—of themselves; *sarve*—all of them; *suparṇāya*—to Garuḍa; *mahā-ātmane*—the powerful.

TRANSLATION

Śukadeva Gosvāmī said: To avoid being eaten by Garuḍa, the serpents had previously made an arrangement with him whereby they would each make a monthly offering of tribute at the base of a tree. Thus every month on schedule, O mighty-armed King Parīkṣit, each serpent would duly make his offering to that powerful carrier of Viṣṇu as a purchase of protection.

PURPORT

Śrīla Śrīdhara Svāmī has given an alternate explanation of this verse. *Upahāryaiḥ* may also be translated as "by those who are to be eaten," and *sarpa-janaiḥ* as "those human beings who were dominated by or who belonged to the serpent race." According to this reading, a group of human beings had fallen under the control of the serpents and were prone to be eaten by them. To avoid this, the human beings would make a monthly offering to the serpents, who in turn would offer a portion of that offering to Garuḍa so that *he* would not eat *them.* The particular translation given above is based on the commentary of Śrīla Sanātana Gosvāmī and the translation by Śrīla Prabhupāda in his *Kṛṣṇa, the Supreme Personality of Godhead.* In any case, all the *ācāryas* agree that the serpents purchased protection from Garuḍa.

TEXT 4

विषवीर्यमदाविष्टः काद्रवेयस्तु कालियः ।
कदर्थीकृत्य गरुडं स्वयं तं बुभुजे बलिम् ॥ ४ ॥

viṣa-vīrya-madāviṣṭaḥ
kādraveyas tu kāliyaḥ
kadarthī-kṛtya garuḍaṁ
svayaṁ taṁ bubhuje balim

viṣa—because of his poison; *vīrya*—and his strength; *mada*—in intoxication; *āviṣṭaḥ*—absorbed; *kādraveyaḥ*—the son of Kadru; *tu*—on the other hand; *kāliyaḥ*—Kāliya; *kadarthī-kṛtya*—disregarding; *garuḍam*—Garuḍa; *svayam*—himself; *tam*—that; *bubhuje*—ate; *balim*—the offering.

TRANSLATION

Although all the other serpents were dutifully making offerings to Garuḍa, one serpent—the arrogant Kāliya, son of Kadru—would eat all these offerings before Garuḍa could claim them. Thus Kāliya directly defied the carrier of Lord Viṣṇu.

TEXT 5

तच्छ्रुत्वा कुपितो राजन् भगवान् भगवत्प्रियः ।
विजिघांसुर्महावेगः कालियं समुपाद्रवत् ॥ ५ ॥

tac chrutvā kupito rājan
bhagavān bhagavat-priyaḥ
vijighāṁsur mahā-vegaḥ
kāliyaṁ samapādravat

tat—that; *śrutvā*—hearing; *kupitaḥ*—angered; *rājan*—O King; *bhagavān*—the powerful Garuḍa; *bhagavat-priyaḥ*—the dear devotee of the Supreme Personality of Godhead; *vijighāṁsuḥ*—desiring to kill; *mahā-vegaḥ*—the greatly swift; *kāliyam*—to Kāliya; *samupādravat*—he rushed.

TRANSLATION

O King, the greatly powerful Garuḍa, who is very dear to the Supreme Lord, became angry when he heard of this. Desiring to kill Kāliya, he rushed toward the serpent with tremendous speed.

PURPORT

Śrīla Sanātana Gosvāmī explains that the word *mahā-vega* indicates that the great speed of Garuḍa cannot be checked by anyone.

TEXT 6

तमापतन्तं तरसा विषायुधः
प्रत्यभ्ययादुत्थितनैकमस्तकः ।
दद्भिः सुपर्णं व्यदशद्ददायुधः
करालजिह्वोच्छ्वसितोग्रलोचनः ॥ ६ ॥

tam āpatantaṁ tarasā viṣāyudhaḥ
pratyabhyayād utthita-naika-mastakaḥ
dadbhiḥ suparṇaṁ vyadaśad dad-āyudhaḥ
karāla-jihvocchvasitogra-locanaḥ

tam—him, Garuḍa; *āpatantam*—attacking; *tarasā*—swiftly; *viṣa*—of poison; *āyudhaḥ*—who possessed the weapon; *prati*—towards; *abhyayāt*—ran; *utthita*—raised; *na eka*—many; *mastakaḥ*—his heads; *dadbhiḥ*—with his fangs; *suparṇam*—Garuḍa; *vyadaśat*—he bit; *dat-āyudhaḥ*—whose fangs were weapons; *karāla*—fearsome; *jihvā*—his tongues; *ucchvasita*—expanded; *ugra*—and terrible; *locanaḥ*—his eyes.

TRANSLATION

As Garuḍa swiftly fell upon him, Kāliya, who had the weapon of poison, raised his numerous heads to counterattack. Showing his ferocious tongues and expanding his horrible eyes, Kāliya then bit Garuḍa with the weapons of his fangs.

PURPORT

The *ācāryas* explain that Kāliya used his weapon of poison at a distance by spitting venom upon his enemy and at short range by biting him with his terrible fangs.

TEXT 7

तं ताक्ष्‍र्यपुत्रः स निरस्य मन्युमान्
प्रचण्डवेगो मधुसूदनासनः ।
पक्षेण सव्येन हिरण्यरोचिषा
जघान कद्रुसुतमुग्रविक्रमः ॥ ७ ॥

taṁ tārkṣya-putraḥ sa nirasya manyumān
pracaṇḍa-vego madhusūdanāsanaḥ

pakṣeṇa savyena hiraṇya-rociṣā
jaghāna kadru-sutam ugra-vikramaḥ

tam—him, Kāliya; *tārkṣya-putraḥ*—the son of Kaśyapa; *saḥ*—he, Garuḍa; *nirasya*—warding off; *manyu-mān*—full of anger; *pracaṇḍa-vegaḥ*—moving with terrible swiftness; *madhusūdana-āsanaḥ*—the carrier of Lord Madhusūdana, Kṛṣṇa; *pakṣeṇa*—with his wing; *savyena*—left; *hiraṇya*—like gold; *rociṣā*—the effulgence of which; *jaghāna*—he struck; *kadru-sutam*—the son of Kadru (Kāliya); *ugra*—mighty; *vikramaḥ*—his prowess.

TRANSLATION

The angry son of Tārkṣya moved with overwhelming speed in repelling Kāliya's attack. That terribly powerful carrier of Lord Madhusūdana struck the son of Kadru with his left wing, which shone like gold.

TEXT 8

सुपर्णपक्षाभिहतः कालियोऽतीव विह्वलः ।
ह्रदं विवेश कालिन्द्यास्तदगम्यं दुरासदम् ॥ ८ ॥

suparṇa-pakṣābhihataḥ
kāliyo'tīva vihvalaḥ
hradaṁ viveśa kālindyās
tad-agamyaṁ durāsadam

suparṇa—of Garuḍa; *pakṣa*—by the wing; *abhihataḥ*—beaten; *kāliyaḥ*—Kāliya; *atīva*—extremely; *vihvalaḥ*—distraught; *hradam*—a lake; *viveśa*—he entered; *kālindyāḥ*—of the river Yamunā; *tat-agamyam*—unapproachable by Garuḍa; *durāsadam*—difficult to enter.

TRANSLATION

Beaten by Garuḍa's wing, Kāliya was extremely distraught, and thus he took shelter of a lake adjoining the river Yamunā. Garuḍa could not enter this lake. Indeed, he could not even approach it.

TEXT 9

तत्रैकदा जलचरं गरुडो भक्ष्यमीप्सितम् ।
निवारितः सौभरिणा प्रसह्य क्षुधितोऽहरत् ॥ ९ ॥

tatraikadā jala-caraṁ
garuḍo bhakṣyam īpsitam
nivāritaḥ saubhariṇā
prasahya kṣudhito'harat

tatra—there (in that lake); *ekadā*—once; *jala-caram*—an aquatic creature; *garuḍaḥ*—Garuḍa; *bhakṣyam*—his proper food; *īpsitam*—desired; *nivāritaḥ*—forbidden; *saubhariṇā*—by Saubhari Muni; *prasahya*—taking courage; *kṣudhitaḥ*—feeling hunger; *aharat*—he took.

TRANSLATION

In that very lake Garuḍa had once desired to eat a fish—fish being, after all, his normal food. Although forbidden by the sage Saubhari, who was meditating there within the water, Garuḍa took courage and, feeling hungry, seized the fish.

PURPORT

Śukadeva Gosvāmī is now explaining why Garuḍa could not approach the lake in the Yamunā River. It is the nature of birds to eat fish, and thus, by the arrangement of the Lord, the great bird Garuḍa does not commit any offense by nourishing himself with fish. On the other hand, Saubhari Muni's forbidding a much greater personality to eat his normal food did constitute an offense. According to Śrīla Viśvanātha Cakravartī Ṭhākura, Saubhari committed two offenses: first, he dared to give an order to a supremely exalted soul like Garuḍa, and second, he obstructed Garuḍa from satisfying his desire.

TEXT 10

मीनान् सुदुःखितान् दृष्ट्वा दीनान्मीनपतौ हते ।
कृपया सौभरिः प्राह तत्रत्यक्षेममाचरन् ॥ १० ॥

mīnān su-duḥkhitān dṛṣṭvā
dīnān mīna-patau hate
kṛpayā saubhariḥ prāha
tatratya-kṣemam ācaran

mīnān—the fish; *su-duḥkhitān*—most unhappy; *dṛṣṭvā*—seeing; *dīnān*—wretched; *mīna-patau*—the lord of the fish; *hate*—being killed; *kṛpayā*—out of compassion; *saubhariḥ*—Saubhari; *prāha*—spoke; *tatratya*—for those living there; *kṣemam*—the welfare; *ācaran*—trying to enact.

TRANSLATION

Seeing how the unfortunate fish in that lake had become most unhappy at the death of their leader, Saubhari uttered the following curse under the impression that he was mercifully acting for the benefit of the lake's residents.

PURPORT

In this regard Śrīla Viśvanātha Cakravartī Ṭhākura explains that when our so-called compassion does not tally with the order of the Supreme Lord, it merely causes a disturbance. Because Saubhari had forbidden Garuḍa's coming to that lake, Kāliya moved in and made his headquarters there, and this spelled doom for all the lake's residents.

TEXT 11

अत्र प्रविश्य गरुडो यदि मत्स्यान् स खादति।
सद्यः प्राणैर्वियुज्येत सत्यमेतद् ब्रवीम्यहम् ॥ ११ ॥

atra praviśya garuḍo
yadi matsyān sa khādati
sadyaḥ prāṇair viyujyeta
satyam etad bravīmy aham

atra—in this lake; *praviśya*—entering; *garuḍaḥ*—Garuḍa; *yadi*—if; *matsyān*—the fish; *saḥ*—he; *khādati*—eats; *sadyaḥ*—immediately; *prāṇaiḥ*—of his force of life; *viyujyeta*—will become deprived; *satyam*—truthfully; *etat*—this; *bravīmi*—am speaking; *aham*—I.

TRANSLATION

If Garuḍa ever again enters this lake and eats the fish here, he will immediately lose his life. What I am saying is the truth.

PURPORT

The *ācāryas* explain in this regard that because of Saubhari Muni's material attachment and affection for a fish, he failed to see the situation from the spiritual viewpoint. The Ninth Canto of *Śrīmad-Bhāgavatam* describes his falldown for this offense. Because of false pride, Saubhari Muni lost his power of austerity, and with it his spiritual beauty and happiness. When Garuḍa came to the Yamunā, Saubhari Muni thought, "Although he may be a personal associate of the Supreme Lord, I will still curse him and even kill him if he disobeys my order." Such an offensive attitude against an exalted Vaiṣṇava will certainly destroy one's auspicious position in life.

As the Ninth Canto describes, Saubhari Muni married many beautiful women, and suffered greatly in their association. But because he had once become glorious by taking shelter of the Yamunā River in Śrī Vṛndāvana, he was ultimately delivered.

TEXT 12

तत् कालियः परं वेद नान्यः कश्चन लेलिहः ।
अवात्सीद् गरुडाद् भीतः कृष्णेन च विवासितः ॥ १२ ॥

tat kāliyaḥ paraṁ veda
nānyaḥ kaścana lelihaḥ
avātsīd garuḍād bhītaḥ
kṛṣṇena ca vivāsitaḥ

tam—that; *kāliyaḥ*—Kāliya; *param*—only; *veda*—knew; *na*—not; *anyaḥ*—other; *kaścana*—any; *lelihaḥ*—serpent; *avātsīt*—he dwelt; *garuḍāt*—of Garuḍa; *bhītaḥ*—afraid; *kṛṣṇena*—by Kṛṣṇa; *ca*—and; *vivāsitaḥ*—expelled.

TRANSLATION

Of all the serpents, only Kāliya came to know of this affair, and in fear of Garuḍa he took up residence in that Yamunā lake. Later Lord Kṛṣṇa drove him out.

TEXTS 13–14

कृष्णं ह्रदाद् विनिष्क्रान्तं दिव्यस्रग्गन्धवाससम् ।
महामणिगणाकीर्णं जाम्बूनदपरिष्कृतम् ॥ १३ ॥
उपलभ्योत्थिताः सर्वे लब्धप्राणा इवासवः ।
प्रमोदनिभृतात्मानो गोपाः प्रीत्याभिरेभिरे ॥ १४ ॥

kṛṣṇaṁ hradād viniṣkrāntaṁ
divya-srag-gandha-vāsasam
mahā-maṇi-gaṇākīrṇaṁ
jāmbūnada-pariṣkṛtam

upalabhyotthitāḥ sarve
labdha-prāṇā ivāsavaḥ
pramoda-nibhṛtātmāno
gopāḥ prītyābhirebhire

kṛṣṇam—Lord Kṛṣṇa; *hradāt*—from out of the lake; *viniṣkrāntam*—rising up; *divya*—divine; *srak*—wearing garlands; *gandha*—fragrances; *vāsasam*—and garments; *mahā-maṇi-gaṇa*—by many fine jewels; *ākīrṇam*—covered; *jāmbūnada*—with gold; *pariṣkṛtam*—decorated; *upalabhya*—seeing; *utthitāḥ*—rising up; *sarve*—all of them; *labdha-prāṇāḥ*—which have regained their vital force; *iva*—just as; *asavaḥ*—senses; *pramoda*—with joy; *nibhṛta-ātmānaḥ*—being filled; *gopāḥ*—the cowherds; *prītyā*—with affection; *abhirebhire*—embraced Him.

TRANSLATION

[Resuming his description of Kṛṣṇa's chastisement of Kāliya, Śukadeva Gosvāmī continued:] Kṛṣṇa rose up out of the lake wearing divine garlands, fragrances and garments, covered with many fine jewels, and decorated with gold. When the cowherds saw Him they all stood up immediately, just like an unconscious person's senses coming back to life. Filled with great joy, they affectionately embraced Him.

TEXT 15

यशोदा रोहिणी नन्दो गोप्यो गोपाश्च कौरव ।
कृष्णं समेत्य लब्धेहा आसन् शुष्का नगा अपि ॥ १५ ॥

yaśodā rohiṇī nando
gopyo gopāś ca kaurava
kṛṣṇaṁ sametya labdhehā
āsan śuṣkā nagā api

yaśodā rohiṇī nandaḥ—Yaśodā, Rohiṇī and Nanda Mahārāja; *gopyaḥ*—the cowherd ladies; *gopāḥ*—the cowherd men; *ca*—and; *kaurava*—O Parīkṣit, descendant of Kuru; *kṛṣṇam*—Lord Kṛṣṇa; *sametya*—meeting; *labdha*—having regained; *īhāḥ*—their conscious functions; *āsan*—they became; *śuṣkāḥ*—dried up; *nagāḥ*—the trees; *api*—even.

TRANSLATION

Having regained their vital functions, Yaśodā, Rohiṇī, Nanda and all the other cowherd women and men went up to Kṛṣṇa. O descendant of Kuru, even the dried-up trees came back to life.

TEXT 16

रामश्चाच्युतमालिंग्य जहासास्यानुभाववित् ।
प्रेम्णा तमंकमारोप्य पुनः पुनरुदैक्षत ।
गावो वृषा वत्सतर्यो लेभिरे परमां मुदम् ॥ १६ ॥

rāmaś cācyutam āliṅgya
jahāsāsyānubhāva-vit
premṇā tam aṅkam āropya
punaḥ punar udaikṣata
gāvo vṛṣā vatsataryo
lebhire paramāṁ mudam

rāmaḥ—Lord Balarāma; *ca*—and; *acyutam*—Kṛṣṇa, the infallible Supreme Personality of Godhead; *āliṅgya*—embracing; *jahāsa*—laughed; *asya*—His; *anubhāva-vit*—knowing well the omnipotence; *premṇā*—out of love; *tam*—Him; *aṅkam*—up on His own lap; *āropya*—raising; *punaḥ punaḥ*—again and again; *udaikṣata*—looked upon; *gāvaḥ*—the cows; *vṛṣāḥ*—the bulls; *vatsataryaḥ*—the female calves; *lebhire*—they attained; *paramām*—supreme; *mudam*—pleasure.

TRANSLATION

Lord Balarāma embraced His infallible brother and laughed, knowing well the extent of Kṛṣṇa's potency. Out of great feelings of love, Balarāma lifted Kṛṣṇa up on His lap and repeatedly looked at Him. The cows, bulls and young female calves also achieved the highest pleasure.

TEXT 17

नन्दं विप्राः समागत्य गुरवः सकलत्रकाः ।
ऊचुस्ते कालियग्रस्तो दिष्ट्या मुक्तस्तवात्मजः ॥ १७ ॥

nandaṁ viprāḥ samāgatya
guravaḥ sa-kalatrakāḥ

ūcus te kāliya-grasto
diṣṭyā muktas tavātmajaḥ

nandam—to Nanda Mahārāja; *viprāḥ*—the *brāhmaṇas; samāgatya*—coming up; *guravaḥ*—respectable personalities; *sa-kalatrakāḥ*—along with their wives; *ūcuḥ*—said; *te*—they; *kāliya-grastaḥ*—seized by Kāliya; *diṣṭyā*—by providence; *muktaḥ*—freed; *tava*—your; *ātma-jaḥ*—son.

TRANSLATION

All the respectable brāhmaṇas, together with their wives, came forward to greet Nanda Mahārāja. They said to him, "Your son was in the grips of Kāliya, but by the grace of providence He is now free."

TEXT 18

देहि दानं द्विजातीनां कृष्णनिर्मुक्तिहेतवे ।
नन्दः प्रीतमना राजन् गाः सुवर्णं तदादिशत् ॥ १८ ॥

dehi dānaṁ dvi-jātīnāṁ
kṛṣṇa-nirmukti-hetave
nandaḥ prīta-manā rājan
gāḥ suvarṇaṁ tadādiśat

dehi—you should give; *dānam*—charity; *dvi-jātīnām*—to the *brāhmaṇas; kṛṣṇa-nirmukti*—the safety of Kṛṣṇa; *hetave*—for the purpose of; *nandaḥ*—Nanda Mahārāja; *prīta-manāḥ*—satisfied within his mind; *rājan*—O King Parīkṣit; *gāḥ*—cows; *suvarṇam*—gold; *tadā*—then; *ādiśat*—gave.

TRANSLATION

The brāhmaṇas then advised Nanda Mahārāja, "To assure that your son Kṛṣṇa will always be free from danger, you should give charity to the brāhmaṇas." With a satisfied mind, O King, Nanda Mahārāja then very gladly gave them gifts of cows and gold.

TEXT 19

यशोदापि महाभागा नष्टलब्धप्रजा सती ।
परिष्वज्यांकमारोप्य मुमोचाश्रुकलां मुहुः ॥ १९ ॥

yaśodāpi mahā-bhāgā
naṣṭa-labdha-prajā satī

pariṣvajyāṅkam āropya
mumocāśru-kalāṁ muhuḥ

yaśodā—mother Yaśodā; *api*—and; *mahā-bhāgā*—the greatly fortunate; *naṣṭa*—having lost; *labdha*—and regained; *prajā*—her son; *satī*—the chaste lady; *pariṣvajya*—embracing; *aṅkam*—upon her lap; *āropya*—raising; *mumoca*—she released; *aśru*—of tears; *kalām*—a torrent; *muhuḥ*—repeatedly.

TRANSLATION

The greatly fortunate mother Yaśodā, having lost her son and then regained Him, placed Him on her lap. That chaste lady cried constant torrents of tears as she repeatedly embraced Him.

TEXT 20

तां रात्रिं तत्र राजेन्द्र क्षुत्तृड्भ्यां श्रमकर्षिताः ।
ऊषुर्व्रजौकसो गावः कालिन्द्या उपकूलतः ॥ २० ॥

tāṁ rātriṁ tatra rājendra
kṣut-tṛḍbhyāṁ śrama-karṣitāḥ
ūṣur vrajaukaso gāvaḥ
kālindyā upakūlataḥ

tām—that; *rātrim*—night; *tatra*—there; *rāja-indra*—O most exalted of kings; *kṣut-tṛḍbhyām*—by hunger and thirst; *śrama*—and by fatigue; *karṣitāḥ*—weakened; *ūṣuḥ*—they remained; *vraja-okasaḥ*—the people of Vṛndāvana; *gāvaḥ*—and the cows; *kālindyāḥ*—of the Yamunā; *upakūlataḥ*—near the shore.

TRANSLATION

O best of kings [Parīkṣit], because the residents of Vṛndāvana were feeling very weak from hunger, thirst and fatigue, they and the cows spent the night where they were, lying down near the bank of the Kālindī.

PURPORT

Śrīla Jīva Gosvāmī points out that although the people were weak from hunger and thirst, they did not drink the milk from the cows present there because they feared it had been contaminated by the serpent's poison. The residents of Vṛndāvana were so overjoyed to get back their beloved Kṛṣṇa that they did not want to go back to their houses. They wanted to stay with Kṛṣṇa on the bank of the Yamunā so that they could continuously see Him. Thus they decided to take rest near the riverbank.

TEXT 21

तदा शुचिवनोद्भूतो दावाग्निः सर्वतो व्रजम् ।
सुप्तं निशीथ आवृत्य प्रदग्धुमुपचक्रमे ॥ २१ ॥

tadā śuci-vanodbhūto
dāvāgniḥ sarvato vrajam
suptaṁ niśītha āvṛtya
pradagdhum upacakrame

tadā—then; *śuci*—of the summer; *vana*—in the forest; *udbhūtaḥ*—arising; *dāva-agniḥ*—a conflagration; *sarvataḥ*—on all sides; *vrajam*—the people of Vṛndāvana; *suptam*—sleeping; *niśīthe*—in the middle of the night; *āvṛtya*—surrounding; *pradagdhum*—to burn; *upacakrame*—began.

TRANSLATION

During the night, while all the people of Vṛndāvana were asleep, a great fire blazed up within the dry summer forest. The fire surrounded the inhabitants of Vraja on all sides and began to scorch them.

PURPORT

Śrīla Sanātana Gosvāmī and Śrīla Viśvanātha Cakravartī Ṭhākura have commented that perhaps a loyal friend of Kāliya had assumed the form of a forest fire to avenge his friend, or perhaps the forest fire was manifest by a demon who was a follower of Kaṁsa's.

TEXT 22

तत उत्थाय सम्भ्रान्ता दह्यमाना व्रजौकसः ।
कृष्णं ययुस्ते शरणं मायामनुजमीश्वरम् ॥ २२ ॥

tata utthāya sambhrāntā
dahyamānā vrajaukasaḥ
kṛṣṇaṁ yayus te śaraṇaṁ
māyā-manujam īśvaram

tataḥ—then; *utthāya*—waking up; *sambhrāntāḥ*—agitated; *dahyamānāḥ*—about to be burned; *vraja-okasaḥ*—the people of Vraja; *kṛṣṇam*—to Kṛṣṇa; *yayuḥ*—went; *te*—they; *śaraṇam*—for shelter; *māyā*—by His potency; *manujam*—appearing like a human being; *īśvaram*—the Supreme Personality of Godhead.

TRANSLATION

Then the residents of Vṛndāvana woke up, extremely disturbed by the great fire threatening to burn them. Thus they took shelter of Kṛṣṇa, the Supreme Lord, who by His spiritual potency appeared like an ordinary human being.

PURPORT

The *śruti,* or Vedic *mantras,* state, *svarūpa-bhūtayā nitya-śaktyā māyākhyayā*: "The Lord's eternal potency named *māyā* is innate in His original form." Thus within the eternal spiritual body of the Supreme Lord there is infinite potency, which effortlessly manipulates all existence according to the omniscient desire of the Absolute Truth. The residents of Vṛndāvana took shelter of Kṛṣṇa, thinking, "This blessed boy will certainly be empowered by God to save us." They remembered the words of the sage Garga Muni, spoken at the birth ceremony of Lord Kṛṣṇa: *anena sarva-durgāṇi yūyam añjas tariṣyatha.* "By His power you will easily be able to cross over all obstacles." (*Bhāg.* 10.8.16) Therefore the residents of Vṛndāvana, who had full faith in Kṛṣṇa, took shelter of the Lord in hopes of being saved from the impending disaster threatened by the forest fire.

TEXT 23

कृष्ण कृष्ण महाभाग हे रामामितविक्रम।
एष घोरतमो वह्निस्तावकान् ग्रसते हि नः ॥ २३ ॥

kṛṣṇa kṛṣṇa mahā-bhaga
he rāmāmita-vikrama
eṣa ghoratamo vahnis
tāvakān grasate hi naḥ

kṛṣṇa—O Kṛṣṇa; *kṛṣṇa*—O Kṛṣṇa; *mahā-bhāga*—O Lord of all opulence; *he rāma*—O Lord Balarāma, source of all happiness; *amita-vikrama*—You whose power is unlimited; *eṣaḥ*—this; *ghora-tamaḥ*—most terrible; *vahniḥ*—fire; *tāvakān*—who are Yours; *grasate*—is devouring; *hi*—indeed; *naḥ*—us.

TRANSLATION

[Vṛndāvana's residents said:] Kṛṣṇa, Kṛṣṇa, O Lord of all opulence! O Rāma, possessor of unlimited power! This most terrible fire is about to devour us, Your devotees!

TEXT 24

सुदुस्तरान्नः स्वान् पाहि कालाग्नेः सुहृदः प्रभो ।
न शक्नुमस्त्वच्चरणं सन्त्यक्तुमकुतोभयम् ॥ २४ ॥

su-dustarān naḥ svān pāhi
kālāgneḥ suhṛdaḥ prabho
na śaknumas tvac-caraṇaṁ
santyaktum akuto-bhayam

su-dustarāt—from the insurmountable; *naḥ*—us; *svān*—Your own devotees; *pāhi*—please protect; *kāla-agneḥ*—from the fire of death; *suhṛdaḥ*—Your true friends; *prabho*—O supreme master; *na śaknumaḥ*—we are incapable; *tvat-caraṇam*—Your feet; *santyaktum*—to give up; *akutaḥ-bhayam*—which drive away all fear.

TRANSLATION

O Lord, we are Your true friends and devotees. Please protect us from this insurmountable fire of death. We can never give up Your lotus feet, which drive away all fear.

PURPORT

The residents of Vṛndāvana told Kṛṣṇa, "If this deadly fire overcomes us, we will be separated from Your lotus feet, and this is unbearable for us. Therefore, just so that we can go on serving Your lotus feet, please protect us."

TEXT 25

इत्थं स्वजनवैक्लव्यं निरीक्ष्य जगदीश्वरः ।
तमग्निमपिबत्तीव्रमनन्तोऽनन्तशक्तिधृक् ॥ २५ ॥

itthaṁ sva-jana-vaiklavyaṁ
nirīkṣya jagad-īśvaraḥ
tam agnim apibat tīvram
ananto'nanta-śakti-dhṛk

ittham—in this manner; *sva-jana*—of His own devotees; *vaiklavyam*—the disturbed condition; *nirīkṣya*—seeing; *jagat-īśvaraḥ*—the Lord of the universe; *tam*—that; *agnim*—fire; *apibat*—drank; *tīvram*—terrible; *anantaḥ*—the unlimited Lord; *ananta-śakti-dhṛk*—the possessor of unlimited potencies.

TRANSLATION

Seeing His devotees so disturbed, Śrī Kṛṣṇa, the infinite Lord of the universe and possessor of infinite power, then swallowed the terrible forest fire.

Thus end the purports of the humble servants of His Divine Grace A.C. Bhaktivedanta Swami Prabhupāda to the Tenth Canto, Seventeenth Chapter, of the Śrīmad-Bhāgavatam, *entitled "The History of Kāliya."*

CHAPTER EIGHTEEN

Lord Balarāma Slays the Demon Pralamba

The killing of Pralambāsura is described in this chapter. While playing happily in Vṛndāvana, Lord Baladeva climbed up on the shoulders of the demon Pralamba and struck his head with His fist, destroying him.

Śrī Vṛndāvana, where Kṛṣṇa and Balarāma enacted Their pastimes, was even during the summer decorated with all the qualities of spring. At that time Lord Śrī Kṛṣṇa would become absorbed in various sports, surrounded by Balarāma and all the cowherd boys. One day they were intently dancing, singing and playing when a demon named Pralamba entered their midst, disguised as a cowherd boy. The omniscient Lord Kṛṣṇa saw through the disguise, but even as He thought of how to kill the demon, He treated him as a friend.

Kṛṣṇa then suggested to His young friends and Baladeva that they play a game involving contending parties. Taking the role of leaders, Kṛṣṇa and Balarāma divided the boys into two groups and determined that the losers would have to carry the winners on their shoulders. Thus when Śrīdāmā and Vṛṣabha, members of Balarāma's party, were victorious, Kṛṣṇa and another boy in His party carried them on their shoulders. Pralambāsura thought that the unconquerable Lord Śrī Kṛṣṇa would be too great an opponent to contend with, so the demon fought with Balarāma instead and was defeated. Taking Lord Balarāma on his back, Pralambāsura began to walk away very swiftly. But Balarāma became as heavy as Mount Sumeru, and the demon, unable to carry Him, had to reveal his true, demoniac form. When Balarāma saw this terrible form, He struck the demon a ferocious blow on the head with His fist. This blow shattered Pralambāsura's head just as lightning bolts hurled by the king of the demigods shatter mountains. The demon repeatedly vomited blood and then fell upon the ground. When the cowherd boys saw Lord Balarāma return, they joyfully embraced and congratulated Him as the demigods showered garlands of flowers from the heavens and glorified Him.

TEXT 1

श्रीशुक उवाच
अथ कृष्णः परिवृतो ज्ञातिभिर्मुदितात्मभिः ।
अनुगीयमानो न्यविशद् व्रजं गोकुलमण्डितम् ॥ १ ॥

śrī-śuka uvāca
atha kṛṣṇaḥ parivṛto
jñātibhir muditātmabhiḥ
anugīyamāno nyaviśad
vrajaṁ gokula-maṇḍitam

śrī-śukaḥ uvāca—Śrī Śukadeva Gosvāmī said; *atha*—next; *kṛṣṇaḥ*—Lord Kṛṣṇa; *parivṛtaḥ*—surrounded; *jñātibhiḥ*—by His companions; *mudita-ātmabhiḥ*—who were joyful by nature; *anugīyamānaḥ*—His glories being chanted; *nyaviśat*—entered; *vrajam*—Vraja; *go-kula*—by the herds of cows; *maṇḍitam*—decorated.

TRANSLATION

Śukadeva Gosvāmī said: Surrounded by His blissful companions, who constantly chanted His glories, Śrī Kṛṣṇa then entered the village of Vraja, which was decorated with herds of cows.

TEXT 2

व्रजे विक्रीडतोरेवं गोपालच्छद्ममायया ।
ग्रीष्मो नामर्तुरभवन्नातिप्रेयाञ्छरीरिणाम् ॥ २ ॥

vraje vikrīḍator evaṁ
gopāla-cchadma-māyayā
grīṣmo nāmartur abhavan
nāti-preyāñ charīriṇām

vraje—in Vṛndāvana; *vikrīḍatoḥ*—while the two of Them were sporting; *evam*—in this way; *gopāla*—as cowherd boys; *chadma*—of the disguise; *māyayā*—by the illusion; *grīṣmaḥ*—summer; *nāma*—thus designated; *ṛtuḥ*—the season; *abhavat*—came about; *na*—not; *ati-preyān*—very much favored; *śarīriṇām*—by embodied beings.

TRANSLATION

While Kṛṣṇa and Balarāma were thus enjoying life in Vṛndāvana in the guise of ordinary cowherd boys, the summer season gradually appeared. This season is not very pleasing to embodied souls.

PURPORT

In Chapter Eighteen, of *Kṛṣṇa, the Supreme Personality of Godhead,* Śrīla Prabhupāda comments as follows: "The summer season in India is not very much welcomed because of the excessive heat, but in Vṛndāvana everyone was pleased because summer there appeared just like spring."

TEXT 3

स च वृन्दावनगुणैर्वसन्त इव लक्षितः ।
यत्रास्ते भगवान् साक्षाद् रामेण सह केशवः ॥ ३ ॥

sa ca vṛndāvana-guṇair
vasanta iva lakṣitaḥ
yatrāste bhagavān sākṣād
rāmeṇa saha keśavaḥ

saḥ—this (hot season); *ca*—nevertheless; *vṛndāvana*—of Śrī Vṛndāvana; *guṇaiḥ*—by the transcendental qualities; *vasantaḥ*—springtime; *iva*—as if; *lakṣitaḥ*—manifesting symptoms; *yatra*—in which (Vṛndāvana); *āste*—remains; *bhagavān*—the Supreme Personality of Godhead; *sākṣāt*—personally; *rāmeṇa saha*—together with Lord Balarāma; *keśavaḥ*—Lord Śrī Kṛṣṇa.

TRANSLATION

Nevertheless, because the Supreme Personality of Godhead was personally staying in Vṛndāvana along with Balarāma, summer manifested the qualities of spring. Such are the features of the land of Vṛndāvana.

TEXT 4

यत्र निर्झरनिर्ह्रादनिवृत्तस्वनझिल्लिकम् ।
शश्वत्तच्छीकरर्जीषद्रुममण्डलमण्डितम् ॥ ४ ॥

yatra nirjhara-nirhrāda-
nivṛtta-svana-jhillikam

śaśvat tac-chīkararjīṣa-
druma-maṇḍala-maṇḍitam

yatra—in which (Vṛndāvana); *nirjhara*—of the waterfalls; *nirhrāda*—by the resounding; *nivṛtta*—stopped; *svana*—the sound; *jhillikam*—of the crickets; *śaśvat*—constant; *tat*—of those (waterfalls); *śīkara*—by the drops of water; *ṛjīṣa*—moistened; *druma*—of trees; *maṇḍala*—with the groups; *maṇḍitam*—decorated.

TRANSLATION

In Vṛndāvana, the loud sound of waterfalls covered the crickets' noise, and clusters of trees constantly moistened by spray from those waterfalls beautified the entire area.

PURPORT

This and the following three verses describe how Vṛndāvana manifested the features of spring, even during the summer season.

TEXT 5

सरित्सरःप्रस्रवणोर्मिवायुना
कह्लारकञ्जोत्पलरेणुहारिणा ।
न विद्यते यत्र वनौकसां दवो
निदाघवह्न्यर्कभवोऽतिशाद्वले ॥ ५ ॥

sarit-saraḥ-prasravaṇormi-vāyunā
kahlāra-kañjotpala-reṇu-hāriṇā
na vidyate yatra vanaukasāṁ davo
nidāgha-vahny-arka-bhavo'ti-śādvale

sarit—of the rivers; *saraḥ*—and the lakes; *prasravaṇa*—(coming into contact with) the currents; *ūrmi*—and waves; *vāyunā*—by the wind; *kahlāra-kañja-utpala*—of the *kahlāra, kañja* and *utpala* lotuses; *reṇu*—the pollen; *hāriṇā*—which was taking away; *na vidyate*—there was not; *yatra*—in which; *vana-okasām*—for the residents of the forest; *davaḥ*—tormenting heat; *nidāgha*—of the summer season; *vahni*—by forest fires; *arka*—and the sun; *bhavaḥ*—generated; *ati-śādvale*—where there was an abundance of green grass.

TRANSLATION

The wind wafting over the waves of the lakes and flowing rivers carried away the pollen of many varieties of lotuses and water lilies and then cooled the entire Vṛndāvana area. Thus the residents there did not suffer from the heat generated by the blazing summer sun and seasonal forest fires. Indeed, Vṛndāvana was abundant with fresh green grass.

TEXT 6

अगाधतोयह्रदिनीतटोर्मिभिर्
द्रवत्पुरीष्याः पुलिनैः समन्ततः ।
न यत्र चण्डांशुकरा विषोल्बणा
भुवो रसं शाद्वलितं च गृह्णते ॥ ६ ॥

agādha-toya-hradinī-taṭormibhir
dravat-purīṣyāḥ pulinaiḥ samantataḥ
na yatra caṇḍāṁśu-karā viṣolbaṇā
bhuvo rasaṁ śādvalitaṁ ca gṛhṇate

agādha—very deep; *toya*—whose water; *hradinī*—of the rivers; *taṭa*—upon the shores; *ūrmibhiḥ*—by the waves; *dravat*—liquefied; *purīṣyāḥ*—whose mud; *pulinaiḥ*—by the sandy banks; *samantataḥ*—on all sides; *na*—not; *yatra*—upon which; *caṇḍa*—of the sun; *aṁśu-karāḥ*—the rays; *viṣa*—like poison; *ulbaṇāḥ*—fierce; *bhuvaḥ*—of the earth; *rasam*—the juice; *śādvalitam*—the greenness; *ca*—and; *gṛhṇate*—take away.

TRANSLATION

With their flowing waves the deep rivers drenched their banks, making them damp and muddy. Thus the rays of the sun, which were as fierce as poison, could not evaporate the earth's sap or parch its green grass.

TEXT 7

वनं कुसुमितं श्रीमन्नदच्चित्रमृगद्विजम् ।
गायन्मयूरभ्रमरं कूजत्कोकिलसारसम् ॥ ७ ॥

vanaṁ kusumitaṁ śrīman
nadac-citra-mṛga-dvijam

gāyan mayūra-bhramaraṁ
kūjat-kokila-sārasam

vanam—the forest; *kusumitam*—full of flowers; *śrīmat*—very beautiful; *nadat*—making sounds; *citra*—variegated; *mṛga*—animals; *dvijam*—and birds; *gāyan*—singing; *mayūra*—peacocks; *bhramaram*—and bees; *kūjat*—cooing; *kokila*—cuckoos; *sārasam*—and cranes.

TRANSLATION

Flowers beautifully decorated the forest of Vṛndāvana, and many varieties of animals and birds filled it with sound. The peacocks and bees sang, and the cuckoos and cranes cooed.

TEXT 8

क्रीडिष्यमाणस्तत् कृष्णो भगवान् बलसंयुतः ।
वेणुं विरणयन् गोपैर्गोधनैः संवृतोऽविशत् ॥ ८ ॥

krīḍiṣyamāṇas tat kṛṣṇo
bhagavān bala-saṁyutaḥ
veṇuṁ viraṇayan gopair
go-dhanaiḥ saṁvṛto'viśat

krīḍiṣyamāṇaḥ—intending to play; *tat*—that (Vṛndāvana forest); *kṛṣṇaḥ*—Kṛṣṇa; *bhagavān*—the Supreme Personality of Godhead; *bala-saṁyutaḥ*—accompanied by Balarāma; *veṇum*—His flute; *viraṇayan*—sounding; *gopaiḥ*—by the cowherd boys; *go-dhanaiḥ*—and the cows, who are their wealth; *saṁvṛtaḥ*—surrounded; *aviśat*—He entered.

TRANSLATION

Intending to engage in pastimes, Lord Kṛṣṇa, the Supreme Personality of Godhead, accompanied by Lord Balarāma and surrounded by the cowherd boys and the cows, entered the forest of Vṛndāvana as He played His flute.

TEXT 9

प्रवालबर्हस्तबकस्रग्धातुकृतभूषणाः ।
रामकृष्णादयो गोपा ननृतुर्युयुधुर्जगुः ॥ ९ ॥

pravāla-barha-stabaka-
srag-dhātu-kṛta-bhūṣaṇāḥ
rāma-kṛṣṇādayo gopā
nanṛtur yuyudhur jaguḥ

pravāla—newly grown leaves; *barha*—peacock feathers; *stabaka*—bunches of small flowers; *srak*—garlands; *dhātu*—and colored minerals; *kṛta-bhūṣaṇāḥ*—wearing as their ornaments; *rāma-kṛṣṇa-ādayaḥ*—headed by Lord Balarāma and Lord Kṛṣṇa; *gopāḥ*—the cowherd boys; *nanṛtuḥ*—danced; *yuyudhuḥ*—fought; *jaguḥ*—sang.

TRANSLATION

Decorating themselves with newly grown leaves, along with peacock feathers, garlands, clusters of flower buds, and colored minerals, Balarāma, Kṛṣṇa and Their cowherd friends danced, wrestled and sang.

TEXT 10

कृष्णस्य नृत्यतः केचिज्जगुः केचिदवादयन् ।
वेणुपाणितलैः शृंगैः प्रशशंसुरथापरे ॥ १० ॥

kṛṣṇasya nṛtyataḥ kecij
jaguḥ kecid avādayan
veṇu-pāṇitalaiḥ śṛṅgaiḥ
praśaśaṁsur athāpare

kṛṣṇasya nṛtyataḥ—while Kṛṣṇa was dancing; *kecit*—some of them; *jaguḥ*—sang; *kecit*—some; *avādayan*—accompanied musically; *veṇu*—with flutes; *pāṇi-talaiḥ*—and hand cymbals; *śṛṅgaiḥ*—with buffalo horns; *praśaśaṁsuḥ*—offered praise; *atha*—and; *apare*—others.

TRANSLATION

As Kṛṣṇa danced, some of the boys accompanied Him by singing, and others by playing flutes, hand cymbals and buffalo horns, while still others praised His dancing.

PURPORT

Wanting to encourage Śrī Kṛṣṇa, some of the cowherd boys openly praised His dancing.

TEXT 11

गोपजातिप्रतिच्छन्ना देवा गोपालरूपिणौ ।
ईडिरे कृष्णरामौ च नटा इव नटं नृप ॥ ११ ॥

gopa-jāti-praticchannā
devā gopāla-rūpiṇau
īḍire kṛṣṇa-rāmau ca
naṭā iva naṭaṁ nṛpa

gopa-jāti—as members of the cowherd community; *praticchannāḥ*—disguised; *devāḥ*—demigods; *gopāla-rūpiṇau*—who had assumed the forms of cowherd boys; *īḍire*—they worshiped; *kṛṣṇa-rāmau*—Lord Kṛṣṇa and Lord Rāma; *ca*—and; *naṭāḥ*—professional dancers; *iva*—just as; *naṭam*—another dancer; *nṛpa*—O King.

TRANSLATION

O King, demigods disguised themselves as members of the cowherd community and, just as dramatic dancers praise another dancer, worshiped Kṛṣṇa and Balarāma, who were also appearing as cowherd boys.

TEXT 12

भ्रमणैर्लङ्घनैः क्षेपैरास्फोटनविकर्षणैः ।
चिक्रीडतुर्नियुद्धेन काकपक्षधरौ क्वचित् ॥ १२ ॥

bhramaṇair laṅghanaiḥ kṣepair
āsphoṭana-vikarṣaṇaiḥ
cikrīḍatur niyuddhena
kāka-pakṣa-dharau kvacit

bhramaṇaiḥ—with whirling about; *laṅghanaiḥ*—jumping; *kṣepaiḥ*—throwing; *āsphoṭana*—slapping; *vikarṣaṇaiḥ*—and dragging; *cikrīḍatuḥ*—They (Kṛṣṇa and Balarāma) played; *niyuddhena*—with fighting; *kāka-pakṣa*—the locks of hair on the sides of Their heads; *dharau*—holding; *kvacit*—sometimes.

TRANSLATION

Kṛṣṇa and Balarāma played with their cowherd boyfriends by whirling about, leaping, hurling, slapping and fighting. Sometimes Kṛṣṇa and Balarāma would pull the hair on the boys' heads.

PURPORT

The *ācāryas* have explained this verse as follows: The word *bhramaṇaiḥ* indicates that the boys, pretending they were machines, would sometimes whirl about until they became dizzy. They would also sometimes jump about (*laṅghanaiḥ*). The word *kṣepaiḥ* indicates that sometimes they would hurl objects like balls or stones and that sometimes they would grab each other by the arms and throw one another about. *Āsphoṭana* means that sometimes they would slap one another's shoulders or backs, and *vikarṣaṇaiḥ* indicates they would drag one another about in the midst of their play. By the word *niyuddhena* arm wrestling and other types of friendly fighting are indicated, and the word *kāka-pakṣa-dharau* means that Kṛṣṇa and Balarāma would sometimes grab the hair on the other boys' heads in a playful manner.

TEXT 13

क्वचिन्नृत्यत्सु चान्येषु गायकौ वादकौ स्वयम् ।
शशंसतुर्महाराज साधु साध्विति वादिनौ ॥ १३ ॥

kvacin nṛtyatsu cānyeṣu
gāyakau vādakau svayam
śaśaṁsatur mahā-rāja
sādhu sādhv iti vādinau

kvacit—sometimes; *nṛtyatsu*—while they were dancing; *ca*—and; *anyeṣu*—others; *gāyakau*—the two of Them (Kṛṣṇa and Balarāma) singing; *vādakau*—both playing musical instruments; *svayam*—Themselves; *śaśaṁsatuḥ*—They praised; *mahā-rāja*—O great King; *sādhu sādhu iti*—"very good, very good"; *vādinau*—speaking.

TRANSLATION

While the other boys were dancing, O King, Kṛṣṇa and Balarāma would sometimes accompany them with song and instrumental music, and sometimes the two Lords would praise the boys, saying, "Very good! Very good!"

TEXT 14

क्वचिद् बिल्वैः क्वचित्कुम्भैः क्वचामलकमुष्टिभिः ।
अस्पृश्यनेत्रबन्धाद्यैः क्वचिन्मृगखगेहया ॥ १४ ॥

kvacid bilvaiḥ kvacit kumbhaiḥ
kvacāmalaka-muṣṭibhiḥ
aspṛśya-netra-bandhādyaiḥ
kvacin mṛga-khagehayā

kvacit—sometimes; *bilvaiḥ*—with *bilva* fruits; *kvacit*—sometimes; *kumbhaiḥ*—with *kumbha* fruits; *kvaca*—and sometimes; *āmalaka-muṣṭibhiḥ*—with palmfuls of *āmalaka* fruits; *aspṛśya*—with games such as trying to touch one another; *netra-bandha*—trying to identify another when one is blindfolded; *ādyaiḥ*—and so on; *kvacit*—sometimes; *mṛga*—like animals; *khaga*—and birds; *īhayā*—acting.

TRANSLATION

Sometimes the cowherd boys would play with bilva or kumbha fruits, and sometimes with handfuls of āmalaka fruits. At other times they would play the games of trying to touch one another or of trying to identify somebody while one is blindfolded, and sometimes they would imitate animals and birds.

PURPORT

Śrīla Sanātana Gosvāmī explains that the word *ādyaiḥ,* "by other such sports," indicates such games as chasing one another and building bridges. Another pastime would occur at noon, while Lord Kṛṣṇa was taking rest. Nearby, the young cowherd girls would be passing by, singing, and Kṛṣṇa's boyfriends would pretend to inquire from them about the price of milk. Then the boys would steal yogurt and other items from them and run away. Kṛṣṇa, Balarāma and Their friends would also play games in which they would cross the river in boats.

Śrīla Viśvanātha Cakravartī Ṭhākura further explains that the boys would play with fruits by throwing a few in the air and then throwing others to try to hit them. The word *netra-bandha* indicates a game in which one boy would approach a blindfolded boy from behind and place his palms over the blindfolded boy's eyes. Then, simply by the feel of his palms, the blindfolded boy would have to guess who the other boy was. In all such games the boys put up stakes for the winner, such as flutes or walking sticks. Sometimes the boys would imitate the various fighting methods of the forest animals, and at other times they would chirp like birds.

TEXT 15

क्वचिच्च दर्दुरप्लावैर्विविधैरुपहासकैः ।
कदाचित् स्पन्दोलिकया कर्हिचिन्नृपचेष्टया ॥ १५ ॥

kvacic ca dardura-plāvair
vividhair upahāsakaiḥ
kadācit syandolikayā
karhicin nṛpa-ceṣṭayā

kvacit—sometimes; *ca*—and; *dardura*—like frogs; *plāvaiḥ*—with jumping; *vividhaiḥ*—various; *upahāsakaiḥ*—with jokes; *kadācit*—sometimes; *syandolikayā*—with riding in swings; *karhicit*—and sometimes; *nṛpa-ceṣṭayā*—with pretending to be kings.

TRANSLATION

They would sometimes jump around like frogs, sometimes play various jokes, sometimes ride in swings and sometimes imitate monarchs.

PURPORT

Śrīla Viśvanātha Cakravartī Ṭhākura explains the word *nṛpa-ceṣṭayā* as follows: In Vṛndāvana there was a particular place on the riverbank where people who wanted to cross the Yamunā would pay a small tax. At times the cowherd boys would assemble in this area and prevent the young girls of Vṛndāvana from crossing the river, insisting that they had to pay a customs duty first. Such activities were full of joking and laughter.

TEXT 16

एवं तौ लोकसिद्धाभिः क्रीडाभिश्चेरतुर्वने ।
नद्यद्रिद्रोणिकुञ्जेषु काननेषु सरःसु च ॥ १६ ॥

evaṁ tau loka-siddhābhiḥ
krīḍābhiś ceratur vane
nady-adri-droṇi-kuñjeṣu
kānaneṣu saraḥsu ca

evam—in this way; *tau*—the two of Them, Kṛṣṇa and Balarāma; *loka-siddhābhiḥ*—which are well known in human society; *krīḍābhiḥ*—with games; *ceratuḥ*—They wandered; *vane*—in the forest; *nadī*—among the rivers; *adri*—mountains; *droṇi*—valleys; *kuñjeṣu*—and groves; *kānaneṣu*—in the smaller forests; *saraḥsu*—along the lakes; *ca*—and.

TRANSLATION

In this way Kṛṣṇa and Balarāma played all sorts of well-known games as They wandered among the rivers, hills, valleys, bushes, trees and lakes of Vṛndāvana.

TEXT 17

पशूंश्चारयतोर्गोपैस्तद्वने रामकृष्णयोः ।
गोपरूपी प्रलम्बोऽगादसुरस्तज्जिहीर्षया ॥ १७ ॥

paśūṁś cārayator gopais
tad-vane rāma-kṛṣṇayoḥ
gopa-rūpī pralambo'gād
asuras taj-jihīrṣayā

paśūn—the animals; *cārayatoḥ*—while the two of Them were herding; *gopaiḥ*—along with the cowherd boys; *tat-vane*—in that forest, Vṛndāvana; *rāma-kṛṣṇayoḥ*—Lord Rāma and Lord Kṛṣṇa; *gopa-rūpī*—assuming the form of a cowherd boy; *pralambaḥ*—Pralamba; *agāt*—came; *asuraḥ*—the demon; *tat*—Them; *jihīrṣayā*—with the desire of kidnapping.

TRANSLATION

While Rāma, Kṛṣṇa and Their cowherd friends were thus tending the cows in that Vṛndāvana forest, the demon Pralamba entered their midst. He had assumed the form of a cowherd boy with the intention of kidnapping Kṛṣṇa and Balarāma.

PURPORT

Having described how Kṛṣṇa and Balarāma acted just like ordinary boys, Śukadeva Gosvāmī will now reveal one of the Lord's transcendental pastimes that is beyond the range of human activity. According to Śrīla Viśvanātha Cakravartī Ṭhākura, the demon Pralamba disguised himself as a particular cowherd boy who on that day had remained at home with duties to perform.

TEXT 18

तं विद्वानपि दाशार्हो भगवान् सर्वदर्शनः ।
अन्वमोदत तत्सख्यं वधं तस्य विचिन्तयन् ॥ १८ ॥

taṁ vidvān api dāśārho
bhagavān sarva-darśanaḥ
anvamodata tat-sakhyaṁ
vadhaṁ tasya vicintayan

tam—him, Pralambāsura; *vidvān*—knowing quite well; *api*—even though; *dāśārhaḥ*—the descendant of Daśārha; *bhagavān*—the Supreme Personality of Godhead; *sarva-darśanaḥ*—the omniscient; *anvamodata*—accepted; *tat*—with him; *sakhyam*—friendship; *vadham*—the killing; *tasya*—of him; *vicintayan*—meditating upon.

TRANSLATION

Since the Supreme Lord Kṛṣṇa, who had appeared in the Daśārha dynasty, sees everything, He understood who the demon was. Still, the Lord pretended to accept the demon as a friend, while at the same time seriously considering how to kill him.

TEXT 19

तत्रोपाहूय गोपालान् कृष्णः प्राह विहारवित् ।
हे गोपा विहरिष्यामो द्वन्द्वीभूय यथायथम् ॥ १९ ॥

tatropāhūya gopālān
kṛṣṇaḥ prāha vihāra-vit
he gopā vihariṣyāmo
dvandvī-bhūya yathā-yatham

tatra—thereupon; *upāhūya*—calling; *gopālān*—the cowherd boys; *kṛṣṇaḥ*—Lord Kṛṣṇa; *prāha*—spoke; *vihāra-vit*—the knower of all sports and games; *he gopāḥ*—O cowherd boys; *vihariṣyāmaḥ*—let us play; *dvandvī-bhūya*—dividing into two groups; *yathā-yatham*—suitably.

TRANSLATION

Kṛṣṇa, who knows all sports and games, then called together the cowherd boys and spoke as follows: "Hey cowherd boys! Let's play now! We'll divide ourselves into two even teams."

PURPORT

The word *yathā-yatham* means that Kṛṣṇa naturally wanted the two teams to be evenly matched so that there would be a good game. In addition to the pleasure of sporting, the purpose of the game was to kill the demon Pralamba.

TEXT 20

तत्र चक्रुः परिवृढौ गोपा रामजनार्दनौ ।
कृष्णसङ्घट्टिनः केचिदासन् रामस्य चापरे ॥ २० ॥

tatra cakruḥ parivṛḍhau
gopā rāma-janārdanau
kṛṣṇa-saṅghaṭṭinaḥ kecid
āsan rāmasya cāpare

tatra—in that game; *cakruḥ*—they made; *parivṛḍhau*—the two leaders; *gopāḥ*—the cowherd boys; *rāma-janārdanau*—Lord Balarāma and Kṛṣṇa; *kṛṣṇa-saṅghaṭṭinaḥ*—members of Kṛṣṇa's party; *kecit*—some of them; *āsan*—became; *rāmasya*—of Balarāma; *ca*—and; *apare*—others.

TRANSLATION

The cowherd boys chose Kṛṣṇa and Balarāma as the leaders of the two parties. Some of the boys were on Kṛṣṇa's side, and others joined Balarāma.

TEXT 21

आचेरुर्विविधाः क्रीडा वाह्यवाहकलक्षणाः ।
यत्रारोहन्ति जेतारो वहन्ति च पराजिताः ॥ २१ ॥

ācerur vividhāḥ krīḍā
vāhya-vāhaka-lakṣaṇāḥ
yatrārohanti jetāro
vahanti ca parājitāḥ

āceruḥ—they performed; *vividhāḥ*—various; *krīḍāḥ*—sports; *vāhya*—by the carried; *vāhaka*—the carrier; *lakṣaṇāḥ*—characterized; *yatra*—in which; *ārohanti*—climb; *jetāraḥ*—the winners; *vahanti*—carry; *ca*—and; *parājitāḥ*—the defeated.

TRANSLATION

The boys played various games involving carriers and passengers. In these games the winners would climb up on the backs of the losers, who would have to carry them.

PURPORT

Śrīla Sanātana Gosvāmī quotes the following relevant verse from the *Viṣṇu Purāṇa* (5.9.12):

hariṇākrīḍanaṁ nāma
bāla-krīḍaṇakaṁ tataḥ
prakrīḍatā hi te sarve
dvau dvau yugapad utpatan

"They then played the childhood game known as *hariṇākrīḍanam,* in which each boy paired off with an opponent and all the boys simultaneously attacked their respective rivals."

TEXT 22

वहन्तो वाह्यमानाश्च चारयन्तश्च गोधनम् ।
भाण्डीरकं नाम वटं जग्मुः कृष्णपुरोगमाः ॥ २२ ॥

vahanto vāhyamānāś ca
cārayantaś ca go-dhanam
bhāṇḍīrakaṁ nāma vaṭaṁ
jagmuḥ kṛṣṇa-purogamāḥ

vahantaḥ—carrying; *vāhyamānāḥ*—being carried; *ca*—and; *cārayantaḥ*—tending; *ca*—also; *go-dhanam*—the cows; *bhāṇḍīrakam nāma*—named Bhāṇḍīraka; *vaṭam*—to the banyan tree; *jagmuḥ*—they went; *kṛṣṇa-puraḥ-gamāḥ*—led by Lord Kṛṣṇa.

TRANSLATION

Thus carrying and being carried by one another, and at the same time tending the cows, the boys followed Kṛṣṇa to a banyan tree known as Bhāṇḍīraka.

PURPORT

Śrīla Sanātana Gosvāmī quotes the following verses from *Śrī Harivaṁśa* (*Viṣṇu-parva* 11.18–22), which describe the banyan tree:

dadarśa vipulodagra-
śākhinaṁ śākhināṁ varam
sthitaṁ dharaṇyāṁ meghābhaṁ
nibiḍaṁ dala-sañcayaiḥ

gaganārdhocchritākāraṁ
parvatābhoga-dhāriṇam
nīla-citrāṅga-varṇaiś ca
sevitaṁ bahubhiḥ khagaiḥ

phalaiḥ pravālaiś ca ghanaiḥ
sendracāpa-ghanopamam
bhavanākāra-viṭapaṁ
latā-puṣpa-sumaṇḍitam

viśāla-mūlāvanataṁ
pāvanāmbhoda-dhāriṇam
ādhipatyam ivānyeṣāṁ
tasya deśasya śākhinām

kurvāṇaṁ śubha-karmāṇaṁ
nirāvarṣam anātapam
nyagrodhaṁ parvatāgrābhaṁ
bhāṇḍīraṁ nāma nāmataḥ

"They saw that best of all trees, which had many long branches. With its dense covering of leaves, it resembled a cloud sitting on the earth. Indeed, its form was so large that it appeared like a mountain covering half the sky. Many birds with charming blue wings frequented that great tree, whose dense fruits and leaves made it seem like a cloud accompanied by a rainbow or like a house decorated with creepers and flowers. It spread its broad roots downward and carried upon itself the sanctified clouds. That banyan tree was like the lordly master of all other trees in that vicinity, as it performed the all-auspicious functions of warding off the rain and the heat of the sun. Such was the appearance of that *nyagrodha* tree known as Bhāṇḍīra, which seemed just like the peak of a great mountain."

TEXT 23

रामसङ्घट्टिनो यर्हि श्रीदामवृषभादयः ।
क्रीडायां जयिनस्तांस्तानूहुः कृष्णादयो नृप ॥ २३ ॥

rāma-saṅghaṭṭino yarhi
śrīdāma-vṛṣabhādayaḥ
krīḍāyāṁ jayinas tāṁs tān
ūhuḥ kṛṣṇādayo nṛpa

rāma-saṅghaṭṭinaḥ—the members of Lord Balarāma's party; *yarhi*—when; *śrīdāma-vṛṣabha-ādayaḥ*—Śrīdāmā, Vṛṣabha and others (such as Subala); *krīḍāyām*—in the games; *jayinaḥ*—victorious; *tān tān*—each of them; *ūhuḥ*—carried; *kṛṣṇa-ādayaḥ*—Kṛṣṇa and the members of His party; *nṛpa*—O King.

TRANSLATION

My dear King Parīkṣit, when Śrīdāmā, Vṛṣabha and the other members of Lord Balarāma's party were victorious in these games, Kṛṣṇa and His followers had to carry them.

TEXT 24

उवाह कृष्णो भगवान् श्रीदामानं पराजितः ।
वृषभं भद्रसेनस्तु प्रलम्बो रोहिणीसुतम् ॥ २४ ॥

uvāha kṛṣṇo bhagavān
śrīdāmānaṁ parājitaḥ
vṛṣabhaṁ bhadrasenas tu
pralambo rohiṇī-sutam

uvāha—carried; *kṛṣṇaḥ*—Lord Śrī Kṛṣṇa; *bhagavān*—the Supreme Personality of Godhead; *śrīdāmānam*—His devotee and friend Śrīdāmā; *parājitaḥ*—being defeated; *vṛṣabham*—Vṛṣabha; *bhadrasenaḥ*—Bhadrasena; *tu*—and; *pralambaḥ*—Pralamba; *rohiṇī-sutam*—the son of Rohiṇī (Balarāma).

TRANSLATION

Defeated, the Supreme Lord Kṛṣṇa carried Śrīdāmā. Bhadrasena carried Vṛṣabha, and Pralamba carried Balarāma, the son of Rohiṇī.

PURPORT

One may ask how Bhagavān, the Supreme Lord, can be defeated by His boyfriends. The answer is that in His original form, God has a most playful nature and occasionally enjoys submitting to the strength or desire of His loving friends. A father may sometimes playfully fall down on the ground when struck by his beloved little child. These acts of love give pleasure to all parties. Thus Śrīdāmā agreed to ride on Lord Kṛṣṇa's shoulders to please his beloved friend, who happened to be Bhagavān, the Supreme Personality of Godhead.

TEXT 25

अविषह्यं मन्यमानः कृष्णं दानवपुंगवः ।
वहन् द्रुततरं प्रागादवरोहणतः परम् ॥ २५ ॥

aviṣahyaṁ manyamānaḥ
kṛṣṇaṁ dānava-puṅgavaḥ
vahan drutataraṁ prāgād
avarohaṇataḥ param

aviṣahyam—invincible; *manyamānaḥ*—considering; *kṛṣṇam*—Lord Kṛṣṇa; *dānava-puṅgavaḥ*—that foremost demon; *vahan*—carrying; *druta-taram*—very quickly; *prāgāt*—he went off; *avarohaṇataḥ param*—beyond the place marked for climbing down.

TRANSLATION

Considering Lord Kṛṣṇa invincible, that foremost demon [Pralamba] quickly carried Balarāma far beyond the spot where he was supposed to put his passenger down.

PURPORT

Pralamba wanted to carry Balarāma out of Lord Kṛṣṇa's sight so that he could cruelly attack Him.

TEXT 26

तमुद्वहन् धरणिधरेन्द्रगौरवं
महासुरो विगतरयो निजं वपुः ।
स आस्थितः पुरटपरिच्छदो बभौ
तडिद्द्युमानुडुपतिवाडिवाम्बुदः ॥ २६ ॥

tam udvahan dharaṇi-dharendra-gauravaṁ
mahāsuro vigata-rayo nijaṁ vapuḥ
sa āsthitaḥ puraṭa-paricchado babhau
taḍid-dyumān uḍupati-vāḍ ivāmbudaḥ

tam—Him, Lord Baladeva; *udvahan*—carrying high; *dharaṇi-dhara-indra*—like the king of the mountains, Sumeru; *gauravam*—whose weight; *mahā-asuraḥ*—the great demon; *vigata-rayaḥ*—losing his momentum; *nijam*—his original; *vapuḥ*—body; *saḥ*—he; *āsthitaḥ*—becoming situated in; *puraṭa*—golden; *paricchadaḥ*—having ornaments; *babhau*—he shone; *taḍit*—like lightning; *dyu-mān*—flashing; *uḍu-pati*—the moon; *vāṭ*—carrying; *iva*—just as; *ambu-daḥ*—a cloud.

TRANSLATION

As the great demon carried Balarāma, the Lord became as heavy as massive Mount Sumeru, and Pralamba had to slow down. He then resumed his actual form—an effulgent body that was covered with golden ornaments and that resembled a cloud flashing with lightning and carrying the moon.

PURPORT

Here the demon Pralamba is compared to a cloud, his golden ornaments to lightning within that cloud, and Lord Balarāma to the moon shining through it. Great demons can assume various forms by exerting their mystic power, but when the Lord's spiritual potency curtails their power, they can no longer maintain an artificial form and must again manifest their actual, demoniac body. Lord Balarāma suddenly became as heavy as a great mountain, and although the demon tried to carry Him high on his shoulders, he could not go on.

TEXT 27

निरीक्ष्य तद्वपुरलमम्बरे चरत्
प्रदीप्तदृग् भ्रुकुटितटोग्रदंष्ट्रकम्।
ज्वलच्छिखं कटककिरीटकुण्डल-
त्विषाद्भुतं हलधर ईषदत्रसत् ॥ २७॥

nirīkṣya tad-vapur alam ambare carat
pradīpta-dṛg bhru-kuṭi-taṭogra-daṁṣṭrakam
jvalac-chikhaṁ kaṭaka-kirīṭa-kuṇḍala-
tviṣādbhutaṁ haladhara īṣad atrasat

nirīkṣya—seeing; *tat*—of Pralambāsura; *vapuḥ*—the body; *alam*—quickly; *ambare*—in the sky; *carat*—moving; *pradīpta*—blazing; *dṛk*—his eyes; *bhru-kuṭi*—of his frown upon his eyebrows; *taṭa*—on the edge; *ugra*—terrible; *daṁṣṭrakam*—his teeth; *jvalat*—fiery; *śikham*—hair; *kaṭaka*—of his armlets; *kirīṭa*—crown; *kuṇḍala*—and earrings; *tviṣā*—by the effulgence; *adbhutam*—astonishing; *hala-dharaḥ*—Lord Balarāma, the carrier of the plow weapon; *īṣat*—a little; *atrasat*—became frightened.

TRANSLATION

When Lord Balarāma, who carries the plow weapon, saw the gigantic body of the demon as he moved swiftly in the sky—with his blazing eyes, fiery hair, terrible teeth reaching toward his scowling brows, and an amazing effulgence generated by his armlets, crown and earrings—the Lord seemed to become a little frightened.

PURPORT

Śrīla Sanātana Gosvāmī explains Lord Baladeva's so-called fear as follows: Balarāma was playfully acting out the role of an ordinary cowherd boy, and to maintain the mood of this pastime He appeared slightly disturbed by the horrible demoniac body. Also, because the demon had appeared as a cowherd boyfriend of Kṛṣṇa's, and because Kṛṣṇa had accepted him as a friend, Baladeva was slightly apprehensive about killing him. Balarāma could also have been worried that since this cowherd boy was actually a demon in disguise, at that very moment another such demon might have been attacking Lord Kṛṣṇa Himself. Thus the omniscient and omnipotent Supreme Lord Balarāma exhibited the pastime of becoming slightly nervous in the presence of the horrible demon Pralamba.

TEXT 28

अथागतस्मृतिरभयो रिपुं बलो
विहाय सार्थमिव हरन्तमात्मनः ।
रुषाहनच्छिरसि दृढेन मुष्टिना
सुराधिपो गिरिमिव वज्ररंहसा ॥ २८ ॥

athāgata-smṛtir abhayo ripuṁ balo
vihāya sārtham iva harantam ātmanaḥ
ruṣāhanac chirasi dṛḍhena muṣṭinā
surādhipo girim iva vajra-raṁhasā

atha—then; *āgata-smṛtiḥ*—remembering Himself; *abhayaḥ*—without fear; *ripum*—His enemy; *balaḥ*—Lord Balarāma; *vihāya*—leaving aside;

sārtham—the company; *iva*—indeed; *harantam*—kidnapping; *ātmanaḥ*—Himself; *ruṣā*—angrily; *ahanat*—He struck; *śirasi*—upon the head; *dṛḍhena*—hard; *muṣṭinā*—with His fist; *sura-adhipaḥ*—the king of the demigods, Indra; *girim*—a mountain; *iva*—just as; *vajra*—of his thunderbolt weapon; *raṁhasā*—with the swiftness.

TRANSLATION

Remembering the actual situation, the fearless Balarāma understood that the demon was trying to kidnap Him and take Him away from His companions. The Lord then became furious and struck the demon's head with His hard fist, just as Indra, the king of the demigods, strikes a mountain with his thunderbolt weapon.

PURPORT

Lord Balarāma's powerful fist came crashing down upon the demon's head, just as a huge lightning bolt comes crashing into a mountain, cracking its stone surface into pieces. The words *vihāya sārtham iva* may also be divided *vihāyasā artham iva,* meaning that the demon was flying in the sky on the cosmic path, *vihāyas,* with the purpose of carrying off Balarāma, who was his *artham,* or object of pursuit.

TEXT 29

स आहतः सपदि विशीर्णमस्तको
मुखाद् वमन् रुधिरमपस्मृतोऽसुरः ।
महारवं व्यसुरपतत् समीरयन्
गिरिर्यथा मघवत आयुधाहतः ॥ २९ ॥

sa āhataḥ sapadi viśīrṇa-mastako
mukhād vaman rudhiram apasmṛto'suraḥ
mahā-ravaṁ vyasur apatat samīrayan
girir yathā maghavata āyudhāhataḥ

saḥ—he, Pralambāsura; *āhataḥ*—struck; *sapadi*—at once; *viśīrṇa*—split; *mastakaḥ*—his head; *mukhāt*—from his mouth; *vaman*—vomiting; *rudhiram*—blood; *apasmṛtaḥ*—unconscious; *asuraḥ*—the demon; *mahā-ravam*—a great noise; *vyasuḥ*—lifeless; *apatat*—he fell; *samīrayan*—sounding; *giriḥ*—a mountain; *yathā*—as; *maghavataḥ*—of Lord Indra; *āyudha*—by the weapon; *āhataḥ*—hit.

TRANSLATION

Thus smashed by Balarāma's fist, Pralamba's head immediately cracked open. The demon vomited blood from his mouth and lost all consciousness, and then with a great noise he fell lifeless on the ground, like a mountain devastated by Indra.

TEXT 30

दृष्ट्वा प्रलम्बं निहतं बलेन बलशालिना ।
गोपाः सुविस्मिता आसन् साधु साध्विति वादिनः ॥ ३० ॥

dṛṣṭvā pralambaṁ nihataṁ
balena bala-śālinā
gopāḥ su-vismitā āsan
sādhu sādhv iti vādinaḥ

dṛṣṭvā—seeing; *pralambam*—Pralambāsura; *nihatam*—killed; *balena*—by Lord Balarāma; *bala-śālinā*—who is by nature very powerful; *gopāḥ*—the cowherd boys; *su-vismitāḥ*—most astonished; *āsan*—became; *sādhu sādhu*—"very wonderful, very wonderful"; *iti*—these words; *vādinaḥ*—speaking.

TRANSLATION

The cowherd boys were most astonished to see how the powerful Balarāma had killed the demon Pralamba, and they exclaimed, "Excellent! Excellent!"

TEXT 31

आशिषोऽभिगृणन्तस्तं प्रशशंसुस्तदर्हणम् ।
प्रेत्यागतमिवालिंग्य प्रेमविह्वलचेतसः ॥ ३१ ॥

āśiṣo'bhigṛṇantas taṁ
praśaśaṁsus tad-arhaṇam
pretyāgatam ivāliṅgya
prema-vihvala-cetasaḥ

āśiṣaḥ—benedictions; *abhigṛṇantaḥ*—offering profusely; *tam*—to Him; *praśaśaṁsuḥ*—they praised; *tat-arhaṇam*—Him who was worthy of such; *pretya*—having died; *āgatam*—come back; *iva*—as if; *āliṅgya*—embracing; *prema*—out of love; *vihvala*—overwhelmed; *cetasaḥ*—their minds.

TRANSLATION

They offered Balarāma profuse benedictions and then glorified Him, who deserves all glorification. Their minds overwhelmed with ecstatic love, they embraced Him as if He had come back from the dead.

TEXT 32

पापे प्रलम्बे निहते देवाः परमनिर्वृताः ।
अभ्यवर्षन् बलं माल्यैः शशंसुः साधु साध्विति ॥ ३२ ॥

pāpe pralambe nihate
devāḥ parama-nirvṛtāḥ
abhyavarṣan balaṁ mālyaiḥ
śaśaṁsuḥ sādhu sādhv iti

pāpe—the sinful; *pralambe*—Pralambāsura; *nihate*—being killed; *devāḥ*—the demigods; *parama*—extremely; *nirvṛtāḥ*—satisfied; *abhyavarṣan*—showered; *balam*—Lord Balarāma; *mālyaiḥ*—with flower garlands; *śaśaṁsuḥ*—they offered prayers; *sādhu sādhu iti*—crying "excellent, excellent."

TRANSLATION

The sinful Pralamba having been killed, the demigods felt extremely happy, and they showered flower garlands upon Lord Balarāma and praised the excellence of His deed.

Thus end the purports of the humble servants of His Divine Grace A.C. Bhaktivedanta Swami Prabhupāda to the Tenth Canto, Eighteenth Chapter, of the Śrīmad-Bhāgavatam, *entitled "Lord Balarāma Slays the Demon Pralamba."*

CHAPTER NINETEEN

Swallowing the Forest Fire

This chapter describes how Lord Kṛṣṇa saved the cows and the cowherd boys from a great fire in the Muñjāraṇya forest.

One day the cowherd boys became absorbed in sporting and allowed the cows to wander into a dense forest. Suddenly a forest fire blazed up, and to escape its flames the cows took refuge in a grove of sharp canes. When the cowherd boys missed their animals, they went searching for them, following their hoofprints and the trail of blades of grass and other plants they had trampled or had broken with their teeth. Finally the boys found the cows and removed them from the cane forest, but by that time the forest fire had grown strong and was threatening both the boys and the cows. Thus the cowherd boys took shelter of Śrī Kṛṣṇa, the master of all mystic power, who told them to close their eyes. They did so, and in a moment He had swallowed up the fierce forest fire and brought them all back to the Bhāṇḍīra tree mentioned in the last chapter. Seeing this wonderful display of mystic potency, the cowherd boys thought Kṛṣṇa must be a demigod, and they began to praise Him. Then they all returned home.

TEXT 1

श्रीशुक उवाच
क्रीडासक्तेषु गोपेषु तद्गावो दूरचारिणीः ।
स्वैरं चरन्त्यो विविशुस्तृणलोभेन गह्वरम् ॥ १ ॥

śrī-śuka uvāca
krīḍāsakteṣu gopeṣu
tad-gāvo dūra-cāriṇīḥ
svairaṁ carantyo viviśus
tṛṇa-lobhena gahvaram

śrī-śukaḥ uvāca—Śrī Śukadeva Gosvāmī said; *krīḍā*—in their playing; *āsakteṣu*—while they were completely absorbed; *gopeṣu*—the cowherd boys; *tat-gāvaḥ*—their cows; *dūra-cāriṇīḥ*—wandering far away; *svairam*—

independently; *carantyaḥ*—grazing; *viviśuḥ*—they entered; *tṛṇa*—for grass; *lobhena*—out of greed; *gahvaram*—a dense forest.

TRANSLATION

Śukadeva Gosvāmī said: While the cowherd boys were completely absorbed in playing, their cows wandered far away. They hungered for more grass, and with no one to watch them they entered a dense forest.

TEXT 2

अजा गावो महिष्यश्च निर्विशन्त्यो वनाद् वनम् ।
ईषीकाटवीं निर्विविशुः क्रन्दन्त्यो दावतर्षिताः ॥ २ ॥

ajā gāvo mahiṣyaś ca
nirviśantyo vanād vanam
īṣīkāṭavīṁ nirviviśuḥ
krandantyo dāva-tarṣitāḥ

ajāḥ—the goats; *gāvaḥ*—the cows; *mahiṣyaḥ*—the buffalo; *ca*—and; *nirviśantyaḥ*—entering; *vanāt*—from one forest; *vanam*—to another forest; *īṣīkā-aṭavīm*—a forest of canes; *nirviviśuḥ*—they entered; *krandantyaḥ*—crying out; *dāva*—because of a forest fire; *tarṣitāḥ*—thirsty.

TRANSLATION

Passing from one part of the great forest to another, the goats, cows and buffalo eventually entered an area overgrown with sharp canes. The heat of a nearby forest fire made them thirsty, and they cried out in distress.

TEXT 3

तेऽपश्यन्तः पशून् गोपाः कृष्णरामादयस्तदा ।
जातानुतापा न विदुर्विचिन्वन्तो गवां गतिम् ॥ ३ ॥

te 'paśyantaḥ paśūn gopāḥ
kṛṣṇa-rāmādayas tadā
jātānutāpā na vidur
vicinvanto gavāṁ gatim

te—they; *apaśyantaḥ*—not seeing; *paśūn*—the animals; *gopāḥ*—the cowherd boys; *kṛṣṇa-rāma-ādayaḥ*—led by Kṛṣṇa and Rāma; *tadā*—then; *jāta-anutāpāḥ*—feeling remorse; *na viduḥ*—they did not know; *vicinvantaḥ*—searching out; *gavām*—of the cows; *gatim*—the path.

TRANSLATION

Not seeing the cows before them, Kṛṣṇa, Rāma and Their cowherd friends suddenly felt repentant for having neglected them. The boys searched all around, but could not discover where they had gone.

TEXT 4

तृणैस्तत्खुरदच्छिन्नैर्गोष्पदैरंकितैर्गवाम् ।
मार्गमन्वगमन् सर्वे नष्टाजीव्या विचेतसः ॥ ४ ॥

tṛṇais tat-khura-dac-chinnair
goṣ-padair aṅkitair gavām
mārgam anvagaman sarve
naṣṭājīvyā vicetasaḥ

tṛṇaiḥ—by the blades of grass; *tat*—of those cows; *khura*—by the hooves; *dat*—and the teeth; *chinnaiḥ*—which were broken; *goḥ-padaiḥ*—with the hoofprints; *aṅkitaiḥ*—(by places in the ground) which were marked; *gavām*—of the cows; *mārgam*—the path; *anvagaman*—they followed; *sarve*—all of them; *nasta-ājīvyāḥ*—having lost their livelihood; *vicetasaḥ*—in anxiety.

TRANSLATION

Then the boys began tracing out the cows' path by noting their hoofprints and the blades of grass the cows had broken with their hooves and teeth. All the cowherd boys were in great anxiety because they had lost their source of livelihood.

TEXT 5

मुञ्जाटव्यां भ्रष्टमार्गं क्रन्दमानं स्वगोधनम् ।
सम्प्राप्य तृषिताः श्रान्तास्ततस्ते संन्यवर्तयन् ॥ ५ ॥

muñjāṭavyāṁ bhraṣṭa-mārgaṁ
krandamānaṁ sva-godhanam

samprāpya tṛṣitāḥ śrāntās
tatas te sannyavartayan

muñjā-aṭavyām—in the Muñjā forest; *bhraṣṭa-mārgam*—who had lost their way; *krandamānam*—crying; *sva*—their own; *go-dhanam*—cows (and other animals); *samprāpya*—finding; *tṛṣitāḥ*—who were thirsty; *śrāntāḥ*—and tired; *tataḥ*—then; *te*—they, the cowherd boys; *sannyavartayan*—turned them all back.

TRANSLATION

Within the Muñjā forest the cowherd boys finally found their valuable cows, who had lost their way and were crying. Then the boys, thirsty and tired, herded the cows onto the path back home.

TEXT 6

ता आहूता भगवता मेघगम्भीरया गिरा ।
स्वनाम्नां निनदं श्रुत्वा प्रतिनेदुः प्रहर्षिताः ॥ ६ ॥

tā āhūtā bhagavatā
megha-gambhīrayā girā
sva-nāmnāṁ ninadaṁ śrutvā
pratineduḥ praharṣitāḥ

tāḥ—they; *āhūtāḥ*—called; *bhagavatā*—by the Supreme Personality of Godhead; *megha-gambhīrayā*—as deep as a cloud; *girā*—with His voice; *sva-nāmnām*—of their own names; *ninadam*—the sound; *śrutvā*—hearing; *pratineduḥ*—they replied; *praharṣitāḥ*—greatly enlivened.

TRANSLATION

The Supreme Personality of Godhead called out to the animals in a voice that resounded like a rumbling cloud. Hearing the sound of their own names, the cows were overjoyed and called out to the Lord in reply.

TEXT 7

ततः समन्ताद्दवधूमकेतुर्
यदृच्छयाभूत् क्षयकृद् वनौकसाम् ।
समीरितः सारथिनोल्बणोल्मुकैर्
विलेलिहानः स्थिरजंगमान्महान् ॥ ७ ॥

tataḥ samantād dava-dhūmaketur
yadṛcchayābhūt kṣaya-kṛd vanaukasām
samīritaḥ sārathinolbaṇolmukair
vilelihānaḥ sthira-jaṅgamān mahān

tataḥ—then; *samantāt*—on all sides; *dava-dhūmaketuḥ*—a terrible forest fire; *yadṛcchayā*—suddenly; *abhūt*—appeared; *kṣaya-kṛt*—threatening destruction; *vana-okasām*—for all those present in the forest; *samīritaḥ*—driven; *sārathinā*—by its chariot driver, the wind; *ulbaṇa*—terrible; *ulmukaiḥ*—with meteorlike sparks; *vilelihānaḥ*—licking; *sthira-jaṅgamān*—all moving and nonmoving creatures; *mahān*—very great.

TRANSLATION

Suddenly a great forest fire appeared on all sides, threatening to destroy all the forest creatures. Like a chariot driver, the wind swept the fire onward, and terrible sparks shot in all directions. Indeed, the great fire extended its tongues of flame toward all moving and nonmoving creatures.

PURPORT

Just as Kṛṣṇa, Balarāma and the cowherd boys were about to take their cows back home, the forest fire previously mentioned raged out of control and surrounded all of them.

TEXT 8

तमापतन्तं परितो दवाग्निं
गोपाश्च गावः प्रसमीक्ष्य भीताः ।
ऊचुश्च कृष्णं सबलं प्रपन्ना
यथा हरिं मृत्युभयार्दिता जनाः ॥ ८ ॥

tam āpatantaṁ parito davāgniṁ
gopāś ca gāvaḥ prasamīkṣya bhītāḥ
ūcuś ca kṛṣṇaṁ sa-balaṁ prapannā
yathā hariṁ mṛtyu-bhayārditā janāḥ

tam—that; *āpatantam*—setting upon them; *paritaḥ*—on all sides; *dava-agnim*—the forest fire; *gopāḥ*—the cowherd boys; *ca*—and; *gāvaḥ*—the cows; *prasamīkṣya*—intensely watching; *bhītāḥ*—afraid; *ūcuḥ*—they addressed; *ca*—and; *kṛṣṇam*—Lord Kṛṣṇa; *sa-balam*—and Lord Balarāma; *prapannāḥ*—taking shelter; *yathā*—as; *harim*—the Supreme Personality of Godhead; *mṛtyu*—of death; *bhaya*—by fear; *arditāḥ*—troubled; *janāḥ*—persons.

TRANSLATION

As the cows and cowherd boys stared at the forest fire attacking them on all sides, they became fearful. The boys then approached Kṛṣṇa and Balarāma for shelter, just as those who are disturbed by fear of death approach the Supreme Personality of Godhead. The boys addressed Them as follows.

TEXT 9

कृष्ण कृष्ण महावीर हे रामामोघविक्रम ।
दावाग्निना दह्यमानान् प्रपन्नांस्त्रातुमर्हथः ॥ ९ ॥

kṛṣṇa kṛṣṇa mahā-vīra
he rāmāmogha vikrama
dāvāgninā dahyamānān
prapannāṁs trātum arhathaḥ

kṛṣṇa kṛṣṇa—O Kṛṣṇa, Kṛṣṇa; *mahā-vīra*—O most powerful one; *he rāma*—O Rāma; *amogha-vikrama*—You whose prowess is never thwarted; *dāva-agninā*—by the forest fire; *dahyamānān*—who are being burned; *prapannān*—who are surrendered; *trātum arhathaḥ*—please save.

TRANSLATION

[The cowherd boys said:] O Kṛṣṇa! Kṛṣṇa! Most powerful one! O Rāma! You whose prowess never fails! Please save Your devotees, who are about to be burned by this forest fire and have come to take shelter of You!

TEXT 10

नूनं त्वद्बान्धवाः कृष्ण न चार्हन्त्यवसादितुम् ।
वयं हि सर्वधर्मज्ञ त्वन्नाथास्त्वत्परायणाः ॥ १० ॥

nūnaṁ tvad-bāndhavāḥ kṛṣṇa
na cārhanty avasāditum

vayaṁ hi sarva-dharma-jña
tvan-nāthās tvat-parāyaṇāḥ

nūnam—certainly; *tvat*—Your; *bāndhavāḥ*—friends; *kṛṣṇa*—our dear Śrī Kṛṣṇa; *na*—never; *ca*—and; *arhanti*—deserve; *avasāditum*—to suffer destruction; *vayam*—we; *hi*—moreover; *sarva-dharma-jña*—O perfect knower of the nature of all beings; *tvat-nāthāḥ*—having You as our Lord; *tvat-parāyaṇāḥ*—devoted to You.

TRANSLATION

Kṛṣṇa! Certainly Your own friends shouldn't be destroyed. O knower of the nature of all things, we have accepted You as our Lord, and we are souls surrendered unto You!

TEXT 11

श्रीशुक उवाच
वचो निशम्य कृपणं बन्धूनां भगवान् हरिः ।
निमीलयत मा भैष्ट लोचनानीत्यभाषत ॥ ११ ॥

śrī-śuka uvāca
vaco niśamya kṛpaṇaṁ
bandhūnāṁ bhagavān hariḥ
nimīlayata mā bhaiṣṭa
locanānīty abhāṣata

śrī-śukaḥ uvāca—Śrī Śukadeva Gosvāmī said; *vacaḥ*—the words; *niśamya*—hearing; *kṛpaṇam*—pitiful; *bandhūnām*—of His friends; *bhagavān*—the Supreme Personality of Godhead; *hariḥ*—Hari; *nimīlayata*—just close; *mā bhaiṣṭa*—do not be afraid; *locanāni*—your eyes; *iti*—thus; *abhāṣata*—He spoke.

TRANSLATION

Śukadeva Gosvāmī said: Hearing these pitiful words from His friends, the Supreme Lord Kṛṣṇa told them, "Just close your eyes and do not be afraid."

PURPORT

This verse clearly reveals the simple, sublime relationship between Kṛṣṇa and His pure devotees. The Absolute Truth, the supreme almighty Lord, is actually a young, blissful cowherd boy named Kṛṣṇa. God is youthful, and His mentality is playful. When He saw that His beloved friends were terrified of the forest fire, He simply told them to close their eyes and not be afraid. Then Lord Kṛṣṇa acted, as described in the next verse.

TEXT 12

तथेति मीलिताक्षेषु भगवानग्निमुल्बणम् ।
पीत्वा मुखेन तान् कृच्छ्राद्योगाधीशो व्यमोचयत् ॥ १२ ॥

tatheti mīlitākṣeṣu
bhagavān agnim ulbaṇam
pītvā mukhena tān kṛcchrād
yogādhīśo vyamocayat

tathā—all right; *iti*—thus speaking; *mīlita*—closing; *akṣeṣu*—their eyes; *bhagavān*—the Supreme Lord; *agnim*—the fire; *ulbaṇam*—terrible; *pītvā*—drinking; *mukhena*—with His mouth; *tān*—them; *kṛcchrāt*—from the danger; *yoga-adhīśaḥ*—the supreme controller of all mystic power; *vyamocayat*—delivered.

TRANSLATION

"All right," the boys replied, and immediately closed their eyes. Then the Supreme Lord, the master of all mystic power, opened His mouth and swallowed the terrible fire, saving His friends from danger.

PURPORT

The cowherd boys were suffering from extreme fatigue, hunger and thirst, and were about to be consumed by a horrible forest fire. All this is indicated here by the word *kṛcchrāt*.

TEXT 13

ततश्च तेऽक्षीण्युन्मील्य पुनर्भाण्डीरमापिताः ।
निशम्य विस्मिता आसन्नात्मानं गाश्च मोचिताः ॥ १३ ॥

tataś ca te'kṣīṇy unmīlya
punar bhāṇḍīram āpitāḥ
niśamya vismitā āsann
ātmānaṁ gāś ca mocitāḥ

tataḥ—then; *ca*—and; *te*—they; *akṣīṇi*—their eyes; *unmīlya*—opening; *punaḥ*—again; *bhāṇḍīram*—to Bhāṇḍīra; *āpitāḥ*—brought; *niśamya*—seeing; *vismitāḥ*—amazed; *āsan*—they became; *ātmānam*—themselves; *gāḥ*—the cows; *ca*—and; *mocitāḥ*—saved.

TRANSLATION

The cowherd boys opened their eyes and were amazed to find not only that they and the cows had been saved from the terrible fire but that they had all been brought back to the Bhāṇḍīra tree.

TEXT 14

कृष्णस्य योगवीर्यं तद् योगमायानुभावितम् ।
दावाग्नेरात्मनः क्षेमं वीक्ष्य ते मेनिरेऽमरम् ॥ १४ ॥

kṛṣṇasya yoga-vīryaṁ tad
yoga-māyānubhāvitam
dāvāgner ātmanaḥ kṣemaṁ
vīkṣya te menire'maram

kṛṣṇasya—of Lord Kṛṣṇa; *yoga-vīryam*—the mystic power; *tat*—that; *yoga-māyā*—by His internal power of illusion; *anubhāvitam*—effected; *dāva-agneḥ*—from the forest fire; *ātmanaḥ*—of themselves; *kṣemam*—the deliverance; *vīkṣya*—seeing; *te*—they; *menire*—thought; *amaram*—a demigod.

TRANSLATION

When the cowherd boys saw that they had been saved from the forest fire by the Lord's mystic power, which is manifested by His internal potency, they began to think that Kṛṣṇa must be a demigod.

PURPORT

The cowherd boys of Vṛndāvana simply loved Kṛṣṇa as their only friend and exclusive object of devotion. To increase their ecstasy, Kṛṣṇa displayed to them His mystic potency and saved them from a terrible forest fire.

The cowherd boys could never give up their ecstatic loving friendship with Kṛṣṇa. Therefore, rather than considering Kṛṣṇa to be God, after they saw His extraordinary power they thought that perhaps He was a demigod. But since Lord Kṛṣṇa was their beloved friend, they were on the same level with Him, and thus they thought that they too must be demigods. In this way Kṛṣṇa's cowherd friends became overwhelmed with ecstasy.

TEXT 15

गाः सन्निवर्त्य सायाह्ने सहरामो जनार्दनः ।
वेणुं विरणयन् गोष्ठमगाद् गोपैरभिष्टुतः ॥ १५ ॥

gāḥ sannivartya sāyāhne
saha-rāmo janārdanaḥ
veṇuṁ viraṇayan goṣṭham
agād gopair abhiṣṭutaḥ

gāḥ—the cows; *sannivartya*—turning back; *sāya-ahne*—in the late afternoon; *saha-rāmaḥ*—together with Lord Balarāma; *janārdanaḥ*—Śrī Kṛṣṇa; *veṇum*—His flute; *viraṇayan*—playing in a specific way; *goṣṭham*—to the cowherd village; *agāt*—He went; *gopaiḥ*—by the cowherd boys; *abhiṣṭutaḥ*—being praised.

TRANSLATION

It was now late in the afternoon, and Lord Kṛṣṇa, accompanied by Balarāma, turned the cows back toward home. Playing His flute in a special way, Kṛṣṇa returned to the cowherd village in the company of His cowherd friends, who chanted His glories.

TEXT 16

गोपीनां परमानन्द आसीद् गोविन्ददर्शने ।
क्षणं युगशतमिव यासां येन विनाभवत् ॥ १६ ॥

gopīnāṁ paramānanda
āsīd govinda-darśane
kṣaṇaṁ yuga-śatam iva
yāsāṁ yena vinābhavat

gopīnām—for the young cowherd girls; *parama-ānandaḥ*—the greatest happiness; *āsīt*—arose; *govinda-darśane*—in seeing Govinda; *kṣaṇam*—a moment; *yuga-śatam*—a hundred millenniums; *iva*—just as; *yāsām*—for whom; *yena*—whom (Kṛṣṇa); *vinā*—without; *abhavat*—became.

TRANSLATION

The young gopīs took the greatest pleasure in seeing Govinda come home, since for them even a moment without His association seemed like a hundred ages.

PURPORT

After saving the cowherd boys from the blazing forest fire, Kṛṣṇa saved the cowherd girls from the blazing fire of separation from Him. The *gopīs,* headed by Śrīmatī Rādhārāṇī, have the greatest love for Kṛṣṇa, and even a single moment's separation from Him seems like millions of years to them. The *gopīs* are the greatest devotees of God, and their specific pastimes with Kṛṣṇa will be described later in this work.

Thus end the purports of the humble servants of His Divine Grace A.C. Bhaktivedanta Swami Prabhupāda to the Tenth Canto, Nineteenth Chapter, of the Śrīmad-Bhāgavatam, *entitled "Swallowing the Forest Fire."*

CHAPTER TWENTY

The Rainy Season and Autumn in Vṛndāvana

To enhance the description of Lord Kṛṣṇa's pastimes, Śrī Śukadeva Gosvāmī describes in this chapter the beauty of Vṛndāvana during autumn and the rainy season. In the course of his presentation he gives various charming instructions in metaphorical terms.

TEXT 1

श्रीशुक उवाच
तयोस्तदद्भुतं कर्म दावाग्नेर्मोक्षमात्मनः ।
गोपाः स्त्रीभ्यः समाचख्युः प्रलम्बवधमेव च ॥ १ ॥

śrī-śuka uvāca
tayos tad adbhutaṁ karma
dāvāgner mokṣam ātmanaḥ
gopāḥ strībhyaḥ samācakhyuḥ
pralamba-vadham eva ca

śrī-śukaḥ uvāca—Śrī Śukadeva Gosvāmī said; *tayoḥ*—of the two of Them, Lord Kṛṣṇa and Lord Balarāma; *tat*—that; *adbhutam*—amazing; *karma*—action; *dāva-agneḥ*—from the forest fire; *mokṣam*—the deliverance; *ātmanaḥ*—of themselves; *gopāḥ*—the cowherd boys; *strībhyaḥ*—to the ladies; *samācakhyuḥ*—they described in detail; *pralamba-vadham*—the killing of Pralambāsura; *eva*—indeed; *ca*—also.

TRANSLATION

Śukadeva Gosvāmī said:To the ladies of Vṛndāvana, the cowherd boys then related in full detail Kṛṣṇa's and Balarāma's wonderful activities of delivering them from the forest fire and killing the demon Pralamba.

TEXT 2

गोपवृद्धाश्च गोप्यश्च तदुपाकर्ण्य विस्मिताः ।
मेनिरे देवप्रवरौ कृष्णरामौ व्रजं गतौ ॥ २ ॥

gopa-vṛddhāś ca gopyaś ca
tad upākarṇya vismitāḥ
menire deva-pravarau
kṛṣṇa-rāmau vrajaṁ gatau

gopa-vṛddhāḥ—the elder cowherd men; *ca*—and; *gopyaḥ*—the cowherd ladies; *ca*—also; *tat*—that; *upākarṇya*—hearing; *vismitāḥ*—surprised; *menire*—they considered; *deva-pravarau*—two eminent demigods; *kṛṣṇa-rāmau*—the brothers Kṛṣṇa and Balarāma; *vrajam*—to Vṛndāvana; *gatau*—come.

TRANSLATION

The elder cowherd men and ladies were amazed to hear this account, and they concluded that Kṛṣṇa and Balarāma must be exalted demigods who had appeared in Vṛndāvana.

TEXT 3

ततः प्रावर्तत प्रावृट् सर्वसत्त्वसमुद्भवा ।
विद्योतमानपरिधिर्विस्फूर्जितनभस्तला ॥ ३ ॥

tataḥ prāvartata prāvṛṭ
sarva-sattva-samudbhavā
vidyotamāna-paridhir
visphūrjita-nabhas-talā

tataḥ—then; *prāvartata*—began; *prāvṛṭ*—the rainy season; *sarva-sattva*—of all living beings; *samudbhavā*—the source of generation; *vidyotamāna*—flashing with lightning; *paridhiḥ*—its horizon; *visphūrjita*—agitated (by thunder); *nabhaḥ-talā*—the sky.

TRANSLATION

Then the rainy season began, giving life and sustenance to all living beings. The sky began to rumble with thunder, and lightning flashed on the horizon.

TEXT 4

सान्द्रनीलाम्बुदैर्व्योम सविद्युत्स्तनयित्नुभिः ।
अस्पष्टज्योतिराच्छन्नं ब्रह्मेव सगुणं बभौ ॥ ४ ॥

sāndra-nīlāmbudair vyoma
sa-vidyut-stanayitnubhiḥ
aspaṣṭa-jyotir ācchannaṁ
brahmeva sa-guṇaṁ babhau

sāndra—dense; *nīla*—blue; *ambudaiḥ*—by the clouds; *vyoma*—the sky; *sa-vidyut*—along with lightning; *stanayitnubhiḥ*—and thunder; *aspaṣṭa*—diffuse; *jyotiḥ*—its illumination; *ācchannam*—covered; *brahma*—the spirit soul; *iva*—as if; *sa-guṇam*—with the material qualities of nature; *babhau*—was manifest.

TRANSLATION

The sky was then covered by dense blue clouds accompanied by lightning and thunder. Thus the sky and its natural illumination were covered in the same way that the spirit soul is covered by the three modes of material nature.

PURPORT

Lightning is compared to the mode of goodness, thunder to the mode of passion, and clouds to the mode of ignorance. Thus the cloudy sky at the onset of the rainy season is analogous to the pure spirit soul when he becomes disturbed by the modes of nature, for at that time he is covered and his original brilliant nature is only dimly reflected through the haze of the material qualities.

TEXT 5

अष्टौ मासान्निपीतं यद् भूम्याश्चोदमयं वसु ।
स्वगोभिर्मोक्तुमारेभे पर्जन्यः काल आगते ॥ ५ ॥

aṣṭau māsān nipītaṁ yad
bhūmyāś coda-mayaṁ vasu
sva-gobhir moktum ārebhe
parjanyaḥ kāla āgate

aṣṭau—eight; *māsān*—during months; *nipītam*—drunk; *yat*—which; *bhūmyāḥ*—of the earth; *ca*—and; *uda-mayam*—consisting of water; *vasu*—the wealth; *sva-gobhiḥ*—by his own rays; *moktum*—to release; *ārebhe*—began; *parjanyaḥ*—the sun; *kāle*—the proper time; *āgate*—when it arrived.

TRANSLATION

With its rays, the sun had for eight months drunk up the earth's wealth in the form of water. Now that the proper time had arrived, the sun began releasing this accumulated wealth.

PURPORT

The *ācāryas* compare the sun's evaporating the earth's wealth of water to a king's collecting taxes. In Chapter Twenty, of *Kṛṣṇa, the Supreme Personality of Godhead,* Śrīla Prabhupāda explains this analogy as follows: "Clouds are accumulated water drawn from the land by the sunshine. Continually for eight months the sun evaporates all kinds of water from the surface of the globe, and this water is accumulated in the shape of clouds, which are distributed as water when there is need. Similarly, a government exacts various taxes from the citizens, which the citizens are able to pay by their different material activities: agriculture, trade and industry. Thus the government can also exact taxes in the form of income tax and sales tax. This is compared to the sun drawing water from the earth. When there is again need of water on the surface of the globe, the same sunshine converts the water into clouds and distributes it all over the globe. Similarly, the taxes collected by the government must be distributed to the people as educational work, public work, sanitation work and so on. This is very essential for a good government. The government should not simply exact taxes for useless squandering; the tax collection should be utilized for the public welfare of the state."

TEXT 6

तडिद्वन्तो महामेघाश्चण्डश्वसनवेपिताः ।
प्रीणनं जीवनं ह्यस्य मुमुचुः करुणा इव ॥ ६ ॥

taḍidvanto mahā-meghāś
caṇḍa-śvasana-vepitāḥ
prīṇanaṁ jīvanaṁ hy asya
mumucuḥ karuṇā iva

taḍit-vantaḥ—displaying lightning; *mahā-meghāḥ*—the great clouds; *caṇḍa*—fierce; *śvasana*—by the wind; *vepitāḥ*—shaken; *prīṇanam*—the gratification; *jīvanam*—their life (their water); *hi*—indeed; *asya*—of this world; *mumucuḥ*—they released; *karuṇāḥ*—merciful personalities; *iva*—just as.

TRANSLATION

Flashing with lightning, great clouds were shaken and swept about by fierce winds. Just like merciful persons, the clouds gave their lives for the pleasure of this world.

PURPORT

Just as great, compassionate personalities sometimes give their lives or wealth for the happiness of society, the rain clouds poured down their rain upon the parched earth. Although the clouds were thus dissipated, they freely provided rainfall for the happiness of the earth.

In *Kṛṣṇa, the Supreme Personality of Godhead,* Śrīla Prabhupāda comments as follows on this verse: "During the rainy season, there are strong winds blustering all over the country and carrying clouds from one place to another to distribute water . When water is urgently needed after the summer season, the clouds are just like a rich man who, in times of need, distributes his money even by exhausting his whole treasury. So the clouds exhaust themselves by distributing water all over the surface of the globe."

"When Mahārāja Daśaratha, the father of Lord Rāmacandra, used to fight with his enemies, it was said that he approached them just like a farmer uprooting unnecessary plants and trees. And when there was need of giving charity, he used to distribute money exactly as the cloud distributes rain. The distribution of rain by clouds is so sumptuous that it is compared to the distribution of wealth by a great, munificent person. The clouds' downpour is so sufficient that the rains even fall on rocks and hills and on the oceans and seas, where there is no need for water. A clouds is like a charitable person who opens his treasury for distribution and does not discriminate whether the charity is needed or not. He gives in charity openhandedly."

Metaphorically speaking, the lightning in rain clouds is the light by which they see the distressed condition of the earth, and the blowing winds are their heavy breathing, such as that found in a distressed person. Distressed to see the condition of the earth, the clouds tremble in the wind like a compassionate person. Thus they pour down their rain.

TEXT 7

तपःकृशा देवमीढा आसीद् वर्षीयसी मही ।
यथैव काम्यतपसस्तनुः सम्प्राप्य तत्फलम् ॥ ७ ॥

tapaḥ-kṛśā deva-mīḍhā
āsīd varṣīyasī mahī
yathaiva kāmya-tapasas
tanuḥ samprāpya tat-phalam

tapaḥ-kṛśā—emaciated by the summer heat; *deva-mīḍhā*—mercifully sprinkled by the god of rain; *āsīt*—became; *varṣīyasī*—fully nourished; *mahī*—the earth; *yathā eva*—just as; *kāmya*—based on sense gratification; *tapasaḥ*—of one whose austerities; *tanuḥ*—the body; *samprāpya*—after obtaining; *tat*—of those austere practices; *phalam*—the fruit.

TRANSLATION

The earth had been emaciated by the summer heat, but she became fully nourished again when moistened by the god of rain. Thus the earth was like a person whose body has been emaciated by austerities undergone for a material purpose, but who again becomes fully nourished when he achieves the fruit of those austerities.

PURPORT

In *Kṛṣṇa, the Supreme Personality of Godhead,* Śrīla Prabhupāda comments on this verse as follows: "Before the rainfall, the whole surface of the globe becomes almost depleted of all kinds of energies and appears very lean. After the rainfall, the whole surface of the earth becomes green with vegetation and appears very healthy and strong. Here, a comparison is made to the person undergoing austerities for fulfillment of a material desire. The flourishing condition of the earth after a rainy season is compared to the fulfillment of material desires. Sometimes, when a country is subjugated by an undesirable government, persons and parties undergo severe penances and austerities to get control of the government, and when they attain control they flourish by giving themselves generous salaries. This also is like the flourishing of the earth in the rainy season. Actually, one should undergo severe austerities and penances only to achieve spiritual happiness. In the *Śrīmad-Bhāgavatam* it is recommended that *tapasya,* or austerities, should be accepted only for realizing the Supreme Lord. By accepting austerity in devotional service, one regains his spiritual life, and as soon as one regains his spiritual life, he enjoys unlimited spiritual bliss. But if someone undertakes austerities and penances for some material gain, then, as stated in the *Bhagavad-gītā,* the results are temporary and are desired only by persons of less intelligence."

TEXT 8

निशामुखेषु खद्योतास्तमसा भान्ति न ग्रहाः ।
यथा पापेन पाषण्डा न हि वेदाः कलौ युगे ॥ ८ ॥

niśā-mukheṣu khadyotās
tamasā bhānti na grahāḥ
yathā pāpena pāṣaṇḍā
na hi vedāḥ kalau yuge

niśā-mukheṣu—during the moments of evening twilight; *khadyotāḥ*—the glowworms; *tamasā*—because of the darkness; *bhānti*—shine; *na*—not; *grahāḥ*—the planets; *yathā*—as; *pāpena*—because of sinful activities; *pāṣaṇḍāḥ*—atheistic doctrines; *na*—and not; *hi*—certainly; *vedāḥ*—the *Vedas; kalau yuge*—in the age of Kali.

TRANSLATION

In the evening twilight during the rainy season, the darkness allowed the glowworms but not the stars to shine forth, just as in the age of Kali the predominance of sinful activities allows atheistic doctrines to overshadow the true knowledge of the Vedas.

PURPORT

Śrīla Prabhupāda comments as follows: "During the rainy season, in the evening there are many glowworms visible about the tops of trees, hither and thither, and they glitter just like lights. But the luminaries of the sky— the stars and the moon—are not visible. Similarly, in the age of Kali, persons who are atheists or miscreants become very prominently visible, whereas persons who are actually following the Vedic principles for spiritual emancipation are practically obscured. This age, Kali-yuga, is compared to the cloudy season of the living entities. In this age, real knowledge is covered by the influence of the material advancement of civilization. The cheap mental speculators, atheists and manufacturers of so-called religious principles become prominent like the glowworms, whereas persons strictly following the Vedic principles, or scriptural injunctions, become covered by the clouds of this age.

"People should learn to take advantage of the actual luminaries of the sky—the sun, moon and stars—instead of the glowworms' light. Actually, the glowworms cannot give any light in the darkness of night. As clouds sometimes clear, even in the rainy season, and the moon, stars and sun become visible, so even in this Kali-yuga there are sometimes advantages. The Vedic movement of Lord Caitanya— the distributiion of the chanting of the Hare Kṛṣṇa *mantra*—is understood in this way. People seriously anxious to find real life should take advantage of this movement instead of looking toward the so-called light of mental speculators and atheists."

TEXT 9

श्रुत्वा पर्जन्यनिनदं मण्डुकाः ससृजुर्गिरः ।
तूष्णीं शयानाः प्राग् यद्वद् ब्राह्मणा नियमात्यये ॥ ९ ॥

śrutvā parjanya-ninadaṁ
maṇḍukāḥ sasṛjur giraḥ
tūṣṇīṁ śayānāḥ prāg yadvad
brāhmaṇā niyamātyaye

śrutvā—hearing; *parjanya*—of the rain clouds; *ninadam*—the resounding; *maṇḍukāḥ*—the frogs; *sasṛjuḥ*—emitted; *giraḥ*—their sounds; *tūṣṇīm*—silently; *śayānāḥ*—lying; *prāk*—previously; *yadvat*—just as; *brāhmaṇāḥ*—*brāhmaṇa* students; *niyama-atyaye*—after finishing their morning duties.

TRANSLATION

The frogs, who had all along been lying silent, suddenly began croaking when they heard the rumbling of the rain clouds, in the same way that brāhmaṇa students, who perform their morning duties in silence, begin reciting their lessons when called by their teacher.

PURPORT

Śrīla Prabhupāda comments: "After the first rainfall, when there is a thundering sound in the clouds, all the frogs begin to croak, like students suddenly engaged in reading their studies. Students are generally supposed to rise early in the morning. They do not usually arise of their own accord, however, but only when there is a bell sounded in the temple or in the cultural institution.

By the order of the spiritual master they immediately rise, and after finishing their morning duties they sit down to study the *Vedas* or chant Vedic *mantras.* Similarly, everyone is sleeping in the darkness of Kali-yuga, but when there is a great *ācārya,* by his calling only everyone takes to the study of the *Vedas* to acquire actual knowledge."

TEXT 10

आसन्नुत्पथगामिन्यः क्षुद्रनद्योऽनुशुष्यतीः ।
पुंसो यथास्वतन्त्रस्य देहद्रविणसम्पदः ॥ १० ॥

āsann utpatha-gāminyaḥ
kṣudra-nadyo 'nuśuṣyatīḥ
puṁso yathāsvatantrasya
deha-draviṇa-sampadaḥ

āsan—they became; *utpatha-gāminyaḥ*—strayed from their courses; *kṣudra*—insignificant; *nadyaḥ*—the rivers; *anuśuṣyatīḥ*—drying up; *puṁsaḥ*—of a person; *yathā*—as; *asvatantrasya*—who is not independent (that is, who is under the control of his senses); *deha*—the body; *draviṇa*—physical property; *sampadaḥ*—and riches.

TRANSLATION

With the advent of the rainy season, the insignificant streams, which had become dry, began to swell and then strayed from their proper courses, like the body, property and money of a man controlled by the urges of his senses.

PURPORT

Śrīla Prabhupāda comments: "During the rainy season, many small ponds, lakes and rivulets become filled with water; otherwise the rest of the year they remain dry. Similarly, materialistic persons are dry, but sometimes, when they are in a so-called opulent position, with a home or children or a little bank balance, they appear to be flourishing, but immediately afterwards they become dry again, like the small rivulets and ponds. The poet Vidyāpati said that in the society of friends, family, children, wife, and so on, there is certainly some pleasure, but that pleasure is compared to a drop of water in the desert. Everyone is hankering after happiness, just as in the desert everyone is hankering after water. If in the desert there is a drop of water, it may of course be said that the water is there, but the benefit from that drop of water is very insignificant. In our materialistic way of life, which is just like a desert, we are hankering after an ocean of happiness, but in the form of society, friends and mundane love we are getting no more than a drop of water. Our satisfaction is never achieved, as the small rivulets, lakes and ponds are never filled with water in the dry season."

TEXT 11

हरिता हरिभिः शष्पैरिन्द्रगोपैश्च लोहिता ।
उच्छिलीन्ध्रकृतच्छाया नृणां श्रीरिव भूरभूत् ॥ ११ ॥

haritā haribhiḥ śaṣpair
indragopaiś ca lohitā
ucchilīndhra-kṛta-cchāyā
nṛṇāṁ śrīr iva bhūr abhūt

haritāḥ—greenish; *haribhiḥ*—which is green; *śaṣpaiḥ*—because of the newly grown grass; *indragopaiḥ*—because of the *indragopa* insects; *ca*—and; *lohitā*—reddish; *ucchilīndhra*—by the mushrooms; *kṛta*—afforded; *chāyā*—shelter; *nṛṇām*—of men; *śrīḥ*—the opulence; *iva*—just as; *bhūḥ*—the earth; *abhūt*—became.

TRANSLATION

The newly grown grass made the earth emerald green, the indragopa insects added a reddish hue, and white mushrooms added further color and circles of shade. Thus the earth appeared like a person who has suddenly become rich.

PURPORT

Śrīla Śrīdhara Svāmī comments that the word *nṛṇām* indicates men of the royal order. Thus the colorful display of dark green fields decorated with bright red insects and white mushroom umbrellas can be compared to a royal parade displaying the military strength of a king.

TEXT 12

क्षेत्राणि शष्यसम्पद्भिः कर्षकाणां मुदं ददुः ।
मानिनामनुतापं वै दैवाधीनमजानताम् ॥ १२ ॥

kṣetrāṇi śaṣya-sampadbhiḥ
karṣakāṇāṁ mudaṁ daduḥ
māninām anutāpaṁ vai
daivādhīnam ajānatām

kṣetrāṇi—the fields; *śaṣya-sampadbhiḥ*—with their wealth of grains; *karṣakāṇām*—to the farmers; *mudam*—joy; *daduḥ*—gave; *māninām*—to others who are falsely proud; *anutāpam*—remorse; *vai*—indeed; *daiva-adhīnam*—the control of destiny; *ajānatām*—not understanding.

TRANSLATION

With their wealth of grains, the fields gave joy to the farmers. But those fields created remorse in the hearts of those who were too proud to engage in farming and who failed to understand how everything is under the control of the Supreme.

PURPORT

It is common for people living in large cities to become miserable and disgusted when there is ample rainfall. They do not understand or have forgotten that the rain is nourishing the crops they will eat. Although they certainly enjoy eating, they do not appreciate that with the rain the Supreme Lord is feeding not only human beings but also plants, animals and the earth itself.

Modern, sophisticated people often look down their noses at those engaged in agricultural work. In fact, in American slang, a simple, unintelligent person is sometimes called "a farmer." There are also government agencies that restrict agricultural production because certain capitalists fear the effect on market prices. Because of various artificial and manipulative practices in modern governments, we find widespread food shortages throughout the world—even in the United States, among the poverty-stricken—and at the same time we find the governments paying farmers not to plant crops. Sometimes these governments throw huge amounts of food into the ocean. Thus the administration of the arrogant and ignorant, those who are too proud to obey the laws of God or too ignorant to recognize them, will always cause frustration among the people, whereas a God conscious government will provide abundance and happiness for all.

TEXT 13

जलस्थलौकसः सर्वे नववारिनिषेवया ।
अबिभ्रन् रुचिरं रूपं यथा हरिनिषेवया ॥ १३ ॥

jala-sthalaukasaḥ sarve
nava-vāri-niṣevayā
abibhran ruciraṁ rūpaṁ
yathā hari-niṣevayā

jala—of the water; *sthala*—and the land; *okasaḥ*—the residents; *sarve*—all; *nava*—new; *vāri*—of the water; *niṣevayā*—by taking recourse; *abibhran*—they took on; *ruciram*—attractive; *rūpam*—form; *yathā*—just as; *hari-niṣevayā*—by rendering devotional service to the Supreme Personality of Godhead.

TRANSLATION

As all creatures of the land and water took advantage of the newly fallen rainwater, their forms became attractive and pleasing, just as a devotee becomes beautiful by engaging in the service of the Supreme Lord.

PURPORT

Śrīla Prabhupāda comments as follows: "We have practical experience of this with our students in the International Society for Krishna Consciousness. Before becoming students, they were dirty-looking, although they had naturally beautiful personal features; but due to having no information of Kṛṣṇa consciousness they appeared very dirty and wretched. Since they have taken to Kṛṣṇa consciousness, their health has improved, and by following the rules and regulations their bodily luster has increased. When they are dressed with saffron-colored cloth, with *tilaka* on their foreheads and beads in their hands and on their necks, they look exactly as if they have come directly from Vaikuṇṭha."

TEXT 14

सरिद्भिः संगतः सिन्धुश्चुक्षोभ श्वसनोर्मिमान्।
अपक्वयोगिनश्चित्तं कामाक्तं गुणयुग् यथा ॥ १४॥

saridbhiḥ saṅgataḥ sindhuś
cukṣobha śvasanormimān
apakva-yoginaś cittaṁ
kāmāktaṁ guṇa-yug yathā

saridbhiḥ—with the rivers; *saṅgataḥ*—on account of meeting; *sindhuḥ*—the ocean; *cukṣobha*—became agitated; *śvasana*—blown by the wind; *ūrmi-mān*—having waves; *apakva*—immature; *yoginaḥ*—of a *yogī; cittam*—the mind; *kāma-aktam*—tainted with lust; *guṇa-yuk*—maintaining connection with objects of sense gratification; *yathā*—just as.

TRANSLATION

Where the rivers joined the ocean it became agitated, its waves blown about by the wind, just as the mind of an immature yogī becomes agitated because he is still tainted by lust and attached to the objects of sense gratification.

TEXT 15

गिरयो वर्षधाराभिर्हन्यमाना न विव्यथुः ।
अभिभूयमाना व्यसनैर्यथाधोक्षजचेतसः ॥ १५ ॥

girayo varṣa-dhārābhir
hanyamānā na vivyathuḥ
abhibhūyamānā vyasanair
yathādhokṣaja-cetasaḥ

girayaḥ—the mountains; *varṣa-dhārābhiḥ*—by the rain-bearing clouds; *hanyamānāḥ*—being struck; *na vivyathuḥ*—did not shake; *abhibhūyamānāḥ*—being attacked; *vyasanaiḥ*—by dangers; *yathā*—as; *adhokṣaja-cetasaḥ*—those whose minds are absorbed in the Supreme Lord.

TRANSLATION

Just as devotees whose minds are absorbed in the Personality of Godhead remain peaceful even when attacked by all sorts of dangers, the mountains in the rainy season were not at all disturbed by the repeated striking of the rain-bearing clouds.

PURPORT

When splashed by torrents of rain, the mountains are not shaken; rather, they are cleansed of dirt and become resplendent and beautiful. Similarly, an advanced devotee of the Supreme Lord is not shaken from his devotional program by disturbing conditions, which instead cleanse his heart of the dust of attachment to this world. Thus the devotee becomes beautiful and resplendent by tolerating difficult conditions. In fact, a devotee accepts all reverses in life as the mercy of Lord Kṛṣṇa, realizing that all suffering is due to the sufferer's own previous misdeeds.

TEXT 16

मार्गा बभूवुः सन्दिग्धास्तृणैश्छन्ना ह्यसंस्कृताः ।
नाभ्यस्यमानाः श्रुतयो द्विजैः कालेन चाहताः ॥ १६ ॥

mārgā babhūvuḥ sandigdhās
tṛṇaiś channā hy asaṁskṛtāḥ
nābhyasyamānāḥ śrutayo
dvijaiḥ kālena cāhatāḥ

mārgāḥ—the roads; *babhūvuḥ*—became; *sandigdhāḥ*—obscured; *tṛṇaiḥ*—by grass; *channāḥ*—covered over; *hi*—indeed; *asaṁskṛtāḥ*—not cleansed; *na abhyasyamānāḥ*—not being studied; *śrutayaḥ*—the scriptures; *dvijaiḥ*—by the *brāhmaṇas; kālena*—by the effects of time; *ca*—and; *āhatāḥ*—corrupted.

TRANSLATION

During the rainy season the roads, not being cleansed, became covered with grass and debris and were thus difficult to make out. These roads were like religious scriptures that brāhmaṇas no longer study and that thus become corrupted and covered over with the passage of time.

TEXT 17

लोकबन्धुषु मेघेषु विद्युतश्चलसौहृदाः ।
स्थैर्यं न चक्रुः कामिन्यः पुरुषेषु गुणिष्विव ॥ १७ ॥

loka-bandhuṣu megheṣu
vidyutaś cala-sauhṛdāḥ
sthairyaṁ na cakruḥ kāminyaḥ
puruṣeṣu guṇiṣv iva

loka—of all the world; *bandhuṣu*—who are the friends; *megheṣu*—among the clouds; *vidyutaḥ*—the lightning; *cala-sauhṛdāḥ*—fickle in their friendship; *sthairyam*—steadiness; *na cakruḥ*—did not maintain; *kāminyaḥ*—lusty women; *puruṣeṣu*—among men; *guṇiṣu*—who are virtuous; *iva*—as.

TRANSLATION

Though the clouds are the well-wishing friends of all living beings, the lightning, fickle in its affinities, moved from one group of clouds to another, like lusty women unfaithful even to virtuous men.

PURPORT

Śrīla Prabhupāda comments: "During the rainy season, lightning appears in one group of clouds and then immediately in another group of clouds. This phenomenon is compared to a lusty woman who does not fix her mind on one man. A cloud is compared to a qualified person because it pours rain and gives sustenance to many people; a man who is qualified similarly gives sustenance to many living creatures, such as family members or many workers in business. Unfortunately, his whole life can be disturbed by a wife who divorces him; when the husband is disturbed, the whole family is ruined, the children are dispersed or the business is closed, and everything is affected. It is therefore recommended that a woman desiring to advance in Kṛṣṇa consciousness peacefully live with a husband and that the couple not separate under any condition. The husband and wife should control sex indulgence and concentrate their minds on Kṛṣṇa consciousness so their life may be successful. After all, in the material world a man requires a woman, and a woman requires a man. When they are combined, they should live peacefully in Kṛṣṇa consciousness and should not be restless like the lightning, flashing from one group of clouds to another."

TEXT 18

धनुर्वियति माहेन्द्रं निर्गुणं च गुणिन्यभात् ।
व्यक्ते गुणव्यतिकरेऽगुणवान् पुरुषो यथा ॥ १८ ॥

dhanur viyati māhendraṁ
nirguṇaṁ ca guṇiny abhāt
vyakte guṇa-vyatikare
'guṇavān puruṣo yathā

dhanuḥ—the bow (rainbow); *viyati*—within the sky; *māhā-indram*—of Lord Indra; *nirguṇam*—without qualities (or without a bowstring); *ca*—although; *guṇini*—within the sky, which has definite qualities like sound; *abhāt*—appeared; *vyakte*—within the manifest material nature; *guṇa-vyatikare*—

which consists of the interactions of material qualities; *aguṇa-vān*—He who has no contact with material qualities; *puruṣaḥ*—the Supreme Personality; *yathā*—just as.

TRANSLATION

When the curved bow of Indra [the rainbow] appeared in the sky, which had the quality of thundering sound, it was unlike ordinary bows because it did not rest upon a string. Similarly, when the Supreme Lord appears in this world, which is the interaction of the material qualities, He is unlike ordinary persons because He remains free from all material qualities and independent of all material conditions.

PURPORT

Śrīla Prabhupāda comments as follows: "Sometimes, in addition to the roaring thunder of the clouds, there is an appearance of a rainbow, which stands as a bow without a string. Uually, a bow stays in the curved position because it is tied at its two ends by the bowstring; but in the rainbow there is no such string, and yet it rests in the sky so beautifully. Similarly, when the Supreme Personality of Godhead descends to this material world, He appears just like an ordinary human being, but He is not resting on any material condition. In the *Bhagavad-gītā,* the Lord says that He appears by His internal potency, which is free from the bondage of the external potency. What is bondage for the ordinary creature is freedom for the Personality of Godhead."

TEXT 19

न रराजोडुपश्छन्नः स्वज्योत्स्नाराजितैर्घनैः ।
अहंमत्या भासितया स्वभासा पुरुषो यथा ॥ १९ ॥

na rarājoḍupaś channaḥ
sva-jyotsnā-rājitair ghanaiḥ
ahaṁ-matyā bhāsitayā
sva-bhāsā puruṣo yathā

na rarāja—did not shine forth; *uḍupaḥ*—the moon; *channaḥ*—covered; *sva-jyotsnā*—by its own light; *rājitaiḥ*—which are illuminated; *ghanaiḥ*—by the clouds; *aham-matyā*—by false ego; *bhāsitayā*—which is illuminated; *sva-bhāsā*—by his own luster; *puruṣaḥ*—the living entity; *yathā*—as.

TRANSLATION

During the rainy season the moon was prevented from appearing directly by the covering of the clouds, which were themselves illumined by the moon's rays. Similarly, the living being in material existence is prevented from appearing directly by the covering of the false ego, which is itself illumined by the consciousness of the pure soul.

PURPORT

The analogy given here is excellent. During the rainy season we cannot see the moon in the sky, because the moon is covered by clouds. These clouds, however, are radiant with the glow of the moon's own rays. Similarly, in our conditioned, material existence we cannot directly perceive the soul, because our consciousness is covered by the false ego, which is the false identification with the material world and the material body. Yet it is the soul's own consciousness that illumines the false ego.

As the *Gītā* describes, the energy of the soul is consciousness, and when this consciousness manifests through the screen of false ego, it appears as dull, material consciousness, in which there is no direct vision of the soul or God. In the material world, even great philosophers ultimately resort to hazy ambiguities when speaking about the Absolute Truth, just as the cloudy sky manifests only in a dull and indirect way the iridescent light of the moon.

In material life, our false ego is often enthusiastic, hopeful and apparently aware of various material affairs, and such consciousness encourages us to push on in material existence. But in truth we are merely experiencing the dull reflection of our original, pure consciousness, which is Kṛṣṇa consciousness—direct perception of the soul and God. Not realizing that the false ego merely hampers and dulls our real, spiritual consciousness, which is fully enlightened and blissful, we mistakenly think that material consciousness is full of knowledge and happiness. This is comparable to thinking that the luminous clouds are lighting up the night sky, while in fact it is the moonshine that illumines the sky, and the clouds that merely dull and hamper the moonshine. The clouds appear luminous because they are filtering and impeding the brilliant rays of the moon. Similarly, at times material consciousness appears pleasurable or enlightened because it is screening or filtering the original, blissful and enlightened consciousness coming directly from the soul. If we can understand the ingenious analogy given in this verse, we can easily advance in Kṛṣṇa consciousness.

TEXT 20

मेघागमोत्सवा हृष्टाः प्रत्यनन्दञ् छिखण्डिनः ।
गृहेषु तप्तनिर्विण्णा यथाच्युतजनागमे ॥ २० ॥

meghāgamotsavā hṛṣṭāḥ
pratyanandañ chikhaṇḍinaḥ
gṛheṣu tapta-nirviṇṇā
yathācyuta-janāgame

megha—of clouds; *āgama*—because of the arrival; *utsavāḥ*—who celebrate a festival; *hṛṣṭāḥ*—becoming joyful; *pratyanandan*—they cried out in greeting; *śikhaṇḍinaḥ*—the peacocks; *gṛheṣu*—within their homes; *tapta*—those who are distressed; *nirviṇṇāḥ*—and then become happy; *yathā*—just as; *acyuta*—of the infallible Personality of Godhead; *jana*—of the devotees; *āgame*—upon the arrival.

TRANSLATION

The peacocks became festive and cried out a joyful greeting when they saw the clouds arrive, just as people distressed in household life feel pleasure when the pure devotees of the infallible Supreme Lord visit them.

PURPORT

After the dry summer season, the peacocks become jubilant with the arrival of the first thundering rain clouds, and thus they dance in great happiness. Śrīla Prabhupāda comments, "We have practical experience that many of our students were dry and morose previous to their coming to Kṛṣṇa consciousness, but having come in contact with devotees they are now dancing like jubilant peacocks."

TEXT 21

पीत्वापः पादपाः पद्भिरासन्नानात्ममूर्तयः ।
प्राक्क्षामास्तपसा श्रान्ता यथा कामानुसेवया ॥ २१ ॥

pītvāpaḥ pādapāḥ padbhir
āsan nānātma-mūrtayaḥ
prāk kṣāmās tapasā śrāntā
yathā kāmānusevayā

pītvā—having drunk; *āpaḥ*—water; *pāda-pāḥ*—the trees; *padbhiḥ*—with their feet; *āsan*—assumed; *nānā*—various; *ātma-mūrtayaḥ*—bodily features; *prāk*—previously; *kṣāmāḥ*—emaciated; *tapasā*—by austerities; *śrāntāḥ*—fatigued; *yathā*—as; *kāma-anusevayā*—by enjoying acquired desired objects.

TRANSLATION

The trees had grown thin and dry, but after they drank the newly fallen rainwater through their feet, their various bodily features blossomed. Similarly, one whose body has grown thin and weak from austerity again exhibits his healthy bodily features upon enjoying the material objects gained through that austerity.

PURPORT

The word *pāda* means foot, and *pā* means drinking. Trees are called *pādapa* because they drink through their roots, which are likened to feet. Upon drinking the newly fallen rainwater, the trees in Vṛndāvana began to manifest new leaves, sprouts and blossoms, and they thus enjoyed new growth. Similarly, materialistic persons often perform severe austerities to acquire the object of their desire. For example, politicians in America undergo grueling austerities while traveling about the countryside campaigning for election. Businessmen also will often deny personal comfort to make their business successful. Such austere persons, upon acquiring the fruits of their austerity, again become healthy and satisfied, like trees eagerly drinking rainwater after enduring the austerity of a dry, hot summer.

TEXT 22

सरःस्वशान्तरोधःसु न्यूषुरंगापि सारसाः ।
गृहेष्वशान्तकृत्येषु ग्राम्या इव दुराशयाः ॥ २२ ॥

saraḥsv aśānta-rodhaḥsu
nyūṣur aṅgāpi sārasāḥ
gṛheṣv aśānta-kṛtyeṣu
grāmyā iva durāśayāḥ

saraḥsu—upon the lakes; *aśānta*—disturbed; *rodhaḥsu*—whose banks; *nyūṣuḥ*—continued to dwell; *aṅga*—my dear King; *api*—indeed; *sārasāḥ*—the cranes; *gṛheṣu*—in their homes; *aśānta*—feverish; *kṛtyeṣu*—where activities are performed; *grāmyāḥ*—materialistic men; *iva*—indeed; *durāśayāḥ*—whose minds are contaminated.

TRANSLATION

The cranes continued dwelling on the shores of the lakes, although the shores were agitated during the rainy season, just as materialistic persons with contaminated minds always remain at home, despite the many disturbances there.

PURPORT

During the rainy season there are often mud slides around the shores of lakes, and thorny bushes, stones and other debris sometimes accumulate there. Despite all these inconveniences, ducks and cranes continue meandering around the lakeshores. Similarly, innumerable painful occurrences are always disturbing family life, but a materialistic man never even considers leaving his family in the hands of his grown sons and going away for spiritual improvement. He regards such an idea as shocking and uncivilized, because he is completely ignorant of the Absolute Truth and his relationship to that Truth.

TEXT 23

जलौघैर्निरभिद्यन्त सेतवो वर्षतीश्वरे ।
पाषण्डिनामसद्वादैर्वेदमार्गाः कलौ यथा ॥ २३ ॥

jalaughair nirabhidyanta
setavo varṣatīśvare
pāṣaṇḍinām asad-vādair
veda-mārgāḥ kalau yathā

jala-oghaiḥ—by the floodwater; *nirabhidyanta*—became broken; *setavaḥ*—the dikes; *varṣati*—when he is showering rain; *īśvare*—Lord Indra; *pāṣaṇḍinām*—of the atheists; *asat-vādaiḥ*—by the false theories; *veda-mārgāḥ*—the paths of the *Vedas;* *kalau*—in the Kali-yuga; *yathā*—as.

TRANSLATION

When Indra sent forth his rains, the floodwaters broke through the irrigation dikes in the agricultural fields, just as in the Kali-yuga the atheists' false theories break down the boundaries of Vedic injunctions.

TEXT 24

व्यमुञ्चन् वायुभिर्नुन्ना भूतेभ्यश्चामृतं घनाः ।
यथाशिषो विश्पतयः काले काले द्विजेरिताः ॥ २४ ॥

vyamuñcan vāyubhir nunnā
bhūtebhyaś cāmṛtaṁ ghanāḥ
yathāśiṣo viś-patayaḥ
kāle kāle dvijeritāḥ

vyamuñcan—they released; *vāyubhiḥ*—by the winds; *nunnāḥ*—impelled; *bhūtebhyaḥ*—to all living beings; *ca*—and; *amṛtam*—their nectarean water; *ghanāḥ*—the clouds; *yathā*—as; *āśiṣaḥ*—charitable benedictions; *viṭ-patayaḥ*—kings; *kāle kāle*—from time to time; *dvija*—by the *brāhmaṇas; īritāḥ*—encouraged.

TRANSLATION

The clouds, impelled by the winds, released their nectarean water for the benefit of all living beings, just as kings, instructed by their brāhmaṇa priests, dispense charity to the citizens.

PURPORT

Śrīla Prabhupāda comments: "In the rainy season, the clouds, tossed by the wind, deliver water, that is welcomed like nectar. When the Vedic followers, the *brāhmaṇas,* inspire rich men like kings and the wealthy mercantile community to give charity in the performance of great sacrifices, the distribution of such wealth is also nectarean. The four sections of human society, namely the *brāhmaṇas,* the *kṣatriyas,* the *vaiśyas* and the *śūdras,* are meant to live peacefully in a cooperative mood; this is possible when they are guided by expert Vedic *brāhmaṇas* who perform sacrifices and distribute wealth equally."

TEXT 25

एवं वनं तद् वर्षिष्ठं पक्वखर्जुरजम्बुमत् ।
गोगोपालैर्वृतो रन्तुं सबलः प्राविशद्धरिः ॥ २५ ॥

evaṁ vanaṁ tad varṣiṣṭhaṁ
pakva-kharjura-jambumat

go-gopālair vṛto rantuṁ
sa-balaḥ prāviśad dhariḥ

evam—thus; *vanam*—forest; *tat*—that; *varṣiṣṭham*—most resplendent; *pakva*—ripe; *kharjura*—dates; *jambu*—and *jambu* fruits; *mat*—having; *go*—by the cows; *gopālaiḥ*—and the cowherd boys; *vṛtaḥ*—surrounded; *rantum*—with the purpose of playing; *sa-balaḥ*—accompanied by Lord Balarāma; *prāviśat*—He entered; *hariḥ*—Lord Kṛṣṇa.

TRANSLATION

When the Vṛndāvana forest had thus become resplendent, filled with ripe dates and jambu fruits, Lord Kṛṣṇa, surrounded by His cows and cowherd boyfriends and accompanied by Śrī Balarāma, entered that forest to enjoy.

TEXT 26

धेनवो मन्दगामिन्य ऊधोभारेण भूयसा ।
ययुर्भगवताहूता द्रुतं प्रीत्या स्नुतस्तनाः ॥ २६ ॥

dhenavo manda-gāminya
ūdho-bhāreṇa bhūyasā
yayur bhagavatāhūtā
drutaṁ prītyā snuta-stanāḥ

dhenavaḥ—the cows; *manda-gāminyaḥ*—moving slowly; *ūdhaḥ*—of their udders; *bhāreṇa*—because of the weight; *bhūyasā*—very great; *yayuḥ*—they went; *bhagavatā*—by the Lord; *āhūtāḥ*—being called; *drutam*—quickly; *prītyā*—out of affection; *snuta*—wet; *stanāḥ*—their udders.

TRANSLATION

The cows had to move slowly because of their weighty milk bags, but they quickly ran to the Supreme Personality of Godhead as soon as He called them, their affection for Him causing their udders to become wet.

PURPORT

Śrīla Prabhupāda comments, "The cows, being fed by new grasses, became very healthy, and their milk bags were all very full. When Lord Kṛṣṇa called them by name, they immediately came to Him out of affection, and in their joyful condition the milk flowed from their bags."

TEXT 27

वनौकसः प्रमुदिता वनराजीर्मधुच्युतः ।
जलधारा गिरेर्नादादासन्ना ददृशे गुहाः ॥ २७ ॥

vanaukasaḥ pramuditā
vana-rājīr madhu-cyutaḥ
jala-dhārā girer nādād
āsannā dadṛśe guhāḥ

vana-okasaḥ—the aborigine girls of the forest; *pramuditāḥ*—joyful; *vana-rājīḥ*—the trees of the forest; *madhu-cyutaḥ*—dripping sweet sap; *jala-dhārāḥ*—waterfalls; *gireḥ*—on the mountains; *nādāt*—from their resounding; *āsannāḥ*—nearby; *dadṛśe*—He observed; *guhāḥ*—caves.

TRANSLATION

The Lord saw the joyful aborigine girls of the forest, the trees dripping sweet sap, and the mountain waterfalls, whose resounding indicated that there were caves nearby.

TEXT 28

क्वचिद् वनस्पतिक्रोडे गुहायां चाभिवर्षति ।
निर्विश्य भगवान् रेमे कन्दमूलफलाशनः ॥ २८ ॥

kvacid vanaspati-kroḍe
guhāyāṁ cābhivarṣati
nirviśya bhagavān reme
kanda-mūla-phalāśanaḥ

kvacit—sometimes; *vanaspati*—of a tree; *kroḍe*—in the hollow; *guhāyām*—in a cave; *ca*—or; *abhivarṣati*—when it was raining; *nirviśya*—entering; *bhagavān*—the Supreme Lord; *reme*—enjoyed; *kanda-mūla*—roots; *phala*—and fruits; *aśanaḥ*—eating.

TRANSLATION

When it rained, the Lord would sometimes enter a cave or the hollow of a tree to play and to eat roots and fruits.

PURPORT

Śrīla Sanātana Gosvāmī explains that during the rainy season bulbs and roots are very tender and palatable, and Lord Kṛṣṇa would eat them along with wild fruits found in the forest. Lord Kṛṣṇa and His young boyfriends would sit in the hollow of a tree or within a cave and enjoy pastimes while waiting for the rain to stop.

TEXT 29

दध्योदनं समानीतं शिलायां सलिलान्तिके ।
सम्भोजनीयैर्बुभुजे गोपैः संकर्षणान्वितः ॥ २९ ॥

dadhy-odanaṁ samānītaṁ
śilāyāṁ salilāntike
sambhojanīyair bubhuje
gopaiḥ saṅkarṣaṇānvitaḥ

dadhi-odanam—boiled rice mixed with yogurt; *samānītam*—sent; *śilāyām*—on a stone; *salila-antike*—near the water; *sambhojanīyaiḥ*—who would take meals with Him; *bubhuje*—He ate; *gopaiḥ*—together with the cowherd boys; *saṅkarṣaṇa-anvitaḥ*—in the company of Lord Balarāma.

TRANSLATION

Lord Kṛṣṇa would take His meal of boiled rice and yogurt, sent from home, in the company of Lord Saṅkarṣaṇa and the cowherd boys who regularly ate with Him. They would all sit down to eat on a large stone near the water.

TEXTS 30–31

शाद्वलोपरि संविश्य चर्वतो मीलितेक्षणान् ।
तृप्तान् वृषान् वत्सतरान् गाश्च स्वोधोभरश्रमाः ॥ ३० ॥
प्रावृट्श्रियं च तां वीक्ष्य सर्वकालसुखावहाम् ।
भगवान् पूजयां चक्रे आत्मशक्त्युपबृंहिताम् ॥ ३१ ॥

śādvalopari saṁviśya
carvato mīlitekṣaṇān
tṛptān vṛṣān vatsatarān
gāś ca svodho-bhara-śramāḥ

prāvṛṭ-śriyaṁ ca tāṁ vīkṣya
sarva-kāla-sukhāvahām
bhagavān pūjayāṁ cakre
ātma-śakty-upabṛṁhitām

śādvala—a grassy patch; *upari*—upon; *saṁviśya*—sitting; *carvataḥ*—who were grazing; *mīlita*—closed; *īkṣaṇān*—their eyes; *tṛptān*—satisfied; *vṛṣān*—the bulls; *vatsatarān*—the calves; *gāḥ*—the cows; *ca*—and; *sva*—their own; *ūdhaḥ*—of the milk bags; *bhara*—by the weight; *śramāḥ*—fatigued; *prāvṛṭ*—of the rainy season; *śriyam*—the opulence; *ca*—and; *tām*—that; *vīkṣya*—seeing; *sarva-kāla*—always; *sukha*—pleasure; *āvahām*—giving; *bhagavān*—the Supreme Personality of Godhead; *pūjayām cakre*—honored; *ātma-śakti*—from His internal potency; *upabṛṁhitām*—expanded.

TRANSLATION

Lord Kṛṣṇa watched the contented bulls, calves and cows sitting on the green grass and grazing with closed eyes, and He saw that the cows were tired from the burden of their heavy milk bags. Thus observing the beauty and opulence of Vṛndāvana's rainy season, a perennial source of great happiness, the Lord offered all respect to that season, which was expanded from His own internal potency.

PURPORT

The lush beauty of the rainy season in Vṛndāvana is meant to enhance the pleasure pastimes of Śrī Kṛṣṇa. Thus, to set the scene for the Lord's loving affairs, His internal potency makes all the arrangements described in this chapter.

TEXT 32

एवं निवसतोस्तस्मिन् रामकेशवयोर्व्रजे ।
शरत् समभवद् व्यभ्रा स्वच्छाम्ब्वपरुषानिला ॥ ३२ ॥

evaṁ nivasatos tasmin
rāma-keśavayor vraje
śarat samabhavad vyabhrā
svacchāmbv-aparuṣānilā

evam—in this manner; *nivasatoḥ*—while the two of Them were dwelling; *tasmin*—in that; *rāma-keśavayoḥ*—Lord Rāma and Lord Keśava; *vraje*—in

Vṛndāvana; *śarat*—the fall season; *samabhavat*—became fully manifest; *vyabhrā*—free from clouds in the sky; *svaccha-ambu*—in which the water was clear; *aparuṣa-anilā*—and the wind was gentle.

TRANSLATION

While Lord Rāma and Lord Keśava were thus dwelling in Vṛndāvana, the fall season arrived, when the sky is cloudless, the water clear and the wind gentle.

TEXT 33

शरदा नीरजोत्पत्त्या नीराणि प्रकृतिं ययुः ।
भ्रष्टानामिव चेतांसि पुनर्योगनिषेवया ॥ ३३ ॥

śaradā nīrajotpattyā
nīrāṇi prakṛtiṁ yayuḥ
bhraṣṭānām iva cetāṁsi
punar yoga-niṣevayā

śaradā—by the effect of the autumn season; *nīraja*—the lotus flowers; *utpattyā*—which regenerates; *nīrāṇi*—the bodies of water; *prakṛtim*—to their natural state (of cleanliness); *yayuḥ*—returned; *bhraṣṭānām*—of those who are fallen; *iva*—just as; *cetāṁsi*—the minds; *punaḥ*—once again; *yoga*—of devotional service; *niṣevayā*—by practice.

TRANSLATION

The autumn season, which regenerated the lotus flowers, also restored the various bodies of water to their original purity, just as the process of devotional service purifies the minds of the fallen yogīs when they return to it.

TEXT 34

व्योम्नोऽब्भ्रं भूतशाबल्यं भुवः पंकमपां मलम् ।
शरज्जहाराश्रमिणां कृष्णे भक्तिर्यथाशुभम् ॥ ३४ ॥

vyomno 'bbhraṁ bhūta-śābalyaṁ
bhuvaḥ paṅkam apāṁ malam
śaraj jahārāśramiṇāṁ
kṛṣṇe bhaktir yathāśubham

vyomnaḥ—in the sky; *ap-bhram*—the clouds; *bhūta*—of the animals; *śābalyam*—the crowded condition; *bhuvaḥ*—of the earth; *paṅkam*—the muddy covering; *apām*—of the water; *malam*—the contamination; *śarat*—the autumn season; *jahāra*—removed; *āśramiṇām*—of the members of the four different spiritual orders of human society; *kṛṣṇe*—for Lord Kṛṣṇa; *bhaktiḥ*—devotional service; *yathā*—just as; *aśubham*—all inauspiciousness.

TRANSLATION

Autumn cleared the sky of clouds, let the animals get out of their crowded living conditions, cleaned the earth of its covering of mud, and purified the water of contamination, in the same way that loving service rendered to Lord Kṛṣṇa frees the members of the four spiritual orders from their respective troubles.

PURPORT

Every human being must perform the prescribed duties corresponding to one of the four spiritual orders of life. These divisions are 1) celibate student life, *brahmacarya;* 2) married life, *gṛhastha;* 3) retired life, *vānaprastha;* and 4) renounced life, *sannyāsa.* A *brahmacārī* must perform many menial duties during his student life, but as he becomes advanced in loving service to Kṛṣṇa, his superiors recognize his spiritual status and elevate him to higher duties. The innumerable obligations performed on behalf of wife and children constantly harass a householder, but as he becomes advanced in loving service to Kṛṣṇa, he is automatically elevated by the laws of nature to more enjoyable, spiritual occupations, and he somehow minimizes material duties.

Those in the *vānaprastha,* or retired, order of life also perform many duties, and these can also be replaced by ecstatic loving service to Kṛṣṇa. Similarly, renounced life has many natural difficulties, not the least of which is that *sannyāsīs,* or renounced men, are inclined to meditate on the impersonal aspect of the Absolute Truth. As stated in the *Bhagavad-gītā* (12.5), *kleśo'dhikataras teṣām avyaktāsakta-cetasām:* "For those whose minds are attached to the unmanifested, impersonal feature of the Lord, advancement is exceedingly painful." But as soon as a *sannyāsī* takes to preaching the glories of Kṛṣṇa in every town and village, his life becomes a blissful sequence of beautiful spiritual realizations.

In the autumn season the sky returns to its natural blue color. The vanishing of the clouds is like the vanishing of troublesome duties in *brahmacārī* life.

Just after summer comes the rainy season, when the animals sometimes become disturbed by the torrential storms and thus huddle together. But the autumn season signals the time for the animals to go to their respective areas and live more peacefully. This represents a householder's becoming free from the harassment of family duties and being able to devote more of his time to spiritual responsibilities, which are the real goal of life both for himself and his family. The removal of the muddy layer on the earth is like the removal of the inconveniences of *vānaprastha* life, and the purification of the water is like the sanctification of *sannyāsa* life by one's preaching the glories of Kṛṣṇa without sex desire.

TEXT 35

सर्वस्वं जलदा हित्वा विरेजुः शुभ्रवर्चसः ।
यथा त्यक्तैषणाः शान्ता मुनयो मुक्तकिल्बिषाः ॥ ३५ ॥

sarva-svaṁ jaladā hitvā
virejuḥ śubhra-varcasaḥ
yathā tyaktaiṣaṇāḥ śāntā
munayo mukta-kilbiṣāḥ

sarva-svam—everything they possess; *jala-dāḥ*—the clouds; *hitvā*—having given up; *virejuḥ*—shone forth; *śubhra*—pure; *varcasaḥ*—their effulgence; *yathā*—just as; *tyakta-eṣaṇāḥ*—who have given up all desires; *śāntāḥ*—pacified; *munayaḥ*—sages; *mukta-kilbiṣāḥ*—freed from evil propensities.

TRANSLATION

The clouds, having given up all they possessed, shone forth with purified effulgence, just like peaceful sages who have given up all material desires and are thus free of all sinful propensities.

PURPORT

When the clouds are filled with water, they are dark and cover the sun's rays, just as the material mind of an impure man covers the soul shining within. But when the clouds pour down their rain, they become white and then brilliantly reflect the shining sun, just as a man who gives up all material desires and sinful propensities becomes purified and then brilliantly reflects his own soul and the Supreme Soul within.

TEXT 36

गिरयो मुमुचुस्तोयं क्वचिन्न मुमुचुः शिवम्।
यथा ज्ञानामृतं काले ज्ञानिनो ददते न वा ॥ ३६ ॥

girayo mumucus toyaṁ
kvacin na mumucuḥ śivam
yathā jñānāmṛtaṁ kāle
jñānino dadate na vā

girayaḥ—the mountains; *mumucuḥ*—released; *toyam*—their water; *kvacit*—sometimes; *na mumucuḥ*—they did not release; *śivam*—pure; *yathā*—just as; *jñāna*—of transcendental knowledge; *amṛtam*—the nectar; *kāle*—at the appropriate time; *jñāninaḥ*—experts in spiritual knowledge; *dadate*—bestow; *na vā*—or not.

TRANSLATION

During this season the mountains sometimes released their pure water and sometimes did not, just as experts in transcendental science sometimes give the nectar of transcendental knowledge and sometimes do not.

PURPORT

The first part of this chapter described the rainy season, and the second part has been dealing with the autumn season, which begins when the rain stops. During the rainy season water always flows from the mountains, but during the autumn the water sometimes flows and sometimes does not. Similarly, great saintly teachers sometimes speak expansively on spiritual knowledge, and sometimes they are silent. The self-realized soul is closely in touch with the Supreme Soul, and according to His desires a competent spiritual scientist may or may not describe the Absolute Truth, depending on the specific circumstances.

TEXT 37

नैवाविदन् क्षीयमाणं जलं गाधजलेचराः।
यथायुरन्वहं क्षय्यं नरा मूढाः कुटुम्बिनः ॥ ३७ ॥

naivāvidan kṣīyamāṇaṁ
jalaṁ gādha-jale-carāḥ

yathāyur anv-ahaṁ kṣayyaṁ
narā mūḍhāḥ kuṭumbinaḥ

na—not; *eva*—indeed; *avidan*—appreciated; *kṣīyamāṇam*—diminishing; *jalam*—the water; *gādha-jale*—in shallow water; *carāḥ*—those who move; *yathā*—as; *āyuḥ*—their life span; *anu-aham*—every day; *kṣayyam*—diminishing; *narāḥ*—men; *mūḍhāḥ*—foolish; *kuṭumbinaḥ*—living with family members.

TRANSLATION

The fish swimming in the increasingly shallow water did not at all understand that the water was diminishing, just as foolish family men cannot see how the time they have left to live is diminishing with every passing day.

PURPORT

After the rainy season the water gradually goes down, but stupid fish do not understand this; thus they are often stranded on the lakeshores and riverbanks. Similarly, those infatuated with family life do not understand that the remainder of their life is constantly decreasing; thus they fail to perfect their Kṛṣṇa consciousness and are stranded in the cycle of birth and death.

TEXT 38

गाधवारिचरास्तापमविन्दञ्छरदर्कजम् ।
यथा दरिद्रः कृपणः कुटुंब्यविजितेन्द्रियः ॥ ३८ ॥

gādha-vāri-carās tāpam
avindañ charad-arka-jam
yathā daridraḥ kṛpaṇaḥ
kuṭumby avijitendriyaḥ

gādha-vāri-carāḥ—those who were moving in shallow water; *tāpam*—suffering; *avindan*—experienced; *śarat-arka-jam*—due to the sun in the autumn season; *yathā*—as; *daridraḥ*—a poor person; *kṛpaṇaḥ*—miserly; *kuṭumbī*—absorbed in family life; *avijita-indriyaḥ*—who has not controlled the senses.

TRANSLATION

Just as a miserly, poverty-stricken person overly absorbed in family life suffers because he cannot control his senses, the fish swimming in the shallow water had to suffer the heat of the autumn sun.

PURPORT

Although, as described in the previous verse, unintelligent fish are not aware of the diminishing water, one may think these fish are still happy according to the old proverb "Ignorance is bliss." But even the ignorant fish are scorched by the autumn sun. Similarly, although an attached family man may consider his ignorance of spiritual life blissful, he is constantly disturbed by the problems of family life, and, indeed, his uncontrolled senses lead him into a situation of unrelieved anguish.

TEXT 39

शनैः शनैर्जहुः पंकं स्थलान्यामं च वीरुधः ।
यथाहंममतां धीराः शरीरादिष्वनात्मसु ॥ ३९ ॥

śanaiḥ śanair jahuḥ paṅkaṁ
sthalāny āmaṁ ca vīrudhaḥ
yathāhaṁ-mamatāṁ dhīrāḥ
śarīrādiṣv anātmasu

śanaiḥ śanaiḥ—very gradually; *jahuḥ*—gave up; *paṅkam*—their mud; *sthalāni*—the places of land; *āmam*—their unripe condition; *ca*—and; *vīrudhaḥ*—the plants; *yathā*—as; *aham-mamatām*—egotism and possessiveness; *dhīrāḥ*—sober sages; *śarīra-ādiṣu*—focused upon the material body and other external objects; *anātmasu*—which are completely distinct from the real self.

TRANSLATION

Gradually the different areas of land gave up their muddy condition and the plants grew past their unripe stage, in the same way that sober sages give up egotism and possessiveness. These are based on things different from the real self—namely, the material body and its by-products.

PURPORT

The word *ādiṣu* in this verse indicates the by-products of the body, such as children, home and wealth.

TEXT 40

निश्चलाम्बुरभूत्तूष्णीं समुद्रः शरदागमे ।
आत्मन्युपरते सम्यङ् मुनिर्व्युपरतागमः ॥ ४० ॥

niścalāmbur abhūt tūṣṇīṁ
samudraḥ śarad-āgame
ātmany uparate samyaṅ
munir vyuparatāgamaḥ

niścala—motionless; *ambuḥ*—its water; *abhūt*—became; *tūṣṇīm*—quiet; *samudraḥ*—the ocean; *śarat*—of the fall season; *āgame*—with the coming; *ātmani*—when the self; *uparate*—has desisted from material activities; *samyak*—completely; *muniḥ*—a sage; *vyuparata*—giving up; *āgamaḥ*—recitation of the Vedic *mantras.*

TRANSLATION

With the arrival of autumn, the ocean and the lakes became silent, their water still, just like a sage who has desisted from all material activities and given up his recitation of Vedic mantras.

PURPORT

One recites ordinary Vedic *mantras* for material promotion, mystic power and impersonal salvation. But when a sage is completely free of personal desire, he vibrates the transcendental glories of the Supreme Lord exclusively.

TEXT 41

केदारेभ्यस्त्वपोऽगृह्णन् कर्षका दृढसेतुभिः ।
यथा प्राणैः स्रवज्ज्ञानं तन्निरोधेन योगिनः ॥ ४१ ॥

kedārebhyas tv apo'gṛhṇan
karṣakā dṛḍha-setubhiḥ
yathā prāṇaiḥ sravaj jñānaṁ
tan-nirodhena yoginaḥ

kedārebhyaḥ—from the flooded fields of rice paddy; *tu*—and; *apaḥ*—the water; *agṛhṇan*—took; *karṣakāḥ*—the farmers; *dṛḍha*—strong; *setubhiḥ*—with dikes; *yathā*—as; *prāṇaiḥ*—through the senses; *sravat*—flowing out; *jñānam*—consciousness; *tat*—of those senses; *nirodhena*—by the strict control; *yoginaḥ*—*yogīs.*

TRANSLATION

In the same way that the practitioners of yoga bring their senses under strict control to check their consciousness from flowing out through the

agitated senses, the farmers erected strong mud banks to keep the water within their rice fields from draining out.

PURPORT

Śrīla Prabhupāda comments: "In autumn, farmers save the water within the fields by building strong walls so that the water contained within the field cannot run out. There is hardly any hope for new rainfall; therefore they want to save whatever is in the field. Similarly, a person who is actually advanced in self-realization protects his energy by controlling the senses. It is advised that after the age of fifty, one should retire from family life and conserve the energy of the body for utilization in the advancement of Kṛṣṇa consciousness. Unless one is able to control the senses and engage them in the transcendental loving service of Mukunda, there is no possibility of salvation."

TEXT 42

शरदर्कांशुजांस्तापान् भूतानामुडुपोऽहरत् ।
देहाभिमानजं बोधो मुकुन्दो व्रजयोषिताम् ॥ ४२ ॥

śarad-arkāṁśu-jāṁs tāpān
bhūtānām uḍupo'harat
dehābhimāna-jaṁ bodho
mukundo vraja-yoṣitām

śarat-arka—of the autumn sun; *aṁśu*—from the rays; *jān*—generated; *tāpān*—suffering; *bhūtānām*—of all creatures; *uḍupaḥ*—the moon; *aharat*—has taken away; *deha*—with the material body; *abhimāna-jam*—based on false identification; *bodhaḥ*—wisdom; *mukundaḥ*—Lord Kṛṣṇa; *vraja-yoṣitām*—of the women of Vṛndāvana.

TRANSLATION

The autumn moon relieved all creatures of the suffering caused by the sun's rays, just as wisdom relieves a person of the misery caused by his identifying with his material body and as Lord Mukunda relieves Vṛndāvana's ladies of the distress caused by their separation from Him.

TEXT 43

खमशोभत निर्मेघं शरद्विमलतारकम् ।
सत्त्वयुक्तं यथा चित्तं शब्दब्रह्मार्थदर्शनम् ॥ ४३ ॥

kham aśobhata nirmeghaṁ
śarad-vimala-tārakam
sattva-yuktaṁ yathā cittaṁ
śabda-brahmārtha-darśanam

kham—the sky; *aśobhata*—shone brilliantly; *nirmegham*—free from clouds; *śarat*—in the fall; *vimala*—clear; *tārakam*—and starry; *sattva-yuktam*—endowed with (spiritual) goodness; *yathā*—just as; *cittam*—the mind; *śabda-brahma*—of the Vedic scripture; *artha*—the purport; *darśanam*—which directly experiences.

TRANSLATION

Free of clouds and filled with clearly visible stars, the autumn sky shone brilliantly, just like the spiritual consciousness of one who has directly experienced the purport of the Vedic scriptures.

PURPORT

The clear and starry autumn sky can also be compared to the pure heart of the devotee. The spiritual nature is always brilliant, clean and blissful, and this spiritual nature, called *vaikuṇṭha,* immediately satisfies all the desires of the soul. This is the secret of Kṛṣṇa consciousness.

TEXT 44

अखण्डमण्डलो व्योम्नि रराजोडुगणैः शशी ।
यथा यदुपतिः कृष्णो वृष्णिचक्रावृतो भुवि ॥ ४४ ॥

akhaṇḍa-maṇḍalo vyomni
rarājoḍu-gaṇaiḥ śaśī
yathā yadu-patiḥ kṛṣṇo
vṛṣṇi-cakrāvṛto bhuvi

akhaṇḍa—unbroken; *maṇḍalaḥ*—its sphere; *vyomni*—in the sky; *rarāja*—shone forth; *uḍu-gaṇaiḥ*—along with the stars; *śaśī*—the moon; *yathā*—as; *yadu-patiḥ*—the master of the Yadu dynasty; *kṛṣṇaḥ*—Lord Kṛṣṇa; *vṛṣṇi-cakra*—by the circle of Vṛṣṇis; *āvṛtaḥ*—surrounded; *bhuvi*—upon the earth.

TRANSLATION

The full moon shone in the sky, surrounded by stars, just as Śrī Kṛṣṇa, the Lord of the Yadu dynasty, shone brilliantly on the earth, surrounded by all the Vṛṣṇis.

PURPORT

Śrīla Sanātana Gosvāmī explains that in Vṛndāvana the full moon is eternally risen, and this full moon is like the full manifestation of the Absolute Truth, Śrī Kṛṣṇa. When He was manifest on earth, Lord Kṛṣṇa was surrounded by prominent members of the Vṛṣṇi dynasty such as Nanda, Upananda, Vasudeva and Akrūra.

TEXT 45

आश्लिष्य समशीतोष्णं प्रसूनवनमारुतम् ।
जनास्तापं जहुर्गोप्यो न कृष्णहृतचेतसः ॥ ४५ ॥

āśliṣya sama-śītoṣṇaṁ
prasūna-vana-mārutam
janās tāpaṁ jahur gopyo
na kṛṣṇa-hṛta-cetasaḥ

āśliṣya—embracing; *sama*—equal; *śīta-uṣṇam*—between cold and heat; *prasūna-vana*—of the forest of flowers; *mārutam*—the wind; *janāḥ*—the people in general; *tāpam*—suffering; *jahuḥ*—were able to abandon; *gopyaḥ*—the *gopīs; na*—not; *kṛṣṇa*—by Lord Kṛṣṇa; *hṛta*—stolen; *cetasaḥ*—whose hearts.

TRANSLATION

Except for the gopīs, whose hearts had been stolen by Kṛṣṇa, the people could forget their suffering by embracing the wind coming from the flower-filled forest. This wind was neither hot nor cold.

TEXT 46

गावो मृगाः खगा नार्यः पुष्पिण्यः शरदाभवन् ।
अन्वीयमानाः स्ववृषैः फलैरीशक्रिया इव ॥ ४६ ॥

gāvo mṛgāḥ khagā nāryaḥ
puṣpiṇyaḥ śaradābhavan
anvīyamānāḥ sva-vṛṣaiḥ
phalair īśa-kriyā iva

gāvaḥ—the cows; *mṛgāḥ*—the female deer; *khagāḥ*—the female birds; *nāryaḥ*—the women; *puṣpiṇyaḥ*—in their fertile periods; *śaradā*—because of the autumn; *abhavan*—became; *anvīyamānāḥ*—followed; *sva-vṛṣaiḥ*—by their respective mates; *phalaiḥ*—by good results; *īśa-kriyāḥ*—activities performed in service to the Supreme Lord; *iva*—as.

TRANSLATION

By the influence of the autumn season, all the cows, doe, women and female birds became fertile and were followed by their respective mates in search of sexual enjoyment, just as activities performed for the service of the Supreme Lord are automatically followed by all beneficial results.

PURPORT

Śrīla Prabhupāda comments, "On the arrival of the autumn season, all the cows, deer, birds and females in general become pregnant, because in that season generally all the husbands become impelled by sex desire. This is exactly like the transcendentalists who, by the grace of the Supreme Lord, are bestowed with the benediction of their destinations in life. Śrīla Rūpa Gosvāmī has instructed in his *Upadeśāmṛta* that one should perform devotional service with great enthusiasm, patience and conviction and should follow the rules and regulations, keep oneself clean from material contamination and stay in the association of devotees. By following these principles, one is sure to achieve the desired result of devotional service. For he who patiently follows the regulative principles of devotional service, the time will come when he will achieve the result, as the wives reap results by becoming pregnant."

TEXT 47

उदहृष्यन् वारिजानि सूर्योत्थाने कुमुद् विना ।
राज्ञा तु निर्भया लोका यथा दस्यून् विना नृप ॥ ४७ ॥

udahṛṣyan vārijāni
sūryotthāne kumud vinā
rājñā tu nirbhayā lokā
yathā dasyūn vinā nṛpa

udahṛṣyan—blossomed abundantly; *vāri-jāni*—the lotuses; *sūrya*—the sun; *utthāne*—when it had arisen; *kumut*—the night-blooming *kumut* lotus; *vinā*—except; *rājñā*—because of the presence of a king; *tu*—indeed; *nirbhayāḥ*—fearless; *lokāḥ*—the populace; *yathā*—as; *dasyūn*—the thieves; *vinā*—except for; *nṛpa*—O King.

TRANSLATION

O King Parīkṣit, when the autumn sun rose, all the lotus flowers blossomed happily, except the night-blooming kumut, just as in the presence of a strong ruler everyone becomes fearless, except the thieves.

TEXT 48

पुरग्रामेष्वाग्रयणैरिन्द्रियैश्च महोत्सवैः ।
बभौ भूः पक्वशष्याढ्या कलाभ्यां नितरां हरेः ॥ ४८ ॥

pura-grāmeṣv āgrayaṇair
indriyaiś ca mahotsavaiḥ
babhau bhūḥ pakva-śaṣyāḍhyā
kalābhyāṁ nitarāṁ hareḥ

pura—in the towns; *grāmeṣu*—and villages; *āgrayaṇaiḥ*—with performances of the Vedic sacrifice for tasting the first grains of the new harvest; *indriyaiḥ*—with other (worldly) celebrations; *ca*—and; *mahā-utsavaiḥ*—great celebrations; *babhau*—shone; *bhūḥ*—the earth; *pakva*—ripe; *śaṣya*—with her grains; *āḍhyā*—rich; *kalā*—she who is the expansion of the Lord; *ābhyām*—with those two (Kṛṣṇa and Balarāma); *nitarām*—very much; *hareḥ*—of the Supreme Personality of Godhead.

TRANSLATION

In all the towns and villages people held great festivals, performing the Vedic fire sacrifice for honoring and tasting the first grains of the new harvest, along with similar celebrations that followed local custom and tradition. Thus the earth, rich with newly grown grain and especially beautified by the presence of Kṛṣṇa and Balarāma, shone beautifully as an expansion of the Supreme Lord.

PURPORT

The word *āgrayaṇaiḥ* refers to a particular authorized Vedic sacrifice, and the word *indriyaiḥ* refers to folk ceremonies that have somewhat worldly objectives.

Śrīla Prabhupāda comments as follows: "During autumn, the fields become filled with ripened grain. At that time, the people become happy over the harvest and observe various ceremonies, such as Navānna—the offering of new grains to the Supreme Personality of Godhead. The new grains are first offered to the Deities in various temples, and all are invited to take sweet rice made with these new grains. There are other religious ceremonies and methods of worship, particularly in Bengal, where the greatest of all such ceremonies is held, called Durgā-pūjā."

TEXT 49

वणिङ्मुनिनृपस्नाता निर्गम्यार्थान् प्रपेदिरे ।
वर्षरुद्धा यथा सिद्धाः स्वपिण्डान् काल आगते ॥ ४९ ॥

vaṇiṅ-muni-nṛpa-snātā
nirgamyārthān prapedire
varṣa-ruddhā yathā siddhāḥ
sva-piṇḍān kāla āgate

vaṇik—the merchants; *muni*—renunciant sages; *nṛpa*—kings; *snātāḥ*—and *brahmacārī* students; *nirgamya*—going out; *arthān*—their desired objects; *prapedire*—obtained; *varṣa*—by the rain; *ruddhāḥ*—checked; *yathā*—as; *siddhāḥ*—perfected persons; *sva-piṇḍān*—the forms they aspire for; *kāle*—when the time; *āgate*—has come.

TRANSLATION

The merchants, sages, kings and brahmacārī students, kept in by the rain, were at last free to go out and attain their desired objects, just as those who achieve perfection in this life can, when the proper time comes, leave the material body and attain their respective forms.

PURPORT

Śrīla Prabhupāda comments, "In Vṛndāvana the autumn season was very beautiful then because of the presence of the Supreme Personality of Godhead, Kṛṣṇa and Balarāma. The mercantile community, the royal order and the great sages were free to move to achieve their desired benedictions. Similarly, the transcendentalists, when freed from the encagement of the material body, also achieved their desired goal. During the rainy season, the mercantile community cannot move from one place to another and so do not get their desired profit. Nor can the royal order go from one place to another to collect taxes from the people. As for saintly persons who must travel to preach transcendental knowledge, they also are restrained by the rainy season. But during the autumn, all of them leave their confines. In the case of the transcendentalist, be he a *jñānī*, a *yogī* or a devotee, because of the material body he cannot actually enjoy spiritual achievement. But as soon as he gives up the body, or after death, the *jñānī* merges into the spiritual effulgence of the Supreme Lord, the *yogī* transfers himself to the various higher planets, and the devotee goes to the planet of the Supreme Lord, Goloka Vṛndāvana, or the Vaikuṇṭhas, and thus enjoys his eternal spiritual life."

Thus end the purports of the humble servants of His Divine Grace A.C. Bhaktivedanta Swami Prabhupāda to the Tenth Canto, Twentieth Chapter, of the Śrīmad-Bhāgavatam, *entitled "The Rainy Season and Autumn in Vṛndāvana."*

CHAPTER TWENTY-ONE

The Gopīs Glorify the Song of Kṛṣṇa's Flute

This chapter describes how Lord Śrī Kṛṣṇa entered the enchanting forest of Vṛndāvana upon the arrival of autumn, and the praises the young cowherd girls sang when they heard the vibration of His flute.

As Lord Kṛṣṇa, Lord Balarāma and Their cowherd friends entered the forest to graze the cows, Kṛṣṇa began playing His flute. The *gopīs* heard the enchanting flute-song and understood that Kṛṣṇa was entering the forest. Then they narrated to each other the Lord's various activities.

The *gopīs* declared: "To see Lord Kṛṣṇa playing His flute while taking the cows to pasture is the highest perfection for the eyes. What pious activities has this flute performed that enable him to freely drink the nectar of Śrī Kṛṣṇa's lips—a blessing we cowherd girls find difficult to achieve? Hearing the song of Kṛṣṇa's flute, the peacocks dance, and all the other creatures become stunned when they see them. Demigoddesses traveling through the sky in their airplanes are vexed by Cupid, and their garments become loose. The ears of the cows stand on end as they drink the nectar of this flute-song, and their calves simply stand stunned, the milk they have been drinking from their mothers' udders still in their mouths. The birds take shelter of the branches of the trees and close their eyes, listening to the song of Kṛṣṇa's flute with rapt attention. The flowing rivers become perturbed by conjugal attraction for Kṛṣṇa and, stopping their flow, embrace Kṛṣṇa's lotus feet with the arms of their waves, while the clouds serve as parasols to shade Kṛṣṇa's head from the hot sun. The aborigine women of the Śabara race, seeing the grass stained by the red *kuṅkuma* adorning the Lord's lotus feet, smear this vermilion powder upon their breasts and faces to alleviate the distress created by Cupid. Govardhana Hill offers grass and various kinds of fruits and bulbous roots in worship of Lord Śrī Kṛṣṇa. All the nonmoving living beings take on the characteristics of moving creatures, and the moving living beings become stationary. These things are all very wonderful."

TEXT 1

श्रीशुक उवाच
इत्थं शरत्स्वच्छजलं पद्माकरसुगन्धिना ।
न्यविशद् वायुना वातं सगोगोपालकोऽच्युतः ॥ १ ॥

śrī-śuka uvāca
itthaṁ śarat-svaccha-jalaṁ
padmākara-sugandhinā
nyaviśad vāyunā vātaṁ
sa-go-gopālako'cyutaḥ

śrī-śukaḥ uvāca—Śrī Śukadeva Gosvāmī said; *ittham*—in this way; *śarat*—of the fall season; *svaccha*—clear; *jalam*—having water; *padma-ākara*—from the lake filled with lotus flowers; *su-gandhinā*—with the sweet fragrance; *nyaviśat*—He entered; *vāyunā*—by the breeze; *vātam*—ventilated; *sa*—with; *go*—the cows; *gopālakaḥ*—and the cowherd boys; *acyutaḥ*—the infallible Supreme Personality of Godhead.

TRANSLATION

Śukadeva Gosvāmī said: Thus the Vṛndāvana forest was filled with transparent autumnal waters and cooled by breezes perfumed with the fragrance of lotus flowers growing in the clear lakes. The infallible Lord, accompanied by His cows and cowherd boyfriends, entered that Vṛndāvana forest.

TEXT 2

कुसुमितवनराजिशुष्मिभृंग-
द्विजकुलघुष्टसरःसरिन्महीध्रम् ।
मधुपतिरवगाह्य चारयन् गाः
सहपशुपालबलश्चुकूज वेणुम् ॥ २ ॥

kusumita-vanarāji-śuṣmi-bhṛṅga
dvija-kula-ghuṣṭa-saraḥ-sarin-mahīdhram
madhupatir avagāhya cārayan gāḥ
saha-paśu-pāla-balaś cukūja veṇum

kusumita—flowering; *vana-rāji*—among the groups of trees; *śuṣmi*—maddened; *bhṛṅga*—with bees; *dvija*—of birds; *kula*—and flocks; *ghuṣṭa*—

resounding; *saraḥ*—its lakes; *sarit*—rivers; *mahīdhram*—and hills; *madhu-patiḥ*—the Lord of Madhu (Kṛṣṇa); *avagāhya*—entering; *cārayan*—while tending; *gāḥ*—the cows; *saha-paśu-pāla-balaḥ*—in the company of the cowherd boys and Lord Balarāma; *cukūja*—vibrated; *veṇum*—His flute.

TRANSLATION

The lakes, rivers and hills of Vṛndāvana resounded with the sounds of maddened bees and flocks of birds moving about the flowering trees. In the company of the cowherd boys and Balarāma, Madhupati [Śrī Kṛṣṇa] entered that forest, and while herding the cows He began to vibrate His flute.

PURPORT

As suggested by the words *cukūja veṇum,* Lord Kṛṣṇa skillfully blended the sound of His flute with the lovely sounds of Vṛndāvana's multicolored birds. Thus an irresistible, heavenly vibration was created.

TEXT 3

तद् व्रजस्त्रिय आश्रुत्य वेणुगीतं स्मरोदयम् ।
काश्चित् परोक्षं कृष्णस्य स्वसखीभ्योऽन्ववर्णयन् ॥ ३ ॥

tad vraja-striya āśrutya
veṇu-gītaṁ smarodayam
kāścit parokṣaṁ kṛṣṇasya
sva-sakhībhyo 'nvavarṇayan

tat—that; *vraja-striyaḥ*—the ladies in the cowherd village; *āśrutya*—hearing; *veṇu-gītam*—the song of the flute; *smara-udayam*—which gives rise to the influence of Cupid; *kāścit*—some of them; *parokṣam*—privately; *kṛṣṇasya*—about Kṛṣṇa; *sva-sakhībhyaḥ*—to their intimate companions; *an-vavarṇayan*—described.

TRANSLATION

When the young ladies in the cowherd village of Vraja heard the song of Kṛṣṇa's flute, which arouses the influence of Cupid, some of them privately began describing Kṛṣṇa's qualities to their intimate friends.

TEXT 4

तद् वर्णयितुमारब्धाः स्मरन्त्यः कृष्णचेष्टितम् ।
नाशकन् स्मरवेगेन विक्षिप्तमनसो नृप ॥ ४ ॥

tad varṇayitum ārabdhāḥ
smarantyaḥ kṛṣṇa-ceṣṭitam
nāśakan smara-vegena
vikṣipta-manaso nṛpa

tat—that; *varṇayitum*—to describe; *ārabdhāḥ*—beginning; *smarantyaḥ*—remembering; *kṛṣṇa-ceṣṭitam*—the activities of Kṛṣṇa; *na aśakan*—they were incapable; *smara-vegena*—by the force of Cupid; *vikṣipta*—agitated; *manasaḥ*—whose minds; *nṛpa*—O King Parīkṣit.

TRANSLATION

The cowherd girls began to speak about Kṛṣṇa, but when they remembered His activities, O King, the power of Cupid disturbed their minds, and thus they could not speak.

TEXT 5

बर्हापीडं नटवरवपुः कर्णयोः कर्णिकारं
बिभ्रद् वासः कनककपिशं वैजयन्तीं च मालाम् ।
रन्ध्रान् वेणोरधरसुधयापूरयन् गोपवृन्दैर्
वृन्दारण्यं स्वपदरमणं प्राविशद् गीतकीर्तिः ॥ ५ ॥

barhāpīḍaṁ naṭa-vara-vapuḥ karṇayoḥ karṇikāraṁ
bibhrad vāsaḥ kanaka-kapiśaṁ vaijayantīṁ ca mālām
randhrān veṇor adhara-sudhayāpūrayan gopa-vṛndair
vṛndāraṇyaṁ sva-pada-ramaṇaṁ prāviśad gīta-kīrtiḥ

barha—a peacock feather; *āpīḍam*—as the decoration of His head; *naṭa-vara*—of the best of dancers; *vapuḥ*—the transcendental body; *karṇayoḥ*—on the ears; *karṇikāram*—a particular kind of blue lotuslike flower; *bibhrat*—wearing; *vāsaḥ*—garments; *kanaka*—like gold; *kapiśam*—yellowish; *vaijayantīm*—named Vaijayantī; *ca*—and; *mālām*—the garland; *randhrān*—the holes; *veṇoḥ*—of His flute; *adhara*—of His lips; *sudhayā*—with the nectar; *āpūrayan*—filling up; *gopa-vṛndaiḥ*—by the cowherd boys; *vṛndā-araṇyam*—the forest of Vṛndāvana; *sva-pada*—because of the marks of His lotus feet; *ramaṇam*—enchanting; *prāviśat*—He entered; *gīta*—being sung; *kīrtiḥ*—His glories.

TRANSLATION

Wearing a peacock-feather ornament upon His head, blue karṇikāra flowers on His ears, a yellow garment as brilliant as gold, and the Vaijayantī garland, Lord Kṛṣṇa exhibited His transcendental form as the greatest of dancers as He entered the forest of Vṛndāvana, beautifying it with the marks of His footprints. He filled the holes of His flute with the nectar of His lips, and the cowherd boys sang His glories.

PURPORT

The *gopīs* remembered all the transcendental qualities of Kṛṣṇa mentioned in this verse. Kṛṣṇa's artful way of dressing and the beautiful blue flowers placed over His ears excited the *gopīs'* romantic desires, and as He poured the nectar of His lips into His flute, they simply lost themselves in ecstatic love for Him.

TEXT 6

इति वेणुरवं राजन् सर्वभूतमनोहरम् ।
श्रुत्वा व्रजस्त्रियः सर्वा वर्णयन्त्योऽभिरेभिरे ॥ ६ ॥

iti veṇu-ravaṁ rājan
sarva-bhūta-manoharam
śrutvā vraja-striyaḥ sarvā
varṇayantyo 'bhirebhire

iti—thus; *veṇu-ravam*—the vibration of the flute; *rājan*—O King Parīkṣit; *sarva-bhūta*—of all living beings; *manaḥ-haram*—stealing the minds; *śrutvā*—hearing; *vraja-striyaḥ*—the ladies standing in the village of Vraja; *sarvāḥ*—all of them; *varṇayantyaḥ*—engaged in describing; *abhirebhire*—embraced one another.

TRANSLATION

O King, when the young ladies in Vraja heard the sound of Kṛṣṇa's flute, which captivates the minds of all living beings, they all embraced one another and began describing it.

PURPORT

The word *iti* here indicates that after becoming speechless by remembering Kṛṣṇa, the cowherd damsels then regained their composure and were thus able to ecstatically describe the sound of Kṛṣṇa's flute. As a few *gopīs* began to exclaim, and the other *gopīs* realized that they shared the same ecstatic love within their hearts, all of them started embracing one another, overwhelmed with conjugal love for young Kṛṣṇa.

TEXT 7

श्रीगोप्य ऊचुः
अक्षण्वतां फलमिदं न परं विदामः
सख्यः पशूननुविवेशयतोर्वयस्यैः ।
वक्त्रं व्रजेशसुतयोरनुवेणुजुष्टं
यैर्वा निपीतमनुरक्तकटाक्षमोक्षम् ॥ ७॥

śrī-gopya ūcuḥ
akṣaṇvatāṁ phalam idaṁ na paraṁ vidāmaḥ
sakhyaḥ paśūn anuviveśayator vayasyaiḥ
vaktraṁ vrajeśa-sutayor anaveṇu-juṣṭaṁ
yair vā nipītam anurakta-kaṭākṣa-mokṣam

śrī-gopyaḥ ūcuḥ—the *gopīs* said; *akṣaṇvatām*—of those who have eyes; *phalam*—the fruit; *idam*—this; *na*—not; *param*—other; *vidāmaḥ*—we know; *sakhyaḥ*—O friends; *paśūn*—the cows; *anuviveśayatoḥ*—causing to enter one forest after another; *vayasyaiḥ*—with Their friends of the same age; *vaktram*—the faces; *vraja-īśa*—of Mahārāja Nanda; *sutayoḥ*—of the two sons; *anu-veṇu-juṣṭam*—possessed of flutes; *yaiḥ*—by which; *vā*—or; *nipītam*—imbibed; *anurakta*—loving; *kaṭa-akṣa*—glances; *mokṣam*—giving off.

TRANSLATION

The cowherd girls said: O friends, those eyes that see the beautiful faces of the sons of Mahārāja Nanda are certainly fortunate. As these two sons enter the forest, surrounded by Their friends, driving the cows before Them, They hold Their flutes to Their mouths and glance lovingly upon the residents of Vṛndāvana. For those who have eyes, we think there is no greater object of vision.

PURPORT

This translation is quoted from Śrīla Prabhupāda's *Caitanya-caritāmṛta* (*Ādi-līlā* 4.155).

Śrīla Viśvanātha Cakravartī Ṭhākura has commented as follows: "The *gopīs* meant to say,'O friends, if you simply remain in the shackles of family life in this material world, what will you ever get to see? The creator has granted us these eyes, so let us see the most wonderful thing there is to see, Kṛṣṇa.'"

The *gopīs* were aware that their mothers or other elder persons might hear their romantic words and disapprove, and thus they said, *akṣaṇvatāṁ phalam:* "To see Kṛṣṇa is the goal for all persons and not simply ourselves." In other words, the *gopīs* indicated that since Kṛṣṇa is the supreme object of love for everyone, why couldn't they also love Him in spiritual ecstasy?

According to the *ācāryas,* a different *gopī* spoke this and each of the following verses (through Text 19).

TEXT 8

चूतप्रवालबर्हस्तबकोत्पलाब्ज-
मालानुपृक्तपरिधानविचित्रवेशौ ।
मध्ये विरेजतुरलं पशुपालगोष्ठ्यां
रंगे यथा नटवरौ क्वच गायमानौ ॥ ८ ॥

cūta-pravāla-barha-stabakotpalābja
mālānupṛkta-paridhāna-vicitra-veśau
madhye virejatur alaṁ paśu-pāla-goṣṭhyāṁ
raṅge yathā naṭa-varau kvaca gāyamānau

cūta—of a mango tree; *pravāla*—with young sprouts; *barha*—peacock feathers; *stabaka*—bunches of flowers; *utpala*—lotuses; *abja*—and lilies; *mālā*—with garlands; *anupṛkta*—touched; *paridhāna*—Their garments; *vicitra*—with great variety; *veśau*—being dressed; *madhye*—in the midst; *virejatuḥ*—the two of Them shone forth; *alam*—magnificently; *paśu-pāla*—of the cowherd boys; *goṣṭhyām*—within the assembly; *raṅge*—upon a stage; *yathā*—just as; *naṭa-varau*—two most excellent dancers; *kvaca*—sometimes; *gāyamānau*—Themselves singing.

TRANSLATION

Dressed in a charming variety of garments, upon which Their garlands rest, and decorating Themselves with peacock feathers, lotuses, lilies, newly grown mango sprouts and clusters of flower buds, Kṛṣṇa and Balarāma shine forth magnificently among the assembly of cowherd boys.

They look just like the best of dancers appearing on a dramatic stage, and sometimes They sing.

PURPORT

The *gopīs* continue singing their ecstatic song as they remember the pastimes of Lord Kṛṣṇa. The *gopīs* wanted to go to the forest where Kṛṣṇa was performing His pastimes and, while remaining concealed, peer through the leaves of the creepers and see the wonder of Kṛṣṇa and Balarāma dancing and singing with Their boyfriends. This was their desire, but because they could not go, they sang this song in ecstatic love.

TEXT 9

गोप्यः किमाचरदयं कुशलं स्म वेणुर्
दामोदराधरसुधामपि गोपिकानाम् ।
भुंक्ते स्वयं यदवशिष्टरसं ह्रदिन्यो
हृष्यत्त्वचोऽश्रु मुमुचुस्तरवो यथार्याः ॥ ९ ॥

gopyaḥ kim ācarad ayaṁ kuśalaṁ sma veṇur
dāmodarādhara-sudhām api gopikānām
bhuṅkte svayaṁ yad avaśiṣṭa-rasaṁ hradinyo
hṛṣyat-tvaco 'śru mumucus taravo yathāryāḥ

gopyaḥ—O *gopīs; kim*—what; *ācarat*—performed; *ayam*—this; *kuśalam*—auspicious activities; *sma*—certainly; *veṇuḥ*—the flute; *dāmodara*—of Kṛṣṇa; *adhara-sudhām*—the nectar of the lips; *api*—even; *gopikānām*—which is owed to the *gopīs; bhuṅkte*—enjoys; *svayam*—independently; *yat*—from which; *avaśiṣṭa*—remaining; *rasam*—the taste only; *hradinyaḥ*—the rivers; *hṛṣyat*—feeling jubilant; *tvacaḥ*—whose bodies; *aśru*—tears; *mumucuḥ*—shed; *taravaḥ*—the trees; *yathā*—exactly like; *āryāḥ*—old forefathers.

TRANSLATION

My dear gopīs, what auspicious activities must the flute have performed to enjoy the nectar of Kṛṣṇa's lips independently and leave only a taste for us gopīs, for whom that nectar is actually meant! The forefathers of the flute, the bamboo trees, shed tears of pleasure. His mother, the river on whose bank the bamboo was born, feels jubilation, and therefore her blooming lotus flowers are standing like hair on her body.

PURPORT

This translation is quoted from Śrīla Prabhupāda's *Caitanya-caritāmṛta* (*Antya* 16.140).

In the guise of releasing flowing sap, the bamboo trees are actually crying tears of ecstasy upon seeing their child become an exalted devotee-flute of the Supreme Personality of Godhead, Śrī Kṛṣṇa.

Sanātana Gosvāmī gives an alternate explanation: The trees are crying because they are unhappy at not being able to play with Kṛṣṇa themselves. One may object that the trees in Vṛndāvana should not lament for that which is impossible for them to obtain, just as a beggar certainly doesn't lament because he is forbidden to meet the king. But the trees are actually just like intelligent persons who suffer when they cannot obtain the goal of life. Thus the trees are crying because they cannot get the nectar of Kṛṣṇa's lips.

TEXT 10

वृन्दावनं सखि भुवो वितनोति कीर्तिं
यद्देवकीसुतपदाम्बुजलब्धलक्ष्मि ।
गोविन्दवेणुमनु मत्तमयूरनृत्यं
प्रेक्ष्याद्रिसान्ववरतान्यसमस्तसत्त्वम् ॥ १० ॥

vṛndāvanaṁ sakhi bhuvo vitanoti kīrtiṁ
yad devakī-suta-padāmbuja-labdha-lakṣmi
govinda-veṇum anu matta-mayūra-nṛtyaṁ
prekṣyādri- sānv-avaratānya-samasta-sattvam

vṛndāvanam—Vṛndāvana; *sakhi*—O friend; *bhuvaḥ*—of the earth; *vitanoti*—spreads; *kīrtim*—the glories; *yat*—because; *devakī-suta*—of the son of Devakī; *pada-ambuja*—from the lotus feet; *labdha*—received; *lakṣmi*—the treasure; *govinda-veṇum*—the flute of Govinda; *anu*—upon hearing; *matta*—maddened; *mayūra*—of the peacocks; *nṛtyam*—in which there is the dancing; *prekṣya*—seeing; *adri-sānu*—upon the peaks of the hills; *avarata*—stunned; *anya*—other; *samasta*—all; *sattvam*—creatures.

TRANSLATION

O friend, Vṛndāvana is spreading the glory of the earth, having obtained the treasure of the lotus feet of Kṛṣṇa, the son of Devakī. The peacocks dance madly when they hear Govinda's flute, and when other creatures see them from the hilltops, they all become stunned.

PURPORT

Śrīla Śrīdhara Svāmī explains that because activities such as those described in this verse do not occur in any other world, the earth is unique. In fact, the earth's glories are being spread by wonderful Vṛndāvana because it is the place of Kṛṣṇa's pastimes.

The name Devakī also refers to mother Yaśodā, as stated in the *Bṛhad-viṣṇu Purāṇa:*

dve nāmnī nanda-bhāryāyā
yaśodā devakīti ca
ataḥ sakhyam abhūt tasyā
devakyā śauri-jāyayā

"The wife of Nanda had two names, Yaśodā and also Devakī. Therefore it was natural that she [the wife of Nanda] develop friendship with Devakī, the wife of Śauri [Vasudeva]."

Śrīla Viśvanātha Cakravartī Ṭhākura explains *kṛṣṇa-līlā* as follows: "In Vṛndāvana, the peacocks request Kṛṣṇa, 'Govinda, please make us dance.' Thus Kṛṣṇa plays His flute, and they surround Him in a circle and dance in time with the rhythm of His melody. And while standing in the midst of their dancing, He also sings and dances. Then those peacocks, who are fully satisfied with His musical performance, out of gratitude offer for His pleasure their own divine feathers. In the usual manner of musical performers, Kṛṣṇa gladly accepts these presentations and places a feather upon the turban atop His head. Gentle animals such as deer and doves greatly relish the transcendental entertainment presented by Kṛṣṇa, and to get a good view they flock to the peaks of hills. Then, as they watch the breathtaking program, they become stunned in ecstasy."

Śrīla Sanātana Gosvāmī comments that because in Vṛndāvana Kṛṣṇa goes barefoot and can thus directly mark the earth with the symbols of His lotus feet, that transcendental land is even more glorious than Vaikuṇṭha, where Viṣṇu wears slippers.

TEXT 11

धन्याः स्म मूढगतयोऽपि हरिण्य एता
या नन्दनन्दनमुपात्तविचित्रवेशम् ।
आकर्ण्य वेणुरणितं सहकृष्णसाराः
पूजां दधुर्विरचितां प्रणयावलोकैः ॥ ११ ॥

dhanyāḥ sma mūḍha-gatayo'pi hariṇya etā
yā nanda-nandanam upātta-vicitra-veśam
ākarṇya veṇu-raṇitaṁ saha-kṛṣṇa-sārāḥ
pūjāṁ dadhur viracitāṁ praṇayāvalokaiḥ

dhanyāḥ—fortunate, blessed; *sma*—certainly; *mūḍha-gatayaḥ*—having taken birth in an ignorant animal species; *api*—although; *hariṇyaḥ*—she-deer; *etāḥ*—these; *yāḥ*—who; *nanda-nandanam*—the son of Mahārāja Nanda; *upātta-vicitra-veśam*—dressed very attractively; *ākarṇya*—hearing; *veṇu-raṇitam*—the sound of His flute; *saha-kṛṣṇa-sārāḥ*—accompanied by the black deer (their husbands); *pūjām dadhuḥ*—they worshiped; *viracitām*—performed; *praṇaya-avalokaiḥ*—by their affectionate glances.

TRANSLATION

Blessed are all these foolish deer because they have approached Mahārāja Nanda's son, who is gorgeously dressed and is playing on His flute. Indeed, both the doe and the bucks worship the Lord with looks of love and affection.

PURPORT

This translation is quoted from Śrīla Prabhupāda's *Caitanya-caritāmṛta* (*Madhya* 17.36).

According to the ācāryas, the *gopīs* were thinking as follows: "The female deer can approach Kṛṣṇa along with their husbands because Kṛṣṇa is the ultimate object of affection for the male deer. Because of their affection for Kṛṣṇa, they are encouraged by seeing their wives attracted to Him and thus consider their household lives fortunate. Indeed, they become joyful upon seeing how their wives are searching after Kṛṣṇa, and, following along, they urge their wives to go to the Lord. On the other hand, our husbands are jealous of Kṛṣṇa, and because of their lack of devotion to Him they cannot even stand to smell His fragrance. Therefore what is the use of our lives?"

TEXT 12

कृष्णं निरीक्ष्य वनितोत्सवरूपशीलं
श्रुत्वा च तत्क्वणितवेणुविविक्तगीतम् ।
देव्यो विमानगतयः स्मरनुन्नसारा
भ्रश्यत्प्रसूनकबरा मुमुहुर्विनीव्यः ॥ १२ ॥

kṛṣṇaṁ nirīkṣya vanitotsava-rūpa-śīlaṁ
śrutvā ca tat-kvaṇita-veṇu-vivikta-gītam
devyo vimāna-gatayaḥ smara-nunna-sārā
bhraśyat-prasūna-kabarā mumuhur vinīvyaḥ

kṛṣṇam—Lord Kṛṣṇa; *nirīkṣya*—observing; *vanitā*—for all women; *utsava*—a festival; *rūpa*—whose beauty; *śīlam*—and character; *śrutvā*—hearing; *ca*—and; *tat*—by Him; *kvaṇita*—vibrated; *veṇu*—of the flute; *vivikta*—clear; *gītam*—song; *devyaḥ*—the wives of the demigods; *vimāna-gatayaḥ*—traveling in their airplanes; *smara*—by Cupid; *nunna*—agitated; *sārāḥ*—their hearts; *bhraśyat*—slipping; *prasūna-kabarāḥ*—the flowers tied in their hair; *mumuhuḥ*—they became bewildered; *vinīvyaḥ*—their belts loosening.

TRANSLATION

Kṛṣṇa's beauty and character create a festival for all women. Indeed, when the demigods' wives flying in airplanes with their husbands catch sight of Him and hear His resonant flute-song, their hearts are shaken by Cupid, and they become so bewildered that the flowers fall out of their hair and their belts loosen.

PURPORT

In *Kṛṣṇa, the Supreme Personality of Godhead,* Śrīla Prabhupāda comments: "[This verse indicates] that the transcendental sound of the flute of Kṛṣṇa extended to all corners of the universe. Also, it is significant that the *gopīs* knew about the different kinds of airplanes flying in the sky."

In fact, even while sitting on the laps of their demigod husbands, the demigoddesses became agitated by hearing the sounds of Kṛṣṇa's flute. Thus the *gopīs* thought that they themselves should not be blamed for their ecstatic conjugal attraction for Kṛṣṇa, who after all was a cowherd boy from their own village and thus a natural object of their love. If even demigoddesses became mad after Kṛṣṇa, how could poor, earthly cowherd girls from Kṛṣṇa's own village avoid having their hearts completely conquered by His loving glances and the sounds of His flute?

The *gopīs* also considered that the demigods, although noting their wives' attraction to Kṛṣṇa, did not become envious. The demigods are actually very refined in culture and intelligence, and therefore when flying in their airplanes they regularly take their wives along to see Kṛṣṇa. The *gopīs* thought, "Our husbands, on the other hand, are envious. Therefore even the inferior deer are better off than we, and the demigoddesses are also very fortunate, whereas we poor human beings in an intermediate position are most unfortunate."

TEXT 13

गावश्च कृष्णमुखनिर्गतवेणुगीत-
पीयूषमुत्तभितकर्णपुटैः पिबन्त्यः ।
शावाः स्नुतस्तनपयःकवलाः स्म तस्थुर्
गोविन्दमात्मनि दृशाश्रुकलाः स्पृशन्त्यः ॥ १३ ॥

gāvaś ca kṛṣṇa-mukha-nirgata-veṇu-gīta
pīyūṣam uttabhita-karṇa-puṭaiḥ pibantyaḥ
śāvāḥ snuta-stana-payaḥ-kavalāḥ sma tasthur
govindam ātmani dṛśāśru-kalāḥ spṛśantyaḥ

gāvaḥ—the cows; *ca*—and; *kṛṣṇa-mukha*—from the mouth of Lord Kṛṣṇa; *nirgata*—emitted; *veṇu*—of the flute; *gīta*—of the song; *pīyūṣam*—the nectar; *uttabhita*—raised high; *karṇa*—with their ears; *puṭaiḥ*—which were acting as vessels; *pibantyaḥ*—drinking; *śāvāḥ*—the calves; *snuta*—exuding; *stana*—from their udders; *payaḥ*—the milk; *kavalāḥ*—whose mouthfuls; *sma*—indeed; *tasthuḥ*—stood still; *govindam*—Lord Kṛṣṇa; *ātmani*—within their minds; *dṛśā*—with their vision; *aśru-kalāḥ*—their eyes full of tears; *spṛśantyaḥ*—touching.

TRANSLATION

Using their upraised ears as vessels, the cows are drinking the nectar of the flute-song flowing out of Kṛṣṇa's mouth. The calves, their mouths full of milk from their mothers' moist nipples, stand still as they take Govinda within themselves through their tear-filled eyes and embrace Him within their hearts.

TEXT 14

प्रायो बताम्ब विहगा मुनयो वनेऽस्मिन्
कृष्णेक्षितं तदुदितं कलवेणुगीतम् ।
आरुह्य ये द्रुमभुजान् रुचिरप्रवालान्
शृण्वन्ति मीलितदृशो विगतान्यवाचः ॥ १४ ॥

prāyo batāmba vihagā munayo vane'smin
kṛṣṇekṣitaṁ tad-uditaṁ kala-veṇu-gītam
āruhya ye druma-bhujān rucira-pravālān
śṛṇvanti mīlita-dṛśo vigatānya-vācaḥ

prāyaḥ—almost; *bata*—certainly; *amba*—O mother; *vihagāḥ*—the birds; *munayaḥ*—great sages; *vane*—in the forest; *asmin*—this; *kṛṣṇa-īkṣitam*—in order to see Kṛṣṇa; *tat-uditam*—created by Him; *kala-veṇu-gītam*—sweet vibrations made by playing the flute; *āruhya*—rising; *ye*—who; *druma-bhujān*—to the branches of the trees; *rucira-pravālān*—having beautiful creepers and twigs; *śṛṇvanti*—they hear; *mīlita-dṛśaḥ*—closing their eyes; *vigata-anya-vācaḥ*—stopping all other sounds.

TRANSLATION

O mother, in this forest all the birds have risen onto the beautiful branches of the trees to see Kṛṣṇa. With closed eyes they are simply listening in silence to the sweet vibrations of His flute, and they are not attracted by any other sound. Surely these birds are on the same level as great sages.

PURPORT

The birds resemble sages because they live in the forest, keep their eyes closed, observe silence and remain motionless. Significantly, it is stated here that even great sages become maddened by the sound of Kṛṣṇa's flute, which is a completely spiritual vibration.

The word *rucira-pravālān* indicates that even the branches of the trees are transformed in ecstasy when struck by the vibration of Kṛṣṇa's flute-song. Indra, Brahmā, Śiva and Viṣṇu, being primordial gods, travel throughout the universe and have extensive knowledge of the science of music, and yet even these great personalities have never heard or composed music like that which emanates from Kṛṣṇa's flute. Indeed, the birds are so moved by the blissful sound that in their ecstasy they close their eyes and cling to the branches to avoid falling off the trees.

Śrīla Viśvanātha Cakravartī Ṭhākura explains that the *gopīs* would sometimes address each other as *amba,* "mother."

TEXT 15

नद्यस्तदा तदुपधार्य मुकुन्दगीतम्
आवर्तलक्षितमनोभवभग्नवेगाः ।
आलिंगनस्थगितमूर्मिभुजैर्मुरारेर्
गृह्णन्ति पादयुगलं कमलोपहाराः ॥ १५ ॥

nadyas tadā tad upadhārya mukunda-gītam
āvarta-lakṣita-manobhava-bhagna-vegāḥ
āliṅgana-sthagitam ūrmi-bhujair murārer
gṛhṇanti pāda-yugalaṁ kamalopahārāḥ

nadyaḥ—the rivers; *tadā*—then; *tat*—that; *upadhārya*—perceiving; *mukunda*—of Lord Kṛṣṇa; *gītam*—the song of His flute; *āvarta*—by their whirlpools; *lakṣita*—manifest; *manaḥ-bhava*—by their conjugal desire; *bhagna*—broken; *vegāḥ*—their currents; *āliṅgana*—by their embrace; *sthagitam*—held stationary; *ūrmi-bhujaiḥ*—by the arms of their waves; *murāreḥ*—of Lord Murāri; *gṛhṇanti*—they seize; *pāda-yugalam*—the two lotus feet; *kamala-upahārāḥ*—carrying offerings of lotus flowers.

TRANSLATION

When the rivers hear the flute-song of Kṛṣṇa, their minds begin to desire Him, and thus the flow of their currents is broken and their waters are agitated, moving around in whirlpools. Then with the arms of their waves the rivers embrace Murāri's lotus feet and, holding on to them, present offerings of lotus flowers.

PURPORT

Even such sacred bodies of water as the Yamunā and the Mānasa-gaṅgā are enchanted by the flute-song, and thus they are disturbed by conjugal attraction for young Kṛṣṇa. The *gopīs* are implying that since many different types of living beings are overwhelmed by conjugal love for Kṛṣṇa, why should the *gopīs* be criticized for their intense desire to serve Kṛṣṇa in the conjugal relationship?

TEXT 16

दृष्ट्वातपे व्रजपशून् सह रामगोपैः
सञ्चारयन्तमनु वेणुमुदीरयन्तम् ।

प्रेमप्रवृद्ध उदितः कुसुमावलीभिः
सख्युर्व्यधात् स्ववपुषाम्बुद आतपत्रम् ॥ १६ ॥

dṛṣṭvātape vraja-paśūn saha rāma-gopaiḥ
sañcārayantam anu veṇum udīrayantam
prema-pravṛddha uditaḥ kusumāvalībhiḥ
sakhyur vyadhāt sva-vapuṣāmbuda ātapatram

dṛṣṭvā—seeing; *ātape*—in the full heat of the sun; *vraja-paśūn*—the domestic animals of Vraja; *saha*—together with; *rāma-gopaiḥ*—Lord Balarāma and the cowherd boys; *sañcārayantam*—herding together; *anu*—repeatedly; *veṇum*—His flute; *udīrayantam*—loudly playing; *prema*—out of love; *pravṛddhaḥ*—expanded; *uditaḥ*—rising high; *kusuma-āvalībhiḥ*—(with droplets of water vapor, which are like) groups of flowers; *sakhyuḥ*—for his friend; *vyadhāt*—he constructed; *sva-vapuṣā*—out of his own body; *ambudaḥ*—the cloud; *ātapatram*—an umbrella.

TRANSLATION

In the company of Balarāma and the cowherd boys, Lord Kṛṣṇa is continually vibrating His flute as He herds all the animals of Vraja, even under the full heat of the summer sun. Seeing this, the cloud in the sky has expanded himself out of love. He is rising high and constructing out of his own body, with its multitude of flower-like droplets of water, an umbrella for the sake of his friend.

PURPORT

Śrīla Prabhupāda states in his *Kṛṣṇa, the Supreme Personality of Godhead:* "The scorching heat of the autumn sunshine was sometimes intolerable, and therefore the clouds in the sky appeared in sympathy above Kṛṣṇa and Balarāma and Their boyfriends while They engaged in blowing Their flutes. The clouds served as a soothing umbrella over Their heads just to make friendship with Kṛṣṇa."

TEXT 17

पूर्णाः पुलिन्द्य उरुगायपदाब्जराग-
श्रीकुंकुमेन दयितास्तनमण्डितेन ।
तद्दर्शनस्मररुजस्तृणरूषितेन
लिम्पन्त्य आननकुचेषु जहुस्तदाधिम् ॥ १७ ॥

pūrṇāḥ pulindya urugāya-padābja-rāga
śrī-kuṅkumena dayitā-stana-maṇḍitena
tad-darśana-smara-rujas tṛṇa-rūṣitena
limpantya ānana-kuceṣu jahus tad-ādhim

pūrṇāḥ—fully satisfied; *pulindyaḥ*—the wives of the Śabara tribe; *urugāya*—of Lord Kṛṣṇa; *pada-abja*—from the lotus feet; *rāga*—of reddish color; *śrī-kuṅkumena*—by the transcendental *kuṅkuma* powder; *dayitā*—of His girlfriends; *stana*—the breasts; *maṇḍitena*—which had decorated; *tat*—of that; *darśana*—by the sight; *smara*—of Cupid; *rujaḥ*—feeling the torment; *tṛṇa*—upon the blades of grass; *rūṣitena*—attached; *limpantyaḥ*—smearing; *ānana*—upon their faces; *kuceṣu*—and breasts; *jahuḥ*—they gave up; *tat*—that; *ādhim*—mental pain.

TRANSLATION

The aborigine women of the Vṛndāvana area become disturbed by lust when they see the grass marked with reddish kuṅkuma powder. Endowed with the color of Kṛṣṇa's lotus feet, this powder originally decorated the breasts of His beloveds, and when the aborigine women smear it on their faces and breasts, they give up all their anxiety.

PURPORT

Śrīla Prabhupāda explains this verse as follows: "The wanton aborigine girls also became fully satisfied when they smeared their faces and breasts with the dust of Vṛndāvana, which was reddish from the touch of Kṛṣṇa's lotus feet. The aborigine girls had very full breasts, and they were also very lusty, but when their lovers felt their breasts, they were not very satisfied. When they came out into the midst of the forest, they saw that while Kṛṣṇa was walking, some of the leaves and creepers of Vṛndāvana turned reddish from the *kuṅkuma* powder that fell from His lotus feet. His lotus feet were held by the *gopīs* on their breasts, which were also smeared with *kuṅkuma* powder, but when Kṛṣṇa traveled in the Vṛndāvana forest with Balarāma and His boyfriends, the reddish powder fell on the ground of the Vṛndāvana forest. So the lusty aborigine girls, while looking toward Kṛṣṇa playing His flute, saw the reddish *kuṅkuma* on the ground and immediately took it and smeared it over their faces and breasts. In this way they became fully satisfied, although they were not satisfied when their lovers touched their breasts. All material lusty desires can be immediately satisfied if one comes in contact with Kṛṣṇa consciousness."

TEXT 18

हन्तायमद्रिरबला हरिदासवर्यो
यद् रामकृष्णचरणस्परशप्रमोदः ।
मानं तनोति सहगोगणयोस्तयोर्यत्
पानीयसूयवसकन्दरकन्दमूलैः ॥ १८ ॥

hantāyam adrir abalā hari-dāsa-varyo
yad rāma-kṛṣṇa-caraṇa-sparaśa-pramodaḥ
mānaṁ tanoti saha-go-gaṇayos tayor yat
pānīya-sūyavasa-kandara-kandamūlaiḥ

hanta—oh; *ayam*—this; *adriḥ*—hill; *abalāḥ*—O friends; *hari-dāsa-varyaḥ*—the best among the servants of the Lord; *yat*—because; *rāma-kṛṣṇa-caraṇa*—of the lotus feet of Lord Kṛṣṇa and Balarāma; *sparaśa*—by the touch; *pramodaḥ*—jubilant; *mānam*—respect; *tanoti*—offers; *saha*—with; *go-gaṇayoḥ*—the cows, calves and cowherd boys; *tayoḥ*—to Them (Śrī Kṛṣṇa and Balarāma); *yat*—because; *pānīya*—with drinking water; *sūyavasa*—very soft grass; *kandara*—caves; *kanda-mūlaiḥ*—and edible roots.

TRANSLATION

Of all the devotees, this Govardhana Hill is the best! O my friends, this hill supplies Kṛṣṇa and Balarāma, along with Their calves, cows and cowherd friends, with all kinds of necessities—water for drinking, very soft grass, caves, fruits, flowers and vegetables. In this way the hill offers respects to the Lord. Being touched by the lotus feet of Kṛṣṇa and Balarāma, Govardhana Hill appears very jubilant.

PURPORT

This translation is quoted from Śrīla Prabhupāda's *Caitanya-caritāmṛta* (*Madhya* 18.34).

Śrīla Viśvanātha Cakravartī Ṭhākura explains the opulence of Govardhana Hill as follows: *Pānīya* refers to the fragrant, cool water from the Govardhana waterfalls, which Kṛṣṇa and Balarāma drink and use to wash Their feet and mouths. Govardhana also offers other beverages, such as honey, mango juice and *pīlu* juice. *Sūyavasa* indicates *dūrvā* grass, used to make the religious offering of *arghya.* Govardhana also has grass that is fragrant, soft and conducive to the strong growth of cows and increased production of milk. Thus this grass is used for feeding the transcendental herds. *Kandara* refers to the caves where Kṛṣṇa, Balarāma and Their friends play, sit and lie down. These caves give pleasure when the weather is too hot or too cold, or when it is raining. Govardhana also features soft roots for eating, jewels for ornamenting the body, flat places for sitting, and lamps and mirrors in the form of smooth stones, glistening water and other natural substances.

TEXT 19

गा गोपकैरनुवनं नयतोरुदार-
वेणुस्वनैः कलपदैस्तनुभृत्सु सख्यः ।
अस्पन्दनं गतिमतां पुलकस्तरुणां
निर्योगपाशकृतलक्षणयोर्विचित्रम् ॥ १९ ॥

gā gopakair anu-vanaṁ nayator udāra
veṇu-svanaiḥ kala-padais tanu-bhṛtsu sakhyaḥ
aspandanaṁ gati-matāṁ pulakas tarūṇāṁ
niryoga-pāśa-kṛta-lakṣaṇayor vicitram

gāḥ—the cows; *gopakaiḥ*—with the cowherd boys; *anu-vanam*—to each forest; *nayatoḥ*—leading; *udāra*—very liberal; *veṇu-svanaiḥ*—by the vibrations of the Lord's flute; *kala-padaiḥ*—having sweet tones; *tanu-bhṛtsu*—among the living entities; *sakhyaḥ*—O friends; *aspandanam*—the lack of movement; *gati-matām*—of those living entities that can move; *pulakaḥ*—the ecstatic jubilation; *tarūṇām*—of the otherwise nonmoving trees; *niryoga-pāśa*—the ropes for binding the rear legs of the cows; *kṛta-lakṣaṇayoḥ*—of those two (Kṛṣṇa and Balarāma), who are characterized by; *vicitram*—wonderful.

TRANSLATION

My dear friends, as Kṛṣṇa and Balarāma pass through the forest with Their cowherd friends, leading Their cows, They carry ropes to bind the cows' rear legs at the time of milking. When Lord Kṛṣṇa plays on His flute, the sweet music causes the moving living entities to become stunned and the nonmoving trees to tremble with ecstasy. These things are certainly very wonderful.

PURPORT

Kṛṣṇa and Balarāma would sometimes wear Their cowherding ropes on Their heads and sometimes carry them on Their shoulders, and thus They were beautifully decorated with all the equipment of cowherd boys.

Śrīla Viśvanātha Cakravartī Ṭhākura explains that the ropes of Kṛṣṇa and Balarāma are made of yellow cloth and have clusters of pearls at both ends. Sometimes They wear these ropes around Their turbans, and the ropes thus become wonderful decorations.

TEXT 20

एवंविधा भगवतो या वृन्दावनचारिणः ।
वर्णयन्त्यो मिथो गोप्यः क्रीडास्तन्मयतां ययुः ॥ २० ॥

evaṁ-vidhā bhagavato
yā vṛndāvana-cāriṇaḥ
varṇayantyo mitho gopyaḥ
krīḍās tan-mayatāṁ yayuḥ

evam-vidhāḥ—such; *bhagavataḥ*—of the Supreme Personality of Godhead; *yāḥ*—which; *vṛndāvana-cāriṇaḥ*—who was wandering in the Vṛndāvana forest; *varṇayantyaḥ*—engaged in describing; *mithaḥ*—among one another; *gopyaḥ*—the *gopīs; krīḍaḥ*—the pastimes; *tat-mayatām*—fullness in ecstatic meditation upon Him; *yayuḥ*—they attained.

TRANSLATION

Thus narrating to one another the playful pastimes of the Supreme Personality of Godhead as He wandered about in the Vṛndāvana forest, the gopīs became fully absorbed in thoughts of Him.

PURPORT

In this regard Śrīla Prabhupāda comments, "This is the perfect example of Kṛṣṇa consciousness: to somehow or other remain always engrossed in thoughts of Kṛṣṇa. The vivid example is always present in the behavior of the *gopis;* therefore Lord Caitanya declared that no one can worship the Supreme Lord by any method that is better than the method of the *gopīs.* The *gopīs* were not born in very high *brāhmaṇa* or *kṣatriya* families; they were born in the families of *vaiśyas,* and not in big mercantile communities but in the families of cowherd men. They were not very well educated, although they heard all sorts of knowledge from the *brāhmaṇas,* the authorities of Vedic knowledge. The *gopīs'* only purpose was to remain always absorbed in thoughts of Kṛṣṇa."

Thus end the purports of the humble servants of His Divine Grace A.C. Bhaktivedanta Swami Prabhupāda to the Tenth Canto, Twenty-first Chapter, of the Śrīmad-Bhāgavatam, *entitled "The Gopīs Glorify the Song of Kṛṣṇa's Flute."*

CHAPTER TWENTY-TWO

Kṛṣṇa Steals the Garments of the Unmarried Gopīs

This chapter describes how the marriageable daughters of the cowherd men worshiped Kātyāyanī to get Lord Śrī Kṛṣṇa as their husband, and how Kṛṣṇa stole the garments of the young girls and gave the girls benedictions.

During the month of Mārgaśīrṣa, every day early in the morning the young daughters of the cowherds would take one another's hands and, singing of Kṛṣṇa's transcendental qualities, go to the Yamunā to bathe. Desiring to obtain Kṛṣṇa as their husband, they would then worship the goddess Kātyāyanī with incense, flowers and other items.

One day, the young *gopīs* left their garments on the shore as usual and began playing in the water while chanting of Lord Kṛṣṇa's activities. Suddenly Kṛṣṇa Himself came there, took away all the garments and climbed a nearby *kadamba* tree. Wanting to tease the *gopīs,* Kṛṣṇa said, "I understand how fatigued you *gopīs* are from your austerities, so please come onto the shore and take back your clothes."

The *gopīs* then pretended to become angry and said the cold water of the Yamunā was giving them great pain. If Kṛṣṇa did not give them back their garments, they said, they would inform King Kaṁsa of all that had happened. But if He did give the clothes back, they would willingly carry out His orders in the mood of humble servants.

Śrī Kṛṣṇa replied that He had no fear of King Kaṁsa, and that if the girls really intended to follow His command and be His maidservants, they should each immediately come onto the shore and take their respective garments. The girls, trembling from the cold, climbed out of the water with their two hands covering their private parts. Kṛṣṇa, who felt great affection for them, again spoke: "Because while executing a vow you bathed in the water naked, you have committed an offense against the demigods, and to counteract it you should offer obeisances with joined palms. Then your vow of austerity will achieve its full result."

The *gopīs* followed this instruction and, folding their hands in respect, offered obeisances to Śrī Kṛṣṇa. Satisfied, He gave them back their clothing. But the young girls had become so attracted to Him that they could not leave. Understanding their minds, Kṛṣṇa said that He knew they had worshiped Kātyāyanī to get Him as their husband. Because they had offered their hearts to Him, their desires would never again become tainted by the mood of materialistic enjoyment, just as fried barleycorns can no longer grow into shoots. Next autumn, He told them, their most cherished desire would be fulfilled.

Then the *gopīs,* fully satisfied, returned to Vraja, and Śrī Kṛṣṇa and His cowherd friends went off to a distant place to graze the cows.

Sometime later, when the boys felt disturbed by the great heat of summer, they took shelter at the base of a tree that stood just like an umbrella. The Lord then said that the life of a tree is most excellent, for even while feeling pain a tree continues to protect others from heat, rain, snow and so on. With its leaves, flowers, fruits, shade, roots, bark, wood, fragrance, sap, ashes, pulp and sprouts, a tree fulfills the desires of everyone. This kind of life is ideal. Indeed, said Kṛṣṇa, the perfection of life is to act with one's vital energy, wealth, intelligence and words for the benefit of all.

After the Lord had glorified the trees in this way, the entire company went to the Yamunā, where the cowherd boys let the cows drink the sweet water and also drank some themselves.

TEXT 1

श्रीशुक उवाच
हेमन्ते प्रथमे मासि नन्दव्रजकुमारिकाः ।
चेरुर्हविष्यं भुञ्जानाः कात्यायन्यर्चनव्रतम् ॥ १ ॥

śrī-śuka uvāca
hemante prathame māsi
nanda-vraja-kamārikāḥ
cerur haviṣyaṁ bhuñjānāḥ
kātyāyany-arcana-vratam

śrī-śukaḥ uvāca—Śrī Śukadeva Gosvāmī said; *hemante*—during the winter; *prathame*—in the first; *māsi*—month; *nanda-vraja*—of the cowherd village of Nanda Mahārāja; *kumārikāḥ*—the unmarried young girls; *ceruḥ*—performed; *haviṣyam*—unseasoned *khichrī; bhuñjānāḥ*—subsisting on; *kātyāyanī*—of the goddess Kātyāyanī; *arcana-vratam*—the vow of worship.

TRANSLATION

Śukadeva Gosvāmī said: During the first month of the winter season, the young unmarried girls of Gokula observed the vow of worshiping Goddess Kātyāyanī. For the entire month they ate only unspiced khichrī.

PURPORT

The word *hemante* refers to the month of Mārgaśīrṣa—from approximately the middle of November to the middle of December, according to the Western calendar. In Chapter Twenty-two of *Kṛṣṇa, the Supreme Personality of Godhead,* Śrīla Prabhupāda comments that the *gopīs* "first ate *haviṣyānna,* a kind of food prepared by boiling together mung *dāl* and rice without any spices or turmeric. According to Vedic injunction, this kind of food is recommended to purify the body before one enacts a ritualistic ceremony."

TEXTS 2–3

आप्लुत्याम्भसि कालिन्द्या जलान्ते चोदितेऽरुणे ।
कृत्वा प्रतिकृतिं देवीमानर्चुर्नृप सैकतीम् ॥ २ ॥
गन्धैर्माल्यैः सुरभिभिर्बलिभिर्धूपदीपकैः ।
उच्चावचैश्चोपहारैः प्रवालफलतण्डुलैः ॥ ३ ॥

āplutyāmbhasi kālindyā
jalānte codite'ruṇe
kṛtvā pratikṛtiṁ devīm
ānarcur nṛpa saikatīm

gandhair mālyaiḥ surabhibhir
balibhir dhūpa-dīpakaiḥ
uccāvacaiś copahāraiḥ
pravāla-phala-taṇḍulaiḥ

āplutya—bathing; *ambhasi*—in the water; *kālindyāḥ*—of the Yamunā; *jala-ante*—on the shore of the river; *ca*—and; *udite*—as was arising; *aruṇe*—the dawn; *kṛtvā*—making; *prati-kṛtim*—a deity; *devīm*—the goddess; *ānarcuḥ*—they worshiped; *nṛpa*—O King Parīkṣit; *saikatīm*—made of earth; *gandhaiḥ*—with sandalwood pulp and other fragrant articles; *mālyaiḥ*—with garlands; *surabhibhiḥ*—fragrant; *balibhiḥ*—with gifts; *dhūpa-dīpakaiḥ*—with incense and lamps; *ucca-avacaiḥ*—opulent and also simple; *ca*—and;

upahāraiḥ—with presentations; *pravāla*—newly grown leaves; *phala*—fruit; *taṇḍulaiḥ*—and betel nuts.

TRANSLATION

My dear King, after they had bathed in the water of the Yamunā just as the sun was rising, the gopīs made an earthen deity of Goddess Durgā on the riverbank. Then they worshiped her with such aromatic substances as sandalwood pulp, along with other items both opulent and simple, including lamps, fruits, betel nuts, newly grown leaves, and fragrant garlands and incense.

PURPORT

The word *balibhiḥ* in this verse indicates offerings of clothing, ornaments, food and so on.

TEXT 4

कात्यायनि महामाये महायोगिन्यधीश्वरि ।
नन्दगोपसुतं देवि पतिं मे कुरु ते नमः ।
इति मन्त्रं जपन्त्यस्ताः पूजां चक्रुः कमारिकाः ॥ ४ ॥

kātyāyani mahā-māye
mahā-yoginy adhīśvari
nanda-gopa-sutaṁ devi
patiṁ me kuru te namaḥ
iti mantraṁ japantyas tāḥ
pūjāṁ cakruḥ kumārikāḥ

kātyāyanī—O Goddess Kātyāyanī; *mahā-māye*—O great potency; *mahā-yogini*—O possessor of great mystic power; *adhīśvari*—O mighty controller; *nanda-gopa-sutam*—the son of Mahārāja Nanda; *devi*—O goddess; *patim*—the husband; *me*—my; *kuru*—please make; *te*—unto you; *namaḥ*—my obeisances; *iti*—with these words; *mantram*—the hymn; *japantyaḥ*—chanting; *tāḥ*—they; *pūjām*—worship; *cakruḥ*—performed; *kumārikāḥ*—the unmarried girls.

TRANSLATION

Each of the young unmarried girls performed her worship while chanting the following mantra. "O Goddess Kātyāyanī, O great potency of

the Lord, O possessor of great mystic power and mighty controller of all, please make the son of Nanda Mahārāja my husband. I offer my obeisances unto you."

PURPORT

According to various *ācāryas,* the goddess Durgā mentioned in this verse is not the illusory energy of Kṛṣṇa called Māyā but rather the internal potency of the Lord known as Yoga-māyā. The distinction between the internal and external, or illusory, potency of the Lord is described in the *Nārada-pañcarātra,* in the conversation between Śruti and Vidyā:

jānāty ekāparā kāntaṁ
saivā durgā tad-ātmikā
yā parā paramā śaktir
mahā-viṣṇu-svarūpiṇī

yasyā vijñāna-mātreṇa
parāṇāṁ paramātmanaḥ
muhūrtād deva-devasya
prāptir bhavati nānyathā

ekeyaṁ prema-sarvasva
svabhāvā gokuleśvarī
anayā su-labho jñeya
ādi-devo'khileśvaraḥ

asyā āvārika-śaktir
mahā-māyākhileśvarī
yayā mugdaṁ jagat sarvaṁ
sarve dehābhimāninaḥ

"The Lord's inferior potency, known as Durgā, is dedicated to His loving service. Being the Lord's potency, this inferior energy is nondifferent from Him. There is another, superior potency, whose form is on the same spiritual level as that of God Himself. Simply by scientifically understanding this supreme potency, one can immediately achieve the Supreme Soul of all souls, who is the Lord of all lords. There is no other process to achieve Him. That supreme potency of the Lord is known as Gokuleśvarī, the goddess of Gokula. Her nature is to be completely absorbed in love of God, and through Her one can easily obtain the primeval God, the Lord of all that be. This internal potency of the Lord has a covering potency, known as Mahā-māyā, who rules the material world. In fact she bewilders the entire universe, and thus everyone within the universe falsely identifies himself with the material body."

From the above we can understand that the internal and external, or superior and inferior, potencies of the Supreme Lord are personified as Yoga-māyā and Mahā-māyā, respectively. The name Durgā is sometimes used to refer to the internal, superior potency, as stated in the *Pañcarātra*: "In all *mantras* used to worship Kṛṣṇa, the presiding deity is known as Durgā." Thus in the transcendental sound vibrations glorifying and worshiping the Absolute Truth, Kṛṣṇa, the presiding deity of the particular *mantra* or hymn is called Durgā. The name Durgā therefore refers also to that personality who functions as the internal potency of the Lord and who is thus on the platform of *śuddha-sattva,* pure transcendental existence. This internal potency is understood to be Kṛṣṇa's sister, known also as Ekānaṁśā or Subhadrā. This is the Durgā who was worshiped by the *gopīs* in Vṛndāvana. Several *ācāryas* have pointed out that ordinary people are sometimes bewildered and think that the names Mahā-māyā and Durgā refer exclusively to the external potency of the Lord.

Even if we accept hypothetically that the *gopīs* were worshiping the external Māyā, there is no fault on their part, since in their pastimes of loving Kṛṣṇa they were acting as ordinary members of society. Śrīla Prabhupāda comments in this regard: "The Vaiṣṇavas generally do not worship any demigods. Śrīla Narottama dāsa Ṭhākura has strictly forbidden all worship of the demigods for anyone who wants to advance in pure devotional service. Yet the *gopīs,* who are beyond compare in their affection for Kṛṣṇa, were seen to worship Durgā. The worshipers of demigods also sometimes mention that the *gopīs* also worshiped Goddess Durgā, but we must understand the purpose of the *gopīs.* Generally, people worship Goddess Durgā for some material benediction. Here, the *gopīs* could adopt any means to satisfy or serve Kṛṣṇa. That was the superexcellent characteristic of the *gopīs.* They worshiped Goddess Durgā completely for one month in order to have Kṛṣṇa as their husband. Every day they prayed for Kṛṣṇa, the son of Nanda Mahārāja, to become their husband."

The conclusion is that a sincere devotee of Kṛṣṇa will never imagine any material quality to exist in the transcendental *gopīs,* who are the most exalted devotees of the Lord. The only motivation in all their activities was simply to love and satisfy Kṛṣṇa, and if we foolishly consider their activities to be mundane in any way, it will be impossible for us to understand Kṛṣṇa consciousness.

TEXT 5

एवं मासं व्रतं चेरुः कुमार्यः कृष्णचेतसः ।
भद्रकालीं समानर्चुर्भूयान्नन्दसुतः पतिः ॥ ५ ॥

evaṁ māsaṁ vratam ceruḥ
kumāryaḥ kṛṣṇa-cetasaḥ
bhadrakālīṁ samānarcur
bhūyān nanda-sutaḥ patiḥ

evam—in this manner; *māsam*—an entire month; *vratam*—their vow; *ceruḥ*—they executed; *kumāryaḥ*—the girls; *kṛṣṇa-cetasaḥ*—their minds absorbed in Kṛṣṇa; *bhadra-kālīm*—the goddess Kātyāyanī; *samānarcuḥ*—they properly worshiped; *bhūyāt*—may He become; *nanda-sutaḥ*—the son of King Nanda; *patiḥ*—my husband.

TRANSLATION

Thus for an entire month the girls carried out their vow and properly worshiped the goddess Bhadrakālī, fully absorbing their minds in Kṛṣṇa and meditating upon the following thought: "May the son of King Nanda become my husband."

TEXT 6

ऊषस्युत्थाय गोत्रैः स्वैरन्योन्याबद्धबाहवः ।
कृष्णमुच्चैर्जगुर्यान्त्यः कालिन्द्यां स्नातुमन्वहम् ॥ ६ ॥

ūṣasy utthāya gotraiḥ svair
anyonyābaddha-bāhavaḥ
kṛṣṇam uccair jagur yāntyaḥ
kālindyāṁ snātum anvaham

ūṣasi—at dawn; *utthāya*—rising; *gotraiḥ*—by their names; *svaiḥ*—proper; *anyonya*—one with another; *ābaddha*—holding; *bāhavaḥ*—their hands; *kṛṣṇam*—in glorification of Kṛṣṇa; *uccaiḥ*—loudly; *jaguḥ*—they sang; *yāntyaḥ*—while going; *kālindyām*—to the Yamunā; *snātum*—in order to bathe; *anu-aham*—each day.

TRANSLATION

Each day they rose at dawn. Calling out to one another by name, they all held hands and loudly sang the glories of Kṛṣṇa while going to the Kālindī to take their bath.

TEXT 7

नद्याः कदाचिदागत्य तीरे निक्षिप्य पूर्ववत् ।
वासांसि कृष्णं गायन्त्यो विजह्रुः सलिले मुदा ॥ ७ ॥

nadyāḥ kadācid āgatya
tīre nikṣipya pūrva-vat
vāsāṁsi kṛṣṇaṁ gāyantyo
vijahruḥ salile mudā

nadyāḥ—of the river; *kadācit*—once; *āgatya*—coming; *tīre*—to the shore; *nikṣipya*—throwing down; *pūrva-vat*—as previously; *vāsāṁsi*—their clothing; *kṛṣṇam*—about Kṛṣṇa; *gāyantyaḥ*—singing; *vijahruḥ*—they played; *salile*—in the water; *mudā*—with pleasure.

TRANSLATION

One day they came to the riverbank and, putting aside their clothing as they had done before, happily played in the water while singing the glories of Kṛṣṇa.

PURPORT

According to Śrīla Viśvanātha Cakravartī Ṭhākura, this incident occurred on the day the young *gopīs* completed their vow, which was a full-moon day. To celebrate the successful completion of their vow, the girls invited young Rādhārāṇī—the daughter of Vṛṣabhānu and the special object of their affection—along with other important *gopīs,* and brought them all to the river to bathe. Their playing in the water was meant to serve as the *avabhṛtha-snāna,* the ceremonial bath taken immediately upon the completion of a Vedic sacrifice.

Śrīla Prabhupāda comments as follows: "It is an old system among Indian girls and women that when they take bath in the river they place their garments on the bank and dip into the water completely naked. The portion of the river where the girls and women bathe was strictly prohibited to any male, and this is still the system. The Supreme Personality of Godhead, knowing the minds of the unmarried young *gopīs,* awarded them their desired objective. They had prayed for Kṛṣṇa to become their husband, and Kṛṣṇa wanted to fulfill their desires."

TEXT 8

भगवांस्तदभिप्रेत्य कृष्णो योगेश्वरेश्वरः ।
वयस्यैरावृतस्तत्र गतस्तत्कर्मसिद्धये ॥ ८ ॥

bhagavāṁs tad abhipretya
kṛṣno yogeśvareśvaraḥ
vayasyair āvṛtas tatra
gatas tat-karma-siddhaye

bhagavān—the Supreme Personality of Godhead; *tat*—that; *abhipretya*—seeing; *kṛṣṇaḥ*—Lord Kṛṣṇa; *yoga-īśvara-īśvaraḥ*—the master of all masters of mystic power; *vayasyaiḥ*—by young companions; *āvṛtaḥ*—surrounded; *tatra*—there; *gataḥ*—went; *tat*—of those girls; *karma*—the ritualistic activities; *siddhaye*—for assuring the result.

TRANSLATION

Lord Kṛṣṇa, the Supreme Personality of Godhead and master of all masters of mystic yoga, was aware of what the gopīs were doing, and thus He went there surrounded by His young companions to award the gopīs the perfection of their endeavor.

PURPORT

As the master of all masters of mystic power, Lord Kṛṣṇa could easily understand the desires of the *gopīs,* and He could also fulfill them. The *gopīs,* like all young girls from respectable families, considered the embarrassment of appearing naked before a young boy to be worse than giving up their lives. Yet Lord Kṛṣṇa made them come out of the water and bow down to Him. Although the bodily forms of the *gopīs* were all fully developed, and although Kṛṣṇa met them in a secluded place and brought them fully under His control, because the Lord is completely transcendental there was not a trace of material desire in His mind. Lord Kṛṣṇa is the ocean of transcendental bliss, and He wanted to share His bliss with the *gopīs* on the spiritual platform, completely free of ordinary lust.

Śrīla Viśvanātha Cakravartī Ṭhākura explains that the companions of Kṛṣṇa mentioned here were mere toddlers two or three years old. They were completely naked and were unaware of the difference between male and female. When Kṛṣṇa went out to herd the cows, they followed Him because they were so attached to Him that they could not bear to be without His association.

TEXT 9

तासां वासांस्युपादाय नीपमारुह्य सत्वरः ।
हसद्भिः प्रहसन् बालैः परिहासमुवाच ह ॥ ९ ॥

tāsāṁ vāsāṁsy upādāya
nīpam āruhya satvaraḥ
hasadbhiḥ prahasan bālaiḥ
parihāsam uvāca ha

tāsām—of those girls; *vāsāṁsi*—the garments; *upādāya*—taking; *nīpam*—a *kadamba* tree; *āruhya*—climbing; *satvaraḥ*—quickly; *hasadbhiḥ*—who were laughing; *prahasan*—Himself laughing loudly; *bālaiḥ*—with the boys; *parihāsam*—joking words; *uvāca ha*—He spoke.

TRANSLATION

Taking the girls' garments, He quickly climbed to the top of a kadamba tree. Then, as He laughed loudly and His companions also laughed, He addressed the girls jokingly.

TEXT 10

अत्रागत्याबलाः कामं स्वं स्वं वासः प्रगृह्यताम् ।
सत्यं ब्रुवाणि नो नर्म यद् यूयं व्रतकर्शिताः ॥ १० ॥

atrāgatyābalāḥ kāmaṁ
svaṁ svaṁ vāsaḥ pragṛhyatām
satyaṁ bruvāṇi no narma
yad yūyaṁ vrata-karśitāḥ

atra—here; *āgatya*—coming; *abalāḥ*—O girls; *kāmam*—as you wish; *svam svam*—each your own; *vāsaḥ*—clothing; *pragṛhyatām*—please take; *satyam*—the truth; *bruvāṇi*—I am speaking; *na*—not; *u*—rather; *narma*—jest; *yat*—because; *yūyam*—you; *vrata*—by your vow of austerity; *karśitāḥ*—fatigued.

TRANSLATION

[Lord Kṛṣṇa said:] My dear girls, you may each come here as you wish and take back your garments. I'm telling you the truth and am not joking with you, since I see you're fatigued from executing austere vows.

TEXT 11

न मयोदितपूर्वं वा अनृतं तदिमे विदुः ।
एकैकशः प्रतीच्छध्वं सहैवेति सुमध्यमाः ॥ ११ ॥

na mayodita-pūrvaṁ vā
anṛtaṁ tad ime viduḥ
ekaikaśaḥ pratīcchadhvaṁ
sahaiveti su-madhyamāḥ

na—never; *mayā*—by Me; *udita*—spoken; *pūrvam*—previously; *vai*—definitely; *anṛtam*—anything false; *tat*—that; *ime*—these young boys; *viduḥ*—know; *eka-ekaśaḥ*—one by one; *pratīcchadhvam*—pick out (your garments); *saha*—or all together; *eva*—indeed; *iti*—thus; *su-madhyamāḥ*—O slender-waisted girls.

TRANSLATION

I have never before spoken a lie, and these boys know it. Therefore, O slender-waisted girls, please come forward, either one by one or all together, and pick out your clothes.

TEXT 12

तस्य तत्क्ष्वेलितं दृष्ट्वा गोप्यः प्रेमपरिप्लुताः ।
व्रीडिताः प्रेक्ष्य चान्योन्यं जातहासा न निर्ययुः ॥ १२ ॥

tasya tat kṣvelitaṁ dṛṣṭvā
gopyaḥ prema-pariplutāḥ
vrīḍitāḥ prekṣya cānyonyaṁ
jāta-hāsā na niryayuḥ

tasya—His; *tat*—that; *kṣvelitam*—joking behavior; *dṛṣṭvā*—seeing; *gopyaḥ*—the *gopīs; prema-pariplutāḥ*—fully immersed in pure love of Godhead; *vrīḍitāḥ*—embarrassed; *prekṣya*—glancing; *ca*—and; *anyonyam*—

upon one another; *jāta-hāsāḥ*—beginning to laugh; *na niryayuḥ*—they did not come out.

TRANSLATION

Seeing how Kṛṣṇa was joking with them, the gopīs became fully immersed in love for Him, and as they glanced at each other they began to laugh and joke among themselves, even in their embarrassment. But still they did not come out of the water.

PURPORT

Śrīla Viśvanātha Cakravartī Ṭhākura explains this verse as follows:

"The *gopīs* were from most respectable families, and they might have argued with Kṛṣṇa:'Why don't You simply leave our clothes on the bank of the river and go away?'

"Kṛṣṇa might have replied,'But there are so many of you that some of the girls might take clothes belonging to another.'

"The *gopīs* would reply,'We are honest and never steal anything. We never touch another's property.'

"Then Kṛṣṇa would say,'If that's true, then simply come and get your clothes. What is the difficulty?'

"When the *gopīs* saw Kṛṣṇa's determination, they were filled with loving ecstasy. Although embarrassed, they were overjoyed to receive such attention from Kṛṣṇa. He was joking with them as if they were His wives or girlfriends, and the *gopīs'* only desire was to achieve such a relationship with Him. At the same time, they were embarrassed to be seen naked by Him. But still they could not help laughing at His joking words and even began to joke among themselves, one *gopī* urging another,'Go ahead, you go first, and let us see if Kṛṣṇa plays any tricks on you. Then we will go later.'"

TEXT 13

एवं ब्रुवति गोविन्दे नर्मणाक्षिप्तचेतसः ।
आकण्ठमग्नाः शीतोदे वेपमानास्तमब्रुवन् ॥ १३ ॥

evaṁ bruvati govinde
narmaṇākṣipta-cetasaḥ
ā-kaṇṭha-magnāḥ śītode
vepamānās tam abruvan

evam—thus; *bruvati*—speaking; *govinde*—Lord Govinda; *narmaṇā*—by His joking words; *ākṣipta*—agitated; *cetasaḥ*—their minds; *ā-kaṇṭha*—up to their necks; *magnāḥ*—submerged; *śīta*—cold; *ude*—in the water; *vepamānāḥ*—shivering; *tam*—to Him; *abruvan*—they spoke.

TRANSLATION

As Śrī Govinda spoke to the gopīs in this way, His joking words completely captivated their minds. Submerged up to their necks in the cold water, they began to shiver. Thus they addressed Him as follows.

PURPORT

Śrīla Viśvanātha Cakravartī Ṭhākura gives the following example of joking between Kṛṣṇa and the *gopīs.*

Kṛṣṇa: O birdlike girls, if you do not come here, then with these garments caught in the branches I will make a swing and a hammock. I need to lie down, since I have spent the entire night awake and am now becoming sleepy.

Gopīs: Our dear cowherd boy, Your cows, greedy for grass, have gone into a cave. So You must quickly go there to herd them back on the proper path.

Kṛṣṇa: Come now, My dear cowherd girls, you must quickly go from here to Vraja and perform your household duties. Don't become a disturbance to your parents and other elders.

Gopīs: Our dear Kṛṣṇa, we will not go home for an entire month, for it is by the order of our parents and other elders that we are executing this vow of fasting, the Kātyāyanī-vrata.

Kṛṣṇa: My dear austere ladies, I too, by the strength of seeing you, have now developed a surprising mood of detachment from family life. I wish to stay here for a month and execute the vow of dwelling in the clouds. And if you show mercy to Me, I can come down from here and observe the vow of fasting in your company.

The *gopīs* were completely captivated by Kṛṣṇa's joking words, but out of shyness they submerged themselves in the water up to their necks. Shaking from the cold, they addressed Kṛṣṇa as follows.

TEXT 14

मानयं भोः कृथास्त्वां तु नन्दगोपसुतं प्रियम् ।
जानीमोऽगं व्रजश्लाघ्यं देहि वासांसि वेपिताः ॥ १४ ॥

mānayaṁ bhoḥ kṛthās tvāṁ tu
nanda-gopa-sutaṁ priyam
jānīmo'ṅga vraja-ślāghyaṁ
dehi vāsāṁsi vepitāḥ

mā—do not; *anayam*—injustice; *bhoḥ*—our dear Kṛṣṇa; *kṛthāḥ*—do; *tvām*—You; *tu*—on the other hand; *nanda-gopa*—of Mahārāja Nanda; *sutam*—the son; *priyam*—loved; *jānīmaḥ*—we know; *aṅga*—O dear one; *vraja-ślāghyam*—renowned throughout Vraja; *dehi*—please give; *vāsāṁsi*—our garments; *vepitāḥ*—(to us) who are shivering.

TRANSLATION

[The gopīs said:] Dear Kṛṣṇa, don't be unfair! We know that You are the respectable son of Nanda and that You are honored by everyone in Vraja. You are also very dear to us. Please give us back our clothes. We are shivering in the cold water.

TEXT 15

श्यामसुन्दर ते दास्यः करवाम तवोदितम् ।
देहि वासांसि धर्मज्ञ नो चेद् राज्ञे ब्रुवाम हे ॥ १५ ॥

śyāmasundara te dāsyaḥ
karavāma tavoditam
dehi vāsāṁsi dharma-jña
no ced rājñe bruvāma he

śyāmasundara—O Lord Śyāmasundara; *te*—Your; *dāsyaḥ*—maidservants; *karavāma*—we shall do; *tava*—by You; *uditam*—what is spoken; *dehi*—please give; *vāsāṁsi*—our clothing; *dharma-jña*—O knower of religion; *na*—not; *u*—indeed; *cet*—if; *rājñe*—to the king; *bruvāmaḥ*—we shall tell; *he*—O Kṛṣṇa.

TRANSLATION

O Śyāmasundara, we are Your maidservants and must do whatever You say. But give us back our clothing. You know what the religious principles are, and if You don't give us our clothes we will have to tell the king. Please!

TEXT 16

श्रीभगवानुवाच
भवत्यो यदि मे दास्यो मयोक्तं वा करिष्यथ ।
अत्रागत्य स्ववासांसि प्रतीच्छत शुचिस्मिताः ।
नो चेन्नाहं प्रदास्ये किं क्रुद्धो राजा करिष्यति ॥ १६ ॥

śrī-bhagavān uvāca
bhavatyo yadi me dāsyo
mayoktaṁ vā kariṣyatha
atrāgatya sva-vāsāṁsi
pratīcchata śuci-smitāḥ
no cen nāhaṁ pradāsye kiṁ
kruddho rājā kariṣyati

śrī-bhagavān uvāca—the Supreme Personality of Godhead said; *bhavatyaḥ*—you; *yadi*—if; *me*—My; *dāsyaḥ*—servants; *mayā*—by Me; *uktam*—what has been spoken; *vā*—or; *kariṣyatha*—you will do; *atra*—here; *āgatya*—coming; *sva-vāsāṁsi*—your own garments; *pratīcchata*—pick out; *śuci*—fresh; *smitāḥ*—whose smiles; *na u*—not; *cet*—if; *na*—not; *aham*—I; *pradāsye*—will give; *kim*—what; *kruddhaḥ*—angry; *rājā*—the king; *kariṣyati*—will be able to do.

TRANSLATION

The Supreme Personality of Godhead said: If you girls are actually My maidservants, and if you will really do what I say, then come here with your innocent smiles and let each girl pick out her clothes. If you don't do what I say, I won't give them back to you. And even if the king becomes angry, what can he do?

PURPORT

Śrīla Prabhupāda comments, "When the *gopīs* saw that Kṛṣṇa was strong and determined, they had no alternative but to abide by His order."

TEXT 17

ततो जलाशयात् सर्वा दारिकाः शीतवेपिताः ।
पाणिभ्यां योनिमाच्छाद्य प्रोत्तेरुः शीतकर्शिताः ॥ १७ ॥

tato jalāśayāt sarvā
dārikāḥ śīta-vepitāḥ
pāṇibhyāṁ yonim ācchādya
protteruḥ śīta-karśitāḥ

tataḥ—then; *jala-āśayāt*—out of the river; *sarvāḥ*—all; *dārikāḥ*—the young girls; *śīta-vepitāḥ*—shivering from the cold; *pāṇibhyām*—with their hands; *yonim*—their pubic area; *ācchādya*—covering; *protteruḥ*—they came up; *śīta-karśitāḥ*—pained by the cold.

TRANSLATION

Then, shivering from the painful cold, all the young girls rose up out of the water, covering their pubic area with their hands.

PURPORT

The *gopīs* had assured Kṛṣṇa that they were His eternal servants and would do whatever He said, and thus they were now defeated by their own words. If they delayed any longer, they thought, some other man might come along, and this would be unbearable for them. The *gopīs* loved Kṛṣṇa so much that even in that awkward situation their attachment to Him was increasing more and more, and they were very eager to stay in His company. Thus they did not even consider drowning themselves in the river because of the embarrassing situation.

They concluded that they could do nothing but go forward to their beloved Kṛṣṇa, putting aside their embarrassment. Thus the *gopīs* assured each other that there was no alternative and rose up out of the water to meet Him.

TEXT 18

भगवानाहता वीक्ष्य शुद्धभावप्रसादितः ।
स्कन्धे निधाय वासांसि प्रीतः प्रोवाच सस्मितम्॥ १८ ॥

bhagavān āhatā vīkṣya
śuddha-bhāva-prasāditaḥ
skandhe nidhāya vāsāṁsi
prītaḥ provāca sa-smitam

bhagavān—the Supreme Lord; *āhatāḥ*—struck; *vīkṣya*—seeing; *śuddha*—pure; *bhāva*—by their loving affection; *prasāditaḥ*—satisfied; *skandhe*—

upon His shoulder; *nidhāya*—placing; *vāsāṁsi*—their garments; *prītaḥ*—lovingly; *provāca*—spoke; *sa-smitam*—while smiling.

TRANSLATION

When the Supreme Lord saw how the gopīs were struck with embarrassment, He was satisfied by their pure loving affection. Putting their clothes on His shoulder, the Lord smiled and spoke to them with affection.

PURPORT

Śrīla Prabhupāda comments: "The *gopīs'* simple presentation was so pure that Lord Kṛṣṇa immediately became pleased with them. All the unmarried *gopīs* who prayed to Kātyāyanī to have Kṛṣṇa as their husband were thus satisfied. A woman cannot be naked before any male except her husband. The unmarried *gopīs* desired Kṛṣṇa as their husband, and He fulfilled their desire in this way."

For aristocratic girls like the *gopīs,* standing naked before a young boy was worse than death, and yet they decided to give up everything for the pleasure of Lord Kṛṣṇa. He wanted to see the power of their love for Him, and He was completely satisfied by their unalloyed devotion.

TEXT 19

यूयं विवस्त्रा यदपो धृतव्रता
व्यगाहतैतत्तदु देवहेलनम् ।
बद्ध्वाञ्जलिं मूर्ध्न्यपनुत्तयेऽंहसः
कृत्वा नमोऽधोवसनं प्रगृह्यताम् ॥ १९ ॥

yūyaṁ vivastrā yad apo dhṛta-vratā
vyagāhataitat tad u deva-helanam
baddhvāñjaliṁ mūrdhny apanuttaye'ṁhasaḥ
kṛtvā namo'dho-vasanaṁ pragṛhyatām

yūyam—you; *vivastrāḥ*—naked; *yat*—because; *apaḥ*—in the water; *dhṛta-vratāḥ*—while executing a Vedic ritualistic vow; *vyagāhata*—bathed; *etat tat*—this; *u*—indeed; *deva-helanam*—an offense against Varuṇa and the other gods; *baddhvā añjalim*—with palms joined together; *mūrdhni*—upon your heads; *apanuttaye*—for counteracting; *aṁhasaḥ*—your sinful action; *kṛtvā namaḥ*—paying obeisances; *adhaḥ-vasanam*—your lower garments; *pragṛhyatām*—please take back.

TRANSLATION

[Lord Kṛṣṇa said:] You girls bathed naked while executing your vow, and that is certainly an offense against the demigods. To counteract your sin you should offer obeisances while placing your joined palms above your heads. Then you should take back your lower garments.

PURPORT

Kṛṣṇa wanted to see the full surrender of the *gopīs,* and thus He ordered them to offer obeisances with their palms joined above their heads. In other words, the *gopīs* could no longer cover their bodies. We should not foolishly think that Lord Kṛṣṇa is an ordinary lusty boy enjoying the naked beauty of the *gopīs.* Kṛṣṇa is the Supreme Absolute Truth, and He was acting to fulfill the loving desire of the young cowherd girls of Vṛndāvana. In this world we would certainly become lusty in a situation like this. But to compare ourselves to God is a great offense, and because of this offense we will not be able to understand Kṛṣṇa's transcendental position, for we will wrongly take Him to be materially conditioned like ourselves. To lose transcendental sight of Kṛṣṇa is certainly a great disaster for one trying to relish the bliss of the Absolute Truth.

TEXT 20

इत्यच्युतेनाभिहितं व्रजाबला
मत्वा विवस्त्राप्लवनं व्रतच्युतिम् ।
तत्पूर्तिकामास्तदशेषकर्मणां
साक्षात्कृतं नेमुरवद्यमृग् यतः ॥ २० ॥

ity acyutenābhihitaṁ vrajābalā
matvā vivastrāplavanaṁ vrata-cyutim
tat-pūrti-kāmās tad-aśeṣa-karmaṇāṁ
sākṣāt-kṛtaṁ nemur avadya-mṛg yataḥ

iti—in these words; *acyutena*—by the infallible Supreme Lord; *abhihitam*—indicated; *vraja-abalāḥ*—the girls of Vraja; *matvā*—considering; *vivastra*—naked; *āplavanam*—the bathing; *vraja-cyutim*—a falldown from their vow; *tat-pūrti*—the successful completion of that; *kāmāḥ*—intently desiring;

tat—of that performance; *aśeṣa-karmarṇām*—and of unlimited other pious activities; *sākṣāt-kṛtam*—to the directly manifest fruit; *nemuḥ*—they offered their obeisances; *avadya-mṛk*—the cleanser of all sins; *yataḥ*—because.

TRANSLATION

Thus the young girls of Vṛndāvana, considering what Lord Acyuta had told them, accepted that they had suffered a falldown from their vow by bathing naked in the river. But they still desired to successfully complete their vow, and since Lord Kṛṣṇa is Himself the ultimate result of all pious activities, they offered their obeisances to Him to cleanse away all their sins.

PURPORT

The transcendental position of Kṛṣṇa consciousness is clearly described here. The *gopīs* decided that it was better to renounce their so-called family tradition and traditional morality and simply surrender unto the Supreme Lord Kṛṣṇa. This does not mean that the Kṛṣṇa consciousness movement advocates immoral activities. In fact, the devotees of ISKCON practice the highest standard of restraint and morality, but at the same time we recognize the transcendental position of Kṛṣṇa. Lord Kṛṣṇa is God and therefore has no material desire to enjoy young girls in sexual affairs. As will be seen in this chapter, Lord Kṛṣṇa was not at all attracted to enjoying the *gopīs;* rather He was attracted to their love and wanted to satisfy them.

The greatest offense is to imitate the activities of Lord Kṛṣṇa. In India there is a group called *prākṛta-sahajiyā,* who imitate these affairs of Kṛṣṇa and try to enjoy naked young girls in the name of worshiping Kṛṣṇa. The ISKCON movement sternly rejects this mockery of religion, because the greatest offense is for a human being to ludicrously imitate the Supreme Personality of Godhead. In the ISKCON movement there are no cheap incarnations, and it is not possible for a devotee of this movement to promote himself to the position of Kṛṣṇa.

Five hundred years ago Kṛṣṇa appeared as Lord Caitanya Mahāprabhu, who practiced strict celibacy throughout His student life and at the age of twenty-four took *sannyāsa,* a lifelong vow of celibacy. Caitanya Mahāprabhu rigidly avoided contact with women in order to carry out His vow of loving service to Kṛṣṇa. When Kṛṣṇa personally appeared five thousand years ago, He exhibited these wonderful pastimes, which attract our attention. We should not become envious or shocked when we hear that God can perform such pastimes. Our shock is due to our ignorance, because if we tried to perform these activities our bodies would be afflicted by lust. Lord Kṛṣṇa, however, is the Supreme Absolute Truth and is therefore never disturbed by any material desire whatsoever. Thus, this incident—in which the *gopīs* gave up normal standards of morality and, raising their hands to their head, bowed down in compliance with Kṛṣṇa's order—is an example of pure devotional surrender and not a discrepancy in religious principles.

In fact, the *gopīs'* surrender is the perfection of all religion, as Śrīla Prabhupāda describes in *Kṛṣṇa, the Supreme Personality of Godhead:* "The *gopīs* were all simple souls, and whatever Kṛṣṇa said, they took to be true. In order to be freed from the wrath of Varuṇadeva, as well as to fulfill the desired end of their vows and ultimately to please their worshipable Lord, Kṛṣṇa, they immediately abided by His order. Thus they became the greatest lovers of Kṛṣṇa, and His most obedient servitors."

"Nothing can compare to the Kṛṣṇa consciousness of the *gopīs.* Actually, the *gopīs* did not care for Varuṇa or any other demigod; they only wanted to satisfy Kṛṣṇa."

TEXT 21

तास्तथावनता दृष्ट्वा भगवान् देवकीसुतः ।
वासांसि ताभ्यः प्रायच्छत्करुणस्तेन तोषितः ॥ २१ ॥

tās tathāvanatā dṛṣṭvā
bhagavān devakī-sutaḥ
vāsāṁsi tābhyaḥ prāyacchat
karuṇas tena toṣitaḥ

tāḥ—then; *tathā*—thus; *avanatāḥ*—bowed down; *dṛṣṭvā*—seeing; *bhagavān*—the Supreme Personality of Godhead; *devakī-sutaḥ*—Kṛṣṇa, the son of Devakī; *vāsāṁsi*—the garments; *tābhyaḥ*—to them; *prāyacchat*—He returned; *karuṇaḥ*—compassionate; *tena*—by that act; *toṣitaḥ*—satisfied.

TRANSLATION

Seeing them bow down like that, the Supreme Personality of Godhead, the son of Devakī, gave them back their garments, feeling compassionate toward them and satisfied by their act.

TEXT 22

दृढं प्रलब्धास्त्रपया च हापिताः
प्रस्तोभिताः क्रीडनवच्च कारिताः ।
वस्त्राणि चैवापहृतान्यथाप्यमुं
ता नाभ्यसूयन् प्रियसंगनिर्वृताः ॥ २२ ॥

dṛḍhaṁ pralabdhās trapayā ca hāpitāḥ
prastobhitāḥ krīḍana-vac ca kāritāḥ
vastrāṇi caivāpahṛtāny athāpy amuṁ
tā nābhyasūyan priya-saṅga-nirvṛtāḥ

dṛḍham—thoroughly; *pralabdhāḥ*—cheated; *trapayā*—of their shame; *ca*—and; *hāpitāḥ*—deprived; *prastobhitāḥ*—laughed at; *krīḍana-vat*—just like toy dolls; *ca*—and; *kāritāḥ*—made to act; *vastrāṇi*—their clothing; *ca*—and; *eva*—indeed; *apahṛtāni*—stolen; *atha api*—nevertheless; *amum*—toward Him; *tāḥ*—they; *na abhyasūyan*—did not feel inimical; *priya*—of their beloved; *saṅga*—by the association; *nirvṛtāḥ*—joyful.

TRANSLATION

Although the gopīs had been thoroughly cheated, deprived of their modesty, ridiculed and made to act just like toy dolls, and although their clothing had been stolen, they did not feel at all inimical toward Śrī Kṛṣṇa. Rather, they were simply joyful to have this opportunity to associate with their beloved.

PURPORT

Śrīla Prabhupāda comments, "This attitude of the *gopīs* is described by Lord Caitanya Mahāprabhu when He prays,'My dear Lord Kṛṣṇa, You may embrace Me or trample Me under Your feet, or You may make Me brokenhearted by never being present before Me. Whatever You like, You can do, because You have complete freedom to act. But in spite of all of Your dealings, You are My Lord eternally, and I have no other worshipable object.' This is the attitude of the *gopīs* toward Kṛṣṇa."

TEXT 23

परिधाय स्ववासांसि प्रेष्ठसंगमसज्जिताः ।
गृहीतचित्ता नो चेलुस्तस्मिन् लज्जायितेक्षणाः ॥ २३ ॥

paridhāya sva-vāsāṁsi
preṣṭha-saṅgama-sajjitāḥ
gṛhīta-cittā no celus
tasmin lajjāyitekṣaṇāḥ

paridhāya—putting on; *sva-vāsāṁsi*—their own garments; *preṣṭha*—of their beloved; *saṅgama*—by this association; *sajjitāḥ*—becoming completely attached to Him; *gṛhīta*—taken away; *cittāḥ*—whose minds; *na*—could not; *u*—indeed; *celuḥ*—move; *tasmin*—upon Him; *lajjāyita*—full of shyness; *īkṣaṇāḥ*—whose glances.

TRANSLATION

The gopīs were addicted to associating with their beloved Kṛṣṇa, and thus they became captivated by Him. Thus, even after putting their clothes on they did not move. They simply remained where they were, shyly glancing at Him.

PURPORT

By association with their beloved Kṛṣṇa, the *gopīs* had become more attached to Him than ever. Just as Kṛṣṇa had stolen their clothes, He had also stolen their minds and their love. The *gopīs* interpreted the whole incident as proof that Kṛṣṇa was also attached to them. Otherwise, why would He have gone to the trouble of playing with them in this way? Because they thought that Kṛṣṇa was now attached to them, they glanced at Him with shyness, and being stunned by the rising of their ecstatic love, they could not move from where they stood. Kṛṣṇa had overcome their shyness and forced them to come out of the water naked, but now, having dressed properly, they again became shy in His presence. In fact, this incident increased their humbleness before Kṛṣṇa. They did not want Kṛṣṇa to see them staring at Him, but they cautiously took the opportunity to glance at the Lord.

TEXT 24

तासां विज्ञाय भगवान् स्वपादस्पर्शकाम्यया।
धृतव्रतानां संकल्पमाह दामोदरोऽबला: ॥ २४ ॥

tāsāṁ vijñāya bhagavān
sva-pāda-sparśa-kāmyayā

dhṛta-vratānāṁ saṅkalpam
āha dāmodaro'balāḥ

tāsām—of these girls; *vijñāya*—understanding; *bhagavān*—the Supreme Personality of Godhead; *sva-pāda*—of His own feet; *sparśa*—for the touch; *kāmyayā*—with the desire; *dhṛta-vratānām*—who had taken their vow; *saṅkalpam*—the motivation; *āha*—spoke; *dāmodaraḥ*—Lord Dāmodara; *abalāḥ*—to the girls.

TRANSLATION

The Supreme Lord understood the determination of the gopīs in executing their strict vow. The Lord also knew that the girls desired to touch His lotus feet, and thus Lord Dāmodara, Kṛṣṇa, spoke to them as follows.

TEXT 25

संकल्पो विदितः साध्व्यो भवतीनां मदर्चनम् ।
मयानुमोदितः सोऽसौ सत्यो भवितुमर्हति ॥ २५ ॥

saṅkalpo viditaḥ sādhvyo
bhavatīnāṁ mad-arcanam
mayānumoditaḥ so'sau
satyo bhavitum arhati

saṅkalpaḥ—the motivation; *viditaḥ*—understood; *sādhvyaḥ*—O pious girls; *bhavatīnām*—your; *mat-arcanam*—worship of Me; *mayā*—by Me; *anumoditaḥ*—approved of; *saḥ asau*—that; *satyaḥ*—true; *bhavitum*—to become; *arhati*—must.

TRANSLATION

[Lord Kṛṣṇa said:] O saintly girls, I understand that your real motive in this austerity has been to worship Me. That intent of yours is approved of by Me, and indeed it must come to pass.

PURPORT

Just as Kṛṣṇa is free of all impure desire, so are the *gopīs.* Their attempt to gain Kṛṣṇa as their husband was therefore motivated not by a desire for personal sense gratification but by their overwhelming desire to serve Kṛṣṇa and to please Him. Because of their intense love, the *gopīs* did not see Kṛṣṇa as God but rather as the most wonderful boy in all creation, and being beautiful young girls, they desired only to please Him by loving service. Lord Kṛṣṇa understood the pure desire of the *gopīs* and was thus satisfied. The Lord could certainly not be satisfied by ordinary lust, but He was moved by the intense loving devotion of the cowherd girls of Vṛndāvana.

TEXT 26

न मय्यावेशितधियां कामः कामाय कल्पते ।
भर्जिता क्वथिता धानाः प्रायो बीजाय नेशते ॥ २६ ॥

na mayy āveśita-dhiyāṁ
kāmaḥ kāmāya kalpate
bharjitā kvathitā dhānāḥ
prāyo bījāya neśate

na—not; *mayi*—in Me; *āveśita*—fully absorbed; *dhiyām*—of those whose consciousness; *kāmaḥ*—desire; *kāmāya*—to material lust; *kalpate*—leads; *bharjitāḥ*—burned; *kvathitāḥ*—cooked; *dhānāḥ*—grains; *prāyaḥ*—for the most part; *bījāya*—new growth; *na iṣyate*—are not capable of causing.

TRANSLATION

The desire of those who fix their minds on Me does not lead to material desire for sense gratification, just as barleycorns burned by the sun and then cooked can no longer grow into new sprouts.

PURPORT

The words *mayy āveśita-dhiyām* are very significant here. Unless one has achieved an advanced degree of devotion, one cannot fix the mind and intelligence on Kṛṣṇa, since Kṛṣṇa is pure spiritual existence. Self-realization is a state not of desirelessness but rather of purified desire, wherein one desires only the pleasure of Lord Kṛṣṇa. The *gopīs* were certainly attracted to Kṛṣṇa in a mood of conjugal love, and yet, having fixed their minds and indeed their entire existence completely on Kṛṣṇa, their conjugal desire could never manifest as material lust; rather, it became the most exalted form of love of Godhead ever seen within the universe.

TEXT 27

याताबला व्रजं सिद्धा मयेमा रंस्यथ क्षपाः ।
यदुद्दिश्य व्रतमिदं चेरुरार्यार्चनं सतीः ॥ २ ७ ॥

yātābalā vrajaṁ siddhā
mayemā raṁsyatha kṣapāḥ
yad uddiśya vratam idaṁ
cerur āryārcanaṁ satīḥ

yāta—go now; *abalāḥ*—My dear girls; *vrajam*—to Vraja; *siddhāḥ*—having achieved your desire; *mayā*—with Me; *imāḥ*—these; *raṁsyatha*—you will enjoy; *kṣapāḥ*—the nights; *yat*—which; *uddiśya*—having in mind; *vratam*—vow; *idam*—this; *ceruḥ*—you executed; *āryā*—of Goddess Kātyāyanī; *arcanam*—the worship; *satīḥ*—being pure.

TRANSLATION

Go now, girls, and return to Vraja. Your desire is fulfilled, for in My company you will enjoy the coming nights. After all, this was the purpose of your vow to worship Goddess Kātyāyanī, O pure-hearted ones.

TEXT 28

श्रीशुक उवाच
इत्यादिष्टा भगवता लब्धकामाः कुमारिकाः ।
ध्यायन्त्यस्तत्पदाम्भोजं कृच्छ्रान्निर्विविशुर्व्रजम् ॥ २८ ॥

śrī-śuka uvāca
ity ādiṣṭā bhagavatā
labdha-kāmāḥ kumārikāḥ
dhyāyantyas tat-padāmbhojaṁ
kṛcchrān nirviviśur vrajam

śrī-śukaḥ uvāca—Śrī Śukadeva Gosvāmī said; *iti*—thus; *ādiṣṭāḥ*—instructed; *bhagavatā*—by the Supreme Personality of Godhead; *labdha*—having obtained; *kāmāḥ*—their desire; *kumārikāḥ*—the young girls; *dhyāyantyaḥ*—meditating; *tat*—His; *pada-ambhojam*—upon the lotus feet; *kṛcchrāt*—with difficulty; *nirviviśuḥ*—they returned; *vrajam*—to the cowherd village.

TRANSLATION

Śukadeva Gosvāmī said: Thus instructed by the Supreme Personality of Godhead, the young girls, their desire now fulfilled, could bring themselves only with great difficulty to return to the village of Vraja, meditating all the while upon His lotus feet.

PURPORT

The *gopīs'* desire was fulfilled because Lord Kṛṣṇa had agreed to act as their husband. A young girl can never spend the night with any man except her husband, and thus when Kṛṣṇa agreed to engage the girls in the nocturnal *rāsa* dance during the coming autumn season, in effect He was agreeing to reciprocate their love for Him in the role of a husband.

TEXT 29

अथ गोपैः परिवृतो भगवान् देवकीसुतः ।
वृन्दावनाद् गतो दूरं चारयन् गाः सहाग्रजः ॥ २९ ॥

atha gopaiḥ parivṛto
bhagavān devakī-sutaḥ
vṛndāvanād gato dūraṁ
cārayan gāḥ sahāgrajaḥ

atha—some time later; *gopaiḥ*—by the cowherd boys; *parivṛtaḥ*—surrounded; *bhagavān*—the Supreme Lord; *devakī-sutaḥ*—the son of Devakī; *vṛndāvanāt*—from Vṛndāvana; *gataḥ*—He went; *dūram*—a distance; *cārayan*—grazing; *gāḥ*—the cows; *saha-agrajaḥ*—together with His brother Balarāma.

TRANSLATION

Some time later Lord Kṛṣṇa, the son of Devakī, surrounded by His cowherd friends and accompanied by His elder brother, Balarāma, went a good distance away from Vṛndāvana, herding the cows.

PURPORT

Having described how Lord Kṛṣṇa stole the garments of the young *gopīs,* Śukadeva Gosvāmī now begins introducing the description of Lord Kṛṣṇa's blessings upon the wives of some ritualistic *brāhmaṇas.*

TEXT 30

निदाघार्कातपे तिग्मे छायाभिः स्वाभिरात्मनः ।
आतपत्रायितान् वीक्ष्य द्रुमानाह व्रजौकसः ॥ ३० ॥

nidāghārkātape tigme
chāyābhiḥ svābhir ātmanaḥ
ātapatrāyitān vīkṣya
drumān āha vrajaukasaḥ

nidāgha—of the hot season; *arka*—of the sun; *ātape*—in the heat; *tigme*—fierce; *chāyābhiḥ*—with the shade; *svābhiḥ*—their own; *ātmanaḥ*—for Himself; *ātapatrāyitān*—serving as umbrellas; *vīkṣya*—observing; *drumān*—the trees; *aha*—He said; *vraja-okasaḥ*—to the boys of Vraja.

TRANSLATION

When the sun's heat became intense, Lord Kṛṣṇa saw that the trees were acting as umbrellas by shading Him, and thus He spoke as follows to His boyfriends.

TEXTS 31–32

हे स्तोककृष्ण हे अंशो श्रीदामन् सुबलार्जुन ।
विशाल वृषभौजस्विन् देवप्रस्थ वरूथप ॥ ३१ ॥
पश्यतैतान्महाभागान् परार्थैकान्तजीवितान् ।
वातवर्षातपहिमान् सहन्तो वारयन्ति नः ॥ ३२ ॥

he stoka-kṛṣṇa he aṁśo
śrīdāman subalārjuna
viśāla vṛṣabhaujasvin
devaprastha varūthapa

paśyataitān mahā-bhāgān
parārthaikānta-jīvitān
vāta-varṣātapa-himān
sahanto vārayanti naḥ

he stoka-kṛṣṇa—O Stoka-Kṛṣṇa; *he aṁśo*—O Aṁśu; *śrīdāman subala arjuna*—O Śrīdāmā, Subala and Arjuna; *viśāla vṛṣabha ojasvin*—O Viśāla, Vṛṣabha and Ojasvī; *devaprastha varūthapa*—O Devaprastha and Varūthapa;

paśyata—just see; *etān*—these; *mahā-bhāgān*—most fortunate; *para-artha*—for the benefit of others; *ekānta*—exclusively; *jīvitān*—whose life; *vāta*—the wind; *varṣa*—rain; *ātapa*—heat of the sun; *himān*—and snow; *sahantaḥ*—tolerating; *vārayanti*—keep off; *naḥ*—for us.

TRANSLATION

[Lord Kṛṣṇa said:] O Stoka Kṛṣṇa and Aṁśu, O Śrīdāmā, Subala and Arjuna, O Vṛṣabha, Ojasvī, Devaprastha and Varūthapa, just see these greatly fortunate trees, whose lives are completely dedicated to the benefit of others. Even while tolerating the wind, rain, heat and snow, they protect us from these elements.

PURPORT

Lord Kṛṣṇa was preparing to bestow His mercy on the wives of the hard-hearted ritualistic *brāhmaṇas,* and in these verses the Lord indicates that even trees who are dedicated to the welfare of others are superior to *brāhmaṇas* who are not. Certainly the members of the Kṛṣṇa consciousness movement should soberly study this point.

TEXT 33

अहो एषां वरं जन्म सर्वप्राण्युपजीवनम् ।
सुजनस्येव येषां वै विमुखा यान्ति नार्थिनः ॥ ३३ ॥

aho eṣāṁ varaṁ janma
sarva-prāṇy-upajīvanam
su-janasyeva yeṣāṁ vai
vimukhā yānti nārthinaḥ

aho—oh, just see; *eṣām*—of these trees; *varam*—superior; *janma*—birth; *sarva*—for all; *prāṇi*—living entities; *upajīvinam*—who provide maintenance; *su-janasya iva*—like a great personality; *yeṣām*—from whom; *vai*—certainly; *vimukhāḥ*—disappointed; *yānti*—go away; *na*—never; *arthinaḥ*—those who are asking for something.

TRANSLATION

Just see how these trees are maintaining every living entity! Their birth is successful. Their behavior is just like that of great personalities, for anyone who asks anything from a tree never goes away disappointed.

PURPORT

This translation is quoted from Śrīla Prabhupāda's *Caitanya-caritāmṛta* (*Ādi* 9.46).

TEXT 34

पत्रपुष्पफलच्छायामूलवल्कलदारुभिः ।
गन्धनिर्यासभस्मास्थितोक्मैः कामान् वितन्वते ॥ ३४ ॥

patra-puṣpa-phala-cchāyā-
mūla-valkala-dārubhiḥ
gandha-niryāsa-bhasmāsthi-
tokmaiḥ kāmān vitanvate

patra—by their leaves; *puṣpa*—flowers; *phala*—fruits; *chāyā*—shade; *mūla*—roots; *valkala*—bark; *dārubhiḥ*—and wood; *gandha*—by their fragrance; *niryāsa*—sap; *bhasma*—ashes; *asthi*—pulp; *tokmaiḥ*—and young shoots; *kāmān*—desirable things; *vitanvate*—they award.

TRANSLATION

These trees fulfill one's desires with their leaves, flowers and fruits, their shade, roots, bark and wood, and also with their fragrance, sap, ashes, pulp and shoots.

TEXT 35

एतावज्जन्मसाफल्यं देहिनामिह देहिषु ।
प्राणैरर्थैर्धिया वाचा श्रेयआचरणं सदा ॥ ३५ ॥

etāvaj janma-sāphalyaṁ
dehinām iha dehiṣu
prāṇair arthair dhiyā vācā
śreya-ācaraṇaṁ sadā

etāvat—up to this; *janma*—of birth; *sāphalyam*—perfection; *dehinām*—of every living being; *iha*—in this world; *dehiṣu*—toward those who are embodied; *prāṇaiḥ*—by life; *arthaiḥ*—by wealth; *dhiyā*—by intelligence; *vācā*—by words; *śreyaḥ*—eternal good fortune; *ācaraṇam*—acting practically; *sadā*—always.

TRANSLATION

It is the duty of every living being to perform welfare activities for the benefit of others with his life, wealth, intelligence and words.

PURPORT

This translation is quoted from Śrīla Prabhupāda's *Caitanya-caritāmṛta* (*Ādi* 9.42).

TEXT 36

इति प्रवालस्तबकफलपुष्पदलोत्करैः ।
तरूणां नम्रशाखानां मध्यतो यमुनां गतः ॥ ३६ ॥

iti pravāla-stabaka-
phala-puṣpa-dalotkaraiḥ
tarūṇāṁ namra-śākhānāṁ
madhyato yamunāṁ gataḥ

iti—thus speaking; *pravāla*—of new branches; *stabaka*—by the clusters; *phala*—of fruit; *puṣpa*—flowers; *dala*—and leaves; *utkaraiḥ*—by the abundance; *tarūṇām*—of the trees; *namra*—bowed down; *śākhānām*—whose branches; *madhyataḥ*—from within the midst; *yamunām*—the Yamunā River; *gataḥ*—He came upon.

TRANSLATION

Thus moving among the trees, whose branches were bent low by their abundance of twigs, fruits, flowers and leaves, Lord Kṛṣṇa came to the Yamunā River.

TEXT 37

तत्र गाः पाययित्वापः सुमृष्टाः शीतलाः शिवाः ।
ततो नृप स्वयं गोपाः कामं स्वादु पपुर्जलम् ॥ ३७ ॥

tatra gāḥ pāyayitvāpaḥ
su-mṛṣṭāḥ śītalāḥ śivāḥ
tato nṛpa svayaṁ gopāḥ
kāmaṁ svādu papur jalam

tatra—there; *gāḥ*—the cows; *pāyayitvā*—making drink; *apaḥ*—the water; *su-mṛṣṭāḥ*—very clear; *śītalāḥ*—cool; *śivāḥ*—wholesome; *tataḥ*—then; *nṛpa*—O King Parīkṣit; *svayam*—themselves; *gopāḥ*—the cowherd boys; *kāmam*—freely; *svādu*—sweet-tasting; *papuḥ*—they drank; *jalam*—the water.

TRANSLATION

The cowherd boys let the cows drink the clear, cool and wholesome water of the Yamunā. O King Parīkṣit, the cowherd boys themselves also drank that sweet water to their full satisfaction.

TEXT 38

तस्या उपवने कामं चारयन्तः पशून्नृप ।
कृष्णरामावुपागम्य क्षुधार्ता इदमब्रुवन् ॥ ३८ ॥

tasyā upavane kāmaṁ
cārayantaḥ paśūn nṛpa
kṛṣṇa-rāmāv upāgamya
kṣudh-ārtā idam abruvan

tasyāḥ—along the Yamunā; *upavane*—within a small forest; *kāmam*—here and there, as they wished; *cārayantaḥ*—tending; *paśūn*—the animals; *nṛpa*—O King; *kṛṣṇa-rāmau*—Lord Kṛṣṇa and Lord Rāma; *upāgamya*—approaching; *kṣut-ārtāḥ*—disturbed by hunger; *idam*—this; *abruvan*—they (the cowherd boys) said.

TRANSLATION

Then, O King, the cowherd boys began herding the animals in a leisurely way within a small forest along the Yamunā. But soon they became afflicted by hunger and, approaching Kṛṣṇa and Balarāma, spoke as follows.

PURPORT

Śrīla Jīva Gosvāmī explains that the cowherd boys were concerned that Kṛṣṇa would be hungry, and thus they feigned their own hunger so that Kṛṣṇa and Balarāma would make suitable arrangements to eat.

Thus end the purports of the humble servants of His Divine Grace A.C. Bhaktivedanta Swami Prabhupāda to the Tenth Canto, Twenty-second Chapter, of the Śrīmad-Bhāgavatam, *entitled "Kṛṣṇa Steals the Garments of the Unmarried Gopīs."*

CHAPTER TWENTY- THREE

The Brāhmaṇas' Wives Blessed

This chapter describes how Lord Śrī Kṛṣṇa, after inducing the cowherd boys to beg for food, showed mercy to the wives of some *brāhmaṇas* performing a sacrifice and made the *brāhmaṇas* themselves feel remorse.

When the cowherd boys became very hungry, they asked Śrī Kṛṣṇa about obtaining food, and He sent them to beg some from a group of *brāhmaṇas* who were performing a sacrifice nearby. But these *brāhmaṇas* ignored the boys, thinking Śrī Kṛṣṇa an ordinary human being. The boys returned disappointed, but the Lord sent them off again, advising them to ask the *brāhmaṇas'* wives for the food. These ladies had heard of Kṛṣṇa's transcendental qualities and were very much attached to Him. Thus as soon as they learned He was nearby, they went to Him in great haste, bringing all four varieties of food. In this way they offered themselves to Śrī Kṛṣṇa.

Kṛṣṇa told the women that while one can develop transcendental love for Him by seeing His Deity form in the temple, meditating upon Him and chanting His glories, one cannot achieve this result simply by being in His physical presence. He advised them that since they were housewives, their particular duty was to help their husbands perform sacrifices. He therefore instructed them to return to their homes.

When the ladies went back home, their *brāhmaṇa* husbands at once felt remorse, and they lamented, "For anyone inimical to Kṛṣṇa, his three births —seminal, brahminical and sacrificial—are all condemned. On the other hand, these womenfolk, who have not undergone the purificatory processes of the brahminical class or performed any austerity or pious rituals, have through devotion for Kṛṣṇa easily cut off the bondage of death."

"Since Lord Kṛṣṇa's every desire is completely fulfilled, His begging for food was simply an act of mercy toward us *brāhmaṇas.* All the fruits of Vedic sacrifice—and indeed all things on earth—are His opulences, yet out of ignorance we could not appreciate this fact."

Having spoken thus, all the *brāhmaṇas* offered their obeisances to Lord Śrī Kṛṣṇa, hoping to counteract their offense. Nonetheless, out of fear of King Kaṁsa they did not go to see the Lord in person.

TEXT 1

श्रीगोपा ऊचुः
राम राम महाबाहो कृष्ण दुष्टनिबर्हण ।
एषा वै बाधते क्षुन्नस्तच्छान्तिं कर्तुमर्हथः ॥ १ ॥

śrī-gopa ūcuḥ
rāma rāma mahā-bāho
kṛṣṇa duṣṭa-nibarhaṇa
eṣā vai bādhate kṣun nas
tac-chāntiṁ kartum arhathaḥ

śrī-gopāḥ ūcuḥ—the cowherd boys said; *rāma rāma*—O Lord Rāma, Lord Rāma; *mahā-bāho*—O mighty-armed one; *kṛṣṇa*—O Lord Kṛṣṇa; *duṣṭa*—of the wicked; *nibarhaṇa*—O destroyer; *eṣā*—this; *vai*—indeed; *bādhate*—is causing distress; *kṣut*—hunger; *naḥ*—to us; *tat-śāntim*—its counteraction; *kartum arhathaḥ*—You ought to do.

TRANSLATION

The cowherd boys said: O Rāma, Rāma, mighty-armed one! O Kṛṣṇa, chastiser of the wicked! We are being harassed by hunger, and You should do something about it.

PURPORT

The cowherd boys jokingly implied that since Śrī Kṛṣṇa is the subduer of all bad things, the Lord should subdue their hunger by arranging for them to eat. In this statement by the cowherd boys, we observe the intimate loving friendship they enjoyed with the Supreme Personality of Godhead.

TEXT 2

श्रीशुक उवाच
इति विज्ञापितो गोपैर्भगवान् देवकीसुतः ।
भक्ताया विप्रभार्यायाः प्रसीदन्निदमब्रवीत् ॥ २ ॥

śrī-śuka uvāca
iti vijñāpito gopair
bhagavān devakī-sutaḥ

bhaktāyā vipra-bhāryāyāḥ
prasīdann idam abravīt

śrī-śukaḥ uvāca—Śrī Śukadeva Gosvāmī said; *iti*—thus; *vijñāpitaḥ*—informed; *gopaiḥ*—by the cowherd boys; *bhagavān*—the Supreme Personality of Godhead; *devakī-sutaḥ*—the son of Devakī; *bhaktāyāḥ*—His devotees; *vipra-bhāryāyāḥ*—the wives of the *brāhmaṇas; prasīdan*—desiring to satisfy; *idam*—this; *abravīt*—He spoke.

TRANSLATION

Śukadeva Gosvāmī said: Thus entreated by the cowherd boys, the Supreme Personality of Godhead, the son of Devakī, replied as follows, desiring to please certain of His devotees who were brāhmaṇas' wives.

TEXT 3

प्रयात देवयजनं ब्राह्मणा ब्रह्मवादिनः ।
सत्रमांगिरसं नाम ह्यासते स्वर्गकाम्यया ॥ ३ ॥

prayāta deva-yajanaṁ
brāhmaṇā brahma-vādinaḥ
satram āṅgirasaṁ nāma
hy āsate svarga-kāmyayā

prayāta—please go; *deva-yajanam*—to the sacrificial arena; *brāhmaṇāḥ*—*brāhmaṇas; brahma-vādinaḥ*—followers of the Vedic injunctions; *satram*—a sacrifice; *āṅgirasam nāma*—known as Āṅgirasa; *hi*—indeed; *āsate*—they are now performing; *svarga-kāmyayā*—with the motive of promotion to heaven.

TRANSLATION

[Lord Kṛṣṇa said:] Please go to the sacrificial arena where a group of brāhmaṇas, learned in the Vedic injunctions, are now performing the Āṅgirasa sacrifice to gain promotion to heaven.

TEXT 4

तत्र गत्वौदनं गोपा याचतास्मद्विसर्जिताः ।
कीर्तयन्तो भगवत आर्यस्य मम चाभिधाम् ॥ ४ ॥

tatra gatvaudanaṁ gopā
yācatāsmad-visarjitāḥ
kīrtayanto bhagavata
āryasya mama cābhidhām

tatra—there; *gatvā*—going; *odanam*—food; *gopāḥ*—My dear cowherd boys; *yācata*—just request; *asmat*—by Us; *visarjitāḥ*—dispatched; *kīrtayantaḥ*—announcing; *bhagavataḥ*—of the Supreme Lord; *āryasya*—the elder; *mama*—My; *ca*—also; *abhidhām*—name.

TRANSLATION

When you go there, My dear cowherd boys, simply request some food. Declare to them the name of My elder brother, the Supreme Lord Balarāma, and also My name, and explain that you have been sent by Us.

PURPORT

Lord Kṛṣṇa encouraged His boyfriends to request charity without being embarrassed. In case the boys felt they had no right to personally approach such respectable *brāhmaṇas,* the Lord told them to mention the names of Balarāma and Kṛṣṇa, the holy names of God.

TEXT 5

इत्यादिष्टा भगवता गत्वायाचन्त ते तथा ।
कृताञ्जलिपुटा विप्रान् दण्डवत् पतिता भुवि ॥ ५ ॥

ity ādiṣṭā bhagavatā
gatvā yācanta te tathā
kṛtāñjali-puṭā viprān
daṇḍa-vat patitā bhuvi

iti—in these words; *ādiṣṭāḥ*—ordered; *bhagavatā*—by the Supreme Lord Kṛṣṇa; *gatvā*—going; *ayācanta*—begged; *te*—they; *tathā*—in that manner; *kṛta-añjali-puṭāḥ*—joining their palms in humble supplication; *viprān*—to the *brāhmaṇas; daṇḍa-vat*—like sticks; *patitāḥ*—falling; *bhuvi*—upon the ground.

TRANSLATION

Thus instructed by the Supreme Personality of Godhead, the cowherd boys went there and submitted their request. They stood before the

brāhmaṇas with palms joined in supplication and then fell flat on the ground to offer respect.

TEXT 6

हे भूमिदेवाः शृणुत कृष्णस्यादेशकारिणः ।
प्राप्ताञ्जानीत भद्रं वो गोपान्नो रामचोदितान् ॥ ६ ॥

he bhūmi-devāḥ śṛṇuta
kṛṣṇasyādeśa-kāriṇaḥ
prāptāñ jānīta bhadraṁ vo
gopān no rāma-coditān

he bhūmi-devāḥ—O earthly gods; *śṛṇuta*—please hear us; *kṛṣṇasya ādeśa*—of the order of Kṛṣṇa; *kāriṇaḥ*—the executors; *prāptān*—arrived; *jānīta*—please recognize; *bhadram*—all good; *vaḥ*—unto you; *gopān*—cowherd boys; *naḥ*—us; *rāma-coditān*—sent by Lord Rāma.

TRANSLATION

[The cowherd boys said:] O earthly gods, please hear us. We cowherd boys are executing the orders of Kṛṣṇa, and we have been sent here by Balarāma. We wish all good for you. Please acknowledge our arrival.

PURPORT

The term *bhūmi-devāḥ,* "gods on earth," refers here to the *brāhmaṇas,* who are supposed to closely represent the will of the Supreme Lord. The philosophy of Kṛṣṇa consciousness is not a primitive polytheistic doctrine holding that human beings on the earth are gods. Rather, it is a science that traces the descent of authority from the Absolute Truth Himself, Śrī Kṛṣṇa. The authority and power of God naturally extend along with the extension of His creation, and on the earth the Lord's will and authority are represented by purified, enlightened men called *brāhmaṇas.*

This account will illustrate that the ritualistic *brāhmaṇas* approached by the cowherd boys were not at all properly enlightened and thus could not appreciate the position of Kṛṣṇa and Balarāma or that of Their intimate associates. In fact, this pastime exposes the pretentious position of so-called *brāhmaṇas* who are not faithful devotees of the Supreme Lord.

TEXT 7

गाश्चारयन्ताववि‍दूर ओदनं
रामाच्युतौ वो लषतो बुभुक्षितौ ।
तयोर्द्विजा ओदनमर्थिनोर्यदि
श्रद्धा च वो यच्छत धर्मवित्तमाः ॥ ७ ॥

gāś cārayantāv avidūra odanaṁ
rāmācyutau vo laṣato bubhukṣitau
tayor dvijā odanam arthinor yadi
śraddhā ca vo yacchata dharma-vittamāḥ

gāḥ—Their cows; *cārayantau*—grazing; *avidūre*—not far away; *odanam*—food; *rāma-acyutau*—Lord Rāma and Lord Acyuta; *vaḥ*—from you; *laṣataḥ*—are desiring; *bubhukṣitau*—being hungry; *tayoḥ*—for Them; *dvijāḥ*—O *brāhmaṇas; odanam*—food; *arthinoḥ*—begging; *yadi*—if; *śraddhā*—any faith; *ca*—and; *vaḥ*—on your part; *yacchata*—please give; *dharma-vit-tamāḥ*—O best knowers of the principles of religion.

TRANSLATION

Lord Rāma and Lord Acyuta are tending Their cows not far from here. They are hungry and want you to give Them some of your food. Therefore, O brāhmaṇas, O best of the knowers of religion, if you have faith please give some food to Them.

PURPORT

The cowherd boys doubted the generosity of the *brāhmaṇas,* and thus they used the word *bubhukṣitau,* meaning that Kṛṣṇa and Balarāma were hungry. The boys expected the *brāhmaṇas* to know the Vedic injunction *annasya kṣuditaṁ pātram*: "Anyone who is hungry is a fit candidate for receiving food in charity." But if the *brāhmaṇas* would not recognize the authority of Kṛṣṇa and Balarāma, their title *dvija* would be taken to mean merely "born from two parents" (*dvi*—from two, *ja*—born) rather than "twice-born." When the *brāhmaṇas* did not respond to the cowherd boys' initial request, the boys addressed the *brāhmaṇas,* with a slight trace of sarcasm, as *dharma-vit-tamāḥ,* "O best of the knowers of religion."

TEXT 8

दीक्षायाः पशुसंस्थायाः सौत्रामण्याश्च सत्तमाः ।
अन्यत्र दीक्षितस्यापि नान्नमश्नन् हि दुष्यति ॥ ८ ॥

dīkṣāyāḥ paśu-saṁsthāyāḥ
sautrāmaṇyāś ca sattamāḥ
anyatra dīkṣitasyāpi
nānnam aśnan hi duṣyati

dīkṣāyāḥ—beginning with the initiation for a sacrifice; *paśu-saṁsthāyāḥ*—until sacrificing the animal; *sautrāmaṇyāḥ*—outside of the sacrifice known as Sautrāmaṇi; *ca*—and; *sat-tamāḥ*—O purest ones; *anyatra*—elsewhere; *dīkṣitasya*—of one who has been initiated for the sacrifice; *api*—even; *na*—not; *annam*—food; *aśnan*—eating; *hi*—indeed; *duṣyati*—creates offense.

TRANSLATION

Except during the interval between the initiation of the performer of a sacrifice and the actual sacrifice of the animal, O most pure brāhmaṇas, it is not contaminating for even the initiated to partake of food, at least in sacrifices other than the Sautrāmaṇi.

PURPORT

The cowherd boys anticipated the possible objection from the *brāhmaṇas* that they couldn't give the boys any food because they themselves had not yet eaten, and that a priest initiated to perform a sacrifice should not eat. Therefore the boys humbly informed the *brāhmaṇas* about various technicalities of ritualistic sacrifice. The cowherd boys were not unaware of the formalities of Vedic culture, but their real intention was simply to render loving service to Lord Kṛṣṇa.

TEXT 9

इति ते भगवद्याच्ञां शृण्वन्तोऽपि न शुश्रुवुः ।
क्षुद्राशा भूरिकर्माणो बालिशा वृद्धमानिनः ॥ ९ ॥

iti te bhagavad-yācñāṁ
śṛṇvanto 'pi na śuśruvuḥ
kṣudrāśā bhūri-karmāṇo
bāliśā vṛddha-māninaḥ

iti—thus; *te*—they, the *brāhmaṇas; bhagavat*—of the Supreme Personality of Godhead; *yācñām*—the supplication; *śṛṇvantaḥ*—hearing; *api*—although; *na śuśruvuḥ*—they did not hear; *kṣudra-āśāḥ*—full of petty desire; *bhūri-karmāṇaḥ*—entangled in elaborate ritualistic activities; *bāliśāḥ*—childish fools; *vṛddha-māninaḥ*—presuming themselves to be wise men.

TRANSLATION

The brāhmaṇas heard this supplication from the Supreme Personality of Godhead, yet they refused to pay heed. Indeed, they were full of petty desires and entangled in elaborate rituals. Though presuming themselves advanced in Vedic learning, they were actually inexperienced fools.

PURPORT

These childish *brāhmaṇas* were full of petty desires, such as the desire to attain to material heaven, and therefore they could not recognize the golden transcendental opportunity offered them by the arrival of Kṛṣṇa's personal boyfriends. Presently, throughout the world, people are madly pursuing material advancement and thus cannot hear the message of the Supreme Lord Kṛṣṇa that is being broadcast through the missionary activities of the Kṛṣṇa consciousness movement. Times have hardly changed, and proud, materialistic priests are still prevalent on the earth.

TEXTS 10–11

देशः कालः पृथग् द्रव्यं मन्त्रतन्त्रर्त्विजोऽग्नयः ।
देवता यजमानश्च क्रतुर्धर्मश्च यन्मयः ॥ १० ॥
तं ब्रह्म परमं साक्षाद् भगवन्तमधोक्षजम् ।
मनुष्यदृष्ट्या दुष्प्रज्ञा मर्त्यात्मानो न मेनिरे ॥ ११ ॥

deśaḥ kālaḥ pṛthag dravyaṁ
mantra-tantrartvijo'gnayaḥ
devatā yajamānaś ca
kratur dharmaś ca yan-mayaḥ

taṁ brahma paramaṁ sākṣād
bhagavantam adhokṣajam
manuṣya-dṛṣṭyā duṣprajñā
martyātmāno na menire

deśaḥ—the place; *kālaḥ*—time; *pṛthak dravyam*—particular items of paraphernalia; *mantra*—Vedic hymns; *tantra*—prescribed rituals; *ṛtvijaḥ*—priests; *agnayaḥ*—sacrificial fires; *devatāḥ*—the presiding demigods; *yajamānaḥ*—the performer of the sacrifice; *ca*—and; *kratuḥ*—the offering; *dharmaḥ*—the invisible power of fruitive results; *ca*—and; *yat*—whom; *mayaḥ*—constituting; *tam*—Him; *brahma paramam*—the Supreme Absolute Truth; *sākṣāt*—directly manifest; *bhagavantam*—the Personality of Godhead; *adhokṣajam*—who is transcendental to material senses; *manuṣya-dṛṣṭyā*—seeing Him as an ordinary man; *duṣprajñāḥ*—perverted in their intelligence; *martya-ātmānaḥ*—falsely identifying themselves with the material body; *na menire*—they did not properly honor.

TRANSLATION

Although the ingredients of sacrificial performance—the place, time, particular paraphernalia, mantras, rituals, priests, fires, demigods, performer, offering and the as yet unseen beneficial results—are all simply aspects of His opulences, the brāhmaṇas saw Lord Kṛṣṇa as an ordinary human because of their perverted intelligence. They failed to recognize that He is the Supreme Absolute Truth, the directly manifest Personality of Godhead, whom the material senses cannot ordinarily perceive. Thus bewildered by their false identification with the mortal body, they did not show Him proper respect.

PURPORT

The ritualistic *brāhmaṇas* could not understand why the sacrificial food should be offered to Lord Kṛṣṇa, whom they considered an ordinary human being. Just as a person with rose-colored glasses sees the entire world as rose-colored, a conditioned soul with mundane vision sees even God Himself as mundane and thus loses the opportunity to go back home, back to Godhead.

TEXT 12

न ते यदोमिति प्रोचुर्न नेति च परन्तप ।
गोपा निराशाः प्रत्येत्य तथोचुः कृष्णरामयोः ॥ १२ ॥

na te yad om iti procur
na neti ca parantapa
gopā nirāśāḥ pratyetya
tathocuḥ kṛṣṇa-rāmayoḥ

na—not; *te*—they; *yat*—when; *om*—"so be it"; *iti*—thus; *procuḥ*—did speak; *na*—not; *na*—"no"; *iti*—thus; *ca*—either; *parantapa*—O chastiser of the enemies, Parīkṣit Mahārāja; *gopāḥ*—the cowherd boys; *nirāśāḥ*—discouraged; *pratyetya*—returning; *tathā*—thus; *ūcuḥ*—described; *kṛṣṇa-rāmayoḥ*—to Lord Kṛṣṇa and Lord Rāma.

TRANSLATION

When the brāhmaṇas failed to reply even with a simple yes or no, O chastiser of the enemy [Parīkṣit], the cowherd boys returned disappointed to Kṛṣṇa and Rāma and reported this to Them.

TEXT 13

तदुपाकर्ण्य भगवान् प्रहस्य जगदीश्वरः ।
व्याजहार पुनर्गोपान् दर्शयन् लौकिकीं गतिम् ॥ १३ ॥

tad upākarṇya bhagavān
prahasya jagad-īśvaraḥ
vyājahāra punar gopān
darśayan laukikīṁ gatim

tat—that; *upākarṇya*—hearing; *bhagavān*—the Supreme Lord; *prahasya*—laughing; *jagat-īśvaraḥ*—the controller of the entire universe; *vyājahāra*—addressed; *punaḥ*—again; *gopān*—the cowherd boys; *darśayan*—showing; *laukikīm*—of the ordinary world; *gatim*—the way.

TRANSLATION

Hearing what had happened, the Supreme Personality of Godhead, the Lord of the universe, simply laughed. Then He again addressed the cowherd boys, showing them the way men act in this world.

PURPORT

By laughing, Lord Kṛṣṇa indicated to the cowherd boys that they need not be angry at the ritualistic *brāhmaṇas* but should understand that one who begs will often be refused.

TEXT 14

मां ज्ञापयत पत्नीभ्यः ससंकर्षणमागतम् ।
दास्यन्ति काममन्नं वः स्निग्धा मय्युषिता धिया ॥ १४ ॥

māṁ jñāpayata patnībhyaḥ
sa-saṅkarṣaṇam āgatam
dāsyanti kāmam annaṁ vaḥ
snigdhā mayy uṣitā dhiyā

mām—Me; *jñāpayata*—please announce; *patnībhyaḥ*—to the wives; *sa-saṅkarṣaṇam*—together with Lord Balarāma; *āgatam*—arrived; *dāsyanti*—they will give; *kāmam*—as much as you desire; *annam*—food; *vaḥ*—to you; *snigdhāḥ*—affectionate; *mayi*—in Me; *uṣitāḥ*—residing; *dhiyā*—with their intelligence.

TRANSLATION

[Lord Kṛṣṇa said:] Tell the wives of the brāhmaṇas that I have come here with Lord Saṅkarṣaṇa. They will certainly give you all the food you want, for they are most affectionate toward Me and, indeed, with their intelligence reside in Me alone.

PURPORT

While physically the wives of the *brāhmaṇas* remained at home, within their minds they resided in the Supreme Lord Kṛṣṇa because of intense affection for Him. Śrīla Viśvanātha Cakravartī Ṭhākura explains that the reason Lord Kṛṣṇa did not have the cowherd boys tell the *brāhmaṇas'* wives He was hungry is that He knew this would severely distress these devoted ladies. Simply out of affection for Lord Kṛṣṇa, however, the wives would be happy to give all the food requested of them. They would not heed their husbands' prohibitions, since they resided within the Lord through their transcendental intelligence.

TEXT 15

गत्वाथ पत्नीशालायां दृष्ट्वासीनाः स्वलंकृताः ।
नत्वा द्विजसतीर्गोपाः प्रश्रिता इदमब्रुवन् ॥ १५ ॥

gatvātha patnī-śālāyāṁ
dṛṣṭvāsīnāḥ sv-alaṅkṛtāḥ
natvā dvija-satīr gopāḥ
praśritā idam abruvan

gatvā—going; *atha*—then; *patnī-śālāyām*—in the house of the wives of the *brāhmaṇas; dṛṣṭvā*—seeing them; *asīnāḥ*—sitting; *su-alaṅkṛtāḥ*—nicely ornamented; *natvā*—bowing down to offer obeisances; *dvija-satīḥ*—to the chaste wives of the *brāhmaṇas; gopāḥ*—the cowherd boys; *praśritāḥ*—humbly; *idam*—this; *abruvan*—spoke.

TRANSLATION

The cowherd boys then went to the house where the brāhmaṇas' wives were staying. There the boys saw those chaste ladies sitting, nicely decorated with fine ornaments. Bowing down to the brāhmaṇa ladies, the boys addressed them in all humility.

TEXT 16

नमो वो विप्रपत्नीभ्यो निबोधत वचांसि नः ।
इतोऽविदूरे चरता कृष्णेनेहेषिता वयम् ॥ १६ ॥

namo vo vipra-patnībhyo
nibodhata vacāṁsi naḥ
ito'vidūre caratā
kṛṣṇeneheṣitā vayam

namaḥ—obeisances; *vaḥ*—unto you; *vipra-patnībhyaḥ*—the wives of the *brāhmaṇas; nibodhata*—please hear; *vacāṁsi*—words; *naḥ*—our; *itaḥ*—from here; *avidūre*—not distant; *caratā*—who is going; *kṛṣṇena*—by Lord Kṛṣṇa; *iha*—here; *iṣitāḥ*—sent; *vayam*—we.

TRANSLATION

[The cowherd boys said:] Obeisances unto you, O wives of the learned brāhmaṇas. Kindly hear our words. We have been sent here by Lord Kṛṣṇa, who is passing by not far from here.

TEXT 17

गाश्चारयन् स गोपालैः सरामो दूरमागतः ।
बुभुक्षितस्य तस्यान्नं सानुगस्य प्रदीयताम् ॥ १७॥

gāś cārayan sa gopālaiḥ
sa-rāmo dūram āgataḥ
bubhukṣitasya tasyānnaṁ
sānugasya pradīyatām

gāḥ—the cows; *cārayan*—tending; *saḥ*—He; *gopālaiḥ*—in the company of the cowherd boys; *sa-rāmaḥ*—together with Lord Balarāma; *dūram*—from far away; *āgataḥ*—has come; *bubhukṣitasya*—who is hungry; *tasya*—for Him; *annam*—food; *sa-anugasya*—together with His companions; *pradīyatām*—should be given.

TRANSLATION

He has come a long way with the cowherd boys and Lord Balarāma, tending the cows. Now He is hungry, so some food should be given for Him and His companions.

TEXT 18

श्रुत्वाच्युतमुपायातं नित्यं तद्दर्शनोत्सुकाः ।
तत्कथाक्षिप्तमनसो बभूवुर्जातसम्भ्रमाः ॥ १८ ॥

śrutvācyutam upāyātaṁ
nityaṁ tad-darśanotsukāḥ
tat-kathākṣipta-manaso
babhūvur jāta-sambhramāḥ

śrutvā—hearing; *acyutam*—Lord Kṛṣṇa; *upāyātam*—come nearby; *nityam*—constantly; *tat-darśana*—for the sight of Him; *utsukāḥ*—eager; *tat-kathā*—by descriptions of Him; *ākṣpita*—enchanted; *manasaḥ*—their minds; *babhūvuḥ*—they became; *jāta-sambhramāḥ*—excited.

TRANSLATION

The wives of the brāhmaṇas were always eager to see Kṛṣṇa, for their minds had been enchanted by descriptions of Him. Thus as soon as they heard that He had come, they became very excited.

TEXT 19

चतुर्विधं बहुगुणमन्नमादाय भाजनैः ।
अभिसस्रुः प्रियं सर्वाः समुद्रमिव निम्नगाः ॥ १९ ॥

catur-vidhaṁ bahu-guṇam
annam ādāya bhājanaiḥ
abhisasruḥ priyaṁ sarvāḥ
samudram iva nimnagāḥ

catuḥ-vidham—of the four varieties (that which is chewed, that which is swallowed, that which is licked and that which is sucked); *bahu-guṇam*—endowed with many rich tastes and fragrances; *annam*—food; *ādāya*—bringing; *bhājanaiḥ*—in large vessels; *abhisasruḥ*—they went forward; *priyam*—to their beloved; *sarvāḥ*—all of them; *samudram*—to the ocean; *iva*—just as; *nimna-gāḥ*—the rivers.

TRANSLATION

Taking along in large vessels the four kinds of foods, full of fine tastes and aromas, all the ladies went forth to meet their beloved, just as rivers flow toward the sea.

PURPORT

Śrīla Viśvanātha Cakravartī Ṭhākura explains that the wives of the *brāhmaṇas* experienced conjugal feelings toward Kṛṣṇa, as if He were their paramour; thus they could not be checked as they rushed to see Him.

TEXT 20–21

निषिध्यमानाः पतिभिर्भ्रातृभिर्बन्धुभिः सुतैः ।
भगवत्युत्तमश्लोके दीर्घश्रुतधृताशयाः ॥ २० ॥
यमुनोपवनेऽशोकनवपल्लवमण्डिते ।
विचरन्तं वृतं गोपैः साग्रजं ददृशुः स्त्रियः ॥ २१ ॥

niṣidhyamānāḥ patibhir
bhrātṛbhir bandhubhiḥ sutaiḥ
bhagavaty uttama-śloke
dīrgha-śruta-dhṛtāśayāḥ

yamunopavane'śoka
nava-pallava-maṇḍite
vicarantaṁ vṛtaṁ gopaiḥ
sāgrajaṁ dadṛśuḥ striyaḥ

niṣidhyamānāḥ—being forbidden; *patibhiḥ*—by their husbands; *bhrātṛbhiḥ*—by their brothers; *bandhubhiḥ*—by other relatives; *sutaiḥ*—and by their sons; *bhagavati*—directed toward the Supreme Personality of Godhead; *uttama-śloke*—who is praised with transcendental hymns; *dīrgha*—for a long time; *śruta*—because of hearing; *dhṛta*—acquired; *āśayāḥ*—

whose expectations; *yamunā-upavane*—in a garden along the river Yamunā; *aśoka-nava-pallava*—by the buds of the *aśoka* trees; *maṇḍite*—decorated; *vicarantam*—wandering; *vṛtam*—surrounded; *gopaiḥ*—by the cowherd boys; *sa-agrajam*—together with His elder brother; *dadṛśuḥ*—they saw; *striyaḥ*—the ladies.

TRANSLATION

Although their husbands, brothers, sons and other relatives tried to forbid them from going, their hope of seeing Kṛṣṇa, cultivated by extensive hearing of His transcendental qualities, won out. Along the river Yamunā, within a garden decorated with buds of aśoka trees, they caught sight of Him strolling along in the company of the cowherd boys and His elder brother, Balarāma.

TEXT 22

श्यामं हिरण्यपरिधिं वनमाल्यबर्ह-
धातुप्रवालनटवेषमनुव्रतांसे ।
विन्यस्तहस्तमितरेण धुनानमब्जं
कर्णोत्पलालककपोलमुखाब्जहासम् ॥ २२ ॥

śyāmaṁ hiraṇya-paridhiṁ vanamālya-barha-
dhātu-pravāla-naṭa-veṣam anuvratāṁse
vinyasta-hastam itareṇa dhunānam abjaṁ
karṇotpalālaka-kapola-mukhābja-hāsam

śyāmam—dark blue in complexion; *hiraṇya*—golden; *paridhim*—whose garment; *vana-mālya*—with a forest garland; *barha*—peacock feather; *dhātu*—colored minerals; *pravāla*—and sprigs of buds; *naṭa*—like a dancer upon the stage; *veṣam*—dressed; *anuvrata*—of a friend; *aṁse*—upon the shoulder; *vinyasta*—placed; *hastam*—His hand; *itareṇa*—with the other; *dhunānam*—twirling; *abjam*—a lotus; *karṇa*—upon His ears; *utpala*—lilies; *alaka-kapola*—with hair extending over His cheeks; *mukha-abja*—upon His lotuslike face; *hāsam*—having a smile.

TRANSLATION

His complexion was dark blue and His garment golden. Wearing a peacock feather, colored minerals, sprigs of flower buds, and a garland of forest flowers and leaves, He was dressed just like a dramatic dancer. He

rested one hand upon the shoulder of a friend and with the other twirled a lotus. Lilies graced His ears, His hair hung down over His cheeks, and His lotuslike face was smiling.

TEXT 23

प्रायःश्रुतप्रियतमोदयकर्णपूरैर्
यस्मिन्निमग्नमनसस्तमथाक्षिरन्ध्रैः ।
अन्तः प्रवेश्य सुचिरं परिरभ्य तापं
प्राज्ञं यथाभिमतयो विजहुर्नरेन्द्र ॥ २३ ॥

prāyaḥ-śruta-priyatamodaya-karṇa-pūrair
yasmin nimagna-manasas tam athākṣi-randraiḥ
antaḥ praveśya su-ciraṁ parirabhya tāpaṁ
prājñaṁ yathābhimatayo vijahur narendra

prāyaḥ—repeatedly; *śruta*—heard; *priya-tama*—of their dearmost; *udaya*—the glories; *karṇa-pūraiḥ*—which were the ornaments of their ears; *yasmin*—in whom; *nimagna*—submerged; *manasaḥ*—their minds; *tam*—Him; *atha*—then; *akṣi-randhraiḥ*—through the apertures of their eyes; *antaḥ*—within; *praveśya*—making enter; *su-ciram*—for a long time; *parirabhya*—embracing; *tāpam*—their distress; *prājñam*—the inner consciousness; *yathā*—as; *abhimatayaḥ*—the functions of false ego; *vijahuḥ*—they gave up; *nara-indra*—O ruler of men.

TRANSLATION

O ruler of men, for a long time those brāhmaṇa ladies had heard about Kṛṣṇa, their beloved, and His glories had become the constant ornaments of their ears. Indeed, their minds were always absorbed in Him. Through the apertures of their eyes they now forced Him to enter within their hearts, and then they embraced Him within for a long time. In this way they finally gave up the pain of separation from Him, just as sages give up the anxiety of false ego by embracing their innermost consciousness.

TEXT 24

तास्तथा त्यक्तसर्वाशाः प्राप्ता आत्मदिदृक्षया ।
विज्ञायाखिलदृग्द्रष्टा प्राह प्रहसिताननः ॥ २४ ॥

tās tathā tyakta-sarvāśāḥ
prāptā ātma-didṛkṣayā
vijñāyākhila-dṛg-draṣṭā
prāha prahasitānanaḥ

tāḥ—those ladies; *tathā*—in such a state; *tyakta-sarva-āśāḥ*—having given up all material desires; *prāptāḥ*—arrived; *ātma-didṛkṣayā*—with the desire of seeing Himself; *vijñāya*—understanding; *akhila-dṛk*—of the vision of all creatures; *draṣṭā*—the seer; *prāha*—He spoke; *prahasita-ānanaḥ*—with a smile upon His face.

TRANSLATION

Lord Kṛṣṇa, who witnesses the thoughts of all creatures, understood how those ladies had abandoned all worldly hopes and come there simply to see Him. Thus He addressed them as follows with a smile upon His face.

TEXT 25

स्वागतं वो महाभागा आस्यतां करवाम किम्।
यन्नो दिदृक्षया प्राप्ता उपपन्नमिदं हि वः ॥ २५ ॥

svāgataṁ vo mahā-bhāgā
āsyatāṁ karavāma kim
yan no didṛkṣayā prāptā
upapannam idaṁ hi vaḥ

su-āgatam—auspicious welcome; *vaḥ*—for you; *mahā-bhāgāḥ*—O fortunate ladies; *āsyatām*—please come sit; *karavāma*—I can do, *kim*—what; *yat*—because; *naḥ*—Us; *didṛkṣayā*—with the desire of seeing; *prāptāḥ*—you have come; *upapannam*—fitting; *idam*—this; *hi*—certainly; *vaḥ*—on your part.

TRANSLATION

[Lord Kṛṣṇa said:] Welcome, O most fortunate ladies. Please sit down and make yourselves comfortable. What can I do for you? That you have come here to see Me is most appropriate.

PURPORT

Just as Śrī Kṛṣṇa welcomed the *gopīs* who came to dance with Him at night, He similarly welcomed the *brāhmaṇas'* wives, whose pure love for Him was proved by their overcoming many hindrances to see the Lord. The word *upapannam* indicates that although these ladies had rejected their husbands' orders, their behavior was not at all inappropriate, since their husbands had obviously tried to obstruct their loving service to Lord Kṛṣṇa.

TEXT 26

नन्वद्धा मयि कुर्वन्ति कुशलाः स्वार्थदर्शिनः ।
अहैतुक्यव्यवहितां भक्तिमात्मप्रिये यथा ॥ २६ ॥

nanv addhā mayi kurvanti
kuśalāḥ svārtha-darśinaḥ
ahaituky avyavahitāṁ
bhaktim ātma-priye yathā

nanu—certainly; *addhā*—directly; *mayi*—unto Me; *kurvanti*—they perform; *kuśalāḥ*—those who are expert; *sva-artha*—their own true benefit; *darśinaḥ*—who perceive; *ahaitukī*—unmotivated; *avyavahitām*—uninterrupted; *bhaktim*—devotional service; *ātma*—to the soul; *priye*—who am most dear; *yathā*—properly.

TRANSLATION

Certainly expert personalities, who can see their own true interest, render unmotivated and uninterrupted devotional service directly unto Me, for I am most dear to the soul.

PURPORT

The Supreme Lord informed the *brāhmaṇas'* wives that not only they but all people who recognize their true self-interest take to the spiritual process of loving service to the Lord. Lord Kṛṣṇa is *ātma-priya,* the real object of love for everyone. Although each individual has his own taste and freedom, ultimately every living being is a spiritual spark of the Supreme Personality of Godhead; thus everyone's primary loving attraction is constitutionally meant for Lord Śrī Kṛṣṇa. Loving service to the Lord should be *ahaitukī,* without personal motive, and *avyavahitā,* unobstructed by mental speculation, selfish desire or any quirk of time and circumstance.

TEXT 27

प्राणबुद्धिमनःस्वात्मदारापत्यधनादयः ।
यत्सम्पर्कात् प्रिया आसंस्ततः कोऽन्वपरः प्रियः ॥ २७ ॥

prāṇa-buddhi-manaḥ-svātma
dārāpatya-dhanādayaḥ
yat-samparkāt priyā āsaṁs
tataḥ ko nv aparaḥ priyaḥ

prāṇa—one's vital force; *buddhi*—intelligence; *manaḥ*—mind; *sva*—relatives; *ātma*—body; *dāra*—wife; *apatya*—children; *dhana*—wealth; *ādayaḥ*—and so forth; *yat*—with which (self); *samparkāt*—because of contact; *priyāḥ*—dear; *āsan*—have become; *tataḥ*—than that; *kaḥ*—what; *nu*—indeed; *aparaḥ*—other; *priyaḥ*—dear object.

TRANSLATION

It is only by contact with the self that one's vital breath, intelligence, mind, friends, body, wife, children, wealth and so on are dear. Therefore what object can possibly be more dear than one's own self?

PURPORT

The word *yat-samparkāt* in this verse refers to contact with the individual self and ultimately with the Supreme Self, the Lord, who is the origin of the individual living being. By developing Kṛṣṇa consciousness, one automatically becomes self-realized, and thus one's vital strength, intelligence, mind, relatives, body, family and wealth all become enhanced and brilliant by the central influence of Kṛṣṇa consciousness. This happens because Kṛṣṇa consciousness is the optimum efficient conjunction of the individual self, who is pure consciousness, with the Supreme Self and supreme consciousness, Kṛṣṇa.

TEXT 28

तद् यात देवयजनं पतयो वो द्विजातयः ।
स्वसत्रं पारयिष्यन्ति युष्माभिर्गृहमेधिनः ॥ २८ ॥

tad yāta deva-yajanaṁ
patayo vo dvijātayaḥ
sva-satraṁ pārayiṣyanti
yuṣmābhir gṛha-medhinaḥ

tat—therefore; *yāta*—go; *deva-yajanam*—to the sacrificial arena; *patayaḥ*—the husbands; *vaḥ*—your; *dvi-jātayaḥ*—the *brāhmaṇas; sva-satram*—their own sacrifices; *pārayiṣyanti*—will be able to finish; *yuṣmābhiḥ*—together with you; *gṛha-medhinaḥ*—the householders.

TRANSLATION

You should thus return to the sacrificial arena, because your husbands, the learned brāhmaṇas, are householders and need your assistance to finish their respective sacrifices.

TEXT 29

श्रीपत्न्य ऊचुः
मैवं विभोऽर्हति भवान् गदितुं नृशंसं
सत्यं कुरुष्व निगमं तव पादमूलम् ।
प्राप्ता वयं तुलसिदाम पदावसृष्टं
केशैर्निवोढुमतिलंग्य समस्तबन्धून् ॥ २९ ॥

śrī-patnya ūcuḥ
maivaṁ vibho'rhati bhavān gadituṁ nṛ-śaṁsaṁ
satyaṁ kuruṣva nigamaṁ tava pāda-mūlam
prāptā vayaṁ tulasi-dāma padāvasṛṣṭaṁ
keśair nivoḍhum atilaṅghya samasta-bandhūn

śrī-patnyaḥ ūcuḥ—the wives of the *brāhmaṇas* said; *mā*—not; *evam*—like this; *vibho*—O almighty Lord; *arhati*—ought; *bhavān*—You; *gaditum*—to speak; *nṛ-śaṁsam*—harshly; *satyam*—true; *kuruṣva*—please make; *nigamam*—the promise given in the revealed scripture; *tava*—Your; *pāda-mūlam*—the base of the lotus feet; *prāptāḥ*—having obtained; *vayam*—we; *tulasi-dāma*—the garland of *tulasī* leaves; *padā*—by Your foot; *avasṛṣṭam*—neglectfully kicked away; *keśaiḥ*—upon our hair; *nivoḍhum*—in order to carry; *atilaṅghya*—rejecting; *samasta*—all; *bandhūn*—relations.

TRANSLATION

The wives of the brāhmaṇas replied: O almighty one, please do not speak such cruel words. Rather, You should fulfill Your promise that You always reciprocate with Your devotees in kind. Now that we have attained Your lotus feet, we simply wish to remain here in the forest so we may carry upon our heads the garlands of tulasī leaves You may neglectfully kick away with Your lotus feet. We are ready to give up all material relationships.

PURPORT

Here the *brāhmaṇas'* wives are saying something similar to what the *gopīs* say at the beginning of the *rāsa* dance (*Bhāg.* 10.29.31), when Lord Kṛṣṇa tells them to go home as well. Like this verse, the *gopīs'* statement begins with the words *maivaṁ vibho'rhati bhavān gadituṁ nṛ-śaṁsam.*

Nigama refers to the Vedic literature, which states that one who surrenders at the lotus feet of the Lord does not return to this material world. Thus the *brāhmaṇas'* wives appealed to the Lord that since they had surrendered to Him, it was unfair for Him to order them to return to their materialistic husbands.

According to Śrīla Viśvanātha Cakravartī Ṭhākura, Lord Kṛṣṇa might have pointed out to the *brāhmaṇas'* wives, "You young ladies are members of the aristocratic *brāhmaṇa* community, so how can you surrender at the feet of a mere cowherd boy?"

To this the ladies might have replied, "Since we have already surrendered at Your lotus feet, and since we desire to become Your servants, we are obviously not maintaining a false identification as members of the so-called *brāhmaṇa* community. You can easily ascertain this from our words."

Lord Kṛṣṇa might have replied, "I am a cowherd boy, and My proper maidservants and girlfriends are the cowherd girls, the *gopīs.*"

The wives might have answered, "True, let them be so. Let them shine forth if You are embarrassed in front of Your relatives to make *brāhmaṇa* ladies Your maidservants. We certainly don't want to embarrass You. We will not go to Your village but will rather remain in Vṛndāvana, like presiding deities of the forest. We simply desire to perfect our lives by even a slight trace of connection with You."

Thus by the spiritual insight of Śrīla Viśvanātha Cakravartī Ṭhākura, we learn that the *brāhmaṇas'* wives offered to remain at a distance and simply take the *tulasī* leaves that would fall from the lotus feet of Kṛṣṇa or be crushed by the feet of His girlfriends when He would embrace them.

The ladies offered to carry these *tulasī* leaves upon their heads. Thus renouncing the desire to become Kṛṣṇa's intimate girlfriends or maidservants (a position they knew was difficult to achieve), the young *brāhmaṇa* ladies begged to remain in Vṛndāvana forest. If the Lord had then asked "Then what will your family members say?" they would have replied "We have already transcended our so-called relatives because we are seeing You, the Supreme Lord, face to face."

TEXT 30

गृह्णन्ति नो न पतयः पितरौ सुता वा
न भ्रातृबन्धुसुहृदः कुत एव चान्ये ।
तस्माद् भवत्प्रपदयोः पतितात्मनां नो
नान्या भवेद् गतिररिन्दम तद् विधेहि ॥ ३० ॥

gṛhṇanti no na patayaḥ pitarau sutā vā
na bhrātṛ-bandhu-suhṛdaḥ kuta eva cānye
tasmād bhavat-prapadayoḥ patitātmanāṁ no
nānyā bhaved gatir arindama tad vidhehi

gṛhṇanti—they will accept; *naḥ*—us; *na*—not; *patayaḥ*—our husbands; *pitarau*—fathers; *sutāḥ*—sons; *vā*—or; *na*—not; *bhrātṛ*—brothers; *bandhu*—other relatives; *suhṛdaḥ*—and friends; *kutaḥ*—how then; *eva*—indeed; *ca*—and; *anye*—other people; *tasmāt*—therefore; *bhavat*—Your; *prapadayoḥ*—at the tips of the lotus feet; *patita*—fallen; *ātmanām*—whose bodies; *naḥ*—for us; *na*—not; *anyā*—any other; *bhavet*—there can be; *gatiḥ*—destination; *arim-dama*—O chastiser of enemies; *tat*—that; *vidhehi*—kindly bestow upon us.

TRANSLATION

Our husbands, fathers, sons, brothers, other relatives and friends will no longer take us back, and how could anyone else be willing to give us shelter? Therefore, since we have thrown ourselves at Your lotus feet and have no other destination, please, O chastiser of enemies, grant our desire.

PURPORT

Śrīla Viśvanātha Cakravartī Ṭhākura comments as follows: "From their very youth the *brāhmaṇas'* wives had heard about Lord Kṛṣṇa's beauty, qualities and sweetness from the womenfolk of Vṛndāvana village, and also from the flower ladies, the betel-nut sellers and others. Consequently they always felt ecstatic love for Kṛṣṇa and were indifferent to their household duties. Their husbands, seeing them as deviant, doubted them and avoided dealing with them as far as possible. Now the wives of the *brāhmaṇas* were ready to formally reject their so-called families and neighbors, and out of great agitation they were crying and placing their heads upon Lord Kṛṣṇa's lotus feet, offering obeisances. In this way, with choking voices, they spoke the above verse. They begged that Lord Kṛṣṇa bestow upon them the benediction that He be their only destination, that He, the chastiser of enemies, subdue all *their* enemies —those difficulties obstructing them from attaining the Lord."

The wives of the *brāhmaṇas* simply wanted to serve Lord Kṛṣṇa, and this is pure Kṛṣṇa consciousness in ecstatic love of Godhead.

TEXT 31

श्रीभगवानुवाच
पतयो नाभ्यसूयेरन् पितृभ्रातृसुतादयः ।
लोकाश्च वो मयोपेता देवा अप्यनुमन्वते ॥ ३१ ॥

śrī-bhagavān uvāca
patayo nābhyasūyeran
pitṛ-bhrātṛ-sutādayaḥ
lokāś ca vo mayopetā
devā apy anumanvate

śrī-bhagavān uvāca—the Supreme Personality of Godhead said; *patayaḥ* —your husbands; *na abhyasūyeran*—will not feel inimical; *pitṛ-bhrātṛ-suta-ādayaḥ*—your fathers, brothers, sons and others; *lokāḥ*—the general populace; *ca*—also; *vaḥ*—toward you; *mayā*—by Me; *upetāḥ*—advised; *devāḥ* —the demigods; *api*—even; *anumanvate*—regard favorably.

TRANSLATION

The Supreme Personality of Godhead replied: Rest assured that your husbands will not be inimical toward you, nor will your fathers, brothers, sons, other relatives or the general populace. I will personally advise them of the situation. Indeed, even the demigods will express their approval.

TEXT 32

न प्रीतयेऽनुरागाय ह्यंगसंगो नृणामिह ।
तन्मनो मयि युञ्जाना अचिरान्मामवाप्स्यथ ॥ ३२ ॥

na prītaye'nurāgāya
hy aṅga-saṅgo nṛṇām iha
tan mano mayi yuñjānā
acirān mām avāpsyatha

na—not; *prītaye*—for satisfaction; *anurāgāya*—for loving attraction; *hi*—certainly; *aṅga-saṅgaḥ*—physical association; *nṛṇām*—for people; *iha*—in this world; *tat*—therefore; *manaḥ*—your minds; *mayi*—upon Me; *yuñjānāḥ*—fixing; *acirāt*—very quickly; *mām*—Me; *avāpsyatha*—you will achieve.

TRANSLATION

For you to remain in My bodily association would certainly not please people in this world, nor would it be the best way for you to increase your love for Me. Rather, you should fix your minds on Me, and very soon you will achieve Me.

PURPORT

The Lord pointed out that people in general would not appreciate a loving affair between Lord Kṛṣṇa, who superficially was appearing as a cowherd boy, and the wives from the *brāhmaṇa* community. Also, the *brāhmaṇa* ladies' own devotion and love would increase most efficiently in separation. In other words, it would be best all around if they continued to fix their minds on Lord Kṛṣṇa and thus went on with the process they had been practicing throughout their lives. The Lord and His bona fide representative, the spiritual master, expertly engage the Lord's devotees in different types of service so that all of them can quickly return to His lotus feet.

TEXT 33

श्रवणाद्दर्शनाद् ध्यानान्मयि भावोऽनुकीर्तनात् ।
न तथा सन्निकर्षेण प्रतियात ततो गृहान् ॥ ३३ ॥

śravaṇād darśanād dhyānān
mayi bhāvo'nukīrtanāt
na tathā sannikarṣeṇa
pratiyāta tato gṛhān

śravaṇāt—by hearing; *darśanāt*—by seeing the Deity form; *dhyānāt*—by meditation; *mayi*—for Me; *bhāvaḥ*—love; *anukīrtanāt*—by chanting My names and qualities; *na*—not; *tathā*—in the same way; *sannikarṣeṇa*—by literal proximity; *pratiyāta*—return; *tataḥ*—therefore; *gṛhān*—to your homes.

TRANSLATION

It is by hearing about Me, seeing My Deity form, meditating upon Me and chanting My names and glories that love for Me develops, not by physical proximity. Therefore please go back to your homes.

TEXT 34

श्रीशुक उवाच
इत्युक्ता द्विजपत्न्यस्ता यज्ञवाटं पुनर्गताः ।
ते चानसूयवस्ताभिः स्त्रीभिः सत्रमपारयन् ॥ ३४ ॥

śrī-śuka uvāca
ity uktā dvija-patnyas tā
yajña-vāṭaṁ punar gatāḥ
te cānasūyavas tābhiḥ
strībhiḥ satram apārayan

śrī-śukaḥ uvāca—Śrī Śukadeva Gosvāmī said; *iti*—with these words; *uktāḥ*—spoken to; *dvija-patnyaḥ*—the wives of the *brāhmaṇas; tāḥ*—they; *yajña-vāṭam*—to the place of sacrifice; *punaḥ*—again; *gatāḥ*—went; *te*—they, their husbands; *ca*—and; *anasūyavaḥ*—not inimical; *tābhiḥ*—together with them; *strībhiḥ*—their wives; *satram*—the sacrificial performance; *apārayan*—they completed.

TRANSLATION

Śrīla Śukadeva Gosvāmī said: Thus instructed, the wives of the brāhmaṇas returned to the place of sacrifice. The brāhmaṇas did not find any fault with their wives, and together with them they finished the sacrifice.

PURPORT

The wives of the *brāhmaṇas* obeyed Lord Kṛṣṇa's order and returned to the sacrificial arena of their husbands, whereas the *gopīs,* although ordered by Kṛṣṇa to go home, remained in the forest to dance with Him through the full-moon night. Both the *gopīs* and the *brāhmaṇas'* wives achieved pure love of Godhead.

TEXT 35

तत्रैका विधृता भर्त्रा भगवन्तं यथाश्रुतम् ।
हृदोपगुह्य विजहौ देहं कर्मानुबन्धनम् ॥ ३५ ॥

tatraikā vidhṛtā bhartrā
bhagavantaṁ yathā-śrutam
hṛdopaguhya vijahau
dehaṁ karmānubandhanam

tatra—there; *ekā*—one of them; *vidhṛtā*—held back by force; *bhartrā*—by her husband; *bhagavantam*—the Supreme Lord, Śrī Kṛṣṇa; *yathā-śrutam*—as she heard about Him from the others; *hṛdā*—within her heart; *upaguhya*—embracing; *vijahau*—she gave up; *deham*—her material body; *karma-anubandhanam*—which is simply the basis of bondage to material activity.

TRANSLATION

One of the ladies had been forcibly kept back by her husband. When she heard the others describe the Supreme Lord Kṛṣṇa, she embraced Him within her heart and gave up her material body, the basis of bondage to material activity.

PURPORT

The lady described here was especially devoted to Lord Kṛṣṇa. Upon giving up her material body, she immediately attained a spiritual body and left the sacrificial arena to join the Supreme Personality of Godhead.

TEXT 36

भगवानपि गोविन्दस्तेनैवान्नेन गोपकान् ।
चतुर्विधेनाशयित्वा स्वयं च बुभुजे प्रभुः ॥ ३६ ॥

bhagavān api govindas
tenaivānnena gopakān
catur-vidhenāśayitvā
svayaṁ ca bubhuje prabhuḥ

bhagavān—the Supreme Personality of Godhead; *api*—moreover; *govindaḥ*—Lord Govinda; *tena*—with that; *eva*—very same; *annena*—food; *gopakān*—the cowherd boys; *catuḥ-vidhena*—of four varieties; *aśayitvā*—feeding; *svayam*—Himself; *ca*—and; *bubhuje*—partook; *prabhuḥ*—the Almighty.

TRANSLATION

Govinda, the Supreme Personality of Godhead, fed the cowherd boys with that food of four varieties. Then the all-powerful Lord Himself partook of the preparations.

TEXT 37

एवं लीलानरवपुर्नृलोकमनुशीलयन् ।
रेमे गोगोपगोपीनां रमयन् रूपवाक्कृतैः ॥ ३७ ॥

evaṁ līlā-nara-vapur
nṛ-lokam anuśīlayan
reme go-gopa-gopīnāṁ
ramayan rūpa-vāk-kṛtaiḥ

evam—in this manner; *līlā*—for pastimes; *nara*—appearing as a human being; *vapuḥ*—whose transcendental body; *nṛ-lokam*—human society; *anuśīlayan*—imitating; *reme*—He took pleasure; *go*—the cows; *gopa*—cowherd boys; *gopīnām*—the cowherd girls; *ramayan*—pleasing; *rūpa*—with His beauty; *vāk*—words; *kṛtaiḥ*—and actions.

TRANSLATION

Thus the Supreme Lord, appearing like a human being to perform His pastimes, imitated the ways of human society. He enjoyed pleasing His cows, cowherd boyfriends and cowherd girlfriends with His beauty, words and actions.

TEXT 38

अथानुस्मृत्य विप्रास्ते अन्वतप्यन् कृतागसः ।
यद् विश्वेश्वरयोर्याच्ञामहन्म नृविडम्बयोः ॥ ३८ ॥

athānusmṛtya viprās te
anvatapyan kṛtāgasaḥ
yad viśveśvarayor yācñām
ahanma nṛ-viḍambayoḥ

atha—then; *anusmṛtya*—coming to their senses; *viprāḥ*—the *brāhmaṇas; te*—they; *anvatapyan*—felt great remorse; *kṛta-agasaḥ*—having committed sinful offenses; *yat*—because; *viśva-īśvarayoḥ*—of the two Lords of the universe, Kṛṣṇa and Balarāma; *yācñām*—the humble supplication; *ahanma*—we transgressed; *nṛ-viḍambayoḥ*—of those who were deceptively appearing as human beings.

TRANSLATION

The brāhmaṇas then came to their senses and began to feel great remorse. They thought, "We have sinned, for we have denied the request of the two Lords of the universe, who deceptively appeared as ordinary human beings."

PURPORT

Lord Kṛṣṇa and Lord Balarāma did not try to deceive the *brāhmaṇas:* They straightforwardly requested food from them. Rather, the *brāhmaṇas* deceived themselves, as indicated by the Sanskrit word *nṛ-viḍambayoḥ,* which means that Kṛṣṇa and Balarāma are bewildering for an ordinary human being who considers Them also to be human. Still, because the wives of the *brāhmaṇas* were great devotees of the Lord, the foolish *brāhmaṇas* received spiritual benefit and finally came to their senses.

TEXT 39

दृष्ट्वा स्त्रीणां भगवति कृष्णे भक्तिमलौकिकीम्।
आत्मानं च तया हीनमनुतप्ता व्यगर्हयन् ॥ ३९ ॥

dṛṣṭvā strīṇāṁ bhagavati
kṛṣṇe bhaktim alaukikīm
ātmānaṁ ca tayā hīnam
anutaptā vyagarhayan

dṛṣṭvā—observing; *strīṇām*—of their wives; *bhagavati*—for the Supreme Personality of Godhead; *kṛṣṇe*—Śrī Kṛṣṇa; *bhaktim*—the pure devotion; *alaukikīm*—transcendental to this world; *ātmānam*—themselves; *ca*—and; *tayā*—of that; *hīnam*—devoid; *anutaptāḥ*—lamenting; *vyagarhayan*—they condemned.

TRANSLATION

Taking note of their wives' pure, transcendental devotion for Lord Kṛṣṇa, the Supreme Personality of Godhead, and seeing their own lack of devotion, the brāhmaṇas felt most sorrowful and began to condemn themselves.

TEXT 40

धिग् जन्म नस्त्रिवृद् यत्तद्धिग् व्रतं धिग् बहुज्ञताम् ।
धिक्कुलं धिक्क्रियादाक्ष्यं विमुखा ये त्वधोक्षजे ॥ ४० ॥

dhig janma nas tri-vṛd yat tad
dhig vrataṁ dhig bahu-jñatām
dhik kulaṁ dhik kriyā-dākṣyaṁ
vimukhā ye tv adhokṣaje

dhik—to hell; *janma*—with the birth; *naḥ*—our; *tri-vṛt*—threefold (the first from the physical parents, the second at the time of brahminical initiation, and the third at the time of initiation into the performances of Vedic sacrifice); *yat tat*—whatever; *dhik*—to hell; *vratam*—with our vow (of celibacy); *dhik*—to hell; *bahu-jñatām*—with our extensive knowledge; *dhik*—to hell; *kulam*—with our aristocratic lineage; *dhik*—to hell; *kriyā-dākṣyam*—with our expertise in ritualistic activities; *vimukhāḥ*—inimical; *ye*—who; *tu*—however; *adhokṣaje*—to the transcendental Personality of Godhead.

TRANSLATION

[The brāhmaṇas said:] To hell with our threefold birth, our vow of celibacy and our extensive learning! To hell with our aristocratic background and our expertise in the rituals of sacrifice! These are all condemned because we were inimical to the transcendental Personality of Godhead.

PURPORT

As explained in the definitions above, the words *tri-vṛd janma,* or "threefold birth," refer to 1) physical birth, 2) brahminical initiation and 3) initiation into the performance of Vedic sacrifice. Everything is useless if one is ignorant of the Absolute Truth, the Supreme Lord Kṛṣṇa.

TEXT 41

नूनं भगवतो माया योगिनामपि मोहिनी ।
यद् वयं गुरवो नृणां स्वार्थे मुह्यामहे द्विजाः ॥ ४१ ॥

nūnaṁ bhagavato māyā
yoginām api mohinī

yad vayaṁ guravo nṝṇāṁ
svārthe muhyāmahe dvijāḥ

nūnam—indeed; *bhagavataḥ*—of the Supreme Lord; *māyā*—the illusory potency; *yoginām*—for great mystics; *api*—even; *mohinī*—is bewildering; *yat*—since; *vayam*—we; *guravaḥ*—the spiritual masters; *nṝṇām*—of society in general; *sva-arthe*—about our own real interest; *muhyāmahe*—have become bewildered; *dvijāḥ*—*brāhmaṇas.*

TRANSLATION

The illusory potency of the Supreme Lord certainly bewilders even the great mystics, what to speak of us. As brāhmaṇas we are supposed to be the spiritual masters of all classes of men, yet we have been bewildered about our own real interest.

TEXT 42

अहो पश्यत नारीणामपि कृष्णे जगद्गुरौ ।
दुरन्तभावं योऽविध्यन्मृत्युपाशान् गृहाभिधान् ॥ ४२ ॥

aho paśyata nārīṇām
api kṛṣṇe jagad-gurau
duranta-bhāvaṁ yo'vidhyan
mṛtyu-pāśān gṛhābhidhān

aho paśyata—just see; *nārīṇām*—of these women; *api*—even; *kṛṣṇe*—for Lord Kṛṣṇa; *jagat-gurau*—the spiritual master of the entire universe; *duranta*—unlimited; *bhāvam*—the devotion; *yaḥ*—which; *avidhyat*—has broken; *mṛtyu*—of death; *pāśān*—the bonds; *gṛha-abhidhān*—known as family life.

TRANSLATION

Just see the unlimited love these women have developed for Lord Kṛṣṇa, the spiritual master of the entire universe! This love has broken for them the very bonds of death—their attachment to family life.

PURPORT

Superficially, the husbands, fathers, fathers-in-law and so on were the ladies' *gurus,* or teachers. Yet the women had become perfect in Kṛṣṇa consciousness, whereas the men had fallen into the darkness of ignorance.

According to Śrīla Viśvanātha Cakravartī Ṭhākura, upon returning home the ladies showed transcendental ecstatic symptoms, such as trembling of the body, shedding of tears, standing of the bodily hairs on end, discoloration of the complexion, crying out "O pleasure of my life, O Kṛṣṇa!" with faltering words, and so forth.

Śrīla Viśvanātha Cakravartī goes on to state that while one may object that it is not fitting for a woman to love anyone other than her husband, here the husbands themselves point out that they are *gurus* only in imitation of the Supreme Lord, who is *jagad-guru,* the universal teacher and spiritual master. The husbands noted that the women, having perfected their transcendental attachment for Kṛṣṇa, did not have even a trace of attachment left for home, husband, children and so forth. Therefore from that day on the husbands accepted those ladies as their worshipable spiritual masters and no longer thought of them as their wives or property.

TEXTS 43–44

नासां द्विजातिसंस्कारो न निवासो गुरावपि ।
न तपो नात्ममीमांसा न शौचं न क्रियाः शुभाः ॥ ४३ ॥
तथापि ह्युत्तमःश्लोके कृष्णे योगेश्वरेश्वरे ।
भक्तिर्दृढा न चास्माकं संस्कारादिमतामपि ॥ ४४ ॥

nāsāṁ dvijāti-saṁskāro
na nivāso gurāv api
na tapo nātma-mīmāṁsā
na śaucaṁ na kriyāḥ śubhāḥ

tathāpi hy uttamaḥ-śloke
kṛṣṇe yogeśvareśvare
bhaktir dṛḍhā na cāsmākaṁ
saṁskārādimatām api

na—there is not; *āsām*—on their part; *dvijāti-saṁskāraḥ*—the purificatory rituals pertaining to the twice-born classes of society; *na*—nor; *nivāsaḥ*—residence; *gurau*—in the *āśrama* of a spiritual master (that is, training as a *brahmacārī*); *api*—even; *na*—no; *tapaḥ*—execution of austerities; *na*—no; *ātma-mīmāṁsā*—philosophical inquiry into the reality of the self; *na*—no; *śaucam*—rituals of cleanliness; *na*—no; *kriyāḥ*—ritualistic activities; *śubhāḥ*—pious; *tathā api*—nevertheless; *hi*—indeed; *uttamaḥ-śloke*—

whose glories are chanted by the exalted *mantras* of the *Vedas; kṛṣṇe*—for Lord Kṛṣṇa; *yoga-īśvara-īśvare*—the supreme master of all masters of mystic power; *bhaktiḥ*—pure devotional service; *dṛḍhā*—firm; *na*—not; *ca*—on the other hand; *asmākam*—of us; *saṁskāra-ādi-matām*—who possess such purification and so forth; *api*—even though.

TRANSLATION

These women have never undergone the purificatory rites of the twice-born classes, nor have they lived as brahmacārīs in the āśrama of a spiritual master, nor have they executed austerities, speculated on the nature of the self, followed the formalities of cleanliness or engaged in pious rituals. Nevertheless, they have firm devotion for Lord Kṛṣṇa, whose glories are chanted by the exalted hymns of the Vedas and who is the supreme master of all masters of mystic power. We, on the other hand, have no such devotion for the Lord, although we have executed all these processes.

PURPORT

According to Śrīla Śrīdhara Svāmī, the husbands were not aware that their wives had occasionally associated with residents of Vṛndāvana, such as the flower ladies, and had heard about the beauty and qualities of Kṛṣṇa. The *brāhmaṇas* were astonished at their wives' loving devotion for Lord Kṛṣṇa, not realizing that this devotion had developed as a result of hearing and chanting about the Lord in the association of His pure devotees.

TEXT 45

ननु स्वार्थविमूढानां प्रमत्तानां गृहेहया ।
अहो नः स्मारयामास गोपवाक्यैः सतां गतिः ॥ ४५ ॥

nanu svārtha-vimūḍhānāṁ
pramattānāṁ gṛhehayā
aho naḥ smārayām āsa
gopa-vākyaiḥ satāṁ gatiḥ

nanu—indeed; *sva-artha*—about their own true benefit; *vimūḍhānām*—who were bewildered; *pramattānām*—who were intoxicated; *gṛha-īhayā*—with their household endeavors; *aho*—ah; *naḥ*—us; *smārayām āsa*—He reminded about; *gopa-vākyaiḥ*—by the words of cowherds; *satām*—of the transcendental souls; *gatiḥ*—the ultimate destination.

TRANSLATION

Indeed, infatuated as we are with our household affairs, we have deviated completely from the real aim of our life. But now just see how the Lord, through the words of these simple cowherd boys, has reminded us of the ultimate destination of all true transcendentalists.

TEXT 46

अन्यथा पूर्णकामस्य कैवल्याद्यशिषां पतेः ।
ईशितव्यैः किमस्माभिरीशस्यैतद् विडम्बनम् ॥ ४६ ॥

anyathā pūrṇa-kāmasya
kaivalyādy-āśiṣāṁ pateḥ
īśitavyaiḥ kim asmābhir
īśasyaitad viḍambanam

anyathā—otherwise; *pūrṇa-kāmasya*—of Him whose every possible desire is fulfilled; *kaivalya*—of liberation; *ādi*—and others; *āśiṣām*—benedictions; *pateḥ*—the master; *īśitavyaiḥ*—with those who are meant to be controlled; *kim*—what; *asmābhiḥ*—with us; *īśasya*—of Him who is the absolute controller; *etat*—this; *viḍambanam*—pretense.

TRANSLATION

Otherwise, why would the supreme controller—whose every desire is already fulfilled and who is the master of liberation and all other transcendental benedictions—enact this pretense with us, who are always to be controlled by Him?

PURPORT

Although Lord Kṛṣṇa is the Absolute Truth, He humbly sent His cowherd boyfriends to beg food from the *brāhmaṇas.* In so doing, He exposed the *brāhmaṇas'* foolish arrogance and established the glories of His own transcendental beauty by attracting their very wives to surrender at His lotus feet.

TEXT 47

हित्वान्यान् भजते यं श्रीः पादस्पर्शाशयासकृत्।
स्वात्मदोषापवर्गेण तद्याच्ञा जनमोहिनी ॥ ४७ ॥

hitvānyān bhajate yaṁ śrīḥ
pāda-sparśāśayāsakṛt
svātma-doṣāpavargeṇa
tad-yācñā jana-mohinī

hitvā—giving up; *anyān*—others; *bhajate*—worships; *yam*—which Lord; *śrīḥ*—the goddess of fortune; *pāda-sparśa*—for the touch of His lotus feet; *āśayā*—with the desire; *asakṛt*—constantly; *sva-ātma*—of herself; *doṣa*—the faults (of fickleness and pride); *apavargeṇa*—putting aside; *tat*—His; *yācñā*—begging; *jana*—ordinary humans; *mohinī*—bewildering.

TRANSLATION

Hoping for the touch of His lotus feet, the goddess of fortune perpetually worships Him alone, leaving aside all others and renouncing her pride and fickleness. That He begs is certainly astonishing to everyone.

PURPORT

The supreme master of the goddess of fortune herself obviously does not have to beg for food, as pointed out here by the *brāhmaṇas,* who are finally manifesting real spiritual intelligence.

TEXTS 48–49

देशः कालः पृथग् द्रव्यं मन्त्रतन्त्रर्त्विजोऽग्नयः ।
देवता यजमानश्च क्रतुर्धर्मश्च यन्मयः ॥ ४८ ॥
स एव भगवान् साक्षाद् विष्णुर्योगेश्वरेश्वरः ।
जातो यदुष्वित्याशृण्म ह्यपि मूढा न विद्महे ॥ ४९ ॥

deśaḥ kālaḥ pṛthag dravyaṁ
mantra-tantrartvijo'gnayaḥ
devatā yajamānaś ca
kratur dharmaś ca yan-mayaḥ

sa eva bhagavān sākṣād
viṣṇur yogeśvareśvaraḥ
jāto yaduṣv ity āśṛṇma
hy api mūḍhā na vidmahe

deśaḥ—the place; *kālaḥ*—time; *pṛthak dravyam*—particular items of paraphernalia; *mantra*—Vedic hymns; *tantra*—prescribed rituals; *ṛtvijaḥ*—

priests; *agnayaḥ*—and the sacrificial fires; *devatā*—the presiding demigods; *yajamānaḥ*—the performer; *ca*—and; *kratuḥ*—the offering; *dharmaḥ*—the pious reaction; *ca*—and; *yat*—whom; *mayaḥ*—constituting; *saḥ*—He; *eva*—indeed; *bhagavān*—the Supreme Personality of Godhead; *sākṣāt*—directly; *viṣṇuḥ*—Lord Viṣṇu; *yoga-īśvara-īśvaraḥ*—the Lord of all mystic controllers; *jātaḥ*—taken birth; *yaduṣu*—among the Yadu dynasty; *iti*—thus; *āśṛṇma*—we have heard; *hi*—certainly; *api*—nevertheless; *mūḍhāḥ*—foolish; *na vidmahe*—we could not understand.

TRANSLATION

All the aspects of sacrifice—the auspicious place and time, the various items of paraphernalia, the Vedic hymns, the prescribed rituals, the priests and sacrificial fires, the demigods, the patron of the sacrifice, the sacrificial offering and the pious results obtained—all are simply manifestations of His opulences. Yet even though we had heard that the Supreme Personality of Godhead, Viṣṇu, the Lord of all mystic controllers, had taken birth in the Yadu dynasty, we were so foolish that we could not recognize Śrī Kṛṣṇa to be none other than Him.

TEXT 50

तस्मै नमो भगवते कृष्णायाकुण्ठमेधसे ।
यन्मायामोहितधियो भ्रमामः कर्मवर्त्मसु ॥ ५० ॥

tasmai namo bhagavate
kṛṣṇāyākuṇṭha-medhase
yan-māyā-mohita-dhiyo
bhramāmaḥ karma-vartmasu

tasmai—unto Him; *namaḥ*—obeisances; *bhagavate*—unto the Supreme Personality of Godhead; *kṛṣṇāya*—Lord Kṛṣṇa; *akuṇṭha-medhase*—whose intelligence is never restricted; *yat-māyā*—by whose illusory potency; *mohita*—bewildered; *dhiyaḥ*—whose minds; *bhramāmaḥ*—we are wandering; *karma-vartmasu*—upon the paths of fruitive activity.

TRANSLATION

Let us offer our obeisances unto Lord Kṛṣṇa, the Supreme Personality of Godhead. His intelligence is never bewildered, whereas we, confused by His power of illusion, are simply wandering about on the paths of fruitive work.

TEXT 51

स वै न आद्यः पुरुषः स्वमायामोहितात्मनाम् ।
अविज्ञातानुभावानां क्षन्तुमर्हत्यतिक्रमम् ॥ ५१ ॥

sa vai na ādyaḥ puruṣaḥ
sva-māyā-mohitātmanām
avijñātānubhāvānāṁ
kṣantum arhaty atikramam

saḥ—He; *vai*—indeed; *naḥ*—our; *ādyaḥ*—the primeval Lord; *puruṣaḥ*—the Supreme Personality of Godhead; *sva-mayā-mohita-ātmanām*—of those whose minds have been bewildered by His illusory potency; *avijñāta*—who did not understand; *anubhāvānām*—His influence; *kṣantum*—to forgive; *arhati*—should; *atikramam*—the offense.

TRANSLATION

We were bewildered by Lord Kṛṣṇa's illusory potency and thus could not understand His influence as the original Personality of Godhead. Now we hope He will kindly forgive our offense.

TEXT 52

इति स्वाघमनुस्मृत्य कृष्णे ते कृतहेलनाः ।
दिदृक्षवो व्रजमथ कंसाद् भीता न चाचलन् ॥ ५२ ॥

iti svāgham anusmṛtya
kṛṣṇe te kṛta-helanāḥ
didṛkṣavo vrajam atha
kaṁsād bhītā na cācalan

iti—thus; *sva-agham*—their own offense; *anusmṛtya*—thinking back upon; *kṛṣṇe*—against Lord Kṛṣṇa; *te*—they; *kṛta-helanāḥ*—having shown contempt; *didṛkṣavaḥ*—wishing to see; *vrajam*—to the village of Nanda Mahārāja; *atha*—then; *kaṁsāt*—of Kaṁsa; *bhītāḥ*—afraid; *na*—not; *ca*—and; *acalan*—they went.

TRANSLATION

Thus reflecting on the sin they had committed by neglecting Lord Kṛṣṇa, they became very eager to see Him. But being afraid of King Kaṁsa, they did not dare go to Vraja.

PURPORT

Realizing their offense against Lord Kṛṣṇa, and finally appreciating His almighty position, the *brāhmaṇas* naturally wanted to rush to Vraja and surrender at the lotus feet of the Lord. But they were afraid that Kaṁsa would certainly kill them when his spies reported that they had gone to Kṛṣṇa. The *brāhmaṇas'* wives were absorbed in ecstatic Kṛṣṇa consciousness and thus went to Kṛṣṇa anyway, just as the *gopīs,* simply to dance with the Lord, traveled in the dead of night through a forest inhabited by wild animals. But the *brāhmaṇas* were not on such an advanced platform of Kṛṣṇa consciousness and thus, overcome by fear of Kaṁsa, could not see the Lord face to face.

Thus end the purports of the humble servants of His Divine Grace A.C. Bhaktivedanta Swami Prabhupāda to the Tenth Canto, Twenty-third Chapter, of the Śrīmad-Bhāgavatam, *entitled "The Brāhmaṇas' Wives Blessed."*

CHAPTER TWENTY- FOUR

Worshiping Govardhana Hill

In this chapter Lord Śrī Kṛṣṇa crushes the pride of Indra by prohibiting a sacrifice intended for him and initiating a substitute sacrifice in worship of Govardhana Hill.

When Śrī Kṛṣṇa saw the cowherd men busily preparing for a sacrifice to Indra, He inquired about it from their king, Nanda. Nanda explained that the rain given by Indra enables all living entities to maintain their lives, and therefore this sacrifice would be executed to satisfy him. Kṛṣṇa responded, "It is because of *karma* alone that living entities take their birth in a certain body, experience varieties of happiness and suffering in that body, and then give it up as the *karma* pertaining to it runs out. Thus it is *karma* alone that is our enemy, our friend, our *guru* and our lord, and Indra can do nothing to alter the happiness and distress of anyone, for everyone is tightly bound by his karmic reactions. The material modes of goodness, passion and ignorance bring about the creation, maintenance and destruction of this world. The clouds give forth rain when they are impelled by the mode of passion, and cowherds prosper by protecting the cows. Furthermore, the cowherds' proper residence is in the forest and on the hills. Therefore you should offer worship to the cows, the *brāhmaṇas* and Govardhana Hill."

After Kṛṣṇa spoke thus, He arranged for the cowherd men to worship Govardhana with the paraphernalia collected for the sacrifice to Indra. He then assumed a huge, unprecedented transcendental form and devoured all the food and other offerings presented to Govardhana. As He did so He proclaimed to the cowherd community that although they had worshiped Indra for so long, he had never appeared in person, whereas Govardhana himself had now manifested before their eyes and eaten their offerings of foodstuffs. Therefore they should all now offer obeisances to Govardhana Hill. Then Lord Kṛṣṇa joined the cowherds in offering obeisances to His own newly assumed form.

TEXT 1

श्रीशुक उवाच

भगवानपि तत्रैव बलदेवेन संयुतः ।
अपश्यन्निवसन् गोपानिन्द्रयागकृतोद्यमान् ॥ १ ॥

śrī-śuka uvāca
bhagavān api tatraiva
baladevena saṁyutaḥ
apaśyan nivasan gopān
indra-yāga-kṛtodyamān

śrī-śukaḥ uvāca—Śrī Śukadeva Gosvāmī said; *bhagavān*—the Supreme Personality of Godhead; *api*—also; *tatra eva*—in that same place; *baladevena*—by Lord Balarāma; *saṁyutaḥ*—joined; *apaśyat*—saw; *nivasan*—staying; *gopān*—the cowherd men; *indra*—for Indra, the King of heaven; *yāga*—for the sake of a sacrifice; *kṛta*—making; *udyamān*—great endeavor.

TRANSLATION

Śukadeva Gosvāmī said: While staying in that very place with His brother Baladeva, Lord Kṛṣṇa happened to see the cowherd men busily arranging for a sacrifice to Indra.

PURPORT

According to Śrīla Śrīdhara Svāmī and other *ācāryas,* the words *tatra eva* in this verse indicate that Lord Kṛṣṇa stayed in the village of the *brāhmaṇas* whose wives had satisfied Him by their devotion. Thus He gave His mercy to those *brāhmaṇas* as well as to their chaste wives, who had no one to associate with except their husbands. In that place the cowherd men, headed by Lord Kṛṣṇa's father, Nanda Mahārāja, were somehow or other preparing an elaborate sacrifice to Lord Indra, and Lord Kṛṣṇa reacted as follows.

TEXT 2

तदभिज्ञोऽपि भगवान् सर्वात्मा सर्वदर्शनः ।
प्रश्रयावनतोऽपृच्छद् वृद्धान्नन्दपुरोगमान् ॥ २ ॥

tad-abhijño'pi bhagavān
sarvātmā sarva-darśanaḥ

praśrayāvanato'pṛcchad
vṛddhān nanda-purogamān

tat-abhijñaḥ—being in full knowledge about it; *api*—although; *bhagavān*—the Supreme Lord; *sarva-ātmā*—the Supersoul within everyone's heart; *sarva-darśanaḥ*—the omniscient Personality of Godhead; *praśraya-avanataḥ*—bowing down humbly; *apṛcchat*—He inquired; *vṛddhān*—from the elders; *nanda-puraḥ-gamān*—headed by Mahārāja Nanda.

TRANSLATION

Being the omniscient Supersoul, the Supreme Lord Kṛṣṇa already understood the situation, yet He still humbly inquired from the elders, headed by His father, Nanda Mahārāja.

PURPORT

Lord Kṛṣṇa was eager to enact His pastime of lifting Govardhana Hill and defeating the false pride of Indra, and thus He cleverly inquired from His father about the imminent sacrifice.

TEXT 3

कथ्यतां मे पितः कोऽयं सम्भ्रमो व उपागतः ।
किं फलं कस्य वोद्देशः केन वा साध्यते मखः ॥ ३ ॥

kathyatāṁ me pitaḥ ko'yaṁ
sambhramo va upāgataḥ
kiṁ phalaṁ kasya voddeśaḥ
kena vā sādhyate makhaḥ

kathyatām—let it be explained; *me*—to Me; *pitaḥ*—My dear father; *kaḥ*—what; *ayam*—this; *sambhramaḥ*—flurry of activity; *vaḥ*—upon you; *upāgataḥ*—come; *kim*—what; *phalam*—the consequence; *kasya*—for whose; *vā*—and; *uddeśaḥ*—sake; *kena*—by what means; *vā*—and; *sādhyate*—is to be accomplished; *makhaḥ*—this sacrifice.

TRANSLATION

[Lord Kṛṣṇa said:] My dear father, kindly explain to Me what this great endeavor of yours is all about. What is it meant to accomplish? If this is a ritual sacrifice, then for whose satisfaction is it intended and by what means is it going to be executed?

TEXT 4

एतद् ब्रूहि महान् कामो मह्यं शुश्रूषवे पितः ।
न हि गोप्यं हि साधूनां कृत्यं सर्वात्मनामिह ।
अस्त्यस्वपरदृष्टीनाममित्रोदास्तविद्विषाम् ॥ ४ ॥

etad brūhi mahān kāmo
mahyaṁ śuśrūṣave pitaḥ
na hi gopyaṁ hi sādhūnāṁ
kṛtyaṁ sarvātmanām iha
asty asva-para-dṛṣṭīnām
amitrodāsta-vidviṣām

etat—this; *brūhi*—please speak; *mahān*—great; *kāmaḥ*—desire; *mahyam*—to Me; *śuśrūṣave*—who am ready to hear faithfully; *pitaḥ*—O father; *na*—not; *hi*—indeed; *gopyam*—to be kept secret; *hi*—certainly; *sādhūnām*—of saintly persons; *kṛtyam*—the activities; *sarva-ātmanām*—who see everyone as equal to themselves; *iha*—in this world; *asti*—there is; *asva-para-dṛṣṭīnām*—who do not distinguish between what is their own and what is another's; *amitra-udāsta-vidviṣām*—who do not distinguish between friends, neutral parties and enemies.

TRANSLATION

Please tell Me about it, O father. I have a great desire to know and am ready to hear in good faith. Certainly, no secrets are to be kept by saintly personalities, who see all others as equal to themselves, who have no conception of "mine" or "another's" and who do not consider who is a friend, who is an enemy and who is neutral.

PURPORT

Lord Kṛṣṇa's father might have thought that his son was a mere child and thus could not properly question the validity of a Vedic sacrifice. But the Lord's clever statement here would certainly have convinced Nanda that Śrī Kṛṣṇa was making a serious, not a whimsical, inquiry and that a serious answer should thus be given.

TEXT 5

उदासीनोऽरिवद् वर्ज्य आत्मवत् सुहृदुच्यते ॥ ५ ॥

udāsīno'ri-vad varjya
ātma-vat suhṛd ucyate

udāsīnaḥ—one who is indifferent; *ari-vat*—just like an enemy; *varjyaḥ*—is to be avoided; *ātma-vat*—like one's own self; *suhṛt*—a friend; *ucyate*—is said to be.

TRANSLATION

One who is neutral may be avoided like an enemy, but a friend should be considered like one's own self.

PURPORT

Even if Nanda Mahārāja did not see friends, enemies and neutral parties as entirely equal, Lord Kṛṣṇa, being Nanda Mahārāja's son, was certainly a most trustworthy friend and should therefore not be left out of intimate discussions. In other words, Nanda Mahārāja might have thought that as a householder he could not act on the highest saintly platform, and thus Lord Kṛṣṇa furnished additional reasons why His father should trust Him and reveal the entire purpose of the sacrifice.

According to Śrīla Jīva Gosvāmī, Nanda Mahārāja stood silent, doubting his position of parental aloofness, since Garga Muni had predicted that his son would be "equal to Nārāyaṇa in His qualities," and the young boy had already conquered and killed many powerful demons.

TEXT 6

ज्ञात्वाज्ञात्वा च कर्माणि जनोऽयमनुतिष्ठति ।
विदुषः कर्मसिद्धिः स्याद्यथा नाविदुषो भवेत् ॥ ६ ॥

jñātvājñātvā ca karmāṇi
jano'yam anutiṣṭhati
viduṣaḥ karma-siddhiḥ syād
yathā nāviduṣo bhavet

jñātvā—understanding; *ajñātvā*—not understanding; *ca*—also; *karmāṇi*—activities; *janaḥ*—the common people; *ayam*—these; *anutiṣṭhati*—perform; *viduṣaḥ*—for one who is wise; *karma-siddhiḥ*—achievement of the intended goal of activity; *syāt*—arises; *yathā*—as; *na*—not; *aviduṣaḥ*—for one who is foolish; *bhavet*—occurs.

TRANSLATION

When people in this world perform activities, sometimes they understand what they are doing and sometimes they don't. Those who know what they are doing achieve success in their work, whereas ignorant people do not.

PURPORT

The Lord here informs His father that people should perform a particular ceremony or activity only after thoroughly understanding it through discussion with friends. We should not be blind followers of tradition. If a person doesn't even know what he's doing, how can he be successful in his work? This, essentially, is the Lord's argument in this verse. Since Śrī Kṛṣṇa, as the young child of Nanda, would naturally be expected to show enthusiasm for His father's religious activities, it was the father's duty to give the son a thorough explanation of the ceremony.

TEXT 7

तत्र तावत् क्रियायोगो भवतां किं विचारितः ।
अथवा लौकिकस्तन्मे पृच्छतः साधु भण्यताम् ॥ ७ ॥

tatra tāvat kriyā-yogo
bhavatāṁ kiṁ vicāritaḥ
atha vā laukikas tan me
pṛcchataḥ sādhu bhaṇyatām

tatra tāvat—that being the case; *kriyā-yogaḥ*—this fruitive endeavor; *bhavatām*—of yours; *kim*—whether; *vicāritaḥ*—learned from the scriptures; *atha vā*—or else; *laukikaḥ*—of ordinary custom; *tat*—that; *me*—to Me; *pṛcchataḥ*—who am inquiring; *sādhu*—clearly; *bhaṇyatām*—it should be explained.

TRANSLATION

Such being the case, this ritualistic endeavor of yours should be clearly explained to Me. Is it a ceremony based on scriptural injunction, or simply a custom of ordinary society?

TEXT 8

श्रीनन्द उवाच
पर्जन्यो भगवानिन्द्रो मेघास्तस्यात्ममूर्तयः ।
तेऽभिवर्षन्ति भूतानां प्रीणनं जीवनं पयः ॥ ८ ॥

śrī-nanda uvāca
parjanyo bhagavān indro
meghās tasyātma-mūrtayaḥ
te'bhivarṣanti bhūtānāṁ
prīṇanaṁ jīvanaṁ payaḥ

śrī-nandaḥ uvāca—Śrī Nanda Mahārāja said; *parjanyaḥ*—the rain; *bhagavān*—the great lord; *indraḥ*—Indra; *meghāḥ*—the clouds; *tasya*—his; *ātma-mūrtayaḥ*—personal representatives; *te*—they; *abhivarṣanti*—directly give rain; *bhūtānām*—for all living entities; *prīṇanam*—the gratification; *jīvanam*—the life-giving force; *payaḥ*—(like) milk.

TRANSLATION

Nanda Mahārāja replied: The great Lord Indra is the controller of the rain. The clouds are his personal representatives, and they directly provide rainwater, which gives happiness and sustenance to all creatures.

PURPORT

Without clean rainwater, the earth could not possibly provide food or drink for anyone, nor could there be cleanliness. Thus it would be difficult to overestimate the value of rain.

TEXT 9

तं तात वयमन्ये च वार्मुचां पतिमीश्वरम् ।
द्रव्यैस्तद्रेतसा सिद्धैर्यजन्ते क्रतुभिर्नराः ॥ ९ ॥

taṁ tāta vayam anye ca
vārmucāṁ patim īśvaram
dravyais tad-retasā siddhair
yajante kratubhir narāḥ

tam—him; *tāta*—my dear son; *vayam*—we; *anye*—others; *ca*—also; *vāḥ-mucām*—of the clouds; *patim*—the master; *īśvaram*—the powerful controller; *dravyaiḥ*—with various items; *tat-retasā*—by his liquid discharge; *siddhaiḥ*—produced; *yajante*—they worship; *kratubhiḥ*—by fire sacrifices; *narāḥ*—men.

TRANSLATION

Not only we, my dear son, but also many other men worship him, the lord and master of the rain-giving clouds. We offer him grain and other paraphernalia of worship produced through his own discharge in the form of rain.

PURPORT

Nanda Mahārāja patiently tried to explain the "facts of life" to his young son, Śrī Kṛṣṇa, but in fact Nanda and all the residents of Vṛndāvana would learn an astonishing lesson, as explained in this chapter.

TEXT 10

तच्छेषेणोपजीवन्ति त्रिवर्गफलहेतवे ।
पुंसां पुरुषकाराणां पर्जन्यः फलभावनः ॥ १० ॥

tac-cheṣeṇopajīvanti
tri-varga-phala-hetave
puṁsāṁ puruṣa-kārāṇāṁ
parjanyaḥ phala-bhāvanaḥ

tat—of that sacrifice; *śeṣeṇa*—by the remnants; *upajīvanti*—they sustain their lives; *tri-varga*—consisting of the three aims of human life (religiosity, economic development and sense gratification); *phala-hetave*—for the sake of fruit; *puṁsām*—for persons; *puruṣa-kārāṇām*—engaged in human endeavor; *parjanyaḥ*—Lord Indra; *phala-bhāvanaḥ*—the means of effecting the intended goals.

TRANSLATION

By accepting the remnants of sacrifices performed to Indra, people sustain their lives and accomplish the threefold aims of religiosity, economic development and sense gratification. Thus Lord Indra is the agent responsible for the fruitive success of industrious people.

PURPORT

One might object that people sustain themselves by farming, industry and so on. But as previously mentioned, all human and nonhuman endeavor depends on food and drink, which cannot be produced without ample rain. By the word *tri-varga* Nanda further points out that the prosperity achieved through sacrifice for Indra is meant not merely for sense gratification but also for religiosity and economic development. Unless people are well fed, it is difficult for them to execute their duties, and without performance of duty, it is very difficult to be religious.

TEXT 11

य एनं विसृजेद्धर्मं परम्पर्यागतं नरः ।
कामाद् द्वेषाद् भयाल्लोभात्स वै नाप्नोति शोभनम् ॥ ११ ॥

ya enaṁ visṛjed dharmaṁ
paramparyāgataṁ naraḥ
kāmād dveṣād bhayāl lobhāt
sa vai nāpnoti śobhanam

yaḥ—anyone who; *enam*—this; *visṛjet*—rejects; *dharmam*—the religious principle; *paramparya*—from traditional authority; *āgatam*—received; *naraḥ*—a person; *kāmāt*—because of lust; *dveṣāt*—because of enmity; *bhayāt*—because of fear; *lobhāt*—or because of greed; *saḥ*—he; *vai*—certainly; *na āpnoti*—cannot achieve; *śobhanam*—auspiciousness.

TRANSLATION

This religious principle is based on sound tradition. Anyone who rejects it out of lust, enmity, fear or greed will certainly fail to achieve good fortune.

PURPORT

If a person neglects his religious duties because of lust, envy, fear or greed, his life will never be brilliant or perfect.

TEXT 12

श्रीशुक उवाच
वचो निशम्य नन्दस्य तथान्येषां व्रजौकसाम् ।
इन्द्राय मन्युं जनयन् पितरं प्राह केशवः ॥ १२ ॥

śrī-śuka uvāca
vaco niśamya nandasya
tathānyeṣāṁ vrajaukasām
indrāya manyuṁ janayan
pitaraṁ prāha keśavaḥ

śrī śukaḥ uvāca—Śrī Śukadeva Gosvāmī said; *vacaḥ*—the words; *niśamya*—hearing; *nandasya*—of Mahārāja Nanda; *tathā*—and also; *anyeṣām*—of the others; *vraja-okasām*—the residents of Vraja; *indrāya*—in Lord Indra; *manyum*—anger; *janayan*—generating; *pitaram*—to His father; *prāha*—spoke; *keśavaḥ*—Lord Keśava.

TRANSLATION

Śukadeva Gosvāmī said: When Lord Keśava [Kṛṣṇa] heard the statements of His father, Nanda, and other senior residents of Vraja, He addressed His father as follows, to arouse anger in Lord Indra.

PURPORT

Śrīla Śrīdhara Svāmī explains that Lord Kṛṣṇa's intention was not simply to insult a demigod, but rather to knock down the great mountain of false pride that had arisen within the Lord's tiny servant, who was supposed to represent the Lord as Indra. By lifting Govardhana Hill Lord Kṛṣṇa would thus initiate a blissful annual festival called Govardhana-pūjā, and He would further enjoy the pleasant pastime of dwelling for several days beneath the hill with all His loving devotees.

TEXT 13

श्रीभगवानुवाच
कर्मणा जायते जन्तुः कर्मणैव प्रलीयते।
सुखं दुःखं भयं क्षेमं कर्मणैवाभिपद्यते ॥ १३ ॥

śrī-bhagavān uvāca
karmaṇā jāyate jantuḥ
karmaṇaiva pralīyate
sukhaṁ duḥkhaṁ bhayaṁ kṣemaṁ
karmaṇaivābhipadyate

śrī-bhagavān uvāca—the Supreme Personality of Godhead said; *karmaṇā*—by the force of *karma; jāyate*—takes birth; *jantuḥ*—the living entity; *kar-*

maṇā—by *karma; eva*—alone; *pralīyate*—he meets his destruction; *sukham* —happiness; *duḥkham*—unhappiness; *bhayam*—fear; *kṣemam*—security; *karmaṇā eva*—by *karma* alone; *abhipadyate*—are obtained.

TRANSLATION

Lord Kṛṣṇa said: It is by the force of karma that a living entity takes birth, and it is by karma alone that he meets his destruction. His happiness, distress, fear and sense of security all arise as the effects of karma.

PURPORT

Lord Kṛṣṇa minimized the importance of the demigods by speaking the philosophy known as Karma-vāda or Karma-mīmāṁsā, which, basically, is atheism with a belief in reincarnation. According to this philosophy, there are subtle laws of nature that reward or punish us according to how we act: "As you sow, so shall you reap." In a future life one reaps the fruit of his present work, and this is the sum and substance of reality. Lord Kṛṣṇa, being God Himself, could hardly be a serious proponent of this mediocre philosophy. In the role of a young boy He was simply teasing His pure devotees by preaching it.

Śrīla Jīva Gosvāmī points out that Lord Kṛṣṇa was thinking, "Why are these eternal associates of Mine, appearing as My father and other relatives and friends, so caught up in this worship of Indra?" Thus although the Lord's main purpose was to take away the false pride of Indra, He also wanted to remind His eternal devotees that they need not divert their attention to other so-called gods, since in fact His devotees were already living with the Supreme Absolute Truth, the almighty Lord Himself.

TEXT 14

अस्ति चेदीश्वरः कश्चित् फलरूप्यन्यकर्मणाम् ।
कर्तारं भजते सोऽपि न ह्यकर्तुः प्रभुर्हि सः ॥ १४ ॥

asti ced īśvaraḥ kaścit
phala-rūpy anya-karmaṇām
kartāraṁ bhajate so'pi
na hy akartuḥ prabhur hi saḥ

asti—there is; *cet*—if hypothetically; *īśvaraḥ*—a supreme controller; *kaścit*—someone; *phala-rūpī*—serving to award fruitive results; *anya-karmaṇām*—of the activities of other persons; *kartāram*—the performer of activity; *bhajate*—depends upon; *saḥ*—He; *api*—even; *na*—not; *hi*—after all; *akartuḥ*—of one who performs no activity; *prabhuḥ*—the master; *hi*—certainly; *saḥ*—He.

TRANSLATION

Even if there is some supreme controller who awards all others the results of their activities, He must also depend upon a performer's engaging in activity. After all, there is no question of being the bestower of fruitive results unless fruitive activities have actually been performed.

PURPORT

Here Lord Kṛṣṇa argues that if there is a supreme controller, He must depend on a performer of activity to reciprocate with and must therefore also be subject to the laws of *karma,* being obliged to award happiness and distress to conditioned souls according to the laws of good and evil.

This superficial argument neglects the obvious point that the laws of nature that prescribe the good and bad results of pious and impious acts are themselves creations of the all-good Supreme Lord. Being the creator and sustainer of these laws, the Lord is not subject to them. Furthermore, the Lord is not dependent on the work of the conditioned souls, since He is satisfied and complete within Himself. Out of His all-merciful nature He awards the results appropriate to our activities. That which we call destiny, fate or *karma* is an elaborate and subtle system of rewards and punishments meant for gradually encouraging conditioned souls to evolve to the stage of perfect consciousness, which is their original, constitutional nature.

The Supreme Personality of Godhead has so dexterously formulated and applied the laws of material nature governing punishment and reward for human behavior that the living being is discouraged from sin and encouraged toward goodness without suffering any significant interference with his free will as an eternal soul.

In contrast to the material nature, the Lord exhibits His essential nature in the spiritual world, where He reciprocates the eternal love of His pure devotees. Such loving affairs are based completely on the mutual freedom of the Lord and His devotees, not on a mechanical reciprocity of coinciding selfish interests. The Supreme Lord, assisted by His pure devotees, repeatedly offers the conditioned souls of this world the opportunity to give up their bizarre attempt at exploiting the material universe and go back home, back to Godhead, for an eternal life of bliss and knowledge. Considering all these points, the atheistic arguments given here by Lord Kṛṣṇa in a playful mood are not to be taken seriously.

TEXT 15

किमिन्द्रेणेह भूतानां स्वस्वकर्मानुवर्तिनाम् ।
अनीशेनान्यथा कर्तुं स्वभावविहितं नृणाम्॥ १५॥

kim indreṇeha bhūtānāṁ
sva-sva-karmānuvartinām
anīśenānyathā kartuṁ
svabhāva-vihitaṁ nṛṇām

kim—what; *indreṇa*—with Indra; *iha*—here; *bhūtānām*—for living entities; *sva-sva*—each their own; *karma*—of fruitive action; *anuvartinām*—who are experiencing the consequences; *anīśena*—(Indra) who is incapable; *anyathā*—otherwise; *kartum*—to make; *svabhāva*—by their conditioned natures; *vihitam*—that which is ordained; *nṛṇām*—for men.

TRANSLATION

Living beings in this world are forced to experience the consequences of their own particular previous work. Since Lord Indra cannot in any way change the destiny of human beings, which is born of their own nature, why should people worship him?

PURPORT

Lord Kṛṣṇa's argument here is not a negation of free will. If one accepts the existence of *karma* as a system of laws awarding reactions for our present activities, then we ourselves, according to our nature, will decide our future. Our happiness and distress in this life have already been adjudicated and fixed according to our previous activities, and not even the demigods can change that. They must award us the prosperity or poverty, sickness or health, happiness or distress due us by our previous work. However, we still retain the freedom to select a pious or impious mode of activity in this life, and the choice we make will determine our future suffering and enjoyment.

For example, if I was pious in my last life, in this life the demigods may award me great material wealth. But I am free to spend my riches for good or for bad purposes, and my choice will determine my future life. Thus, although no one can change the karmic results due him in this life, everyone still retains his free will, by which he determines what his future situation will be. Lord Kṛṣṇa's argument here is quite interesting; however, it neglects the overriding consideration that we are all eternal servants of God and must satisfy Him by all that we do.

TEXT 16

स्वभावतन्त्रो हि जनः स्वभावमनुवर्तते।
स्वभावस्थमिदं सर्वं सदेवासुरमानुषम् ॥ १६ ॥

svabhāva-tantro hi janaḥ
svabhāvam anuvartate
svabhāva-stham idaṁ sarvaṁ
sa-devāsura-mānuṣam

svabhāva—of his conditioned nature; *tantraḥ*—under the control; *hi*—indeed; *janaḥ*—a person; *svabhāvam*—his nature; *anuvartate*—he follows; *svabhāva-stham*—based on conditioned propensities; *idam*—this world; *sarvam*—entire; *sa*—together with; *deva*—the demigods; *asura*—the demons; *mānuṣam*—and humankind.

TRANSLATION

Every individual is under the control of his own conditioned nature, and thus he must follow that nature. This entire universe, with all its demigods, demons and human beings, is based on the conditioned nature of the living entities.

PURPORT

Lord Kṛṣṇa here elaborates upon the argument given in the previous verse. Since everything depends on *svabhāva,* or one's conditioned nature, why bother worshiping God or the demigods? This argument would be sublime if *svabhāva,* or conditioned nature, were all-powerful. But unfortunately it is not. There is a supreme controller and we must worship Him, as Lord Kṛṣṇa will emphatically reveal in this chapter of the *Śrīmad-Bhāgavatam.* For now, however, He is content to tease His relatives.

TEXT 17

देहानुच्चावचाञ्जन्तुः प्राप्योत्सृजति कर्मणा।
शत्रुर्मित्रमुदासीनः कर्मैव गुरुरीश्वरः ॥ १७ ॥

dehān uccāvacāñ jantuḥ
prāpyotsṛjati karmaṇā
śatrur mitram udāsīnaḥ
karmaiva gurur īśvaraḥ

dehān—material bodies; *ucca-avacān*—high- and low-class; *jantuḥ*—the conditioned living entity; *prāpya*—obtaining; *utsṛjati*—gives up; *karmaṇā*—by the reactions of his material activities; *śatruḥ*—his enemy; *mitram*—friend; *udāsīnaḥ*—and neutral party; *karma*—material work; *eva*—alone; *guruḥ*—his spiritual master; *īśvaraḥ*—his lord.

TRANSLATION

Because it is karma that causes the conditioned living entity to accept and then give up different high- and low-grade material bodies, this karma is his enemy, friend and neutral witness, his spiritual master and controlling lord.

PURPORT

Even the demigods are bound and limited by the laws of *karma.* That Indra himself is subordinate to the laws of *karma* is explicitly stated in the *Brahma-saṁhitā* (5.54): *yas tv indra-gopam atha vendram aho sva-karma-bandhānurūpa-phala-bhājanam ātanoti.* The Supreme Lord, Govinda, awards all creatures the appropriate results of their work. This is as true for mighty Indra, the lord of the material heavens, as it is for the germ called *indra-gopa.* The *Bhagavad-gītā* (7.20) also states, *kāmais tais tair hṛta-jñānāḥ prapadyante'nya-devatāḥ.* Only those who have lost their intelligence because of various material desires surrender unto demigods rather than worship the Supreme Lord. In fact, the demigods cannot award benefits to anyone independently, as stated by Lord Kṛṣṇa in the *Gītā: mayaiva vihitān hi tān.* All benefits are ultimately issued by the Lord Himself.

Thus it is not altogether incorrect to say that demigod worship is useless, since even the demigods are under the laws of *karma.* In fact, this is the case. But Lord Kṛṣṇa, the Supreme Absolute Truth, is not subordinate to the law of *karma;* rather, He can independently offer or withhold His favor. This is confirmed in the verse from the *Brahma-saṁhitā* quoted above, the third line of which is *karmāṇi nirdahati kintu ca bhakti-bhājām:* "The Supreme Lord burns up all the accumulated *karma* of those engaged in His loving service." Not only is Lord Kṛṣṇa above the laws of material action and reaction, but He can immediately dissolve these laws for anyone who satisfies Him through loving service. Thus the almighty God is supreme in absolute freedom, and by surrendering to Him we can escape the bonds of *karma* and stop accepting their dismal rule as supreme.

TEXT 18

तस्मात्सम्पूजयेत्कर्म स्वभावस्थः स्वकर्मकृत्।
अञ्जसा येन वर्तेत तदेवास्य हि दैवतम् ॥ १८ ॥

tasmāt sampūjayet karma
svabhāva-sthaḥ sva-karma-kṛt
anjasā yena varteta
tad evāsya hi daivatam

tasmāt—therefore; *sampūjayet*—one should fully worship; *karma*—his prescribed activity; *svabhāva*—in the position corresponding to his own conditioned nature; *sthaḥ*—remaining; *sva-karma*—his own prescribed duty; *kṛt*—performing; *añjasā*—without difficulty; *yena*—by which; *varteta*—one lives; *tat*—that; *eva*—certainly; *asya*—his; *hi*—indeed; *daivatam*—worshipable deity.

TRANSLATION

Therefore one should seriously worship work itself. A person should remain in the position corresponding to his nature and should perform his own duty. Indeed, that by which we may live nicely is really our worshipable deity.

PURPORT

Lord Kṛṣṇa here proposes the modern if absurd philosophy that our work or occupation is really God and that we should therefore simply worship our work. Upon close scrutiny, we observe that our work is nothing more than the interaction of the material body with material nature, as Lord Kṛṣṇa Himself states, in a more serious mood, in the *Bhagavad-gītā* (3.28): *guṇā guṇeṣu vartanta. Karma-mīmāṁsā* philosophy accepts that good activity in this life will give us a better next life. If this is true, there must be some type of conscious soul different from the body. And if that is the case, why should a transcendental soul worship the interaction of the temporary body with material nature? If the words *sampūjayet karma* here mean that one should worship the laws of *karma* governing our activities, then one may astutely ask what it means to worship laws and, indeed, what might be the origin of such laws and who is maintaining them. To say that laws have created or are maintaining the world is a meaningless proposition, since there is nothing about the nature of a law that indicates it could generate the existential situation it is supposed to govern. In fact, worship is meant for Kṛṣṇa Himself, and this real conclusion will be clearly revealed in this chapter.

TEXT 19

आजीव्यैकतरं भावं यस्त्वन्यमुपजीवति ।
न तस्माद् विन्दते क्षेमं जारान्नार्यसती यथा ॥ १९ ॥

ājīvyaikataraṁ bhāvaṁ
yas tv anyam upajīvati
na tasmād vindate kṣemaṁ
jārān nāry asatī yathā

ājīvya—sustaining his life; *ekataram*—one; *bhāvam*—entity; *yaḥ*—who; *tu*—but; *anyam*—another; *upajīvati*—resorts to; *na*—not; *tasmāt*—from that one; *vindate*—gains; *kṣemam*—real benefit; *jārāt*—from a paramour; *nārī*—a woman; *asatī*—who is unchaste; *yathā*—as.

TRANSLATION

If one thing is actually sustaining our life but we take shelter of something else, how can we achieve any real benefit? We would be like an unfaithful woman, who can never achieve any actual benefit by consorting with her paramour.

PURPORT

The word *kṣemam* means actual prosperity, not merely the accumulation of money. Here Lord Kṛṣṇa boldly argues that just as a woman can never achieve actual dignity or enlightenment from an illicit lover, the residents of Vṛndāvana will never be happy by neglecting the real source of their prosperity and worshiping Indra instead. According to Śrīla Jīva Gosvāmī, the audacity that child Kṛṣṇa displayed before His father and other elders should be understood as an exhibition of transcendental anger aroused when He saw His eternal devotees worshiping an insignificant demigod.

TEXT 20

वर्तेत ब्रह्मणा विप्रो राजन्यो रक्षया भुवः ।
वैश्यस्तु वार्तया जीवेच्छूद्रस्तु द्विजसेवया ॥ २० ॥

varteta brahmaṇā vipro
rājanyo rakṣayā bhuvaḥ
vaiśyas tu vārtayā jīvec
chūdras tu dvija-sevayā

varteta—lives; *brahmaṇā*—by the *Vedas; vipraḥ*—the *brāhmaṇa; rājanyaḥ*—the member of the ruling class; *rakṣayā*—by protection; *bhuvaḥ*—of the earth; *vaiśyaḥ*—the *vaiśya; tu*—on the other hand; *vārtayā*—by trade; *jīvet*—lives; *śūdraḥ*—the *śūdra; tu*—and; *dvija-sevayā*—by serving the twice-born *brāhmaṇas, kṣatriyas* and *vaiśyas.*

TRANSLATION

The brāhmaṇa maintains his life by studying and teaching the Vedas, the member of the royal order by protecting the earth, the vaiśya by trade, and the śūdra by serving the higher, twice-born classes.

PURPORT

After glorifying *karma,* or work, Lord Kṛṣṇa now explains what He means by prescribed duties born of one's nature. He was not referring to any whimsical activity, but rather to the religious duties prescribed in the *varṇāśrama,* or Vedic social system.

TEXT 21

कृषिवाणिज्यगोरक्षा कुसीदं तूर्यमुच्यते ।
वार्ता चतुर्विधा तत्र वयं गोवृत्तयोऽनिशम् ॥ २१ ॥

kṛṣi-vāṇijya-go-rakṣā
kusīdaṁ tūryam ucyate
vārtā catur-vidhā tatra
vayaṁ go-vṛttayo'niśam

kṛṣi—farming; *vāṇijya*—commerce; *go-rakṣā*—and protecting cows; *kusīdam*—banking; *tūryam*—the fourth; *ucyate*—is said; *vārtā*—the occupational duty; *catuḥ-vidhā*—fourfold; *tatra*—among these; *vayam*—we; *go-vṛttayaḥ*—engaged in protecting the cows; *aniśam*—without cessation.

TRANSLATION

The occupational duties of the vaiśya are conceived in four divisions: farming, commerce, cow protection and moneylending. Out of these, we as a community are always engaged in cow protection.

TEXT 22

सत्त्वं रजस्तम इति स्थित्युत्पत्त्यन्तहेतवः ।
रजसोत्पद्यते विश्वमन्योन्यं विविधं जगत् ॥ २२ ॥

sattvaṁ rajas tama iti
sthity-utpatty-anta-hetavaḥ
rajasotpadyate viśvam
anyonyaṁ vividhaṁ jagat

sattvam—goodness; *rajaḥ*—passion; *tamaḥ*—and ignorance; *iti*—thus; *sthiti*—of maintenance; *utpatti*—creation; *anta*—and destruction; *hetavaḥ*—the causes; *rajasā*—by the mode of passion; *utpadyate*—is generated; *viśvam*—this universe; *anyonyam*—by combination of male and female; *vividham*—becomes variegated; *jagat*—the world.

TRANSLATION

The causes of creation, maintenance and destruction are the three modes of nature—namely goodness, passion and ignorance. In particular, the mode of passion creates this universe and through sexual combination causes it to become full of variety.

PURPORT

Anticipating the possible objection that a livelihood based on cows certainly depends on Lord Indra, who supplies rain, Lord Kṛṣṇa here introduces a mechanistic theory of existence known as atheistic Sāṅkhya. The tendency to attribute exclusive causality to the apparently mechanistic functions of nature is an old tendency indeed. Five thousand years ago Lord Kṛṣṇa referred to a doctrine already well known in human society.

TEXT 23

रजसा चोदिता मेघा वर्षन्त्यम्बूनि सर्वतः ।
प्रजास्तैरेव सिध्यन्ति महेन्द्रः किं करिष्यति ॥ २३ ॥

rajasā coditā meghā
varṣanty ambūni sarvataḥ
prajās tair eva sidhyanti
mahendraḥ kiṁ kariṣyati

rajasā—by passion; *coditāḥ*—impelled; *meghāḥ*—the clouds; *varṣanti*—pour down; *ambūni*—their water; *sarvataḥ*—everywhere; *prajāḥ*—the population; *taiḥ*—by that water; *eva*—simply; *sidhyanti*—maintain their existence; *mahā-indraḥ*—the great Indra; *kim*—what; *kariṣyati*—can do.

TRANSLATION

Impelled by the material mode of passion, the clouds pour down their rain everywhere, and by this rain all creatures gain their sustenance. What has the great Indra to do with this arrangement?

PURPORT

Lord Kṛṣṇa continues His mechanistic explanation of existence, concluding *mahendraḥ kiṁ kariṣyati:* "Who needs the great Indra, since the rain, sent by the clouds, which in turn are impelled by the mode of passion, is actually producing everyone's food?" The word *sarvataḥ* indicates that the clouds magnanimously send their rain even on the ocean, rocks and barren land, where there is no apparent necessity for such sweet water.

TEXT 24

न नः पुरो जनपदा न ग्रामा न गृहा वयम् ।
वनौकसस्तात नित्यं वनशैलनिवासिनः ॥ २४ ॥

na naḥ purojanapadā
na grāmā na gṛhā vayam
vanaukasas tāta nityaṁ
vana-śaila-nivāsinaḥ

na—not; *naḥ*—for us; *puraḥ*—the cities; *jana-padāḥ*—developed inhabited area; *na*—not; *grāmāḥ*—villages; *na*—not; *gṛhāḥ*—living in permanent homes; *vayam*—we; *vana-okasaḥ*—dwelling in the forests; *tāta* —My dear father; *nityam*—always; *vana*—in the forests; *śaila*—and on the hills; *nivāsinaḥ*—living.

TRANSLATION

My dear father, our home is not in the cities or towns or villages. Being forest dwellers, we always live in the forest and on the hills.

PURPORT

Lord Kṛṣṇa here points out that the residents of Vṛndāvana should recognize their relationship with Govardhana Hill and with the forests of Vṛndāvana, and not worry about a distant demigod like Indra. Having concluded His argument, Lord Kṛṣṇa makes a radical proposal in the following verse.

TEXT 25

तस्माद् गवां ब्राह्मणानामद्रेश्चारभ्यतां मखः ।
य इन्द्रयागसम्भारास्तैरयं साध्यतां मखः ॥ २५ ॥

tasmād gavāṁ brāhmaṇānām
adreś cārabhyatāṁ makhaḥ
ya indra-yāga-sambhārās
tair ayaṁ sādhyatām makhaḥ

tasmāt—therefore; *gavām*—of the cows; *brāhmaṇānām*—of the *brāhmaṇas; adreḥ*—and of the hill (Govardhana); *ca*—also; *ārabhyatām*—let it begin; *makhaḥ*—the sacrifice; *ye*—which; *indra-yāga*—for the sacrifice to Indra; *sambhārāḥ*—the ingredients; *taiḥ*—by them; *ayam*—this; *sādhyatām* —may it be carried out; *makhaḥ*—the sacrifice.

TRANSLATION

Therefore may a sacrifice for the pleasure of the cows, the brāhmaṇas and Govardhana Hill begin! With all the paraphernalia collected for worshiping Indra, let this sacrifice be performed instead.

PURPORT

Lord Kṛṣṇa is famous as *go-brāhmaṇa-hita,* the well-wishing friend of the cows and the *brāhmaṇas.* Lord Kṛṣṇa specifically included the local *brāhmaṇas* in His proposal because He is always devoted to those who are devoted to the godly Vedic culture.

TEXT 26

पच्यन्तां विविधाः पाकाः सूपान्ताः पायसादयः ।
संयावापूपशष्कुल्यः सर्वदोहश्च गृह्यताम् ॥२६॥

pacyantāṁ vividhāḥ pākāḥ
sūpāntāḥ pāyasādayaḥ
saṁyāvāpūpa-śaṣkulyaḥ
sarva-dohaś ca gṛhyatām

pacyantām—let the people cook; *vividhāḥ*—many varieties; *pākāḥ*—of cooked foods; *sūpa-antāḥ*—ending with liquid vegetable preparations; *pāyasa-ādayaḥ*—beginning with sweet rice; *saṁyāva-āpūpa*—fried and baked cakes; *śaṣkulyaḥ*—large, round cakes made from rice flour; *sarva*—all; *dohaḥ*—what is obtained by milking the cows; *ca*—and; *gṛhyatām*—let it be taken.

TRANSLATION

Let many different kinds of food be cooked, from sweet rice to vegetable soups! Many kinds of fancy cakes, both baked and fried, should be prepared. And all the available milk products should be taken for this sacrifice.

PURPORT

The word *sūpa* indicates bean broth and also liquid vegetables. Thus to celebrate the Govardhana-pūjā, Lord Kṛṣṇa called for hot preparations such as soup, cold preparations like sweet rice, and all types of milk products.

TEXT 27

हूयन्तामग्नयः सम्यग् ब्राह्मणैर्ब्रह्मवादिभिः ।
अन्नं बहुगुणं तेभ्यो देयं वो धेनुदक्षिणाः ॥२७॥

hūyantām agnayaḥ samyag
brāhmaṇair brahma-vādibhiḥ
annaṁ bahu-guṇaṁ tebhyo
deyaṁ vo dhenu-dakṣiṇāḥ

hūyantām—should be invoked; *agnayaḥ*—the sacrificial fires; *samyak*—in the proper manner; *brāhmaṇaiḥ*—by the *brāhmaṇas; brahma-vādibhiḥ*—

who are learned in the *Vedas; annam*—food; *bahu-guṇam*—well prepared; *tebhyaḥ*—to them; *deyam*—should be given; *vaḥ*—by you; *dhenu-dakṣiṇāḥ*—cows and other gifts as remuneration.

TRANSLATION

The brāhmaṇas who are learned in the Vedic mantras must properly invoke the sacrificial fires. Then you should feed the priests with nicely prepared food and reward them with cows and other gifts.

PURPORT

According to Śrīla Śrīdhara Svāmī, Lord Śrī Kṛṣṇa instructed His father and other residents of Vṛndāvana in the technical details of this Vedic sacrifice to assure the quality of the sacrifice and also to inspire Nanda and the others with faith in the concept of such a sacrifice. Thus the Lord mentioned that there must be orthodox *brāhmaṇas,* regular sacrificial fires and proper distribution of charity. And things were to be done in the order given by the Lord.

TEXT 28

अन्येभ्यश्चाश्वचाण्डालपतितेभ्यो यथार्हतः ।
यवसं च गवां दत्त्वा गिरये दीयतां बलिः ॥ २८ ॥

anyebhyaś cāśva-cāṇḍāla-
patitebhyo yathārhataḥ
yavasaṁ ca gavāṁ dattvā
giraye dīyatāṁ baliḥ

anyebhyaḥ—to the others; *ca*—also; *ā-śva-cāṇḍāla*—even down to the dogs and the dog-eaters; *patitebhyaḥ*—to such fallen persons; *yathā*—as; *arhataḥ*—is proper in each case; *yavasam*—grass; *ca*—and; *gavām*—to the cows; *dattvā*—having given; *giraye*—to the mountain called Govardhana; *dīyatām*—should be presented; *baliḥ*—respectful offerings.

TRANSLATION

After giving the appropriate food to everyone else, including such fallen souls as dogs and dog-eaters, you should give grass to the cows and then present your respectful offerings to Govardhana Hill.

TEXT 29

स्वलंकृता भुक्तवन्तः स्वनुलिप्ताः सुवाससः ।
प्रदक्षिणां च कुरुत गोविप्रानलपर्वतान् ॥ २९ ॥

sv-alaṅkṛtā bhuktavantaḥ
sv-anuliptāḥ su-vāsasaḥ
pradakṣiṇāṁ ca kuruta
go-viprānala-parvatān

su-alaṅkṛtāḥ—handsomely adorned; *bhuktavantaḥ*—having eaten to your satisfaction; *su-anuliptāḥ*—anointed with auspicious sandalwood pulp; *su-vāsasaḥ*—wearing fine garments; *pradakṣiṇām*—circumambulation; *ca*—and; *kuruta*—you should perform; *go*—of the cows; *vipra*—the *brāhmaṇas; anala*—the sacrificial fires; *parvatān*—and the hill, Govardhana.

TRANSLATION

After everyone has eaten to his satisfaction, you should all dress and decorate yourselves handsomely, smear your bodies with sandalwood paste and then circumambulate the cows, the brāhmaṇas, the sacrificial fires and Govardhana Hill.

PURPORT

Lord Kṛṣṇa wanted all the human beings and even the animals to eat nice *bhagavat-prasādam,* sanctified foods offered to the Lord. To enthuse His relatives with a festive mood, He requested them to dress beautifully with fine clothes and ornaments and to refresh their bodies with luxurious sandalwood paste. The essential activity, however, was the circumambulation of the holy *brāhmaṇas*, cows, sacrificial fires and especially Govardhana Hill.

TEXT 30

एतन्मम मतं तात क्रियतां यदि रोचते ।
अयं गोब्राह्मणाद्रीणां मह्यं च दयितो मखः ॥ ३० ॥

etan mama mataṁ tāta
kriyatāṁ yadi rocate
ayaṁ go-brāhmaṇādrīṇāṁ
mahyaṁ ca dayito makhaḥ

etat—this; *mama*—My; *matam*—idea; *tāta*—O father; *kriyatām*—may it be carried out; *yadi*—if; *rocate*—it is pleasing; *ayam*—this; *go-brāhmaṇa-adrīṇām*—for the cows, *brāhmaṇas* and Govardhana Hill; *mahyam*—for Me; *ca*—also; *dayitaḥ*—cherished; *makhaḥ*—sacrifice.

TRANSLATION

This is My idea, O father, and you may carry it out if it appeals to you. Such a sacrifice will be very dear to the cows, the brāhmaṇas and Govardhana Hill, and also to Me.

PURPORT

Whatever is pleasing to the *brāhmaṇas,* the cows and the Supreme Lord Himself is auspicious and beneficial for the entire world. Spiritually blind "modern" people do not understand this and instead adopt a "scientific" approach to life that is rapidly destroying the entire earth.

TEXT 31

श्रीशुक उवाच
कालात्मना भगवता शक्रदर्पजिघांसया ।
प्रोक्तं निशम्य नन्दाद्याः साध्वगृह्णन्त तद्वचः ॥ ३१ ॥

śrī-śuka uvāca
kālātmanā bhagavatā
śakra-darpa-jighāṁsayā
proktaṁ niśamya nandādyāḥ
sādhv agṛhṇanta tad-vacaḥ

śrī-śukaḥ uvāca—Śrī Śukadeva Gosvāmī said; *kāla-ātmanā*—manifesting as the force of time; *bhagavatā*—by the Supreme Personality of Godhead; *śakra*—of Indra; *darpa*—the pride; *jighāṁsayā*—with a desire to destroy; *proktam*—what was spoken; *niśamya*—hearing; *nanda-ādyāḥ*—Nanda and the other elder cowherd men; *sādhu*—as excellent; *agṛhṇanta*—they accepted; *tat-vacaḥ*—His words.

TRANSLATION

Śukadeva Gosvāmī said: Lord Kṛṣṇa, who is Himself powerful time, desired to destroy the false pride of Lord Indra. When Nanda and the other senior men of Vṛndāvana heard Śrī Kṛṣṇa's statement, they accepted His words as proper.

TEXTS 32–33

तथा च व्यदधुः सर्वं यथाह मधुसूदनः ।
वाचयित्वा स्वस्त्ययनं तद्द्रव्येण गिरिद्विजान् ॥ ३२ ॥
उपहृत्य बलीन् सम्यगादृता यवसं गवाम् ।
गोधनानि पुरस्कृत्य गिरिं चक्रुः प्रदक्षिणम् ॥ ३३ ॥

tathā ca vyadadhuḥ sarvaṁ
yathāha madhusūdanaḥ
vācayitvā svasty-ayanaṁ
tad-dravyeṇa giri-dvijān

upahṛtya balīn samyag
ādṛtā yavasaṁ gavām
go-dhanāni puraskṛtya
giriṁ cakruḥ pradakṣiṇam

tathā—thus; *ca*—and; *vyadadhuḥ*—they executed; *sarvam*—everything; *yathā*—as; *āha*—He spoke; *madhusūdanaḥ*—Lord Kṛṣṇa; *vācayitvā*—making (the *brāhmaṇas*) recite; *svasti-ayanam*—the auspicious chants; *tat-dravyeṇa*—with the paraphernalia intended for Indra's sacrifice; *giri*—to the hill; *dvijān*—and the *brāhmaṇas; upahṛtya*—offering; *balīn*—the presentations of tribute; *samyak*—all together; *ādṛtāḥ*—respectfully; *yavasam*—grass; *gavām*—to the cows; *go-dhanāni*—the bulls, cows and calves; *puraskṛtya*—placing in front; *girim*—of the hill; *cakruḥ*—they performed; *pradakṣiṇam*—circumambulation.

TRANSLATION

The cowherd community then did all that Madhusūdana had suggested. They arranged for the brāhmaṇas to recite the auspicious Vedic mantras, and using the paraphernalia that had been intended for Indra's sacrifice, they presented offerings to Govardhana Hill and the brāhmaṇas with reverential respect. They also gave grass to the cows. Then, placing the cows, bulls and calves in front of them, they circumambulated Govardhana.

PURPORT

The residents of Vṛndāvana were simply devoted to Lord Kṛṣṇa; that was the sum and substance of their existence. Being the Lord's eternal associates, they were ultimately not concerned with Lord Indra or ritualistic sacrifice, and they were certainly not interested in the mechanistic philosophy that Kṛṣṇa had just spoken to them. They simply loved Kṛṣṇa, and out of intense affection they did exactly what He had requested.

Their simple loving mentality was not small-mindedness or ignorance, since they were devoted to the Supreme Absolute Truth, who contains within Himself all existence. Thus the residents of Vṛndāvana constantly experienced the highest, essential truth underlying all other truths—and that is Śrī Kṛṣṇa Himself, the cause of all causes and that which sustains the existence of all that exists. The residents of Vṛndāvana were overwhelmed in loving service to that Supreme Absolute Truth; therefore they were the most fortunate, most intelligent and most pragmatic of all living beings.

TEXT 34

अनांस्यनडुद्युक्तानि ते चारुह्य स्वलंकृताः ।
गोप्यश्च कृष्णवीर्याणि गायन्त्यः सद्विजाशिषः ॥ ३४ ॥

anāṁsy anaḍud-yuktāni
te cāruhya sv-alaṅkṛtāḥ
gopyaś ca kṛṣṇa-vīryāṇi
gāyantyaḥ sa-dvijāśiṣaḥ

anāṁsi—wagons; *anaḍut-yuktāni*—yoked with oxen; *te*—they; *ca*—and; *āruhya*—riding; *su-alaṅkṛtāḥ*—nicely ornamented; *gopyaḥ*—the cowherd women; *ca*—and; *kṛṣṇa-vīryāṇi*—the glories of Lord Kṛṣṇa; *gāyantyaḥ*—singing; *sa*—together with; *dvija*—of the *brāhmaṇas; āśiṣaḥ*—the benedictions.

TRANSLATION

As the beautifully ornamented cowherd ladies followed along, riding on wagons drawn by oxen, they sang the glories of Lord Kṛṣṇa, and their songs mingled with the brāhmaṇas' chanting of benedictions.

TEXT 35

कृष्णस्त्वन्यतमं रूपं गोपविश्रम्भणं गतः ।
शैलोऽस्मीति ब्रुवन् भूरि बलिमादद् बृहद्वपुः ॥ ३५ ॥

kṛṣṇas tv anyatamaṁ rūpaṁ
gopa-viśrambhaṇaṁ gataḥ
śailo'smīti bruvan bhūri
balim ādad bṛhad-vapuḥ

kṛṣṇaḥ—Lord Kṛṣṇa; *tu*—and then; *anyatamam*—another; *rūpam*—transcendental form; *gopa-viśrambhaṇam*—for generating the faith of the cowherds; *gataḥ*—assumed; *śailaḥ*—the mountain; *asmi*—I am; *iti*—these words; *bruvan*—saying; *bhūri*—abundant; *balim*—the offerings; *ādat*—He devoured; *bṛhat-vapuḥ*—in His huge form.

TRANSLATION

Kṛṣṇa then assumed an unprecedented, huge form to instill faith in the cowherd men. Declaring "I am Govardhana Mountain!" He ate the abundant offerings.

PURPORT

In Chapter Twenty-four of *Kṛṣṇa, the Supreme Personality of Godhead,* Śrīla Prabhupāda writes: "When everything was complete, Kṛṣṇa assumed a great transcendental form and declared to the inhabitants of Vṛndāvana that He was Himself Govardhana Hill in order to convince the devotees that Govardhana Hill and Kṛṣṇa Himself are identical. Then Kṛṣṇa began to eat all the food offered there. The identity of Kṛṣṇa and Govardhana Hill is still honored, and great devotees take rocks from Govardhana Hill and worship them exactly as they worship the Deity of Kṛṣṇa in the temples. The followers of the Krsna consciousness movement may therefore collect small rocks or pebbles from Govardhana Hill and worship them at home, because this worship is as good as Deity worship."

Lord Kṛṣṇa had induced the residents of Vṛndāvana to assume a significant risk on His behalf. He convinced them to neglect a sacrifice to what is, after all, the powerful government of the universe and to worship a hill called Govardhana instead. The cowherd community did all this simply out of love for Kṛṣṇa, and now to convince them that their decision was correct, Lord Kṛṣṇa appeared in an unprecedented, huge transcendental form and demonstrated that He Himself was Govardhana Hill.

TEXT 36

तस्मै नमो व्रजजनैः सह चक्र आत्मनात्मने ।
अहो पश्यत शैलोऽसौ रूपी नोऽनुग्रहं व्यधात् ॥ ३६ ॥

tasmai namo vraja-janaiḥ
saha cakra ātmanātmane
aho paśyata śailo'sau
rūpī no'nugrahaṁ vyadhāt

tasmai—to Him; *namaḥ*—obeisances; *vraja-janaiḥ*—with the people of Vraja; *saha*—together; *cakre*—He made; *ātmanā*—by Himself; *ātmane*—to Himself; *aho*—ah; *paśyata*—just see; *śailaḥ*—hill; *asau*—this; *rūpī*—manifest in person; *naḥ*—upon us; *anugraham*—mercy; *vyadhāt*—has bestowed.

TRANSLATION

Together with the people of Vraja, the Lord bowed down to this form of Govardhana Hill, thus in effect offering obeisances to Himself. Then He said, "Just see how this hill has appeared in person and bestowed mercy upon us!"

PURPORT

It is clear from this verse that Lord Kṛṣṇa had expanded Himself and was appearing in His normal form among the festival-goers of Vṛndāvana while simultaneously manifesting Himself as the great form of Govardhana Hill. Thus, in His form as a child, Kṛṣṇa led the residents of Vṛndāvana in bowing down to His new incarnation as Govardhana Hill, and to all He pointed out the great mercy bestowed by this divine form of Govardhana. Lord Kṛṣṇa's amazing transcendental activities were certainly in keeping with the festive atmosphere.

TEXT 37

एषोऽवजानतो मर्त्यान् कामरूपी वनौकसः ।
हन्ति ह्यस्मै नमस्यामः शर्मणे आत्मनो गवाम् ॥ ३७ ॥

eṣo'vajānato martyān
kāma-rūpī vanaukasaḥ
hanti hy asmai namasyāmaḥ
śarmaṇe ātmano gavām

eṣaḥ—this one; *avajānataḥ*—those who are neglectful; *martyān*—mortals; *kāma-rūpī*—assuming any form at will (such as that of the snakes who live upon the hill); *vana-okasaḥ*—residents of the forest; *hanti*—will kill; *hi*

—certainly; *asmai*—to him; *namasyāmaḥ*—let us pay our obeisances; *śarmaṇe*—for the protection; *ātmanaḥ*—of ourselves; *gavām*—and of the cows.

TRANSLATION

"This Govardhana Hill, assuming any form he wishes, will kill any residents of the forest who neglect him. Therefore let us pay our obeisances to him for the safety of ourselves and our cows."

PURPORT

Kāma-rūpī indicates that the form of Govardhana can manifest as poisonous snakes, wild animals, falling rocks and so on, all of which are competent to kill a human being.

According to Śrīla Śrīdhara Svāmī, the Lord presented six theoretical points in this chapter: 1) that *karma* alone is sufficient to determine one's destiny; 2) that one's conditioned nature is the supreme controller; 3) that the modes of nature are the supreme controller; 4) that the Supreme Lord is simply a dependent aspect of *karma;* 5) that He is under the control of *karma;* and 6) that one's occupation is the actual worshipable deity.

The Lord presented these arguments not because He believed them but rather because He wanted to stop the impending sacrifice to Indra and divert it to Himself in the form of Govardhana Hill. In this way the Lord desired to agitate that falsely proud demigod.

TEXT 38

इत्यद्रिगोद्विजमखं वासुदेवप्रचोदिताः ।
यथा विधाय ते गोपा सहकृष्णा व्रजं ययुः ॥ ३८ ॥

ity adri-go-dvija-makhaṁ
vāsudeva-pracoditāḥ
yathā vidhāya te gopā
saha-kṛṣṇā vrajaṁ yayuḥ

iti—in this manner; *adri*—to Govardhana Hill; *go*—the cows; *dvija*—and the *brāhmaṇas; makham*—the great sacrifice; *vāsudeva*—by Lord Kṛṣṇa; *pracoditāḥ*—urged; *yathā*—properly; *vidhāya*—executing; *te*—they; *gopāḥ*—the cowherds; *saha-kṛṣṇāḥ*—together with Lord Kṛṣṇa; *vrajam*—to Vraja; *yayuḥ*—they went.

TRANSLATION

The members of the cowherd community, having thus been inspired by Lord Vāsudeva to properly execute the sacrifice to Govardhana Hill, the cows and the brāhmaṇas, returned with Lord Kṛṣṇa to their village, Vraja.

PURPORT

Although the Govardhana-pūjā was performed in a blissful and successful way, the matter was hardly finished. Lord Indra is, after all, tremendously powerful, and he received the news of the Govardhana sacrifice with burning anger. What ensued will be described in the following chapter.

Thus end the purports of the humble servants of His Divine Grace A.C. Bhaktivedanta Swami Prabhupāda to the Tenth Canto, Twenty-fourth Chapter, of the Śrīmad-Bhāgavatam, *entitled "Worshiping Govardhana Hill."*

CHAPTER TWENTY- FIVE

Lord Kṛṣṇa Lifts Govardhana Hill

This chapter describes how Lord Indra was overcome by anger when the residents of Vraja canceled his sacrifice, how he tried to punish them by sending forth a devastating rainfall to Vṛndāvana, and how Lord Śrī Kṛṣṇa protected Gokula by lifting Govardhana Hill and for seven days using it as an umbrella to ward off the rain.

Indra, angered at the disruption of the sacrifice meant for him and falsely presuming himself the supreme controller, said, "People often give up the pursuit of transcendental knowledge—the means for self-realization—and imagine that they can cross over the ocean of material existence by mundane fruitive sacrifices. Similarly, these cowherd men have become intoxicated by pride and have offended me by taking shelter of an ignorant, ordinary child—Kṛṣṇa."

To remove this supposed pride of the residents of Vraja, Indra sent the clouds known as Sāṁvartaka, whose function is to facilitate the destruction of the world. He sent them to harass the Vrajavāsīs with downpours of rain and hail. The cowherd community was very disturbed by this and approached Kṛṣṇa for shelter. Understanding that this trouble was the work of Indra, Kṛṣṇa decided to smash to pieces Indra's false prestige, and thus He lifted Govardhana Hill with one hand. He then invited the entire cowherd community to take shelter in the dry space beneath the mountain. For seven successive days He held up the hill, until Indra finally understood Kṛṣṇa's mystic power and ordered the clouds to withdraw.

When the cowherd villagers emerged from beneath the mountain, Kṛṣṇa put Govardhana Hill back in its proper place. The cowherds were in ecstasy, showing loving symptoms such as flowing tears and bodily hairs standing on end. They embraced Kṛṣṇa and offered Him benedictions according to their respective positions, while the demigods in heaven rained down flowers and sang the Lord's praises.

TEXT 1

श्रीशुक उवाच
इन्द्रस्तदात्मनः पूजां विज्ञाय विहतां नृप ।
गोपेभ्यः कृष्णनाथेभ्यो नन्दादिभ्यश्चुकोप ह ॥ १ ॥

śrī-śuka uvāca
indras tadātmanaḥ pūjāṁ
vijñāya vihatāṁ nṛpa
gopebhyaḥ kṛṣṇa-nāthebhyo
nandādibhyaś cukopa ha

śrī-śukaḥ uvāca—Śrī Śukadeva Gosvāmī said; *indraḥ*—Lord Indra; *tadā*—then; *ātmanaḥ*—his own; *pūjām*—worship; *vijñāya*—understanding; *vihatām*—diverted; *nṛpa*—O King (Parīkṣit); *gopebhyaḥ*—at the cowherds; *kṛṣṇa-nāthebhyaḥ*—who took Kṛṣṇa as their Lord; *nanda-ādibhyaḥ*—headed by Nanda Mahārāja; *cukopa ha*—he became angry.

TRANSLATION

Śukadeva Gosvāmī said: My dear King Parīkṣit, when Indra understood that his sacrifice had been put aside, he became furious with Nanda Mahārāja and the other cowherd men, who were accepting Kṛṣṇa as their Lord.

PURPORT

At the very beginning of this chapter Śukadeva Gosvāmī reveals the foolishness of Indra and the absurdity of his anger. Indra was frustrated because the residents of Vṛndāvana accepted Śrī Kṛṣṇa as their Lord. But the simple fact is that Śrī Kṛṣṇa *is* the Lord, not only of the residents of Vṛndāvana but of all that exists, including Indra himself. Thus Indra's petulant reaction was ridiculous. As the common saying goes, "Pride goes before a fall."

TEXT 2

गणं सांवर्तकं नाम मेघानां चान्तकारीणाम् ।
इन्द्रः प्रचोदयत् क्रुद्धो वाक्यं चाहेशमान्युत ॥ २ ॥

gaṇaṁ sāṁvartakaṁ nāma
meghānāṁ cānta-kāriṇām

indraḥ pracodayat kruddho
vākyaṁ cāheśa-māny uta

gaṇam—the group; *sāṁvartakam nāma*—named Sāṁvartaka; *meghānām*—of clouds; *ca*—and; *anta-kāriṇām*—who effect the end of the universe; *indraḥ*—Indra; *pracodayat*—sent forth; *kruddhaḥ*—angry; *vākyam*—words; *ca*—and; *āha*—spoke; *īśa-mānī*—falsely thinking himself the supreme controller; *uta*—indeed.

TRANSLATION

Angry Indra sent forth the clouds of universal destruction, known as Sāṁvartaka. Imagining himself the supreme controller, he spoke as follows.

PURPORT

The word *īśa-mānī* here is very significant. Indra arrogantly considered himself to be the Lord, and thus he exhibited the typical attitude of a conditioned soul. Many thinkers in the twentieth century have noted the exaggerated sense of individual prestige characteristic of our culture; indeed, writers have even coined the phrase "the me generation." Everyone in this world is more or less guilty of the syndrome called *īśa-māna,* or proudly considering oneself the Lord.

TEXT 3

अहो श्रीमदमाहात्म्यं गोपानां काननौकसाम् ।
कृष्णं मर्त्यमुपाश्रित्य ये चक्रुर्देवहेलनम् ॥ ३ ॥

aho śrī-mada-māhātmyaṁ
gopānāṁ kānanaukasām
kṛṣṇaṁ martyam upāśritya
ye cakrur deva-helanam

aho—just see; *śrī*—because of opulence; *mada*—of intoxication; *māhātmyam*—the great extent; *gopānām*—of the cowherds; *kānana*—in the forest; *okasām*—who dwell; *kṛṣṇam*—Kṛṣṇa; *martyam*—an ordinary human; *upāśritya*—taking shelter of; *ye*—who; *cakruḥ*—have committed; *deva*—against the demigods; *helanam*—offense.

TRANSLATION

[Indra said:] Just see how these cowherd men living in the forest have become so greatly intoxicated by their prosperity! They have surrendered to an ordinary human being, Kṛṣṇa, and thus they have offended the gods.

PURPORT

Of course, Indra was really saying that the cowherd men had offended him, Indra, by taking shelter of Kṛṣṇa, whom Indra considered to be *martya,* a mortal. This was certainly a gross miscalculation on Indra's part.

TEXT 4

यथादृढैः कर्ममयैः क्रतुभिर्नामनौनिभैः ।
विद्यामान्वीक्षिकीं हित्वा तितीर्षन्ति भवार्णवम् ॥ ४ ॥

yathādṛḍhaiḥ karma-mayaiḥ
kratubhir nāma-nau-nibhaiḥ
vidyām ānvīkṣikīṁ hitvā
titīrṣanti bhavārṇavam

yathā—as; *adṛḍhaiḥ*—which are inadequate; *karma-mayaiḥ*—based on fruitive activity; *kratubhiḥ*—by ritual sacrifices; *nāma*—in name only; *nau-nibhaiḥ*—which serve as boats; *vidyām*—knowledge; *ānvīkṣikīm*—spiritual; *hitvā*—abandoning; *titīrṣanti*—they try to cross beyond; *bhava-arṇavam*—the ocean of material existence.

TRANSLATION

Their taking shelter of Kṛṣṇa is just like the foolish attempt of men who abandon transcendental knowledge of the self and instead try to cross over the great ocean of material existence in the false boats of fruitive, ritual sacrifices.

TEXT 5

वाचालं बालिशं स्तब्धमज्ञं पण्डितमानिनम् ।
कृष्णं मर्त्यमुपाश्रित्य गोपा मे चक्रुरप्रियम् ॥ ५ ॥

vācālaṁ bāliśaṁ stabdham
ajñaṁ paṇḍita-māninam

kṛṣṇaṁ martyam upāśritya
gopā me cakrur apriyam

vācālaṁ—overtalkative; *bāliśam*—child; *stabdham*—arrogant; *ajñam*—foolish; *paṇḍita-māninam*—thinking Himself wise; *kṛṣṇam*—Kṛṣṇa; *martyam*—a human being; *upāśritya*—taking shelter of; *gopāḥ*—the cowherds; *me*—against me; *cakruḥ*—have acted; *apriyam*—unfavorably.

TRANSLATION

These cowherd men have acted inimically toward me by taking shelter of this ordinary human being, Kṛṣṇa, who thinks Himself very wise but who is simply a foolish, arrogant, overtalkative child.

PURPORT

According to Śrīla Śrīdhara Svāmī, through the insults of Indra Goddess Sarasvatī is actually praising Kṛṣṇa. The *ācārya* explains: "*Bāliśam* means 'free from pretension, just like a child.' *Stabdham* means that He bows down to no one because there is no one for Him to offer homage to, *ajñam* means that there is nothing more for Him to know because He is omniscient, *paṇḍita-māninam* means that He is highly honored by the knowers of the Absolute Truth, and *kṛṣṇam* means He is the Supreme Absolute Truth, whose transcendental form is full of eternity and ecstasy. *Martyam* means that although He is the Absolute Truth, He nevertheless appears in this world as a human being out of affection for His devotees."

Indra wanted to rebuke Kṛṣṇa as *vācālam* because the Lord had presented many audacious arguments in the line of Karma-mīmāṁsā and Sāṅkhya philosophy even though He did not accept these arguments; thus Indra called the Lord *bāliśa,* "foolish." Indra called Him *stabdha* because He had spoken boldly even in the presence of His own father. Thus although Indra attempted to criticize Śrī Kṛṣṇa, the Lord's transcendental character is in fact impeccable, and this chapter will demonstrate how Indra came to recognize the position of the Lord.

TEXT 6

एषां श्रियावलिप्तानां कृष्णेनाध्मापितात्मनाम् ।
धुनुत श्रीमदस्तम्भं पशून्नयत सङ्क्षयम् ॥ ६ ॥

eṣāṁ śriyāvaliptānāṁ
kṛṣṇenādhmāpitātmanām
dhunuta śrī-mada-stambhaṁ
paśūn nayata saṅkṣayam

eṣām—of them; *śriyā*—by their opulences; *avaliptānām*—who are intoxicated; *kṛṣṇena*—by Kṛṣṇa; *ādhmāpita*—fortified; *ātmanām*—whose hearts; *dhunuta*—remove; *śrī*—based on their wealth; *mada*—being maddened; *stambham*—their false pride; *paśūn*—their animals; *nayata*—bring; *saṅkṣayam*—to destruction.

TRANSLATION

[To the clouds of destruction King Indra said:] The prosperity of these people has made them mad with pride, and their arrogance is backed up by Kṛṣṇa. Now go and remove their pride and bring their animals to destruction.

PURPORT

It is clear from this verse that the residents of Vṛndāvana had become highly prosperous simply by protecting cows, since Indra wanted to destroy their so-called pride based on wealth by killing their animals. Well-tended cows produce large quantities of milk, from which come cheese, butter, yogurt, ghee and so on. These foods are delicious by themselves and also enhance other foods, such as fruits, vegetables and grains. Bread and vegetables are delicious with butter, and fruit is especially appetizing when mixed with cream or yogurt. Dairy products are always desirable in civilized society, and the surplus can be traded for many valuable commodities. Thus, simply by a Vedic dairy enterprise, the residents of Vṛndāvana were wealthy, healthy and happy, even in the material sense, and most of all they were eternal associates of the Supreme Lord Kṛṣṇa.

TEXT 7

अहं चैरावतं नागमारुह्यानुव्रजे व्रजम् ।
मरुद्गणैर्महावेगैर्नन्दगोष्ठजिघांसया ॥ ७ ॥

ahaṁ cairāvataṁ nāgam
āruhyānuvraje vrajam

marud-gaṇair mahā-vegair
nanda-goṣṭha-jighāṁsayā

aham—I; *ca*—also; *airāvatam*—named Airāvata; *nāgam*—my elephant; *āruhya*—riding; *anuvraje*—will follow along; *vrajam*—to Vraja; *marut-gaṇaiḥ*—accompanied by the wind gods; *mahā-vegaiḥ*—who move with great power; *nanda-goṣṭha*—the cowherd community of Nanda Mahārāja; *jighāṁsayā*—with the intent of destroying.

TRANSLATION

I will follow you to Vraja, riding on my elephant Airāvata and taking with me the swift and powerful wind-gods to decimate the cowherd village of Nanda Mahārāja.

PURPORT

The Sāṁvartaka clouds were frightened by Indra's powerful mood and thus carried out his order, as described in the following verse.

TEXT 8

श्रीशुक उवाच
इत्थं मघवताज्ञप्ता मेघा निर्मुक्तबन्धनाः ।
नन्दगोकुलमासारैः पीडयामासुरोजसा ॥ ८ ॥

śrī-śuka uvāca
itthaṁ maghavatājñaptā
meghā nirmukta-bandhanāḥ
nanda-gokulam āsāraiḥ
pīḍayām āsur ojasā

śrī-śukaḥ uvāca—Śrī Śukadeva Gosvāmī said; *ittham*—in this manner; *maghavatā*—by Indra; *ājñaptāḥ*—ordered; *meghāḥ*—the clouds; *nirmukta-bandhanāḥ*—released from their bonds (although they were supposed to be kept in check until the time for the destruction of the world); *nanda-gokulam*—the cowherd pastures of Nanda Mahārāja; *āsāraiḥ*—by great downpours of rain; *pīḍayām āsuḥ*—they tormented; *ojasā*—with all their power.

TRANSLATION

Śukadeva Gosvāmī said: On Indra's order the clouds of universal destruction, released untimely from their bonds, went to the cowherd

pastures of Nanda Mahārāja. There they began to torment the inhabitants by powerfully pouring down torrents of rain upon them.

PURPORT

The Sāṁvartaka clouds could cover the entire earth with a single vast ocean. With great strength, these clouds began flooding the simple land of Vraja.

TEXT 9

विद्योतमाना विद्युद्भिः स्तनन्तः स्तनयित्नुभिः ।
तीव्रैर्मरुद्गणैर्नुन्ना ववृषुर्जलशर्कराः ॥ ९ ॥

vidyotamānā vidyudbhiḥ
stanantaḥ stanayitnubhiḥ
tīvrair marud-gaṇair nunnā
vavṛṣur jala-śarkarāḥ

vidyotamānāḥ—being illuminated; *vidyudbhiḥ*—by bolts of lightning; *stanantaḥ*—roaring; *stanayitnubhiḥ*—with thunder; *tīvraiḥ*—fearsome; *marut-gaṇaiḥ*—by the wind-gods; *nunnāḥ*—propelled; *vavṛṣuḥ*—they poured down; *jala-śarkarāḥ*—hailstones.

TRANSLATION

Propelled by the fearsome wind-gods, the clouds blazed with lightning bolts and roared with thunder as they hurled down hailstones.

PURPORT

Śrīla Śrīdhara Svāmī explains that the word *marud-gaṇaiḥ* indicates the seven great winds, such as Āvaha, who presides over the region of Bhuvarloka, and Pravaha, who holds the planets in their places.

TEXT 10

स्थूणास्थूला वर्षधारा मुञ्चत्स्वभ्रेष्वभीक्ष्णशः ।
जलौघैः प्लाव्यमाना भूर्नादृश्यत नतोन्नतम् ॥ १० ॥

sthūṇā-sthūlā varṣa-dhārā
muñcatsv abhreṣv abhīkṣṇaśaḥ
jalaughaiḥ plāvyamānā bhūr
nādṛśyata natonnatam

sthūṇā—like columns; *sthūlāḥ*—massive; *varsa-dhārāḥ*—downpours of rain; *muñcatsu*—releasing; *abhreṣu*—the clouds; *abhīkṣṇaśaḥ*—incessantly; *jala-oghaiḥ*—by the flood of water; *plāvyamānā*—being submerged; *bhūḥ*—the earth; *na adṛśyata*—could not be seen; *nataunnatam*—low or high.

TRANSLATION

As the clouds released torrents of rain as thick as massive columns, the earth was submerged in the flood, and high ground could no longer be distinguished from low.

TEXT 11

अत्यासारातिवातेन पशवो जातवेपनाः ।
गोपा गोप्यश्च शीतार्ता गोविन्दं शरणं ययुः ॥ ११ ॥

aty-āsārāti-vātena
paśavo jāta-vepanāḥ
gopā gopyaś ca śītārtā
govindaṁ śaraṇaṁ yayuḥ

ati-āsāra—by the excessive rainfall; *ati-vātena*—and the excessive wind; *paśavaḥ*—the cows and other animals; *jāta-vepanāḥ*—trembling; *gopāḥ*—the cowherd men; *gopyaḥ*—the cowherd ladies; *ca*—also; *śīta*—by the cold; *ārtāḥ*—distressed; *govindam*—to Lord Govinda; *śaraṇam*—for shelter; *yayuḥ*—they went.

TRANSLATION

The cows and other animals, shivering from the excessive rain and wind, and the cowherd men and ladies, pained by the cold, all approached Lord Govinda for shelter.

TEXT 12

शिरः सुतांश्च कायेन प्रच्छाद्यासारपीडिताः ।
वेपमाना भगवतः पादमूलमुपाययुः ॥ १२ ॥

śiraḥ sutāṁś ca kāyena
pracchādyāsāra-pīḍitāḥ
vepamānā bhagavataḥ
pāda-mūlam upāyayuḥ

śiraḥ—their heads; *sutān*—their children; *ca*—and; *kāyena*—by their bodies; *pracchādya*—covering; *āsāra-pīḍitāḥ*—distressed by the rainfall; *vepamānāḥ*—trembling; *bhagavataḥ*—of the Supreme Personality of Godhead; *pāda-mūlam*—the base of the lotus feet; *upāyayuḥ*—they approached.

TRANSLATION

Trembling from the distress brought about by the severe rainfall, and trying to cover their heads and calves with their own bodies, the cows approached the lotus feet of the Supreme Personality of Godhead.

TEXT 13

कृष्ण कृष्ण महाभाग त्वन्नाथं गोकुलं प्रभो ।
त्रातुमर्हसि देवान्नः कुपिताद् भक्तवत्सल ॥ १३ ॥

kṛṣṇa kṛṣṇa mahā-bhāga
tvan-nāthaṁ gokulaṁ prabho
trātum arhasi devān naḥ
kupitād bhakta-vatsala

kṛṣṇa kṛṣṇa—O Kṛṣṇa, Kṛṣṇa; *mahā-bhāga*—O all-fortunate one; *tvat-nātham*—whose master is Yourself; *go-kulam*—the community of cows; *prabho*—O Lord; *trātum arhasi*—kindly protect; *devāt*—from the demigod Indra; *naḥ*—us; *kupitāt*—who is angry; *bhakta-vatsala*—O You who are very affectionate to Your devotees.

TRANSLATION

[The cowherd men and women addressed the Lord:] Kṛṣṇa, Kṛṣṇa, O most fortunate one, please deliver the cows from the wrath of Indra! O Lord, You are so affectionate to Your devotees. Please save us also.

PURPORT

At the time of Lord Kṛṣṇa's birth, Garga Muni had predicted, *anena sarva-durgāṇi yūyam añjas tariṣyathā* (*Bhāg.* 10.8.16): "By His grace you will easily cross beyond all difficulties." The residents of Vṛndāvana were confident that in such a great emergency Lord Śrī Nārāyaṇa would empower Kṛṣṇa to protect them. They accepted Kṛṣṇa as everything, and Kṛṣṇa reciprocated their love.

TEXT 14

शिलावर्षातिवातेन हन्यमानमचेतनम् ।
निरीक्ष्य भगवान्मेने कुपितेन्द्रकृतं हरिः ॥ १४ ॥

śilā-varṣāti-vātena
hanyamānam acetanam
nirīkṣya bhagavān mene
kupitendra-kṛtaṁ hariḥ

śilā—of (hail)stones; *varṣa*—by the rain; *ati-vātena*—and by the extreme wind; *hanyamānam*—being attacked; *acetanam*—unconscious; *nirīkṣya*—seeing; *bhagavān*—the Supreme Personality of Godhead; *mene*—considered; *kupita*—angry; *indra*—by Indra; *kṛtam*—done; *hariḥ*—Lord Hari.

TRANSLATION

Seeing the inhabitants of His Gokula rendered practically unconscious by the onslaught of hail and blasting wind, the Supreme Lord Hari understood that this was the work of angry Indra.

PURPORT

Śrīla Viśvanātha Cakravartī Ṭhākura explains that the severe distress Indra apparently inflicted upon the residents of Vṛndāvana was an arrangement made by Śrī Kṛṣṇa's pastime potency to enhance the loving dealings between the residents and the Lord. The *ācārya* gives the analogy that for a hungry person, the pain of hunger increases the happiness he feels when he finally eats excellent food, and thus hunger can be said to enhance the pleasure of eating. Similarly, the residents of Vṛndāvana, although not experiencing ordinary, material anxiety, felt a type of distress at the activities of Indra and thus intensified their meditation on Kṛṣṇa. When the Lord finally acted, the result was wonderful.

TEXT 15

अपर्त्वत्युल्बणं वर्षमतिवातं शिलामयम् ।
स्वयागे विहतेऽस्माभिरिन्द्रो नाशाय वर्षति ॥ १५ ॥

apartv aty-ulbaṇaṁ varṣam
ati-vātaṁ śilā-mayam
sva-yāge vihate'smābhir
indro nāśāya varṣati

apa-ṛtu—out of season; *ati-ulbaṇam*—unusually fierce; *varṣam*—rain; *ati-vātam*—accompanied by great wind; *śilā-mayam*—full of hailstones; *sva-yāge*—his sacrifice; *vihate*—having been stopped; *asmābhiḥ*—by Ourselves; *indraḥ*—King Indra; *nāśāya*—for destruction; *varṣati*—is raining.

TRANSLATION

[Śrī Kṛṣṇa said to Himself:] Because We have stopped his sacrifice, Indra has caused this unusually fierce, unseasonable rain, together with terrible winds and hail.

TEXT 16

तत्र प्रतिविधिं सम्यगात्मयोगेन साधये ।
लोकेशमानिनां मौढ्याद्धनिष्ये श्रीमदं तमः ॥ १६ ॥

tatra pratividhiṁ samyag
ātma-yogena sādhaye
lokeśa-māninām mauḍhyād
dhaniṣye śrī-madaṁ tamaḥ

tatra—in that regard; *prati-vidhim*—counteracting measures; *samyak*—properly; *ātma-yogena*—by My mystic power; *sādhaye*—I shall arrange; *loka-īśa*—lords of the world; *māninām*—of those who falsely consider themselves; *mauḍhyāt*—out of foolishness; *haniṣye*—I shall defeat; *śrī-madam*—their pride in opulence; *tamaḥ*—the ignorance.

TRANSLATION

By My mystic power I will completely counteract this disturbance caused by Indra. Demigods like Indra are proud of their opulence, and out of foolishness they falsely consider themselves the Lord of the universe. I will now destroy such ignorance.

TEXT 17

न हि सद्भावयुक्तानां सुराणामीशविस्मयः ।
मत्तोऽसतां मानभंगः प्रशमायोपकल्पते ॥ १७ ॥

na hi sad-bhāva-yuktānāṁ
surāṇām īśa-vismayaḥ

matto'satāṁ māna-bhaṅgaḥ
praśamāyopakalpate

na—not; *hi*—certainly; *sat-bhāva*—with the mode of goodness; *yuk-tānām*—who are endowed; *surāṇām*—of the demigods; *īśa*—as controlling lords; *vismayaḥ*—false identification; *mattaḥ*—by Me; *asatām*—of the impure; *māna*—of the false prestige; *bhaṅgaḥ*—the eradication; *praśamāya*—for relieving them; *upakalpate*—is intended.

TRANSLATION

Since the demigods are endowed with the mode of goodness, the false pride of considering oneself the Lord should certainly not affect them. When I break the false prestige of those bereft of goodness, My purpose is to bring them relief.

PURPORT

The demigods are supposed to be *sad-bhāva-yukta,* endowed with spiritual existence, since they are deputed servants of the Supreme Lord. In the *Bhagavad-gītā* (4.24) it is stated:

brahmārpaṇaṁ brahma havir
brahmāgnau brahmaṇā hutam
brahmaiva tena gantavyaṁ
brahma-karma-samādhinā

"That which is duly offered to the Lord becomes spiritualized." The demigods engage in the devotional service of the Lord by managing various departments of cosmic administration. Therefore as demigods, or as servants of the Lord, their existence is pure (*sad-bhāva*). When the demigods fail to live up to the high position given them by the Lord and deviate from proper behavior, they are not acting as demigods but rather as conditioned souls.

Māna, or false prestige, is certainly an anxiety-ridden burden for the conditioned soul. A falsely proud person is not truly peaceful or satisfied, because his understanding of himself is false and inflated. When a servant of the Lord becomes *asat,* or irreligious, the Lord saves him from impiety by breaking the false prestige that has led him to be offensive or sinful. As stated by the Lord Himself, *yasyāham anugṛhṇāmi hariṣye tad-dhanaṁ śanaiḥ:* "I give My blessings to a person by taking away his so-called opulence."

Of course, the advanced stage of devotional service to the Lord, as described by Rūpa Gosvāmī, is *yukta-vairāgya,* utilizing the opulence of this world to execute the Lord's mission. Obviously the things of this world can be used wonderfully to spread the glories of God and to create a godly society, and a more advanced devotee will not be seduced by material paraphernalia but will dutifully and honestly engage it solely for the pleasure of the Lord. In this particular case, Lord Indra forgot that he was a humble servant of God, and Lord Kṛṣṇa therefore arranged to bring this bewildered demigod to his senses.

TEXT 18

तस्मान्मच्छरणं गोष्ठं मन्नाथं मत्परिग्रहम् ।
गोपाये स्वात्मयोगेन सोऽयं मे व्रत आहितः ॥ १८ ॥

tasmān mac-charaṇaṁ goṣṭhaṁ
man-nāthaṁ mat-parigraham
gopāye svātma-yogena
so'yaṁ me vrata āhitaḥ

tasmāt—therefore; *mat-śaraṇam*—having taken shelter of Me; *goṣṭham*—the cowherd community; *mat-nātham*—who have Me as their master; *mat-parigraham*—My own family; *gopāye*—I shall protect; *sva-ātma-yogena*—by My personal mystic power; *saḥ ayam*—this; *me*—by Me; *vrataḥ*—vow; *āhitaḥ*—has been taken.

TRANSLATION

I must therefore protect the cowherd community by My transcendental potency, for I am their shelter, I am their master, and indeed they are My own family. After all, I have taken a vow to protect My devotees.

PURPORT

The word *mac-charaṇam* indicates not only that Lord Kṛṣṇa was the sole shelter for the vraja-jana, the people of Vṛndāvana, but also that Lord Kṛṣṇa had established His home among them. Śrīla Viśvanātha Cakravartī Ṭhākura quotes from the *Anekārtha-varga* dictionary, *śaraṇaṁ gṛha-rakṣitroḥ*: "The word *śaraṇam* can represent either home or protector." The residents of Vṛndāvana adopted Kṛṣṇa as their beloved child, friend, lover and life itself, and the Lord reciprocated their feelings. Thus Śrī Kṛṣṇa lived among these fortunate people, moving in their houses and fields; naturally He would protect such intimate devotees from all types of danger.

TEXT 19

इत्युक्त्वैकेन हस्तेन कृत्वा गोवर्धनाचलम् ।
दधार लीलया विष्णुश्छत्राकमिव बालकः ॥ १९ ॥

ity uktvaikena hastena
kṛtvā govardhanācalam
dadhāra līlayā viṣṇuś
chatrākam iva bālakaḥ

iti—thus; *uktvā*—having spoken; *ekena*—with one; *hastena*—hand; *kṛtvā*—taking; *govardhana-acalam*—Govardhana Hill; *dadhāra*—He held it; *līlayā*—very easily; *viṣṇuḥ*—Lord Viṣṇu; *chatrākam*—a mushroom; *iva*—just as; *bālakaḥ*—a child.

TRANSLATION

Having said this, Lord Kṛṣṇa, who is Viṣṇu Himself, picked up Govardhana Hill with one hand and held it aloft just as easily as a child holds up a mushroom.

PURPORT

It is confirmed in the *Hari-vaṁśa* that Śrī Kṛṣṇa picked up the Govardhana Mountain with His left hand: *sa dhṛtaḥ saṅgato meghair giriḥ savyena pāṇinā.* "With His left hand He picked up that mountain, which was touching the clouds." According to Śrīla Viśvanātha Cakravartī Ṭhākura, when Lord Kṛṣṇa was preparing to lift Govardhana Hill, a partial expansion of His Yoga-māyā potency named Saṁhārikī temporarily removed all the rain from the sky so that as He ran very swiftly from the porch of His house to the mountain, neither His turban nor other garments became wet.

TEXT 20

अथाह भगवान् गोपान् हेऽम्ब तात व्रजौकसः ।
यथोपजोषं विशत गिरिगर्तं सगोधनाः ॥ २० ॥

athāha bhagavān gopān
he'mba tāta vrajaukasaḥ
yathopajoṣaṁ viśata
giri-gartaṁ sa-go-dhanāḥ

atha—then; *āha*—addressed; *bhagavān*—the Supreme Lord; *gopān*—the cowherds; *he*—O; *amba*—mother; *tāta*—O father; *vraja-okasaḥ*—O residents of Vraja; *yathā-upajoṣam*—as suits your pleasure; *viśata*—please enter; *giri*—this hill; *gartam*—the empty space below; *sa-godhanāḥ*—together with your cows.

TRANSLATION

The Lord then addressed the cowherd community: O Mother, O Father, O residents of Vraja, if you wish you may now come under this hill with your cows.

PURPORT

Śrīla Viśvanātha Cakravartī Ṭhākura provides the following insight in this regard: Ordinarily a large cowherd community, which included many thousands of cows, calves, bulls and so on, could not fit under the base of a medium-sized hill like Śrī Govardhana. However, because the hill was in ecstasy, being touched by the hand of the Supreme Personality of Godhead, it acquired inconceivable power and even felt the hundreds of deadly thunderbolts thrown upon its back by angry Indra to be offerings of soft, fragrant flowers. At times Śrī Govardhana was not even aware that the thunderbolts were striking. From the *Hari-vaṁśa* the *ācārya* has also quoted Śrī Kṛṣṇa Himself as saying, *trai-lokyam apy utsahate rakṣituṁ kiṁ punar vrajam*: "Śrī Govardhana can give shelter to all the three worlds, what to speak of the simple land of Vraja."

When Indra's attack began and Kṛṣṇa lifted the hill, the deer, wild hogs, and other animals and birds standing on the hill's flanks climbed up to its peaks, and even they did not experience the slightest distress.

TEXT 21

न त्रास इह वः कार्यो मद्धस्ताद्रिनिपातनात् ।
वातवर्षभयेनालं तत्त्राणं विहितं हि वः ॥ २१ ॥

na trāsa iha vaḥ kāryo
mad-dhastādri-nipātanāt
vāta-varṣa-bhayenālaṁ
tat-trāṇaṁ vihitaṁ hi vaḥ

na—not; *trāsaḥ*—fear; *iha*—in this matter; *vaḥ*—by you; *kāryaḥ*—should be felt; *mat-hasta*—from My hand; *adri*—of the mountain; *nipātanāt*

—of the falling; *vāta*—of the wind; *varṣa*—and the rain; *bhayena*—with fear; *alam*—enough; *tat-trāṇam*—the deliverance from that; *vihitam*—has been provided; *hi*—certainly; *vaḥ*—for you.

TRANSLATION

You should have no fear that this mountain will fall from My hand. And don't be afraid of the wind and rain, for your deliverance from these afflictions has already been arranged.

TEXT 22

तथा निर्विविशुर्गर्तं कृष्णाश्वासितमानसः ।
यथावकाशं सधनाः सव्रजाः सोपजीविनः ॥ २२ ॥

tathā nirviviśur gartaṁ
kṛṣṇāśvāsita-mānasaḥ
yathāvakāśaṁ sa-dhanāḥ
sa-vrajāḥ sopajīvinaḥ

tathā—thus; *nirviviśuḥ*—they entered; *gartam*—the hollow; *kṛṣṇa*—by Lord Kṛṣṇa; *āśvāsita*—pacified; *mānasaḥ*—their minds; *yathā-avakāśam*—comfortably; *sa-dhanāḥ*—with their cows; *sa-vrajāḥ*—and with their wagons; *sa-upajīvinaḥ*—together with their dependents (such as their servants and *brāhmaṇa* priests).

TRANSLATION

Their minds thus pacified by Lord Kṛṣṇa, they all entered beneath the hill, where they found ample room for themselves and all their cows, wagons, servants and priests, and for all other members of the community as well.

PURPORT

All the domestic animals of Vṛndāvana were brought beneath Govardhana Hill for shelter.

TEXT 23

क्षुत्तृड्व्यथां सुखापेक्षां हित्वा तैर्व्रजवासिभिः ।
वीक्ष्यमाणो दधाराद्रिं सप्ताहं नाचलत्पदात् ॥ २३ ॥

kṣut-tṛḍ-vyathāṁ sukhāpekṣāṁ
hitvā tair vraja-vāsibhiḥ
vīkṣyamāṇo dadhārādriṁ
saptāhaṁ nācalat padāt

kṣut—of hunger; *tṛṭ*—and thirst; *vyathām*—the pain; *sukha*—of personal happiness; *apekṣām*—all consideration; *hitvā*—putting aside; *taiḥ*—by them; *vraja-vāsibhiḥ*—the residents of Vraja; *vīkṣyamāṇaḥ*—being glanced upon; *dadhāra*—He held; *adrim*—the mountain; *sapta-aham*—for seven days; *na acalat*—He did not move; *padāt*—from that place.

TRANSLATION

Lord Kṛṣṇa, forgetting hunger and thirst and putting aside all considerations of personal pleasure, stood there holding up the hill for seven days as the people of Vraja gazed upon Him.

PURPORT

According to the *Viṣṇu Purāṇa:*

vrajaika-vāsibhir harṣa-
vismitākṣair nirīkṣitaḥ
gopa-gopī-janair hṛṣṭaiḥ
prīti-visphāritekṣaṇaiḥ
saṁstūyamāna-caritaḥ
kṛṣṇaḥ śailam adhārayat

"Lord Kṛṣṇa held up the mountain while His praises were chanted by the residents of Vraja, all of whom now had the opportunity to dwell together with Him, and who glanced at Him with joyful and amazed eyes. Thus the cowherd men and women were all elated, and out of loving affection they opened their eyes wide."

By continuously drinking the nectar of the beauty and sweetness of Śrī Kṛṣṇa, the residents of Vṛndāvana felt no hunger, thirst or fatigue, and Lord Kṛṣṇa, by seeing their beautiful forms, also forgot about eating, drinking and sleeping. Śrīla Viśvanātha Cakravartī Ṭhākura points out that seven days of continuous rain from the Sāṁvartaka clouds failed to flood the district of Mathurā because the Supreme Lord, simply by His potency, immediately dried up the water as it fell to the ground. Thus Kṛṣṇa's lifting of Govardhana Hill is full of fascinating details and has for thousands of years remained one of His most famous pastimes.

TEXT 24

कृष्णयोगानुभावं तं निशम्येन्द्रोऽतिविस्मितः ।
निस्तम्भो भ्रष्टसंकल्पः स्वान्मेघान् संन्यवारयत् ॥२४॥

kṛṣṇa-yogānubhāvaṁ taṁ
niśamyendro 'ti-vismitaḥ
nistambho bhraṣṭa-saṅkalpaḥ
svān meghān sannyavārayat

kṛṣṇa—of Lord Kṛṣṇa; *yoga*—of the mystic power; *anubhāvam*—the influence; *tam*—that; *niśamya*—seeing; *indraḥ*—Lord Indra; *ati-vismitaḥ*—most amazed; *nistambhaḥ*—whose false pride was brought down; *bhraṣṭa*—ruined; *saṅkalpaḥ*—whose determination; *svān*—his own; *meghān*—clouds; *sannyavārayat*—stopped.

TRANSLATION

When Indra observed this exhibition of Lord Kṛṣṇa's mystic power, he became most astonished. Pulled down from his platform of false pride, and his intentions thwarted, he ordered his clouds to desist.

TEXT 25

खं व्यभ्रमुदितादित्यं वातवर्षं च दारुणम् ।
निशम्योपरतं गोपान् गोवर्धनधरोऽब्रवीत् ॥ २५ ॥

khaṁ vyabhram uditādityaṁ
vāta-varṣaṁ ca dāruṇam
niśamyoparataṁ gopān
govardhana-dharo 'bravīt

kham—the sky; *vi-abhram*—empty of clouds; *udita*—arisen; *ādityam*—with the sun; *vāta-varṣam*—the wind and rain; *ca*—and; *dāruṇam*—fierce; *niśamya*—seeing; *uparatam*—ceased; *gopān*—to the cowherds; *govardhana-dharaḥ*—the lifter of Govardhana Hill; *abravīt*—spoke.

TRANSLATION

Seeing that the fierce wind and rain had now ceased, the sky had become clear of rainclouds, and the sun had risen, Lord Kṛṣṇa, the lifter of Govardhana Hill, spoke to the cowherd community as follows.

TEXT 26

निर्यात त्यजत त्रासं गोपाः सस्त्रीधनार्भकाः ।
उपारतं वातवर्षं व्युदप्रायाश्च निम्नगाः ॥ २६ ॥

niryāta tyajata trāsaṁ
gopāḥ sa-strī-dhanārbhakāḥ
upāratam̐ vāta-varṣaṁ
vyuda-prāyāś ca nimnagāḥ

niryāta—please go out; *tyajata*—give up; *trāsam*—your fear; *gopāḥ*—O cowherd men; *sa*—together with; *strī*—your women; *dhana*—property; *arbhakāḥ*—and children; *upāratam*—finished; *vāta-varṣam*—the wind and rain; *vi-uda*—without water; *prāyāḥ*—practically; *ca*—and; *nimnagāḥ*—the rivers.

TRANSLATION

[Lord Kṛṣṇa said:] My dear cowherd men, please go out with your wives, children and possessions. Give up your fear. The wind and rain have stopped, and the rivers' high waters have subsided.

TEXT 27

ततस्ते निर्ययुर्गोपाः स्वं स्वमादाय गोधनम् ।
शकटोढोपकरणं स्त्रीबालस्थविराः शनैः ॥ २७ ॥

tatas te niryayur gopāḥ
svaṁ svam ādāya go-dhanam
śakaṭoḍhopakaraṇaṁ
strī-bāla-sthavirāḥ śanaiḥ

tataḥ—then; *te*—they; *niryayuḥ*—went out; *gopāḥ*—the cowherd men; *svam svam*—each his own; *ādāya*—taking; *go-dhanam*—their cows; *śakaṭa*—upon their wagons; *ūḍha*—loaded; *upakaraṇam*—their paraphernalia; *strī*—the women; *bāla*—children; *sthavirāḥ*—and old people; *śanaiḥ*—slowly.

TRANSLATION

After collecting their respective cows and loading their paraphernalia into their wagons, the cowherd men went out. The women, children and elderly persons gradually followed them.

TEXT 28

भगवानपि तं शैलं स्वस्थाने पूर्ववत्प्रभुः ।
पश्यतां सर्वभूतानां स्थापयामास लीलया ॥ २८ ॥

bhagavān api taṁ śailaṁ
sva-sthāne pūrva-vat prabhuḥ
paśyatāṁ sarva-bhūtānāṁ
sthāpayām āsa līlayā

bhagavān—the Supreme Personality of Godhead; *api*—and; *tam*—that; *śailam*—hill; *sva-sthāne*—upon its place; *pūrva-vat*—as originally; *prabhuḥ*—the almighty Lord; *paśyatām*—while they were looking on; *sarva-bhūtānām*—all the living creatures; *sthāpayām āsa*—He put; *līlayā*—with ease.

TRANSLATION

While all living creatures looked on, the Supreme Personality of Godhead put down the hill in its original place, just as it had stood before.

TEXT 29

तं प्रेमवेगान्निर्भृता व्रजौकसो
यथा समीयुः परिरम्भणादिभिः ।
गोप्यश्च सस्नेहमपूजयन्मुदा
दध्यक्षताद्भिर्युयुजुः सदाशिषः ॥ २९ ॥

taṁ prema-vegān nirbhṛtā vrajaukaso
yathā samīyuḥ parirambhaṇādibhiḥ
gopyaś ca sa-sneham apūjayan mudā
dadhy-akṣatādbhir yuyujuḥ sad-āśiṣaḥ

tam—to Him; *prema*—of their pure love; *vegāt*—by the force; *nirbhṛtāḥ*—fulfilled; *vraja-okasaḥ*—the residents of Vraja; *yathā*—each according to his position; *samīyuḥ*—came forward; *parirambhaṇa-ādibhiḥ*—with embracing and so forth; *gopyaḥ*—the cowherd ladies; *ca*—and; *sa-sneham*—with great affection; *apūjayan*—showed their respect; *mudā*—joyfully; *dadhi*—with yogurt; *akṣata*—unbroken grains; *adbhiḥ*—and water; *yuyujuḥ*—they presented; *sat*—excellent; *āśiṣaḥ*—benedictions.

TRANSLATION

All the residents of Vṛndāvana were overwhelmed with ecstatic love, and they came forward and greeted Śrī Kṛṣṇa according to their individual relationships with Him—some embracing Him, others bowing down to Him, and so forth. The cowherd women presented water mixed with yogurt and unbroken barleycorns as a token of honor, and they showered auspicious benedictions upon Him.

PURPORT

Śrīla Viśvanātha Cakravartī Ṭhākura explains that each of the residents of Vṛndāvana regarded Kṛṣṇa in his own way—as an inferior, younger member of the community; as an equal; or as a superior—and they dealt with Him accordingly. Kṛṣṇa's superiors offered auspicious benedictions, lovingly smelled His head, kissed Him, rubbed His arms and fingers, and inquired with parental affection as to whether He was tired or pained. Kṛṣṇa's equals laughed or joked with Him, and those who were younger fell at His feet, massaged His feet, and so on.

The word *ca* in this verse indicates that the wives of the *brāhmaṇas* joined with the cowherd ladies to offer auspicious items like yogurt and unbroken grains. Lord Kṛṣṇa received benedictions such as this: "May You subdue the wicked, protect the decent people, give pleasure to Your parents and be enriched with all wealth and opulence."

TEXT 30

यशोदा रोहिणी नन्दो रामश्च बलिनां वरः ।
कृष्णमालिंग्य युयुजुराशिषः स्नेहकातराः ॥ ३० ॥

yaśodā rohiṇī nando
rāmaś ca balināṁ varaḥ
kṛṣṇam āliṅgya yuyujur
āśiṣaḥ sneha-kātarāḥ

yaśodā—mother Yaśodā; *rohiṇī*—Rohiṇī; *nandaḥ*—Nanda Mahārāja; *rāmaḥ*—Balarāma; *ca*—also; *balinām*—of the strong; *varaḥ*—the greatest; *kṛṣṇam*—Kṛṣṇa; *āliṅgya*—embracing; *yuyujuḥ*—they all offered; *āśiṣaḥ*—benedictions; *sneha*—by their affection for Him; *kātarāḥ*—beside themselves.

TRANSLATION

Mother Yaśodā, mother Rohiṇī, Nanda Mahārāja and Balarāma, the greatest of the strong, all embraced Kṛṣṇa. Overwhelmed with affection, they offered Him their blessings.

TEXT 31

दिवि देवगणाः सिद्धाः साध्या गन्धर्वचारणाः ।
तुष्टुवुर्मुमुचुस्तुष्टाः पुष्पवर्षाणि पार्थिव ॥ ३१ ॥

divi deva-gaṇāḥ siddhāḥ
sādhyā gandharva-cāraṇāḥ
tuṣṭuvur mumucus tuṣṭāḥ
puṣpa-varṣāṇi pārthiva

divi—in the heavens; *deva-gaṇāḥ*—the demigods; *siddhāḥ*—the Siddhas; *sādhyāḥ*—the Sādhyas; *gandharva-cāraṇāḥ*—the Gandharvas and Cāraṇas; *tuṣṭuvuḥ*—they recited the Lord's praises; *mumucuḥ*—they released; *tuṣṭāḥ*—being satisfied; *puṣpa-varṣāṇi*—downpours of flowers; *pārthiva*—O King (Parīkṣit).

TRANSLATION

In the heavens, O King, all the demigods, including the Siddhas, Sādhyas, Gandharvas and Cāraṇas, sang the praises of Lord Kṛṣṇa and showered down flowers in great satisfaction.

PURPORT

The demigods in heaven were just as jubilant as the residents of Vṛndāvana, and thus a great universal festival took place.

TEXT 32

शंखदुन्दुभयो नेदुर्दिवि देवप्रचोदिताः ।
जगुर्गन्धर्वपतयस्तुम्बुरुप्रमुखा नृप ॥ ३२ ॥

śaṅkha-dundubhayo nedur
divi deva-pracoditāḥ
jagur gandharva-patayas
tumburu-pramukhā nṛpa

śaṅkha—conchshells; *dundubhayaḥ*—and kettledrums; *neduḥ*—resounded; *divi*—in the heavenly planets; *deva-pracoditāḥ*—played by the demigods; *jaguḥ*—sang; *gandharva-patayaḥ*—the chiefs of the Gandharvas; *tumburu-pramukhāḥ*—led by Tumburu; *nṛpa*—my dear King.

TRANSLATION

My dear Parīkṣit, the demigods in heaven resoundingly played their conchshells and kettledrums, and the best of the Gandharvas, led by Tumburu, began to sing.

TEXT 33

ततोऽनुरक्तैः पशुपैः परिश्रितो
राजन् स्वगोष्ठं सबलोऽव्रजद्धरिः ।
तथाविधान्यस्य कृतानि गोपिका
गायन्त्य ईयुर्मुदिता हृदिस्पृशः ॥ ३३ ॥

tato 'nuraktaiḥ paśupaiḥ pariśrito
rājan sva-goṣṭhaṁ sa-balo 'vrajad dhariḥ
tathā-vidhāny asya kṛtāni gopikā
gāyantya īyur muditā hṛdi-spṛśaḥ

tataḥ—then; *anuraktaiḥ*—loving; *paśu-paiḥ*—by the cowherd boys; *pariśritaḥ*—surrounded; *rājan*—O King; *sva-goṣṭham*—to the place where He was tending His own cows; *sa-balaḥ*—together with Lord Balarāma; *avrajat*—went off; *hariḥ*—Kṛṣṇa; *tathā-vidhāni*—such as this (lifting of Govardhana); *asya*—of Him; *kṛtāni*—the activities; *gopikāḥ*—the cowherd girls; *gāyantyaḥ*—singing; *īyuḥ*—they went; *muditāḥ*—happily; *hṛdi-spṛśaḥ*—of Him who touched them within their hearts.

TRANSLATION

Surrounded by His loving cowherd boyfriends and Lord Balarāma, Kṛṣṇa then went off to the place where He had been tending His cows. The cowherd girls returned to their homes, singing joyfully about the lifting of Govardhana Hill and other glorious deeds performed by Lord Kṛṣṇa, who had so deeply touched their hearts.

PURPORT

Before returning to their homes, the *gopīs* shared intimate association with their lover, Śrī Kṛṣṇa, by exchanging secret glances. Ordinarily they could not publicly talk about Kṛṣṇa, since they were chaste young girls in a religious village, but now they took advantage of this wonderful exhibition by the Lord and freely sang of His beautiful qualities. It is natural that a young man wants to do something wonderful in the presence of a beautiful young girl. The *gopīs* were the most beautiful and pure-hearted young girls, and Śrī Kṛṣṇa performed the most wonderful activities in their presence. Thus He entered deep within their tender hearts, enlivening their eternal devotion to Him.

Thus end the purports of the humble servants of His Divine Grace A.C. Bhaktivedanta Swami Prabhupāda to the Tenth Canto, Twenty-fifth Chapter, of the Śrīmad-Bhāgavatam, *entitled "Lord Kṛṣṇa Lifts Govardhana Hill."*

CHAPTER TWENTY-SIX

Wonderful Kṛṣṇa

In this chapter Nanda Mahārāja describes Kṛṣṇa's opulences to the cowherd men, as Nanda had heard of them from Garga Muni.

The cowherd men, unaware of Lord Kṛṣṇa's power, were amazed to see His various extraordinary activities. The men approached Nanda Mahārāja and told him that after seeing how Kṛṣṇa, a boy only seven years old, had lifted a mountain, and how He had previously killed the demoness Pūtanā and generated extreme attraction in the hearts of everyone in Vṛndāvana, the men had become doubtful and bewildered about how Śrī Kṛṣṇa could possibly have taken birth in the unsuitable environment of a cowherd community. Nanda replied by relating to them what Garga Muni had told him about Śrī Kṛṣṇa.

Garga Muni had said that in the previous three ages Nanda's boy had manifested Himself in white, red and yellow forms, whereas now, in the Dvāpara age, He had assumed His darkish-blue form, *kṛṣṇa-rūpa.* Because He descended as the son of Vasudeva, one of His many names is Vāsudeva, and He has innumerable other names indicating His many qualities and activities.

Garga Muni had predicted that Kṛṣṇa would prevent all sorts of catastrophes in Gokula, spread unlimited auspiciousness, and increase the ecstasy of the cowherd men and women. In a previous age He had provided protection for the saintly *brāhmaṇas* when they were harassed by low-class dacoits and there was no proper ruler in society. As the demons in the higher planets can never defeat the demigods who have Lord Viṣṇu on their side, no enemy can ever defeat those who love Kṛṣṇa. In His affinity for His devotees and in His opulence and power, Kṛṣṇa is just like Lord Nārāyaṇa Himself.

Overjoyed and awestruck by Garga Muni's statements, the cowherd men concluded that Kṛṣṇa must be an empowered representative of the Supreme Lord, Nārāyaṇa. Thus they worshiped Him and Nanda Mahārāja.

TEXT 1

श्रीशुक उवाच

एवंविधानि कर्माणि गोपाः कृष्णस्य वीक्ष्य ते ।
अतद्वीर्यविदः प्रोचुः समभ्येत्य सुविस्मिताः ॥ १ ॥

śrī-śuka uvāca
evaṁ-vidhāni karmāṇi
gopāḥ kṛṣṇasya vīkṣya te
atad-vīrya-vidaḥ procuḥ
samabhyetya su-vismitāḥ

śrī-śukaḥ uvāca—Śrī Śukadeva Gosvāmī said; *evam-vidhāni*—like this; *karmāṇi*—activities; *gopāḥ*—the cowherd men; *kṛṣṇasya*—of Lord Kṛṣṇa; *vīkṣya*—seeing; *te*—they; *atat-vīrya-vidaḥ*—unable to understand His power; *procuḥ*—they spoke; *samabhyetya*—approaching (Nanda Mahārāja); *su-vismitāḥ*—very astonished.

TRANSLATION

Śukadeva Gosvāmī said: The cowherd men were astonished when they saw Kṛṣṇa's activities, such as lifting Govardhana Hill. Unable to understand His transcendental potency, they approached Nanda Mahārāja and spoke as follows.

PURPORT

Śrīla Viśvanātha Cakravartī Ṭhākura explains this verse as follows: "During Lord Kṛṣṇa's pastime of lifting Śrī Govardhana Hill, the cowherd men simply enjoyed the spiritual bliss of the Lord's activities without analyzing them. But afterwards, when they had returned to their homes, perplexity arose within their hearts. Thus they thought,'Now we have directly seen child Kṛṣṇa lift Govardhana Hill, and we remember how He killed Pūtanā and other demons, extinguished the forest fire, and so on. At the time, we thought that these extraordinary acts occurred because of a benediction from the *brāhmaṇas* or because of Nanda Mahārāja's great fortune, or that perhaps this boy had achieved the mercy of Lord Nārāyaṇa and was thus empowered by Him."

"'But all these presumptions are false, because an ordinary seven-year old boy could never hold up the king of mountains for seven whole days. Kṛṣṇa is not a human being. He must be the Supreme Lord Himself."

"'But on the other hand, child Kṛṣṇa loves it when we coddle Him, and He becomes morose when we—His uncles and well-wishers, simply worldly cowherd men—do not give Him attention. He appears to become hungry and thirsty, steals yogurt and milk, sometimes plays tricks, tells lies, chatters childishly and tends the calves. If He is actually the Supreme Lord, why would He do these things? Don't they indicate that He is an ordinary human child?"

"'We are totally unable to establish the truth of His identity. Therefore let us go and inquire from the highly intelligent King of Vraja, Nanda Mahārāja, and he shall free us from our doubts.'"

According to Śrīla Viśvanātha Cakravartī Ṭhākura, the cowherd men thus made up their minds, and then they entered Nanda Mahārāja's great assembly hall and questioned him as described in the following verse.

TEXT 2

बालकस्य यदेतानि कर्माण्यत्यद्‌भुतानि वै ।
कथमर्हत्यसौ जन्म ग्राम्येष्वात्मजुगुप्सितम् ॥ २ ॥

bālakasya yad etāni
karmāṇy aty-adbhutāni vai
katham arhaty asau janma
grāmyeṣv ātma-jugupsitam

bālakasya—of the boy; *yat*—because; *etāni*—these; *karmāṇi*—activities; *ati-adbhutāni*—most amazing; *vai*—certainly; *katham*—how; *arhati*—should deserve; *asau*—He; *janma*—birth; *grāmyeṣu*—among worldly men; *ātma*—for Himself; *jugupsitam*—contemptible.

TRANSLATION

[The cowherd men said:] Since this boy performs such extraordinary activities, how could He warrant a birth among worldly men like us—a birth that for Him would seem contemptible?

PURPORT

An ordinary living being cannot avoid unpleasant circumstances, but the supreme controller can always make perfect arrangements for His pleasure.

TEXT 3

यः सप्तहायनो बालः करेणैकेन लीलया ।
कथं बिभ्रद् गिरिवरं पुष्करं गजराडिव ॥ ३ ॥

yaḥ sapta-hāyano bālaḥ
kareṇaikena līlayā
kathaṁ bibhrad giri-varaṁ
puṣkaraṁ gaja-rāḍ iva

yaḥ—who; *sapta-hāyanaḥ*—seven years of age; *bālaḥ*—a boy; *kareṇa*—with a hand; *ekena*—one; *līlayā*—playfully; *katham*—how; *bibhrat*—He held up; *giri-varam*—the best of mountains, Govardhana; *puṣkaram*—a lotus flower; *gaja-rāṭ*—a mighty elephant; *iva*—as.

TRANSLATION

How could this seven-year-old boy playfully hold up the great hill Govardhana with one hand, just as a mighty elephant holds up a lotus flower?

TEXT 4

तोकेनामीलिताक्षेण पूतनाया महौजसः ।
पीतः स्तनः सह प्राणैः कालेनेव वयस्तनोः ॥ ४ ॥

tokenāmīlitākṣeṇa
pūtanāyā mahaujasaḥ
pītaḥ stanaḥ saha prāṇaiḥ
kāleneva vayas tanoḥ

tokena—by the young child; *ā-mīlita*—almost closed; *akṣeṇa*—whose eyes; *pūtanāyāḥ*—of the witch Pūtanā; *mahā-ojasaḥ*—whose power was very great; *pītaḥ*—drunk; *stanaḥ*—the breast; *saha*—along with; *prāṇaiḥ*—her life air; *kālena*—by the force of time; *iva*—as; *vayaḥ*—the life span; *tanoḥ*—of a material body.

TRANSLATION

As a mere infant who had hardly yet opened His eyes, He drank the breast milk of the powerful demoness Pūtanā and then sucked out her very life air as well, just as the force of time sucks out the youth of one's body.

PURPORT

The word *vayaḥ* in this verse indicates youth or life span in general. With irresistible power, time takes away our life, and that time is actually Lord Kṛṣṇa Himself. Thus in the case of the powerful witch Pūtanā, Lord Kṛṣṇa accelerated the time process and within an instant withdrew the duration of her life. Here the cowherd men mean to say, "How could a mere infant who could barely open His eyes so easily kill a very powerful demoness?"

TEXT 5

हिन्वतोऽधः शयानस्य मास्यस्य चरणावुदक् ।
अनोऽपतद् विपर्यस्तं रुदतः प्रपदाहतम् ॥ ५ ॥

hinvato'dhaḥ śayānasya
māsyasya caraṇāv udak
ano'patad viparyastaṁ
rudataḥ prapadāhatam

hinvataḥ—moving; *adhaḥ*—beneath; *śayānasya*—of Him who was lying; *māsyasya*—the child only a few months old; *caraṇau*—His two feet; *udak*—upwards; *anaḥ*—the cart; *apatat*—fell; *viparyastam*—turned upside-down; *rudataḥ*—of Him who was crying; *prapada*—by the tip of the foot; *āhatam*—struck.

TRANSLATION

Once, when only three months old, little Kṛṣṇa was crying and kicking up His feet as He lay beneath a huge cart. Then the cart fell and turned upside-down simply because it was struck by the tip of His toe.

TEXT 6

एकहायन आसीनो ह्रियमाणो विहायसा ।
दैत्येन यस्तृणावर्तमहन् कण्ठग्रहातुरम् ॥ ६ ॥

eka-hāyana āsīno
hriyamāṇo vihāyasā
daityena yas tṛṇāvartam
ahan kaṇṭha-grahāturam

eka-hāyanaḥ—one year old; *āsīnaḥ*—sitting; *hriyamāṇaḥ*—being taken away; *vihāyasā*—in the sky; *daityena*—by the demon; *yaḥ*—who; *tṛṇāvartam*—named Tṛṇāvarta; *ahan*—killed; *kaṇṭha*—his neck; *graha*—by being seized; *āturam*—tormented.

TRANSLATION

At the age of one, while sitting peacefully He was taken up into the sky by the demon Tṛṇāvarta. But baby Kṛṣṇa grabbed the demon's neck, causing him great pain, and thus killed him.

PURPORT

The cowherd men, who loved Kṛṣṇa as an ordinary child, were astonished by all these activities. A newborn infant cannot ordinarily kill a powerful witch, and one would hardly think that a one-year-old baby could kill a demon who has kidnapped him and carried him up into the sky. But Kṛṣṇa did all of these wonderful things, and the cowherd men were enhancing their love for Him by remembering and discussing His activities.

TEXT 7

क्वचिद्धैयंगवस्तैन्ये मात्रा बद्ध उदूखले ।
गच्छन्नर्जुनयोर्मध्ये बाहुभ्यां तावपातयत् ॥ ७ ॥

kvacid dhaiyaṅgava-stainye
mātrā baddha udūkhale
gacchann arjunayor madhye
bāhubhyāṁ tāv apātayat

kvacit—once; *haiyaṅgava*—butter; *stainye*—engaged in stealing; *mātrā*—by His mother; *baddhaḥ*—bound up; *udūkhale*—to a large mortar; *gacchan*—moving; *arjunayoḥ*—the twin *arjuna* trees; *madhye*—between; *bāhubhyām*—by His hands; *tau apātayat*—He made them fall.

TRANSLATION

Once, His mother tied Him with ropes to a mortar because she had caught Him stealing butter. Then, crawling on His hands, He dragged the mortar between a pair of arjuna trees and pulled them down.

PURPORT

The two *arjuna* trees were old and thick, and they towered above little Kṛṣṇa's courtyard. Nevertheless, they were pulled down quite easily by the naughty child.

TEXT 8

वने सञ्चारयन् वत्सान् सरामो बालकैर्वृतः ।
हन्तुकामं बकं दोर्भ्यां मुखतोऽरिमपाटयत् ॥ ८ ॥

vane sañcārayan vatsān
sa-rāmo bālakair vṛtaḥ

hantu-kāmaṁ bakaṁ dorbhyāṁ
mukhato'rim apāṭayat

vane—in the forest; *sañcārayan*—grazing; *vatsān*—the calves; *sarāmaḥ*—together with Lord Balarāma; *bālakaiḥ*—by the cowherd boys; *vṛtaḥ*—surrounded; *hantu-kāmam*—desiring to kill; *bakam*—the demon Baka; *dorbhyām*—with His arms; *mukhataḥ*—from the mouth; *arim*—the enemy; *apāṭayat*—tore apart.

TRANSLATION

Another time, when Kṛṣṇa was tending the calves in the forest together with Balarāma and the cowherd boys, the demon Bakāsura came with the intention of killing Kṛṣṇa. But Kṛṣṇa seized this inimical demon by the mouth and tore him apart.

TEXT 9

वत्सेषु वत्सरूपेण प्रविशन्तं जिघांसया ।
हत्वा न्यपातयत्तेन कपित्थानि च लीलया ॥ ९ ॥

vatseṣu vatsa-rūpeṇa
praviśantaṁ jighāṁsayā
hatvā nyapātayat tena
kapitthāni ca līlayā

vatseṣu—among the calves; *vatsa-rūpeṇa*—appearing as if another calf; *praviśantam*—who had entered; *jighāṁsayā*—wanting to kill; *hatvā*—killing him; *nyapātayat*—He made to fall; *tena*—by him; *kapitthāni*—the *kapittha* fruits; *ca*—and; *līlayā*—as a sport.

TRANSLATION

Desiring to kill Kṛṣṇa, the demon Vatsa disguised himself as a calf and entered among Kṛṣṇa's calves. But Kṛṣṇa killed the demon and, using his body, enjoyed the sport of knocking kapittha fruits down from the trees.

TEXT 10

हत्वा रासभदैतेयं तद्बन्धूंश्च बलान्वितः ।
चक्रे तालवनं क्षेमं परिपक्वफलान्वितम् ॥ १० ॥

hatvā rāsabha-daiteyaṁ
tad-bandhūṁś ca balānvitaḥ
cakre tāla-vanaṁ kṣemaṁ
paripakva-phalānvitam

hatvā—killing; *rāsabha*—who appeared as a jackass; *daiteyam*—the descendant of Diti; *tat-bandhūn*—the demon's companions; *ca*—and; *bala-anvitaḥ*—accompanied by Balarāma; *cakre*—He made; *tāla-vanam*—the Tālavana forest; *kṣemam*—auspicious; *paripakva*—fully ripened; *phala*—with fruits; *anvitam*—filled.

TRANSLATION

Together with Lord Balarāma, Kṛṣṇa killed the jackass demon and all his friends, thereby securing the safety of the Tālavana forest, which abounded with fully ripened palm fruits.

PURPORT

Long, long ago, the powerful demons Hiraṇyakaśipu and Hiraṇyākṣa were born of the goddess Diti. Therefore demons are commonly called *daiteyas* or *daityas,* meaning "descendants of Diti." Dhenukāsura, the ass demon, terrorized the Tāla forest with his friends, but Śrī Kṛṣṇa and Śrī Balarāma killed them just as modern governments kill terrorists who harass innocent people.

TEXT 11

प्रलम्बं घातयित्वोग्रं बलेन बलशालिना ।
अमोचयद् व्रजपशून् गोपांश्चारण्यवह्नितः ॥ ११ ॥

pralambaṁ ghātayitvograṁ
balena bala-śālinā
amocayad vraja-paśūn
gopāṁś cāraṇya-vahnitaḥ

pralambam—the demon named Pralamba; *ghāyayitvā*—arranging to be killed; *ugram*—terrible; *balena*—by Lord Balarāma; *bala-śālinā*—who is very powerful; *amocayat*—He liberated; *vraja-paśūn*—the animals of Vraja; *gopān*—the cowherd boys; *ca*—and; *āraṇya*—of the forest; *vahnitaḥ*—from the fire.

TRANSLATION

After arranging for the mighty Lord Balarāma to kill the terrible demon Pralamba, Kṛṣṇa saved Vraja's cowherd boys and their animals from a forest fire.

TEXT 12

आशीविषतमाहीन्द्रं दमित्वा विमदं ह्रदात् ।
प्रसह्योद्वास्य यमुनां चक्रेऽसौ निर्विषोदकाम् ॥ १२ ॥

āśī-viṣatamāhīndraṁ
damitvā vimadaṁ hradāt
prasahyodvāsya yamunāṁ
cakre'sau nirviṣodakām

āśī—of his fangs; *viṣa-tama*—having the most powerful poison; *ahi*—of the snakes; *indram*—the chief; *damitvā*—subduing; *vimadam*—whose pride was removed; *hradāt*—from the lake; *prasahya*—by force; *udvāsya*—sending him away; *yamunām*—the river Yamunā; *cakre*—made; *asau*—He; *nirviṣa*—free from poison; *udakām*—its water.

TRANSLATION

Kṛṣṇa chastised the most poisonous serpent, Kāliya, and after humbling him He drove him forcibly from the lake of the Yamunā. In this way the Lord made the water of that river free of the snake's powerful poison.

TEXT 13

दुस्त्यजश्चानुरागोऽस्मिन् सर्वेषां नो व्रजौकसाम्।
नन्द ते तनयेऽस्मासु तस्याप्यौत्पत्तिकः कथम् ॥ १३ ॥

dustyajaś cānurāgo'smin
sarveṣāṁ no vrajaukasām
nanda te tanaye'smāsu
tasyāpy autpattikaḥ katham

dustyajaḥ—impossible to give up; *ca*—and; *anurāgaḥ*—loving affection; *asmin*—for Him; *sarveṣām*—on the part of all; *naḥ*—us; *vraja-okasām*—the residents of Vraja; *nanda*—dear Nanda Mahārāja; *te*—your; *tanaye*—for the son; *asmāsu*—toward us; *tasya*—on His part; *api*—also; *autpattikaḥ*—natural; *katham*—how.

TRANSLATION

Dear Nanda, how is it that we and all the other residents of Vraja cannot give up our constant affection for your son? And how is it that He is so spontaneously attracted to us?

PURPORT

The very word *kṛṣṇa* means "the all-attractive one." The residents of Vṛndāvana could not give up their constant love (*anurāga*) for Lord Kṛṣṇa. Their attitude toward Him was not particularly theistic, because they were unsure whether He was God or not. But He attracted all their love precisely because as God He is the all-attractive person, the supreme object of our love.

The cowherd men also asked, "How is it that young Kṛṣṇa feels such constant love for us?" In fact the Supreme Lord loves all living beings, who are eternally His children. At the end of the *Bhagavad-gītā,* Lord Kṛṣṇa dramatically declares His affection for Arjuna and urges Arjuna to reciprocate that love by surrendering to Him. Śrī Caitanya Mahāprabhu, in His prayers to Lord Kṛṣṇa, states, *etādṛśī tava kṛpā bhagavan mamāpi durdaivam īdṛśam ihājani nānurāgaḥ*: "My Lord, You are so merciful toward Me, but I am so unfortunate that love for You has not awakened within Me." (*Śikṣāṣṭaka* 2) In this statement Śrī Caitanya Mahāprabhu also uses the word *anurāga.* Our misfortune is that we cannot reciprocate the *anurāga,* or loving affection, that the Lord feels for us. Although we are infinitesimal and insignificant and the Lord is infinitely attractive, somehow we do not give Him our love. We must accept responsibility for this foolish decision, since to surrender to God or not is the essential expression of our free will.

The Kṛṣṇa consciousness movement provides an efficient, systematic program to help conditioned souls revive their original, blissful consciousness, which is love of God, Kṛṣṇa consciousness. The intricacies of Kṛṣṇa consciousness are so wonderful that even Kṛṣṇa's eternal associates, the residents of Vṛndāvana, are astonished by them, as shown by these verses.

TEXT 14

क्व सप्तहायनो बालः क्व महाद्रिविधारणम् ।
ततो नो जायते शंका व्रजनाथ तवात्मजे ॥ १४ ॥

kva sapta-hāyano bālaḥ
kva mahādri-vidhāraṇam
tato no jāyate śaṅkā
vraja-nātha tavātmaje

kva—where, in comparison; *sapta-hāyanaḥ*—seven years old; *bālaḥ*—this boy; *kva*—where; *mahā-adri*—of the great mountain; *vidhāraṇam*—the lifting; *tataḥ*—thus; *naḥ*—for us; *jāyate*—arises; *śaṅkā*—doubt; *vraja-nātha*—O master of Vraja; *tava*—your; *ātmaje*—concerning the son.

TRANSLATION

On the one hand this boy is only seven years old, and on the other we see that He has lifted the great hill Govardhana. Therefore, O King of Vraja, a doubt about your son arises within us.

TEXT 15

श्रीनन्द उवाच
श्रूयतां मे वचो गोपा व्येतु शंका च वोऽर्भके ।
एनं कुमारमुद्दिश्य गर्गो मे यदुवाच ह ॥ १५ ॥

śrī-nanda uvāca
śrūyatāṁ me vaco gopā
vyetu śaṅkā ca vo'rbhake
enam kumāram uddiśya
gargo me yad uvāca ha

śrī-nandaḥ uvāca—Śrī Nanda Mahārāja said; *śrūyatām*—please hear; *me*—my; *vacaḥ*—words; *gopāḥ*—my dear cowherd men; *vyetu*—let it go away; *śaṅkā*—the doubt; *ca*—and; *vaḥ*—your; *arbhake*—concerning the boy; *enam*—this; *kumāram*—to the child; *uddiśya*—referring; *gargaḥ*—the sage Garga; *me*—to me; *yat*—which; *uvāca*—spoke; *ha*—in the past.

TRANSLATION

Nanda Mahārāja replied: O cowherd men, just hear my words and let all your doubts concerning my son be gone. Some time ago Garga Muni spoke to me as follows about this boy.

PURPORT

Śrīla Śrīdhara Svāmī comments, "The words previously heard from Gargācārya awakened Nanda Mahārāja to the truth about Kṛṣṇa, and thus, by Nanda's constantly remembering His activities, all thoughts about their being impossible ceased in him. Now he is instructing the cowherd men with these same words."

TEXT 16

वर्णास्त्रयः किलास्यासन् गृह्णतोऽनुयुगं तनूः ।
शुक्लो रक्तस्तथा पीत इदानीं कृष्णतां गतः ॥ १६ ॥

varṇās trayaḥ kilāsyāsan
gṛhṇato'nu-yugaṁ tanūḥ
śuklo raktas tathā pīta
idānīṁ kṛṣṇatāṁ gataḥ

varṇāḥ trayaḥ—three colors; *kila*—indeed; *asya*—by your son Kṛṣṇa; *āsan*—were assumed; *gṛhṇataḥ*—accepting; *anu-yugam tanūḥ*—transcendental bodies according to the different *yugas; śuklaḥ*—sometimes white; *raktaḥ*—sometimes red; *tathā*—as well as; *pītaḥ*—sometimes yellow; *idānīm kṛṣṇatām gataḥ*—at the present moment He has assumed a blackish color.

TRANSLATION

[Garga Muni had said:] Your son Kṛṣṇa appears as an incarnation in every millennium. In the past He assumed three different colors—white, red and yellow—and now He has appeared in a blackish color.

PURPORT

This and the next six verses (17 through 22) are taken from the eighth chapter of this canto, in which Garga Muni instructs Nanda Mahārāja about Nanda's son Kṛṣṇa. The translations found herein for these verses are based on those of His Divine Grace A.C. Bhaktivedanta Swami Prabhupāda. In Chapter Eight, where the verses originally appear, the reader will find extensive purports by Śrīla Prabhupāda.

TEXT 17

प्रागयं वसुदेवस्य क्वचिज्जातस्तवात्मजः ।
वासुदेव इति श्रीमानभिज्ञाः सम्प्रचक्षते ॥ १७ ॥

prāg ayaṁ vasudevasya
kvacij jātas tavātmajaḥ
vāsudeva iti śrīmān
abhijñāḥ sampracakṣate

prāk—before; *ayam*—this child; *vasudevasya*—of Vasudeva; *kvacit*—sometimes; *jātaḥ*—was born; *tava*—your; *ātmajaḥ*—Kṛṣṇa, who has taken birth as your child; *vāsudevaḥ*—therefore He may be given the name Vāsudeva; *iti*—thus; *śrīmān*—very beautiful; *abhijñāḥ*—those who are learned; *sampracakṣate*—also say that Kṛṣṇa is Vāsudeva.

TRANSLATION

For many reasons, this beautiful son of yours sometimes appeared previously as the son of Vasudeva. Therefore, those who are learned sometimes call this child Vāsudeva.

TEXT 18

बहूनि सन्ति नामानि रूपाणि च सुतस्य ते ।
गुणकर्मानुरूपाणि तान्यहं वेद नो जनाः ॥ १८ ॥

bahūni santi nāmāni
rūpāṇi ca sutasya te
guṇa-karmānurūpāṇi
tāny ahaṁ veda no janāḥ

bahūni—various; *santi*—there are; *nāmāni*—names; rūpāṇi—forms; *ca*—also; *sutasya*—of the son; *te*—your; *guṇa-karma-anurūpāṇi*—according to His attributes and activities; *tāni*—them; *aham*—I; *veda*—know; *na u janāḥ*—not ordinary persons.

TRANSLATION

For this son of yours there are many forms and names according to His transcendental qualities and activities. These are known to me, but people in general do not understand them.

TEXT 19

एष वः श्रेय आधास्यद् गोपगोकुलनन्दनः ।
अनेन सर्वदुर्गाणि यूयमञ्जस्तरिष्यथ ॥ १९ ॥

eṣa vaḥ śreya ādhāsyad
gopa-gokula-nandanaḥ
anena sarva-durgāṇi
yūyam añjas tariṣyatha

eṣaḥ—this child; *vaḥ*—for all of you people; *śreyaḥ ādhāsyat*—will act all-auspiciously; *gopa-gokula-nandanaḥ*—just like a cowherd boy born in a family of cowherd men as the son of the estate of Gokula; *anena*—by Him; *sarva-durgāṇi*—all kinds of miserable conditions; *yūyam*—all of you; *añjaḥ*—easily; *tariṣyatha*—will overcome.

TRANSLATION

To increase the transcendental bliss of the cowherd men of Gokula, this child will always act auspiciously for you. And by His grace only, you will surpass all difficulties.

TEXT 20

पुरानेन व्रजपते साधवो दस्युपीडिताः ।
अराजके रक्ष्यमाणा जिग्युर्दस्यून् समेधिताः ॥ २० ॥

purānena vraja-pate
sādhavo dasyu-pīḍitāḥ
arājake rakṣyamāṇā
jigyur dasyūn samedhitāḥ

purā—formerly; *anena*—by Kṛṣṇa; *vraja-pate*—O King of Vraja; *sādhavaḥ*—those who were honest; *dasyu-pīḍitāḥ*—being disturbed by rogues and thieves; *arājake*—when there was an irregular government; *rakṣyamāṇāḥ*—were protected; *jigyuḥ*—conquered; *dasyūn*—the rogues and thieves; *samedhitāḥ*—flourished.

TRANSLATION

O Nanda Mahārāja, as recorded in history, when there was an irregular, incapable government, Indra having been dethroned, and when honest people were being harassed and disturbed by thieves, this child appeared in order to curb the rogues and to protect the people and enable them to flourish.

TEXT 21

य एतस्मिन्महाभागे प्रीतिं कुर्वन्ति मानवाः ।
नारयोऽभिभवन्त्येतान् विष्णुपक्षानिवासुराः ॥ २१ ॥

ya etasmin mahā-bhāge
prītiṁ kurvanti mānavāḥ
nārayo'bhibhavanty etān
viṣṇu-pakṣān ivāsurāḥ

ye—those persons who; *etasmin*—unto this child; *mahā-bhāge*—most auspicious; *prītim*—affection; *kurvanti*—execute; *mānavāḥ*—such persons; *na*—not; *arayaḥ*—their enemies; *abhibhavanti*—do overcome; *etān*—those who are attached to Kṛṣṇa; *viṣṇu-pakṣān*—the demigods, who always have Lord Viṣṇu on their side; *iva*—like; *asurāḥ*—the demons.

TRANSLATION

Demons cannot harm the demigods, who always have Lord Viṣṇu on their side. Similarly, any person or group attached to all-auspicious Kṛṣṇa cannot be defeated by enemies.

PURPORT

Śrīla Prabhupāda has especially indicated in this connection that just as Lord Kṛṣṇa's associates could not be defeated by Kaṁsa, so His modern-day devotees will not be defeated by their demoniac opponents, nor will the Lord's devotees be defeated by the internal enemies—the lusty, materialistic senses.

TEXT 22

तस्मान्नन्द कुमारोऽयं नारायणसमो गुणैः ।
श्रिया कीर्त्यानुभावेन तत्कर्मसु न विस्मयः ॥ २२ ॥

tasmān nanda kumāro'yaṁ
nārāyaṇa-samo guṇaiḥ
śriyā kīrtyānubhāvena
tat-karmasu na vismayaḥ

tasmāt—therefore; *nanda*—O Nanda Mahārāja; *kumāraḥ*—child; *ayam*—this; *nārāyaṇa-samaḥ*—is as good as Nārāyaṇa; *guṇaiḥ*—by His qualities; *śriyā*—by His opulence; *kīrtyā*—especially by His name and fame; *anub-*

hāvena—and by His influence; *tat*—His; *karmasu*—concerning the activities; *na*—there is no; *vismayaḥ*—surprise.

TRANSLATION

Therefore, O Nanda Mahārāja, this child of yours is as good as Nārāyaṇa. In His transcendental qualities, opulence, name, fame and influence, He is exactly like Nārāyaṇa. Thus you should not be astonished by His activities.

PURPORT

Nanda here reports to the cowherd men the concluding remarks of Garga Muni, who spoke at the secret birth ceremony of Lord Kṛṣṇa.

TEXT 23

इत्यद्धा मां समादिश्य गर्गे च स्वगृहं गते ।
मन्ये नारायणस्यांशं कृष्णमक्लिष्टकारिणम् ॥ २३ ॥

ity addhā māṁ samādiśya
garge ca sva-gṛhaṁ gate
manye nārāyaṇasyāṁśaṁ
kṛṣṇam akliṣṭa-kāriṇam

iti—thus speaking; *addhā*—directly; *mām*—me; *samādiśya*—advising; *garge*—Gargācārya; *ca*—and; *sva-gṛham*—to his home; *gate*—going; *manye*—I consider; *nārāyaṇasya*—of the Supreme Personality of Godhead, Nārāyaṇa; *aṁśam*—an empowered expansion; *kṛṣṇam*—Kṛṣṇa; *akliṣṭa-kāriṇam*—who keeps us free from misery.

TRANSLATION

[Nanda Mahārāja continued:] After Garga Ṛṣi spoke these words to me and returned home, I began to consider that Kṛṣṇa, who keeps us free from trouble, is actually an expansion of Lord Nārāyaṇa.

TEXT 24

इति नन्दवचः श्रुत्वा गर्गगीतं व्रजौकसः ।
मुदिता नन्दमानर्चुः कृष्णं च गतविस्मयाः ॥ २४ ॥

iti nanda-vacaḥ śrutvā
garga-gītaṁ taṁ vrajaukasaḥ

muditā nandam ānarcuḥ
kṛṣṇaṁ ca gata-vismayāḥ

iti—thus; *nanda-vacaḥ*—the words of Nanda Mahārāja; *śrutvā*—hearing; *garga-gītam*—the statements of Garga Ṛṣi; *vraja-okasaḥ*—the residents of Vraja; *muditāḥ*—enlivened; *nandam*—Nanda Mahārāja; *ānarcuḥ*—they honored; *kṛṣṇam*—Lord Kṛṣṇa; *ca*—and; *gata*—gone; *vismayāḥ*—their perplexity.

TRANSLATION

[Śukadeva Gosvāmī continued:] Having heard Nanda Mahārāja relate the statements of Garga Muni, the residents of Vṛndāvana became enlivened. Their perplexity was gone, and they worshiped Nanda and Lord Kṛṣṇa with great respect.

PURPORT

Śrīla Jīva Gosvāmī explains that in this verse the word *ānarcuḥ* indicates that the residents of Vṛndāvana honored Nanda and Kṛṣṇa with such offerings as fragrances, garlands and garments brought from their homes. Śrīla Viśvanātha Cakravartī Ṭhākura adds that the residents of Vṛndāvana honored Nanda and Kṛṣṇa with loving offerings of jewels and gold coins. Apparently, Lord Kṛṣṇa was playing in the forest when this conversation took place, so when He returned home the residents of Vṛndāvana encouraged Him by decorating Him with beautiful yellow garments, necklaces, armlets, earrings and crowns, and by shouting, "All glories, all glories to the jewel of Vṛndāvana!"

TEXT 25

देवे वर्षति यज्ञविप्लवरुषा वज्राश्मवर्षानिलैः
सीदत्पालपशुस्त्रियात्मशरणं दृष्ट्वानुकम्प्युत्स्मयन् ।
उत्पाट्यैककरेण शैलमबलो लीलोच्छिलीन्ध्रं यथा
बिभ्रद् गोष्ठमपान्महेन्द्रमदभित् प्रीयान्न इन्द्रो गवाम् ॥ २५ ॥

deve varṣati yajña-viplava-ruṣā vajrāśma-varṣānilaiḥ
sīdat-pāla-paśu-striy ātma-śaraṇaṁ dṛṣṭvānukampy utsmayan
utpāṭyaika-kareṇa śailam abalo līlocchilīndhraṁ yathā
bibhrad goṣṭham apān mahendra-mada-bhit prīyān na indro gavām

deve—when the demigod Indra; *varṣati*—caused rain; *yajña*—of his sacrifice; *viplava*—due to the disturbances; *ruṣā*—out of anger; *vajra*—with lightning bolts; *aśma-varṣa*—hail; *anilaiḥ*—and winds; *sīdat*—suffering; *pāla*—the cowherds; *paśu*—animals; *stri*—and women; *ātma*—Himself; *śaraṇam*—being their only shelter; *dṛṣṭvā*—seeing; *anukampī*—very compassionate by nature; *utsmayan*—smiling broadly; *utpāṭya*—picking up; *eka-kareṇa*—in one hand; *śailam*—the hill, Govardhana; *abalaḥ*—a small child; *līlā*—in play; *ucchilīndhram*—a mushroom; *yathā*—just as; *bibhrat*—He held; *goṣṭham*—the cowherd community; *apāt*—He protected; *mahā-indra*—of King Indra; *mada*—of the false pride; *bhit*—the destroyer; *prīyāt*—may He be satisfied; *naḥ*—with us; *indraḥ*—the Lord; *gavām*—of the cows.

TRANSLATION

Indra became angry when his sacrifice was disrupted, and thus he caused rain and hail to fall on Gokula, accompanied by lightning and powerful winds, all of which brought great suffering to the cowherds, animals and women there. When Lord Kṛṣṇa, who is by nature always compassionate, saw the condition of those who had only Him as their shelter, He smiled broadly and lifted Govardhana Hill with one hand, just as a small child picks up a mushroom to play with it. In this way He protected the cowherd community. May He, Govinda, the Lord of the cows and the destroyer of Indra's false pride, be pleased with us.

PURPORT

The word *indra* means "lord" or "king." Thus in this verse Kṛṣṇa is pointedly called *indro gavām,* "the Lord of the cows." In fact, He is the real Indra, the real ruler, of everyone, and the demigods are merely His servants, representing His supreme will.

It is apparent from this and the previous verses in this chapter that Lord Kṛṣṇa's lifting of Govardhana Hill made quite an impression on the simple cowherd men of Vṛndāvana, and they repeatedly remembered this feat. Certainly anyone who soberly and objectively considers the activities of young Kṛṣṇa will surrender to Him and become His eternal devotee in loving devotional service. That is the rational conclusion one should come to after reading this chapter.

Thus end the purports of the humble servants of His Divine Grace A.C. Bhaktivedanta Swami Prabhupāda to the Tenth Canto, Twenty-sixth Chapter, of the Śrīmad-Bhāgavatam, *entitled "Wonderful Kṛṣṇa."*

CHAPTER TWENTY-SEVEN

Lord Indra and Mother Surabhi Offer Prayers

This chapter describes how the Surabhi cow and Indra, having seen the amazing power of Lord Kṛṣṇa, performed a bathing ceremony for Him.

Ashamed of having attacked Vṛndāvana with a violent storm, Indra secretly came before Lord Kṛṣṇa, offered obeisances and praised Him. Indra stated that although Śrī Kṛṣṇa is never caught in the current of material illusion, which is born of ignorance, He nevertheless accepts a humanlike body and performs various activities to establish religious principles and chastise the wicked. By this means He crushes the false prestige of those who presume themselves great controllers. Indra went on to declare that Kṛṣṇa is the father, *guru* and Lord of all living entities, and that in the form of time He is the agent of their punishment.

Satisfied with Indra's prayers, Śrī Kṛṣṇa told him that He had stopped the *indra-yajña* so that Indra, puffed up as he was with false pride, would remember the Lord. Persons intoxicated by material opulence never see Him standing before them with the rod of punishment in His hand. Therefore if Lord Kṛṣṇa desires the actual good fortune of some person, He brings him down from his position of opulence.

Lord Kṛṣṇa ordered Indra to return to his proper position in heaven and to serve there without egotism. Indra, along with the cow Surabhi, then performed a bathing ceremony for Kṛṣṇa, using the water of the heavenly Ganges and the milk of mother Surabhi. Indra and the cow took this opportunity to bestow upon the Lord the name Govinda, and the demigods showered flowers and recited various prayers.

TEXT 1

श्रीशुक उवाच

गोवर्धने धृते शैले आसाराद् रक्षिते व्रजे ।
गोलोकादाव्रजत् कृष्णं सुरभिः शक्र एव च ॥१॥

śrī-śuka uvāca
govardhane dhṛte śaile
āsārād rakṣite vraje
go-lokād āvrajat kṛṣṇaṁ
surabhiḥ śakra eva ca

śrī-śukaḥ uvāca—Śrī Śukadeva Gosvāmī said; *govardhane*—Govardhana; *dhṛte*—having been held; *śaile*—the hill; *āsārāt*—from the rainfall; *rakṣite*—having been protected; *vraje*—Vraja; *go-lokāt*—from the planet of the cows; *āvrajat*—came; *kṛṣṇam*—to Kṛṣṇa; *surabhiḥ*—mother Surabhi; *śakraḥ*—Indra; *eva*—also; *ca*—and.

TRANSLATION

Śukadeva Gosvāmī said: After Kṛṣṇa had lifted Govardhana Hill and thus protected the inhabitants of Vraja from the terrible rainfall, Surabhi, the mother of the cows, came from her planet to see Kṛṣṇa. She was accompanied by Indra.

PURPORT

The word *go-lokāt* here indicates the material planet called Goloka, which is filled with exceptional cows. Surabhi went joyfully to see Lord Kṛṣṇa, but Indra went fearfully. As indicated by this verse, Lord Kṛṣṇa had to adopt extraordinary measures to protect His Vṛndāvana associates from Indra's obnoxious and offensive attack. Certainly Indra was ashamed, and also nervous about his future. Having acted improperly, he had fearfully gone to seek the shelter of Lord Brahmā, who then ordered him to take along Surabhi from the material Goloka planet and go to see Kṛṣṇa.

TEXT 2

विविक्त उपसंगम्य व्रीडीतः कृतहेलनः ।
पस्पर्श पादयोरेनं किरीटेनार्कवर्चसा ॥ २ ॥

vivikta upasaṅgamya
vrīḍitaḥ kṛta-helanaḥ
pasparśa pādayor enaṁ
kirīṭenārka-varcasā

vivikte—in a solitary place; *upasaṅgamya*—approaching; *vrīḍitaḥ*—ashamed; *kṛta-helanaḥ*—having committed offense; *pasparśa*—he touched;

pādayoḥ—upon His feet; *enam*—Him; *kirīṭena*—with his helmet; *arka*—like the sun; *varcasā*—the effulgence of which.

TRANSLATION

Indra was very ashamed of having offended the Lord. Approaching Him in a solitary place, Indra fell down and lay his helmet, whose effulgence was as brilliant as the sun, upon the Lord's lotus feet.

PURPORT

The specific "solitary place" where Indra approached Śrī Kṛṣṇa is mentioned by the sage Śrī Vaiśampāyana in the *Hari-vaṁśa* (*Viṣṇu-parva* 19.3): *sa dadarśopaviṣṭaṁ vai govardhana-śilā-tale.* "He saw Him [Kṛṣṇa] sitting at the base of Govardhana Hill."

From the commentaries of the *ācāryas* we understand that Lord Kṛṣṇa wanted to provide a solitary meeting for Indra so that he would not be further humiliated. Indra came to surrender and beg forgiveness, and the Lord allowed him to do so privately.

TEXT 3

दृष्टश्रुतानुभावोऽस्य कृष्णस्यामिततेजसः ।
नष्टत्रिलोकेशमद इदमाह कृताञ्जलिः ॥ ३ ॥

dṛṣṭa-śrutānubhāvo'sya
kṛṣṇasyāmita-tejasaḥ
naṣṭa-tri-lokeśa-mada
idam āha kṛtāñjaliḥ

dṛṣṭa—seen; *śruta*—heard; *anubhāvaḥ*—the power; *asya*—of this; *kṛṣṇasya*—Lord Kṛṣṇa; *amita*—immeasurable; *tejasaḥ*—whose potencies; *naṣṭa*—destroyed; *tri-loka*—of the three worlds; *īśa*—of being the lord; *madaḥ*—his intoxication; *idam*—these words; *āha*—spoke; *kṛta-añjaliḥ*—joining his palms in supplication.

TRANSLATION

Indra had now heard of and seen the transcendental power of omnipotent Kṛṣṇa, and his false pride in being the lord of the three worlds was thus defeated. Holding his hands together in supplication, he addressed the Lord as follows.

TEXT 4

इन्द्र उवाच
विशुद्धसत्त्वं तव धाम शान्तं
तपोमयं ध्वस्तरजस्तमस्कम् ।
मायामयोऽयं गुणसम्प्रवाहो
न विद्यते तेऽग्रहणानुबन्धः ॥ ४ ॥

indra uvāca
viśuddha-sattvaṁ tava dhāma śāntaṁ
tapo-mayaṁ dhvasta-rajas-tamaskam
māyā-mayo'yaṁ guṇa-sampravāho
na vidyate te 'grahaṇānubandhaḥ

indraḥ uvāca—Indra said; *viśuddha-sattvam*—manifesting transcendental goodness; *tava*—Your; *dhāma*—form; *śāntam*—changeless; *tapaḥ-mayam*—full of knowledge; *dhvasta*—destroyed; *rajaḥ*—the mode of passion; *tamaskam*—and the mode of ignorance; *māyā-mayaḥ*—based on illusion; *ayam*—this; *guṇa*—of the modes of material nature; *sampravāhaḥ*—the great flux; *na vidyate*—is not present; *te*—within You; *agrahaṇa*—ignorance; *anubandhaḥ*—which is due to.

TRANSLATION

King Indra said: Your transcendental form, a manifestation of pure goodness, is undisturbed by change, shining with knowledge and devoid of passion and ignorance. In You does not exist the mighty flow of the modes of material nature, which is based on illusion and ignorance.

PURPORT

The great *Bhāgavatam* commentator Śrīla Śrīdhara Svāmī has masterfully explained the Sanskrit elements of this profound verse.

The Sanskrit word *dhāma* has several meanings: a) dwelling place, house, abode and so on; b) a favorite thing or person; delight; or pleasure; c) form or appearance; d) power, strength, majesty, glory, splendor or light.

Concerning the first set of meanings, the *Vedānta-sūtra* states that the Absolute Truth is the source and resting place of all existence, and in the first verse of the *Bhāgavatam* that Absolute Truth is said to be Kṛṣṇa. Although Lord Kṛṣṇa exists in His own *dhāma,* or abode, called Kṛṣṇaloka, He Himself is the abode of all existence, as Arjuna confirms in the *Bhagavad-gītā,* where he addresses Kṛṣṇa as *paraṁ dhāma,* "the supreme abode."

The very name Kṛṣṇa indicates the all-attractive person, and thus Lord Kṛṣṇa, the source of all beauty and pleasure, is certainly "the favorite thing or person; delight; and pleasure." Ultimately these terms can refer only to Kṛṣṇa.

Dhāma also refers to form or appearance, and as Indra offered these prayers he was in fact directly seeing the form of Kṛṣṇa before him.

As clearly explained in the Vedic literature, Lord Kṛṣṇa's power, strength, majesty, splendor and effulgence are all contained within His transcendental body and thus attest to the infinite glories of the Lord.

Śrīla Śrīdhara Svāmī has brilliantly summarized all these meanings of the word *dhāma* by giving the Sanskrit term *svarūpa* as a synonym. The word *svarūpa* means "one's own form or shape" and also "one's own condition, character or nature." Since Lord Kṛṣṇa, being pure spirit, is nondifferent from His body, there is absolutely no difference between the Lord and His visible form. By contrast, in this material world we conditioned souls are all distinctly different from our bodies, whether those bodies be male, female, black, white or whatever. All of us are eternal souls, different from our temporary, flimsy bodies.

When the word *svarūpa* is applied to us, it especially indicates our spiritual form, because our "own form" is in fact our "own condition, character or nature" eternally. Thus the liberated condition in which one's outward form is one's deepest spiritual nature is called *svarūpa.* Primarily, however, this term refers to the Supreme Personality of Godhead, Śrī Kṛṣṇa. This is all indicated in this verse by the words *tava dhāma,* as explained by Śrīdhara Svāmī.

Śrīdhara Svāmī has explained that here the word *śāntam* means "always in the same form." *Śāntam* can also mean "undisturbed, free from passion, or purified." According to Vedic philosophy, all change in this world is caused by the influence of passion and ignorance. The passionate mode is creative, and the ignorant mode is destructive, whereas the mode of goodness, *sattva,* is serene and sustaining. In many ways this verse emphasizes that Lord Kṛṣṇa is free from the modes of nature. The words *viśuddha-sattvam, śāntam, dhvasta-rajas-tamaskam* and *guṇa-sampravāho na vidyate te* all indicate this. Unlike Kṛṣṇa, we change from one body to another because of our involvement with the modes of nature; the various transformations of material forms are impelled by the modes of nature, which are themselves set in motion by the influence of time. Therefore one who is free from the material modes of nature is changeless and eternally satisfied in blissful spiritual existence. Thus the word *śāntam* indicates that the Lord is undisturbed by change, since He is free from the material modes of nature.

According to this verse, the powerful flow of the material modes of nature —namely passion, stupidity and mundane piety—are based on *agrahaṇa,* which Śrīla Śrīdhara Svāmī has translated as "ignorance." Since the Sanskrit root *grah* means "to take, accept, grasp or comprehend," *grahaṇa* means "grasp" exactly in the sense of "to grasp an idea or fact." Therefore *agrahaṇa* here means one's failure to understand one's spiritual position, and this failure causes one to fall into the violent currents of material existence.

An additional meaning of the word *agrahaṇa* is derived when it is divided into the compound *agra-haṇa. Agra* means "the first, top or best," and *hana* means "killing." The best part of our existence is the pure soul, which is eternal, in contradistinction to the temporary, material body and mind. Thus one who chooses material existence over Kṛṣṇa consciousness is in fact killing the best part of himself, the soul, which in its pure state can enjoy Kṛṣṇa consciousness unlimitedly.

Śrīla Śrīdhara Svāmī has translated *tapo-mayam* as "full of knowledge." The word *tapas,* generally indicating "austerity," is derived from the Sanskrit verb *tap,* whose meaning can be summarized as indicating the various functions of the sun. *Tap* means "to burn, to shine, to heat and so on." The Supreme Lord is eternally perfect, and therefore here *tapo-mayam* does not indicate that His transcendental body is meant for austerities, since austerities are performed by conditioned souls to purify themselves or to acquire a particular power. An omnipotent, perfect being neither purifies Himself nor acquires power: He is eternally pure and all-powerful. Therefore Śrīdhara Svāmī has intelligently understood that in this case the word *tapas* refers to the illuminating function of the sun and thus indicates that the Lord's self-effulgent body is omniscient. Light is a common symbol of knowledge. The Lord's spiritual effulgence does not merely illuminate physically, as in the case of a candle or light bulb; more importantly, the Lord's body illuminates our consciousness with perfect knowledge because the Lord's effulgence is itself perfect knowledge.

We offer our respectful obeisances at the lotus feet of Śrīla Śrīdhara Svāmī and thank him for his enlightening comments on this verse.

TEXT 5

कुतो नु तद्धेतव ईश तत्कृता
लोभादयो येऽबुधलिंगभावाः ।

तथापि दण्डं भगवान् बिभर्ति
धर्मस्य गुप्त्यै खलनिग्रहाय ॥ ५ ॥

kuto nu tad-dhetava īśa tat-kṛtā
lobhādayo ye'budha-linga-bhāvāḥ
tathāpi daṇḍaṁ bhagavān bibharti
dharmasya guptyai khala-nigrahāya

kutaḥ—how; *nu*—certainly; *tat*—of that (existence of the material body); *hetavaḥ*—the causes; *īśa*—O Lord; *tat-kṛtāḥ*—produced by one's connection with the material body; *lobha-ādayaḥ*—greed and so forth; *ye*—which; *abudha*—of an ignorant person; *linga-bhāvāḥ*—symptoms; *tathā api*—nevertheless; *daṇḍam*—punishment; *bhagavān*—the Supreme Personality of Godhead; *bibharti*—wields; *dharmasya*—of the principles of religion; *guptyai*—for the protection; *khala*—of wicked persons; *nigrahāya*—for the chastisement.

TRANSLATION

How, then, could there exist in You the symptoms of an ignorant person—such as greed, lust, anger and envy—which are produced by one's previous involvement in material existence and which cause one to become further entangled in material existence? And yet as the Supreme Lord You impose punishment to protect religious principles and curb down the wicked.

PURPORT

This complex philosophical statement by Indra may be analyzed as follows: In the first line of this verse, Indra refers to the main idea expressed at the end of the previous verse—namely, that the great currents of material existence, which are based on ignorance, cannot possibly exist within the Supreme Lord. The words *tad-dhetavaḥ* and *tat-kṛtāḥ* indicate that something causes the modes of nature to manifest, and that they in turn become the cause of that which caused them. In the second line of this verse, we find that it is material feelings such as greed, lust, envy and anger that cause the modes of nature to manifest and that are themselves caused by the modes of nature.

The explanation of this seeming paradox is as follows: When the conditioned soul decides to associate with the material qualities, he becomes contaminated by those qualities. As stated in the *Gītā* (13.22), *kāraṇaṁ guṇa-saṅgo'sya sad-asad-yoni-janmasu.* For example, in the presence of a seductive woman, a man may give in to his lower instincts and try to enjoy sex with her. By his deciding to associate with the lower qualities of nature, those qualities manifest in him very powerfully. He is overwhelmed with lust and driven to try again and again to satisfy his burning desire. Because his mind has been infected by lust, all that he does, thinks and speaks will be influenced by his strong attachment to sex. In other words, by choosing to associate with the lusty qualities of nature, he has caused them to powerfully manifest within himself, and eventually those lusty qualities themselves will cause him to accept another material body suitable for affairs governed by those qualities.

The lower qualities, such as lust, greed, anger and envy, are *abudha-liṅga-bhāvāḥ,* symptoms of ignorance. Indeed, as indicated by Śrīla Śrīdhara Svāmī in his commentary, the manifestation of the modes of nature is synonymous with the manifestation of a particular material body. It is clearly explained throughout the Vedic literature that the conditioned soul receives a particular body, gives it up and then accepts another simply because of his involvement with the modes of nature (*kāraṇaṁ guṇa-saṅgo'sya*). Thus to say that one is participating in the modes of nature is to say that one is accepting particular types of bodies suitable for the particular material qualities one is involved with.

An ignorant bystander might have simplistically interpreted Kṛṣṇa's pastime of lifting Govardhana Hill as follows: The residents of Vṛndāvana were obliged by Vedic principles to make certain offerings to the god of heaven, Indra. Child Kṛṣṇa, ignoring the position of Indra, usurped these offerings and took them for His own pleasure. When Indra tried to punish Kṛṣṇa and His associates, the Lord frustrated Indra's attempt, humiliated him, and exhausted his pride and resources.

But this superficial interpretation is refuted in this verse. Here Lord Indra addresses Śrī Kṛṣṇa as *bhagavān,* indicating that He is not an ordinary child but in fact God. Therefore Kṛṣṇa's punishing Indra was part of His mission of protecting religious principles and curbing down the envious; it was not a display of material anger or of greed for the offerings meant for Indra. Śrī Kṛṣṇa is pure spiritual existence, and His simple, sublime desire is to engage all living beings in the perfect, blissful life of Kṛṣṇa consciousness. Kṛṣṇa's desire to make us Kṛṣṇa conscious is not egotistical, since ultimately Kṛṣṇa is everything and Kṛṣṇa consciousness is objectively the best consciousness. Lord Indra is really the humble servant of Kṛṣṇa, a fact he is now beginning to remember.

do so, their materialistic leaders, oblivious of the will of the Supreme Lord, will undoubtedly be chastised by cataclysmic events, and the people who elected such leaders, being responsible for their leaders' acts, will share in the suffering.

It is ironic that in modern democracies not only do the leaders consider themselves universal controllers, but the mass of people, considering the leaders merely *their* representatives rather than the representatives of God, also consider themselves, as a people, to be the controllers of their nation. Thus the chastisement mentioned in this verse has become unprecedentedly applicable to people in general in the modern world.

Modern man should not simply make himself a lesson of nature by falling down from his proud position; rather he should submissively execute the will of the all-attractive Personality of Godhead, the Absolute Truth, Śrī Kṛṣṇa, and usher in a new era of sanity, tranquillity and widespread enlightenment.

TEXT 8

स त्वं ममैश्वर्यमदप्लुतस्य
कृतागसस्तेऽविदुषः प्रभावम् ।
क्षन्तुं प्रभोऽथार्हसि मूढचेतसो
मैवं पुनर्भून्मतिरीश मेऽसती ॥ ८ ॥

sa tvaṁ mamaiśvarya-mada-plutasya
kṛtāgasas te'viduṣaḥ prabhāvam
kṣantuṁ prabho'thārhasi mūḍha-cetaso
maivaṁ punar bhūn matir īśa me'satī

saḥ—He; *tvam*—Yourself; *mama*—of me; *aiśvarya*—of rulership; *mada*—in the intoxication; *plutasya*—who is submerged; *kṛta*—having committed; *āgasaḥ*—sinful offense; *te*—Your; *aviduṣaḥ*—not knowing; *prabhāvam*—the transcendental influence; *kṣantum*—to forgive; *prabho*—O master; *atha*—therefore; *arhasi*—You should; *mūḍha*—foolish; *cetasaḥ*—whose intelligence; *mā*—never; *evam*—thus; *punaḥ*—again; *bhūt*—may it be; *matiḥ*—consciousness; *īśa*—O Lord; *me*—my; *asatī*—impure.

TRANSLATION

Engrossed in pride over my ruling power, ignorant of Your majesty, I offended You. O Lord, may You forgive me. My intelligence was bewildered, but let my consciousness never again be so impure.

PURPORT

Although Lord Kṛṣṇa protected the residents of Vraja by lifting Govardhana Hill, He had not yet punished Indra himself, and Indra feared that at any moment Śrī Kṛṣṇa might call the son of Vivasvān, Yamarāja, who punishes impudent persons who defy the laws of God.

Indra was quite fearful and thus begged the Lord's forgiveness on the plea that he could be purified only by Kṛṣṇa's mercy—that he was too stubborn to learn a good lesson through mere punishment.

In fact, despite Indra's humility in this case, his heart was not completely purified. Later on in this canto we find that when Lord Kṛṣṇa once took a *pārijāta* flower from Indra's kingdom, poor Indra again reacted violently against the Supreme Personality of Godhead. Thus, we should aspire to go back to our eternal home in the kingdom of Kṛṣṇa, and should not become entangled in the imperfect life of the material gods.

TEXT 9

तवावतारोऽयमधोक्षजेह
भुवो भराणामुरुभारजन्मनाम् ।
चमूपतीनामभवाय देव
भवाय युष्मच्चरणानुवर्तिनाम् ॥ ९ ॥

tavāvatāro'yam adhokṣajeha
bhuvo bharāṇām uru-bhāra-janmanām
camū-patīnām abhavāya deva
bhavāya yuṣmac-caraṇānuvartinām

tava—Your; *avatāraḥ*—descent; *ayam*—this; *adhokṣaja*—O transcendental Lord; *iha*—into this world; *bhuvaḥ*—of the earth; *bharāṇām*—who constitute a great burden; *uru-bhāra*—to many disturbances; *janmanām*—who have given rise; *camū-patīnām*—of military leaders; *abhavāya*—for the destruction; *deva*—O Supreme Personality of Godhead; *bhavāya*—for the auspicious benefit; *yuṣmat*—Your; *caraṇa*—lotus feet; *anuvartinām*—of those who serve.

TRANSLATION

You descend into this world, O transcendent Lord, to destroy the warlords who burden the earth and create many terrible disturbances. O

Lord, you simultaneously act for the welfare of those who faithfully serve Your lotus feet.

PURPORT

This verse utilizes an attractive poetic device. Lord Kṛṣṇa's descent into the world is said to be for the *abhava,* literally "nonexistence" or "destruction," of the demoniac warlords, and simultaneously for the *bhava,* or "existence, prosperity," of those who faithfully serve the Lord's lotus feet.

True existence, indicated here by the word *bhava,* is *sac-cid-ānanda,* eternal and full of bliss and knowledge. To an uninformed observer, it may appear that Śrī Kṛṣṇa is simply rewarding His followers and punishing His enemies the way any ordinary person might do. This specific doubt about the Lord is raised extensively in the Sixth Canto in connection with Kṛṣṇa's taking the side of the faithful demigods against the faithless demons in a particular cosmic war. In that canto the Vaiṣṇava authorities clearly explain that in fact Lord Kṛṣṇa is the father and Lord of all living beings and that all His activities are therefore meant for the benefit of all existence. Lord Kṛṣṇa does not really cause the nonexistence of anyone; rather He curbs the foolish, destructive, material ways of those who defy the laws of God. These laws are created to ensure the prosperity, harmony and happiness of the entire creation, and their violation is an unjustifiable disturbance.

Certainly Indra hoped that Lord Kṛṣṇa would count him among the devotees and not the demons, although considering Indra's actions one might doubt where his loyalties actually lay. Indra was aware of this possible doubt and thus, as we find in the next verse, he tried his best to surrender to the Supreme Lord.

TEXT 10

नमस्तुभ्यं भगवते पुरुषाय महात्मने ।
वासुदेवाय कृष्णाय सात्वतां पतये नमः ॥ १० ॥

namas tubhyaṁ bhagavate
puruṣāya mahātmane
vāsudevāya kṛṣṇāya
sātvatāṁ pataye namaḥ

namaḥ—obeisances; *tubhyam*—unto You; *bhagavate*—the Supreme Personality of Godhead; *puruṣāya*—the Lord dwelling within the hearts of all;

mahā-ātmane—the great Soul; *vāsudevāya*—to Him who dwells everywhere; *kṛṣṇāya*—Śrī Kṛṣṇa; *sātvatām*—of the Yadu dynasty; *pataye*—to the master; *namaḥ*—obeisances.

TRANSLATION

Obeisances unto You, the Supreme Personality of Godhead, the great Soul, who are all-pervading and who reside in the hearts of all. My obeisances unto You, Kṛṣṇa, the chief of the Yadu dynasty.

TEXT 11

स्वच्छन्दोपात्तदेहाय विशुद्धज्ञानमूर्तये ।
सर्वस्मै सर्वबीजाय सर्वभूतात्मने नमः ॥ ११ ॥

svacchandopātta-dehāya
viśuddha-jñāna-mūrtaye
sarvasmai sarva-bījāya
sarva-bhūtātmane namaḥ

sva—of His own (devotees); *chanda*—according to the desire; *upātta*—who assumes; *dehāya*—His transcendental bodies; *viśuddha*—perfectly pure; *jñāna*—knowledge; *mūrtaye*—whose form; *sarvasmai*—to Him who is everything; *sarva-bījāya*—who is the seed of all; *sarva-bhūta*—of all created beings; *ātmane*—who is the indwelling Soul; *namaḥ*—obeisances.

TRANSLATION

Unto Him who assumes transcendental bodies according to the desires of His devotees, unto Him whose form is itself pure consciousness, unto Him who is everything, who is the seed of everything and who is the Soul of all creatures, I offer my obeisances.

PURPORT

We could hardly construe from the first line of this verse that God is somehow impersonal but assumes a personal material body. It is clearly said here that the Lord assumes different forms according to *svacchanda*—according to His own desire or according to the desires of His devotees. An impersonal God could hardly reciprocate with the personal desires of Its devotees, nor could an impersonal God Itself have desires, since desire is characteristic of personality. Therefore, the Lord's manifesting different forms in a personal way, responding to personal desires, indicates that He is eternally a person and manifests His different transcendental bodies as an expression of His own eternal nature.

The word *viśuddha-jñāna-mūrtaye* is most significant. *Mūrti* means the form of the Deity, and it is specifically stated here that the Lord's form is itself completely pure consciousness. Consciousness is the primary spiritual element, distinct from any of the material elements, and even distinct from the subtle or psychological material elements—mundane mind, intelligence and false ego—which are simply a psychic covering over pure consciousness. Since the Lord's form is made of pure consciousness, it can hardly be understood as a material body like the mortal bags of flesh and bones we carry around in this world.

In the last two lines of this verse, there is poetic emphasis on the word *sarva,* "everything." The Lord is everything: He is the seed of everything and He is the Soul of every creature. Therefore, let us join with Indra in offering our obeisances to the Lord.

TEXT 12

मयेदं भगवन् गोष्ठनाशायासारवायुभिः ।
चेष्टितं विहते यज्ञे मानिना तीव्रमन्युना ॥ १२ ॥

mayedaṁ bhagavan goṣṭha-
nāśāyāsāra-vāyubhiḥ
ceṣṭitaṁ vihate yajñe
māninā tīvra-manyunā

mayā—by me; *idam*—this; *bhagavan*—O Lord; *goṣṭha*—of Your cowherd community; *nāśāya*—for the destruction; *āsāra*—by hard rain; *vāyubhiḥ*—and wind; *ceṣṭitam*—enacted; *vihate*—when it was disrupted; *yajñe*—my sacrifice; *māninā*—(by me) who was falsely proud; *tīvra*—fierce; *manyunā*—whose anger.

TRANSLATION

My dear Lord, when my sacrifice was disrupted I became fiercely angry because of false pride. Thus I tried to destroy Your cowherd community with severe rain and wind.

TEXT 13

त्वयेशानुगृहीतोऽस्मि ध्वस्तस्तम्भो वृथोद्यमः ।
ईश्वरं गुरुमात्मानं त्वामहं शरणं गतः ॥ १३ ॥

tvayeśānugṛhīto'smi
dhvasta-stambho vṛthodyamaḥ
īśvaraṁ gurum ātmānaṁ
tvām ahaṁ śaraṇaṁ gataḥ

tvayā—by You; *īśa*—O Lord; *anugṛhītaḥ*—shown mercy; *asmi*—I am; *dhvasta*—shattered; *stambhaḥ*—my false pride; *vṛthā*—fruitless; *udyamaḥ*—my attempt; *īśvaram*—the Supreme Lord; *gurum*—the spiritual master; *ātmānam*—the true Self; *tvām*—to You; *aham*—I; *śaraṇam*—for shelter; *gataḥ*—have come.

TRANSLATION

O Lord, You have shown mercy to me by shattering my false pride and defeating my attempt [to punish Vṛndāvana]. To You, the Supreme Lord, spiritual master and Supreme Soul, I have now come for shelter.

TEXT 14

श्रीशुक उवाच
एवं संकीर्तितः कृष्णो मघोना भगवानमुम् ।
मेघगम्भीरया वाचा प्रहसन्निदमब्रवीत् ॥ १४॥

śrī-śuka uvāca
evaṁ saṅkīrtitaḥ kṛṣṇo
maghonā bhagavān amum
megha-gambhīrayā vācā
prahasann idam abravīt

śrī-śukaḥ uvāca—Śrī Śukadeva Gosvāmī said; *evam*—in this manner; *saṅkīrtitaḥ*—glorified; *kṛṣṇaḥ*—Lord Kṛṣṇa; *maghonā*—by Indra; *bhagavān*—the Supreme Personality of Godhead; *amum*—to him; *megha*—like the clouds; *gambhīrayā*—grave; *vācā*—with words; *prahasan*—smiling; *idam*—the following; *abravīt*—spoke.

TRANSLATION

Śukadeva Gosvāmī said: Thus glorified by Indra, Lord Kṛṣṇa, the Supreme Personality of Godhead, smiled and then spoke to him as follows in a voice resonant like the clouds.

PURPORT

Although in this pastime Lord Kṛṣṇa appeared to be a small boy, the words *megha-gambhīrayā vācā* indicate that He spoke to Indra with the deep, resonant voice of the Supreme Lord.

TEXT 15

श्रीभगवानुवाच
मया तेऽकारि मघवन्मखभंगोऽनुगृह्णता ।
मदनुस्मृतये नित्यं मत्तस्येन्द्रश्रिया भृशम् ॥ १५ ॥

śrī-bhagavān uvāca
mayā te'kāri maghavan
makha-bhaṅgo'nugṛhṇatā
mad-anusmṛtaye nityaṁ
mattasyendra-śriyā bhṛśam

śrī-bhagavān uvāca—the Supreme Personality of Godhead said; *mayā*—by Me; *te*—unto you; *akāri*—has been done; *maghavan*—My dear Indra; *makha*—of your sacrifice; *bhaṅgaḥ*—the stopping; *anugṛhṇatā*—acting to show mercy to you; *mat-anusmṛtaye*—for the sake of remembrance of Me; *nityam*—constant; *mattasya*—of one intoxicated; *indra-śriyā*—with the opulence of Indra; *bhṛśam*—greatly.

TRANSLATION

The Supreme Personality of Godhead said: My dear Indra, it was out of mercy that I stopped the sacrifice meant for you. You were greatly intoxicated by your opulence as King of heaven, and I wanted you to always remember Me.

PURPORT

According to Śrīdhara Svāmī, Indra and Lord Kṛṣṇa here exchange a heart-to-heart talk. Indra revealed his mind to the Lord, and now Lord Kṛṣṇa similarly reveals His own intention.

In text 11 of this chapter, Indra emphatically declared that Lord Kṛṣṇa is in fact everything, and thus, according to Indra's own criteria, forgetting Lord Kṛṣṇa is clearly a state of insanity. When the Supreme Lord reminds us of His supreme existence, He is not proudly advertising Himself like a mundane politician or entertainer. The Lord is self-satisfied in His own infinite existence and is trying, lovingly, to bring us back to our own perfect existence as His eternal associates.

From God's point of view even the mighty King of heaven, Indra, is a mere child—and a naughty child at that—and thus the Lord, being a caring father, punished His child and brought him back to the sanity of Kṛṣṇa consciousness.

TEXT 16

मामैश्वर्यश्रीमदान्धो दण्डपाणिं न पश्यति ।
तं भ्रंशयामि सम्पद्भ्यो यस्य चेच्छाम्यनुग्रहम् ॥ १६ ॥

mām aiśvarya-śrī-madāndho
daṇḍa pāṇiṁ na paśyati
taṁ bhraṁśayāmi sampadbhyo
yasya cecchāmy anugraham

mām—Me; *aiśvarya*—of his power; *śrī*—and opulence; *mada*—by the intoxication; *andhaḥ*—rendered blind; *daṇḍa*—with the rod of punishment; *pāṇim*—in My hand; *na paśyati*—one does not see; *tam*—him; *bhraṁśayāmi*—I make fall; *sampadbhyaḥ*—from his material assets; *yasya*—for whom; *ca*—and; *icchāmi*—I desire; *anugraham*—benefit.

TRANSLATION

A man blinded by intoxication with his power and opulence cannot see Me nearby with the rod of punishment in My hand. If I desire his real welfare, I drag him down from his materially fortunate position.

PURPORT

One may argue, "God should desire everyone's real welfare; therefore why should Lord Kṛṣṇa state in this verse that He removes the intoxicating opulence of one who is about to receive His mercy, rather than simply stating that He will remove everyone's opulence and bless everyone?" On the other hand, we may point out that irrevocable death occurs for everyone, and thus Lord Kṛṣṇa *does* take away everyone's opulence and everyone's false pride. However, if we apply the Lord's statement to events within one's immediate life, before death, we may refer to Kṛṣṇa's statement in the *Bhagavad-gītā* (4.11): *ye yathā māṁ prapadyante tāṁs tathaiva bhajāmy aham.* "As people surrender to Me, I reward them accordingly." Lord Kṛṣṇa desires everyone's welfare, but when

He says here *yasya cecchāmy anugraham,* "for one whose welfare I desire," it is understood that the Lord refers to those who by their own activities and thoughts have manifested a desire to achieve spiritual benefit. Lord Kṛṣṇa wants everyone to be happy in Kṛṣṇa consciousness, but when He sees that a specific person also desires spiritual happiness, the Lord especially desires it for that person. This is a natural act of reciprocation consistent with the Lord's statement *samo'haṁ sarva-bhūteṣu*: "I am equal in My attitude to all living beings." (Bg. 9.29)

TEXT 17

गम्यतां शक्र भद्रं वः क्रियतां मेऽनुशासनम् ।
स्थीयतां स्वाधिकारेषु युक्तैर्वः स्तम्भवर्जितैः ॥ १७ ॥

gamyatāṁ śakra bhadraṁ vaḥ
kriyatāṁ me'nuśāsanam
sthīyatāṁ svādhikāreṣu
yuktair vaḥ stambha-varjitaiḥ

gamyatām—you may go; *śakra*—O Indra; *bhadram*—good fortune; *vaḥ*—unto you; *kriyatām*—you should execute; *me*—My; *anuśāsanam*—order; *sthīyatām*—you may remain; *sva*—in your own; *adhikāreṣu*—responsibilities; *yuktaiḥ*—soberly engaged; *vaḥ*—you; *stambha*—false pride; *varjitaiḥ*—devoid of.

TRANSLATION

Indra, you may now go. Execute My order and remain in your appointed position as King of heaven. But be sober, without false pride.

PURPORT

Lord Kṛṣṇa here addresses Indra in the plural form (*vaḥ*) because this grave instruction was meant to be a lesson for all the demigods.

TEXT 18

अथाह सुरभिः कृष्णमभिवन्द्य मनस्विनी ।
स्वसन्तानैरुपामन्त्र्य गोपरूपिणमीश्वरम् ॥ १८ ॥

athāha surabhiḥ kṛṣṇam
abhivandya manasvinī

sva-santānair upāmantrya
gopa-rūpiṇam īśvaram

atha—then; *āha*—spoke; *surabhiḥ*—the mother of the cows, Surabhi; *kṛṣṇam*—to Kṛṣṇa; *abhivandya*—offering respects; *manasvinī*—peaceful in mind; *sva-santānaiḥ*—together with her progeny, the cows; *upāmantrya*—begging for His attention; *gopa-rūpiṇam*—appearing as a cowherd boy; *īśvaram*—the Supreme Lord.

TRANSLATION

Mother Surabhi, along with her progeny, the cows, then offered her obeisances to Lord Kṛṣṇa. Respectfully requesting His attention, the gentle lady addressed the Supreme Personality of Godhead, who was present before her as a cowherd boy.

PURPORT

The statement here that the heavenly cow Surabhi approached Lord Kṛṣṇa along with her progeny (*sva-santānaiḥ*) is a reference to the transcendental cows who play with Lord Kṛṣṇa in Vṛndāvana. Although Lord Kṛṣṇa's cows are transcendental, the heavenly cow Surabhi affectionately saw them, as indeed Lord Kṛṣṇa Himself did, as related to her. Since Lord Kṛṣṇa was appearing in the form of a cowherd boy, the whole situation was quite congenial, and Surabhi took the opportunity to offer the following prayers.

TEXT 19

सुरभिरुवाच
कृष्ण कृष्ण महायोगिन् विश्वात्मन् विश्वसम्भव।
भवता लोकनाथेन सनाथा वयमच्युत ॥ १९ ॥

surabhir uvāca
kṛṣṇa kṛṣṇa mahā-yogin
viśvātman viśva-sambhava
bhavatā loka-nāthena
sa-nāthā vayam acyuta

surabhiḥ uvāca—Surabhi said; *kṛṣṇa kṛṣṇa*—O Kṛṣṇa, Kṛṣṇa; *mahā yogin*—O greatest of mystics; *viśva-ātman*—O Soul of the universe; *viśva-sambhava*—O origin of the universe; *bhavatā*—by You; *loka nāthena*—the master of the world; *sa-nāthāḥ*—having a master; *vayam*—we; *acyuta*—O infallible one.

TRANSLATION

Mother Surabhi said: O Kṛṣṇa, Kṛṣṇa, greatest of mystics! O Soul and origin of the universe! You are the master of the world, and by Your grace, O infallible Lord, we have You as our master.

PURPORT

Śrīla Viśvanātha Cakravartī Ṭhākura points out here that mother Surabhi is feeling great ecstasy as she repeats the words "Kṛṣṇa, Kṛṣṇa." Kṛṣṇa lifted Govardhana Hill by His mystic power and thus protected the cows of Vṛndāvana, whereas her so-called master, Indra, had tried to kill them. Thus Surabhi now clearly understands that it is not the demigods but rather the Supreme God, Kṛṣṇa Himself, who is her real master forever.

TEXT 20

त्वं नः परमकं दैवं त्वं न इन्द्रो जगत्पते ।
भवाय भव गोविप्रदेवानां ये च साधवः ॥ २० ॥

tvaṁ naḥ paramakaṁ daivaṁ
tvaṁ na indro jagat-pate
bhavāya bhava go-vipra
devānāṁ ye ca sādhavaḥ

tvam—You; *naḥ*—our; *paramakam*—supreme; *daivam*—worshipable Deity; *tvam*—You; *naḥ*—our; *indraḥ*—Lord Indra; *jagat-pate*—O master of the universe; *bhavāya*—for the welfare; *bhava*—please be; *go*—of the cows; *vipra*—the *brāhmaṇas; devānām*—and the demigods; *ye*—who; *ca*—and; *sādhavaḥ*—saintly persons.

TRANSLATION

You are our worshipable Deity. Therefore, O Lord of the universe, for the benefit of the cows, the brāhmaṇas, the demigods and all other saintly persons, please become our Indra.

PURPORT

The Supreme Lord is self-sufficient: He can do everything Himself. The Lord appointed one of His innumerable children to the position of Indra, the lord of the cosmic heaven. But Indra abused his authority, and now Surabhi requests Lord Kṛṣṇa, the Absolute Truth, to directly become her Lord, her Indra. We should carefully perform our duties without false pride; thus we will not become obsolete and embarrassed, as in the present case of King Indra, who actually attacked Lord Kṛṣṇa and His Vṛndāvana devotees.

TEXT 21

इन्द्रं नस्त्वाभिषेक्ष्यामो ब्रह्मणा चोदिता वयम्।
अवतीर्णोऽसि विश्वात्मन् भूमेर्भारापनुत्तये ॥ २१ ॥

indraṁ nas tvābhiṣekṣyāmo
brahmaṇā coditā vayam
avatīrṇo'si viśvātman
bhūmer bhārāpanuttaye

indram—as Indra; *naḥ*—our; *tvā*—to You; *abhiṣekṣyāmaḥ*—we shall perform the bathing ceremony of coronation; *brahmaṇā*—by Lord Brahmā; *coditāḥ*—ordered; *vayam*—we; *avatīrṇaḥ asi*—You have descended; *viśva-ātman*—O Soul of the universe; *bhūmeḥ*—of the earth; *bhāra*—the burden; *apanuttaye*—in order to alleviate.

TRANSLATION

As ordered by Lord Brahmā, we shall perform Your bathing ceremony to coronate You as Indra. O Soul of the universe, You descend to this world to relieve the burden of the earth.

PURPORT

Surabhi makes it quite clear in this verse that she has had enough of the leadership of imperfect demigods like Purandara (Indra), and now she is determined to directly serve the Supreme Lord. Since Brahmā has ordered her, her attempt to coronate Lord Kṛṣṇa as her personal Lord is authorized by higher authority. Moreover, Lord Kṛṣṇa Himself comes down to the earth to relieve the burden of self-destructive, mundane administration, and thus it is perfectly consistent with the Lord's own purpose that He become the Lord of Surabhi. Since the Lord rules millions of universes, He can certainly take care of mother Surabhi.

In fact, Surabhi wanted to bathe the Lord for her own purification, and she earnestly makes her proposal to Viśvātmā, the Soul of the universe, Śrī Kṛṣṇa.

TEXTS 22–23

श्रीशुक उवाच
एवं कृष्णमुपामन्त्र्य सुरभिः पयसात्मनः ।
जलैराकाशगंगाया ऐरावतकरोद्धृतैः ॥ २२ ॥
इन्द्रः सुरर्षिभिः साकं चोदितो देवमातृभिः ।
अभ्यसिञ्चत दाशार्हं गोविन्द इति चाभ्यधात् ॥ २३ ॥

śrī-śuka uvāca
evaṁ kṛṣṇam upāmantrya
surabhiḥ payasātmanaḥ
jalair ākāśa-gaṅgāyā
airāvata-karoddhṛtaiḥ

indraḥ surarṣibhiḥ sākaṁ
codito deva-mātṛbhiḥ
abhyasiñcata dāśārhaṁ
govinda iti cābhyadhāt

śrī-śukaḥ uvāca—Śrī Śukadeva Gosvāmī said; *evam*—thus; *kṛṣṇam*—Lord Kṛṣṇa; *upāmantrya*—requesting; *surabhiḥ*—mother Surabhi; *payasā*—with milk; *ātmanaḥ*—her own; *jalaiḥ*—with the water; *ākāśa-gaṅgāyāḥ*—of the Ganges flowing through the heavenly region (known as the Mandākinī); *airāvata*—of Indra's carrier, the elephant Airāvata; *kara*—by the trunk; *uddhṛtaiḥ*—carried; *indraḥ*—Lord Indra; *sura*—by the demigods; *ṛṣibhiḥ*—and the great sages; *sākam*—accompanied; *coditaḥ*—inspired; *deva*—of the demigods; *mātṛbhiḥ*—by the mothers (headed by Aditi); *abhyasiñcata*—he bathed; *dāśārham*—Lord Kṛṣṇa, the descendant of King Daśārha; *govindaḥ iti*—as Govinda; *ca*—and; *abhyadhāt*—he named the Lord.

TRANSLATION

Śukadeva Gosvāmī said: Having thus appealed to Lord Kṛṣṇa, mother Surabhi performed His bathing ceremony with her own milk, and Indra, ordered by Aditi and other mothers of the demigods, anointed the Lord with heavenly Gaṅgā water from the trunk of Indra's elephant carrier, Airāvata. Thus, in the company of the demigods and great sages, Indra coronated Lord Kṛṣṇa, the descendant of Daśārha, and gave Him the name Govinda.

PURPORT

According to the *ācāryas,* because Indra was embarrassed by his blunder of attacking Vṛndāvana, he was reluctant to worship the Lord. Therefore the heavenly mothers, such as Aditi, encouraged him to go ahead and do so. Feeling authorized by the encouragement of demigods less offensive than he, Indra then bathed the Lord. Indra discovered that the beautiful cowherd boy named Kṛṣṇa is indeed the Supreme Personality of Godhead.

TEXT 24

तत्रागतास्तुम्बुरुनारदादयो
गन्धर्वविद्याधरसिद्धचारणाः ।
जगुर्यशो लोकमलापहं हरेः
सुरांगनाः सन्ननृतुर्मुदान्विताः ॥ २४ ॥

tatrāgatās tumburu-nāradādayo
gandharva-vidyādhara-siddha-cāraṇāḥ
jagur yaśo loka-malāpahaṁ hareḥ
surāṅganāḥ sannanṛtur mudānvitāḥ

tatra—to that place; *āgatāḥ*—coming; *tumburu*—the Gandharva named Tumburu; *nārada*—Nārada Muni; *ādayaḥ*—and other demigods; *gandharva-vidyādhara-siddha-cāraṇāḥ*—the Gandharvas, Vidyādharas, Siddhas and Cāraṇas; *jaguḥ*—sang; *yaśaḥ*—the glories; *loka*—of the entire world; *mala*—the contamination; *apaham*—which eradicate; *hareḥ*—of Lord Hari; *sura*—of the demigods; *aṅganāḥ*—the wives; *sannanṛtuḥ*—danced together; *mudā anvitāḥ*—filled with joy.

TRANSLATION

Tumburu, Nārada and other Gandharvas, along with the Vidyādharas, Siddhas and Cāraṇas, came there to sing the glories of Lord Hari, which purify the entire world. And the wives of the demigods, filled with joy, danced together in the Lord's honor.

TEXT 25

तं तुष्टुवुर्देवनिकायकेतवो
ह्यवाकिरंश्चाद्भुतपुष्पवृष्टिभिः ।

लोकाः परां निर्वृतिमाप्नुवंस्त्रयो
गावस्तदा गामनयन् पयोद्रुताम् ॥ २५ ॥

taṁ tuṣṭuvur deva-nikāya-ketavo
hy avākiraṁś cādbhuta-puṣpa-vṛṣṭibhiḥ
lokāḥ parāṁ nirvṛtim āpnuvaṁs trayo
gāvas tadā gām anayan payo-drutām

tam—Him; *tuṣṭuvuḥ*—praised; *deva-nikāya*—of all the demigods; *ketavaḥ*—the most eminent; *hi*—indeed; *avākiran*—they covered Him; *ca*—and; *adbhuta*—amazing; *puṣpa*—of flowers; *vṛṣṭibhiḥ*—with showers; *lokāḥ*—the worlds; *parām*—supreme; *nirvṛtim*—satisfaction; *āpnuvan*—experienced; *trayaḥ*—three; *gāvaḥ*—the cows; *tadā*—then; *gām*—the earth; *anayan*—brought; *payaḥ*—with their milk; *drutām*—to saturation.

TRANSLATION

The most eminent demigods chanted the praises of the Lord and scattered wonderful showers of flowers all around Him. All three worlds felt supreme satisfaction, and the cows drenched the surface of the earth with their milk.

PURPORT

The word *ketavaḥ* means, literally, "banners." The leading demigods are the emblems, or banners, of the demigod race, and they took the lead in glorifying the Lord and covering Him with an amazing shower of multicolored, fragrant flowers.

TEXT 26

नानारसौघाः सरितो वृक्षा आसन्मधुस्रवाः ।
अकृष्टपच्यौषधयो गिरयोऽबिभ्रनुन्मणीन् ॥ २६ ॥

nānā-rasaughāḥ sarito
vṛkṣā āsan madhu-sravāḥ
akṛṣṭa-pacyauṣadhayo
girayo'bibhran un maṇīn

nānā—various; *rasa*—liquids; *oghāḥ*—flooding; *saritaḥ*—the rivers; *vṛkṣāḥ*—the trees; *āsan*—became; *madhu*—with sweet sap; *sravāḥ*—flowing; *akṛṣṭa*—even without cultivation; *pacya*—ripened; *oṣadhayaḥ*—the plants; *girayaḥ*—the mountains; *abibhran*—carried; *ut*—above the ground; *maṇīn*—jewels.

TRANSLATION

Rivers flowed with various kinds of tasty liquids, trees exuded honey, edible plants came to maturity without cultivation, and hills gave forth jewels formerly hidden in their interiors.

TEXT 27

कृष्णेऽभिषिक्त एतानि सर्वाणि कुरुनन्दन।
निर्वैराण्यभवंस्तात क्रूराण्यपि निसर्गतः ॥ २७॥

kṛṣṇe'bhiṣikta etāni
sarvāṇi kuru-nandana
nirvairāṇy abhavaṁs tāta
krūrāṇy api nisargataḥ

kṛṣṇe—Lord Kṛṣṇa; *abhiṣikte*—having been bathed; *etāni*—these; *sarvāṇi*—all; *kuru-nandana*—O beloved of the Kuru dynasty; *nirvairāṇi*—free from enmity; *abhavan*—became; *tāta*—my dear Parīkṣit; *krūrāṇi*—vicious; *api*—although; *nisargataḥ*—by nature.

TRANSLATION

O Parīkṣit, beloved of the Kuru dynasty, upon the ceremonial bathing of Lord Kṛṣṇa, all living creatures, even those cruel by nature, became entirely free of enmity.

PURPORT

Those corrupted by a type of sophisticated cynicism may mock these descriptions of a paradisiacal world situation effected simply by worshiping the Supreme Lord. Unfortunately, modern man has created a hell on earth in his cynical rejection of heaven on earth, which is actually possible through Kṛṣṇa consciousness. The situation described here, created simply by the auspicious bathing ceremony of the Lord, is an authentic historical incident. Since history repeats itself, there is hope that the Kṛṣṇa consciousness movement may again bring the world community to the brilliant reality of self-realized existence.

TEXT 28

इति गोगोकुलपतिं गोविन्दमभिषिच्य सः ।
अनुज्ञातो ययौ शक्रो वृतो देवादिभिर्दिवम् ॥ २८ ॥

iti go-gokula-patiṁ
govindam abhiṣicya saḥ
anujñāto yayau śakro
vṛto devādibhir divam

iti—thus; *go*—of the cows; *go-kula*—and of the community of cowherds; *patim*—the master; *govindam*—Lord Kṛṣṇa; *abhiṣicya*—bathing; *saḥ*—he, Indra; *anujñātaḥ*—given permission; *yayau*—went; *śakraḥ*—King Indra; *vṛtaḥ*—surrounded; *deva-ādibhiḥ*—by the demigods and others; *divam*—to heaven.

TRANSLATION

After he had ceremonially bathed Lord Govinda, who is the master of the cows and the cowherd community, King Indra took the Lord's permission and, surrounded by the demigods and other higher beings, returned to his heavenly abode.

Thus end the purports of the humble servants of His Divine Grace A.C. Bhaktivedanta Swami Prabhupāda to the Tenth Canto, Twenty-seventh Chapter, of the Śrīmad-Bhāgavatam, *entitled "Lord Indra and Mother Surabhi Offer Prayers."*

CHAPTER TWENTY-EIGHT

Kṛṣṇa Rescues Nanda Mahārāja from the Abode of Varuṇa

This chapter describes how Lord Kṛṣṇa brought Nanda Mahārāja back from the abode of Varuṇa and how the cowherd men saw Vaikuṇṭha.

The king of the cowherds, Nanda Mahārāja, observed the prescribed fast on the eleventh day of the lunar month and then considered how to break his fast properly on the twelfth day. By circumstance only a few more minutes remained, and so he decided to take his bath at the very end of the night, although astrologically that was an inauspicious time. Thus he entered the water of the Yamunā. A servant of Varuṇa, the demigod of the ocean, noticed Nanda Mahārāja entering the water at a time forbidden by scripture and took him away to the demigod's abode. In the early morning the cowherd men unsuccessfully searched for Nanda, but Lord Kṛṣṇa immediately understood the situation and went to see Varuṇa. Varuṇa worshiped Kṛṣṇa with great and variegated festivity. Afterwards he begged the Lord to forgive his servant for having foolishly arrested the king of the cowherds.

Nanda was amazed to see the influence Śrī Kṛṣṇa exerted in the court of Varuṇadeva, and after returning home he described his experiences to his friends and relatives. They all thought Kṛṣṇa must be the Supreme Personality of Godhead Himself and wanted to see His supreme abode. Thereupon the omniscient Personality of Godhead arranged for them to bathe in the same lake where Akrūra would have his vision of the Absolute Truth. There the Lord revealed to them Brahmaloka, which is realized by great sages in their mystic trance.

TEXT 1

श्रीबादरायणिरुवाच

एकादश्यां निराहारः समभ्यर्च्य जनार्दनम् ।
स्नातुं नन्दस्तु कालिन्द्यां द्वादश्यां जलमाविशत् ॥ १ ॥

śrī-bādarāyaṇir uvāca
ekādaśyāṁ nirāhāraḥ
samabhyarcya janārdanam
snātuṁ nandas tu kālindyāṁ
dvādaśyāṁ jalam āviśat

śrī-bādarāyaṇiḥ uvāca—Śrī Bādarāyaṇi (Śukadeva Gosvāmī) said; *ekādaśyām*—on Ekādaśī (the eleventh day of the lunar month); *nirāhāraḥ*—fasting; *samabhyarcya*—having worshiped; *janārdanam*—Lord Janārdana, the Supreme Personality of Godhead; *snātum*—in order to bathe (before breaking the fast at its prescribed completion); *nandaḥ*—Nanda Mahārāja; *tu*—but; *kālindyām*—in the river Yamunā; *dvādaśyām*—on the twelfth day; *jalam*—the water; *āviśat*—entered.

TRANSLATION

Śrī Bādarāyaṇi said: Having worshiped Lord Janārdana and fasted on the Ekādaśī day, Nanda Mahārāja entered the water of the Kālindī on the Dvādaśī to take his bath.

TEXT 2

तं गृहीत्वानयद् भृत्यो वरुणस्यासुरोऽन्तिकम् ।
अवज्ञायासुरीं वेलां प्रविष्टमुदकं निशि ॥ २ ॥

taṁ gṛhītvānayad bhṛtyo
varuṇasyāsuro 'ntikam
avajñāyāsurīṁ velāṁ
praviṣṭam udakaṁ niśi

tam—him; *gṛhītvā*—seizing; *anayat*—brought; *bhṛtyaḥ*—a servant: *varuṇasya*—of Varuṇa, the lord of the sea; *asuraḥ*—demon; *antikam*—to the presence (of his master); *avajñāya*—who had disregarded; *āsurīm*—the inauspicious; *velām*—time; *praviṣṭam*—having entered; *udakam*—the water; *niśi*—during the night.

TRANSLATION

Because Nanda Mahārāja entered the water in the dark of night, disregarding that the time was inauspicious, a demoniac servant of Varuṇa seized him and brought him to his master.

PURPORT

Nanda Mahārāja was intent on breaking his fast during the Dvādaśī day, of which there remained only a few minutes. Thus he entered the water to bathe at an inauspicious time, before the first dawn light.

The servant of Varuṇa who arrested Nanda Mahārāja is stated here to be an *asura,* or demon, for obvious reasons. First, the servant was foolishly ignorant of Nanda Mahārāja's position as the pastime father of the Supreme Absolute Truth. Also, Nanda Mahārāja's intention was to carry out the injunctions of scripture; therefore Varuṇa's servant should not have arrested Nanda on the technical grounds that he bathed in the Yamunā at an inauspicious time. Later in this chapter Varuṇa himself will say, *ajānatā māmakena mūḍhena*: "This was done by my ignorant servant, who is a fool." This foolish servant did not understand the position of Kṛṣṇa or Nanda Mahārāja or devotional service to the Lord.

In conclusion, it is clear that Lord Kṛṣṇa wanted to give His personal audience to Varuṇa and simultaneously accomplish other didactic purposes. Thus this wonderful pastime will now unfold.

TEXT 3

चुक्रुशुस्तमपश्यन्तः कृष्ण रामेति गोपकाः ।
भगवांस्तदुपश्रुत्य पितरं वरुणाहृतम् ।
तदन्तिकं गतो राजन् स्वानामभयदो विभुः ॥ ३ ॥

cukruśus tam apaśyantaḥ
kṛṣṇa rāmeti gopakāḥ
bhagavāṁs tad upaśrutya
pitaraṁ varuṇāhṛtam
tad-antikaṁ gato rājan
svānām abhaya-do vibhuḥ

cukruśuḥ—they called out loudly; *tam*—him, Nanda; *apaśyantaḥ*—not seeing; *kṛṣṇa*—O Kṛṣṇa; *rāma*—O Rāma; *iti*—thus; *gopakāḥ*—the cowherd men; *bhagavān*—the Supreme Lord, Kṛṣṇa; *tat*—that; *upaśrutya*—hearing; *pitaram*—His father; *varuṇa*—by Varuṇa; *āhṛtam*—taken away; *tat*—of Varuṇa; *antikam*—to the presence; *gataḥ*—went; *rājan*—my dear King Parīkṣit; *svānām*—of His own devotees; *abhaya*—of fearlessness; *daḥ*—the giver; *vibhuḥ*—the almighty Lord.

TRANSLATION

O King, not seeing Nanda Mahārāja, the cowherd men loudly cried out, "O Kṛṣṇa! O Rāma!" Lord Kṛṣṇa heard their cries and understood that His father had been captured by Varuṇa. Therefore the almighty Lord, who makes His devotees fearless, went to the court of Varuṇadeva.

PURPORT

Viśvanātha Cakravartī Ṭhākura explains that when Nanda Mahārāja went to bathe in the river, he was accompanied by several cowherd men. When Nanda did not come out of the water, they began to cry out, and Lord Kṛṣṇa immediately came there. Understanding the situation, Śrī Kṛṣṇa entered the water and went to the court of the demigod Varuṇa, determined to free His father and the other cowherd men from fear of a mere demigod.

TEXT 4

प्राप्तं वीक्ष्य हृषीकेशं लोकपालः सपर्यया ।
महत्या पूजयित्वाह तद्दर्शनमहोत्सवः ॥ ४ ॥

prāptaṁ vīkṣya hṛṣīkeśaṁ
loka-pālaḥ saparyayā
mahatyā pūjayitvāha
tad-darśana-mahotsavaḥ

prāptam—arrived; *vīkṣya*—seeing; *hṛṣīkeśam*—Lord Kṛṣṇa, the controller of the senses; *loka*—of that planet (the watery regions); *pālaḥ*—the presiding deity (Varuṇa); *saparyayā*—with respectful offerings; *mahatyā*—elaborate; *pūjayitvā*—worshiping; *āha*—spoke; *tat*—of Lord Kṛṣṇa; *darśana*—from the sight; *mahā*—great; *utsavaḥ*—jubilant pleasure.

TRANSLATION

Seeing that the Lord, Hṛṣīkeśa, had arrived, the demigod Varuṇa worshiped Him with elaborate offerings. Varuṇa was in a state of great jubilation upon seeing the Lord, and he spoke as follows.

TEXT 5

श्रीवरुण उवाच

अद्य मे निभृतो देहोऽद्यैवार्थोऽधिगतः प्रभो ।
त्वत्पादभाजो भगवन्नवापुः पारमध्वनः ॥ ५ ॥

śrī-varuṇa uvāca
adya me nibhṛto deho
'dyaivārtho'dhigataḥ prabho
tvat-pāda-bhājo bhagavann
avāpuḥ pāram adhvanaḥ

śrī-varuṇaḥ uvāca—Śrī Varuṇa said; *adya*—today; *me*—by me; *nibhṛtaḥ*—is carried successfully; *dehaḥ*—my material body; *adya*—today; *eva*—indeed; *arthaḥ*—the goal of life; *adhigataḥ*—is experienced; *prabho*—O Lord; *tvat*—Your; *pāda*—the lotus feet; *bhājaḥ*—those who serve; *bhagavan*—O Supreme Personality; *avāpuḥ*—have achieved; *pāram*—the state of transcendence; *adhvanaḥ*—of the path (of material existence).

TRANSLATION

Śrī Varuṇa said: Now my body has fulfilled its function. Indeed, now the goal of my life is achieved, O Lord. Those who accept Your lotus feet, O Personality of Godhead, can transcend the path of material existence.

PURPORT

Varuṇa ecstatically exclaims here that since he has now seen the infinitely gorgeous body of Lord Kṛṣṇa, the trouble of assuming a material body has now been supremely justified. Indeed, the *artha,* the goal or real value of Varuṇa's life, has now been achieved. Because Lord Kṛṣṇa's form is transcendental, those who accept His lotus feet go beyond the boundary of material existence, and thus only the spiritually unaware would presume that the Lord's lotus feet are material.

TEXT 6

नमस्तुभ्यं भगवते ब्रह्मणे परमात्मने ।
न यत्र श्रूयते माया लोकसृष्टिविकल्पना ॥ ६ ॥

namas tubhyaṁ bhagavate
brahmaṇe paramātmane
na yatra śrūyate māyā
loka-sṛṣṭi-vikalpanā

namaḥ—obeisances; *tubhyam*—unto You; *bhagavate*—unto the Supreme Personality of Godhead; *brahmaṇe*—the Absolute Truth; *parama-ātmane*—the Supreme Soul; *na*—not; *yatra*—in whom; *śrūyate*—is heard of; *māyā*—the illusory, material energy; *loka*—of this world; *sṛṣṭi*—the creation; *vikalpanā*—which arranges.

TRANSLATION

My obeisances unto You, the Supreme Personality of Godhead, the Absolute Truth, the Supreme Soul, within whom there is no trace of the illusory energy, which orchestrates the creation of this world.

PURPORT

The word *śrūyate* is significant here. *Śruti,* or Vedic literature, consists of authorized statements made by the Lord Himself or His enlightened representatives. Thus neither the Lord nor recognized spiritual authorities would ever say that within the Absolute Truth, the Personality of Godhead, there is the fault of illusion. Śrīla Śrīdhara Svāmī points out that the word *brahmaṇe* here indicates the Lord is full in Himself, and that the term *paramātmane* indicates He is the controller of all living entities. Thus within the supreme being, complete in Himself and omnipotent, we do not find any jurisdiction of the material, illusory energy.

TEXT 7

अजानता मामकेन मूढेनाकार्यवेदिना ।
आनीतोऽयं तव पिता तद् भवान् क्षन्तुमर्हति ॥ ७ ॥

ajānatā māmakena
mūḍhenākārya-vedinā
ānīto'yaṁ tava pitā
tad bhavān kṣantum arhati

ajānatā—by one who was ignorant; *māmakena*—by my servant; *mūḍhena*—foolish; *akārya-vedinā*—not knowing his proper duty; *ānītaḥ*—was brought; *ayam*—this person; *tava*—Your; *pitā*—father; *tat*—that; *bhavān*—Your good self; *kṣantum arhati*—should please forgive.

TRANSLATION

Your father, who is sitting here, was brought to me by a foolish, ignorant servant of mine who did not understand his proper duty. Therefore, please forgive us.

PURPORT

The word *ayam,* "this one here," clearly indicates that Kṛṣṇa's father, Nanda Mahārāja, was present as Varuṇa was speaking. In fact, Viśvanātha Cakravartī Ṭhākura states that Varuṇa had seated Śrī Nanda on a jeweled throne and had personally worshiped him out of respect.

Technically, Nanda Mahārāja was correct in entering the water just before sunrise. The following explanation is given by Śrīla Jīva Gosvāmī in his commentary on the first verse of this chapter: After an especially short Ekādaśī, measuring only eighteen hours, about six hours of the lunar day in which the fast had to be broken, namely the Dvādaśī, had already expired before the dawn. Since at sunrise the proper time for breaking the fast would have passed, Nanda Mahārāja decided to enter the water at an otherwise inauspicious time.

Of course, Varuṇa's servant should have been aware of these technical details, which are meant for strict followers of the Vedic rituals. Above and beyond that, Nanda Mahārāja was acting as the Supreme Lord's father and was therefore a most sacred person, beyond the touch of insignificant cosmic bureaucrats like the foolish servant of Varuṇa.

TEXT 8

ममाप्यनुग्रहं कृष्ण कर्तुमर्हस्यशेषदृक् ।
गोविन्द नीयतामेष पिता ते पितृवत्सल ॥ ८ ॥

mamāpy anugrahaṁ kṛṣṇa
kartum arhasy aśeṣa-dṛk
govinda nīyatām eṣa
pitā te pitṛ-vatsala

mama—to me; *api*—even; *anugraham*—mercy; *kṛṣṇa*—O Lord Kṛṣṇa; *kartum arhasi*—please do; *aśeṣa*—of everything; *dṛk*—O You who see; *govinda*—O Govinda; *nīyatām*—may he be taken; *eṣaḥ*—this; *pitā*—father; *te*—Your; *pitṛ-vatsala*—O You who are most affectionate to Your parents.

TRANSLATION

O Kṛṣṇa, O seer of everything, please give Your mercy even to me. O Govinda, You are most affectionate to Your father. Please take him home.

TEXT 9

श्रीशुक उवाच
एवं प्रसादितः कृष्णो भगवानीश्वरेश्वरः ।
आदायागात् स्वपितरं बन्धूनां चावहन्मुदम् ॥ ९ ॥

śrī-śuka uvāca
evaṁ prasāditaḥ kṛṣṇo
bhagavān īśvareśvaraḥ
ādāyāgāt sva-pitaraṁ
bandhūnāṁ cāvahan mudam

śrī-śukaḥ uvāca—Śrī Śukadeva Gosvāmī said; *evam*—thus; *prasāditaḥ*—satisfied; *kṛṣṇaḥ*—Lord Kṛṣṇa; *bhagavān*—the Supreme Personality of Godhead; *īśvara*—of all controllers; *īśvaraḥ*—the supreme controller; *ādāya*—taking; *agāt*—went; *sva-pitaram*—His father; *bandhūnām*—to His relatives; *ca*—and; *āvahan*—bringing; *mudam*—pleasure.

TRANSLATION

Śukadeva Gosvāmī said: Thus satisfied by Lord Varuṇa, Śrī Kṛṣṇa, the Supreme Personality of Godhead, Lord of lords, took His father and returned home, where their relatives were overjoyed to see them.

PURPORT

In this pastime, Lord Kṛṣṇa gives a sublime demonstration of His position as the Supreme Lord of all lords. Varuṇa, the demigod of the seas, is most powerful, yet he was happy to worship even Lord Kṛṣṇa's father, what to speak of Kṛṣṇa Himself.

TEXT 10

नन्दस्त्वतीन्द्रियं दृष्ट्वा लोकपालमहोदयम् ।
कृष्णे च सन्नतिं तेषां ज्ञातिभ्यो विस्मितोऽब्रवीत् ॥ १० ॥

nandas tv atīndriyaṁ dṛṣṭvā
loka-pāla-mahodayam
kṛṣṇe ca sannatiṁ teṣāṁ
jñātibhyo vismito'bravīt

nandaḥ—Nanda Mahārāja; *tu*—and; *atīndriyam*—not seen before; *dṛṣṭvā*—seeing; *loka-pāla*—of the controlling deity of the (ocean) planet, Varuṇa; *mahā-udayam*—the great opulence; *kṛṣṇe*—unto Kṛṣṇa; *ca*—and; *sannatim*—the offering of obeisances; *teṣām*—by them (Varuṇa and his followers); *jñātibhyaḥ*—to his friends and relatives; *vismitaḥ*—amazed; *abravīt*—spoke.

TRANSLATION

Nanda Mahārāja had been astonished to see for the first time the great opulence of Varuṇa, the ruler of the ocean planet, and also to see how Varuṇa and his servants had offered such humble respect to Kṛṣṇa. Nanda described all this to his fellow cowherd men.

TEXT 11

ते चौत्सुक्यधियो राजन्मत्वा गोपास्तमीश्वरम् ।
अपि नः स्वगतिं सूक्ष्मामुपाधास्यदधीश्वरः ॥ ११ ॥

te cautsukya-dhiyo rājan
matvā gopās tam īśvaram
api naḥ sva-gatiṁ sūkṣmām
upādhāsyad adhīśvaraḥ

te—they; *ca*—and; *autsukya*—full of eagerness; *dhiyaḥ*—their minds; *rājan*—O King Parīkṣit; *matvā*—thinking; *gopāḥ*—the cowherd men; *tam*—Him; *īśvaram*—the Supreme Lord; *api*—perhaps; *naḥ*—to us; *sva-gatim*—His own abode; *sūkṣmām*—transcendental; *upādhāsyat*—is going to bestow; *adhīśvaraḥ*—the supreme controller.

TRANSLATION

[Hearing about Kṛṣṇa's pastimes with Varuṇa,] the cowherd men considered that Kṛṣṇa must be the Supreme Lord, and their minds, O King, were filled with eagerness. They thought, "Will the Supreme Lord bestow upon us His transcendental abode?"

PURPORT

The cowherd men were filled with excitement upon hearing how Kṛṣṇa had gone to the abode of Varuṇa to rescue His father. Suddenly realizing that they were in fact dealing with the Supreme Personality of Godhead, they joyfully conjectured among themselves about their auspicious destination after finishing their present life.

TEXT 12

इति स्वानां स भगवान् विज्ञायाखिलदृक् स्वयम्।
संकल्पसिद्धये तेषां कृपयैतदचिन्तयत् ॥ १२॥

iti svānāṁ sa bhagavān
vijñāyākhila-dṛk svayam
saṅkalpa-siddhaye teṣāṁ
kṛpayaitad acintayat

iti—such; *svānām*—of His personal devotees; *saḥ*—He; *bhagavān*—the Supreme Personality of Godhead; *vijñāya*—understanding; *akhila-dṛk*—the seer of everything; *svayam*—Himself; *saṅkalpa*—of the imagined desire; *siddhaye*—for the realization; *teṣām*—their; *kṛpayā*—compassionately; *etat*—this (as follows in the next verse); *acintayat*—thought.

TRANSLATION

Because He sees everything, Lord Kṛṣṇa, the Supreme Personality of Godhead, automatically understood what the cowherd men were conjecturing. Wanting to show His compassion to them by fulfilling their desires, the Lord thought as follows.

TEXT 13

जनो वै लोक एतस्मिन्नविद्याकामकर्मभिः ।
उच्चावचासु गतिषु न वेद स्वां गतिं भ्रमन् ॥ १३॥

jano vai loka etasminn
avidyā-kāma-karmabhiḥ
uccāvacāsu gatiṣu
na veda svāṁ gatiṁ bhraman

janaḥ—people; *vai*—certainly; *loke*—in the world; *etasmin*—this; *avidyā*—without knowledge; *kāma*—because of desires; *karmabhiḥ*—by activities; *ucca*—among superior; *avacāsu*—and inferior; *gatiṣu*—destinations;

na veda—does not recognize; *svām*—his own; *gatim*—destination; *bhraman*—wandering.

TRANSLATION

[Lord Kṛṣṇa thought:] Certainly people in this world are wandering among higher and lower destinations, which they achieve through activities performed according to their desires and without full knowledge. Thus people do not know their real destination.

PURPORT

Śrīla Jīva Gosvāmī has elaborately explained how this verse applies to the eternally liberated residents of Śrī Vṛndāvana, the Lord's abode. One of the fundamental philosophical principles of the *Śrīmad-Bhāgavatam* is the distinction between two types of illusion, Yoga-māyā and Mahā-māyā, the spiritual and material states of existence, respectively. Although Kṛṣṇa is God, the omnipotent, omniscient Supreme Being, His intimate associates in the spiritual world love Him so much that they see Him as their beloved child, friend, lover and so on. So that their ecstatic love can transcend the boundaries of mere reverence, they forget that Kṛṣṇa is the Supreme God of all the universes, and thus their pure, intimate love expands unlimitedly. One may consider their activities of treating Kṛṣṇa as a helpless child, a handsome boyfriend, or a playmate to be a manifestation of *avidyā,* ignorance of Lord Kṛṣṇa's position as God, but the residents of Vṛndāvana are in fact ignoring the secondary majesty of Kṛṣṇa and focusing intensely on His infinite beauty, which is the essence of His existence.

In fact, describing Lord Kṛṣṇa as the supreme controller and God is almost a type of political analysis, referring as it does to a hierarchy of power and control. Such analysis of levels of power and hierarchies of rule is significant in a context in which one entity is not fully surrendered, in love, to a higher entity. In other words, control becomes visible, or is consciously felt as control, when there is resistance to that control. To cite a simple example: A pious, law-abiding citizen sees a policeman as a friend and well-wisher, whereas a criminal sees him as a threatening symbol of punishment. Those who are enthusiastic about government policies feel not that the government is controlling them but rather that it is helping them.

Thus Lord Kṛṣṇa is seen as a "controller," and hence as "the Supreme God," by those who are not fully enchanted by His beauty and pastimes. Those fully in love with Lord Kṛṣṇa focus on His sublime, attractive features and, because of the nature of their relationship with Him, do not much notice His controlling power.

A simple proof that the residents of Vraja have transcended lower states of God consciousness rather than failed to attain them is the fact that throughout the pastimes of the Lord they often "remember" that Kṛṣṇa is God. Usually they are astonished at this remembrance, having been fully absorbed in seeing Kṛṣṇa as their friend, lover and so on.

The word *kāma* is conventionally used to indicate a material desire, or else a spiritual desire so intense that it becomes somehow analogous to intense material desires. Still, the fundamental distinction remains: material desire is selfish and self-gratificatory; spiritual desire is free of selfishness, being wholly for the pleasure of the other, the Lord. Thus the residents of Vṛndāvana executed their daily activities solely for the pleasure of their beloved Kṛṣṇa.

It should be remembered that the entire purpose of Kṛṣṇa's descent into this world is to attract living beings back home, back to Godhead. Two things are required for this: that His pastimes display the beauty of spiritual perfection, and that they somehow seem relevant and hence interesting to the conditioned souls of this world. The *Bhāgavatam* often states that Lord Kṛṣṇa plays just like a youthful actor, and He undoubtedly engages His eternal devotees in the dramatic presentation. Thus Lord Kṛṣṇa here muses to Himself that people in this world certainly do not know their ultimate destination, and with an obvious touch of the facetious He also thinks in this way about His own eternally liberated associates, who were playing in this world like ordinary members of a cowherd village.

Apart from the double meaning obviously present in this verse when it is applied to Kṛṣṇa's liberated associates, Kṛṣṇa here makes an entirely direct and pointedly critical observation about ordinary people. When applied to conditioned souls who are actually wandering throughout the universe, His statement that people are acting out of ignorance and lust is not mitigated by any deeper, spiritual meaning. People in general are simply ignorant, and they do not seriously consider their ultimate destination. As usual, Lord Śrī Kṛṣṇa is able to say many profound and complex things in a few simple words. How fortunate we are that God is not a dry field of energy, a transcendent, effulgent blob, or nothing at all—as various people would have it. In fact, He is the most wonderful Personality of Godhead, full of absolute personal qualities, and certainly whatever we can do, He can do better, as evidenced by His brilliant way of speaking.

TEXT 14

इति सञ्चिन्त्य भगवान्महाकारुणिको हरिः ।
दर्शयामास लोकं स्वं गोपानां तमसः परम् ॥ १४॥

iti sañcintya bhagavān
mahā-kāruṇiko hariḥ
darśayām āsa lokaṁ svaṁ
gopānāṁ tamasaḥ param

iti—in these words; *sañcintya*—considering to Himself; *bhagavān*—the Supreme Personality of Godhead; *mahā-kāruṇikaḥ*—the most merciful; *hariḥ*—Lord Hari; *darśayām āsa*—showed; *lokam*—the planet, Vaikuṇṭha; *svam*—His own; *gopānām*—to the cowherd men; *tamasaḥ*—material darkness; *param*—beyond.

TRANSLATION

Thus deeply considering the situation, the all-merciful Supreme Personality of Godhead Hari revealed to the cowherd men His abode, which is beyond material darkness.

PURPORT

It is clear from this verse that the Absolute Truth dwells in His own eternal abode. Everyone of us tries to live as comfortably as possible, surrounding ourselves with peace and beauty. How can we, in the name of "logic," begrudge the Supreme Lord, our creator, the supremely beautiful and comfortable abode known by people in general as the kingdom of God?

TEXT 15

सत्यं ज्ञानमनन्तं यद् ब्रह्मज्योतिः सनातनम् ।
यद्धि पश्यन्ति मुनयो गुणापाये समाहिताः ॥ १५ ॥

satyaṁ jñānam anantaṁ yad
brahma-jyotiḥ sanātanam
yad dhi paśyanti munayo
guṇāpāye samāhitāḥ

satyam—indestructible; *jñānam*—knowledge; *anantam*—unlimited; *yat*—which; *brahma*—the absolute; *jyotiḥ*—effulgence; *sanātanam*—eternal;

yat—which; *hi*—indeed; *paśyanti*—see; *munayaḥ*—sages; *guṇa*—the modes of material nature; *apāye*—when they subside; *samāhitāḥ*—absorbed in trance.

TRANSLATION

Lord Kṛṣṇa revealed the indestructible spiritual effulgence, which is unlimited, conscious and eternal. Sages see that spiritual existence in trance, when their consciousness is free of the modes of material nature.

PURPORT

In text 14 Lord Kṛṣṇa revealed to the residents of Vṛndāvana His own abode, the spiritual planet of Kṛṣṇaloka. This and innumerable other Vaikuṇṭha planets float in an infinite ocean of spiritual light called the *brahmajyoti.* That spiritual light is in fact the spiritual sky, which Kṛṣṇa also, quite naturally, revealed to the residents of Vṛndāvana. For example, if we want to show the moon to a child, we say, "Look up in the sky. See the moon over there in the sky." Similarly, Lord Kṛṣṇa revealed the vast spiritual sky to the residents of Vṛndāvana, but as emphasized in text 14 and in the following text, 16, the actual destination of the Lord's associates was His own spiritual planet.

TEXT 16

ते तु ब्रह्महृदं नीता मग्नाः कृष्णेन चोद्धृताः ।
ददृशुर्ब्रह्मणो लोकं यत्राक्रूरोऽध्यगात् पुरा ॥ १६ ॥

te tu brahma-hradaṁ nītā
magnāḥ kṛṣṇena coddhṛtāḥ
dadṛśur brahmaṇo lokaṁ
yatrākrūro'dhyagāt purā

te—they; *tu*—and; *brahma-hradam*—to the lake known as Brahma-hrada; *nītāḥ*—brought; *magnāḥ*—submerged; *kṛṣṇena*—by Kṛṣṇa; *ca*—and; *uddhṛtāḥ*—lifted out; *dadṛśuḥ*—they saw; *brahmaṇaḥ*—of the Absolute Truth; *lokam*—the transcendental planet; *yatra*—where; *akrūraḥ*—Akrūra; *adhyagāt*—saw; *purā*—previously.

TRANSLATION

The cowherd men were brought by Lord Kṛṣṇa to the Brahma-hrada, made to submerge in the water, and then lifted up. From the same vantage

point that Akrūra saw the spiritual world, the cowherd men saw the planet of the Absolute Truth.

PURPORT

The unlimited extension of spiritual light, called the *brahmajyoti* in text 15, is compared to a lake called Brahma-hrada. Lord Kṛṣṇa submerged the cowherd men in that lake in the sense that He submerged them in the awareness of the impersonal Brahman. But then, as indicated by the word *uddhṛtāḥ,* He lifted them up to a higher understanding, that of the Personality of Godhead in His own planet. As clearly stated here, *dadṛśur brahmaṇo lokam:* They saw, just as Akrūra did, the transcendental abode of the Absolute Truth.

The evolution of consciousness may be briefly summarized as follows: In ordinary consciousness we perceive and are attracted to the variety of material things. Rising to the first stage of spiritual consciousness, we transcend material variety and focus instead on the undifferentiated One, which lies behind and gives existence to the many. Finally, rising to Kṛṣṇa consciousness, we find that the absolute, spiritual One contains its own eternal variety. In fact, since this world is a mere shadow of eternal existence, we would expect to find spiritual variety within the One, and indeed we do find it in the sacred text of *Śrīmad-Bhāgavatam.*

Astute readers may note that the pastime involving Akrūra takes place later in the *Bhāgavatam,* after the present affair with the cowherd men. The reason Śukadeva Gosvāmī says Akrūra saw Vaikuṇṭha *purā,* "previously," is that all these incidents took place many years before the conversation between Śukadeva Gosvāmī and Mahārāja Parīkṣit.

TEXT 17

नन्दादयस्तु तं दृष्ट्वा परमानन्दनिवृताः ।
कृष्णं च तत्र च्छन्दोभिः स्तूयमानं सुविस्मिताः ॥ १७ ॥

nandādayas tu taṁ dṛṣṭvā
paramānanda-nivṛtāḥ
kṛṣṇaṁ ca tatra cchandobhiḥ
stūyamānaṁ su-vismitāḥ

nanda-ādayaḥ—the cowherd men headed by Nanda Mahārāja; *tu*—and; *tam*—that; *dṛṣṭvā*—seeing; *parama*—supreme; *ānanda*—by ecstasy; *nivṛtāḥ*—overwhelmed with joy; *kṛṣṇam*—Lord Kṛṣṇa; *ca*—and; *tatra*—

there; *chandobhiḥ*—by the Vedic hymns; *stūyamānam*—being praised; *su*—very much; *vismitāḥ*—surprised.

TRANSLATION

Nanda Mahārāja and the other cowherd men felt the greatest happiness when they saw that transcendental abode. They were especially amazed to see Kṛṣṇa Himself there, surrounded by the personified Vedas, who were offering Him prayers.

PURPORT

Although the residents of Vṛndāvana considered themselves ordinary persons, Lord Kṛṣṇa wanted them to know of their extraordinary good fortune. Thus, within a lake in the Yamunā River the Lord showed them His personal abode. The cowherd men were amazed to see that the kingdom of God had exactly the same spiritual atmosphere as their own earthly Vṛndāvana and that, just as in their Vṛndāvana Lord Kṛṣṇa was personally present, in their unique vision He was present as the Lord of the spiritual world.

As Śrīla Bhaktisiddhānta Sarasvatī Ṭhākura points out, these verses emphasize that Lord Kṛṣṇa did not merely show the cowherd men a sample Vaikuṇṭha planet but that He specifically revealed His Kṛṣṇaloka, the greatest of eternal abodes and the natural home of the residents of Vṛndāvana, who loved Kṛṣṇa more than anyone else did.

Thus end the purports of the humble servants of His Divine Grace A.C. Bhaktivedanta Swami Prabhupāda to the Tenth Canto, Twenty-eighth Chapter, of the Śrīmad-Bhāgavatam, *entitled "Kṛṣṇa Rescues Nanda Mahārāja from the Abode of Varuṇa."*

CHAPTER TWENTY NINE

Kṛṣṇa and the Gopīs Meet for the Rāsa Dance

This chapter describes how Lord Śrī Kṛṣṇa, intending to enjoy the *rāsa* dance, engaged in arguments and counterarguments with the *gopīs.* Then there is a description of the beginning of the *rāsa* dance and the Lord's pastime of disappearing from the midst of the *gopīs.*

Remembering the promise He had made to the *gopīs* when He had stolen their clothes, Lord Kṛṣṇa employed His Yoga-māyā potency and manifested within Himself the desire to enjoy pastimes during an autumn night. Thus He began to play His flute. When the *gopīs* heard the flute's sound, the impulses of Cupid were violently aroused within them, and they immediately abandoned all their household duties and hastily went to Kṛṣṇa. All the *gopīs* had purely spiritual bodies, but when some of the *gopīs'* husbands and other family members stopped the young girls from going, Lord Kṛṣṇa arranged for them to temporarily exhibit material bodies, which they then left at the sides of their husbands. In this way they deceived their relatives and went off to meet Kṛṣṇa.

When the *gopīs* came before Lord Kṛṣṇa, He asked, "Why have you come? It is not good for you to travel to such a place in the dead of the night, for this forest is full of violent creatures. Your husbands and children will soon come searching after you to bring you home and engage you again in your household duties. After all, the prime religious duty of a woman is to serve her husband and children. For a respectable woman to consort with a paramour is totally contemptible and sure to obstruct her progress to heaven. Moreover, one develops pure love for Me not by physical proximity but by hearing topics connected with Me, by viewing My Deity form in the temple, by meditating upon Me and by faithfully chanting My glories. Therefore, all of you would do best to return home."

The *gopīs* were crestfallen to hear this, and after crying a little they replied, with a bit of anger, "It is very unfair for You to reject young girls who have abandoned everything in their lives and come to You with the exclusive desire to serve You. By serving our husbands and children we receive only pain, whereas by serving You, the dearmost Soul of all living beings, we will perfectly fulfill the true religious duty of the self. What woman will not deviate from her prescribed duties as soon as she hears Your flute-song and sees Your form, which enchants the three worlds? Just as the Supreme Lord Viṣṇu protects the demigods, You destroy the unhappiness of the people of Vṛndāvana. Therefore You should immediately relieve the torment we have felt because of separation from You."

Wanting to please the *gopīs,* Lord Kṛṣṇa, who is always satisfied in Himself, responded to their appeals by playing with them in various pastimes. But when this show of attention made them a little proud, He humbled them by suddenly disappearing from the arena of the *rāsa* dance.

TEXT 1

श्रीबादरायणिरुवाच
भगवानपि ता रात्रीः शारदोत्फुल्लमल्लिकाः ।
वीक्ष्य रन्तुं मनश्चक्रे योगमायामुपाश्रितः ॥ १ ॥

śrī-bādarāyaṇir uvāca
bhagavān api tā rātrīḥ
śāradotphulla-mallikāḥ
vīkṣya rantuṁ manaś cakre
yoga-māyām upāśritaḥ

śrī-bādarāyaṇiḥ uvāca—Śrī Śukadeva, the son of Śrīla Badarāyaṇa Vedavyāsa, said; *bhagavān*—Kṛṣṇa, the Supreme Personality of Godhead; *api*—although; *tāḥ*—those; *rātrīḥ*—nights; *śārada*—of autumn: *utphulla*—blossoming; *mallikāḥ*—the jasmine flowers; *vīkṣya*—seeing: *rantum*—to enjoy love; *manaḥ cakre*—He made up His mind; *yoga-māyām*—His spiritual potency that makes the impossible possible; *upāśritaḥ*—resorting to.

TRANSLATION

Śrī Bādarāyaṇi said: Śrī Kṛṣṇa is the Supreme Personality of Godhead, full in all opulences, yet upon seeing those autumn nights scented with blossoming jasmine flowers, He turned His mind toward loving affairs. To fulfill His purposes He employed His internal potency.

PURPORT

As we begin the famous narration of Lord Kṛṣṇa's *rāsa* dance, a dance of love with beautiful young girls, questions will inevitably arise in the minds of ordinary people regarding the propriety of God's romantic dancing with many young girls in the middle of a full-moon autumn night. In his description of the Lord's *rāsa* dance in *Kṛṣṇa, the Supreme Personality of Godhead,* Śrīla Prabhupāda painstakingly explains the spiritual purity of these transcendental activities. Those advanced in the science of Kṛṣṇa—the great teachers, or *ācāryas*—leave no doubt that Lord Kṛṣṇa is full and satisfied in Himself, free of all material desire, which is, after all, a sense of incompleteness or lack.

Materialistic persons and impersonal philosophers stubbornly reject the bona fide explanation of Śrī Kṛṣṇa's transcendental nature. There is no reason to deny the beautiful reality of an absolute person able to perform absolute romantic activities, of which our so-called romance is merely a shadow or perverted reflection. The irrational insistence that material activities cannot be a reflection of the perfect, spiritual activities performed by God reflects the unimaginative emotional disposition of those who oppose the reality of Śrī Kṛṣṇa. This psychological disposition of the nondevotees, which leads them to fervently deny the very existence of the absolute person, unfortunately boils down to what may be succinctly described as envy, since the overwhelming majority of the impersonal critics eagerly pursue their own romantic affairs, which they consider quite real and even "spiritual."

The actual supreme lover is Lord Kṛṣṇa. The *Vedānta-sūtra* begins by declaring that the Absolute Truth is the source of everything, and even Western philosophy was born in a somewhat awkward attempt at finding the original One behind the apparent many of material existence. Conjugal love, one of the most intense and demanding aspects of human existence, can hardly have nothing at all to do with supreme reality.

In fact, the conjugal love experienced by human beings is a mere reflection of spiritual reality, in which the same love exists in an absolute, pristine state. Thus it is clearly stated here that when Kṛṣṇa decided to enjoy the romantic atmosphere of autumn, "He resorted to His spiritual potency" (*yoga-māyām upāśritaḥ*). The spiritual nature of Lord Kṛṣṇa's conjugal affairs is a major theme in this section of the *Śrīmad-Bhāgavatam.*

A woman is attractive because of the sweet sound of her voice, her beauty and gentleness, her enchanting fragrance and tenderness, and also because of her cleverness and skill in music and dance. The most attractive ladies of all are the young *gopīs* of Vṛndāvana, who are Lord Kṛṣṇa's internal potency, and this chapter tells how He enjoyed their brilliant feminine qualities—even though, as Śrīla Viśvanātha Cakravartī Ṭhākura has mentioned, Lord Kṛṣṇa was an eight-year-old boy when these events took place.

Ordinary people prefer God simply to be a witness of their romantic affairs. When a boy desires a girl or a girl desires a boy, sometimes they pray to God for their enjoyment. Such people are shocked and dismayed to find out that the Lord can enjoy His own loving affairs with His own transcendental senses. In truth, Śrī Kṛṣṇa is the original Cupid, and His exciting conjugal pastimes will be described in this section of the *Bhāgavatam.*

When Lord Kṛṣṇa descends to the earth, His spiritual body seems to take birth and grow as He displays His variegated pastimes. The Lord could hardly allow His boyhood to pass without exhibiting the supreme loving affairs between a young boy and young girls. Thus Viśvanātha Cakravartī Ṭhākura quotes Śrīla Rūpa Gosvāmī as follows: *kaiśoraṁ saphalī-karoti kalayan kuñje vihāraṁ hariḥ.* "Lord Hari perfects His youth by arranging loving pastimes in the groves of the Vṛndāvana forest."

TEXT 2

तदोडुराजः ककुभः करैर्मुखं
प्राच्या विलिम्पन्नरुणेन शन्तमैः ।
स चर्षणीनामुदगाच्छुचो मृजन्
प्रियः प्रियाया इव दीर्घदर्शनः ॥ २ ॥

tadoḍurājaḥ kakubhaḥ karair mukhaṁ
prācyā vilimpann aruṇena śantamaiḥ
sa carṣaṇīnām udagāc chuco mṛjan
priyaḥ priyāyā iva dīrgha-darśanaḥ

tadā—at that time; *uḍu-rājaḥ*—the moon, king of the stars; *kakubhaḥ*—of the horizon; *karaiḥ*—with his "hands" (rays); *mukham*—the face; *prācyāḥ*—western; *vilimpan*—smearing; *aruṇena*—with reddish color; *śam-tamaiḥ*—(his rays) which give great comfort; *saḥ*—he; *carṣaṇīnām*—of all those who watched; *udagāt*—rose; *śucaḥ*—the unhappiness; *mṛjan*—wiping away; *priyaḥ*—a beloved husband; *priyāyāḥ*—of his beloved wife; *iva*—as; *dīrgha*—after a long time; *darśanaḥ*—being seen again.

TRANSLATION

The moon then rose, anointing the face of the Western horizon with the reddish hue of his comforting rays, and thus dispelling the pain of all who watched him rise. The moon was like a beloved husband who returns after a long absence and adorns the face of his beloved wife with red kuṅkuma.

PURPORT

Young Kṛṣṇa engaged His internal potency, and she immediately created an exciting atmosphere for conjugal love.

TEXT 3

दृष्ट्वा कुमुद्वन्तमखण्डमण्डलं
रमाननाभं नवकुंकुमारुणम् ।
वनं च तत्कोमलगोभी रञ्जितं
जगौ कलं वामदृशां मनोहरम् ॥ ३ ॥

dṛṣṭvā kumudvantam akhaṇḍa-maṇḍalaṁ
ramānanābhaṁ nava-kuṅkumāruṇam
vanaṁ ca tat-komala-gobhī rañjitaṁ
jagau kalaṁ vāma-dṛśāṁ manoharam

dṛṣṭvā—observing; *kamut-vantam*—causing the night-blooming *kumuda* lotuses to open; *akhaṇḍa*—unbroken; *maṇḍalam*—the disk of whose face; *ramā*—of the goddess of fortune; *ānana*—(resembling) the face; *ābham*—whose light; *nava*—new; *kuṅkuma*—with vermilion powder; *aruṇam*—reddened; *vanam*—the forest; *ca*—and; *tat*—of that moon; *komala*—gentle; *gobhiḥ*—by the rays; *rañjitam*—colored; *jagau*—He played His flute; *kalam*—sweetly; *vāma-dṛśām*—for the girls who had charming eyes; *manaḥ-haram*—enchanting.

TRANSLATION

Lord Kṛṣṇa saw the unbroken disk of the full moon glowing with the red effulgence of newly applied vermilion, as if it were the face of the goddess of fortune. He also saw the kumuda lotuses opening in response to the moon's presence and the forest gently illumined by its rays. Thus the Lord began to play sweetly on His flute, attracting the minds of the beautiful-eyed gopīs.

PURPORT

The word *jagau* in this verse indicates that Lord Kṛṣṇa played songs on His flute, as confirmed in text 40 by the words *kā stry aṅga te kala-padāyata-veṇu-gīta.* The word *ramā* may indicate not only Lord Viṣṇu's consort but also Śrīmatī Rādhārāṇī, the original goddess of fortune. Lord Kṛṣṇa appeared in the dynasty of the moon god, and the moon plays a prominent role here in preparing for the Lord's entrance into the midst of the *rāsa* dance.

TEXT 4

निशम्य गीतां तदनंगवर्धनं
व्रजस्त्रियः कृष्णगृहीतमानसाः ।
आजग्मुरन्योन्यमलक्षितोद्यमाः
स यत्र कान्तो जवलोलकुण्डलाः ॥ ४ ॥

niśamya gītaṁ tad anaṅga-vardhanaṁ
vraja-striyaḥ kṛṣṇa-gṛhīta-mānasāḥ
ājagmur anyonyam alakṣitodyamāḥ
sa yatra kānto java-lola-kuṇḍalāḥ

niśamya—hearing; *gītam*—the music; *tat*—that; *anaṅga*—Cupid; *vardhanam*—which fortifies; *vraja-striyaḥ*—the young women of Vraja; *kṛṣṇa*—by Kṛṣṇa; *gṛhīta*—seized; *mānasāḥ*—whose minds; *ājagmuḥ*—they went; *anyonyam*—to one another; *alakṣita*—unnoticed; *udyamāḥ*—their going forward; *saḥ*—He; *yatra*—where; *kāntaḥ*—their boyfriend; *java*—because of their haste; *lola*—swinging; *kuṇḍalāḥ*—whose earrings.

TRANSLATION

When the young women of Vṛndāvana heard Kṛṣṇa's flute-song, which arouses romantic feelings, their minds were captivated by the Lord. They went to where their lover waited, each unknown to the others, moving so quickly that their earrings swung back and forth.

PURPORT

Apparently each *gopī* went secretly, hoping to avoid advertising to her rivals the fact that young Kṛṣṇa was in the mood for romantic affairs. Śrīla Viśvanātha Cakravartī poetically describes the situation as follows:

"Kṛṣṇa instigated a terrible act of thievery in Vṛndāvana when He played on His flute. The song of His flute entered through the ears of the *gopīs,* into the inner treasure-chamber of their hearts. That wonderful music stole all their most valuable possessions—their sobriety, shyness, fear and discrimination, along with their very minds—and in a split second this music delivered all these goods to Kṛṣṇa. Now each *gopī* went to beg the Lord to return her personal property. Each beautiful young girl was thinking,'I have to capture that great thief,' and thus they went forward, each unknown to the others."

TEXT 5

दुहन्त्योऽभिययुः काश्चिद्दोहं हित्वा समुत्सुकाः ।
पयोऽधिश्रित्य संयावमनुद्वास्यापरा ययुः ॥ ५ ॥

duhantyo'bhiyayuḥ kāścid
dohaṁ hitvā samutsukāḥ
payo'dhiśritya saṁyāvam
anudvāsyāparā yayuḥ

duhantyaḥ—in the middle of milking the cows; *abhiyayuḥ*—went away; *kāścit*—some of them; *doham*—the milking; *hitvā*—abandoning; *samutsukāḥ*—extremely eager; *payaḥ*—milk; *adhiśritya*—having placed on the stove; *saṁyāvam*—cakes made of flour; *anudvāsya*—without removing from the oven; *aparāḥ*—others; *yayuḥ*—went.

TRANSLATION

Some of the gopīs were milking cows when they heard Kṛṣṇa's flute. They stopped milking and went off to meet Him. Some left milk curdling on the stove, and others left cakes burning in the oven.

PURPORT

The eagerness of these cowherd girls, so lovingly devoted to young Kṛṣṇa, is shown here.

TEXTS 6–7

परिवेषयन्त्यस्तद्धित्वा पाययन्त्यः शिशून् पयः ।
शुश्रूषन्त्यः पतीन् काश्चिदश्नन्त्योऽपास्य भोजनम् ॥ ६ ॥
लिम्पन्त्यः प्रमृजन्त्योऽन्या अञ्जन्त्यः काश्च लोचने ।
व्यत्यस्तवस्त्राभरणाः काश्चित्कृष्णान्तिकं ययुः ॥ ७ ॥

pariveṣayantyas tad dhitvā
pāyayantyaḥ śiśūn payaḥ
śuśrūṣantyaḥ patīn kāścid
aśnantyo'pāsya bhojanam

limpantyaḥ pramṛjantyo'nyā
añjantyaḥ kāśca locane
vyatyasta-vastrābharaṇāḥ
kāścit kṛṣṇāntikaṁ yayuḥ

pariveṣayantyaḥ—getting dressed; *tat*—that; *hitvā*—putting aside; *pāyayantyaḥ*—making drink; *śiśūn*—their children; *payaḥ*—milk; *śuśrūṣantyaḥ*—rendering personal service; *patīn*—to their husbands; *kāścit*—some of them; *aśnantyaḥ*—eating; *apāsya*—leaving aside; *bhojanam*—their meals; *limpantyaḥ*—applying cosmetics; *pramṛjantyaḥ*—cleansing themselves with oils; *anyāḥ*—others; *añjantyaḥ*—applying *kajjala; kāśca*—some; *locane*—on their eyes; *vyatyasta*—in disarray; *vastra*—their clothing; *ābharaṇāḥ*—and ornaments; *kāścit*—some of them; *kṛṣṇa-antikam*—to the proximity of Lord Kṛṣṇa; *yayuḥ*—went.

TRANSLATION

Some of them were getting dressed, feeding milk to their infants or rendering personal service to their husbands, but they all gave up these duties and went to meet Kṛṣṇa. Other gopīs were taking their evening meals, washing themselves, putting on cosmetics or applying kajjala to their eyes. But all the gopīs stopped these activities at once and, though their clothes and ornaments were in complete disarray, rushed off to Kṛṣṇa.

TEXT 8

ता वार्यमाणाः पतिभिः पितृभिर्भ्रातृबन्धुभिः ।
गोविन्दापहृतात्मानो न न्यवर्तन्त मोहिताः ॥ ८ ॥

tā vāryamāṇāḥ patibhiḥ
pitṛbhir bhrātṛ-bandhubhiḥ
govindāpahṛtātmāno
na nyavartanta mohitāḥ

tāḥ—they; *vāryamāṇāḥ*—being checked; *patibhiḥ*—by their husbands; *pitṛbhiḥ*—by their fathers; *bhrātṛ*—brothers; *bandhubhiḥ*—and other relatives; *govinda*—by Lord Kṛṣṇa; *apahṛta*—stolen away; *ātmānaḥ*—their very selves; *na nyavartanta*—they did not turn back; *mohitāḥ*—enchanted.

TRANSLATION

Their husbands, fathers, brothers and other relatives tried to stop them, but Kṛṣṇa had already stolen their hearts. Enchanted by the sound of His flute, they refused to turn back.

PURPORT

Some of the young *gopīs* were married, and their husbands tried to stop them. The unmarried girls had to deal with their fathers and brothers and other relatives. None of these relatives would have ordinarily allowed even the young girls' dead bodies to go alone into the forest at night, but Lord Kṛṣṇa had already engaged His internal potency, and thus the entire romantic episode unfolded without interference.

TEXT 9

अन्तर्गृहगताः काश्चिद् गोप्योऽलब्धविनिर्गमाः ।
कृष्णं तद्भावनायुक्ता दध्युर्मीलितलोचनाः ॥ ९ ॥

antar-gṛha-gatāḥ kāścid
gopyo 'labdha-vinirgamāḥ
kṛṣṇaṁ tad-bhāvanā-yuktā
dadhyur mīlita-locanāḥ

antaḥ-gṛha—within their homes; *gatāḥ*—present; *kāścit*—some; *gopyaḥ*—*gopīs; alabdha*—not obtaining; *vinirgamāḥ*—any exit; *kṛṣṇam*—upon Śrī Kṛṣṇa; *tat-bhāvanā*—with ecstatic love for Him; *yuktāḥ*—fully endowed; *dadhyuḥ*—they meditated; *mīlita*—closed; *locanāḥ*—their eyes.

TRANSLATION

Some of the gopīs, however, could not manage to get out of their houses, and instead they remained home with eyes closed, meditating upon Him in pure love.

PURPORT

Throughout the Tenth Canto, Śrīla Viśvanātha Cakravartī Ṭhākura gives elaborate poetic commentaries on Lord Kṛṣṇa's pastimes. It is not always possible to include these extensive descriptions, but we will quote in its entirety his comments on this verse. It is our sincere recommendation to the learned Vaiṣṇava community that a qualified devotee of the Lord present the entire commentary of Śrīla Viśvanātha Cakravartī on the Tenth Canto as a separate book, which will undoubtedly be appreciated by devotees and nondevotees alike. The *ācārya's* comments on this verse are as follows:

"In this context we will make our analysis according to the method described in Śrīla Rūpa Gosvāmī's *Ujjvala-nīlamaṇi.* There are two categories of *gopīs:* the eternally perfect (the *nitya-siddhas*) and those who have become perfect by practicing *bhakti-yoga* (the *sādhana-siddhas*). The *sādhana-siddhas* are of two categories: those who belong to special groups and those who do not. And there are also two classes of the *gopīs* belonging to special groups: namely the *śruti-cārīs,* who come from the group of the personified *Vedas,* and the *ṛṣi-cārīs,* who come from the group of sages who saw Lord Rāmacandra in the Daṇḍakāraṇya forest."

"This same fourfold categorization of the *gopīs* is given in the *Padma Purāṇa:*

gopyas tu śrutayo jñeyā
ṛṣi-jā gopa-kanyakāḥ
deva-kanyāś ca rājendra
na mānuṣyāḥ kathañcana

'It is understood that some of the *gopīs* are personified Vedic literatures, while others are reborn sages, daughters of cowherds, or demigod maidens. But by no means, my dear King, are any of them ordinary humans.' Here we are informed that although the *gopīs* appeared to be human cowherd girls, they actually were not. Thus the contention that they are mortals is refuted."

"The daughters of cowherds, referred to here as *gopa-kanyās,* must be eternally perfect, since we never hear of them having executed any *sādhana.* Their apparent *sādhana* of worshiping Goddess Kātyāyanī in the role of *gopīs* merely manifests their manner of playing like human beings, and the *Bhāgavatam* narrates the account of this worship only to show how they had fully taken on the role of cowherd girls."

"That the *gopa-kanyā gopīs* are actually *nitya-siddhas,* eternally perfect devotees of the Lord, is established by a statement in *Brahma-saṁhitā* (5.37) —*ānanda-cinmaya-rasa-pratibhāvitābhiḥ*—which proves that they are the Lord's spiritual pleasure potency. Similarly, we have the words of the *Gautamīya-tantra, hlādinī yā mahā-śaktiḥ.* Further corroboration of their eternal perfection is that these *gopīs,* being coeternal with Lord Kṛṣṇa, their lover, are mentioned along with Him in the eighteen-syllable *mantra,* the ten-syllable *mantra* and others, and also that the worship of these *mantras,* and also the *śrutis* that present them, have been in existence since beginningless time."

The *deva-kanyās,* daughters of the demigods, who are mentioned in the verse beginning *sambhavas tv amara-striyaḥ,* are explained in *Śrī Ujjvala-nīlamaṇi* as partial expansions of the *gopīs* who are eternally perfect. That the *śruti-cārī gopīs,* the personified *Vedas,* are *sādhana-siddha* is understood from the following words of theirs quoted in the *Bṛhad-vāmana Purāṇa:*

kandarpa-koṭi-lāvaṇye
tvayi dṛṣṭe manāṁsi naḥ
kāminī-bhāvam āsādya
smara-kṣubdhānya-saṁśayāḥ

yathā tval-loka-vāsinyaḥ
kāma-tattvena gopikāḥ
bhajanti ramaṇaṁ matvā
cikīrṣājaninas tathā

'Since we have seen Your face, which possesses the beauty of millions of Cupids, our minds have become lusty after You like those of young girls, and we have forgotten all other allurements. We have developed the desire to act toward You as do the *gopīs* who dwell on Your transcendental planet and who manifest the nature of Cupid by worshiping You with the idea that You are their paramour.'

"The *ṛṣi-cārī gopīs* are also *sādhana-siddha,* as stated in *Ujjvala-nīlamaṇi: gopālopāsakāḥ pūrvam aprāptābhīṣṭa-siddhayaḥ.* Previously they were all *mahārṣis* living in the Daṇḍaka forest. We find evidence for this in the *Padma Purāṇa, Uttara-khaṇḍa:*

dṛṣṭvā rāmaṁ hariṁ tatra
bhoktum aicchan su-vigraham
te sarve strītvam āpannāḥ
samudbhūtāś ca gokule
hariṁ samprāpya kāmena
tato muktā bhavārṇavāt

This verse says that upon seeing Lord Rāmacandra, the sages in the Daṇḍaka forest desired to enjoy Lord Hari (Kṛṣṇa). In other words, the sight of Lord Rāma's beauty reminded them of Lord Hari, Gopāla, their personal object of worship, and they then wanted to enjoy with Him. But out of embarrassment they did not act on that desire, whereupon Lord Śrī Rāma, who is like a desire tree, gave His mercy to them, even though they had not voiced their request. Thus their desire was fulfilled, as stated by the words beginning *te sarve.* By means of their lusty attraction they became freed from the ocean of material existence, the cycle of birth and death, and coincidentally they got the association of Hari in conjugal love.

"In the present verse of the *Bhāgavatam* we understand that it was the *gopīs* who had children who were kept forcibly at home. This fact is clear from verses yet to come: *mātaraḥ pitaraḥ putrāḥ* (*Bhāg.* 10.29.20), *yat-paty-apatya-suhṛdām anuvṛttir aṅga* (*Bhāg.* 10.29.32) and *pati-sutānvaya-bhrātṛ-bāndhavān* (*Bhāg.* 10.31.16). In his comments on the Tenth Canto, Śrīla Kavi-karṇapūra Gosvāmī mentions this fact. Without trying to repeat all his thoughts on this verse, we will give the gist of his purport:

"'Upon seeing the personal form of Lord Śrī Rāmacandra, the sages who were worshipers of Lord Gopāla immediately became elevated to the mature platform of spontaneous devotion, automatically reaching the stages of firm faith, attraction and attachment. But they had not yet completely freed themselves of all material contamination; therefore Śrī Yoga-māyā-devi arranged for them to take birth from the wombs of *gopīs* and become cowherd girls. By associating with the eternally perfect *gopīs,* some of these new *gopīs* fully manifested *pūrva-raga* loving attraction for Kṛṣṇa as soon as they reached puberty. (This kind of attraction develops even before one meets the beloved.) When these new *gopīs* got the direct audience of Kṛṣṇa and physically associated with Him, all their remaining contamination became burned up, and they achieved the advanced stages of *prema, sneha* and so on."

"'Even though they were in the company of their cowherd husbands, by the power of Yoga-māyā the *gopīs* remained unsullied by sexual contact with them; rather, they were situated in purely spiritual bodies that Kṛṣṇa enjoyed. On the night they heard the sound of Kṛṣṇa's flute, their husbands tried to stop them, but by the merciful assistance of Yoga-māyā the *sādhana-siddha gopīs* were able to go forth to their beloved, together with the *nitya-siddha gopīs."*

"'Other *gopīs,* however, because of not getting the good fortune of associating with the *nitya-siddha gopīs* and other advanced *gopīs,* had not achieved the stage of *prema,* and so their contamination was not completely burned away. They entered the company of their cowherd husbands and, after sexual union with them, gave birth to children. But a short time later even these *gopīs* developed their *pūrva-raga* by hankering intensely for the physical association of Kṛṣṇa—a hankering they acquired by associating with the advanced *gopīs.* Becoming worthy recipients of the mercy of the perfected *gopīs,* they assumed transcendental bodies fit to be enjoyed by Kṛṣṇa, and when Yoga-māyā failed to help them overcome their husbands' attempts to keep them from going out, they felt themselves cast into the worst calamity. Viewing their husbands, brothers, fathers and other family members as enemies, they came close to dying. Just as other women might remember their mothers or other relatives at the time of death, these *gopīs* remembered the sole friend of their very life, Kṛṣṇa, as stated in the present verse of the *Bhāgavatam,* beginning with the word *antar.*"

"'It is implied that those ladies were not able to exit because they were held back by their husbands, who were standing before them with sticks in their hands, scolding them. Although these *gopīs* were perpetually absorbed in love for Kṛṣṇa, at that particular time they meditated upon Him and cried out within: "Alas, alas, O only friend of our life! O ocean of the artistic skills of Vṛndāvana forest! Please let us become your girlfriends in some future life, because at this time we cannot see Your lotuslike face with our eyes. So be it; we shall look upon You with our minds." Each of them lamenting to herself in this way, the *gopīs* stood with their eyes shut and meditated deeply upon Him.'"

TEXTS 10–11

दुःसहप्रेष्ठविरहतीव्रतापधुताशुभाः ।
ध्यानप्राप्ताच्युताश्लेषनिर्वृत्या क्षीणमंगलाः ॥ १० ॥
तमेव परमात्मानं जारबुद्ध्यापि संगताः ।
जहुर्गुणमयं देहं सद्यः प्रक्षीणबन्धनाः ॥ ११ ॥

duḥsaha-preṣṭha-viraha-
tīvra-tāpa-dhutāśubhāḥ
dhyāna-prāptācyutāśleṣa-
nirvṛtyā kṣīṇa-maṅgalāḥ

tam eva paramātmānaṁ
jāra-buddhyāpi saṅgatāḥ
jahur guṇa-mayaṁ dehaṁ
sadyaḥ prakṣīṇa-bandhanāḥ

duḥsaha—intolerable; *preṣṭha*—from their beloved; *viraha*—from separation; *tīvra*—intense; *tāpa*—by the burning pain; *dhuta*—removed; *aśubhāḥ*—all inauspicious things in their hearts; *dhyāna*—by meditation; *prāpta*—obtained; *acyuta*—of the infallible Lord Śrī Kṛṣṇa; *āśleṣa*—caused by the embrace; *nirvṛtyā*—by the joy; *kṣīṇa*—reduced to nil; *maṅgalāḥ*—their auspicious karmic reactions; *tam*—Him; *eva*—even though; *parama-ātmānam*—the Supersoul; *jāra*—a paramour; *buddhyā*—thinking Him to be; *api*—nevertheless; *saṅgatāḥ*—getting His direct association; *jahuḥ*—they gave up; *guṇa-mayam*—composed of the modes of material nature; *deham*—their bodies; *sadyaḥ*—immediately; *prakṣīṇa*—thoroughly counteracted; *bandhanāḥ*—all their bondage of *karma.*

TRANSLATION

For those gopīs who could not go to see Kṛṣṇa, intolerable separation from their beloved caused an intense agony that burned away all impious karma. By meditating upon Him they realized His embrace, and the ecstasy they then felt exhausted their material piety. Although Lord Kṛṣṇa is the Supreme Soul, these girls simply thought of Him as their male lover and associated with Him in that intimate mood. Thus their karmic bondage was nullified and they abandoned their gross material bodies.

PURPORT

Śrīla Viśvanātha Cakravartī comments upon this verse as follows: "Here Śukadeva Gosvāmī speaks in a peculiar way: he presents the intimate object the *gopīs* attained as if it were an external idea, thus keeping its true nature secret from outsiders, while at the same time he reveals to the confidential devotees well versed in the scientific conclusions of devotional service the internal meaning that is his real purport. Thus to outsiders Śukadeva says that Kṛṣṇa gave the *gopīs* liberation, but to the confidential hearers Śukadeva reveals that when the *gopīs* experienced separation from their beloved there arose in them both immeasurable unhappiness and immeasurable happiness, and that they gradually achieved their desired goal."

"Thus the verse can be understood as follows: Because of their intolerable separation from their beloved, the *gopīs* felt terrible agony, by which they caused all inauspicious things to tremble. In other words, when people in general hear of the *gopīs'* extreme agony in separation from their beloved, they abandon thousands of inauspicious things—things even as fearsome as the subterranean fires of millions of universes or the powerful poison swallowed by Lord Śiva. More specifically, those who hear of the *gopīs'* love in separation give up their terrible false ego and, thinking themselves defeated, are shaken. When the *gopīs* meditated on Lord Acyuta, He became manifest and personally came to them, and they experienced great joy by embracing His body, which was full of transcendental love for them. The *gopīs* also experienced great joy by exhibiting personal characteristics and a sense of identification appropriate to such love. That joy made all their good fortune, both material and spiritual, seem paltry by comparison."

"The implication is that when other persons see how happy the *gopīs* became upon embracing Kṛṣṇa when He manifested Himself directly before them, these other persons feel that thousands of so-called auspicious objects are insignificant by comparison, including all the sense gratificatory pleasures found in millions of universes and even the supersensory pleasure of spiritual bliss (*brahmānanda*). Thus hearing of the *gopīs'* distress and the joy that arose, respectively, out of their separation from the Supreme Lord and their union with Him, anyone can get rid of all the reactions of his past activities, both sinful and pious. Vaiṣṇavas certainly do not think that sinful and pious reactions can be destroyed only by being lived out, since, after all, neither separation from the Supreme Lord nor direct association with Him are in the category of *karma.* This kind of elimination of karmic reactions occurs in the stage of *bhajana,* for those who have come to the level of *anartha-nivṛtti.*"

"And thus the *gopīs* thought of Kṛṣṇa—the Paramātmā, or supreme worthy object of all love—as their paramour. Even though such a concept is ordinarily contemptible, the *gopīs* realized Kṛṣṇa in an even fuller sense than did Rukmiṇī and His other queens, who thought of Him most respectfully as their husband. That thinking of the Lord as one's paramour is superior to thinking of Him as one's husband is proved by the fact that unbridled pure love is superior to domesticated love. This idea is borne out by the following words of Śrī Uddhava: *yā dustyajaṁ sva-janam ārya-pathaṁ ca hitvā.* 'These ladies of Vraja abandoned their families and their advanced religious principles, even though to do so is very difficult.' (*Bhāg.* 10.47.61)

"In His pastimes on earth Kṛṣṇa often turns the most lowly things into the most elevated. As Bhīṣma stated, Kṛṣṇa's pastime of acting as Arjuna's chariot driver was even more elevated than the pastimes in which He acted as a mighty King of kings: *vijaya-ratha-kuṭumba ātta-totre/ dhṛta-haya-raśmini tac-chriyeskṣaṇīye.* 'I concentrate upon the chariot driver of Arjuna, who stood with a whip in His right hand and a bridle rope in His left, and who was very careful to protect Arjuna's chariot by all means.' (*Bhāg.* 1.9.39) Similarly, in the Lord's appearance as Kṛṣṇa we see that the normally inferior conjugal *rāsa* becomes better than the normally superior mood of *śānta-rasa,* as also the attitude of loving a paramour becomes superior to the loving exchange between legitimate spouses, and lowly *guñjā* necklaces, red oxide paste and peacock feathers become better than the most excellent jeweled ornaments."

"But, it may be objected, it is not fitting for the Supreme Lord to sport with women whose bodies have already been enjoyed by other men. This objection is replied to by the words beginning *jahuḥ.* The word *deham* is used here in the singular form to indicate unity of category, even though the *gopīs* are many. Some authorities say that by the power of Yoga-māyā these *gopīs'* bodies disappeared in a way no one noticed, but other authorities say that the 'body' referred to in this context is the inferior body, composed of the modes of material nature. Thus by the prominence of the adjective *guṇa-mayam,* it is understood that before the *gopīs* heard the sound of Kṛṣṇa's flute their bodies had been twofold, material and spiritual, and upon hearing the flute they gave up the material bodies, which their husbands had enjoyed. We may analyze this as follows:

"When devotees begin prosecuting devotional service in accordance with the instructions of a bona fide spiritual master, they engage their ears and other senses in pure devotion by hearing of the Lord, chanting His glories, remembering Him, offering obeisances to Him, giving Him personal attendance, and so forth. Thus the devotees make the Lord's transcendental qualities the objects of their senses, as stated by the Lord Himself: *nirguṇo mad-apāśrayaḥ.* (*Bhāg.* 11.25.26) In this way the devotees' bodies transcend the material modes. Yet sometimes the devotees may take as their sense objects mundane sounds and so on, and that is material. Thus a devotee's body can have two aspects, transcendental and material."

"According to one's level of devotional service, to that degree the transcendental aspects of one's body become prominent and the material aspects diminish. This transformation is described in the following verse from the *Bhāgavatam* (11.2.42):

bhaktiḥ pareśānubhavo viraktir
anyatra caiṣa trika eka-kālaḥ
prapadyamānasya yathāśnataḥ syus
tuṣṭiḥ puṣṭiḥ kṣud-apāyo'nu-ghāsam

'Devotion, direct experience of the Supreme Lord, and detachment from other things — these three occur simultaneously for one who has taken shelter of the Supreme Personality of Godhead, in the same way that pleasure, nourishment and relief from hunger come simultaneously and increasingly, with each bite, for a person engaged in eating.' When one achieves totally pure love of God, the material portions of the body disappear and the body becomes completely spiritual. Nonetheless, so as not to disturb the false opinions of atheists and so as to protect the confidentiality of devotional service, the Supreme Lord usually has His illusory energy exhibit the demise of the gross body. An example of this is the disappearance of the Yādavas during the Mauṣala-līlā.

"Sometimes, however, to proclaim the excellence of *bhakti-yoga,* Kṛṣṇa will allow a devotee to go back to Godhead in his selfsame body, as in the case of Dhruva Mahārāja. We can cite evidence for this point from the Twenty-fifth Chapter of the Eleventh Canto, text 32:

yeneme nirjitāḥ saumya
guṇā jīvena citta-jāḥ
bhakti-yogena man-niṣṭho
mad-bhāvāya prapadyate

'A living entity who conquers the modes of material nature, which are manifested from the mind, can dedicate himself to Me [Kṛṣṇa] by the process of devotional service and thus attain pure love for Me.' Here the Lord states that the defeat and destruction of that which is composed of the modes of material nature can be brought about only by the process of devotional service.

"Therefore, what we should understand from the present verse of the *Bhāgavatam* is that the *gopīs* who could not go to see Kṛṣṇa had their inauspicious, material bodies removed or burned up, while their auspicious, spiritual bodies, far from being destroyed, simply grew more prominent because of the ecstasy the *gopīs* felt by embracing Kṛṣṇa in meditation. Thus their bondage was completely destroyed: by the help of Yoga-māyā they got free from ignorance and also from the prohibitions of their husbands and other relatives."

"We should not make the mistake of explaining this falling away of the *gopīs'* bodies as being a result of their dying. As the Lord Himself states (*Bhāg.* 10.47.37):

yā mayā krīḍatā rātryāṁ
vane'smin vraja āsthitāḥ
alabdha-rāsāḥ kalyāṇyo
māpur mad-vīrya-cintayā

'Some of those all-auspcious *gopīs* could not directly join Me in enjoying the *rāsa* dance on that night in this Vṛndāvana forest, yet still they achieved My association by remembering My transcendental pastimes.' By using the word *kalyāṇyaḥ* in this verse, the Lord implies,'Even though these *gopīs* wanted to give up their bodies because of their husbands' prohibitions and the torment of separation from Me, for them to die at the very beginning of the most auspicious festival of the *rāsa* dance would have been displeasing to Me and thus inauspicious. So they did not die.'

"More evidence that the *gopīs* who were prevented from going to see Kṛṣṇa did not physically die is provided by a statement of Śrī Śukadeva's later in this canto (10.47.38): *tā ūcur uddhavaṁ prītās tat-sandeśāgata-smṛtīḥ.* 'Then they [the *gopīs*] replied to Uddhava, feeling satisfied because His message had reminded them of Kṛṣṇa.' Here we understand that the *gopīs* speaking to Uddhava were the ones who had not had the chance to participate directly in the *rāsa* dance because of being held captive in their homes. Thus the conclusion is that they gave up their material bodies without dying. Parched by the intense heat of separation, their material bodies gave up their materiality and became purely spiritual, just like the bodies of such great devotees as Dhruva Mahārāja. This is the meaning of the *gopīs*' giving up their bodies.'

"The following analogy illustrates the statuses of the various *gopīs:* By observing seven or eight ripe mangoes on a tree, we can ascertain that all the fruits on the tree are ripe. Then we can pick them all and bring them home, where in due course the sun's rays and other agents will make them fine-looking, fragrant and delicious—fit to be offered to the king for his enjoyment. When the time comes for the king to take his meal, a discriminating servant can choose those fruits ready to offer him. From the appearance of the fruits the servant can tell which are ripe in the middle but still raw on the outside and thus not yet fit for the king. By the application of a special heating process, these remaining fruits will become ripe in two or three days, and then they too will be ready to offer to the king."

"Similarly, among the *muni-cārī gopīs* who took birth in Gokula, those who completely gave up the materiality of their bodies and very early in life achieved purely spiritual bodies were able to remain untouched by any other man; thus Yoga-māyā allowed them to join the *nitya-siddha* and other advanced *gopīs* when they went to meet Kṛṣṇa. Other *muni-cārī gopīs* still retained some connection with the external material body, but even they, after being parched by the heat of separation from Śrī Kṛṣṇa, gave up the materiality of their bodies and assumed perfectly transcendental bodies, purified of all taint of contact with other men. On the night of the *rāsa* dance, Yoga-māyā sent some of these *gopīs* out behind those who had already gone out; others, who Yoga-māyā saw still had a slight amount of contamination, she kept back to further purify with the heat of separation, and then she sent them out on some other night."

"After enjoying the pleasures of the *rāsa* dance and other pastimes with Kṛṣṇa, the *muni-cārī gopīs* who had participated went back to their homes when the night was over, as did the *nitya-siddha* and other advanced *gopīs.* But now Yoga-māyā protected these *muni-cārī gopīs* from the material association of their husbands; in other words, these *gopīs* were devoid of any selfish attachment for husband, children and so on. Since these *gopīs* were thoroughly immersed in the great ocean of love for Kṛṣṇa, their breasts dried up so that they could not feed their infants, and to their family members they appeared as if haunted by ghosts. In conclusion, it is not unseemly that the *gopīs* who were previously in material association joined in the *rāsa* dance."

"Some authorities, however, maintain that the *gopīs* who were kept back in their houses did not have children. According to them, whenever such words as *apatya* ('children') are used in verses yet to come, these words refer to the children of co-wives, to adopted children or to nephews and nieces."

TEXT 12

श्रीपरीक्षिदुवाच
कृष्णं विदुः परं कान्तं न तु ब्रह्मतया मुने।
गुणप्रवाहोपरमस्तासां गुणधियां कथम् ॥ १२॥

śrī-parīkṣid uvāca
kṛṣṇaṁ viduḥ paraṁ kāntaṁ
na tu brahmatayā mune
guṇa-pravāhoparamas
tāsāṁ guṇa-dhiyāṁ katham

śrī-parīkṣit uvāca—Śrī Parīkṣit said; *kṛṣṇam*—Lord Kṛṣṇa; *viduḥ*—they knew; *param*—only; *kāntam*—as their beloved; *na*—not; *tu*—but; *brahmatayā*—as the Absolute Truth; *mune*—O sage, Śukadeva; *guṇa*—of the three modes of material nature; *pravāha*—of the mighty current; *uparamaḥ*—the cessation; *tāsām*—for them; *guṇa-dhiyām*—whose mentality was caught up in those modes; *katham*—how.

TRANSLATION

Śrī Parīkṣit Mahārāja said: O sage, the gopīs knew Kṛṣṇa only as their lover, not as the Supreme Absolute Truth. So how could these girls, their

minds caught up in the waves of the modes of nature, free themselves from material attachment?

PURPORT

King Parīkṣit was sitting in an assembly of great sages and other important personalities, listening to the words of Śukadeva Gosvāmī. According to Śrīla Viśvanātha Cakravartī, as Śukadeva began speaking of the *gopīs'* conjugal love for Kṛṣṇa, the King noticed the expressions on the faces of some of the more materialistic persons present there and realized the doubt lurking in their hearts. Therefore, although the King thoroughly knew the purport of Śukadeva's words, he presented himself as experiencing personal doubt so that he could eradicate the doubt of others. That is why he asked this question.

TEXT 13

श्रीशुक उवाच
उक्तं पुरस्तादेतत्ते चैद्यः सिद्धिं यथा गतः ।
द्विषन्नपि हृषीकेशं किमुताधोक्षजप्रियाः ॥ १३ ॥

śrī-śuka uvāca
uktaṁ purastād etat te
caidyaḥ siddhiṁ yathā gataḥ
dviṣann api hṛṣīkeśaṁ
kim utādhokṣaja-priyāḥ

śrī-śukaḥ uvāca—Śukadeva Gosvāmī said; *uktam*—spoken; *purastāt*—previously; *etat*—this; *te*—to you; *caidyaḥ*—the King of Cedi, Śiśupāla; *siddhim*—perfection; *yathā*—as; *gataḥ*—he attained; *dviṣan*—hating; *api*—even; *hṛṣīkeśam*—the Supreme Lord Hṛṣīkeśa; *kim uta*—what to speak then; *adhokṣaja*—to the transcendental Lord, who lies beyond the purview of ordinary senses; *priyāḥ*—of those devotees who are very dear.

TRANSLATION

Śukadeva Gosvāmī said: This point was explained to you previously. Since even Śiśupāla, who hated Kṛṣṇa, achieved perfection, then what to speak of the Lord's dear devotees.

PURPORT

Although the spiritual nature of conditioned souls may be covered by illusion, Lord Kṛṣṇa's spiritual nature is omnipotent and is never covered by any other power. In fact, all other powers are His energy and thus function according to His will. The *Brahma-saṁhitā* (5.44) states, *sṛṣṭi sthiti-pralaya-sādhana-śaktir ekā/ chāyeva yasya bhuvanāni bibharti durgā/ icchānurūpam api yasya ca ceṣṭate sā*: "The mighty Durgā, who creates, maintains and annihilates the material worlds, is the potency of the Supreme Lord, and she moves like His shadow, according to His desire." Thus because the Lord's spiritual influence does not depend on whether someone understands Him or not, the *gopīs'* spontaneous love for Kṛṣṇa guaranteed their spiritual perfection.

The great Madhvācārya quotes the following relevant passages from the *Skanda Purāṇa:*

kṛṣṇa-kāmās tadā gopyas
tyaktvā dehaṁ divaṁ gatāḥ
samyak kṛṣṇaṁ para-brahma
jñātvā kālāt paraṁ yayuḥ

"At that time the *gopīs,* who desired Kṛṣṇa, gave up their bodies and went to the spiritual world. Because they properly understood Kṛṣṇa to be the Supreme Absolute Truth, they transcended the influence of time."

pūrvaṁ ca jñāna-saṁyuktās
tatrāpi prāyaśas tathā
atas tāsāṁ paraṁ brahma
gatir āsīn na kāmataḥ

"In their previous lives most of the *gopīs* were already fully endowed with transcendental knowledge. It is because of this knowledge, not their lust, that they were able to attain the Supreme Brahman."

na tu jñānam ṛte mokṣo
nānyaḥ pantheti hi śrutiḥ
kāma-yuktā tadā bhaktir
jñānaṁ cāto vimukti-gāḥ

"The *Vedas* declare that without spiritual knowledge there is no valid path to liberation. Because these apparently lusty *gopīs* possessed devotion and knowledge, they achieved liberation."

ato mokṣe'pi tāsāṁ ca
kāmo bhaktyānuvartate
mukti-śabdodito caidya-
prabhṛtau dveṣa-bhāginaḥ

"Thus even in their attainment of liberation,'lust' followed as a manifestation of their pure devotion. After all, what we call liberation was experienced even by envious persons like Śiśupāla."

bhakti-mārgī pṛthaṅ muktim
agād viṣṇu-prasādataḥ
kāmas tv aśubha-kṛc cāpi
bhaktyā viṣṇoḥ prasāda-kṛt

"By the mercy of Lord Viṣṇu, one who follows the path of devotional service gains liberation as a by-product, and such a person's lusty desire, which would normally invoke misfortune, instead invokes the mercy of Viṣṇu when exhibited in pure devotion."

dveṣi-jīva-yutaṁ cāpi
bhaktaṁ viṣṇur vimocayet
aho'ti-karuṇā viṣṇoḥ
śiśupālasya mokṣaṇāt

"Lord Viṣṇu will save even a devotee possessed of an envious life. Just see the extreme mercy of the Lord, as shown by His granting liberation to Śiśupāla!"

Śiśupāla was Lord Kṛṣṇa's cousin. He was mortified when the Lord stole the gorgeous young Rukmiṇī, whom Śiśupāla himself was hell-bent on marrying. For various other reasons also, Śiśupāla was consumed with envy of Lord Kṛṣṇa, and finally he insanely offended Him in a great assembly called the Rājasūya sacrifice. At that time Kṛṣṇa nonchalantly cut off Śiśupāla's head and gave him liberation. Everyone present saw the effulgent soul of Śiśupāla rise out of his dead body and merge into the existence of the Lord. The Seventh Canto explains that Śiśupāla was an incarnation of a gatekeeper in the spiritual world cursed to take birth on the earth as a demon. Since even Śiśupāla was liberated by the Lord, who took into consideration the whole situation, then what to speak of the *gopīs,* who loved Kṛṣṇa more than anything.

TEXT 14

नृणां निःश्रेयसार्थाय व्यक्तिर्भगवतो नृप।
अव्ययस्याप्रमेयस्य निर्गुणस्य गुणात्मनः ॥ १४ ॥

nṛṇāṁ niḥśreyasārthāya
vyaktir bhagavato nṛpa
avyayasyāprameyasya
nirguṇasya guṇātmanaḥ

nṛṇām—for humanity; *niḥśreyasa*—of the highest benefit; *arthāya*—for the purpose; *vyaktiḥ*—the personal appearance; *bhagavataḥ*—of the Supreme Lord; *nṛpa*—O King; *avyayasya*—of Him who is inexhaustible; *aprameyasya*—immeasurable; *nirguṇasya*—untouched by material qualities; *guṇa-ātmanaḥ*—the controller of the material modes.

TRANSLATION

O King, the Supreme Lord is inexhaustible and immeasurable, and He is untouched by the material modes because He is their controller. His personal appearance in this world is meant for bestowing the highest benefit on humanity.

PURPORT

Since Lord Kṛṣṇa descends to benefit mankind in general, why would He neglect innocent young girls who loved Him more than anyone else did? Although the Lord awards Himself to His pure devotees, He is *avyaya,* inexhaustible, because He is *aprameya,* immeasurable. He is also *nirguṇa,* free of material qualities, and thus those who intimately associate with Him are on the same spiritual platform. He is *guṇātmā,* the controller or original personality behind the modes of nature, and it is specifically for this reason that He is free of them. In other words, because the modes of nature are His energy, they cannot act upon Him.

TEXT 15

कामं क्रोधं भयं स्नेहमैक्यं सौहृदमेव च ।
नित्यं हरौ विदधतो यान्ति तन्मयतां हि ते ॥ १५ ॥

kāmaṁ krodhaṁ bhayaṁ sneham
aikyaṁ sauhṛdam eva ca

nityaṁ harau vidadhato
yānti tan-mayatāṁ hi te

kāmam—lust; *krodham*—anger; *bhayam*—fear; *sneham*—loving affection; *aikyam*—unity; *sauhṛdam*—friendship; *eva ca*—also; *nityam*—always; *harau*—for Lord Hari; *vidadhataḥ*—exhibiting; *yānti*—they achieve; *tat-mayatām*—absorption in Him; *hi*—indeed; *te*—such persons.

TRANSLATION

Persons who constantly direct their lust, anger, fear, protective affection, feeling of impersonal oneness or friendship toward Lord Hari are sure to become absorbed in thought of Him.

PURPORT

Lord Kṛṣṇa is pure spiritual existence, and those who somehow or other become attached to Him, absorbed in thoughts of Him, rise to the spiritual platform. This is the absolute nature of the Lord's personal association.

With this verse Śukadeva Gosvāmī answers King Parīkṣit's question about the gopīs. After all, Śukadeva has begun to narrate Kṛṣṇa's most intimate pastime, the rāsa dance, and Parīkṣit is cooperating to remove the doubts of others who are hearing or who in the future may hear this astonishing story. Śrīla Madhvācārya has quoted a statement from the Skanda Purāṇa that emphatically declares persons like the gopīs to be liberated souls, beyond the pale of material illusion:

bhaktyā hi nitya-kāmitvaṁ
na tu muktiṁ vinā bhavet
ataḥ kāmitayā vāpi
muktir bhaktimatāṁ harau

"Eternal conjugal attraction to Kṛṣṇa, expressed in pure devotional service, cannot develop in one who is not already liberated. Thus those who are devoted to Lord Hari, even in conjugal attraction, are already liberated."

"Śrīla Madhvācārya then quotes from the *Padma Purāṇa* to clarify the essential point that one cannot be liberated simply by lusting after Lord Kṛṣṇa but rather only by possessing conjugal attraction in *pure devotional service:*

sneha-bhaktāḥ sadā devāḥ
kāmitvenāpsara-striyaḥ
kāścit kāścin na kāmena
bhaktyā kevalayaiva tu

"The demigods are always affectionately devoted to the Lord, and the young ladies of heaven called Apsarās have lusty feelings toward Him, although some of them have pure devotion for Him untainted by material lust. Only these latter Apsarās are ready for liberation, because without bona fide devotional service one cannot possibly achieve liberation."

Thus devotional service is not *yogyam,* or appropriate, unless free from material lust. One should not take cheaply the *gopīs'* achievement of personal association with Lord Kṛṣṇa in a conjugal relationship. To show the gravity of direct relationship with the Lord, Śrīla Madhvācārya has quoted the following verses from the *Varāha Purāṇa:*

patitvena śriyopāsyo
brahmaṇā me piteti ca
pitāmahatayānyeṣāṁ
tridaśānāṁ janārdanaḥ

"The goddess Lakṣmī worships Lord Janārdana as her husband, Lord Brahmā worships Him as his father, and the other demigods worship Him as their grandfather."

prapitāmaho me bhagavān
iti sarva-janasya tu
guruḥ śrī-brahmaṇo viṣṇuḥ
surāṇāṁ ca guror guruḥ

"Thus people in general should think,'The Supreme Lord is my great-grandfather.' Lord Viṣṇu is the spiritual master of Brahmā and thus the *guru* of the *guru* of the demigods."

gurur brahmāsya jagato
daivaṁ viṣṇuḥ sanātanaḥ
ity evopāsanaṁ kāryaṁ
nānyathā tu kathañcana

"Brahmā is the spiritual master of this universe, and Viṣṇu is the eternally worshipable Deity. With this understanding, and not otherwise, one should worship the Lord."

The above injunctions apply to *sarva-jana,* "all people in general." Thus one should follow these injunctions until one achieves the exalted platform of intimate relationship with the Supreme Lord. There is abundant evidence that the *gopīs* of Vṛndāvana were highly elevated, liberated souls, and thus their pastimes with Kṛṣṇa are pure, spiritual affairs. Keeping this in mind, we can truly understand this chapter of the *Śrīmad-Bhāgavatam.*

TEXT 16

न चैवं विस्मयः कार्यो भवता भगवत्यजे ।
योगेश्वरेश्वरे कृष्णे यत एतद्विमुच्यते ॥ १६ ॥

na caivaṁ vismayaḥ kāryo
bhavatā bhagavaty aje
yogeśvareśvare kṛṣṇe
yata etad vimucyate

na ca—nor; *evam*—like this; *vismayaḥ*—astonishment; *kāryaḥ*—should be had; *bhavatā*—by you; *bhagavati*—in regard to the Supreme Personality of Godhead; *aje*—who is unborn; *yoga-īśvara*—of the masters of *yoga; īśvare*—the ultimate master; *kṛṣṇe*—Lord Kṛṣṇa; *yataḥ*—by whom; *etat*—this (world); *vimucyate*—becomes liberated.

TRANSLATION

You should not be so astonished by Kṛṣṇa, the unborn master of all masters of mystic power, the Supreme Personality of Godhead. After all, it is the Lord who liberates this world.

PURPORT

Parīkṣit Mahārāja should not have been so astonished that Lord Kṛṣṇa's so-called romantic affairs are in fact meant to liberate the entire universe. After all, that is the Lord's purpose—to bring all conditioned souls back home, back to Godhead, for an eternal life of bliss and knowledge. The Lord's conjugal affairs with the *gopīs* fit in very nicely with that program because we who are actually lusty in material consciousness can be purified and liberated by hearing of them.

In the First Canto of *Śrīmad-Bhāgavatam* (1.5.33), Nārada Muni states:

āmayo yaś ca bhūtānāṁ
jāyate yena su-vrata
tad eva hy āmayaṁ dravyaṁ
na punāti cikitsitam

"O good soul, does not a thing applied therapeutically cure a disease that was caused by that very same thing?" Thus Kṛṣṇa's romantic affairs, being pure, spiritual activities, will cure those who hear about them of the disease of material lust.

TEXT 17

ता दृष्ट्वान्तिकमायाता भगवान् व्रजयोषितः ।
अवदद्वदतां श्रेष्ठो वाचः पेशैर्विमोहयन् ॥ १७ ॥

tā dṛṣṭvāntikam āyātā
bhagavān vraja-yoṣitaḥ
avadad vadatāṁ śreṣṭho
vācaḥ peśair vimohayan

tāḥ—them; *dṛṣṭvā*—seeing; *antikam*—nearby; *āyātāḥ*—arrived; *bhagavān*—the Supreme Lord; *vraja-yoṣitaḥ*—the girls of Vraja; *avadat*—He spoke; *vadatām*—of speakers; *śreṣṭhaḥ*—the best; *vācaḥ*—of language; *peśaiḥ*—with decorations; *vimohayan*—bewildering.

TRANSLATION

Seeing that the girls of Vraja had arrived, Lord Kṛṣṇa, the best of speakers, greeted them with charming words that bewildered their minds.

PURPORT

Having established the spiritual nature of the *gopīs'* love for Kṛṣṇa, Śukadeva Gosvāmī proceeds with his narration.

TEXT 18

श्रीभगवानुवाच
स्वागतं वो महाभागाः प्रियं किं करवाणि वः ।
व्रजस्यानामयं कच्चिद् ब्रूतागमनकारणम् ॥ १८ ॥

śrī-bhagavān uvāca
svāgataṁ vo mahā-bhāgāḥ
priyaṁ kiṁ karavāṇi vaḥ
vrajasyānāmayaṁ kaccid
brūtāgamana-kāraṇam

śrī-bhagavān uvāca—the Supreme Personality of Godhead said; *su-āgatam*—welcome; *vaḥ*—to you; *mahā-bhāgāḥ*—O most fortunate ladies; *priyam*—pleasing; *kim*—what; *karavāṇi*—may I do; *vaḥ*—for you; *vrajasya*—of Vraja; *anāmayam*—the well-being; *kaccit*—whether; *brūta*—please tell; *āgamana*—for your coming; *kāraṇam*—the reason.

TRANSLATION

Lord Kṛṣṇa said: O most fortunate ladies, welcome. What may I do to please you? Is everything well in Vraja? Please tell Me the reason for your coming here.

PURPORT

Lord Kṛṣṇa knew perfectly well why the *gopīs* had come. In fact, He had called them with the romantic melodies of His flute. So Kṛṣṇa was simply teasing the *gopīs* by asking them, "Why have you come here so quickly? Is something wrong in town? Why have you come here, anyway? What do you want?"

The *gopīs* were Kṛṣṇa's young lovers, and therefore these questions certainly bewildered them, for they had responded to Kṛṣṇa's call with the simple mentality of enjoying conjugal love with Him.

TEXT 19

रजन्येषा घोररूपा घोरसत्त्वनिषेविता ।
प्रतियात व्रजं नेह स्थेयं स्त्रीभिः सुमध्यमाः ॥ १९ ॥

rajany eṣā ghora-rūpā
ghora-sattva-niṣevitā
pratiyāta vrajaṁ neha
stheyaṁ strībhiḥ su-madhyamāḥ

rajanī—night; *eṣā*—this; *ghora-rūpā*—fearsome in appearance; *ghora-sattva*—by fearsome creatures; *niṣevitā*—populated; *pratiyāta*—please return; *vrajam*—to the cowherd village of Vraja; *na*—not; *iha*—here; *stheyam*—should stay; *strībhiḥ*—women; *su-madhyamāḥ*—O slender-waisted girls.

TRANSLATION

This night is quite frightening, and frightening creatures are lurking about. Return to Vraja, slender-waisted girls. This is not a proper place for women.

PURPORT

Śrīla Viśvanātha Cakravartī Ṭhākura has written the following charming commentary on this verse:

"[The *gopīs* thought,] 'Alas, alas, even after shattering our family responsibilities, our sobriety and our shame and enjoying us day after day, and after now dragging us here by the sound of His flute, He is asking us why we have come!'

"As the *gopīs* cast sidelong glances at one another, the Lord said,'If you try to tell Me that you have come to get night-blooming flowers to use in the worship of God, and that it is these flowers you are looking at with your sidelong glances, I will have to reject your excuse as unacceptable, since neither the time, place nor persons involved are appropriate.'

"This is the Lord's meaning in the verse beginning *rajanī.* He might have said, 'Even though there is abundant moonlight, this time of night is very fearsome because many snakes, scorpions and other dangerous creatures too small for you to see are lying beneath the creepers, roots and twigs. Therefore this time is unsuitable for gathering flowers. And not only the time but also this place is unsuitable for you to gather flowers, because at night terrible creatures such as tigers are abroad here. Therefore you should go back to Vraja.'

"'But,' the *gopīs* may object, 'let us just rest for a few minutes, and then we will go.'

"Then the Lord might reply, 'Women shouldn't remain in this kind of place.' In other words, 'Because of the time and place, it is wrong for persons like yourselves to stay here even for a moment.'

"Furthermore, by the word *su-madhyamāḥ,* 'O slender-waisted ones,' the Lord implied, 'You are beautiful young girls, and I am a beautiful young boy. Because you are all very chaste and I am a *brahmacārī,* as confirmed by the words *kṛṣṇo brahmacārī* in the *śruti* [*Gopāla-tāpanī Upaniṣad*], there should be no fault in our being in the same place. Nonetheless, the mind can never be trusted — neither yours nor My own.'

"The Lord's inner eagerness thus hinted at is obvious if we read His words between the lines, as follows: 'If out of shyness you cannot tell Me the reason you've come, then don't speak. I already know it anyway, so just listen as I tell it to you.' Thus the Lord speaks the words beginning *rajanī.*"

The following statement by Kṛṣṇa is based on an alternative meaning of the verse derived when the Sanskrit words are separated in a different way. The alternative separation, according to Śrīla Viśvanātha Cakravartī, would be *rajanī eṣā aghora-rūpā aghora-sattva-niṣevitā/ pratiyāta vrajaṁ na iha stheyaṁ stribhiḥ su-madhyamāḥ.* Through Śrīla Viśvanātha's commentary Kṛṣṇa now explains the meaning of this division of words.

"'The pervasive moonshine has made this night appear not at all fearsome, and therefore this forest is populated by harmless creatures such as deer (*aghora-sattvaiḥ*), or else by animals such as tigers that are harmless because of Vṛndāvana's naturally nonviolent atmosphere. Consequently this night should not frighten you.' Or else Kṛṣṇa may have meant, 'You should not be afraid of your own husbands and other relatives because, the night being populated by fearsome animals, they will not come near this place. Therefore please do not go back to Vraja [*na pratiyāta*], but stay here in My company [*iha stheyam*].'

"The *gopīs* may ask the Lord, 'How are You staying here?'

"The Lord answers, 'With women.'

"But are You satisfied to keep just any women in Your company?'

"The Lord replies to this with the word *su-madhyamāḥ,* meaning, 'Only women who are young and beautiful, who have slender waists—namely yourselves—should stay here with Me, and not others.' Thus we can appreciate that Kṛṣṇa's statements are full of considerate as well as neglectful sentiments."

Kṛṣṇa's words are certainly brilliant, because according to the rules of Sanskrit grammar they may be understood in either of two opposite ways. In the first case, as translated above, Lord Kṛṣṇa continues to tease the *gopīs* by telling them the night is dangerous and inauspicious and that they should go home. But Kṛṣṇa is simultaneously saying exactly the opposite—namely, that there is absolutely no reason for the *gopīs* to fear coming to the Lord, that the night is quite auspicious and that the girls should under no circumstances go back home. Thus Lord Kṛṣṇa simultaneously teases and enchants the *gopīs* with His words.

TEXT 20

मातरः पितरः पुत्रा भ्रातरः पतयश्च वः ।
विचिन्वन्ति ह्यपश्यन्तो मा कृढ्वं बन्धुसाध्वसम्॥ २०॥

mātaraḥ pitaraḥ putrā
bhrātaraḥ patayaś ca vaḥ
vicinvanti hy apaśyanto
mā kṛḍhvaṁ bandhu-sādhvasam

mātaraḥ—mothers; *pitaraḥ*—fathers; *putrāḥ*—sons; *bhrātaraḥ*—brothers; *patayaḥ*—husbands; *ca*—and; *vaḥ*—your; *vincinvanti*—are searching; *hi*—certainly; *apaśyantaḥ*—not seeing; *mā kṛḍhvam*—do not create; *bandhu*—for your family members; *sādhvasam*—anxiety.

TRANSLATION

Not finding you at home, your mothers, fathers, sons, brothers and husbands are certainly searching for you. Don't cause anxiety for your family members.

TEXTS 21–22

दृष्टं वनं कुसुमितं राकेशकररञ्जितम् ।
यमुनानिललीलैजत्तरुपल्लवशोभितम् ॥ २१ ॥
तद्यात मा चिरं गोष्ठं शुश्रूषध्वं पतीन् सतीः ।
क्रन्दन्ति वत्सा बालाश्च तान् पाययत दुह्यत ॥ २२ ॥

dṛṣṭaṁ vanaṁ kusumitaṁ
rākeśa-kara-rañjitam
yamunānila-līlaijat
taru-pallava-śobhitam

tad yāta mā ciraṁ goṣṭhaṁ
śuśrūṣadhvaṁ patīn satīḥ
krandanti vatsā bālāś ca
tān pāyayata duhyata

dṛṣṭam—seen; *vanam*—the forest; *kusumitam*—full of flowers; *rākā-īśa*—of the moon, the lord of the presiding goddess of the full-moon day; *kara*—by the hand; *rañjitam*—made resplendent; *yamunā*—coming from the Yamunā River; *anila*—by the wind; *līlā*—playfully; *ejat*—trembling; *taru*—of the trees; *pallava*—with the leaves; *śobhitam*—beautified; *tat*—therefore; *yāta*—go back; *mā ciram*—without delay; *goṣṭham*—to the cowherd village; *śuśrūṣadhvam*—you must serve; *patīn*—your husbands; *satīḥ*—O chaste women; *krandanti*—are crying; *vatsāḥ*—the calves; *bālāḥ*—the children; *ca*—and; *tān*—them; *pāyayata*—breast-feed; *duhyata*—feed with cow's milk.

TRANSLATION

Now you have seen this Vṛndāvana forest, full of flowers and resplendent with the light of the full moon. You have seen the beauty of the trees, with their leaves trembling in the gentle breeze coming from the Yamunā. So now go back to the cowherd village. Don't delay. O chaste ladies, serve your husbands and give milk to your crying babies and calves.

PURPORT

Śrīla Viśvanātha Cakravartī Ṭhākura further explains text 22 as follows: "Lord Kṛṣṇa says, 'Therefore don't wait a long time before going, but go immediately.' The word *satīḥ* means that the *gopīs* are loyal to their husbands; therefore Kṛṣṇa indicates that the *gopīs* should serve their husbands so the latter can accomplish their religious duties, and that the *gopīs* should also be considered worshipable because of their chastity. All this Kṛṣṇa says to the *gopīs* who are married. And now to the unmarried girls He says, 'The calves are crying, so see to it that they get milk.' To the *muni-cārī gopīs* He says, 'Your babies are crying, so feed them milk.'"

Śrīla Viśvanātha Cakravartī Ṭhākura further reveals the hidden meaning of these two verses as follows: "In text 21 Kṛṣṇa might have said, 'This Vṛndāvana is the very best of places, and moreover this is a full-moon night. Furthermore, we have the Yamunā on all sides, and there are cool, gentle, fragrant breezes blowing. These are all transcendental opulences that stimulate loving exchanges, and since I am also here as the foremost ecstatic opulence—the object of love—let us now test how much expertise you can show in relishing *rasas.*'

"In text 22 He means to say, 'Thus for a long time, for the entire duration of this night, don't leave, but rather stay here and enjoy with Me. Don't go serve your husbands and the gentle women—your mothers-in-law and so forth. It would not be fitting for you to waste such beauty and youth, which are gifts of the creator. Nor should you milk the cows or give milk to the calves and babies. What do you, who are so full of ecstatic attraction for Me, have to do with these affairs?'"

Śrīla Viśvanātha Cakravartī Ṭhākura also explains that the *gopīs* could not really be sure exactly what Kṛṣṇa was doing—whether He was merely joking, inviting them to stay or instructing them to return home. Thus as Śrī Kṛṣṇa spoke about the beauty of the forest, the *gopīs* felt embarrassed and bewildered and looked upward at the trees, and as He spoke about the Yamunā they looked all around at the river. Their absolute purity and simplicity, along with their absolute devotion to Lord Kṛṣṇa in the conjugal mood, created the most beautiful pastimes ever exhibited in this universe.

TEXT 23

अथ वा मदभिस्नेहाद् भवत्यो यन्त्रिताशयाः ।
आगता ह्युपपन्नं वः प्रीयन्ते मयि जन्तवः ॥ २३ ॥

atha vā mad-abhisnehād
bhavatyo yantritāśayāḥ
āgatā hy upapannaṁ vaḥ
prīyante mayi jantavaḥ

atha vā—or else; *mat-abhisnehāt*—because of love for Me; *bhavatyaḥ*—you; *yantrita*—subjugated; *aśayāḥ*—your hearts; *āgatāḥ*—have come; *hi*—indeed; *upapannam*—fitting; *vaḥ*—on your part; *prīyante*—have affection; *mayi*—for Me; *jantavaḥ*—all living beings.

TRANSLATION

On the other hand, perhaps you have come here out of your great love for Me, which has taken control of your hearts. This is of course quite commendable on your part, since all living entities possess natural affection for Me.

TEXT 24

भर्तुः शुश्रूषणं स्त्रीणां परो धर्मो ह्यमायया ।
तद्बन्धूनां च कल्याणः प्रजानां चानुपोषणम् ॥ २४ ॥

bhartuḥ śuśrūṣaṇaṁ strīṇāṁ
paro dharmo hy amāyayā
tad-bandhūnāṁ ca kalyāṇaḥ
prajānāṁ cānupoṣaṇam

bhartuḥ—of one's husband; *śuśrūṣaṇam*—faithful service; *strīṇām*—for women; *paraḥ*—the highest; *dharmaḥ*—religious duty; *hi*—indeed; *amāyayā*—without duplicity; *tat-bandhūnām*—to the relatives of their husbands; *ca*—and; *kalyāṇaḥ*—doing good; *prajānām*—of their offspring; *ca*—and; *anupoṣaṇam*—the care.

TRANSLATION

The highest religious duty for a woman is to sincerely serve her husband, behave well toward her husband's family and take good care of her children.

PURPORT

Śrīla Jīva Gosvāmī astutely points out here that the *gopīs'* real, eternal husband is Lord Kṛṣṇa, not their so-called husbands at home, who falsely considered the *gopīs* their property. Thus a strict interpretation of the word *amāyayā,* "without illusion," reveals that the supreme religious duty for the *gopīs* is to serve Śrī Kṛṣṇa, their real lover.

TEXT 25

दुःशीलो दुर्भगो वृद्धो जडो रोग्यधनोऽपि वा ।
पतिः स्त्रीभिर्न हातव्यो लोकेप्सुभिरपातकी ॥ २५ ॥

duḥśīlo durbhago vṛddho
jaḍo rogy adhano'pi vā
patiḥ strībhir na hātavyo
lokepsubhir apātakī

duḥśīlaḥ—of bad character; *durbhagaḥ*—unfortunate; *vṛddhaḥ*—old; *jaḍaḥ*—retarded; *rogī*—sickly; *adhanaḥ*—poor; *api vā*—even; *patiḥ*—the husband; *strībhiḥ*—by women; *na hātavyaḥ*—should not be rejected; *loka*—a good destination in the next life; *īpsubhiḥ*—who desire; *apātakī*—(if he is) not fallen.

TRANSLATION

Women who desire a good destination in the next life should never abandon a husband who has not fallen from his religious standards, even if he is obnoxious, unfortunate, old, unintelligent, sickly or poor.

PURPORT

Śrīla Viśvanātha Cakravartī quotes a similar statement from *smṛti-śāstra*: *patiṁ tv apatitaṁ bhajet.* "One should serve a master who is not fallen." Sometimes the foolish argument is given that even if a husband falls down from spiritual principles, his wife should continue to follow him since he is her "*guru.*" In fact, since Kṛṣṇa consciousness cannot be subordinated to any other religious principle, a *guru* who engages his follower in materialistic, sinful activities loses his status as a *guru.* Śrīla Prabhupāda stated that the system of monarchy collapsed in Europe because the monarchs abused and exploited their position. Similarly, in the Western world men have abused and exploited women, and now there is a popular movement in which women reject the authority of their husbands. Ideally, men should be staunch in spiritual life and give pure, sincere guidance to the women under their care.

The *gopīs,* of course, being on the highest platform of spiritual perfection, were transcendental to all positive and negative religious considerations. In other words, they were the eternal lovers of the Absolute Truth.

TEXT 26

अस्वर्ग्यमयशस्यं च फल्गु कृच्छ्रं भयावहम्।
जुगुप्सितं च सर्वत्र ह्यौपपत्यं कुलस्त्रियः ॥ २६ ॥

asvargyam ayaśasyaṁ ca
phalgu kṛcchraṁ bhayāvaham
jugupsitaṁ ca sarvatra
hy aupapatyaṁ kula-striyaḥ

asvargyam—not leading to heaven; *ayaśasyam*—unfavorable for a good reputation; *ca*—and; *phalgu*—insignificant; *kṛcchram*—difficult: *bhaya-āvaham*—creating fear; *jugupsitam*—contemptible; *ca*—and: *sarvatra*—in all cases; *hi*—indeed; *aupapatyam*—adulterous affairs; *kula-striyaḥ*—for a woman coming from a respectable family.

TRANSLATION

For a woman from a respectable family, petty adulterous affairs are always condemned. They bar her from heaven, ruin her reputation and bring her difficulty and fear.

TEXT 27

श्रवणाद्दर्शनाद्ध्यानान्मयि भावोऽनुकीर्तनात्।
न तथा सन्निकर्षेण प्रतियात ततो गृहान् ॥ २७ ॥

śravaṇād darśanād dhyānān
mayi bhāvo'nukīrtanāt
na tathā sannikarṣeṇa
pratiyāta tato gṛhān

śravaṇāt—by hearing (My glories); *darśanāt*—by viewing (My Deity form in the temple); *dhyānāt*—by meditation; *mayi*—for Me; *bhāvaḥ*—love; *anukīrtanāt*—by subsequent chanting; *na*—not; *tathā*—in the same way; *sannikarṣeṇa*—by physical proximity; *pratiyāta*—please return; *tataḥ*—therefore; *gṛhān*—to your homes.

TRANSLATION

Transcendental love for Me arises by the devotional processes of hearing about Me, seeing My Deity form, meditating on Me and faithfully chanting My glories. The same result is not achieved by mere physical proximity. So please go back to your homes.

PURPORT

Lord Kṛṣṇa is certainly presenting formidable arguments.

TEXT 28

श्रीशुक उवाच
इति विप्रियमाकर्ण्य गोप्यो गोविन्दभाषितम् ।
विषण्णा भग्नसंकल्पाश्चिन्तामापुर्दुरत्ययाम् ॥ २८ ॥

śrī-śuka uvāca
iti vipriyam ākarṇya
gopyo govinda-bhāṣitam
viṣaṇṇā bhagna-saṅkalpāś
cintām āpur duratyayām

śrī-śukaḥ uvāca—Śukadeva Gosvāmī said; *iti*—thus; *vipriyam*—unpleasant; *ākarṇya*—hearing; *gopyaḥ*—the *gopīs; govinda-bhāṣitam*—the words spoken by Govinda; *viṣaṇṇāḥ*—becoming morose; *bhagna*—thwarted; *saṅkalpāḥ*—their strong desires; *cintām*—anxiety; *āpuḥ*—they experienced; *duratyayām*—insurmountable.

TRANSLATION

Śukadeva Gosvāmī said: Hearing these unpleasant words spoken by Govinda, the gopīs became morose. Their great hopes were frustrated and they felt insurmountable anxiety.

PURPORT

The *gopīs* did not know what to do. They considered falling at Kṛṣṇa's feet and crying for His mercy, or perhaps remaining aloof and going back to their homes. But they could do neither of these things and so felt great anxiety.

TEXT 29

कृत्वा मुखान्यव शुचः श्वसनेन शुष्यद्
बिम्बाधराणि चरणेन भुवः लिखन्त्यः ।
अस्त्रैरुपात्तमसिभिः कुचकुंकुमानि
तस्थुर्मृजन्त्य उरुदुःखभराः स्म तूष्णीम् ॥ २९ ॥

kṛtvā mukhāny ava śucaḥ śvasanena śuṣyad
bimbādharāṇi caraṇena bhuvaḥ likhantyaḥ
asrair upātta-masibhiḥ kuca-kuṅkumāni
tasthur mṛjantya uru-duḥkha-bharāḥ sma tūṣṇīm

kṛtvā—placing; *mukhāni*—their faces; *ava*—downward; *śucaḥ*—out of sorrow; *śvasanena*—by sighing; *śuṣyat*—drying up; *bimba*—(appearing like) red *bimba* fruits; *adharāṇi*—their lips; *caraṇena*—with their toes; *bhuvaḥ*—the ground; *likhantyaḥ*—scratching; *asraiḥ*—with their tears; *upātta*—which carried; *masibhiḥ*—the *kajjala* from their eyes; *kuca*—on the breasts; *kuṅkumāni*—the vermilion powder; *tasthuḥ*—they stood still; *mṛjantyaḥ*—washing away; *uru*—excessive; *duḥkha*—of unhappiness; *bharāḥ*—feeling the burden; *sma*—indeed; *tūṣṇīm*—silently.

TRANSLATION

Their heads hanging down and their heavy, sorrowful breathing drying up their reddened lips, the gopīs scratched the ground with their toes. Tears flowed from their eyes, carrying their kajjala and washing away the vermilion smeared on their breasts. Thus they stood, silently bearing the burden of their unhappiness.

PURPORT

The *gopīs* felt, "If Kṛṣṇa has not been conquered by our love, then our love must not be genuine. And if we cannot properly love Kṛṣṇa, what is the use of our lives?" Their reddish lips were drying up because of the hot breathing that arose from their unhappiness. When the hot sun dries ripe red *bimba* fruits, dark spots appear on them and they grow soft. The beautiful lips of the *gopīs* similarly changed in appearance. They stood silently before Kṛṣṇa, unable to speak.

TEXT 30

प्रेष्ठं प्रियेतरमिव प्रतिभाषमाणं
कृष्णं तदर्थविनिवर्तितसर्वकामाः ।
नेत्रे विमृज्य रुदितोपहते स्म किञ्चित्
संरम्भगद्गदगिरोऽब्रुवतानुरक्ताः ॥ ३० ॥

preṣṭhaṁ priyetaram iva pratibhāṣamāṇaṁ
kṛṣṇaṁ tad-artha-vinivartita-sarva-kāmāḥ
netre vimṛjya ruditopahate sma kiñcit
saṁrambha-gadgada-giro'bruvatānuraktāḥ

preṣṭham—their beloved; *priya-itaram*—just the opposite of a beloved; *iva*—as if; *pratibhāṣamāṇam*—addressing them; *kṛṣṇam*—Lord Kṛṣṇa; *tat-artha*—for His sake; *vinivartita*—desisted from; *sarva*—all; *kāmāḥ*—their material desires; *netre*—their eyes; *vimṛjya*—wiping; *rudita*—their crying; *upahate*—having stopped; *sma*—then; *kiñcit*—something; *saṁrambha*—with agitation; *gadgada*—choking up; *giraḥ*—their voices; *abruvata*—they spoke; *anuraktāḥ*—firmly attached.

TRANSLATION

Although Kṛṣṇa was their beloved, and although they had abandoned all other objects of desire for His sake, He had been speaking to them unfavorably. Nonetheless, they remained unflinching in their attachment to Him. Stopping their crying, they wiped their eyes and began to speak, their voices stammering with agitation.

PURPORT

The *gopīs* now replied to Śrī Kṛṣṇa, their voices choking up with anger caused by their intense love for Him and their unwillingness to give Him up. They would not allow Him to reject them.

TEXT 31

श्रीगोप्य ऊचुः
मैवं विभोऽर्हति भवान् गदितुं नृशंसं
सन्त्यज्य सर्वविषयांस्तव पादमूलम् ।

भक्ता भजस्व दुरवग्रह मा त्यजास्मान्
देवो यथादिपुरुषो भजते मुमुक्षून् ॥ ३१ ॥

śrī-gopya ūcuḥ
maivaṁ vibho'rhati bhavān gadituṁ nṛ-śaṁsaṁ
santyajya sarva-viṣayāṁs tava pāda-mūlam
bhaktā bhajasva duravagraha mā tyajāsmān
devo yathādi-puruṣo bhajate mumukṣūn

śrī-gopyaḥ ūcuḥ—the beautiful *gopīs* said; *mā*—not; *evam*—in this way; *vibho*—O all-powerful one; *arhati*—should; *bhavān*—Your good self; *gaditum*—speak; *nṛ-śaṁsam*—cruelly; *santyajya*—renouncing completely; *sarva*—all; *viṣayān*—varieties of sense gratification; *tava*—Your; *pāda-mūlam*—feet; *bhaktāḥ*—worshiping; *bhajasva*—please reciprocate with; *duravagraha*—O stubborn one; *mā tyaja*—do not reject; *asmān*—us; *devāḥ*—the Supreme Personality of Godhead; *yathā*—just as; *ādi-puruṣaḥ*—the primeval Lord, Nārāyaṇa; *bhajate*—reciprocates; *mumukṣūn*—with those who desire liberation.

TRANSLATION

The beautiful gopīs said: O all-powerful one, You should not speak in this cruel way. Do not reject us, who have renounced all material enjoyment to render devotional service to Your lotus feet. Reciprocate with us, O stubborn one, just as the primeval Lord, Śrī Nārāyaṇa, reciprocates with His devotees in their endeavors for liberation.

TEXT 32

यत्पत्यपत्यसुहृदामनुवृत्तिरंग
स्त्रीणां स्वधर्म इति धर्मविदा त्वयोक्तम् ।
अस्त्वेवमेतदुपदेशपदे त्वयीशे
प्रेष्ठो भवांस्तनुभृतां किल बन्धुरात्मा ॥ ३२ ॥

yat paty-apatya-suhṛdām anuvṛttir aṅga
strīṇāṁ sva-dharma iti dharma-vidā tvayoktam
astv evam etad upadeśa-pade tvayīśe
preṣṭho bhavāṁs tanu-bhṛtāṁ kila bandhur ātmā

yat—which; *pati*—of husbands; *apatya*—children; *suhṛdām*—and well-wishing relatives and friends; *anuvṛttiḥ*—the following; *aṅga*—our dear Kṛṣṇa; *strīṇām*—of women; *sva-dharmaḥ*—the proper religious duty; *iti*—thus; *dharma-vidā*—by the knower of religion; *tvayā*—You; *uktam*—spoken; *astu*—let it be; *evam*—like that; *etat*—this; *upadeśa*—of this instruction; *pade*—to the real object; *tvayi*—You; *īśe*—O Lord; *preṣṭhaḥ*—the dearmost; *bhavān*—You; *tanu-bhṛtām*—for all embodied living beings; *kila*—certainly; *bandhuḥ*—the close relative; *ātmā*—the very Self.

TRANSLATION

Our dear Kṛṣṇa, as an expert in religion You have advised us that the proper religious duty for women is to faithfully serve their husbands, children and other relatives. We agree that this principle is valid, but actually this service should be rendered to You. After all, O Lord, You are the dearmost friend of all embodied souls. You are their most intimate relative and indeed their very Self.

PURPORT

Śrī Kṛṣṇa is the Soul of all souls, their dearmost friend and well-wisher. As stated in the Eleventh Canto of the *Bhāgavatam* (11.5.41):

devarṣi-bhūtāpta-nṛṇāṁ pitṝṇāṁ
na kiṅkaro nāyam ṛṇī ca rājan
sarvātmanā yaḥ śaraṇaṁ śaraṇyaṁ
gato mukundaṁ parihṛtya kartam

"O King, one who has given up all material duties and has taken full shelter of the lotus feet of Mukunda, who offers shelter to all, is not indebted to the demigods, great sages, ordinary living beings, relatives, friends, mankind or even one's forefathers who have passed away. Since all such classes of living entities are part and parcel of the Supreme Lord, one who has surrendered to the Lord's service has no need to serve such persons separately." Authority descends from the author of all existence, the Supreme Lord. Natural figures of authority such as husbands, mothers, government leaders and sages gain their power and authority from the Supreme Lord and should thus represent the Absolute Truth to those who follow them. If one wholeheartedly engages in loving service to the original, Supreme Truth, one need not indirectly serve the Absolute Truth through the above-mentioned secondary authorities.

Even a soul surrendered to God, however, continues to serve the spiritual master, who is a direct, not an indirect, representative of the Supreme Lord. A bona fide *ācārya,* or spiritual master, is the transparent medium leading the disciple to the lotus feet of Kṛṣṇa. All indirect authorities become obsolete when one is directly in touch with the Absolute Truth. The *gopīs* wanted to explain this basic point to Kṛṣṇa, and some of the bolder young girls among them attempted to defeat Śrī Kṛṣṇa with His own statements, as exemplified in this verse.

TEXT 33

कुर्वन्ति हि त्वयि रतिं कुशलाः स्व आत्मन्
नित्यप्रिये पतिसुतादिभिरार्तिदैः किम् ।
तन्नः प्रसीद परमेश्वर मा स्म छिन्द्या
आशां धृतां त्वयि चिरादरविन्दनेत्र ॥ ३३ ॥

kurvanti hi tvayi ratiṁ kuśalāḥ sva ātman
nitya-priye pati-sutādibhir ārti-daiḥ kim
tan naḥ prasīda parameśvara mā sma chindyā
āśāṁ dhṛtāṁ tvayi cirād aravinda-netra

kurvanti—they show; *hi*—indeed; *tvayi*—for You; *ratim*—attraction; *kuśalāḥ*—expert persons; *sve*—for their own; *ātman*—Self; *nitya*—eternally; *priye*—who is dear; *pati*—with our husbands; *suta*—children; *ādibhiḥ*—and other relations; *ārti-daiḥ*—who only give trouble; *kim*—what; *tat*—therefore; *naḥ*—to us; *prasīda*—be merciful; *parama-īśvara*—O supreme controller; *mā sma chindyāḥ*—please do not cut down; *āśām*—our hopes; *dhṛtām*—sustained; *tvayi*—for You; *cirāt*—for a long time; *aravinda-netra*—O lotus-eyed one.

TRANSLATION

Expert transcendentalists always direct their affection toward You because they recognize You as their true Self and eternal beloved. What use do we have for these husbands, children and relatives of ours, who simply give us trouble? Therefore, O supreme controller, grant us Your mercy. O lotus-eyed one, please do not cut down our long-cherished hope to have Your association.

TEXT 34

चित्तं सुखेन भवतापहृतं गृहेषु
यन्निर्विशत्युत करावपि गृह्यकृत्ये ।
पादौ पदं न चलतस्तव पादमूलाद्
यामः कथं व्रजमथो करवाम किं वा ॥ ३४ ॥

cittaṁ sukhena bhavatāpahṛtaṁ gṛheṣu
yan nirviśaty uta karāv api gṛhya-kṛtye
pādau padaṁ na calatas tava pāda-mūlād
yāmaḥ kathaṁ vrajam atho karavāma kiṁ vā

cittam—our minds; *sukhena*—easily; *bhavatā*—by You; *apahṛtam*—were stolen; *gṛheṣu*—in our households; *yat*—which; *nirviśati*—were absorbed; *uta*—moreover; *karau*—our hands; *api*—as well; *gṛhya-kṛtye*—in household work; *pādau*—our feet; *padam*—one step; *na calataḥ*—are not moving; *tava*—Your; *pāda-mūlāt*—away from the feet; *yāmaḥ*—we shall go; *katham*—how; *vrajam*—back to Vraja; *atha u*—and then; *karavāma*—we shall do; *kim*—what; *vā*—furthermore.

TRANSLATION

Until today our minds were absorbed in household affairs, but You easily stole both our minds and our hands away from our housework. Now our feet won't move one step from Your lotus feet. How can we go back to Vraja? What would we do there?

PURPORT

Śrī Kṛṣṇa had blown into His flute, and the intoxicating music that had come out of its holes had stolen the minds of the young *gopī* girls. Now they had come to see Kṛṣṇa to demand back their stolen property, but they could regain their minds only if Śrī Kṛṣṇa accepted them and engaged with them in conjugal affairs.

Śrī Kṛṣṇa might have replied, "But My dear *gopīs,* just go home for now. Let Me consider the situation for a day or two, and then I will give you back your minds." In reply to this possible argument, the *gopīs* state, "Our feet refuse to move even one step. So please give us back our minds and accept us, and then we will go."

TEXT 35

सिञ्चांग नस्त्वदधरामृतपूरकेण
हासावलोककलगीतजहृच्छयाग्निम्।
नो चेद्वयं विरहजाग्न्युपयुक्तदेहा
ध्यानेन याम पदयोः पदवीं सखे ते ॥ ३५ ॥

siñcāṅga nas tvad-adharāmṛta-pūrakeṇa
hāsāvaloka-kala-gīta-ja-hṛc-chayāgnim
no ced vayaṁ virahajāgny-upayukta-dehā
dhyānena yāma padayoḥ padavīṁ sakhe te

siñca—please pour; *aṅga*—our dear Kṛṣṇa; *naḥ*—our; *tvat*—Your; *adhara*—of the lips; *amṛta*—of the nectar; *pūrakeṇa*—with the flood; *hāsa*—smiling; *avaloka*—by Your glances; *kala*—melodious; *gīta*—and the song (of Your flute); *ja*—generated; *hṛt-śaya*—situated within our hearts; *agnim*—the fire; *na u cet*—if not; *vayam*—we; *viraha*—from separation; *ja*—born; *agni*—within the fire; *upayukta*—placing; *dehāḥ*—our bodies; *dhyānena*—by meditation; *yāma*—we shall go; *padayoḥ*—of the feet; *padavīm*—to the place; *sakhe*—O friend; *te*—Your.

TRANSLATION

Dear Kṛṣṇa, please pour the nectar of Your lips upon the fire within our hearts—a fire You ignited with Your smiling glances and the sweet song of Your flute. If You do not, we will consign our bodies to the fire of separation from You, O friend, and thus like yogīs attain to the abode of Your lotus feet by meditation.

TEXT 36

यर्ह्यम्बुजाक्ष तव पादतलं रमाया
दत्तक्षणं क्वचिदरण्यजनप्रियस्य ।
अस्प्राक्ष्म तत्प्रभृति नान्यसमक्षमञ्जः
स्थातुंस्त्वयाभिरमिता बत पारयामः ॥ ३६ ॥

yarhy ambujākṣa tava pāda-talaṁ ramāyā
datta-kṣaṇaṁ kvacid araṇya-jana-priyasya
asprākṣma tat-prabhṛti nānya-samakṣam añjaḥ
sthātuṁs tvayābhiramitā bata pārayāmaḥ

yarhi—when; *ambuja*—like lotuses; *akṣa*—O You whose eyes; *tava*—Your; *pāda*—of the feet; *talam*—at the base; *ramāyāḥ*—for the goddess of fortune, Śrīmatī Lakṣmīdevī; *datta*—affording; *kṣaṇam*—a festival; *kvacit*—sometimes; *araṇya*—who dwell in the forest; *jana*—the people; *priyasya*—who hold dear; *asprākṣma*—we shall touch; *tat-prabhṛti*—from that moment forward; *na*—never; *anya*—of any other man; *samakṣam*—in the presence; *añjaḥ*—directly; *sthātum*—to stand; *tvayā*—by You; *abhiramitāḥ*—filled with joy; *bata*—certainly; *pārayāmaḥ*—will we be able.

TRANSLATION

O lotus-eyed one, the goddess of fortune considers it a festive occasion whenever she touches the soles of Your lotus feet. You are very dear to the residents of the forest, and therefore we will also touch those lotus feet. From that time on we will be unable even to stand in the presence of any other man, for we will have been fully satisfied by You.

TEXT 37

श्रीर्यत्पदाम्बुजरजश्चकमे तुलस्या
लब्ध्वापि वक्षसि पदं किल भृत्यजुष्टम्।
यस्याः स्ववीक्षण उतान्यसुरप्रयासस्
तद्वद्वयं च तव पादरजः प्रपन्नाः ॥ ३७ ॥

śrīr yat padāmbuja-rajaś cakame tulasyā
labdhvāpi vakṣasi padaṁ kila bhṛtya-juṣṭam
yasyāḥ sva-vīkṣaṇa utānya-sura-prayāsas
tadvad vayaṁ ca tava pāda-rajaḥ prapannāḥ

śrīḥ—the goddess of fortune, wife of Lord Nārāyaṇa; *yat*—as; *pada-ambuja*—of the lotus feet; *rajaḥ*—the dust; *cakame*—desired; *tulasyā*—together with Tulasī-devī; *labdhvā*—having obtained; *api*—even; *vakṣasi*—upon His chest; *padam*—her position; *kila*—indeed; *bhṛtya*—by servants; *juṣṭam*—served; *yasyāḥ*—whose (Lakṣmī's); *sva*—upon themselves; *vīkṣaṇe*—for the sake of the glance; *uta*—on the other hand; *anya*—of the other; *sura*—demigods; *prayāsaḥ*—the endeavor; *tadvat*—in the same way; *vayam*—we; *ca*—also; *tava*—Your; *pāda*—of the feet; *rajaḥ*—the dust; *prapannāḥ*—have approached for shelter.

TRANSLATION

Goddess Lakṣmī, whose glance is sought after by the demigods with great endeavor, has achieved the unique position of always remaining on the chest of her Lord, Nārāyaṇa. Still, she desires the dust of His lotus feet, even though she has to share that dust with Tulasī-devī and indeed with the Lord's many other servants. Similarly, we have approached the dust of Your lotus feet for shelter.

PURPORT

The *gopīs* here point out that the dust of the Lord's feet is so ecstatic and enlivening that the goddess of fortune wants to abandon her unique position on His chest to share with many other devotees a position at His feet. Thus the *gopīs* urge Lord Kṛṣṇa not to be guilty of a double standard. Since the Lord gave the goddess of fortune a place on His chest and also allowed her to seek the dust of His lotus feet, Kṛṣṇa should certainly give the same opportunity to His most loving devotees, the *gopīs*. "After all" the *gopīs* plead, "seeking the dust of Your lotus feet is perfectly justified, and You should encourage us in this endeavor and not try to send us away."

TEXT 38

तन्नः प्रसीद वृजिनार्दन तेऽङ्घ्रिमूलं
प्राप्ता विसृज्य वसतीस्त्वदुपासनाशाः ।
त्वत्सुन्दरस्मितनिरीक्षणतीव्रकाम-
तप्तात्मनां पुरुषभूषण देहि दास्यम् ॥३८॥

tan naḥ prasīda vṛjinārdana te'ṅghri-mūlaṁ
prāptā visṛjya vasatīs tvad-upāsanāśāḥ
tvat-sundara-smita-nirīkṣaṇa-tīvra-kāma
taptātmanāṁ puruṣa-bhūṣaṇa dehi dāsyam

tat—therefore; *naḥ*—to us; *prasīda*—please show Your mercy; *vṛjina*—of all distress; *ardana*—O vanquisher; *te*—Your; *aṅghri-mūlam*—feet; *prāptāḥ*—we have approached; *visṛjya*—renouncing; *vasatīḥ*—our homes; *tvat-upāsanā*—the worship of You; *āśāḥ*—hoping for; *tvat*—Your; *sundara*—beautiful; *smita*—smiling; *nirīkṣaṇa*—because of the glances; *tīvra*—intense; *kāma*—by the lust; *tapta*—burned; *ātmanām*—whose hearts; *puruṣa*—of all men; *bhūṣaṇa*—O ornament; *dehi*—please grant; *dāsyam*—servitude.

TRANSLATION

Therefore, O vanquisher of all distress, please show us mercy. To approach Your lotus feet we abandoned our families and homes, and we have no desire other than to serve You. Our hearts are burning with intense desires generated by Your beautiful smiling glances. O jewel among men, please make us Your maidservants.

PURPORT

When Śrī Kṛṣṇa was born, the sage Garga predicted that He would manifest all the opulences of the Supreme Lord Nārāyaṇa. The *gopīs* now appeal to the Lord to fulfill this prediction by being merciful and granting them direct service, just as Lord Nārāyaṇa awards direct service to His loving devotees. The *gopīs* emphasize that they did not give up their families and homes with the hope of securing a higher pleasure from Kṛṣṇa. They are simply begging for service, revealing their pure-hearted devotion. The *gopīs* think, "If in the course of Your pursuing Your happiness we somehow or other become happy by seeing Your face, what is the harm in that?"

Śrīla Viśvanātha Cakravartī comments on the words *puruṣa-bhūṣaṇa,* "O jewel among men." The Ṭhākura states that the *gopīs* meant to say, "O jewel of all males, please decorate our golden bodies with the dark blue gems of Your limbs."

TEXT 39

वीक्ष्यालकावृतमुखं तव कुण्डलश्री-
गण्डस्थलाधरसुधं हसितावलोकम् ।
दत्ताभयं च भुजदण्डयुगं विलोक्य
वक्षः श्रियैकरमणं च भवाम दास्यः ॥ ३९ ॥

vīkṣyālakāvṛta-mukhaṁ tava kuṇḍala-śrī
gaṇḍa-sthalādhara-sudhaṁ hasitāvalokam
dattābhayaṁ ca bhuja-daṇḍa-yugaṁ vilokya
vakṣaḥ śriyaika-ramaṇaṁ ca bhavāma dāsyaḥ

vīkṣya—seeing; *alaka*—by Your hair; *āvṛta*—covered; *mukham*—face; *tava*—Your; *kuṇḍala*—of Your earrings; *śrī*—with the beauty; *gaṇḍa-sthala*—having the cheeks; *adhara*—of Your lips; *sudham*—and the nectar; *hasita*—smiling; *avalokam*—with glances; *datta*—bestowing; *abhayam*—fearlessness; *ca*—and; *bhuja-daṇḍa*—of Your mighty arms; *yugam*—the pair; *vilokya*—glancing upon; *vakṣaḥ*—Your chest; *śrī*—of the goddess of fortune; *eka*—the only; *ramaṇam*—source of pleasure; *ca*—and; *bhavāma*—we must become; *dāsyaḥ*—Your maidservants.

TRANSLATION

Seeing Your face encircled by curling locks of hair, Your cheeks beautified by earrings, Your lips full of nectar, and Your smiling glance, and also seeing Your two imposing arms, which take away our fear, and Your chest, which is the only source of pleasure for the goddess of fortune, we must become Your maidservants.

PURPORT

Śrīla Viśvanātha Cakravartī Ṭhākura envisions the *gopīs'* dealings with Kṛṣṇa as follows:

"Kṛṣṇa says, 'You want to become My servants; so do I have to buy you with some payment, or are you giving yourselves freely?'

"The *gopīs* reply, 'Since the beginning of our youthful womanhood You have been purchasing us with a payment millions and millions of times more than enough. That payment is Your gemlike smiling glance, which constitutes a great treasure we have never heard about or seen anywhere else.'

"'When You put Your golden turban on Your head, Your maidservant will act as Your valet, pulling up the turban bit by bit until it is in just the right position. And even while You shake a chastising finger at her, trying hard to prohibit her, she will put her hand beneath Your turban and take the opportunity to glance at Your face. Thus we, Your maidservants, will relish with our eyes Your abundant sweetness.'

"Kṛṣṇa says, 'Your husbands will not tolerate this behavior of ours. They will complain bitterly to King Kaṁsa, thus producing a fearful situation for Me and for you as well.'

"The *gopīs* say, 'But Kṛṣṇa, Your two mighty arms make us fearless, just as they did when You held up Govardhana Hill to protect us from the pride of Mahendra. Those arms will certainly kill that beast Kaṁsa.'

"'But being a religious person, I cannot make others' wives My maidservants.'

"'O dear crest jewel of religious personalities, You may say that You refuse to make the cowherds' wives Your maidservants, but by force You have already taken Lakṣmī, the wife of Nārāyaṇa, from Vaikuṇṭha and are carrying her around on Your chest. Out of shame she has assumed the form of a golden line on Your chest, and she takes her only pleasure there.

"Besides, within all the fourteen worlds and even above these worlds—in Vaikuṇṭhaloka, beyond this universe—You never reject any beautiful woman, no matter who she is or whom she belongs to. We know this quite well."

TEXT 40

का स्त्र्यंग ते कलपदायतवेणुगीत-
सम्मोहितार्यचरितान्न चलेत्त्रिलोक्याम् ।
त्रैलोक्यसौभगमिदं च निरीक्ष्य रूपं
यद् गोद्विजद्रुममृगाः पुलकान्यबिभ्रन् ॥ ४० ॥

kā stry aṅga te kala-padāyata-veṇu-gīta-
sammohitārya-caritān na calet tri-lokyām
trailokya-saubhagam idaṁ ca nirīkṣya rūpaṁ
yad go-dvija-druma-mṛgāḥ pulakāny abibhran

kā—which; *strī*—woman; *aṅga*—dear Kṛṣṇa; *te*—Your; *kala*—sweet-sounding; *pada*—having stanzas; *āyata*—drawn-out; *veṇu*—of Your flute; *gīta*—by the song; *sammohitā*—completely bewildered; *ārya*—of civilized people; *caritāt*—from the proper behavior; *na calet*—does not deviate; *tri-lokyām*—within the three worlds; *trai-lokya*—of all the three worlds; *saub-hagam*—the cause of auspiciousness; *idam*—this; *ca*—and; *nirīkṣya*—seeing; *rūpam*—the personal beauty; *yat*—because of which; *go*—the cows; *dvija*—birds; *druma*—trees; *mṛgāḥ*—and deer; *pulakāni*—bodily hair standing on end; *abibhran*—they bore.

TRANSLATION

Dear Kṛṣṇa, what woman in all the three worlds wouldn't deviate from religious behavior when bewildered by the sweet, drawn-out melody of Your flute? Your beauty makes all three worlds auspicious. Indeed, even the cows, birds, trees and deer manifest the ecstatic symptom of bodily hair standing on end when they see Your beautiful form.

TEXT 41

व्यक्तं भवान् व्रजभयार्तिहरोऽभिजातो
देवो यथादिपुरुषः सुरलोकगोप्ता ।

तन्नो निधेहि करपंकजमार्तबन्धो
तप्तस्तनेषु च शिरःसु च किंकरीणाम्॥ ४१॥

vyaktaṁ bhavān vraja-bhayārti-haro'bhijāto
devo yathādi-puruṣaḥ sura-loka-goptā
tan no nidhehi kara-paṅkajam ārta-bandho
tapta-staneṣu ca śiraḥsu ca kiṅkarīṇām

vyaktam—obviously; *bhavān*—You; *vraja*—of the people of Vraja; *bhaya*—of the fear; *ārti*—and distress; *haraḥ*—as the remover; *abhijātaḥ*—have taken birth; *devaḥ*—the Supreme Personality of Godhead; *yathā*—just as; *ādi-puruṣaḥ*—the primeval Lord; *sura-loka*—of the planets of the demigods; *goptā*—the protector; *tat*—therefore; *naḥ*—of us; *nidhehi*—kindly place; *kara*—Your hand; *paṅkajam*—lotuslike; *ārta*—of the distressed; *bandho*—O friend; *tapta*—burning; *staneṣu*—on the breasts; *ca*—and; *śiraḥsu*—on the heads; *ca*—also; *kiṅkarīṇām*—of Your maidservants.

TRANSLATION

Clearly You have taken birth in this world to relieve the fear and distress of the people of Vraja, just as the Supreme Personality of Godhead, the primeval Lord, protects the domain of the demigods. Therefore, O friend of the distressed, kindly place Your lotus hand on Your maidservants' heads and burning breasts.

TEXT 42

श्रीशुक उवाच
इति विक्लवितं तासां श्रुत्वा योगेश्वरेश्वरः।
प्रहस्य सदयं गोपीरात्मारामोऽप्यरीरमत् ॥ ४२॥

śrī-śuka uvāca
iti viklavitaṁ tāsāṁ
śrutvā yogeśvareśvaraḥ
prahasya sa-dayaṁ gopīr
ātmārāmo'py arīramat

śrī-śukaḥ uvāca—Śukadeva Gosvāmī said; *iti*—in these words; *viklavitam*—the despondent expressions of; *tāsām*—of them; *śrutvā*—having heard; *yoga-īśvara-īśvaraḥ*—the Lord of all lords of mystic power; *prahasya*—laughing; *sa-dayam*—mercifully; *gopīḥ*—the *gopīs; ātma ārāmaḥ*—self-satisfied; *api*—even though; *arīramat*—He satisfied.

TRANSLATION

Śukadeva Gosvāmī said: Smiling upon hearing these despondent words from the gopīs, Lord Kṛṣṇa, the supreme master of all masters of mystic yoga, mercifully enjoyed with them, although He is self-satisfied.

TEXT 43

ताभिः समेताभिरुदारचेष्टितः
प्रियेक्षणोत्फुल्लमुखीभिरच्युतः ।
उदारहासद्विजकुन्ददीधतिर्
व्यरोचतैणांक इवोडुभिर्वृतः ॥ ४३ ॥

tābhiḥ sametābhir udāra-ceṣṭitaḥ
priyekṣaṇotphulla-mukhībhir acyutaḥ
udāra-hāsa-dvija-kunda-dīdhatir
vyarocataiṇāṅka ivoḍubhir vṛtaḥ

tābhiḥ—with them; *sametābhiḥ*—who were all joined together; *udāra*—magnanimous; *ceṣṭitaḥ*—He whose activities; *priya*—affectionate; *īkṣaṇa*—by His glances; *utphulla*—blossoming; *mukhībhiḥ*—whose faces; *acyutaḥ*—the infallible Lord; *udāra*—with broad; *hāsa*—smiles; *dvija*—of His teeth; *kunda*—(like) jasmine flowers; *dīdhatiḥ*—showing the effulgence; *vyarocata*—He appeared splendid; *eṇa-aṅkaḥ*—the moon, who bears marks resembling a black deer; *iva*—like; *uḍubhiḥ*—by stars; *vṛtaḥ*—surrounded.

TRANSLATION

Among the assembled gopīs, the infallible Lord Kṛṣṇa appeared just like the moon surrounded by stars. He whose activities are so magnanimous made their faces blossom with His affectionate glances, and His broad smiles revealed the effulgence of His jasmine-budlike teeth.

PURPORT

The word *acyuta* here indicates that Lord Kṛṣṇa did not fail to give pleasure to each and every *gopī* in the nocturnal assembly.

TEXT 44

उपगीयमान उद्गायन् वनिताशतयूथपः ।
मालां बिभ्रद्वैजयन्तीं व्यचरन्मण्डयन् वनम् ॥ ४४ ॥

upagīyamāna udgāyan
vanitā-śata-yūthapaḥ
mālāṁ bibhrad vaijayantīṁ
vyacaran maṇḍayan vanam

upagīyamānaḥ—being sung about; *udgāyan*—singing loudly Himself; *vanitā*—of women; *śata*—hundreds; *yūthapaḥ*—the commander; *mālām*—the garland; *bibhrat*—wearing; *vaijayantīm*—known as Vaijayantī (which consists of flowers of five different colors); *vyacaran*—moving about; *maṇḍayan*—beautifying; *vanam*—the forest.

TRANSLATION

As the gopīs sang His praises, that leader of hundreds of women sang loudly in reply. He moved among them, wearing His Vaijayantī garland, beautifying the Vṛndāvana forest.

PURPORT

According to Śrīla Jīva Gosvāmī, Lord Kṛṣṇa sang many wonderful melodies and meters, and the *gopīs* accompanied Him, following His lead. Kṛṣṇa's singing on this occasion is described in the *Śrī Viṣṇu Purāṇa:*

kṛṣṇaḥ śarac-candramasaṁ
kaumudīṁ kumudākaram
jagau gopī-janas tv ekaṁ
kṛṣṇa-nāma punaḥ punaḥ

"Kṛṣṇa sang the glories of the autumn moon, the moonshine and the lotus-filled river, while the *gopīs* simply sang His name repeatedly."

TEXTS 45–46

नद्याः पुलिनमाविश्य गोपीभिर्हिमवालुकम् ।
जुष्टं तत्तरलानन्दिकुमुदामोदवायुना ॥ ४५ ॥

बाहुप्रसारपरिरम्भकरालकोरु-
नीवीस्तनालभननर्मनखाग्रपातैः ।
क्ष्वेल्यावलोकहसितैर्व्रजसुन्दरीणाम्
उत्तम्भयन् रतिपतिं रमयां चकार ॥ ४६ ॥

nadyāḥ pulinam āviśya
gopībhir hima-vālukam
juṣṭaṁ tat-taralānandi
kumudāmoda-vāyunā

bāhu-prasāra-parirambha-karālakoru
nīvī-stanālabhana-narma-nakhāgra-pātaiḥ
kṣvelyāvaloka-hasitair vraja-sundarīṇām
uttambhayan rati-patiṁ ramayāṁ cakāra

nadyāḥ—of the river; *pulinam*—the bank; *āviśya*—entering upon; *gopībhiḥ*—together with the *gopīs; hima*—cool; *vālukam*—by its sand; *juṣṭam*—served; *tat*—of it; *tarala*—by the waves; *ānandi*—made joyful; *kumuda*—of the lotuses; *āmoda*—(carrying) the fragrance; *vāyunā*—by the wind; *bāhu*—of His arms; *prasāra*—with the throwing; *pari-rambha*—with embraces; *kara*—of their hands; *alaka*—hair; *ūru*—thighs; *nīvī*—belts; *stana*—and breasts; *ālabhana*—with the touching; *narma*—in sport; *nakha*—of fingernails; *agra-pātaiḥ*—with the striking; *kṣvelyā*—with playful conversation; *avaloka*—glancing; *hasitaiḥ*—and laughter; *vraja-sundarīṇām*—for the beautiful young girls of Vraja; *ut-tambhayan*—inciting; *rati-patim*—Cupid; *ramayām cakāra*—He took pleasure.

TRANSLATION

Śrī Kṛṣṇa went with the gopīs to the bank of the Yamunā, where the sand was cooling and the wind, enlivened by the river's waves, bore the fragrance of lotuses. There Kṛṣṇa threw His arms around the gopīs and embraced them. He aroused Cupid in the beautiful young ladies of Vraja by touching their hands, hair, thighs, belts and breasts, by playfully scratching them with His fingernails, and also by joking with them, glancing at them and laughing with them. In this way the Lord enjoyed His pastimes.

TEXT 47

एवं भगवतः कृष्णाल्लब्धमाना महात्मनः ।
आत्मानं मेनिरे स्त्रीणां मानिन्यो ह्यधिकं भुवि ॥ ४७ ॥

evaṁ bhagavataḥ kṛṣṇāl
labdha-mānā mahātmanaḥ
ātmānaṁ menire strīṇāṁ
māninyo hy adhikaṁ bhuvi

evam—in this way; *bhagavataḥ*—from the Personality of Godhead; *kṛṣṇāt*—Lord Kṛṣṇa; *labdha*—receiving; *mānāḥ*—special respect; *mahā-ātmanaḥ*—from the Supreme Soul; *ātmānam*—themselves; *menire*—they considered; *strīṇām*—among all women; *māninyaḥ*—becoming proud; *hi*—indeed; *adhikam*—the best; *bhuvi*—on the earth.

TRANSLATION

The gopīs became proud of themselves for having received such special attention from Kṛṣṇa, the Supreme Personality of Godhead, and each of them thought herself the best woman on earth.

PURPORT

The gopīs were proud because they had attained as their lover the greatest of all personalities. So in a sense they were proud of Kṛṣṇa. Also, the pride of the *gopīs* was a pretense created by Kṛṣṇa's pastime potency in order to intensify their love for Him through separation. In this connection, Śrīla Viśvanātha Cakravartī quotes Bharata Muni's *Nāṭyaśāstra: na vinā vipralambhena sambhogaḥ puṣṭim aśnute.* "Direct contact is not fully appreciated until separation has been experienced."

TEXT 48

तासां तत्सौभगमदं वीक्ष्य मानं च केशवः ।
प्रशमाय प्रसादाय तत्रैवान्तरधीयत ॥ ४८ ॥

tāsāṁ tat-saubhaga-madaṁ
vīkṣya mānaṁ ca keśavaḥ
praśamāya prasādāya
tatraivāntaradhīyata

tāsām—of them; *tat*—that; *saubhaga*—due to their good fortune; *madam*—intoxicated state; *vīkṣya*—observing; *mānam*—the false pride; *ca*—and; *keśavaḥ*—Lord Kṛṣṇa; *praśamāya*—in order to diminish it; *prasādāya*—to show them favor; *tatra eva*—right there; *antaradhīyata*—He disappeared.

TRANSLATION

Lord Keśava, seeing the gopīs too proud of their good fortune, wanted to relieve them of this pride and show them further mercy. Thus He immediately disappeared.

PURPORT

The word *prasādāya* here is significant. Lord Kṛṣṇa was not going to neglect the *gopīs;* rather, He would increase the power of their loving affairs by making another spectacular arrangement. After all, the *gopīs* were basically proud of Kṛṣṇa. He also made this arrangement, as we shall see, to show special favor to the beautiful young daughter of King Vṛṣabhānu.

Thus end the purports of the humble servants of His Divine Grace A.C. Bhaktivedanta Swami Prabhupāda to the Tenth Canto, Twenty-ninth Chapter, of the Śrīmad-Bhāgavatam, *entitled "Kṛṣṇa and the Gopīs Meet for the Rāsa Dance."*

CHAPTER THIRTY

The Gopīs Search for Kṛṣṇa

This chapter describes how the *gopīs,* tormented through the long night by separation from Kṛṣṇa, wandered like madwomen from forest to forest in search of Him.

When Śrī Kṛṣṇa suddenly disappeared from the arena of the *rāsa* dance, the *gopīs,* their minds fully absorbed in thoughts of Him, began looking for Him in the various forests. From all the moving and nonmoving creatures they asked for news of Kṛṣṇa's whereabouts. Finally they became so distraught that they began imitating His pastimes.

Later, while wandering in a corner of the forest, the *gopīs* saw Śrī Kṛṣṇa's footprints, which appeared mixed with Śrīmatī Rādhārāṇī's. Seeing these footprints perturbed them greatly, and they declared that surely Śrīmatī Rādhārāṇī must have worshiped Kṛṣṇa with unusual excellence, since She had been privileged to associate with Him in seclusion. Further along the path the *gopīs* came to a place where they could no longer see Śrīmatī Rādhārāṇī's footprints; they then concluded that Kṛṣṇa must have taken Rādhārāṇī onto His shoulders. In another place they noticed that Kṛṣṇa's footprints were showing only the toes, and thus the *gopīs* concluded He had been picking flowers with which to decorate His beloved. In yet another spot the *gopīs* saw signs that led them to imagine that Śrī Kṛṣṇa had been tying the locks of Śrīmatī Rādhārāṇī's hair. All these thoughts brought pain to the *gopīs'* minds.

Because of the special attention She received from Kṛṣṇa, Śrī Rādhā began to consider Herself the most fortunate of women. She told Him that She could walk no further and that He would have to carry Her on His shoulders. But just then Lord Kṛṣṇa disappeared from Her sight. Śrīmatī Rādhārāṇī, extremely troubled, then began looking everywhere for Him, and when She finally met Her *gopī* girlfriends She related to them what had happened. All the *gopīs* then went out to look for Kṛṣṇa in the forest, going as far as the moonlight reached. But in the end they were unsuccessful, so they went back to the shore of the Yamunā and simply sang Kṛṣṇa's glories in utter helplessness.

TEXT 1

श्रीशुक उवाच
अन्तर्हिते भगवति सहसैव व्रजांगनाः ।
अतप्यंस्तमचक्षाणाः करिण्य इव यूथपम्॥ १ ॥

śrī-śuka uvāca
antarhite bhagavati
sahasaiva vrajāṅganāḥ
atapyaṁs tam acakṣāṇāḥ
kariṇya iva yūthapam

śrī-śukaḥ uvāca—Śukadeva Gosvāmī said; *antarhite*—when He disappeared; *bhagavati*—the Supreme Personality of Godhead; *sahasā eva*—quite suddenly; *vraja-aṅganāḥ*—the young ladies of Vraja; *atapyan*—felt great remorse; *tam*—Him; *acakṣāṇāḥ*—not seeing; *kariṇyaḥ*—female elephants; *iva*—just as; *yūthapam*—their male leader.

TRANSLATION

Śukadeva Gosvāmī said: When Lord Kṛṣṇa disappeared so suddenly, the gopīs felt great sorrow at losing sight of Him, like a group of female elephants who have lost their mate.

TEXT 2

गत्यानुरागस्मितविभ्रमेक्षितैर्
मनोरमालापविहारविभ्रमैः ।
आक्षिप्तचित्ताः प्रमदा रमापतेस्
तास्ता विचेष्टा जगृहुस्तदात्मिकाः ॥ २ ॥

gatyānurāga-smita-vibhramekṣitair
mano-ramālāpa-vihāra-vibhramaiḥ
ākṣipta-cittāḥ pramadā ramā-pates
tās tā viceṣṭā jagṛhus tad-ātmikāḥ

gatyā—by His movements; *anurāga*—affectionate; *smita*—smiles; *vibhrama*—playful; *īkṣitaiḥ*—and glances; *manaḥ-rama*—charming; *ālāpa*—by His talking; *vihāra*—playing; *vibhramaiḥ*—and other allurements;

ākṣipta—overwhelmed; *cittāḥ*—whose hearts; *pramadāḥ*—the girls; *ramā-pateḥ*—of the husband of Ramā, the goddess of fortune, or of the master of beauty and opulence; *tāḥ tāḥ*—each of those; *viceṣṭāḥ*—wonderful activities; *jagṛhuḥ*—they enacted; *tat-ātmikāḥ*—absorbed in Him.

TRANSLATION

As the cowherd women remembered Lord Kṛṣṇa, their hearts were overwhelmed by His movements and loving smiles, His playful glances and enchanting talks, and by the many other pastimes He would enjoy with them. Thus absorbed in thoughts of Kṛṣṇa, the Lord of Ramā, the gopīs began acting out His various transcendental pastimes.

PURPORT

Śrīla Viśvanātha Cakravartī Ṭhākura describes the following charming exchange between Kṛṣṇa and the *gopīs:*

"Kṛṣṇa said to a *gopī,* 'My dear land lily, are you going to offer your honey to this very thirsty honeybee or not?'

"The *gopī* replied, 'My dear bee, the husband of the lilies is the sun, not the bee, so why are You claiming that my honey belongs to You?'

"But My dear lily, the very nature of you lilies is that you don't give your honey to your husband, the sun, but rather to your paramour, the bee.' The *gopī,* defeated by the words of Kṛṣṇa, laughed and then gave Him her lips as honey to drink."

Śrīla Viśvanātha Cakravartī also describes the following conversation:

"Kṛṣṇa said to a *gopī,* 'Ah, I can understand that as you approached this *nīpa* tree standing here, you were bitten by an audacious snake. Its venom has already reached your chest, but since you are a respectable maiden you haven't asked Me to cure you. Still I've come, being merciful by nature. Now, while I massage your body with My hands, I'll chant a *mantra* to counteract the serpent's poison.'

"The *gopī* said, 'But, my dear snake charmer, no snake has bitten me. Go massage the body of some girl who actually has suffered a snakebite.'

"'Come now, My dear respectable girl, from your trembling voice I can tell that you are experiencing a feverish reaction to poisoning. Knowing this, if I don't take care of you I'll be guilty of killing an innocent woman. So let Me treat you.'

"With this, Kṛṣṇa applied His fingernails to the *gopī's* chest."

TEXT 3

गतिस्मितप्रेक्षणभाषणादिषु
प्रियाः प्रियस्य प्रतिरूढमूर्तयः ।
असावहं त्वित्यबलास्तदात्मिका
न्यवेदिषुः कृष्णविहारविभ्रमाः ॥ ३ ॥

gati-smita-prekṣaṇa-bhāṣaṇādiṣu
priyāḥ priyasya pratirūḍha-mūrtayaḥ
asāv ahaṁ tv ity abalās tad-ātmikā
nyavediṣuḥ kṛṣṇa-vihāra-vibhramāḥ

gati—in His movements; *smita*—smiling; *prekṣaṇa*—beholding; *bhāṣaṇā*—talking; *ādiṣu*—and so on; *priyāḥ*—the dear *gopīs; priyasya*—of their beloved; *pratirūḍha*—fully absorbed; *mūrtayaḥ*—their bodies; *asau*—He; *aham*—I; *tu*—actually; *iti*—speaking thus; *abalāḥ*—the women; *tat-ātmikāḥ*—identifying with Him; *nyavediṣuḥ*—they announced; *kṛṣṇa-vihāra*—caused by the pastimes of Kṛṣṇa; *vibhramāḥ*—whose intoxication.

TRANSLATION

Because the beloved gopīs were absorbed in thoughts of their beloved Kṛṣṇa, their bodies imitated His way of moving and smiling, His way of beholding them, His speech and His other distinctive features. Deeply immersed in thinking of Him and maddened by remembering His pastimes, they declared to one another, "I am Kṛṣṇa!"

PURPORT

Spontaneously, the *gopīs* began moving like Kṛṣṇa: they smiled as He would smile, glanced boldly as He would and spoke as He would. The *gopīs* were completely absorbed in the existence of Kṛṣṇa and mad with love at their sudden separation from Him, and thus their dedication to Him attained absolute perfection.

TEXT 4

गायन्त्य उच्चैरमुमेव संहता
विचिक्युरुन्मत्तकवद् वनाद् वनम् ।
पप्रच्छुराकाशवदन्तरं बहिर्
भूतेषु सन्तं पुरुषं वनस्पतीन् ॥ ४ ॥

gāyantya uccair amum eva saṁhatā
vicikyur unmattaka-vad vanād vanam
papracchur ākāśa-vad antaraṁ bahir
bhūteṣu santaṁ puruṣaṁ vanaspatīn

gāyantyaḥ—singing; *uccaiḥ*—loudly; *amum*—about Him; *eva*—indeed; *saṁhatāḥ*—together in a group; *vicikyuḥ*—they searched; *unmattaka-vat*—like madwomen; *vanāt vanam*—from one area of the forest to another; *papracchuḥ*—they inquired; *ākāśa-vat*—like the sky; *antaram*—internally; *bahiḥ*—and externally; *bhūteṣu*—in all created beings; *santam*—present; *puruṣam*—the Supreme Person; *vanaspatīn*—from the trees.

TRANSLATION

Singing loudly of Kṛṣṇa, they searched for Him throughout the Vṛndāvana forest like a band of madwomen. They even asked the trees about Him, who as the Supersoul is present inside and outside of all created things, just like the sky.

PURPORT

Lost in the madness of love for Kṛṣṇa, the *gopīs* inquired about Him from even the trees in Vṛndāvana. Of course, there is no actual separation from Lord Kṛṣṇa, since He is the all-pervading Supersoul.

TEXT 5

दृष्टो वः कच्चिदश्वत्थ प्लक्ष न्यग्रोध नो मनः ।
नन्दसूनुर्गतो हृत्वा प्रेमहासावलोकनैः ॥ ५ ॥

dṛṣṭo vaḥ kaccid aśvattha
plakṣa nyagrodha no manaḥ
nanda-sūnur gato hṛtvā
prema-hāsāvalokanaiḥ

dṛṣṭaḥ—has been seen; *vaḥ*—by you; *kaccit*—whether; *aśvattha*—O *aśvattha* (holy fig tree); *plakṣa*—O *plakṣa* (waved-leaf fig tree); *nyagrodha*—O *nyagrodha* (banyan tree); *naḥ*—our; *manaḥ*—minds; *nanda*—of Mahārāja Nanda; *sūnuḥ*—the son; *gataḥ*—has gone away; *hṛtvā*—after stealing; *prema*—loving; *hāsa*—with His smiles; *avalokanaiḥ*—and glances.

TRANSLATION

[The gopīs said:] O aśvattha tree, O plakṣa, O nyagrodha, have you seen Kṛṣṇa? That son of Nanda Mahārāja has gone away after stealing our minds with His loving smiles and glances.

TEXT 6

कच्चित्कुरबकाशोकनागपुन्नागचम्पकाः ।
रामानुजो मानिनीनामितो दर्पहरस्मितः ॥ ६ ॥

kaccit kurabakāśoka-
nāga-punnāga-campakāḥ
rāmānujo māninīnām
ito darpa-hara-smitaḥ

kaccit—whether; *kurabaka-aśoka-nāga-punnāga-campakāḥ*—O *kurabaka* (red amaranth), *aśoka, nāga, punnāga* and *campaka* trees; *rāma*—of Balarāma; *anujaḥ*—the younger brother; *māninīnām*—of women, who are proud by nature; *itaḥ*—passing by here; *darpa*—the pride; *hara*—removing; *smitaḥ*—whose smile.

TRANSLATION

O kurabaka tree, O aśoka, O nāga, punnāga and campaka, has Balarāma's younger brother, whose smile removes the audacity of all proud women, passed this way?

PURPORT

As soon as the *gopīs* saw that a particular tree would not answer them, they impatiently left it and rushed off to another to make further inquiries.

TEXT 7

कच्चित्तुलसि कल्याणि गोविन्दचरणप्रिये ।
सह त्वालिकुलैर्बिभ्रद् दृष्टस्तेऽतिप्रियोऽच्युतः ॥ ७ ॥

kaccit tulasi kalyāṇi
govinda-caraṇa-priye
saha tvāli-kulair bibhrad
dṛṣṭas te'ti-priyo'cyutaḥ

kaccit—whether; *tulasi*—O *tulasī* plant; *kalyāṇi*—O kind one; *govinda*—of Lord Kṛṣṇa; *caraṇa*—the feet; *priye*—you to whom are dear; *saha*—together with; *tvā*—you; *ali*—of bees; *kulaiḥ*—swarms; *bibhrat*—carrying; *dṛṣṭaḥ*—seen; *te*—by you; *ati-priyaḥ*—very dear; *acyutaḥ*—Lord Acyuta.

TRANSLATION

O most kind tulasī, to whom the feet of Govinda are so dear, have you seen that infallible one walk by, wearing you and encircled by swarms of bees?

PURPORT

The *ācāryas* explain here that the word *caraṇa* is a term of respect, as in the expression *evaṁ vadanty ācārya-caraṇāḥ.* The bees humming around the garland worn by Śrī Govinda were attracted by the fragrance of the *tulasī mañjarīs* offered to Him. The *gopīs* felt that the trees had not replied because they were male, but that *tulasī,* being female, would sympathize with their plight.

TEXT 8

मालत्यदर्शि वः कच्चिन्मल्लिके जातियूथिके ।
प्रीतिं वो जनयन् यातः करस्पर्शेन माधवः ॥ ८ ॥

mālaty adarśi vaḥ kaccin
mallike jāti-yūthike
prītiṁ vo janayan yātaḥ
kara-sparśena mādhavaḥ

mālati—O *mālatī* plant (a kind of white jasmine); *adarśi*—has been seen; *vaḥ*—by you; *kaccit*—whether; *mallike*—O *mallikā* (a different kind of jasmine); *jāti*—O *jāti* (another kind of white jasmine); *yūthike*—O *yūthikā* (yet another jasmine); *prītim*—pleasure; *vaḥ*—for you; *janayan*—generating; *yātaḥ*—has gone by; *kara*—of His hand; *sparśena*—by the touch; *mādhavaḥ*—Kṛṣṇa, the embodiment of the spring season.

TRANSLATION

O mālati, O mallikā, O jāti and yūthikā, has Mādhava gone by here, giving you pleasure with the touch of His hand?

PURPORT

When even *tulasī* herself did not answer the *gopīs,* they approached the fragrant jasmine flowers. The *gopīs,* seeing the jasmine vines humbly bowing down, assumed that these plants must have seen Lord Kṛṣṇa and were therefore showing humility in their ecstasy.

TEXT 9

चूतप्रियालपनसासनकोविदार-
जम्ब्वर्कबिल्वबकुलाम्रकदम्बनीपाः ।
येऽन्ये परार्थभवका यमुनोपकूलाः
शंसन्तु कृष्णपदवीं रहितात्मनां नः ॥ ९ ॥

cūta-priyāla-panasāsana-kovidāra
jambv-arka-bilva-bakulāmra-kadamba-nīpāḥ
ye'nye parārtha-bhavakā yamunopakūlāḥ
śaṁsantu kṛṣṇa-padavīṁ rahitātmanāṁ naḥ

cūta—O mango creeper; *priyāla*—O *priyāla* tree (a kind of *śāla* tree); *panasa*—O jackfruit tree; *āsana*—O *āsana* tree (a yellow *śāla*); *kovidāra*—O *kovidāra* tree; *jambu*—O rose-apple tree; *arka*—O *arka* plant; *bilva*—O *bel*-fruit tree; *bakula*—O mimosa tree; *āmra*—O mango tree; *kadamba*—O *kadamba* tree; *nīpāḥ*—O *nīpa* (a smaller kind of *kadamba*); *ye*—who; *anye*—others; *para*—of others; *artha*—for the sake; *bhavakāḥ*—whose existence; *yamunā-upakūlāḥ*—living near the bank of the river Yamunā; *śaṁsantu*—kindly tell; *kṛṣṇa-padavīm*—the path Kṛṣṇa has taken; *rahita*—who have been deprived; *ātmanām*—of our minds; *naḥ*—to us.

TRANSLATION

O cūta, O priyāla, O panasa, āsana and kovidāra, O jambu, O arka, O bilva, bakula and āmra, O kadamba and nīpa and all you other plants and trees living by the banks of the Yamunā who have dedicated your very existence to the welfare of others, we gopīs have lost our minds, so please tell us where Kṛṣṇa has gone.

PURPORT

According to Śrīla Jīva Gosvāmī, the *cūta* is a mango creeper, whereas the *āmra* is a mango tree. He goes on to explain that the *nīpa,* though not a very prominent tree, bears large flowers, and that the *gopīs'* desperation to find Kṛṣṇa is clearly shown by the fact that they approached the insignificant *arka* plant.

Śrīla Viśvanātha Cakravartī gives the following information about Vṛndāvana's trees: "The *nīpa* is 'the dust *kadamba,*' and it has large flowers. The *kadamba* proper has smaller flowers and a very pleasant fragrance. The *kovidāra* is a particular kind of *kañcanāra* [mountain ebony tree]. Even though the *arka* plant is very insignificant, it always grows near Lord Gopīśvara [the Śiva deity in Vṛndāvana forest] because it is dear to him."

TEXT 10

किं ते कृतं क्षिति तपो बत केशवाङ्घ्रि-
स्पर्शोत्सवोत्पुलकिताङ्गरुहैर्विभासि ।
अप्यङ्घ्रिसम्भव उरुक्रमविक्रमाद् वा
आहो वराहवपुषः परिरम्भणेन ॥ १० ॥

kiṁ te kṛtaṁ kṣiti tapo bata keśavāṅghri-
sparśotsavotpulakitāṅga-nahair vibhāsi
apy aṅghri-sambhava urukrama-vikramād vā
āho varāha-vapuṣaḥ parirambhaṇena

kim—what; *te*—by you; *kṛtam*—performed; *kṣiti*—O earth; *tapaḥ*—austerity; *bata*—indeed; *keśava*—of Lord Kṛṣṇa; *aṅghri*—by the feet; *sparśa*—on account of being touched; *utsava*—due to the joyful experience; *utpulakita*—standing on end in jubilation; *aṅga-ruhaiḥ*—with your bodily hairs (the grass and growing plants on your surface); *vibhāsi*—you appear beautiful; *api*—perhaps; *aṅghri*—by the feet (of Kṛṣṇa present now on your surface); *sambhavaḥ*—generated; *urukrama*—of Lord Vāmana-deva, Lord Kṛṣṇa's dwarf incarnation, who covered the entire universe in three mighty steps; *vikramāt*—because of the stepping; *vā*—or; *āha u*—or else perhaps; *varāha*—of Lord Kṛṣṇa's incarnation as a boar; *vapuṣaḥ*—by the body; *parirambhaṇena*—because of the embrace.

TRANSLATION

O mother earth, what austerity did you perform to attain the touch of Lord Keśava's lotus feet, which has brought you such great joy that your bodily hairs are standing on end? You appear very beautiful in this

condition. Was it during the Lord's current appearance that you acquired this ecstatic symptom, or was it perhaps much earlier, when He stepped upon you in His form of the dwarf Vāmana-deva, or even earlier, when He embraced you in His form of the boar Varāhadeva?

PURPORT

Śrīla Viśvanātha Cakravartī explains the thoughts of the *gopīs* as follows: "'Perhaps the trees and plants [mentioned in the previous verses] did not hear our question because they were in trance, meditating on Lord Viṣṇu. Or perhaps, since they will not tell us where Kṛṣṇa has gone, they are hardhearted even though they live in a holy place. Anyway, what is the use of unnecessarily criticizing the residents of a holy place? We cannot tell if they really know where Kṛṣṇa has gone. So let us find someone who definitely knows where He is.' Thus the *gopīs* concluded that since Lord Kṛṣṇa had to be *somewhere* on the earth, the earth herself must know His whereabouts."

"Then the *gopīs* thought, 'Since Kṛṣṇa always walks on the earth, she is never separated from Him and thus cannot understand how much His parents, girlfriends and servants suffer in His absence. Let us ask her what austerities she has performed to gain the great fortune of being constantly touched by the feet of Lord Keśava.'"

TEXT 11

अप्येणपत्न्युपगतः प्रिययेह गात्रैस्
तन्वन् दृशां सखि सुनिर्वृतिमच्युतो वः ।
कान्तांगसंगकुचकुंकुमरञ्जितायाः
कुन्दस्रजः कुलपतेरिह वाति गन्धः ॥ ११ ॥

apy eṇa-patny upagataḥ priyayeha gātrais
tanvan dṛśāṁ sakhi su-nirvṛtim acyuto vaḥ
kāntāṅga-saṅga-kuca-kuṅkuma-rañjitāyāḥ
kunda-srajaḥ kula-pater iha vāti gandhaḥ

api—whether; *eṇa*—of the deer; *patni*—O wife; *upagataḥ*—has been encountered; *priyayā*—together with His beloved; *iha*—here; *gātraiḥ*—by His bodily limbs; *tanvan*—producing; *dṛśām*—of the eyes; *sakhi*—O friend; *su-nirvṛtim*—great pleasure; *acyutaḥ*—the infallible Lord Kṛṣṇa; *vaḥ*—your; *kāntā*—of His girlfriend; *aṅga-saṅga*—because of the physical contact; *kuca*

—on the breast; *kuṅkuma*—by the vermilion powder; *rañjitāyāḥ*—colored; *kunda*—of jasmine flowers; *srajaḥ*—of the garland; *kula*—of the group (of *gopīs*); *pateḥ*—of the master; *iha*—around here; *vāti*—is blowing; *gandhaḥ*—the fragrance.

TRANSLATION

O friend, wife of the deer, has Lord Acyuta been here with His beloved, bringing great joy to your eyes? Indeed, blowing this way is the fragrance of His garland of kunda flowers, which was smeared with the kuṅkuma from the breasts of His girlfriend when He embraced Her.

PURPORT

Śrīla Viśvanātha Cakravartī provides the following charming commentary on this verse:

"The *gopīs* spoke to a doe, 'O friend, wife of the deer, from the bliss in your clear eyes we can tell that Śrī Kṛṣṇa has expanded your joy with the beauty of His limbs, His face and so forth. You are eager to realize the ecstasy of seeing Kṛṣṇa, and thus your eyes are following Him. In fact, He is never lost to you.'

"Then the *gopīs,* seeing the doe continue to walk in her natural way, exclaimed, 'Oh, are you telling us that you have seen Kṛṣṇa? Look! As this deer walks she constantly turns her head back to us, as if to say, "I will show Him to you; just follow me and I will show you Kṛṣṇa." In this merciless Vṛndāvana, she is the only merciful person.'

"As the *gopīs* follow the doe they happen to lose sight of her, and they cry out, 'Oh, why can't we see the deer who is showing us the way to Kṛṣṇa?'

"One *gopī* suggests that Kṛṣṇa must be somewhere in the vicinity and that the deer, being afraid of Him, must have hidden herself to avoid the possible mistake of revealing His presence. Conjecturing in this way, the *gopīs* detect a fragrance that has by chance blown their way, and they repeatedly declare with great joy, 'Yes! Yes! This is it! By Kṛṣṇa's physical contact with His girlfriend, His jasmine garland was smeared with the *kuṅkuma* powder on Her breasts, and the fragrances of all these things are reaching us.' Thus the *gopīs* smelled the aroma of the two lovers' bodies, of Kṛṣṇa's jasmine garland, and of the cosmetic powder on the breasts of His lover."

TEXT 12

बाहुं प्रियांस उपधाय गृहीतपद्मो
रामानुजस्तुलसिकालिकुलैर्मदान्धैः ।

अन्वीयमान इह वस्तरवः प्रणामं
किं वाभिनन्दति चरन् प्रणयावलोकैः ॥ १२ ॥

bāhuṁ priyāṁsa upadhāya gṛhīta-padmo
rāmānujas tulasikāli-kulair madāndhaiḥ
anvīyamāna iha vas taravaḥ praṇāmaṁ
kiṁ vābhinandati caran praṇayāvalokaiḥ

bāhum—His arm; *priyā*—of His beloved; *aṁse*—on the shoulder; *upadhāya*—placing; *gṛhīta*—holding; *padmaḥ*—a lotus; *rāma-anujaḥ*—Kṛṣṇa, the younger brother of Balarāma; *tulasikā*—swarming around the *tulasī mañjarīs* (which are ornamenting His garland); *ali-kulaiḥ*—by the many bees; *mada*—with intoxication; *andhaiḥ*—who are blind; *anvīyamānaḥ*—being followed; *iha*—here; *vaḥ*—your; *taravaḥ*—O trees; *praṇāmam*—the bowing down; *kim vā*—whether; *abhinandati*—has acknowledged; *caran*—while walking by; *praṇaya*—imbued with love; *avalokaiḥ*—with His glances.

TRANSLATION

O trees, we see that you are bowing down. When the younger brother of Rāma walked by here, followed by intoxicated bees swarming around the tulasī mañjarīs decorating His garland, did He acknowledge your obeisances with His affectionate glances? He must have been resting His arm on the shoulder of His beloved and carrying a lotus flower in His free hand.

PURPORT

The *gopīs* saw that the trees, bent over with abundant fruits and flowers, were offering obeisances to Lord Kṛṣṇa. The *gopīs* supposed Kṛṣṇa must have recently passed that way, since the trees were still bowing down. Because Śrī Kṛṣṇa had left the *gopīs* to go with His favorite consort, they were jealous and thus imagined that He had become fatigued from His loving affairs and was resting His left arm on the soft shoulder of His beloved. The *gopīs* further imagined that Kṛṣṇa must have been carrying a blue lotus in His right hand to drive away the bees eagerly trying to attack His beloved's face after smelling its aroma. The scene was so beautiful, the *gopīs* imagined, that the maddened bees had left the *tulasī* garden to follow the two lovers.

TEXT 13

पृच्छतेमा लता बाहूनप्याश्लिष्टा वनस्पतेः ।
नूनं तत्करजस्पृष्टा बिभ्रत्युत्पुलकान्यहो ॥ १३ ॥

pṛcchatemā latā bāhūn
apy āśliṣṭā vanaspateḥ
nūnaṁ tat-karaja-spṛṣṭā
bibhraty utpulakāny aho

pṛcchata—just ask; *imāḥ*—from these; *latāḥ*—creepers; *bāhūn*—the arms (branches); *api*—even though; *āśliṣṭāḥ*—embracing; *vanaspateḥ*—of the tree; *nūnam*—certainly; *tat*—of Him, Kṛṣṇa; *kara-ja*—by the fingernails; *spṛṣṭāḥ*—touched; *bibhrati*—they are bearing; *utpulakāni*—joyful eruptions on the skin; *aho*—just see.

TRANSLATION

Let us ask these creepers about Kṛṣṇa. Even though they are embracing the arms of their husband, this tree, they certainly must have been touched by Kṛṣṇa's fingernails, since out of joy they are manifesting eruptions on their skin.

PURPORT

The *gopīs* reasoned that the creepers would not show signs of rapture merely by physical contact with their husband, a tree. Thus the *gopīs* concluded that although the creepers were embracing the strong limbs of their husband, they must have been touched by Lord Kṛṣṇa as He moved through the forest.

TEXT 14

इत्युन्मत्तवचो गोप्यः कृष्णान्वेषणकातराः ।
लीला भगवतस्तास्ता ह्यनुचक्रुस्तदात्मिकाः ॥ १४ ॥

ity unmatta-vaco gopyaḥ
kṛṣṇānveṣaṇa-kātarāḥ
līlā bhagavatas tās tā
hy anucakrus tad-ātmikāḥ

iti—thus; *unmatta*—maddened; *vacaḥ*—speaking words; *gopyaḥ*—the *gopīs; kṛṣṇa-anveṣaṇa*—by searching for Kṛṣṇa; *kātarāḥ*—distraught; *līlāḥ*

—the transcendental pastimes; *bhagavataḥ*—of Him, the Supreme Personality of Godhead; *tāḥ tāḥ*—each of them; *hi*—indeed; *anucakruḥ*—they acted out; *tat-ātmikāḥ*—becoming absorbed in thought of Him.

TRANSLATION

Having spoken these words, the gopīs, distraught from searching for Kṛṣṇa, began to act out His various pastimes, fully absorbed in thoughts of Him.

TEXT 15

कस्याचित्पूतनायन्त्याः कृष्णायन्त्यपिबत्स्तनम् ।
तोकयित्वा रुदत्यन्या पदाहन् शकटायतीम् ॥ १५ ॥

kasyācit pūtanāyantyāḥ
kṛṣṇāyanty apibat stanam
tokayitvā rudaty anyā
padāhan śakaṭāyatīm

kasyācit—of one of the *gopīs; pūtanāyantyāḥ*—who was acting like the witch Pūtanā; *kṛṣṇāyantī*—another, who was acting like Kṛṣṇa; *apibat*—drank; *stanam*—from the breast; *tokayitvā*—acting like an infant; *rudatī*—crying; *anyā*—another; *padā*—with her foot; *ahan*—struck; *śakaṭā-yatīm*—another, who was imitating a cart.

TRANSLATION

One gopī imitated Pūtanā, while another acted like infant Kṛṣṇa and pretended to suck her breast. Another gopī, crying in imitation of infant Kṛṣṇa, kicked a gopī who was taking the role of the cart demon, Śakaṭāsura.

TEXT 16

दैत्यायित्वा जहारान्यामेको कृष्णार्भभावनाम् ।
रिंगयामास काप्यङ्घ्री कर्षन्ती घोषनिःस्वनैः ॥ १६ ॥

daityāyitvā jahārānyām
eko kṛṣṇārbha-bhāvanām
riṅgayām āsa kāpy aṅghrī
karṣantī ghoṣa-niḥsvanaiḥ

daityāyitvā—imitating a demon (namely Tṛṇāvarta); *jahāra*—carried away; *anyām*—another *gopī; ekā*—one *gopī; kṛṣṇa-arbha*—of the infant Kṛṣṇa; *bhāvanām*—who was assuming the mood; *riṅgayām āsa*—crawled about; *kā api*—one of them; *aṅghrī*—her two feet; *karṣantī*—dragging; *ghoṣa*—of tinkling bells; *niḥsvanaiḥ*—with the sounding.

TRANSLATION

One gopī took the role of Tṛṇāvarta and carried away another, who was acting like infant Kṛṣṇa, while yet another gopī crawled about, her ankle bells tinkling as she pulled her feet.

PURPORT

The *gopīs* started imitating all of Śrī Kṛṣṇa's pastimes, beginning from His earliest activities as a baby.

TEXT 17

कृष्णरामायिते द्वे तु गोपायन्त्यश्च काश्चन ।
वत्सायतीं हन्ति चान्या तत्रैका तु बकायतीम् ॥ १७ ॥

kṛṣṇa-rāmāyite dve tu
gopāyantyaś ca kāścana
vatsāyatīṁ hanti cānyā
tatraikā tu bakāyatīm

kṛṣṇa-rāmāyite—acting like Lord Kṛṣṇa and Lord Balarāma; *dve*—two *gopīs; tu*—and; *gopāyantyaḥ*—acting like Their cowherd boyfriends; *ca*—and; *kāścana*—some; *vatsāyatīm*—who was imitating the calf demon, Vatsāsura; *hanti*—killed; *ca*—and; *anyā*—another; *tatra*—there; *ekā*—one; *tu*—moreover; *bakāyatīm*—another, who was imitating the crane demon, Bakāsura.

TRANSLATION

Two gopīs acted like Rāma and Kṛṣṇa in the midst of several others, who took the role of cowherd boys. One gopī enacted Kṛṣṇa's killing of the demon Vatsāsura, represented by another gopī, and a pair of gopīs acted out the killing of Bakāsura.

TEXT 18

आहूय दूरगा यद्वत्कृष्णस्तमनुवर्ततीम् ।
वेणुं क्वणन्तीं क्रीडन्तीमन्याः शंसन्ति साध्विति ॥ १८ ॥

āhūya dūra-gā yadvat
kṛṣṇas tam anuvartatīm
veṇuṁ kvaṇantīṁ krīḍantīm
anyāḥ śaṁsanti sādhv iti

āhūya—calling; *dūra*—who were far away; *gāḥ*—the cows; *yadvat*—just as; *kṛṣṇaḥ*—Kṛṣṇa; *tam*—him; *anuvartatīm*—one *gopī* who was imitating; *veṇum*—the flute; *kvaṇantīm*—vibrating; *krīḍantīm*—playing games; *anyāḥ*—the other *gopīs; śaṁsanti*—praised; *sādhu iti*—"excellent!"

TRANSLATION

When one gopī perfectly imitated how Kṛṣṇa would call the cows who had wandered far away, how He would play His flute and how He would engage in various sports, the others congratulated her with exclamations of "Well done! Well done!"

TEXT 19

कस्याञ्चित्स्वभुजं न्यस्य
चलन्त्याहापरा ननु ।
कृष्णोऽहं पश्यत गतिं
ललितामिति तन्मनाः ॥ १९ ॥

kasyāñcit sva-bhujaṁ nyasya
calanty āhāparā nanu
kṛṣṇo 'haṁ paśyata gatiṁ
lalitām iti tan-manāḥ

kasyāñcit—of one of them; *sva-bhujam*—her arm; *nyasya*—placing (on the shoulder); *calantī*—walking about; *āha*—stated; *aparā*—another; *nanu*—indeed; *kṛṣṇaḥ*—Kṛṣṇa; *aham*—I am; *paśyata*—just see; *gatim*—my movements; *lalitām*—graceful; *iti*—with these words; *tat*—in Him; *manāḥ*—with her mind fully absorbed.

TRANSLATION

Another gopī, her mind fixed on Kṛṣṇa, walked about with her arm resting on the shoulder of a friend and declared, "I am Kṛṣṇa! Just see how gracefully I move!"

TEXT 20

मा भैष्ट वातवर्षाभ्यां तत्त्राणं विहितं मया ।
इत्युक्त्वैकेन हस्तेन यतन्त्युन्निदधेऽम्बरम् ॥ २० ॥

mā bhaiṣṭa vāta-varṣābhyāṁ
tat-trāṇaṁ vihitaṁ mayā
ity uktvaikena hastena
yatanty unnidadhe'mbaram

mā bhaiṣṭa—don't any of you fear; *vāta*—the wind; *varṣābhyām*—and rain; *tat*—from that; *trāṇam*—your deliverance; *vihitam*—has been arranged; *mayā*—by me; *iti*—thus; *uktvā*—speaking; *ekena*—with one; *hastena*—hand; *yatantī*—endeavoring; *unnidadhe*—she lifted; *ambaram*—her upper garment.

TRANSLATION

"Don't be afraid of the wind and rain," said one gopī. "I will save you." And with that she lifted her shawl above her head.

PURPORT

Here a *gopī* enacts Lord Kṛṣṇa's pastime of lifting Govardhana Hill.

TEXT 21

आरुह्यैका पदाक्रम्य शिरस्याहापरां नृप ।
दुष्टाहे गच्छ जातोऽहं खलानां ननु दण्डकृत् ॥ २१ ॥

āruhyaikā padākramya
śirasy āhāparāṁ nṛpa
duṣṭāhe gaccha jāto'haṁ
khalānām nanu daṇḍa-kṛt

āruhya—rising up; *ekā*—one of the *gopīs; padā*—with her foot; *ākramya*—climbing above; *śirasi*—the head; *āha*—said; *aparām*—to another; *nṛpa*—O King (Parīkṣit); *duṣṭa*—wicked; *ahe*—O snake; *gaccha*—go away; *jātaḥ*—have taken birth; *aham*—I; *khalānām*—on those who are envious; *nanu*—indeed; *daṇḍa*—of punishment; *kṛt*—as the imposer.

TRANSLATION

[Śukadeva Gosvāmī continued:] O King, one gopī climbed on another's shoulders and, putting her foot on the other's head, said, "Go away from here, O wicked snake! You should know that I have taken birth in this world just to punish the envious."

PURPORT

Here the *gopīs* enact Kṛṣṇa's chastisement of Kāliya.

TEXT 22

तत्रैकोवाच हे गोपा दावाग्निं पश्यतोल्बणम् ।
चक्षूंष्याश्वपिदध्वं वो विधास्ये क्षेममञ्जसा ॥ २२ ॥

tatraikovāca he gopā
dāvāgniṁ paśyatolbaṇam
cakṣūṁṣy āśv apidadhvaṁ vo
vidhāsye kṣemam añjasā

tatra—there; *ekā*—one of them; *uvāca*—said; *he gopāḥ*—O cowherd boys; *dāva-agnim*—the forest fire; *paśyata*—see; *ulbaṇam*—fierce: *cakṣūṁṣi*—your eyes; *āśu*—quickly; *apidadhvam*—just close; *vaḥ*—your; *vidhāsye*—I will arrange; *kṣemam*—protection; *añjasā*—with ease.

TRANSLATION

Then another gopī spoke up: My dear cowherd boys, look at this raging forest fire! Quickly close your eyes and I will easily protect you.

TEXT 23

बद्धान्यया स्रजा काचित्तन्वी तत्र उलूखले ।
बध्नामि भाण्डभेत्तारं हैयंगवमुषं त्विति ।
भीता सुदृक् पिधायास्यं भेजे भीतिविडम्बनम् ॥ २३ ॥

baddhānyayā srajā kācit
tanvī tatra ulūkhale
badhnāmi bhāṇḍa-bhettāraṁ
haiyaṅgava-muṣaṁ tv iti
bhītā su-dṛk pidhāyāsyaṁ
bheje bhīti-viḍambanam

baddhā—tied up; *anyayā*—by another *gopī; srajā*—with a flower garland; *kācit*—one *gopī; tanvī*—slender; *tatra*—there; *ulūkhale*—to the grinding mortar; *badhnāmi*—I am binding; *bhāṇḍa*—of the storage pots; *bhettāram*—the breaker; *haiyam-gava*—of the butter saved from the previous day's milk; *muṣam*—the stealer; *tu*—indeed; *iti*—thus speaking; *bhītā*—afraid; *su-dṛk*—with beautiful eyes; *pidhāya*—covering; *āsyam*—her face; *bheje*—assumed; *bhīti*—of fear; *viḍambanam*—the pretense.

TRANSLATION

One gopī tied up her slender companion with a flower garland and said, "Now I will bind this boy who has broken the butter pots and stolen the butter." The second gopī then covered her face and beautiful eyes, pretending to be afraid.

TEXT 24

एवं कृष्णं पृच्छमाना वृन्दावनलतास्तरून् ।
व्यचक्षत वनोद्देशे पदानि परमात्मनः ॥ २४ ॥

evaṁ kṛṣṇaṁ pṛcchamānā
vṛndāvana-latās tarūn
vyacakṣata vanoddeśe
padāni paramātmanaḥ

evam—in this manner; *kṛṣṇam*—about Kṛṣṇa; *pṛcchamānāḥ*—inquiring; *vṛndāvana*—of the Vṛndāvana forest; *latāḥ*—from the creepers; *tarūn*—and the trees; *vyacakṣata*—they saw; *vana*—of the forest; *uddeśe*—in one spot; *padāni*—the footprints; *parama-ātmanaḥ*—of the Supersoul.

TRANSLATION

While the gopīs were thus imitating Kṛṣṇa's pastimes and asking Vṛndāvana's creepers and trees where Kṛṣṇa, the Supreme Soul, might be, they happened to see His footprints in a corner of the forest.

TEXT 25

पदानि व्यक्तमेतानि नन्दसूनोर्महात्मनः ।
लक्ष्यन्ते हि ध्वजाम्भोजवज्रांकुशयवादिभिः ॥ २५ ॥

padāni vyaktam etāni
nanda-sūnor mahātmanaḥ
lakṣyante hi dhvajāmbhoja-
vajrāṅkuśa-yavādibhiḥ

padāni—the footprints; *vyaktam*—clearly; *etāni*—these; *nanda-sūnoḥ*—of the son of Nanda Mahārāja; *mahā-ātmanaḥ*—the great soul; *lakṣyante*—are ascertained; *hi*—indeed; *dhvaja*—by the flag; *ambhoja*—lotus; *vajra*—thunderbolt; *aṅkuśa*—elephant goad; *yava-ādibhiḥ*—barleycorn, etc.

TRANSLATION

[The gopīs said:] The marks of a flag, lotus, thunderbolt, elephant goad, barleycorn and so forth on these footprints clearly distinguish them as belonging to that great soul, the son of Nanda Mahārāja.

PURPORT

Śrīla Viśvanātha Cakravartī Ṭhākura, in his commentary on this verse, gives the following scriptural information about the symbolic markings on the lotus feet of Kṛṣṇa:

"In the following verses the *Skanda Purāṇa* states the particular places on His feet where Kṛṣṇa carries the mark of the flag and also other marks, and the reasons for these marks:

dakṣiṇasya padāṅguṣṭha-
mūle cakraṁ bibharty ajaḥ
tatra bhakta-janasyāri-
ṣaḍ-varga-cchedanāya saḥ

'At the base of the large toe on His right foot, the unborn Lord carries the mark of a disc, which cuts down the six [mental] enemies of His devotees.'

madhyamāṅguli-mūle ca
dhatte kamalam acyutaḥ
dhyātṛ-citta-dvirephāṇāṁ
lobhanāyāti-śobhanām

'At the bottom of the middle toe of that same foot Lord Acyuta has a lotus flower, which increases the greed for Him in the minds of the beelike devotees who meditate on His feet.'

kaniṣṭha-mūlato vajraṁ
bhakta-pāpādri-bhedanam
pārṣṇi-madhye'ṅkuśaṁ bhakta
cittebha-vaśa-kāriṇam

'At the base of His small toe is a thunderbolt, which smashes the mountains of His devotees' reactions to past sins, and in the middle of His heel is the mark of an elephant goad, which brings the elephants of His devotees' minds under control.'

bhoga-sampan-mayaṁ dhatte
yavam aṅguṣṭha-parvaṇi

'The joint of His right large toe bears the mark of a barleycorn, representing all kinds of enjoyable opulences.'

"The *Skanda Purāṇa* also states:

vajraṁ vai dakṣiṇe pārśve
aṅkuśo vai tad-agrataḥ

'A thunderbolt is found on the right side of His right foot, and an elephant goad below that.'

"The *ācāryas* of the Vaiṣṇava *sampradāya* explain that since the particular feet under discussion are Lord Kṛṣṇa's, we should know that the thunderbolt is at the base of His small toe and the elephant goad below the thunderbolt. An elephant goad on the heel belongs rather to Lord Nārāyaṇa and other *viṣṇu-tattva* expansions.

"Thus the *Skanda Purāṇa* describes six marks on Kṛṣṇa's right foot—the disc, flag, lotus, thunderbolt, elephant goad and barleycorn. And the *Vaiṣṇava-toṣaṇī* mentions even more marks—a vertical line beginning at the middle of His foot and continuing as far as the juncture between His big toe and second toe; an umbrella below the disc; at the base of the middle of His foot, a group of four *svastikas* in the four cardinal directions; at the four points where each *svastika* meets the next, four rose apples; and in the middle of the *svastikas,* an octagon. This makes eleven marks on Kṛṣṇa's right foot."

Śrīla Viśvanātha Cakravartī describes the marks on Kṛṣṇa's left foot as follows: "At the base of the large toe is a conchshell with its mouth facing the toe. At the base of the middle toe are two concentric circles, representing the inner and outer sky. Below this mark is Cupid's unstrung bow, at the base of the bow is a triangle, and surrounding the triangle is a group of four waterpots. At the base of the triangle is a half-moon with two more triangles touching its points, and below the half-moon is a fish.

"All together, then, there are nineteen distinguishing marks on the soles of Lord Kṛṣṇa's lotus feet."

TEXT 26

तैस्तैः पदैस्तत्पदवीमन्विच्छन्त्योऽग्रतोऽबलाः ।
वध्वाः पदैः सुपृक्तानि विलोक्यार्ताः समब्रुवन् ॥ २६ ॥

tais taiḥ padais tat-padavīm
anvicchantyo'grato 'balāḥ
vadhvāḥ padaiḥ su-pṛktāni
vilokyārtāḥ samabruvan

taiḥ taiḥ—by those various; *padaiḥ*—footprints; *tat*—His; *padavīm*—path; *anvicchantyaḥ*—tracing out; *agrataḥ*—forward; *abalāḥ*—the girls; *vadhvāḥ*—of His special consort; *padaiḥ*—with the footprints; *supṛktāni*—thoroughly intermingled; *vilokya*—noticing; *ārtāḥ*—distressed; *samabruvan*—they spoke.

TRANSLATION

The gopīs began following Kṛṣṇa's path, as shown by His many footprints, but when they saw that these prints were thoroughly intermixed with those of His dearmost consort, they became perturbed and spoke as follows.

TEXT 27

कस्याः पदानि चैतानि याताया नन्दसूनुना ।
अंसन्यस्तप्रकोष्ठायाः करेणोः करिणा यथा ॥ २७ ॥

kasyāḥ padāni caitāni
yātāyā nanda-sūnunā
aṁsa-nyasta-prakoṣṭhāyāḥ
kareṇoḥ kariṇā yathā

kasyāḥ—of one certain *gopī; padāni*—the footprints; *ca*—also; *etāni*—these; *yātāyāḥ*—who was going; *nanda-sūnunā*—together with the son of Nanda Mahārāja; *aṁsa*—upon whose shoulder; *nyasta*—placed; *prakoṣṭhāyāḥ*—His forearm; *kareṇoḥ*—of a she-elephant; *kariṇā*—by the he-elephant; *yathā*—as.

TRANSLATION

[The gopīs said:] Here we see the footprints of some gopī who must have been walking along with the son of Nanda Mahārāja. He must have put His arm on Her shoulder, just as an elephant rests His trunk on the shoulder of an accompanying she-elephant.

TEXT 28

अनयाराधितो नूनं भगवान् हरिरीश्वरः ।
यन् नो विहाय गोविन्दः प्रीतो यामनयद् रहः ॥ २८ ॥

anayārādhito nūnaṁ
bhagavān harir īśvaraḥ
yan no vihāya govindaḥ
prīto yām anayad rahaḥ

anayā—by Her; *ārādhitaḥ*—perfectly worshiped; *nūnam*—certainly; *bhagavān*—the Personality of Godhead; *hariḥ*—Lord Kṛṣṇa; *īśvaraḥ*—the supreme controller; *yat*—inasmuch as; *naḥ*—us; *vihāya*—rejecting; *govindaḥ*—Lord Govinda; *prītaḥ*—pleased; *yām*—whom; *anayat*—led; *rahaḥ*—to a secluded place.

TRANSLATION

Certainly this particular gopī has perfectly worshiped the all-powerful Personality of Godhead, Govinda, since He was so pleased with Her that He abandoned the rest of us and brought Her to a secluded place.

PURPORT

Śrīla Viśvanātha Cakravartī explains that the word *ārādhitaḥ* refers to Śrīmatī Rādhārāṇī. He comments, "The sage Śukadeva Gosvāmī has tried with all endeavor to keep Her name hidden, but now it automatically shines forth from the moon of his mouth. That he has spoken Her name is indeed Her mercy, and thus the word *ārādhitaḥ* is like the rumbling of a kettledrum sounded to announce Her great good fortune."

Although the *gopīs* spoke as if jealous of Śrīmatī Rādhārāṇī, they were actually ecstatic to see that She had captured Śrī Kṛṣṇa.

Śrīla Viśvanātha Cakravartī quotes the following detailed description of Śrīmatī Rādhārāṇī's footprints, as given by Śrīla Rūpa Gosvāmī in his *Śrī Ujjvala-nīlamaṇi:* "At the base of the large toe of Her left foot is the mark of a barleycorn, below that mark is a disc, below the disc is an umbrella, and below the umbrella is a bracelet. A vertical line extends from the middle of Her foot to the juncture of Her large and second toes. At the base of the middle toe is a lotus, below that is a flag with a banner, and below the flag is a creeper, together with a flower. At the base of Her small toe is an elephant goad, and upon Her heel is a half-moon. Thus there are eleven marks on Her left foot."

"At the base of the large toe of Her right foot is a conchshell, and below that a spear. At the base of the small toe of Her right foot is a sacrificial altar, below that an earring, and below the earring a spear. Along the base of the second, third, fourth and small toes is the mark of a mountain, below which is a chariot, and on the heel is a fish."

"Thus all together there are nineteen distinguishing marks on the soles of Śrīmatī Rādhārāṇī's lotus feet."

TEXT 29

धन्या अहो अमी आल्यो गोविन्दाङ्घ्र्यब्जरेणवः ।
यान् ब्रह्मेशौ रमा देवी दधुर्मूर्ध्न्यघनुत्तये ॥ २९ ॥

dhanyā aho amī ālyo
govindāṅghry-abja-reṇavaḥ
yān brahmeśau ramā devī
dadhur mūrdhny agha-nuttaye

dhanyāḥ—sanctified; *aho*—ah; *amī*—these; *ālyaḥ*—O *gopīs; govinda*—of Govinda; *aṅghri-abja*—of the lotuslike feet; *reṇavaḥ*—the particles of dust; *yān*—which; *brahmā*—Lord Brahmā; *īśau*—and Lord Śiva; *ramā devī*—Ramādevī, the wife of Lord Viṣṇu; *dadhuḥ*—take; *mūrdhni*—on their heads; *agha*—of their sinful reactions; *nuttaye*—for the dispelling.

TRANSLATION

O girls! The dust of Govinda's lotus feet is so sacred that even Brahmā, Śiva and the goddess Ramā take that dust upon their heads to dispel sinful reactions.

PURPORT

According to Śrīla Viśvanātha Cakravartī, who quotes from *śāstra,* each day in the late afternoon, as Kṛṣṇa returned from the cow pastures with His cowherd boyfriends, great demigods like Brahmā and Śiva would come down from heaven and take the dust of His feet.

Great personalities like the goddess Ramā (the wife of Viṣṇu), Śiva and Brahmā are not at all sinful. But in the ecstasy of pure Kṛṣṇa consciousness they feel themselves fallen and impure. Thus, desiring to purify themselves, they blissfully take the dust of the Lord's lotus feet on their heads.

TEXT 30

तस्या अमूनि नः क्षोभं कुर्वन्त्युच्चैः पदानि यत्
यैकापहृत्य गोपीनां रहो भुंक्तेऽच्युताधरम् ।
न लक्ष्यन्ते पदान्यत्र तस्या नूनं तृणांकुरैः
खिद्यत्सुजाताङ्घ्रितलामुन्निन्ये प्रेयसीं प्रियः ॥ ३० ॥

tasyā amūni naḥ kṣobhaṁ
kurvanty uccaiḥ padāni yat
yaikāpahṛtya gopīnāṁ
raho bhuṅkte'cyutādharam

na lakṣyante padāny atra
tasyā nūnaṁ tṛṇāṅkuraiḥ
khidyat-sujātāṅghri-talām
unninye preyasīṁ priyaḥ

tasyāḥ—of Her; *amūni*—these; *naḥ*—for us; *kṣobham*—agitation; *kurvanti*—create; *uccaiḥ*—exceedingly; *padāni*—the footprints; *yat*—because; *yā*—who; *ekā*—alone; *apahṛtya*—being taken aside; *gopīnām*—of all the *gopīs; rahaḥ*—in seclusion; *bhuṅkte*—She enjoys; *acyuta*—of Kṛṣṇa; *adharam*—the lips; *na lakṣyante*—are not seen; *padāni*—the feet; *atra*—here; *tasyāḥ*—Her; *nūnam*—certainly; *tṛṇa*—by the blades of grass; *aṅkuraiḥ*—and the growing sprouts; *khidyat*—being caused pain; *sujāta*—tender; *aṅghri*—of whose feet; *talām*—the soles; *unninye*—He has lifted up; *preyasīm*—His beloved; *priyaḥ*—Her dear Kṛṣṇa.

TRANSLATION

These footprints of that special gopī greatly disturb us. Of all the gopīs, She alone was taken away to a secluded place, where She is enjoying the lips of Kṛṣṇa. Look, we can't see Her footprints over here! It's obvious that the grass and sprouts were hurting the tender soles of Her feet, and so the lover lifted up His beloved.

TEXT 31

इमान्यधिकमग्नानि पदानि वहतो वधूम् ।
गोप्यः पश्यत कृष्णस्य भाराक्रान्तस्य कामिनः ।
अत्रावरोपिता कान्ता पुष्पहेतोर्महात्मना ॥ ३१ ॥

imāny adhika-magnāni
padāni vahato vadhūm
gopyaḥ paśyata kṛṣṇasya
bhārākrāntasya kāminaḥ
atrāvaropitā kāntā
puṣpa-hetor mahātmanā

imāni—these; *adhika*—very much; *magnāni*—merged; *padāni*—footprints; *vahataḥ*—of Him who was carrying; *vadhūm*—His consort; *gopyaḥ*—O *gopīs; paśyata*—just see; *kṛṣṇasya*—of Kṛṣṇa; *bhāra*—by the weight; *ākrāntasya*—oppressed; *kāminaḥ*—lusty; *atra*—in this place; *avaropitā*—placed down; *kāntā*—the girlfriend; *puṣpa*—of (gathering) flowers; *hetoḥ*—for the purpose; *mahā-ātmanā*—by the very intelligent.

TRANSLATION

Please observe, my dear gopīs, how in this place lusty Kṛṣṇa's footprints are pressed more deeply into the ground. Carrying the weight of His beloved must have been difficult for Him. And over here that intelligent boy must have put Her down to gather some flowers.

PURPORT

The word *vadhūm* indicates that even though Śrī Kṛṣṇa was not officially married to Rādhārāṇī, He had in fact made Her His bride in the Vṛndāvana forest.

According to Śrīla Viśvanātha Cakravartī Ṭhākura, the *gopīs* use the word *kāminaḥ* here to indicate the following thoughts: "We actually love Śrī Kṛṣṇa, but still He has rejected us. Therefore His private dealings with Rādhārāṇī prove that this young prince of Vraja has carried Her away because of lust. If He were interested in love, He would have accepted us instead of that cowherd girl Rādhārāṇī."

These thoughts reveal the mood of the *gopīs* who are rivals of Śrīmatī Rādhārāṇī. Of course, the *gopīs* who are Her direct allies were jubilant to see Her good fortune.

TEXT 32

अत्र प्रसूनावचयः प्रियार्थे प्रेयसा कृतः ।
प्रपदाक्रमण एते पश्यतासकले पदे ॥ ३२ ॥

atra prasūnāvacayaḥ
priyārthe preyasā kṛtaḥ
prapadākramaṇa ete
paśyatāsakale pade

atra—here; *prasūna*—of flowers; *avacayaḥ*—the gathering; *priyā-arthe*—for the sake of His beloved; *preyasā*—by the beloved Kṛṣṇa; *kṛtaḥ*—done; *prapada*—front of His feet; *ākramaṇe*—with the pressing down; *ete*—these; *paśyata*—just see; *asakale*—incomplete; *pade*—the pair of footprints.

TRANSLATION

Just see how in this place dear Kṛṣṇa collected flowers for His beloved. Here He has left the impression of only the front part of His feet because He was standing on His toes to reach the flowers.

TEXT 33

केशप्रसाधनं त्वत्र कामिन्याः कामिना कृतम् ।
तानि चूडयता कान्तामुपविष्टमिह ध्रुवम् ॥ ३३ ॥

keśa-prasādhanaṁ tv atra
kāminyāḥ kāminā kṛtam
tāni cūḍayatā kāntām
upaviṣṭam iha dhruvam

keśa—of Her hair; *prasādhanam*—the decorative arrangement; *tu*—furthermore; *atra*—here; *kāminyāḥ*—of the lusty girl; *kāminā*—by the lusty boy; *kṛtam*—done; *tāni*—with those (flowers); *cūḍayatā*—by Him who was making a crown; *kāntām*—His consort; *upaviṣṭam*—seated; *iha*—here; *dhruvam*—certainly.

TRANSLATION

Certainly Kṛṣṇa sat down here with His girlfriend to arrange Her hair. The lusty boy must have made a crown for that lusty girl out of the flowers He had collected.

PURPORT

The *ācāryas* explain that Śrī Kṛṣṇa wanted to decorate Rādhārāṇī's hair with the forest flowers He had collected. Therefore They sat down together facing the same direction, with Rādhārāṇī between Kṛṣṇa's knees, and Kṛṣṇa proceeded to arrange Her hair with flowers and make a flower crown for Her, coronating Her as the goddess of the forest. Thus the romantic young boy and girl played and joked together in Vṛndāvana.

TEXT 34

रेमे तया चात्मरत आत्मारामोऽप्यखण्डितः ।
कामिनां दर्शयन् दैन्यं स्त्रीणां चैव दुरात्मताम् ॥ ३४ ॥

reme tayā cātma-rata
ātmārāmo'py akhaṇḍitaḥ
kāminām̐ darśayan dainyam̐
strīṇām̐ caiva durātmatām

reme—He enjoyed; *tayā*—with Her; *ca*—and; *ātma-rataḥ*—He who takes pleasure only within Himself; *ātma-ārāmaḥ*—completely self-satisfied; *api*—although; *akhaṇḍitaḥ*—never incomplete; *kāminām*—of ordinary lusty men; *darśayan*—showing; *dainyam*—the degraded condition; *strīṇām*—of ordinary women; *ca eva*—also; *durātmatām*—the hardheartedness.

TRANSLATION

[Śukadeva Gosvāmī continued:] Lord Kṛṣṇa enjoyed with that gopī, although He enjoys only within, being self-satisfied and complete in Himself. Thus by contrast He showed the wretchedness of ordinary lusty men and hardhearted women.

PURPORT

This verse directly refutes the superficial criticism materialistic people sometimes direct against Lord Kṛṣṇa's pastimes. The philosopher Aristotle claimed that ordinary activities are unworthy of God, and with this idea in mind some people declare that since the activities of Lord Kṛṣṇa resemble those of ordinary human beings, He cannot be the Absolute Truth.

But in this verse Śukadeva Gosvāmī emphatically points out that Lord Kṛṣṇa acts on the liberated platform of spiritual self-satisfaction. This fact is indicated here by the terms *ātma-rata, ātmārāma* and *akhaṇḍita.* It is inconceivable to ordinary people that a handsome young boy and a beautiful young girl enjoying romantic conjugal affairs in the forest moonlight can be engaging in pure activity, free from egoistic desire and lust. Yet while Lord Kṛṣṇa is inconceivable to ordinary persons, those who love Him can easily realize the absolute, pure nature of His activities.

One may argue that "beauty is in the eye of the beholder" and that therefore the devotees of Kṛṣṇa are only imagining the Lord's activities to be pure. This argument ignores many significant facts. For one, the path of Kṛṣṇa consciousness, of developing love for Kṛṣṇa, demands that a devotee strictly follow four regulative principles: no illicit sex, no gambling, no intoxication and no eating of meat, fish or eggs. When one is freed from material lust and rises to the liberated platform, beyond material desire, one realizes the absolute beauty of Lord Kṛṣṇa. This process is not theoretical: it has been practiced and completed by many thousands of great sages, who have left us their shining example and their brilliant teachings concerning the path of Kṛṣṇa consciousness.

Certainly beauty is in the eye of the beholder. However, real beauty is perceived by the soul's eye and not by the lusty eye of the material body. Therefore the Vedic literature repeatedly stresses that only those freed from material desire can see the beauty of Lord Kṛṣṇa with the eye of the pure soul, anointed with love of Godhead. It may finally be noted that upon realizing the pastimes of Lord Kṛṣṇa one becomes free of all tinges of sex desire, a state of mind that can hardly result from meditating upon material sexual affairs.

One final note: The conjugal pastimes of Kṛṣṇa perfectly round out His qualification as the Supreme Absolute Truth. The *Vedānta* states that the Absolute Truth is the source of everything, so certainly the Absolute cannot lack any of the beautiful things of this world. It is only because romantic affairs exist in a pure, spiritual form in the Absolute that they can manifest in a perverted, material form in this world. Thus the apparent beauty of this world is not to be absolutely rejected; rather, beauty should be accepted in its pure, spiritual form.

Since the beginning of time men and women have been inspired to poetic rapture by the art of romance. Unfortunately, romance in this world usually leads to crushing disappointment, brought about by a change of heart or by death. Thus although we may at first find romantic affairs beautiful and enjoyable, they are eventually spoiled by the onslaught of material nature. Still, it is unreasonable to totally reject the concept of romance. Rather, we should accept conjugal attraction in its absolute, perfect, pure form, as it exists within God, without a tinge of material lust or selfishness. That pure conjugal attraction—the supreme beauty and pleasure of the Supreme Truth—is what we are reading about here in the pages of *Śrīmad-Bhāgavatam.*

TEXTS 35–36

इत्येवं दर्शयन्त्यस्ताश्चेरुर्गोप्यो विचेतसः ।
यां गोपीमनयत्कृष्णो विहायान्याः स्त्रियो वने ॥ ३५ ॥
सा च मेने तदात्मानं वरिष्ठं सर्वयोषिताम् ।
हित्वा गोपीः कामयाना मामसौ भजते प्रियः ॥ ३६ ॥

ity evaṁ darśayantyas tāś
cerur gopyo vicetasaḥ
yāṁ gopīm anayat kṛṣṇo
vihāyānyāḥ striyo vane

sā ca mene tadātmānaṁ
variṣṭhaṁ sarva-yoṣitām
hitvā gopīḥ kāma-yānā
mām asau bhajate priyaḥ

iti—thus; *evam*—in this manner; *darśayantyaḥ*—showing; *tāḥ*—they; *ceruḥ*—wandered; *gopyaḥ*—the *gopīs; vicetasaḥ*—completely bewildered; *yām*—which; *gopīm*—*gopī; anayat*—He took; *kṛṣṇaḥ*—Lord Kṛṣṇa; *vihāya*—abandoning; *anyāḥ*—the other; *striyaḥ*—women; *vane*—in the forest; *sā*—She; *ca*—also; *mene*—thought; *tadā*—then; *ātmānam*—Herself; *variṣṭham*—the best; *sarva*—of all; *yoṣitām*—women; *hitvā*—rejecting; *gopīḥ*—the *gopīs; kāma-yānāḥ*—who are impelled by lusty desire; *mām*—Me; *asau*—He; *bhajate*—is accepting; *priyaḥ*—the beloved.

TRANSLATION

As the gopīs wandered about, their minds completely bewildered, they pointed out various signs of Kṛṣṇa's pastimes. The particular gopī whom Kṛṣṇa had led into a secluded forest when He had abandoned all the other young girls began to think Herself the best of women. "My beloved has rejected all the other gopīs," She thought, "even though they are driven by Cupid himself. He has chosen to reciprocate with Me alone."

PURPORT

Previously all the *gopīs* had become proud of their association with Kṛṣṇa and then suddenly lost His association. Only Rādhārāṇī remained with Him. Now She has also become proud of that association and will suffer a similar fate. The Lord arranges all this to reveal the *gopīs'* unparalleled devotion for Him, a devotion whose intensity fully manifests in moments of separation.

TEXT 37

ततो गत्वा वनोद्देशं दृप्ता केशवमब्रवीत् ।
न पारयेऽहं चलितुं नय मां यत्र ते मनः ॥ ३७ ॥

tato gatvā vanoddeśaṁ
dṛptā keśavam abravīt
na pāraye'haṁ calituṁ
naya māṁ yatra te manaḥ

tataḥ—then; *gatvā*—going; *vana*—of the forest; *uddeśam*—to one region; *dṛptā*—becoming proud; *keśavam*—to Kṛṣṇa; *abravīt*—She said; *na pāraye*—am not able; *aham*—I; *calitum*—to move; *naya*—bring; *mām*—Me; *yatra*—where; *te*—Your; *manaḥ*—mind.

TRANSLATION

As the two lovers passed through one part of the Vṛndāvana forest, the special gopī began feeling proud of Herself. She told Lord Keśava, "I cannot walk any further. Please carry Me wherever You want to go."

TEXT 38

एवमुक्तः प्रियामाह स्कन्ध आरुह्यतामिति ।
ततश्चान्तर्दधे कृष्णः सा वधूरन्वतप्यत ॥ ३८ ॥

evam uktaḥ priyām āha
skandha āruhyatām iti
tataś cāntardadhe kṛṣṇaḥ
sā vadhūr anvatapyata

evam—thus; *uktaḥ*—addressed; *priyām*—to His beloved; *āha*—He said; *skandhe*—on My shoulder; *āruhyatām*—please climb; *iti*—these words; *tataḥ*—then; *ca*—and; *antardadhe*—He disappeared; *kṛṣṇaḥ*—Lord Śrī Kṛṣṇa; *sā*—She; *vadhūḥ*—His consort; *anvatapyata*—felt remorse.

TRANSLATION

Thus addressed, Lord Kṛṣṇa replied, "Just climb on My shoulder." But as soon as He said this, He disappeared. His beloved consort then immediately felt great remorse.

PURPORT

Śrīmatī Rādhārāṇī was exhibiting the pride of a beautiful girl who has brought Her boyfriend under control. Thus She told Kṛṣṇa, "Please carry Me wherever You want to go. I can't walk anymore." Śrī Kṛṣṇa now disappears from Her sight, intensifying Her ecstatic love more and more.

TEXT 39

हा नाथ रमण प्रेष्ठ क्वासि क्वासि महाभुज ।
दास्यास्ते कृपणाया मे सखे दर्शय सन्निधिम् ॥ ३९ ॥

hā nātha ramaṇa preṣṭha
kvāsi kvāsi mahā-bhuja
dāsyās te kṛpaṇāyā me
sakhe darśaya sannidhim

hā—O; *nātha*—master; *ramaṇa*—lover; *preṣṭha*—dearmost; *kva asi kva asi*—where are You, where are You; *mahā-bhuja*—O mighty-armed one; *dāsyāḥ*—to the maidservant; *te*—Your; *kṛpaṇāyāḥ*—wretched; *me*—Me; *sakhe*—O friend; *darśaya*—please show; *sannidhim*—Your presence.

TRANSLATION

She cried out: O master! My lover! O dearmost, where are You? Where are You? Please, O mighty-armed one, O friend, show Yourself to Me, Your poor servant!

PURPORT

Śrīla Viśvanātha Cakravartī Ṭhākura describes the following moving exchange:

"Rādhā says, 'My Lord, I am being burned in the great fire of separation from You, and My life air is about to leave My body. Even with the greatest endeavor I cannot maintain My life. But You are the Lord of My life, and so You can quickly save Me simply by glancing upon Me. Please do so immediately. I beg You to save My life, not for My sake but rather for Yours. After giving up all the other *gopīs,* You've brought Me so far to a secluded place in the forest just to enjoy special pleasure with Me. If I die You will not be able to find conjugal happiness anywhere else. You will remember Me and thus lament in Your sorrow.'

"Kṛṣṇa replies, 'So let Me become unhappy. What does that matter to You?'

"'But You are most dear to Me. I will feel Your unhappiness millions of times more than You. Even if I've already died, I still will not be able to tolerate the pain that even one spot on the nails of Your lotus feet may experience. Indeed, to prevent such pain I am ready to throw My life away millions and millions of times. So kindly show Yourself and drive away that unhappiness.'

"'But if Your life air is on the verge of leaving Your body, what can I do to stop that?'

"'Simply by the touch of Your arms, which are a medicinal herb with the power to revive the dead, My body will return to its healthy, normal condition, and My life air will automatically come back and remain in My body.'

"'But You know the forest path Yourself without My help, so why did You order Me, the king's son and a very young and gentle boy who is to be respected? Why did You command, "Take Me wherever You wish"? Why do You anger Me like this?'

"Rādhā cries out, 'Please show Yourself to Your wretched maidservant. Be merciful to Me! Be merciful! When I ordered You, I was overcome by sleepiness. I was so tired from playing with You. Therefore please excuse what Your poor servant said. Please don't be angry. It was only because You treated Me like such a close friend, though I am unworthy, that I spoke like that to You.'

"'All right, My love, I am very pleased with You, so please come to Me.'

"'But I've been blinded by lamentation. I can't see where You are. Please tell Me where You are.'"

TEXT 40

श्रीशुक उवाच
अन्विच्छन्त्यो भगवतो मार्गं गोप्योऽविदूरितः ।
ददृशुः प्रियविश्लेषान्मोहितां दुःखितां सखीम् ॥ ४० ॥

śrī-śuka uvāca
anvicchantyo bhagavato
mārgaṁ gopyo 'vidūritaḥ
dadṛśuḥ priya-viśleṣān
mohitāṁ duḥkhitāṁ sakhīm

śrī-śukaḥ uvāca—Śrī Śukadeva Gosvāmī said; *anvicchantyaḥ*—searching out; *bhagavataḥ*—of the Supreme Personality of Godhead; *mārgam*—the path; *gopyaḥ*—the *gopīs; avidūritaḥ*—not far away; *dadṛśuḥ*—saw; *priya*—from Her beloved; *viśleṣāt*—because of the separation; *mohitām*—bewildered; *duḥkhitām*—unhappy; *sakhīm*—their friend.

TRANSLATION

Śukadeva Gosvāmī said: While continuing to search out Kṛṣṇa's path, the gopīs discovered their unhappy friend close by. She was bewildered by separation from Her lover.

TEXT 41

तया कथितमाकर्ण्य मानप्राप्तिं च माधवात् ।
अवमानं च दौरात्म्याद् विस्मयं परमं ययुः ॥ ४१ ॥

tayā kathitam ākarṇya
māna-prāptiṁ ca mādhavāt
avamānaṁ ca daurātmyād
vismayaṁ paramaṁ yayuḥ

tayā—by Her; *kathitam*—what was related; *ākarṇya*—hearing; *māna*—of respect; *prāptim*—the receiving; *ca*—and; *mādhavāt*—from Lord Kṛṣṇa;

avamānam—the dishonor; *ca*—also; *daurātmyāt*—because of Her impropriety; *vismayam*—amazement; *paramam*—supreme; *yayuḥ*—they experienced.

TRANSLATION

She told them how Mādhava had given Her much respect, but how She then suffered dishonor because of Her misbehavior. The gopīs were extremely amazed to hear this.

PURPORT

It was natural for Rādhārāṇī to ask Kṛṣṇa to carry Her, for this request was consistent with the loving mood of Their relationship. Now, however, in great humility She describes Her behavior as wicked. Hearing of these affairs, the other *gopīs* are astonished.

TEXT 42

ततोऽविशन् वनं चन्द्रज्योत्स्ना यावद् विभाव्यते ।
तमः प्रविष्टमालक्ष्य ततो निववृतुः स्त्रियः ॥ ४२ ॥

tato'viśan vanaṁ candra
jyotsnā yāvad vibhāvyate
tamaḥ praviṣṭam ālakṣya
tato nivavṛtuḥ striyaḥ

tataḥ—then; *aviśan*—they entered; *vanam*—the forest; *candra*—of the moon; *jyotsnā*—the light; *yāvat*—as far; *vibhāvyate*—as was visible; *tamaḥ*—darkness; *praviṣṭam*—entered; *ālakṣya*—noticing; *tataḥ*—thereupon; *nivavṛtuḥ*—they desisted; *striyaḥ*—the women.

TRANSLATION

In search of Kṛṣṇa, the gopīs then entered the depths of the forest as far as the light of the moon shone. But when they found themselves engulfed in darkness, they decided to turn back.

PURPORT

The *gopīs* entered a part of the forest so dense that even the light of the full moon couldn't penetrate it. This scene is also described in the *Viṣṇu Purāṇa:*

praviṣṭo gahanaṁ kṛṣṇaḥ
padam atra na lakṣyate
nivartadhvaṁ śaśāṅkasya
naitad dīdhiti-gocaraḥ

"One *gopī* said, 'Kṛṣṇa has entered such a dark part of the forest that we cannot possibly see His footprints. Therefore let us turn back from this area, which even the light of the moon cannot reach.'"

TEXT 43

तन्मनस्कास्तदालापास्तद्विचेष्टास्तदात्मिकाः ।
तद्गुणानेव गायन्त्यो नात्मगाराणि सस्मरुः ॥ ४३ ॥

tan-manaskās tad-ālāpās
tad-viceṣṭās tad-ātmikāḥ
tad-guṇān eva gāyantyo
nātmāgārāṇi sasmaruḥ

tat-manaskāḥ—their minds filled with thoughts of Him; *tat-ālāpāḥ*—conversing about Him; *tat-viceṣṭāḥ*—imitating His activities; *tat-ātmikāḥ*—filled with His presence; *tat-guṇān*—about His qualities; *eva*—simply; *gāyantyaḥ*—singing; *na*—not; *ātma*—their own; *āgārāṇi*—homes; *sasmaruḥ*—remembered.

TRANSLATION

Their minds absorbed in thoughts of Him, they conversed about Him, acted out His pastimes and felt themselves filled with His presence. They completely forgot about their homes as they loudly sang the glories of Kṛṣṇa's transcendental qualities.

PURPORT

Actually there is no separation from Kṛṣṇa for the pure devotees of the Lord. Although apparently abandoned by Kṛṣṇa, the *gopīs* were actually tightly connected to Him by the spiritual process of *śravaṇaṁ kīrtanaṁ viṣṇoḥ,* hearing and chanting the glories of the Lord.

TEXT 44

पुनः पुलिनमागत्य कालिन्द्याः कृष्णभावनाः ।
समवेता जगुः कृष्णं तदागमनकाङ्क्षिताः ॥ ४४ ॥

punaḥ pulinam āgatya
kālindyāḥ kṛṣṇa-bhāvanāḥ
samavetā jaguḥ kṛṣṇaṁ
tad-āgamana-kāṅkṣitāḥ

punaḥ—again; *pulinam*—to the bank; *āgatya*—coming; *kālindyāḥ*—of the river Yamunā; *kṛṣṇa-bhāvanāḥ*—meditating on Kṛṣṇa; *samavetāḥ*—joined together; *jaguḥ*—they sang; *kṛṣṇam*—about Kṛṣṇa; *tat-āgamana*—His arrival; *kāṅkṣitāḥ*—eagerly desired.

TRANSLATION

The gopīs again came to the bank of the Kālindī. Meditating on Kṛṣṇa and eagerly hoping He would come, they sat down together to sing of Him.

PURPORT

As stated in the *Kaṭha Upaniṣad* (1.2.23), *yam evaiṣa vṛṇute tena labhyaḥ:* "The Supersoul can be realized by that person whom He chooses." Thus the *gopīs* fervently pray that Kṛṣṇa come back to them.

Thus end the purports of the humble servants of His Divine Grace A.C. Bhaktivedanta Swami Prabhupāda to the Tenth Canto, Thirtieth Chapter, of the Śrīmad-Bhāgavatam, *entitled "The Gopīs Search for Kṛṣṇa."*

CHAPTER THIRTY-ONE

The Gopīs' Songs of Separation

This chapter relates how the *gopīs,* overwhelmed by feelings of separation from Kṛṣṇa, sat down on the bank of the Yamunā and began praying for His audience and singing His glories.

Because the *gopīs* had dedicated their minds and very lives to Kṛṣṇa, they were beside themselves with the transcendental pain of separation. But their crying, which appears like evidence of misery, actually shows their exalted state of transcendental bliss. As it is said, *yata dekha vaiṣṇaver vyavahāra duḥkh niścaya jāniha sei paramānanda sukh.* "Whenever one sees a Vaiṣṇava acting unhappy, one should know it for sure that he is actually experiencing the highest spiritual bliss." Thus each of the *gopīs* began addressing Lord Śrī Kṛṣṇa according to her individual mode of ecstasy, and they all prayed for Him for His mercy.

As the pastimes of Kṛṣṇa spontaneously arose in the minds of the *gopīs,* they sang their song, which relieves the agony of those suffering from the burning pain of separation from Kṛṣṇa and which bestows supreme auspiciousness. They sang, "O Lord, O lover, O cheater, when we remember Your smile, Your loving glances and Your pastimes with Your boyhood friends, we become extremely agitated. Remembering Your lotus face, adorned with locks of blackish hair smeared with the dust of the cows, we become irrevocably attached to You. And when we remember how You followed the cows from forest to forest with Your tender feet, we feel great pain."

In their separation from Kṛṣṇa the *gopīs* considered a single moment an entire age. Even when they had previously seen Him they had found the blinking of their eyelids intolerable, for it blocked their vision of Him for a fraction of a second.

The ecstatic sentiments for Lord Kṛṣṇa that the *gopīs* expressed may appear like symptoms of lust, but in reality they are manifestations of their pure desire to satisfy the Supreme Lord's spiritual senses. There is not even the slightest trace of lust in these moods of the *gopīs.*

TEXT 1

गोप्य ऊचुः
जयति तेऽधिकं जन्मना व्रजः
श्रयत इन्दिरा शश्वदत्र हि ।
दयित दृश्यतां दिक्षु तावकास्
त्वयि धृतासवस्त्वां विचिन्वते ॥ १ ॥

gopya ūcuḥ
jayati te'dhikaṁ janmanā vrajaḥ
śrayata indirā śaśvad atra hi
dayita dṛśyatāṁ dikṣu tāvakās
tvayi dhṛtāsavas tvāṁ vicinvate

gopyaḥ ūcuḥ—the *gopīs* said; *jayati*—is glorious; *te*—Your; *adhikam*—exceedingly; *janmanā*—by the birth; *vrajaḥ*—the land of Vraja; *śrayate*—is residing; *indirā*—Lakṣmī, the goddess of fortune; *śaśvat*—perpetually; *atra*—here; *hi*—indeed; *dayita*—O beloved; *dṛśyatām*—may (You) be seen; *dikṣu*—in all directions; *tāvakāḥ*—Your (devotees); *tvayi*—for Your sake; *dhṛta*—sustained; *asavaḥ*—their life airs; *tvām*—for You; *vicinvate*—they are searching.

TRANSLATION

The gopīs said: O beloved, Your birth in the land of Vraja has made it exceedingly glorious, and thus Indirā, the goddess of fortune, always resides here. It is only for Your sake that we, Your devoted servants, maintain our lives. We have been searching everywhere for You, so please show Yourself to us.

PURPORT

Those who are familiar with the art of chanting Sanskrit verses will be able to appreciate the especially exquisite Sanskrit poetry of this chapter. Specifically, the poetic meter of the verses is extraordinarily beautiful, and also, for the most part, in each line the first and seventh syllables begin with the same consonant, as do the second syllables of all four lines.

TEXT 2

शरदुदाशये साधुजातसत्-
सरसिजोदरश्रीमुषा दृशा ।

सुरतनाथ तेऽशुल्कदासिका
वरद निघ्नतो नेह किं वधः ॥ २ ॥

śarad-udāśaye sādhu-jāta-sat-
sarasijodara-śrī-muṣā dṛśā
surata-nātha te'śulka-dāsikā
vara-da nighnato neha kiṁ vadhaḥ

śarat—of the autumn season; *uda-āśaye*—in the reservoir of water; *sādhu*—excellently; *jāta*—grown; *sat*—fine; *sarasi-ja*—of the lotus flowers; *udara*—in the middle; *śrī*—the beauty; *muṣā*—which excels; *dṛśā*—with Your glance; *surata-nātha*—O Lord of love; *te*—Your; *aśulka*—acquired without payment; *dāsikāḥ*—maidservants; *vara-da*—O giver of benedictions; *nighnataḥ*—for You who are killing; *na*—not; *iha*—in this world; *kim*—why; *vadhaḥ*—murder.

TRANSLATION

O Lord of love, in beauty Your glance excels the whorl of the finest, most perfectly formed lotus within the autumn pond. O bestower of benedictions, You are killing the maidservants who have given themselves to You freely, without any price. Isn't this murder?

PURPORT

In the autumn season, the whorl of the lotus has a special beauty, but that unique loveliness is surpassed by the beauty of Kṛṣṇa's glance.

TEXT 3

विषजलाप्ययाद् व्यालराक्षसाद्
वर्षमारुताद्वैद्युतानलात् ।
वृषमयात्मजाद्विश्वतो भयाद्
ऋषभ ते वयं रक्षिता मुहुः ॥ ३ ॥

viṣa-jalāpyayād vyāla-rākṣasād
varṣa-mārutād vaidyutānalāt
vṛṣa-mayātmajād viśvato bhayād
ṛṣabha te vayaṁ rakṣitā muhuḥ

viṣa—poisonous; *jala*—by the water (of the Yamunā, contaminated by Kāliya); *apyayāt*—from destruction; *vyāla*—fearsome; *rākṣasāt*—from the demon (Agha); *varṣa*—from rain (sent by Indra); *mārutāt*—and the windstorm (created by Tṛṇāvarta); *vaidyuta-analāt*—from the thunderbolt (of Indra); *vṛṣa*—from the bull, Ariṣṭāsura; *maya-ātmajāt*—from the son of Maya (Vyomāsura); *viśvataḥ*—from all; *bhayāt*—fear; *ṛṣabha*—O greatest of personalities; *te*—by You; *vayam*—we; *rakṣitāḥ*—have been protected; *muhuḥ*—repeatedly.

TRANSLATION

O greatest of personalities, You have repeatedly saved us from all kinds of danger—from poisoned water, from the terrible man-eater Agha, from the great rains, from the wind demon, from the fiery thunderbolt of Indra, from the bull demon and from the son of Maya Dānava.

PURPORT

Here the *gopīs* imply, "O Kṛṣṇa, You saved us from so many terrible dangers, so now that we are dying of separation from You, won't You save us again?" Śrīla Viśvanātha Cakravartī Ṭhākura explains that the *gopīs* mention Ariṣṭa and Vyoma because, although Kṛṣṇa had not yet killed these demons, the fact that He would kill them in the future was well known, having been predicted by the sages Garga and Bhāguri at the time of the Lord's birth.

TEXT 4

न खलु गोपीकानन्दनो भवान्
अखिलदेहिनामन्तरात्मदृक् ।
विखनसार्थितो विश्वगुप्तये
सख उदेयिवान् सात्वतां कुले ॥ ४ ॥

na khalu gopikā-nandano bhavān
akhila-dehinām antarātma-dṛk
vikhanasārthito viśva-guptaye
sakha udeyivān sātvatāṁ kule

na—not; *khalu*—indeed; *gopikā*—of the *gopī*, Yaśodā; *nandanaḥ*—the son; *bhavān*—Your good self; *akhila*—of all; *dehinām*—embodied living entities; *antaḥ-ātma*—of the inner consciousness; *dṛk*—the seer; *vikhanasā*—by Lord Brahmā; *arthitaḥ*—prayed for; *viśva*—of the universe; *guptaye*—for the protection; *sakhe*—O friend; *udeyivān*—You arose; *sātvatām*—of the Sātvatas; *kule*—in the dynasty.

TRANSLATION

You are not actually the son of the gopī Yaśodā, O friend, but rather the indwelling witness in the hearts of all embodied souls. Because Lord Brahmā prayed for You to come and protect the universe, You have now appeared in the Sātvata dynasty.

PURPORT

The *gopīs* here imply, "Since You have descended to protect the entire universe, how can You neglect Your own devotees?"

TEXT 5

विरचिताभयं वृष्णिधूर्य ते
चरणमीयुषां संसृतेर्भयात् ।
करसरोरुहं कान्त कामदं
शिरसि धेहि नः श्रीकरग्रहम् ॥ ५ ॥

viracitābhayaṁ vṛṣṇi-dhūrya te
caraṇam īyuṣāṁ saṁsṛter bhayāt
kara-saroruhaṁ kānta kāma-daṁ
śirasi dhehi naḥ śrī-kara-graham

viracita—created; *abhayam*—fearlessness; *vṛṣṇi*—of the Vṛṣṇi dynasty; *dhūrya*—O best; *te*—Your; *caraṇam*—feet; *īyuṣām*—of those who approach; *saṁsṛteḥ*—of material existence; *bhayāt*—out of fear; *kara*—Your hand; *saraḥ-ruham*—like a lotus flower; *kānta*—O lover; *kāma*—desires; *dam*—fulfilling; *śirasi*—on the heads; *dhehi*—please place; *naḥ*—of us; *śrī*—of the goddess of fortune, Lakṣmīdevī; *kara*—the hand; *graham*—taking.

TRANSLATION

O best of the Vṛṣṇis, Your lotuslike hand, which holds the hand of the goddess of fortune, grants fearlessness to those who approach Your feet out of fear of material existence. O lover, please place that wish-fulfilling lotus hand on our heads.

TEXT 6

व्रजजनार्तिहन् वीर योषितां
निजजनस्मयध्वंसनस्मित ।

भज सखे भवत्किंकरीः स्म नो
जलरुहाननं चारु दर्शय ॥ ६ ॥

vraja-janārti-han vīra yoṣitāṁ
nija-jana-smaya-dhvaṁsana-smita
bhaja sakhe bhavat-kiṅkarīḥ sma no
jalaruhānanaṁ cāru darśaya

vraja-jana—of the people of Vraja; *ārti*—of the suffering; *han*—O destroyer; *vīra*—O hero; *yoṣitām*—of women; *nija*—Your own; *jana*—of the people; *smaya*—the pride; *dhvaṁsana*—destroying; *smita*—whose smile; *bhaja*—please accept; *sakhe*—O friend; *bhavat*—Your; *kiṅkarīḥ*—maidservants; *sma*—indeed; *naḥ*—us; *jala-ruha*—lotus; *ānanam*—Your face; *cāru*—beautiful; *darśaya*—please show.

TRANSLATION

O You who destroy the suffering of Vraja's people, O hero of all women, Your smile shatters the false pride of Your devotees. Please, dear friend, accept us as Your maidservants and show us Your beautiful lotus face.

TEXT 7

प्रणतदेहिनां पापकर्षणं
तृणचरानुगं श्रीनिकेतनम् ।
फणिफणार्पितं ते पदाम्बुजं
कृणु कुचेषु नः कृन्धि हृच्छयम् ॥ ७ ॥

praṇata-dehināṁ pāpa-karṣaṇaṁ
tṛṇa-carānugaṁ śrī-niketanam
phaṇi-phaṇārpitaṁ te padāmbujaṁ
kṛṇu kuceṣu naḥ kṛndhi hṛc-chayam

praṇata—who are surrendered to You; *dehinām*—of the embodied living beings; *pāpa*—the sins; *karṣaṇam*—which remove; *tṛṇa*—grass; *cara*—who graze (the cows); *anugam*—following; *śrī*—of the goddess of fortune; *niketanam*—the abode; *phaṇi*—of the serpent (Kāliya); *phaṇā*—on the hoods; *arpitam*—placed; *te*—Your; *pada-ambujam*—lotus feet; *kṛṇu*—please put; *kuceṣu*—on the breasts; *naḥ*—our; *kṛndhi*—cut away; *hṛt-śayam*—the lust in our hearts.

TRANSLATION

Your lotus feet destroy the past sins of all embodied souls who surrender to them. Those feet follow after the cows in the pastures and are the eternal abode of the goddess of fortune. Since You once put those feet on the hoods of the great serpent Kāliya, please place them upon our breasts and tear away the lust in our hearts.

PURPORT

In their appeal, the *gopīs* point out that Lord Kṛṣṇa's lotus feet destroy the sins of all surrendered conditioned souls. The Lord is so merciful that He even goes out to herd the cows in the pasturing ground, and thus His lotus feet follow them about in the grass. He has offered His lotus feet to the goddess of fortune and has placed them upon the hoods of the serpent Kāliya. Therefore, considering all this, the Lord should place His lotus feet on the *gopīs'* breasts and satisfy their desire. That is the logic the *gopīs* employ here.

TEXT 8

मधुरया गिरा वल्गुवाक्यया
बुधमनोज्ञया पुष्करेक्षण ।
विधिकरीरिमा वीर मुह्यतीर्
अधरसीधुनाप्याययस्व नः ॥ ८ ॥

madhurayā girā valgu-vākyayā
budha-manojñayā puṣkarekṣaṇa
vidhi-karīr imā vīra muhyatīr
adhara-sīdhunāpyāyayasva naḥ

madhurayā—sweet; *girā*—by Your voice; *valgu*—charming; *vākyayā*—by Your words; *budha*—to the intelligent; *mano-jñayā*—attractive; *puṣkara*—lotus; *īkṣaṇa*—You whose eyes; *vidhi-karīḥ*—maidservants; *imāḥ*—these; *vīra*—O hero; *muhyatīḥ*—becoming bewildered; *adhara*—of Your lips; *sīdhunā*—with the nectar; *āpyāyayasva*—please restore to life; *naḥ*—us.

TRANSLATION

O lotus-eyed one, Your sweet voice and charming words, which attract the minds of the intelligent, are bewildering us more and more. Our dear hero, please revive Your maidservants with the nectar of Your lips.

TEXT 9

तव कथामृतं तप्तजीवनं
कविभिरीडितं कल्मषापहम् ।
श्रवणमंगलं श्रीमदाततं
भुवि गृणन्ति ये भूरिदा जनाः ॥ ९ ॥

tava kathāmṛtaṁ tapta-jīvanaṁ
kavibhir īḍitaṁ kalmaṣāpaham
śravaṇa-maṅgalaṁ śrīmad ātataṁ
bhuvi gṛṇanti ye bhūri-dā janāḥ

tava—Your; *kathā-amṛtam*—the nectar of words; *tapta-jīvanam*—life for those aggrieved in the material world; *kavibhiḥ*—by great thinkers; *īḍitam*—described; *kalmaṣa-apaham*—that which drives away sinful reactions; *śravaṇa-maṅgalam*—giving spiritual benefit when heard; *śrīmat*—filled with spiritual power; *ātatam*—broadcast all over the world; *bhuvi*—in the material world; *gṛṇanti*—chant and spread; *ye*—those who; *bhūri-dāḥ*—most beneficent; *janāḥ*—persons.

TRANSLATION

The nectar of Your words and the descriptions of Your activities are the life and soul of those suffering in this material world. These narrations, transmitted by learned sages, eradicate one's sinful reactions and bestow good fortune upon whoever hears them. These narrations are broadcast all over the world and are filled with spiritual power. Certainly those who spread the message of Godhead are most munificent.

PURPORT

King Pratāparudra recited this verse to Śrī Caitanya Mahāprabhu during Lord Jagannātha's Ratha-yātrā festival. While the Lord was resting in a garden, King Pratāparudra humbly entered and began massaging His legs and lotus feet. Then the King recited the Thirty-first Chapter of the Tenth Canto of the *Śrīmad-Bhāgavatam,* the songs of the *gopīs.* The *Caitanya-caritāmṛta* relates that when Lord Caitanya heard this verse, beginning *tava kathāmṛtam,* He immediately arose in ecstatic love and embraced King Pratāparudra. The incident is described in detail in the *Caitanya-caritāmṛta* (*Madhya* 14.4–18), and in his edition Śrīla Prabhupāda has given extensive commentary on it.

TEXT 10

प्रहसितं प्रिय प्रेमवीक्षणं
विहरणं च ते ध्यानमंगलम् ।
रहसि संविदो या हृदि स्पृशः
कुहक नो मनः क्षोभयन्ति हि ॥ १० ॥

prahasitaṁ priya-prema-vīkṣaṇaṁ
viharaṇaṁ ca te dhyāna-maṅgalam
rahasi saṁvido yā hṛdi spṛśaḥ
kuhaka no manaḥ kṣobhayanti hi

prahasitam—the smiling; *priya*—affectionate; *prema*—with love; *vīkṣaṇam*—glances; *viharaṇam*—intimate pastimes; *ca*—and; *te*—Your; *dhyāna*—by meditation; *maṅgalam*—auspicious; *rahasi*—in solitary places; *saṁvidaḥ*—conversations; *yāḥ*—which; *hṛdi*—the heart; *spṛśaḥ*—touching; *kuhaka*—O cheater; *naḥ*—our; *manaḥ*—minds; *kṣobhayanti*—agitate; *hi*—indeed.

TRANSLATION

Your smiles, Your sweet, loving glances, the intimate pastimes and confidential talks we enjoyed with You—all these are auspicious to meditate upon, and they touch our hearts. But at the same time, O deceiver, they very much agitate our minds.

TEXT 11

चलसि यद् व्रजाच्चारयन् पशून्
नलिनसुन्दरं नाथ ते पदम् ।
शिलतृणांकुरैः सीदतीति नः
कलिलतां मनः कान्त गच्छति ॥ ११ ॥

calasi yad vrajāc cārayan paśūn
nalina-sundaraṁ nātha te padam
śila-tṛṇāṅkuraiḥ sīdatīti naḥ
kalilatāṁ manaḥ kānta gacchati

calasi—You go; *yat*—when; *vrajāt*—from the cowherd village; *cārayan*—herding; *paśūn*—the animals; *nalina*—than a lotus flower; *sundaram*—

more beautiful; *nātha*—O master; *te*—Your; *padam*—feet; *śila*—by sharp edges of grain; *tṛṇa*—grass; *aṅkuraiḥ*—and sprouting plants; *sīdati*—are experiencing pain; *iti*—thus thinking; *naḥ*—us; *kalilatām*—discomfort; *manaḥ*—our minds; *kānta*—O lover; *gacchati*—feel.

TRANSLATION

Dear master, dear lover, when You leave the cowherd village to herd the cows, our minds are disturbed with the thought that Your feet, more beautiful than a lotus, will be pricked by the spiked husks of grain and the rough grass and plants.

TEXT 12

दिनपरिक्षये नीलकुन्तलैर्
वनरुहाननं बिभ्रदावृतम् ।
घनरजस्वलं दर्शयन्मुहुर्
मनसि नः स्मरं वीर यच्छसि ॥ १२ ॥

dina-parikṣaye nīla-kuntalair
vanaruhānanaṁ bibhrad āvṛtam
ghana-rajasvalaṁ darśayan muhur
manasi naḥ smaraṁ vīra yacchasi

dina—of the day; *parikṣaye*—at the finish; *nīla*—dark blue; *kuntalaiḥ*—with locks of hair; *vana-ruha*—lotus; *ānanam*—face; *bibhrat*—exhibiting; *āvṛtam*—covered; *ghana*—thick; *rajaḥ-valam*—smeared with dust; *darśayan*—showing; *muhuḥ*—repeatedly; *manasi*—in the minds; *naḥ*—our; *smaram*—Cupid; *vīra*—O hero; *yacchasi*—You are placing.

TRANSLATION

At the end of the day You repeatedly show us Your lotus face, covered with dark blue locks of hair and thickly powdered with dust. Thus, O hero, You arouse lusty desires in our minds.

TEXT 13

प्रणतकामदं पद्मजार्चितं
धरणिमण्डनं ध्येयमापदि ।

चरणपंकजं शन्तमं च ते
रमण नः स्तनेष्वर्पयाधिहन् ॥१३॥

praṇata-kāma-daṁ padmajārcitaṁ
dharaṇi-maṇḍanaṁ dhyeyam āpadi
caraṇa-paṅkajaṁ śantamaṁ ca te
ramaṇa naḥ staneṣv arpayādhi-han

praṇata—of those who bow down; *kāma*—the desires; *dam*—fulfilling; *padma-ja*—by Lord Brahmā; *arcitam*—worshiped; *dharaṇi*—of the earth; *maṇḍanam*—the ornament; *dhyeyam*—the proper object of meditation; *āpadi*—in time of distress; *caraṇa-paṅkajam*—the lotus feet; *śam-tamam*—giving the highest satisfaction; *ca*—and; *te*—Your; *ramaṇa*—O lover; *naḥ*—our; *staneṣu*—on the breasts; *arpaya*—please place; *ādhi-han*—O destroyer of mental distress.

TRANSLATION

Your lotus feet, which are worshiped by Lord Brahmā, fulfill the desires of all who bow down to them. They are the ornament of the earth, they give the highest satisfaction, and in times of danger they are the appropriate object of meditation. O lover, O destroyer of anxiety, please put those lotus feet upon our breasts.

TEXT 14

सुरतवर्धनं शोकनाशनं
स्वरितवेणुना सुष्ठु चुम्बितम्।
इतररागविस्मारणं नृणां
वितर वीर नस्तेऽधरामृतम् ॥१४॥

surata-vardhanaṁ śoka-nāśanaṁ
svarita-veṇunā suṣṭhu cumbitam
itara-rāga-vismāraṇaṁ nṛṇāṁ
vitara vīra nas te'dharāmṛtam

surata—conjugal happiness; *vardhanam*—which increases; *śoka*—grief; *nāśanam*—which destroys; *svarita*—vibrated; *veṇunā*—by Your flute; *suṣṭhu*—abundantly; *cumbitam*—kissed; *itara*—other; *rāga*—attachments; *vismāraṇam*—causing to forget; *nṛṇām*—men; *vitara*—please spread; *vīra*

—O hero; *naḥ*—upon us; *te*—Your; *adhara*—of the lips; *amṛtam*—the nectar.

TRANSLATION

O hero, kindly distribute to us the nectar of Your lips, which enhances conjugal pleasure and vanquishes grief. That nectar is thoroughly relished by Your vibrating flute and makes people forget any other attachment.

PURPORT

Śrīla Viśvanātha Cakravartī' s charming commentary on this verse is in the form of a dialogue between the *gopīs* and Kṛṣṇa:

"The *gopīs* say, 'O Kṛṣṇa, You exactly resemble Dhanvantari, the best of physicians. So please give us some medicine, for we are suffering from the disease of romantic desire for You. Don't hesitate to give us the medicinal nectar of Your lips freely, without our paying a substantial price. Since You are a great hero in giving charity, You should give it without any payment, even to the most wretched persons. Consider that we are losing our life and that now You can restore us to life by giving us that nectar. After all, You have already given it to Your flute, which is simply a hollow bamboo stick."

"Kṛṣṇa says, 'But the diet of people in this world is the bad one of attachment to wealth, followers, family and so forth. The particular medicine you've requested should not be given to those who have such a bad diet."

"'But this medicine makes one forget all other attachments. So wonderful is this herbal drug that it counteracts bad dietary habits. Please give that nectar to us, O hero, since You are most charitable.'"

TEXT 15

अटति यद् भवानह्नि काननं
त्रुटि युगायते त्वामपश्यताम् ।
कुटिलकुन्तलं श्रीमुखं च ते
जड उदीक्षतां पक्ष्मकृद्दृशाम् ॥ १५ ॥

aṭati yad bhavān ahni kānanaṁ
truṭi yugāyate tvām apaśyatām
kuṭila-kuntalaṁ śrī-mukhaṁ ca te
jaḍa udīkṣatāṁ pakṣma-kṛd dṛśām

aṭati—travel; *yat*—when; *bhavān*—You; *ahni*—during the daytime; *kānanam*—to the forest; *truṭi*—about 1/1700 of a second; *yugāyate*—becomes like an entire millennium; *tvām*—You; *apaśyatām*—for those who do not see; *kuṭila*—curling; *kuntalam*—with locks of hair; *śrī*—beautiful; *mukham*—face; *ca*—and; *te*—Your; *jaḍaḥ*—foolish; *udīkṣatām*—for those who are eagerly looking; *pakṣma*—of lids; *kṛt*—the creator; *dṛśām*—of the eyes.

TRANSLATION

When You go off to the forest during the day, a tiny fraction of a second becomes like a millennium for us because we cannot see You. And even when we can eagerly look upon Your beautiful face, so lovely with its adornment of curly locks, our pleasure is hindered by our eyelids, which were fashioned by the foolish creator.

TEXT 16

पतिसुतान्वयभ्रातृबान्धवान्
अतिविलङ्घ्य तेऽन्त्यच्युतागताः ।
गतिविदस्तवोद्गीतमोहिताः
कितव योषितः कस्त्यजेन्निशि ॥ १६ ॥

pati-sutānvaya-bhrātṛ-bāndhavān
ativilaṅghya te 'nty acyutāgatāḥ
gati-vidas tavodgīta-mohitāḥ
kitava yoṣitaḥ kas tyajen niśi

pati—husbands; *suta*—children; *anvaya*—ancestors; *bhrātṛ*—brothers; *bāndhavān*—and other relatives; *ativilaṅghya*—completely neglecting; *te*—Your; *anti*—into the presence; *acyuta*—O infallible one; *āgatāḥ*—having come; *gati*—of our movements; *vidaḥ*—who understand the purpose; *tava*—Your; *udgīta*—by the loud song (of the flute); *mohitāḥ*—bewildered; *kitava*—O cheater; *yoṣitaḥ*—women; *kaḥ*—who; *tyajet*—would abandon; *niśi*—in the night.

TRANSLATION

Dear Acyuta, You know very well why we have come here. Who but a cheater like You would abandon young women who come to see Him in the middle of the night, enchanted by the loud song of His flute? Just to

see You, we have completely rejected our husbands, children, ancestors, brothers and other relatives.

TEXT 17

रहसि संविदं हृच्छयोदयं
प्रहसिताननं प्रेमवीक्षणम् ।
बृहदुरः श्रियो वीक्ष्य धाम ते
मुहुरतिस्पृहा मुह्यते मनः ॥ १७ ॥

rahasi saṁvidaṁ hṛc-chayodayaṁ
prahasitānanaṁ prema-vīkṣaṇam
bṛhad-uraḥ śriyo vīkṣya dhāma te
muhur ati-spṛhā muhyate manaḥ

rahasi—in private; *saṁvidam*—confidential discussions; *hṛt-śaya*—of lust in the heart; *udayam*—the rise; *prahasita*—smiling; *ānanam*—face; *prema*—loving; *vīkṣaṇam*—glances; *bṛhat*—broad; *uraḥ*—chest; *śriyaḥ*—of the goddess of fortune; *vīkṣya*—seeing; *dhāma*—the abode; *te*—Your; *muhuḥ*—repeatedly; *ati*—excessive; *spṛhā*—hankering; *muhyate*—bewilders; *manaḥ*—the mind.

TRANSLATION

Our minds are repeatedly bewildered as we think of the intimate conversations we had with You in secret, feel the rise of lust in our hearts and remember Your smiling face, Your loving glances and Your broad chest, the resting place of the goddess of fortune. Thus we experience the most severe hankering for You.

TEXT 18

व्रजवनौकसां व्यक्तिरंग ते
वृजिनहन्त्र्यलं विश्वमंगलम् ।
त्यज मनाक् च नस्त्वत्स्पृहात्मनां
स्वजनहृद्रुजां यन्निषूदनम् ॥ १८ ॥

vraja-vanaukasāṁ vyaktir aṅga te
vṛjina-hantry alaṁ viśva-maṅgalam

tyaja manāk ca nas tvat-spṛhātmanāṁ
sva-jana-hṛd-rujāṁ yan niṣūdanam

vraja-vana—in the forests of Vraja; *okasām*—for those who dwell; *vyaktiḥ*—the appearance; *aṅga*—dear one; *te*—Your; *vṛjina*—of distress; *hantrī*—the agent of destruction; *alam*—extremely so; *viśva-maṅgalam*—all-auspicious; *tyaja*—please release; *manāk*—a little; *ca*—and; *naḥ*—to us; *tvat*—for You; *spṛhā*—with hankering; *ātmanām*—whose minds are filled; *sva*—Your own; *jana*—devotees; *hṛt*—in the hearts; *rujām*—of the disease; *yat*—which is; *niṣūdanam*—that which counteracts.

TRANSLATION

O beloved, Your all-auspicious appearance vanquishes the distress of those living in Vraja's forests. Our minds long for Your association. Please give to us just a bit of that medicine, which counteracts the disease in Your devotees' hearts.

PURPORT

According to the *ācāryas,* the *gopīs* repeatedly entreat Lord Kṛṣṇa to place His lotus feet on their breasts. The *gopīs* are not victims of material lust, but rather they are absorbed in pure love of Godhead and thus want to serve Lord Kṛṣṇa's lotus feet by offering their beautiful breasts to Him. Materialistic persons, who are victims of mundane sex desire, will not be able to understand how these conjugal dealings take place on a pure, spiritual platform, and that is the materialists' great misfortune.

TEXT 19

यत्ते सुजातचरणाम्बुरुहं स्तनेषु
भीताः शनैः प्रिय दधीमहि कर्कशेषु ।
तेनाटवीमटसि तद् व्यथते न किं स्वित्
कूर्पादिभिर्भ्रमति धीर्भवदायुषां नः ॥ १९ ॥

yat te sujāta-caraṇāmburuhaṁ staneṣu
bhītāḥ śanaiḥ priya dadhīmahi karkaśeṣu
tenāṭavīm aṭasi tad vyathate na kiṁ svit
kūrpādibhir bhramati dhīr bhavad-āyuṣāṁ naḥ

yat—which; *te*—Your; *su-jāta*—very fine; *caraṇa-ambu-ruham*—lotus feet; *staneṣu*—on the breasts; *bhītāḥ*—being afraid; *śanaiḥ*—gently; *priya*—O dear one; *dadhīmahi*—we place; *karkaśeṣu*—rough; *tena*—with them; *aṭavīm*—the forest; *aṭasi*—You roam; *tat*—they; *vyathate*—are distressed; *na*—not; *kim svit*—we wonder; *kūrpa-ādibhiḥ*—by small stones and so on; *bhramati*—flutters; *dhīḥ*—the mind; *bhavat-āyuṣām*—of those of whom Your Lordship is the very life; *naḥ*—of us.

TRANSLATION

O dearly beloved! Your lotus feet are so soft that we place them gently on our breasts, fearing that Your feet will be hurt. Our life rests only in You. Our minds, therefore, are filled with anxiety that Your tender feet might be wounded by pebbles as You roam about on the forest path.

PURPORT

The translation of this verse is from Śrīla Prabhupāda's English rendering of *Caitanya-caritāmṛta* (*Ādi* 4.173).

Thus end the purports of the humble servants of His Divine Grace A.C. Bhaktivedanta Swami Prabhupāda to the Tenth Canto, Thirty-first Chapter, of the Śrīmad-Bhāgavatam, *entitled "The Gopīs' Songs of Separation."*

CHAPTER THIRTY-TWO

The Reunion

This chapter describes how Śrī Kṛṣṇa manifested Himself in the midst of the *gopīs,* who had become extremely disturbed by their separation from Him. After He consoled them, they expressed to Him their deep feelings of ecstasy.

The *gopīs* having shown in various ways their great eagerness to see Kṛṣṇa, the attractor of Cupid, He appeared before them wearing silken yellow garments and a beautiful flower garland. Some of the *gopīs,* overwhelmed with ecstasy at seeing Him, grasped His hands, others placed His arm on their shoulders, and others accepted the remnants of betel nut He had chewed. Thus they served Him.

One *gopī,* impelled by loving anger toward Kṛṣṇa, bit her lip and looked askance at Him. Because the *gopīs* were so attached to Kṛṣṇa, they were not satiated even by continuously gazing at Him. One of them then placed Kṛṣṇa within her heart, closed her eyes and, embracing Him within herself again and again, became absorbed in transcendental bliss, just like a *yogī.* In this way the pain the *gopīs* had felt because of separation from the Lord was dispelled.

Next Lord Kṛṣṇa went to the bank of the Yamunā in the company of the cowherd girls, His internal potencies. The *gopīs* then made a seat for Kṛṣṇa out of their shawls, and after He had sat down they enjoyed with Him by gesturing amorously. The *gopīs* still felt hurt that Kṛṣṇa had disappeared, so He explained to them why He had done so. He further told them that He had come under the exclusive control of their loving devotion and would ever remain indebted to them.

TEXT 1

श्रीशुक उवाच

इति गोप्यः प्रगायन्त्यः प्रलपन्त्यश्च चित्रधा ।
रुरुदुः सुस्वरं राजन् कृष्णदर्शनलालसाः ॥१॥

śrī-śuka uvāca
iti gopyaḥ pragāyantyaḥ
pralapantyaś ca citradhā

ruruduḥ su-svaraṁ rājan
kṛṣṇa-darśana-lālasāḥ

śrī-śukaḥ uvāca—Śrī Śukadeva Gosvāmī said; *iti*—thus, as related above; *gopyaḥ*—the *gopīs; pragāyantyaḥ*—singing forth; *pralapantyaḥ*—speaking forth; *ca*—and; *citradhā*—in various charming ways; *ruruduḥ*—they cried; *su-svaram*—loudly; *rājan*—O King; *kṛṣṇa-darśana*—for the sight of Kṛṣṇa; *lālasāḥ*—hankering.

TRANSLATION

Śukadeva Gosvāmī said: O King, having thus sung and spoken their hearts out in various charming ways, the gopīs began to weep loudly. They were very eager to see Lord Kṛṣṇa.

TEXT 2

तासामाविरभूच्छौरिः स्मयमानमुखाम्बुजः ।
पीताम्बरधरः स्रग्वी साक्षान्मन्मथमन्मथः ॥ २ ॥

tāsām āvirabhūc chauriḥ
smayamāna-mukhāmbujaḥ
pītāmbara-dharaḥ sragvī
sākṣān manmatha-manmathaḥ

tāsām—before them; *āvirabhūt*—He appeared; *śauriḥ*—Lord Kṛṣṇa; *smayamāna*—smiling; *mukha*—His face; *ambujaḥ*—lotuslike; *pīta*—yellow; *ambara*—a garment; *dharaḥ*—wearing; *srak-vī*—wearing a flower garland; *sākṣāt*—directly; *man-matha*—of Cupid (who bewilders the mind); *man*—of the mind; *mathaḥ*—the bewilderer.

TRANSLATION

Then Lord Kṛṣṇa, a smile on His lotus face, appeared before the gopīs. Wearing a garland and a yellow garment, He directly appeared as one who can bewilder the mind of Cupid, who himself bewilders the minds of ordinary people.

TEXT 3

तं विलोक्यागतं प्रेष्ठं प्रीत्युत्फुल्लदृशोऽबलाः ।
उत्तस्थुर्युगपत्सर्वास्तन्वः प्राणमिवागतम् ॥ ३ ॥

taṁ vilokyāgataṁ preṣṭhaṁ
prīty-utphulla-dṛśo'balāḥ
uttasthur yugapat sarvās
tanvaḥ prāṇam ivāgatam

tam—Him; *vilokya*—seeing; *āgatam*—returned; *preṣṭham*—their dearmost; *prīti*—out of affection; *utphulla*—opening wide; *dṛśaḥ*—their eyes; *abalāḥ*—the girls; *uttasthuḥ*—they stood up; *yugapat*—all at once; *sarvāḥ*—all of them; *tanvaḥ*—of the body; *prāṇam*—the life air; *iva*—as; *āgatam*—returned.

TRANSLATION

When the gopīs saw that their dearmost Kṛṣṇa had returned to them, they all stood up at once, and out of their affection for Him their eyes bloomed wide. It was as if the air of life had reentered their bodies.

TEXT 4

काचित्कराम्बुजं शौरेर्जगृहेऽञ्जलिना मुदा ।
काचिद्दधार तद्बाहुमंसे चन्दनभूषितम् ॥ ४ ॥

kācit karāmbujaṁ śaurer
jagṛhe'ñjalinā mudā
kācid dadhāra tad-bāhum
aṁse candana-bhūṣitam

kācit—one of them; *kara-ambujam*—the lotus hand; *śaureḥ*—of Lord Kṛṣṇa; *jagṛhe*—seized; *añjalinā*—in her folded palms; *mudā*—with joy; *kācit*—another; *dadhāra*—put; *tat-bāhum*—His arm; *aṁse*—on her shoulder; *candana*—with sandalwood paste; *bhūṣitam*—adorned.

TRANSLATION

One gopī joyfully took Kṛṣṇa's hand between her folded palms, and another placed His arm, anointed with sandalwood paste, on her shoulder.

TEXT 5

काचिदञ्जलिनागृह्णात्तन्वी ताम्बूलचर्वितम् ।
एका तदङ्घ्रिकमलं सन्तप्ता स्तनयोरधात् ॥ ५ ॥

kācid añjalināgṛhṇāt
tanvī tāmbūla-carvitam
ekā tad-aṅghri-kamalaṁ
santaptā stanayor adhāt

kācit—one; *añjalinā*—with joined hands; *agṛhṇāt*—took; *tanvī*—slender; *tāmbūla*—of betel nut; *carvitam*—His chewed remnants; *ekā*—one; *tat*—His; *aṅghri*—foot; *kamalam*—lotus; *santaptā*—burning; *stanayoḥ*—on her breasts; *adhāt*—placed.

TRANSLATION

A slender gopī respectfully took in her joined hands the betel nut He had chewed, and another gopī, burning with desire, put His lotus feet on her breasts.

TEXT 6

एका भ्रुकुटिमाबध्य प्रेमसंरम्भविह्वला ।
घ्नन्तीवैक्षत्कटाक्षेपैः सन्दष्टदशनच्छदा ॥ ६ ॥

ekā bhru-kuṭim ābadhya
prema-saṁrambha-vihvalā
ghnantīvaikṣat kaṭākṣepaiḥ
sandaṣṭa-daśana-cchadā

ekā—one more *gopī; bhru-kuṭim*—her eyebrows; *ābadhya*—constricting; *prema*—of her pure love; *saṁrambha*—by the fury; *vihvalā*—beside herself; *ghnantī*—injuring; *iva*—as if; *aikṣat*—she looked; *kaṭa*—of her sidelong glances; *ākṣepaiḥ*—with the insults; *sandaṣṭa*—biting; *daśana*—of her teeth; *chadā*—the covering (her lips).

TRANSLATION

One gopī, beside herself with loving anger, bit her lips and stared at Him with frowning eyebrows, as if to wound Him with her harsh glances.

TEXT 7

अपरानिमिषद्दृग्भ्यां जुषाणा तन्मुखाम्बुजम् ।
आपीतमपि नातृप्यत्सन्तस्तच्चरणं यथा ॥ ७ ॥

aparānimiṣad-dṛgbhyāṁ
juṣāṇā tan-mukhāmbujam
āpītam api nātṛpyat
santas tac-caraṇaṁ yathā

aparā—yet another *gopī; animiṣat*—unblinking; *dṛgbhyām*—with eyes; *juṣāṇā*—relishing; *tat*—His; *mukha-ambujam*—lotus face; *āpītam*—fully tasted; *api*—although; *na atṛpyat*—She did not become satiated; *santaḥ*—mystic saints; *tat-caraṇam*—His feet; *yathā*—as.

TRANSLATION

Another gopī looked with unblinking eyes upon His lotus face, but even after deeply relishing its sweetness She did not feel satiated, just as mystic saints are never satiated when meditating upon the Lord's feet.

PURPORT

Śrīla Viśvanātha Cakravartī Ṭhākura explains that the analogy given here of saintly persons meditating upon the Lord's feet is only partially applicable, since the ecstasy the *gopīs* felt when Kṛṣṇa came back was actually unparalleled. Śrīla Viśvanātha Cakravartī also reveals that this particular *gopī* is the most fortunate of all, Śrīmatī Rādhārāṇī.

TEXT 8

तं काचिन्नेत्ररन्ध्रेण हृदि कृत्वा निमील्य च ।
पुलकांग्युपगुह्यास्ते योगीवानन्दसम्प्लुता ॥ ८ ॥

taṁ kācin netra-randhreṇa
hṛdi kṛtvā nimīlya ca
pulakāṅgy upaguhyāste
yogīvānanda-samplutā

tam—Him; *kācit*—one of them; *netra*—of her eyes; *randhreṇa*—through the aperture; *hṛdi*—in her heart; *kṛtvā*—placing; *nimīlya*—closing; *ca*—and; *pulaka-aṅgī*—the hair on her limbs standing on end; *upaguhya*—embracing; *āste*—she remained; *yogī*—a *yogī; iva*—like; *ānanda*—in ecstasy; *samplutā*—drowned.

TRANSLATION

One gopī took the Lord through the aperture of her eyes and placed Him within her heart. Then, with her eyes closed and her bodily hairs

standing on end, she continuously embraced Him within. Thus immersed in transcendental ecstasy, she resembled a yogī meditating upon the Lord.

PURPORT

Śrīla Viśvanātha Cakravartī Ṭhākura states that the seven *gopīs* mentioned so far in this chapter are the first seven of the eight principal *gopīs,* whose status allowed them to immediately approach Śrī Kṛṣṇa upon His reappearance. The *ācārya* quotes a verse from the *Śrī Vaiṣṇava-toṣaṇī* that gives the names of these seven as Candrāvalī, Śyāmalā, Śaibyā, Padmā, Śrī Rādhā, Lalitā and Viśākhā. The eighth is understood to be Bhadrā. *Śrī Vaiṣṇava-toṣaṇī* itself quotes a verse from the *Skanda Purāṇa* that declares these eight *gopīs* to be the principal among the three billion *gopīs.* Detailed information about the hierarchy of *gopīs* is available in Śrīla Rūpa Gosvāmī's *Ujjvala-nīlamaṇi.*

The *Padma Purāṇa* confirms that Śrī Rādhā is the foremost of the *gopīs:*

yathā rādhā priyā viṣṇos
tasyāḥ kuṇḍaṁ priyaṁ tathā
sarva-gopīṣu saivaikā
viṣṇor atyanta-vallabhā

"Just as Śrīmatī Rādhārāṇī is most dear to Kṛṣṇa, Her bathing pond is similarly dear. Of all the *gopīs,* She is the most beloved of the Lord."

The *Bṛhad-gautamīya-tantra* also names Śrīmatī Rādhārāṇī as Kṛṣṇa's foremost consort:

devī kṛṣṇa-mayī proktā
rādhikā para-devatā
sarva-lakṣmī-mayī sarva
kāntiḥ sammohinī parā

"The transcendental goddess Śrīmatī Rādhārāṇī is the direct counterpart of Lord Śrī Kṛṣṇa. She is the central figure for all the goddesses of fortune. She possesses all attractiveness to attract the all-attractive Personality of Godhead. She is the primeval internal potency of the Lord." (This translation is Śrīla Prabhupāda's English rendering of *Caitanya-caritāmṛta, Ādi* 4.83.)

Additional information about Śrī Rādhā is given in the *Ṛg-pariśiṣṭa* (the supplement to the *Ṛg Veda*): *rādhayā mādhavo devo mādhavenaiva rādhikā/ vibhrājante janeṣu.* "Among all persons, it is Śrī Rādhā in whose company Lord Mādhava is especially glorious, as She is especially glorious in His."

TEXT 9

सर्वास्ताः केशवालोकपरमोत्सवनिर्वृताः ।
जहुर्विरहजं तापं प्राज्ञं प्राप्य यथा जनाः ॥ ९ ॥

sarvās tāḥ keśavāloka-
paramotsava-nirvṛtāḥ
jahur viraha-jaṁ tāpaṁ
prājñaṁ prāpya yathā janāḥ

sarvāḥ—all; *tāḥ*—those *gopīs; keśava*—of Lord Kṛṣṇa; *āloka*—by the sight; *parama*—supreme; *utsava*—of festivity; *nirvṛtāḥ*—feeling joy; *jahuḥ*—they gave up; *viraha-jam*—born of their separation; *tāpam*—the distress; *prājñam*—a spiritually enlightened person; *prāpya*—achieving; *yathā*—as; *janāḥ*—people in general.

TRANSLATION

All the gopīs enjoyed the greatest festivity when they saw their beloved Keśava again. They gave up the distress of separation, just as people in general forget their misery when they gain the association of a spiritually enlightened person.

TEXT 10

ताभिर्विधूतशोकाभिर्भगवानच्युतो वृतः ।
व्यरोचताधिकं तात पुरुषः शक्तिभिर्यथा ॥ १० ॥

tābhir vidhūta-śokābhir
bhagavān acyuto vṛtaḥ
vyarocatādhikaṁ tāta
puruṣaḥ śaktibhir yathā

tābhiḥ—by these *gopīs; vidhūta*—fully cleansed; *śokābhiḥ*—of their distress; *bhagavān*—the Supreme Personality of Godhead; *acyutaḥ*—the infallible Lord; *vṛtaḥ*—surrounded; *vyarocata*—appeared brilliant; *adhikam*—exceedingly; *tāta*—my dear (King Parīkṣit); *puruṣaḥ*—the Supreme Soul; *śaktibhiḥ*—with His transcendental potencies; *yathā*—as.

TRANSLATION

Encircled by the gopīs, who were now relieved of all distress, Lord Acyuta, the Supreme Personality of Godhead, shone forth splendidly. My

dear King, Kṛṣṇa thus appeared like the Supersoul encircled by His spiritual potencies.

PURPORT

The *gopīs* are Lord Kṛṣṇa's internal potency, and therefore when they were relieved and happy again the Lord shone forth even more brilliantly than before, and His transcendental bliss increased. Kṛṣṇa loves the *gopīs* with pure transcendental love, and they love Him in the same pure way. The whole affair, conducted on the transcendental platform, is inconceivable to those bound in material existence.

TEXTS 11–12

ताः समादाय कालिन्द्या निर्विश्य पुलिनं विभुः ।
विकसत्कुन्दमन्दारसुरभ्यनिलषट्पदम् ॥ ११ ॥
शरच्चन्द्रांशुसन्दोहध्वस्तदोषातमः शिवम् ।
कृष्णाया हस्ततरलाचितकोमलवालुकम् ॥ १२ ॥

tāḥ samādāya kālindyā
nirviśya pulinaṁ vibhuḥ
vikasat-kunda-mandāra
surabhy-anila-ṣaṭpadam

śarac-candrāṁśu-sandoha-
dhvasta-doṣā-tamaḥ śivam
kṛṣṇāyā hasta-taralā
cita-komala-vālukam

tāḥ—those *gopīs; samādāya*—taking; *kālindyāḥ*—of the Yamunā; *nirviśya*—entering upon; *pulinam*—the bank; *vibhuḥ*—the almighty Supreme Lord; *vikasat*—blooming; *kunda-mandāra*—of *kunda* and *mandāra* flowers; *surabhi*—fragrant; *anila*—with the breeze; *ṣaṭ-padam*—with bees; *śarat*—autumnal; *candra*—of the moon; *aṁśu*—of the rays; *sandoha*—by the abundance; *dhvasta*—dispelled; *doṣā*—of the night; *tamaḥ*—the darkness; *śivam*—auspicious; *kṛṣṇāyāḥ*—of the river Yamunā; *hasta*—like hands; *tarala*—by her waves; *ācita*—collected; *komala*—soft; *vālukam*—sand.

TRANSLATION

The almighty Lord then took the gopīs with Him to the bank of the Kālindī, who with the hands of her waves had scattered piles of soft sand

upon the shore. In that auspicious place the breeze, bearing the fragrance of blooming kunda and mandāra flowers, attracted many bees, and the abundant rays of the autumn moon dispelled the darkness of night.

TEXT 13

तद्दर्शनाह्लादविधूतहृद्रुजो
मनोरथान्तं श्रुतयो यथा ययुः ।
स्वैरुत्तरीयैः कुचकुंकुमाकिंतैर्
अचीक्लृपन्नासनमात्मबन्धवे ॥ १३ ॥

tad-darśanāhlāda-vidhūta-hṛd-rujo
manorathāntaṁ śrutayo yathā yayuḥ
svair uttarīyaiḥ kuca-kuṅkumāṅkitair
acīklpann āsanam ātma-bandhave

tat—Him, Kṛṣṇa; *darśana*—due to seeing; *āhlāda*—by the ecstasy; *vidhūta*—driven away; *hṛt*—in their hearts; *rujaḥ*—the pain; *manaḥ-ratha*—of their desires; *antam*—the ultimate fulfillment; *śrutayaḥ*—the revealed scriptures; *yathā*—as; *yayuḥ*—they attained; *svaiḥ*—with their own; *uttarīyaiḥ*—covering garments; *kuca*—of their breasts; *kuṅkuma*—with the vermilion powder; *aṅkitaiḥ*—smeared; *acīklpan*—they arranged; *āsanam*—a seat; *ātma*—of their souls; *bandhave*—for the dear friend.

TRANSLATION

Their heartache vanquished by the ecstasy of seeing Kṛṣṇa, the gopīs, like the personified Vedas before them, felt their desires completely fulfilled. For their dear friend Kṛṣṇa they arranged a seat with their shawls, which were smeared with the kuṅkuma powder from their breasts.

PURPORT

In the Eighty-seventh Chapter of this canto (text 23), the *śrutis,* or personified *Vedas,* pray as follows:

striya uragendra-bhoga-bhuja-daṇḍa-viṣakta-dhiyo
vayam api te samāḥ samadṛśo 'ṅghri-saroja-sudhāḥ

"These women fully absorbed their minds in meditation on Lord Kṛṣṇa's powerful arms, which are like the bodies of great serpents. We want to become just like the *gopīs* and render service to His lotus feet." The *śrutis* had seen

Kṛṣṇa during His appearance in the previous day of Brahmā and had become full of the most intense desire to associate with Him. Then in this *kalpa* they became *gopīs.* And since the *Vedas* are eternal in human society, the *śrutis* in this *kalpa* also become full of desire for Kṛṣṇa and in the next *kalpa* will also become *gopīs.* This information is given by Śrīla Viśvanātha Cakravartī Ṭhākura.

TEXT 14

तत्रोपविष्टो भगवान् स ईश्वरो
योगेश्वरान्तर्हृदि कल्पितासनः ।
चकास गोपीपरिषद्गतोऽर्चितस्
त्रैलोक्यलक्ष्म्येकपदं वपुर्दधत् ॥ १४ ॥

tatropaviṣṭo bhagavān sa īśvaro
yogeśvarāntar-hṛdi kalpitāsanaḥ
cakāsa gopī-pariṣad-gato'rcitas
trailokya-lakṣmy-eka-padaṁ vapur dadhat

tatra—there; *upaviṣṭaḥ* — seated; *bhagavān* — the Supreme Personality of Godhead; *saḥ* — He; *īśvaraḥ* — the ultimate controller; *yoga-īśvara* — of the masters of mystic meditation; *antaḥ* — within; *hṛdi* — the hearts; *kalpita* — arranged; *āsanaḥ* — His seat; *cakāsa*—He appeared resplendent; *gopī-pariṣat*—in the assembly of the *gopīs; gataḥ*—present; *arcitaḥ*—worshiped; *trai-lokya*—of the three worlds; *lakṣmī*—of the beauty and other opulences; *eka*—the exclusive; *padam*—reservoir; *vapuḥ*—His transcendental, personal form; *dadhat*—exhibiting.

TRANSLATION

Lord Kṛṣṇa, the Supreme Personality of Godhead, for whom the great masters of mystic meditation arrange a seat within their hearts, took His seat in the assembly of gopīs. His transcendental body, the exclusive abode of beauty and opulence within the three worlds, shone brilliantly as the gopīs worshiped Him.

PURPORT

The masters of mystic meditation include Lord Śiva, Ananta Śeṣa and other exalted personalities, all of whom keep the Lord seated within the lotus of their hearts. This same Lord, conquered by the intense, selfless love of the *gopīs,* agreed to become their boyfriend and dance with them in Vṛndāvana, after sitting upon their fragrant shawls on the bank of the Yamunā River.

TEXT 15

सभाजयित्वा तमनंगदीपनं
सहासलीलेक्षणविभ्रमभ्रुवा ।
संस्पर्शनेनांककृताङ्घ्रिहस्तयोः
संस्तुत्य ईषत्कुपिता बभाषिरे ॥ १५ ॥

sabhājayitvā tam anaṅga-dīpanaṁ
sahāsa-līlekṣaṇa-vibhrama-bhruvā
saṁsparśanenāṅka-kṛtāṅghri-hastayoḥ
saṁstutya īṣat kupitā babhāṣire

sabhājayitvā—honoring; *tam*—Him; *anaṅga*—of lusty desires; *dīpanam*—the inciter; *sa-hāsa*—smiling; *līlā*—playful; *īkṣaṇa*—with glances; *vibhrama*—sporting; *bhruvā*—with their eyebrows; *saṁsparśanena*—with touching; *aṅka*—upon their laps; *kṛta*—placed; *aṅghri*—of His feet; *hastayoḥ*—and hands; *saṁstutya*—offering praise; *īṣat*—somewhat; *kupitāḥ*—angry; *babhāṣire*—they spoke.

TRANSLATION

Śrī Kṛṣṇa had awakened romantic desires within the gopīs, and they honored Him by glancing at Him with playful smiles, gesturing amorously with their eyebrows, and massaging His hands and feet as they held them in their laps. Even while worshiping Him, however, they felt somewhat angry, and thus they addressed Him as follows.

TEXT 16

श्रीगोप्य ऊचुः
भजतोऽनुभजन्त्येक एक एतद्विपर्ययम् ।
नोभयांश्च भजन्त्येक एतन्नो ब्रूहि साधु भोः ॥ १६ ॥

śrī-gopya ūcuḥ
bhajato'nubhajanty eka
eka etad-viparyayam
nobhayāṁś ca bhajanty eka
etan no brūhi sādhu bhoḥ

śrī-gopyaḥ ūcuḥ—the *gopīs* said; *bhajataḥ*—to those who respect them; *anu*—reciprocally; *bhajanti*—show respect; *eke*—some; *eke*—some; *etat*—to this; *viparyayam*—the contrary; *na ubhayān*—with neither; *ca*—and; *bhajanti*—reciprocate; *eke*—some; *etat*—this; *naḥ*—to us; *brūhi*—speak; *sādhu*—properly; *bhoḥ*—O dear one.

TRANSLATION

The gopīs said: Some people reciprocate the affection only of those who are affectionate toward them, while others show affection even to those who are indifferent or inimical. And yet others will not show affection toward anyone. Dear Kṛṣṇa, please properly explain this matter to us.

PURPORT

By this apparently polite question, the *gopīs* want to expose Lord Kṛṣṇa's failure to properly reciprocate their love. They were very disturbed when Śrī Kṛṣṇa left them in the forest, and they want to know why He caused them to suffer in these loving affairs.

TEXT 17

श्रीभगवानुवाच
मिथो भजन्ति ये सख्यः स्वार्थैकान्तोद्यमा हि ते ।
न तत्र सौहृदं धर्मः स्वार्थार्थं तद्धि नान्यथा ॥ १७ ॥

śrī-bhagavān uvāca
mitho bhajanti ye sakhyaḥ
svārthaikāntodyamā hi te
na tatra sauhṛdaṁ dharmaḥ
svārthārthaṁ tad dhi nānyathā

śrī-bhagavān uvāca—the Supreme Personality of Godhead said; *mithaḥ*—mutually; *bhajanti*—reciprocate; *ye*—who; *sakhyaḥ*—friends; *sva-artha*—for their own sake; *eka-anta*—exclusively; *udyamāḥ*—whose endeavor; *hi*—indeed; *te*—they; *na*—not; *tatra*—therein; *sauhṛdam*—true friendship; *dharmaḥ*—true religiosity; *sva-artha*—of their own benefit; *artham*—for the sake; *tat*—that; *hi*—indeed; *na*—not; *anyathā*—otherwise.

TRANSLATION

The Supreme Personality of Godhead said: So-called friends who show affection for each other only to benefit themselves are actually selfish.

They have no true friendship, nor are they following the true principles of religion. Indeed, if they did not expect benefit for themselves, they would not reciprocate.

PURPORT

The Lord here reminds the *gopīs* that in pure loving friendship there is no sense of selfish interest but rather only love for one's friend.

TEXT 18

भजन्त्यभजतो ये वै करुणाः पितरौ यथा।
धर्मो निरपवादोऽत्र सौहृदं च सुमध्यमाः ॥ १८ ॥

bhajanty abhajato ye vai
karuṇāḥ pitarau yathā
dharmo nirapavādo'tra
sauhṛdaṁ ca su-madhyamāḥ

bhajanti—they devotedly serve; *abhajataḥ*—with those who do not reciprocate with them; *ye*—those who; *vai*—indeed; *karuṇāḥ*—merciful; *pitarau*—parents; *yathā*—as; *dharmaḥ*—religious duty; *nirapavādaḥ*—faultless; *atra*—in this; *sauhṛdam*—friendship; *ca*—and; *su-madhyamāḥ*—O slender-waisted ones.

TRANSLATION

My dear slender-waisted gopīs, some people are genuinely merciful or, like parents, naturally affectionate. Such persons, who devotedly serve even those who fail to reciprocate with them, are following the true, faultless path of religion, and they are true well-wishers.

TEXT 19

भजतोऽपि न वै केचिद् भजन्त्यभजतः कुतः ।
आत्मारामा ह्याप्तकामा अकृतज्ञा गुरुद्रुहः ॥ १९ ॥

bhajato'pi na vai kecid
bhajanty abhajataḥ kutaḥ
ātmārāmā hy āpta-kāmā
akṛta-jñā guru-druhaḥ

bhajataḥ—with those who are acting favorably; *api*—even; *na*—not; *vai*—certainly; *kecit*—some; *bhajanti*—reciprocate; *abhajataḥ*—with those who are not acting favorably; *kutaḥ*—what to speak of; *ātma-ārāmāḥ*—the self-satisfied; *hi*—indeed; *āpta-kāmāḥ*—those who have already attained their material desires; *akṛta-jñāḥ*—those who are ungrateful; *guru-druhaḥ*—those who are inimical to superiors.

TRANSLATION

Then there are those individuals who are spiritually self-satisfied, materially fulfilled or by nature ungrateful or simply envious of superiors. Such persons will not love even those who love them, what to speak of those who are inimical.

PURPORT

Some people, being spiritually self-satisfied, do not reciprocate others' affection because they want to avoid entanglement in mundane dealings. Other persons do not reciprocate simply out of envy or arrogance. And still others fail to reciprocate because they are materially satisfied and thus uninterested in new material opportunities. Lord Kṛṣṇa patiently explains all these things to the *gopīs.*

TEXT 20

नाहं तु सख्यो भजतोऽपि जन्तून्
भजाम्यमीषामनुवृत्तिवृत्तये ।
यथाधनो लब्धधने विनष्टे
तच्चिन्तयान्यन्निभृतो न वेद ॥ २० ॥

nāhaṁ tu sakhyo bhajato'pi jantūn
bhajāmy amīṣām anuvṛtti-vṛttaye
yathādhano labdha-dhane vinaṣṭe
tac-cintayānyan nibhṛto na veda

na—do not; *aham*—I; *tu*—on the other hand; *sakhyaḥ*—O friends; *bhajataḥ*—worshiping; *api*—even; *jantūn*—with living beings; *bhajāmi*—reciprocate; *amīṣām*—their; *anuvṛtti*—propensity (for pure love); *vṛttaye*—in order to impel; *yathā*—just as; *adhanaḥ*—a poor man; *labdha*—having obtained; *dhane*—wealth; *vinaṣṭe*—and it being lost; *tat*—of that; *cintayā*—with anxious thought; *anyat*—anything else; *nibhṛtaḥ*—filled; *na veda*—does not know.

TRANSLATION

But the reason I do not immediately reciprocate the affection of living beings even when they worship Me, O gopīs, is that I want to intensify their loving devotion. They then become like a poor man who has gained some wealth and then lost it, and who thus becomes so anxious about it that he can think of nothing else.

PURPORT

Lord Kṛṣṇa states in *Bhagavad-gītā, ye yathā māṁ prapadyante tāṁs tathaiva bhajāmy aham*: "As people approach Me, I reciprocate with them accordingly." Yet even if the Lord is approached by someone with devotion, to intensify the devotee's love the Lord may not immediately reciprocate fully. In fact, the Lord is truly reciprocating. After all, a sincere devotee always prays to the Lord, "Please help me to love You purely." Therefore the Lord's so-called neglect is actually the fulfillment of the devotee's prayer. Lord Kṛṣṇa intensifies our love for Him by apparently separating Himself from us, and the result is that we achieve what we really wanted and prayed for: intense love for the Absolute Truth, Kṛṣṇa. Thus Lord Kṛṣṇa's apparent negligence is actually His thoughtful reciprocation and the fulfillment of our deepest and purest desire.

According to the *ācāryas*, as Lord Kṛṣṇa began to speak this verse the *gopīs* looked at one another with squinting eyes, trying to hide the smiles breaking out on their faces. Even as Lord Kṛṣṇa was speaking, the *gopīs* had begun to realize that He was bringing them to the highest perfection of loving service.

TEXT 21

एवं मदर्थोज्झितलोकवेद-
स्वानां हि वो मय्यनुवृत्तयेऽबला: ।
मयापरोक्षं भजता तिरोहितं
मासूयितुं मार्हथ तत्प्रियं प्रिया: ॥ २१ ॥

evaṁ mad-arthojjhita-loka-veda
svānāṁ hi vo mayy anuvṛttaye'balāḥ
mayāparokṣaṁ bhajatā tirohitaṁ
māsūyituṁ mārhatha tat priyaṁ priyāḥ

evam—thus; *mat*—My; *artha*—for the sake; *ujjhita*—having rejected; *loka*—worldly opinion; *veda*—the opinion of the *Vedas; svānām*—and relatives; *hi*—indeed; *vaḥ*—of you; *mayi*—for Me; *anuvṛttaye*—for the loving propensity; *abalāḥ*—My dear girls; *mayā*—by Me; *aparokṣam*—removed from your sight; *bhajatā*—who is actually reciprocating; *tirohitam*—the disappearance; *mā*—with Me; *asūyitum*—to be inimical; *ma arhatha*—you should not; *tat*—therefore; *priyam*—with your beloved; *priyāḥ*—My dear beloveds.

TRANSLATION

My dear girls, understanding that simply for My sake you had rejected the authority of worldly opinion, of the Vedas and of your relatives, I acted as I did only to increase your attachment to Me. Even when I removed Myself from your sight by suddenly disappearing, I never stopped loving you. Therefore, My beloved gopīs, please do not harbor any bad feelings toward Me, your beloved.

PURPORT

Here the Lord indicates that though the *gopīs* were already perfect in their love for Him, still, to inconceivably increase their perfection and show an example for the world, He acted as He did.

TEXT 22

न पारयेऽहं निरवद्यसंयुजां
स्वसाधुकृत्यं विबुधायुषापि वः ।
या माभजन् दुर्जरगेहशृंखलाः
संवृश्च्य तद्वः प्रतियातु साधुना ॥ २२ ॥

na pāraye'haṁ niravadya-saṁyujāṁ
sva-sādhu-kṛtyaṁ vibudhāyuṣāpi vaḥ
yā mābhajan durjara-geha-śṛṅkhalāḥ
saṁvṛścya tad vaḥ pratiyātu sādhunā

na—not; *pāraye*—am able to make; *aham*—I; *niravadya-saṁyujām*—to those who are completely free from deceit; *sva-sādhu-kṛtyam*—proper compensation; *vibudha-āyuṣā*—with a lifetime as long as that of the demigods; *api*—although; *vaḥ*—to you; *yāḥ*—who; *mā*—Me; *abhajan*—have worshiped; *durjara*—difficult to overcome; *geha-śṛṅkhalāḥ*—the chains of household life; *saṁvṛścya*—cutting; *tat*—that; *vaḥ*—of you; *pratiyātu*—let it be returned; *sādhunā*—by the good activity itself.

TRANSLATION

I am not able to repay My debt for your spotless service, even within a lifetime of Brahmā. Your connection with Me is beyond reproach. You have worshiped Me, cutting off all domestic ties, which are difficult to break. Therefore please let your own glorious deeds be your compensation.

PURPORT

The translation and word meanings for this verse are taken from Śrīla Prabhupāda's English rendering of *Śrī Caitanya-caritāmṛta* (*Ādi* 4.180).

In conclusion, the *gopīs* became eternally glorious by their behavior in the Lord's temporary absence, and the mutual love between them and the Lord was wonderfully enhanced. This is the perfection of Kṛṣṇa and His loving devotees.

Thus end the purports of the humble servants of His Divine Grace A.C. Bhaktivedanta Swami Prabhupāda to the Tenth Canto, Thirty-second Chapter, of the Śrīmad-Bhāgavatam, *entitled "The Reunion."*

CHAPTER THIRTY-THREE

The Rāsa Dance

This chapter describes Lord Śrī Kṛṣṇa's *rāsa* dance, which He enjoyed with His beloved girlfriends in the forests along the Yamunā River.

The Supreme Personality of Godhead, Śrī Kṛṣṇa, is most expert in the knowledge of transcendental moods. In the company of the *gopīs,* who were tightly bound to Him by the ropes of affection and totally dedicated to His service, the Lord expanded Himself into numerous forms. The *gopīs* became intoxicated with their enthusiasm to enjoy the *rāsa* dance, and thus they began satisfying Kṛṣṇa's senses by singing, dancing and gesturing amorously. The sweet voices of the *gopīs* filled all the directions.

Even after Lord Kṛṣṇa manifested Himself in numerous forms, each *gopī* thought He was standing next to her alone. Gradually the *gopīs* became fatigued from the continuous dancing and singing, and each of them placed her arm on the shoulder of the Kṛṣṇa standing beside her. Some *gopīs* smelled and kissed Kṛṣṇa's arm, which bore the fragrance of the lotus and was anointed with sandalwood paste. Others put Kṛṣṇa's hand on their bodies, and yet others gave Kṛṣṇa pleasure by embracing Him lovingly.

Lord Kṛṣṇa, being the Supreme Absolute Truth, is the only actual enjoyer and object of enjoyment. Although He is one without a second, He expands Himself into many forms to increase His personal pastimes. Therefore great scholars say that Kṛṣṇa's *rāsa-līlā* is like a child's playing with His own reflection. Śrī Kṛṣṇa is self-satisfied and fully endowed with inconceivable, transcendental opulences. When He exhibits such pastimes as the *rāsa-līlā,* all living beings, from Brahmā down to the blades of grass, become merged in the ocean of astonishment.

When Mahārāja Parīkṣit heard the narration of Kṛṣṇa's conjugal pastimes with the *gopīs,* which superficially resemble the activities of lusty, wanton persons, he expressed a doubt to the great devotee Śrīla Śukadeva Gosvāmī. Śukadeva dispelled this doubt by stating, "Since Śrī Kṛṣṇa is the absolute enjoyer, such pastimes as these can never be contaminated by any fault. But if anyone other than the Supreme Personality of Godhead tries to enjoy such pastimes, he will suffer the same fate that someone other than Lord Rudra would suffer if he attempted to drink an ocean of poison. Moreover, even one who only thinks of imitating Lord Kṛṣṇa's *rāsa-līlā* will certainly suffer misfortune."

The Supreme Absolute Truth, Śrī Kṛṣṇa, is present within the hearts of all living entities as their indwelling witness. When out of His mercy He exhibits His intimate pastimes to His devotees, these activities are never besmirched by mundane imperfection. Any living being who hears of the spontaneous loving attraction the *gopīs* felt for Lord Kṛṣṇa will have his desires for material sense gratification destroyed at the root and will develop his natural propensity for serving the Supreme Lord, the spiritual master, and the Lord's devotees.

TEXT 1

श्रीशुक उवाच
इत्थं भगवतो गोप्यः श्रुत्वा वाचः सुपेशलाः ।
जहुर्विरहजं तापं तदंगोपचिताशिषः ॥ १ ॥

śrī-śuka uvāca
itthaṁ bhagavato gopyaḥ
śrutvā vācaḥ su-peśalāḥ
jahur viraha-jaṁ tāpaṁ
tad-aṅgopacitāśiṣaḥ

śrī-śukaḥ uvāca—Śrī Śukadeva Gosvāmī said; *ittham*—thus; *bhagavataḥ*—of the Supreme Personality of Godhead; *gopyaḥ*—the cowherd girls; *śrutvā*—hearing; *vācaḥ*—the words; *su-peśalāḥ*—most charming; *jahuḥ*—they gave up; *viraha-jam*—born out of their feelings of separation; *tāpam*—the distress; *tat*—His; *aṅga*—from (touching) the limbs; *upacita*—fulfilled; *āśiṣaḥ*—whose desires.

TRANSLATION

Śukadeva Gosvāmī said: When the cowherd girls heard the Supreme Personality of Godhead speak these most charming words, they forgot their distress caused by separation from Him. Touching His transcendental limbs, they felt all their desires fulfilled.

TEXT 2

तत्रारभत गोविन्दो रासक्रीडामनुव्रतैः ।
स्त्रीरत्नैरन्वितः प्रीतैरन्योन्याबद्धबाहुभिः ॥ २ ॥

tatrārabhata govindo
rāsa-krīḍām anuvrataiḥ
strī-ratnair anvitaḥ prītair
anyonyābaddha-bāhubhiḥ

tatra—there; *ārabhata*—began; *govindaḥ*—Lord Kṛṣṇa; *rāsa-krīḍam*—the pastime of the *rāsa* dance; *anuvrataiḥ*—by the faithful (*gopīs*); *strī*—of women; *ratnaiḥ*—the jewels; *anvitaḥ*—joined; *prītaiḥ*—who were satisfied; *anyonya*—among one another; *ābaddha*—entwining; *bāhubhiḥ*—their arms.

TRANSLATION

There on the Yamunā's banks Lord Govinda then began the pastime of the rāsa dance in the company of those jewels among women, the faithful gopīs, who joyfully linked their arms together.

TEXT 3

रासोत्सवः सम्प्रवृत्तो गोपीमण्डलमण्डितः ।
योगेश्वरेण कृष्णेन तासां मध्ये द्वयोर्द्वयोः ॥
प्रविष्टेन गृहीतानां कण्ठे स्वनिकटं स्त्रियः ।
यं मन्येरन्नभस्तावद्विमानशतसंकुलम् ।
दिवौकसां सदाराणामौत्सुक्यापहृतात्मनाम् ॥ ३ ॥

rāsotsavaḥ sampravṛtto
gopī-maṇḍala-maṇḍitaḥ
yogeśvareṇa kṛṣṇena
tāsāṁ madhye dvayor dvayoḥ
praviṣṭena gṛhītānāṁ
kaṇṭhe sva-nikaṭaṁ striyaḥ

yaṁ manyeran nabhas tāvad
vimāna-śata-saṅkulam
divaukasāṁ sa-dārāṇām
autsukyāpahṛtātmanām

rāsa—of the *rāsa* dance; *utsavaḥ*—the festivity; *sampravṛttaḥ*—commenced; *gopī-maṇḍala*—by the circle of *gopīs; maṇḍitaḥ*—decorated; *yoga*—of mystic power; *īśvareṇa*—by the supreme controller; *kṛṣṇena*—Lord

Kṛṣṇa; *tāsām*—of them; *madhye*—within the midst; *dvayoḥ dvayoḥ*—between each pair; *praviṣṭena*—present; *gṛhīṭānām*—who were held; *kaṇṭhe*—by the necks; *sva-nikaṭam*—next to themselves; *striyaḥ*—the women; *yam*—whom; *manyeran*—considered; *nabhaḥ*—the sky; *tāvat*—at that time; *vimāna*—of airplanes; *śata*—with hundreds; *saṅkulam*—crowded; *diva*—of the heavenly planets; *okasām*—belonging to the inhabitants; *sa*—accompanied; *dārāṇām*—by their wives; *autsukya*—by eagerness; *apahṛta*—carried away; *ātmanām*—their minds.

TRANSLATION

The festive rāsa dance commenced, with the gopīs arrayed in a circle. Lord Kṛṣṇa expanded Himself and entered between each pair of gopīs, and as that master of mystic power placed His arms around their necks, each girl thought He was standing next to her alone. The demigods and their wives were overwhelmed with eagerness to witness the rāsa dance, and they soon crowded the sky with their hundreds of celestial airplanes.

PURPORT

Śrīla Bilvamaṅgala Ṭhākura has written the following verse about the *rāsa* dance:

aṅganām aṅganām antarā mādhavo
mādhavaṁ mādhavaṁ cāntareṇāṅganāḥ
ittham ākalpite maṇḍale madhya-gaḥ
sañjagau veṇunā devakī-nandanaḥ

"Lord Mādhava was situated between each pair of *gopīs,* and a *gopī* was situated between each pair of His manifestations. And Śrī Kṛṣṇa, the son of Devakī, also appeared in the middle of the circle, playing upon His flute and singing."

Śrīla Viśvanātha Cakravartī Ṭhākura points out that the *gopīs,* maddened by love, were unable to understand that Śrī Kṛṣṇa had expanded Himself so He could personally dance with each of them. Each *gopī* saw one manifestation of Kṛṣṇa. The demigods and their wives, however, could see all His different manifestations as they watched the *rāsa* dance from their airplanes, and thus they were completely astonished.

TEXT 4

ततो दुन्दुभयो नेदुर्निपेतुः पुष्पवृष्टयः ।
जगुर्गन्धर्वपतयः सस्त्रीकास्तद्यशोऽमलम् ॥ ४ ॥

tato dundubhayo nedur
nipetuḥ puṣpa-vṛṣṭayaḥ
jagur gandharva-patayaḥ
sa-strīkās tad-yaśo'malam

tataḥ—then; *dundubhayaḥ*—kettledrums; *neduḥ*—resounded; *nipetuḥ*—fell down; *puṣpa*—of flowers; *vṛṣṭayaḥ*—rain; *jaguḥ*—they sang; *gandharva-patayaḥ*—the chief Gandharvas; *sa-strīkāḥ*—along with their wives; *tat*—of Him, Lord Kṛṣṇa; *yaśaḥ*—the glories; *amalam*—spotless.

TRANSLATION

Kettledrums then resounded in the sky while flowers rained down and the chief Gandharvas and their wives sang Lord Kṛṣṇa's spotless glories.

PURPORT

As stated here, Lord Kṛṣṇa's glory in dancing the *rāsa* dance is pure spiritual bliss. The demigods in heaven, in charge of maintaining propriety in the universe, ecstatically accepted the *rāsa* dance as the ultimate religious affair, completely different from the perverted reflection of romance we find in this mundane world.

TEXT 5

वलयानां नूपुराणां किंकिणीनां च योषिताम् ।
सप्रियाणामभूच्छब्दस्तुमुलो रासमण्डले ॥ ५ ॥

valayānāṁ nūpurāṇāṁ
kiṅkiṇīnāṁ ca yoṣitām
sa-priyāṇām abhūc chabdas
tumulo rāsa-maṇḍale

valayānām—of the armlets; *nūpurāṇām*—ankle bells; *kiṅkiṇīnām*—bells worn around the waist; *ca*—and; *yoṣitām*—of the women; *sa-priyāṇām*—who were with their beloved; *abhūt*—there was; *śabdaḥ*—a sound; *tumulaḥ*—tumultuous; *rāsa-maṇḍale*—in the circle of the *rāsa* dance.

TRANSLATION

A tumultuous sound arose from the armlets, ankle bells and waist bells of the gopīs as they sported with their beloved Kṛṣṇa in the circle of the rāsa dance.

TEXT 6

तत्रातिशुशुभे ताभिर्भगवान् देवकीसुतः ।
मध्ये मणीनां हैमानां महामरकतो यथा ॥ ६ ॥

tatrātiśuśubhe tābhir
bhagavān devakī-sutaḥ
madhye maṇīnāṁ haimānāṁ
mahā-marakato yathā

tatra—there; *atiśuśubhe*—appeared most brilliant; *tābhiḥ*—with them; *bhagavān*—the Supreme Lord; *devakī-sutaḥ*—Kṛṣṇa, the son of Devakī; *madhye*—in the midst; *maṇīnām*—of ornaments; *haimānām*—golden; *mahā*—great; *marakataḥ*—a sapphire; *yathā*—as.

TRANSLATION

In the midst of the dancing gopīs, Lord Kṛṣṇa appeared most brilliant, like an exquisite sapphire in the midst of golden ornaments.

PURPORT

Śrīla Bhaktisiddhānta Sarasvatī Ṭhākura states that *Devakī*, besides being the name of Vasudeva's wife, is also a name of mother Yaśodā, as stated in the *Ādi Purāṇa: dve nāmnī nanda-bhāryāyā yaśodā devakīti ca.* "The wife of Nanda has two names—Yaśodā and Devakī."

TEXT 7

पादन्यासैर्भुजविधुतिभिः सस्मितैर्भ्रूविलासैर्
भज्यन्मध्यैश्चलकुचपटैः कुण्डलैर्गण्डलोलैः ।
स्विद्यन्मुख्यः कवररसनाग्रन्थयः कृष्णवध्वो
गायन्त्यस्तं तडित इव ता मेघचक्रे विरेजुः ॥ ७ ॥

pāda-nyāsair bhuja-vidhutibhiḥ sa-smitair bhrū-vilāsair
bhajyan madhyaiś cala-kuca-paṭaiḥ kuṇḍalair gaṇḍa-lolaiḥ
svidyan-mukhyaḥ kavara-rasanāgranthayaḥ kṛṣṇa-vadhvo
gāyantyas taṁ taḍita iva tā megha-cakre virejuḥ

pāda—of their feet; *nyāsaiḥ*—by the placement; *bhuja*—of their hands; *vidhutibhiḥ*—by the gestures; *sa-smitaiḥ*—smiling; *bhrū*—of their eyebrows; *vilāsaiḥ*—by the playful movements; *bhajyan*—bending; *madhyaiḥ*

—by their middles; *cala*—moving; *kuca*—covering their breasts; *paṭaiḥ*—by the cloths; *kuṇḍalaiḥ*—by their earrings; *gaṇḍa*—on their cheeks; *lolaiḥ*—rolling; *svidyan*—perspiring; *mukhyaḥ*—whose faces; *kavara*—the braids of their hair; *rasanā*—and their belts; *āgranthayaḥ*—having tightly tied; *kṛṣṇa-vadhvaḥ*—the consorts of Lord Kṛṣṇa; *gāyantyaḥ*—singing; *tam*—about Him; *taḍitaḥ*—bolts of lightning; *iva*—as if; *tāḥ*—they; *megha-cakre*—in a range of clouds; *virejuḥ*—shone.

TRANSLATION

As the gopīs sang in praise of Kṛṣṇa, their feet danced, their hands gestured, and their eyebrows moved with playful smiles. With their braids and belts tied tight, their waists bending, their faces perspiring, the garments on their breasts moving this way and that, and their earrings swinging on their cheeks, Lord Kṛṣṇa's young consorts shone like streaks of lightning in a mass of clouds.

PURPORT

Śrīla Śrīdhara Svāmī explains that according to the analogy of lightning flashing in clouds, the perspiration on the lovely faces of the *gopīs* resembled drops of mist, and their singing resembled thunder. The word *āgranthayaḥ* may also be read *agranthayaḥ,* meaning "loosened." This would indicate that although the *gopīs* began the dance with their hair and belts tightly drawn, these gradually slackened and loosened.

Śrīla Viśvanātha Cakravartī points out that the *gopīs* were expert at exhibiting *mudrās* (precise hand gestures that express feelings or convey meanings associated with the theme of a performance). Thus sometimes Kṛṣṇa and the *gopīs* would artistically move their interlocked arms together, and sometimes they would separate arms and exhibit *mudrās* to act out the meaning of the songs they were singing.

The word *pāda-nyāsaiḥ* indicates that the *gopīs* artistically and gracefully placed the steps of their dancing feet in an enchanting way, and the words *sa-smitair bhrū-vilāsair* indicate that the romantic movements of their eyebrows, smiling with love, were most charming to behold.

TEXT 8

उच्चैर्जगुर्नृत्यमाना रक्तकंठ्यो रतिप्रियाः ।
कृष्णाभिमर्शमुदिता यद्गीतेनेदमावृतम् ॥ ८ ॥

uccair jagur nṛtyamānā
rakta-kaṇṭhyo rati-priyāḥ
kṛṣṇābhimarśa-muditā
yad-gītenedam āvṛtam

uccaiḥ—loudly; *jaguḥ*—they sang; *nṛtyamānāḥ*—while dancing; *rakta*—colored; *kaṇṭhyaḥ*—their throats; *rati*—conjugal enjoyment; *priyāḥ*—dedicated to; *kṛṣṇa-abhimarśa*—by the touch of Lord Kṛṣṇa; *muditāḥ*—joyful; *yat*—whose; *gītena*—by the singing; *idam*—this entire universe; *āvṛtam*—is pervaded.

TRANSLATION

Eager to enjoy conjugal love, their throats colored with various pigments, the gopīs sang loudly and danced. They were overjoyed by Kṛṣṇa's touch, and they sang songs that filled the entire universe.

PURPORT

According to an authoritative book on music called *Saṅgīta-sāra, tāvanta eva rāgāḥ sūryāvatyo jīva-jātayaḥ, teṣu ṣoḍaśa-sāhasrī purā gopī-kṛtā varā:* "There are as many musical *rāgas* as there are species of life. Among these *rāgas* are sixteen thousand principal ones, which were manifested by the *gopīs.*" Thus the *gopīs* created sixteen thousand different *rāgas,* or musical modes, and these have subsequently been disseminated throughout the world. The words *yad-gītenedam āvṛtam* also indicate that even today devotees throughout the world sing the praises of Kṛṣṇa, following the example of the *gopīs.*

TEXT 9

काचित्समं मुकुन्देन स्वरजातीरमिश्रिताः ।
उन्निन्ये पूजिता तेन प्रीयता साधु साध्विति ।
तदेव ध्रुवमुन्निन्ये तस्यै मानं च बह्वदात् ॥ ९ ॥

kācit samaṁ mukundena
svara-jātīr amiśritāḥ
unninye pūjitā tena
prīyatā sādhu sādhv iti
tad eva dhruvam unninye
tasyai mānaṁ ca bahv adāt

kācit—a certain *gopī; samam*—together; *mukundena*—with Lord Kṛṣṇa; *svara-jātīḥ*—pure musical tones; *amiśritāḥ*—not confused with the sounds vibrated by Kṛṣṇa; *unninye*—she raised; *pūjitā*—honored; *tena*—by Him; *prīyatā*—who was pleased; *sādhu sādhu iti*—saying, "excellent, excellent"; *tat eva*—that same (melody); *dhruvam*—with a particular metrical pattern; *unninye*—vibrated (another *gopī*); *tasyai*—to her; *mānam*—special respect; *ca*—and; *bahu*—much; *adāt*—He gave.

TRANSLATION

One gopī, joining Lord Mukunda in His singing, sang pure melodious tones that rose harmoniously above His. Kṛṣṇa was pleased and showed great appreciation for her performance, saying "Excellent! Excellent!" Then another gopī repeated the same melody, but in a special metrical pattern, and Kṛṣṇa praised her also.

TEXT 10

काचिद् रासपरिश्रान्ता पार्श्वस्थस्य गदाभृतः ।
जग्राह बाहुना स्कन्धं श्लथद्वलयमल्लिका ॥ १० ॥

kācid rāsa-pariśrāntā
pārśva-sthasya gadā-bhṛtaḥ
jagrāha bāhunā skandhaṁ
ślathad-valaya-mallikā

kācit—a certain *gopī; rāsa*—by the *rāsa* dance; *pariśrāntā*—fatigued; *pārśva*—at Her side; *sthasya*—who was standing; *gadā-bhṛtaḥ*—of Lord Kṛṣṇa, holding a baton; *jagrāha*—took hold of; *bāhunā*—with Her arm; *skandham*—the shoulder; *ślathat*—loosening; *valaya*—Her bracelets; *mallikā*—and the flowers (in Her hair).

TRANSLATION

When one gopī grew tired from the rāsa dance, She turned to Kṛṣṇa, standing at Her side holding a baton, and grasped His shoulder with Her arm. The dancing had loosened Her bracelets and the flowers in Her hair.

PURPORT

The previous verse states that Śrī Kṛṣṇa honored the *gopīs* for their dancing and singing, and in this verse we see how the *gopīs* responded by dealing intimately and confidently with Him. Here a tired *gopī* held on to Kṛṣṇa's shoulder with her arm, resting against Him.

Śrīla Jīva Gosvāmī explains that the word *gadā* in this verse indicates a baton suitable for a dancing master. Lord Kṛṣṇa brought this item of paraphernalia to enhance His enjoyment of the *rāsa* dance. Śrīla Viśvanātha Cakravartī states that the *gopī* mentioned here is Śrīmatī Rādhārāṇī, whereas the two *gopīs* mentioned in the previous verse are, in order, Viśākhā and Lalitā.

TEXT 11

तत्रैकांसगतं बाहुं कृष्णस्योत्पलसौरभम् ।
चन्दनालिप्तमाघ्राय हृष्टरोमा चुचुम्ब ह ॥ ११ ॥

tatraikāṁsa-gataṁ bāhuṁ
kṛṣṇasyotpala-saurabham
candanāliptam āghrāya
hṛṣṭa-romā cucumba ha

tatra—there; *ekā*—one (*gopī*); *aṁsa*—upon her shoulder; *gatam*—placed; *bāhum*—the arm; *kṛṣṇasya*—of Lord Kṛṣṇa; *utpala*—like a blue lotus; *saurabham*—the fragrance of which; *candana*—with sandalwood pulp; *āliptam*—smeared; *āghrāya*—smelling; *hṛṣṭa*—standing on end; *romā*—her bodily hairs; *cucumba ha*—she kissed.

TRANSLATION

Upon the shoulder of one gopī Kṛṣṇa placed His arm, whose natural blue-lotus fragrance was mixed with that of the sandalwood pulp anointing it. As the gopī relished that fragrance, her bodily hair stood on end in jubilation, and she kissed His arm.

TEXT 12

कस्याश्चिन्नाट्यविक्षिप्तकुण्डलत्विषमण्डितम् ।
गण्डं गण्डे सन्दधत्याः प्रादात्ताम्बूलचर्वितम् ॥ १२ ॥

kasyāścin nāṭya-vikṣipta
kuṇḍala-tviṣa-maṇḍitam
gaṇḍaṁ gaṇḍe sandadhatyāḥ
prādāt tāmbūla-carvitam

kasyāścit—to a certain *gopī; nāṭya*—by the dancing; *vikṣipta*—shaken; *kuṇḍala*—whose earrings; *tviṣa*—with the glitter; *maṇḍitam*—adorned; *gaṇḍam*—her cheek; *gaṇḍe*—next to His cheek; *sandadhatyāḥ*—who was placing; *prādāt*—He carefully gave; *tāmbūla*—the betel nut; *carvitam*—chewed.

TRANSLATION

Next to Kṛṣṇa's cheek one gopī put her own, beautified by the effulgence of her earrings, which glittered as she danced. Kṛṣṇa then carefully gave her the betel nut He was chewing.

TEXT 13

नृत्यती गायती काचित्कूजन्नूपुरमेखला ।
पार्श्वस्थाच्युतहस्ताब्जं श्रान्ताधात्स्तनयोः शिवम् ॥ १३ ॥

nṛtyatī gāyatī kācit
kūjan nūpura-mekhalā
pārśva-sthācyuta-hastābjaṁ
śrāntādhāt stanayoḥ śivam

nṛtyatī—dancing; *gāyatī*—singing; *kācit*—a certain *gopī; kūjan*—murmuring; *nūpura*—her ankle bells; *mekhalā*—and her belt; *pārśva-stha*—standing at her side; *acyuta*—of Lord Kṛṣṇa; *hasta-abjam*—the lotus hand; *śrāntā*—feeling tired; *adhāt*—placed; *stanayoḥ*—upon her breasts; *śivam*—pleasing.

TRANSLATION

Another gopī became fatigued as she danced and sang, the bells on her ankles and waist tinkling. So she placed upon her breasts the comforting lotus hand of Lord Acyuta, who was standing by her side.

TEXT 14

गोप्यो लब्ध्वाच्युतं कान्तं श्रिय एकान्तवल्लभम् ।
गृहीतकंठ्यस्तद्दोर्भ्यां गायन्त्यस्तं विजह्रिरे ॥ १४ ॥

gopyo labdhvācyutaṁ kāntaṁ
śriya ekānta-vallabham

gṛhīta-kaṇṭhyas tad-dorbhyāṁ
gāyantyas taṁ vijahrire

gopyaḥ—the *gopīs; labdhvā*—having attained; *acyutam*—the infallible Lord; *kāntam*—as their lover; *śriyaḥ*—of the goddess of fortune; *ekānta*—the exclusive; *vallabham*—lover; *gṛhīta*—held; *kaṇṭhyaḥ*—their necks; *tat*—His; *dorbhyām*—by the arms; *gāyantyaḥ*—singing; *tam*—about Him; *vijahrire*—they took pleasure.

TRANSLATION

Having attained as their intimate lover Lord Acyuta, the exclusive consort of the goddess of fortune, the gopīs enjoyed great pleasure. They sang His glories as He held their necks with His arms.

TEXT 15

कर्णोत्पलालकविटंककपोलघर्म-
वक्त्रश्रियो वलयनूपुरघोषवाद्यैः ।
गोप्यः समं भगवता ननृतुः स्वकेश-
स्रस्तस्रजो भ्रमरगायकरासगोष्ठ्याम् ॥ १५ ॥

karṇotpalālaka-viṭaṅka-kapola-gharma-
vaktra-śriyo valaya-nūpura-ghoṣa-vādyaiḥ
gopyaḥ samaṁ bhagavatā nanṛtuḥ sva-keśa-
srasta-srajo bhramara-gāyaka-rāsa-goṣṭhyām

karṇa—upon their ears; *utpala*—with the lotus flowers; *alaka*—by locks of their hair; *viṭaṅka*—decorated; *kapola*—their cheeks; *gharma*—with perspiration; *vaktra*—of their faces; *śriyaḥ*—the beauty; *valaya*—of their armlets; *nūpura*—and ankle bells; *ghoṣa*—of the reverberation; *vādyaiḥ*—with the musical sound; *gopyaḥ*—the *gopīs; samam*—together; *bhagavatā*—with the Personality of Godhead; *nanṛtuḥ*—danced; *sva*—their own; *keśa*—from the hair; *srasta*—scattered; *srajaḥ*—the garlands; *bhramara*—the bees; *gāyaka*—singers; *rāsa*—of the *rāsa* dance; *goṣṭhyām*—in the assembly.

TRANSLATION

Enhancing the beauty of the gopīs' faces were the lotus flowers behind their ears, the locks of hair decorating their cheeks, and drops of

perspiration. The reverberation of their armlets and ankle bells made a loud musical sound, and their chaplets scattered. Thus the gopīs danced with the Supreme Lord in the arena of the rāsa dance as swarms of bees sang in accompaniment.

TEXT 16

एवं परिष्वंगकराभिमर्श-
स्निग्धेक्षणोद्दामविलासहासैः ।
रेमे रमेशो व्रजसुन्दरीभिर्
यथार्भकः स्वप्रतिबिम्बविभ्रमः ॥ १६ ॥

evaṁ pariṣvaṅga-karābhimarśa-
snigdhekṣaṇoddāma-vilāsa-hāsaiḥ
reme rameśo vraja-sundarībhir
yathārbhakaḥ sva-pratibimba-vibhramaḥ

evam—thus; *pariṣvaṅga*—with embracing; *kara*—by His hand; *abhimarśa*—with touching; *snigdha*—affectionate; *īkṣaṇa*—with glances; *uddāma*—broad; *vilāsa*—playful; *hāsaiḥ*—with smiles; *reme*—He took pleasure; *ramā*—of the goddess of fortune; *īśaḥ*—the master; *vraja-sundarībhiḥ*—with the young women of the cowherd community; *yathā*—just as; *arbhakaḥ*—a boy; *sva*—His own; *pratibimba*—with the reflection; *vibhramaḥ*—whose playing.

TRANSLATION

In this way Lord Kṛṣṇa, the original Lord Nārāyaṇa, master of the goddess of fortune, took pleasure in the company of the young women of Vraja by embracing them, caressing them and glancing lovingly at them as He smiled His broad, playful smiles. It was just as if a child were playing with his own reflection.

PURPORT

Śrīla Bhaktisiddhānta Sarasvatī Ṭhākura comments as follows on this verse: "Lord Kṛṣṇa alone is the Supreme Absolute Truth, and His potencies are unlimited. All these potencies, taking personal forms, engage Lord Kṛṣṇa in His pastimes. Just as the opulent manifestation of His one supreme transcendental potency manifests all the countless potencies of the Lord, so in the *rāsa* dance Kṛṣṇa manifests Himself as many times as there are various potencies represented by the *gopīs.* Everything is Kṛṣṇa, but by His desire His spiritual energy Yoga-māyā manifests the *gopīs.* When His internal potency Yoga-māyā thus produces such pastimes for the enhancement of His transcendental emotions, it is just like a young boy playing with His own reflection. But since these pastimes are created by His spiritual potency, they are eternal and self-manifesting."

TEXT 17

तदंगसंगप्रमुदाकुलेन्द्रियाः
केशान् दुकूलं कुचपट्टिकां वा ।
नाञ्जः प्रतिव्योढुमलं व्रजस्त्रियो
विस्रस्तमालाभरणाः कुरूद्वह ॥ १७ ॥

tad-aṅga-saṅga-pramudākulendriyāḥ
keśān dukūlaṁ kuca-paṭṭikāṁ vā
nāñjaḥ prativyoḍhum alaṁ vraja-striyo
visrasta-mālābharaṇāḥ kurūdvaha

tat—with Him; *aṅga-saṅga*—from the bodily contact; *pramudā*—by the joy; *ākula*—overflowing; *indriyāḥ*—whose senses; *keśān*—their hair; *dukūlam*—dresses; *kuca-paṭṭikām*—the garments covering their breasts; *vā*—or; *na*—not; *añjaḥ*—easily; *prativyoḍhum*—to keep properly arranged; *alam*—capable; *vraja-striyaḥ*—the women of Vraja; *visrasta*—scattered; *mālā*—their flower garlands; *ābharaṇāḥ*—and ornaments; *kuru-udvaha*—O most eminent member of the Kuru dynasty.

TRANSLATION

Their senses overwhelmed by the joy of having His physical association, the gopīs could not prevent their hair, their dresses and the cloths covering their breasts from becoming disheveled. Their garlands and ornaments scattered, O hero of the Kuru dynasty.

TEXT 18

कृष्णविक्रीडितं वीक्ष्य मुमुहुः खेचरस्त्रियः ।
कामार्दिताः शशांकश्च सगणो विस्मितोऽभवत् ॥ १८ ॥

kṛṣṇa-vikrīḍitaṁ vīkṣya
mumuhuḥ khe-cara-striyaḥ
kāmārditāḥ śaśāṅkaś ca
sa-gaṇo vismito'bhavat

kṛṣṇa-vikrīḍitam—the playing of Kṛṣṇa; *vīkṣya*—seeing; *mumuhuḥ*—became entranced; *khe-cara*—traveling in the sky; *striyaḥ*—the women (demigoddesses); *kāma*—by lusty desires; *arditāḥ*—agitated; *śaśāṅkaḥ*—the moon; *ca*—also; *sa-gaṇaḥ*—with his followers, the stars; *vismitaḥ*—amazed; *abhavat*—became.

TRANSLATION

The wives of the demigods, observing Kṛṣṇa's playful activities from their airplanes, were entranced and became agitated with lust. Indeed, even the moon and his entourage, the stars, became astonished.

TEXT 19

कृत्वा तावन्तमात्मानं यावतीर्गोपयोषितः ।
रेमे स भगवांस्ताभिरात्मारामोऽपि लीलया ॥ १९ ॥

kṛtvā tāvantam ātmānaṁ
yāvatīr gopa-yoṣitaḥ
reme sa bhagavāṁs tābhir
ātmārāmo'pi līlayā

kṛtvā—making; *tāvantam*—expanded that many times; *ātmānam*—Himself; *yāvatīḥ*—as many as; *gopa-yoṣitaḥ*—cowherd women; *reme*—enjoyed; *saḥ*—He; *bhagavān*—the Supreme Lord; *tābhiḥ*—with them; *ātma-ārāmaḥ*—self-satisfied; *api*—although; *līlayā*—as a pastime.

TRANSLATION

Expanding Himself as many times as there were cowherd women to associate with, the Supreme Lord, though self-satisfied, playfully enjoyed their company.

PURPORT

As Śrīla Viśvanātha Cakravartī points out, it has already been explained that Lord Kṛṣṇa is eternally free from all material desire, perfect on the platform of spiritual self-satisfaction.

TEXT 20

तासां रतिविहारेण श्रान्तानां वदनानि सः ।
प्रामृजत्करुणः प्रेम्णा शन्तमेनांग पाणिना ॥ २० ॥

tāsāṁ rati-vihāreṇa
śrāntānāṁ vadanāni saḥ
prāmṛjat karuṇaḥ premṇā
śantamenāṅga pāṇinā

tāsām—of them, the *gopīs; rati*—of conjugal love; *vihāreṇa*—by the enjoyment; *śrāntānām*—who were fatigued; *vadanāni*—the faces; *saḥ*—He; *prāmṛjat*—wiped; *karuṇaḥ*—merciful; *premṇā*—lovingly; *śantamena*—most comforting; *aṅga*—my dear (King Parīkṣit); *pāṇinā*—with His hand.

TRANSLATION

Seeing that the gopīs were fatigued from conjugal enjoyment, my dear King, merciful Kṛṣṇa lovingly wiped their faces with His comforting hand.

TEXT 21

गोप्यः स्फुरत्पुरटकुण्डलकुन्तलत्विड्-
गण्डश्रिया सुधितहासनिरीक्षणेन ।
मानं दधत्य ऋषभस्य जगुः कृतानि
पुण्यानि तत्कररुहस्पर्शप्रमोदाः ॥ २१ ॥

gopyaḥ sphurat-puraṭa-kuṇḍala-kuntala-tviḍ-
gaṇḍa-śriyā sudhita-hāsa-nirīkṣaṇena
mānaṁ dadhatya ṛṣabhasya jaguḥ kṛtāni
puṇyāni tat-kara-ruha-sparśa-pramodāḥ

gopyaḥ—the *gopīs; sphurat*—shining; *puraṭa*—golden; *kuṇḍala*—of their earrings; *kuntala*—and of the locks of their hair; *tviṭ*—of the effulgence; *gaṇḍa*—of their cheeks; *śriyā*—by the beauty; *sudhita*—made nectarean; *hāsa*—smiling; *nirīkṣaṇena*—by their glances; *mānam*—honor; *dadhatyaḥ*—giving; *ṛṣabhasya*—of their hero; *jaguḥ*—they sang; *kṛtāni*—the activities; *puṇyāni*—auspicious; *tat*—His; *kara-ruha*—of the fingernails; *sparśa*—by the touch; *pramodāḥ*—greatly pleased.

TRANSLATION

The gopīs honored their hero with smiling glances sweetened by the beauty of their cheeks and the effulgence of their curly locks and glittering golden earrings. Overjoyed from the touch of His fingernails, they chanted the glories of His all-auspicious transcendental pastimes.

TEXT 22

ताभिर्युतः श्रममपोहितुमंगसंग-
घृष्टस्रजः स कुचकुंकुमरञ्जितायाः ।
गन्धर्वपालिभिरनुद्रुत आविशद्वाः
श्रान्तो गजीभिरिभराडिव भिन्नसेतुः ॥ २२ ॥

tābhir yutaḥ śramam apohitum aṅga-saṅga-
ghṛṣṭa-srajaḥ sa kuca-kuṅkuma-rañjitāyāḥ
gandharva-pālibhir anudruta āviśad vāḥ
śrānto gajībhir ibha-rāḍ iva bhinna-setuḥ

tābhiḥ—by them; *yutaḥ*—accompanied; *śramam*—fatigue; *apohitum*—to dispel; *aṅga-saṅga*—by their conjugal association; *ghṛṣṭa*—crushed; *srajaḥ*—whose garland; *saḥ*—He; *kuca*—from their breasts; *kuṅkuma*—of the vermilion powder; *rañjitāyāḥ*—which was smeared by the color; *gandharva-pa*—(who appeared like) leaders of the heavenly singers; *alibhiḥ*—by bees; *anudrutaḥ*—swiftly followed; *āviśat*—He entered; *vāḥ*—the water; *śrāntaḥ*—tired; *gajībhiḥ*—together with His female elephant consorts; *ibha-rāṭ*—a lordly elephant; *iva*—as; *bhinna*—having broken; *setuḥ*—the walls of a paddy field.

TRANSLATION

Lord Kṛṣṇa's garland had been crushed during His conjugal dalliance with the gopīs and colored vermilion by the kuṅkuma powder on their breasts. To dispel the fatigue of the gopīs, Kṛṣṇa entered the water of the Yamunā, followed swiftly by bees who were singing like the best of the Gandharvas. He appeared like a lordly elephant entering the water to relax in the company of his consorts. Indeed, the Lord had transgressed all worldly and Vedic morality just as a powerful elephant might break the dikes in a paddy field.

TEXT 23

सोऽम्भस्यलं युवतिभिः परिषिच्यमानः
प्रेम्णेक्षितः प्रहसतीभिरितस्ततोऽङ्ग ।
वैमानिकैः कुसुमवर्षिभिरीड्यमानो
रेमे स्वयं स्वरतिरत्र गजेन्द्रलीलः ॥ २३ ॥

so'mbhasy alaṁ yuvatibhiḥ pariṣicyamānaḥ
premṇekṣitaḥ prahasatībhir itas tato'ṅga
vaimānikaiḥ kusuma-varṣibhir īḍyamāno
reme svayaṁ sva-ratir atra gajendra-līlaḥ

saḥ—He; *ambhasi*—in the water; *alam*—very much; *yuvatibhiḥ*—by the girls; *pariṣicyamānaḥ*—being splashed; *premṇā*—with love; *īkṣitaḥ*—glanced upon; *prahasatībhiḥ*—by them, who were laughing; *itaḥ tataḥ*—here and there; *aṅga*—my dear King; *vaimānikaiḥ*—by those traveling in their airplanes; *kusuma*—flowers; *varṣibhiḥ*—who were raining down; *īḍyamānaḥ*—being worshiped; *reme*—enjoyed; *svayam*—personally; *sva-ratiḥ*—satisfied within Himself; *atra*—here; *gaja-indra*—of a king of the elephants; *līlaḥ*—whose playing.

TRANSLATION

My dear King, in the water Kṛṣṇa found Himself being splashed on all sides by the laughing gopīs, who looked at Him with love. As the demigods worshiped Him by showering flowers from their airplanes, the self-satisfied Lord took pleasure in playing like the king of the elephants.

TEXT 24

ततश्च कृष्णोपवने जलस्थल-
प्रसूनगन्धानिलजुष्टदिक्तटे ।
चचार भृंगप्रमदागणावृतो
यथा मदच्युद् द्विरदः करेणुभिः ॥ २४ ॥

tataś ca kṛṣṇopavane jala-sthala
prasūna-gandhānila-juṣṭa-dik-taṭe
cacāra bhṛṅga-pramadā-gaṇāvṛto
yathā mada-cyud dviradaḥ kareṇubhiḥ

tataḥ—then; *ca*—and; *kṛṣṇā*—of the river Yamunā; *upavane*—in a small forest; *jala*—of the water; *sthala*—and the land; *prasūna*—of flowers; *gandha*—with the fragrance; *anila*—by the wind; *juṣṭa*—joined; *dik-taṭe*—the edges of the directions; *cacāra*—He passed; *bhṛṅga*—of bees; *pramadā*—and women; *gaṇa*—by the groups; *āvṛtaḥ*—surrounded; *yathā*—just as; *mada-cyut*—exuding a secretion from its forehead because of excitement; *dviradaḥ*—an elephant; *kareṇubhiḥ*—with his she-elephants.

TRANSLATION

Then the Lord strolled through a small forest on the bank of the Yamunā. This forest was filled to its limits with breezes carrying the fragrances of all the flowers growing on the land and in the water. Followed by His entourage of bees and beautiful women, Lord Kṛṣṇa appeared like an intoxicated elephant with his she-elephants.

PURPORT

According to Śrīla Viśvanātha Cakravartī, it is implicit here that after playing in the water Lord Kṛṣṇa had His body massaged, and that He then dressed Himself in His favorite clothing before resuming His pastimes with the *gopīs.*

TEXT 25

एवं शशांकांशुविराजिता निशाः
स सत्यकामोऽनुरताबलागणः ।
सिषेव आत्मन्यवरुद्धसौरतः
सर्वाः शरत्काव्यकथारसाश्रयाः ॥ २५ ॥

evaṁ śaśāṅkāṁśu-virājitā niśāḥ
sa satya-kāmo'nuratābalā-gaṇaḥ
siṣeva ātmany avaruddha-saurataḥ
sarvāḥ śarat-kāvya-kathā-rasāśrayāḥ

evam—in this manner; *śaśāṅka*—of the moon; *aṁśu*—by the rays; *virājitāḥ*—made brilliant; *niśāḥ*—the nights; *saḥ*—He; *satya-kāmaḥ*—whose desires are always fulfilled; *anurata*—constantly attached to Him; *abalā-gaṇaḥ*—His many girlfriends; *siṣeve*—He utilized; *ātmani*—within Himself; *avaruddha*—reserved; *sauratah*—conjugal feelings; *sarvāḥ*—all (the nights); *śarat*—of the autumn; *kāvya*—poetic; *kathā*—of narrations; *rasa*—of the transcendental moods; *āśrayāḥ*—the repositories.

TRANSLATION

Although the gopīs were firmly attached to Lord Kṛṣṇa, whose desires are always fulfilled, the Lord was not internally affected by any mundane sex desire. Still, to perform His pastimes the Lord took advantage of all those moonlit autumn nights, which inspire poetic descriptions of transcendental affairs.

PURPORT

It is difficult to translate into English the word *rasa,* which indicates the spiritual bliss derived from one's loving relationship with Lord Kṛṣṇa. That bliss is experienced in the midst of spiritual pastimes with the Lord and His devotees. Śrīla Viśvanātha Cakravartī explains that great Vaiṣṇava poets like Vyāsa, Parāśara, Jayadeva, Līlāśuka (Bilvamaṅgala Ṭhākura), Govardhanācārya and Śrīla Rūpa Gosvāmī have tried in their poetry to describe the conjugal affairs of the Lord. These descriptions are never complete, however, since the Lord's pastimes are unlimited; thus the attempt to glorify such pastimes is still going on and will go on forever. Lord Kṛṣṇa arranged an extraordinary season of beautiful autumn nights to enhance His loving affairs, and those autumn nights have inspired transcendental poets since time immemorial.

TEXTS 26–27

श्रीपरीक्षिदुवाच
संस्थापनाय धर्मस्य प्रशमायेतरस्य च ।
अवतीर्णो हि भगवानंशेन जगदीश्वरः ॥ २६ ॥
स कथं धर्मसेतूनां वक्ता कर्ताभिरक्षिता ।
प्रतीपमाचरद् ब्रह्मन् परदाराभिमर्शनम् ॥ २७ ॥

śrī-parīkṣid uvāca
saṁsthāpanāya dharmasya
praśamāyetarasya ca
avatīrṇo hi bhagavān
aṁśena jagad-īśvaraḥ

sa kathaṁ dharma-setūnāṁ
vaktā kartābhirakṣitā
pratīpam ācarad brahman
para-dārābhimarśanam

śrī-parīkṣit uvāca—Śrī Parīkṣit Mahārāja said; *saṁsthāpanāya*—for the establishment; *dharmasya*—of religious principles; *praśamāya*—for the subduing; *itarasya*—of the opposite; *ca*—and; *avatīrṇaḥ*—descended (upon this earth); *hi*—indeed; *bhagavān*—the Supreme Personality of Godhead; *aṁśena*—with His plenary expansion (Śrī Balarāma); *jagat*—of the entire universe; *īśvaraḥ*—the Lord; *saḥ*—He; *katham*—how; *dharma-setūnām*—of the restrictive codes of moral behavior; *vaktā*—the original speaker; *kartā*—the executor; *abhirakṣitā*—the protector; *pratīpam*—contrary; *ācarat*—behaved; *brahman*—O *brāhmaṇa,* Śukadeva Gosvāmī; *para*—of others; *dāra*—the wives; *abhimarśanam*—touching.

TRANSLATION

Parīkṣit Mahārāja said: O brāhmaṇa, the Supreme Personality of Godhead, the Lord of the universe, has descended to this earth along with His plenary portion to destroy irreligion and reestablish religious principles. Indeed, He is the original speaker, follower and guardian of moral laws. How, then, could He have violated them by touching other men's wives?

PURPORT

As Śukadeva Gosvāmī was speaking, King Parīkṣit noticed that some persons seated in the assembly on the bank of the Ganges were harboring doubt about the Lord's activities. These doubtful persons were *karmīs, jñānīs* and others who were not devotees of the Lord. To clear up their doubts, King Parīkṣit asks this question on their behalf.

TEXT 28

आप्तकामो यदुपतिः कृतवान् वै जुगुप्सितम् ।
किमभिप्राय एतन्नः शंशयं छिन्धि सुव्रत ॥ २८ ॥

āpta-kāmo yadu-patiḥ
kṛtavān vai jugupsitam
kim-abhiprāya etan naḥ
śaṁśayaṁ chindhi su-vrata

āpta-kāmaḥ—self-satisfied; *yadu-patiḥ*—the master of the Yadu dynasty; *kṛtavān*—has performed; *vai*—certainly; *jugupsitam*—that which is contemptible; *kim-abhiprāyaḥ*—with what intent; *etat*—this; *naḥ*—our;

śaṁśayam—doubt; *chindhi*—please cut; *su-vrata*—O faithful upholder of vows.

TRANSLATION

O faithful upholder of vows, please destroy our doubt by explaining to us what purpose the self-satisfied Lord of the Yadus had in mind when He behaved so contemptibly.

PURPORT

It is clear to the enlightened that these doubts will arise in the minds and hearts of persons unfamiliar with the transcendental pastimes of the Lord. Therefore since time immemorial great sages and enlightened kings like Parīkṣit Mahārāja have openly raised these questions to provide the authoritative answer for all posterity.

TEXT 29

श्रीशुक उवाच
धर्मव्यतिक्रमो दृष्ट ईश्वराणां च साहसम्।
तेजीयसां न दोषाय वह्नेः सर्वभुजो यथा ॥ २९ ॥

śrī-śuka uvāca
dharma-vyatikramo dṛṣṭa
īśvarāṇāṁ ca sāhasam
tejīyasāṁ na doṣāya
vahneḥ sarva-bhujo yathā

śrī-śukaḥ uvāca—Śrī Śukadeva Gosvāmī said; *dharma-vyatikramaḥ*—the transgression of religious or moral principles; *dṛṣṭaḥ*—seen; *īśvarāṇām*—of powerful controllers; *ca*—even; *sāhasam*—due to audacity; *tejīyasām*—who are spiritually potent; *na*—does not; *doṣāya*—(lead) to any fault; *vahneḥ*—of fire; *sarva*—everything; *bhujaḥ*—devouring; *yathā*—as.

TRANSLATION

Śukadeva Gosvāmī said: The status of powerful controllers is not harmed by any apparently audacious transgression of morality we may see in them, for they are just like fire, which devours everything fed into it and remains unpolluted.

PURPORT

Great, potent personalities are not ruined by an apparent transgression of moral principles. Śrīdhara Svāmī mentions the examples of Brahmā, Indra, Soma, Viśvāmitra and others. A fire devours all that is fed into it but the fire does not change its nature. Similarly, a great personality does not fall from his position by an irregularity in behavior. In the following verse, however, Śukadeva Gosvāmī makes it clear that if we try to imitate the great personalities ruling the universe, the result will be catastrophic.

TEXT 30

नैतत्समाचरेज्जातु मनसापि ह्यनीश्वरः ।
विनश्यत्याचरन्मौढ्याद्यथारुद्रोऽब्धिजं विषम् ॥ ३० ॥

naitat samācarej jātu
manasāpi hy anīśvaraḥ
vinaśyaty ācaran mauḍhyād
yathārudro'bdhi-jaṁ viṣam

na—not; *etat*—this; *samācaret*—should perform; *jātu*—ever; *manasā*—with the mind; *api*—even; *hi*—certainly; *anīśvaraḥ*—one who is not a controller; *vinaśyati*—he is destroyed; *ācaran*—acting; *mauḍhyāt*—out of foolishness; *yathā*—as; *arudraḥ*—one who is not Lord Rudra; *abdhijam*—generated from the ocean; *viṣam*—poison.

TRANSLATION

One who is not a great controller should never imitate the behavior of ruling personalities, even mentally. If out of foolishness an ordinary person does imitate such behavior, he will simply destroy himself, just as a person who is not Rudra would destroy himself if he tried to drink an ocean of poison.

PURPORT

Lord Śiva, or Rudra, once drank an ocean of poison, and the result was that an attractive blue mark appeared on his neck. But if we were to drink even a drop of such poison, we would die immediately. Just as we should not imitate this pastime of Śiva's, we should not imitate Lord Kṛṣṇa's activities with the *gopīs.* We should clearly understand that while Lord Kṛṣṇa certainly descends to demonstrate religious principles, He also descends to demonstrate that He is God and we are not. That also must be demonstrated. The Lord enjoys with His internal potency and thus attracts us to the spiritual platform. We should not try to imitate Kṛṣṇa, for we will suffer severely.

TEXT 31

ईश्वराणां वचः सत्यं तथैवाचरितं क्वचित् ।
तेषां यत्स्ववचोयुक्तं बुद्धिमांस्तत्समाचरेत् ॥ ३१ ॥

īśvarāṇāṁ vacaḥ satyaṁ
tathaivācaritaṁ kvacit
teṣāṁ yat sva-vaco-yuktaṁ
buddhimāṁs tat samācaret

īśvarāṇām—of the Lord's empowered servants; *vacaḥ*—the words; *satyam*—true; *tathā eva*—also; *ācaritam*—what they do; *kvacit*—sometimes; *teṣām*—of them; *yat*—which; *sva-vacaḥ*—with their own words; *yuktam*—in agreement; *buddhi-mān*—one who is intelligent; *tat*—that; *samācaret*—should perform.

TRANSLATION

The statements of the Lord's empowered servants are always true, and the acts they perform are exemplary when consistent with those statements. Therefore one who is intelligent should carry out their instructions.

PURPORT

The word *īśvara* is usually defined in Sanskrit dictionaries as "lord, master, ruler," and also as "capable, potent to perform." Śrīla Prabhupāda often translated the word *īśvara* as "controller," which brilliantly synthesizes the two fundamental concepts of *īśvara,* namely a master or ruler and a capable or potent person. A master may be incompetent, but a controller is a master or lord who in fact makes things happen. The *parameśvara,* the supreme *īśvara,* the supreme controller, is of course God, Kṛṣṇa, the cause of all causes.

Although people in general, especially in the Western countries, are not aware of the fact, powerful personalities control our universe. The modern, impersonal concept of the universe depicts an almost totally lifeless cosmos in which the earth floats meaninglessly. Thus we are left with the dubious "ultimate purpose" of preserving and reproducing our genetic code, which has its own "ultimate purpose" of adding another link to the meaningless chain of events by again reproducing itself.

In contrast to this sterile, meaningless world concocted by ignorant materialists, the actual universe is full of life—personal life—and in fact full of God, who pervades and supports all that exists. The essence of reality is the Supreme Personality of Godhead and His personal relationship with the innumerable living beings, of whom we are samples. Some of the living beings are trapped in the illusion of materialism, or identification with the material body, while others are liberated, aware of their eternal, spiritual nature. A third class comprises those progressing in self-realization from the materialistic state of ignorance to the enlightened state of Kṛṣṇa consciousness.

Reality is ultimately personal and divine, and therefore it is not surprising that, as the Vedic literature reveals to us, our universe and other universes are managed by great personalities, just as our city, state and country are managed by empowered personalities. When we democratically award a particular politician the right to govern, we vote for him because he has exhibited something we call "leadership" or "ability." We think, "He'll get the job done." In other words, it is only after an individual acquires the power to govern that we vote for him; our vote does not make him a leader but rather recognizes a power in him coming from some other source. Thus, as Lord Kṛṣṇa explains at the end of the Tenth Chapter of the *Bhagavad-gītā,* any living being exhibiting an extraordinary power, ability or authority must have been empowered by the Lord Himself or by the Lord's energy.

Those directly empowered by the Lord are devoted to Him, and thus their power and influence spread goodness throughout the world, whereas those who are empowered by the Lord's illusory potency are in an indirect relationship with Kṛṣṇa because they do not directly reflect His will. Of course, they do reflect His will indirectly, since it is by Kṛṣṇa's arrangement that the laws of nature act upon ignorant living beings, gradually persuading them, through their journey of many lifetimes, to surrender to the Supreme Lord. Thus as politicians create wars, false hopes and innumerable passionate schemes for the materialistic persons who follow them, the politicians are indirectly carrying out the Lord's program of allowing the conditioned souls to experience the bitter fruit of godlessness.

Śrīla Bhaktisiddhānta Sarasvatī Ṭhākura has translated the word *īśvarāṇām* as "those who have become powerful through knowledge and austerity." As one understands the nature and will of God and makes the personal sacrifice required to achieve excellence in spiritual life, one becomes empowered by the Supreme Lord to represent His will, which one has intelligently recognized and accepted.

The Supreme Personality of Godhead kindly descends to earth to show a vivid example of religious behavior. As Lord Kṛṣṇa states in the *Bhagavad-gītā* (3.24), "If I did not execute standard duties, the whole world would be misled and in fact destroyed." Thus the Lord showed, in His different incarnations, how to act properly in this world. A good example is Lord Rāmacandra, who behaved wonderfully as the son of King Daśaratha.

But when Lord Kṛṣṇa Himself descends, He also demonstrates the ultimate religious principle, namely that the Supreme Lord is beyond all other living beings and that no one can imitate His supreme position. This foremost of all religious principles—that the Lord is unique, without equal or superior—was clearly demonstrated in Lord Kṛṣṇa's apparently immoral pastimes with the *gopīs.* No one can imitate these activities without incurring dire consequences, as explained here by Śukadeva Gosvāmī. One who thinks that Lord Kṛṣṇa is an ordinary living being subjected to lust, or who accepts His *rāsa* dance as admirable and tries to imitate it, will certainly be vanquished, as described in text 30 of this chapter.

Finally, a distinction must be made between the Lord and His empowered servants. An empowered servant of the Lord, as in the case of Brahmā, may experience a remnant of reactions to previous activities, according to the law of *karma.* But the Lord is eternally free from any entanglement in the laws of *karma.* He is on a unique platform.

TEXT 32

कुशलाचरितेनैषामिह स्वार्थो न विद्यते ।
विपर्ययेण वानर्थो निरहंकारिणां प्रभो ॥ ३२ ॥

kuśalācaritenaiṣām
iha svārtho na vidyate
viparyayeṇa vānartho
nirahaṅkāriṇāṁ prabho

kuśala—pious; *ācaritena*—by activity; *eṣām*—for them; *iha*—in this world; *sva-arthaḥ*—selfish benefit; *na vidyate*—does not accrue; *viparyayeṇa*—by the opposite; *vā*—or; *anarthaḥ*—undesirable reactions; *nira-haṅkāriṇām*—who are free from false ego; *prabho*—my dear sir.

TRANSLATION

My dear Prabhu, when these great persons who are free from false ego act piously in this world, they have no selfish motives to fulfill, and even when they act in apparent contradiction to the laws of piety, they are not subject to sinful reactions.

TEXT 33

किमुताखिलसत्त्वानां तिर्यङ्मर्त्यदिवौकसाम् ।
ईशितुश्चेशितव्यानां कुशलाकुशलान्वयः ॥ ३३ ॥

kim utākhila-sattvānāṁ
tiryaṅ-martya-divaukasām
īśituś ceśitavyānāṁ
kuśalākuśalānvayaḥ

kim uta—what to speak then; *akhila*—of all; *sattvānām*—created beings; *tiryak*—animals; *martya*—humans; *diva-okasām*—and inhabitants of heaven; *īśutuḥ*—for the controller; *ca*—and; *īśitavyānām*—of those who are controlled; *kuśala*—with piety; *akuśala*—and impiety; *anvayaḥ*—causal connection.

TRANSLATION

How, then, could the Lord of all created beings—animals, men and demigods—have any connection with the piety and impiety that affect His subject creatures?

PURPORT

As explained in text 32, even great personalities empowered by the Lord are free from the laws of *karma.* Then what to speak of the Lord Himself. After all, the law of *karma* is created by Him and is an expression of His omnipotent will. Therefore His activities, which He performs out of His own pure goodness, are never subject to criticism by ordinary living beings.

TEXT 34

यत्पादपंकजपरागनिषेवतृप्ता
योगप्रभावविधुताखिलकर्मबन्धाः ।
स्वैरं चरन्ति मुनयोऽपि न नह्यमानास्
तस्येच्छयात्तवपुषः कुत एव बन्धः ॥ ३४ ॥

yat-pāda-paṅkaja-parāga-niṣeva-tṛptā
yoga-prabhāva-vidhutākhila-karma-bandhāḥ
svairaṁ caranti munayo'pi na nahyamānās
tasyecchayātta-vapuṣaḥ kuta eva bandhaḥ

yat—whose; *pāda-paṅkaja*—of the lotus feet; *parāga*—of the dust; *niṣeva*—by the service; *tṛptāḥ*—satisfied; *yoga-prabhāva*—by the power of yoga; *vidhuta*—washed away; *akhila*—all; *karma*—of fruitive activity; *bandhāḥ*—whose bondage; *svairam*—freely; *caranti*—they act; *munayaḥ*—wise sages; *api*—also; *na*—never; *nahyamānāḥ*—becoming bound up; *tasya*—of Him; *icchayā*—by His desire; *ātta*—accepted; *vapuṣaḥ*—transcendental bodies; *kutaḥ*—where; *eva*—indeed; *bandhaḥ*—bondage.

TRANSLATION

Material activities never entangle the devotees of the Supreme Lord, who are fully satisfied by serving the dust of His lotus feet. Nor do material activities entangle those intelligent sages who have freed themselves from the bondage of all fruitive reactions by the power of yoga. So how could there be any question of bondage for the Lord Himself, who assumes His transcendental forms according to His own sweet will?

TEXT 35

गोपीनां तत्पतीनां च सर्वेषामेव देहिनाम् ।
योऽन्तश्चरति सोऽध्यक्षः क्रीडनेनेह देहभाक् ॥ ३५ ॥

gopīnāṁ tat-patīnāṁ ca
sarveṣām eva dehinām
yo'ntaś carati so'dhyakṣaḥ
krīḍaneneha deha-bhāk

gopīnām—of the *gopīs; tat-patīnām*—of their husbands; *ca*—and; *sarveṣām*—of all; *eva*—indeed; *dehinām*—embodied living beings; *yaḥ*—who; *antaḥ*—within; *carati*—lives; *saḥ*—He; *adhyakṣaḥ*—the overseeing witness; *krīḍanena*—for sport; *iha*—in this world; *deha*—His form; *bhāk*—assuming.

TRANSLATION

He who lives as the overseeing witness within the gopīs and their husbands, and indeed within all embodied living beings, assumes forms in this world to enjoy transcendental pastimes.

PURPORT

We certainly do not assume our bodies to enjoy transcendental pastimes, as the Lord does. We eternal souls have accepted material bodies by force because of our foolish attempt to enjoy this material world. The Lord's forms are all eternal, spiritual existence and cannot be reasonably equated with our temporary flesh.

Since Lord Kṛṣṇa is the Supreme Lord dwelling within the *gopīs,* their so-called husbands and all other living beings, what possible sin could there be on His part if He embraces some of the beings He Himself has created? What fault could there be if the Lord goes with the *gopīs* to a secret place, since He already dwells within the most secret part of every living being, the core of the heart?

TEXT 36

अनुग्रहाय भक्तानां मानुषं देहमास्थितः ।
भजते तादृशीः क्रीडा याः श्रुत्वा तत्परो भवेत् ॥ ३६ ॥

anugrahāya bhaktānāṁ
mānuṣaṁ deham āsthitaḥ
bhajate tādṛśīḥ krīḍā
yāḥ śrutvā tat-paro bhavet

anugrahāya—to show mercy; *bhaktānām*—to His devotees; *mānuṣam*—humanlike; *deham*—a body; *āsthitaḥ*—assuming; *bhajate*—He accepts; *tādṛśīḥ*—such; *kriḍāḥ*—pastimes; *yāḥ*—about which; *śrutvā*—hearing; *tat-paraḥ*—dedicated to Him; *bhavet*—one becomes.

TRANSLATION

When the Lord assumes a humanlike body to show mercy to His devotees, He engages in such pastimes as will attract those who hear about them to become dedicated to Him.

PURPORT

Śrīla Jīva Gosvāmī explains in this connection that when Lord Kṛṣṇa descends to this world in His original two-handed form, out of kindness He manifests that form in a way His devotees conditioned in human society can perceive and understand. Thus here it is stated, *mānuṣaṁ deham āsthitaḥ:* "He assumes a humanlike body." Śrīla Viśvanātha Cakravartī Ṭhākura glorifies the Lord's conjugal pastimes, stating that these romantic affairs have an inconceivable spiritual potency to attract the polluted heart of conditioned souls. It is an undeniable fact that any pure- or simple-hearted person who hears narrations of the loving affairs of Kṛṣṇa will be attracted to the lotus feet of the Lord and gradually become His devotee.

TEXT 37

नासूयन् खलु कृष्णाय मोहितास्तस्य मायया ।
मन्यमानाः स्वपार्श्वस्थान् स्वान् स्वान् दारान् व्रजौकसः ॥ ३७ ॥

nāsūyan khalu kṛṣṇāya
mohitās tasya māyayā
manyamānāḥ sva-pārśva-sthān
svān svān dārān vrajaukasaḥ

na asūyan—were not jealous; *khalu*—even; *kṛṣṇāya*—against Kṛṣṇa; *mohitāḥ*—bewildered; *tasya*—His; *māyayā*—by the spiritual potency of illusion; *manyamānāḥ*—thinking; *sva-pārśva*—at their own sides; *sthān*—standing; *svān svān*—each their own; *dārān*—wives; *vraja-okasaḥ*—the cowherd men of Vraja.

TRANSLATION

The cowherd men, bewildered by Kṛṣṇa's illusory potency, thought their wives had remained home at their sides. Thus they did not harbor any jealous feelings against Him.

PURPORT

Because the *gopīs* loved Kṛṣṇa exclusively, Yoga-māyā protected their relationship with the Lord at all times, even though they were married. Śrīla Viśvanātha Cakravartī quotes from the *Ujjvala-nīlamaṇi* as follows:

māyā-kalpita-tādṛk-strī
śīlanenānusūyubhiḥ

na jātu vraja-devīnāṁ
patibhiḥ saha saṅgamaḥ

"The gopīs' jealous husbands consorted not with their wives but with doubles manufactured by Māyā. Thus these men never actually had any intimate contact with the divine ladies of Vraja." The gopīs are the internal energy of the Lord and can never belong to any other living being. Kṛṣṇa arranged their apparent marriage to other men simply to create the excitement of *parakīya-rasa,* the love between a married woman and her paramour. These activities are absolutely pure because they are the Lord's pastimes, and saintly persons since time immemorial have relished these supreme spiritual events.

TEXT 38

ब्रह्मरात्र उपावृत्ते वासुदेवानुमोदिताः ।
अनिच्छन्त्यो ययुर्गोप्यः स्वगृहान् भगवत्प्रियाः ॥ ३८ ॥

brahma-rātra upāvṛtte
vāsudevānumoditāḥ
anicchantyo yayur gopyaḥ
sva-gṛhān bhagavat-priyāḥ

brahma-rātre—the nighttime of Brahmā; *upāvṛtte*—being completed; *vāsudeva*—by Lord Kṛṣṇa; *anumoditāḥ*—advised; *anicchantyaḥ*—unwilling; *yayuḥ*—went; *gopyaḥ*—the *gopīs; sva-gṛhān*—to their homes; *bhagavat*—of the Supreme Lord; *priyāḥ*—the dear consorts.

TRANSLATION

After an entire night of Brahmā had passed, Lord Kṛṣṇa advised the gopīs to return to their homes. Although they did not wish to do so, the Lord's beloved consorts complied with His command.

PURPORT

In the *Bhagavad-gītā* (8.17) Lord Kṛṣṇa explains, "By human calculation, a thousand ages taken together is the duration of Brahmā's one day. And such also is the duration of his night." Thus one thousand ages entered within a single twelve-hour night when Lord Kṛṣṇa performed His *rāsa* dance. Śrīla Viśvanātha Cakravartī compares this inconceivable compression of time to the fact that many universes fit neatly within the forty-mile range of earthly

Vṛndāvana. Or one may consider that mother Yaśodā could not encircle the small abdomen of child Kṛṣṇa with numerous ropes, and that at another time He manifested many universes within His mouth. The transcendence of spiritual reality above and beyond mundane physics is concisely explained in Śrīla Rūpa Gosvāmī's *Laghu-bhāgavatāmṛta:*

evaṁ prabhoḥ priyāṇāṁ ca
dhāmnaś ca samayasya ca
avicintya-prabhāvatvād
atra kiñcin na durghaṭam

"Nothing is impossible for the Lord, His dear devotees, His transcendental abode or the time of His pastimes, for all these entities are inconceivably powerful."

Śrīla Viśvanātha Cakravartī further explains that the word *vāsudevānu-moditāḥ* indicates that Lord Kṛṣṇa advised the *gopīs,* "To assure the success of these pastimes, you and I should keep them secret." The word *vāsudeva,* a name of Kṛṣṇa, also indicates Lord Kṛṣṇa's plenary expansion who acts as the presiding Deity of consciousness. When the word *vāsudeva* is understood in this context, the word *vāsudevānumoditāḥ* indicates that the presiding Deity of consciousness, Vāsudeva, manifested embarrassment and fear of their elders within the *gopīs'* hearts, and therefore it was only with great reluctance that the young girls returned home.

TEXT 39

विक्रीडितं व्रजवधूभिरिदं च विष्णोः
श्रद्धान्वितोऽनुशृणुयादथ वर्णयेद्यः ।
भक्तिं परां भगवति प्रतिलभ्य कामं
हृद्रोगमाश्वपहिनोत्यचिरेण धीरः ॥ ३९ ॥

vikrīḍitaṁ vraja-vadhūbhir idaṁ ca viṣṇoḥ
śraddhānvito'nuśṛṇuyād atha varṇayed yaḥ
bhaktiṁ parāṁ bhagavati pratilabhya kāmaṁ
hṛd-rogam āśv apahinoty acireṇa dhīraḥ

vikrīḍitam—the sporting; *vraja-vadhūbhiḥ*—with the young women of Vṛndāvana; *idam*—this; *ca*—and; *viṣṇoḥ*—by Lord Viṣṇu; *śraddhā-anvitaḥ*—faithfully; *anuśṛṇuyāt*—hears; *atha*—or; *varṇayet*—describes; *yaḥ*—

who; *bhaktim*—devotional service; *parām*—transcendental; *bhagavati*—unto the Supreme Personality of Godhead; *pratilabhya*—obtaining; *kāmam*—material lust; *hṛt*—in the heart; *rogam*—the disease; *aśu*—quickly; *apahinoti*—he drives away; *acireṇa*—without delay; *dhīraḥ*—sober.

TRANSLATION

Anyone who faithfully hears or describes the Lord's playful affairs with the young gopīs of Vṛndāvana will attain the Lord's pure devotional service. Thus he will quickly become sober and conquer lust, the disease of the heart.

PURPORT

The extraordinary power of Lord Kṛṣṇa's conjugal pastimes is clearly revealed here. Qualitatively, the Lord's spiritual, loving pastimes are the diametric opposite of material, lusty affairs, so much so that simply by hearing about the Lord's pastimes a devotee conquers sex desire. By reading pornographic literature or hearing about material romance, we certainly do not conquer sex desire but rather increase our lust. But hearing or reading about the Lord's conjugal affairs has exactly the opposite effect because they are of the opposite nature, being purely spiritual. Therefore it is by the causeless mercy of Lord Kṛṣṇa that He exhibits His *rāsa-līlā* within this world. If we become attached to this narration, we will experience the bliss of spiritual love and thus reject the perverted reflection of that love, which is called lust. As nicely put by Lord Kṛṣṇa in the *Bhagavad-gītā* (2.59), *paraṁ dṛṣṭvā nivartate:* "Once having directly experienced the Supreme, one will not return to material pleasures."

Thus end the purports of the humble servants of His Divine Grace A.C. Bhaktivedanta Swami Prabhupāda to the Tenth Canto, Thirty-third Chapter, of the Śrīmad-Bhāgavatam, *entitled "The Rāsa Dance."*

CHAPTER THIRTY-FOUR

Nanda Mahārāja Saved and Śaṅkhacūḍa Slain

This chapter describes how Lord Śrī Kṛṣṇa saved His father Nanda from the clutches of a serpent and delivered a Vidyādhara named Sudarśana from the curse of the Āṅgirasa sages.

One day Nanda Mahārāja and the other cowherd men placed their family members on their bullock carts and went to the Ambikāvana forest to worship Lord Śiva. After bathing in the Sarasvatī River and worshiping Lord Sadāśiva, a form of Lord Viṣṇu, they decided to spend the night in the forest. As they slept, a hungry serpent came and began to swallow Nanda Mahārāja. Terrified, Nanda cried out in distress, "O Kṛṣṇa! O my son, please save this surrendered soul!" The cowherd men immediately awoke and began beating the serpent with wooden torches, but the serpent would not release Nanda. Then Lord Kṛṣṇa came and touched the serpent with His lotus foot. The serpent was immediately freed from his reptilian body and appeared in his original form as a demigod. He told them about his previous identity and described how he had been cursed by a group of sages. Then he offered his homage at the lotus feet of Śrī Kṛṣṇa and, on the Lord's order, returned to his own abode.

Later, during the Dola-pūrṇimā festival, Śrī Kṛṣṇa and Baladeva enjoyed pastimes in the forest with the young women of Vraja. The girlfriends of Baladeva and those of Kṛṣṇa joined together and sang about Their transcendental qualities. When the two Lords became absorbed in singing to the point of apparent intoxication, a servant of Kuvera's named Śaṅkhacūḍa boldly came forward and began abducting the *gopīs.* The young girls called out, "Kṛṣṇa, please save us!" and He and Rāma began to chase after Śaṅkhacūḍa. "Don't be afraid!" Kṛṣṇa called out to the *gopīs.* In fear of the Lords, Śaṅkhacūḍa left the *gopīs* aside and ran for his life. Kṛṣṇa chased after him, swiftly approached him and with a blow of His fist removed Śaṅkhacūḍa's jewel, together with his head. Then Kṛṣṇa brought the jewel back and presented it to Lord Baladeva.

TEXT 1

श्रीशुक उवाच
एकदा देवयात्रायां गोपाला जातकौतुकाः ।
अनोभिरनडुद्युक्तैः प्रययुस्तेऽम्बिकावनम् ॥१॥

śrī-śuka uvāca
ekadā deva-yātrāyāṁ
gopālā jāta-kautukāḥ
anobhir anaḍud-yuktaiḥ
prayayus te'mbikā-vanam

śrī-śukaḥ uvāca—Śrī Śukadeva Gosvāmī said; *ekadā*—once; *deva*—(to worship) the demigod, Lord Śiva; *yatrāyām*—on a trip; *gopālāḥ*—the cowherd men; *jāta-kautukāḥ*—eager; *anobhiḥ*—with wagons; *anaḍut*—to oxen; *yuktaiḥ*—yoked; *prayayuḥ*—went forth; *te*—they; *ambikā-vanam*—to the Ambikā forest.

TRANSLATION

Śukadeva Gosvāmī said: One day the cowherd men, eager to take a trip to worship Lord Śiva, traveled by bullock carts to the Ambikā forest.

PURPORT

According to Śrīla Jīva Gosvāmī, the word *ekadā* here indicates the occasion of Śiva-rātri. He further mentions that Ambikāvana is in Gujarat province, near the city of Siddhapura. Śrīla Viśvanātha Cakravartī Ṭhākura adds that the departure of the cowherd men specifically took place on the fourteenth lunar day of the dark fortnight of the month of Phālguna. Śrīla Viśvanātha Cakravartī also quotes authorities who claim that Ambikāvana lies on the bank of the Sarasvatī River, northwest of Mathurā. Ambikāvana is notable because within it are deities of Śrī Śiva and his wife, Goddess Umā.

TEXT 2

तत्र स्नात्वा सरस्वत्यां देवं पशुपतिं विभुम् ।
आनर्चुरर्हणैर्भक्त्या देवीं च नृपतेऽम्बिकाम् ॥ २ ॥

tatra snātvā sarasvatyāṁ
devaṁ paśu-patiṁ vibhum

ānarcur arhaṇair bhaktyā
devīṁ ca nṛpate'mbikām

tatra—there; *snātvā*—bathing; *sarasvatyām*—in the river Sarasvatī; *devam*—the demigod; *paśu-patim*—Lord Śiva; *vibhum*—the powerful; *ānarcuḥ*—they worshiped; *arhaṇaiḥ*—with paraphernalia; *bhaktyā*—devotedly; *devīm*—the goddess; *ca*—and; *nṛ-pate*—O King; *ambikām*—Ambikā.

TRANSLATION

O King, after arriving there, they bathed in the Sarasvatī and then devotedly worshiped with various paraphernalia the powerful Lord Paśupati and his consort, Goddess Ambikā.

TEXT 3

गावो हिरण्यं वासांसि मधु मध्वन्नमादृताः ।
ब्राह्मणेभ्यो ददुः सर्वे देवो नः प्रीयतामिति ॥ ३ ॥

gāvo hiraṇyaṁ vāsāṁsi
madhu madhv-annam ādṛtāḥ
brāhmaṇebhyo daduḥ sarve
devo naḥ prīyatām iti

gāvaḥ—cows; *hiraṇyam*—gold; *vāsāṁsi*—clothing; *madhu*—sweet-tasting; *madhu*—mixed with honey; *annam*—grains; *ādṛtāḥ*—respectfully; *brāhmaṇebhyaḥ*—to the *brāhmaṇas; daduḥ*—they gave; *sarve*—all of them; *devaḥ*—the lord; *naḥ*—with us; *prīyatām*—may be pleased; *iti*—thus praying.

TRANSLATION

The cowherd men gave the brāhmaṇas gifts of cows, gold, clothing and cooked grains mixed with honey. Then the cowherds prayed, "May the lord be pleased with us."

TEXT 4

ऊषुः सरस्वतीतीरे जलं प्राश्य यतव्रताः ।
रजनीं तां महाभागा नन्दसुनन्दकादयः ॥ ४ ॥

ūṣuḥ sarasvatī-tīre
jalaṁ prāśya yata-vratāḥ

rajanīṁ tāṁ mahā-bhāgā
nanda-sunandakādayaḥ

ūṣuḥ—they stayed; *sarasvatī-tīre*—on the bank of the Sarasvatī; *jalam*—water; *prāśya*—subsisting on; *yata-vratāḥ*—taking strict vows; *rajanīm*—the night; *tām*—that; *mahā-bhāgāḥ*—the greatly fortunate ones; *nanda-sunandaka-ādayaḥ*—Nanda, Sunanda and the others.

TRANSLATION

Nanda, Sunanda and the other greatly fortunate cowherds spent that night on the bank of the Sarasvatī, strictly observing their vows. They fasted, taking only water.

PURPORT

Śrīla Viśvanātha Cakravartī explains that Sunanda is the younger brother of Nanda Mahārāja.

TEXT 5

कश्चिन्महानहिस्तस्मिन् विपिनेऽतिबुभुक्षितः ।
यदृच्छयागतो नन्दं शयानमुरगोऽग्रसीत् ॥ ५ ॥

kaścin mahān ahis tasmin
vipine'ti-bubhukṣitaḥ
yadṛcchayāgato nandaṁ
śayānam ura-go'grasīt

kaścit—a certain; *mahān*—great; *ahiḥ*—snake; *tasmin*—in that; *vipine*—area of the forest; *ati-bubhukṣitaḥ*—extremely hungry; *yadṛcchayā*—by chance; *āgataḥ*—came there; *nandam*—Nanda Mahārāja; *śayānam*—who was lying asleep; *ura-gaḥ*—moving on his belly; *agrasīt*—swallowed.

TRANSLATION

During the night a huge and extremely hungry snake appeared in that thicket. Slithering on his belly up to the sleeping Nanda Mahārāja, the snake began swallowing him.

TEXT 6

स चुक्रोशाहिना ग्रस्तः कृष्ण कृष्ण महानयम् ।
सर्पो मां ग्रसते तात प्रपन्नं परिमोचय ॥ ६ ॥

sa cukrośāhinā grastaḥ
kṛṣṇa kṛṣṇa mahān ayam
sarpo māṁ grasate tāta
prapannaṁ parimocaya

saḥ—he, Nanda Mahārāja; *cukrośa*—shouted; *ahinā*—by the snake; *grastaḥ*—seized; *kṛṣṇa kṛṣṇa*—O Kṛṣṇa, Kṛṣṇa; *mahān*—large; *ayam*—this; *sarpaḥ*—serpent; *mām*—me; *grasate*—is swallowing; *tāta*—my dear boy; *prapannam*—who is surrendered; *parimocaya*—please deliver.

TRANSLATION

In the clutches of the snake, Nanda Mahārāja cried out, "Kṛṣṇa, Kṛṣṇa, my dear boy! This huge serpent is swallowing me! Please save me, who am surrendered to You!"

TEXT 7

तस्य चाक्रन्दितं श्रुत्वा गोपालाः सहसोत्थिताः ।
ग्रस्तं च दृष्ट्वा विभ्रान्ताः सर्पं विव्यधुरुल्मुकैः ॥ ७ ॥

tasya cākranditaṁ śrutvā
gopālāḥ sahasotthitāḥ
grastaṁ ca dṛṣṭvā vibhrāntāḥ
sarpaṁ vivyadhur ulmukaiḥ

tasya—his; *ca*—and; *ākranditam*—the crying out; *śrutvā*—hearing; *gopālāḥ*—the cowherds; *sahasā*—suddenly; *utthitāḥ*—rising up; *grastam*—seized; *ca*—and; *dṛṣṭvā*—seeing; *vibhrāntāḥ*—disturbed; *sarpam*—the snake; *vivyadhuḥ*—they beat; *ulmukaiḥ*—with flaming torches.

TRANSLATION

When the cowherd men heard the cries of Nanda, they immediately rose up and saw that he was being swallowed. Distraught, they beat the serpent with blazing torches.

TEXT 8

अलातैर्दह्यमानोऽपि नामुञ्चत्तमुरंगमः ।
तमस्पृशत्पदाभ्येत्य भगवान् सात्वतां पतिः ॥ ८ ॥

alātair dahyamāno'pi
nāmuñcat tam uraṅgamaḥ
tam aspṛśat padābhyetya
bhagavān sātvatāṁ patiḥ

alātaiḥ—by the firebrands; *dahyamānaḥ*—being burned; *api*—although; *na amuñcat*—did not release; *tam*—him; *uraṅgamaḥ*—the snake; *tam*—that snake; *aspṛśat*—touched; *padā*—with His foot; *abhyetya*—coming; *bhagavān*—the Supreme Lord; *sātvatām*—of the devotees; *patiḥ*—the master.

TRANSLATION

But even though the firebrands were burning him, the serpent would not release Nanda Mahārāja. Then the Supreme Lord Kṛṣṇa, master of His devotees, came to the spot and touched the snake with His foot.

TEXT 9

स वै भगवतः श्रीमत्पादस्पर्शहताशुभः ।
भेजे सर्पवपुर्हित्वा रूपं विद्याधरार्चितम् ॥ ९ ॥

sa vai bhagavataḥ śrīmat
pāda-sparśa-hatāśubhaḥ
bheje sarpa-vapur hitvā
rūpaṁ vidyādharārcitam

saḥ—he; *vai*—indeed; *bhagavataḥ*—of the Supreme Personality of Godhead; *śrī-mat*—divine; *pāda*—of the foot; *sparśa*—by the touch; *hata*—destroyed; *aśubhaḥ*—all inauspiciousness; *bheje*—assumed; *sarpa-vapuḥ*—his snake body; *hitvā*—giving up; *rūpam*—a form; *vidyādhara*—by the Vidyādharas; *arcitam*—worshiped.

TRANSLATION

The snake had all his sinful reactions destroyed by the touch of the Supreme Lord's divine foot, and thus he gave up his serpent body and appeared in the form of a worshipable Vidyādhara.

PURPORT

The words *rūpaṁ vidyādharārcitam* indicate that the erstwhile snake appeared in a beautiful form worshipable among the demigods called Vidyādharas. In other words, he appeared as the leader of the Vidyādharas.

TEXT 10

तमपृच्छद्धृषीकेशः प्रणतं समवस्थितम् ।
दीप्यमानेन वपुषा पुरुषं हेममालिनम् ॥ १० ॥

tam apṛcchad dhṛṣīkeśaḥ
praṇataṁ samavasthitam
dīpyamānena vapuṣā
puruṣaṁ hema-mālinam

tam—from him; *apṛcchat*—inquired; *hṛṣīkeśaḥ*—the Supreme Lord Hṛṣīkeśa; *praṇatam*—who was offering obeisances; *samavasthitam*—standing before Him; *dīpyamānena*—brilliantly shining; *vapuṣā*—with his body; *puruṣam*—the personality; *hema*—golden; *mālinam*—wearing necklaces.

TRANSLATION

The Supreme Lord Hṛṣīkeśa then questioned this personality, who was standing before Him with his head bowed, his brilliantly effulgent body bedecked with golden necklaces.

PURPORT

The demigod was about to speak, and Lord Kṛṣṇa wanted to focus everyone's attention on his words. Therefore He personally inquired from the worshipable Vidyādhara, who was standing before Him with his head bowed.

TEXT 11

को भवान् परया लक्ष्म्या रोचतेऽद्भुतदर्शनः ।
कथं जुगुप्सितामेतां गतिं वा प्रापितोऽवशः ॥ ११ ॥

ko bhavān parayā lakṣmyā
rocate'dbhuta-darśanaḥ
kathaṁ jugupsitām etāṁ
gatiṁ vā prāpito'vaśaḥ

kaḥ—who; *bhavān*—your good self; *parayā*—with great; *lakṣmyā*—beauty; *rocate*—shine; *adbhuta*—wonderful; *darśanaḥ*—to see; *katham*—why; *yugupsitām*—terrible; *etām*—this; *gatim*—destination; *vā*—and; *prāpitaḥ*—made to assume; *avaśaḥ*—beyond your control.

TRANSLATION

[Lord Kṛṣṇa said:] My dear sir, you appear so wonderful, glowing with such great beauty. Who are you? And who forced you to assume this terrible body of a snake?

TEXTS 12–13

सर्प उवाच
अहं विद्याधरः कश्चित्सुदर्शन इति श्रुतः ।
श्रिया स्वरूपसम्पत्त्या विमानेनाचरन् दिशः ॥ १२ ॥
ऋषीन् विरूपांगिरसः प्राहसं रूपदर्पितः ।
तैरिमां प्रापितो योनिं प्रलब्धैः स्वेन पाप्मना ॥ १३ ॥

sarpa uvāca
ahaṁ vidyādharaḥ kaścit
sudarśana iti śrutaḥ
śriyā svarūpa-sampattyā
vimānenācaran diśaḥ

ṛṣīn virūpāṅgirasaḥ
prāhasaṁ rūpa-darpitaḥ
tair imāṁ prāpito yoniṁ
pralabdhaiḥ svena pāpmanā

sarpaḥ uvāca—the serpent said; *aham*—I; *vidyādharaḥ*—a Vidyādhara; *kaścit*—certain; *sudarśanaḥ*—Sudarśana; *iti*—thus; *śrutaḥ*—well known; *śriyā*—with opulence; *svarūpa*—of my personal form; *sampattyā*—with the asset; *vimānena*—in my airplane; *ācaran*—wandering; *diśaḥ*—the directions; *ṛṣīn*—sages; *virūpa*—deformed; *āṅgirasaḥ*—of the disciplic succession of Āṅgirā Muni; *prāhasam*—I ridiculed; *rūpa*—because of beauty; *darpitaḥ*—overly conceited; *taiḥ*—by them; *imām*—this; *prāpitaḥ*—made to assume; *yonim*—the birth; *pralabdhaiḥ*—who were laughed at; *svena*—because of my own; *pāpmanā*—sinful action.

TRANSLATION

The serpent replied: I am the well-known Vidyādhara named Sudarśana. I was very opulent and beautiful, and I used to wander freely in all directions in my airplane. Once I saw some homely sages of the

lineage of Aṅgirā Muni. Proud of my beauty, I ridiculed them, and because of my sin they made me assume this lowly form.

TEXT 14

शापो मेऽनुग्रहायैव कृतस्तैः करुणात्मभिः ।
यदहं लोकगुरुणा पदा स्पृष्टो हताशुभः ॥ १४ ॥

śāpo me'nugrahāyaiva
kṛtas taiḥ karuṇātmabhiḥ
yad ahaṁ loka-guruṇā
padā spṛṣṭo hatāśubhaḥ

śāpaḥ—the curse; *me*—my; *anugrahāya*—for the benediction; *eva*—certainly; *kṛtaḥ*—created; *taiḥ*—by them; *karuṇa-ātmabhiḥ*—who are merciful by nature; *yat*—since; *aham*—I; *loka*—of all the worlds; *guruṇā*—by the spiritual master; *padā*—with His foot; *spṛṣṭaḥ*—touched; *hata*—destroyed; *aśubhaḥ*—all inauspiciousness.

TRANSLATION

It was actually for my benefit that those merciful sages cursed me, since now I have been touched by the foot of the supreme spiritual master of all the worlds and have thus been relieved of all inauspiciousness.

TEXT 15

तं त्वाहं भवभीतानां प्रपन्नानां भयापहम् ।
आपृच्छे शापनिर्मुक्तः पादस्पर्शादमीवहन् ॥ १५ ॥

taṁ tvāhaṁ bhava-bhītānāṁ
prapannānāṁ bhayāpaham
āpṛcche śāpa-nirmuktaḥ
pāda-sparśād amīva-han

tam—that same person; *tvā*—You; *aham*—I; *bhava*—of material existence; *bhītānām*—for those who are afraid; *prapannānām*—who are surrendered; *bhaya*—of fear; *apaham*—the remover; *āpṛcche*—I request permission; *śāpa*—from the curse; *nirmuktaḥ*—freed; *pāda-sparśāt*—by the touch of Your foot; *amīva*—of all distress; *han*—O destroyer.

TRANSLATION

My Lord, You destroy all fear for those who, fearing this material world, take shelter of You. By the touch of Your feet I am now freed from the curse of the sages. O destroyer of distress, please let me return to my planet.

PURPORT

According to the *ācāryas,* the word *āpṛcche* indicates that Sudarśana humbly requested the Lord for permission to return to his abode, where he might take up his duties again, certainly in a chastened state of mind.

TEXT 16

प्रपन्नोऽस्मि महायोगिन्महापुरुष सत्पते ।
अनुजानीहि मां देव सर्वलोकेश्वरेश्वर ॥ १६ ॥

prapanno'smi mahā-yogin
mahā-puruṣa sat-pate
anujānīhi māṁ deva
sarva-lokeśvareśvara

prapannaḥ—surrendered; *asmi*—I am; *mahā-yogin*—O greatest of all possessors of mystic power; *mahā-puruṣa*—O greatest of all personalities; *sat-pate*—O master of the devotees; *anujānīhi*—please order; *mām*—me; *deva*—O God; *sarva*—of all; *loka*—of the worlds; *īśvara*—of the controllers; *īśvara*—O supreme controller.

TRANSLATION

O master of mystic power, O great personality, O Lord of the devotees, I surrender to You. Please command me as You will, O supreme God, Lord of all lords of the universe.

TEXT 17

ब्रह्मदण्डाद्विमुक्तोऽहं सद्यस्तेऽच्युत दर्शनात् ।
यन्नाम गृह्णन्नखिलान् श्रोतॄनात्मानमेव च ।
सद्यः पुनाति किं भूयस्तस्य स्पृष्टः पदा हि ते ॥ १७ ॥

brahma-daṇḍād vimukto'haṁ
sadyas te'cyuta darśanāt

yan-nāma gṛhṇann akhilān
śrotṝn ātmānam eva ca
sadyaḥ punāti kiṁ bhūyas
tasya spṛṣṭaḥ padā hi te

brahma—of the *brāhmaṇas; daṇḍāt*—from the punishment; *vimuktaḥ*—freed; *aham*—I am; *sadyaḥ*—immediately; *te*—You; *acyuta*—O infallible Lord; *darśanāt*—by seeing; *yat*—whose; *nāma*—name; *gṛhṇan*—chanting; *akhilān*—all; *śrotṝn*—hearers; *ātmānam*—oneself; *eva*—indeed; *ca*—also; *sadyaḥ*—immediately; *punāti*—purifies; *kim bhūyaḥ*—what more, then; *tasya*—His; *spṛṣṭaḥ*—touched; *padā*—by the foot; *hi*—indeed; *te*—Your.

TRANSLATION

O infallible one, I was immediately freed from the brāhmaṇas' punishment simply by seeing You. Anyone who chants Your name purifies all who hear his chanting, as well as himself. How much more beneficial, then, is the touch of Your lotus feet?

TEXT 18

इत्यनुज्ञाप्य दाशार्हं परिक्रम्याभिवन्द्य च ।
सुदर्शनो दिवं यातः कृच्छ्रान्नन्दश्च मोचितः ॥ १८ ॥

ity anujñāpya dāśārhaṁ
parikramyābhivandya ca
sudarśano divaṁ yātaḥ
kṛcchrān nandaś ca mocitaḥ

iti—thus; *anujñāpya*—taking permission; *dāśārham*—from Lord Kṛṣṇa; *parikramya*—circumambulating; *abhivandya*—offering obeisances; *ca*—and; *sudarśanaḥ*—Sudarśana; *divam*—to heaven; *yātaḥ*—went; *kṛcchrāt*—from his difficulty; *nandaḥ*—Nanda Mahārāja; *ca*—also; *mocitaḥ*—was delivered.

TRANSLATION

Thus receiving the permission of Lord Kṛṣṇa, the demigod Sudarśana circumambulated Him, bowed down to offer Him homage and then returned to his heavenly planet. Nanda Mahārāja was thus delivered from peril.

TEXT 19

निशाम्य कृष्णस्य तदात्मवैभवं
व्रजौकसो विस्मितचेतसस्ततः ।
समाप्य तस्मिन्नियमं पुनर्व्रजं
नृपाययुस्तत्कथयन्त आदृताः ॥ १९ ॥

niśāmya kṛṣṇasya tad ātma-vaibhavaṁ
vrajaukaso vismita-cetasas tataḥ
samāpya tasmin niyamaṁ punar vrajaṁ
nṛpāyayus tat kathayanta ādṛtāḥ

niśāmya—seeing; *kṛṣṇasya*—of Lord Kṛṣṇa; *tat*—that; *ātma*—personal; *vaibhavam*—opulent display of power; *vraja-okasaḥ*—the inhabitants of Vraja; *vismita*—amazed; *cetasaḥ*—in their minds; *tataḥ*—then; *samāpya*—finishing; *tasmin*—at that place; *niyamam*—their vow; *punaḥ*—again; *vrajam*—to the cowherd village; *nṛpa*—O King; *āyayuḥ*—they returned; *tat*—that display; *kathayantaḥ*—describing; *ādṛtāḥ*—with reverence.

TRANSLATION

The inhabitants of Vraja were astonished to see the mighty power of Śrī Kṛṣṇa. Dear King, they then completed their worship of Lord Śiva and returned to Vraja, along the way respectfully describing Kṛṣṇa's powerful acts.

TEXT 20

कदाचिदथ गोविन्दो रामश्चाद्भुतविक्रमः ।
विजह्रतुर्वने रात्र्यां मध्यगौ व्रजयोषिताम् ॥ २० ॥

kadācid atha govindo
rāmaś cādbhuta-vikramaḥ
vijahratur vane rātryāṁ
madhya-gau vraja-yoṣitām

kadācit—on one occasion; *atha*—then; *govindaḥ*—Lord Kṛṣṇa; *rāmaḥ*—Lord Balarāma; *ca*—and; *adbhuta*—wonderful; *vikramaḥ*—whose deeds; *vijahratuḥ*—the two of Them played; *vane*—in the forest; *rātryām*—at night; *madhya-gau*—in the midst; *vraja-yoṣitām*—of the women of the cowherd community.

TRANSLATION

Once Lord Govinda and Lord Rāma, the performers of wonderful feats, were playing in the forest at night with the young girls of Vraja.

PURPORT

This verse introduces a new pastime. According to the *ācāryas,* the occasion mentioned here is the Holikā-pūrṇimā, a day also known as Gaura-pūrṇimā.

TEXT 21

उपगीयमानौ ललितं स्त्रीजनैर्बद्धसौहृदैः ।
स्वलंकृतानुलिप्तांगौ स्रग्विनौ विरजोऽम्बरौ ॥ २१ ॥

upagīyamānau lalitaṁ
strī-janair baddha-sauhṛdaiḥ
sv-alaṅkṛtānuliptāṅgau
sragvinau virajo-'mbarau

upagīyamānau—Their glories being sung; *lalitam*—charmingly; *strī-janaiḥ*—by the womenfolk; *baddha*—bound; *sauhṛdaiḥ*—in affection for Them; *su-alaṅkṛta*—finely decorated; *anulipta*—and anointed with (sandalwood pulp); *aṅgau*—whose limbs; *srak-vinau*—wearing flower garlands; *vi-rajaḥ*—spotless; *ambarau*—whose garments.

TRANSLATION

Kṛṣṇa and Balarāma wore flower garlands and spotless garments, and Their limbs were beautifully decorated and anointed. The women sang Their glories in a charming way, bound to Them by affection.

TEXT 22

निशामुखं मानयन्तावुदितोडुपतारकम् ।
मल्लिकागन्धमत्तालि जुष्टं कुमुदवायुना ॥ २२ ॥

niśā-mukhaṁ mānayantāv
uditoḍupa-tārakam
mallikā-gandha-mattāli-
juṣṭaṁ kumuda-vāyunā

niśā-mukham—the beginning of night; *mānayantau*—the two of Them honoring; *udita*—having risen; *uḍupa*—the moon; *tārakam*—and stars; *mallikā*—of the jasmine flowers; *gandha*—by the fragrance; *matta*—intoxicated; *ali*—by the bees; *juṣṭam*—liked; *kumuda*—from the lotuses; *vāyunā*—with the breeze.

TRANSLATION

The two Lords praised the nightfall, signaled by the rising of the moon and the appearance of stars, a lotus-scented breeze and bees intoxicated by the fragrance of jasmine flowers.

TEXT 23

जगतुः सर्वभूतानां मनःश्रवणमंगलम् ।
तौ कल्पयन्तौ युगपत्स्वरमण्डलमूर्च्छितम् ॥ २३ ॥

jagatuḥ sarva-bhūtānāṁ
manaḥ-śravaṇa-maṅgalam
tau kalpayantau yugapat
svara-maṇḍala-mūrcchitam

jagatuḥ—They sang; *sarva-bhūtānām*—of all living beings; *manaḥ*—for the mind; *śravaṇa*—and ears; *maṅgalam*—happiness; *tau*—the two of Them; *kalpayantau*—producing; *yugapat*—simultaneously; *svara*—of musical tones; *maṇḍala*—by the entire scale; *mūrcchitam*—augmented.

TRANSLATION

Kṛṣṇa and Balarāma sang, producing the entire range of musical sounds simultaneously. Their singing brought happiness to the ears and minds of all living beings.

TEXT 24

गोप्यस्तद्गीतमाकर्ण्य मूर्च्छिता नाविदन्नृप ।
स्रंसद्दुकूलमात्मानं स्रस्तकेशस्रजं ततः ॥ २४ ॥

gopyas tad-gītam ākarṇya
mūrcchitā nāvidan nṛpa
sraṁsad-dukūlam ātmānaṁ
srasta-keśa-srajaṁ tataḥ

gopyaḥ—the *gopīs; tat*—of Them; *gītam*—the singing; *ākarṇya*—hearing; *mūrcchitāḥ*—stunned; *na avidan*—were not aware of; *nṛpa*—my dear King; *sraṁsat*—slipping; *dukūlam*—the fine cloth of their garments; *ātmānam*—themselves; *srasta*—disheveled; *keśa*—their hair; *srajam*—the garlands; *tataḥ*—(slipping) from that.

TRANSLATION

The gopīs became stunned when they heard that song. Forgetting themselves, O King, they did not notice that their fine garments were becoming loose and their hair and garlands disheveled.

TEXT 25

एवं विक्रीडतोः स्वैरं गायतोः सम्प्रमत्तवत् ।
शंखचूड इति ख्यातो धनदानुचरोऽभ्यगात् ॥ २५ ॥

evaṁ vikrīḍatoḥ svairaṁ
gāyatoḥ sampramatta-vat
śaṅkhacūḍa iti khyāto
dhanadānucaro'bhyagāt

evam—thus; *vikrīḍatoḥ*—as the two of Them were playing; *svairam*—as They desired; *gāyatoḥ*—singing; *sampramatta*—to the point of intoxication; *vat*—as if; *śaṅkhacūḍaḥ*—Śaṅkhacūḍa; *iti*—thus; *khyātaḥ*—named; *dhana-da*—of the treasurer of the demigods, Lord Kuvera; *anucaraḥ*—a servant; *abhyagāt*—arrived.

TRANSLATION

While Lord Kṛṣṇa and Lord Balarāma thus played according to Their own sweet will and sang to the point of apparent intoxication, a servant of Kuvera named Śaṅkhacūḍa came upon the scene.

TEXT 26

तयोर्निरीक्षतो राजंस्तन्नाथं प्रमदाजनम् ।
क्रोशन्तं कालयामास दिश्युदीच्यामशंकितः ॥ २६ ॥

tayor nirīkṣato rājaṁs
tan-nāthaṁ pramadā-janam

krośantaṁ kālayām āsa
diśy udīcyām aśaṅkitaḥ

tayoḥ—the two of Them; *nirīkṣatoḥ*—as They looked on; *rājan*—O King; *tat-nātham*—having Them as their Lords; *pramadā-janam*—the assemblage of women; *krośantam*—crying out; *kālayām āsa*—he drove; *diśi*—in the direction; *udīcyām*—northern; *aśaṅkitaḥ*—without fear.

TRANSLATION

O King, even as the two Lords looked on, Śaṅkhacūḍa brazenly began driving the women off toward the north. The women, who had accepted Kṛṣṇa and Balarāma as their Lords, began to cry out to Them.

PURPORT

According to Śrīla Viśvanātha Cakravartī, the demon Śaṅkhacūḍa shook a large stick at the beautiful young girls, thus frightening them and driving them toward the north. He did not actually touch them, as is corroborated by the following verse.

TEXT 27

क्रोशन्तं कृष्ण रामेति विलोक्य स्वपरिग्रहम् ।
यथा गा दस्युना ग्रस्ता भ्रातरावन्वधावताम् ॥ २७ ॥

krośantaṁ kṛṣṇa rāmeti
vilokya sva-parigraham
yathā gā dasyunā grastā
bhrātarāv anvadhāvatām

krośantam—crying out; *kṛṣṇa rāma iti*—"Kṛṣṇa! Rāma!"; *vilokya*—seeing; *sva-parigraham*—Their devotees; *yathā*—just as; *gāḥ*—cows; *dasyunā*—by a thief; *grastāḥ*—seized; *bhrātarau*—the two brothers; *anvadhāvatām*—ran after.

TRANSLATION

Hearing Their devotees crying out "Kṛṣṇa! Rāma!" and seeing that they were just like cows being stolen by a thief, Kṛṣṇa and Balarāma began to run after the demon.

TEXT 28

मा भैष्टेत्यभयारावौ शालहस्तौ तरस्विनौ ।
आसेदतुस्तं तरसा त्वरितं गुह्यकाधमम् ॥ २८ ॥

mā bhaiṣṭety abhayārāvau
śāla-hastau tarasvinau
āsedatus taṁ tarasā
tvaritaṁ guhyakādhamam

mā bhaiṣṭa—do not fear; *iti*—thus calling; *abhaya*—giving fearlessness; *ārāvau*—whose words; *śāla*—stones; *hastau*—in Their hands; *tarasvinau*—moving quickly; *āsedatuḥ*—They approached; *tam*—that demon; *tarasā*—with haste; *tvaritam*—who was moving swiftly; *guhyaka*—of Yakṣas; *adhamam*—the worst.

TRANSLATION

The Lords called out in reply, "Do not fear!" Then They picked up logs of the śala tree and quickly pursued that lowest of Guhyakas, who swiftly ran away.

TEXT 29

स वीक्ष्य तावनुप्राप्तौ कालमृत्यू इवोद्विजन् ।
विषृज्य स्त्रीजनं मूढः प्राद्रवज्जीवितेच्छया ॥ २९ ॥

sa vīkṣya tāv anuprāptau
kāla-mṛtyū ivodvijan
visṛjya strī-janaṁ mūḍhaḥ
prādravaj jīvitecchayā

saḥ—he, Śaṅkhacūḍa; *vīkṣya*—seeing; *tau*—the two; *anuprāptau*—approached; *kāla-mṛtyū*—Time and Death; *iva*—as; *udvijan*—becoming anxious; *visṛjya*—leaving aside; *strī-janam*—the women; *mūḍhaḥ*—confused; *prādravat*—ran away; *jīvita*—his life; *icchayā*—with the desire of preserving.

TRANSLATION

When Śaṅkhacūḍa saw the two of Them coming toward him like the personified forces of Time and Death, he was filled with anxiety. Confused, he abandoned the women and fled for his life.

TEXT 30

तमन्वधावद् गोविन्दो यत्र यत्र स धावति ।
जिहीर्षुस्तच्छिरोरत्नं तस्थौ रक्षन् स्त्रियो बलः ॥ ३० ॥

tam anvadhāvad govindo
yatra yatra sa dhāvati
jihīrṣus tac-chiro-ratnaṁ
tasthau rakṣan striyo balaḥ

tam—after him; *anvadhāvat*—ran; *govindaḥ*—Lord Kṛṣṇa; *yatra yatra*—wherever; *saḥ*—he; *dhāvati*—was running; *jihīrṣuḥ*—desiring to take away; *tat*—his; *śiraḥ*—upon the head; *ratnam*—the jewel; *tasthau*—stood; *rakṣan*—protecting; *striyaḥ*—the women; *balaḥ*—Lord Balarāma.

TRANSLATION

Lord Govinda chased the demon wherever he ran, eager to take his crest jewel. Meanwhile Lord Balarāma stayed with the women to protect them.

PURPORT

Śrīla Viśvanātha Cakravartī explains that the women were fatigued from being driven away, and thus Lord Balarāma protected them and consoled them as they rested. Meanwhile Lord Kṛṣṇa went after the demon.

TEXT 31

अविदूर इवाभ्येत्य शिरस्तस्य दुरात्मनः ।
जहार मुष्टिनैवांग सहचूडामणिं विभुः ॥ ३१ ॥

avidūra ivābhyetya
śiras tasya durātmanaḥ
jahāra muṣṭinaivāṅga
saha-cūḍā-maṇiṁ vibhuḥ

avidūre—nearby; *iva*—as if; *abhyetya*—coming toward; *śiraḥ*—the head; *tasya*—of him; *durātmanaḥ*—the wicked one; *jahāra*—took away; *muṣṭinā*—with His fist; *eva*—simply; *aṅga*—my dear King; *saha*—together with; *cūḍā-maṇim*—the jewel upon his head; *vibhuḥ*—the almighty Lord.

TRANSLATION

The mighty Lord overtook Śaṅkhacūḍa from a great distance as if from nearby, my dear King, and then with His fist the Lord removed the wicked demon's head, together with his crest jewel.

TEXT 32

शंखचूडं निहत्यैवं मणिमादाय भास्वरम् ।
अग्रजायाददात्प्रीत्या पश्यन्तीनां च योषिताम् ॥ ३२ ॥

śaṅkhacūḍaṁ nihatyaivaṁ
maṇim ādāya bhāsvaram
agrajāyādadāt prītyā
paśyantīnāṁ ca yoṣitām

śaṅkhacūḍam—the demon Śaṅkhacūḍa; *nihatya*—killing; *evam*—in this manner; *maṇim*—the jewel; *ādāya*—taking; *bhāsvaram*—brilliant; *agra-jāya*—to His elder brother (Lord Balarāma); *adadāt*—gave; *prītyā*—with satisfaction; *paśyantīnām*—as they were watching; *ca*—and; *yoṣitām*—the women.

TRANSLATION

Having thus killed the demon Śaṅkhacūḍa and taken away his shining jewel, Lord Kṛṣṇa gave it to His elder brother with great satisfaction as the gopīs watched.

PURPORT

Various *gopīs* perhaps thought that Govinda would give one of them the valuable jewel. To prevent rivalry among them, Śrī Kṛṣṇa happily gave the jewel to His older brother, Balarāma.

Thus end the purports of the humble servants of His Divine Grace A.C. Bhaktivedanta Swami Prabhupāda to the Tenth Canto, Thirty-fourth Chapter, of the Śrīmad-Bhāgavatam, *entitled "Nanda Mahārāja Saved and Śaṅkhacūḍa Slain."*

CHAPTER THIRTY- FIVE

The Gopīs Sing of Kṛṣṇa as He Wanders in the Forest

This chapter contains the songs the *gopīs* sing to express their feelings of separation from Kṛṣṇa when He goes to the forest during the day.

As the *gopīs'* mood of separation from Śrī Kṛṣṇa becomes ever more intense, His names, forms, qualities and pastimes begin spontaneously manifesting in their hearts. Thus they join together and sing as follows: "The beauty of Kṛṣṇa attracts the minds of all. When He stands in His threefold-bending way and plays upon His flute, the Siddhas' wives, flying in the sky with their husbands, become attracted to Him and forget external reality. The bulls, cows and other animals in the pasture become stunned in ecstasy, and they stand so still, with the grass unchewed between their teeth, that they appear like figures in a drawing. Indeed, even the unconscious rivers stop flowing.

"Just see! When Kṛṣṇa dresses Himself in forest array and calls the cows' names by blowing on His flute, even the trees and creepers become so ecstatic out of love that their limbs display eruptions and their sap pours down like a torrent of tears. The sound of Kṛṣṇa's flute causes the cranes, swans and other birds in the lakes to close their eyes in deep meditation, the clouds in the sky to gently rumble, imitating the flute's vibration, and even such great authorities in the science of music as Indra, Siva and Brahmā to become astonished. And just as we *gopīs* are anxious to offer everything we have to Kṛṣṇa, so the wives of the black deer follow Him about, imitating us."

"When Kṛṣṇa is returning to Vraja, He constantly plays His flute while His young companions chant His glories, and Brahmā and other chief demigods come to worship His lotus feet."

Thus the *gopīs,* feeling intense separation from Kṛṣṇa, sing of His pastimes.

TEXT 1

श्रीशुक उवाच

गोप्यः कृष्णे वनं याते तमनुद्रुतचेतसः ।

कृष्णलीलाः प्रगायन्त्यो निन्युर्दुःखेन वासरान् ॥ १ ॥

śrī-śuka uvāca
gopyaḥ kṛṣṇe vanaṁ yāte
tam anudruta-cetasaḥ
kṛṣṇa-līlāḥ pragāyantyo
ninyur duḥkhena vāsarān

śrī-śukaḥ uvāca—Śrī Śukadeva Gosvāmī said; *gopyaḥ*—the *gopīs; kṛṣṇe*—Lord Kṛṣṇa; *vanam*—to the forest; *yāte*—having gone; *tam*—after Him; *anudruta*—chasing; *cetasaḥ*—whose minds; *kṛṣṇa-līlāḥ*—the transcendental pastimes of Kṛṣṇa; *pragāyantyaḥ*—singing loudly; *ninyuḥ*—they passed; *duḥkhena*—unhappily; *vāsarān*—the days.

TRANSLATION

Śukadeva Gosvāmī said: Whenever Kṛṣṇa went to the forest, the minds of the gopīs would run after Him, and thus the young girls sadly spent their days singing of His pastimes.

PURPORT

Although the *gopīs* enjoyed direct association with Kṛṣṇa at night in the *rāsa* dance, during the day He went about His normal duties, tending His cows in the forest. At that time the minds of the *gopīs* would run after Him, but the young girls had to stay back in the village and do their own duties. Thus feeling the pain of separation, they would sing about Śrī Kṛṣṇa's transcendental pastimes.

TEXTS 2–3

श्रीगोप्य ऊचुः
वामबाहुकृतवामकपोलो
वल्गितभ्रुरधरार्पितवेणुम् ।
कोमलांगुलिभिराश्रितमार्गं
गोप्य ईरयति यत्र मुकुन्दः ॥ २ ॥
व्योमयानवनिताः सह सिद्धैर्
विस्मितास्तदुपधार्य सलज्जाः ।
काममार्गणसमर्पितचित्ताः
कश्मलं ययुरपस्मृतनीव्यः ॥ ३ ॥

śrī-gopya ūcuḥ
vāma-bāhu-kṛta-vāma-kapolo
valgita-bhrur adharārpita-veṇum
komalāṅgulibhir āśrita-mārgaṁ
gopya īrayati yatra mukundaḥ

vyoma-yāna-vanitāḥ saha siddhair
vismitās tad upadhārya sa-lajjāḥ
kāma-mārgaṇa-samarpita-cittāḥ
kaśmalaṁ yayur apasmṛta-nīvyaḥ

śrī-gopyaḥ ūcuḥ—the *gopīs* said; *vāma*—left; *bāhu*—on His arm; *kṛta*—putting; *vāma*—left; *kapolaḥ*—His cheek; *valgita*—moving; *bhruḥ*—His eyebrows; *adhara*—upon His lips; *arpita*—placed; *veṇum*—His flute; *komala*—tender; *aṅgulibhiḥ*—with His fingers; *āśrita-mārgam*—its holes stopped; *gopyaḥ*—O *gopīs; īrayati*—vibrates; *yatra*—where; *mukundaḥ*—Lord Kṛṣṇa; *vyoma*—in the sky; *yāna*—traveling; *vanitāḥ*—the ladies; *saha*—together with; *siddhaiḥ*—the Siddha demigods; *vismitāḥ*—amazed; *tat*—to that; *upadhārya*—listening; *sa*—with; *lajjāḥ*—embarrassment; *kāma*—of lust; *mārgaṇa*—to the pursuit; *samarpita*—offered; *cittāḥ*—their minds; *kaśmalam*—distress; *yayuḥ*—they experienced; *apasmṛta*—forgetting; *nīvyaḥ*—the belts of their dresses.

TRANSLATION

The gopīs said: When Mukunda vibrates the flute He has placed to His lips, stopping its holes with His tender fingers, He rests His left cheek on His left arm and makes His eyebrows dance. At that time the demigoddesses traveling in the sky with their husbands, the Siddhas, become amazed. As those ladies listen, they are embarrassed to find their minds yielding to the pursuit of lusty desires, and in their distress they are unaware that the belts of their garments are loosening.

PURPORT

Śrīla Jīva Gosvāmī states that this chapter consists of a collection of statements the *gopīs* made at various times as they stood in small groups here and there in Vṛndāvana.

TEXTS 4–5

हन्त चित्रमबलाः शृणुतेदं
हारहास उरसि स्थिरविद्युत् ।
नन्दसूनुरयमार्तजनानां
नर्मदो यर्हि कूजितवेणुः ॥ ४ ॥
वृन्दशो व्रजवृषा मृगगावो
वेणुवाद्यहृतचेतस आरात् ।
दन्तदष्टकवला धृतकर्णा
निद्रिता लिखितचित्रमिवासन् ॥ ५ ॥

hanta citram abalāḥ śṛṇutedaṁ
hāra-hāsa urasi sthira-vidyut
nanda-sūnur ayam ārta-janānāṁ
narma-do yarhi kūjita-veṇuḥ

vṛndaśo vraja-vṛṣā mṛga-gāvo
veṇu-vādya-hṛta-cetasa ārāt
danta-daṣṭa-kavalā dhṛta-karṇā
nidritā likhita-citram ivāsan

hanta—ah; *citram*—wonder; *abalāḥ*—O girls; *śṛṇuta*—hear; *idam*—this; *hāra*—(brilliant) like a necklace; *hāsaḥ*—whose smile; *urasi*—upon the chest; *sthira*—motionless; *vidyut*—lightning; *nanda-sūnuḥ*—son of Nanda Mahārāja; *ayam*—this; *ārta*—troubled; *janānām*—for persons; *narma*—of joy; *daḥ*—the giver; *yarhi*—when; *kūjita*—has vibrated; *veṇuḥ*—His flute; *vṛndaśaḥ*—in groups; *vraja*—kept in the pasture; *vṛṣāḥ*—the bulls; *mṛga*—the deer; *gāvaḥ*—and the cows; *veṇu*—of the flute; *vādya*—by the playing; *hṛta*—stolen away; *cetasaḥ*—their minds; *ārāt*—at a distance; *danta*—by their teeth; *daṣṭa*—bit; *kavalāḥ*—whose mouthfuls; *dhṛta*—holding up; *karṇāḥ*—their ears; *nidritāḥ*—asleep; *likhita*—drawn; *citram*—an illustration; *iva*—as if; *āsan*—they were.

TRANSLATION

O girls! This son of Nanda, who gives joy to the distressed, bears steady lightning on His chest and has a smile like a jeweled necklace. Now please hear something wonderful. When He vibrates His flute, Vraja's bulls, deer and cows, standing in groups at a great distance, are all captivated by the

sound, and they stop chewing the food in their mouths and cock their ears. Stunned, they appear as if asleep, or like figures in a painting.

PURPORT

The word *sthira-vidyut,* "steady lightning," refers to the goddess of fortune, who resides on the chest of the Supreme Lord. When the animals of Vṛndāvana hear the sound of the flute, they become stunned in ecstasy, and thus they stop chewing their food and cannot swallow it. The *gopīs,* in separation from Kṛṣṇa, marvel at the extraordinary effect of the Lord's flute-playing.

Śrīla Śrīdhara Svāmī gives the following explanation of the compound word *hāra-hāsa,* which compares Lord Kṛṣṇa's smile to a necklace: "The word can mean 'He whose smile is brilliantly clear like a jeweled necklace' or 'He whose smile is reflected from His jeweled necklaces,' because while Kṛṣṇa plays the flute He bends His head down and smiles. The word can also mean 'He whose smile, like a jeweled necklace, casts its effulgence upon His chest' or 'He whose necklaces shine brilliantly, just like a smile.'"

TEXTS 6–7

बर्हिणस्तबकधातुपलाशैर्
बद्धमल्लपरिबर्हविडम्बः ।
कर्हिचित्सबल आलि स गोपैर्
गाः समाह्वयति यत्र मुकुन्दः ॥ ६ ॥
तर्हि भग्नगतयः सरितो वै
तत्पदाम्बुजरजोऽनिलनीतम् ।
स्पृहयतीर्वयमिवाबहुपुण्याः
प्रेमवेपितभुजाः स्तिमितापः ॥ ७ ॥

barhiṇa-stabaka-dhātu-palāśair
baddha-malla-paribarha-viḍambaḥ
karhicit sa-bala āli sa gopair
gāḥ samāhvayati yatra mukundaḥ

tarhi bhagna-gatayaḥ sarito vai
tat-padāmbuja-rajo'nila-nītam
spṛhayatīr vayam ivābahu-puṇyāḥ
prema-vepita-bhujāḥ stimitāpaḥ

barhiṇa—of peacocks; *stabaka*—with the tail feathers; *dhātu*—with colored minerals; *palāśaiḥ*—and with leaves; *baddha*—arranged; *malla*—of a wrestler; *paribarha*—the apparel; *viḍambaḥ*—imitating; *karhicit*—sometimes; *sa-balaḥ*—with Balarāma; *āli*—my dear *gopī; saḥ*—He; *gopaiḥ*—with the cowherd boys; *gāḥ*—the cows; *samāhvayati*—calls; *yatra*—when; *mukundaḥ*—Lord Mukunda; *tarhi*—then; *bhagna*—broken; *gatayaḥ*—their movement; *saritaḥ*—the rivers; *vai*—indeed; *tat*—His; *pada-ambuja*—of the lotus feet; *rajaḥ*—the dust; *anila*—by the wind; *nītam*—brought; *spṛhayatīḥ*—hankering for; *vayam*—ourselves; *iva*—just like; *abahu*—slight; *puṇyāḥ*—the piety to whose credit; *prema*—due to love of God; *vepita*—trembling; *bhujāḥ*—whose arms (waves); *stimita*—stopped; *āpaḥ*—whose water.

TRANSLATION

My dear gopī, sometimes Mukunda imitates the appearance of a wrestler by decorating Himself with leaves, peacock feathers and colored minerals. Then, in the company of Balarāma and the cowherd boys, He plays His flute to call the cows. At that time the rivers stop flowing, their water stunned by the ecstasy they feel as they eagerly wait for the wind to bring them the dust of His lotus feet. But like us, the rivers are not very pious, and thus they merely wait with their arms trembling out of love.

PURPORT

The *gopīs* state here that the sound of Kṛṣṇa's flute causes even inanimate objects like rivers to become conscious and then stunned in ecstasy. Just as the *gopīs* could not always be in Kṛṣṇa's physical association, the rivers could not come to the Lord's lotus feet. Although they desired the Lord, their movement was checked by ecstasy, and their "arms," their waves, trembled with love of Godhead.

TEXTS 8–11

अनुचरैः समनुवर्णितवीर्य
आदिपूरुष इवाचलभूतिः ।
वनचरो गिरितटेषु चरन्तीर्
वेणुनाह्वयति गाः स यदा हि ॥ ८ ॥
वनलतास्तरव आत्मनि विष्णुं
व्यञ्जयन्त्य इव पुष्पफलाढ्याः ।

प्रणतभारविटपा मधुधाराः
प्रेमहृष्टतनवो ववृषुः स्म ॥ ९ ॥
दर्शनीयतिलको वनमाला-
दिव्यगन्धतुलसीमधुमत्तैः ।
अलिकुलैरलघु गीतामभीष्टम्
आद्रियन् यर्हि सन्धितवेणुः ॥ १० ॥
सरसि सारसहंसविहंगाश्
चारुगीतहृतचेतस एत्य ।
हरिमुपासत ते यतचित्ता
हन्त मीलितदृशो धृतमौनाः ॥ ११ ॥

anucaraiḥ samanuvarṇita-vīrya
ādi-pūruṣa ivācala-bhūtiḥ
vana-caro giri-taṭeṣu carantīr
veṇunāhvayati gāḥ sa yadā hi

vana-latās tarava ātmani viṣṇuṁ
vyañjayantya iva puṣpa-phalāḍhyāḥ
praṇata-bhāra-viṭapā madhu-dhārāḥ
prema-hṛṣṭa-tanavo vavṛṣuḥ sma

darśanīya-tilako vana-mālā-
divya-gandha-tulasī-madhu-mattaiḥ
ali-kulair alaghu gītam abhīṣṭam
ādriyan yarhi sandhita-veṇuḥ

sarasi sārasa-haṁsa-vihaṅgāś
cāru-gīta-hṛta-cetasa etya
harim upāsata te yata-cittā
hanta mīlita-dṛśo dhṛta-maunāḥ

anucaraiḥ—by His companions; *samanuvarṇita*—being elaborately described; *vīryaḥ*—whose prowess; *ādi-pūruṣaḥ*—the original Personality of Godhead; *iva*—as if; *acala*—unchanging; *bhūtiḥ*—whose opulences; *vana*—in the forest; *carah*—moving about; *giri*—of the mountains; *taṭeṣu*—on the sides; *carantīḥ*—who are grazing; *veṇunā*—with His flute; *āhvayati*—calls; *gāḥ*—the cows; *saḥ*—He; *yadā*—when; *hi*—indeed; *vana-latāḥ*—the forest creepers; *taravaḥ*—and the trees; *ātmani*—within themselves; *viṣṇum*—the Supreme Lord, Viṣṇu; *vyañjayantyaḥ*—revealing; *iva*—as if; *puṣpa*—with flowers; *phala*—and fruits; *āḍhyāḥ*—richly endowed; *praṇata*—bowed down; *bhāra*—because of the weight; *viṭapāḥ*—whose branches; *madhu*—of sweet sap; *dhārāḥ*—torrents; *prema*—out of ecstatic love; *hṛṣṭa*—hairs standing on end; *tanavaḥ*—on whose bodies (trunks); *vavṛṣuḥ sma*—they have rained down; *darśanīya*—of persons who are attractive to see; *tilakaḥ*—the most excellent; *vana-mālā*—upon His garland made of forest flowers; *divya*—divine; *gandha*—whose fragrance; *tulasī*—of the *tulasī* flowers; *madhu*—by the honeylike sweetness; *mattaiḥ*—intoxicated; *ali*—of bees; *kulaiḥ*—by the swarms; *alaghu*—strong; *gītam*—the singing; *abhīṣṭam*—desirable; *ādriyan*—thankfully acknowledging; *yarhi*—when; *sandhita*—placed; *veṇuḥ*—His flute; *sarasi*—in the lake; *sārasa*—the cranes; *haṁsa*—swans; *vihaṅgāḥ*—and other birds; *cāru*—charming; *gīta*—by the song (of His flute); *hṛta*—taken away; *cetasaḥ*—whose minds; *etya*—coming forward; *harim*—Lord Kṛṣṇa; *upāsata*—worship; *te*—they; *yata*—under control; *cittāḥ*—whose minds; *hanta*—ah; *mīlita*—closed; *dṛśaḥ*—their eyes; *dhṛta*—maintaining; *maunāḥ*—silence.

TRANSLATION

Kṛṣṇa moves about the forest in the company of His friends, who vividly chant the glories of His magnificent deeds. He thus appears just like the Supreme Personality of Godhead exhibiting His inexhaustible opulences. When the cows wander onto the mountainsides and Kṛṣṇa calls out to them with the sound of His flute, the trees and creepers in the forest respond by becoming so luxuriant with fruits and flowers that they seem to be manifesting Lord Viṣṇu within their hearts. As their branches bend low with the weight, the filaments on their trunks and vines stand erect out of the ecstasy of love of God, and both the trees and the creepers pour down a rain of sweet sap.

Maddened by the divine, honeylike aroma of the tulasī flowers on the garland Kṛṣṇa wears, swarms of bees sing loudly for Him, and that most beautiful of all persons thankfully acknowledges and acclaims their song by taking His flute to His lips and playing it. The charming flute-song then steals away the minds of the cranes, swans and other lake-dwelling birds. Indeed, they approach Kṛṣṇa, close their eyes and, maintaining strict silence, worship Him by fixing their consciousness upon Him in deep meditation.

PURPORT

Śrīla Viśvanātha Cakravartī Ṭhākura has made several illuminating comments on these verses. He gives the analogy that just as when householder Vaiṣṇavas hear a *saṅkīrtana* party approaching they become ecstatic and offer obeisances, so the trees and creepers in Vṛndāvana became ecstatic when they heard Kṛṣṇa's flute and bowed low with their branches and vines. The word *darśanīya-tilaka* in text 10 indicates not only that the Lord is "the most excellent (to see)," but also that He decorated Himself with attractive reddish *tilaka* taken from the mineral-rich earth of Vṛndāvana forest.

Śrīla Viśvanātha Cakravartī also points out that *tulasī,* although exalted in many ways, is not normally considered an especially fragrant plant. However, early in the morning *tulasī* emits a transcendental fragrance that ordinary people cannot perceive but that transcendental personalities fully appreciate. The bees who are privileged to swarm about the flower garlands worn by the Supreme Personality of Godhead certainly appreciate this fragrance, and Śrīla Viśvanātha Cakravartī quotes from the *Bhāgavatam* (3.15.19) to the effect that the most fragrant plants in Vaikuṇṭha also appreciate the special qualifications of Tulasī-devī.

The word *sandhita-veṇuḥ* in text 10 indicates that Lord Kṛṣṇa placed His flute firmly upon His lips. And the melody emanating from that flute is certainly the most enchanting of sounds, as the *gopīs* describe in this chapter.

TEXTS 12–13

सहबलः स्त्रगवतंसविलासः
सानुषु क्षितिभृतो व्रजदेव्यः ।
हर्षयन् यर्हि वेणुरवेण
जातहर्ष उपरम्भति विश्वम् ॥ १२ ॥
महदतिक्रमणशंकितचेता
मन्दमन्दमनुगर्जति मेघः ।
सुहृदमभ्यवर्षत्सुमनोभिश्
छायया च विदधत्प्रतपत्रम् ॥ १३ ॥

saha-balaḥ srag-avataṁsa-vilāsaḥ
sānuṣu kṣiti-bhṛto vraja-devyaḥ
harṣayan yarhi veṇu-raveṇa
jāta-harṣa uparambhati viśvam

mahad-atikramaṇa-śaṅkita-cetā
manda-mandam anugarjati meghaḥ
suhṛdam abhyavarṣat sumanobhiś
chāyayā ca vidadhat pratapatram

saha-balaḥ—together with Balarāma; *srak*—a flower garland; *avataṁsa*—as the ornament on His head; *vilāsaḥ*—playfully wearing; *sānuṣu*—on the sides; *kṣiti-bhṛtaḥ*—of a mountain; *vraja-devyaḥ*—O goddesses of Vṛndāvana (*gopīs*); *harṣayan*—creating joy; *yarhi*—when; *veṇu*—of His flute; *raveṇa*—by the resounding vibration; *jāta-harṣaḥ*—becoming joyful; *uparambhati*—causes to relish; *viśvam*—the entire world; *mahat*—against a great personality; *atikramaṇa*—of a transgression; *śaṅkita*—fearful; *cetāḥ*—in his mind; *manda-mandam*—very gently; *anugarjati*—thunders in response; *meghaḥ*—the cloud; *suhṛdam*—upon his friend; *abhyavarṣat*—has rained down; *sumanobhiḥ*—with flowers; *chāyayā*—with his shade; *ca*—and; *vidadhat*—providing; *pratapatram*—an umbrella as protection from the sun.

TRANSLATION

O goddesses of Vraja, when Kṛṣṇa is enjoying Himself with Balarāma on the mountain slopes, playfully wearing a flower garland on the top of His head, He engladdens all with the resonant vibrations of His flute. Thus He delights the entire world. At that time the nearby cloud, afraid of offending a great personality, thunders very gently in accompaniment. The cloud showers flowers onto his dear friend Kṛṣṇa and shades Him from the sun like an umbrella.

TEXTS 14–15

विविधगोपचरणेषु विदग्धो
वेणुवाद्य उरुधा निजशिक्षाः ।
तव सुतः सति यदाधरबिम्बे
दत्तवेणुरनयत्स्वरजातीः ॥ १४ ॥
सवनशस्तदुपधार्य सुरेशाः
शक्रशर्वपरमेष्ठिपुरोगाः ।
कवय आनतकन्धरचित्ताः
कश्मलं ययुरनिश्चिततत्त्वाः ॥ १५ ॥

vividha-gopa-caraṇeṣu vidagdho
veṇu-vādya urudhā nija-śikṣāḥ
tava sutaḥ sati yadādhara-bimbe
datta-veṇur anayat svara-jātīḥ

savanaśas tad upadhārya sureśāḥ
śakra-śarva-parameṣṭhi-purogāḥ
kavaya ānata-kandhara-cittāḥ
kaśmalaṁ yayur aniścita-tattvāḥ

vividha—various; *gopa*—of cowherds; *caraṇeṣu*—in the activities; *vidagdhaḥ*—expert; *veṇu*—of the flute; *vādye*—in the matter of playing; *urudhā*—manifold; *nija*—of His own production; *śikṣāḥ*—whose teachings; *tava*—your; *sutaḥ*—son; *sati*—O pious lady (Yaśodā); *yadā*—when; *adhara*—upon His lips; *bimbe*—which are like red *bimba* fruits; *datta*—placing; *veṇuḥ*—His flute; *anayat*—He brought forth; *svara*—of musical sound; *jātīḥ*—the harmonic tones; *savanaśaḥ*—with a variety of low, high and middle pitches; *tat*—that; *upadhārya*—hearing; *sura-īśāḥ*—the principal demigods; *śakra*—Indra; *śarva*—Śiva; *parameṣṭhi*—and Brahmā; *puraḥ-gāḥ*—headed by; *kavayaḥ*—learned scholars; *ānata*—bowed; *kandhara*—their necks; *cittāḥ*—and minds; *kaśmalam yayuḥ*—they became bewildered; *aniścita*—unable to ascertain; *tattvāḥ*—its essence.

TRANSLATION

O pious mother Yaśodā, your son, who is expert in all the arts of herding cows, has invented many new styles of flute-playing. When He takes His flute to His bimba-red lips and sends forth the tones of the harmonic scale in variegated melodies, Brahmā, Śiva, Indra and other chief demigods become confused upon hearing the sound. Although they are the most learned authorities, they cannot ascertain the essence of that music, and thus they bow down their heads and hearts.

PURPORT

The words *tava sutaḥ sati,* "your son, O chaste lady," clearly indicate that at this point mother Yaśodā is among the young *gopīs* as they earnestly describe Lord Kṛṣṇa's glories. According to Śrīla Viśvanātha Cakravartī, among the demigods led by Śakra (Lord Indra) were Upendra, Agni and Yamarāja, among those led by Śarva (Lord Śiva) were Kātyāyanī, Skanda and Gaṇeśa, and among those led by Parameṣṭhī (Lord Brahmā) were the four Kumāras and

Nārada. Thus the best collective intelligence in the universe could not definitively analyze the enchanting musical arrangements of the Supreme Lord.

TEXTS 16–17

निजपदाब्जदलैर्ध्वजवज्र-
नीरजांकुशविचित्रललामैः ।
व्रजभुवः शमयन् खुरतोदं
वर्ष्मधुर्यगतिरीडितवेणुः ॥ १६ ॥
व्रजति तेन वयं सविलास-
वीक्षणार्पितमनोभववेगाः ।
कुजगतिं गमिता न विदामः
कश्मलेन कवरं वसनं वा ॥ १७ ॥

nija-padābja-dalair dhvaja-vajra
nīrajāṅkuśa-vicitra-lalāmaiḥ
vraja-bhuvaḥ śamayan khura-todaṁ
varṣma-dhurya-gatir īḍita-veṇuḥ

vrajati tena vayaṁ sa-vilāsa
vīkṣaṇārpita-manobhava-vegāḥ
kuja-gatiṁ gamitā na vidāmaḥ
kaśmalena kavaraṁ vasanaṁ vā

nija—His own; *pada-abja*—of the lotus feet; *dalaiḥ*—like flower petals; *dhvaja*—of a flag; *vajra*—thunderbolt; *nīraja*—lotus; *aṅkuśa*—and elephant goad; *vicitra*—variegated; *lalāmaiḥ*—by the markings; *vraja*—of Vraja; *bhuvaḥ*—of the ground; *śamayan*—relieving; *khura*—from the hooves (of the cows); *todam*—the pain; *varṣma*—with His body; *dhurya*—like an elephant's; *gatiḥ*—whose movement; *īḍita*—extolled; *veṇuḥ*—whose flute; *vrajati*—He walks; *tena*—by that; *vayam*—we; *savilāsa*—playful; *vīkṣaṇa*—with His glances; *arpita*—bestowed; *manaḥ-bhava*—of lust; *vegāḥ*—whose agitation; *kuja*—like that of trees; *gatim*—whose movement (i.e., complete lack of movement); *gamitāḥ*—attaining; *na vidāmaḥ*—we do not recognize; *kaśmalena*—because of our bewilderment; *kavaram*—the braids of our hair; *vasanam*—our dress; *vā*—or.

TRANSLATION

As Kṛṣṇa strolls through Vraja with His lotus-petal-like feet, marking the ground with the distinctive emblems of flag, thunderbolt, lotus and elephant goad, He relieves the distress the ground feels from the cows' hooves. As He plays His renowned flute, His body moves with the grace of an elephant. Thus we gopīs, who become agitated by Cupid when Kṛṣṇa playfully glances at us, stand as still as trees, unaware that our hair and garments are slackening.

PURPORT

Here mother Yaśodā is no longer in the company of the *gopīs,* who are confidentially describing their conjugal attraction to Śrī Kṛṣṇa. It is clear from the comments of Jīva Gosvāmī and other *ācāryas* that the statements in this chapter were made at various times and places. This is natural, since the *gopīs* were always absorbed in thoughts of Śrī Kṛṣṇa, day and night.

TEXTS 18–19

मणिधरः क्वचिदागणयन् गा
  मालया दयितगन्धतुलस्याः ।
प्रणयिनोऽनुचरस्य कदांसे
  प्रक्षिपन् भुजमगायत यत्र ॥ १८ ॥
क्वणितवेणुरववञ्चितचित्ताः
  कृष्णमन्वसत कृष्णगृहिण्यः ।
गुणगणार्णमनुगत्य हरिण्यो
  गोपिका इव विमुक्तगृहाशाः ॥ १९ ॥

maṇi-dharaḥ kvacid āgaṇayan gā
  mālayā dayita-gandha-tulasyāḥ
praṇayino 'nucarasya kadāṁse
  prakṣipan bhujam agāyata yatra

kvaṇita-veṇu-rava-vañcita-cittāḥ
  kṛṣṇam anvasata kṛṣṇa-gṛhiṇyaḥ
guṇa-gaṇārṇam anugatya hariṇyo
  gopikā iva vimukta-gṛhāśāḥ

maṇi—(a string of) gems; *dharaḥ*—holding; *kvacit*—somewhere; *āgaṇayan*—counting; *gāḥ*—the cows; *mālayā*—with a flower garland; *dayita*—of His beloved; *gandha*—having the fragrance; *tulasyāḥ*—the *tulasī* flowers upon which; *praṇayinaḥ*—loving; *anucarasya*—of a companion; *kadā*—at some time; *aṁse*—on the shoulder; *prakṣipan*—throwing; *bhujam*—His arm; *agāyata*—He sang; *yatra*—when; *kvaṇita*—vibrated; *veṇu*—of His flute; *rava*—by the sound; *vañcita*—stolen; *cittāḥ*—their hearts; *kṛṣṇam*—Kṛṣṇa; *anvasata*—they sat down beside; *kṛṣṇa*—of the black deer; *gṛhiṇyaḥ*—the wives; *guṇa-gaṇa*—of all transcendental qualities; *arṇam*—the ocean; *anugatya*—approaching; *hariṇyaḥ*—the does; *gopikāḥ*—the *gopīs; iva*—just like; *vimukta*—having given up; *gṛha*—for home and family; *āśāḥ*—their hopes.

TRANSLATION

Now Kṛṣṇa is standing somewhere counting His cows on a string of gems. He wears a garland of tulasī flowers that bear the fragrance of His beloved, and He has thrown His arm over the shoulder of an affectionate cowherd boyfriend. As Kṛṣṇa plays His flute and sings, the music attracts the black deer's wives, who approach that ocean of transcendental qualities and sit down beside Him. Just like us cowherd girls, they have given up all hope for happiness in family life.

PURPORT

Śrīla Jīva Gosvāmī explains that in the afternoon Śrī Kṛṣṇa dressed Himself in new clothing and then went out to call the cows home. Śrīla Viśvanātha Cakravartī gives the following information about the transcendental cows of Vṛndāvana: "For each of the four colors of cows—white, red, black and yellow—there are twenty-five subdivisions, making a total of one hundred colors. And such qualities as being colored like sandalwood-pulp *tilaka* [speckled] or having a head shaped like a mṛdaṅga drum create eight further groups. To count these 108 groups of cows, distinguished by color and form, Kṛṣṇa is using a string of 108 jewel-beads."

"Thus when Kṛṣṇa calls out 'Hey Dhavalī [the name of a white cow],' a whole group of white cows come forward, and when He calls 'Haṁsī, Candanī, Gaṅgā, Muktā' and so on, the twenty-four other groups of white cows come. The reddish cows are called Aruṇī, Kuṅkuma, Sarasvatī, etc., the blackish ones Śyāmalā, Dhūmalā, Yamunā, etc., and the yellowish ones Pītā, Piṅgalā, Haritā-likā, etc. Those in the group with *tilaka* marks on their foreheads are called Citritā, Citra-tilakā, Dīrgha-tilakā and Tiryak-tilakā, and there are groups known as Mṛdaṅga-mukhī [*mṛdaṅga*-head], Siṁha-mukhī [lion-head] and so on."

"Thus being called by name, the cows are coming forward, and Kṛṣṇa, thinking that when it is time to bring them back from the forest none should be forgotten, is counting them on His jewel-beads."

TEXTS 20–21

कुन्ददामकृतकौतुकवेषो
गोपगोधनवृतो यमुनायाम् ।
नन्दसूनुरनघे तव वत्सो
नर्मदः प्रणयिणां विजहार ॥ २० ॥
मन्दवायुरुपवात्यनुकूलं
मानयन्मलयजस्पर्शेन ।
वन्दिनस्तमुपदेवगणा ये
वाद्यगीतबलिभिः परिवव्रुः ॥ २१ ॥

kunda-dāma-kṛta-kautuka-veṣo
gopa-godhana-vṛto yamunāyām
nanda-sūnur anaghe tava vatso
narma-daḥ praṇayiṇāṁ vijahāra

manda-vāyur upavāty anukūlaṁ
mānayan malayaja-sparśena
vandinas tam upadeva-gaṇā ye
vādya-gīta-balibhiḥ parivavruḥ

kunda—of jasmine flowers; *dāma*—with a garland; *kṛta*—made; *kautuka*—playful; *veṣaḥ*—His array; *gopa*—by the cowherd boys; *godhana*—and the cows; *vṛtaḥ*—surrounded; *yamunāyām*—along the Yamunā; *nanda-sūnuḥ*—the son of Nanda Mahārāja; *anaghe*—O sinless lady; *tava*—your; *vatsaḥ*—darling child; *narma-daḥ*—amusing; *praṇayiṇām*—His dear companions; *vijahāra*—He has played; *manda*—gentle; *vāyuḥ*—the wind; *upavāti*—blows; *anukūlam*—favorably; *mānayan*—showing honor; *malaya-ja*—of (the fragrance of) sandalwood; *sparśena*—the touch; *vandinaḥ*—those who offer praise; *tam*—Him; *upadeva*—of the minor demigods; *gaṇāḥ*—members of the various categories; *ye*—who; *vādya*—with instrumental music; *gīta*—singing; *balibhiḥ*—and presentation of gifts; *parivavruḥ*—they have encircled.

TRANSLATION

O sinless Yaśodā, your darling child, the son of Mahārāja Nanda, has festively enhanced His attire with a jasmine garland, and He is now playing along the Yamunā in the company of the cows and cowherd boys, amusing His dear companions. The gentle breeze honors Him with its soothing fragrance of sandalwood, while the various Upadevas, standing on all sides like panegyrists, offer their music, singing and gifts of tribute.

PURPORT

Śrīla Jīva Gosvāmī explains that the *gopīs* are again in the courtyard of mother Yaśodā, the queen of Vraja. They are trying to encourage her by describing Kṛṣṇa's return to Vṛndāvana after He has spent the day herding cows and playing.

Śrīla Viśvanātha Cakravartī comments that the Upadevas, the minor demigods mentioned here, include the Gandharvas, who are famous for their celestial music and dancing.

TEXTS 22–23

वत्सलो व्रजगवां यदगध्रो
वन्द्यमानचरणः पथि वृद्धैः ।
कृत्स्नगोधनमुपोह्य दिनान्ते
गीतवेणुरनुगेडितकीर्तिः ॥ २२ ॥
उत्सवं श्रमरुचापि दृशीनाम्
उन्नयन् खुररजश्छुरितस्रक् ।
दित्सयैति सुहृदाशिष एष
देवकीजठरभूरुडुराजः ॥ २३ ॥

vatsalo vraja-gavāṁ yad aga-dhro
vandyamāna-caraṇaḥ pathi vṛddhaiḥ
kṛtsna-go-dhanam upohya dinānte
gīta-veṇur anugeḍita-kīrtiḥ

utsavaṁ śrama-rucāpi dṛśīnām
unnayan khura-rajaś-churita-srak
ditsayaiti suhṛd-āśiṣa eṣa
devakī-jaṭhara-bhūr uḍu-rājaḥ

vatsalaḥ—affectionate; *vraja-gavām*—to the cows of Vraja; *yat*—because; *aga*—of the mountain; *dhraḥ*—the lifter; *vandyamāna*—being worshiped; *caraṇaḥ*—His feet; *pathi*—along the path; *vṛddhaiḥ*—by the exalted demigods; *kṛtsna*—entire; *go-dhanam*—the herd of cows; *upohya*—collecting; *dina*—of the day; *ante*—at the end; *gītā-veṇuḥ*—playing His flute; *anuga*—by His companions; *īḍita*—praised; *kīrtiḥ*—His glories; *utsavam*—a festival; *śrama*—of fatigue; *rucā*—by His coloring; *api*—even; *dṛśīnām*—for the eyes; *unnayan*—raising; *khura*—from the hooves (of the cows); *rajaḥ*—with the dust; *churita*—powdered; *srak*—His garland; *ditsayā*—with the desire; *eti*—He is coming; *suhṛt*—to His friends; *āśiṣaḥ*—their desires; *eṣaḥ*—this; *devakī*—of mother Yaśodā; *jaṭhara*—from the womb; *bhūḥ*—born; *uḍu-rājaḥ*—moon.

TRANSLATION

Out of great affection for the cows of Vraja, Kṛṣṇa became the lifter of Govardhana Hill. At the end of the day, having rounded up all His own cows, He plays a song on His flute, while exalted demigods standing along the path worship His lotus feet and the cowherd boys accompanying Him chant His glories. His garland is powdered by the dust raised by the cows' hooves, and His beauty, enhanced by His fatigue, creates an ecstatic festival for everyone's eyes. Eager to fulfill His friends' desires, Kṛṣṇa is the moon arisen from the womb of mother Yaśodā.

PURPORT

According to the *ācāryas,* at this point the *gopīs* climbed into the watchtowers of Vṛndāvana's houses so they could see Kṛṣṇa as soon as possible when He returned home. Mother Yaśodā was very anxious for her son to come back, and therefore she had the tallest of the beautiful young *gopīs* climb up to see when He would arrive. It is implied here that Kṛṣṇa was somewhat delayed on the way home because His lotus feet were being worshiped by great demigods along the path.

TEXTS 24–25

मदविघूर्णितलोचन ईषत्
मानदः स्वसुहृदां वनमाली ।
बदरपाण्डुवदनो मृदुगण्डं
मण्डयन् कनककुण्डललक्ष्म्या ॥ २४ ॥

यदुपतिर्द्विरदराजविहारो
    यामिनीपतिरिवैष दिनान्ते ।
मुदितवक्त्र उपयाति दुरन्तं
    मोचयन् व्रजगवां दिनतापम् ॥ २५ ॥

mada-vighūrṇita-locana īṣat
māna-daḥ sva-suhṛdāṁ vana-mālī
badara-pāṇḍu-vadano mṛdu-gaṇḍaṁ
maṇḍayan kanaka-kuṇḍala-lakṣmyā

yadu-patir dvirada-rāja-vihāro
yāminī-patir ivaiṣa dinānte
mudita-vaktra upayāti durantaṁ
mocayan vraja-gavāṁ dina-tāpam

mada—by intoxication; *vighūrṇita*—rolling; *locanaḥ*—His eyes; *īṣat*—slightly; *māna-daḥ*—showing honor; *sva-suhṛdām*—to His well-wishing friends; *vana-mālī*—wearing a garland of forest flowers; *badara*—like a *badara* fruit; *pāṇḍu*—whitish; *vadanaḥ*—His face; *mṛdu*—soft; *gaṇḍam*—His cheeks; *maṇḍayan*—ornamenting; *kanaka*—golden; *kuṇḍala*—of His earrings; *lakṣmyā*—with the beauty; *yadu-patiḥ*—the Lord of the Yadu dynasty; *dvirada-rāja*—like a kingly elephant; *vihāraḥ*—His sporting; *yāminī-patiḥ*—the lord of the night (the moon); *iva*—like; *eṣaḥ*—He; *dina-ante*—at the end of the day; *mudita*—joyful; *vaktraḥ*—His face; *upayāti*—is coming; *durantam*—insurmountable; *mocayan*—driving away; *vraja*—of Vraja; *gavām*—of the cows, or of those who are to be shown mercy; *dina*—of the daytime; *tāpam*—the painful heat.

TRANSLATION

As Kṛṣṇa respectfully greets His well-wishing friends, His eyes roll slightly as if from intoxication. He wears a flower garland, and the beauty of His soft cheeks is accentuated by the brilliance of His golden earrings and the whiteness of His face, which has the color of a badara berry. With His cheerful face resembling the moon, lord of the night, the Lord of the Yadus moves with the grace of a regal elephant. Thus He returns in the evening, delivering the cows of Vraja from the heat of the day.

PURPORT

The word *gavām* is constructed from the Sanskrit word *go,* which means "cow" or "senses." Thus Śrī Kṛṣṇa, by coming back to the village of Vraja, relieved the inhabitants of Vṛndāvana from the distress their eyes and other senses felt during the day because of being separated from direct contact with Him.

TEXT 26

श्रीशुक उवाच
एवं व्रजस्त्रियो राजन् कृष्णलीलानुगायतीः ।
रेमिरेऽहःसु तच्चित्तास्तन्मनस्का महोदयाः ॥ २६ ॥

śrī-śuka uvāca
evaṁ vraja-striyo rājan
kṛṣṇa-līlānugāyatīḥ
remire'haḥsu tac-cittās
tan-manaskā mahodayāḥ

śrī-śukaḥ uvāca—Śukadeva Gosvāmī said; *evam*—thus; *vraja-striyaḥ*—the women of Vraja; *rājan*—O King; *kṛṣṇa-līlā*—about the pastimes of Kṛṣṇa; *anugāyatīḥ*—continuously chanting; *remire*—they enjoyed; *ahaḥsu*—during the days; *tat-cittāḥ*—their hearts absorbed in Him; *tat-manaskāḥ*—their minds absorbed in Him; *mahā*—great; *udayāḥ*—experiencing a festivity.

TRANSLATION

Śrī Śukadeva Gosvāmī said: O King, thus during the daytime the women of Vṛndāvana took pleasure in continuously singing about the pastimes of Kṛṣṇa, and those ladies' minds and hearts, absorbed in Him, were filled with great festivity.

PURPORT

This verse definitely confirms that the so-called pain of the heartbroken *gopīs* is actually great spiritual bliss. On the material platform, pain is pain—period. But on the spiritual platform, so-called pain is simply a different variety of spiritual ecstasy. In the Western countries, people take pleasure in mixing different flavors of ice cream to produce wonderful combinations of flavor. Similarly, on the spiritual platform Śrī Kṛṣṇa and His devotees expertly mix the flavors of spiritual bliss, and thus every day was a treat for the *gopīs.*

Thus end the purports of the humble servants of His Divine Grace A.C. Bhaktivedanta Swami Prabhupāda to the Tenth Canto, Thirty-fifth Chapter, of the Śrīmad-Bhāgavatam, *entitled "The Gopīs Sing of Kṛṣṇa as He Wanders in the Forest."*

CHAPTER THIRTY- SIX

The Slaying of Ariṣṭa, the Bull Demon

This chapter describes how Kṛṣṇa killed Ariṣṭāsura and how Kaṁsa reacted when he learned from Nārada that Kṛṣṇa and Balarāma were the sons of Vasudeva.

The demon Ariṣṭa wanted to kill Kṛṣṇa and Balarāma, and thus he assumed the form of a huge bull with sharp horns. Everyone in Kṛṣṇa's cowherd village became terrified when Ariṣṭāsura approached it, but the Lord pacified them, and when the bull demon charged Him He seized him by the horns and threw him about six yards. Though weakened, Ariṣṭa still wanted to attack Kṛṣṇa. Thus, dripping with sweat, he charged the Lord once again. This time Kṛṣṇa grabbed his horns, threw him to the ground and thrashed him like a pile of wet clothing. The demon vomited blood and gave up his life. Then Kṛṣṇa and Rāma, while being honored by the demigods and cowherd boys, returned to the village.

A short time later Nārada Muni, the great sage among the demigods, came to see King Kaṁsa. He informed the King that Kṛṣṇa and Balarāma were not Nanda's sons but rather Vasudeva's. It was out of fear of Kaṁsa that Vasudeva had put the two boys under Nanda's care. Furthermore, said Nārada, Kaṁsa would meet his death at Their hands.

Kaṁsa shook with fear and anger when he heard all this, and in great agitation he began thinking of how to destroy Kṛṣṇa and Balarāma. He called for the demons Cāṇūra and Muṣṭika and instructed them to kill the two brothers in a wrestling match. Then he spoke to Akrūra, who was expert at executing his duties. Taking Akrūra by the hand, Kaṁsa persuaded him to go to Vraja to bring the two boys to Mathurā. Akrūra agreed to carry out Kaṁsa's order and then returned home.

TEXT 1

श्री बादरायणिरुवाच

अथ तर्ह्यागतो गोष्ठमरिष्टो वृषभासुरः ।
महीं महाककुत्कायः कम्पयन् खुरविक्षताम् ॥ १ ॥

śrī bādarāyaṇir uvāca
atha tarhy āgato goṣṭham
ariṣṭo vṛṣabhāsuraḥ
mahīṁ mahā-kakut-kāyaḥ
kampayan khura-vikṣatām

śrī bādarāyaṇiḥ uvāca—Śrī Śukadeva Gosvāmī said; *atha*—next; *tarhi*—then; *āgataḥ*—came; *goṣṭham*—to the cowherd village; *ariṣṭaḥ*—named Ariṣṭa; *vṛṣabha-asuraḥ*—the bull demon; *mahīm*—the earth; *mahā*—great; *kakut*—having a hump; *kāyaḥ*—whose body; *kampayan*—making tremble; *khura*—by his hooves; *vikṣatām*—torn.

TRANSLATION

Śukadeva Goswāmī said: The demon Ariṣṭa then came to the cowherd village. Appearing in the form of a bull with a large hump, he made the earth tremble as he tore it apart with his hooves.

PURPORT

According to the *Śrī Viṣṇu Purāṇa,* Ariṣṭāsura entered Kṛṣṇa's village at twilight, as the Lord prepared to dance with the *gopīs:*

prodoṣārdhe kadācit tu
rāsāsakte janārdane
trāsayan sa-mado goṣṭham
ariṣṭaḥ sampāgataḥ

"Once, midway through the period of dusk, when Lord Janārdana was eager to perform the *rāsa* dance, Ariṣṭāsura madly entered the cowherd village, terrifying everyone."

TEXT 2

रम्भमाणः खरतरं पदा च विलिखन्महीम् ।
उद्यम्य पुच्छं वप्राणि विषाणाग्रेण चोद्धरन् ।
किञ्चित्किञ्चिच्छकृन्मुञ्चन्मूत्रयन् स्तब्धलोचनः ॥ २ ॥

rambhamāṇaḥ kharataraṁ
padā ca vilikhan mahīm
udyamya pucchaṁ vaprāṇi
viṣāṇāgreṇa coddharan

kiñcit kiñcic chakṛn muñcan
mūtrayan stabdha-locanaḥ

rambhamāṇaḥ—bellowing; *khara-taram*—most harshly; *padā*—with his hooves; *ca*—and; *vilikhan*—scraping; *mahīm*—the ground; *udyamya*—raising upward; *puccham*—his tail; *vaprāṇi*—the embankments; *viṣāṇa*—of his horns; *agreṇa*—with the tips; *ca*—and; *uddharan*—lifting and tearing up; *kiñcit kiñcit*—a little; *śakṛt*—stool; *muñcan*—releasing; *mūtrayan*—urinating; *stabdha*—glaring; *locanaḥ*—his eyes.

TRANSLATION

Ariṣṭāsura bellowed very harshly and pawed the ground. With his tail raised and his eyes glaring, he began to tear up the embankments with the tips of his horns, every now and then passing a little stool and urine.

TEXTS 3–4

यस्य निर्ह्रादितेनांग निष्ठुरेण गवां नृणाम् ।
पतन्त्यकालतो गर्भाः स्रवन्ति स्म भयेन वै ॥ ३ ॥
निर्विशन्ति घना यस्य ककुद्यचलशंकया ।
तं तीक्ष्णशृंगमुद्वीक्ष्य गोप्यो गोपाश्च तत्रसुः ॥ ४ ॥

yasya nirhrāditenāṅga
niṣṭhureṇa gavāṁ nṛṇām
patanty akālato garbhāḥ
sravanti sma bhayena vai

nirviśanti ghanā yasya
kakudy acala-śaṅkayā
taṁ tīkṣṇa-śṛṅgam udvīkṣya
gopyo gopāś ca tatrasuḥ

yasya—whose; *nirhrāditena*—by the reverberating sound; *aṅga*—my dear King (Parīkṣit); *niṣṭhureṇa*—rough; *gavām*—of cows; *nṛṇām*—of humans; *patanti*—fall; *akālataḥ*—untimely; *garbhāḥ*—the embryos; *sravanti sma*—are miscarried; *bhayena*—out of fear; *vai*—indeed; *nirviśanti*—enter; *ghanāḥ*—clouds; *yasya*—whose; *kakudi*—onto the hump; *acala*—as a mountain; *śaṅkayā*—by the mistaken identification; *tam*—him; *tīkṣṇa*—sharp; *śṛṅgam*—whose horns; *udvīkṣya*—seeing; *gopyaḥ*—the cowherd women; *gopāḥ*—the cowherd men; *ca*—and; *tatrasuḥ*—became frightened.

TRANSLATION

My dear King, clouds hovered about sharp-horned Ariṣṭāsura's hump, mistaking it for a mountain, and when the cowherd men and ladies caught sight of the demon, they were struck with terror. Indeed, the strident reverberation of his roar so frightened the pregnant cows and women that they lost their fetuses in miscarriages.

PURPORT

The Vedic literature categorizes miscarriages as follows: *a-caturthād bhavet srāvaḥ pātaḥ pañcama-ṣaṣṭhayoḥ/ ata ūrdhvaṁ prasūtiḥ syāt.* "Up to the fourth month a premature delivery is called *srāva,* in the fifth and sixth months it is called *pāta,* and after this it is considered a birth (*prasūti*)."

TEXT 5

पशवो दुद्रुवुर्भीता राजन् सन्त्यज्य गोकुलम् ।
कृष्ण कृष्णेति ते सर्वे गोविन्दं शरणं ययुः ॥ ५ ॥

paśavo dudruvur bhītā
rājan santyajya go-kulam
kṛṣṇa kṛṣṇeti te sarve
govindaṁ śaraṇaṁ yayuḥ

paśavaḥ—the domestic animals; *dudruvuḥ*—ran away; *bhītāḥ*—afraid; *rājan*—O King; *santyajya*—abandoning; *go-kulam*—the dairy pasture; *kṛṣṇa kṛṣṇa iti*—"Kṛṣṇa, Kṛṣṇa"; *te*—they (the inhabitants of Vṛndāvana); *sarve*—all; *govindam*—to Lord Govinda; *śaraṇam*—for shelter; *yayuḥ*—went.

TRANSLATION

The domestic animals fled the pasture in fear, O King, and all the inhabitants rushed to Lord Govinda for shelter, crying, "Kṛṣṇa, Kṛṣṇa!"

TEXT 6

भगवानपि तद्वीक्ष्य गोकुलं भयविद्रुतम् ।
मा भैष्टेति गिराश्वास्य वृषासुरमुपाह्वयत् ॥ ६ ॥

bhagavān api tad vīkṣya
go-kulaṁ bhaya-vidrutam
mā bhaiṣṭeti girāśvāsya
vṛṣāsuram upāhvayat

bhagavān—the Supreme Personality of Godhead; *api*—indeed; *tat*—that; *vīkṣya*—seeing; *go-kulam*—the cowherd community; *bhaya*—out of fear; *vidrutam*—made to flee, or distraught; *mā bhaiṣṭa*—"don't be afraid"; *iti*—thus; *girā*—with words; *āśvāsya*—pacifying; *vṛṣa-asuram*—to the bull demon; *upāhvayat*—He called out.

TRANSLATION

When the Supreme Lord saw the cowherd community distraught and fleeing in fear, He calmed them, saying, "Don't be afraid." Then He called out to the bull demon as follows.

TEXT 7

गोपालैः पशुभिर्मन्द त्रासितैः किमसत्तम ।
मयि शास्तरि दुष्टानां त्वद्विधानां दुरात्मनाम् ॥ ७ ॥

gopālaiḥ paśubhir manda
trāsitaiḥ kim asattama
mayi śāstari duṣṭānāṁ
tvad-vidhānāṁ durātmanām

gopālaiḥ—with the cowherds; *paśubhiḥ*—and with their animals; *manda*—O fool; *trāsitaiḥ*—who are frightened; *kim*—what purpose; *asattama*—O most wicked one; *mayi*—when I (am present); *śāstari*—as the punisher; *duṣṭānām*—of the contaminated; *tvat-vidhānām*—like you; *durātmanām*—miscreants.

TRANSLATION

You fool! What do you think you're doing, you wicked rascal, frightening the cowherd community and their animals when I am here just to punish corrupt miscreants like you!

TEXT 8

इत्यास्फोत्याच्युतोऽरिष्टं तलशब्देन कोपयन् ।
सख्युरंसे भुजाभोगं प्रसार्यावस्थितो हरिः ॥ ८ ॥

ity āsphotyācyuto'riṣṭaṁ
tala-śabdena kopayan
sakhyur aṁse bhujābhogaṁ
prasāryāvasthito hariḥ

iti—speaking thus; *āsphotya*—slapping His arms; *acyutaḥ*—the infallible Lord; *ariṣṭam*—Ariṣṭāsura; *tala*—from His palms; *śabdena*—with the sound; *kopayan*—angering; *sakhyuḥ*—of a friend; *aṁse*—over the shoulder; *bhuja*—His arm; *ābhogam*—(which is like) a serpent's body; *prasārya*—throwing; *avasthitaḥ*—was standing; *hariḥ*—Lord Hari.

TRANSLATION

Having spoken these words, the infallible Lord Hari slapped His arms with His palms, further angering Ariṣṭa with the loud sound. The Lord then casually threw His mighty, serpentine arm over the shoulder of a friend and stood facing the demon.

PURPORT

Lord Kṛṣṇa showed His contempt for the ignorant demon.

TEXT 9

सोऽप्येवं कोपितोऽरिष्टः खुरेणावनिमुल्लिखन्।
उद्यत्पुच्छभ्रमन्मेघः क्रुद्धः कृष्णमुपाद्रवत् ॥ ९ ॥

so'py evaṁ kopito'riṣṭaḥ
khureṇāvanim ullikhan
udyat-puccha-bhraman-meghaḥ
kruddhaḥ kṛṣṇam upādravat

saḥ—he; *api*—indeed; *evam*—in this way; *kopitaḥ*—angered; *ariṣṭaḥ*—Ariṣṭa; *khureṇa*—with his hoof; *avanim*—the earth; *ullikhan*—scratching; *udyat*—raised; *puccha*—within his tail; *bhraman*—wandering; *meghaḥ*—clouds; *kruddhaḥ*—furious; *kṛṣṇam*—toward Lord Kṛṣṇa; *upādravat*—he charged.

TRANSLATION

Thus provoked, Ariṣṭa pawed the ground with one of his hooves and then, with the clouds hovering around his upraised tail, furiously charged Kṛṣṇa.

TEXT 10

अग्रन्यस्तविषाणाग्रः स्तब्धासृग्लोचनोऽच्युतम् ।
कटाक्षिप्याद्रवत्तूर्णमिन्द्रमुक्तोऽशनिर्यथा ॥ १० ॥

agra-nyasta-viṣāṇāgraḥ
stabdhāsṛg-locano'cyutam
kaṭākṣipyādravat tūrṇam
indra-mukto'śanir yathā

agra—forward; *nyasta*—pointing; *viṣāṇa*—of his horns; *agraḥ*—the front; *stabdha*—glaring; *asṛk*—bloody; *locanaḥ*—his eyes; *acyutam*—at Lord Kṛṣṇa; *kaṭa-ākṣipya*—looking sideways; *adravat*—he ran; *tūrṇam*—at full speed; *indra-muktaḥ*—released by King Indra; *aśaniḥ*—a thunderbolt; *yathā*—like.

TRANSLATION

Pointing the tips of his horns straight ahead and glaring menacingly at Lord Kṛṣṇa from the corners of his bloodshot eyes, Ariṣṭa rushed toward Him at full speed, like a thunderbolt hurled by Indra.

TEXT 11

गृहीत्वा शृंगयोस्तं वा अष्टादश पदानि सः ।
प्रत्यपोवाह भगवान् गजः प्रतिगजं यथा ॥ ११ ॥

gṛhītvā śṛṅgayos taṁ vā
aṣṭādaśa padāni saḥ
pratyapovāha bhagavān
gajaḥ prati-gajaṁ yathā

gṛhītvā—seizing; *śṛṅgayoḥ*—by the horns; *tam*—him; *vai*—indeed; *aṣṭādaśa*—eighteen; *padāni*—steps; *saḥ*—He; *pratyapovāha*—threw back; *bhagavān*—the Supreme Lord; *gajaḥ*—an elephant; *prati-gajam*—a rival elephant; *yathā*—like.

TRANSLATION

The Supreme Lord Kṛṣṇa seized Ariṣṭāsura by the horns and threw him back eighteen steps, just as an elephant might do when fighting a rival elephant.

TEXT 12

सोऽपविद्धो भगवता पुनरुत्थाय सत्वरम् ।
आपतत्स्विन्नसर्वांगो निःश्वसन् क्रोधमूर्च्छितः ॥ १२ ॥

so'paviddho bhagavatā
punar utthāya satvaram
āpatat svinna-sarvāṅgo
niḥśvasan krodha-mūrcchitaḥ

saḥ—he; *apaviddhaḥ*—thrown back; *bhagavatā*—by the Lord; *punaḥ*—again; *utthāya*—rising; *satvaram*—quickly; *āpatat*—attacked; *svinna*—sweating; *sarva*—all; *aṅgaḥ*—his limbs; *niḥśvasan*—breathing hard; *krodha*—by anger; *mūrcchitaḥ*—stupefied.

TRANSLATION

Thus repulsed by the Supreme Lord, the bull demon got up and, breathing hard and sweating all over his body, again charged Him in a mindless rage.

TEXT 13

तमापतन्तं स निगृह्य शृंगयोः
पदा समाक्रम्य निपात्य भूतले ।
निष्पीडयामास यथार्द्रमम्बरं
कृत्वा विषाणेन जघान सोऽपतत् ॥ १३ ॥

tam āpatantaṁ sa nigṛhya śṛṅgayoḥ
padā samākramya nipātya bhū-tale
niṣpīḍayām āsa yathārdram ambaraṁ
kṛtvā viṣāṇena jaghāna so'patat

tam—him; *āpatantam*—attacking; *saḥ*—He; *nigṛhya*—seizing; *śṛṅgayoḥ*—by the horns; *padā*—with His foot; *samākramya*—treading; *nipātya*—making him fall; *bhū-tale*—onto the ground; *niṣpīḍayām āsa*—He beat him; *yathā*—like; *ardram*—wet; *ambaram*—a garment; *kṛtvā*—making; *viṣāṇena*—with his horn; *jaghāna*—struck; *saḥ*—he; *apatat*—fell.

TRANSLATION

As Ariṣṭa attacked, Lord Kṛṣṇa seized him by the horns and knocked him to the ground with His foot. The Lord then thrashed him as if he were a wet cloth, and finally He yanked out one of the demon's horns and struck him with it until he lay prostrate.

TEXT 14

असृग् वमन्मूत्रशकृत्समुत्सृजन्
क्षिपंश्च पादाननवस्थितेक्षणः ।
जगाम कृच्छ्रं निरृतेरथ क्षयं
पुष्पैः किरन्तो हरिमीडिरे सुराः ॥ १४ ॥

asṛg vaman mūtra-śakṛt samutsṛjan
kṣipaṁś ca pādān anavasthitekṣaṇaḥ
jagāma kṛcchraṁ nirṛter atha kṣayaṁ
puṣpaiḥ kiranto harim īḍire surāḥ

asṛk—blood; *vaman*—vomiting; *mūtra*—urine; *śakṛt*—and feces; *samutsṛjan*—profusely excreting; *kṣipan*—throwing about; *ca*—and; *pādān*—his legs; *anavasthita*—unsteady; *īkṣaṇaḥ*—his eyes; *jagāma*—he went; *kṛcchram*—with pain; *nirṛteḥ*—of Death; *atha*—then; *kṣayam*—to the abode; *puṣpaiḥ*—flowers; *kirantaḥ*—scattering; *harim*—upon Lord Kṛṣṇa; *īḍire*—worshiped; *surāḥ*—the demigods.

TRANSLATION

Vomiting blood and profusely excreting stool and urine, kicking his legs and rolling his eyes about, Ariṣṭāsura thus went painfully to the abode of Death. The demigods honored Lord Kṛṣṇa by scattering flowers upon Him.

TEXT 15

एवं कुकुद्मिनं हत्वा स्तूयमानः द्विजातिभिः ।
विवेश गोष्ठं सबलो गोपीनां नयनोत्सवः ॥ १५ ॥

evaṁ kukudminaṁ hatvā
stūyamānaḥ dvijātibhiḥ
viveśa goṣṭhaṁ sa-balo
gopīnāṁ nayanotsavaḥ

evam—thus; *kukudminam*—the humped (bull demon); *hatvā*—killing; *stūyamānaḥ*—being praised; *dvijātibhiḥ*—by the *brāhmaṇas; viveśa*—He entered; *goṣṭham*—the cowherd village; *sa-balaḥ*—together with Lord Balarāma; *gopīnām*—of the *gopīs; nayana*—for the eyes; *utsavaḥ*—who is a festival.

TRANSLATION

Having thus killed the bull demon Ariṣṭa, He who is a festival for the gopīs' eyes entered the cowherd village with Balarāma.

PURPORT

This verse exemplifies the sublime contrast of spiritual qualities within Śrī Kṛṣṇa. In one four-line verse we simultaneously learn that Lord Kṛṣṇa killed a powerful and wicked demon and that His boyish beauty gave festive pleasure to His young girlfriends. Lord Kṛṣṇa is as hard as a thunderbolt or as soft as a rose, depending on our attitude toward Him. The demon Ariṣṭa wanted to kill Kṛṣṇa and all His friends, so the Lord beat him into a wet rag and killed him. The *gopīs,* however, loved Kṛṣṇa, and thus the Lord boyishly reciprocated their conjugal feelings.

TEXT 16

अरिष्टे निहते दैत्ये कृष्णेनाद्भुतकर्मणा ।
कंसायाथाह भगवान्नारदो देवदर्शनः ॥ १६ ॥

ariṣṭe nihate daitye
kṛṣṇenādbhuta-karmaṇā
kaṁsāyāthāha bhagavān
nārado deva-darśanaḥ

ariṣṭe—Ariṣṭa; *nihate*—having been killed; *daitye*—the demon; *kṛṣṇena*—by Kṛṣṇa; *adbhuta-karmaṇā*—whose activities are wonderful; *kaṁsāya*—to Kaṁsa; *atha*—then; *āha*—spoke; *bhagavān*—the powerful sage; *nāradaḥ*—Nārada; *deva-darśanaḥ*—whose vision is godly.

TRANSLATION

After Ariṣṭāsura had been killed by Kṛṣṇa, who acts wonderfully, Nārada Muni went to speak to King Kaṁsa. That powerful sage of godly vision addressed the King as follows.

PURPORT

The term *deva-darśana* can be understood in many ways, all of which are consistent with the context and purport of this narration. *Deva* means "God," and *darśanaḥ* means "seeing" or "an audience with a great personality." Thus *deva-darśana,* a name for Nārada Muni, indicates that Nārada has attained the perfection of seeing God, that getting Nārada's audience is as good as getting God's (since Nārada is a pure representative of the Lord), and also that Nārada's audience is as good as that of the demigods, who are also known as *devas.* That there are all these meanings of the term *deva-darśanaḥ* reveals something of the richness of the *Śrīmad-Bhāgavatam's* language.

From the *Purāṇas,* Śrīla Viśvanātha Cakravartī Ṭhākura has quoted twenty verses describing a joking conversation between Rādhā and Kṛṣṇa that took place after Kṛṣṇa had killed the demon Ariṣṭa. This conversation, so kindly quoted by the *ācārya,* describes the origin of Rādhā-kuṇḍa and Śyāma-kuṇḍa, Rādhā's and Kṛṣṇa's bathing ponds. The verses are as follows:

māsmān spṛśādya vṛṣabhārdana hanta mugdhā
ghoro'suro'yam ayi kṛṣṇa tad apy ayaṁ gauḥ
vṛtro yathā dvija ihāsty ayi niṣkṛtiḥ kiṁ
śudhyed bhavāṁs tri-bhuvana-sthita-tīrtha-kṛcchrāt

"The innocent young *gopīs* said, 'Ah, Kṛṣṇa, don't touch us now, O killer of a bull! Alas, even though Ariṣṭa was a terrible demon, still he was a male cow, so You will have to undergo atonement, just as Lord Indra did after killing Vṛtrāsura. But how can You purify Yourself without going to the trouble of visiting every single holy place in the three worlds?'"

kiṁ paryaṭāmi bhuvanāny adhunaiva sarvā
ānīya tīrtha-vitatīḥ karavāṇi tāsu
snānaṁ vilokayata tāvad idaṁ mukundaḥ
procyaiva tatra kṛtavān bata pārṣṇi-ghātam

"[Kṛṣṇa replied,] 'Why should I have to wander throughout the entire universe? I will at once bring all the countless pilgrimage places here and take My bath in them. Just watch!' With this, Lord Mukunda struck His heel on the ground."

pātālato jalam idaṁ kila bhogavatyā
āyātam atra nikhilā api tīrtha-saṅghāḥ
āgacchateti bhagavad-vacasā ta etya
tatraiva rejur atha kṛṣṇa uvāca gopīḥ

"[Then He said,] 'This is the water of the Bhogavatī River, coming from the Pātāla region. And now, O holy places, all of you please come here!' When the Supreme Lord had spoken these words, all the holy places went there and appeared before Him. Kṛṣṇa then addressed the *gopīs* as follows."

tīrthāni paśyata harer vacasā tavaivaṁ
naiva pratīma iti tā atha tīrtha-varyāḥ
procuḥ kṛtāñjali-puṭā lavaṇābdhir asmi
kṣīrābdhir asmi śṛṇutāmara-dīrghikāsmi

"See all the holy places!'

"But the *gopīs* replied, 'We don't see them as You describe.'

"Then those best of holy places, joining their palms in supplication, spoke up:

"I am the Salt ocean.'

"I am the Ocean of Milk.'

"I am the Amara-dīrghikā."

śoṇo'pi sindhur aham asmi bhavāmi tāmra-
parṇī ca puṣkaram ahaṁ ca sarasvatī ca
godāvarī ravi-sutā sarayuḥ prayāgo
revāsmi paśyata jalaṁ kuruta pratītim

"I am the river Śoṇa.'

"I am the Sindhu.'

"I am the Tāmraparṇī.'

"I am the holy place Puṣkara.'

"I am the river Sarasvatī.'

"And we are the Godāvarī, Yamunā and Revā rivers and the confluence of rivers at Prayāga. Just see our waters!"

snātvā tato harir ati-prajagalbha eva
śuddhaḥ saro'py akaravaṁ sthita-sarva-tīrtham
yuṣmābhir ātma-januṣīha kṛto na dharmaḥ
ko'pi kṣitāv atha sakhīr nijagāda rādhā

"After purifying Himself by bathing, Lord Hari became quite arrogant and said, 'I have produced a pond containing all the various holy places, whereas you *gopīs* must never have executed any religious duties on this earth for the pleasure of Lord Brahmā.' Then Śrīmatī Rādhārāṇī addressed Her girlfriends as follows."

kāryaṁ mayāpy ati-manohara-kuṇḍam ekaṁ
tasmād yatadhvam iti tad-vacanena tābhiḥ
śrī-kṛṣṇa-kuṇḍa-taṭa-paścima-diśya-mando
gartaḥ kṛto vṛṣabha-daitya-khurair vyaloki

"I must create an even more beautiful pond. So go to work!' Having heard these words, the *gopīs* saw that Ariṣṭāsura's hooves had dug a shallow ditch just west of Śrī Kṛṣṇa's pond."

tatrārdra-mṛn-mṛdula-gola-tatīḥ prati-sva-
hastoddhṛtā anati-dūra-gatā vidhāya
divyaṁ saraḥ prakaṭitaṁ ghaṭikā-dvayena
tābhir vilokya sarasaṁ smarate sma kṛṣṇaḥ

"At that nearby spot, all the *gopīs* began digging up lumps of soft mud with their hands, and in this way a divine pond manifested in the short span of an hour. Kṛṣṇa was astonished to see the lake they produced."

proce ca tīrtha-salilaiḥ paripūrayaitan
mat-kuṇḍataḥ sarasijākṣi sahālibhis tvam
rādhā tadā na na na neti jagāda yasmāt
tvat-kuṇḍa-nīram uru-go-vadha-pātakāktam

"He said, 'Go ahead, lotus-eyed one. You and Your companions should fill this pond with water from Mine.'

"But Rādhā replied, 'No, no, no, no! This is impossible, since the water of Your pond is contaminated by Your terrible sin of killing a cow."

āhṛtya puṇya-salilaṁ śata-koṭi-kumbhaiḥ
sakhy-arbudena saha mānasa-jāhnavītaḥ
etat saraḥ sva-madhunā paripūrayāmi
tenaiva kīrtim atulāṁ tanavāni loke

"'I will have My countless *gopī* companions bring the pure water of the Mānasa-gaṅgā here in billions of pots. In this way I will fill this lake with My own water and thus make its renown unequaled in the entire world.'"

kṛṣṇeṅgitena sahasaitya samasta-tīrtha-
sakhyas tadīya-saraso dhṛta-divya-mūrtiḥ
tuṣṭāva tatra vṛṣabhānu-sutāṁ praṇamya
bhaktyā kṛtāñjali-puṭaḥ sravad-asra-dhāraḥ

"Lord Kṛṣṇa then gestured to a heavenly personality who was an intimate associate of all the holy places. Suddenly that person rose up out of Kṛṣṇa's pond and bowed down to the daughter of Śrī Vṛṣabhānu [Rādhārāṇī]. Then, with palms joined and tears pouring from his eyes, he began praying to Her in devotion."

devi tvadīya-mahimānam avaiti sarva
śāstrārtha-vin na ca vidhir na haro na lakṣmīḥ
kintv eka eva puruṣārtha-śiromaṇis tvat-
prasveda-mārjana-paraḥ svayam eva kṛṣṇaḥ

"O goddess, even Lord Brahmā himself, the knower of all scriptures, cannot understand Your glories, nor can Lord Śiva or Lakṣmī. Only Kṛṣṇa, the supreme goal of all human endeavor, can understand them, and thus He feels obliged to personally make sure that You can wash away Your perspiration when You are fatigued.'"

yaś cāru-yāvaka-rasena bhavat-padābjam
ārajya nūpuram aho nidadhāti nityam
prāpya tvadīya-nayanābja-taṭa-prasādaṁ
svaṁ manyate parama-dhanyatamaṁ prahṛṣyan

tasyājñayaiva sahasā vayam ājagāma
tat-pārṣṇi-ghāta-kṛta-kuṇḍa-vare vasāmaḥ
tvaṁ cet prasīdasi karoṣi kṛpā-kaṭākṣaṁ
tarhy eva tarṣa-viṭapī phalito bhaven naḥ

"He is always anointing Your lotus feet with nectarean *cāru* and *yāvaka* and decorating them with ankle bells, and He rejoices and feels most fortunate simply by satisfying the tips of the toes of Your lotus feet. On His order we have immediately come here to live in this most excellent pond, which He created by one stroke of His heel. But only if You now feel satisfied with us and bestow upon us Your merciful glance will the tree of our desire bear fruit."

śrutvā stutiṁ nikhila-tīrtha-gaṇasya tuṣṭā
prāha sma tarṣam ayi vedayateti rādhā
yāma tvadīya-sarasīṁ sa-phalā bhavāma
ity eva no vara iti prakaṭaṁ tadocuḥ

"Hearing this prayer spoken by the representative of the full assembly of holy places, Śrī Rādhā was pleased and said, 'So, kindly tell Me your desire.'

"They then told Her plainly, 'Our lives would be successful if we could come to Your pond. That is the benediction we desire.'"

āgacchateti vṛṣabhānu-sutā smitāsyā
provāca kānta-vadanābja-dhṛtākṣi-koṇā
sakhyo'pi tatra kṛta-sammatayaḥ sukhābdhau
magnā virejur akhilā sthira-jaṅgamāś ca

"Glancing at Her beloved from the corners of Her eyes, the daughter of Vṛṣabhānu replied with a smile, 'Please come.' Her *gopī* companions all agreed with Her decision and became immersed in the ocean of happiness. Indeed, the beauty of all creatures, both mobile and stationary, was enhanced."

prāpya prasādam atha te vṛṣabhānujāyāḥ
śrī-kṛṣṇa-kuṇḍa-gata-tīrtha-varāḥ prasahya
bhittveva bhittim ati-vegata eva rādhā-
kuṇḍaṁ vyadhuḥ sva-salilaiḥ paripūrṇam eva

"Thus gaining the grace of Śrīmatī Rādhārāṇī, the holy rivers and lakes in Śrī Kṛṣṇa-kuṇḍa forcibly broke through its boundary walls and swiftly filled Rādhā-kuṇḍa with their waters."

proce hariḥ priyatame tava kuṇḍam etan
mat-kuṇḍato'pi mahimādhikam astu loke
atraiva me salila-kelir ihaiva nityaṁ
snānaṁ yathā tvam asi tadvad idaṁ saro me

"Lord Hari then said, 'My dear Rādhā, may this pond of Yours become even more world-renowned than Mine. I will always come here to bathe and to enjoy My water pastimes. Indeed, this lake is as dear to Me as You are.'"

rādhābravīd aham api sva-sakhībhir etya
snāsyāmy ariṣṭa-śata-mardanam astu tasya
yo'riṣṭa-mardana-sarasy uru-bhaktir atra
snāyād vasen mama sa eva mahā-priyo'stu

"Rādhā replied, 'I will come to bathe in Your pond as well, even though You may kill hundreds of Ariṣṭa demons here. In the future, anyone who has intense devotion for this lake, which is on the spot where You chastised Ariṣṭāsura, and who bathes or resides here is sure to become very dear to Me.'"

rāsotsavaṁ prakurute sma ca tatra rātrau
kṛṣṇāmbudaḥ kṛta-mahā-rasa-harṣa-varṣaḥ

śrī-rādhikā-pravara-vidyud alaṅkṛta-śrīs
trailokya-madhya-vitatī-kṛta-divya-kīrtiḥ

"That night Lord Kṛṣṇa initiated a *rāsa* dance at Rādhā-kuṇḍa, generating a torrent of the greatest mood of splendorous pleasure. Śrī Kṛṣṇa resembled a cloud, and Śrīmatī Rādhārāṇī a brilliant flash of lightning filling the sky with abundant beauty. In this way Their divine glories permeated the expanses of the three worlds."

As a final note, it should be mentioned that Nārada Muni, being a great sage, understood that the killing of Ariṣṭa more or less concluded the pastimes of Kṛṣṇa in Vṛndāvana. Therefore Nārada, anxious to facilitate the transferal of Kṛṣṇa's pastimes to Mathurā, approached Kaṁsa and addressed him as follows.

TEXT 17

यशोदायाः सुतां कन्यां देवक्याः कृष्णमेव च ।
रामं च रोहिणीपुत्रं वसुदेवेन बिभ्यता ।
न्यस्तौ स्वमित्रे नन्दे वै याभ्यां ते पुरुषा हताः ॥ १७ ॥

yaśodāyāḥ sutāṁ kanyāṁ
devakyāḥ kṛṣṇam eva ca
rāmaṁ ca rohiṇī-putraṁ
vasudevena bibhyatā
nyastau sva-mitre nande vai
yābhyāṁ te puruṣā hatāḥ

yaśodāyāḥ—of Yaśodā; *sutām*—the daughter; *kanyām*—the female child; *devakyāḥ*—of Devakī; *kṛṣṇam*—Kṛṣṇa; *eva ca*—also; *rāmam*—Balarāma; *ca*—and; *rohiṇī-putram*—the son of Rohiṇī; *vasudevena*—by Vasudeva; *bibhyatā*—who was afraid; *nyastau*—placed; *sva-mitre*—with his friend; *nande*—Nanda Mahārāja; *vai*—indeed; *yābhyām*—by which two; *te*—your; *puruṣāḥ*—men; *hatāḥ*—have been killed.

TRANSLATION

[Nārada told Kaṁsa:] Yaśodā's child was actually a daughter, and Kṛṣṇa is the son of Devakī. Also, Rāma is the son of Rohiṇī. Out of fear, Vasudeva entrusted Kṛṣṇa and Balarāma to his friend Nanda Mahārāja, and it is these two boys who have killed your men.

PURPORT

Kaṁsa had been led to believe that Kṛṣṇa was the son of Yaśodā and that Devakī's eighth child had been a daughter. The identity of Devakī's eighth child was extremely important to Kaṁsa because a prophecy had foretold that her eighth child would kill him. Here Nārada informs the King that the eighth child of Devakī was the formidable Kṛṣṇa, thus implying that the prophecy should be taken very seriously. Having received this information, Kaṁsa obviously will now do everything in his power to kill Kṛṣṇa and Balarāma.

TEXT 18

निशम्य तद् भोजपतिः कोपात्प्रचलितेन्द्रियः ।
निशातमसिमादत्त वसुदेवजिघांसया ॥ १८ ॥

niśamya tad bhoja-patiḥ
kopāt pracalitendriyaḥ
niśātam asim ādatta
vasudeva-jighāṁsayā

niśamya—hearing; *tat*—that; *bhoja-patiḥ*—the lord of the Bhoja dynasty (Kaṁsa); *kopāt*—out of anger; *pracalita*—disturbed; *indriyaḥ*—his senses; *niśātam*—sharp; *asim*—a sword; *ādatta*—took up; *vasudeva-jighāṁsayā*—with the desire to kill Vasudeva.

TRANSLATION

Upon hearing this, the master of the Bhojas became furious and lost control of his senses. He picked up a sharp sword to kill Vasudeva.

TEXT 19

निवारितो नारदेन तत्सुतौ मृत्युमात्मनः ।
ज्ञात्वा लोहमयैः पाशैर्बबन्ध सह भार्यया ॥ १९ ॥

nivārito nāradena
tat-sutau mṛtyum ātmanaḥ
jñātvā loha-mayaiḥ pāśair
babandha saha bhāryayā

nivāritaḥ—checked; *nāradena*—by Nārada; *tat-sutau*—his two sons; *mṛtyum*—death; *ātmanaḥ*—his own; *jñātvā*—understanding; *loha-mayaiḥ*

—made of iron; *pāśaiḥ*—with shackles; *babandha*—he bound up (Vasudeva); *saha*—together with; *bhāryayā*—his wife.

TRANSLATION

But Nārada restrained Kaṁsa by reminding him that it was the two sons of Vasudeva who would cause his death. Kaṁsa then had Vasudeva and his wife shackled in iron chains.

PURPORT

Kaṁsa realized that there was no use in killing Vasudeva, since it was Vasudeva's sons, Kṛṣṇa and Balarāma, who were to kill him. According to the *ācāryas,* Nārada also advised Kaṁsa that if he killed Vasudeva the two young boys might flee and that it was therefore better not to kill him. Rather, Nārada recommended, Kaṁsa should bring Kṛṣṇa and Balarāma to Kaṁsa's capital city, Mathurā.

Śrīla Viśvanātha Cakravartī points out that Nārada did not act inimically toward the great devotees Vasudeva and Devakī when he revealed this information to Kaṁsa. In fact, as explained in the Eleventh Canto, Vasudeva was grateful to Nārada because he was arranging for Kaṁsa's death at Kṛṣṇa's hands, and further arranging for Kṛṣṇa to come and live in Mathurā, where His loving father could associate with Him.

TEXT 20

प्रतियाते तु देवर्षौ कंस आभाष्य केशिनम् ।
प्रेषयामास हन्येतां भवता रामकेशवौ ॥ २० ॥

pratiyāte tu devarṣau
kaṁsa ābhāṣya keśinam
preṣayām āsa hanyetāṁ
bhavatā rāma-keśavau

pratiyāte—having left; *tu*—then; *deva-ṛṣau*—the sage among the demigods; *kaṁsaḥ*—King Kaṁsa; *ābhāṣya*—addressing; *keśinam*—the demon Keśī; *preṣayām āsa*—he sent him; *hanyetām*—the two should be killed; *bhavatā*—by you; *rāma-keśavau*—Balarāma and Kṛṣṇa.

TRANSLATION

After Nārada left, King Kaṁsa summoned Keśī and ordered him, "Go kill Rāma and Kṛṣṇa."

PURPORT

Before having Kṛṣṇa and Balarāma brought to Mathurā, Kaṁsa tried sending one more demon to Vṛndāvana.

TEXT 21

ततो मुष्टिकचाणूरशलतोशलकादिकान् ।
अमात्यान् हस्तिपांश्चैव समाहूयाह भोजराट् ॥ २१ ॥

tato muṣṭika-cāṇūra
śala-tośalakādikān
amātyān hastipāṁś caiva
samāhūyāha bhoja-rāṭ

tataḥ—then; *muṣṭika-cāṇūra-śala-tośalaka-ādikān*—Muṣṭika, Cāṇūra, Śala, Tośala and others; *amātyān*—his ministers; *hasti-pān*—his elephant-keepers; *ca eva*—also; *samāhūya*—calling together; *āha*—spoke; *bhoja-rāṭ*—the King of the Bhojas.

TRANSLATION

The King of the Bhojas next called for his ministers, headed by Muṣṭika, Cāṇūra, Śala and Tośala, and also for his elephant-keepers. The King addressed them as follows.

TEXTS 22–23

भो भो निशम्यतामेतद्वीरचाणूरमुष्टिकौ ।
नन्दव्रजे किलासाते सुतावानकदुन्दुभेः ॥ २२ ॥
रामकृष्णौ ततो मह्यं मृत्युः किल निदर्शितः ।
भवद्भ्यामिह सम्प्राप्तौ हन्येतां मल्ललीलया ॥ २३ ॥

bho bho niśamyatām etad
vīra-cāṇūra-muṣṭikau
nanda-vraje kilāsāte
sutāv ānakadundubheḥ

rāma-kṛṣṇau tato mahyaṁ
mṛtyuḥ kila nidarśitaḥ
bhavadbhyām iha samprāptau
hanyetāṁ malla-līlayā

bhoḥ bhoḥ—my dear (advisers); *niśamyatām*—please listen; *etat*—to this; *vīra*—O heroes; *cāṇūra-muṣṭikau*—Cāṇūra and Muṣṭika; *nanda-vraje*—in the cowherd village of Nanda; *kila*—indeed; *āsāte*—are living; *sutau*—the two sons; *ānakadundubheḥ*—of Vasudeva; *rāma-kṛṣṇau*—Rāma and Kṛṣṇa; *tataḥ*—from Them; *mahyam*—my; *mṛtyuḥ*—death; *kila*—indeed; *nidarśitaḥ*—has been indicated; *bhavadbhyām*—by you two; *iha*—here; *samprāptau*—brought; *hanyetām*—They should be killed; *malla*—of wrestling; *līlayā*—on the pretext of the sport.

TRANSLATION

My dear heroic Cāṇūra and Muṣṭika, please hear this. Rāma and Kṛṣṇa, the sons of Ānakadundubhi [Vasudeva], are living in Nanda's cowherd village. It has been predicted that these two boys will be the cause of my death. When They are brought here, kill Them on the pretext of engaging Them in a wrestling match.

TEXT 24

मञ्चाः क्रियन्तां विविधा मल्लरंगपरिश्रिताः ।
पौरा जानपदाः सर्वे पश्यन्तु स्वैरसंयुगम् ॥ २४ ॥

mañcāḥ kriyantāṁ vividhā
malla-raṅga-pariśritāḥ
paurā jānapadāḥ sarve
paśyantu svaira-saṁyugam

mañcāḥ—stages; *kriyantām*—should be built; *vividhāḥ*—various; *malla-raṅga*—a wrestling ring; *pariśritāḥ*—surrounding; *paurāḥ*—the residents of the city; *jānapadāḥ*—and the residents of the outlying districts; *sarve*—all; *paśyantu*—should see; *svaira*—voluntarily participated in; *saṁyugam*—the competition.

TRANSLATION

Erect a wrestling ring with many surrounding viewing stands, and bring all the residents of the city and the outlying districts to see the open competition.

PURPORT

The word *mañcāḥ* refers to platforms constructed with large pillars. Kaṁsa wanted a festive atmosphere so that Kṛṣṇa and Balarāma would not be afraid to come.

TEXT 25

महामात्र त्वया भद्र रंगद्वार्युपनीयताम् ।
द्विपः कुवलयापीडो जहि तेन ममाहितौ ॥ २५ ॥

mahāmātra tvayā bhadra
raṅga-dvāry upanīyatām
dvipaḥ kuvalayāpīḍo
jahi tena mamāhitau

mahā-mātra—O elephant-keeper; *tvayā*—by you; *bhadra*—my good man; *raṅga*—of the arena; *dvāri*—to the doorway; *upanīyatām*—should be brought; *dvipaḥ*—the elephant; *kuvalayāpīḍaḥ*—named Kuvalayāpīḍa; *jahi*—destroy; *tena*—with that (elephant); *mama*—my; *ahitau*—enemies.

TRANSLATION

You, elephant-keeper, my good man, should position the elephant Kuvalayāpīḍa at the entrance to the wrestling arena and have him kill my two enemies.

TEXT 26

आरभ्यतां धनुर्यागश्चतुर्दश्यां यथाविधि ।
विशसन्तु पशून्मेध्यान् भूतराजाय मीढुषे ॥ २६ ॥

ārabhyatāṁ dhanur-yāgaś
caturdaśyāṁ yathā-vidhi
viśasantu paśūn medhyān
bhūta-rājāya mīḍhuṣe

ārabhyatām—should be commenced; *dhanuḥ-yāgaḥ*—the bow sacrifice; *caturdaśyām*—on the fourteenth day of the month; *yathā-vidhi*—in accordance with Vedic injunctions; *viśasantu*—offer in sacrifice; *paśūn*—animals; *medhyān*—which are fit to be offered; *bhūta-rājāya*—to Lord Śiva, the lord of ghostly spirits; *mīḍhuṣe*—the giver of benedictions.

TRANSLATION

Commence the bow sacrifice on the Caturdaśī day in accordance with the relevant Vedic injunctions. In ritual slaughter offer the appropriate kinds of animals to the magnanimous Lord Śiva.

TEXT 27

इत्याज्ञाप्यार्थतन्त्रज्ञ आहूय यदुपुंगवम् ।
गृहीत्वा पाणिना पाणिं ततोऽक्रूरमुवाच ह ॥ २७ ॥

ity ājñāpyārtha-tantra-jña
āhūya yadu-puṅgavam
gṛhītvā pāṇinā pāṇiṁ
tato'krūram uvāca ha

iti—with these words; *ājñāpya*—ordering; *artha*—of personal interest and advantage; *tantra*—of the doctrine; *jñaḥ*—the knower; *āhūya*—calling for; *yadu-puṅgavam*—the most eminent of the Yadus; *gṛhītvā*—taking; *pāṇinā*—with his own hand; *pāṇim*—his hand; *tataḥ*—then; *akrūram*—to Akrūra; *uvāca ha*—he said.

TRANSLATION

Having thus commanded his ministers, Kaṁsa next called for Akrūra, the most eminent of the Yadus. Kaṁsa knew the art of securing personal advantage, and thus he took Akrūra's hand in his own and spoke to him as follows.

TEXT 28

भो भो दानपते मह्यं क्रियतां मैत्रमादृतः ।
नान्यस्त्वत्तो हिततमो विद्यते भोजवृष्णिषु ॥ २८ ॥

bho bho dāna-pate mahyaṁ
kriyatāṁ maitram ādṛtaḥ
nānyas tvatto hitatamo
vidyate bhoja-vṛṣṇiṣu

bhoḥ bhoḥ—my dear; *dāna*—of charity; *pate*—master; *mahyam*—for me; *kriyatām*—please do; *maitram*—a friendly favor; *ādṛtaḥ*—out of respect; *na*—none; *anyaḥ*—other; *tvattaḥ*—than yourself; *hita-tamaḥ*—who acts most favorably; *vidyate*—exists; *bhoja-vṛṣṇiṣu*—among the Bhojas and Vṛṣṇis.

TRANSLATION

My dear Akrūra, most charitable one, please do me a friendly favor out of respect. Among the Bhojas and Vṛṣṇis, there is no one else as kind to us as you.

TEXT 29

अतस्त्वामाश्रितः सौम्य कार्यगौरवसाधनम् ।
यथेन्द्रो विष्णुमाश्रित्य स्वार्थमध्यगमद्विभुः ॥ २९ ॥

atas tvām āśritaḥ saumya
kārya-gaurava-sādhanam
yathendro viṣṇum āśritya
svārtham adhyagamad vibhuḥ

ataḥ—therefore; *tvām*—on you; *āśritaḥ*—(I am) depending; *saumya*—O gentle one; *kārya*—prescribed duties; *gaurava*—soberly; *sādhanam*—who executes; *yathā*—as similarly; *indraḥ*—Indra; *viṣṇum*—Lord Viṣṇu; *āśritya*—taking shelter of; *sva-artham*—his goals; *adhyagamat*—achieved; *vibhuḥ*—the powerful King of heaven.

TRANSLATION

Gentle Akrūra, you always carry out your duties soberly, and therefore I am depending on you, just as powerful Indra took shelter of Lord Viṣṇu to achieve his goals.

TEXT 30

गच्छ नन्दव्रजं तत्र सुतावानकदुन्दुभेः ।
आसाते ताविहानेन रथेनानय मा चिरम् ॥ ३० ॥

gaccha nanda-vrajaṁ tatra
sutāv ānakadundubheḥ
āsāte tāv ihānena
rathenānaya mā ciram

gaccha—go; *nanda-vrajam*—to the cowherd village of Nanda; *tatra*—there; *sutau*—the two sons; *ānakadundubheḥ*—of Vasudeva; *āsāte*—are living; *tau*—Them; *iha*—here; *anena*—by this; *rathena*—chariot; *ānaya*—bring; *mā ciram*—without delay.

TRANSLATION

Please go to Nanda's village, where the two sons of Ānakadundubhi are living, and without delay bring Them here on this chariot.

PURPORT

Śrīla Viśvanātha Cakravartī gives the following interesting note: "When King Kaṁsa said 'with this chariot,' he pointed with his index finger to a brand-new, attractive chariot. Kaṁsa thought that since Akrūra was innocent by nature, when he saw this fine, new vehicle he would naturally want to drive it and quickly bring the two boys back. But the actual reason Akrūra went on a new chariot was that it would have been clearly inappropriate for the Supreme Personality of Godhead to mount a chariot that had already been enjoyed by the wicked Kaṁsa."

TEXT 31

निसृष्टः किल मे मृत्युर्देवैर्वैकुण्ठसंश्रयैः ।
तावानय समं गोपैर्नन्दाद्यैः साभ्युपायनैः ॥ ३१ ॥

nisṛṣṭaḥ kila me mṛtyur
devair vaikuṇṭha-saṁśrayaiḥ
tāv ānaya samaṁ gopair
nandādyaiḥ sābhyupāyanaiḥ

nisṛṣṭaḥ—sent; *kila*—indeed; *me*—my; *mṛtyuḥ*—death; *devaiḥ*—by the demigods; *vaikuṇṭha*—of Lord Viṣṇu; *saṁśrayaiḥ*—who take shelter; *tau*—the two of Them; *ānaya*—bring; *samam*—together with; *gopaiḥ*—the cowherd men; *nanda-ādyaiḥ*—headed by Nanda; *sa*—with; *abhyupāyanaiḥ*—gifts.

TRANSLATION

The demigods, who are under the protection of Viṣṇu, have sent these two boys as my death. Bring Them here, and also have Nanda and the other cowherd men come with gifts of tribute.

TEXT 32

घातयिष्य इहानीतौ कालकल्पेन हस्तिना।
यदि मुक्तौ ततो मल्लैर्घातये वैद्युतोपमैः ॥ ३२ ॥

ghātayiṣya ihānītau
kāla-kalpena hastinā
yadi muktau tato mallair
ghātaye vaidyutopamaiḥ

ghātayiṣye—I shall have Them killed; *iha*—here; *ānītau*—brought; *kāla-kalpena*—like death itself; *hastinā*—by the elephant; *yadi*—if; *muktau*—They go free; *tataḥ*—then; *mallaiḥ*—by wrestlers; *ghātaye*—I will have killed; *vaidyuta*—lightning; *upamaiḥ*—just like.

TRANSLATION

After you bring Kṛṣṇa and Balarāma, I will have Them killed by my elephant, who is as powerful as death itself. And if by chance They escape from him, I will have Them killed by my wrestlers, who are as strong as lightning.

TEXT 33

तयोर्निहतयोस्तप्तान् वसुदेवपुरोगमान् ।
तद्बन्धून्निहनिष्यामि वृष्णिभोजदशार्हकान् ॥ ३३ ॥

tayor nihatayos taptān
vasudeva-purogamān
tad-bandhūn nihaniṣyāmi
vṛṣṇi-bhoja-daśārhakān

tayoḥ—the two of Them; *nihatayoḥ*—when They are killed; *taptān*—tormented; *vasudeva-purogamān*—led by Vasudeva; *tad-bandhūn*—Their relatives; *nihaniṣyāmi*—I will kill; *vṛṣṇi-bhoja-daśārhakān*—the Vṛṣṇis, Bhojas and Daśārhas.

TRANSLATION

When these two have been killed, I will kill Vasudeva and all Their lamenting relatives—the Vṛṣṇis, Bhojas and Daśārhas.

PURPORT

Even today there are wicked political leaders throughout the world who make such plans and even carry them out.

TEXT 34

उग्रसेनं च पितरं स्थविरं राज्यकामुकं ।
तद्भ्रातरं देवकं च ये चान्ये विद्विषो मम ॥ ३४ ॥

ugrasenaṁ ca pitaraṁ
sthaviraṁ rājya-kāmukaṁ
tad-bhrātaraṁ devakaṁ ca
ye cānye vidviṣo mama

ugrasenam—King Ugrasena; *ca*—and; *pitaram*—my father; *sthaviram*—old; *rājya*—for the kingdom; *kāmukam*—greedy; *tat-bhrātaram*—his brother; *devakam*—Devaka; *ca*—also; *ye*—who; *ca*—and; *anye*—others; *vidviṣaḥ*—enemies; *mama*—my.

TRANSLATION

I will also kill my old father, Ugrasena, who is greedy for my kingdom, and I will kill his brother Devaka and all my other enemies as well.

TEXT 35

ततश्चैषा मही मित्र भवित्री नष्टकण्टका ॥ ३५ ॥

tataś caiṣā mahī mitra
bhavitrī naṣṭa-kaṇṭakā

tataḥ—then; *ca*—and; *eṣā*—this; *mahī*—earth; *mitra*—O friend; *bhavitrī*—will be; *naṣṭa*—destroyed; *kaṇṭakā*—her thorns.

TRANSLATION

Then, my friend, this earth will be free of thorns.

TEXT 36

जरासन्धो मम गुरुर्द्विविदो दयितः सखा ।
शम्बरो नरको बाणो मय्येव कृतसौहृदाः ।
तैरहं सुरपक्षीयान् हत्वा भोक्ष्ये महीं नृपान् ॥ ३६ ॥

jarāsandho mama gurur
dvivido dayitaḥ sakhā
śambaro narako bāṇo
mayy eva kṛta-sauhṛdāḥ
tair ahaṁ sura-pakṣīyān
hatvā bhokṣye mahīṁ nṛpān

jarāsandhaḥ—Jarāsandha; *mama*—my; *guruḥ*—elder (father-in-law); *dvividaḥ*—Dvivida; *dayitaḥ*—my dear; *sakhā*—friend; *śambaraḥ*—Śambara; *narakaḥ*—Naraka; *bāṇaḥ*—Bāṇa; *mayi*—for me; *eva*—indeed; *kṛta-sauhṛdāḥ*—who have strong friendship; *taiḥ*—with them; *aham*—I; *sura*—of the demigods; *pakṣīyān*—those who are allies; *hatvā*—killing; *bhokṣye*—will enjoy; *mahīm*—the earth; *nṛpān*—the kings.

TRANSLATION

My elder relative Jarāsandha and my dear friend Dvivida are solid well-wishers of mine, as are Śambara, Naraka and Bāṇa. I will use them all to kill off those kings who are allied with the demigods, and then I will rule the earth.

TEXT 37

एतज्ज्ञात्वानय क्षिप्रं रामकृष्णाविहार्भकौ ।
धनुर्मखनिरीक्षार्थं द्रष्टुं यदुपुरश्रियम् ॥ ३७ ॥

etaj jñātvānaya kṣipraṁ
rāma-kṛṣṇāv ihārbhakau
dhanur-makha-nirīkṣārthaṁ
draṣṭuṁ yadu-pura-śriyam

etat—this; *jñātvā*—knowing; *ānaya*—bring; *kṣipram*—quickly; *rāma-kṛṣṇau*—Rāma and Kṛṣṇa; *iha*—here; *arbhakau*—the young boys; *dhanuḥ-makha*—the bow sacrifice; *nirīkṣā-artham*—in order to witness; *draṣṭum*—to see; *yadu-pura*—of the capital city of the Yadu dynasty; *śriyam*—the opulence.

TRANSLATION

Now that you understand my intentions, please go at once and bring Kṛṣṇa and Balarāma to watch the bow sacrifice and see the opulence of the Yadus' capital.

TEXT 38

श्रीअक्रूर उवाच
राजन्मनीषितं सध्र्यक् तव स्वावद्यमार्जनम् ।
सिद्ध्यसिद्ध्योः समं कुर्याद्दैवं हि फलसाधनम् ॥ ३८ ॥

śrī-akrūra uvāca
rājan manīṣitaṁ sadhryak
tava svāvadya-mārjanam
siddhy-asiddhyoḥ samaṁ kuryād
daivaṁ hi phala-sādhanam

śrī-akrūraḥ uvāca—Śrī Akrūra said; *rājan*—O King; *manīṣitam*—the thinking; *sadhryak*—perfect; *tava*—your; *sva*—your own; *avadya*—misfortune; *mārjanam*—which will wash away; *siddhi-asiddhyoḥ*—in both success and failure; *samam*—equal; *kuryāt*—one should act; *daivam*—destiny; *hi*—after all; *phala*—the fruit, result; *sādhanam*—the cause of achieving.

TRANSLATION

Śrī Akrūra said: O King, you have expertly devised a process to free yourself of misfortune. Still, one should be equal in success and failure, since it is certainly destiny that produces the results of one's work.

TEXT 39

मनोरथान् करोत्युच्चैर्जनो दैवहतानपि ।
युज्यते हर्षशोकाभ्यां तथाप्याज्ञां करोमि ते ॥ ३९ ॥

manorathān karoty uccair
jano daiva-hatān api
yujyate harṣa-śokābhyāṁ
tathāpy ājñāṁ karomi te

manaḥ-rathān—his desires; *karoti*—carries out; *uccaiḥ*—fervently; *janaḥ*—the average person; *daiva*—by providence; *hatān*—thwarted; *api*—even though; *yujyate*—he is confronted; *harṣa-śokābhyām*—by happiness and distress; *tathā api*—nonetheless; *ājñām*—order; *karomi*—I will do; *te*—your.

TRANSLATION

An ordinary person is determined to act on his desires even when fate prevents their fulfillment. Therefore he encounters both happiness and distress. Yet even though such is the case, I will execute your order.

PURPORT

Śrīla Viśvanātha Cakravartī explains that although what Akrūra said was courteous and encouraging, his hidden meaning was far different. What he really meant was this: "Your plan is not fit to execute, yet I will carry it out since you are the King and I am your subject, and in any case, you are about to die."

TEXT 40

श्रीशुक उवाच
एवमादिश्य चाक्रूरं मन्त्रिणश्च विसृज्य सः ।
प्रविवेश गृहं कंसस्तथाक्रूरः स्वमालयम् ॥ ४० ॥

śrī-śuka uvāca
evam ādiśya cākrūraṁ
mantriṇaś ca visṛjya saḥ
praviveśa gṛhaṁ kaṁsas
tathākrūraḥ svam ālayam

śrī-śukaḥ uvāca—Śukadeva Gosvāmī said; *evam*—thus; *ādiśya*—instructing; *ca*—and; *akrūram*—Akrūra; *mantriṇaḥ*—his ministers; *ca*—and; *visṛjya*—dismissing; *saḥ*—he; *praviveśa*—entered; *gṛham*—his quarters; *kaṁsaḥ*—Kaṁsa; *tathā*—also; *akrūraḥ*—Akrūra; *svam*—his own; *ālayam*—residence.

TRANSLATION

Śukadeva Gosvāmī said: Having thus instructed Akrūra, King Kaṁsa dismissed his ministers and retired to his quarters, and Akrūra returned home.

Thus end the purports of the humble servants of His Divine Grace A.C. Bhaktivedanta Swami Prabhupāda to the Tenth Canto, Thirty-sixth Chapter, of the Śrīmad-Bhāgavatam, *entitled "The Slaying of Ariṣṭa, the Bull Demon."*

CHAPTER THIRTY-SEVEN

The Killing of the Demons Keśī and Vyoma

This chapter describes the killing of the horse demon, Keśī; Nārada's glorification of Lord Kṛṣṇa's future pastimes; and Kṛṣṇa's killing of Vyomāsura.

On Kaṁsa's order the Keśī demon assumed the form of a huge horse and went to Vraja. As he approached, his loud neighing terrified all the inhabitants, and they began looking for Śrī Kṛṣṇa. When He saw the demon, Kṛṣṇa came forward and challenged him to come near. Keśī charged Kṛṣṇa and tried to strike Him with his front legs, but the Lord seized them, whirled the demon around several times, and then threw him a distance of one hundred bow-lengths. Keśī remained unconscious for some time. When the demon regained consciousness, he furiously charged Kṛṣṇa again, his mouth agape. The Lord then thrust His left arm into the horse demon's mouth, and as Keśī tried to bite the arm, it felt like a red-hot iron rod. Kṛṣṇa's arm expanded more and more, finally choking the demon, and in extreme agony Keśī gave up his life. Lord Kṛṣṇa then removed His arm. He stood calmly, showing no pride at having killed the demon, as the demigods showered down flowers from the sky and glorified the Lord with prayers.

Soon thereafter Nārada Muni, the great sage among the demigods, approached Kṛṣṇa and prayed to Him in various ways, glorifying the Lord's future pastimes. Then Nārada paid his obeisances and departed.

One day, while tending the cows, Kṛṣṇa, Balarāma and the cowherd boys became engrossed in playing hide-and-go-seek. Some of the boys took the role of sheep, some the role of thieves, and others shepherds. The shepherds would search for the sheep when the thieves stole them. Taking advantage of this game, a demon named Vyoma, sent by Kaṁsa, dressed himself like a cowherd boy and joined the band of "thieves." He abducted a few cowherd boys at a time and threw them into a mountain cave, keeping them there by blocking the entrance with a boulder. Gradually Vyomāsura abducted all but four or five cowherd boys. When Kṛṣṇa saw what the demon was doing, He ran after him, grabbed him and killed him just as one would kill a sacrificial animal.

TEXTS 1–2

श्रीशुक उवाच
केशी तु कंसप्रहितः खुरैर्महीं
महाहयो निर्जरयन्मनोजवः ।
सटावधूताभ्रविमानसंकुलं
कुर्वन्नभो हेषितभीषिताखिलः ॥ १ ॥

तं त्रासयन्तं भगवान् स्वगोकुलं
तद्धेषितैर्वालविघूर्णिताम्बुदम् ।
आत्मानमाजौ मृगयन्तमग्रणीर्
उपाह्वयत्स व्यनदन्मृगेन्द्रवत् ॥ २ ॥

śrī-śuka uvāca
keśī tu kaṁsa-prahitaḥ khurair mahīṁ
mahā-hayo nirjarayan mano-javaḥ
saṭāvadhūtābhra-vimāna-saṅkulaṁ
kurvan nabho heṣita-bhīṣitākhilaḥ

taṁ trāsayantaṁ bhagavān sva-gokulaṁ
tad-dheṣitair vāla-vighūrṇitāmbudam
ātmānam ājau mṛgayantam agra-ṇīr
upāhvayat sa vyanadan mṛgendra-vat

śrī-śukaḥ uvāca—Śrī Śukadeva Gosvāmī said; *keśī*—the demon named Keśī; *tu*—and then; *kaṁsa-prahitaḥ*—sent by Kaṁsa; *khuraiḥ*—with his hooves; *mahīm*—the earth; *mahā-hayaḥ*—a huge horse; *nirjarayan*—ripping apart; *manaḥ*—like that of the mind; *javaḥ*—whose speed; *saṭā*—by the hairs of his mane; *avadhūta*—scattered; *abhra*—with the clouds; *vimāna*—and the airplanes (of the demigods); *saṅkulam*—crowded; *kurvan*—making; *nabhaḥ*—the sky; *heṣita*—by his neighing; *bhīṣita*—frightened; *akhilaḥ*—everyone; *tam*—him; *trāsayantam*—terrifying; *bhagavān*—the Supreme Lord; *sva-gokulam*—His cowherd village; *tat-heṣitaiḥ*—by that neighing; *vāla*—by the hairs of his tail; *vighūrṇita*—shaken; *ambudam*—the clouds; *ātmānam*—Himself; *ājau*—for a fight; *mṛgayantam*—searching after; *agra-nīḥ*—coming forward; *upāhvayat*—called out; *saḥ*—he, Keśī; *vyanadan*—roared; *mṛgendra-vat*—like a lion.

TRANSLATION

Śukadeva Gosvāmī said: The demon Keśī, sent by Kaṁsa, appeared in Vraja as a great horse. Running with the speed of the mind, he tore up the earth with his hooves. The hairs of his mane scattered the clouds and the demigods' airplanes throughout the sky, and he terrified everyone present with his loud neighing.

When the Supreme Personality of Godhead saw how the demon was frightening His village of Gokula by neighing terribly and shaking the clouds with his tail, the Lord came forward to meet him. Keśī was searching for Kṛṣṇa to fight, so when the Lord stood before him and challenged him to approach, the horse responded by roaring like a lion.

TEXT 3

स तं निशाम्याभिमुखो मुखेन खं
पिबन्निवाभ्यद्रवदत्यमर्षणः ।
जघान पद्भ्यामरविन्दलोचनं
दुरासदश्चण्डजवो दुरत्ययः ॥ ३ ॥

sa taṁ niśāmyābhimukho mukhena khaṁ
pibann ivābhyadravad aty-amarṣaṇaḥ
jaghāna padbhyām aravinda-locanaṁ
durāsadaś caṇḍa-javo duratyayaḥ

saḥ—he, Keśī; *tam*—Him, Kṛṣṇa; *niśāmya*—seeing; *abhimukhaḥ*—in front of himself; *mukhena*—with his mouth; *kham*—the sky; *piban*—drinking up; *iva*—as if; *abhyadravat*—ran forward; *ati-amarṣaṇaḥ*—very angry; *jaghāna*—he attacked; *padbhyām*—with his two legs; *aravinda-locanam*—the lotus-eyed Lord; *durāsadaḥ*—unapproachable; *caṇḍa*—fierce; *javaḥ*—whose speed; *duratyayaḥ*—unconquerable.

TRANSLATION

Seeing the Lord standing before him, Keśī ran toward Him in extreme rage, his mouth gaping as if to swallow up the sky. Rushing with furious speed, the unconquerable and unapproachable horse demon tried to strike the lotus-eyed Lord with his two front legs.

TEXT 4

तद्वञ्चयित्वा तमधोक्षजो रुषा
प्रगृह्य दोर्भ्यां परिविध्य पादयोः ।
सावज्ञमुत्सृज्य धनुःशतान्तरे
यथोरगं तार्क्ष्यसुतो व्यवस्थितः ॥ ४ ॥

tad vañcayitvā tam adhokṣajo ruṣā
pragṛhya dorbhyāṁ parividhya pādayoḥ
sāvajñam utsṛjya dhanuḥ-śatāntare
yathoragaṁ tārkṣya-suto vyavasthitaḥ

tat—that; *vañcayitvā*—avoiding; *tam*—him; *adhokṣajaḥ*—the transcendental Lord; *ruṣā*—angrily; *pragṛhya*—seizing; *dorbhyām*—with His arms; *parividhya*—whirling around; *pādayoḥ*—by the legs; *sa-avajñam*—contemptuously; *utsṛjya*—discarding; *dhanuḥ*—of bow-lengths; *śata*—one hundred; *antare*—to the distance; *yathā*—as; *uragam*—a snake; *tārkṣya*—of Kardama Muni; *sutaḥ*—the son (Garuḍa); *vyavasthitaḥ*—standing.

TRANSLATION

But the transcendental Lord dodged Keśī's blow and then with His arms angrily seized the demon by the legs, whirled him around in the air and contemptuously threw him the distance of one hundred bow-lengths, just as Garuḍa might throw a snake. Lord Kṛṣṇa then stood there.

TEXT 5

सः लब्धसंज्ञः पुनरुत्थितो रुषा
व्यादाय केशी तरसापतद्धरिम् ।
सोऽप्यस्य वक्त्रे भुजमुत्तरं स्मयन्
प्रवेशयामास यथोरगं बिले ॥ ५ ॥

saḥ labdha-saṁjñaḥ punar utthito ruṣā
vyādāya keśī tarasāpatad dharim
so'py asya vaktre bhujam uttaraṁ smayan
praveśayām āsa yathoragaṁ bile

saḥ—he, Keśī; *labdha*—regaining; *saṁjñaḥ*—consciousness; *punaḥ*—again; *utthitaḥ*—rose up; *ruṣā*—in anger; *vyādāya*—opening (his mouth) wide; *keśī*—Keśī; *tarasā*—rapidly; *apatat*—ran; *harim*—toward Kṛṣṇa; *saḥ*—He, Lord Kṛṣṇa; *api*—and; *asya*—his; *vaktre*—in the mouth; *bhujam*—His arm; *uttaram*—left; *smayan*—smiled; *praveśayām āsa*—placed within; *yathā*—as; *uragam*—a snake; *bile*—(enters) within a hole.

TRANSLATION

Upon regaining consciousness Keśī angrily got up, opened his mouth wide and again rushed to attack Lord Kṛṣṇa. But the Lord just smiled and thrust His left arm into the horse's mouth as easily as one would make a snake enter a hole in the ground.

TEXT 6

दन्ता निपेतुर्भगवद्भुजस्पृशस्
ते केशिनस्तप्तमयस्पृशो यथा ।
बाहुश्च तद्देहगतो महात्मनो
यथामयः संववृधे उपेक्षितः ॥ ६ ॥

dantā nipetur bhagavad-bhuja-spṛśas
te keśinas tapta-maya-spṛśo yathā
bāhuś ca tad-deha-gato mahātmano
yathāmayaḥ saṁvavṛdhe upekṣitaḥ

dantāḥ—the teeth; *nipetuḥ*—fell out; *bhagavat*—of the Supreme Lord; *bhuja*—the arm; *spṛśaḥ*—touching; *te*—they; *keśinaḥ*—of Keśī; *tapta-maya*—red-hot (iron); *spṛśaḥ*—touching; *yathā*—as; *bāhuḥ*—the arm; *ca*—and; *tat*—his, Keśī's; *deha*—body; *gataḥ*—having entered; *mahā-ātmanaḥ*—of the Supreme Soul; *yathā*—like; *āmayaḥ*—a diseased condition (particularly, distension of the stomach); *saṁvavṛdhe*—increased greatly in size; *upekṣitaḥ*—neglected.

TRANSLATION

Keśī's teeth immediately fell out when they touched the Supreme Lord's arm, which to the demon felt as hot as molten iron. Within Keśī's body the Supreme Personality's arm then expanded greatly, like a diseased stomach swelling because of neglect.

PURPORT

Śrīla Viśvanātha Cakravartī points out that although Lord Kṛṣṇa's arm is more tender and cooling than a blue lotus, to Keśī it felt extremely hot, as if made of lightning bolts.

TEXT 7

समेधमानेन स कृष्णबाहुना
निरुद्धवायुश्चरणांश्च विक्षिपन् ।
प्रस्विन्नगात्रः परिवृत्तलोचनः
पपात लण्डं विसृजन् क्षितौ व्यसुः ॥ ७ ॥

samedhamānena sa kṛṣṇa-bāhunā
niruddha-vāyuś caraṇāṁś ca vikṣipan
prasvinna-gātraḥ parivṛtta-locanaḥ
papāta laṇḍaṁ visṛjan kṣitau vyasuḥ

samedhamānena—expanding; *saḥ*—he; *kṛṣṇa-bāhunā*—by Lord Kṛṣṇa's arm; *niruddha*—stopped; *vāyuḥ*—his breathing; *caraṇān*—his legs; *ca*—and; *vikṣipan*—throwing about; *prasvinna*—perspiring; *gātraḥ*—his body; *parivṛtta*—rolling; *locanaḥ*—his eyes; *papāta*—he fell down; *laṇḍam*—feces; *visṛjan*—excreting; *kṣitau*—onto the ground; *vyasuḥ*—lifeless.

TRANSLATION

As Lord Kṛṣṇa's expanding arm completely blocked Keśī's breathing, his legs kicked convulsively, his body became covered with sweat, and his eyes rolled around. The demon then passed stool and fell on the ground, dead.

TEXT 8

तद्देहतः कर्कटिकाफलोपमाद्
व्यसोरपाकृष्य भुजं महाभुजः ।
अविस्मितोऽयत्नहतारिकः सुरैः
प्रसूनवर्षैर्वर्षद्भिरीडितः ॥ ८ ॥

tad-dehataḥ karkaṭikā-phalopamād
vyasor apākṛṣya bhujaṁ mahā-bhujaḥ
avismito'yatna-hatārikaḥ suraiḥ
prasūna-varṣair varṣadbhir īḍitaḥ

tat-dehataḥ—from Keśī's body; *karkaṭikā-phala*—a *karkaṭikā* fruit; *upamāt*—which resembled; *vyasoḥ*—from which the vital airs had departed;

apākṛṣya—withdrawing; *bhujam*—His arm; *mahā-bhujaḥ*—the mighty-armed Lord; *avismitaḥ*—without undue pride; *ayatna*—without effort; *hata*—having killed; *arikaḥ*—His enemy; *suraiḥ*—by the demigods; *prasūna*—of flowers; *varṣaiḥ*—with downpours; *varṣadbhiḥ*—who were raining upon Him; *īḍitaḥ*—worshiped.

TRANSLATION

The mighty-armed Kṛṣṇa withdrew His arm from Keśī's body, which now appeared like a long karkaṭikā fruit. Without the least display of pride at having so effortlessly killed His enemy, the Lord accepted the demigods' worship in the form of flowers rained down from above.

TEXT 9

देवर्षिरुपसंगम्य भागवतप्रवरो नृप ।
कृष्णमक्लिष्टकर्माणं रहस्येतदभाषत ॥ ९ ॥

devarṣir upasaṅgamya
bhāgavata-pravaro nṛpa
kṛṣṇam akliṣṭa-karmāṇaṁ
rahasy etad abhāṣata

deva-ṛṣiḥ—the sage among the demigods (Nārada Muni); *upasaṅgamya*—approaching; *bhāgavata*—of devotees of the Lord; *pravaraḥ*—the most exalted; *nṛpa*—O King (Parīkṣit); *kṛṣṇam*—Lord Kṛṣṇa; *akliṣṭa*—without trouble; *karmāṇam*—whose activities; *rahasi*—in privacy; *etat*—this; *abhāṣata*—said.

TRANSLATION

My dear King, thereafter Lord Kṛṣṇa was approached in a solitary place by the great sage among the demigods, Nārada Muni. That most exalted devotee spoke as follows to the Lord, who effortlessly performs His pastimes.

PURPORT

After speaking with Kaṁsa, Nārada went to see Lord Kṛṣṇa. The Lord's Vṛndāvana pastimes were nearly completed, and Nārada wanted to see those He would enact in Mathurā.

TEXTS 10–11

कृष्ण कृष्णाप्रमेयात्मन् योगेश जगदीश्वर ।
वासुदेवाखिलावास सात्वतां प्रवर प्रभो ॥ १० ॥
त्वमात्मा सर्वभूतानामेको ज्योतिरिवैधसाम् ।
गूढो गुहाशयः साक्षी महापुरुष ईश्वरः ॥ ११ ॥

kṛṣṇa kṛṣṇāprameyātman
yogeśa jagad-īśvara
vāsudevākhilāvāsa
sātvatāṁ pravara prabho

tvam ātmā sarva-bhūtānām
eko jyotir ivaidhasām
gūḍho guhā-śayaḥ sākṣī
mahā-puruṣa īśvaraḥ

kṛṣṇa kṛṣṇa—O Kṛṣṇa, Kṛṣṇa; *aprameya-ātman*—O immeasurable one; *yoga-īśa*—O source of all mystic power; *jagat-īśvara*—O Lord of the universe; *vāsudeva*—O son of Vasudeva; *akhila-āvāsa*—O shelter of all beings; *sātvatām*—of the Yadu dynasty; *pravara*—O You who are the best; *prabho*—O master; *tvam*—You; *ātmā*—the Supreme Soul; *sarva*—of all; *bhūtānām*—created beings; *ekaḥ*—alone; *jyotiḥ*—fire; *iva*—like; *edhasām*—in kindling wood; *gūḍhaḥ*—hidden; *guhā*—within the cave of the heart; *śayaḥ*—sitting; *sākṣī*—the witness; *mahā-puruṣaḥ*—the Supreme Personality of Godhead; *īśvaraḥ*—the supreme controller.

TRANSLATION

[Nārada Muni said:] O Kṛṣṇa, Kṛṣṇa, unlimited Lord, source of all mystic power, Lord of the universe! O Vāsudeva, shelter of all beings and best of the Yadus! O master, You are the Supreme Soul of all created beings, sitting unseen within the cave of the heart like the fire dormant within kindling wood. You are the witness within everyone, the Supreme Personality and the ultimate controlling Deity.

TEXT 12

आत्मनात्माश्रयः पूर्वं मायया ससृजे गुणान् ।
तैरिदं सत्यसंकल्पः सृजस्यत्स्यवसीश्वरः ॥ १२ ॥

ātmanātmāśrayaḥ pūrvaṁ
māyayā sasṛje guṇān
tair idaṁ satya-saṅkalpaḥ
sṛjasy atsy avasīśvaraḥ

ātmanā—by Your personal potency; *ātma*—of the spirit soul; *āśrayaḥ*—the shelter; *pūrvam*—first; *māyayā*—by Your creative energy; *sasṛje*—You produced; *guṇān*—the basic modes of material nature; *taiḥ*—through these; *idam*—this (universe); *satya*—always realized in fact; *saṅkalpaḥ*—whose desires; *sṛjasi*—You create; *atsi*—withdraw; *avasi*—and maintain; *īśvaraḥ*—the controller.

TRANSLATION

You are the shelter of all souls, and being the supreme controller, You fulfill Your desires simply by Your will. By Your personal creative potency You manifested in the beginning the primal modes of material nature, and through their agency You create, maintain and then destroy this universe.

TEXT 13

स त्वं भूधरभूतानां दैत्यप्रमथरक्षसाम् ।
अवतीर्णो विनाशाय साधुनां रक्षणाय च ॥ १३ ॥

sa tvaṁ bhūdhara-bhūtānāṁ
daitya-pramatha-rakṣasām
avatīrṇo vināśāya
sādhūnāṁ rakṣaṇāya ca

saḥ—He; *tvam*—Yourself; *bhū-dhara*—as kings; *bhūtānām*—who are appearing; *daitya-pramatha-rakṣasām*—of various kinds of demons; *avatīrṇaḥ*—You have descended; *vināśāya*—for the destruction; *sādhūnām*—of saintly persons; *rakṣaṇāya*—for the protection; *ca*—and.

TRANSLATION

You, that very same creator, have now descended on the earth to annihilate the Daitya, Pramatha and Rākṣasa demons who are posing as kings, and also to protect the godly.

TEXT 14

दिष्ट्या ते निहतो दैत्यो लीलयायं हयाकृतिः ।
यस्य हेषितसन्त्रस्तास्त्यजन्त्यनिमिषा दिवम् ॥ १४ ॥

diṣṭyā te nihato daityo
līlayāyaṁ hayākṛtiḥ
yasya heṣita-santrastās
tyajanty animiṣā divam

diṣṭyā—by (our) good fortune; *te*—by You; *nihataḥ*—killed; *daityaḥ*—demon; *līlayā*—as a game; *ayam*—this; *haya-ākṛtiḥ*—having the form of a horse; *yasya*—whose; *heṣita*—by the neighing; *santrastāḥ*—terrified; *tyajanti*—abandon; *animiṣāḥ*—the demigods; *divam*—heaven.

TRANSLATION

The horse demon was so terrifying that his neighing frightened the demigods into leaving their heavenly kingdom. But by our good fortune You have enjoyed the sport of killing him.

TEXTS 15–20

चाणूरं मुष्टिकं चैव मल्लानन्यांश्च हस्तिनम् ।
कंसं च निहतं द्रक्ष्ये परश्वोऽहनि ते विभो ॥ १५ ॥
तस्यानु शंखयवनमुराणां नरकस्य च ।
पारिजातापहरणमिन्द्रस्य च पराजयम् ॥ १६ ॥
उद्वाहं वीरकन्यानां वीर्यशुल्कादिलक्षणम् ।
नृगस्य मोक्षणं शापाद् द्वारकायां जगत्पते ॥ १७ ॥
स्यमन्तकस्य च मणेरादानं सह भार्यया ।
मृतपुत्रप्रदानं च ब्राह्मणस्य स्वधामतः ॥ १८ ॥
पौण्ड्रकस्य वधं पश्चात्काशिपुर्याश्च दीपनम् ।
दन्तवक्रस्य निधनं चैद्यस्य च महाक्रतौ ॥ १९ ॥
यानि चान्यानि वीर्याणि द्वारकामावसन् भवान् ।
कर्ता द्रक्ष्याम्यहं तानि गेयानि कविभिर्भुवि ॥ २० ॥

cāṇūraṁ muṣṭikaṁ caiva
mallān anyāṁś ca hastinam

kaṁsaṁ ca nihataṁ drakṣye
paraśvo'hani te vibho

tasyānu śaṅkha-yavana-
murāṇāṁ narakasya ca
pārijātāpaharaṇam
indrasya ca parājayam

udvāhaṁ vīra-kanyānāṁ
vīrya-śulkādi-lakṣaṇam
nṛgasya mokṣaṇaṁ śāpād
dvārakāyāṁ jagat-pate

syamantakasya ca maṇer
ādānaṁ saha bhāryayā
mṛta-putra-pradānaṁ ca
brāhmaṇasya sva-dhāmataḥ

pauṇḍrakasya vadhaṁ paścāt
kāśi-puryāś ca dīpanam
dantavakrasya nidhanaṁ
caidyasya ca mahā-kratau

yāni cānyāni vīryāṇi
dvārakām āvasan bhavān
kartā drakṣyāmy ahaṁ tāni
geyāni kavibhir bhuvi

cāṇūram—Cāṇūra; *muṣṭikam*—Muṣṭika; *ca*—and; *eva*—also; *mallān*—the wrestlers; *anyān*—others; *ca*—and; *hastinam*—the elephant (Kuvalayāpīḍa); *kaṁsam*—King Kaṁsa; *ca*—and; *nihatam*—killed; *drakṣye*—I will see; *para-śvaḥ*—the day after tomorrow; *ahani*—on that day; *te*—by You; *vibho*—O almighty Lord; *tasya anu*—after that; *śaṅkha-yavana-murāṇām*—of the demons Śaṅkha (Pañcajana), Kālayavana and Mura; *narakasya*—of Narakāsura; *ca*—as well; *pārijāta*—of the heavenly *pārijāta* flower; *apaharaṇam*—the stealing; *indrasya*—of Lord Indra; *ca*—and; *parājayam*—the defeat; *udvāham*—the marriage; *vīra*—of heroic kings; *kanyānām*—of the daughters; *vīrya*—by Your valor; *śulka*—as the payment for the brides; *ādi*—and so forth; *lakṣaṇam*—characterized; *nṛgasya*—of King Nṛga; *mokṣaṇam*—the deliverance; *śāpāt*—from his curse; *dvārakāyām*

—in the city of Dvārakā; *jagat-pate*—O master of the universe; *syamantakasya*—named Syamantaka; *ca*—and; *maṇeḥ*—of the jewel; *ādānam*—the taking; *saha*—together with; *bhāryayā*—a wife (Jāmbavatī); *mṛta*—dead; *putra*—of the son; *pradānam*—the presenting; *ca*—and; *brāhmaṇasya*—of a *brāhmaṇa; sva-dhāmataḥ*—from Your own domain (i.e., from the abode of Death); *pauṇḍrakasya*—of Pauṇḍraka; *vadham*—the killing; *paścāt*—after; *kāśi-puryāḥ*—of the city of Kāśī (Benares); *ca*—and; *dīpanam*—the burning; *dantavakrasya*—of Dantavakra; *nidhanam*—the demise; *caidyasya*—of Caidya (Śiśupāla); *ca*—and; *mahā-kratau*—during the great sacrificial performance (the Rājasūya-yajña of Mahārāja Yudhiṣṭhira); *yāni*—which; *ca*—and; *anyāni*—other; *vīryāṇi*—great feats; *dvārakām*—in Dvārakā; *āvasan*—dwelling; *bhavān*—You; *kartā*—are going to perform; *drakṣyāmi*—will see; *aham*—I; *tāni*—them; *geyāni*—to be sung about; *kavibhiḥ*—by poets; *bhuvi*—on this earth.

TRANSLATION

In just two days, O almighty Lord, I will see the deaths of Cāṇūra, Muṣṭika and other wrestlers, along with those of the elephant Kuvalayāpīḍa and King Kaṁsa—all by Your hand. Then I will see You kill Kālayavana, Mura, Naraka and the conch demon, and I will also see You steal the pārijāta flower and defeat Indra. I will then see You marry many daughters of heroic kings after paying for them with Your valor. Then, O Lord of the universe, in Dvārakā You will deliver King Nṛga from a curse and take for Yourself the Syamantaka jewel, together with another wife. You will bring back a brāhmaṇa's dead son from the abode of Your servant Yamarāja, and thereafter You will kill Pauṇḍraka, burn down the city of Kāśī and annihilate Dantavakra and the King of Cedi during the great Rājasūya sacrifice. I shall see all these heroic pastimes, along with many others You will perform during Your residence in Dvārakā. These pastimes are glorified on this earth in the songs of transcendental poets.

TEXT 21

अथ ते कालरूपस्य क्षपयिष्णोरमुष्य वै ।
अक्षौहिणीनां निधनं द्रक्ष्याम्यर्जुनसारथेः ॥ २१ ॥

atha te kāla-rūpasya
kṣapayiṣṇor amuṣya vai

akṣauhiṇīnāṁ nidhanaṁ
drakṣyāmy arjuna-sāratheḥ

atha—then; *te*—by You; *kāla-rūpasya*—who are assuming the form of time; *kṣapayiṣṇoḥ*—who is intending to effect the destruction; *amuṣya*—of (the burden of) this world; *vai*—indeed; *akṣauhiṇīnām*—of entire armies; *nidhanam*—the destruction; *drakṣyāmi*—I will see; *arjuna sāratheḥ*—by the chariot driver of Arjuna.

TRANSLATION

Subsequently I will see You appear as time personified, serving as Arjuna's chariot driver and destroying entire armies of soldiers to rid the earth of her burden.

TEXT 22

विशुद्धविज्ञानघनं स्वसंस्थया
समाप्तसर्वार्थममोघवाञ्छितम् ।
स्वतेजसा नित्यनिवृत्तमाया-
गुणप्रवाहं भगवन्तमीमहि ॥ २२ ॥

viśuddha-vijñāna-ghanaṁ sva-saṁsthayā
samāpta-sarvārtham amogha-vāñchitam
sva-tejasā nitya-nivṛtta-māyā-
guṇa-pravāhaṁ bhagavantam īmahi

viśuddha—perfectly pure; *vijñāna*—spiritual awareness; *ghanam*—full of; *sva-saṁsthayā*—in His original identity; *samāpta*—already fulfilled; *sarva*—in all; *artham*—purposes; *amogha*—never frustrated; *vāñchitam*—whose desires; *sva-tejasā*—by His own potency; *nitya*—eternally; *nivṛtta*—desisting; *māyā*—of the illusory, material energy; *guṇa*—of the manifest modes; *pravāham*—from the flowing interaction; *bhagavantam*—the Supreme Personality of Godhead; *īmahi*—let us approach.

TRANSLATION

Let us approach You, the Supreme Personality of Godhead, for shelter. You are full of perfectly pure spiritual awareness and are always situated in Your original identity. Since Your will is never thwarted, You have already achieved all possible desirable things, and by the power of Your spiritual energy You remain eternally aloof from the flow of the qualities of illusion.

TEXT 23

त्वामीश्वरं स्वाश्रयमात्ममायया
विनिर्मिताशेषविशेषकल्पनम् ।
क्रीडार्थमद्यात्तमनुष्यविग्रहं
नतोऽस्मि धुर्यं यदुवृष्णिसात्वताम् ॥ २३ ॥

tvām īśvaraṁ svāśrayam ātma-māyayā
vinirmitāśeṣa-viśeṣa-kalpanam
krīḍārtham adyātta-manuṣya-vigrahaṁ
nato'smi dhuryaṁ yadu-vṛṣṇi-sātvatām

tvām—to You; *īśvaram*—the supreme controller; *sva-āśrayam*—self-contained; *ātma*—Your own; *māyayā*—by the creative potency; *vinirmita*—constructed; *aśeṣa*—unlimited; *viśeṣa*—particular; *kalpanam*—arrangements; *krīḍā*—of playing; *artham*—for the sake; *adya*—now; *ātta*—taken on; *manuṣya*—among humans; *vigraham*—battle; *nataḥ*—bowed down; *asmi*—I am; *dhuryam*—to the greatest; *yadu-vṛṣṇi-sātvatām*—of the Yadu, Vṛṣṇi and Sātvata dynasties.

TRANSLATION

I bow down to You, the supreme controller, who are dependent only on Yourself. By Your potency You have constructed the unlimited particular arrangements of this universe. Now you have appeared as the greatest hero among the Yadus, Vṛṣṇis and Sātvatas and have chosen to participate in human warfare.

TEXT 24

श्रीशुक उवाच
एवं यदुपतिं कृष्णं भागवतप्रवरो मुनिः ।
प्रणिपत्याभ्यनुज्ञातो ययौ तद्दर्शनोत्सवः ॥ २४ ॥

śrī-śuka uvāca
evaṁ yadu-patiṁ kṛṣṇaṁ
bhāgavata-pravaro muniḥ
praṇipatyābhyanujñāto
yayau tad-darśanotsavaḥ

śrī-śukaḥ uvāca—Śukadeva Gosvāmī said; *evam*—thus; *yadu-patim*—to the chief of the Yadus; *kṛṣṇam*—Lord Kṛṣṇa; *bhāgavata*—of devotees; *pravaraḥ*—most eminent; *muniḥ*—the sage Nārada; *praṇipatya*—respectfully bowing down; *abhyanujñātaḥ*—given leave; *yayau*—went; *tat*—Him, Kṛṣṇa; *darśana*—by having seen; *utsavaḥ*—experiencing great joy.

TRANSLATION

Śukadeva Gosvāmī said: Having thus addressed Lord Kṛṣṇa, the chief of the Yadu dynasty, Nārada bowed down and offered Him obeisances. Then that great sage and most eminent devotee took his leave from the Lord and went away, feeling great joy at having directly seen Him.

TEXT 25

भगवानपि गोविन्दो हत्वा केशिनमाहवे ।
पशूनपालयत्पालैः प्रीतैर्व्रजसुखावहः ॥ २५ ॥

bhagavān api govindo
hatvā keśinam āhave
paśūn apālayat pālaiḥ
prītair vraja-sukhāvahaḥ

bhagavān—the Supreme Lord; *api*—and; *govindaḥ*—Govinda; *hatvā*—having killed; *keśinam*—the demon Keśī; *āhave*—in battle; *paśūn*—the animals; *apālayat*—He tended; *pālaiḥ*—together with the cowherd boys; *prītaiḥ*—who were pleased; *vraja*—to the inhabitants of Vṛndāvana; *sukha*—happiness; *āvahaḥ*—bringing.

TRANSLATION

After killing the demon Keśī in battle, the Supreme Personality of Godhead continued to tend the cows and other animals in the company of His joyful cowherd boyfriends. Thus He brought happiness to all the residents of Vṛndāvana.

TEXT 26

एकदा ते पशून् पालाश्चारयन्तोऽद्रिसानुषु ।
चक्रुर्निलायनक्रीडाश्चोरपालापदेशतः ॥ २६ ॥

ekadā te paśūn pālāś
cārayanto'dri-sānuṣu
cakrur nilāyana-krīḍāś
cora-pālāpadeśataḥ

ekadā—one day; *te*—they; *paśūn*—the animals; *pālāḥ*—the cowherd boys; *cārayantaḥ*—grazing; *adri*—of a mountain; *sānuṣu*—on the sides; *cakruḥ*—they enacted; *nilāyana*—of "stealing and hiding"; *krīḍāḥ*—games; *cora*—of thieves; *pāla*—and protectors; *apadeśataḥ*—playing the roles.

TRANSLATION

One day the cowherd boys, while grazing their animals on the mountain slopes, played the game of stealing and hiding, acting out the roles of rival thieves and herders.

TEXT 27

तत्रासन् कतिचिच्चोराः पालाश्च कतिचिन्नृप।
मेषायिताश्च तत्रैके विजह्रुरकुतोभयाः ॥ २७ ॥

tatrāsan katicic corāḥ
pālāś ca katicin nṛpa
meṣāyitāś ca tatraike
vijahrur akuto-bhayāḥ

tatra—in that; *āsan*—were; *katicit*—some; *corāḥ*—thieves; *pālāḥ*—herders; *ca*—and; *katicit*—some; *nṛpa*—O King (Parīkṣit); *meṣāyitāḥ*—acting as the sheep; *ca*—and; *tatra*—therein; *eke*—some of them; *vijahruḥ*—they played; *akutaḥ-bhayāḥ*—without any fear.

TRANSLATION

In that game, O King, some acted as thieves, others as shepherds and others as sheep. They played their game happily, without fear of danger.

TEXT 28

मयपुत्रो महामायो व्योमो गोपालवेषधृक्।
मेषायितानपोवाह प्रायश्चोरायितो बहून् ॥ २८ ॥

maya-putro mahā-māyo
vyomo gopāla-veṣa-dhṛk

meṣāyitān apovāha
prāyaś corāyito bahūn

maya-putraḥ—a son of the demon Maya; *mahā māyaḥ*—a powerful magician; *vyomaḥ*—named Vyoma; *gopāla*—of a cowherd boy; *veṣa*—the disguise; *dhṛk*—assuming; *meṣāyitān*—those who were acting as sheep; *apovāha*—he took away; *prāyaḥ*—almost all; *corāyitaḥ*—pretending to be playing as a thief; *bahūn*—many.

TRANSLATION

A powerful magician named Vyoma, son of the demon Maya, then appeared on the scene in the guise of a cowherd boy. Pretending to join the game as a thief, he proceeded to steal most of the cowherd boys who were acting as sheep.

TEXT 29

गिरिदर्यां विनिक्षिप्य नीतं नीतं महासुरः ।
शिलया पिदधे द्वारं चतुःपञ्चावशेषिताः ॥ २९ ॥

giri-daryāṁ vinikṣipya
nītaṁ nītaṁ mahāsuraḥ
śilayā pidadhe dvāraṁ
catuḥ-pañcāvaśeṣitāḥ

giri—of a mountain; *daryām*—in a cave; *vinikṣipya*—throwing; *nītam nītam*—gradually bringing them; *mahā-asuraḥ*—the great demon; *śilayā*—with a stone; *pidadhe*—he blocked; *dvāram*—the entrance; *catuḥ-pañca*—four or five; *avaśeṣitāḥ*—remained.

TRANSLATION

Gradually the great demon abducted more and more of the cowherd boys and cast them into a mountain cave, which he sealed shut with a boulder. Finally only four or five boys acting as sheep remained in the game.

TEXT 30

तस्य तत्कर्म विज्ञाय कृष्णः शरणदः सताम् ।
गोपान्नयन्तं जग्राह वृकं हरिरिवौजसा ॥ ३० ॥

tasya tat karma vijñāya
kṛṣṇaḥ śaraṇa-daḥ satām
gopān nayantaṁ jagrāha
vṛkaṁ harir ivaujasā

tasya—of him, Vyomāsura; *tat*—that; *karma*—activity; *vijñāya*—fully understanding; *kṛṣṇaḥ*—Lord Kṛṣṇa; *śaraṇa*—of shelter; *daḥ*—the giver; *satām*—to saintly devotees; *gopān*—cowherd boys; *nayantam*—who was leading; *jagrāha*—He seized; *vṛkam*—a wolf; *hariḥ*—a lion; *iva*—just as; *ojasā*—forcefully.

TRANSLATION

Lord Kṛṣṇa, who shelters all saintly devotees, understood perfectly well what Vyomāsura was doing. Just as a lion grabs a wolf, Kṛṣṇa forcefully seized the demon as he was taking away more cowherd boys.

TEXT 31

स निजं रूपमास्थाय गिरीन्द्रसदृशं बली ।
इच्छन् विमोक्तुमात्मानं नाशक्नोद् ग्रहणातुरः ॥ ३१ ॥

sa nijaṁ rūpam āsthāya
girīndra-sadṛśaṁ balī
icchan vimoktum ātmānaṁ
nāśaknod grahaṇāturaḥ

saḥ—he, the demon; *nijam*—his original; *rūpam*—form; *āsthāya*—assuming; *giri-indra*—a kingly mountain; *sadṛśam*—just like; *balī*—powerful; *icchan*—wanting; *vimoktum*—to free; *ātmānam*—himself; *na aśaknot*—he was not able; *grahaṇa*—by being forcibly held; *āturaḥ*—debilitated.

TRANSLATION

The demon changed into his original form, as big and powerful as a great mountain. But try as he might to free himself, he could not do so, having lost his strength from being held in the Lord's tight grip.

TEXT 32

तं निगृह्याच्युतो दोर्भ्यां पातयित्वा महीतले ।
पश्यतां दिवि देवानां पशुमारममारयत् ॥ ३२ ॥

taṁ nigṛhyācyuto dorbhyāṁ
pātayitvā mahī-tale
paśyatāṁ divi devānāṁ
paśu-māram amārayat

tam—him; *nigṛhya*—holding fast; *acyutaḥ*—Lord Kṛṣṇa; *dorbhyām*—with His arms; *pātayitvā*—making him fall; *mahī-tale*—onto the ground; *paśyatām*—while they were watching; *divi*—in the heavenly planets; *devānām*—the demigods; *paśu-māram*—as a sacrificial animal is slaughtered; *amārayat*—He killed him.

TRANSLATION

Lord Acyuta clutched Vyomāsura between His arms and threw him to the ground. Then, while the demigods in heaven looked on, Kṛṣṇa killed him in the same way that one kills a sacrificial animal.

PURPORT

The *ācāryas* inform us that sacrificial animals were killed by means of strangulation.

TEXT 33

गुहापिधानं निर्भिद्य गोपान्निःसार्य कृच्छ्रतः ।
स्तूयमानः सुरैर्गोपैः प्रविवेश स्वगोकुलम् ॥ ३३ ॥

guhā-pidhānaṁ nirbhidya
gopān niḥsārya kṛcchrataḥ
stūyamānaḥ surair gopaiḥ
praviveśa sva-gokulam

guhā—of the cave; *pidhānam*—the blockage; *nirbhidya*—breaking; *gopān*—the cowherd boys; *niḥsārya*—leading out; *kṛcchrataḥ*—from the dangerous place; *stūyamānaḥ*—being praised; *suraiḥ*—by the demigods; *gopaiḥ*—and by the cowherd boys; *praviveśa*—he entered; *sva*—His own; *gokulam*—cowherd village.

TRANSLATION

Kṛṣṇa then smashed the boulder blocking the cave's entrance and led the trapped cowherd boys to safety. Thereafter, as the demigods and cowherd boys sang His glories, He returned to His cowherd village, Gokula.

Thus end the purports of the humble servants of His Divine Grace A.C. Bhaktivedanta Swami Prabhupāda to the Tenth Canto, Thirty-seventh Chapter, of the Śrīmad-Bhāgavatam, *entitled "The Killing of the Demons Keśī and Vyoma."*

CHAPTER THIRTY- EIGHT

Akrūra's Arrival in Vṛndāvana

This chapter describes Akrūra's trip from Mathurā to Vṛndāvana, his meditation on Kṛṣṇa and Balarāma along the way and the honor the two Lords showed Akrūra upon his arrival.

Early in the morning on the day after Kaṁsa had ordered him to bring Kṛṣṇa and Balarāma to Mathurā, Akrūra prepared his chariot and set off for Gokula. As he traveled, he thought as follows: "I am about to attain the great good fortune of seeing Śrī Kṛṣṇa's lotus feet, which are worshiped by Brahmā, Rudra and the other demigods. Although Kaṁsa is an enemy of the Supreme Lord and His devotees, still, it is by Kaṁsa's grace that I will get this great boon of seeing the Lord. When I first catch sight of His lotus feet, all my sinful reactions will be destroyed at once. I will descend from my chariot and fall at the feet of Kṛṣṇa and Balarāma, and even though I have been sent by Kaṁsa, the omniscient Śrī Kṛṣṇa will certainly harbor no animosity toward me." As Akrūra thus thought to himself, he arrived in Gokula at sunset. Alighting from his chariot in the cowherd pasture, he began rolling about in the dust in great ecstasy.

Then Akrūra continued on to Vraja. When he saw Kṛṣṇa and Balarāma he fell at Their lotus feet, and both the Lords embraced him. Afterward They brought him to Their residence, inquired from him about the comfort of his trip and honored him in various ways—offering him water for washing his feet, *arghya,* a seat and so forth. They relieved him of his fatigue by massaging his feet and served him a delicious banquet. Mahārāja Nanda also honored Akrūra with many sweet words.

TEXT 1

श्रीशुक उवाच

अक्रूरोऽपि च तां रात्रिं मधुपुर्यां महामतिः ।
उषित्वा रथमास्थाय प्रययौ नन्दगोकुलम् ॥ १ ॥

śrī-śuka uvāca
akrūro'pi ca tāṁ rātriṁ
madhu-puryāṁ mahā-matiḥ

uṣitvā ratham āsthāya
prayayau nanda-gokulam

śrī-śukaḥ uvāca—Śukadeva Gosvāmī said; *akrūraḥ*—Akrūra; *api ca*—and; *tām*—that; *rātrim*—night; *madhu-puryām*—in the city of Mathurā; *mahā-matiḥ*—high-minded; *uṣitvā*—remaining; *ratham*—his chariot; *āsthāya*—mounting; *prayayau*—he set off; *nanda-gokulam*—for the cowherd village of Nanda Mahārāja.

TRANSLATION

Śukadeva Gosvāmī said: After passing the night in the city of Mathurā, the high-minded Akrūra mounted his chariot and set off for the cowherd village of Nanda Mahārāja.

PURPORT

King Kaṁsa ordered Akrūra to go to Vṛndāvana on the Ekādaśī of the dark fortnight of the Vedic month of Phālguna. After spending the night in Mathurā, Akrūra left early the next day. That morning Nārada offered his prayers to Kṛṣṇa in Vṛndāvana, and in the afternoon the demon Vyoma was killed there. At dusk Akrūra entered the Lord's village.

TEXT 2

गच्छन् पथि महाभागो भगवत्यम्बुजेक्षणे ।
भक्तिं परामुपगत एवमेतदचिन्तयत् ॥ २ ॥

gacchan pathi mahā-bhāgo
bhagavaty ambujekṣaṇe
bhaktiṁ parām upagata
evam etad acintayat

gacchan—traveling; *pathi*—along the road; *mahā-bhāgaḥ*—the greatly fortunate; *bhagavati*—for the Supreme Personality of Godhead; *ambuja-īkṣaṇe*—the lotus-eyed Lord; *bhaktim*—devotion; *parām*—exceptional; *upagataḥ*—he experienced; *evam*—thus; *etat*—this (as follows); *acintayat*—he thought.

TRANSLATION

As he traveled on the road, the great soul Akrūra felt tremendous

devotion for the lotus-eyed Personality of Godhead, and thus he began to consider as follows.

TEXT 3

किं मयाचरितं भद्रं किं तप्तं परमं तपः ।
किं वाथाप्यर्हते दत्तं यद्द्रक्ष्याम्यद्य केशवम् ॥ ३ ॥

kiṁ mayācaritaṁ bhadraṁ
kiṁ taptaṁ paramaṁ tapaḥ
kiṁ vāthāpy arhate dattaṁ
yad drakṣyāmy adya keśavam

kim—what; *mayā*—by me; *ācaritam*—has been performed; *bhadram*—good works; *kim*—what; *taptam*—suffered; *paramam*—severe; *tapaḥ*—austerity; *kim*—what; *vā*—or else; *atha api*—otherwise; *arhate*—worship performed; *dattam*—charity given; *yat*—by which; *drakṣyāmi*—I am going to see; *adya*—today; *keśavam*—Lord Kṛṣṇa.

TRANSLATION

[Śrī Akrūra thought:] What pious deeds have I done, what severe austerities undergone, what worship performed or charity given so that today I will see Lord Keśava?

TEXT 4

ममैतद्दुर्लभं मन्य उत्तमःश्लोकदर्शनम् ।
विषयात्मनो यथा ब्रह्मकीर्तनं शूद्रजन्मनः ॥ ४ ॥

mamaitad durlabhaṁ manya
uttamaḥ-śloka-darśanam
viṣayātmano yathā brahma-
kīrtanaṁ śūdra-janmanaḥ

mama—my; *etat*—this; *durlabham*—difficult to achieve; *manye*—I consider; *uttamaḥ-śloka*—of the Supreme Lord, who is praised in the best poetry; *darśanam*—the audience; *viṣaya-ātmanaḥ*—for one who is absorbed in sense gratification; *yathā*—just as; *brahma*—of the *Vedas; kīrtanam*—chanting; *śūdra*—as a low-class man; *janmanaḥ*—by one who has taken his birth.

TRANSLATION

Since I am a materialistic person absorbed simply in sense gratification, I think it is as difficult for me to have gotten this opportunity to see Lord Uttamaḥśloka as it would be for one born a śūdra to be allowed to recite the Vedic mantras.

TEXT 5

मैवं ममाधमस्यापि स्यादेवाच्युतदर्शनम् ।
ह्रियमाणः कालनद्या क्वचित्तरति कश्चन ॥ ५ ॥

maivaṁ mamādhamasyāpi
syād evācyuta-darśanam
hriyamāṇaḥ kāla-nadyā
kvacit tarati kaścana

mā evam—I should not think like this; *mama*—for me; *adhamasya*—who am most fallen; *api*—even; *syāt*—it may come about; *eva*—certainly; *acyuta*—of the infallible Lord; *darśanam*—the sight; *hriyamāṇaḥ*—being pulled along; *kāla*—of time; *nadyā*—by the river; *kvacit*—sometimes; *tarati*—crosses to the shore; *kaścana*—someone.

TRANSLATION

But enough of such thoughts! After all, even a fallen soul like me can have the chance to behold the infallible Supreme Lord, for one of the conditioned souls being swept along in the river of time may sometimes reach the shore.

TEXT 6

ममाद्यामंगलं नष्टं फलवांश्चैव मे भवः ।
यन्नमस्ये भगवतो योगिध्येयाङ्घ्रिपंकजम् ॥ ६ ॥

mamādyāmaṅgalaṁ naṣṭaṁ
phalavāṁś caiva me bhavaḥ
yan namasye bhagavato
yogi-dhyeyāṅghri-paṅkajam

mama—my; *adya*—today; *amaṅgalam*—inauspicious sinful reactions; *naṣṭam*—eradicated; *phala-vān*—fruitful; *ca*—and; *eva*—indeed; *me*—

my; *bhavaḥ*—birth; *yat*—since; *namasye*—I am going to offer obeisances; *bhagavataḥ*—of the Supreme Lord; *yogi-dhyeya*—meditated upon by *yogīs;* *aṅghri*—to the feet; *paṅkajam*—lotuslike.

TRANSLATION

Today all my sinful reactions have been eradicated and my birth has become worthwhile, since I will offer my obeisances to the Supreme Lord's lotus feet, which mystic yogīs meditate upon.

TEXT 7

कंसो बताद्याकृत मेऽत्यनुग्रहं
द्रक्ष्येऽङ्घ्रिपद्मं प्रहितोऽमुना हरेः ।
कृतावतारस्य दुरत्ययं तमः
पूर्वेऽतरन् यन्नखमण्डलत्विषा ॥ ७ ॥

kaṁso batādyākṛta me'ty-anugrahaṁ
drakṣye'ṅghri-padmaṁ prahito'munā hareḥ
kṛtāvatārasya duratyayaṁ tamaḥ
pūrve'taran yan-nakha-maṇḍala-tviṣā

kaṁsaḥ—King Kaṁsa; *bata*—indeed; *adya*—today; *akṛta*—has done; *me*—toward me; *ati-anugraham*—an act of extreme kindness; *drakṣye*—I will see; *aṅghri-padmam*—the lotus feet; *prahitaḥ*—sent; *amunā*—by him; *hareḥ*—of the Supreme Personality of Godhead; *kṛta*—who has enacted; *avatārasya*—His descent to this world; *duratyayam*—insurmountable; *tamaḥ*—the darkness of material existence; *pūrve*—persons in the past; *ataran*—transcended; *yat*—whose; *nakha-maṇḍala*—of the orb of the toenails; *tviṣā*—by the effulgence.

TRANSLATION

Indeed, today King Kaṁsa has shown me extreme mercy by sending me to see the lotus feet of Lord Hari, who has now appeared in this world. Simply by the effulgence of His toenails, many souls in the past have transcended the insurmountable darkness of material existence and achieved liberation.

PURPORT

Akrūra noted how ironic it was that the envious, demoniac Kaṁsa had given him an extraordinary blessing by sending him to see the Supreme Lord Kṛṣṇa.

TEXT 8

यदर्चितं ब्रह्मभवादिभिः सुरैः
श्रिया च देव्या मुनिभिः ससात्वतैः ।
गोचारणायानुचरैश्चरद्वने
यद् गोपिकानां कुचकुंकुमांकितम् ॥ ८ ॥

yad arcitaṁ brahma-bhavādibhiḥ suraiḥ
śriyā ca devyā munibhiḥ sa-sātvataiḥ
go-cāraṇāyānucaraiś carad vane
yad gopikānāṁ kuca-kuṅkumāṅkitam

yat—which (lotus feet); *arcitam*—worshiped; *brahma-bhava*—by Brahmā and Śiva; *ādibhiḥ*—and other; *suraiḥ*—demigods; *śriyā*—by Śrī; *ca*—also; *devyā*—the goddess of fortune; *munibhiḥ*—by the sages; *sa-sātvataiḥ*—along with the devotees; *go*—the cows; *cāraṇāya*—for tending; *anucaraiḥ*—together with His companions; *carat*—moving about; *vane*—in the forest; *yat*—which; *gopikānām*—of the cowherd girls; *kuca*—from the breasts; *kuṅkuma*—by the red *kuṅkuma* powder; *aṅkitam*—marked.

TRANSLATION

Those lotus feet are worshiped by Brahmā, Śiva and all the other demigods, by the goddess of fortune, and also by the great sages and Vaiṣṇavas. Upon those lotus feet the Lord walks about the forest while herding the cows with His companions, and those feet are smeared with the kuṅkuma from the gopīs' breasts.

TEXT 9

द्रक्ष्यामि नूनं सुकपोलनासिकं
स्मितावलोकारुणकञ्जलोचनम् ।
मुखं मुकुन्दस्य गुडालकावृतं
प्रदक्षिणं मे प्रचरन्ति वै मृगाः ॥९॥

drakṣyāmi nūnaṁ su-kapola-nāsikaṁ
smitāvalokāruṇa-kañja-locanam
mukhaṁ mukundasya guḍālakāvṛtaṁ
pradakṣiṇaṁ me pracaranti vai mṛgāḥ

drakṣyāmi—I am going to see; *nūnam*—for certain; *su*—beautiful; *kapola*—whose cheeks; *nāsikam*—and nose; *smita*—smiling; *avaloka*—with glances; *aruṇa*—reddish; *kañja*—lotuslike; *locanam*—the eyes; *mukham*—the face; *mukundasya*—of Lord Kṛṣṇa; *guḍa*—twisting; *alaka*—with hair; *āvṛtam*—framed; *pradakṣiṇam*—clockwise circumambulation; *me*—of me; *pracaranti*—are performing; *vai*—indeed; *mṛgāḥ*—the deer.

TRANSLATION

Surely I shall see the face of Lord Mukunda, since the deer are now walking past me on my right. That face, framed by His curly hair, is beautified by His attractive cheeks and nose, His smiling glances and His reddish lotus eyes.

PURPORT

Akrūra saw an auspicious omen—the passing of the deer on his right—and thus felt sure he would see the Supreme Lord Kṛṣṇa.

TEXT 10

अप्यद्य विष्णोर्मनुजत्वमीयुषो
भारावताराय भुवो निजेच्छया ।
लावण्यधाम्नो भवितोपलम्भनं
मह्यं न न स्यात्फलमञ्जसा दृशः ॥ १० ॥

apy adya viṣṇor manujatvam īyuṣo
bhārāvatārāya bhuvo nijecchayā
lāvaṇya-dhāmno bhavitopalambhanaṁ
mahyaṁ na na syāt phalam añjasā dṛśaḥ

api—furthermore; *adya*—today; *viṣṇoḥ*—of the Supreme Lord Viṣṇu; *manujatvam*—the form of a human being; *īyuṣaḥ*—who has assumed; *bhāra*—the burden; *avatārāya*—for diminishing; *bhuvaḥ*—of the earth; *nija*—by His own; *icchayā*—desire; *lāvaṇya*—of beauty; *dhāmnaḥ*—of the abode; *bhavitā*—there will be; *upalambhanam*—the perceiving; *mahyam*—for me;

na—it is not the case; *na syāt*—that it will not happen; *phalam*—the fruit; *añjasā*—directly; *dṛśaḥ*—of sight.

TRANSLATION

I am going to see the Supreme Lord Viṣṇu, the reservoir of all beauty, who by His own sweet will has now assumed a humanlike form to relieve the earth of her burden. Thus there is no denying that my eyes will achieve the perfection of their existence.

TEXT 11

य ईक्षिताहंरहितोऽप्यसत्सतोः
स्वतेजसापास्ततमोभिदाभ्रमः ।
स्वमाययात्मन् रचितैस्तदीक्षया
प्राणाक्षधीभिः सदनेष्वभीयते ॥ ११ ॥

ya īkṣitāhaṁ-rahito'py asat-satoḥ
sva-tejasāpāsta-tamo-bhidā-bhramaḥ
sva-māyayātman racitais tad-īkṣayā
prāṇākṣa-dhībhiḥ sadaneṣv abhīyate

yaḥ—who; *īkṣitā*—the witness; *aham*—false ego; *rahitaḥ*—devoid of; *api*—nevertheless; *asat-satoḥ*—of material products and causes; *sva-tejasā*—by His personal potency; *apāsta*—having dispelled; *tamaḥ*—the darkness of ignorance; *bhidā*—the idea of being separate; *bhramaḥ*—and bewilderment; *sva-māyayā*—by His material creative energy; *ātman*—within Himself; *racitaiḥ*—by those who are produced (the living entities); *tat-īkṣayā*—by His glancing upon that Māyā; *prāṇa*—by the vital airs; *akṣa*—the senses; *dhībhiḥ*—and intelligence; *sadaneṣu*—within the bodies of the living beings; *abhīyate*—His presence is surmised.

TRANSLATION

He is the witness of material cause and effect, yet He is always free from false identification with them. By His internal potency He dispels the darkness of separation and confusion. The individual souls in this world, who are manifested here when He glances upon His material creative energy, indirectly perceive Him in the activities of their life airs, senses and intelligence.

PURPORT

In this verse Akrūra establishes the all-powerful position of the Supreme Lord, whom he is about to see in Vṛndāvana. The false concept of separation from the Lord is described in the Eleventh Canto of the *Bhāgavatam* (11.2.37): *bhayaṁ dvitīyābhiniveśataḥ syād īśād apetasya viparyayo'smṛtiḥ.* Although all existence emanates from the Absolute Truth, Kṛṣṇa, we imagine a "second thing," this material world, to be entirely separate from the Lord's existence. With this mentality, we try to exploit that "second thing" for our sense gratification. Thus the psychological underpinning of material life is the illusion that this world is somehow separate from God and therefore meant for our enjoyment.

It is ironic that the impersonal philosophers, in their radical renunciation of this world, claim it to be utterly false and totally separate from the Absolute. Unfortunately, this artificial attempt to divest this world of its divine nature, or, in other words, its relation to God, does not lead people to utterly reject it but rather to try to enjoy it. While it is true that this world is temporary and thus in one sense illusory, the mechanism of illusion is a spiritual potency of the Supreme Lord. Realizing this, we should immediately desist from any attempt to exploit this world; rather, we should recognize it as God's energy. We will actually give up our material desires only when we understand that this world belongs to God and is therefore not meant for our selfish gratification.

The word *abhīyate* here refers to a process of surmising the presence of the Lord through meditative introspection. This process is also described in the Second Canto of the *Bhāgavatam* (2.2.35):

bhagavān sarva-bhūteṣu
lakṣitaḥ svātmanā hariḥ
dṛśyair buddhy-ādibhir draṣṭā
lakṣaṇair anumāpakaiḥ

"The Personality of Godhead, Lord Śrī Kṛṣṇa, is in every living being along with the individual soul. And this fact is perceived and hypothesized in our acts of seeing and taking help from the intelligence."

Akrūra states that the Lord is free of the egoistic pride afflicting ordinary, embodied souls. Yet the Lord appears to be embodied like everyone else, and therefore someone might object to the statement that He is free of egoism. Śrīla Viśvanātha Cakravartī comments on this puzzle as follows: "How can we distinguish between being free of false ego and being afflicted by it? 'If a living entity is situated in a body,' [argues the objector,] 'he will encounter the unhappiness and confusion that occur within it, just as a person living in a house, whether he be attached to it or not, cannot avoid experiencing the darkness, warmth and cold that occur within it.' This objection is answered as follows: By His internal potency the Lord dispels the darkness of ignorance along with the separateness and bewilderment it produces."

TEXT 12

यस्याखिलामीवहभिः सुमंगलैः
वाचो विमिश्रा गुणकर्मजन्मभिः ।
प्राणन्ति शुम्भन्ति पुनन्ति वै जगत्
यास्तद्विरक्ताः शवशोभना मताः ॥ १२ ॥

yasyākhilāmīva-habhiḥ su-maṅgalaiḥ
vāco vimiśrā guṇa-karma-janmabhiḥ
prāṇanti śumbhanti punanti vai jagat
yās tad-viraktāḥ śava-śobhanā matāḥ

yasya—of whom; *akhila*—all; *amīva*—sins; *habhiḥ*—which destroy; *su-maṅgalaiḥ*—most auspicious; *vācaḥ*—words; *vimiśrāḥ*—joined; *guṇa*—with the qualities; *karma*—activities; *janmabhiḥ*—and incarnations; *prāṇanti*—they give life; *śumbhanti*—make beautiful; *punanti*—and purify; *vai*—indeed; *jagat*—the entire universe; *yāḥ*—which (words); *tat*—of these; *viraktāḥ*—devoid; *śava*—of a corpse; *śobhanāḥ*—(like) the decorating; *matāḥ*—considered.

TRANSLATION

All sins are destroyed and all good fortune is created by the Supreme Lord's qualities, activities and appearances, and words that describe these three things animate, beautify and purify the world. On the other hand, words bereft of His glories are like the decorations on a corpse.

PURPORT

Śrīla Śrīdhara Svāmī brings up the following possible objection: How can one who is devoid of ordinary ego, who is fully self-satisfied, engage in pastimes? The answer is given here. Lord Kṛṣṇa acts on the pure, spiritual platform for the pleasure of His loving devotees, not for any kind of mundane gratification.

TEXT 13

स चावतीर्णः किल सात्वतान्वये
स्वसेतुपालामरवर्यशर्मकृत् ।
यशो वितन्वन् व्रज आस्त ईश्वरो
गायन्ति देवा यदशेषमंगलम् ॥ १३ ॥

sa cāvatīrṇaḥ kila sātvatānvaye
sva-setu-pālāmara-varya-śarma-kṛt
yaśo vitanvan vraja āsta īśvaro
gāyanti devā yad aśeṣa-maṅgalam

saḥ—He; *ca*—and; *avatīrṇaḥ*—having descended; *kila*—indeed; *sātvata*—of the Sātvatas; *anvaye*—in the dynasty; *sva*—His own; *setu*—codes of religion; *pāla*—who maintain; *amara-varya*—of the chief demigods; *śarma*—delight; *kṛt*—creating; *yaśaḥ*—His fame; *vitanvan*—spreading; *vraje*—in Vraja; *āste*—is present; *īśvaraḥ*—the Supreme Lord; *gāyanti*—sing; *devāḥ*—the demigods; *yat*—of which (fame); *aśeṣa-maṅgalam*—all-auspicious.

TRANSLATION

That same Supreme Lord has descended into the dynasty of the Sātvatas to delight the exalted demigods, who maintain the principles of religion He has created. Residing in Vṛndāvana, He spreads His fame, which the demigods glorify in song and which brings auspiciousness to all.

TEXT 14

तं त्वद्य नूनं महतां गतिं गुरुं
त्रैलोक्यकान्तं दृशिमन्महोत्सवम् ।
रूपं दधानं श्रिय ईप्सितास्पदं
द्रक्ष्ये ममासन्नुषसः सुदर्शनाः ॥ १४ ॥

taṁ tv adya nūnaṁ mahatāṁ gatiṁ guruṁ
trailokya-kāntaṁ dṛśiman-mahotsavam
rūpaṁ dadhānaṁ śriya īpsitāspadaṁ
drakṣye mamāsann uṣasaḥ su-darśanāḥ

tam—Him; *tu*—yet; *adya*—today; *nūnam*—certainly; *mahatām*—of great souls; *gatim*—the destination; *gurum*—and the spiritual master; *trai-*

lokya—of all the three worlds; *kāntam*—the real beauty; *dṛśi-mat*—for all who have eyes; *mahā-utsavam*—a great festivity; *rūpam*—His personal form; *dadhānam*—exhibiting; *śriyaḥ*—of the goddess of fortune; *īpsita*—the desired; *āspadam*—place of shelter; *drakṣye*—I shall see; *mama*—my; *āsan*—have become; *uṣasaḥ*—the dawns; *su-darśanāḥ*—auspicious to see.

TRANSLATION

Today I shall certainly see Him, the goal and spiritual master of the great souls. Seeing Him brings jubilation to all who have eyes, for He is the true beauty of the universe. Indeed, His personal form is the shelter desired by the goddess of fortune. Now all the dawns of my life have become auspicious.

TEXT 15

अथावरूढः सपदीशयो रथात्
प्रधानपुंसोश्चरणं स्वलब्धये ।
धिया धृतं योगिभिरप्यहं ध्रुवं
नमस्य आभ्यां च सखीन् वनौकसः ॥ १५ ॥

athāvarūḍhaḥ sapadīśayo rathāt
pradhāna-puṁsoś caraṇaṁ sva-labdhaye
dhiyā dhṛtaṁ yogibhir apy ahaṁ dhruvaṁ
namasya ābhyāṁ ca sakhīn vanaukasaḥ

atha—then; *avarūḍhaḥ*—getting down; *sapadi*—at once; *īśayoḥ*—of the two Lords; *rathāt*—from my chariot; *pradhāna-puṁsoḥ*—of the Supreme Personalities; *caraṇam*—to the feet; *sva-labdhaye*—for the sake of self-realization; *dhiyā*—with their intelligence; *dhṛtam*—held on to; *yogibhiḥ*—by mystic *yogīs; api*—even; *aham*—I; *dhruvam*—surely; *namasye*—will bow down; *ābhyām*—with Them; *ca*—also; *sakhīn*—to the friends; *vana-okasaḥ*—to the residents of the forest.

TRANSLATION

Then I will at once alight from my chariot and bow down to the lotus feet of Kṛṣṇa and Balarāma, the Supreme Personalities of Godhead. Theirs are the same feet that great mystic yogīs striving for self-realization bear

within their minds. I will also offer my obeisances to the Lords' cowherd boyfriends and to all the other residents of Vṛndāvana.

TEXT 16

अप्यङ्घ्रिमूले पतितस्य मे विभुः
शिरस्यधास्यन्निजहस्तपंकजम् ।
दत्ताभयं कालभुजांगरंहसा
प्रोद्वेजितानां शरणैषिणां नृणाम् ॥ १६ ॥

apy aṅghri-mūle patitasya me vibhuḥ
śirasy adhāsyan nija-hasta-paṅkajam
dattābhayaṁ kāla-bhujāṅga-raṁhasā
prodvejitānāṁ śaraṇaiṣiṇāṁ nṛṇām

api—furthermore; *aṅghri*—of His feet; *mūle*—at the base; *patitasya*—who have fallen; *me*—of me; *vibhuḥ*—the almighty Lord; *śirasi*—upon the head; *adhāsyat*—will place; *nija*—His own; *hasta*—hand; *paṅkajam*—lotuslike; *datta*—which grants; *abhayam*—fearlessness; *kāla*—time; *bhuja-aṅga*—of the serpent; *raṁhasā*—by the swift force; *prodvejitānām*—who are greatly disturbed; *śaraṇa*—shelter; *eṣiṇām*—searching for; *nṛṇām*—to persons.

TRANSLATION

And when I have fallen at His feet, the almighty Lord will place His lotus hand upon my head. For those who seek shelter in Him because they are greatly disturbed by the powerful serpent of time, that hand removes all fear.

TEXT 17

समर्हणं यत्र निधाय कौशिकस्
तथा बलिश्चाप जगत्त्रयेन्द्रताम् ।
यद्वा विहारे व्रजयोषितां श्रमं
स्पर्शेन सौगन्धिकगन्ध्यपानुदत् ॥ १७ ॥

samarhaṇaṁ yatra nidhāya kauśikas
tathā baliś cāpa jagat-trayendratām

yad vā vihāre vraja-yoṣitāṁ śramaṁ
sparśena saugandhika-gandhy apānudat

samarhaṇam—the respectful offering; *yatra*—into which; *nidhāya*—by placing; *kauśikaḥ*—Purandara; *tathā*—as well as; *baliḥ*—Bali Mahārāja; *ca*—also; *āpa*—attained; *jagat*—of the worlds; *traya*—three; *indratām*—rulership (as Indra, the King of heaven); *yat*—which (lotus hand of the Lord); *vā*—and; *vihāre*—during the pastimes (of the *rāsa* dance); *vraja-yoṣitām*—of the ladies of Vraja; *śramam*—the fatigue; *sparśena*—by their contact; *saugandhika*—like an aromatic flower; *gandhi*—fragrant; *apānudat*—wiped away.

TRANSLATION

By offering charity to that lotus hand, Purandara and Bali earned the status of Indra, King of heaven, and during the pleasure pastimes of the rāsa dance, when the Lord wiped away the gopīs' perspiration and removed their fatigue, the touch of their faces made that hand as fragrant as a sweet flower.

PURPORT

The *Purāṇas* call the lotus found in the Mānasa-sarovara Lake a *saugandhika.* Lord Kṛṣṇa's lotus hand acquired the fragrance of this flower by coming in contact with the beautiful faces of the *gopīs.* This specific incident, which occurred during the *rāsa-līlā,* is described in the Thirty-Third Chapter of the Tenth Canto.

TEXT 18

न मय्युपैष्यत्यरिबुद्धिमच्युतः
कंसस्य दूतः प्रहितोऽपि विश्वदृक् ।
योऽन्तर्बहिश्चेतस एतदीहितं
क्षेत्रज्ञ ईक्षत्यमलेन चक्षुषा ॥ १८ ॥

na mayy upaiṣyaty ari-buddhim acyutaḥ
kaṁsasya dūtaḥ prahito'pi viśva-dṛk
yo'ntar bahiś cetasa etad īhitaṁ
kṣetra-jña īkṣaty amalena cakṣuṣā

na—not; *mayi*—toward me; *upaiṣyati*—will He develop; *ari*—of being an enemy; *buddhim*—the attitude; *acyutaḥ*—the infallible Lord; *kaṁsasya*—of Kaṁsa; *dūtaḥ*—a messenger; *prahitaḥ*—sent; *api*—although; *viśva*—of everything; *dṛk*—the witness; *yaḥ*—who; *antaḥ*—inside; *bahiḥ*—and outside; *cetasaḥ*—of the heart; *etat*—this; *īhitam*—whatever is done; *kṣetra*—of the field (of the material body); *jñaḥ*—the knower; *īkṣati*—He sees; *amalena*—with perfect; *cakṣuṣā*—vision.

TRANSLATION

The infallible Lord will not consider me an enemy, even though Kaṁsa has sent me here as his messenger. After all, the omniscient Lord is the actual knower of the field of this material body, and with His perfect vision He witnesses, both externally and internally, all the endeavors of the conditioned soul's heart.

PURPORT

Being omniscient, Lord Kṛṣṇa knew that Akrūra was only externally a friend of Kaṁsa. Internally he was an eternal devotee of Lord Kṛṣṇa.

TEXT 19

अप्यङ्घ्रिमूलेऽवहितं कृताञ्जलिं
मामीक्षिता सस्मितमार्द्रया दृशा ।
सपद्यपध्वस्तसमस्तकिल्बिषो
वोढा मुदं वीतविशंक ऊर्जिताम् ॥ १९ ॥

apy aṅghri-mūle'vahitaṁ kṛtāñjaliṁ
mām īkṣitā sa-smitam ārdrayā dṛśā
sapady apadhvasta-samasta-kilbiṣo
voḍhā mudaṁ vīta-viśaṅka ūrjitām

api—and; *aṅghri*—of His feet; *mūle*—at the base; *avahitam*—fixed; *kṛta-añjalim*—with joined palms; *mām*—me; *īkṣitā*—will look upon; *sasmitam*—smiling; *ārdrayā*—with an affectionate; *dṛśā*—glance; *sapadi*—immediately; *apadhvasta*—eradicated; *samasta*—all; *kilbiṣaḥ*—contamination; *voḍhā*—I will achieve; *mudam*—happiness; *vīta*—freed; *viśaṅkaḥ*—from doubt; *ūrjitām*—intense.

TRANSLATION

Thus He will cast His smiling, affectionate glance upon me as I remain fixed with joined palms, fallen in obeisances at His feet. Then all my contamination will at once be dispelled, and I will give up all doubts and feel the most intense bliss.

TEXT 20

सुहृत्तमं ज्ञातिमनन्यदैवतं
दोर्भ्यां बृहद्भ्यां परिरप्स्यतेऽथ माम्।
आत्मा हि तीर्थीक्रियते तदैव मे
बन्धश्च कर्मात्मक उच्छ्वसित्यतः ॥ २० ॥

suhṛttamaṁ jñātim ananya-daivataṁ
dorbhyāṁ bṛhadbhyāṁ parirapsyate'tha mām
ātmā hi tīrthī-kriyate tadaiva me
bandhaś ca karmātmaka ucchvasity ataḥ

suhṛt-tamam—the best of friends; *jñātim*—a family member; *ananya*—exclusive; *daivatam*—(having Him) as my object of worship; *dorbhyām*—with His two arms; *bṛhadbhyām*—large; *parirapsyate*—He will embrace; *atha*—thereupon; *mām*—me; *ātmā*—the body; *hi*—indeed; *tīrthī*—sanctified; *kriyate*—will become; *tadā eva*—exactly then; *me*—my; *bandhaḥ*—the bondage; *ca*—and; *karma-ātmakaḥ*—due to fruitive activity; *ucchvasiti*—will become slackened; *ataḥ*—as a result of this.

TRANSLATION

Recognizing me as an intimate friend and relative, Kṛṣṇa will embrace me with His mighty arms, instantly sanctifying my body and diminishing to nil all my material bondage, which is due to fruitive activities.

TEXT 21

लब्ध्वांगसंगं प्रणतं कृताञ्जलिं
मां वक्ष्यतेऽक्रूर ततेत्युरुश्रवाः ।
तदा वयं जन्मभृतो महीयसा
नैवादृतो यो धिगमुष्य जन्म तत् ॥ २१ ॥

labdhvāṅga-saṅgaṁ praṇataṁ kṛtāñjaliṁ
māṁ vakṣyate'krūra tatety uruśravāḥ
tadā vayaṁ janma-bhṛto mahīyasā
naivādṛto yo dhig amuṣya janma tat

labdhvā—having achieved; *aṅga-saṅgam*—physical contact; *praṇatam*—who am standing with head bowed; *kṛta-añjalim*—with palms joined together in supplication; *mām*—to me; *vakṣyate*—He will speak; *akrūra*—O Akrūra; *tata*—My dear relative; *iti*—in such words; *uruśravāḥ*—Lord Kṛṣṇa, whose fame is vast; *tadā*—then; *vayam*—we; *janma-bhṛtaḥ*—our birth becoming successful; *mahīyasā*—by the greatest of all persons; *na*—not; *eva*—indeed; *ādṛtaḥ*—honored; *yaḥ*—who; *dhik*—to be pitied; *amuṣya*—his; *janma*—birth; *tat*—that.

TRANSLATION

Having been embraced by the all-famous Lord Kṛṣṇa, I will humbly stand before Him with bowed head and joined palms, and He will address me, "My dear Akrūra." At that very moment my life's purpose will be fulfilled. Indeed, the life of anyone whom the Supreme Personality fails to recognize is simply pitiable.

TEXT 22

न तस्य कश्चिद्दयितः सुहृत्तमो
न चाप्रियो द्वेष्य उपेक्ष्य एव वा ।
तथापि भक्तान् भजते यथा तथा
सुरद्रुमो यद्वदुपाश्रितोऽर्थदः ॥ २२ ॥

na tasya kaścid dayitaḥ suhṛttamo
na cāpriyo dveṣya upekṣya eva vā
tathāpi bhaktān bhajate yathā tathā
sura-drumo yadvad upāśrito'rtha-daḥ

na tasya—He does not have; *kaścit*—any; *dayitaḥ*—favorite; *suhṛttamaḥ*—best friend; *na ca*—nor; *apriyaḥ*—unfavored; *dveṣyaḥ*—hated: *upekṣyaḥ*—neglected; *eva*—indeed; *vā*—or; *tathā api*—still; *bhaktān*—with His devotees; *bhajate*—He reciprocates; *yathā*—as they are; *tathā*—accordingly; *sura-drumaḥ*—a heavenly desire tree; *yadvat*—just as; *upāśritaḥ*—taken shelter of; *artha*—desired benefits; *daḥ*—giving.

TRANSLATION

The Supreme Lord has no favorite and no dearmost friend, nor does He consider anyone undesirable, despicable or fit to be neglected. All the same, He lovingly reciprocates with His devotees in whatever manner they worship Him, just as the trees of heaven fulfill the desires of whoever approaches them.

PURPORT

The Lord says something similar in the *Bhagavad-gītā* (9.29):

samo'haṁ sarva-bhūteṣu
na me dveṣyo'sti na priyaḥ
ye bhajanti tu māṁ bhaktyā
mayi te teṣu cāpy aham

"I envy no one, nor am I partial to anyone. I am equal to all. But whoever renders service unto Me in devotion is a friend and is in Me, and I am also a friend to him."

Similarly, Lord Caitanya was as hard as a thunderbolt for those who envied Him, and as soft as a rose for those who understood His divine mission.

TEXT 23

किं चाग्रजो मावनतं यदूत्तमः
स्मयन् परिष्वज्य गृहीतमञ्जलौ ।
गृहं प्रवेष्याप्तसमस्तसत्कृतं
सम्प्रक्ष्यते कंसकृतं स्वबन्धुषु ॥ २३ ॥

kiṁ cāgrajo māvanataṁ yadūttamaḥ
smayan pariṣvajya gṛhītam añjalau
gṛhaṁ praveṣyāpta-samasta-satkṛtaṁ
samprakṣyate kaṁsa-kṛtaṁ sva-bandhuṣu

kim ca—furthermore; *agra-jaḥ*—His elder brother (Lord Balarāma); *mā*—me; *avanatam*—who am standing with head bowed; *yadu-uttamaḥ*—the most exalted of the Yadus; *smayan*—smiling; *pariṣvajya*—embracing; *gṛhītam*—taken hold of; *añjalau*—by my joined palms; *gṛham*—His house; *praveṣya*—bringing into; *āpta*—who will have received; *samasta*—all; *sat-kṛtam*—signs of respect; *samprakṣyate*—He will inquire; *kaṁsa*—by Kaṁsa; *kṛtam*—what has been done; *sva-bandhuṣu*—to His family members.

TRANSLATION

And then Lord Kṛṣṇa's elder brother, the foremost of the Yadus, will grasp my joined hands while I am still standing with my head bowed, and after embracing me He will take me to His house. There He will honor me with all items of ritual welcome and inquire from me about how Kaṁsa has been treating His family members.

TEXT 24

श्रीशुक उवाच
इति सञ्चिन्तयन् कृष्णं श्वफल्कतनयोऽध्वनि ।
रथेन गोकुलं प्राप्तः सूर्यश्चास्तगिरिं नृप ॥ २४ ॥

śrī-śuka uvāca
iti sañcintayan kṛṣṇaṁ
śvaphalka-tanayo'dhvani
rathena gokulaṁ prāptaḥ
sūryaś cāsta-giriṁ nṛpa

śrī-śukaḥ uvāca—Śukadeva Gosvāmī said; *iti*—thus; *sañcintayan*—thinking deeply; *kṛṣṇam*—about Lord Kṛṣṇa; *śvaphalka-tanayaḥ*—Akrūra, the son of Śvaphalka; *adhvani*—on the road; *rathena*—by his chariot; *gokulam*—the village of Gokula; *prāptaḥ*—reached; *sūryaḥ*—the sun; *ca*—and; *asta-girim*—the mountain behind which the sun sets; *nṛpa*—O King (Parīkṣit).

TRANSLATION

Śukadeva Gosvāmī continued: My dear King, while the son of Śvaphalka, traveling on the road, thus meditated deeply on Śrī Kṛṣṇa, he reached Gokula as the sun was beginning to set.

PURPORT

Śrīla Śrīdhara Svāmī comments that although Akrūra did not even notice the road, being deeply absorbed in meditation on Lord Kṛṣṇa, he still reached Gokula on his chariot.

TEXT 25

पदानि तस्याखिललोकपाल-
किरीटजुष्टामलपादरेणोः ।

दद‍र्श गोष्ठे क्षितिकौतुकानि
विलक्षितान्यब्जयवांकुशाद्यैः ॥ २५ ॥

padāni tasyākhila-loka-pāla-
kirīṭa-juṣṭāmala-pāda-reṇoḥ
dadarśa goṣṭhe kṣiti-kautukāni
vilakṣitāny abja-yavāṅkuśādyaiḥ

padāni—the footprints; *tasya*—of Him; *akhila*—all; *loka*—of the planets; *pāla*—by the superintendents; *kirīṭa*—upon their crowns; *juṣṭa*—placed; *amala*—pure; *pāda*—of His feet; *reṇoḥ*—the dust; *dadarśa*—he (Akrūra) saw; *goṣṭhe*—in the cow pasture; *kṣiti*—the earth; *kautakāni*—wonderfully decorating; *vilakṣitāni*—distinguishable; *abja*—by the lotus; *yava*—barleycorn; *aṅkuśa*—elephant goad; *ādyaiḥ*—and so on.

TRANSLATION

In the cowherd pasture Akrūra saw the footprints of those feet whose pure dust the rulers of all the planets in the universe hold on their crowns. Those footprints of the Lord, distinguished by such marks as the lotus, barleycorn and elephant goad, made the ground wonderfully beautiful.

TEXT 26

तद्दर्शनाह्लादविवृद्धसम्भ्रमः
प्रेम्णोर्ध्वरोमाश्रुकलाकुलेक्षणः ।
रथादवस्कन्द्य स तेष्वचेष्टत
प्रभोरमून्यङ्घ्रिरजांस्यहो इति ॥ २६ ॥

tad-darśanāhlāda-vivṛddha-sambhramaḥ
premṇordhva-romāśru-kalākulekṣaṇaḥ
rathād avaskandya sa teṣv aceṣṭata
prabhor amūny aṅghri-rajāṁsy aho iti

tat—of Lord Kṛṣṇa's footprints; *darśana*—from the sight; *āhlāda*—by the ecstasy; *vivṛddha*—greatly increased; *sambhramaḥ*—whose agitation; *premṇā*—out of pure love; *ūrdhva*—standing erect; *roma*—whose bodily hairs; *aśru-kalā*—with teardrops; *ākula*—filled; *īkṣaṇaḥ*—whose eyes; *rathāt*—from the chariot; *avaskandya*—getting down; *saḥ*—he, Akrūra; *teṣu*—among those (footprints); *aceṣṭata*—rolled about; *prabhoḥ*—of my master;

amūni—these; *aṅghri*—from the feet; *rajāṁsi*—particles of dust; *aho*—ah; *iti*—with these words.

TRANSLATION

Increasingly agitated by ecstasy at seeing the Lord's footprints, his bodily hairs standing on end because of his pure love, and his eyes filled with tears, Akrūra jumped down from his chariot and began rolling about among those footprints, exclaiming, "Ah, this is the dust from my master's feet!"

TEXT 27

देहंभृतामियानर्थो हित्वा दम्भं भियं शुचम् ।
सन्देशाद्यो हरेर्लिंगदर्शनश्रवणादिभिः ॥ २७ ॥

deham-bhṛtām iyān artho
hitvā dambhaṁ bhiyaṁ śucam
sandeśād yo harer liṅga-
darśana-śravaṇādibhiḥ

deham-bhṛtām—of embodied beings; *iyān*—this much; *arthaḥ*—the goal of life; *hitvā*—giving up; *dambham*—pride; *bhiyam*—fear; *śucam*—and sorrow; *sandeśāt*—beginning from his being ordered (by Kaṁsa); *yaḥ*—which; *hareḥ*—of Lord Kṛṣṇa; *liṅga*—the signs; *darśana*—with the seeing; *śravaṇa*—hearing about; *ādibhiḥ*—and so on.

TRANSLATION

The very goal of life for all embodied beings is this ecstasy, which Akrūra experienced when, upon receiving Kaṁsa's order, he put aside all pride, fear and lamentation and absorbed himself in seeing, hearing and describing the things that reminded him of Lord Kṛṣṇa.

PURPORT

Śrīla Viśvanātha Cakravartī explains that Akrūra gave up fear by openly showing his love and reverence for Kṛṣṇa, even though he or his family might have been punished by the angry Kaṁsa. Akrūra gave up his pride in being an aristocratic member of society and worshiped the cowherd residents of the simple village of Vṛndāvana. And he gave up lamenting for his house, wife and family, which were in danger from King Kaṁsa. Giving up all these things, he rolled in the dust of the lotus feet of God.

TEXTS 28–33

दद‍र्श कृष्णं रामं च व्रजे गोदोहनं गतौ ।
पीतनीलाम्बरधरौ शरदम्बुरुहेक्षणौ ॥ २८ ॥
किशोरौ श्यामलश्वेतौ श्रीनिकेतौ बृहद्‍भुजौ ।
सुमुखौ सुन्दरवरौ बलद्विरदविक्रमौ ॥ २९ ॥
ध्वजवज्रांकुशाम्भोजैश्चिह्नितैरङ्घ्रिभिर्व्रजम् ।
शोभयन्तौ महात्मानौ सानुक्रोशस्मितेक्षणौ ॥ ३० ॥
उदाररुचिरक्रीडौ स्रग्विणौ वनमालिनौ ।
पुण्यगन्धानुलिप्तांगौ स्नातौ विरजवाससौ ॥ ३१ ॥
प्रधानपुरुषावाद्यौ जगद्धेतू जगत्पती ।
अवतीर्णौ जगत्यर्थे स्वांशेन बलकेशवौ ॥ ३२ ॥
दिशो वितिमिरा राजन् कुर्वाणौ प्रभया स्वया ।
यथा मारकतः शैलो रौप्यश्च कनकाचितौ ॥ ३३ ॥

dadarśa kṛṣṇaṁ rāmaṁ ca
vraje go-dohanaṁ gatau
pīta-nīlāmbara-dharau
śarad-amburuhekṣaṇau

kiśorau śyāmala-śvetau
śrī-niketau bṛhad-bhujau
su-mukhau sundara-varau
bala-dvirada-vikramau

dhvaja-vajrāṅkuśāmbhojaiś
cihnitair aṅghribhir vrajam
śobhayantau mahātmānau
sānukrośa-smitekṣaṇau

udāra-rucira-krīḍau
sragviṇau vana-mālinau
puṇya-gandhānuliptāṅgau
snātau viraja-vāsasau

pradhāna-puruṣāv ādyau
jagad-dhetū jagat-patī

avatīrṇau jagaty-arthe
svāṁśena bala-keśavau

diśo vitimirā rājan
kurvāṇau prabhayā svayā
yathā mārakataḥ śailo
raupyaś ca kanakācitau

dadarśa—he saw; *kṛṣṇam rāmam ca*—Lord Kṛṣṇa and Lord Balarāma; *vraje*—in the village of Vraja; *go*—the cows; *dohanam*—to the place of milking; *gatau*—gone; *pīta-nīla*—yellow and blue; *ambara*—clothes; *dharau*—wearing; *śarat*—of the autumn season; *amburuha*—like lotuses; *īkṣaṇau*—whose eyes; *kiśorau*—the two youths; *śyāmala-śvetau*—dark-blue and white; *śrī-niketau*—the shelters of the goddess of fortune; *bṛhat*—mighty; *bhujau*—whose arms; *su-mukhau*—with attractive faces; *sundara-varau*—the most beautiful; *bala*—young; *dvirada*—like an elephant; *vikramau*—whose walking; *dhvaja*—by the flag; *vajra*—lightning bolt; *aṅkuśa*—elephant goad; *ambhojaiḥ*—and lotus; *cihnitaiḥ*—marked; *aṅghribhiḥ*—with Their feet; *vrajam*—the cow pasture; *śobhayantau*—beautifying; *mahā-ātmānau*—great souls; *sa-anukrośa*—compassionate; *smita*—and smiling; *īkṣaṇau*—whose glances; *udāra*—magnanimous; *rucira*—and attractive; *krīḍau*—whose pastimes; *srak-vinau*—wearing jeweled necklaces; *vana-mālinau*—and wearing flower garlands; *puṇya*—auspicious; *gandha*—with fragrant substances; *anulipta*—anointed; *aṅgau*—whose limbs; *snātau*—freshly bathed; *viraja*—spotless; *vāsasau*—whose garments; *pradhāna*—the most exalted; *puruṣau*—two persons; *ādyau*—primeval; *jagat-dhetū*—the causes of the universe; *jagat-patī*—the masters of the universe; *avatīrṇau*—having descended; *jagati-arthe*—for the benefit of the universe; *sva-aṁśena*—in Their distinct forms; *bala-keśavau*—Balarāma and Keśava; *diśaḥ*—all the directions; *vitimirāḥ*—free from darkness; *rājan*—O King; *kurvāṇau*—making; *prabhayā*—with the effulgence; *svayā*—Their own; *yathā*—as; *mārakataḥ*—made of emerald; *śailaḥ*—a mountain; *raupyaḥ*—one made of silver; *ca*—and; *kanaka*—with gold; *acitau*—both decorated.

TRANSLATION

Akrūra then saw Kṛṣṇa and Balarāma in the village of Vraja, going to milk the cows. Kṛṣṇa wore yellow garments, Balarāma blue, and Their eyes resembled autumnal lotuses. One of Those two mighty-armed youths, the shelters of the goddess of fortune, had a dark-blue complexion, and the

other's was white. With Their fine-featured faces They were the most beautiful of all persons. As They walked with the gait of young elephants, glancing about with compassionate smiles, Those two exalted personalities beautified the cow pasture with the impressions of Their feet, which bore the marks of the flag, lightning bolt, elephant goad and lotus. The two Lords, whose pastimes are most magnanimous and attractive, were ornamented with jeweled necklaces and flower garlands, anointed with auspicious, fragrant substances, freshly bathed, and dressed in spotless raiment. They were the primeval Supreme Personalities, the masters and original causes of the universes, who had for the welfare of the earth now descended in Their distinct forms of Keśava and Balarāma. O King Parīkṣit, They resembled two gold-bedecked mountains, one of emerald and the other of silver, as with Their effulgence They dispelled the sky's darkness in all directions.

TEXT 34

रथात्तूर्णमवप्लुत्य सोऽक्रूरः स्नेहविह्वलः ।
पपात चरणोपान्ते दण्डवद् रामकृष्णयोः ॥ ३४ ॥

rathāt tūrṇam avaplutya
so'krūraḥ sneha-vihvalaḥ
papāta caraṇopānte
daṇḍa-vad rāma-kṛṣṇayoḥ

rathāt—from his chariot; *tūrṇam*—quickly; *avaplutya*—climbing down; *saḥ*—he; *akrūraḥ*—Akrūra; *sneha*—by affection; *vihvalaḥ*—overcome; *papāta*—fell; *caraṇa-upānte*—next to the feet; *daṇḍa-vat*—flat like a rod; *rāma-kṛṣṇayoḥ*—of Balarāma and Kṛṣṇa.

TRANSLATION

Akrūra, overwhelmed with affection, quickly jumped down from his chariot and fell at the feet of Kṛṣṇa and Balarāma like a rod.

TEXT 35

भगवद्दर्शनाह्लादबाष्पपर्याकुलेक्षणः ।
पुलकाचितांग औत्कण्ठयात्स्वाख्याने नाशकन्नृप ॥ ३५ ॥

bhagavad-darśanāhlāda-
bāṣpa-paryākulekṣaṇaḥ

pulakācitāṅga autkaṇṭhyāt
svākhyāne nāśakan nṛpa

bhagavat—the Supreme Personality of Godhead; *darśana*—because of seeing; *āhlāda*—due to the joy; *bāṣpa*—with tears; *paryākula*—overflowing; *īkṣaṇaḥ*—whose eyes; *pulaka*—with eruptions; *ācita*—marked; *aṅgaḥ*—whose limbs; *autkaṇṭhyāt*—from eagerness; *sva-ākhyāne*—to announce himself; *na aśakat*—he was not able; *nṛpa*—O King.

TRANSLATION

The joy of seeing the Supreme Lord flooded Akrūra's eyes with tears and decorated his limbs with eruptions of ecstasy. He felt such eagerness that he could not speak to present himself, O King.

TEXT 36

भगवांस्तमभिप्रेत्य रथांगाकिंतपाणिना ।
परिरेभेऽभ्युपाकृष्य प्रीतः प्रणतवत्सलः ॥ ३६ ॥

bhagavāṁs tam abhipretya
rathāṅgāṅkita-pāṇinā
parirebhe'bhyupākṛṣya
prītaḥ praṇata-vatsalaḥ

bhagavān—the Supreme Lord; *tam*—him, Akrūra; *abhipretya*—recognizing; *ratha-aṅga*—with a chariot wheel; *aṅkita*—marked; *pāṇinā*—by His hand; *parirebhe*—He embraced; *abhyupākṛṣya*—pulling near; *prītaḥ*—pleased; *praṇata*—to those who are surrendered; *vatsalaḥ*—who is benignly disposed.

TRANSLATION

Recognizing Akrūra, Lord Kṛṣṇa drew him close with His hand, which bears the sign of the chariot wheel, and then embraced him. Kṛṣṇa felt pleased, for He is always benignly disposed toward His surrendered devotees.

PURPORT

According to the *ācāryas*, by extending His hand, marked with the chariot wheel, or *cakra*, Lord Kṛṣṇa indicated His ability to kill Kaṁsa.

TEXTS 37–38

संकर्षणश्च प्रणतमुपगुह्य महामनाः ।
गृहीत्वा पाणिना पाणी अनयत्सानुजो गृहम् ॥ ३७ ॥
पृष्ट्वाथ स्वागतं तस्मै निवेद्य च वरासनम् ।
प्रक्षाल्य विधिवत्पादौ मधुपर्कार्हणमाहरत् ॥ ३८ ॥

saṅkarṣaṇaś ca praṇatam
upaguhya mahā-manāḥ
gṛhītvā pāṇinā pāṇī
anayat sānujo gṛham

pṛṣṭvātha sv-āgataṁ tasmai
nivedya ca varāsanam
prakṣālya vidhi-vat pādau
madhu-parkārhaṇam āharat

saṅkarṣaṇaḥ—Lord Balarāma; *ca*—and; *praṇatam*—who was standing with his head bowed; *upaguhya*—embracing; *mahā-manāḥ*—magnanimous; *gṛhītvā*—taking hold of; *pāṇinā*—with His hand; *pāṇī*—his two hands; *anayat*—He took; *sa-anujaḥ*—with His younger brother (Lord Kṛṣṇa); *gṛham*—to His residence; *pṛṣṭvā*—inquiring; *atha*—then; *su-āgatam*—about the comfort of his trip; *tasmai*—to him; *nivedya*—offering; *ca*—and; *vara*—excellent; *āsanam*—a seat; *prakṣālya*—washing; *vidhi-vat*—in accordance with scriptural injunctions; *pādau*—his feet; *madhu-parka*—honey mixed with milk; *arhaṇam*—as a respectful offering; *āharat*—He brought.

TRANSLATION

As Akrūra stood with his head bowed, Lord Saṅkarṣaṇa [Balarāma] grasped his joined hands, and then Balarāma took him to His house in the company of Lord Kṛṣṇa. After inquiring from Akrūra whether his trip had been comfortable, Balarāma offered him a first-class seat, bathed his feet in accordance with the injunctions of scripture and respectfully served him milk with honey.

TEXT 39

निवेद्य गां चातिथये संवाह्य श्रान्तमादृतः ।
अन्नं बहुगुणं मेध्यं श्रद्धयोपाहरद्विभुः ॥ ३९ ॥

nivedya gāṁ cātithaye
saṁvāhya śrāntam ādṛtaḥ
annaṁ bahu-guṇaṁ medhyaṁ
śraddhayopāharad vibhuḥ

nivedya—presenting in charity; *gām*—a cow; *ca*—and; *atithaye*—to the guest; *saṁvāhya*—massaging; *śrāntam*—who was tired; *ādṛtaḥ*—with great respect; *annam*—cooked food; *bahu-guṇam*—of various tastes; *medhyam*—suitable for offering; *śraddhayā*—faithfully; *upāharat*—offered; *vibhuḥ*—the almighty Lord.

TRANSLATION

The almighty Lord Balarāma presented Akrūra with the gift of a cow, massaged his feet to relieve him of fatigue and then with great respect and faith fed him suitably prepared food of various fine tastes.

PURPORT

According to Śrīla Viśvanātha Cakravartī, Akrūra went to Kṛṣṇa's and Balarāma's house on the twelfth lunar day, on which one should not break a fast at night. However, Akrūra dispensed with this formality because he was eager to receive food in the Lord's house.

TEXT 40

तस्मै भुक्तवते प्रीत्या रामः परमधर्मवित् ।
मुखवासैर्गन्धमाल्यैः परां प्रीतिं व्यधात्पुनः ॥ ४० ॥

tasmai bhuktavate prītyā
rāmaḥ parama-dharma-vit
mukha-vāsair gandha-mālyaiḥ
parāṁ prītiṁ vyadhāt punaḥ

tasmai—to him; *bhuktavate*—who had finished eating; *prītyā*—affectionately; *rāmaḥ*—Lord Balarāma; *parama*—the supreme; *dharma-vit*—knower of religious principles; *mukha-vāsaiḥ*—with aromatic herbs for sweetening the mouth; *gandha*—with perfume; *mālyaiḥ*—and flower garlands; *parām*—the highest; *prītim*—satisfaction; *vyadhāt*—arranged; *punaḥ*—further.

TRANSLATION

When Akrūra had eaten to his satisfaction, Lord Balarāma, the supreme knower of religious duties, offered him aromatic herbs for sweetening his mouth, along with fragrances and flower garlands. Thus Akrūra once again enjoyed the highest pleasure.

TEXT 41

पप्रच्छ सत्कृतं नन्दः कथं स्थ निरनुग्रहे ।
कंसे जीवति दाशार्ह सौनपाला इवावयः ॥ ४१ ॥

papraccha sat-kṛtaṁ nandaḥ
kathaṁ stha niranugrahe
kaṁse jīvati dāśārha
sauna-pālā ivāvayaḥ

papraccha—asked; *sat-kṛtam*—who had been honored; *nandaḥ*—Nanda Mahārāja; *katham*—how; *stha*—you are living; *niranugrahe*—the merciless; *kaṁse*—Kaṁsa; *jīvati*—while he is alive; *dāśārha*—O descendant of Daśārha; *sauna*—an animal slaughterer; *pālāḥ*—whose keeper; *iva*—just like; *avayaḥ*—sheep.

TRANSLATION

Nanda Mahārāja asked Akrūra: O descendant of Daśārha, how are all of you maintaining yourselves while that merciless Kaṁsa remains alive? You are just like sheep under the care of a butcher.

TEXT 42

योऽवधीत्स्वस्वसुस्तोकान् क्रोशन्त्या असुतृप् खलः ।
किं नु स्वित्तत्प्रजानां वः कुशलं विमृशामहे ॥ ४२ ॥

yo'vadhīt sva-svasus tokān
krośantyā asu-tṛp khalaḥ
kiṁ nu svit tat-prajānāṁ vaḥ
kuśalaṁ vimṛśāmahe

yaḥ—who; *avadhīt*—killed; *sva*—of his own; *svasuḥ*—sister; *tokān*—the babies; *krośantyāḥ*—who was crying; *asu-tṛp*—self-indulgent; *khalaḥ*—

cruel; *kim nu*—what then; *svit*—indeed; *tat*—his; *prajānām*—of the subjects; *vaḥ*—you; *kuśalam*—well-being; *vimṛśāmahe*—we should conjecture.

TRANSLATION

That cruel, self-serving Kaṁsa murdered the infants of his own sister in her presence, even as she cried in anguish. So why should we even ask about the well-being of you, his subjects?

TEXT 43

इत्थं सूनृतया वाचा नन्देन सुसभाजितः ।
अक्रूरः परिपृष्टेन जहावध्वपरिश्रमम् ॥ ४३ ॥

itthaṁ sūnṛtayā vācā
nandena su-sabhājitaḥ
akrūraḥ paripṛṣṭena
jahāv adhva-pariśramam

ittham—thus; *sū-nṛtayā*—very true and pleasing; *vācā*—with words; *nandena*—by Nanda Mahārāja; *su*—well; *sabhājitaḥ*—honored; *akrūraḥ*—Akrūra; *paripṛṣṭena*—by the inquiry; *jahau*—put aside; *adhva*—of the road; *pariśramam*—his fatigue.

TRANSLATION

Honored by Nanda Mahārāja with these true and pleasing words of inquiry, Akrūra forgot the fatigue of his journey.

Thus end the purports of the humble servants of His Divine Grace A.C. Bhaktivedanta Swami Prabhupāda to the Tenth Canto, Thirty-eighth Chapter, of the Śrīmad-Bhāgavatam, *entitled "Akrūra's Arrival in Vṛndāvana."*

CHAPTER THIRTY- NINE

Akrūra's Vision

This chapter describes how Akrūra informed Lord Kṛṣṇa and Lord Balarāma of Kaṁsa's plans and his activities in Mathurā; what the *gopīs* cried out in distress when Kṛṣṇa left for Mathurā; and also the vision of Lord Viṣṇu's abode that Akrūra saw within the water of the Yamunā.

When Kṛṣṇa and Balarāma offered Akrūra great respect and comfortably seated him on a couch, he felt that all the desires he had reflected on while traveling to Vṛndāvana were now fulfilled. After the evening meal, Kṛṣṇa asked Akrūra whether his trip had been peaceful and whether he was well. The Lord also inquired about how Kaṁsa was behaving toward their family members, and finally He asked why Akrūra had come.

Akrūra described how Kaṁsa had been persecuting the Yādavas, what Nārada had told Kaṁsa and how Kaṁsa had been treating Vasudeva cruelly. Akrūra also spoke of Kaṁsa's desire to bring Kṛṣṇa and Balarāma to Mathurā to kill Them on the pretext of Their seeing the bow sacrifice and engaging in a wrestling match. Kṛṣṇa and Balarāma laughed out loud when They heard this. They went to Their father, Nanda, and informed him of Kaṁsa's orders. Nanda then issued an order to all the residents of Vraja that they should collect various offerings for the King and prepare to go to Mathurā.

The young *gopīs* were extremely upset to hear that Kṛṣṇa and Balarāma would be going to Mathurā. They lost all external awareness and began to remember Kṛṣṇa's pastimes. Condemning the creator for separating them from Him, they began to lament. They said that Akrūra did not deserve his name (*a,* "not"; *krūra,* "cruel"), since he was so cruel to be taking away their dearmost Kṛṣṇa. "It must be that fate is against us," they lamented, "because otherwise the elders of Vraja would have forbidden Kṛṣṇa to leave. So let us forget our shyness and try to stop Lord Mādhava from going." With these words the young cowherd girls began to chant Kṛṣṇa's names and cry.

But even as they wept, Akrūra began taking Kṛṣṇa and Balarāma to Mathurā in his chariot. The cowherd men of Gokula followed behind on their wagons, and the young *gopīs* also walked behind for some distance, but then they became placated by Kṛṣṇa's glances and gestures and pacified by a message from Him that said "I will return." With their minds completely absorbed in Kṛṣṇa, the cowherd girls stood as still as figures in a painting until they could no longer see the chariot's flag or the dust cloud being raised on the road. Then, chanting Kṛṣṇa's glories all the while, they despondently returned to their homes.

Akrūra halted the chariot at the bank of the Yamunā so Kṛṣṇa and Balarāma could perform a ritual of purification and drink some water. After the two Lords had gotten back into the chariot, Akrūra took Their permission to bathe in the Yamunā. As he recited Vedic *mantras,* he was startled to see the two Lords standing in the water. Akrūra came out of the river and returned to the chariot—where he saw the Lords still sitting. Then he returned to the water to find out if the two figures he had seen there were real or not.

What Akrūra saw in the water was four-armed Lord Vāsudeva. His complexion was dark blue like a fresh raincloud, He wore yellow garments and He lay on the lap of thousand-hooded Ananta Śeṣa. Lord Vāsudeva was receiving the prayers of perfected beings, celestial serpents and demons, and He was encircled by His personal attendants. Serving Him were His many potencies, such as Śrī, Puṣṭi and Ilā, while Brahmā and other demigods sang His praises. Akrūra rejoiced at this vision and, joining his palms in supplication, began to pray to the Supreme Lord in a voice choked with emotion.

TEXT 1

श्रीशुक उवाच

सुखोपविष्टः पर्यंके रमकृष्णोरुमानितः ।
लेभे मनोरथान् सर्वान् पथि यान् स चकार ह ॥ १ ॥

śrī-śuka uvāca
sukhopaviṣṭaḥ paryaṅke
rama-kṛṣṇoru-mānitaḥ
lebhe manorathān sarvān
pathi yān sa cakāra ha

śrī-śukaḥ uvāca—Śukadeva Gosvāmī said; *sukha*—comfortably; *upaviṣṭaḥ*—seated; *paryaṅke*—on a couch; *rāma-kṛṣṇa*—by Lord Balarāma and Lord Kṛṣṇa; *uru*—very much; *mānitaḥ*—honored; *lebhe*—he attained; *manaḥ-rathān*—his desires; *sarvān*—all; *pathi*—on the road; *yān*—which; *saḥ*—he; *cakāra ha*—had manifested.

TRANSLATION

Śukadeva Gosvāmī said: Having been honored so much by Lord Balarāma and Lord Kṛṣṇa, Akrūra, seated comfortably on a couch, felt that all the desires he had contemplated on the road were now fulfilled.

TEXT 2

किमलभ्यं भगवति प्रसन्ने श्रीनिकेतने ।
तथापि तत्परा राजन्न हि वाञ्छन्ति किञ्चन ॥ २ ॥

kim alabhyaṁ bhagavati
prasanne śrī-niketane
tathāpi tat-parā rājan
na hi vāñchanti kiñcana

kim—what; *alabhyam*—is unattainable; *bhagavati*—the Supreme Lord; *prasanne*—being satisfied; *śrī*—of the goddess of fortune; *niketane*—the resting place; *tathā api*—nevertheless; *tat-parāḥ*—those who are devoted to Him; *rājan*—O King (Parīkṣit); *na*—do not; *hi*—indeed; *vāñchanti*—desire; *kiñcana*—anything.

TRANSLATION

My dear King, what is unattainable for one who has satisfied the Supreme Personality of Godhead, the shelter of the goddess of fortune? Even so, those who are dedicated to His devotional service never want anything from Him.

TEXT 3

सायन्तनाशनं कृत्वा भगवान् देवकीसुतः ।
सुहृत्सु वृत्तं कंसस्य पप्रच्छान्यच्चिकीर्षितम् ॥ ३ ॥

sāyantanāśanaṁ kṛtvā
bhagavān devakī-sutaḥ
suhṛtsu vṛttaṁ kaṁsasya
papracchānyac cikīrṣitam

sāyantana—of the evening; *aśanam*—the dining; *kṛtvā*—having done; *bhagavān*—the Supreme Lord; *devakī-sutaḥ*—the son of Devakī; *suhṛtsu*—

toward His well-wishing relatives and friends; *vṛttam*—about the behavior; *kaṁsasya*—of Kaṁsa; *papraccha*—He inquired; *anyat*—other; *cikīrṣitam*—intentions.

TRANSLATION

After the evening meal, Lord Kṛṣṇa, the son of Devakī, asked Akrūra how Kaṁsa was treating their dear relatives and friends and what the King was planning to do.

TEXT 4

श्रीभगवानुवाच
तात सौम्यागतः कच्चित्स्वागतं भद्रमस्तु वः ।
अपि स्वज्ञातिबन्धूनामनमीवमनामयम् ॥ ४ ॥

śrī-bhagavān uvāca
tāta saumyāgataḥ kaccit
sv-āgataṁ bhadram astu vaḥ
api sva-jñāti-bandhūnām
anamīvam anāmayam

śrī-bhagavān uvāca—the Supreme Personality of Godhead said; *tāta*—O uncle; *saumya*—O gentle one; *āgataḥ*—arrived; *kaccit*—whether; *su-āgatam*—welcome; *bhadram*—all good; *astu*—may there be; *vaḥ*—for you; *api*—whether; *sva*—for your well-wishing friends; *jñāti*—intimate relatives; *bandhūnām*—and other family members; *anamīvam*—freedom from unhappiness; *anāmayam*—freedom from disease.

TRANSLATION

The Supreme Lord said: My dear, gentle Uncle Akrūra, was your trip here comfortable? May all good fortune be yours. Are our well-wishing friends and our relatives, both close and distant, happy and in good health?

TEXT 5

किं नु नः कुशलं पृच्छे एधमाने कुलामये ।
कंसे मातुलनाम्नांग स्वानां नस्तत्प्रजासु च ॥ ५ ॥

kiṁ nu naḥ kuśalaṁ pṛcche
edhamāne kulāmaye

kaṁse mātula-nāmnāṅga
svānāṁ nas tat-prajāsu ca

kim—what; *nu*—rather; *naḥ*—our; *kuśalam*—about the well-being; *pṛcche*—I should inquire; *edhamāne*—when he is prospering; *kula*—of our family; *āmaye*—the disease; *kaṁse*—King Kaṁsa; *mātula-nāmnā*—by the name "maternal uncle"; *aṅga*—my dear; *svānām*—of the relatives; *naḥ*—our; *tat*—his; *prajāsu*—of the citizens; *ca*—and.

TRANSLATION

But, my dear Akrūra, as long as King Kaṁsa—that disease of our family who goes by the name "maternal uncle"—is still prospering, why should I even bother to ask about the well-being of our family members and his other subjects?

TEXT 6

अहो अस्मदभूद् भूरि पित्रोर्वृजिनमार्ययोः ।
यद्धेतोः पुत्रमरणं यद्धेतोर्बन्धनं तयोः ॥ ६ ॥

aho asmad abhūd bhūri
pitror vṛjinam āryayoḥ
yad-dhetoḥ putra-maraṇaṁ
yad-dhetor bandhanaṁ tayoḥ

aho—ah; *asmat*—because of Me; *abhūt*—there was; *bhūri*—great; *pitroḥ*—for My parents; *vṛjinam*—suffering; *āryayoḥ*—for the offenseless ones; *yat-hetoḥ*—because of whom; *putra*—of their sons; *maraṇam*—the death; *yat-hetoḥ*—because of whom; *bandhanam*—bondage; *tayoḥ*—their.

TRANSLATION

Just see how much suffering I have caused My offenseless parents! Because of Me their sons were killed and they themselves imprisoned.

PURPORT

Because Kaṁsa had heard a prophecy that the eighth son of Devakī would kill him, he tried to kill all her children. For the same reason, he imprisoned her and her husband, Vasudeva.

TEXT 7

दिष्ट्याद्य दर्शनं स्वानां मह्यं वः सौम्य काङ्क्षितम् ।
सञ्जातं वर्ण्यतां तात तवागमनकारणम् ॥ ७ ॥

diṣṭyādya darśanaṁ svānāṁ
mahyaṁ vaḥ saumya kāṅkṣitam
sañjātaṁ varṇyatāṁ tāta
tavāgamana-kāraṇam

diṣṭyā—by good fortune; *adya*—today; *darśanam*—the sight; *svānām*—of My close relative; *mahyam*—for Me; *vaḥ*—yourself; *saumya*—O gentle one; *kāṅkṣitam*—desired; *sañjātam*—has come about; *varṇyatām*—please explain; *tāta*—O uncle; *tava*—your; *āgamana*—for the coming; *kāraṇam*—the reason.

TRANSLATION

By good fortune We have today fulfilled Our desire to see you, Our dear relative. O gentle uncle, please tell Us why you have come.

TEXT 8

श्रीशुक उवाच
पृष्टो भगवता सर्वं वर्णयामास माधवः ।
वैरानुबन्धं यदुषु वसुदेववधोद्यमम् ॥ ८ ॥

śrī-śuka uvāca
pṛṣṭo bhagavatā sarvaṁ
varṇayām āsa mādhavaḥ
vairānubandhaṁ yaduṣu
vasudeva-vadhodyamam

śrī-śukaḥ uvāca—Śukadeva Gosvāmī said; *pṛṣṭaḥ*—requested; *bhagavatā*—by the Supreme Lord; *sarvam*—everything; *varṇayām āsa*—described; *mādhavaḥ*—Akrūra, descendant of Madhu; *vaira-anubandham*—the inimical attitude; *yaduṣu*—toward the Yadus; *vasudeva*—Vasudeva; *vadha*—to murder; *udyamam*—the attempt.

TRANSLATION

Śukadeva Gosvāmī said: In response to the Supreme Lord's request, Akrūra, the descendant of Madhu, described the whole situation, including

King Kaṁsa's enmity toward the Yadus and his attempt to murder Vasudeva.

TEXT 9

यत्सन्देशो यदर्थं वा दूतः सम्प्रेषितः स्वयम् ।
यदुक्तं नारदेनास्य स्वजन्मानकदुन्दुभेः ॥ ९ ॥

yat-sandeśo yad-arthaṁ vā
dūtaḥ sampreṣitaḥ svayam
yad uktaṁ nāradenāsya
sva-janmānakadundubheḥ

yat—having which; *sandeśaḥ*—message; *yat*—which; *artham*—purpose; *vā*—and; *dūtaḥ*—as a messenger; *sampreṣitaḥ*—sent; *svayam*—himself (Akrūra); *yat*—what; *uktam*—was spoken; *nāradena*—by Nārada; *asya*—to him (Kaṁsa); *sva*—His (Kṛṣṇa's); *janma*—birth; *ānakadundubheḥ*—from Vasudeva.

TRANSLATION

Akrūra relayed the message he had been sent to deliver. He also described Kaṁsa's real intentions and how Nārada had informed Kaṁsa that Kṛṣṇa had been born as the son of Vasudeva.

TEXT 10

श्रुत्वाक्रूरवचः कृष्णो बलश्च परवीरहा ।
प्रहस्य नन्दं पितरं राज्ञा दिष्टं विजज्ञतुः ॥ १० ॥

śrutvākrūra-vacaḥ kṛṣṇo
balaś ca para-vīra-hā
prahasya nandaṁ pitaraṁ
rājñā diṣṭaṁ vijajñatuḥ

śrutvā—hearing; *akrūra-vacaḥ*—Akrūra's words; *kṛṣṇaḥ*—Lord Kṛṣṇa; *balaḥ*—Lord Balarāma; *ca*—and; *para-vīra*—of opposing heroes; *hā*—the destroyer; *prahasya*—laughing; *nandam*—to Nanda Mahārāja; *pitaram*—Their father; *rājñā*—by the King; *diṣṭam*—the order given; *vijajñatuḥ*—They informed.

TRANSLATION

Lord Kṛṣṇa and Lord Balarāma, the vanquisher of heroic opponents, laughed when They heard Akrūra's words. The Lords then informed Their father, Nanda Mahārāja, of King Kaṁsa's orders.

TEXTS 11–12

गोपान् समादिशत्सोऽपि गृह्यतां सर्वगोरसः ।
उपायनानि गृह्णीध्वं युज्यन्तां शकटानि च ॥ ११ ॥
यास्यामः श्वो मधुपुरीं दास्यामो नृपते रसान् ।
द्रक्ष्यामः सुमहत्पर्व यान्ति जानपदाः किल ।
एवमाघोषयत्क्षत्रा नन्दगोपः स्वगोकुले ॥ १२ ॥

gopān samādiśat so'pi
gṛhyatāṁ sarva-go-rasaḥ
upāyanāni gṛhṇīdhvaṁ
yujyantāṁ śakaṭāni ca

yāsyāmaḥ śvo madhu-purīṁ
dāsyāmo nṛpate rasān
drakṣyāmaḥ su-mahat parva
yānti jānapadāḥ kila
evam āghoṣayat kṣatrā
nanda-gopaḥ sva-gokule

gopān—the cowherd men; *samādiśat*—ordered; *saḥ*—he (Nanda Mahārāja); *api*—also; *gṛhyatām*—have collected; *sarva*—all; *go-rasaḥ*—the milk products; *upāyanāni*—excellent gifts; *gṛhṇīdhvam*—take; *yujyantām*—yoke; *śakaṭāni*—the wagons; *ca*—and; *yāsyāmaḥ*—we shall go; *śvaḥ*—tomorrow; *madhu-purīm*—to Mathurā; *dāsyāmaḥ*—we shall give; *nṛpateḥ*—to the King; *rasān*—our milk products; *drakṣyāmaḥ*—we shall see; *su-mahat*—a very great; *parva*—festival; *yānti*—are going; *jānapadāḥ*—the residents of all the outlying districts; *kila*—indeed; *evam*—thus; *āghoṣayat*—he had announced; *kṣatrā*—by the village constable; *nanda-gopaḥ*—Nanda Mahārāja; *sva-gokule*—to the people of his Gokula.

TRANSLATION

Nanda Mahārāja then issued orders to the cowherd men by having the village constable make the following announcement throughout Nanda's

domain of Vraja: "Go collect all the available milk products. Bring valuable gifts and yoke your wagons. Tomorrow we shall go to Mathurā, present our milk products to the King and see a very great festival. The residents of all the outlying districts are also going."

PURPORT

Nanda wanted to bring ghee and other milk products as taxes for the King.

TEXT 13

गोप्यस्तास्तदुपश्रुत्य बभूवुर्व्यथिता भृशम् ।
रामकृष्णौ पुरीं नेतुमक्रूरं व्रजमागतम् ॥ १३ ॥

gopyas tās tad upaśrutya
babhūvur vyathitā bhṛśam
rāma-kṛṣṇau purīṁ netum
akrūraṁ vrajam āgatam

gopyaḥ—the cowherd girls; *tāḥ*—they; *tat*—then; *upaśrutya*—hearing; *babhūvuḥ*—became; *vyathitāḥ*—distressed; *bhṛśam*—extremely; *rāma-kṛṣṇau*—Balarāma and Kṛṣṇa; *purīm*—to the city; *netum*—to take; *akrūram*—Akrūra; *vrajam*—to Vṛndāvana; *āgatam*—come.

TRANSLATION

When the young gopīs heard that Akrūra had come to Vraja to take Kṛṣṇa and Balarāma to the city, they became extremely distressed.

TEXT 14

काश्चित्तत्कृतहृत्तापश्वासम्लानमुखश्रियः ।
स्रंसद्दुकूलवलयकेशग्रन्थ्यश्च काश्चन ॥ १४ ॥

kāścit tat-kṛta-hṛt-tāpa
śvāsa-mlāna-mukha-śriyaḥ
sraṁsad-dukūla-valaya
keśa-granthyaś ca kāścana

kāścit—some of them; *tat*—by that (hearing); *kṛta*—created; *hṛt*—in their hearts; *tāpa*—from the torment; *śvāsa*—by the sighing; *mlāna*—made pale; *mukha*—of their faces; *śriyaḥ*—the luster; *sraṁsat*—loosening; *dukūla*

—their dresses; *valaya*—bracelets; *keśa*—in their hair; *granthyaḥ*—the knots; *ca*—and; *kāścana*—others.

TRANSLATION

Some gopīs felt so pained at heart that their faces turned pale from their heavy breathing. Others were so anguished that their dresses, bracelets and braids became loose.

TEXT 15

अन्याश्च तदनुध्याननिवृत्ताशेषवृत्तयः ।
नाभ्यजानन्निमं लोकमात्मलोकं गता इव ॥ १५ ॥

anyāś ca tad-anudhyāna
nivṛttāśeṣa-vṛttayaḥ
nābhyajānann imaṁ lokam
ātma-lokaṁ gatā iva

anyāḥ—others; *ca*—and; *tat*—on Him; *anudhyāna*—by fixed meditation; *nivṛtta*—ceased; *aśeṣa*—all; *vṛttayaḥ*—their sensory functions; *na abhyajānan*—they were unaware; *imam*—of this; *lokam*—world; *ātma*—of self-realization; *lokam*—the realm; *gatāḥ*—those who have attained; *iva*—just as.

TRANSLATION

Other gopīs entirely stopped their sensory activities and became fixed in meditation on Kṛṣṇa. They lost all awareness of the external world, just like those who attain the platform of self-realization.

PURPORT

The *gopīs* were in fact already on the platform of self-realization. The *Caitanya-caritāmṛta* (*Madhya* 20.108) states, *jīvera svarūpa haya kṛṣṇera nitya-dāsa:* "The self, or individual soul, is an eternal servant of Kṛṣṇa." Thus because they were rendering the most intense loving service to the Lord, the *gopīs* were situated at the highest stage of self-realization.

TEXT 16

स्मरन्त्यश्चापराः शौरेरनुरागस्मितेरिताः ।
हृदिस्पृशश्चित्रपदा गिरः सम्मुमुहुः स्त्रियः ॥ १६ ॥

smarantyaś cāparāḥ śaurer
anurāga-smiteritāḥ
hṛdi-spṛśaś citra-padā
giraḥ sammumuhuḥ striyaḥ

smarantyaḥ—remembering; *ca*—and; *aparāḥ*—others; *śaureḥ*—of Kṛṣṇa; *anurāga*—affectionate; *smita*—by His smile; *īritāḥ*—sent; *hṛdi*—the heart; *spṛśaḥ*—touching; *citra*—wonderful; *padāḥ*—with phrases; *giraḥ*—the speech; *sammumuhuḥ*—fainted; *striyaḥ*—women.

TRANSLATION

And still other young women fainted simply by remembering the words of Lord Śauri [Kṛṣṇa]. These words, decorated with wonderful phrases and expressed with affectionate smiles, would deeply touch the young girls' hearts.

TEXTS 17–18

गतिं सुललितां चेष्टां स्निग्धहासावलोकनम् ।
शोकापहानि नर्माणि प्रोद्दामचरितानि च ॥ १७ ॥
चिन्तयन्त्यो मुकुन्दस्य भीता विरहकातराः ।
समेताः सङ्घशः प्रोचुरश्रुमुख्योऽच्युताशयाः ॥ १८ ॥

gatiṁ su-lalitāṁ ceṣṭāṁ
snigdha-hāsāvalokanam
śokāpahāni narmāṇi
proddāma-caritāni ca

cintayantyo mukundasya
bhītā viraha-kātarāḥ
sametāḥ saṅghaśaḥ procur
aśru-mukhyo 'cyutāśayāḥ

gatim—the movements; *su-lalitām*—very charming; *ceṣṭām*—the activities; *snigdha*—affectionate; *hāsa*—smiling; *avalokanam*—the glances; *śoka*—unhappiness; *apahāni*—which remove; *narmāṇi*—the joking words; *proddāma*—mighty; *caritāni*—the deeds; *ca*—and; *cintayantyaḥ*—thinking about; *mukundasya*—of Lord Kṛṣṇa; *bhītāḥ*—afraid; *viraha*—because of separation; *kātarāḥ*—greatly distressed; *sametāḥ*—joining together;

saṅghaśaḥ—in groups; *procuḥ*—they spoke; *aśru*—with tears; *mukhyaḥ*—their faces; *acyuta-āśayāḥ*—their minds absorbed in Lord Acyuta.

TRANSLATION

The gopīs were frightened at the prospect of even the briefest separation from Lord Mukunda, so now, as they remembered His graceful gait, His pastimes, His affectionate, smiling glances, His heroic deeds and His joking words, which would relieve their distress, they were beside themselves with anxiety at the thought of the great separation about to come. They gathered in groups and spoke to one another, their faces covered with tears and their minds fully absorbed in Acyuta.

TEXT 19

श्रीगोप्य ऊचुः

अहो विधातस्तव न क्वचिद्दया
संयोज्य मैत्र्या प्रणयेन देहिनः ।
तांश्चाकृतार्थान् वियुनङ्क्ष्यपार्थकं
विक्रीडितं तेऽर्भकचेष्टितं यथा ॥ १९ ॥

śrī-gopya ūcuḥ
aho vidhātas tava na kvacid dayā
saṁyojya maitryā praṇayena dehinaḥ
tāṁś cākṛtārthān viyunaṅkṣy apārthakaṁ
vikrīḍitaṁ te'rbhaka-ceṣṭitaṁ yathā

śrī-gopyaḥ ūcuḥ—the *gopīs* said; *aho*—O; *vidhātaḥ*—Providence; *tava*—your; *na*—there is not; *kvacit*—anywhere; *dayā*—mercy; *saṁyojya*—bringing together; *maitryā*—with friendship; *praṇayena*—and with love; *dehinaḥ*—embodied living beings; *tān*—them; *ca*—and; *akṛta*—unfulfilled; *arthān*—their aims; *viyunaṅkṣi*—you separate; *apārthakam*—uselessly; *vikrīḍitam*—play; *te*—your; *arbhaka*—of a child; *ceṣṭitam*—the activity; *yathā*—as.

TRANSLATION

The gopīs said: O Providence, you have no mercy! You bring embodied creatures together in friendship and love and then senselessly separate them before they fulfill their desires. This whimsical play of yours is like a child's game.

TEXT 20

यस्त्वं प्रदर्श्यासितकुन्तलावृतं
मुकुन्दवक्त्रं सुकपोलमुन्नसम् ।
शोकापनोदस्मितलेशसुन्दरं
करोषि पारोक्ष्यमसाधु ते कृतम् ॥ २० ॥

yas tvaṁ pradarśyāsita-kuntalāvṛtaṁ
mukunda-vaktraṁ su-kapolam un-nasam
śokāpanoda-smita-leśa-sundaraṁ
karoṣi pārokṣyam asādhu te kṛtam

yaḥ—who; *tvam*—you; *pradarśya*—showing; *asita*—black; *kuntala*—by locks; *āvṛtam*—framed; *mukunda*—of Kṛṣṇa; *vaktram*—the face; *su-kapolam*—with fine cheeks; *ut-nasam*—and raised nose; *śoka*—misery; *apanoda*—eradicating; *smita*—with His smile; *leśa*—slight; *sundaram*—beautiful; *karoṣi*—you make; *pārokṣyam*—invisible; *asādhu*—not good; *te*—by you; *kṛtam*—done.

TRANSLATION

Having shown us Mukunda's face, framed by dark locks and beautified by His fine cheeks, raised nose and gentle smiles, which eradicate all misery, you are now making that face invisible. This behavior of yours is not at all good.

TEXT 21

क्रूरस्त्वमक्रूरसमाख्यया स्म नश्
चक्षुर्हि दत्तं हरसे बताज्ञवत् ।
येनैकदेशेऽखिलसर्गसौष्ठवं
त्वदीयमद्राक्ष्म वयं मधुद्विषः ॥ २१ ॥

krūras tvam akrūra-samākhyayā sma naś
cakṣur hi dattaṁ harase batājña-vat
yenaika-deśe'khila-sarga-sauṣṭhavaṁ
tvadīyam adrākṣma vayaṁ madhu-dviṣaḥ

krūraḥ—cruel; *tvam*—you (are); *akrūra-samākhyayā*—by the name Akrūra (which means "not cruel"); *sma*—certainly; *naḥ*—our; *cakṣuḥ*—

eyes; *hi*—indeed; *dattam*—given; *harase*—you are taking; *bata*—alas; *ajña*—a fool; *vat*—just like; *yena*—with which (eyes); *eka*—in one; *deśe*—place; *akhila*—of all; *sarga*—the creation; *sauṣṭhavam*—the perfection; *tvadīyam*—your; *adrākṣma*—have seen; *vayam*—we; *madhudviṣaḥ*—of Lord Kṛṣṇa, enemy of the demon Madhu.

TRANSLATION

O Providence, though you come here with the name Akrūra, you are indeed cruel, for like a fool you are taking away what you once gave us—those eyes with which we have seen, even in one feature of Lord Madhudviṣa's form, the perfection of your entire creation.

PURPORT

The *gopīs* did not care to see anything but Kṛṣṇa; therefore if Kṛṣṇa left Vṛndāvana, their eyes would have no function. Thus Kṛṣṇa's departure was blinding these poor girls, and in their distress they berated Akrūra, whose name means "not cruel," as cruel indeed.

TEXT 22

न नन्दसूनुः क्षणभंगसौहृदः
समीक्षते नः स्वकृतातुरा बत ।
विहाय गेहान् स्वजनान् सुतान् पतींस्
तद्दास्यमद्धोपगता नवप्रियः ॥ २२ ॥

na nanda-sūnuḥ kṣaṇa-bhaṅga-sauhṛdaḥ
samīkṣate naḥ sva-kṛtāturā bata
vihāya gehān sva-janān sutān patīṁs
tad-dāsyam addhopagatā nava-priyaḥ

na—does not; *nanda-sūnuḥ*—the son of Nanda Mahārāja; *kṣaṇa*—in a moment; *bhaṅga*—the breaking; *sauhṛdaḥ*—of whose friendship; *samīkṣate*—look upon; *naḥ*—us; *sva*—by Him; *kṛta*—made; *āturāḥ*—under His control; *bata*—alas; *vihāya*—giving up; *gehān*—our homes; *sva-janān*—relatives; *sutān*—children; *patīn*—husbands; *tat*—to Him; *dāsyam*—servitude; *addhā*—directly; *upagatāḥ*—who have taken up; *nava*—ever new; *priyaḥ*—whose lovers.

TRANSLATION

Alas, Nanda's son, who breaks loving friendships in a second, will not even look directly at us. Forcibly brought under His control, we abandoned our homes, relatives, children and husbands just to serve Him, but He is always looking for new lovers.

TEXT 23

सुखं प्रभाता रजनीयमाशिषः
सत्या बभूवुः पुरयोषितां ध्रुवम् ।
याः संप्रविष्टस्य मुखं व्रजस्पतेः
पास्यन्त्यपांगोत्कलितस्मितासवम् ॥ २३ ॥

sukhaṁ prabhātā rajanīyam āśiṣaḥ
satyā babhūvuḥ pura-yoṣitāṁ dhruvam
yāḥ saṁpraviṣṭasya mukhaṁ vrajas-pateḥ
pāsyanty apāṅgotkalita-smitāsavam

sukham—happy; *prabhātā*—its dawn; *rajanī*—the night; *iyam*—this; *āśiṣaḥ*—the hopes; *satyāḥ*—true; *babhūvuḥ*—have become; *pura*—of the city; *yoṣitām*—of the women; *dhruvam*—certainly; *yāḥ*—who; *saṁpraviṣṭasya*—of Him who has entered (Mathurā); *mukham*—the face; *vrajaḥ-pateḥ*—of the master of Vraja; *pāsyanti*—they will drink; *apāṅga*—upon the corners of His eyes; *utkalita*—expanded; *smita*—a smile; *āsavam*—nectar.

TRANSLATION

The dawn following this night will certainly be auspicious for the women of Mathurā. All their hopes will now be fulfilled, for as the Lord of Vraja enters their city, they will be able to drink from His face the nectar of the smile emanating from the corners of His eyes.

TEXT 24

तासां मुकुन्दो मधुमञ्जुभाषितैर्
गृहीतचित्तः परवान्मनस्व्यपि ।
कथं पुनर्नः प्रतियास्यतेऽबला
ग्राम्याः सलज्जस्मितविभ्रमैर्भ्रमन् ॥ २४ ॥

tāsāṁ mukundo madhu-mañju-bhāṣitair
gṛhīta-cittaḥ para-vān manasvy api
kathaṁ punar naḥ pratiyāsyate'balā
grāmyāḥ salajja-smita-vibhramair bhraman

tāsām—their; *mukundaḥ*—Kṛṣṇa; *madhu*—like honey; *mañju*—sweet; *bhāṣitaiḥ*—by the words; *gṛhīta*—seized; *cittaḥ*—whose mind; *paravān*—subservient; *manasvī*—intelligent; *api*—although; *katham*—how; *punaḥ*—again; *naḥ*—to us; *pratiyāsyate*—will He return; *abalāḥ*—O girls; *grāmyāḥ*—who are rustic; *sa-lajja*—shyly; *smita*—smiling; *vibhramaiḥ*—by their enchantments; *bhraman*—becoming bewildered.

TRANSLATION

O gopīs, although our Mukunda is intelligent and very obedient to His parents, once He has fallen under the spell of the honey-sweet words of the women of Mathurā and been enchanted by their alluring, shy smiles, how will He ever return to us unsophisticated village girls?

TEXT 25

अद्य ध्रुवं तत्र दृशो भविष्यते
दाशार्हभोजान्धकवृष्णिसात्वताम् ।
महोत्सवः श्रीरमणं गुणास्पदं
द्रक्ष्यन्ति ये चाध्वनि देवकीसुतम् ॥ २५ ॥

adya dhruvaṁ tatra dṛśo bhaviṣyate
dāśārha-bhojāndhaka-vṛṣṇi-sātvatām
mahotsavaḥ śrī-ramaṇaṁ guṇāspadaṁ
drakṣyanti ye cādhvani devakī-sutam

adya—today; *dhruvam*—certainly; *tatra*—there; *dṛśaḥ*—for the eyes; *bhaviṣyate*—there will be; *dāśārha-bhoja-andhaka-vṛṣṇi-sātvatām*—of the members of the Dāśārha, Bhoja, Andhaka, Vṛṣṇi and Sātvata clans; *mahā-utsavaḥ*—a great festivity; *śrī*—of the goddess of fortune; *ramaṇam*—the darling; *guṇa*—of all transcendental qualities; *āspadam*—the reservoir; *drakṣyanti*—they will see; *ye*—those who; *ca*—also; *adhvani*—on the road; *devakī-sutam*—Kṛṣṇa, the son of Devakī.

TRANSLATION

When the Dāśārhas, Bhojas, Andhakas, Vṛṣṇis and Sātvatas see the son of Devakī in Mathurā, they will certainly enjoy a great festival for their eyes, as will all those who see Him traveling along the road to the city. After all, He is the darling of the goddess of fortune and the reservoir of all transcendental qualities.

TEXT 26

मैतद्विधस्याकरुणस्य नाम भूद्
अक्रूर इत्येतदतीव दारुणः ।
योऽसावनाश्वास्य सुदुःखितं जनं
प्रियात्प्रियं नेष्यति पारमध्वनः ॥ २६ ॥

maitad-vidhasyākaruṇasya nāma bhūd
akrūra ity etad atīva dāruṇaḥ
yo'sāv anāśvāsya su-duḥkhitam janaṁ
priyāt priyaṁ neṣyati pāram adhvanaḥ

mā—should not; *etat-vidhasya*—of such; *akaruṇasya*—an unkind person; *nāma*—the name; *bhūt*—be; *akrūraḥ iti*—"Akrūra"; *etat*—this; *atīva*—extremely; *dāruṇaḥ*—cruel; *yaḥ*—who; *asau*—he; *anāśvāsya*—not consoling; *su-duḥkhitam*—who are very miserable; *janam*—people; *priyāt*—than the most dear; *priyam*—dear (Kṛṣṇa); *neṣyati*—will take; *pāram adhvanaḥ*—beyond our sight.

TRANSLATION

He who is doing this merciless deed should not be called Akrūra. He is so extremely cruel that without even trying to console the sorrowful residents of Vraja, he is taking away Kṛṣṇa, who is more dear to us than life itself.

TEXT 27

अनार्द्रधीरेष समास्थितो रथं
तमन्वमी च त्वरयन्ति दुर्मदाः ।
गोपा अनोभिः स्थविरैरुपेक्षितं
दैवं च नोऽद्य प्रतिकूलमीहते ॥ २७ ॥

anārdra-dhīr eṣa samāsthito rathaṁ
tam anv amī ca tvarayanti durmadāḥ
gopā anobhiḥ sthavirair upekṣitaṁ
daivaṁ ca no'dya pratikūlam īhate

anārdra-dhīḥ—hard-hearted; *eṣaḥ*—this (Kṛṣṇa); *samāsthitaḥ*—having mounted; *ratham*—the chariot; *tam*—Him; *anu*—following; *amī*—these; *ca*—and; *tvarayanti*—hurry; *durmadāḥ*—befooled; *gopāḥ*—cowherds; *anobhiḥ*—in their bullock carts; *sthaviraiḥ*—by the elders; *upekṣitam*—disregarded; *daivam*—fate; *ca*—and; *naḥ*—with us; *adya*—today; *pratikūlam*—unfavorably; *īhate*—is acting.

TRANSLATION

Hard-hearted Kṛṣṇa has already mounted the chariot, and now the foolish cowherds are hurrying after Him in their bullock carts. Even the elders are saying nothing to stop Him. Today fate is working against us.

PURPORT

Śrīla Śrīdhara Svāmī reveals what the *gopīs* thought: "These foolish cowherd men and elders are not even trying to stop Kṛṣṇa. Don't they realize they are committing suicide? They are helping Kṛṣṇa go to Mathurā, but they will have to come back to Vṛndāvana and will certainly die in His absence. The whole world has become nonsensical."

TEXT 28

निवारयामः समुपेत्य माधवं
किं नोऽकरिष्यन् कुलवृद्धबान्धवाः ।
मुकुन्दसंगान्निमिषार्धदुस्त्यजाद्
दैवेन विध्वंसितदीनचेतसाम् ॥ २८ ॥

nivārayāmaḥ samupetya mādhavaṁ
kiṁ no'kariṣyan kula-vṛddha-bāndhavāḥ
mukunda-saṅgān nimiṣārdha-dustyajād
daivena vidhvaṁsita-dīna-cetasām

nivārayāmaḥ—let us stop; *samupetya*—going up to Him; *mādhavam*—Kṛṣṇa; *kim*—what; *naḥ*—to us; *akariṣyan*—will do; *kula*—of the family; *vṛddha*—the elders; *bāndhavāḥ*—and our relatives; *mukunda-saṅgāt*—

from the association of Lord Mukunda; *nimiṣa*—of the wink of an eye; *ardha*—for one half; *dustyajāt*—which is impossible to give up; *daivena*—by fate; *vidhvaṁsita*—separated; *dīna*—wretched; *cetasām*—whose hearts.

TRANSLATION

Let us directly approach Mādhava and stop Him from going. What can our family elders and other relatives do to us? Now that fate is separating us from Mukunda, our hearts are already wretched, for we cannot bear to give up His association even for a fraction of a second.

PURPORT

Śrīla Viśvanātha Cakravartī describes what the *gopīs* thought: "Let us go right up to Kṛṣṇa and pull at His clothes and hands and insist that He get down from His chariot and stay here with us. We will tell Him, 'Don't bring upon Yourself the sinful reaction for murdering so many women!'"

"But if we do that," said other *gopīs,* "our relatives and the village elders will discover our secret love for Kṛṣṇa and abandon us."

"But what can they do to us?"

"Yes, our lives are already wretched now that Kṛṣṇa is leaving. We have nothing to lose."

"That's right. We will remain in the Vṛndāvana forest just like presiding goddesses, and then we can fulfill our true desire—to stay with Kṛṣṇa in the forest."

"Yes, and even if the elders and our relatives punish us by beating us or locking us up, we can still live happily with the knowledge that Kṛṣṇa is residing in our village. Some of our girlfriends who are not imprisoned will cleverly find a way to bring us the remnants of Kṛṣṇa's food, and then we can remain alive. But if Kṛṣṇa is not stopped, we will certainly die."

TEXT 29

यस्यानुरागललितस्मितवल्गुमन्त्र-
लीलावलोकपरिरम्भणरासगोष्ठाम् ।
नीताः स्म नः क्षणमिव क्षणदा विना तं
गोप्यः कथं न्वतितरेम तमो दुरन्तम् ॥ २९ ॥

yasyānurāga-lalita-smita-valgu-mantra
līlāvaloka-parirambhaṇa-rāsa-goṣṭhām

nītāḥ sma naḥ kṣaṇam iva kṣaṇadā vinā taṁ
gopyaḥ kathaṁ nv atitarema tamo durantam

yasya—whose; *anurāga*—with loving affection; *lalita*—charming; *smita*—(where there were) smiles; *valgu*—attractive; *mantra*—intimate discussions; *līlā*—playful; *avaloka*—glances; *parirambhaṇa*—and embraces; *rāsa*—of the *rāsa* dance; *goṣṭhām*—to the assembly; *nītāḥ sma*—who were brought; *naḥ*—for us; *kṣaṇam*—a moment; *iva*—like; *kṣaṇadāḥ*—the nights; *vinā*—without; *tam*—Him; *gopyaḥ*—O *gopīs; katham*—how; *nu*—indeed; *atitarema*—will we cross over; *tamaḥ*—the darkness; *durantam*—insurmountable.

TRANSLATION

When He brought us to the assembly of the rāsa dance, where we enjoyed His affectionate and charming smiles, His delightful secret talks, His playful glances and His embraces, we passed many nights as if they were a single moment. O gopīs, how can we possibly cross over the insurmountable darkness of His absence?

PURPORT

For the *gopīs,* a long time in Kṛṣṇa's association passed like a moment, and a single moment in His absence seemed like a very long time.

TEXT 30

योऽह्नः क्षये व्रजमनन्तसखः परीतो
गोपैर्विशन् खुररजश्छुरितालकस्रक् ।
वेणुं क्वणन् स्मितकटाक्षनिरीक्षणेन
चित्तं क्षिणोत्यमुमृते नु कथं भवेम ॥ ३० ॥

yo 'hnaḥ kṣaye vrajam ananta-sakhaḥ parīto
gopair viśan khura-rajaś-churitālaka-srak
veṇuṁ kvaṇan smita-kaṭākṣa-nirīkṣaṇena
cittaṁ kṣiṇoty amum ṛte nu kathaṁ bhavema

yaḥ—who; *ahnaḥ*—of the day; *kṣaye*—at the demise; *vrajam*—the village of Vraja; *ananta*—of Ananta, Lord Balarāma; *sakhaḥ*—the friend, Kṛṣṇa; *parītaḥ*—accompanied on all sides; *gopaiḥ*—by the cowherd boys; *viśan*—entering; *khura*—of the hoofprints (of the cows); *rajaḥ*—with the dust; *chu-*

rita—smeared; *alaka*—the locks of His hair; *srak*—and His garlands; *veṇum*—His flute; *kvaṇan*—playing; *smita*—smiling; *kaṭa-akṣa*—from the corners of His eyes; *nirīkṣaṇena*—with glances; *cittam*—our minds; *kṣiṇoti*—He destroys; *amum*—Him; *ṛte*—without; *nu*—indeed; *katham*—how; *bhavema*—we can exist.

TRANSLATION

How can we exist without Ananta's friend Kṛṣṇa, who in the evening would return to Vraja in the company of the cowherd boys, His hair and garland powdered with the dust raised by the cows' hooves? As He played His flute, He would captivate our minds with His smiling sidelong glances.

TEXT 31

श्रीशुक उवाच
एवं ब्रुवाणा विरहातुरा भृशं
व्रजस्त्रियः कृष्णविषक्तमानसाः ।
विसृज्य लज्जां रुरुदुः स्म सुस्वरं
गोविन्द दामोदर माधवेति ॥ ३१ ॥

śrī-śuka uvāca
evaṁ bruvāṇā virahāturā bhṛśaṁ
vraja-striyaḥ kṛṣṇa-viṣakta-mānasāḥ
visṛjya lajjāṁ ruruduḥ sma su-svaraṁ
govinda dāmodara mādhaveti

śrī-śukaḥ uvāca—Śukadeva Gosvāmī said; *evam*—thus; *bruvāṇāḥ*—speaking; *viraha*—by feelings of separation; *āturāḥ*—distraught; *bhṛśam*—thoroughly; *vraja-striyaḥ*—the ladies of Vraja; *kṛṣṇa*—to Kṛṣṇa; *viṣakta*—attached; *mānasāḥ*—their minds; *visṛjya*—abandoning; *lajjām*—shame; *ruruduḥ sma*—they cried; *su-svaram*—loudly; *govinda dāmodara mādhava iti*—O Govinda, O Dāmodara, O Mādhava.

TRANSLATION

Śukadeva Gosvāmī said: After speaking these words, the ladies of Vraja, who were so attached to Kṛṣṇa, felt extremely agitated by their imminent separation from Him. They forgot all shame and loudly cried out, "O Govinda! O Dāmodara! O Mādhava!"

PURPORT

For a long time the *gopīs* had carefully hidden their conjugal love for Kṛṣṇa. But now that Kṛṣṇa was leaving, the *gopīs* were so distressed that they could no longer hide their feelings.

TEXT 32

स्त्रीणामेवं रुदन्तीनामुदिते सवितर्यथ ।
अक्रूरश्चोदयामास कृतमैत्रादिको रथम् ॥ ३२ ॥

strīṇām evaṁ rudantīnām
udite savitary atha
akrūraś codayām āsa
kṛta-maitrādiko ratham

strīṇām—the women; *evam*—in this manner; *rudantīnām*—while they were crying; *udite*—rising; *savitari*—the sun; *atha*—then; *akrūraḥ*—Akrūra; *codayām āsa*—started; *kṛta*—having performed; *maitra-ādikaḥ*—his morning worship and other regular duties; *ratham*—the chariot.

TRANSLATION

But even as the gopīs cried out in this way, Akrūra, having at sunrise performed His morning worship and other duties, began to drive the chariot.

PURPORT

According to some Vaiṣṇava authorities, Akrūra offended the *gopīs* by not consoling them when he took Kṛṣṇa to Mathurā, and because of this offense Akrūra was later forced to leave Dvārakā and be separated from Kṛṣṇa during the episode of the Syamantaka jewel. At that time Akrūra had to take up an ignoble residence in Vārāṇasī.

Apparently, mother Yaśodā and the other residents of Vṛndāvana were not crying like the *gopīs*, for they sincerely believed Kṛṣṇa would be coming back within a few days.

TEXT 33

गोपास्तमन्वसज्जन्त नन्दाद्याः शकटैस्ततः ।
आदायोपायनं भूरि कुम्भान् गोरससम्भृतान् ॥ ३३ ॥

gopās tam anvasajjanta
nandādyāḥ śakaṭais tataḥ
ādāyopāyanaṁ bhūri
kumbhān go-rasa-sambhṛtān

gopāḥ—the cowherd men; *tam*—Him; *anvasajjanta*—followed; *nanda-ādyāḥ*—headed by Nanda; *śakaṭaiḥ*—in their wagons; *tataḥ*—then; *ādāya*—having taken; *upāyanam*—offerings; *bhūri*—abundant; *kumbhān*—clay pots; *go-rasa*—with milk products; *sambhṛtān*—filled.

TRANSLATION

Led by Nanda Mahārāja, the cowherd men followed behind Lord Kṛṣṇa in their wagons. The men brought along many offerings for the King, including clay pots filled with ghee and other milk products.

TEXT 34

गोप्यश्च दयितं कृष्णमनुव्रज्यानुरञ्जिताः ।
प्रत्यादेशं भगवतः काङ्क्षन्त्यश्चावतस्थिरे ॥ ३४ ॥

gopyaś ca dayitaṁ kṛṣṇam
anuvrajyānurañjitāḥ
pratyādeśaṁ bhagavataḥ
kāṅkṣantyaś cāvatasthire

gopyaḥ—the *gopīs; ca*—and; *dayitam*—their beloved; *kṛṣṇam*—Kṛṣṇa; *anuvrajya*—following; *anurañjitāḥ*—pleased; *pratyādeśam*—some instruction in reply; *bhagavataḥ*—from the Lord; *kāṅkṣantyaḥ*—hoping for; *ca*—and; *avatasthire*—they stood.

TRANSLATION

[With His glances] Lord Kṛṣṇa somewhat pacified the gopīs, and they also followed behind for some time. Then, hoping He would give them some instruction, they stood still.

TEXT 35

तास्तथा तप्यतीर्वीक्ष्य स्वप्रस्थाने यदूत्तमः ।
सान्त्वयामास सप्रेमैरायास्य इति दौत्यकैः ॥ ३५ ॥

tās tathā tapyatīr vīkṣya
sva-prasthāne yadūttamaḥ
sāntvayām asa sa-premair
āyāsya iti dautyakaiḥ

tāḥ—them (the *gopīs*); *tathā*—thus; *tapyatīḥ*—lamenting; *vīkṣya*—seeing; *sva-prasthāne*—as He was leaving; *yadu-uttamaḥ*—the greatest of the Yadus; *sāntvayām āsa*—He consoled them; *sa-premaiḥ*—full of love; *āyāsye iti*—"I will return"; *dautyakaiḥ*—with words sent through a messenger.

TRANSLATION

As He departed, that best of the Yadus saw how the gopīs were lamenting, and thus He consoled them by sending a messenger with this loving promise: "I will return."

TEXT 36

यावदालक्ष्यते केतुर्यावद् रेणू रथस्य च ।
अनुप्रस्थापितात्मानो लेख्यानीवोपलक्षिताः ॥ ३६ ॥

yāvad ālakṣyate ketur
yāvad reṇū rathasya ca
anuprasthāpitātmāno
lekhyānīvopalakṣitāḥ

yāvat—as long as; *ālakṣyate*—was visible; *ketuḥ*—the flag; *yāvat*—as long as; *reṇuḥ*—the dust; *rathasya*—of the chariot; *ca*—and; *anuprasthāpita*—sending after; *ātmānaḥ*—their minds; *lekhyāni*—painted figures; *iva*—like; *upalakṣitāḥ*—they appeared.

TRANSLATION

Sending their minds after Kṛṣṇa, the gopīs stood as motionless as figures in a painting. They remained there as long as the flag atop the chariot was visible, and even until they could no longer see the dust raised by the chariot wheels.

TEXT 37

ता निराशा निववृतुर्गोविन्दविनिवर्तने ।
विशोका अहनी निन्युर्गायन्त्यः प्रियचेष्टितम् ॥ ३७ ॥

tā nirāśā nivavṛtur
govinda-vinivartane
viśokā ahanī ninyur
gāyantyaḥ priya-ceṣṭitam

tāḥ—they; *nirāśāḥ*—without hope; *nivavṛtuḥ*—turned back; *govinda-vinivartane*—of Govinda's returning; *viśokāḥ*—extremely sorrowful; *ahanī*—the days and nights; *ninyuḥ*—they spent; *gāyantyaḥ*—chanting; *priya*—of their beloved; *ceṣṭitam*—about the activities.

TRANSLATION

The gopīs then turned back, without hope that Govinda would ever return to them. Full of sorrow, they began to spend their days and nights chanting about the pastimes of their beloved.

TEXT 38

भगवानपि सम्प्राप्तो रामाक्रूरयुतो नृप ।
रथेन वायुवेगेन कालिन्दीमघनाशिनीम् ॥ ३८ ॥

bhagavān api samprāpto
rāmākrūra-yuto nṛpa
rathena vāyu-vegena
kālindīm agha-nāśinīm

bhagavān—the Supreme Lord; *api*—and; *samprāptaḥ*—arrived; *rāma-akrūra-yutaḥ*—together with Balarāma and Akrūra; *nṛpa*—O King (Parīkṣit); *rathena*—by the chariot; *vāyu*—like the wind; *vegena*—swift; *kālindīm*—at the river Kālindī (Yamunā); *agha*—sins; *nāśinīm*—which destroys.

TRANSLATION

My dear King, the Supreme Lord Kṛṣṇa, traveling as swiftly as the wind in that chariot with Lord Balarāma and Akrūra, arrived at the river Kālindī, which destroys all sins.

PURPORT

Śrīla Jīva Gosvāmī comments that Lord Kṛṣṇa secretly lamented His separation from the *gopīs.* These transcendental feelings of the Lord are part of His supreme pleasure potency.

TEXT 39

तत्रोपस्पृश्य पानीयं पीत्वा मृष्टं मणिप्रभम् ।
वृक्षषण्डमुपव्रज्य सरामो रथमाविशत् ॥ ३९ ॥

tatropaspṛśya pānīyaṁ
pītvā mṛṣṭaṁ maṇi-prabham
vṛkṣa-ṣaṇḍam upavrajya
sa-rāmo ratham āviśat

tatra—there; *upaspṛśya*—touching the water; *pānīyam*—in His hand; *pītvā*—drinking; *mṛṣṭam*—sweet; *maṇi*—like jewels; *prabham*—effulgent; *vṛkṣa*—of trees; *ṣaṇḍam*—a grove; *upavrajya*—moving up to; *sa-rāmaḥ*—with Balarāma; *ratham*—the chariot; *āviśat*—He mounted.

TRANSLATION

The river's sweet water was more effulgent than brilliant jewels. After Lord Kṛṣṇa had touched it for purification, He drank some from His hand. Then He had the chariot moved near a grove of trees and climbed back on, along with Balarāma.

TEXT 40

अक्रूरस्तावुपामन्त्र्य निवेश्य च रथोपरि ।
कालिन्द्या ह्रदमागत्य स्नानं विधिवदाचरत् ॥ ४० ॥

akrūras tāv upāmantrya
niveśya ca rathopari
kālindyā hradam āgatya
snānaṁ vidhi-vad ācarat

akrūraḥ—Akrūra; *tau*—from the two of Them; *upāmantrya*—taking permission; *niveśya*—having Them sit down; *ca*—and; *ratha-upari*—on the chariot; *kālindyāḥ*—of the Yamunā; *hradam*—to a pond; *āgatya*—going; *snānam*—his bath; *vidhi-vat*—in accordance with scriptural injunction; *ācarat*—he performed.

TRANSLATION

Akrūra asked the two Lords to take Their seats on the chariot. Then, taking Their permission, he went to a pool in the Yamunā and took his bath as enjoined in the scriptures.

TEXT 41

निमज्ज्य तस्मिन् सलिले जपन् ब्रह्म सनातनम् ।
तावेव ददृशेऽक्रूरो रामकृष्णौ समन्वितौ ॥ ४१ ॥

nimajjya tasmin salile
japan brahma sanātanam
tāv eva dadṛśe 'krūro
rāma-kṛṣṇau samanvitau

nimajjya—immersing himself; *tasmin*—in that; *salile*—water; *japan*—reciting; *brahma*—Vedic *mantras; sanātanam*—eternal; *tau*—Them; *eva*—indeed; *dadṛśe*—saw; *akrūraḥ*—Akrūra; *rāma-kṛṣṇau*—Balarāma and Kṛṣṇa; *samanvitau*—together.

TRANSLATION

While immersing himself in the water and reciting eternal mantras from the Vedas, Akrūra suddenly saw Balarāma and Kṛṣṇa before him.

TEXTS 42–43

तौ रथस्थौ कथमिह सुतावानकदुन्दुभेः ।
तर्हि स्वित्स्यन्दने न स्त इत्युन्मज्ज्य व्यचष्ट सः ॥ ४२ ॥
तत्रापि च यथापूर्वमासीनौ पुनरेव सः ।
न्यमज्जद्दर्शनं यन्मे मृषा किं सलिले तयोः ॥ ४३ ॥

tau ratha-sthau katham iha
sutāv ānakadundubheḥ
tarhi svit syandane na sta
ity unmajjya vyacaṣṭa saḥ

tatrāpi ca yathā-pūrvam
āsīnau punar eva saḥ
nyamajjad darśanaṁ yan me
mṛṣā kiṁ salile tayoḥ

tau—They; *ratha-sthau*—present on the chariot; *katham*—how; *iha*—here; *sutau*—the two sons; *ānakadundubheḥ*—of Vasudeva; *tarhi*—then; *svit*—whether; *syandane*—on the chariot; *na staḥ*—They are not there; *iti*—thinking this; *unmajjya*—rising from the water; *vyacaṣṭa*—saw; *saḥ*—he;

tatra api—in the same place; *ca*—and; *yathā*—as; *pūrvam*—previously; *āsīnau*—sitting; *punaḥ*—again; *eva*—indeed; *saḥ*—he; *nyamajjat*—entered the water; *darśanam*—the vision; *yat*—if; *me*—my; *mṛṣā*—false; *kim*—perhaps; *salile*—in the water; *tayoḥ*—of Them.

TRANSLATION

Akrūra thought, "How can the two sons of Ānakadundubhi, who are sitting in the chariot, be standing here in the water? They must have left the chariot." But when he came out of the river, there They were on the chariot, just as before. Asking himself "Was the vision I had of Them in the water an illusion?" Akrūra reentered the pool.

TEXTS 44–45

भूयस्तत्रापि सोऽद्राक्षीत्स्तूयमानमहीश्वरम् ।
सिद्धचारणगन्धर्वैरसुरैर्नतकन्धरैः ॥ ४४ ॥
सहस्रशिरसं देवं सहस्रफणमौलिनम् ।
नीलाम्बरं विसश्वेतं शृंगैः श्वेतमिव स्थितम् ॥ ४५ ॥

bhūyas tatrāpi so'drākṣīt
stūyamānam ahīśvaram
siddha-cāraṇa-gandharvair
asurair nata-kandharaiḥ

sahasra-śirasaṁ devaṁ
sahasra-phaṇa-maulinam
nīlāmbaraṁ visa-śvetaṁ
śṛṅgaiḥ śvetam iva sthitam

bhūyaḥ—again; *tatra api*—in that same place; *saḥ*—he; *adrākṣīt*—saw; *stūyamānam*—being praised; *ahi-īśvaram*—the Lord of serpents (Ananta Śeṣa, the plenary expansion of Lord Balarāma who serves as the bed of Viṣṇu); *siddha-cāraṇa-gandharvaiḥ*—by Siddhas, Cāraṇas and Gandharvas; *asuraiḥ*—and by demons; *nata*—bowed; *kandharaiḥ*—whose necks; *sahasra*—thousands; *śirasam*—having heads; *devam*—the Supreme Lord; *sahasra*—thousands; *phaṇa*—having hoods; *maulinam*—and helmets; *nīla*—blue; *ambaram*—whose clothing; *visa*—like the filaments of a lotus stem; *śvetam*—white; *śṛṅgaiḥ*—with its peaks; *śvetam*—Kailāsa Mountain; *iva*—as if; *sthitam*—situated.

TRANSLATION

There Akrūra now saw Ananta Śeṣa, the Lord of the serpents, receiving praise from Siddhas, Cāraṇas, Gandharvas and demons, who all had their heads bowed. The Personality of Godhead whom Akrūra saw had thousands of heads, thousands of hoods and thousands of helmets. His blue garment and His fair complexion, as white as the filaments of a lotus stem, made Him appear like white Kailāsa Mountain with its many peaks.

TEXTS 46–48

तस्योत्संगे घनश्यामं पीतकौशेयवाससम् ।
पुरुषं चतुर्भुजं शान्तं पद्मपत्रारुणेक्षणम् ॥ ४६ ॥
चारुप्रसन्नवदनं चारुहासनिरीक्षणम् ।
सुभ्रून्नसं चारुकर्णं सुकपोलारुणाधरम् ॥ ४७ ॥
प्रलम्बपीवरभुजं तुंगांसोरःस्थलश्रियम् ।
कम्बुकण्ठं निम्ननाभिं वलिमत्पल्लवोदरम् ॥ ४८ ॥

tasyotsaṅge ghana-śyāmaṁ
pīta-kauśeya-vāsasam
puruṣaṁ catur-bhujaṁ śāntaṁ
padma-patrāruṇekṣaṇam

cāru-prasanna-vadanaṁ
cāru-hāsa-nirīkṣaṇam
su-bhrūnnasaṁ cāru-karṇaṁ
su-kapolāruṇādharam

pralamba-pīvara-bhujaṁ
tuṅgāṁsoraḥ-sthala-śriyam
kambu-kaṇṭhaṁ nimna-nābhiṁ
valimat-pallavodaram

tasya—of Him (Ananta Śeṣa); *utsaṅge*—on the lap; *ghana*—like a rain cloud; *śyāmam*—dark blue; *pīta*—yellow; *kauśeya*—silk; *vāsasam*—whose garment; *puruṣam*—the Supreme Lord; *catuḥ-bhujam*—with four arms; *śāntam*—peaceful; *padma*—of a lotus; *patra*—like the leaves; *aruṇa*—reddish; *īkṣaṇam*—whose eyes; *cāru*—attractive; *prasanna*—cheerful; *vadanam*—whose face; *cāru*—attractive; *hāsa*—smiling; *nirīkṣaṇam*—whose glance; *su*—beautiful; *bhrū*—whose eyebrows; *ut*—raised; *nasam*

—whose nose; *cāru*—attractive; *karṇam*—whose ears; *su*—beautiful; *kapola*—whose cheeks; *aruṇa*—reddish; *adharam*—whose lips; *pralamba*—extended; *pīvara*—stout; *bhujam*—whose arms; *tuṅga*—raised; *aṁsa*—by His shoulders; *uraḥ-sthala*—and chest; *śriyam*—beautified; *kambu*—like a conchshell; *kaṇṭham*—whose throat; *nimna*—low; *nābhim*—whose navel; *vali*—lines; *mat*—having; *pallava*—like a leaf; *udaram*—whose abdomen.

TRANSLATION

Akrūra then saw the Supreme Personality of Godhead lying peacefully on the lap of Lord Ananta Śeṣa. The complexion of that Supreme Person was like a dark-blue cloud. He wore yellow garments and had four arms and reddish lotus-petal eyes. His face looked attractive and cheerful with its smiling, endearing glance and lovely eyebrows, its raised nose and finely formed ears, and its beautiful cheeks and reddish lips. The Lord's broad shoulders and expansive chest were beautiful, and His arms long and stout. His neck resembled a conchshell, His navel was deep, and His abdomen bore lines like those on a banyan leaf.

TEXTS 49–50

बृहत्कटितटश्रोणिकरभोरुद्वयान्वितम् ।
चारुजानुयुगं चारुजङ्घायुगलसंयुतम् ॥ ४९ ॥
तुंगगुल्फारुणनखव्रातदीधितिभिर्वृतम् ।
नवांगुल्यंगुष्ठदलैर्विलसत्पादपंकजम् ॥ ५० ॥

bṛhat-kaṭi-taṭa-śroṇi
karabhoru-dvayānvitam
cāru-jānu-yugaṁ cāru
jaṅghā-yugala-saṁyutam

tuṅga-gulphāruṇa-nakha
vrāta-dīdhitibhir vṛtam
navāṅguly-aṅguṣṭha-dalair
vilasat-pāda-paṅkajam

bṛhat—large; *kaṭi-taṭa*—whose loins; *śroṇi*—and hips; *karabha*—like an elephant's trunk; *ūru*—of thighs; *dvaya*—a pair; *anvitam*—having; *cāru*—attractive; *jānu-yugam*—whose two knees; *cāru*—attractive; *jaṅghā*—of shanks; *yugala*—a pair; *saṁyutam*—having; *tuṅga*—high; *gulpha*—whose ankles; *aruṇa*—reddish; *nakha-vrāta*—from whose toenails; *dīdhitibhiḥ*—with effulgent rays; *vṛtam*—surrounded; *nava*—soft; *aṅguli-aṅguṣṭha*—the two big toes and other toes; *dalaiḥ*—like flower petals; *vilasat*—glowing; *pāda-paṅkajam*—whose lotus feet.

TRANSLATION

He had large loins and hips, thighs like an elephant's trunk, and shapely knees and shanks. His raised ankles reflected the brilliant effulgence emanating from the nails on His petallike toes, which beautified His lotus feet.

TEXTS 51–52

सुमहार्हमणिव्रातकिरीटकटकांगदैः ।
कटिसूत्रब्रह्मसूत्रहारनूपुरकुण्डलैः ॥ ५१ ॥
भ्राजमानं पद्मकरं शंखचक्रगदाधरम् ।
श्रीवत्सवक्षसं भ्राजत्कौस्तुभं वनमालिनम् ॥ ५२ ॥

su-mahārha-maṇi-vrāta
kirīṭa-kaṭakāṅgadaiḥ
kaṭi-sūtra-brahma-sūtra
hāra-nūpura-kuṇḍalaiḥ

bhrājamānaṁ padma-karaṁ
śaṅkha-cakra-gadā-dharam
śrīvatsa-vakṣasaṁ bhrājat
kaustubhaṁ vana-mālinam

su-mahā—greatly; *arha*—precious; *maṇi-vrāta*—having many gems; *kirīṭa*—with helmets; *kaṭaka*—bracelets; *aṅgadaiḥ*—and armlets; *kaṭi-sūtra*—with belt; *brahma-sūtra*—sacred thread; *hāra*—necklaces; *nūpura*—ankle bells; *kuṇḍalaiḥ*—and earrings; *bhrājamānam*—effulgent; *padma*—carrying a lotus; *karam*—whose hand; *śaṅkha*—a conchshell; *cakra*—discus; *gadā*—and club; *dharam*—holding; *śrīvatsa*—carrying the mark known as Śrīvatsa; *vakṣasam*—whose chest; *bhrājat*—brilliant; *kaustubham*—with the Kaustubha gem; *vana-mālinam*—with a flower garland.

TRANSLATION

Adorned with a helmet, bracelets and armlets, which were all bedecked with many priceless jewels, and also with a belt, a sacred thread, necklaces,

ankle bells and earrings, the Lord shone with dazzling effulgence. In one hand He held a lotus flower, in the others a conchshell, discus and club. Gracing His chest were the Śrīvatsa mark, the brilliant Kaustubha gem and a flower garland.

TEXTS 53–55

सुनन्दनन्दप्रमुखैः पर्षदैः सनकादिभिः ।
सुरेशैर्ब्रह्मरुद्राद्यैर्नवभिश्च द्विजोत्तमैः ॥ ५३ ॥
प्रह्लादनारदवसुप्रमुखैर्भागवतोत्तमैः ।
स्तूयमानं पृथग्भावैर्वचोभिरमलात्मभिः ॥ ५४ ॥
श्रिया पुष्ट्या गिरा कान्त्या कीर्त्या तुष्ट्येलयोर्जया ।
विद्ययाविद्यया शक्त्या मायया च निषेवितम् ॥ ५५ ॥

sunanda-nanda-pramukhaiḥ
parṣadaiḥ sanakādibhiḥ
sureśair brahma-rudrādyair
navabhiś ca dvijottamaiḥ

prahrāda-nārada-vasu
pramukhair bhāgavatottamaiḥ
stūyamānaṁ pṛthag-bhāvair
vacobhir amalātmabhiḥ

śriyā puṣṭyā girā kāntyā
kīrtyā tuṣṭyelayorjayā
vidyayāvidyayā śaktyā
māyayā ca niṣevitam

sunanda-nanda-pramukhaiḥ—headed by Sunanda and Nanda; *parṣadaiḥ*—by His personal attendants; *sanaka-ādibhiḥ*—by Sanaka Kumāra and his brothers; *sura-īśaiḥ*—by the chief demigods; *brahma-rudra-ādyaiḥ*—headed by Brahmā and Rudra; *navabhiḥ*—nine; *ca*—and; *dvija-uttamaiḥ*—by the chief *brāhmaṇas* (headed by Marīci); *prahrāda-nārada-vasu-pramukhaiḥ*—headed by Prahlāda, Nārada and Uparicara Vasu; *bhāgavata-uttamaiḥ*—by the most exalted devotees; *stūyamānam*—being praised; *pṛthak-bhāvaiḥ*—by each in a different loving attitude; *vacobhiḥ*—with words; *amala-ātmabhiḥ*—sanctified; *śriyā puṣṭyā girā kāntyā kīrtyā tuṣṭyā ilayā ūrjayā*—by His internal potencies Śrī, Puṣṭi, Gīr, Kānti, Kīrti, Tuṣṭi, Ilā and Ūrjā; *vidyayā avidyayā*—by His potencies of knowledge and ignorance; *śaktyā*—by His internal pleasure potency; *māyayā*—by His material creative potency; *ca*—and; *niṣevitam*—being served.

TRANSLATION

Encircling the Lord and worshiping Him were Nanda, Sunanda and His other personal attendants; Sanaka and the other Kumāras; Brahmā, Rudra and other chief demigods; the nine chief brāhmaṇas; and the best of the saintly devotees, headed by Prahlāda, Nārada and Uparicara Vasu. Each of these great personalities was worshiping the Lord by chanting sanctified words of praise in his own unique mood. Also in attendance were the Lord's principal internal potencies—Śrī, Puṣṭi, Gīr, Kānti, Kīrti, Tuṣṭi, Ilā and Ūrjā—as were His material potencies Vidyā, Avidyā and Māyā, and His internal pleasure potency, Śakti.

PURPORT

Śrīla Viśvanātha Cakravartī explains the Lord's potencies mentioned in these verses: "Śrī is the potency of wealth; Puṣṭi that of strength; Gīr, knowledge; Kānti, beauty; Kīrti, fame; and Tuṣṭi, renunciation. These are the Lord's six opulences. Ilā is His *bhū-śakti,* also known as *sandhinī,* the internal potency of whom the element earth is an expansion. Ūrjā is His internal potency for performing pastimes; she expands as the *tulasī* plant in this world. Vidyā and Avidyā [knowledge and ignorance] are external potencies who cause the living entities' liberation and bondage, respectively. Śakti is His internal pleasure potency, *hlādinī,* and Māyā is an internal potency who is the basis of Vidyā and Avidyā. The word *ca* implies the presence of the Lord's marginal energy, the *jīva-śakti,* who is subordinate to Māyā. Lord Viṣṇu was being served by all these personified potencies."

TEXTS 56–57

विलोक्य सुभृशं प्रीतो भक्त्या परमया युतः ।
हृष्यत्तनूरुहो भावपरिक्लिन्नात्मलोचनः ॥ ५६ ॥
गिरा गद्गदयास्तौषीत्सत्त्वमालम्ब्य सात्वतः ।
प्रणम्य मूर्ध्नावहितः कृताञ्जलिपुटः शनैः ॥ ५७ ॥

vilokya su-bhṛśaṁ prīto
bhaktyā paramayā yutaḥ

hṛṣyat-tanūruho bhāva-
pariklinnātma-locanaḥ

girā gadgadayāstauṣīt
sattvam ālambya sātvataḥ
praṇamya mūrdhnāvahitaḥ
kṛtāñjali-puṭaḥ śanaiḥ

vilokya—(Akrūra) seeing; *su-bhṛśam*—greatly; *prītaḥ*—pleased; *bhaktyā*—with devotion; *paramayā*—supreme; *yutaḥ*—enthused; *hṛṣyat*—standing on end; *tanū-ruhaḥ*—the hairs of his body; *bhāva*—out of loving ecstasy; *pariklinna*—wet; *ātma*—his body; *locanaḥ*—and eyes; *girā*—with words; *gadgadayā*—choking; *astauṣīt*—He offered homage; *sattvam*—soberness; *ālambya*—taking hold of; *sātvataḥ*—the great devotee; *praṇamya*—bowing down; *mūrdhnā*—with his head; *avahitaḥ*—attentively; *kṛta-añjali-puṭaḥ*—joining his palms in supplication; *śanaiḥ*—slowly.

TRANSLATION

As the great devotee Akrūra beheld all this, he became extremely pleased and felt enthused with transcendental devotion. His intense ecstasy caused His bodily hairs to stand on end and tears to flow from his eyes, drenching his entire body. Somehow managing to steady himself, Akrūra bowed his head to the ground. Then he joined his palms in supplication and, in a voice choked with emotion, very slowly and attentively began to pray.

Thus end the purports of the humble servants of His Divine Grace A.C. Bhaktivedanta Swami Prabhupāda to the Tenth Canto, Thirty-ninth Chapter, of the Śrīmad-Bhāgavatam, *entitled "Akrūra's Vision."*

CHAPTER FORTY

The Prayers of Akrūra

This chapter relates Akrūra's prayers to the Supreme Personality of Godhead.

Akrūra prayed, "Brahmā, who created this visible world, emanated from the lotus navel of the Supreme Lord. The five elements of physical nature, the five corresponding objects of perception, the ten senses, the ego, the total nature, the primeval creator and the demigods all originate from His bodily limbs. He cannot be known by sensory knowledge, and thus even Brahmā and the other demigods are ignorant of His real identity."

"Different classes of people worship the Supreme Personality of Godhead in different ways. Fruitive workers worship Him by performing Vedic sacrifices, philosophers by renouncing material work and pursuing spiritual knowledge, *yogīs* by meditating, Śaivites by worshiping Lord Śiva, Vaiṣṇavas by following the injunctions of such scriptures as the *Pañcarātra,* and other saintly persons by worshiping Him as the original form of the self, of the material substance and of the controlling demigods. Just as rivers flow from various directions into the ocean, the worship of those who dedicate themselves to these various entities finds its ultimate purpose within the Supreme Lord Viṣṇu."

"The form of the total universe, the Virāṭ-rūpa, is imagined to be the form of Lord Viṣṇu. Like aquatics moving about in water or like tiny insects burrowing in an *udumbara* fruit, all living beings move about within the Lord. These living beings, bewildered by His Māyā, wander along the path of material work, falsely identifying with body, home and so forth. Under the sway of illusion, a foolish person may overlook a reservoir of water covered by grass and leaves and instead run after a mirage. Similarly, living beings caught in the grip of ignorance abandon Lord Viṣṇu and become attached to their bodies, homes and so on. Such faithful servants of their senses cannot take shelter of the Supreme Lord's lotus feet. Only if, by His mercy, they get the association of saintly devotees will their material entanglement end. Only then can they develop Kṛṣṇa consciousness by serving the Lord's pure devotees."

TEXT 1

श्रीअक्रूर उवाच
नतोऽस्म्यहं त्वाखिलहेतुहेतुं
नारायणं पूरुषमाद्यमव्ययम् ।
यन्नाभिजातादरविन्दकोषाद्
ब्रह्माविरासीद्यत एष लोकः ॥ १ ॥

śrī-akrūra uvāca
nato'smy ahaṁ tvākhila-hetu-hetuṁ
nārāyaṇaṁ pūruṣam ādyam avyayam
yan-nābhi-jātād aravinda-koṣād
brahmāvirāsīd yata eṣa lokaḥ

śrī-akrūraḥ uvāca—Śrī Akrūra said; *nataḥ*—bowed down; *asmi*—am; *aham*—I; *tvā*—to You; *akhila*—of all; *hetu*—causes; *hetum*—the cause; *nārāyaṇam*—Lord Nārāyaṇa; *pūruṣam*—the Supreme Person; *ādyam*—original; *avyayam*—inexhaustible; *yat*—from whose; *nābhi*—navel; *jātāt*—which was generated; *aravinda*—of a lotus plant; *koṣāt*—from the whorl; *brahmā*—Brahmā; *avirāsīt*—appeared; *yataḥ*—from whom; *eṣaḥ*—this; *lokaḥ*—world.

TRANSLATION

Śrī Akrūra said: I bow down to You, the cause of all causes, the original and inexhaustible Supreme Person, Nārāyaṇa. From the whorl of the lotus born from Your navel, Brahmā appeared, and by his agency this universe has come into being.

TEXT 2

भूस्तोयमग्निः पवनं खमादिर्
महानजादिर्मन इन्द्रियाणि ।
सर्वेन्द्रियार्था विबुधाश्च सर्वे
ये हेतवस्ते जगतोऽंगभूताः ॥ २ ॥

bhūs toyam agniḥ pavanaṁ kham ādir
mahān ajādir mana indriyāṇi
sarvendriyārthā vibudhāś ca sarve
ye hetavas te jagato'ṅga-bhūtāḥ

bhūḥ—earth; *toyam*—water; *agniḥ*—fire; *pavanam*—air; *kham*—ether; *ādiḥ*—and its source, false ego; *mahān*—the *mahat-tattva; ajā*—the total material nature; *ādiḥ*—her source, the Supreme Lord; *manaḥ*—the mind; *indriyāṇi*—the senses; *sarva-indriya*—of all the senses; *arthāḥ*—the objects; *vibudhāḥ*—the demigods; *ca*—and; *sarve*—all; *ye*—which; *hetavaḥ*—causes; *te*—Your; *jagataḥ*—of the universe; *aṅga*—from the body; *bhūtāḥ*—generated.

TRANSLATION

Earth; water; fire; air; ether and its source, false ego; the mahat-tattva; the total material nature and her source, the Supreme Lord's puruṣa expansion; the mind; the senses; the sense objects; and the senses' presiding deities—all these causes of the cosmic manifestation are born from Your transcendental body.

TEXT 3

नैते स्वरूपं विदुरात्मनस्ते
ह्यजादयोऽनात्मतया गृहीताः ।
अजोऽनुबद्धः स गुणैरजाया
गुणात्परं वेद न ते स्वरूपम् ॥ ३ ॥

naite svarūpaṁ vidur ātmanas te
hy ajādayo 'nātmatayā gṛhītāḥ
ajo 'nubaddhaḥ sa guṇair ajāyā
guṇāt paraṁ veda na te svarūpam

na—do not; *ete*—these (elements of creation); *svarūpam*—the true identity; *viduḥ*—know; *ātmanaḥ*—of the Supreme Soul; *te*—You; *hi*—indeed; *ajā-ādayaḥ*—headed by the total material nature; *anātmatayā*—by the status of being nonliving matter; *gṛhītāḥ*—seized; *ajaḥ*—Lord Brahmā; *anubaddhaḥ*—bound up; *saḥ*—he; *guṇaiḥ*—by the modes; *ajāyāḥ*—of material nature; *guṇāt*—to these modes; *param*—transcendental; *veda na*—he does not know; *te*—Your; *svarūpam*—true form.

TRANSLATION

The total material nature and these other elements of creation certainly cannot know You as You are, for they are manifested in the realm of dull matter. Since You are beyond the modes of nature, even Lord Brahmā, who is bound up in these modes, does not know Your true identity.

PURPORT

God is transcendental to material nature. Unless we also transcend the limited consciousness of material existence, we cannot know Him. Even the greatest living entity in the universe, Brahmā, cannot understand the Supreme unless he comes to the platform of pure Kṛṣṇa consciousness.

TEXT 4

त्वां योगिनो यजन्त्यद्धा महापुरुषमीश्वरम् ।
साध्यात्मं साधिभूतं च साधिदैवं च साधवः ॥ ४ ॥

tvāṁ yogino yajanty addhā
mahā-puruṣam īśvaram
sādhyātmaṁ sādhibhūtaṁ ca
sādhidaivaṁ ca sādhavaḥ

tvām—for You; *yoginaḥ*—*yogīs; yajanti*—perform sacrifice; *addhā*—certainly; *mahā-puruṣam*—for the Supreme Personality; *īśvaram*—the Godhead; *sa-adhyātmam*—(the witness of) the living entities; *sa-adhibhūtam*—of the material elements; *ca*—and; *sa-adhidaivam*—of the controlling demigods; *ca*—and; *sādhavaḥ*—purified persons.

TRANSLATION

Pure yogīs worship You, the Supreme Personality of Godhead, by conceiving of You in the threefold form comprising the living entities, the material elements that constitute the living entities' bodies, and the controlling deities of those elements.

TEXT 5

त्रय्या च विद्यया केचित्त्वां वै वैतानिका द्विजाः ।
यजन्ते विततैर्यज्ञैर्नानारूपामराख्यया ॥ ५ ॥

trayyā ca vidyayā kecit
tvāṁ vai vaitānikā dvijāḥ
yajante vitatair yajñair
nānā-rūpāmarākhyayā

trayyā—of the three *Vedas; ca*—and; *vidyayā*—by the *mantras; kecit*—some; *tvām*—You; *vai*—indeed; *vaitānikāḥ*—who respect the regulations of the three sacred fires; *dvijāḥ*—*brāhmaṇas; yajante*—worship; *vitataiḥ*—elaborate; *yajñaiḥ*—with ritual sacrifices; *nānā*—various; *rūpa*—having forms; *amara*—of demigods; *ākhyayā*—by the designations.

TRANSLATION

Brāhmaṇas who follow the regulations concerning the three sacred fires worship You by chanting mantras from the three Vedas and performing elaborate fire sacrifices for the various demigods, who have many forms and names.

PURPORT

Akrūra has now described how those who follow the paths of Sāṅkhya, *yoga* and the three *Vedas* worship the Supreme Lord in different ways. In the various places where the *Vedas* appear to recommend that one worship Indra, Varuṇa and other demigods, these demigods are stated to be supreme. But at the same time the *Vedas* state that there is one supreme controller, the Absolute Truth. That is Śrī Kṛṣṇa, the Personality of Godhead, who expands His potency through material creation into the forms of the demigods. Thus worship of the demigods goes to Him through the indirect method of *karma-kāṇḍa,* or fruitive religious rituals. Ultimately, however, one who wants to achieve eternal perfection should worship the Lord directly, in full Kṛṣṇa consciousness.

TEXT 6

एके त्वाखिलकर्माणि संन्यस्योपशमं गताः ।
ज्ञानिनो ज्ञानयज्ञेन यजन्ति ज्ञानविग्रहम् ॥ ६ ॥

eke tvākhila-karmāṇi
sannyasyopaśamaṁ gatāḥ
jñānino jñāna-yajñena
yajanti jñāna-vigraham

eke—some; *tvā*—to You; *akhila*—all; *karmāṇi*—activities; *sannyasya*—resigning; *upaśamam*—peace; *gatāḥ*—attaining; *jñāninaḥ*—pursuers of knowledge; *jñāna-yajñena*—by the sacrifice of cultivating knowledge; *yajanti*—they worship; *jñāna-vigraham*—the embodiment of knowledge.

TRANSLATION

In pursuit of spiritual knowledge, some persons renounce all material activities and, having thus become peaceful, perform the sacrifice of philosophic investigation to worship You, the original form of all knowledge.

PURPORT

Modern philosophers pursue knowledge without bothering to worship the Supreme Personality of Godhead, and thus they naturally end up with meager, if not trivial, results.

TEXT 7

अन्ये च संस्कृतात्मानो विधिनाभिहितेन ते ।
यजन्ति त्वन्मयास्त्वां वै बहुमूर्त्येकमूर्तिकम् ॥ ७॥

anye ca saṁskṛtātmāno
vidhinābhihitena te
yajanti tvan-mayās tvāṁ vai
bahu-mūrty-eka-mūrtikam

anye—others; *ca*—and; *saṁskṛta*—purified; *ātmānaḥ*—whose intelligence; *vidhinā*—by the injunctions (of such scriptures as the *Pañcarātra*); *abhihitena*—presented; *te*—by You; *yajanti*—worship; *tvat-mayāḥ*—filled with thought of You; *tvām*—You; *vai*—indeed; *bahu-mūrti*—having many forms; *eka-mūrtikam*—having one form.

TRANSLATION

And yet others—those whose intelligence is pure—follow the injunctions of Vaiṣṇava scriptures promulgated by You. Absorbing their minds in thought of You, they worship You as the one Supreme Lord manifesting in multiple forms.

PURPORT

The word *saṁskṛtātmānaḥ,* "they whose intelligence is pure," is significant here. It implies that the worshipers mentioned before have not completely purified their intelligence of material contamination and thus worship the Lord indirectly. Those who are purified, however, directly worship the Lord, either as the Supreme Personality of Godhead, Lord Kṛṣṇa, or as one of His various plenary forms, such as Vāsudeva, Saṅkarṣaṇa, Pradyumna or Aniruddha, as indicated here.

TEXT 8

त्वामेवान्ये शिवोक्तेन मार्गेण शिवरूपिणम् ।
बह्वाचार्यविभेदेन भगवन्तमुपासते ॥ ८ ॥

tvām evānye śivoktena
mārgeṇa śiva-rūpiṇam
bahv-ācārya-vibhedena
bhagavantam upāsate

tvām—You; *eva*—also; *anye*—others; *śiva*—by Lord Śiva; *uktena*—spoken; *mārgeṇa*—by the path; *śiva-rūpiṇam*—in the form of Lord Śiva; *bahu-ācārya*—of many teachers; *vibhedena*—following the different presentations; *bhagavantam*—the Supreme Lord; *upāsate*—they worship.

TRANSLATION

There are still others, who worship You, the Supreme Lord, in the form of Lord Śiva. They follow the path described by him and interpreted in various ways by many teachers.

PURPORT

The words *tvām eva,* "You also," indicate that the path of worshiping Lord Śiva is indirect and therefore inferior. Akrūra himself is following the superior method by directly worshiping Kṛṣṇa, or Viṣṇu, with his prayers.

TEXT 9

सर्व एव यजन्ति त्वां सर्वदेवमयेश्वरम् ।
येऽप्यन्यदेवताभक्ता यद्यप्यन्यधियः प्रभो ॥ ९ ॥

sarva eva yajanti tvāṁ
sarva-deva-mayeśvaram
ye 'py anya-devatā-bhaktā
yady apy anya-dhiyaḥ prabho

sarve—all; *eva*—indeed; *yajanti*—worship; *tvam*—You; *sarva-deva*—all the demigods; *maya*—O You who comprise; *īśvaram*—the Supreme Lord;

ye—they; *api*—even; *anya*—of other; *devatā*—deities; *bhaktāḥ*—devotees; *yadi api*—although; *anya*—turned elsewhere; *dhiyaḥ*—their attention; *prabho*—O master.

TRANSLATION

But all these people, my Lord, even those who have turned their attention away from You and are worshiping other deities, are actually worshiping You alone, O embodiment of all the demigods.

PURPORT

The idea here is that even those who worship the demigods are indirectly worshiping the Supreme Lord Viṣṇu. The understanding of such worshipers, however, is imperfect.

TEXT 10

यथाद्रिप्रभवा नद्यः पर्जन्यापूरिताः प्रभो ।
विशन्ति सर्वतः सिन्धुं तद्वत्त्वां गतयोऽन्ततः ॥ १० ॥

yathādri-prabhavā nadyaḥ
parjanyāpūritāḥ prabho
viśanti sarvataḥ sindhuṁ
tadvat tvāṁ gatayo'ntataḥ

yathā—as; *adri*—from the mountains; *prabhavāḥ*—born; *nadyaḥ*—rivers; *parjanya*—by the rain; *āpūritāḥ*—filled; *prabho*—O master; *viśanti*—enter; *sarvataḥ*—from all sides; *sindhum*—the ocean; *tadvat*—similarly; *tvām*—You; *gatayaḥ*—these paths; *antataḥ*—finally.

TRANSLATION

As rivers born from the mountains and filled by the rain flow from all sides into the sea, so do all these paths in the end reach You, O master.

PURPORT

Lord Kṛṣṇa Himself speaks on this issue of worship in the *Bhagavad-gītā* (9.23–25):

ye'py anya-devatā-bhaktā
yajante śraddhayānvitāḥ

te'pi mām eva kaunteya
yayanty avidhi-pūrvakam

ahaṁ hi sarva-yajñānāṁ
bhoktā ca prabhur eva ca
na tu mām abhijānanti
tattvenātaś cyavanti te

yānti deva-vratā devān
pitṝn yānti pitṛ-vratāḥ
bhūtāni yānti bhūtejyā
yānti mad-yājino'pi mām

"Those who are devotees of other gods and who worship them with faith actually worship only Me, O son of Kuntī, but they do so in a wrong way. I am the only enjoyer and master of all sacrifices. Therefore, those who do not recognize My true transcendental nature fall down. Those who worship the demigods will take birth among the demigods; those who worship the ancestors go to the ancestors; those who worship ghosts and spirits will take birth among such beings; and those who worship Me will live with Me."

TEXT 11

सत्त्वं रजस्तम इति भवतः प्रकृतेर्गुणाः ।
तेषु हि प्राकृताः प्रोता आब्रह्मस्थावरादयः ॥ ११ ॥

sattvaṁ rajas tama iti
bhavataḥ prakṛter guṇāḥ
teṣu hi prākṛtāḥ protā
ā-brahma-sthāvarādayaḥ

sattvam—goodness; *rajaḥ*—passion; *tamaḥ*—ignorance; *iti*—thus known; *bhavataḥ*—Your; *prakṛteḥ*—of the material nature; *guṇāḥ*—the qualities; *teṣu*—to them; *hi*—certainly; *prākṛtāḥ*—the conditioned living entities; *protāḥ*—woven; *ā-brahma*—up to Lord Brahmā; *sthāvara-ādayaḥ*—starting with the nonmoving creatures.

TRANSLATION

Goodness, passion and ignorance, the qualities of Your material nature, entangle all conditioned living beings, from Brahmā down to the nonmoving creatures.

TEXT 12

तुभ्यं नमस्ते त्वविषक्तदृष्टये
सर्वात्मने सर्वधियां च साक्षिणे ।
गुणप्रवाहोऽयमविद्यया कृतः
प्रवर्तते देवनृतिर्यगात्मसु ॥ १२ ॥

tubhyaṁ namas te tv aviṣakta-dṛṣṭaye
sarvātmane sarva-dhiyāṁ ca sākṣiṇe
guṇa-pravāho'yam avidyayā kṛtaḥ
pravartate deva-nṛ-tiryag-ātmasu

tubhyam—to You; *namaḥ*—obeisances; *te*—Your; *tu*—and; *aviṣakta*—aloof; *dṛṣṭaye*—whose vision; *sarva-ātmane*—to the Soul of all; *sarva*—of everyone; *dhiyām*—of the consciousness; *ca*—and; *sākṣiṇe*—to the witness; *guṇa*—of the material modes; *pravāhaḥ*—the flow; *ayam*—this; *avidyayā*—by the force of ignorance; *kṛtaḥ*—created; *pravartate*—goes on; *deva*—as demigods; *nṛ*—humans; *tiryak*—and animals; *ātmasu*—among those who assume the identities.

TRANSLATION

I offer My obeisances to You, who as the Supreme Soul of all beings witness everyone's consciousness with unbiased vision. The current of Your material modes, produced by the force of ignorance, flows strongly among the living beings who assume identities as demigods, humans and animals.

TEXTS 13–14

अग्निर्मुखं तेऽवनिरङ्घ्रिरीक्षणं
सूर्यो नभो नाभिरथो दिशः श्रुतिः ।
द्यौः कं सुरेन्द्रास्तव बाहवोऽर्णवाः
कुक्षिर्मरुत्प्राणबलं प्रकल्पितम् ॥ १३ ॥

रोमाणि वृक्षौषधयः शिरोरुहा
मेघाः परस्यास्थिनखानि तेऽद्रयः ।
निमेषणं रात्र्यहनी प्रजापतिर्
मेढ्रस्तु वृष्टिस्तव वीर्यमिष्यते ॥ १४ ॥

agnir mukhaṁ te'vanir aṅghrir īkṣaṇaṁ
sūryo nabho nābhir atho diśaḥ śrutiḥ
dyauḥ kaṁ surendrās tava bāhavo'rṇavāḥ
kukṣir marut prāṇa-balaṁ prakalpitam

romāṇi vṛkṣauṣadhayaḥ śiroruhā
meghāḥ parasyāsthi-nakhāni te'drayaḥ
nimeṣaṇaṁ rātry-ahanī prajāpatir
meḍhras tu vṛṣṭis tava vīryam iṣyate

agniḥ—fire; *mukham*—face; *te*—Your; *avaniḥ*—the earth; *aṅghriḥ*—feet; *ikṣaṇam*—eye; *sūryaḥ*—the sun; *nabhaḥ*—the sky; *nābhiḥ*—navel; *atha u*—and also; *diśaḥ*—the directions; *śrutiḥ*—sense of hearing; *dyauḥ*—heaven; *kam*—head; *sura-indrāḥ*—the chief demigods; *tava*—Your; *bāhavaḥ*—arms; *arṇavāḥ*—the oceans; *kukṣiḥ*—abdomen; *marut*—the wind; *prāṇa*—vital air; *balam*—and physical strength; *prakalpitam*—conceived; *romāṇi*—bodily hairs; *vṛkṣa*—the trees; *oṣadhayaḥ*—the plants; *śiraḥ-ruhāḥ*—the hair on Your head; *meghāḥ*—the clouds; *parasya*—of the Supreme; *asthi*—bones; *nakhāni*—and nails; *te*—of You; *adrayaḥ*—the mountains; *nimeṣaṇam*—the blinking of Your eyes; *rātri-ahanī*—day and night; *prajāpatiḥ*—the progenitor of mankind; *meḍhraḥ*—genitals; *tu*—and; *vṛṣṭiḥ*—the rain; *tava*—Your; *vīryam*—semen; *iṣyate*—is considered.

TRANSLATION

Fire is said to be Your face, the earth Your feet, the sun Your eye, and the sky Your navel. The directions are Your sense of hearing, the chief demigods Your arms, and the oceans Your abdomen. Heaven is thought to be Your head, and the wind Your vital air and physical strength. The trees and plants are the hairs on Your body, the clouds the hair on Your head, and the mountains the bones and nails of You, the Supreme. The passage of day and night is the blinking of Your eyes, the progenitor of mankind Your genitals, and the rain Your semen.

TEXT 15

त्वय्यव्ययात्मन् पुरुषे प्रकल्पिता
लोकाः सपाला बहुजीवसंकुलाः ।
यथा जले सञ्जिहते जलौकसो
ऽप्युदुम्बरे वा मशका मनोमये ॥ १५ ॥

tvayy avyayātman puruṣe prakalpitā
lokāḥ sa-pālā bahu-jīva-saṅkulāḥ
yathā jale sañjihate jalaukaso
'py udumbare vā maśakā mano-maye

tvayi—within You; *avyaya-ātman*—their inexhaustible one; *puruṣe*—the Supreme Personality of Godhead; *prakalpitāḥ*—created; *lokāḥ*—the worlds; *sa-pālāḥ*—together with their protecting demigods; *bahu*—with many; *jīva*—living beings; *saṅkulāḥ*—crowded; *yathā*—just as; *jale*—in water; *sañjihate*—move about; *jala-okasaḥ*—aquatic animals; *api*—indeed; *udumbare*—in an *udumbara* fruit (a kind of fig); *vā*—or; *maśakāḥ*—small biting insects; *manaḥ*—the mind (and other senses); *maye*—(in You) who comprise.

TRANSLATION

All the worlds, with their presiding demigods and teeming populations, originate in You, the inexhaustible Supreme Personality of Godhead. These worlds travel within You, the basis of the mind and senses, just as aquatics swim in the sea or tiny insects burrow within an udumbara fruit.

TEXT 16

यानि यानीह रूपाणि क्रीडनार्थं बिभर्षि हि।
तैरामृष्टशुचो लोका मुदा गायन्ति ते यशः ॥ १६ ॥

yāni yānīha rūpāṇi
krīḍanārthaṁ bibharṣi hi
tair āmṛṣṭa-śuco lokā
mudā gāyanti te yaśaḥ

yāni yāni—which various; *iha*—in this material world; *rūpāṇi*—forms; *krīḍana*—of play; *artham*—for the sake; *bibharṣi*—You manifest; *hi*—indeed; *taiḥ*—by them; *āmṛṣṭa*—cleansed; *śucaḥ*—of their unhappiness; *lokāḥ*—people; *mudā*—joyfully; *gāyanti*—sing; *te*—Your; *yaśaḥ*—glories.

TRANSLATION

To enjoy Your pastimes You manifest Yourself in various forms in this material world, and these incarnations cleanse away all the unhappiness of those who joyfully chant Your glories.

TEXTS 17–18

नमः कारणमत्स्याय प्रलयाब्धिचराय च ।
हयशीर्ष्णे नमस्तुभ्यं मधुकैटभमृत्यवे ॥ १७ ॥
अकूपाराय बृहते नमो मन्दरधारिणे ।
क्षित्युद्धारविहाराय नमः शूकरमूर्तये ॥ १८ ॥

namaḥ kāraṇa-matsyāya
pralayābdhi-carāya ca
hayaśīrṣṇe namas tubhyaṁ
madhu-kaiṭabha-mṛtyave

akūpārāya bṛhate
namo mandara-dhāriṇe
kṣity-uddhāra-vihārāya
namaḥ śūkara-mūrtaye

namaḥ—obeisances; *kāraṇa*—who is the original cause of creation; *matsyāya*—to the Supreme Lord's appearance as a fish; *pralaya*—of annihilation; *abdhi*—in the ocean; *carāya*—who moved about; *ca*—and; *haya-śīrṣṇe*—to the incarnation who appeared with the head of a horse; *namaḥ*—obeisances; *tubhyam*—to You; *madhu-kaiṭabha*—of the demons Madhu and Kaiṭabha; *mṛtyave*—to the killer; *akūpārāya*—to the tortoise; *bṛhate*—huge; *namaḥ*—obeisances; *mandara*—of Mandara Mountain; *dhāriṇe*—to the holder; *kṣiti*—of the earth; *uddhāra*—the lifting up; *vihārāya*—whose pleasure; *namaḥ*—obeisances; *śūkara*—of a boar; *mūrtaye*—to the form.

TRANSLATION

I offer my obeisances to You, the cause of the creation, Lord Matsya, who swam about in the ocean of dissolution, to Lord Hayagrīva, the killer of Madhu and Kaiṭabha, to the immense tortoise [Lord Kūrma], who supported Mandara Mountain, and to the boar incarnation [Lord Varāha], who enjoyed lifting the earth.

PURPORT

The *Viśva-kośa* dictionary states that the word *akūpārāya* indicates the king of tortoises.

TEXT 19

नमस्तेऽद्भुतसिंहाय साधुलोकभयापह ।
वामनाय नमस्तुभ्यं क्रान्तत्रिभुवनाय च ॥ १९ ॥

namas te'dbhuta-siṁhāya
sādhu-loka-bhayāpaha
vāmanāya namas tubhyaṁ
krānta-tribhuvanāya ca

namaḥ—obeisances; *te*—to You; *adbhuta*—amazing; *siṁhāya*—to the lion; *sādhu-loka*—of all saintly devotees; *bhaya*—of the fear; *apaha*—O remover; *vāmanāya*—to the dwarf; *namaḥ*—obeisances; *tubhyam*—to You; *krānta*—who stepped over; *tri-bhuvanāya*—the three planetary systems of the universe; *ca*—and.

TRANSLATION

Obeisances to You, the amazing lion [Lord Nṛsiṁha], who remove Your saintly devotees' fear, and to the dwarf Vāmana, who stepped over the three worlds.

TEXT 20

नमो भृगूणां पतये दृप्तक्षत्रवनच्छिदे ।
नमस्ते रघुवर्याय रावणान्तकराय च ॥ २० ॥

namo bhṛgūṇāṁ pataye
dṛpta-kṣatra-vana-cchide
namas te raghu-varyāya
rāvaṇānta-karāya ca

namaḥ—obeisances; *bhṛgūṇām*—of the descendants of Bhṛgu; *pataye*—to the chief (Lord Paraśurāma); *dṛpta*—conceited; *kṣatra*—of the members of the royal order; *vana*—the forest; *chide*—who cut down; *namaḥ*—obeisances; *te*—to You; *raghu-varyāya*—the best of the descendants of Raghu; *rāvaṇa*—of Rāvaṇa; *anta-karāya*—who put an end; *ca*—and.

TRANSLATION

Obeisances to You, Lord of the Bhṛgus, who cut down the forest of the conceited royal order, and to Lord Rāma, the best of the Raghu dynasty, who put an end to the demon Rāvaṇa.

TEXT 21

नमस्ते वासुदेवाय नमः संकर्षणाय च ।
प्रद्युम्नायानिरुद्धाय सात्वतां पतये नमः ॥ २१ ॥

namas te vāsudevāya
namaḥ saṅkarṣaṇāya ca
pradyumnāyāniruddhāya
sātvatāṁ pataye namaḥ

namaḥ—obeisances; *te*—unto You; *vāsudevāya*—Lord Śrī Vāsudeva; *namaḥ*—obeisances; *saṅkarṣaṇāya*—to Lord Saṅkarṣaṇa; *ca*—and; *pradyumnāya*—to Lord Pradyumna; *aniruddhāya*—and to Lord Aniruddha; *sātvatām*—of the Yādavas; *pataye*—to the chief; *namaḥ*—obeisances.

TRANSLATION

Obeisances to You, Lord of the Sātvatas, and to Your forms of Vāsudeva, Saṅkarṣaṇa, Pradyumna and Aniruddha.

TEXT 22

नमो बुद्धाय शुद्धाय दैत्यदानवमोहिने ।
म्लेच्छप्रायक्षत्रहन्त्रे नमस्ते कल्किरूपिणे ॥ २२ ॥

namo buddhāya śuddhāya
daitya-dānava-mohine
mleccha-prāya-kṣatra-hantre
namas te kalki-rūpiṇe

namaḥ—obeisances; *buddhāya*—to Lord Buddha; *śuddhāya*—the pure; *daitya-dānava*—of the demoniac descendants of Diti and Dānu; *mohine*—to the bewilderer; *mleccha*—of the outcaste meat-eaters; *prāya*—resembling; *kṣatra*—kings; *hantre*—to the killer; *namaḥ*—obeisances; *te*—to You; *kalki-rūpiṇe*—in the form of Kalki.

TRANSLATION

Obeisances to Your form as the faultless Lord Buddha, who will bewilder the Daityas and Dānavas, and to Lord Kalki, the annihilator of the meat-eaters posing as kings.

TEXT 23

भगवन् जीवलोकोऽयं मोहितस्तव मायया ।
अहं ममेत्यसद्ग्राहो भ्राम्यते कर्मवर्त्मसु ॥ २३ ॥

bhagavan jīva-loko'yaṁ
mohitas tava māyayā
ahaṁ mamety asad-grāho
bhrāmyate karma-vartmasu

bhagavan—O Supreme Lord; *jīva*—of living entities; *lokaḥ*—the world; *ayam*—this; *mohitaḥ*—bewildered; *tava*—Your; *māyayā*—by the illusory energy; *aham mama iti*—based on the conceptions of "I" and "my"; *asat*—false; *grāhaḥ*—whose conception; *bhrāmyate*—is made to wander; *karma*—of fruitive work; *vartmasu*—along the paths.

TRANSLATION

O Supreme Lord, the living entities in this world are bewildered by Your illusory energy. Becoming involved in the false concepts of "I" and "my," they are forced to wander along the paths of fruitive work.

TEXT 24

अहं चात्मात्मजागारदारार्थस्वजनादिषु ।
भ्रमामि स्वप्नकल्पेषु मूढः सत्यधिया विभो ॥ २४ ॥

ahaṁ cātmātmajāgāra-
dārārtha-svajanādiṣu
bhramāmi svapna-kalpeṣu
mūḍhaḥ satya-dhiyā vibho

aham—I; *ca*—also; *ātma*—concerning my body; *ātma-ja*—children; *agāra*—home; *dāra*—wife; *artha*—wealth; *sva-jana*—followers; *ādiṣu*—and so on; *bhramāmi*—am deluded; *svapna*—a dream; *kalpeṣu*—who are just like; *mūḍhaḥ*—foolish; *satya*—that they are real; *dhiyā*—with the idea; *vibho*—O almighty Lord.

TRANSLATION

I too am deluded in this way, O almighty Lord, foolishly thinking my body, children, home, wife, money and followers to be real, though they are actually as unreal as a dream.

TEXT 25

अनित्यानात्मदुःखेषु विपर्ययमतिर्ह्यहम् ।
द्वन्द्वारामस्तमोविष्टो न जाने त्वात्मनः प्रियम् ॥ २५ ॥

anityānātma-duḥkheṣu
viparyaya-matir hy aham
dvandvārāmas tamo-viṣṭo
na jāne tvātmanaḥ priyam

anitya—not eternal; *anātma*—not the real self; *duḥkheṣu*—in the sources of misery; *viparyaya*—backwards; *matiḥ*—whose mentality; *hi*—indeed; *aham*—I; *dvandva*—in duality; *ārāmaḥ*—taking pleasure; *tamaḥ*—in ignorance; *viṣṭaḥ*—absorbed; *na jāne*—I fail to recognize; *tvā*—You; *ātmanaḥ*—of myself; *priyam*—the dearmost.

TRANSLATION

Thus mistaking the temporary for the eternal, my body for my self, and sources of misery for sources of happiness, I have tried to take pleasure in material dualities. Covered in this way by ignorance, I could not recognize You as the real object of my love.

TEXT 26

यथाबुधो जलं हित्वा प्रतिच्छन्नं तदुद्भवैः ।
अभ्येति मृगतृष्णां वै तद्वत्त्वाहं पराङ्मुखः ॥ २६ ॥

yathābudho jalaṁ hitvā
praticchannaṁ tad-udbhavaiḥ
abhyeti mṛga-tṛṣṇāṁ vai
tadvat tvāhaṁ parāṅ-mukhaḥ

yathā—as; *abudhaḥ*—someone who is unintelligent; *jalam*—water; *hitvā*—overlooking; *praticchannam*—covered; *tat-udbhavaiḥ*—by the plants growing in it; *abhyeti*—approaches; *mṛga-tṛṣṇām*—a mirage; *vai*—indeed; *tadvat*—in that same way; *tvā*—You; *aham*—I; *parāk-mukhaḥ*—turned away.

TRANSLATION

Just as a fool overlooks a body of water covered by the vegetation growing in it and chases a mirage, so I have turned away from You.

TEXT 27

नोत्सहेऽहं कृपणधीः काममकर्महतं मनः ।
रोद्धुं प्रमाथिभिश्चाक्षैर्ह्रियमाणमितस्ततः ॥ २७ ॥

notsahe'haṁ kṛpaṇa-dhīḥ
kāma-karma-hataṁ manaḥ
roddhuṁ pramāthibhiś cākṣair
hriyamāṇam itas tataḥ

na utsahe—am not able to find the strength; *aham*—I; *kṛpaṇa*—crippled; *dhīḥ*—whose intelligence; *kāma*—by material desires; *karma*—and material activities; *hatam*—disturbed; *manaḥ*—my mind; *roddhum*—to keep in check; *pramāthibhiḥ*—which are very powerful and willful; *ca*—and; *akṣaiḥ*—by the senses; *hriyamāṇam*—being dragged; *itaḥ tataḥ*—here and there.

TRANSLATION

My intelligence is so crippled that I cannot find the strength to curb my mind, which is disturbed by material desires and activities and constantly dragged here and there by my obstinate senses.

TEXT 28

सोऽहं तवाङ्घ्र्युपगतोऽस्म्यसतां दुरापं
तच्चाप्यहं भवदनुग्रह ईश मन्ये ।
पुंसो भवेद्यर्हि संसरणापवर्गस्
त्वय्यब्जनाभ सदुपासनया मतिः स्यात् ॥ २८ ॥

so'haṁ tavāṅghry-upagato'smy asatāṁ durāpaṁ
tac cāpy ahaṁ bhavad-anugraha īśa manye

puṁso bhaved yarhi saṁsaraṇāpavargas
tvayy abja-nābha sad-upāsanayā matiḥ syāt

saḥ—being such; *aham*—I; *tava*—Your; *aṅghri*—feet; *upagataḥ asmi* —am approaching; *asatām*—for those who are impure; *durāpam*—impossible to attain; *tat*—that; *ca*—and; *api*—also; *aham*—I; *bhavat*—Your; *anugrahaḥ*—mercy; *īśa*—O Lord; *manye*—think; *puṁsaḥ*—of a person; *bhavet* —occurs; *yarhi*—when; *saṁsaraṇa*—of his rotation in the cycle of material existence; *apavargaḥ*—the cessation; *tvayi*—of You; *abja*—like a lotus; *nābha*—O You whose navel; *sat*—of pure devotees; *upāsanayā*—by worship; *matiḥ*—consciousness; *syāt*—develops.

TRANSLATION

Being thus fallen, I am approaching Your feet for shelter, O Lord, because although the impure can never attain Your feet, I think it is nevertheless possible by Your mercy. Only when one's material life has ceased, O lotus-naveled Lord, can one develop consciousness of You by serving Your pure devotees.

TEXT 29

नमो विज्ञानमात्राय सर्वप्रत्ययहेतवे ।
पुरुषेशप्रधानाय ब्रह्मणेऽनन्तशक्तये ॥ २९ ॥

namo vijñāna-mātrāya
sarva-pratyaya-hetave
puruṣeśa-pradhānāya
brahmaṇe'nanta-śaktaye

namaḥ—obeisances; *vijñāna*—of pure knowledge; *mātrāya*—to the embodiment; *sarva*—of all; *pratyaya*—forms of knowledge; *hetave*—to the source; *puruṣa*—of a person; *īśa*—the controlling forces; *pradhānāya*—to Him who predominates; *brahmaṇe*—to the Supreme Absolute Truth; *ananta* —unlimited; *śaktaye*—whose potencies.

TRANSLATION

Obeisances to the Supreme Absolute Truth, the possessor of unlimited energies. He is the embodiment of pure, transcendental knowledge, the source of all kinds of awareness, and the predominator of the forces of nature that rule over the living being.

TEXT 30

नमस्ते वासुदेवाय सर्वभूतक्षयाय च ।
हृषीकेश नमस्तुभ्यं प्रपन्नं पाहि मां प्रभो ॥ ३० ॥

namas te vāsudevāya
sarva-bhūta-kṣayāya ca
hṛṣīkeśa namas tubhyaṁ
prapannaṁ pāhi māṁ prabho

namaḥ—obeisances; *te*—to You; *vāsudevāya*—the son of Vasudeva; *sarva*—of all; *bhūta*—living beings; *kṣayāya*—the residence; *ca*—and; *hṛṣīka-īśa*—O Lord of the mind and senses; *namaḥ*—obeisances; *tubhyam*—to You; *prapannam*—who am surrendered; *pāhi*—please protect; *mām*—me; *prabho*—O master.

TRANSLATION

O son of Vasudeva, obeisances to You, within whom all living beings reside. O Lord of the mind and senses, again I offer You my obeisances. O master, please protect me, who am surrendered unto You.

Thus end the purports of the humble servants of His Divine Grace A.C. Bhaktivedanta Swami Prabhupāda to the Tenth Canto, Fortieth Chapter, of the Śrīmad-Bhāgavatam, *entitled "The Prayers of Akrūra."*

CHAPTER FORTY- ONE

Kṛṣṇa and Balarāma Enter Mathurā

This chapter describes how Lord Kṛṣṇa entered the city of Mathurā, killed a washerman and bestowed benedictions upon a weaver and a garland-maker named Sudāmā.

After showing His Viṣṇu form to Akrūra in the waters of the Yamunā and receiving Akrūra's prayers, Lord Kṛṣṇa withdrew that vision just as an actor winds up his performance. Akrūra emerged from the water and in great amazement approached the Lord, who asked him whether he had seen something wonderful while bathing. Akrūra replied, "Whatever wonderful things there are in the realms of water, earth or sky, all have their existence within You. Thus when one has seen You, nothing remains unseen." Akrūra then began driving the chariot again.

Kṛṣṇa, Balarāma and Akrūra reached Mathurā late in the afternoon. After meeting up with Nanda Mahārāja and the other cowherds, who had gone on ahead, Kṛṣṇa asked Akrūra to return home, promising to visit him there after He had killed Kaṁsa. Akrūra unhappily bid the Lord goodbye, went to King Kaṁsa to inform him that Kṛṣṇa and Balarāma had come, and went home.

Kṛṣṇa and Balarāma took the cowherd boys with Them to see the splendorous city. As they all entered Mathurā, the women of the city eagerly came out of their houses to see Kṛṣṇa. They had often heard about Him and had long since developed a deep attraction for Him. But now that they were actually seeing Him, they were overwhelmed with happiness, and all their distress due to His absence was eradicated.

Kṛṣṇa and Balarāma then came upon Kaṁsa's wicked washerman. Kṛṣṇa asked him for some of the first-class garments he was carrying, but he refused and even chastised the two Lords. At this Kṛṣṇa became very angry and beheaded the man with His fingertips. The washerman's assistants, seeing his untimely end, dropped their bundles of clothes on the spot and ran off in all directions. Kṛṣṇa and Balarāma then took some of the garments They especially fancied.

Next a weaver approached the two Lords and arrayed Them suitably, for which service he received from Kṛṣṇa opulence in this life and liberation in the next. Kṛṣṇa and Balarāma then went to the house of the garland-maker Sudāmā. Sudāmā offered Them his full obeisances, worshiped Them by bathing Their feet and offering Them such items as *arghya* and sandalwood paste, and chanted prayers in Their honor. Then he adorned Them with garlands of fragrant flowers. Pleased, the Lords offered him whatever benedictions he wished, and then They moved on.

TEXT 1

श्रीशुक उवाच

स्तुवतस्तस्य भगवान् दर्शयित्वा जले वपुः ।
भूयः समाहरत्कृष्णो नटो नाट्यमिवात्मनः ॥ १ ॥

śrī-śuka uvāca
stuvatas tasya bhagavān
darśayitvā jale vapuḥ
bhūyaḥ samāharat kṛṣṇo
naṭo nāṭyam ivātmanaḥ

śrī-śukaḥ uvāca—Śukadeva Gosvāmī said; *stuvataḥ*—while praying; *tasya*—he, Akrūra; *bhagavān*—the Supreme Lord; *darśayitvā*—having shown; *jale*—in the water; *vapuḥ*—His personal form; *bhūyaḥ*—again; *samāharat*—withdrew; *kṛṣṇaḥ*—Śrī Kṛṣṇa; *naṭaḥ*—an actor; *nāṭyam*—the performance; *iva*—as; *ātmanaḥ*—his own.

TRANSLATION

Śukadeva Gosvāmī said: While Akrūra was still offering prayers, the Supreme Lord Kṛṣṇa withdrew His form that He had revealed in the water, just as an actor winds up his performance.

PURPORT

Lord Kṛṣṇa withdrew from Akrūra's sight the Viṣṇu form along with the vision of the spiritual sky and its eternal inhabitants.

TEXT 2

सोऽपि चान्तर्हितं वीक्ष्य जलादुन्मज्य सत्वरः ।
कृत्वा चावश्यकं सर्वं विस्मितो रथमागमत् ॥ २ ॥

so'pi cāntarhitaṁ vīkṣya
jalād unmajya satvaraḥ
kṛtvā cāvaśyakaṁ sarvaṁ
vismito ratham āgamat

saḥ—he, Akrūra; *api*—indeed; *ca*—and; *antarhitam*—disappeared; *vīkṣya*—seeing; *jalāt*—from the water; *unmajya*—emerging; *satvaraḥ*—quickly; *kṛtvā*—performing; *ca*—and; *āvaśyakam*—his prescribed duties; *sarvam*—all; *vismitaḥ*—surprised; *ratham*—to the chariot; *āgamat*—went.

TRANSLATION

When Akrūra saw the vision disappear, he came out of the water and quickly finished his various ritual duties. He then returned to the chariot, astonished.

TEXT 3

तमपृच्छद्धृषीकेशः किं ते दृष्टमिवाद्भुतम् ।
भूमौ वियति तोये वा तथा त्वां लक्षयामहे ॥ ३ ॥

tam apṛcchad dhṛṣīkeśaḥ
kiṁ te dṛṣṭam ivādbhutam
bhūmau viyati toye vā
tathā tvāṁ lakṣayāmahe

tam—of him; *apṛcchat*—asked; *hṛṣīkeśaḥ*—Lord Kṛṣṇa; *kim*—whether; *te*—by you; *dṛṣṭam*—seen; *iva*—indeed; *adbhutam*—something exceptional; *bhūmau*—on the earth; *viyati*—in the sky; *toye*—in the water; *va*—or; *tathā*—so; *tvām*—you; *lakṣayāmahe*—We surmise.

TRANSLATION

Lord Kṛṣṇa asked Akrūra: Have you seen something wonderful on the earth, in the sky or in the water? From your appearance, We think you have.

TEXT 4

श्रीअक्रूर उवाच
अद्भुतानीह यावन्ति भूमौ वियति वा जले ।
त्वयि विश्वात्मके तानि किं मेऽदृष्टं विपश्यतः ॥ ४ ॥

śrī-akrūra uvāca
adbhutānīha yāvanti
bhūmau viyati vā jale
tvayi viśvātmake tāni
kiṁ me'dṛṣṭaṁ vipaśyataḥ

śrī-akrūraḥ uvāca—Śrī Akrūra said; *adbhutāni*—wonderful things; *iha*—in this world; *yāvanti*—whatever; *bhūmau*—on the earth; *viyati*—in the sky; *vā*—or; *jale*—in the water; *tvayi*—in You; *viśva-ātmake*—who comprise everything; *tāni*—they; *kim*—what; *me*—by me; *adṛṣṭam*—not seen; *vipaśyataḥ*—seeing (You).

TRANSLATION

Śrī Akrūra said: Whatever wonderful things the earth, sky or water contain, all exist in You. Since You encompass everything, when I am seeing You, what have I not seen?

TEXT 5

यत्राद्भुतानि सर्वाणि भूमौ वियति वा जले ।
तं त्वानुपश्यतो ब्रह्मन् किं मे दृष्टमिहाद्भुतम् ॥ ५ ॥

yatrādbhutāni sarvāṇi
bhūmau viyati vā jale
taṁ tvānupaśyato brahman
kiṁ me dṛṣṭam ihādbhutam

yatra—in whom; *adbhutāni*—amazing things; *sarvāṇi*—all; *bhūmau*—on the earth; *viyati*—in the sky; *vā*—or; *jale*—in the water; *tam*—that person; *tvā*—You; *anupaśyataḥ*—seeing; *brahman*—O Supreme Absolute Truth; *kim*—what; *me*—by me; *dṛṣṭam*—seen; *iha*—in this world; *adbhutam*—amazing.

TRANSLATION

And now that I am seeing You, O Supreme Absolute Truth, in whom reside all amazing things on the earth, in the sky and in the water, what amazing things could I see in this world?

PURPORT

Akrūra has now realized that Lord Kṛṣṇa is not merely his nephew.

TEXT 6

इत्युक्त्वा चोदयामास स्यन्दनं गान्दिनीसुतः ।
मथुरामनयद् रामं कृष्णं चैव दिनात्यये ॥ ६ ॥

ity uktvā codayām āsa
syandanaṁ gāndinī-sutaḥ
mathurām anayad rāmaṁ
kṛṣṇaṁ caiva dinātyaye

iti—thus; *uktvā*—saying; *codayām āsa*—drove forward; *syandanam*—the chariot; *gāndinī-sutaḥ*—the son of Gāndinī, Akrūra; *mathurām*—to Mathurā; *anayat*—he brought; *rāmam*—Lord Balarāma; *kṛṣṇam*—Lord Kṛṣṇa; *ca*—and; *eva*—also; *dina*—of the day; *atyaye*—at the end.

TRANSLATION

With these words, Akrūra, the son of Gāndinī, began driving the chariot onward. At the end of the day he arrived in Mathurā with Lord Balarāma and Lord Kṛṣṇa.

TEXT 7

मार्गे ग्रामजना राजंस्तत्र तत्रोपसंगताः ।
वसुदेवसुतौ वीक्ष्य प्रीता दृष्टिं न चाददुः ॥ ७ ॥

mārge grāma-janā rājaṁs
tatra tatropasaṅgatāḥ
vasudeva-sutau vīkṣya
prītā dṛṣṭiṁ na cādaduḥ

mārge—on the road; *grāma*—of the villages; *janāḥ*—the people; *rājan*—O King (Parīkṣit); *tatra tatra*—here and there; *upasaṅgatāḥ*—approaching; *vasudeva-sutau*—at the two sons of Vasudeva; *vīkṣya*—looking; *prītāḥ*—pleased; *dṛṣṭim*—their vision; *na*—not; *ca*—and; *ādaduḥ*—could take back.

TRANSLATION

Wherever they passed along the road, O King, the village people came forward and looked upon the two sons of Vasudeva with great pleasure. In fact, the villagers could not withdraw their eyes from Them.

TEXT 8

तावद् व्रजौकसस्तत्र नन्दगोपादयोऽग्रतः ।
पुरोपवनमासाद्य प्रतीक्षन्तोऽवतस्थिरे ॥ ८ ॥

tāvad vrajaukasas tatra
nanda-gopādayo'grataḥ
puropavanam āsādya
pratīkṣanto'vatasthire

tāvat—by then; *vraja-okasaḥ*—the inhabitants of Vraja; *tatra*—there; *nanda-gopa-ādayaḥ*—headed by Nanda, the king of the cowherds; *agrataḥ*—before; *pura*—of the city; *upavanam*—a garden; *āsādya*—coming upon; *pratīkṣantaḥ*—waiting; *avatasthire*—they stayed there.

TRANSLATION

Nanda Mahārāja and the other residents of Vṛndāvana, having reached Mathurā ahead of the chariot, had stopped at a garden on the outskirts of the city to wait for Kṛṣṇa and Balarāma.

PURPORT

Nanda and the others reached Mathurā first because the chariot carrying Kṛṣṇa and Balarāma was delayed by Akrūra's bathing.

TEXT 9

तान् समेत्याह भगवानक्रूरं जगदीश्वरः ।
गृहीत्वा पाणिना पाणिं प्रश्रितं प्रहसन्निव ॥ ९ ॥

tān sametyāha bhagavān
akrūraṁ jagad-īśvaraḥ
gṛhītvā pāṇinā pāṇiṁ
praśritaṁ prahasann iva

tān—with them; *sametya*—meeting; *āha*—said; *bhagavān*—the Supreme Personality of Godhead; *akrūram*—to Akrūra; *jagat-īśvaraḥ*—the Lord of the universe; *gṛhītvā*—taking; *pāṇinā*—with His hand; *pāṇim*—his hand; *praśritam*—who was humble; *prahasan*—smiling; *iva*—indeed.

TRANSLATION

After joining Nanda and the others, the Supreme Lord Kṛṣṇa, the controller of the universe, took humble Akrūra's hand in His own and, smiling, spoke as follows.

TEXT 10

भवान् प्रविशतामग्रे सहयानः पुरीं गृहम् ।
वयं त्विहावमुच्याथ ततो द्रक्ष्यामहे पुरीम् ॥ १० ॥

bhavān praviśatām agre
saha-yānaḥ purīṁ gṛham
vayaṁ tv ihāvamucyātha
tato drakṣyāmahe purīm

bhavān—you; *praviśatām*—should enter; *agre*—ahead; *saha*—together with; *yānaḥ*—the vehicle; *purīm*—the city; *gṛham*—and your home; *vayam*—we; *tu*—on the other hand; *iha*—here; *avamucya*—getting down; *atha*—then; *tataḥ*—afterwards; *drakṣyāmahe*—will see; *purīm*—the city.

TRANSLATION

[Lord Kṛṣṇa said:] Take the chariot and enter the city ahead of us. Then go home. After resting here a while, we will go to see the city.

TEXT 11

श्रीअक्रूर उवाच
नाहं भवद्भ्यां रहितः प्रवेक्ष्ये मथुरां प्रभो ।
त्यक्तुं नार्हसि मां नाथ भक्तं ते भक्तवत्सल ॥ ११ ॥

śrī-akrūra uvāca
nāhaṁ bhavadbhyāṁ rahitaḥ
pravekṣye mathurāṁ prabho
tyaktuṁ nārhasi māṁ nātha
bhaktaṁ te bhakta-vatsala

śrī-akrūraḥ uvāca—Śrī Akrūra said; *na*—cannot; *aham*—I; *bhavadbhyām*—of the two of You; *rahitaḥ*—deprived; *pravekṣye*—enter; *mathurām*—Mathurā; *prabho*—O master; *tyaktum*—abandon; *na arhasi*—You should not; *mām*—me; *nātha*—O Lord; *bhaktam*—devotee; *te*—Your; *bhakta-vat-sala*—O You who have parental affection for Your devotees.

TRANSLATION

Śrī Akrūra said: O master, without the two of You I shall not enter Mathurā. I am Your devotee, O Lord, so it is not fair for You to abandon me, since You are always affectionate to Your devotees.

TEXT 12

आगच्छ याम गेहान्नः सनाथान् कुर्वधोक्षज ।
सहाग्रजः सगोपालैः सुहृद्भिश्च सुहृत्तम ॥ १२ ॥

āgaccha yāma gehān naḥ
sa-nāthān kurv adhokṣaja
sahāgrajaḥ sa-gopālaiḥ
suhṛdbhiś ca suhṛttama

āgaccha—please come; *yāma*—let us go; *gehān*—to the house; *naḥ*—our; *sa*—having; *nāthān*—a master; *kuru*—please make it; *adhokṣaja*—O transcendental Lord; *saha*—with; *agra-jaḥ*—Your elder brother; *sa-gopālaiḥ*—with the cowherd men; *suhṛdbhiḥ*—with Your friends; *ca*—and; *suhṛt-tama*—O supreme well-wisher.

TRANSLATION

Come, let us go to my house with Your elder brother, the cowherd men and Your companions. O best of friends, O transcendental Lord, in this way please grace my house with its master.

TEXT 13

पुनीहि पादरजसा गृहान्नो गृहमेधिनाम् ।
यच्छौचेनानुतृप्यन्ति पितरः साग्नयः सुराः ॥ १३ ॥

punīhi pāda-rajasā
gṛhān no gṛha-medhinām
yac-chaucenānutṛpyanti
pitaraḥ sāgnayaḥ surāḥ

punīhi—please purify; *pāda*—of Your feet; *rajasā*—with the dust; *gṛhān*—the home; *naḥ*—of us; *gṛha-medhinām*—who are attached to household ritual duties; *yat*—by which; *śaucena*—purification; *anutṛpyanti*—will become satisfied; *pitaraḥ*—my forefathers; *sa*—together with; *agnayaḥ*—the sacrificial fires; *surāḥ*—and the demigods.

TRANSLATION

I am simply an ordinary householder attached to ritual sacrifices, so please purify my home with the dust of Your lotus feet. By that act of purification, my forefathers, the sacrificial fires and the demigods will all become satisfied.

TEXT 14

अवनिज्याङ्घ्रियुगलमासीत्श्लोक्यो बलिर्महान् ।
ऐश्वर्यमतुलं लेभे गतिं चैकान्तिनां तु या ॥ १४ ॥

avanijyāṅghri-yugalam
āsīt ślokyo balir mahān
aiśvaryam atulaṁ lebhe
gatiṁ caikāntināṁ tu yā

avanijya—bathing; *aṅghri-yugalam*—the two feet; *āsīt*—became; *ślokyaḥ*—glorious; *baliḥ*—King Bali; *mahān*—the great; *aiśvaryam*—power; *atulam*—unequaled; *lebhe*—he achieved; *gatīm*—the destination; *ca*—and; *ekāntinām*—of the unalloyed devotees of the Lord; *tu*—indeed; *yā*—which.

TRANSLATION

By bathing Your feet, the exalted Bali Mahārāja attained not only glorious fame and unequaled power but also the final destination of pure devotees.

TEXT 15

आपस्तेऽङ्घ्र्यवनेजन्यस्त्रींल्ँ लोकान् शुचयोऽपुनन् ।
शिरसाधत्त याः शर्वः स्वर्याताः सगरात्मजाः ॥ १५ ॥

āpas te'ṅghry-avanejanyas
trīl̐ lokān śucayo'punan
śirasādhatta yāḥ śarvaḥ
svar yātāḥ sagarātmajāḥ

āpaḥ—the water (namely, the river Ganges); *te*—Your; *aṅghri*—of the feet; *avanejanyaḥ*—coming from the bathing; *trīn*—the three; *lokān*—worlds; *śucayaḥ*—being purely spiritual; *apunan*—has purified; *śirasā*—on his head; *ādhatta*—has taken; *yāḥ*—which; *śarvaḥ*—Lord Siva; *svaḥ*—to heaven; *yātāḥ*—went; *sagara-ātmajāḥ*—the sons of King Sagara.

TRANSLATION

The water of the river Ganges has purified the three worlds, having become transcendental by bathing Your feet. Lord Śiva accepted that water on his head, and by that water's grace the sons of King Sagara attained to heaven.

TEXT 16

देवदेव जगन्नाथ पुण्यश्रवणकीर्तन ।
यदूत्तमोत्तमःश्लोक नारायण नमोऽस्तु ते ॥ १६ ॥

deva-deva jagan-nātha
puṇya-śravaṇa-kīrtana
yadūttamottamaḥ-śloka
nārāyaṇa namo'stu te

deva-deva—O Lord of lords; *jagat-nātha*—O master of the universe; *puṇya*—pious; *śravaṇa*—hearing; *kīrtana*—and chanting (about whom); *yadu-uttama*—O best of the Yadus; *uttamaḥ-śloka*—O You who are glorified in excellent verses; *nārāyaṇa*—O Supreme Lord Nārāyaṇa; *namaḥ*—obeisances; *astu*—let there be; *te*—unto You.

TRANSLATION

O Lord of lords, master of the universe, O You whose glories it is most pious to hear and chant! O best of the Yadus, O You whose fame is recounted in excellent poetry! O Supreme Lord Nārāyaṇa, I offer You my obeisances.

TEXT 17

श्रीभगवानुवाच

आयास्ये भवतो गेहमहमार्यसमन्वितः ।
यदुचक्रद्रुहं हत्वा वितरिष्ये सुहृत्प्रियम् ॥ १७ ॥

śrī-bhagavān uvāca
āyāsye bhavato geham
aham ārya-samanvitaḥ
yadu-cakra-druhaṁ hatvā
vitariṣye suhṛt-priyam

śrī-bhagavān uvāca—the Supreme Lord said; *āyāsye*—will come; *bhavataḥ*—to your; *geham*—house; *aham*—I; *ārya*—by My elder (brother, Balarāma); *samanvitaḥ*—accompanied; *yadu-cakra*—of the circle of Yadus; *druham*—the enemy (Kaṁsa); *hatvā*—killing; *vitariṣye*—I will grant; *suhṛt*—to My well-wishers; *priyam*—satisfaction.

TRANSLATION

The Supreme Lord said: I will come to Your house with My elder brother, but first I must satisfy My friends and well-wishers by killing the enemy of the Yadu clan.

PURPORT

Akrūra glorified Kṛṣṇa in text 16 as *yadūttama,* "the best of the Yadus." Śrī Kṛṣṇa here confirms this by saying, in effect, "Since I am the best of the Yadus, I must kill the enemy of the Yadus, Kaṁsa, and then I will come to your house."

TEXT 18

श्रीशुक उवाच
एवमुक्तो भगवता सोऽक्रूरो विमना इव।
पुरीं प्रविष्टः कंसाय कर्मावेद्य गृहं ययौ ॥ १८ ॥

śrī-śuka uvāca
evam ukto bhagavatā
so'krūro vimanā iva
purīṁ praviṣṭaḥ kaṁsāya
karmāvedya gṛhaṁ yayau

śrī-śukaḥ uvāca—Śukadeva Gosvāmī said; *evam*—thus; *uktaḥ*—addressed; *bhagavatā*—by the Lord; *saḥ*—he; *akrūraḥ*—Akrūra; *vimanāḥ*—disheartened; *iva*—somewhat; *purīm*—the city; *praviṣṭaḥ*—entering; *kaṁsāya*—to Kaṁsa; *karma*—about his activities; *āvedya*—informing; *gṛham*—to his home; *yayau*—went.

TRANSLATION

Śukadeva Gosvāmī said: Thus addressed by the Lord, Akrūra entered the city with a heavy heart. He informed King Kaṁsa of the success of his mission and then went home.

TEXT 19

अथापराह्णे भगवान् कृष्णः संकर्षणान्वितः ।
मथुरां प्राविशद् गोपैर्दिदृक्षुः परिवारितः ॥ १९ ॥

athāparāhne bhagavān
kṛṣṇaḥ saṅkarṣaṇānvitaḥ
mathurāṁ prāviśad gopair
didṛkṣuḥ parivāritaḥ

atha—then; *apara-ahne*—in the afternoon; *bhagavān*—the Supreme Lord; *kṛṣṇaḥ*—Kṛṣṇa; *saṅkarṣaṇa-anvitaḥ*—together with Lord Balarāma; *mathurām*—Mathurā; *prāviśat*—entered; *gopaiḥ*—by the cowherd boys; *didṛkṣuḥ*—wanting to see; *parivāritaḥ*—joined.

TRANSLATION

Lord Kṛṣṇa desired to see Mathurā, so toward evening He took Lord Balarāma and the cowherd boys with Him and entered the city.

TEXTS 20–23

ददर्श तां स्फाटिकतुंगगोपुर-
द्वारां बृहद्धेमकपाटतोरणाम् ।
ताम्रारकोष्ठां परिखादुरासदाम्
उद्यानरम्योपवनोपशोभिताम् ॥ २० ॥
सौवर्णशृंगाटकहर्म्यनिष्कुटैः
श्रेणीसभाभिर्भवनैरुपस्कृताम् ।
वैदूर्यवज्रामलनीलविद्रुमैर्
मुक्ताहरिद्भिर्वलभीषु वेदिषु ॥ २१ ॥
जुष्टेषु जालामुखरन्ध्रकुट्टिमेष्व्
आविष्टपारावतबर्हिनादिताम् ।

संसिक्तरथ्यापणमार्गचत्वरां
प्रकीर्णमाल्यांकुरलाजतण्डुलाम् ॥ २२ ॥
आपूर्णकुम्भैर्दधिचन्दनोक्षितैः
प्रसूनदीपावलिभिः सपल्लवैः ।
सवृन्दरम्भाक्रमुकैः सकेतुभिः
स्वलंकृतद्वारगृहां सपट्टिकैः ॥ २३ ॥

dadarśa tāṁ sphāṭika-tuṅga-gopura-
dvārāṁ bṛhad-dhema-kapāṭa-toraṇām
tāmrāra-koṣṭhāṁ parikhā-durāsadām
udyāna-ramyopavanopaśobhitām

sauvarṇa-śṛṅgāṭaka-harmya-niṣkuṭaiḥ
śreṇī-sabhābhir bhavanair upaskṛtām
vaidūrya-vajrāmala-nīla-vidrumair
muktā-haridbhir valabhīṣu vediṣu

juṣṭeṣu jālāmukha-randhra-kuṭṭimeṣv
āviṣṭa-pārāvata-barhi-nāditām
saṁsikta-rathyāpaṇa-mārga-catvarāṁ
prakīrṇa-mālyāṅkura-lāja-taṇḍulām

āpūrṇa-kumbhair dadhi-candanokṣitaiḥ
prasūna-dīpāvalibhiḥ sa-pallavaiḥ
sa-vṛnda-rambhā-kramukaiḥ sa-ketubhiḥ
sv-alaṅkṛta-dvāra-gṛhāṁ sa-paṭṭikaiḥ

dadarśa—He saw; *tām*—that (city); *sphāṭika*—of crystal; *tuṅga*—high; *gopura*—whose main gates; *dvārām*—and household gates; *bṛhat*—immense; *hema*—gold; *kapāṭa*—whose doors; *toraṇām*—and ornamental arches; *tāmra*—of copper; *āra*—and brass; *koṣṭhām*—whose storehouses; *parikhā*—with its canals; *durāsadām*—inviolable; *udyāna*—with public gardens; *ramya*—attractive; *upavana*—and parks; *upaśobhitām*—beautified; *sauvarṇa*—gold; *śṛṅgāṭaka*—with crossways; *harmya*—mansions; *niṣkuṭaiḥ*—and pleasure gardens; *śreṇī*—of guilds; *sabhābhiḥ*—with the assembly halls; *bhavanaiḥ*—and with houses; *upaskṛtām*—ornamented; *vaidūrya*—with *vaidūrya* gems; *vajra*—diamonds; *amala*—crystal quartz; *nīla*—sapphires; *vidrumaiḥ*—and coral; *muktā*—with pearls; *haridbhiḥ*—and emeralds; *valabhīṣu*—on the wood panels decorating the rafters in front of the houses; *vediṣu*—on columned balconies; *juṣṭeṣu*—bedecked; *jāla-āmukha*—of lattice windows; *randhra*—in the openings; *kuṭṭimeṣu*—and on gem-studded floors; *āviṣṭa*—sitting; *pārāvata*—with the pet doves; *barhi*—and the peacocks; *nāditām*—resounding; *saṁsikta*—sprinkled with water; *rathyā*—with royal avenues; *āpaṇa*—commercial streets; *mārga*—other roads; *catvarām*—and courtyards; *prakīrṇa*—scattered; *mālya*—with flower garlands; *aṅkura*—new sprouts; *lāja*—parched grains; *taṇḍulām*—and rice; *āpūrṇa*—full; *kumbhaiḥ*—with pots; *dadhi*—with yogurt; *candana*—and sandalwood paste; *ukṣitaiḥ*—smeared; *prasūna*—with flower petals; *dīpa-āvalibhiḥ*—and rows of lamps; *sa-pallavaiḥ*—with leaves; *sa-vṛnda*—with bunches of flowers; *rambhā*—with trunks of banana trees; *kramukaiḥ*—and trunks of betel-nut trees; *sa-ketubhiḥ*—with flags; *su-alaṅkṛta*—nicely decorated; *dvāra*—with doors; *gṛhām*—whose houses; *sa-paṭṭikaiḥ*—with ribbons.

TRANSLATION

The Lord saw Mathurā, with its tall gates and household entrances made of crystal, its immense archways and main doors of gold, its granaries and other storehouses of copper and brass, and its impregnable moats. Beautifying the city were pleasant gardens and parks. The main intersections were fashioned of gold, and there were mansions with private pleasure gardens, along with guildhalls and many other buildings. Mathurā resounded with the calls of peacocks and pet turtledoves, who sat in the small openings of the lattice windows and on the gem-studded floors, and also on the columned balconies and on the ornate rafters in front of the houses. These balconies and rafters were adorned with vaidūrya stones, diamonds, crystal quartz, sapphires, coral, pearls and emeralds. All the royal avenues and commercial streets were sprinkled with water, as were the side roads and courtyards, and flower garlands, newly grown sprouts, parched grains and rice had been scattered about everywhere. Gracing the houses' doorways were elaborately decorated pots filled with water, which were bedecked with mango leaves, smeared with yogurt and sandalwood paste, and encircled by flower petals and ribbons. Near the pots were flags, rows of lamps, bunches of flowers and the trunks of banana and betel-nut trees.

PURPORT

Śrīla Viśvanātha Cakravartī Ṭhākura gives this description of the elaborately decorated pots: "On either side of each doorway, above the scattered rice, is a pot. Encircling each pot are flower petals, on its neck are ribbons and in its mouth are leaves of mango and other trees. Above each pot, on a gold plate, are rows of lamps. A trunk of a banana tree stands on either side of each pot, and a betel-nut tree trunk stands in front and also behind. Flags lean against the pots."

TEXT 24

तां सम्प्रविष्टौ वसुदेवनन्दनौ
वृतौ वयस्यैर्नरदेववर्त्मना ।
द्रष्टुं समीयुस्त्वरिताः पुरस्त्रियो
हर्म्याणि चैवारुरुहुर्नृपोत्सुकाः ॥ २४ ॥

tāṁ sampraviṣṭau vasudeva-nandanau
vṛtau vayasyair naradeva-vartmanā
draṣṭuṁ samīyus tvaritāḥ pura-striyo
harmyāṇi caivāruruhur nṛpotsukāḥ

tām—that (Mathurā); *sampraviṣṭau*—entering; *vasudeva*—of Vasudeva; *nandanau*—the two sons; *vṛtau*—surrounded; *vayasyaiḥ*—by Their young friends; *nara-deva*—of the King; *vartmanā*—by the road; *draṣṭum*—to see; *samīyuḥ*—came forward together; *tvaritāḥ*—hurriedly; *pura*—of the city; *striyaḥ*—the women; *harmyāṇi*—their houses; *ca*—and; *eva*—also; *āru-ruhuḥ*—they climbed on top of; *nṛpa*—O King (Parīkṣit); *utsukāḥ*—eager.

TRANSLATION

The women of Mathurā hurriedly assembled and went forth to see the two sons of Vasudeva as They entered the city on the King's road, surrounded by Their cowherd boyfriends. Some of the women, my dear King, eagerly climbed to the roofs of their houses to see Them.

TEXT 25

काश्चिद्विपर्यग्धृतवस्त्रभूषणा
विस्मृत्य चैकं युगलेष्वथापराः ।
कृतैकपत्रश्रवणैकनूपुरा
नांक्त्वा द्वितीयं त्वपराश्च लोचनम् ॥ २५ ॥

kāścid viparyag-dhṛta-vastra-bhūṣaṇā
vismṛtya caikaṁ yugaleṣv athāparāḥ
kṛtaika-patra-śravaṇaika-nūpurā
nāṅktvā dvitīyaṁ tv aparāś ca locanam

kāścit—some of them; *viparyak*—backwards; *dhṛta*—putting on; *vastra*—their clothes; *bhūṣaṇāḥ*—and ornaments; *vismṛtya*—forgetting; *ca*—and; *ekam*—one; *yugaleṣu*—of the pairs; *atha*—and; *aparāḥ*—others; *kṛta*—placing; *eka*—only one; *patra*—earring; *śravaṇa*—on their ears; *eka*—or one; *nūpurāḥ*—set of ankle bells; *na aṅktvā*—not anointing; *dvitīyam*—the second; *tu*—but; *aparāḥ*—other ladies; *ca*—and; *locanam*—an eye.

TRANSLATION

Some of the ladies put their clothes and ornaments on backwards, others forgot one of their earrings or ankle bells, and others applied makeup to one eye but not the other.

PURPORT

The ladies were very eager to see Kṛṣṇa, and in their haste and excitement they forgot themselves.

TEXT 26

अश्नन्त्य एकास्तदपास्य सोत्सवा
अभ्यज्यमाना अकृतोपमज्जनाः ।
स्वपन्त्य उत्थाय निशम्य निःस्वनं
प्रपाययन्त्योऽर्भमपोह्य मातरः ॥ २६ ॥

aśnantya ekās tad apāsya sotsavā
abhyajyamānā akṛtopamajjanāḥ
svapantya utthāya niśamya niḥsvanaṁ
prapāyayantyo'rbham apohya mātaraḥ

aśnantyaḥ—taking meals; *ekāḥ*—some; *tat*—that; *apāsya*—abandoning; *sa-utsavāḥ*—joyfully; *abhyajyamānāḥ*—being massaged; *akṛta*—not finishing; *upamajjanāḥ*—their bathing; *svapantyaḥ*—sleeping; *utthāya*—getting up; *niśamya*—having heard; *niḥsvanam*—the loud sounds; *prapāyayantyaḥ*—giving milk; *arbham*—to an infant; *apohya*—put aside; *mātaraḥ*—mothers.

TRANSLATION

Those who were taking their meals abandoned them, others went out without finishing their baths or massages, women who were sleeping at once rose when they heard the commotion, and mothers breast-feeding their infants simply put them aside.

TEXT 27

मनांसि तासामरविन्दलोचनः
प्रगल्भलीलाहसितावलोकैः ।
जहार मत्तद्विरदेन्द्रविक्रमो
दृशां ददच्छ्रीरमणात्मनोत्सवम् ॥ २७ ॥

manāṁsi tāsām aravinda-locanaḥ
pragalbha-līlā-hasitāvalokaiḥ
jahāra matta-dviradendra-vikramo
dṛśāṁ dadac chrī-ramaṇātmanotsavam

manāṁsi—the minds; *tāsām*—their; *aravinda*—like lotuses; *locanaḥ*—He whose eyes; *pragalbha*—bold; *līlā*—with His pastimes; *hasita*—smiling; *avalokaiḥ*—with His glances; *jahāra*—He took away; *matta*—in rut; *dvirada-indra*—(like) a lordly elephant; *vikramaḥ*—whose gait; *dṛśām*—to their eyes; *dadat*—affording; *śrī*—of the goddess of fortune; *ramaṇa*—which is the source of pleasure; *ātmanā*—with His body; *utsavam*—a festival.

TRANSLATION

The lotus-eyed Lord, smiling as He recalled His bold pastimes, captivated those ladies' minds with His glances. He walked with the gait of a lordly elephant in rut, creating a festival for their eyes with His transcendental body, which is the source of pleasure for the divine goddess of fortune.

TEXT 28

दृष्ट्वा मुहुः श्रुतमनुद्रुतचेतसस्तं
तत्प्रेक्षणोत्स्मितसुधोक्षणलब्धमानाः ।
आनन्दमूर्तिमुपगुह्य दृशात्मलब्धं
हृष्यत्त्वचो जहुरनन्तमरिन्दमाधिम् ॥ २८ ॥

dṛṣṭvā muhuḥ śrutam anudruta-cetasas taṁ
tat-prekṣaṇotsmita-sudhokṣaṇa-labdha-mānāḥ
ānanda-mūrtim upaguhya dṛśātma-labdhaṁ
hṛṣyat-tvaco jahur anantam arindamādhim

dṛṣṭvā—seeing; *muhuḥ*—repeatedly; *śrutam*—heard about; *anudruta*—melted; *cetasaḥ*—whose hearts; *tam*—Him; *tat*—His; *prekṣaṇa*—of the glances; *ut-smita*—and the broad smiles; *sudhā*—by the nectar; *ukṣaṇa*—from the sprinkling; *labdha*—receiving; *mānāḥ*—honor; *ānanda*—of ecstasy; *mūrtim*—the personal form; *upaguhya*—embracing; *dṛśā*—through their eyes; *ātma*—within themselves; *labdham*—gained; *hṛṣyat*—erupting; *tvacaḥ*—their skin; *jahuḥ*—they gave up; *anantam*—unlimited; *arim-dama*—O subduer of enemies (Parīkṣit); *ādhim*—mental distress.

TRANSLATION

The ladies of Mathurā had repeatedly heard about Kṛṣṇa, and thus as soon as they saw Him their hearts melted. They felt honored that He was sprinkling upon them the nectar of His glances and broad smiles. Taking Him into their hearts through their eyes, they embraced Him, the embodiment of all ecstasy, and as their bodily hairs stood on end, O subduer of enemies, they forgot the unlimited distress caused by His absence.

TEXT 29

प्रासादशिखरारूढाः प्रीत्युत्फुल्लमुखाम्बुजाः ।
अभ्यवर्षन् सौमनस्यैः प्रमदा बलकेशवौ ॥ २९ ॥

prāsāda-śikharārūḍhāḥ
prīty-utphulla-mukhāmbujāḥ
abhyavarṣan saumanasyaiḥ
pramadā bala-keśavau

prāsāda—of the mansions; *śikhara*—to the roofs; *ārūḍhāḥ*—having climbed; *prīti*—with affection; *utphulla*—blooming; *mukha*—their faces; *ambujāḥ*—which were like lotuses; *abhyavarṣan*—they showered; *saumanasyaiḥ*—with flowers; *pramadāḥ*—the attractive women; *bala-keśavau*—Balarāma and Kṛṣṇa.

TRANSLATION

Their lotus faces blooming with affection, the ladies who had climbed to the roofs of the mansions rained down showers of flowers upon Lord Balarāma and Lord Kṛṣṇa.

TEXT 30

दध्यक्षतैः सोदपात्रैः स्रग्गन्धैरभ्युपायनैः ।
तावानर्चुः प्रमुदितास्तत्र तत्र द्विजातयः ॥ ३० ॥

dadhy-akṣataiḥ soda-pātraiḥ
srag-gandhair abhyupāyanaiḥ
tāv ānarcuḥ pramuditās
tatra tatra dvijātayaḥ

dadhi—with yogurt; *akṣataiḥ*—unbroken barleycorns; *sa*—and; *uda-pātraiḥ*—with pots filled with water; *srak*—with garlands; *gandhaiḥ*—and fragrant substances; *abhyupāyanaiḥ*—and also with other items of worship; *tau*—the two of Them; *ānarcuḥ*—worshiped; *pramuditāḥ*—joyful; *tatra tatra*—in various places; *dvi-jātayaḥ*—*brāhmaṇas.*

TRANSLATION

Brāhmaṇas standing along the way honored the two Lords with presentations of yogurt, unbroken barleycorns, pots full of water, garlands, fragrant substances such as sandalwood paste, and other items of worship.

TEXT 31

ऊचुः पौरा अहो गोप्यस्तपः किमचरन्महत् ।
या ह्येतावनुपश्यन्ति नरलोकमहोत्सवौ ॥ ३१ ॥

ūcuḥ paurā aho gopyas
tapaḥ kim acaran mahat
yā hy etāv anupaśyanti
nara-loka-mahotsavau

ūcuḥ—said; *paurāḥ*—the women of the city; *aho*—ah; *gopyaḥ*—the cowherd girls (of Vṛndāvana); *tapaḥ*—austerity; *kim*—what; *acaran*—have executed; *mahat*—great; *yāḥ*—who; *hi*—indeed; *etau*—these two; *anu-*

paśyanti—constantly see; *nara-loka*—for human society; *mahā-utsavau*—who are the greatest source of pleasure.

TRANSLATION

The women of Mathurā exclaimed: Oh, what severe austerities the gopīs must have performed to be able to regularly see Kṛṣṇa and Balarāma, who are the greatest source of pleasure for all mankind!

TEXT 32

रजकं कञ्चिदायान्तं रंगकारं गदाग्रजः ।
दृष्ट्वायाचत वासांसि धौतान्यत्युत्तमानि च ॥ ३२ ॥

rajakaṁ kañcid āyāntaṁ
raṅga-kāraṁ gadāgrajaḥ
dṛṣṭvāyācata vāsāṁsi
dhautāny aty-uttamāni ca

rajakam—washerman; *kañcit*—a certain; *āyāntam*—approaching; *raṅga-kāram*—engaged in dyeing; *gada-agrajaḥ*—Lord Śrī Kṛṣṇa, the elder brother of Gada; *dṛṣṭvā*—seeing; *ayācata*—requested; *vāsāṁsi*—garments; *dhautāni*—cleaned; *ati-uttamāni*—first class; *ca*—and.

TRANSLATION

Seeing a washerman approaching who had been dyeing some clothes, Kṛṣṇa asked him for the finest laundered garments he had.

TEXT 33

देह्यावयोः समुचितान्यंग वासांसि चार्हतोः ।
भविष्यति परं श्रेयो दातुस्ते नात्र संशयः ॥ ३३ ॥

dehy āvayoḥ samucitāny
aṅga vāsāṁsi cārhatoḥ
bhaviṣyati paraṁ śreyo
dātus te nātra saṁśayaḥ

dehi—please give; *āvayoḥ*—to Us two; *samucitāni*—suitable; *aṅga*—My dear; *vāsāṁsi*—clothes; *ca*—and; *arhatoḥ*—to the two who are deserving; *bhaviṣyati*—there will be; *param*—supreme; *śreyaḥ*—benefit; *dātuḥ*—

for the giver; *te*—you; *na*—there is not; *atra*—in this matter; *saṁśayaḥ*—doubt.

TRANSLATION

[Lord Kṛṣṇa said:] Please give suitable garments to the two of Us, who certainly deserve them. If you grant this charity, you will undoubtedly receive the greatest benefit.

TEXT 34

स याचितो भगवता परिपूर्णेन सर्वतः ।
साक्षेपं रुषितः प्राह भृत्यो राज्ञः सुदुर्मदः ॥ ३४ ॥

sa yācito bhagavatā
paripūrṇena sarvataḥ
sākṣepaṁ ruṣitaḥ prāha
bhṛtyo rājñaḥ su-durmadaḥ

saḥ—he; *yācitaḥ*—requested; *bhagavatā*—by the Supreme Lord; *paripūrṇena*—who is absolutely complete; *sarvataḥ*—in all respects; *sa-ākṣepam*—insultingly; *ruṣitaḥ*—angered; *prāha*—he spoke; *bhṛtyaḥ*—the servant; *rājñaḥ*—of the King; *su*—very much; *durmadaḥ*—falsely proud.

TRANSLATION

Thus requested by the Supreme Lord, who is perfectly complete in all respects, that arrogant servant of the King became angry and replied insultingly.

TEXT 35

ईदृशान्येव वासांसी नित्यं गिरिवनेचराः ।
परिधत्त किमुद्वृत्ता राजद्रव्याण्यभीप्सथ ॥ ३५ ॥

īdṛśāny eva vāsāṁsi
nityaṁ giri-vane-carāḥ
paridhatta kim udvṛttā
rāja-dravyāṇy abhīpsatha

īdṛśāni—of this sort; *eva*—indeed; *vāsāṁsi*—garments; *nityam*—always; *giri*—on the mountains; *vane*—and in the forests; *carāḥ*—those who travel; *paridhatta*—would put on; *kim*—whether; *udvṛttāḥ*—impudent; *rāja*—the King's; *dravyāṇi*—things; *abhīpsatha*—You want.

TRANSLATION

[The washerman said:] You impudent boys! You're accustomed to roaming the mountains and forests, and yet You would dare put on such clothes as these! These are the King's possessions You're asking for!

TEXT 36

याताशु बालिशा मैवं प्रार्थ्यं यदि जिजीविषा ।
बध्नन्ति घ्नन्ति लुम्पन्ति दृप्तं राजकुलानि वै ॥ ३६ ॥

yātāśu bāliśā maivaṁ
prārthyaṁ yadi jijīviṣā
badhnanti ghnanti lumpanti
dṛptaṁ rāja-kulāni vai

yāta—go; *āśu*—quickly; *bāliśāḥ*—fools; *mā*—do not; *evam*—like this; *prārthyam*—beg; *yadi*—if; *jijīviṣā*—You have the desire to live; *badhnanti*—they tie up; *ghnanti*—kill; *lumpanti*—and loot (his house); *dṛptam*—one who is bold; *rāja-kulāni*—the King's men; *vai*—indeed.

TRANSLATION

Fools, get out of here quickly! Don't beg like this if You want to stay alive. When someone is too bold, the King's men arrest him and kill him and take all his property.

TEXT 37

एवं विकत्थमानस्य कुपितो देवकीसुतः ।
रजकस्य कराग्रेण शिरः कायादपातयत् ॥ ३७ ॥

evaṁ vikatthamānasya
kupito devakī-sutaḥ
rajakasya karāgreṇa
śiraḥ kāyād apātayat

evam—thus; *vikatthamānasya*—who was brazenly speaking; *kupitaḥ*—angered; *devakī-sutaḥ*—Kṛṣṇa, the son of Devakī; *rajakasya*—of the washerman; *kara*—of one hand; *agreṇa*—with the front; *śiraḥ*—the head; *kāyāt*—from his body; *apātayat*—made fall.

TRANSLATION

As the washerman thus spoke brazenly, the son of Devakī became angry, and then merely with His fingertips He separated the man's head from his body.

TEXT 38

तस्यानुजीविनः सर्वे वासःकोशान् विसृज्य वै ।
दुद्रुवुः सर्वतो मार्गं वासांसि जगृहेऽच्युतः ॥ ३८ ॥

tasyānujīvinaḥ sarve
vāsaḥ-kośān visṛjya vai
dudruvuḥ sarvato mārgaṁ
vāsāṁsi jagṛhe'cyutaḥ

tasya—his; *anujīvinaḥ*—employees; *sarve*—all; *vāsaḥ*—of clothes; *kośān*—the bundles; *visṛjya*—leaving behind; *vai*—indeed; *dadruvuḥ*—they fled; *sarvataḥ*—in all directions; *mārgam*—down the road; *vāsāṁsi*—garments; *jagṛhe*—took; *acyutaḥ*—Lord Kṛṣṇa.

TRANSLATION

The washerman's assistants all dropped their bundles of clothes and fled down the road, scattering in all directions. Lord Kṛṣṇa then took the clothes.

TEXT 39

वसित्वात्मप्रिये वस्त्रे कृष्णः संकर्षणस्तथा ।
शेषाण्यादत्त गोपेभ्यो विसृज्य भुवि कानिचित् ॥ ३९ ॥

vasitvātma-priye vastre
kṛṣṇaḥ saṅkarṣaṇas tathā
śeṣāṇy ādatta gopebhyo
visṛjya bhuvi kānicit

vasitvā—dressing Himself; *ātma-priye*—which He liked; *vastre*—in a pair of garments; *kṛṣṇaḥ*—Kṛṣṇa; *saṅkarṣaṇaḥ*—Balarāma; *tathā*—also; *śeṣāṇi*

—the rest; *ādatta*—He gave; *gopebhyaḥ*—to the cowherd boys; *visṛjya*—throwing away; *bhuvi*—on the ground; *kānicit*—several.

TRANSLATION

Kṛṣṇa and Balarāma put on pairs of garments that especially pleased Them, and then Kṛṣṇa distributed the remaining clothes among the cowherd boys, leaving some scattered on the ground.

TEXT 40

ततस्तु वायकः प्रीतस्तयोर्वेषमकल्पयत् ।
विचित्रवर्णैश्चैलेयैराकल्पैरनुरूपतः ॥ ४० ॥

tatas tu vāyakaḥ prītas
tayor veṣam akalpayat
vicitra-varṇaiś caileyair
ākalpair anurūpataḥ

tataḥ—then; *tu*—moreover; *vāyakaḥ*—a weaver; *prītaḥ*—affectionate; *tayoḥ*—for the two of Them; *veṣam*—dress; *akalpayat*—arranged; *vicitra*—various; *varṇaiḥ*—with colors; *caileyaiḥ*—made of cloth; *ākalpaiḥ*—with ornaments; *anurūpataḥ*—suitably.

TRANSLATION

Thereupon a weaver came forward and, feeling affection for the Lords, nicely adorned Their attire with cloth ornaments of various colors.

PURPORT

Śrīla Jīva Gosvāmī explains that the weaver adorned the Lords with cloth armlets and earrings that looked just like jewels. The word *anurūpataḥ* indicates that the colors matched nicely.

TEXT 41

नानालक्षणवेषाभ्यां कृष्णरामौ विरेजतुः ।
स्वलंकृतौ बालगजौ पर्वणीव सितेतरौ ॥ ४१ ॥

nānā-lakṣaṇa-veṣābhyāṁ
kṛṣṇa-rāmau virejatuḥ

sv-alaṅkṛtau bāla-gajau
parvaṇīva sitetarau

nānā—various; *lakṣaṇa*—having fine qualities; *veṣābhyām*—with Their individual clothes; *kṛṣṇa-rāmau*—Kṛṣṇa and Balarāma; *virejatuḥ*—appeared resplendent; *su-alaṅkṛtau*—nicely decorated; *bāla*—young; *gajau*—elephants; *parvaṇi*—during a festival; *iva*—as if; *sita*—white; *itarau*—and the opposite (black).

TRANSLATION

Kṛṣṇa and Balarāma looked resplendent, each in His own unique, wonderfully ornamented outfit. They resembled a pair of young elephants, one white and the other black, decorated for a festive occasion.

TEXT 42

तस्य प्रसन्नो भगवान् प्रादात्सारूप्यमात्मनः ।
श्रियं च परमां लोके बलैश्वर्यस्मृतीन्द्रियम् ॥ ४२ ॥

tasya prasanno bhagavān
prādāt sārūpyam ātmanaḥ
śriyaṁ ca paramāṁ loke
balaiśvarya-smṛtīndriyam

tasya—with him; *prasannaḥ*—satisfied; *bhagavān*—the Supreme Lord; *prādāt*—granted; *sārūpyam*—the liberation of having the same form; *ātmanaḥ*—as Himself; *śriyam*—opulence; *ca*—and; *paramām*—supreme; *loke*—in this world; *bala*—physical strength; *aiśvarya*—influence; *smṛti*—strength of memory; *indriyam*—dexterity of the senses.

TRANSLATION

Pleased with the weaver, the Supreme Lord Kṛṣṇa blessed him that after death he would achieve the liberation of attaining a form like the Lord's, and that while in this world he would enjoy supreme opulence, physical strength, influence, memory and sensory vigor.

TEXT 43

ततः सुदाम्नो भवनं मालाकारस्य जग्मतुः ।
तौ दृष्ट्वा स समुत्थाय ननाम शिरसा भुवि ॥ ४३ ॥

tataḥ sudāmno bhavanaṁ
mālā-kārasya jagmatuḥ
tau dṛṣṭvā sa samutthāya
nanāma śirasā bhuvi

tataḥ—then; *sudāmnaḥ*—of Sudāmā; *bhavanam*—to the home; *mālā-kārasya*—of the garland-maker; *jagmatuḥ*—the two of Them went; *tau*—Them; *dṛṣṭvā*—seeing; *saḥ*—he; *samutthāya*—standing up; *nanāma*—bowed down; *śirasā*—with his head; *bhuvi*—on the ground.

TRANSLATION

The two Lords then went to the house of the garland-maker Sudāmā. When Sudāmā saw Them he at once stood up and then bowed down, placing his head on the ground.

TEXT 44

तयोरासनमानीय पाद्यं चार्घ्यार्हणादिभिः ।
पूजां सानुगयोश्चक्रे स्रक्ताम्बूलानुलेपनैः ॥ ४४ ॥

tayor āsanam ānīya
pādyaṁ cārghyārhaṇādibhiḥ
pūjāṁ sānugayoś cakre
srak-tāmbūlānulepanaiḥ

tayoḥ—for Them; *āsanam*—seats; *ānīya*—bringing; *pādyam*—water to wash the feet; *ca*—and; *arghya*—with water to wash the hands; *arhaṇa*—presents; *ādibhiḥ*—and so on; *pūjām*—worship; *sa-anugayoḥ*—of the two, together with Their companions; *cakre*—he performed; *srak*—with garlands; *tāmbūla*—betel-nut preparation (*pān*); *anulepanaiḥ*—and sandalwood paste.

TRANSLATION

After offering Them seats and bathing Their feet, Sudāmā worshiped Them and Their companions with arghya, garlands, pān, sandalwood paste and other presentations.

TEXT 45

प्राह नः सार्थकं जन्म पावितं च कुलं प्रभो ।
पितृदेवर्षयो मह्यं तुष्टा ह्यागमनेन वाम् ॥ ४५ ॥

prāha naḥ sārthakaṁ janma
pāvitaṁ ca kulaṁ prabho
pitṛ-devarṣayo mahyaṁ
tuṣṭā hy āgamanena vām

prāha—he said; *naḥ*—our; *sa-arthakam*—worthwhile; *janma*—the birth; *pāvitam*—purified; *ca*—and; *kulam*—the family; *prabho*—O Lord; *pitṛ*—my forefathers; *deva*—the demigods; *ṛṣayaḥ*—and the great sages; *mahyam*—with me; *tuṣṭāḥ*—are satisfied; *hi*—indeed; *āgamanena*—by the arrival; *vām*—of You two.

TRANSLATION

[Sudāmā said:] O Lord, my birth is now sanctified and my family free of contamination. Now that You both have come here, my forefathers, the demigods and the great sages are certainly all satisfied with me.

TEXT 46

भवन्तौ किल विश्वस्य जगतः कारणं परम्।
अवतीर्णाविहांशेन क्षेमाय च भवाय च ॥ ४६ ॥

bhavantau kila viśvasya
jagataḥ kāraṇaṁ param
avatīrṇāv ihāṁśena
kṣemāya ca bhavāya ca

bhavantau—You two; *kila*—indeed; *viśvasya*—of the entire; *jagataḥ*—universe; *kāraṇam*—the cause; *param*—ultimate; *avatīrṇau*—having descended; *iha*—here; *aṁśena*—with Your plenary portions; *kṣemāya*—for the benefit; *ca*—and; *bhavāya*—for the prosperity; *ca*—also.

TRANSLATION

You two Lords are the ultimate cause of this entire universe. To bestow sustenance and prosperity upon this realm, You have descended with Your plenary expansions.

TEXT 47

न हि वां विषमा दृष्टिः सुहृदोर्जगदात्मनोः।
समयोः सर्वभूतेषु भजन्तं भजतोरपि ॥ ४७ ॥

na hi vāṁ viṣamā dṛṣṭiḥ
suhṛdor jagad-ātmanoḥ
samayoḥ sarva-bhūteṣu
bhajantaṁ bhajator api

na—there is not; *hi*—indeed; *vām*—on Your part; *viṣamā*—biased; *dṛṣṭiḥ*—vision; *suhṛdoḥ*—who are well-wishing friends; *jagat*—of the universe; *ātmanoḥ*—the Soul; *samayoḥ*—equal; *sarva*—to all; *bhūteṣu*—living beings; *bhajantam*—those who worship You; *bhajatoḥ*—reciprocating with; *api*—even.

TRANSLATION

Because You are the well-wishing friends and Supreme Soul of the whole universe, You regard all with unbiased vision. Therefore, although You reciprocate Your devotees' loving worship, You always remain equally disposed toward all living beings.

TEXT 48

तावाज्ञापयतं भृत्यं किमहं करवाणि वाम्।
पुंसोऽत्यनुग्रहो ह्येष भवद्भिर्यन्नियुज्यते ॥ ४८ ॥

tāv ājñāpayataṁ bhṛtyaṁ
kim ahaṁ karavāṇi vām
puṁso'ty-anugraho hy eṣa
bhavadbhir yan niyujyate

tau—They; *ājñāpayatam*—should please order; *bhṛtyam*—Their servant; *kim*—what; *aham*—I; *karavāṇi*—should do; *vām*—for You; *puṁsaḥ*—for any person; *ati*—extreme; *anugrahaḥ*—mercy; *hi*—indeed; *eṣaḥ*—this; *bhavadbhiḥ*—by You; *yat*—in which; *niyujyate*—he is engaged.

TRANSLATION

Please order me, Your servant, to do whatever You wish. To be engaged by You in some service is certainly a great blessing for anyone.

TEXT 49

इत्यभिप्रेत्य राजेन्द्र सुदामा प्रीतमानसः ।
शस्तैः सुगन्धैः कुसुमैर्माला विरचिता ददौ ॥ ४९ ॥

ity abhipretya rājendra
sudāmā prīta-mānasaḥ
śastaiḥ su-gandhaiḥ kusumair
mālā viracitā dadau

iti—thus speaking; *abhipretya*—understanding Their intention; *rāja-indra*—O best of kings (Parīkṣit); *sudāmā*—Sudāmā; *prīta-mānasaḥ*—pleased at heart; *śastaiḥ*—fresh; *su-gandhaiḥ*—and fragrant; *kusumaiḥ*—with flowers; *malaḥ*—garlands; *viracitāḥ*—made; *dadau*—he gave.

TRANSLATION

[Śukadeva Gosvāmī continued:] O best of kings, having spoken these words, Sudāmā could understand what Kṛṣṇa and Balarāma wanted. Thus with great pleasure he presented Them with garlands of fresh, fragrant flowers.

TEXT 50

ताभिः स्वलंकृतौ प्रीतौ कृष्णरामौ सहानुगौ ।
प्रणताय प्रपन्नाय ददतुर्वरदौ वरान् ॥ ५० ॥

tābhiḥ sv-alaṅkṛtau prītau
kṛṣṇa-rāmau sahānugau
praṇatāya prapannāya
dadatur vara-dau varān

tābhiḥ—with those (garlands); *su-alaṅkṛtau*—beautifully ornamented; *prītau*—satisfied; *kṛṣṇa-rāmau*—Kṛṣṇa and Balarāma; *saha*—along with; *anugau*—Their companions; *praṇatāya*—who was bowing down; *prapannāya*—to the surrendered (Sudāmā); *dadatuḥ*—They gave; *varadau*—the two givers of benedictions; *varān*—a choice of benedictions.

TRANSLATION

Beautifully adorned with these garlands, Kṛṣṇa and Balarāma were delighted, and so were Their companions. The two Lords then offered the surrendered Sudāmā, who was bowing down before Them, whatever benedictions he desired.

TEXT 51

सोऽपि वव्रेऽचलां भक्तिं तस्मिन्नेवाखिलात्मनि।
तद्भक्तेषु च सौहार्दं भूतेषु च दयां पराम् ॥ ५१ ॥

so'pi vavre'calāṁ bhaktiṁ
tasminn evākhilātmani
tad-bhakteṣu ca sauhārdaṁ
bhūteṣu ca dayāṁ parām

saḥ—he; *api*—and; *vavre*—chose; *acalām*—unshakable; *bhaktim*—devotion; *tasmin*—to Him; *eva*—alone; *akhila*—of everything; *ātmani*—the Supreme Soul; *tat*—toward His; *bhakteṣu*—devotees; *ca*—and; *sauhārdam*—friendship; *bhūteṣu*—toward living beings in general; *ca*—and; *dayām*—mercy; *parām*—transcendental.

TRANSLATION

Sudāmā chose unshakable devotion for Kṛṣṇa, the Supreme Soul of all existence; friendship with His devotees; and transcendental compassion for all living beings.

TEXT 52

इति तस्मै वरं दत्त्वा श्रियं चान्वयवर्धिनीम्।
बलमायुर्यशः कान्तिं निर्जगाम सहाग्रजः ॥ ५२ ॥

iti tasmai varaṁ dattvā
śriyaṁ cānvaya-vardhinīm
balam āyur yaśaḥ kāntiṁ
nirjagāma sahāgrajaḥ

iti—thus; *tasmai*—to him; *varam*—the benediction; *dattvā*—giving; *śriyam*—opulence; *ca*—and; *anvaya*—his family; *vardhinīm*—expanding; *balam*—strength; *āyuḥ*—long life; *yaśaḥ*—fame; *kāntim*—beauty; *nirjagāma*—He left; *saha*—together with; *agra-jaḥ*—His elder brother, Lord Balarāma.

TRANSLATION

Not only did Lord Kṛṣṇa grant Sudāmā these benedictions, but He also awarded him strength, long life, fame, beauty and ever-increasing prosperity for his family. Then Kṛṣṇa and His elder brother took Their leave.

PURPORT

We can see a clear difference between Lord Kṛṣṇa's dealings with the nasty washerman and His dealings with the devoted florist Sudāmā. The Lord is as hard as a thunderbolt for those who defy Him and as soft as a rose for those who surrender to Him. Therefore we should all sincerely surrender to Lord Kṛṣṇa, since that is clearly in our self-interest.

Thus end the purports of the humble servants of His Divine Grace A.C. Bhaktivedanta Swami Prabhupāda to the Tenth Canto, Forty-first Chapter, of the Śrīmad-Bhāgavatam, *entitled "Kṛṣṇa and Balarāma Enter Mathurā."*

CHAPTER FORTY- TWO

The Breaking of the Sacrificial Bow

This chapter describes the benediction Trivakrā received, the breaking of the sacrificial bow, the destruction of Kaṁsa's soldiers, the inauspicious omens Kaṁsa saw and the festivities at the wrestling arena.

After leaving Sudāmā's house, Lord Kṛṣṇa came upon Trivakrā, a young hunchbacked maidservant of Kaṁsa's who was carrying a tray of fine ointments. The Lord asked her who she was and requested some ointment from her. Entranced by His beauty and joking words, Trivakrā gave both Kṛṣṇa and Balarāma a good deal of ointment. In return, Kṛṣṇa stepped on her toes with His lotus feet, took hold of her chin and lifted, thus straightening her spine. The now beautiful and charming Trivakrā then grabbed the edge of Kṛṣṇa's upper cloth and asked Him to come to her house. Kṛṣṇa replied that after He had taken care of some business He would certainly come and relieve her mental torment. Then the two Lords continued Their sightseeing tour of Mathurā.

As Kṛṣṇa and Balarāma walked along the King's road, the merchants worshiped Them with various offerings. Kṛṣṇa asked where the bow sacrifice was to take place, and when He arrived at the arena He saw the wonderful bow, which resembled Lord Indra's. Despite the guards' protests, Kṛṣṇa forcibly picked up the bow, easily strung it and in an instant broke it in half, producing an ear-splitting sound that filled the heavens and struck terror in the heart of Kaṁsa. The many guards attacked Kṛṣṇa, crying out "Seize Him! Kill Him!" But Kṛṣṇa and Balarāma simply picked up the two halves of the bow and beat the guards to death. Next the Lords annihilated a company of soldiers sent by Kaṁsa, and then They left the arena and continued Their tour.

When the people of the city saw the amazing prowess and beauty of Kṛṣṇa and Balarāma, they thought They must be two chief demigods. Indeed, as the residents of Mathurā gazed upon the Lords, they enjoyed all the blessings the *gopīs* had predicted.

At sunset Kṛṣṇa and Balarāma returned to the cowherds' camp for Their evening meal. They then passed the night resting comfortably. But King Kaṁsa was not so fortunate. When he heard how Kṛṣṇa and Balarāma had easily broken the mighty bow and destroyed his soldiers, he spent the night in great anxiety. Both while awake and while dreaming he saw many ill omens portending his imminent death, and his fear ruined any chance for rest.

At dawn the wrestling festival began. Crowds of people from the city and outlying districts entered the arena and took their seats in the lavishly decorated galleries. Kaṁsa, his heart trembling, sat down on the royal dais and invited Nanda Mahārāja and the other cowherd men to come sit in their places, and they did so after offering him their gifts. The musical overture then began as the sounds of the wrestlers slapping their arms resounded.

TEXT 1

श्रीशुक उवाच
अथ व्रजन् राजपथेन माधवः
स्त्रियं गृहीतांगविलेपभाजनाम् ।
विलोक्य कुब्जां युवतीं वराननां
पप्रच्छ यान्तीं प्रहसन् रसप्रदः ॥ १ ॥

śrī-śuka uvāca
atha vrajan rāja-pathena mādhavaḥ
striyaṁ gṛhītāṅga-vilepa-bhājanām
vilokya kubjāṁ yuvatīṁ varānanāṁ
papraccha yāntīṁ prahasan rasa-pradaḥ

śrī-śukaḥ uvāca—Śukadeva Gosvāmī said; *atha*—then; *vrajan*—walking; *rāja-pathena*—along the King's road; *mādhavaḥ*—Kṛṣṇa; *striyam*—a woman; *gṛhīta*—holding; *aṅga*—for the body; *vilepa*—with ointments; *bhājanām*—a tray; *vilokya*—seeing; *kubjām*—hunchbacked; *yuvatīm*—young; *vara-ānanām*—with an attractive face; *papraccha*—He inquired; *yāntīm*—going; *prahasan*—smiling; *rasa*—of the pleasure of love; *pradaḥ*—the bestower.

TRANSLATION

Śukadeva Gosvāmī said: As He walked down the King's road, Lord Mādhava then saw a young hunchback woman with an attractive face, who carried a tray of fragrant ointments as she walked along. The bestower of the ecstasy of love smiled and inquired from her as follows.

PURPORT

According to Śrīla Viśvanātha Cakravartī Ṭhākura, the young hunchbacked girl was actually a partial expansion of the Lord's wife Satyabhāmā. Satyabhāmā is the Lord's internal energy known as Bhū-śakti, and this expansion of hers, known as Pṛthivī, represents the earth, which was bent down by the great burden of countless wicked rulers. Lord Kṛṣṇa descended to remove these wicked rulers, and thus His pastime of straightening out the hunchback Trivakrā, as explained in these verses, represents His rectifying the burdened condition of the earth. At the same time, the Lord awarded Trivakrā a conjugal relationship with Himself.

In addition to the given meaning, the word *rasa-pradaḥ* indicates that the Lord amused His cowherd boyfriends by His dealings with the young hunchback.

TEXT 2

का त्वं वरोर्वेतदु हानुलेपनं
कस्यांगने वा कथयस्व साधु नः ।
देह्यावयोरंगविलेपमुत्तमं
श्रेयस्ततस्ते न चिराद् भविष्यति ॥ २ ॥

kā tvaṁ varorv etad u hānulepanaṁ
kasyāṅgane vā kathayasva sādhu naḥ
dehy āvayor aṅga-vilepam uttamaṁ
śreyas tatas te na cirād bhaviṣyati

kā—who; *tvam*—you; *vara-ūru*—O beautiful-thighed one; *etat*—this; *u ha*—ah, indeed; *anulepanam*—ointment; *kasya*—for whom; *aṅgane*—My dear woman; *vā*—or; *kathayasva*—please tell; *sādhu*—honestly; *naḥ*—Us; *dehi*—please give; *āvayoḥ*—to Us two; *aṅga-vilepam*—body ointment; *uttamam*—excellent; *śreyaḥ*—benefit; *tataḥ*—thereafter; *te*—your; *na cirāt*—soon; *bhaviṣyati*—will be.

TRANSLATION

[Lord Kṛṣṇa said:] Who are you, O beautiful-thighed one? Ah, ointment! Who is it for, my dear lady? Please tell Us truthfully. Give Us both some of your finest ointment and you will soon gain a great boon.

PURPORT

The Lord jokingly addressed the lady as *varoru,* "O beautiful-thighed one." His joke was not malicious, since He was actually about to make her beautiful.

TEXT 3

सैरन्ध्र्युवाच
दास्यस्म्यहं सुन्दर कंससम्मता
त्रिवक्रनामा ह्यनुलेपकर्मणि ।
मद्भावितं भोजपतेरतिप्रियं
विना युवां कोऽन्यतमस्तदर्हति ॥ ३ ॥

sairandhry uvāca
dāsy asmy ahaṁ sundara kaṁsa-sammatā
trivakra-nāmā hy anulepa-karmaṇi
mad-bhāvitaṁ bhoja-pater ati-priyaṁ
vinā yuvāṁ ko'nyatamas tad arhati

sairandhrī uvāca—the maidservant said; *dāsī*—a servant; *asmi*—am; *aham*—I; *sundara*—O handsome one; *kaṁsa*—by Kaṁsa; *sammatā*—respected; *trivakra-nāmā*—known as Trivakrā ("bent in three places"); *hi*—indeed; *anulepa*—with ointments; *karmaṇi*—for my work; *mat*—by me; *bhāvitam*—prepared; *bhoja-pateḥ*—to the chief of the Bhojas; *ati-priyam*—very dear; *vinā*—except for; *yuvām*—You two; *kaḥ*—who; *anyatamaḥ*—else; *tat*—that; *arhati*—deserves.

TRANSLATION

The maidservant replied: O handsome one, I am a servant of King Kaṁsa, who highly regards me for the ointments I make. My name is Trivakrā. Who else but You two deserve my ointments, which the lord of the Bhojas likes so much?

PURPORT

Śrīla Viśvanātha Cakravartī explains that Trivakrā, who is also known as Kubjā, used the singular address *sundara,* "O handsome one," to hint that she felt conjugal desire for Kṛṣṇa alone, and she used the dual form *yuvām,* "for both of You," to try to hide her conjugal sentiment. The hunchback's name, Trivakrā, indicates that her body was bent at the neck, chest and waist.

TEXT 4

रूपपेशलमाधुर्यहसितालापवीक्षितैः ।
धर्षितात्मा ददौ सान्द्रमुभयोरनुलेपनम् ॥ ४ ॥

rūpa-peśala-mādhurya
hasitālāpa-vīkṣitaiḥ
dharṣitātmā dadau sāndram
ubhayor anulepanam

rūpa—by His beauty; *peśala*—charm; *mādhurya*—sweetness; *hasita*—smiles; *ālāpa*—talking; *vīkṣitaiḥ*—and glances; *dharṣita*—overwhelmed; *ātmā*—her mind; *dadau*—she gave; *sāndram*—plentiful; *ubhayoḥ*—to both of Them; *anulepanam*—ointment.

TRANSLATION

Her mind overwhelmed by Kṛṣṇa's beauty, charm, sweetness, smiles, words and glances, Trivakrā gave both Kṛṣṇa and Balarāma generous amounts of ointment.

PURPORT

This incident is also described in the *Viṣṇu Purāṇa* (5.20.7):

śrutvā tam āha sā kṛṣṇaṁ
gṛhyatām iti sādaram
anulepanaṁ pradadau
gātra-yogyam athobhayoḥ

"Hearing this, she respectfully replied to Lord Kṛṣṇa, 'Please take it,' and gave both of Them ointment suitable for applying to Their bodies."

TEXT 5

ततस्तावंगरागेण स्ववर्णेतरशोभिना ।
सम्प्राप्तपरभागेन शुशुभातेऽनुरञ्जितौ ॥ ५ ॥

tatas tāv aṅga-rāgeṇa
sva-varṇetara-śobhinā
samprāpta-para-bhāgena
śuśubhāte 'nurañjitau

tataḥ—then; *tau*—They; *aṅga*—of Their bodies; *rāgeṇa*—with the coloring cosmetics; *sva*—Their own; *varṇa*—with colors; *itara*—other than; *śobhinā*—adorning; *samprāpta*—which exhibited; *para*—the highest; *bhagena*—excellence; *śuśubhāte*—They appeared beautiful; *anurañjitau*—anointed.

TRANSLATION

Anointed with these most excellent cosmetics, which adorned Them with hues that contrasted with Their complexions, the two Lords appeared extremely beautiful.

PURPORT

The *ācāryas* suggest that Kṛṣṇa spread yellow ointment upon His body, and Balarāma blue ointment upon His.

TEXT 6

प्रसन्नो भगवान् कुब्जां त्रिवक्रां रुचिराननाम् ।
ऋज्वीं कर्तुं मनश्चक्रे दर्शयन् दर्शने फलम् ॥ ६ ॥

prasanno bhagavān kubjāṁ
trivakrāṁ rucirānanām
ṛjvīṁ kartuṁ manaś cakre
darśayan darśane phalam

prasannaḥ—satisfied; *bhagavān*—the Supreme Lord; *kubjām*—the hunchback; *trivakrā*—Trivakrā; *rucira*—attractive; *ānanām*—whose face; *ṛjvīm*—straight; *kartum*—to make; *manaḥ cakre*—He decided; *darśayan*—showing; *darśane*—of seeing Him; *phalam*—the result.

TRANSLATION

Lord Kṛṣṇa was pleased with Trivakrā, so He decided to straighten that hunchbacked girl with the lovely face just to demonstrate the result of seeing Him.

TEXT 7

पद्भ्यामाक्रम्य प्रपदे द्व्यंगुल्युत्तानपाणिना ।
प्रगृह्य चिबुकेऽध्यात्ममुदनीनमदच्युतः ॥ ७ ॥

padbhyām ākramya prapade
dvy-aṅguly-uttāna-pāṇinā
pragṛhya cibuke'dhyātmam
udanīnamad acyutaḥ

padbhyām—with both His feet; *ākramya*—pressing down; *prapade*—on her toes; *dvi*—having two; *aṅguli*—fingers; *uttāna*—pointing upwards; *pāṇinā*—with His hands; *pragṛhya*—taking hold of; *cibuke*—her chin; *adhyātmam*—her body; *udanīnamat*—He raised; *acyutaḥ*—Lord Kṛṣṇa.

TRANSLATION

Pressing down on her toes with both His feet, Lord Acyuta placed one upward-pointing finger of each hand under her chin and straightened up her body.

TEXT 8

सा तदर्जुसमानांगी बृहच्छ्रोणिपयोधरा ।
मुकुन्दस्पर्शनात्सद्यो बभूव प्रमदोत्तमा ॥ ८ ॥

sā tadarju-samānāṅgī
bṛhac-chroṇi-payodharā
mukunda-sparśanāt sadyo
babhūva pramadottamā

sā—she; *tadā*—then; *ṛju*—straight; *samāna*—even; *aṅgī*—her limbs; *bṛhat*—large; *śroṇi*—her hips; *payaḥ-dharā*—and breasts; *mukunda-sparśanāt*—by the touch of Lord Mukunda; *sadyaḥ*—suddenly; *babhūva*—became; *pramadā*—a woman; *uttamā*—most perfect.

TRANSLATION

Simply by Lord Mukunda's touch, Trivakrā was suddenly transformed into an exquisitely beautiful woman with straight, evenly proportioned limbs and large hips and breasts.

TEXT 9

ततो रूपगुणौदार्यसम्पन्ना प्राह केशवम् ।
उत्तरीयान्तमाकृष्य स्मयन्ती जातहृच्छया ॥ ९ ॥

tato rūpa-guṇaudārya-
sampannā prāha keśavam
uttarīyāntam ākṛṣya
smayantī jāta-hṛc-chayā

tataḥ—then; *rūpa*—with beauty; *guṇa*—good character; *audārya*—and generosity; *sampannā*—endowed; *prāha*—she addressed; *keśavam*—Lord Kṛṣṇa; *uttarīya*—of His upper garment; *antam*—the end; *ākṛṣya*—pulling; *smayantī*—smiling; *jāta*—having developed; *hṛt-śayā*—lusty feelings.

TRANSLATION

Now endowed with beauty, character and generosity, Trivakrā began to feel lusty desires for Lord Keśava. Taking hold of the end of His upper cloth, she smiled and addressed Him as follows.

TEXT 10

एहि वीर गृहं यामो न त्वां त्यक्तुमिहोत्सहे ।
त्वयोन्मथितचित्तायाः प्रसीद पुरुषर्षभ ॥ १० ॥

ehi vīra gṛhaṁ yāmo
na tvāṁ tyaktum ihotsahe
tvayonmathita-cittāyāḥ
prasīda puruṣarṣabha

ehi—come; *vīra*—O hero; *gṛham*—to my house; *yāmaḥ*—let us go; *na*—not; *tvām*—You; *tyaktum*—to leave; *iha*—here; *utsahe*—I can bear; *tvayā*—by You; *unmathita*—agitated; *cittāyāḥ*—on her whose mind; *prasīda*—please have mercy; *puruṣa-ṛṣabha*—O best of men.

TRANSLATION

[Trivakrā said:] Come, O hero, let us go to my house. I cannot bear to leave You here. O best of males, please take pity on me, since You have agitated my mind.

PURPORT

Śrīla Viśvanātha Cakravartī supplies the following conversation:
Kṛṣṇa: Is it for the purpose of dining that you're inviting Me to your house?
Trivakrā: I simply can't leave You here.

Kṛṣṇa: But people here on the King's road will misconstrue what you're saying and laugh. Therefore please don't speak like this.

Trivakrā: I can't help being agitated. You made the mistake of touching me. It's not my fault.

TEXT 11

एवं स्त्रिया याच्यमानः कृष्णो रामस्य पश्यतः ।
मुखं वीक्ष्यानु गोपानां प्रहसंस्तामुवाच ह ॥ ११ ॥

evaṁ striyā yācyamānaḥ
kṛṣṇo rāmasya paśyataḥ
mukhaṁ vīkṣyānu gopānāṁ
prahasaṁs tām uvāca ha

evam—in this way; *striyā*—by the woman; *yācya nānaḥ*—being begged; *kṛṣṇaḥ*—Lord Kṛṣṇa; *rāmasya*—of Balarāma; *paśyataḥ*—who was looking on; *mukham*—at the face; *vīkṣya*—glancing; *anu*—then; *gopānām*—of the cowherd boys; *prahasan*—laughing; *tām*—to her; *uvāca ha*—He said.

TRANSLATION

Thus entreated by the woman, Lord Kṛṣṇa first glanced at the face of Balarāma, who was watching the incident, and then at the faces of the cowherd boys. Then with a laugh Kṛṣṇa replied to her as follows.

TEXT 12

एष्यामि ते गृहं सुभ्रु पुंसामाधिविकर्शनम् ।
साधितार्थोऽगृहाणां नः पान्थानां त्वं परायणम् ॥ १२ ॥

eṣyāmi te gṛhaṁ su-bhru
puṁsām ādhi-vikarśanam
sādhitārtho 'gṛhāṇāṁ naḥ
pānthānāṁ tvaṁ parāyaṇam

eṣyāmi—I will go; *te*—your; *gṛham*—to the house; *su-bhru*—O you who have beautiful eyebrows; *puṁsām*—of men; *ādhi*—the mental distress; *vikarśanam*—which eradicates; *sādhita*—having accomplished; *arthaḥ*—My purpose; *agṛhāṇām*—who have no home; *naḥ*—for Us; *pānthānām*—who are traveling on the road; *tvam*—you; *para*—the best; *ayaṇam*—shelter.

TRANSLATION

[Lord Kṛṣṇa said:] O lady with beautiful eyebrows, as soon as I fulfill My purpose I will certainly visit your house, where men can relieve their anxiety. Indeed, you are the best refuge for Us homeless travelers.

PURPORT

By the word *agṛhāṇām,* Śrī Kṛṣṇa indicated not only that He had no fixed residence but also that He was not yet married.

TEXT 13

विसृज्य माध्व्या वाण्या ताम् व्रजन्मार्गे वणिक्पथैः ।
नानोपायनताम्बूलस्रग्गन्धैः साग्रजोऽर्चितः ॥ १३ ॥

visṛjya mādhvyā vāṇyā tām
vrajan mārge vaṇikpathaiḥ
nānopāyana-tāmbūla-
srag-gandhaiḥ sāgrajo'rcitaḥ

visṛjya—leaving; *mādhvyā*—sweet; *vāṇyā*—with words; *tām*—her; *vrajan*—walking; *mārge*—along the road; *vaṇik-pathaiḥ*—by the merchants; *nānā*—with various; *upāyana*—respectful offerings; *tāmbūla*—betel nut; *srak*—garlands; *gandhaiḥ*—and fragrant substances; *sa*—together with; *agra-jaḥ*—His elder brother; *arcitaḥ*—worshiped.

TRANSLATION

Leaving her with these sweet words, Lord Kṛṣṇa walked further down the road. The merchants along the way worshiped Him and His elder brother by presenting Them with various respectful offerings, including pān, garlands and fragrant substances.

TEXT 14

तद्दर्शनस्मरक्षोभादात्मानं नाविदन् स्त्रियः ।
विस्रस्तवासःकवरवलया लेख्यमूर्तयः ॥ १४ ॥

tad-darśana-smara-kṣobhād
ātmānaṁ nāvidan striyaḥ
visrasta-vāsaḥ-kavara
valayā lekhya-mūrtayaḥ

tat—Him; *darśana*—because of seeing; *smara*—due to the effects of Cupid; *kṣobhāt*—by their agitation; *ātmānam*—themselves; *na avidan*—could not recognize; *striyaḥ*—the women; *visrasta*—disheveled; *vāsaḥ*—their clothes; *kavara*—the locks of their hair; *valayāḥ*—and their bangles; *lekhya*—(as if) drawn in a picture; *mūrtayaḥ*—their forms.

TRANSLATION

The sight of Kṛṣṇa aroused Cupid in the hearts of the city women. Thus agitated, they forgot themselves. Their clothes, braids and bangles became disheveled, and they stood as still as figures in a painting.

PURPORT

Śrīla Viśvanātha Cakravartī states that since the women of Mathurā immediately experienced symptoms of conjugal attraction when they saw Kṛṣṇa, they were the most advanced devotees in the city. The ten effects of Cupid are described as follows: *cakṣū-rāgaḥ prathamaṁ cittāsaṅgas tato'tha saṅkalpaḥ nidrā-cchedas tanutā viṣaya-nivṛttis trapā-nāśaḥ/ unmādo mūrcchā mṛtir ity etāḥ smara-daśā daśaiva syuḥ.* "First comes attraction expressed through the eyes, then intense attachment in the mind, then determination, loss of sleep, becoming emaciated, disinterest in external things, shamelessness, madness, becoming stunned and death. These are the ten stages of Cupid's effects."

Śrīla Viśvanātha Cakravartī also points out that devotees who possess pure love of Godhead generally do not exhibit the symptom of death, since this is inauspicious in relation to Kṛṣṇa. They do, however, manifest the other nine symptoms, culminating in becoming stunned in ecstasy.

TEXT 15

ततः पौरान् पृच्छमानो धनुषः स्थानमच्युतः ।
तस्मिन् प्रविष्टो ददृशे धनुरैन्द्रमिवाद्भुतम् ॥ १५ ॥

tataḥ paurān pṛcchamāno
dhanuṣaḥ sthānam acyutaḥ
tasmin praviṣṭo dadṛśe
dhanur aindram ivādbhutam

tataḥ—then; *paurān*—from the city residents; *pṛcchamānaḥ*—inquiring about; *dhanuṣaḥ*—of the bow; *sthānam*—the place; *acyutaḥ*—the infallible Supreme Lord; *tasmin*—there; *praviṣṭaḥ*—entering; *dadṛśe*—He saw;

dhanuḥ—the bow; *aindram*—that of Lord Indra; *iva*—like; *adbhutam*—amazing.

TRANSLATION

Lord Kṛṣṇa then asked the local people where the arena was in which the bow sacrifice would take place. When He went there He saw the amazing bow, which resembled Lord Indra's.

TEXT 16

पुरुषैर्बहुभिर्गुप्तमर्चितं परमर्द्धिमत् ।
वार्यमाणो नृभिः कृष्णः प्रसह्य धनुराददे ॥ १६ ॥

puruṣair bahubhir guptam
arcitaṁ paramarddhimat
vāryamāṇo nṛbhiḥ kṛṣṇaḥ
prasahya dhanur ādade

puruṣaiḥ—by men; *bahubhiḥ*—many; *guptam*—guarded; *arcitam*—being worshiped; *parama*—supreme; *ṛddhi*—opulence; *mat*—possessing; *vāryamāṇaḥ*—warded off; *nṛbhiḥ*—by the guards; *kṛṣṇaḥ*—Lord Kṛṣṇa; *prasahya*—by force; *dhanuḥ*—the bow; *ādade*—picked up.

TRANSLATION

That most opulent bow was guarded by a large company of men, who were respectfully worshiping it. Kṛṣṇa pushed His way forward and, despite the guards' attempts to stop Him, picked it up.

TEXT 17

करेण वामेन सलीलमुद्धृतं
सज्यं च कृत्वा निमिषेण पश्यताम् ।
नृणां विकृष्य प्रबभञ्ज मध्यतो
यथेक्षुदण्डं मदकर्युरुक्रमः ॥ १७ ॥

kareṇa vāmena sa-līlam uddhṛtaṁ
sajyaṁ ca kṛtvā nimiṣeṇa paśyatām
nṛṇāṁ vikṛṣya prababhañja madhyato
yathekṣu-daṇḍaṁ mada-kary urukramaḥ

kareṇa—with His hand; *vāmena*—left; *sa-līlam*—playfully; *uddhṛtam*—lifted; *sajyam*—the stringing; *ca*—and; *kṛtvā*—doing; *nimiṣeṇa*—in the wink of an eye; *paśyatām*—as they watched; *nṛṇām*—the guards; *vikṛṣya*—pulling it taut; *prababhañja*—He broke it; *madhyataḥ*—in the middle; *yathā*—as; *ikṣu*—of sugarcane; *daṇḍam*—a stick; *mada-karī*—an excited elephant; *urukramaḥ*—Lord Kṛṣṇa.

TRANSLATION

Easily lifting the bow with His left hand, Lord Urukrama strung it in a fraction of a second as the King's guards looked on. He then powerfully pulled the string and snapped the bow in half, just as an excited elephant might break a stalk of sugar cane.

TEXT 18

धनुषो भज्यमानस्य शब्दः खं रोदसी दिशः ।
पूरयामास यं श्रुत्वा कंसस्त्रासमुपागमत् ॥ १८ ॥

dhanuṣo bhajyamānasya
śabdaḥ khaṁ rodasī diśaḥ
pūrayām āsa yaṁ śrutvā
kaṁsas trāsam upāgamat

dhanuṣaḥ—of the bow; *bhajyamānasya*—which was breaking; *śabdaḥ*—the sound; *kham*—the earth; *rodasī*—the sky; *diśaḥ*—and all the directions; *pūrayām āsa*—filled; *yam*—which; *śrutvā*—hearing; *kaṁsaḥ*—King Kaṁsa; *trāsam*—fear; *upāgamat*—experienced.

TRANSLATION

The sound of the bow's breaking filled the earth and sky in all directions. Upon hearing it, Kaṁsa was struck with terror.

TEXT 19

तद्रक्षिणः सानुचरं कुपिता आततायिनः ।
गृहीतुकामा आवव्रुर्गृह्यतां वध्यतामिति ॥ १९ ॥

tad-rakṣiṇaḥ sānucaraṁ
kupitā ātatāyinaḥ

gṛhītu-kāmā āvavrur
gṛhyatāṁ vadhyatām iti

tat—its; *rakṣiṇaḥ*—guards; *sa*—along with; *anucaram*—His companions; *kupitāḥ*—angered; *ātatāyinaḥ*—holding weapons; *gṛhītu*—to catch; *kāmāḥ*—wanting; *āvavruḥ*—surrounded; *gṛhyatām*—seize Him; *vadhyatām*—kill Him; *iti*—thus saying.

TRANSLATION

The enraged guards then took up their weapons and, wanting to seize Kṛṣṇa and His companions, surrounded them and shouted, "Grab Him! Kill Him!"

TEXT 20

अथ तान् दुरभिप्रायान् विलोक्य बलकेशवौ ।
क्रुद्धौ धन्वन आदाय शकले तांश्च जघ्नतुः ॥ २० ॥

atha tān durabhiprāyān
vilokya bala-keśavau
kruddhau dhanvana ādāya
śakale tāṁś ca jaghnatuḥ

atha—thereupon; *tān*—them; *durabhiprāyān*—with evil intent; *vilokya*—seeing; *bala-keśavau*—Balarāma and Kṛṣṇa; *kruddhau*—angry; *dhanvanaḥ*—of the bow; *ādāya*—taking; *śakale*—the two broken pieces; *tān*—them; *ca*—and; *jaghnatuḥ*—struck.

TRANSLATION

Seeing the guards coming upon Them with evil intent, Balarāma and Keśava took up the two halves of the bow and began striking them down.

TEXT 21

बलं च कंसप्रहितं हत्वा शालामुखात्ततः ।
निष्क्रम्य चेरतुर्हृष्टौ निरीक्ष्य पुरसम्पदः ॥ २१ ॥

balaṁ ca kaṁsa-prahitaṁ
hatvā śālā-mukhāt tataḥ

niṣkramya ceratur hṛṣṭau
nirīkṣya pura-sampadaḥ

balam—an armed force; *ca*—and; *kaṁsa-prahitam*—sent by Kaṁsa; *hatvā*—having killed; *śālā*—of the sacrificial arena; *mukhāt*—by the gate; *tataḥ*—then; *niṣkramya*—exciting; *ceratuḥ*—the two of Them walked along; *hṛṣṭau*—happy; *nirīkṣya*—observing; *pura*—of the city; *sampadaḥ*—the riches.

TRANSLATION

After also killing a contingent of soldiers sent by Kaṁsa, Kṛṣṇa and Balarāma left the sacrificial arena by its main gate and continued Their walk about the city, happily looking at the opulent sights.

TEXT 22

तयोस्तदद्भुतं वीर्यं निशाम्य पुरवासिनः ।
तेजः प्रागल्भ्यं रूपं च मेनिरे विबुधोत्तमौ ॥ २२ ॥

tayos tad adbhutaṁ vīryaṁ
niśāmya pura-vāsinaḥ
tejaḥ prāgalbhyaṁ rūpaṁ ca
menire vibudhottamau

tayoḥ—of Them; *tat*—that; *adbhutam*—amazing; *vīryam*—heroic deed; *niśāmya*—seeing; *pura-vāsinaḥ*—the residents of the city; *tejaḥ*—Their strength; *prāgalbhyam*—boldness; *rūpam*—beauty; *ca*—and; *menire*—they considered; *vibudha*—of demigods; *uttamau*—two of the best.

TRANSLATION

Having witnessed the amazing deed Kṛṣṇa and Balarāma had performed, and seeing Their strength, boldness and beauty, the people of the city thought They must be two prominent demigods.

TEXT 23

तयोर्विचरतोः स्वैरमादित्योऽस्तमुपेयिवान् ।
कृष्णरामौ वृतौ गोपैः पुराच्छकटमीयतुः ॥ २३ ॥

tayor vicaratoḥ svairam
ādityo'stam upeyivān

kṛṣṇa-rāmau vṛtau gopaiḥ
purāc chakaṭam īyatuḥ

tayoḥ—as They; *vicaratoḥ*—moved about; *svairam*—at Their will; *ādityaḥ*—the sun; *astam*—its setting; *upeyivān*—approached; *kṛṣṇa-rāmau*—Kṛṣṇa and Balarāma; *vṛtau*—accompanied; *gopaiḥ*—by the cowherd boys; *purāt*—from the city; *śakaṭam*—to the place where the wagons had been unharnessed; *īyatuḥ*—went.

TRANSLATION

As They strolled about at will, the sun began to set, so They left the city with the cowherd boys and returned to the cowherds' wagon encampment.

TEXT 24

गोप्यो मुकुन्दविगमे विरहातुरा या
आशासताशिष ऋता मधुपुर्यभूवन् ।
सम्पश्यतां पुरुषभूषणगात्रलक्ष्मीं
हित्वेतरान्नु भजतश्चकमेऽयनं श्रीः ॥ २४॥

gopyo mukunda-vigame virahāturā yā
āśāsatāśiṣa ṛtā madhu-pury abhūvan
sampaśyatāṁ puruṣa-bhūṣaṇa-gātra-lakṣmīṁ
hitvetarān nu bhajataś cakame'yanaṁ śrīḥ

gopyaḥ—the *gopīs; mukunda-vigame*—when Lord Mukunda was departing; *viraha*—by feelings of separation; *āturāḥ*—tormented; *yāḥ*—which; *āśāsata*—they had spoken; *āśiṣaḥ*—the benedictions; *ṛtāḥ*—true; *madhu-puri*—in Mathurā; *abhūvan*—have become; *sampaśyatām*—for those who are fully seeing; *puruṣa*—of men; *bhūṣaṇa*—of the ornament; *gātra*—of His body; *lakṣmīm*—the beauty; *hitvā*—abandoning; *itarān*—others; *nu*—indeed; *bhajataḥ*—who were worshiping her; *cakame*—hankered for; *ayanam*—shelter; *śrīḥ*—the goddess of fortune.

TRANSLATION

At the time of Mukunda's [Kṛṣṇa's] departure from Vṛndāvana, the gopīs had foretold that the residents of Mathurā would enjoy many benedictions, and now the gopīs' predictions were coming true, for those

residents were gazing upon the beauty of Kṛṣṇa, the jewel among men. Indeed, the goddess of fortune desired the shelter of that beauty so much that she abandoned many other men, although they worshiped her.

TEXT 25

अवनिक्ताङ्घ्रियुगलौ भुक्त्वा क्षीरोपसेचनम्।
ऊषतुस्तां सुखं रात्रिं ज्ञात्वा कंसचिकीर्षितम्॥ २५॥

avaniktāṅghri-yugalau
bhuktvā kṣīropasecanam
ūṣatus tāṁ sukhaṁ rātriṁ
jñātvā kaṁsa-cikīrṣitam

avanikta—bathed; *aṅghri-yugalau*—the two feet of each of Them; *bhuktvā*—eating; *kṣīra-upasecanam*—boiled rice sprinkled with milk; *ūṣatuḥ*—They stayed there; *tām*—for that; *sukham*—comfortably; *rātrim*—night; *jñātvā*—knowing; *kaṁsa-cikīrṣitam*—what Kaṁsa intended to do.

TRANSLATION

After Kṛṣṇa's and Balarāma's feet were bathed, the two Lords ate rice with milk. Then, although knowing what Kaṁsa intended to do, They spent the night there comfortably.

TEXTS 26–27

कंसस्तु धनुषो भंगं रक्षिणां स्वबलस्य च।
वधं निशम्य गोविन्दरामविक्रीडितं परम् ॥ २६॥
दीर्घप्रजागरो भीतो दुर्निमित्तानि दुर्मतिः ।
बहून्यचष्टोभयथा मृत्योर्दौत्यकराणि च ॥ २७॥

kaṁsas tu dhanuṣo bhaṅgaṁ
rakṣiṇāṁ sva-balasya ca
vadhaṁ niśamya govinda-
rāma-vikrīḍitaṁ param

dīrgha-prajāgaro bhīto
durnimittāni durmatiḥ
bahūny acaṣṭobhayathā
mṛtyor dautya-karāṇi ca

kaṁsaḥ—King Kaṁsa; *tu*—but; *dhanuṣaḥ*—of the bow; *bhaṅgam*—the breaking; *rakṣiṇām*—of the guards; *sva*—his; *balasya*—of the army; *ca*—and; *vadham*—the killing; *niśamya*—hearing of; *govinda-rāma*—of Kṛṣṇa and Balarāma; *vikrīḍitam*—the playing; *param*—merely; *dīrgha*—for a long time; *prajāgaraḥ*—remaining awake; *bhītaḥ*—afraid; *durnimittāni*—bad omens; *durmatiḥ*—the wicked-minded; *bahūni*—many; *acaṣṭa*—saw; *ubhayathā*—in both states (sleep and wakefulness); *mṛtyoḥ*—of death; *dautya-karāṇi*—the messengers; *ca*—and.

TRANSLATION

Wicked King Kaṁsa, on the other hand, was terrified, having heard how Kṛṣṇa and Balarāma had broken the bow and killed his guards and soldiers, all simply as a game. He remained awake for a long time, and both while awake and while dreaming he saw many bad omens, messengers of death.

TEXTS 28–31

अदर्शनं स्वशिरसः प्रतिरूपे च सत्यपि ।
असत्यपि द्वितीये च द्वैरूप्यं ज्योतिषां तथा ॥ २८ ॥
छिद्रप्रतीतिश्छायायां प्राणघोषानुपश्रुतिः ।
स्वर्णप्रतीतिर्वृक्षेषु स्वपदानामदर्शनम् ॥ २९ ॥
स्वप्ने प्रेतपरिष्वंगः खरयानं विषादनम् ।
यायान्नलदमाल्येकस्तैलाभ्यक्तो दिगम्बरः ॥ ३० ॥
अन्यानि चेत्थंभूतानि स्वप्नजागरितानि च ।
पश्यन्मरणसन्त्रस्तो निद्रां लेभे न चिन्तया ॥ ३१ ॥

adarśanaṁ sva-śirasaḥ
pratirūpe ca saty api
asaty api dvitīye ca
dvai-rūpyaṁ jyotiṣāṁ tathā

chidra-pratītiś chāyāyāṁ
prāṇa-ghoṣānupaśrutiḥ
svarṇa-pratītir vṛkṣeṣu
sva-padānām adarśanam

svapne preta-pariṣvaṅgaḥ
khara-yānaṁ viṣādanam

yāyān nalada-māly ekas
tailābhyakto dig-ambaraḥ

anyāni cettham̐-bhūtāni
svapna-jāgaritāni ca
paśyan maraṇa-santrasto
nidrām̐ lebhe na cintayā

adarśanam—the invisibility; *sva*—of his own; *śirasaḥ*—head; *pratirūpe*—his reflection; *ca*—and; *sati*—being present; *api*—even; *asati*—there not being; *api*—even; *dvitīye*—a cause for duplication; *ca*—and; *dvai-rūpyam*—double image; *jyotiṣām*—of the heavenly bodies; *tathā*—also; *chidra*—of a hole; *pratītiḥ*—the seeing; *chāyāyām*—in his shadow; *prāṇa*—of his life air; *ghoṣa*—of the reverberation; *anupaśrutiḥ*—the failure to hear; *svarṇa*—of a golden color; *pratītiḥ*—the perception; *vṛkṣeṣu*—on trees; *sva*—his own; *padānām*—footprints; *adarśanam*—not seeing; *svapne*—while asleep; *preta*—by ghostly spirits; *pariṣvaṅgaḥ*—being embraced; *khara*—upon a donkey; *yānam*—traveling; *viṣa*—poison; *adanam*—swallowing; *yāyāt*—was going about; *nalada*—of spikenards, rose-purple flowers native to India; *mālī*—wearing a garland; *ekaḥ*—someone; *taila*—with oil; *abhyaktaḥ*—smeared; *dik-ambaraḥ*—naked; *anyāni*—other (omens); *ca*—and; *ittham-bhūtāni*—like these; *svapna*—while asleep; *jāgaritāni*—while awake; *ca*—also; *paśyan*—seeing; *maraṇa*—of death; *santrastaḥ*—terrified; *nidrām*—sleep; *lebhe*—he could achieve; *na*—not; *cintayā*—because of his anxiety.

TRANSLATION

When he looked at his reflection he could not see his head; for no reason the moon and stars appeared double; he saw a hole in his shadow; he could not hear the sound of his life air; trees seemed covered with a golden hue; and he could not see his footprints. He dreamt that he was being embraced by ghosts, riding a donkey and drinking poison, and also that a naked man smeared with oil was passing by wearing a garland of nalada flowers. Seeing these and other such omens both while dreaming and while awake, Kaṁsa was terrified by the prospect of death, and out of anxiety he could not sleep.

TEXT 32

व्युष्टायां निशि कौरव्य सूर्ये चाद्भ्यः समुत्थिते ।
कारयामास वै कंसो मल्लक्रीडामहोत्सवम् ॥ ३२ ॥

vyuṣṭāyāṁ niśi kauravya
sūrye cādbhyaḥ samutthite
kārayām āsa vai kaṁso
malla-krīḍā-mahotsavam

vyuṣṭāyām—having passed; *niśi*—the night; *kauravya*—O descendant of Kuru (Parīkṣit); *sūrye*—the sun; *ca*—and; *adbhyaḥ*—from the water; *samutthite*—rising; *kārayām āsa*—had carried out; *vai*—indeed; *kaṁsaḥ*—Kaṁsa; *malla*—of wrestlers; *krīḍā*—of the sport; *mahā-utsavam*—the great festival.

TRANSLATION

When the night had finally passed and the sun rose up again from the water, Kaṁsa set about arranging for the grand wrestling festival.

TEXT 33

आनर्चुः पुरुषा रंगं तूर्यभेर्यश्च जघ्निरे ।
मञ्चाश्चालंकृताः स्रग्भिः पताकाचैलतोरणैः ॥ ३३ ॥

ānarcuḥ puruṣā raṅgaṁ
tūrya-bheryaś ca jaghnire
mañcāś cālaṅkṛtāḥ sragbhiḥ
patākā-caila-toraṇaiḥ

ānarcuḥ—worshiped; *puruṣāḥ*—the King's men; *raṅgam*—the arena; *tūrya*—musical instruments; *bheryaḥ*—drums; *ca*—and; *jaghnire*—they vibrated; *mañcāḥ*—the viewing platforms; *ca*—and; *alaṅkṛtāḥ*—were decorated; *sragbhiḥ*—with garlands; *patākā*—with flags; *caila*—cloth ribbons; *toraṇaiḥ*—and gateways.

TRANSLATION

The King's men performed the ritual worship of the wrestling arena, sounded their drums and other instruments and decorated the viewing galleries with garlands, flags, ribbons and arches.

TEXT 34

तेषु पौरा जानपदा ब्रह्मक्षत्रपुरोगमाः ।
यथोपजोषं विविशू राजानश्च कृतासनाः ॥ ३४ ॥

teṣu paurā jānapadā
brahma-kṣatra-purogamāḥ
yathopajoṣaṁ viviśū
rājānaś ca kṛtāsanāḥ

teṣu—upon these (platforms); *paurāḥ*—the city-dwellers; *jānapadāḥ*—and the people of the suburbs; *brahma*—by the *brāhmaṇas; kṣatra*—and the *kṣatriyas; puraḥ-gamāḥ*—headed; *yathā-upajoṣam*—as suited their comfort; *viviśuḥ*—came and sat; *rājānaḥ*—the kings; *ca*—also; *kṛta*—given; *āsanāḥ*—special seats.

TRANSLATION

The city-dwellers and residents of the outlying districts, led by brāhmaṇas and kṣatriyas, came and sat down comfortably in the galleries. The royal guests received special seats.

TEXT 35

कंसः परिवृतोऽमात्यै राजमञ्च उपाविशत् ।
मण्डलेश्वरमध्यस्थो हृदयेन विदूयता ॥ ३५ ॥

kaṁsaḥ parivṛto'mātyai
rāja-mañca upāviśat
maṇḍaleśvara-madhya-stho
hṛdayena vidūyatā

kaṁsaḥ—Kaṁsa; *parivṛtaḥ*—surrounded; *amātyaiḥ*—by his ministers; *rāja-mañce*—on the King's platform; *upāviśat*—sat; *maṇḍala-īśvara*—of secondary rulers of various regions; *madhya*—in the midst; *sthaḥ*—situated; *hṛdayena*—with his heart; *vidūyatā*—trembling.

TRANSLATION

Surrounded by his ministers, Kaṁsa took his seat on the imperial dais. But even as he sat amidst his various provincial rulers, his heart trembled.

TEXT 36

वाद्यमानेषु तूर्येषु मल्लतालोत्तरेषु च ।
मल्लाः स्वलंकृताः दृप्ताः सोपाध्यायाः समासत ॥ ३६ ॥

vādyamāneṣu tūryeṣu
malla-tālottareṣu ca
mallāḥ sv-alaṅkṛtāḥ dṛptāḥ
sopādhyāyāḥ samāsata

vādyamāneṣu—as they were being played; *tūryeṣu*—the musical instruments; *malla*—suitable for wrestling; *tāla*—with meters; *uttareṣu*—prominent; *ca*—and; *mallāḥ*—the wrestlers; *su-alaṅkṛtāḥ*—well ornamented; *dṛptāḥ*—proud; *sa-upādhyāyāḥ*—together with their instructors; *samāsata*—came and sat down.

TRANSLATION

While the musical instruments loudly played in the rhythmic meters appropriate for wrestling matches, the lavishly ornamented wrestlers proudly entered the arena with their coaches and sat down.

TEXT 37

चाणूरो मुष्टिकः कूटः शलस्तोशल एव च ।
त आसेदुरुपस्थानं वल्गुवाद्यप्रहर्षिताः ॥ ३७ ॥

cāṇūro muṣṭikaḥ kūṭaḥ
śalas tośala eva ca
ta āsedur upasthānaṁ
valgu-vādya-praharṣitāḥ

cāṇūraḥ muṣṭikaḥ kūṭaḥ—the wrestlers Cāṇūra, Muṣṭika and Kūṭa; *śalaḥ tośalaḥ*—Śala and Tośala; *eva ca*—also; *te*—they; *āseduḥ*—sat down; *upasthānam*—on the mat of the wrestling ring; *valgu*—pleasing; *vādya*—by the music; *praharṣitāḥ*—enthused.

TRANSLATION

Enthused by the pleasing music, Cāṇūra, Muṣṭika, Kūṭa, Śala and Tośala sat down on the wrestling mat.

TEXT 38

नन्दगोपादयो गोपा भोजराजसमाहुताः ।
निवेदितोपायनास्त एकस्मिन्मञ्च आविशन् ॥ ३८ ॥

nanda-gopādayo gopā
bhoja-rāja-samāhutāḥ
niveditopāyanās ta
ekasmin mañca āviśan

nanda-gopa-ādayaḥ—headed by Nanda Gopa; *gopāḥ*—the cowherds; *bhoja-rāja*—by Kaṁsa, King of the Bhojas; *samāhutāḥ*—called forward; *nivedita*—presenting; *upāyanāḥ*—their offerings; *te*—they; *ekasmin*—in one; *mañce*—viewing gallery; *āviśan*—sat down.

TRANSLATION

Nanda Mahārāja and the other cowherds, summoned by the King of the Bhojas, presented him with their offerings and then took their seats in one of the galleries.

PURPORT

According to Śrīla Viśvanātha Cakravartī, the word *samāhutāḥ* indicates that King Kaṁsa respectfully called the leaders of Vraja forward so that they could make their offerings to the central government. According to the *ācārya,* Kaṁsa assured Nanda as follows: "My dear King of Vraja, you are the most important of my village rulers. Yet even though you have come to Mathurā from your cowherd village, you have not come to visit me. Is that because you are frightened? Don't think that your two sons are bad because They broke the bow. I invited Them here because I heard They were extremely powerful, and I've arranged this wrestling match as a test of Their strength. So please come forward without hesitation. Don't be afraid."

Śrīla Viśvanātha Cakravartī further states that Nanda Mahārāja noticed his two sons were not present. Apparently, out of disrespect for King Kaṁsa's order, They had taken the morning off and gone elsewhere.

Thus Kaṁsa delegated some cowherd men to go look for Them and advise Them to behave properly and come back to the wrestling arena. The *ācārya* also states that the reason Nanda and the other cowherd men sat in the galleries was that they could not find any sitting places on the royal dais.

Thus end the purports of the humble servants of His Divine Grace A.C. Bhaktivedanta Swami Prabhupāda to the Tenth Canto, Forty-second Chapter, of the Śrīmad-Bhāgavatam, *entitled "The Breaking of the Sacrificial Bow."*

CHAPTER FORTY-THREE

Kṛṣṇa Kills the Elephant Kuvalayāpīḍa

This chapter tells how Lord Kṛṣṇa killed the lordly elephant Kuvalayāpīḍa, how Kṛṣṇa and Balarāma entered the wrestling arena and what Kṛṣṇa said to the wrestler Cāṇūra.

After finishing Their early-morning rituals, Kṛṣṇa and Balarāma heard kettledrums heralding the start of the wrestling match, and They went to see the festivities. At the gate of the wrestling arena They encountered an elephant named Kuvalayāpīḍa, who attacked Kṛṣṇa at the urging of his keeper. The mighty elephant grabbed at Kṛṣṇa with his trunk, but the Lord struck back and then disappeared from the beast's sight among his legs. Enraged at not being able to see Kṛṣṇa, Kuvalayāpīḍa sought Him out with his sense of smell and seized Him. But the Lord pulled loose. In this way Kṛṣṇa teased and tormented Kuvalayāpīḍa, finally yanking out one of his tusks and beating him and his keepers to death.

Sprinkled with the elephant's blood and carrying one of his tusks on His shoulder as a weapon, Lord Kṛṣṇa appeared unprecedentedly beautiful as He entered the wrestling arena. There the various classes of people saw Him in different ways, according to their specific relationship with Him.

When King Kaṁsa heard how Kṛṣṇa and Balarāma had killed Kuvalayāpīḍa, he realized They were invincible and became filled with anxiety. The members of the audience, on the other hand, became joyful as they reminded one another about the Lords' amazing pastimes. The people declared that Kṛṣṇa and Balarāma must be two expansions of the Supreme Lord Nārāyaṇa who had descended into the house of Vasudeva.

Cāṇūra then stepped forward and challenged Kṛṣṇa and Balarāma to wrestle, saying King Kaṁsa wished to see such a match. Kṛṣṇa replied, "Although We are merely nomadic forest folk, We are nonetheless subjects of the King; thus We will not hesitate to please him with an exhibition of wrestling." As soon as Cāṇūra heard this, he suggested that Kṛṣṇa should wrestle him and that Balarāma should wrestle Muṣṭika.

TEXT 1

श्रीशुक उवाच
अथ कृष्णश्च रामश्च कृतशौचौ परन्तप।
मल्लदुन्दुभिनिर्घोषं श्रुत्वा द्रष्टुमुपेयतुः ॥ १ ॥

śrī-śuka uvāca
atha kṛṣṇaś ca rāmaś ca
kṛta-śaucau parantapa
malla-dundubhi-nirghoṣaṁ
śrutvā draṣṭum upeyatuḥ

śrī-śukaḥ uvāca—Śrī Śukadeva Gosvāmī said; *atha*—next; *kṛṣṇaḥ*—Kṛṣṇa; *ca*—and; *rāmaḥ*—Balarāma; *ca*—also; *kṛta*—having carried out; *śaucau*—purification; *param-tapa*—O chastiser of enemies; *malla*—of the wrestling match; *dundubhi*—of the kettledrums; *nirghoṣam*—the resounding vibration; *śrutvā*—hearing; *draṣṭum*—to see; *upeyatuḥ*—They approached.

TRANSLATION

Śukadeva Gosvāmī said: O chastiser of enemies, Kṛṣṇa and Balarāma, having executed all necessary purification, then heard the kettledrums resounding at the wrestling arena, and They went there to see what was happening.

PURPORT

Śrīla Śrīdhara Svāmī explains the words *kṛta-śaucau,* "having executed all necessary purification," as follows: "Two days previously, Kṛṣṇa and Balarāma had executed Their purification, Their relief from offense [by performing heroic deeds]. The Lords reasoned: 'Even after We have made Our power known by breaking the bow and by performing other feats, Our parents have still not secured freedom. Kaṁsa is again trying to kill them. Therefore, although he is Our maternal uncle, it will not be wrong for Us to kill him.' They assured Their offenselessness by this reasoning."

TEXT 2

रंगद्वारं समासाद्य तस्मिन्नागमवस्थितम् ।
अपश्यत्कुवलयापीडं कृष्णोऽम्बष्ठप्रचोदितम् ॥ २ ॥

raṅga-dvāraṁ samāsādya
tasmin nāgam avasthitam
apaśyat kuvalayāpīḍaṁ
kṛṣṇo'mbaṣṭha-pracoditam

raṅga—of the arena; *dvāram*—the gate; *samāsādya*—reaching; *tasmin*—in that place; *nāgam*—an elephant; *avasthitam*—standing; *apaśyat*—He saw; *kuvalayāpīḍam*—named Kuvalayāpīḍa; *kṛṣṇaḥ*—Lord Kṛṣṇa; *ambaṣṭha*—by his keeper; *pracoditam*—urged on.

TRANSLATION

When Lord Kṛṣṇa reached the entrance to the arena, He saw the elephant Kuvalayāpīḍa blocking His way at the urging of his keeper.

PURPORT

The elephant-keeper revealed his malicious intent by blocking Lord Kṛṣṇa's entrance into the arena.

TEXT 3

बद्ध्वा परिकरं शौरिः समुह्य कुटिलालकान्।
उवाच हस्तिपं वाचा मेघनादगभीरया ॥ ३ ॥

baddhvā parikaraṁ śauriḥ
samuhya kuṭilālakān
uvāca hastipaṁ vācā
megha-nāda-gabhīrayā

baddhvā—binding; *parikaram*—His clothes; *śauriḥ*—Lord Kṛṣṇa; *samuhya*—tying together; *kuṭila*—curled; *alakān*—the locks of His hair; *uvāca*—He spoke; *hasti-pam*—to the elephant-keeper; *vācā*—with words; *megha*—of a cloud; *nāda*—like the sound; *gabhīrayā*—grave.

TRANSLATION

Securely binding up His clothes and tying back His curly locks, Lord Kṛṣṇa addressed the elephant-keeper with words as grave as the rumbling of a cloud.

PURPORT

Lord Kṛṣṇa was obviously preparing for a fight. According to Śrīla Viśvanātha Cakravartī Ṭhākura, the Lord put aside His jacket, tightened His belt and tied back His hair.

TEXT 4

अम्बष्ठाम्बष्ठ मार्गं नौ देह्यपक्रम मा चिरम् ।
नो चेत्सकुञ्जरं त्वाद्य नयामि यमसादनम् ॥ ४॥

ambaṣṭhāmbaṣṭha mārgaṁ nau
dehy apakrama mā ciram
no cet sa-kuñjaraṁ tvādya
nayāmi yama-sādanam

ambaṣṭha ambaṣṭha—O elephant-keeper, elephant-keeper; *mārgam*—way; *nau*—to Us; *dehi*—give; *apakrama*—move aside; *mā ciram*—without delay; *na u cet*—if not; *sa-kuñjaram*—together with your elephant; *tvā*—you; *adya*—today; *nayāmi*—I will send; *yama*—of the lord of death; *sādanam*—to the abode.

TRANSLATION

[Lord Kṛṣṇa said:] O driver, driver, move aside at once and let Us pass! If you don't, this very day I will send both you and your elephant to the abode of Yamarāja!

TEXT 5

एवं निर्भर्त्सितोऽम्बष्ठः कुपितः कोपितं गजम् ।
चोदयामास कृष्णाय कालान्तकयमोपमम् ॥ ५॥

evaṁ nirbhartsito'mbaṣṭhaḥ
kupitaḥ kopitaṁ gajam
codayām āsa kṛṣṇāya
kālāntaka-yamopamam

evam—thus; *nirbhartsitaḥ*—threatened; *ambaṣṭhaḥ*—the elephant-keeper; *kupitaḥ*—angered; *kopitam*—the enraged; *gajam*—elephant; *codayām āsa*—he goaded; *kṛṣṇāya*—toward Kṛṣṇa; *kāla*—time; *antaka*—death; *yama*—and Yamarāja; *upamam*—comparable to.

TRANSLATION

Thus threatened, the elephant-keeper became angry. He goaded his furious elephant, who appeared equal to time, death and Yamarāja, into attacking Lord Kṛṣṇa.

TEXT 6

करीन्द्रस्तमभिद्रुत्य करेण तरसाग्रहीत् ।
कराद्विगलितः सोऽमुं निहत्याङ्घ्रिष्वलीयत ॥ ६ ॥

karīndras tam abhidrutya
kareṇa tarasāgrahīt
karād vigalitaḥ so'muṁ
nihatyāṅghriṣv alīyata

kari—of elephants; *indraḥ*—the lord; *tam*—Him; *abhidrutya*—running toward; *kareṇa*—with his trunk; *tarasā*—violently; *agrahīt*—seized; *karāt*—from the trunk; *vigalitaḥ*—slipping away; *saḥ*—He, Kṛṣṇa; *amum*—him, Kuvalayāpīḍa; *nihatya*—striking; *aṅghriṣu*—among his legs; *alīyata*—He disappeared.

TRANSLATION

The lord of the elephants charged Kṛṣṇa and violently seized Him with his trunk. But Kṛṣṇa slipped away, struck him a blow and disappeared from his view among his legs.

PURPORT

Lord Kṛṣṇa struck the elephant with His fist and then disappeared among his legs.

TEXT 7

संक्रुद्धस्तमचक्षाणो घ्राणदृष्टिः स केशवम् ।
परामृशत्पुष्करेण स प्रसह्य विनिर्गतः ॥ ७ ॥

saṅkruddhas tam acakṣāṇo
ghrāṇa-dṛṣṭiḥ sa keśavam
parāmṛśat puṣkareṇa
sa prasahya vinirgataḥ

saṅkruddhaḥ—infuriated; *tam*—Him; *acakṣāṇaḥ*—not seeing; *ghrāṇa*—by his sense of smell; *dṛṣṭiḥ*—whose vision; *saḥ*—he, the elephant; *keśavam*—Lord Keśava; *parāmṛśat*—took hold of; *puṣkareṇa*—with the end of his trunk; *saḥ*—He, Kṛṣṇa; *prasahya*—by force; *vinirgataḥ*—came free.

TRANSLATION

Infuriated at being unable to see Lord Keśava, the elephant sought Him out with his sense of smell. Once again Kuvalayāpīḍa seized the Lord with the end of his trunk, only to have the Lord forcefully free Himself.

PURPORT

Lord Kṛṣṇa allowed the elephant to seize Him so that the beast would be encouraged to keep fighting. Once Kuvalayāpīḍa had thus become proud, Lord Kṛṣṇa again thwarted him with His superior potency.

TEXT 8

पुच्छे प्रगृह्यातिबलं धनुषः पञ्चविंशतिम् ।
विचकर्ष यथा नागं सुपर्ण इव लीलया ॥ ८ ॥

pucche pragṛhyāti-balaṁ
dhanuṣaḥ pañca-viṁśatim
vicakarṣa yathā nāgaṁ
suparṇa iva līlayā

pucche—by his tail; *pragṛhya*—grabbing him; *ati-balam*—the extremely powerful (elephant); *dhanuṣaḥ*—bow-lengths; *pañca-viṁśatim*—twenty-five; *vicakarṣa*—He dragged; *yathā*—as; *nāgam*—a snake; *suparṇaḥ*—Garuḍa; *iva*—as; *līlayā*—playfully.

TRANSLATION

Lord Kṛṣṇa then grabbed the powerful Kuvalayāpīḍa by the tail and playfully dragged him twenty-five bow-lengths as easily as Garuḍa might drag a snake.

TEXT 9

स पर्यावर्तमानेन सव्यदक्षिणतोऽच्युतः ।
बभ्राम भ्राम्यमाणेन गोवत्सेनेव बालकः ॥ ९ ॥

sa paryāvartamānena
savya-dakṣiṇato'cyutaḥ
babhrāma bhrāmyamāṇena
go-vatseneva bālakaḥ

saḥ—He; *paryāvartamānena*—with him (the elephant) who was being moved around; *savya-dakṣiṇataḥ*—to the left and then the right; *acyutaḥ*—Lord Kṛṣṇa; *babhrāma*—moved also; *bhrāmyamāṇena*—together with him who was being moved; *go-vatsena*—with a calf; *iva*—just as; *bālakaḥ*—a young boy.

TRANSLATION

As Lord Acyuta held on to the elephant's tail, the animal tried to twist away to the left and to the right, making the Lord swerve in the opposite direction, as a young boy would swerve when pulling a calf by the tail.

TEXT 10

ततोऽभिमुखमभ्येत्य पाणिनाहत्य वारणम् ।
प्राद्रवन् पातयामास स्पृश्यमानः पदे पदे ॥ १० ॥

tato'bhimukham abhyetya
pāṇināhatya vāraṇam
prādravan pātayām āsa
spṛśyamānaḥ pade pade

tataḥ—then; *abhimukham*—face to face; *abhyetya*—coming; *pāṇinā*—with His hand; *āhatya*—slapping; *vāraṇam*—the elephant; *prādravan*—running away; *pātayām āsa*—He made him fall; *spṛśyamānaḥ*—being touched; *pade pade*—with each step.

TRANSLATION

Kṛṣṇa then came face to face with the elephant and slapped him and ran away. Kuvalayāpīḍa pursued the Lord, managing to touch Him again and again with each step, but Kṛṣṇa outmaneuvered the elephant and made him trip and fall.

TEXT 11

स धावन् क्रीडया भूमौ पतित्वा सहसोत्थितः ।
तं मत्वा पतितं क्रुद्धो दन्ताभ्यां सोऽहनत्क्षितिम् ॥ ११ ॥

sa dhāvan krīḍayā bhūmau
patitvā sahasotthitaḥ
taṁ matvā patitaṁ kruddho
dantābhyāṁ so'hanat kṣitim

saḥ—He; *dhāvan*—running; *krīḍayā*—playfully; *bhūmau*—on the ground; *patitvā*—falling; *sahasā*—suddenly; *utthitaḥ*—getting up; *tam*—Him; *matvā*—thinking; *patitam*—fallen; *kruddhaḥ*—angry; *dantābhyām*—with his tusks; *saḥ*—he, Kuvalayāpīḍa; *ahanat*—struck; *kṣitim*—the earth.

TRANSLATION

As Kṛṣṇa dodged about, He playfully fell on the ground and quickly got up again. The raging elephant, thinking Kṛṣṇa was down, tried to gore Him with his tusks but struck the earth instead.

TEXT 12

स्वविक्रमे प्रतिहते कुञ्जरेन्द्रोऽत्यमर्षितः ।
चोद्यमानो महामात्रैः कृष्णमभ्यद्रवद् रुषा ॥ १२ ॥

sva-vikrame pratihate
kuñjarendro'ty-amarṣitaḥ
codyamāno mahāmātraiḥ
kṛṣṇam abhyadravad ruṣā

sva—his; *vikrame*—prowess; *pratihate*—being thwarted; *kuñjara-indraḥ*—the lord of elephants; *ati*—extreme; *amarṣitaḥ*—with frustrated anger; *codyamānaḥ*—urged on; *mahāmātraiḥ*—by the elephant-keepers; *kṛṣṇam*—at Kṛṣṇa; *abhyadravat*—he charged; *ruṣā*—furiously.

TRANSLATION

His prowess foiled, the lordly elephant Kuvalayāpīḍa went into a frenzied rage out of frustration. But the elephant-keepers goaded him on, and he furiously charged Kṛṣṇa once again.

TEXT 13

तमापतन्तमासाद्य भगवान्मधुसूदनः ।
निगृह्य पाणिना हस्तं पातयामास भूतले ॥ १३ ॥

tam āpatantam āsādya
bhagavān madhusūdanaḥ
nigṛhya pāṇinā hastaṁ
pātayām āsa bhū-tale

tam—him; *āpatantam*—attacking; *āsādya*—confronting; *bhagavān*—the Supreme Lord; *madhu-sūdanaḥ*—the killer of the demon Madhu; *nigṛhya*—firmly seizing; *pāṇinā*—with His hand; *hastam*—his trunk; *pātayām āsa*—He made him fall; *bhū-tale*—onto the ground.

TRANSLATION

The Supreme Lord, killer of the demon Madhu, confronted the elephant as he attacked. Seizing his trunk with one hand, Kṛṣṇa threw him to the ground.

TEXT 14

पतितस्य पदाक्रम्य मृगेन्द्र इव लीलया ।
दन्तमुत्पाट्य तेनेभं हस्तिपांश्चाहनद्धरिः ॥ १४ ॥

patitasya padākramya
mṛgendra iva līlayā
dantam utpāṭya tenebhaṁ
hastipāṁś cāhanad dhariḥ

patitasya—of the fallen (elephant); *padā*—with His foot; *ākramya*—climbing upon him; *mṛgendraḥ*—a lion; *iva*—as if; *līlayā*—with ease; *dantam*—one of his tusks; *utpāṭya*—pulling out; *tena*—with it; *ibham*—the elephant; *hasti-pān*—the elephant-keepers; *ca*—also; *ahanat*—killed; *hariḥ*—Lord Kṛṣṇa.

TRANSLATION

Lord Hari then climbed onto the elephant with the ease of a mighty lion, pulled out a tusk, and with it killed the beast and his keepers.

TEXT 15

मृतकं द्विपमुत्सृज्य दन्तपाणिः समाविशत् ।
अंसन्यस्तविषाणोऽसृङ्मदबिन्दुभिरङ्कितः ।
विरूढस्वेदकणिकावदनाम्बुरुहो बभौ ॥ १५ ॥

mṛtakaṁ dvipam utsṛjya
danta-pāṇiḥ samāviśat
aṁsa-nyasta-viṣāṇo'sṛṅ-
mada-bindubhir aṅkitaḥ
virūḍha-sveda-kaṇikā
vadanāmburuho babhau

mṛtakam—dead; *dvipam*—the elephant; *utsṛjya*—discarding; *danta*—his tusk; *pāṇiḥ*—in His hand; *samāviśat*—He entered (the arena); *aṁsa*—upon His shoulder; *nyasta*—placing; *viṣāṇaḥ*—the tusk; *asṛk*—of blood; *mada*—and the elephant's sweat; *bindubhiḥ*—with drops; *aṅkitaḥ*—sprinkled; *virūḍha*—exuding; *sveda*—of (His own) perspiration; *kaṇikā*—with fine drops; *vadana*—His face; *ambu-ruhaḥ*—lotuslike; *babhau*—shone.

TRANSLATION

Leaving the dead elephant aside, Lord Kṛṣṇa held on to the tusk and entered the wrestling arena. With the tusk resting on His shoulder, drops of the elephant's blood and sweat sprinkled all over Him, and His lotus face covered with fine drops of His own perspiration, the Lord shone with great beauty.

TEXT 16

वृतौ गोपैः कतिपयैर्बलदेवजनार्दनौ ।
रंगं विविशतू राजन् गजदन्तवरायुधौ ॥ १६ ॥

vṛtau gopaiḥ katipayair
baladeva-janārdanau
raṅgaṁ viviśatū rājan
gaja-danta-varāyudhau

vṛtau—surrounded; *gopaiḥ*—by cowherd boys; *katipayaiḥ*—several; *baladeva-janārdanau*—Balarāma and Kṛṣṇa; *raṅgam*—the arena; *viviśatuḥ*—entered; *rājan*—O King (Parīkṣit); *gaja-danta*—the elephant's tusks; *vara*—chosen; *āyudhau*—whose weapons.

TRANSLATION

My dear King, Lord Baladeva and Lord Janārdana, each carrying one of the elephant's tusks as His chosen weapon, entered the arena with several cowherd boys.

TEXT 17

मल्लानामशनिर्नृणां नरवरः स्त्रीणां स्मरो मूर्तिमान्
गोपानां स्वजनोऽसतां क्षितिभुजां शास्ता स्वपित्रोः शिशुः ।
मृत्युर्भोजपतेर्विराडविदुषां तत्त्वं परं योगिनां
वृष्णीनां परदेवतेति विदितो रंगं गतः साग्रजः ॥ १७ ॥

mallānām aśanir nṛṇāṁ nara-varaḥ strīṇāṁ smaro mūrtimān
gopānāṁ sva-jano'satāṁ kṣiti-bhujāṁ śāstā sva-pitroḥ śiśuḥ
mṛtyur bhoja-pater virāḍ aviduṣāṁ tattvaṁ paraṁ yogināṁ
vṛṣṇīnāṁ para-devateti vidito raṅgaṁ gataḥ sāgrajaḥ

mallānām—for the wrestlers; *aśaniḥ*—lightning; *nṛṇām*—for the males; *nara-varaḥ*—the best of men; *strīṇām*—for the women; *smaraḥ*—Cupid; *mūrti-mān*—incarnate; *gopānām*—for the cowherds; *sva-janaḥ*—their relative; *asatām*—impious; *kṣiti-bhujām*—for the kings; *śāstā*—a punisher; *sva-pitroḥ*—for His parents; *śiśuḥ*—a child; *mṛtyuḥ*—death; *bhoja-pateḥ*—for the King of the Bhojas, Kaṁsa; *virāṭ*—the totality of the material universe; *aviduṣām*—for the unintelligent; *tattvam*—the Truth; *param*—Supreme; *yoginām*—for the *yogīs; vṛṣṇīnām*—for the members of the Vṛṣṇi dynasty; *para-devatā*—their most worshipable Deity; *iti*—in these ways; *viditaḥ*—understood; *raṅgam*—the arena; *gataḥ*—He entered; *sa*—along with; *agrajaḥ*—His elder brother.

TRANSLATION

The various groups of people in the arena regarded Kṛṣṇa in different ways when He entered it with His elder brother. The wrestlers saw Kṛṣṇa as a lightning bolt, the men of Mathurā as the best of males, the women as Cupid in person, the cowherd men as their relative, the impious rulers as a chastiser, His parents as their child, the King of the Bhojas as death, the unintelligent as the Supreme Lord's universal form, the yogīs as the Absolute Truth and the Vṛṣṇis as their supreme worshipable Deity.

PURPORT

Śrīla Śrīdhara Svāmī quotes the following verse, which explains the ten attitudes toward Kṛṣṇa described here:

raudro'dbhutaś ca śṛṅgāro
hāsyaṁ vīro dayā tathā

bhayānakaś ca bībhatsaḥ
śāntaḥ sa-prema-bhaktikaḥ

"[There are ten different moods:] fury [perceived by the wrestlers], wonder [by the men], conjugal attraction [the women], laughter [the cowherds], chivalry [the kings], mercy [His parents], terror [Kaṁsa], ghastliness [the unintelligent], peaceful neutrality [the *yogīs*] and loving devotion [the Vṛṣṇis]."

Śrīla Viśvanātha Cakravartī points out that people like the wrestlers, Kaṁsa and the impious rulers perceive Kṛṣṇa as dangerous, angry or threatening because they fail to understand the actual position of the Personality of Godhead. Actually, Lord Kṛṣṇa is everyone's friend and well-wisher, but because we rebel against Him, He chastises us, and thus we may perceive Him as threatening. Kṛṣṇa, or God, is actually merciful, and when He punishes us, that is also His mercy.

Śrīla Bhaktisiddhānta Sarasvatī Ṭhākura quotes the following Vedic statement: *raso vai saḥ rasaṁ hy evāyaṁ labdhvānandī bhavati.* "He Himself is *rasa,* the taste or mellow of a particular relationship. And certainly one who achieves this *rasa* becomes *ānandī,* filled with bliss." (*Taittirīya Upaniṣad* 2.7.1)

Śrīla Bhaktisiddhānta Sarasvatī quotes a further verse to explain the word *rasa:*

vyatītya bhāvanā-vartma
yaś camatkāra-bhāra-bhūḥ
hṛdi sattvojjvale bāḍhaṁ
svadate sa raso mataḥ

"That which is beyond imagination, heavy with wonder and relished in the heart shining with goodness—such is known as *rasa.*"

As Śrīla Rūpa Gosvāmī elaborately explains in his *Bhakti-rasāmṛta-sindhu,* there are five main *rasas*—neutrality, servitude, friendship, parental love and conjugal love—and seven secondary *rasas*—amazement, humor, chivalry, compassion, fury, fear and dread. Thus altogether there are twelve *rasas,* and the supreme object of them all is Śrī Kṛṣṇa Himself. In other words, our love and affection are actually meant for Śrī Kṛṣṇa. Unfortunately, out of ignorance we stubbornly try to squeeze happiness and love out of material relationships, which are not directly connected to Kṛṣṇa, and thus life becomes a constant frustration. The solution is simple: surrender to Kṛṣṇa, love Kṛṣṇa, love Kṛṣṇa's devotees and be happy forever.

TEXT 18

हतं कुवलयापीडं दृष्ट्वा तावपि दुर्जयौ ।
कंसो मनस्यपि तदा भृशमुद्विविजे नृप ॥ १८ ॥

hataṁ kuvalayāpīḍaṁ
dṛṣṭvā tāv api durjayau
kaṁso manasy api tadā
bhṛśam udvivije nṛpa

hatam—killed; *kuvalayāpīḍam*—the elephant Kuvalayāpīḍa; *dṛṣṭvā*—seeing; *tau*—the two of Them, Kṛṣṇa and Balarāma; *api*—and; *durjayau*—invincible; *kaṁsaḥ*—King Kaṁsa; *manasi*—in his mind; *api*—indeed; *tadā*—then; *bhṛśam*—exceedingly; *udvivije*—became anxious; *nṛpa*—O King (Parīkṣit).

TRANSLATION

When Kaṁsa saw that Kuvalayāpīḍa was dead and the two brothers were invincible, he was overwhelmed with anxiety, O King.

TEXT 19

तौ रेजतू रंगगतौ महाभुजौ
विचित्रवेषाभरणस्त्रगम्बरौ ।
यथा नटावुत्तमवेषधारिणौ
मनः क्षिपन्तौ प्रभया निरीक्षताम् ॥ १९ ॥

tau rejatū raṅga-gatau mahā-bhujau
vicitra-veṣābharaṇa-srag-ambarau
yathā naṭāv uttama-veṣa-dhāriṇau
manaḥ kṣipantau prabhayā nirīkṣatām

tau—the two of Them; *rejatuḥ*—shone; *raṅga-gatau*—present in the arena; *mahā-bhujau*—the mighty-armed Lords; *vicitra*—variegated; *veṣa*—whose style of dress; *ābharaṇa*—ornaments; *srak*—garlands; *ambarau*—and garments; *yathā*—like; *naṭau*—two actors; *uttama*—excellent; *veṣa*—costumes; *dhāriṇau*—wearing; *manaḥ*—the minds; *kṣipantau*—striking; *prabhayā*—with Their effulgences; *nirīkṣatām*—of those who looked on.

TRANSLATION

Arrayed with variegated ornaments, garlands and garments, just like a pair of excellently costumed actors, the two mighty-armed Lords shone splendidly in the arena. Indeed, They overpowered the minds of all onlookers with Their effulgences.

TEXT 20

निरीक्ष्य तावुत्तमपूरुषौ जना
मञ्चस्थिता नागरराष्ट्रका नृप ।
प्रहर्षवेगोत्कलितेक्षणानना:
पपुर्न तृप्ता नयनैस्तदाननम् ॥ २० ॥

nirīkṣya tāv uttama-pūruṣau janā
mañca-sthitā nāgara-rāṣṭrakā nṛpa
praharṣa-vegotkalitekṣaṇānanāḥ
papur na tṛptā nayanais tad-ānanam

nirīkṣya—seeing; *tau*—both of Them; *uttama-pūruṣau*—the Supreme Personalities; *janāḥ*—the people; *mañca*—in the viewing galleries; *sthitāḥ*—sitting; *nāgara*—the city-dwellers; *rāṣṭrakāḥ*—and the people from outlying districts; *nṛpa*—O King; *praharṣa*—of their joy; *vega*—by the force; *utkalita*—made to expand widely; *īkṣaṇa*—their eyes; *ānanāḥ*—and faces; *papuḥ*—they drank; *na*—not; *tṛptāḥ*—satiated; *nayanaiḥ*—with their eyes; *tat*—of Them; *ānanam*—the faces.

TRANSLATION

O King, as the citizens of the city and the people from outlying districts gazed upon those two Supreme Personalities from their seats in the galleries, the force of the people's happiness caused their eyes to open wide and their faces to blossom. They drank in the vision of the Lords' faces without becoming satiated.

TEXTS 21–22

पिबन्त इव चक्षुर्भ्यां लिहन्त इव जिह्वया ।
जिघ्रन्त इव नासाभ्यां श्लिष्यन्त इव बाहुभिः ॥ २१ ॥
ऊचुः परस्परं ते वै यथादृष्टं यथाश्रुतम् ।
तद्रूपगुणमाधुर्यप्रागल्भ्यस्मारिता इव ॥ २२ ॥

pibanta iva cakṣurbhyāṁ
lihanta iva jihvayā
jighranta iva nāsābhyāṁ
śliṣyanta iva bāhubhiḥ

ūcuḥ parasparaṁ te vai
yathā-dṛṣṭaṁ yathā-śrutam
tad-rūpa-guṇa-mādhurya-
prāgalbhya-smāritā iva

pibantaḥ—drinking; *iva*—as if; *cakṣurbhyām*—with their eyes; *lihantaḥ*—licking; *iva*—as if; *jihvayā*—with their tongues; *jighrantaḥ*—smelling; *iva*—as if; *nāsābhyām*—with their nostrils; *śliṣyantaḥ*—embracing; *iva*—as if; *bāhubhiḥ*—with their arms; *ūcuḥ*—they spoke; *parasparam*—among one another; *te*—they; *vai*—indeed; *yathā*—just as; *dṛṣṭam*—they had seen; *yathā*—just as; *śrutam*—they had heard; *tat*—Their; *rūpa*—of the beauty; *guṇa*—qualities; *mādhurya*—charm; *prāgalbhya*—and bravery; *smāritāḥ*—reminded; *iva*—as if.

TRANSLATION

The people seemed to be drinking Kṛṣṇa and Balarāma with their eyes, licking Them with their tongues, smelling Them with their nostrils and embracing Them with their arms. Reminded of the Lords' beauty, character, charm and bravery, the members of the audience began describing these features to one another according to what they had seen and heard.

PURPORT

Naturally, those who assembled in Mathurā for the wrestling festival had heard the latest news of Kṛṣṇa's and Balarāma's adventures in the city—how the Lords had broken the sacrificial bow, defeated the police and killed the elephant Kuvalayāpīḍa. And now that the people were seeing Kṛṣṇa and Balarāma enter the arena, their greatest expectations were confirmed. Kṛṣṇa is the embodiment of all beauty, fame and opulence, and therefore those assembled in the wrestling arena became fully satisfied by glorifying what they had heard of Him and were now seeing.

TEXT 23

एतौ भगवतः साक्षाद्धरेर्नारायणस्य हि।
अवतीर्णाविहांशेन वसुदेवस्य वेश्मनि ॥ २३ ॥

etau bhagavataḥ sākṣād
dharer nārāyaṇasya hi
avatīrṇāv ihāṁśena
vasudevasya veśmani

etau—these two; *bhagavataḥ*—of the Supreme Lord; *sākṣāt*—directly; *hareḥ*—of Lord Hari; *nārāyaṇasya*—Nārāyaṇa; *hi*—certainly; *avatīrṇau*—have descended; *iha*—to this world; *aṁśena*—as expansions; *vasudevasya*—of Vasudeva; *veśmani*—in the home.

TRANSLATION

[The people said:] These two boys are certainly expansions of the Supreme Lord Nārāyaṇa who have descended to this world in the home of Vasudeva.

TEXT 24

एष वै किल देवक्यां जातो नीतश्च गोकुलम्।
कालमेतं वसन् गूढो ववृधे नन्दवेश्मनि ॥ २४ ॥

eṣa vai kila devakyāṁ
jāto nītaś ca gokulam
kālam etaṁ vasan gūḍho
vavṛdhe nanda-veśmani

eṣaḥ—this (Kṛṣṇa); *vai*—certainly; *kila*—indeed; *devakyām*—from the womb of Devakī; *jātaḥ*—born; *nītaḥ*—brought; *ca*—and; *gokulam*—to Gokula; *kālam*—time; *etam*—this much; *vasan*—living; *gūḍhaḥ*—hidden; *vavṛdhe*—He grew up; *nanda-veśmani*—in the house of Nanda Mahārāja.

TRANSLATION

This one [Kṛṣṇa] took birth from mother Devakī and was brought to Gokula, where He has remained concealed all this time, growing up in the house of King Nanda.

TEXT 25

पूतनानेन नीतान्तं चक्रवातश्च दानवः ।
अर्जुनौ गुह्यकः केशी धेनुकोऽन्ये च तद्विधाः ॥ २५ ॥

pūtanānena nītāntaṁ
cakravātaś ca dānavaḥ
arjunau guhyakaḥ keśī
dhenuko'nye ca tad-vidhāḥ

pūtanā—the witch Pūtanā; *anena*—by Him; *nītā*—brought; *antam*—to her end; *cakravātaḥ*—whirlwind; *ca*—and; *dānavaḥ*—the demon; *arjunau*—the twin Arjuna trees; *guhyakaḥ*—the demon Śaṅkhacūḍa; *keśī*—the horse demon, Keśī; *dhenukaḥ*—the jackass demon, Dhenuka; *anye*—others; *ca*—and; *tat-vidhāḥ*—like them.

TRANSLATION

He made Pūtanā and the whirlwind demon meet with death, pulled down the twin Arjuna trees, and killed Śaṅkhacūḍa, Keśī, Dhenuka and similar demons.

TEXTS 26–27

गावः सपाला एतेन दावाग्नेः परिमोचिताः ।
कालियो दमितः सर्प इन्द्रश्च विमदः कृतः ॥ २६ ॥
सप्ताहमेकहस्तेन धृतोऽद्रिप्रवरोऽमुना ।
वर्षवाताशनिभ्यश्च परित्रातं च गोकुलम् ॥ २७ ॥

gāvaḥ sa-pālā etena
dāvāgneḥ parimocitāḥ
kāliyo damitaḥ sarpa
indraś ca vimadaḥ kṛtaḥ

saptāham eka-hastena
dhṛto'dri-pravaro'munā
varṣa-vātāśanibhyaś ca
paritrātaṁ ca gokulam

gāvaḥ—the cows; *sa*—together with; *pālāḥ*—their tenders; *etena*—by Him; *dāva-agneḥ*—from the forest fire; *parimocitāḥ*—saved; *kāliyaḥ*—

Kāliya; *damitaḥ*—subdued; *sarpaḥ*—the serpent; *indraḥ*—Indra; *ca*—and; *vimadaḥ*—prideless; *kṛtaḥ*—made; *sapta-aham*—for seven days; *eka-hastena*—with one hand; *dhṛtaḥ*—held; *adri*—of mountains; *pravaraḥ*—the most eminent; *amunā*—by Him; *varṣa*—from rain; *vāta*—wind; *aśanibhyaḥ*—and hail; *ca*—also; *paritrātam*—delivered; *ca*—and; *gokulam*—the residents of Gokula.

TRANSLATION

He saved the cows and the cowherds from a forest fire and subdued the serpent Kāliya. He removed Lord Indra's false pride by holding up the best of mountains with one hand for an entire week, thus protecting the inhabitants of Gokula from rain, wind and hail.

TEXT 28

गोप्योऽस्य नित्यमुदितहसितप्रेक्षणं मुखम् ।
पश्यन्त्यो विविधांस्तापांस्तरन्ति स्माश्रमं मुदा ॥ २८ ॥

gopyo'sya nitya-mudita-
hasita-prekṣaṇaṁ mukham
paśyantyo vividhāṁs tāpāṁs
taranti smāśramaṁ mudā

gopyaḥ—the young *gopīs; asya*—His; *nitya*—always; *mudita*—cheerful; *hasita*—smiling; *prekṣaṇam*—whose glance; *mukham*—the face; *paśyantyaḥ*—seeing; *vividhān*—of various kinds; *tāpān*—distress; *taranti sma*—transcended; *aśramam*—free from fatigue; *mudā*—happily.

TRANSLATION

The gopīs overcame all kinds of distress and experienced great happiness by seeing His face, which is always cheerful with smiling glances and ever free of fatigue.

TEXT 29

वदन्त्यनेन वंशोऽयं यदोः सुबहुविश्रुतः ।
श्रियं यशो महत्वं च लप्स्यते परिरक्षितः ॥ २९ ॥

vadanty anena vaṁśo'yaṁ
yadoḥ su-bahu-viśrutaḥ

śriyaṁ yaśo mahatvaṁ ca
lapsyate parirakṣitaḥ

vadanti—they say; *anena*—by Him; *vaṁśaḥ*—the dynasty; *ayam*—this; *yadoḥ*—descending from King Yadu; *su-bahu*—very much; *viśrutaḥ*—famous; *śriyam*—riches; *yaśaḥ*—glory; *mahatvam*—power; *ca*—and; *lapsyate*—it will achieve; *parirakṣitaḥ*—protected on all sides.

TRANSLATION

It is said that under His full protection the Yadu dynasty will become extremely famous and attain wealth, glory and power.

TEXT 30

अयं चास्याग्रजः श्रीमान् रामः कमललोचनः ।
प्रलम्बो निहतो येन वत्सको ये बकादयः ॥ ३० ॥

ayaṁ cāsyāgrajaḥ śrīmān
rāmaḥ kamala-locanaḥ
pralambo nihato yena
vatsako ye bakādayaḥ

ayam—this; *ca*—and; *asya*—His; *agra-jaḥ*—elder brother; *śrī-mān*—the possessor of all opulences; *rāmaḥ*—Lord Balarāma; *kamala-locanaḥ*—the lotus-eyed; *pralambaḥ*—the demon Pralamba; *nihataḥ*—killed; *yena*—by whom; *vatsakaḥ*—Vatsāsura; *ye*—who; *baka*—Bakāsura; *ādayaḥ*—and others.

TRANSLATION

This lotus-eyed elder brother of His, Lord Balarāma, is the proprietor of all transcendental opulences. He has killed Pralamba, Vatsaka, Baka and other demons.

PURPORT

In fact two of the demons mentioned here were killed by Kṛṣṇa, not Balarāma. The reason for the mistake is that as news of Kṛṣṇa's exploits spread among ordinary people, the facts became somewhat muddled. The same tendency can be observed in modern newspapers.

TEXT 31

जनेष्वेवं ब्रुवाणेषु तूर्येषु निनदत्सु च ।
कृष्णरामौ समाभाष्य चाणूरो वाक्यमब्रवीत् ॥ ३१ ॥

janeṣv evaṁ bruvāṇeṣu
tūryeṣu ninadatsu ca
kṛṣṇa-rāmau samābhāṣya
cāṇūro vākyam abravīt

janeṣu—as the people; *evam*—thus; *bruvāṇeṣu*—were speaking; *tūryeṣu*—as the musical instruments; *ninadatsu*—were resounding; *ca*—and; *kṛṣṇa-rāmau*—Kṛṣṇa and Balarāma; *samābhāṣya*—addressing; *cāṇūraḥ*—the demonic wrestler Cāṇūra; *vākyam*—words; *abravīt*—said.

TRANSLATION

While the people talked in this way and the musical instruments resounded, the wrestler Cāṇūra addressed Kṛṣṇa and Balarāma with the following words.

PURPORT

Cāṇūra could not tolerate that the audience was praising Kṛṣṇa so highly. Therefore he had to say something to the two brothers.

TEXT 32

हे नन्दसूनो हे राम भवन्तौ वीरसम्मतौ ।
नियुद्धकुशलौ श्रुत्वा राज्ञाहूतौ दिदृक्षुणा ॥ ३२ ॥

he nanda-sūno he rāma
bhavantau vīra-sammatau
niyuddha-kuśalau śrutvā
rājñāhūtau didṛkṣuṇā

he nanda-sūno—O son of Nanda; *he rāma*—O Rāma; *bhavantau*—You two; *vīra*—by heroes; *sammatau*—are well respected; *niyuddha*—in wrestling; *kuśalau*—skillful; *śrutvā*—hearing; *rājñā*—by the King; *āhūtau*—called for; *didṛkṣuṇā*—who wanted to see.

TRANSLATION

[Cāṇūra said:] O son of Nanda, O Rāma, You two are well respected by courageous men and are both skillful at wrestling. Having heard of Your prowess, the King has called You here, wanting to see for himself.

TEXT 33

प्रियं राज्ञः प्रकुर्वत्यः श्रेयो विन्दन्ति वै प्रजाः ।
मनसा कर्मणा वाचा विपरीतमतोऽन्यथा ॥ ३३ ॥

priyaṁ rājñaḥ prakurvatyaḥ
śreyo vindanti vai prajāḥ
manasā karmaṇā vācā
viparītam ato'nyathā

priyam—the pleasure; *rājñaḥ*—of the King; *prakurvatyaḥ*—executing; *śreyaḥ*—good fortune; *vindanti*—acquire; *vai*—indeed; *prajāḥ*—citizens; *manasā*—with their minds; *karmaṇā*—with their deeds; *vācā*—with their words; *viparītam*—opposite; *ataḥ*—to this; *anyathā*—otherwise.

TRANSLATION

Subjects of the King who try to please him with their thoughts, acts and words are sure to achieve good fortune, but those who fail to do so will suffer the opposite fate.

TEXT 34

नित्यं प्रमुदिता गोपा वत्सपाला यथास्फुटम् ।
वनेषु मल्लयुद्धेन क्रीडन्तश्चारयन्ति गाः ॥ ३४ ॥

nityaṁ pramuditā gopā
vatsa-pālā yathā-sphuṭam
vaneṣu malla-yuddhena
krīḍantaś cārayanti gāḥ

nityam—always; *pramuditāḥ*—very happy; *gopāḥ*—cowherds; *vatsapālāḥ*—tending the calves; *yathā-sphuṭam*—obviously; *vaneṣu*—in the various forests; *malla-yuddhena*—with wrestling; *krīḍantaḥ*—playing; *cārayanti*—they graze; *gāḥ*—the cows.

TRANSLATION

It is well known that cowherd boys are always joyful as they tend their calves, and that the boys playfully wrestle with each other while grazing their animals in the various forests.

PURPORT

Here Cāṇūra explains how the two brothers came to be expert at wrestling.

TEXT 35

तस्माद् राज्ञः प्रियं यूयं वयं च करवाम हे।
भूतानि नः प्रसीदन्ति सर्वभूतमयो नृपः ॥ ३५ ॥

tasmād rājñaḥ priyaṁ yūyaṁ
vayaṁ ca karavāma he
bhūtāni naḥ prasīdanti
sarva-bhūta-mayo nṛpaḥ

tasmāt—therefore; *rājñaḥ*—the King's; *priyam*—pleasure; *yūyam*—You two; *vayam*—we; *ca*—also; *karavāma he*—let us do; *bhūtāni*—all living beings; *naḥ*—with us; *prasīdanti*—will be satisfied; *sarva-bhūta*—all beings; *mayaḥ*—comprising; *nṛpaḥ*—the king.

TRANSLATION

Therefore let's do what the King wants. Everyone will be pleased with us, for the king embodies all living beings.

TEXT 36

तन्निशम्याब्रवीत्कृष्णो देशकालोचितं वचः।
नियुद्धमात्मनोऽभीष्टं मन्यमानोऽभिनन्द्य च ॥ ३६ ॥

tan niśamyābravīt kṛṣṇo
deśa-kālocitaṁ vacaḥ
niyuddham ātmano'bhīṣṭaṁ
manyamāno'bhinandya ca

tat—that; *niśamya*—hearing; *abravīt*—spoke; *kṛṣṇaḥ*—Lord Kṛṣṇa; *deśa*—for the place; *kāla*—and time; *ucitam*—appropriate; *vacaḥ*—words;

niyuddham—wrestling; *ātmanaḥ*—to Himself; *abhīṣṭam*—desirable; *manyamānaḥ*—considering; *abhinandya*—welcoming; *ca*—and.

TRANSLATION

Hearing this, Lord Kṛṣṇa, who liked to wrestle and welcomed the challenge, replied with words appropriate to the time and place.

TEXT 37

प्रजा भोजपतेरस्य वयं चापि वनेचराः ।
करवाम प्रियं नित्यं तन्नः परमनुग्रहः ॥ ३७ ॥

prajā bhoja-pater asya
vayaṁ cāpi vane-carāḥ
karavāma priyaṁ nityaṁ
tan naḥ param anugrahaḥ

prajāḥ—subjects; *bhoja-pateḥ*—of the King of the Bhojas; *asya*—of him; *vayam*—We; *ca*—also; *api*—even though; *vane-carāḥ*—wandering in the forest; *karavāma*—We must execute; *priyam*—his pleasure; *nityam*—always; *tat*—that; *naḥ*—for Us; *param*—the greatest; *anugrahaḥ*—benefit.

TRANSLATION

[Lord Kṛṣṇa said:] Although forest-dwellers, We are also subjects of the Bhoja king. We must gratify his desires, for such behavior will confer upon Us the greatest benefit.

TEXT 38

बाला वयं तुल्यबलैः क्रीडिष्यामो यथोचितम् ।
भवेन्नियुद्धं माधर्मः स्पृशेन्मल्लसभासदः ॥ ३८ ॥

bālā vayaṁ tulya-balaiḥ
krīḍiṣyāmo yathocitam
bhaven niyuddhaṁ mādharmaḥ
spṛśen malla-sabhā-sadaḥ

bālāḥ—young boys; *vayam*—We; *tulya*—equal; *balaiḥ*—with those whose strength; *krīḍiṣyāmaḥ*—We will play; *yathā ucitam*—in a fitting manner; *bhavet*—should occur; *niyuddham*—the wrestling match; *mā*—not;

adharmaḥ—irreligion; *spṛśet*—should touch; *malla-sabhā*—of the assembly in the wrestling arena; *sadaḥ*—the members.

TRANSLATION

We are just young boys and should play with those of equal strength. The wrestling match must go on properly so that irreligion does not taint the respectable members of the audience.

TEXT 39

चाणूर उवाच
न बालो न किशोरस्त्वं बलश्च बलिनां वरः ।
लीलयेभो हतो येन सहस्रद्विपसत्त्वभृत् ॥ ३९ ॥

cāṇūra uvāca
na bālo na kiśoras tvaṁ
balaś ca balināṁ varaḥ
līlayebho hato yena
sahasra-dvipa-sattva-bhṛt

cāṇūraḥ uvāca—Cāṇūra said; *na*—not; *bālaḥ*—a boy; *na*—not; *kiśoraḥ*—a youth; *tvam*—You; *balaḥ*—Balarāma; *ca*—and; *balinām*—of the strong; *varaḥ*—the best; *līlayā*—as play; *ibhaḥ*—the elephant; *hataḥ*—killed; *yena*—by whom; *sahasra*—of one thousand; *dvipa*—elephants; *sattva*—of the strength; *bhṛt*—the bearer.

TRANSLATION

Cāṇūra said: You aren't really a child or even a young man, and neither is Balarāma, the strongest of the strong. After all, You playfully killed an elephant who had the strength of a thousand other elephants.

TEXT 40

तस्माद् भवद्‌भ्यां बलिभिर्योद्धव्यं नानयोऽत्र वै ।
मयि विक्रम वार्ष्णेय बलेन सह मुष्टिकः ॥ ४० ॥

tasmād bhavadbhyāṁ balibhir
yoddhavyaṁ nānayo'tra vai
mayi vikrama vārṣṇeya
balena saha muṣṭikaḥ

tasmāt—therefore; *bhavadbhyām*—You two; *balibhiḥ*—with those who are strong; *yoddhavyam*—should fight; *na*—there is not; *anayaḥ*—injustice; *atra*—in this; *vai*—certainly; *mayi*—to me; *vikrama*—(show) Your prowess; *vārṣṇeya*—O descendant of Vṛṣṇi; *balena saha*—with Balarāma; *muṣṭikaḥ*—Muṣṭika (should fight).

TRANSLATION

Therefore You two should fight powerful wrestlers. There's certainly nothing unfair about that. You, O descendant of Vṛṣṇi, can show Your prowess against me, and Balarāma can fight with Muṣṭika.

Thus end the purports of the humble servants of His Divine Grace A.C. Bhaktivedanta Swami Prabhupāda to the Tenth Canto, Forty-third Chapter, of the Śrīmad-Bhāgavatam, *entitled "Kṛṣṇa Kills the Elephant Kuvalayāpīḍa."*

CHAPTER FORTY-FOUR

The Killing of Kaṁsa

This chapter tells how Kṛṣṇa and Balarāma killed the wrestlers, how Kṛṣṇa killed Kaṁsa and consoled Kaṁsa's wives, and how the two Lords were reunited with Their mother and father.

Deciding to wrestle, Lord Kṛṣṇa faced off against Cāṇūra, and Lord Baladeva took on Muṣṭika. Battling arm to arm, head to head, knee to knee and chest to chest, the opponents attacked each other so fiercely that they appeared to be harming even their own bodies. The ladies in the arena, seeing the violent battle, began to condemn the King and all the members of the assembly: "A respectable audience should never have allowed a wrestling match between such huge wrestlers, whose limbs are as tough as lightning bolts, and such tender young boys, who are just entering youth. An intelligent person should never enter an assembly if he sees injustice being done there." Because Vasudeva and Devakī did not fully understand the power of Kṛṣṇa and Balarāma, they became extremely unhappy when they heard the women of the audience speak these words.

Śrī Kṛṣṇa then grabbed Cāṇūra's arms, whirled him around several times and threw him to the ground, killing him. Muṣṭika met a similar fate: after being struck powerfully by Lord Baladeva's palm, he began vomiting blood and then fell down dead. Thereupon the wrestlers named Kūṭa, Śala and Tośala came forward, but Kṛṣṇa and Balarāma easily killed them with the blows of Their fists and feet. The remaining wrestlers, fearing for their lives, all fled.

Except for Kaṁsa, everyone present cheered Kṛṣṇa and Balarāma. The King, in a rage, stopped the festive music and ordered that Vasudeva, Nanda, Ugrasena and all the cowherds be severely punished and that Kṛṣṇa and Balarāma be driven from the assembly. Kṛṣṇa became furious when He heard Kaṁsa speak this way, and He instantly leapt onto the lofty royal dais. He grabbed Kaṁsa by the hair, hurled him down onto the floor of the wrestling ring and threw Himself on top of him. In this way, Kaṁsa met his death. Because out of fear Kaṁsa had always thought of Kṛṣṇa, after his death he gained the liberation of having a form like the Lord's.

Kaṁsa's eight brothers then attacked Kṛṣṇa, but Balarāma easily killed each of them with His club, just as a lion kills defenseless animals. Kettledrums resounded in the sky as the joyful demigods rained down flowers and chanted the glories of Lord Kṛṣṇa and Lord Balarāma.

The wives of Kaṁsa, grieving for their husband, lamented that he had died because of his violence toward other living beings and his lack of respect for Kṛṣṇa, the Supreme Soul, who creates, maintains and destroys the entire universe. The Lord consoled the widows, had the funeral rites performed for Kaṁsa and his brothers and then released His mother and father from bondage. Kṛṣṇa offered obeisances at His parents' feet, but they, now understanding Him to be the Supreme Personality of Godhead, did not embrace Him.

TEXT 1

श्रीशुक उवाच
एवं चर्चितसंकल्पो भगवान्मधुसूदनः ।
आससादाथ चाणूरं मुष्टिकं रोहिणीसुतः ॥ १ ॥

śrī-śuka uvāca
evaṁ carcita-saṅkalpo
bhagavān madhusūdanaḥ
āsasādātha cāṇūraṁ
muṣṭtikaṁ rohiṇī-sutaḥ

śrī-śukaḥ uvāca—Śukadeva Gosvāmī said; *evam*—thus; *carcita*—fixing; *saṅkalpaḥ*—His determination; *bhagavān*—the Supreme Lord; *madhusūdanaḥ*—Kṛṣṇa; *āsasāda*—confronted; *atha*—then; *cāṇūram*—Cāṇūra; *muṣṭikam*—Muṣṭika; *rohiṇī-sutaḥ*—the son of Rohiṇī, Lord Balarāma.

TRANSLATION

Śukadeva Gosvāmī said: Thus addressed, Lord Kṛṣṇa made up His mind to accept the challenge. He paired off with Cāṇūra, and Lord Balarāma with Muṣṭika.

TEXT 2

हस्ताभ्यां हस्तयोर्बद्ध्वा पद्भ्यामेव च पादयोः ।
विचकर्षतुरन्योन्यं प्रसह्य विजिगीषया ॥ २ ॥

hastābhyāṁ hastayor baddhvā
padbhyām eva ca pādayoḥ
vicakarṣatur anyonyaṁ
prasahya vijigīṣayā

hastābhyām—with their hands; *hastayoḥ*—by the hands; *baddhvā*—seizing; *padbhyām*—with their legs; *eva ca*—also; *pādayoḥ*—by the legs; *vicakarṣatuḥ*—they (Kṛṣṇa paired with Cāṇūra, and Balarāma with Muṣṭika) dragged; *anyonyam*—each other; *prasahya*—with force; *vijigīṣayā*—with desire for victory.

TRANSLATION

Seizing each other's hands and locking legs with each other, the opponents struggled powerfully, eager for victory.

TEXT 3

अरत्नी द्वे अरत्निभ्यां जानुभ्यां चैव जानुनी ।
शिरः शीर्ष्णोरसोरस्तावन्योन्यमभिजघ्नतुः ॥ ३ ॥

aratnī dve aratnibhyāṁ
jānubhyāṁ caiva jānunī
śiraḥ śīrṣṇorasoras tāv
anyonyam abhijaghnatuḥ

aratnī—against the opponent's fists; *dve*—two; *aratnibhyām*—their fists; *jānubhyām*—their knees; *ca eva*—also; *jānunī*—against the opponent's knees; *śiraḥ*—head; *śīrṣṇā*—with head; *urasā*—with chest; *uraḥ*—chest; *tau*—they in pairs; *anyonyam*—each other; *abhijaghnatuḥ*—struck.

TRANSLATION

They each struck fists against fists, knees against knees, head against head and chest against chest.

PURPORT

The word *aratni* in this verse may indicate the elbow as well as the fist. Thus blows were perhaps also struck with the elbow, a technique seen today in various martial arts.

TEXT 4

परिभ्रामणविक्षेपपरिरम्भावपातनैः ।
उत्सर्पणापसर्पणैश्चान्योन्यं प्रत्यरुन्धताम् ॥ ४ ॥

paribhrāmaṇa-vikṣepa-
parirambhāvapātanaiḥ
utsarpaṇāpasarpaṇaiś
cānyonyaṁ pratyarundhatām

paribhrāmaṇa—with wheeling the other about; *vikṣepa*—shoving; *pari-rambha*—crushing; *avapātanaiḥ*—and throwing down; *utsarpaṇa*—releasing and running in front; *apasarpaṇaiḥ*—going behind; *ca*—and; *anyonyam*—each other; *pratyarundhatām*—they resisted.

TRANSLATION

Each fighter contended with his opponent by dragging him about in circles, shoving and crushing him, throwing him down and running before and behind him.

PURPORT

Śrīla Śrīdhara Svāmī explains that the word *parirambha* indicates crushing one's opponent with one's arms.

TEXT 5

उत्थापनैरुन्नयनैश्चालनैः स्थापनैरपि ।
परस्परं जिगीषन्तावपचक्रतुरात्मनः ॥ ५ ॥

utthāpanair unnayanaiś
cālanaiḥ sthāpanair api
parasparaṁ jigīṣantāv
apacakratur ātmanaḥ

utthāpanaiḥ—with lifting up; *unnayanaiḥ*—carrying; *cālanaiḥ*—pushing away; *sthāpanaiḥ*—holding stationary; *api*—also; *parasparam*—each other; *jigīṣantau*—wanting victory; *apacakratuḥ*—they harmed; *ātmanaḥ*—(even) themselves.

TRANSLATION

Forcefully lifting and carrying each other, pushing each other away and holding each other down, the fighters hurt even their own bodies in their great eagerness for victory.

PURPORT

Śrīla Jīva Gosvāmī explains that although Kṛṣṇa and Balarāma did not, of course, harm Themselves, it appeared that way to Cāṇūra, Muṣṭika and others of mundane vision. In other words, the Lords were fully absorbed in the pastime of being wrestlers.

TEXT 6

तद् बलाबलवद्युद्धं समेताः सर्वयोषितः ।
ऊचुः परस्परं राजन् सानुकम्पा वरूथशः ॥ ६ ॥

tad balābalavad yuddhaṁ
sametāḥ sarva-yoṣitaḥ
ūcuḥ parasparaṁ rājan
sānukampā varūthaśaḥ

tat—that; *bala-abala*—the strong and the weak; *vat*—involving; *yuddham*—fight; *sametāḥ*—assembled; *sarva*—all; *yoṣitaḥ*—the women; *ūcuḥ*—said; *parasparam*—to one another; *rājan*—O King (Parīkṣit); *sa-anukampāḥ*—feeling compassion; *varūthaśaḥ*—in groups.

TRANSLATION

My dear King, all the women present, considering the match an unfair fight between the strong and the weak, felt extreme anxiety due to compassion. They assembled in groups around the arena and spoke to one another as follows.

TEXT 7

महानयं बताधर्म एषां राजसभासदाम् ।
ये बलाबलवद्युद्धं राज्ञोऽन्विच्छन्ति पश्यतः ॥ ७ ॥

mahān ayaṁ batādharma
eṣāṁ rāja-sabhā-sadām

ye balābalavad yuddhaṁ
rājño'nvicchanti paśyataḥ

mahān—great; *ayam*—this; *bata*—alas; *adharmaḥ*—act of irreligion; *eṣām*—on the part of these; *rāja-sabhā*—in the King's assembly; *sadām*—persons present; *ye*—who; *bala-abala-vat*—between strong and weak; *yuddham*—a fight; *rājñaḥ*—while the King; *anvicchanti*—they also desire; *paśyataḥ*—is watching.

TRANSLATION

[The women said:] Alas, what a greatly irreligious act the members of this royal assembly are committing! As the King watches this fight between the strong and the weak, they also want to see it.

PURPORT

The idea the ladies are expressing is that even if the King somehow wanted to see such an unfair match, why should the respectable members of the assembly also desire to see it? These feelings are natural. Even nowadays, if in a public place we find a violent fight going on between a very strong, large person and a weaker, smaller person, we are aroused to indignation. Compassionate women are especially offended and enraged by such unfair violence.

TEXT 8

क्व वज्रसारसर्वांगौ मल्लौ शैलेन्द्रसन्निभौ ।
क्व चातिसुकुमारांगौ किशोरौ नाप्तयौवनौ ॥ ८ ॥

kva vajra-sāra-sarvāṅgau
mallau śailendra-sannibhau
kva cāti-sukumārāṅgau
kiśorau nāpta-yauvanau

kva—where, on the one hand; *vajra*—of lightning; *sāra*—with the strength; *sarva*—all; *aṅgau*—whose limbs; *mallau*—two wrestlers; *śaila*—mountains; *indra*—like the chief; *sannibhau*—whose appearance; *kva*—where; *ca*—and, on the other hand; *ati*—very; *su-kumāra*—tender; *aṅgau*—whose limbs; *kiśorau*—two youths; *na āpta*—not having yet attained; *yauvanau*—Their maturity.

TRANSLATION

What comparison can there be between these two professional wrestlers, with limbs as strong as lightning bolts and bodies resembling mighty mountains, and these two young, immature boys with exceedingly tender limbs?

TEXT 9

धर्मव्यतिक्रमो ह्यस्य समाजस्य ध्रुवं भवेत्।
यत्राधर्मः समुत्तिष्ठेन्न स्थेयं तत्र कर्हिचित् ॥ ९॥

dharma-vyatikramo hy asya
samājasya dhruvaṁ bhavet
yatrādharmaḥ samuttiṣṭhen
na stheyaṁ tatra karhicit

dharma—of religious principles; *vyatikramaḥ*—transgression; *hi*—indeed; *asya*—by this; *samājasya*—company; *dhruvam*—certainly; *bhavet*—must be; *yatra*—wherein; *adharmaḥ*—irreligion; *samuttiṣṭhet*—has fully arisen; *na stheyam*—one should not remain; *tatra*—there; *karhicit*—for any duration of time at all.

TRANSLATION

Religious principles have certainly been violated in this assembly. One should not remain for even a moment in a place where irreligion is flourishing.

TEXT 10

न सभां प्रविशेत्प्राज्ञः सभ्यदोषाननुस्मरन्।
अब्रुवन् विब्रुवन्नज्ञो नरः किल्बिषमश्नुते ॥ १०॥

na sabhāṁ praviśet prājñaḥ
sabhya-doṣān anusmaran
abruvan vibruvann ajño
naraḥ kilbiṣam aśnute

na—not; *sabhām*—an assembly; *praviśet*—should enter; *prājñaḥ*—the wise person; *sabhya*—of the assembly members; *doṣān*—sinful discrepancies; *anusmaran*—keeping in mind; *abruvan*—not speaking; *vibruvan*—speaking wrongly; *ajñaḥ*—ignorant (or pretending to be so); *naraḥ*—a man; *kilbiṣam*—sin; *aśnute*—incurs.

TRANSLATION

A wise person should not enter an assembly if he knows the participants there are committing acts of impropriety. And if, having entered such an assembly, he fails to speak the truth, speaks falsely or pleads ignorance, he will certainly incur sin.

TEXT 11

वल्गतः शत्रुमभितः कृष्णस्य वदनाम्बुजम् ।
वीक्ष्यतां श्रमवार्युप्तं पद्मकोशमिवाम्बुभिः ॥ ११ ॥

valgataḥ śatrum abhitaḥ
kṛṣṇasya vadanāmbujam
vīkṣyatāṁ śrama-vāry-uptaṁ
padma-kośam ivāmbubhiḥ

valgataḥ—leaping; *śatrum*—of His enemy; *abhitaḥ*—on all sides; *kṛṣṇasya*—of Kṛṣṇa; *vadana*—the face; *ambujam*—lotuslike; *vīkṣyatām*—you should see; *śrama*—of fatigue; *vāri*—with the moisture; *uptam*—covered; *padma*—of a lotus flower; *kośam*—the whorl; *iva*—like; *ambubhiḥ*—with droplets of water.

TRANSLATION

Just see the lotus face of Kṛṣṇa as He darts around His foe! That face, covered with drops of perspiration brought on by the strenuous fight, resembles a lotus covered with dew.

TEXT 12

किं न पश्यत रामस्य मुखमाताम्रलोचनम् ।
मुष्टिकं प्रति सामर्षं हाससंरम्भशोभितम् ॥ १२ ॥

kiṁ na paśyata rāmasya
mukham ātāmra-locanam
muṣṭikaṁ prati sāmarṣaṁ
hāsa-saṁrambha-śobhitam

kim—why; *na paśyata*—do you not see; *rāmasya*—of Lord Balarāma; *mukham*—the face; *ātāmra*—like copper; *locanam*—with eyes; *muṣṭikam*—Muṣṭika; *prati*—toward; *sa-amarṣam*—with anger; *hāsa*—by His laughter; *saṁrambha*—and His absorption; *śobhitam*—beautified.

TRANSLATION

Don't you see the face of Lord Balarāma, with its eyes copper-red from His anger toward Muṣṭika and its beauty enhanced by His laughter and His absorption in the fight?

TEXT 13

पुण्या बत व्रजभुवो यदयं नृलिंग-
गूढः पुराणपुरुषो वनचित्रमाल्यः ।
गाः पालयन् सहबलः क्वणयंश्च वेणुं
विक्रीडयाञ्चति गिरित्ररमार्चिताङ्घ्रिः ॥ १३ ॥

puṇyā bata vraja-bhuvo yad ayaṁ nṛ-liṅga
gūḍhaḥ purāṇa-puruṣo vana-citra-mālyaḥ
gāḥ pālayan saha-balaḥ kvaṇayaṁś ca veṇuṁ
vikrīḍayāñcati giritra-ramārcitāṅghriḥ

puṇyāḥ—pious; *bata*—indeed; *vraja-bhuvaḥ*—the various regions of the land of Vraja; *yat*—in which; *ayam*—this; *nṛ*—human; *liṅga*—by characteristics; *gūḍhaḥ*—disguised; *purāṇa-puruṣaḥ*—the primeval Personality of Godhead; *vana*—composed of flowers and other items of the forest; *citra*—of wonderful variety; *mālyaḥ*—whose garlands; *gāḥ*—the cows; *pālayan*—herding; *saha*—together with; *balaḥ*—Lord Balarāma; *kvaṇayan*—vibrating; *ca*—and; *veṇum*—His flute; *vikrīḍayā*—with various pastimes; *añcati*—He moves about; *giritra*—by Lord Śiva; *ramā*—and the goddess of fortune; *arcita*—worshiped; *aṅghriḥ*—His feet.

TRANSLATION

How pious are the tracts of land in Vraja, for there the primeval Personality of Godhead, disguising Himself with human traits, wanders about, enacting His many pastimes! Adorned with wonderfully variegated forest garlands, He whose feet are worshiped by Lord Śiva and Goddess Ramā vibrates His flute as He tends the cows in the company of Balarāma.

PURPORT

In this verse the devoted ladies in the audience point out the difference between Mathurā and Vṛndāvana. They want to indicate that in Vṛndāvana Kṛṣṇa simply enjoys with His girlfriends and boyfriends, whereas here in Mathurā the Lord is subjected to harassment by the bullying tactics of professional wrestlers. Thus the ladies are condemning the city of Mathurā because of their pain at seeing Kṛṣṇa in what they consider an unfair wrestling match. Of course, Mathurā is also one of the Lord's eternal abodes, but here the women in the assembly express their love in a critical mood.

TEXT 14

गोप्यस्तपः किमचरन् यदमुष्य रूपं
लावण्यसारमसमोर्ध्वमनन्यसिद्धम् ।
दृग्भिः पिबन्त्यनुसवाभिनवं दुरापम्
एकान्तधाम यशसः श्रीय ऐश्वरस्य ॥ १४ ॥

gopyas tapaḥ kim acaran yad amuṣya rūpaṁ
lāvaṇya-sāram asamordhvam ananya-siddham
dṛgbhiḥ pibanty anusavābhinavaṁ durāpam
ekānta-dhāma yaśasaḥ śriya aiśvarasya

gopyaḥ—the *gopīs; tapaḥ*—austerities; *kim*—what; *acaran*—performed; *yat*—from which; *amuṣya*—of such a one (Lord Kṛṣṇa); *rūpam*—the form; *lāvaṇya-sāram*—the essence of loveliness; *asama-ūrdhvam*—not paralleled or surpassed; *ananya-siddham*—not perfected by any other ornament (self-perfect); *dṛgbhiḥ*—by the eyes; *pibanti*—they drink; *anusava-abhinavam*—constantly new; *durāpam*—difficult to obtain; *ekānta-dhāma*—the only abode; *yaśasaḥ*—of fame; *śriyaḥ*—of beauty; *aiśvarasya*—of opulence.

TRANSLATION

What austerities must the gopīs have performed! With their eyes they always drink the nectar of Lord Kṛṣṇa's form, which is the essence of loveliness and is not to be equaled or surpassed. That loveliness is the only abode of beauty, fame and opulence. It is self-perfect, ever fresh and extremely rare.

PURPORT

The word meanings and translation for this verse are from Śrīla Prabhupāda's *Caitanya-caritāmṛta* (*Ādi* 4.156).

TEXT 15

या दोहनेऽवहनने मथनोपलेप-
प्रेंखेंखनार्भरुदितोक्षणमार्जनादौ ।
गायन्ति चैनमनुरक्तधियोऽश्रुकण्ठ्यो
धन्या व्रजस्त्रिय उरुक्रमचित्तयानाः ॥ १५ ॥

yā dohane'vahanane mathanopalepa
preṅkheṅkhanārbha-ruditokṣaṇa-mārjanādau
gāyanti cainam anurakta-dhiyo'śru-kaṇṭhyo
dhanyā vraja-striya urukrama-citta-yānāḥ

yaḥ—who (the *gopīs*); *dohane*—while milking; *avahanane*—threshing; *mathana*—churning; *upalepa*—smearing; *preṅkha*—on swings; *iṅkhana*—swinging; *arbha-rudita*—(taking care of) crying babies; *ukṣaṇa*—sprinkling; *mārjana*—cleaning; *ādau*—and so on; *gāyanti*—they sing; *ca*—and; *enam*—about Him; *anurakta*—very much attached; *dhiyaḥ*—whose minds; *aśru*—with tears; *kaṇṭhyaḥ*—whose throats; *dhanyāḥ*—fortunate; *vraja-striyaḥ*—the ladies of Vraja; *urukrama*—of Lord Kṛṣṇa; *citta*—by consciousness; *yānāḥ*—whose acquisition of all desired objects.

TRANSLATION

The ladies of Vraja are the most fortunate of women because, with their minds fully attached to Kṛṣṇa and their throats always choked up with tears, they constantly sing about Him while milking the cows, winnowing grain, churning butter, gathering cow dung for fuel, riding on swings, taking care of their crying babies, sprinkling the ground with water, cleaning their houses, and so on. By their exalted Kṛṣṇa consciousness they automatically acquire all desirable things.

TEXT 16

प्रातर्व्रजाद् व्रजत आविशतश्च सायं
गोभिः समं क्वणयतोऽस्य निशम्य वेणुम् ।

निर्गम्य तूर्णमबलाः पथि भूरिपुण्याः
पश्यन्ति सस्मितमुखं सदयावलोकम् ॥ १६ ॥

prātar vrajād vrajata āviśataś ca sāyaṁ
gobhiḥ samaṁ kvaṇayato'sya niśamya veṇum
nirgamya tūrṇam abalāḥ pathi bhūri-puṇyāḥ
paśyanti sa-smita-mukhaṁ sa-dayāvalokam

prātaḥ—in the early morning; *vrajāt*—from Vraja; *vrajataḥ*—of Him who is going; *āviśataḥ*—entering; *ca*—and; *sāyam*—in the evening; *gobhiḥ samam*—together with the cows; *kvaṇayataḥ*—who is playing; *asya*—His; *niśamya*—hearing; *veṇum*—the flute; *nirgamya*—coming out; *tūrṇam*—quickly; *abalāḥ*—the women; *pathi*—on the road; *bhūri*—extremely; *puṇyāḥ*—pious; *paśyanti*—they see; *sa*—with; *smita*—smiling; *mukham*—face; *sa-daya*—merciful; *avalokam*—with glances.

TRANSLATION

When the gopīs hear Kṛṣṇa playing His flute as He leaves Vraja in the morning with His cows or returns with them at sunset, the young girls quickly come out of their houses to see Him. They must have performed many pious activities to be able to see Him as He walks on the road, His smiling face mercifully glancing upon them.

TEXT 17

एवं प्रभाषमाणासु स्त्रीषु योगेश्वरो हरिः ।
शत्रुं हन्तुं मनश्चक्रे भगवान् भरतर्षभ ॥ १७ ॥

evaṁ prabhāṣamāṇāsu
strīṣu yogeśvaro hariḥ
śatruṁ hantuṁ manaś cakre
bhagavān bharatarṣabha

evam—in this manner; *prabhāṣamāṇāsu*—while they were speaking; *strīṣu*—the women; *yoga-īśvaraḥ*—the master of all mystic power; *hariḥ*—Lord Kṛṣṇa; *śatrum*—His enemy; *hantum*—to kill; *manaḥ cakre*—made up His mind; *bhagavān*—the Supreme Lord; *bharata-ṛṣabha*—O hero of the Bhāratas.

TRANSLATION

[Śukadeva Gosvāmī continued:] As the women spoke thus, O hero of the Bhāratas, Lord Kṛṣṇa, the master of all mystic power, made up His mind to kill His opponent.

TEXT 18

सभयाः स्त्रीगिरः श्रुत्वा पुत्रस्नेहशुचातुरौ ।
पितरावन्वतप्येतां पुत्रयोरबुधौ बलम् ॥१८॥

sa-bhayāḥ strī-giraḥ śrutvā
putra-sneha-śucāturau
pitarāv anvatapyetāṁ
putrayor abudhau balam

sa-bhayāḥ—fearful; *strī*—of the women; *giraḥ*—the words; *śrutvā*—hearing; *putra*—for their sons; *sneha*—by their affection; *śuca*—with sorrow; *āturau*—overwhelmed; *pitarau*—Their parents (Devakī and Vasudeva); *anvatapyetām*—felt remorse; *putrayoḥ*—of their two sons; *abudhau*—not knowing; *balam*—the strength.

TRANSLATION

Out of affection for the two Lords, Their parents [Devakī and Vasudeva] became overwhelmed with sorrow when they heard the women's fearful statements. They grieved, not knowing their sons' strength.

PURPORT

Naturally, Kṛṣṇa's parents would lament in this situation, thinking "Why didn't we keep our sons at home? Why did we allow Them to participate in this corrupt exhibition?"

TEXT 19

तैस्तैर्नियुद्धविधिभिर्विविधैरच्युतेतरौ ।
युयुधाते यथान्योन्यं तथैव बलमुष्टिकौ ॥ १९ ॥

tais tair niyuddha-vidhibhir
vividhair acyutetarau
yuyudhāte yathānyonyaṁ
tathaiva bala-muṣṭikau

taiḥ taiḥ—with all these; *niyuddha*—of wrestling; *vidhibhiḥ*—techniques; *vividhaiḥ*—various; *acyuta-itarau*—Lord Acyuta and His opponent; *yuyudhāte*—fought; *yathā*—as; *anyonyam*—with each other; *tathā eva*—just so; *bala-muṣṭikau*—Lord Balarāma and Muṣṭika.

TRANSLATION

Lord Balarāma and Muṣṭika, expertly displaying numerous wrestling techniques, battled each other in the same way that Lord Kṛṣṇa and His opponent did.

TEXT 20

भगवद्गात्रनिष्पातैर्वज्रनिष्पेषनिष्ठुरैः ।
चाणूरो भज्यमानांगो मुहुर्ग्लानिमवाप ह ॥ २० ॥

bhagavad-gātra-niṣpātair
vajra-niṣpeṣa-niṣṭhuraiḥ
cāṇūro bhajyamānāṅgo
muhur glānim avāpa ha

bhagavat—of the Supreme Lord; *gātra*—by the limbs; *niṣpātaiḥ*—due to the blows; *vajra*—of lightning; *niṣpeṣa*—like a crushing stroke; *niṣṭhuraiḥ*—hard; *cāṇūraḥ*—Cāṇūra; *bhajyamāna*—being broken; *aṅgaḥ*—his entire body; *muhuḥ*—more and more; *glānim*—pain and fatigue; *avāpa ha*—felt.

TRANSLATION

The harsh blows from the Supreme Lord's limbs fell like crushing lightning bolts upon Cāṇūra, breaking every part of his body and causing him more and more pain and fatigue.

PURPORT

Cāṇūra's elbows, arms, knees and other limbs were all weakening.

TEXT 21

स श्येनवेग उत्पत्य मुष्टीकृत्य करावुभौ ।
भगवन्तं वासुदेवं क्रुद्धो वक्षस्यबाधत ॥ २१ ॥

sa śyena-vega utpatya
muṣṭī-kṛtya karāv ubhau

bhagavantaṁ vāsudevaṁ
kruddho vakṣasy abādhata

saḥ—he, Cāṇūra; *śyena*—of a hawk; *vegaḥ*—with the speed; *utpatya*—falling upon Him; *muṣṭī*—into fists; *kṛtya*—making; *karau*—his hands; *ubhau*—both; *bhagavantam*—the Supreme Lord; *vāsudevam*—Kṛṣṇa; *kruddhaḥ*—angry; *vakṣasi*—upon His chest; *abādhata*—struck.

TRANSLATION

Furious, Cāṇūra attacked Lord Vāsudeva with the speed of a hawk and struck His chest with both fists.

PURPORT

It appears that Cāṇūra, realizing he was being defeated, became furious and made a final attempt to defeat Lord Kṛṣṇa. The demon certainly had the spirit of a good fighter, but if he hoped for victory, he was certainly in the wrong place at the wrong time with the wrong person.

TEXTS 22–23

नाचलत्तत्प्रहारेण मालाहत इव द्विपः ।
बाह्वोर्निगृह्य चाणूरं बहुशो भ्रामयन् हरिः ॥ २२ ॥
भूपृष्ठे पोथयामास तरसा क्षीणजीवितम् ।
विस्रस्ताकल्पकेशस्रगिन्द्रध्वज इवापतत् ॥ २३ ॥

nācalat tat-prahāreṇa
mālāhata iva dvipaḥ
bāhvor nigṛhya cāṇūraṁ
bahuśo bhrāmayan hariḥ

bhū-pṛṣṭhe pothayām āsa
tarasā kṣīṇa jīvitam
visrastākalpa-keśa-srag
indra-dhvaja ivāpatat

na acalat—He (Lord Kṛṣṇa) did not move; *tat-prahāreṇa*—because of his blows; *mālā*—with a garland; *āhata*—struck; *iva*—as; *dvipaḥ*—an elephant; *bāhvoḥ*—by the two arms; *nigṛhya*—seizing; *cāṇūram*—Cāṇūra; *bahuśaḥ*—several times; *bhrāmayan*—whirling him around; *hariḥ*—Lord Kṛṣṇa; *bhū*

—of the earth; *pṛṣṭhe*—onto the surface; *pothayām āsa*—hurled; *tarasā*—forcefully; *kṣīṇa*—becoming lost; *jīvitam*—his life; *visrasta*—scattered; *ākalpa*—his clothing; *keśa*—hair; *srak*—and flower garland; *indra-dhvajaḥ*—a tall festival column; *iva*—as if; *apatat*—he fell.

TRANSLATION

No more shaken by the demon's mighty blows than an elephant struck with a flower garland, Lord Kṛṣṇa grabbed Cāṇūra by his arms, swung him around several times and hurled him onto the ground with great force. His clothes, hair and garland scattering, the wrestler fell down dead, like a huge festival column collapsing.

PURPORT

Śrīla Śrīdhara Svāmī explains the words *indra-dhvaja* as follows: "In Bengal, on the occasion of a certain festival, people erect a tall column in the form of a man and decorate it with flags, banners, etc. He [Cāṇūra] fell just as such a pole might fall."

TEXTS 24–25

तथैव मुष्टिकः पूर्वं स्वमुष्ट्याभिहतेन वै ।
बलभद्रेण बलिना तलेनाभिहतो भृशम् ॥ २४ ॥
प्रवेपितः स रुधिरमुद्वमन्मुखतोऽर्दितः ।
व्यसुः पपातोर्व्युपस्थे वाताहत इवाङ्घ्रिपः ॥ २५ ॥

tathaiva muṣṭikaḥ pūrvaṁ
sva-muṣṭyābhihatena vai
balabhadreṇa balinā
talenābhihato bhṛśam

pravepitaḥ sa rudhiram
udvaman mukhato'rditaḥ
vyasuḥ papātorvy-upasthe
vātāhata ivāṅghripaḥ

tathā—also; *eva*—similarly; *muṣṭikaḥ*—Muṣṭika; *pūrvam*—previously; *sva-muṣṭyā*—with his fist; *abhihatena*—who had been struck; *vai*—indeed; *balabhadreṇa*—by Lord Balarāma; *balinā*—the powerful; *talena*—with His palm; *abhihataḥ*—struck; *bhṛśam*—violently; *pravepitaḥ*—trembling; *saḥ*

—he, Muṣṭika; *rudhiram*—blood; *udvaman*—vomiting; *mukhataḥ*—from his mouth; *arditaḥ*—tormented; *vyasuḥ*—lifeless; *papāta*—he fell; *urvī*—of the earth; *upasthe*—onto the lap; *vāta*—by the wind; *āhataḥ*—struck down; *iva*—like; *aṅghripaḥ*—a tree.

TRANSLATION

Similarly, Muṣṭika struck Lord Balabhadra with his fist and was slain. Receiving a violent blow from the mighty Lord's palm, the demon trembled all over in great pain, vomited blood and then fell lifeless onto the ground, like a tree blown down by the wind.

TEXT 26

ततः कूटमनुप्राप्तं रामः प्रहरतां वरः ।
अवधील्लीलया राजन् सावज्ञं वाममुष्टिना ॥ २६ ॥

tataḥ kūṭam anuprāptaṁ
rāmaḥ praharatāṁ varaḥ
avadhīl līlayā rājan
sāvajñaṁ vāma-muṣṭinā

tataḥ—then; *kūṭam*—the demonic wrestler Kūṭa; *anuprāptam*—appearing on the scene; *rāmaḥ*—Lord Balarāma; *praharatām*—of fighters; *varaḥ*—the best; *avadhīt*—killed; *līlayā*—playfully; *rājan*—O King, Parīkṣit; *sa-avajñam*—neglectfully; *vāma*—left; *muṣṭinā*—with His fist.

TRANSLATION

Confronted next by the wrestler Kūṭa, Lord Balarāma, the best of fighters, playfully and nonchalantly killed him with His left fist, O King.

TEXT 27

तर्ह्येव हि शलः कृष्णप्रपदाहतशीर्षकः ।
द्विधा विदीर्णस्तोशलक उभावपि निपेततुः ॥ २७ ॥

tarhy eva hi śalaḥ kṛṣṇa-
prapadāhata-śīrṣakaḥ
dvidhā vidīrṇas tośalaka
ubhāv api nipetatuḥ

tarhi eva—and then; *hi*—indeed; *śalaḥ*—the wrestler Śala; *kṛṣṇa*—of Lord Kṛṣṇa; *prapada*—by the toes; *āhata*—struck; *śīrṣakaḥ*—his head; *dvidhā*—in two; *vidīrnaḥ*—torn; *tośalaka*—Tośala; *ubhau api*—both of them; *nipetatuḥ*—fell down.

TRANSLATION

Then Kṛṣṇa struck the wrestler Śala in the head with His toes and tore him in half. The Lord dealt with Tośala in the same way, and both wrestlers fell down dead.

TEXT 28

चाणूरे मुष्टिके कूटे शले तोशलके हते ।
शेषाः प्रदुद्रुवुर्मल्लाः सर्वे प्राणपरीप्सवः ॥ २८ ॥

cāṇūre muṣṭike kūṭe
śale tośalake hate
śeṣāḥ pradudruvur mallāḥ
sarve prāṇa-parīpsavaḥ

cāṇūre muṣṭike kūṭe—Cāṇūra, Muṣṭika and Kūṭa; *śale tośalake*—Śala and Tośala; *hate*—being killed; *śeṣāḥ*—those remaining; *pradudruvuḥ*—ran away; *mallāḥ*—wrestlers; *sarve*—all; *prāṇa*—their lives; *parīpsavaḥ*—hoping to save.

TRANSLATION

Cāṇūra, Muṣṭika, Kūṭa, Śala and Tośala having been killed, the remaining wrestlers all fled for their lives.

TEXT 29

गोपान् वयस्यानाकृष्य तैः संसृज्य विजह्रतुः ।
वाद्यमानेषु तूर्येषु वल्गन्तौ रुतनूपुरौ ॥ २९ ॥

gopān vayasyān ākṛṣya
taiḥ saṁsṛjya vijahratuḥ
vādyamāneṣu tūryeṣu
valgantau ruta-nūpurau

gopān—the cowherd boys; *vayasyān*—Their young friends; *ākṛṣya*—gathering together; *taiḥ*—with them; *saṁsṛjya*—joining up; *vijahratuḥ*—

They sported; *vādyamāneṣu*—while they played; *tūryeṣu*—the musical instruments; *valgantau*—the two of Them dancing about; *ruta*—resounding; *nūpurau*—Their ankle bells.

TRANSLATION

Kṛṣṇa and Balarāma then called Their young cowherd boyfriends to join Them, and in their company the Lords danced about and sported, Their ankle bells resounding as musical instruments played.

PURPORT

Nowadays we see that in championship boxing matches, as soon as there is a victory, all the friends and relatives of the victorious boxer rush into the ring to congratulate him, and often the champion will dance about in great happiness. Exactly in this mood, Kṛṣṇa and Balarāma danced about, celebrating Their victory with Their friends and relatives.

TEXT 30

जनाः प्रजहृषुः सर्वे कर्मणा रामकृष्णयोः ।
ऋते कंसं विप्रमुख्याः साधवः साधु साध्विति ॥ ३० ॥

janāḥ prajahṛṣuḥ sarve
karmaṇā rāma-kṛṣṇayoḥ
ṛte kaṁsaṁ vipra-mukhyāḥ
sādhavaḥ sādhu sādhv iti

janāḥ—the people; *prajahṛṣuḥ*—rejoiced; *sarve*—all; *karmaṇā*—at the deed; *rāma-kṛṣṇayoḥ*—of Balarāma and Kṛṣṇa; *ṛte*—except; *kaṁsam*—Kaṁsa; *vipra*—of the *brāhmaṇas; mukhyāḥ*—the best; *sādhavaḥ*—the saintly persons; *sādhu sādhu iti*—(exclaimed) "Excellent! Excellent!"

TRANSLATION

Everyone except Kaṁsa rejoiced at the wonderful feat Kṛṣṇa and Balarāma had performed. The exalted brāhmaṇas and great saints exclaimed, "Excellent! Excellent!"

PURPORT

It is understood that as the best of the *brāhmaṇas* and saints were exclaiming "Excellent! Excellent!" the worst of the *brāhmaṇas,* namely Kaṁsa's priests, were seriously grieving.

TEXT 31

हतेषु मल्लवर्येषु विद्रुतेषु च भोजराट् ।
न्यवारयत्स्वतूर्याणि वाक्यं चेदमुवाच ह ॥ ३१ ॥

hateṣu malla-varyeṣu
vidruteṣu ca bhoja-rāṭ
nyavārayat sva-tūryāṇi
vākyaṁ cedam uvāca ha

hateṣu—being killed; *malla-varyeṣu*—the best wrestlers; *vidruteṣu*—having run away; *ca*—and; *bhoja-rāṭ*—the Bhoja king, Kaṁsa; *nyavārayat*—stopped; *sva*—his own; *tūryāṇi*—musical instruments; *vākyam*—words; *ca*—and; *idam*—these; *uvāca ha*—spoke.

TRANSLATION

The Bhoja king, seeing that his best wrestlers had all been killed or had fled, stopped the musical performance originally meant for his pleasure and spoke the following words.

TEXT 32

निःसारयत दुर्वृत्तौ वसुदेवात्मजौ पुरात् ।
धनं हरत गोपानां नन्दं बध्नीत दुर्मतिम् ॥ ३२ ॥

niḥsārayata durvṛttau
vasudevātmajau purāt
dhanaṁ harata gopānāṁ
nandaṁ badhnīta durmatim

niḥsārayata—expel; *durvṛttau*—who behave wickedly; *vasudeva-ātma-jau*—the two sons of Vasudeva; *purāt*—from the city; *dhanam*—the wealth; *harata*—take away; *gopānām*—of the cowherds; *nandam*—Nanda Mahārāja; *badhnīta*—tie up; *durmatim*—the fool, whose heart is crooked.

TRANSLATION

[Kaṁsa said:] Drive the two wicked sons of Vasudeva out of the city! Confiscate the cowherds' property and arrest that fool Nanda!

TEXT 33

वसुदेवस्तु दुर्मेधा हन्यतामाश्वसत्तमः ।
उग्रसेनः पिता चापि सानुगः परपक्षगः ॥ ३३ ॥

vasudevas tu durmedhā
hanyatām āśv asattamaḥ
ugrasenaḥ pitā cāpi
sānugaḥ para-pakṣa-gaḥ

vasudevaḥ—Vasudeva; *tu*—and furthermore; *durmedhā*—the foolish-minded; *hanyatām*—should be killed; *āśu*—immediately; *asat-tamaḥ*—the worst of the impure; *ugrasenaḥ*—Ugrasena; *pitā*—my father; *ca api*—also; *sa*—together with; *anugaḥ*—his followers; *para*—of the enemy; *pakṣa-gaḥ*—taking the side.

TRANSLATION

Kill that most evil fool Vasudeva! And also kill my father, Ugrasena, along with his followers, who have all sided with our enemies!

TEXT 34

एवं विकत्थमाने वै कंसे प्रकुपितोऽव्ययः ।
लघिम्नोत्पत्य तरसा मञ्चमुत्तुंगमारुहत् ॥ ३४ ॥

evaṁ vikatthamāne vai
kaṁse prakupito 'vyayaḥ
laghimnotpatya tarasā
mañcam uttuṅgam āruhat

evam—thus; *vikatthamāne*—exclaiming with audacity; *vai*—indeed; *kaṁse*—Kaṁsa; *prakupitaḥ*—becoming extremely angry; *avyayaḥ*—the infallible Lord; *laghimnā*—with ease; *utpatya*—jumping up; *tarasā*—swiftly; *mañcam*—the royal platform; *uttuṅgam*—tall; *āruhat*—climbed onto.

TRANSLATION

As Kaṁsa thus raved so audaciously, the infallible Lord Kṛṣṇa, intensely angry, quickly and easily jumped up onto the high royal dais.

TEXT 35

तमाविशन्तमालोक्य मृत्युमात्मन आसनात् ।
मनस्वी सहसोत्थाय जगृहे सोऽसिचर्मणी ॥ ३५ ॥

tam āviśantam ālokya
mṛtyum ātmana āsanāt
manasvī sahasotthāya
jagṛhe so'si-carmaṇī

tam—Him, Kṛṣṇa; *āviśantam*—entering (into his private sitting area); *ālokya*—seeing; *mṛtyum*—death; *ātmanaḥ*—his own; *āsanāt*—from his seat; *manasvī*—the intelligent; *sahasā*—immediately; *utthāya*—standing up; *jagṛhe*—took up; *saḥ*—he; *asi*—his sword; *carmaṇī*—and his shield.

TRANSLATION

Seeing Lord Kṛṣṇa approaching like death personified, the quick-witted Kaṁsa instantly rose from his seat and took up his sword and shield.

TEXT 36

तं खड्गपाणिं विचरन्तमाशु
श्येनं यथा दक्षिणसव्यमम्बरे ।
समग्रहीद्दुर्विषहोग्रतेजा
यथोरगं तार्क्ष्यसुतः प्रसह्य ॥ ३६ ॥

taṁ khaḍga-pāṇiṁ vicarantam āśu
śyenaṁ yathā dakṣiṇa-savyam ambare
samagrahīd durviṣahogra-tejā
yathoragaṁ tārkṣya-sutaḥ prasahya

tam—him, Kaṁsa; *khaḍga*—with sword; *pāṇim*—in his hand; *vicarantam*—moving about; *āśu*—quickly; *śyenam*—a hawk; *yathā*—like; *dakṣiṇa-savyam*—right and left; *ambare*—in the sky; *samagrahīt*—seized; *durviṣaha*—irresistible; *ugra*—and fearsome; *tejāḥ*—whose strength; *yathā*—as; *uragam*—a snake; *tārkṣya-sutaḥ*—the son of Tārkṣya, Garuḍa; *prasahya*—by force.

TRANSLATION

Sword in hand, Kaṁsa moved quickly from side to side like a hawk in the sky. But Lord Kṛṣṇa, whose fearsome strength is irresistible, powerfully seized the demon just as the son of Tārkṣya might capture a snake.

TEXT 37

प्रगृह्य केशेषु चलत्किरीटं
निपात्य रंगोपरि तुंगमञ्चात् ।
तस्योपरिष्टात्स्वयमब्जनाभः
पपात विश्वाश्रय आत्मतन्त्रः ॥ ३७ ॥

pragṛhya keśeṣu calat-kirīṭaṁ
nipātya raṅgopari tuṅga-mañcāt
tasyopariṣṭāt svayam abja-nābhaḥ
papāta viśvāśraya ātma-tantraḥ

pragṛhya—grabbing; *keśeṣu*—by the hair; *calat*—knocking off; *kirīṭam*—whose crown; *nipātya*—throwing down; *raṅga-upari*—onto the surface of the wrestling ring; *tuṅga*—high; *mañcāt*—from the platform; *tasya*—of him; *upariṣṭāt*—on top; *svayam*—Himself; *abja-nābhaḥ*—the lotus-naveled Supreme Lord; *papāta*—threw; *viśva*—of the entire universe; *āśrayaḥ*—the support; *ātma-tantraḥ*—independent.

TRANSLATION

Grabbing Kaṁsa by the hair and knocking off his crown, the lotus-naveled Lord threw him off the elevated dais onto the wrestling mat. Then the independent Lord, the support of the entire universe, threw Himself upon the King.

PURPORT

In *Kṛṣṇa, the Supreme Personality of Godhead,* Śrīla Prabhupāda describes the death of Kaṁsa as follows: "Kṛṣṇa at once straddled his chest and began to strike him over and over again. Simply from the strokes of Kṛṣṇa's fist, Kaṁsa lost his vital force."

TEXT 38

तं सम्परेतं विचकर्ष भूमौ
हरिर्यथेभं जगतो विपश्यतः ।

हा हेति शब्दः सुमहांस्तदाभूद्
उदीरितः सर्वजनैर्नरेन्द्र ॥ ३८ ॥

taṁ samparetaṁ vicakarṣa bhūmau
harir yathebhaṁ jagato vipaśyataḥ
hā heti śabdaḥ su-mahāṁs tadābhūd
udīritaḥ sarva-janair narendra

tam—him; *samparetam*—dead; *vicakarṣa*—dragged; *bhūmau*—along the ground; *hariḥ*—a lion; *yathā*—as; *ibham*—an elephant; *jagataḥ*—all the people; *vipaśyataḥ*—as they looked on; *hā hā iti*—"Oh, oh!"; *śabdaḥ*—the sound; *su-mahān*—mighty; *tadā*—then; *abhūt*—arose; *udīritaḥ*—spoken; *sarva-janaiḥ*—by all the people; *nara-indra*—O ruler of men (King Parīkṣit).

TRANSLATION

As a lion drags a dead elephant, the Lord then dragged Kaṁsa's dead body along the ground in full view of everyone present. O King, all the people in the arena tumultuously cried out, "Oh! Oh!"

PURPORT

Śrīla Viśvanātha Cakravartī explains that many people in the audience thought Kaṁsa had simply been knocked unconscious when thrown from the lofty dais. Therefore Lord Kṛṣṇa dragged his corpse so everyone would realize that the evil King was indeed dead. Thus the exclamation *hā hā* indicates how surprised the people were that the King was suddenly dead and gone.

The audience's astonishment is also mentioned in the *Viṣṇu Purāṇa:*

tato hāhā-kṛtaṁ sarvam
āsīt tad-raṅga-maṇḍalam
avajñayā hataṁ dṛṣṭvā
kṛṣṇena mathureśvaram

"Then the entire arena became filled with cries of astonishment as the people saw that the master of Mathurā had been contemptuously killed by Kṛṣṇa."

TEXT 39

स नित्यदोद्विग्नधिया तमीश्वरं
पिबन्नदन् वा विचरन् स्वपन् श्वसन् ।

ददर्श चक्रायुधमग्रतो यतस्
तदेव रूपं दुरवापमाप ॥ ३९ ॥

sa nityadodvigna-dhiyā tam īśvaraṁ
pibann adan vā vicaran svapan śvasan
dadarśa cakrāyudham agrato yatas
tad eva rūpaṁ duravāpam āpa

saḥ—he, Kaṁsa; *nityadā*—constantly; *udvigna*—anxious; *dhiyā*—with mind; *tam*—Him; *īśvaram*—the Supreme Lord; *piban*—while drinking; *adan*—eating; *vā*—or; *vicaran*—walking; *svapan*—sleeping; *śvasan*—breathing; *dadarśa*—saw; *cakra*—the disc weapon; *āyudham*—in His hand; *agrataḥ*—before himself; *yataḥ*—because; *tat*—that; *eva*—same; *rūpam*—personal form; *duravāpam*—very difficult to achieve; *āpa*—he achieved.

TRANSLATION

Kaṁsa had always been disturbed by the thought that the Supreme Lord was to kill him. Therefore when drinking, eating, moving about, sleeping or simply breathing, the King had always seen the Lord before him with the disc weapon in His hand. Thus Kaṁsa achieved the rare boon of attaining a form like the Lord's.

PURPORT

Although born out of fear, Kaṁsa's constant meditation on the Supreme Lord eradicated all his offenses, and therefore the demon was liberated upon his death at the Lord's hands.

TEXT 40

तस्यानुजा भ्रातरोऽष्टौ कंकन्यग्रोधकादयः ।
अभ्यधावन्नतिक्रुद्धा भ्रातुर्निर्वेशकारिणः ॥ ४० ॥

tasyānujā bhrātaro'ṣṭau
kaṅka-nyagrodhakādayaḥ
abhyadhāvann ati-kruddhā
bhrātur nirveśa-kāriṇaḥ

tasya—of him, Kaṁsa; *anujāḥ*—younger; *bhrātaraḥ*—the brothers; *aṣṭau*—eight; *kaṅka-nyagrodhaka-ādayaḥ*—Kaṅka, Nyagrodhaka and the others; *abhyadhāvan*—ran forward to attack; *ati-kruddhāḥ*—infuriated; *bhrātuḥ*—to their brother; *nirveśa*—repayment of the debt; *kāriṇaḥ*—doing.

TRANSLATION

Kaṁsa's eight younger brothers, led by Kaṅka and Nyagrodhaka, then attacked the Lords in a rage, seeking to avenge their brother's death.

TEXT 41

तथातिरभसांस्तांस्तु संयत्तान् रोहिणीसुतः ।
अहन् परिघमुद्यम्य पशूनिव मृगाधिपः ॥ ४१ ॥

tathāti-rabhasāṁs tāṁs tu
saṁyattān rohiṇī-sutaḥ
ahan parigham udyamya
paśūn iva mṛgādhipaḥ

tathā—in this manner; *ati-rabhasān*—running very swiftly; *tān*—they; *tu*—and; *saṁyattān*—ready to strike; *rohiṇī-sutaḥ*—the son of Rohiṇī, Lord Balarāma; *ahan*—beat down; *parigham*—His club; *udyamya*—wielding; *paśūn*—animals; *iva*—as; *mṛga-adhipaḥ*—the lion, king of animals.

TRANSLATION

As they ran swiftly toward the two Lords, ready to strike, the son of Rohiṇī slew them with His club just as a lion easily kills other animals.

TEXT 42

नेदुर्दुन्दुभयो व्योम्नि ब्रह्मेशाद्या विभूतयः ।
पुष्पैः किरन्तस्तं प्रीताः शशंसुर्ननृतुः स्त्रियः ॥ ४२ ॥

nedur dundubhayo vyomni
brahmeśādyā vibhūtayaḥ
puṣpaiḥ kirantas taṁ prītāḥ
śaśaṁsur nanṛtuḥ striyaḥ

neduḥ—resounded; *dundubhayaḥ*—kettledrums; *vyomni*—in the sky; *brahma-īśa-ādyāḥ*—Brahmā, Śiva and other demigods; *vibhūtayaḥ*—His expansions; *puṣpaiḥ*—flowers; *kirantaḥ*—scattering down; *tam*—upon Him; *prītāḥ*—pleased; *śaśaṁsuḥ*—they chanted His praises; *nanṛtuḥ*—danced; *striyaḥ*—their wives.

TRANSLATION

Kettledrums resounded in the sky as Brahmā, Śiva and other demigods, the Lord's expansions, rained down flowers upon Him with pleasure. They chanted His praises, and their wives danced.

TEXT 43

तेषां स्त्रियो महाराज सुहृन्मरणदुःखिताः ।
तत्राभीयुर्विनिघ्नन्त्यः शीर्षाण्यश्रुविलोचनाः ॥ ४३ ॥

teṣāṁ striyo mahā-rāja
suhṛn-maraṇa-duḥkhitāḥ
tatrābhīyur vinighnantyaḥ
śīrṣāṇy aśru-vilocanāḥ

teṣām—of them (Kaṁsa and his brothers); *striyaḥ*—the wives; *mahārāja*—O King (Parīkṣit); *suhṛt*—of their well-wishers (their husbands); *maraṇa*—because of the death; *duḥkhitāḥ*—sorrowful; *tatra*—that place; *abhīyuḥ*—approached; *vinighnantyaḥ*—beating; *śīrṣāṇi*—their heads; *aśru*—with tears; *vilocanāḥ*—their eyes.

TRANSLATION

My dear King, the wives of Kaṁsa and his brothers, aggrieved by the death of their well-wishing husbands, came forward with tearful eyes, beating their heads.

TEXT 44

शयानान् वीरशयायां पतीनालिंग्य शोचतीः ।
विलेपुः सुस्वरं नार्यो विसृजन्त्यो मुहुः शुचः ॥ ४४ ॥

śayānān vīra-śayāyāṁ
patīn āliṅgya śocatīḥ
vilepuḥ su-svaraṁ nāryo
visṛjantyo muhuḥ śucaḥ

śayānān—lying; *vīra*—of a hero; *śayāyām*—upon the bed (the ground); *patīn*—their husbands; *āliṅgya*—embracing; *śocatīḥ*—feeling sorrow; *vilepuḥ*—lamented; *su-svaram*—loudly; *nāryaḥ*—the women; *visṛjantyaḥ*—shedding; *muhuḥ*—repeatedly; *śucaḥ*—tears.

TRANSLATION

Embracing their husbands, who lay on a hero's final bed, the sorrowful women loudly lamented while shedding constant tears.

TEXT 45

हा नाथ प्रिय धर्मज्ञ करुणानाथवत्सल ।
त्वया हतेन निहता वयं ते सगृहप्रजाः ॥ ४५ ॥

hā nātha priya dharma-jña
karuṇānātha-vatsala
tvayā hatena nihatā
vayaṁ te sa-gṛha-prajāḥ

ha—alas; *nātha*—O master; *priya*—O dear one; *dharma-jña*—O knower of religious principles; *karuṇa*—O kind one; *anātha*—to those who have no protector; *vatsala*—O you who are compassionate; *tvayā*—by you; *hatena*—being killed; *nihatāḥ*—are killed; *vayam*—we; *te*—your; *sa*—together with; *gṛha*—the home; *prajāḥ*—and offspring.

TRANSLATION

[The women cried out:] Alas, O master, O dear one, O knower of religious principles! O kind and compassionate protector of the shelterless! By your being slain we have also been slain, together with your household and offspring.

TEXT 46

त्वया विरहिता पत्या पुरीयं पुरुषर्षभ ।
न शोभते वयमिव निवृत्तोत्सवमंगला ॥ ४६ ॥

tvayā virahitā patyā
purīyaṁ puruṣarṣabha
na śobhate vayam iva
nivṛttotsava-maṅgalā

tvayā—of you; *virahitā*—bereft; *patyā*—the master; *purī*—the city; *iyam*—this; *puruṣa*—of men; *ṛṣabha*—O most heroic one; *na śobhate*—does not appear beautiful; *vayam*—us; *iva*—just like; *nivṛtta*—ceased; *utsava*—festivity; *maṅgalā*—and auspiciousness.

TRANSLATION

O great hero among men, bereft of you, its master, this city has lost its beauty, just as we have, and all festivity and good fortune within it have come to an end.

TEXT 47

अनागसां त्वं भूतानां कृतवान् द्रोहमुल्बणम् ।
तेनेमां भो दशां नीतो भूतध्रुक्को लभेत शम् ॥ ४७ ॥

anāgasāṁ tvaṁ bhūtānāṁ
kṛtavān droham ulbaṇam
tenemāṁ bho daśāṁ nīto
bhūta-dhruk ko labheta śam

anāgasām—sinless; *tvam*—you; *bhūtānām*—against creatures; *kṛtavān*—have committed; *droham*—violence; *ulbaṇam*—terrible; *tena*—by that; *imām*—to this; *bho*—O dear one; *daśām*—condition; *nītaḥ*—brought; *bhūta*—to living beings; *dhruk*—causing harm; *kaḥ*—who; *labheta*—can achieve; *śam*—happiness.

TRANSLATION

O dear one, you have been brought to this state because of the terrible violence you committed against innocent creatures. How can one who harms others attain happiness?

PURPORT

Having expressed their sentimental grief, the ladies now speak practical wisdom. They are beginning to see things realistically because their minds were purified by the agony of the recent events and by the association of Lord Kṛṣṇa.

TEXT 48

सर्वेषामिह भूतानामेष हि प्रभवाप्ययः ।
गोप्ता च तदवध्यायी न क्वचित्सुखमेधते ॥ ४८ ॥

sarveṣām iha bhūtānām
eṣa hi prabhavāpyayaḥ

goptā ca tad-avadhyāyī
na kvacit sukham edhate

sarveṣām—of all; *iha*—in this world; *bhūtānām*—living beings; *eṣaḥ*—this (Śrī Kṛṣṇa); *hi*—certainly; *prabhava*—the origin; *apyayaḥ*—and disappearance; *goptā*—the maintainer; *ca*—and; *tat*—of Him; *avadhyāyī*—one who is neglectful; *na kvacit*—never; *sukham*—happily; *edhate*—prospers.

TRANSLATION

Lord Kṛṣṇa causes the appearance and disappearance of all beings in this world, and He is their maintainer as well. One who disrespects Him can never prosper happily.

TEXT 49

श्रीशुक उवाच
राजयोषित आश्वास्य भगवाल्ँ लोकभावनः ।
यामाहुर्लौकिकीं संस्थां हतानां समकारयत् ॥ ४९ ॥

śrī-śuka uvāca
rāja-yoṣita āśvāsya
bhagavāl̐ loka-bhāvanaḥ
yām āhur laukikīṁ saṁsthāṁ
hatānāṁ samakārayat

śrī-śukaḥ uvāca—Śukadeva Gosvāmī said; *rāja*—of the King (and his brothers); *yoṣitaḥ*—the wives; *āśvāsya*—consoling; *bhagavān*—the Supreme Lord; *loka*—of all the worlds; *bhāvanaḥ*—the sustainer; *yām*—which; *āhuḥ*—they (Vedic authorities) enjoin; *laukikīm saṁsthām*—funeral rites; *hatānām*—for the deceased; *samakārayat*—He arranged to be performed.

TRANSLATION

Śukadeva Gosvāmī said: After consoling the royal ladies, Lord Kṛṣṇa, sustainer of all the worlds, arranged for the prescribed funeral rites to be performed.

TEXT 50

मातरं पितरं चैव मोचयित्वाथ बन्धनात् ।
कृष्णरामौ ववन्दाते शिरसा स्पृश्य पादयोः ॥ ५० ॥

mātaraṁ pitaraṁ caiva
mocayitvātha bandhanāt
kṛṣṇa-rāmau vavandāte
śirasā spṛśya pādayoḥ

mātaram—Their mother; *pitaram*—father; *ca*—and; *eva*—also; *mocayitvā*—releasing; *atha*—then; *bandhanāt*—from their fetters; *kṛṣṇa-rāmau*—Kṛṣṇa and Balarāma; *vavandāte*—paid obeisances; *śirasā*—with Their heads; *spṛśya*—touching; *pādayoḥ*—their feet.

TRANSLATION

Then Kṛṣṇa and Balarāma released Their mother and father from bondage and offered obeisances to them, touching their feet with Their heads.

TEXT 51

देवकी वसुदेवश्च विज्ञाय जगदीश्वरौ ।
कृतसंवन्दनौ पुत्रौ सस्वजाते न शङ्कितौ ॥ ५१ ॥

devakī vasudevaś ca
vijñāya jagad-īśvarau
kṛta-saṁvandanau putrau
sasvajāte na śaṅkitau

devakī—Devakī; *vasudevaḥ*—Vasudeva; *ca*—and; *vijñāya*—recognizing; *jagat*—of the universe; *īśvarau*—as the two Lords; *kṛta*—paying; *saṁvandanau*—full respects (by standing with joined palms); *putrau*—their two sons; *sasvajāte na*—they did not embrace; *śaṅkitau*—apprehensive.

TRANSLATION

Devakī and Vasudeva, now knowing Kṛṣṇa and Balarāma to be the Lords of the universe, simply stood with joined palms. Being apprehensive, they did not embrace their sons.

Thus end the purports of the humble servants of His Divine Grace A.C. Bhaktivedanta Swami Prabhupāda to the Tenth Canto, Forty-fourth Chapter, of the Śrīmad-Bhāgavatam, *entitled "The Killing of Kaṁsa."*

Appendixes

His Divine Grace
A. C. Bhaktivedanta Swami Prabhupāda

His Divine Grace A.C. Bhaktivedanta Swami Prabhupāda appeared in this world in 1896 in Calcutta, India. He first met his spiritual master, Śrīla Bhaktisiddhānta Sarasvatī Gosvāmī, in Calcutta in 1922. Śrīla Bhaktisiddhānta Sarasvatī, a prominent religious scholar and the founder of sixty-four Gauḍīya Maṭhas (Vedic institutes) in India, liked this educated young man and convinced him to dedicate his life to teaching Vedic knowledge. Śrīla Prabhupāda became his student and, in 1933, his formally initiated disciple.

At their first meeting, Śrīla Bhaktisiddhānta Sarasvatī requested Śrīla Prabhupāda to broadcast Vedic knowledge in English. In the years that followed, Śrīla Prabhupāda wrote a commentary on the *Bhagavad-gītā,* assisted the Gauḍīya Maṭha in its work, and, in 1944, started *Back to Godhead,* an English fortnightly magazine. Single-handedly, Śrīla Prabhupāda edited it, typed the manuscripts, checked the galley proofs, and even distributed the individual copies. The magazine is now being continued by his disciples all over the world.

In 1950 Śrīla Prabhupāda retired from married life, adopting the *vānaprastha* (retired) order to devote more time to his studies and writing. He traveled to the holy city of Vṛndāvana, where he lived in humble circumstances in the historic temple of Rādhā-Dāmodara. There he engaged for several years in deep study and writing. He accepted the renounced order of life (*sannyāsa*) in 1959. At Rādhā-Dāmodara, Śrīla Prabhupāda began work on his life's masterpiece: a multivolume commentated translation of the eighteen-thousand-verse *Śrīmad-Bhāgavatam* (*Bhāgavata Purāṇa*). He also wrote *Easy Journey to Other Planets.*

After publishing three volumes of the *Bhāgavatam,* Śrīla Prabhupāda came to the United States, in September 1965, to fulfill the mission of his spiritual master. Subsequently, His Divine Grace wrote more than sixty volumes of authoritative commentated translations and summary studies of the philosophical and religious classics of India.

When he first arrived by freighter in New York City, Śrīla Prabhupāda was practically penniless. It was after almost a year of great difficulty that he established the International Society for Krishna Consciousness in July of 1966. Before he passed away on November 14, 1977, he had guided the Society and seen it grow to a worldwide confederation of more than one hundred *ashrams,* schools, temples, institutes, and farm communities.

In 1972 His Divine Grace introduced the Vedic system of primary and secondary education in the West by founding the *gurukula* school in Dallas, Texas. Since then his disciples have established similar schools throughout the United States and the rest of the world.

Śrīla Prabhupāda also inspired the construction of several large international cultural centers in India. The center at Śrīdhāma Māyāpur is the site for a planned spiritual city, an ambitious project for which construction will extend over many years to come. In Vṛndāvana are the magnificent Kṛṣṇa-Balarāma Temple and International Guesthouse, *gurukula* school, and Śrīla Prabhupāda Memorial and Museum. There is also a major cultural and educational center in Mumbai. There are beautiful temples in Delhi, Bangalore, Ahmedabad and Vadodara besides many other centers throughout India.

Śrīla Prabhupāda's most significant contribution, however, is his books. Highly respected by scholars for their authority, depth, and clarity, they are used as textbooks in numerous college courses. His writings have been translated into over fifty languages. The Bhaktivedanta Book Trust, established in 1972 exclusively to publish the works of His Divine Grace, has thus become the world's largest publisher of books in the field of Indian religion and philosophy.

In just twelve years, despite his advanced age, Śrīla Prabhupāda circled the globe fourteen times on lecture tours that took him to six continents. In spite of such a vigorous schedule, Śrīla Prabhupāda continued to write prolifically. His writings constitute a veritable library of Vedic philosophy, religion, literature, and culture.

References

The purports of *Śrīmad-Bhāgavatam* are all confirmed by standard Vedic authorities. The following authentic scriptures are cited in this volume. For specific page references, consult the general index.

Bhagavad-gītā

Bhakti-rasāmṛta-sindhu

Brahma-saṁhitā

Bṛhad-viṣṇu Purāṇa

Caitanya-caritāmṛta

Gopāla-tāpanī Upaniṣad

Hari-vaṁśa

Kṛṣṇa, the Supreme Personality of Godhead

Nārada-pañcarātra

Nārada Purāṇa

Nṛsiṁha Purāṇa

Padma Purāṇa

Rādhā-kṛṣṇa-gaṇoddeśa-dīpikā

Śrīmad-Bhāgavatam

Taittirīya Upaniṣad

Upadeśāmṛta

Varāha Purāṇa

Viṣṇu Purāṇa

Glossary

A

Ācārya—a spiritual master who teaches by his own example, and who sets the proper religious example for all human beings.

Anartha-nivṛtti—a stage in the progressive development of devotion to Lord Kṛṣṇa in which one is freed from unwanted desires and karmic reactions; cleansing the heart of all unwanted things.

Aniruddha—a grandson of Lord Kṛṣṇa; also one of the four original expansions of Lord Kṛṣṇa in the spiritual world.

B

Bakāsura—a demon who was shaped like a huge duck and who tried to kill Kṛṣṇa.

Bali Māhāraja—the king of the demons who gave three paces of land to Vamanadeva, the dwarf incarnation of Lord Viṣṇu, and thereby became a great devotee by surrendering everything to Him.

Bhagavad-gītā—a seven-hundred verse record of a conversation between Lord Kṛṣṇa and His disciple, Arjuna, from the *Bhīṣma Parva* of the *Mahābhārata* of Vedavyāsa. The conversation took place between two armies minutes before the start of an immense fratricidal battle. Kṛṣṇa teaches the science of the Absolute Truth and the importance of devotional service to the despondent Arjuna, and it contains the essence of all Vedic wisdom. Śrīla Prabhupāda's annotated English translation is called *Bhagavad-gītā As It Is*; This most essential text of spiritual knowledge, The Song of the Lord, contains Kṛṣṇa's instructions to Arjuna at Kurukṣetra. It is found in the *Mahābhārata*. The *Mahābhārata* is classified as *smṛti-śāstra*, a supplement of the *śruti-śāstra*. *Śruti*, the core Vedic literature, includes the four *Vedas* (*Ṛg, Sāma, Yajur* and *Atharva*) and the *Upaniṣads*. *Śruti* advances the understanding of the absolute. *Bhagavad-gītā* is also known as *Gītopaniṣad*, or a *śruti* text spoken by the Supreme Personality of Godhead Himself. Therefore, Śrīla Prabhupāda wrote in a letter, the *Gītā* should be taken as *śruti*. But they take it as *smṛti* because it is part of the *smṛti* (*Mahābhārata*). In one sense it is both *śruti* and *smṛti.* In only 700 verses, the *Bhagavad-gītā* summarizes all Vedic knowledge about the soul, God, *sanātana-dharma*, sacrifice, *yoga*, *karma*, reincarnation, the modes of material nature, *Vedānta* and pure devotion.

Bhajana—this term generally indicates the service and worship of the Supreme Lord executed by Vaiṣṇavas—from the neophytes up to those who are fully God-realized. The main form that this service takes is the hearing and chanting of the holy name. Otherwise, the term refers to the singing of devotional songs about Kṛṣṇa, usually accompanied by musical instruments.

Bhakti-yoga—the system of cultivation of pure devotional service to the Supreme Personality of Godhead, Lord Kṛṣṇa, which is not tinged by sense gratification or philosophical speculation. It consists of nine *aṅgas* or parts: (1) *śravaṇaṁ*–hearing about the transcendental holy name, form, and other qualities of the Lord (2) *kīrtanaṁ*– chanting about these qualities, (3) *viṣṇoḥ smaraṇaṁ*–remembering them, (4) *pāda-sevanam*–serving the lotus feet of the Lord, (5) *arcanaṁ*–worshipping the Deity of the Lord, (6) *vandanaṁ*–offering prayers to the Lord, (7) *dāsyaṁ* –serving His mission, (8) *sakhyam*–making friends with the Lord, and (9) *ātma-nivedanam*–surrendering everything unto Him.

Brahmā—the first created living being and secondary creator of the material universe. Directed by Lord Viṣṇu, he creates all life forms in the universes. He also rules the mode of passion. Twelve of his hours equal 4,320,000,000 earth-years, and his life span is more than 311 trillion of our years. The first living being in the universe, Brahmā was born, not of a womb, but the lotus that grows from Lord Viṣṇu's navel. He is the fore-father and guru of the demigods, the giver of the *Vedas*, and the director of the *vaikṛta* or secondary phase of cosmic creation by which all species of plants, animals, human beings and demigods come into existence.

Brāhmaṇa—a member of the intellectual, priestly class; a person wise in Vedic knowledge, fixed in goodness and knowledge of Brahman, the Absolute Truth; one of the four orders of Vedic society. Their occupation consists of learning and teaching Vedic literature, learning and teaching Deity worship, and receiving and giving charity.

Brahma-rākṣasa—a man-eating demon who was a fallen *brāhmaṇa* in his last life; the ghost of a sinful *brāhmana*.

C

Caitanya-caritāmṛta—translated as "the character of the living force in immortality," it is the authorized biography of Lord Caitanya Mahāprabhu written in the late sixteenth century by Śrīla Kṛṣṇadāsa Kavirāja Gosvāmī, presenting the Lord's pastimes and teachings. It is written in Bengali, with many Sanskrit verses, and is considered the postgraduate study of spiritual knowledge. Ideally, one begins with *Bhagavad-gītā* and advances through *Śrīmad-Bhāgavatam* to the *Śrī Caitanya-caritāmṛta.*

D

Daśārha—the founder of one of the branches of the Yadu clan.

Durgā—Lord Śiva's wife in a fierce form, riding a tiger. The goddess is empowered by the Supreme Lord to preside over the material nature, and bewilder the souls situated there into misconceiving themselves to be their material bodies and enjoyers and controllers of the mundane creation. She is very powerful, superseded only by Lord Viṣṇu Himself, and is the external manifestation of the Lord's internal potency, *Yoga-māyā.* Once a fallen soul takes to the path of God consciousness, she continues to offer various material allurements to test his sincerity and determination to serve the Lord. Once the Lord accepts the struggling soul she can no longer influence that soul and it is thus liberated.

Dvādaśī—the twelfth day after the full or new moon, thus the day after Ekādaśī, when one breaks one's fast by eating grains.

E

Ekādaśī—Directly presided over by Lord Hari, Ekādaśī is a holy day for Vaiṣṇavas. It falls on the eleventh day after both the full and new moon days. Abstinence from grains and beans is prescribed. One should utilize this day for fasting and increasing one's devotion to Lord Kṛṣṇa by intensifying the chanting of the Hare Kṛṣṇa *mantra* and other devotional activities.

G

Gandharvas—the celestial demigod dancers, singers, and musicians of the heavenly planets.

Gargamuni—the family priest for the Yadu dynasty.

Garuḍa—Lord Viṣṇu's eternal carrier, a great devotee, and the son of Aditi and Kaśyapa who takes the form of an eagle. He is often found atop a pole facing the entrance of Viṣṇu temples. The emblem of Garuḍa is always on the chariot of Lord Kṛṣṇa.

Gopīs—the cowherd girls of Vraja, who are generally the counterparts of Śrī Kṛṣṇa's *hlādini-śākti*, Śrīmatī Rādhārāṇī, and His most surrendered and confidential devotees. They assist Her as maidservants in Her conjugal pastimes with the Supreme Personality of Godhead.

H

Hiraṇyakaśipu—a powerful demon and great atheist who tormented his son Prahlāda Mahārāja, a great devotee, and was killed by Lord Nṛsiṁhadeva, the half man-half lion form of Lord Viṣṇu.

Hiraṇyākṣa—the demoniac son of Kaśyapa, younger brother of Hiraṇyakaśipu who was killed by Lord Varāha.

I

Indra—the chief demigod of heaven, presiding deity of rain, and the father of Arjuna. He is the son of Aditi.

J

Jīva Gosvāmī—one of the Six Gosvāmīs of Vṛndāvana and the nephew of Rupa and Sanātana Gosvāmīs. He grew up absorbed in the worship of Kṛṣṇa and Balarāma. Lord Caitanya instructed him in a dream to proceed to Navadvīpa, and there he toured that sacred place in the association of Śrī Nityānanda Prabhu. He became a disciple of Rūpa Gosvāmī and wrote eighteen major works on Vaiṣṇava philosophy, comprising more than 400,000 verses. He is considered by many philosophers and Sanskrit scholars to be the greatest scholar who ever lived.

Jñānī—one who is engaged in the cultivation of knowledge, especially by philosophical speculation. Upon attaining perfection, a *jñānī* surrenders to Kṛṣṇa;

K

Kajjala—a preparation of lampblack used to darken the edges of the eyelids; kohl.

Kaṁsa—a demoniac king of the Bhoja dynasty and maternal uncle of Kṛṣṇa, the son of Ugrasena. He imprisoned his father and took charge of the kingdom. He killed the first six children of Devakī, and was ultimately killed by Lord Śrī Kṛṣṇa.

Karma—1. material action performed according to scriptural regulations; 2. action pertaining to the development of the material body; 3. any material action which will incur a subsequent reaction and 4. the material reaction one incurs due to fruitive activities. The soul receives due reaction to work by taking his next birth in a lower species, or the human species, or a higher species. Or the soul may be liberated from birth and death altogether. All this depends upon whether the *karma* performed within this lifetime is ignorant, passionate, good or transcendental.

Karmī—a fruitive laborer, one who is attached to the fruits of work, a materialist who works hard to enjoy material life.

Kātyāyanī—the material energy personified, another name for Durgā.

Kavi-karṇapūra Gosvāmī—a noted sixteenth-century author of Sanskrit poems and plays. He is one of the leading followers of Śrī Caitanya Mahāprabhu.

Kṛṣṇa-līlā—the transcendental pastimes of Lord Kṛṣṇa.

Kṣatriya—second of the four social orders of the *varṇāśrama* system; a warrior who is inclined to fight and lead others; the administrative or protective occupation.

Kuṅkuma—a sweetly-flavored reddish cosmetic powder which is thrown on the bodies of worshipable persons, also used by married women to decorate their foreheads.

L

Lakṣmī—the goddess of fortune and the eternal consort of the Supreme Lord as Lord Nārayaṇa, who resides in the unlimited spiritual realm of Vaikuṇṭha.

M

Mahat-tattva—the original, undifferentiated form of the total material energy, from which the material world is manifested when the three modes of material nature are activated by the glance of Mahā-Viṣṇu.

Maha-Viṣṇu—the expansion of the Supreme Lord Viṣṇu reclining on Ādi-Sesa, from whom all material universes emanate.

Mahendra—Lord Indra, the King of heaven.

Mānasa-gaṅgā—a sacred river that flows in Vṛndāvana along a part of the base of Govardhana Hill.

Mañjarī—the small, purplish flowers of the *tulasī* plant. Mañjarīs, along with *tulasī* leaves are offered to the Supreme Personality of Godhead Kṛṣṇa or Viṣṇu and His expansions.

Mantra—a transcendental sound or Vedic hymn, a prayer or chant; a pure sound vibration when repeated over and over delivers the mind from its material inclinations and illusion. The Vedic scriptures are composed of many thousands of *mantras*.

Mathurā—Lord Kṛṣṇa's abode, and birth place, surrounding Vṛndāvana. Lord Krsṇa displayed many of His pastimes here after leaving Vṛndāvana. At the end of Lord Kṛṣṇa's manifest *līlā*, Vajranābha, His grandson, was put in charge of this sacred city.

Mauṣala-līlā—the pastimes of the annihilation of the Yadu dynasty and Lord Kṛṣṇa's disappearance.

N

Nārāyaṇa—the majestic four-armed expansion of the Supreme Personality of Godhead who is the resting place of all living entities, and presides over the Vaikuṇṭha planets.

P

Pañcarātra—Vedic literatures such as *Nārada-pañcarātra* which describe the process of Deity worship.

Paraśurāma—the incarnation of Lord Kṛṣṇa, who appeared in ancient times to overthrow the warrior class when they had become degraded, and destroyed twenty-one consecutive generations of lawless members of the ruling class. He taught the science of weapons to Droṇa and Karṇa.

Pradyumna—one of the four original expansions of Lord Kṛṣṇa in the spiritual world; also the first son of Lord Kṛṣṇa by Rukminī. He fought against Śālva in the fight for Dvārakā.

Prema-bhakti—pure love of Lord Kṛṣṇa, the highest stage in the progressive development of pure devotional service.

Purāṇas— Literally, very old; the eighteen major and eighteen minor ancient Vedic literatures compiled about five thousand years ago in India by Śrīla Vyāsadeva that are histories of this and other planets; literatures supplementary to the *Vedas*, discussing such topics as the creation of the universe, incarnations of the Supreme Lord and demigods, and the history of dynasties of saintly kings. The eighteen principal *Purāṇas* discuss ten primary subject matters: (1) the primary creation, (2) the secondary creation, (3) the planetary systems, (4) protection and maintenance by the *avatāras*, (5) the Manus. (6) dynasties of great kings, (7) noble character and activities of great kings, (8) dissolution of the universe and liberation of the living entity, (9) the *jīva* (the spirit soul), (10) the Supreme Lord.

Puruṣa—the enjoyer, or male; the living entity or the Supreme Lord; Viṣṇu, the incarnation of the Lord for material creation; the male or controlling principle. This term may be applied to both, the individual living being and the Supreme Personality of Godhead.

R

Rāmacandra—the incarnation of the Supreme Personality of Godhead as the perfect king, and the killer of the ten-headed demon king Rāvaṇa. Rāma was exiled to the forest on the order of His father, Mahārāja Daśaratha. His wife Sītā was kidnapped by Rāvaṇa, but by employing a huge army of monkeys, who were the powerful and intelligent offspring of demigods, He regained his wife in battle, and eventually His ancestral kingdom too. This history is recorded in the great epic *Rāmāyaṇa* written by the sage Vālmīki.

Rāsa dance—Lord Kṛṣṇa's pleasure dance with the cowherd maidens of Vṛndāvana, Vrajabhūmi. It is a pure exchange of spiritual love between the Lord and His most advanced, confidential servitors.

Rūpa Gosvāmī—chief of the six *gosvāmīs* of Vṛndāvana who were authorized by Lord Caitanya Mahāprabhu to establish and distribute the philosophy of Kṛṣṇa consciousness. He extensively researched the scriptures, and established the philosophy taught by Lord Caitanya on an unshakable foundation. Gauḍīya Vaiṣṇavas are known as Rūpānugas, followers of Rūpa Gosvāmī.

S

Sādhana—the beginning phase of devotional service consisting of regulated practice.

Sanātana Gosvāmī—one of the Six Gosvāmīs of Vṛndāvana who was authorized by Lord Caitanya Mahāprabhu to establish and distribute the philosophy of Kṛṣṇa consciousness. He was the older brother of Rūpa Gosvāmī who accepted him as his spiritual master. He and Rūpa Gosvāmī were both ministers to the Muslim ruler in Bengal, but renounced everything for the service of Lord Caitanya. The two brothers were ordered by Śrī Caitanya to write books establishing the philosophy of Gauḍīya Vaiṣṇavism and to excavate the holy places in Vṛndāvana.

Saṅkarṣaṇa—one of the four original expansions of Lord Kṛṣṇa in the spiritual world; also, another name of Balarāma.

Sāṅkhya— analytical discrimination between spirit and matter and the path of devotional service as described by Lord Kapila, the son of Devahūti.

Saṅkīrtana—congregational or public glorification of the Supreme Lord Kṛṣṇa through chanting of His holy names, and glorification of His fame and pastimes.

Śānta-rasa—passive love of God; the relationship with the Supreme Lord in neutrality.

Satyaloka—Lord Brahmā's abode, the highest planet in the material universe; also called Brahmaloka.

Sautrāmaṇi—a particular Vedic fire sacrifice offered to Lord Indra.

Śeṣa Nāga—an expansion of Lord Balarāma or Saṅkarṣaṇa who takes the form of a many-hooded serpent and serves as Lord Viṣṇu's couch and other paraphernalia. He also holds the unlimited number of universes on His hoods.

Siddha—a perfected person or mystic; a demigod from Siddhaloka; one who has realized the Brahman effulgence; a perfect devotee.

Śiva—also known as Hara, Mahādeva, Maheśvara, Āśutoṣa (one who is easily pleased), Giriśa (lord of the mountains) and Gopīśvara, he is the *guṇa-avatāra* who is the superintendent of the mode of ignorance (*tamoguṇa*) and who takes charge of destroying the universe at the time of annihilation. He is also considered the greatest Vaiṣṇava, or devotee, of Lord

Kṛṣṇa. He is confused by some with the Supreme Lord.

Sneha—affection for Kṛṣṇa, at which stage the lover cannot be without the beloved.

Śrīdhara Svāmī—the author of the earliest extant Vaiṣṇava commentaries on *Bhagavad-gītā* and *Śrīmad-Bhāgavatam*. A spiritual master in the line of Śri Viśṇusvāmi, he taught pure Vaiṣṇava philosophy. He was a devotee of Lord Nṛsiṁhadeva, and his works were highly regarded by Lord Caitanya, especially his *Śrīmad-Bhāgavatam* gloss, *Bhāvārtha-dīpikā*. Lord Caitanya commented that anyone who wanted to write a commentary on *Srīmad-Bhagavatam* must follow the commentary of Srīdhara Svāmī.

Śrīvatsa—the sign on the chest of Lord Viṣṇu and Nārāyaṇa, indicating the goddess of fortune, Lakṣmī.

Śruti—knowledge via hearing; the original Vedic scriptures (the *Vedas* and *Upaniṣads*) given directly by the Supreme Lord.

Śūdra—a member of the fourth social order, laborer class, in the traditional Vedic social system. They render service to the three higher classes, namely the *brāhmaṇas*, the *kṣatriyas*, and the *vaiśyas*.

T

Tilaka—sacred clay markings placed on the forehead and other parts of the body to designate one as a follower of Viṣṇu, Rāma, Śiva etc.

Tulasī—a pure devotee of Kṛṣṇa in the form of a basil plant, worshipped by Vaiṣṇavas and other followers of Vedic culture, and very dear to Lord Kṛṣṇa. Its leaves and *mañjarīs* (buds) are always offered to His lotus feet.

U

Ujjvala-nīlamaṇi—a Sanskrit work that describes the complete science of *mādhurya-rasa*, the conjugal relationship with Lord Kṛṣṇa. It was compiled by Śrīla Rūpa Gosvāmī in the sixteenth century.

V

Vaijayantī—a garland containing flowers of five colors and reaching down to the knees. It is worn by Lord Kṛṣṇa.

Vaikuṇṭha—the eternal planets of the spiritual world, the abode of Lord Nārāyaṇa, which lies beyond the coverings of the material universe. Literally, "the place with no anxiety."

Vaiṣṇava—a devotee of the Supreme Lord, Viṣṇu, or Kṛṣṇa.

Vaiśya—member of the mercantile and agricultural class in the Vedic *varṇāśrama* system; the third Vedic social order.

Vāmanadeva—the Supreme Lord's incarnation as a dwarf *brāhmaṇa* to reclaim the heavenly kingdom, which the king of the demons Bali Mahārāja had conquered. Bali Mahārāja surrendered all his possessions to Lord Vāmanadeva, and became celebrated as one of the *mahājanas*, or great spiritual authorities.

Vedānta-sūtra—also known as *Brahma-sūtra*, it is Śrīla Vyāsadeva's conclusive summary of Vedic philosophical knowledge, written in brief codes. All apparent contradictory statements of the vast literature of the *Vedas* are resolved in this work. There are four divisions: (1) reconciliation of all scriptures (2) the consistent reconciliation of apparently conflicting hymns (3) the means or process of attaining the goal (spiritual realization) and (4) the object (or desired fruit) achieved by the spiritual process. The codes of the *Vedānta-sūtra* are very terse, and without a fuller explanation or commentary, their meaning is difficult to grasp. In India all the five main schools of *Vedānta* have explained the *sūtras* through their respective *bhāṣyas* (commentaries). The natural commentary on the *Vedānta-sūtra* is the *Śrīmad-Bhāgavatam*.

Vedas—the original *Veda* was divided into four by Śrīla Vyāsadeva. The four original Vedic scriptures, *Saṁhitās* (*Ṛg, Sāma, Atharva* and *Yajur*) and the 108 *Upaniṣads, Mahābhārata, Vedānta-sūtra*, etc. The system of eternal wisdom compiled by Śrīla Vyāsadeva, the literary incarnation of the Supreme Lord, for the gradual upliftment of all mankind from the state of bondage to the state of liberation. The word *veda* literally means "knowledge", and thus in a wider sense it refers to the whole body of Indian Sanskrit religious literature that is in harmony with the philosophical conclusions found in the original four Vedic *Saṁhitās* and *Upaniṣads*. The message of the transcendental realm that has come down to this phenomenal world through the medium of sound is known as the *Veda*. Being the very words of Godhead Himself, the *Vedas* have existed from eternity. Lord Kṛṣṇa originally revealed the *Vedas* to Brahmā, the first soul to appear in the realm of physical nature, and by him they were subsequently made available to other souls through the channel of spiritual disciplic succession; *Veda, Vedas,* Vedic knowledge. The Sanskrit root of the word *Veda* is *vid*, knowledge. This root is widespread even in modern Western language: e.g. *video* (from the Latin word to see) and idea (Gr. *ida*). The term Vedic refers to the teachings of the Vedic literatures. From these literatures we learn that this universe, along with countless others, was produced from the breath of Mahā-Viṣṇu some 155,250,000,000,000 years ago. The Lord's divine breath simultaneously transmitted all the knowledge mankind requires to meet his material needs and revive his dormant God consciousness. This knowledge is called *Veda*. Caturmukha (four-faced) Brahmā, the first created being within this universe, received *Veda* from Viṣṇu. Brahmā, acting as an obedient servant of the Supreme Lord, populated the planetary systems with all species of life. He spoke four *Vedas*, one from each of his mouths, to guide human beings in their spiritual and material progress. The *Vedas* are thus traced to the very beginning of the cosmos. Some of the most basic Vedic teachings are: (1) every living creature is an eternal soul covered by a material body; (2) as long as the souls are bewildered by *māyā* (the illusion of identifying the self with the body) they must reincarnate from body to body, life after life; (3) to accept a material body means to suffer the four-fold pangs of birth, old age, disease and death; (4) depending upon the quality of work (*karma*) in the human form, a soul may take its next birth in a subhuman species, or the human species, or a superhuman species, or it may be freed from birth and death altogether; (5) *karma* dedicated in sacrifice to Viṣṇu as directed by Vedic injunctions elevates and liberates the soul.

Viṣṇu— literally, the all-pervading God; the Supreme Personality of Godhead in His four-armed expansion in Vaikuṇṭha. A plenary expansion of the original Supreme Personality of Godhead, Śrī Kṛṣṇa, He supervises the maintenance of the created universe, and enters into the material universe before creation. He is worshiped by all the demigods and sages, and described throughout the *Vedas* as the summum bonum of all knowledge.

Viśvanātha Cakravartī Ṭhākura—a great *ācārya* in the Caitanya school of Vaiṣṇavism, and the most prominent *ācārya* after Narottama dāsa Ṭhākura. He wrote twenty-four books on the science of *bhakti*, including commentaries on *Śrīmad-Bhāgavatam* and *Bhagavad-gītā*. He established the Gokulānanda Temple in Vṛndāvana. In his final years he lived at Rādhā-kuṇḍa.

Y

Yamarāja—the demigod in charge of death and punishing the sinful. He is the son of the sun-god and the brother of the sacred river Yamunā.

Yoga— literally, connection; the discipline of self-realization. a spiritual discipline meant for linking one's consciousness with the Supreme Lord, Kṛṣṇa; one of the six systems of Vedic philosophy, taught by Patañjali. Through the process of *bhakti-yoga*, the consciousness of the individual soul connects with its source, Kṛṣṇa.

Yogamāyā—the internal, spiritual energy of the Supreme Lord, to which the external energy, *mahāmayā*, is subordinate, and which hides Him from non-devotees.

Yogī—a transcendentalist who practices one of the many authorized forms of *yoga* or processes of spiritual purification; one who practices the eight-fold mystic *yoga* process to gain mystic *siddhis* or Paramātmā realization.

Sanskrit Pronunciation Guide

Throughout the centuries, the Sanskrit language has been written in a variety of alphabets. The mode of writing most widely used throughout India, however, is called *devanāgarī*, which means, literally, the writing used in "the cities of the demigods." The *devanāgarī* alphabet consists of forty-eight characters: thirteen vowels and thirty-five consonants. Ancient Sanskrit grammarians arranged this alphabet according to practical linguistic principles, and this order has been accepted by all Western scholars. The system of transliteration used in this book conforms to a system that scholars have accepted to indicate the pronunciation of each Sanskrit sound.

Vowels

अ a आ ā इ i ई ī उ u ऊ ū ऋ ṛ ॠ ṝ ऌ ḷ
ए e ऐ ai ओ o औ au

Consonants

Gutturals:	क ka	ख kha	ग ga	घ gha	ङ ṅa
Palatals:	च ca	छ cha	ज ja	झ jha	ञ ña
Cerebrals:	ट ṭa	ठ ṭha	ड ḍa	ढ ḍha	ण ṇa
Dentals:	त ta	थ tha	द da	ध dha	न na
Labials:	प pa	फ pha	ब ba	भ bha	म ma
Semivowels:	य ya	र ra	ल la	व va	
Sibilants:	श śa	ष ṣa	स sa		
Aspirate:	ह ha	Anusvāra: ं ṁ	Visarga: ः ḥ		

Numerals

०–0 १–1 २–2 ३–3 ४–4 ५–5 ६–6 ७–7 ८–8 ९–9

The vowels are written as follows after a consonant:

ा ā ि i ी ī ु u ू ū ृ ṛ ॄ ṝ े e ै ai ो o ौ au

For example : क ka का kā कि ki की kī कु ku कू kū
कृ kṛ कॄ kṝ के ke कै kai को ko कौ kau

Generally two or more consonants in conjunction are written together in a special form, as for example: क्ष **kṣa** त्र **tra**

The vowel "a" is implied after a consonant with no vowel symbol.

The symbol virāma (्) indicates that there is no final vowel: क्

The vowels are pronounced as follows:.

a	—	as in b**u**t
ā	—	as in f**a**r but held twice as long as **a**
ai	—	as in **ai**sle
au	—	as in h**ow**
e	—	as in th**ey**
i	—	as in p**i**n
ī	—	as in pique but held twice as long as **i**
ḷ	—	as in **lree**
o	—	as in **go**
ṛ	—	as in **ri**m
ṝ	—	as in **ree**d but held twice as long as **ṛ**
u	—	as in p**u**sh
ū	—	as in r**u**le but held twice as long as **u**

The consonants are pronounced as follows:

Gutturals
(pronounced from the throat)

k	—	as in **k**ite
kh	—	as in Ec**kh**art
g	—	as in **g**ive
gh	—	as in di**g-h**ard
ṅ	—	as in si**ng**

Cerebrals
(pronounced with the tip of the tongue against the roof of the mouth)

ṭ	—	as in **t**ub
ṭh	—	as in ligh**t-h**eart
ḍ	—	as in **d**ove
ḍh	—	as in re**d-h**ot
ṇ	—	as in si**ng**

Labials
(pronounced with the lips)

p	—	as in **p**ine
ph	—	as in u**p-h**ill
b	—	as in **b**ird
bh	—	as in ru**b-h**ard
m	—	as in **m**other

Palatals
(pronounced with the middle of the tongue against the palate)

c	—	as in **ch**air
ch	—	as in staun**ch-h**eart
j	—	as in **j**oy
jh	—	as in he**dgeh**og
ñ	—	as in ca**ny**on

Dentals
(pronounced like the cerebrals but with the tongue against the teeth)

t	—	as in **t**ub
th	—	as in ligh**t-h**eart
d	—	as in **d**ove
dh	—	as in re**d-h**ot
n	—	as in **n**ut

Semivowels

y	—	as in **y**es
r	—	as in **r**un
l	—	as in **l**ight
v	—	as in **v**ine, except when preceded in the same syllable by a consonant, then like in s**w**an

Aspirate

h	—	as in **h**ome

Sibilants

ś	—	as in the German word *sprechen*
ṣ	—	as in **sh**ine
s	—	as in **s**un

Anusvāra

ṁ	—	a resonant nasal sound as in the French word *bon*

Visarga

ḥ	—	a final **h**-sound: **aḥ** is pronounced like **aha**; **iḥ** like **ihi**.

There is no strong accentuation of syllables in Sanskrit, or pausing between words in a line, only a flowing of short and long syllables (the long twice as long as the short). A long syllable is one whose vowel is long (**ā, ai, au, e , ī, o, ṝ, ū**) or whose short vowel is followed by more than one consonant (including **ḥ** and **ṁ**). Aspirated consonants (consonants followed by an **h**) count as single consonants.

Index of Sanskrit Verses

This index constitutes a complete listing of the first and third lines of each of the Sanskrit poetry verses of this volume of *Śrīmad-Bhāgavatam*, arranged in English alphabetical order. The first column gives the Sanskrit transliteration; the second, the chapter-verse reference. Apostrophes are alphabetized as a's.

A

B

C

D

E

H

I

L

M

N

R

S

T

U

V

Y

Index of Verses Quoted

This index lists the verses quoted in the purports of this volume of *Śrīmad-Bhāgavatam.* Numerals in boldface type refer to the first or third lines of verses quoted in full; numerals in roman type refer to partially quoted verses.

General Index

The references to the translations and purports of the verses of *Śrīmad-Bhāgavatam* are presented in the following format: "xx.yy (para n)", where 'xx' is the chapter number, 'yy' is the verse number (text number) and 'n' is the paragraph number in the purport. Numerals in the boldface type indicate the translations and those in regular type indicate the purports. Numerals in the mixed type indicate both translation and purports. While counting the paragraphs in the purports, please remember that, the new paragraph begins (in the purport) only where the first word is indented.

A

Abhava defined, 27.9 (para 1)
Abhīyate defined, 38.11 (para 3)
Aborigine girls in Vṛndāvana, **20.27**, **21.17**
Abortion, 14.51
Absolute Truth
  all existence resting on, 27.4 (para 3)
  compared to moon, 20.19 (para 2)
  ignorance of, as debilitating, 23.40
  illusion absent in, **28.6**
  Kṛṣṇa as, **14.23**, 14.23 (para 4), **14.32**, **16.40**, 19.11, 22.19, 22.20 (para 3), 23.6 (para 1), **23.11**, 23.46, 24.32–33 (para 2), 27.4 (para 3), 29.13 (para 2), 38.11 (para 1)
  materialists &, 20.22
  nondevotees &, 14.3 (para 3)
  as personal, 14.19
  pervasiveness of, 24.32–33 (para 2)
  representing, 29.32 (para 1)
  as source of everything, 29.1 (para 3), 30.34 (para 5)
  understanding, mental speculation &, 14.3 (para 1)
  See also: Kṛṣṇa; Supreme Lord
Abudha-liṅga-bhāvah defined, 27.5 (para 3)
Ācārya(s). See: Spiritual master(s); *specific spiritual masters*
Activities & knowledge, **24.6**
Acyuta defined, 29.43
Acyuta, Lord. *See:* Kṛṣṇa
Adhokṣaja, Lord
  Kṛṣṇa as, **14.12**
  See also: Kṛṣṇa
Ādi-kavi
  defined, 14.2 (para 4)
Ādi-kavi (continued)
  See also: Brahmā
Ādi Purāṇa quoted on names of Yaśodā, 33.6
Ādiṣu defined, 20.39
Aditi, **27.22–23**
Adultery, **29.26**
Adya defined, 15.8 (para 1)
Affection, types of, **32.17–19**
Age of Kali. *See:* Kali-yuga
Aghāsura, **14.46**, **14.48**, 15.1 (para 1), **31.3**
Agrahaṇa defined, 27.4 (para 10&11)
Agṛhāṇām, 42.12
Agricultural production
  government restrictions on, 20.12 (para 2)
  See also: Farmers
Aguṇasya defined, 14.6 (para 1)
Ahaitukī defined, 23.26
Air
  as component of universe, **14.11**
  of life, **38.11**
Airāvata
  as Indra's elephant, **25.6–7**
  Kṛṣṇa bathed by, **27.22–23**
Airplanes of demigods, **21.12**
Aja defined, 14.13
Ajasra-sukha defined, 14.23 (para 2)
Ajita defined, 14.3 (para 3)
Ajñam defined, 25.5 (para 1)
Akrūra
  arrival of, in Gokula (Vṛndāvana), **38.24–26**
  arrival of, in Mathurā, **41.6**
  & austerities, **38.3**
  at Balarāma's house, **38.37–38**, **39.10**
  bewilderment of, **39.42–43**
  & Bhoja dynasty, **36.28**
  chariot used by, 36.30
  & charity, **38.3**

B

C

D

F

G

H

I

J

K

L

M

N

O

P

Q

R

S

T

U

W